Principles of Tort Law

Presenting the law of tort as a body of principles, this authoritative textbook leads students to an incisive and clear understanding of the subject. Each tort is carefully structured and examined within a consistent analytical framework that guides students through its preconditions, elements, defences and remedies. Clear summaries and comparisons accompany the detailed exposition, and further support is provided by numerous diagrams and tables, which clarify complex aspects of the law. Critical discussion of legal judgments encourages students to develop strong analytical and case-reading skills, whilst key reform proposals and leading cases from other jurisdictions illustrate different potential solutions to conundrums in tort law. A rich companion website, featuring ten additional chapters and sections on more advanced areas of tort law, completes the learning package. Written specifically for students, the text is also ideal for practitioners, litigants, policymakers and law reformers seeking a comprehensive and accurate understanding of the law.

Rachael Mulheron is a professor at the Department of Law, Queen Mary University of London, where she has taught since 2004. Her principal fields of academic research concern tort law and class actions jurisprudence. She publishes regularly in both areas, and has frequently assisted various law reform commissions, government departments, and law firms, on tort-related and collective redress-related matters. Professor Mulheron also undertakes extensive law reform work, in her capacity as a member of the Civil Justice Council of England and Wales. For example, in 2015, she chaired a Working Party to make recommendations to the Government as to the redrafting of the legislation governing contingency fees (or 'damages-based agreements'). Prior to her academic career, Professor Mulheron practised as a litigation solicitor in Brisbane, Australia, both in general practice (as a trainee solicitor), and then predominantly in construction law.

Principles of Tort Law

Rachael Mulheron
Professor of Law, Queen Mary University of London

CAMBRIDGE
UNIVERSITY PRESS

University Printing House, Cambridge CB2 8BS, United Kingdom

Cambridge University Press is part of the University of Cambridge.

It furthers the University's mission by disseminating knowledge in the pursuit of education, learning and research at the highest international levels of excellence.

www.cambridge.org
Information on this title: www.cambridge.org/9781107151369

First published 2016
Printed in the United Kingdom by Clays, St Ives plc

A catalogue record for this publication is available from the British Library

ISBN 978-1-107-15136-9 Hardback
ISBN 978-1-316-60566-0 Paperback

Additional resources for this publication at www.cambridge.org/mulheron

Summary contents

Pages preceded by ➊ indicate that the relevant content is locatable in the materials available at the Online Torts Hub (available at www.Cambridge.org/Mulheron).

Detailed contents

Foreword

There are few areas of the law which are as rewarding to study and have as practical an impact on our daily lives as, to borrow from Professor Mulheron, the 'motley bunch of causes of action which fall within English Tort Law!' Not only does detailed study provide an in-depth insight into the development of the common law and of the incremental, precedent-based, common law method in action, it also raises challenging questions of principle. Questions concerning the role that tort law plays in our legal system and wider society, the extent to which the law should impose liability for harm on individuals and the circumstances when it should do so, whether it is underpinned by an overarching principle or by a variety of principles, remain matters of interest and debate. And from a practical perspective, the boundaries of tort law help shape the contours of everyday life. Whether we consider the steps manufacturers must take to ensure that their products are safe for sale or – as in *Donoghue v Stevenson* – consumption, the steps that professionals, such as doctors or lawyers, must take to treat their patients or advise their clients appropriately, or that employers must take to secure the safety of their workers, the law of tort provides the framework.

In this new book, *Principles of Tort Law*, Professor Mulheron, drawing on her extensive experience of the field both in practice in Australia and teaching tort law at Queen Mary University of London, provides a clear, detailed and challenging account of the law of tort. By utilising the method taken by the American Law Institute in its famous Restatements of the Law of Tort – statement of principle followed by detailed exegesis drawing on relevant case law, statutory provision and, where relevant, comparative jurisprudence – she presents a meticulous analysis in a thoroughly accessible manner. This work is a most welcome contribution to the field, one that will be of great benefit to students, practitioners, academics and judges and to anyone interested in gaining a proper understanding of the fundamental nature of this central part of the law. I cannot commend it highly enough.

The Right Honourable Lord Dyson,
Master of the Rolls

Preface

This book aims to do what it 'says on the tin' – to state the corpus of Tort law as a body of principles. Tort lawyers commonly talk of 'the principles of Tort', and yet, when examining case after case, that ethos can easily become lost, in amongst factual distinctions, common law complexities, statutory interventions and appellate cases which frequently contain multiple judgments of differing ratio.

My interest in writing a book which addresses this area of law as a set of principles, with an in-depth underlying analysis, was motivated by four influences:

i. Teaching undergraduate Torts students has enriched my understanding of just how important it is to delve into, and isolate, the principles which we, as academics, seek to convey to those students who are encountering the subject for the first time. Questions such as, 'When should we use *Bolam* and when should we use *Bolitho*?'; 'Is *Donoghue v Stevenson's* ratio still relevant?'; 'Is the test of foreseeability the same for duty of care, breach, and remoteness?', and literally hundreds of similar-type queries and discussion points, have been an important genesis for this book.

   It is intended that this text will, primarily, have utility to the student who is studying Tort law. Students may take on board some of the principles per chapter, and omit others, in accordance with the depth and direction of study being undertaken. The book has been written in a style that incorporates presentational tools to assist the student in his or her studies, by employing frameworks for analysis per chapter, tables of legal analysis, diagrammatic depictions of the parties' relationships in leading cases, boxes illustrating comparative judicial reasoning, and the like.

ii. Whilst in legal practice, I was frequently engaged in Tort litigation, and came to realise that exposition of principle in concise, but in-depth, treatment, is the nadir of what this area of the law should seek to achieve. After all, Tort law is there to serve society in all of its guises, to enable claimants to seek (usually compensatory) redress for their grievances, and to provide defendants with a logical set of defences to such actions. Its complexity and (occasional) opaqueness should not obscure the fact that the law should be capable of being understood by 'the reasonable person on the London underground' (an identity of such importance in Tort law!).

iii. The subject-matter of Tort law is undeniably interesting, and very relevant to everyday life, and hence, a work that seeks to espouse the principles of Tort will be of interest to a wider readership than the student body to which it is principally directed. Notably, it is envisaged that this book will also have utility for those audiences (e.g., judiciary, legal practitioners, legislators and academics) who are already familiar with Tort law, but who are grappling with particular issues and points of complexity associated with distinct principles.

iv. Lastly, one of the key features of Tort law is the extent to which legal and public policy influences, and informs, the development of jurisprudence in this area. Whilst it is called a set of 'principles', much discussion surrounding Tort law is directed to what the Law *should* be – and an explicit acknowledgement and elucidation of that fact is one of the driving interests which motivated the writing of this book. For this reason, key law reform commission opinion is canvassed in those areas in which, for policy reasons, those commissions suggested that the law should perhaps change. Occasionally, comparative vignettes are also referenced in chapters, to show how similar problems in Tort law can yield differing solutions, depending upon differing judicial (or legislative) attitudes in other jurisdictions.

It is an ancillary aim of the book to promote and activate a debate, among policy-makers, reformers, judiciary and academics, about the utility of a *Restatement*-type project of English Tort law. I do not envisage that Tort law should be codified, in the sense that a 'blank sheet of paper' should be the starting point of Tort law for this jurisdiction. Rather, the depth and nuances of the common law of Tort (with occasional statutory enactments), and the jurisprudence generated over its long and distinguished history, are worth preserving in all of its grand complexity. However, as the analysis in this book demonstrates, there are pockets of uncertainty, of unsettled law, of appellate judgments which differ and where 'the circle cannot be squared', and of law reform proposals which remain unenacted. The text of principles and analysis undertaken herein could serve as a useful reference point for a future *Restatement* project, should that be considered desirable.

Grateful thanks are due to many people, whose guidance, input, interest, and insights throughout this long journey have been extremely valuable and much appreciated. The support and encouragement provided by my publishers, particularly by Ms Valerie Appleby and Ms Kim Hughes; by my parents whose constant belief in the value of the project were both vital and sustaining in the long years that this project has taken; and by my family and friends whose patience with, and interest in, the book were always much appreciated, are all (inadequately, but with heartfelt gratitude) acknowledged herein. Grateful thanks are also due to my colleagues at the Department of Law at Queen Mary University of London, Mr Ian Yeats and Ms Margaret Cunningham, both of whom, in combination, kindly provided very helpful feedback on numerous draft chapters; to several colleagues in practice who provided useful insights and/or materials along the way, especially: Mr David Body, former partner of Irwin Mitchell solicitors; Ms Beverley Barton, Ms Martha Castaneda-Wilcox and Ms Susan Scott, all of Practical Law; Mr John Brown, litigation partner of McCarthy Tetrault LLP, Toronto, Canada; Dr Duncan Fairgrieve, Director of Projects at the British Institute of International and Comparative Law; Mr Peter Farr, Chief Executive of the Civil Justice Council of England and Wales; Mr Robert Gapes, partner of Simpson Grier Solicitors, Auckland; His Honour Judge David Grant, of the Technology and Construction Court; Mr Gregory Jones QC; Prof Vince Morabito of Monash University, Australia; Mr John Spencer, foundation partner of Spencer Solicitors; and Ms Anne Ware, partner of Kennedys Lawyers (whose feedback on the chapter entitled 'Defective Products' was highly insightful and helpful). I also wish to record my deep gratitude to Mr Justice Ross Cranston FBA, whose support and encouragement for the worth of the project was unwavering during the years that it has taken to complete. I am also grateful to the various anonymous reviewers who provided feedback on various chapters during the publishing process, and whose insights were very helpful. Finally, the careful production of the case table was primarily due to the unstinting efforts of Ms Holly Abbott, to whom I am deeply indebted. It goes without saying that any errors in either the manuscript, or in the preliminary tables, are solely my own.

Finally, I would like to convey my thanks to all the copyediting and typesetting team at Cambridge University Press and associated entities (especially Rachel Cox, Deborah Hey, and Preeti Saani) for providing valuable editorial and other assistance in order to bring this book to fruition.

The ongoing development of Tort law, particularly in case law, is inevitable and under constant review. To the best of my knowledge, the law is stated as at 31 July 2015, although some reference to later 2015 cases has been possible during the final preparation of the manuscript.

Rachael Mulheron

How to use this book

Print and online chapters

Principles of Tort Law is comprised of 28 chapters in total, 18 of which are print chapters and a further 10 of which are available as online chapters at the accompanying Online Torts Hub (available at www.Cambridge.org/Mulheron).

The print chapters focus upon those particular areas which tend to arise commonly in Torts curricula in England and Wales. In addition to a detailed consideration of the tort of Negligence, the print chapters also cover particular manifestations of negligence (*viz*, the Occupiers' Liability Act regimes, and the law associated with Public Authority liability) and some separate torts altogether (*viz*, Defamation, Private Nuisance, the Rule in *Rylands v Fletcher* and the torts encompassed by Trespass to the Person). Vicarious liability, a strict liability doctrine which forms an important part of the modern Torts curriculum, is also included as a print chapter.

The online chapters, on the other hand, deal with torts, or issues arising from Tort Law, which do not feature as commonly in Torts curricula, but which nevertheless may arise for student consideration from time to time. Of course, some Torts curricula do incorporate the study of particular manifestations of negligence, such as the statutory regimes enacted for defective products and for damage caused by animals, and also consider wider torts such as Public Nuisance, Privacy or the statutory tort of Harassment. The online chapters fully cater for that type of Torts curriculum. Additionally, the often tricky concepts associated with multiple defendants in Tort, and the issues to do with when a tortious cause of action 'accrues', limitation periods, and when a defendant's liability in tort ends, are also dealt with in the online chapters. The online content may also assist students who are studying aspects of Tort as part of other law modules (such as Media Law, Public Authorities and the Law, or Medical Negligence Law), or who are studying such issues for the purposes of mooting, writing research essays, legal advice clinic work and the like.

Occasionally, a section of a print chapter is excised from that chapter and is available online. For example, some of the categories of defendants for whom a duty of care has been a legal issue (e.g., barristers, parental liability for their children's negligence, parental liability to their children and regulators/inspectors/certifiers) are contained in Chapter 2 as online content only.

The system of principle numbering

The numbering of the print chapters follows sequentially throughout the book, from Chapter 1, 'The Role of Modern Tort Law', to Chapter 18, 'Vicarious Liability'. The online chapters appear in the Table of Contents – and for the convenience of readers, their content is also included in the Tables of Cases and Legislation.

The principles in the print chapters adopt the numbering of the particular chapter, so that each principle has a unique identifier. For example, for Chapter 8, 'Causation of Damage', the principles commence at §8.1, and follow sequentially throughout the chapter, until the final principle of that chapter, §8.34.

The principles in the online chapters adopt their numbering from an acronym of the particular chapter, so that, again, each principle has a unique identifier. For example, principle 12 in each of the online chapters is designated as follows: §DP.12, for the 'Defective Products' chapter; §AN.12, for the 'Liability for Animals' chapter; §EM.12, for the 'Employers' Liability' chapter; §SD.12, for the 'Breach of Statutory Duty' chapter; §HA.12, for the 'Statutory Tort of Harassment' chapter; §WD.12, for 'The Rule in *Wilkinson v Downton*' chapter; §PR.12, for the 'Privacy' chapter; §PU.12, for the 'Public Nuisance' chapter; §MD.12, for the 'Multiple Defendants' chapter; and §BE.12, for the 'Beginning and End of Liability' chapter.

Where, within a print chapter, a small section of the chapter is available online, the principles in that online-only section uses a separate referencing system, whereby the principle adopts the chapter number, but uses an alphabetical identifier. For example, as noted above, Chapter 2 is a print chapter, but contains some small sections of online content. For the first online section in that chapter concerning 'Barristers', the principle in that section is numbered as §2.A. The next online section in that chapter concerns 'Parental liability for their children's negligence', in which the relevant principles are numbered as §2.B and §2.C. The next online principle in Chapter 2 is under the section, 'Parental liability to their children', and is numbered as §2.D.

Hence, each principle in the book, whether contained in the print chapters or the online chapters, has a unique identifier which directs the reader to its precise location.

The system of page numbering

As mentioned above, the online chapters appear in the Table of Contents – and for the convenience of readers, their content is also included in the Tables of Cases and Legislation. The online content of the book is paginated sequentially from 1 to 476, as evident from the materials available at the accompanying Online Torts Hub.

Hence, in the Table of Contents, Table of Cases, Table of Legislation, and Index, an entry appearing at, say, p 20 of the print book will be designated merely as '20'; whereas an entry appearing at p 20 of the online part of the book will be designated as ◐ 20, to signify that it is to p 20 of the online content that a reader must refer.

Table of cases

The full citation of each case is locatable at the corresponding page reference which appears in the table below. Pages preceded by 🌐 indicate that the relevant case is locatable in the materials available at the Online Torts Hub (available at www.Cambridge.org/Mulheron).

Table of legislation

Pages preceded by indicate that the relevant statutory provision is locatable in the materials available at the Online Torts Hub (available at www.Cambridge.org/Mulheron).

ENGLAND AND WALES

Statutes

Rules of court

AUSTRALIA

STATE

Statutes

EUROPE

Directives

TREATY

JERSEY

NEW ZEALAND

NORTHERN IRELAND

SCOTLAND

UNITED STATES

INTERNATIONAL CONVENTIONS

Abbreviations

General

[10]	paragraph 10
10	page 10
AG	Attorney General
AHA	Area Health Authority
aka	also known as
Art, Arts	Article, Articles
Ass	Assurance
Assn	Association
Aus or Aust	Australian
BBC	British Broadcasting Corp
BC	Borough Council, or British Columbia (depending upon the context)
Bros	Brothers
CC	County Council, City Council, or Chief Constable (depending upon the context)
Civ	Civil
CN	Contributory negligence
Co	Company
Comm	Commission
Commr	Commissioner
Co-op	Co-operative
Corp	Corporation
CPS	Crown Prosecution Service
CP	Consultation Paper
dB	decibel/s
Dept	Department
DP	Discussion Paper
edn	Edition
Govt	Government
HA	Health Authority
HHJ	His/Her Honour Judge
HMP	Her Majesty's Prison
HMRC	Her Majesty's Revenue and Customs
Hosp	Hospital
Ins	Insurance
Intl	International
J	Justice
LBC	London Borough Council
Litig	Litigation
LJ	Law Journal or Lord Justice (depending upon the context)
LRC	Law Reform Commission
L Rev	Law Review
MBC	Metropolitan Borough Council
MC	Municipal Council
MOD	Ministry of Defence
MR	Master of the Rolls
NLJ	New Law Journal
NHS	National Health Service
P	President
PCC	Press Complaints Commission
PD	Practice Direction
pp	pinpoint
PSLA	damages for pain, suffering and loss of amenity
PTSD	post-traumatic stress disorder
r, rr	rule, rules
reg	regulation
RSC	Rules of the Supreme Court
Rwy	Railway
Sec	Secretary
Soc	Society
s, ss	section, sections
TC	Town Council
US	United States
WHO	World Health Organisation

Legislation

CPA	Consumer Protection Act 1987
CPR	Civil Procedure Rules 1998
ECHR	European Convention on Human Rights
FAA	Fatal Accidents Act 1976
HRA	Human Rights Act 1998
LR(MP) Act	Law Reform (Miscellaneous Provisions) Act 1934
OLA 1957	Occupiers' Liability Act 1957

OLA 1984 Occupiers' Liability Act 1984
UCTA Unfair Contract Terms Act 1977

Courts

ABCA Alberta Court of Appeal
ABQB, or Alta QB Alberta Court of Queen's Bench
ACTSC Australian Capital Territory Supreme Court
Alta SC App Div Alberta Supreme Court Appeal Division
Alta TD Alberta Trial Division
BCCA British Columbia Court of Appeal
BCSC British Columbia Supreme Court
CA Court of Appeal
Ch Chancery Court
Cal Sup Ct California Supreme Court
CSIH Scottish Court of Session (Inner House)
CSOH Scottish Court of Session (Outer House)
Div Ct High Court of Justice Divisional Court
ECJ European Court of Justice
ECtHR European Court of Human Rights
EWCA Civ England and Wales Court of Appeal (Civil Division)
EWHC England and Wales High Court
EW Misc England and Wales Courts – Miscellaneous (via Bailii)
Exch Ct Exchequer Court
FCA Federal Court of Australia
FCAFC Federal Court of Australia, Full Court
FJHC Fiji High Court
HCA High Court of Australia
HKCFA Hong Kong Court of Final Appeal
HKCFI Hong Kong Court of First Instance
HKDC Hong Kong District Court
HL House of Lords
IEHC High Court of Ireland
IESC Supreme Court of Ireland
INSC India Supreme Court
KB England and Wales High Court (King's Bench Division)
LRKB Law Reports, King's Bench
Man CA Manitoba Court of Appeal
MLJU Malaysia Federal Court of Appeal
MLJU(HC) High Court of Malaysia
NICA Northern Ireland Court of Appeal
NICh High Court of Justice, Northern Ireland, Chancery Division
NIQB High Court of Justice, Northern Ireland, Queen's Bench Division
NSWSC New South Wales Supreme Court
NSWCA New South Wales Court of Appeal
NTSC Northern Territory Supreme Court
NZCA New Zealand Court of Appeal
NZSC New Zealand Supreme Court
Ont SCJ Ontario Superior Court of Justice
PC Privy Council
QB England and Wales High Court (Queen's Bench Division)
QB (TCC) High Court of Justice, Queen's Bench Division, Technology and Construction Court
QCA Queensland Court of Appeal
QSC Queensland Supreme Court
SASC South Australian Supreme Court
SC Supreme Court (United Kingdom)
SCC Supreme Court of Canada
Scot CS Scottish Court of Sessions Decisions
SGHC Singapore High Court
SGCA Singapore Court of Appeal
Tas SC Tasmanian Supreme Court
UKEAT United Kingdom Employment Appeals Tribunal
UKFTT United Kingdom First Tier Tribunal (Tax Chamber)
UKHL United Kingdom House of Lords
UKPC United Kingdom Privy Council
UKSC United Kingdom Supreme Court
Ves Sen Vesey Senior's Chancery Reports
Vic SC Victorian Supreme Court
Vic CA Victorian Court of Appeal
WADC Western Australian District Court
WASC Western Australia Supreme Court
WASCA Western Australia Supreme Court, Court of Appeal
ZASCA South African Supreme Court, Court of Appeal

Law Reports

A 2d Atlantic Reporter, Second Series (United States)
AC Law Reports, Appeal Cases (Third Series)
ACD Administrative Court Digest
ACWS (3d) All Canada Weekly Summaries, Third Series

AER All England Law Reports
All ER All England Law Reports
All ER(D) All England Direct Law Reports (Digests)
All ER Rep Ext All England Law Reports Reprint Australian Extension Volumes
ALJR Australian Law Journal Reports
ALR Australian Law Reports
App Cas Law Reports, Appeal Cases (Second Series)
AR Alberta Reports
ATR Australian Tax Reports
B & Ad Barnewall and Adolphus' King's Bench Reports
B & C Barnewall and Cresswell's King's Bench Reports
BCC British Company Law Cases
BCLC Butterworths Company Law Cases
Bing Bingham's Common Pleas Reports
Bing NC Bingham's New Cases, English Common Pleas
BLR Building Law Reports
BMLR Butterworths Medico-Legal Reports
B & S Best and Smith's Queen's Bench Reports
Burr Burrows King's Bench Reports (tempore Mansfield)
C & L Connor and Lawson's Irish Chancery Reports
Cal 3d Californian Reports (Third Series)
Cal Rptr Californian Reporter
Camp Campbell's Nisi Prius Cases
Car and P, or C & P Carrington and Payne's Nisi Prius Reports
CB (NS) Common Bench Reports, New Series
CCL Rep Community Care Law Reports
CCLT Canadian Cases on the Law of Torts
Ch Law Reports, Chancery Division (3rd Series)
CL Current Law Monthly Digest (UK)
CLC CCH Commercial Law Cases
CLR Commonwealth Law Reports
CLY Current Law Yearbook
CMLR Common Market Law Reports
CM & R Crompton, Messon and Roscoe's Exchequer Reports
Co Rep Coke's King's Bench Reports
Con LR Construction Law Reports
Cr & M Crompton and Meeson's Exchequer Reports
Cr App R Criminal Appeal Reports
Dears Dearsley's Crown Cases Reserved
Dears & B Dearsley and Bell's Crown Cases Reserved
De G & Sm De Gex and Smale's Chancery Reports
Dick Dickens Chancery Reports
DLR Dominion Law Reports
E & B Ellis and Blackburn's Queen's Bench Reports
Ed CR Education Case Reports
EGLR Estates Gazette Law Reports
EHRR European Human Rights Reports
ELR Education Law Reports
EMLR Entertainment and Media Law Reports
Env LR Environmental Law Reports
ER English Reports
Ex, or Ct Exch Law Reports, Exchequer Division
F 2d Federal Reporter, Second Series
F & F Foster and Finlayson's Nisi Prius Reports
Fam Law Reports, Family Division
FCR Butterworths Family Court Reports
FLR Family Law Reports (England and Wales)
FSR Fleet Street Reports
Hare Hare's Chancery Reports
HLC (Clark's) Clark and Finnelly's House of Lords Reports, New Series
HLR Housing Law Reports
H & C Hurlstone & Coltman's Exchequer Reports
Hurl & N, or H&N Hurlstone & Norman's Exchequer Reports
H & Tw Hall and Twell's Chancery Reports
ICR Industrial Court Reports
IR, or Ir R Irish Reports
Ir Jur Rep Irish Jurist Reports
IRLR Industrial Relations Law Reports
JP Justice of the Peace Reports
KB Law Reports, King's Bench
KIR Knight's Industrial Reports
LD Raym Lord Raymond's King's Bench and Common Pleas Reports
LGR Local Government Reports
LJCP Law Journal Reports, Common Pleas New Series
LJQB Law Journal Reports, Queen's Bench New Series

Lloyd's Rep	Lloyd's Law Reports
Lloyd's Rep Med	Lloyd's Law Reports (Medical)
Lloyd's Rep PN	Lloyd's Law Reports (Professional Negligence)
Lofft	Lofft's King's Bench Reports
LR	Law Reports (First Series)
LRCP	Law Reports, Common Pleas
LR Eq	Law Reports, Equity Cases
LR Ex	Law Reports, Exchequer Cases
LRKB	Law Reports King's Bench
LT Rep	Law Times Reports (England and Wales)
L & TR	Landlord and Tenant Reports
M & S	Maule and Selwyn's King's Bench Reports
M & W	Meeson and Welsby's Exchequer Reports (England and Wales)
Med LR	Medical Law Reports
Mod	Modern Reports (England and Wales)
NBR	New Brunswick Reports
NE	North Eastern Reporter
NI	Northern Ireland Law Reports
NJ Super	New Jersey Supreme Court Reports
NPC	New Property Cases
NY	New York Reports
NYS	New York Supplement
NZAR	New Zealand Administrative Reports
NZLR	New Zealand Law Reports
OAC	Ontario Appeal Cases
OR	Ontario Reports
P 2d	Pacific Reporter (Second Series) (United States)
P	Law Reports, Probate
PD	Law Reports, Probate, Divorce and Admiralty Division
P 2d	Pacific Reporter, Second Series
PIQR	Personal Injuries and Quantum Reports
PNLR	Professional Negligence and Liability Reports
PTSR	The Public and Third Sector Reports
QB	Law Reports, Queen's Bench (3rd Series)
Qd R	Queensland Reports
RPC	Reports of Patent, Design and Trade Mark Cases
RTR	Road Traffic Reports
SA	South African Law Reports
SASR	South Australian State Reports
SC	Session Cases (Scotland)
SC(HL)	Session Cases, House of Lords (Scotland)
SCLR	Scottish Civil Law Reports
Scot CS	Scottish Court of Session Decisions
SCR	Supreme Court Reports (Canada)
SJLB	Solicitors' Journal Law Brief (UK)
SLT	Scots Law Times
SR(NSW)	New South Wales State Reports
Taunt	Taunton's Common Pleas Reports
TCLR	Technology and Construction Law Reports
TLR	Times Law Reports
VLR	Victorian Law Reports
VR	Victorian Reports
Wils KB	Wilson's King's Bench and Common Pleas Reports
WLR	Weekly Law Reports
WN	Weekly Notes of Cases
WTLR	Wills and Trusts Law Reports
WWR	Western Weekly Reports

Notes on mode of citation

1. In each case citation, the court is referred to in parentheses in all instances where it is not obvious from the report series or mode of citation which court made the decision. Neutral citations have been used wherever available.
2. The expression 'English law' should be understood to include the law of Wales (unless indicated otherwise).
3. Throughout this book, 'C' denotes 'claimant'; and 'D' denotes 'defendant'; and the plural of each is denoted by 'Cs' and 'Ds', respectively.
4. Throughout this book, the masculine personal pronoun is used, for the sake of convenience and, as and where appropriate, should be taken to denote the feminine pronoun.
5. The scholarship and opinion of many entities (including law reform commissions) and persons are referenced throughout this book. All reasonable efforts have been made to reference and to pinpoint as accurately and fulsomely as possible. It should be noted that wherever quotations appear, and in the interests of brevity, footnotes within those quotations have not been reproduced, and the conventional usage of 'footnotes omitted' should be assumed throughout.
6. Wherever available, paragraph numbers are used as pinpoints in preference to page numbers.

1

The role of modern Tort law

WHAT IS A TORT?

§1.1 A tort is a wrongful act or omission, for which compensation or other remedy can be awarded to C (the claimant, or the person aggrieved) against D (the defendant, or tortfeasor). The corpus of Tort law, in general, excludes wrongs which are remediable as a breach of contract (albeit that some claims may give rise to concurrent liability in contract and in tort), a crime (albeit that occasionally a tort may also be a crime), an equitable cause of action, or a restitutionary cause of action.

The word 'tort' is derived from the Old French, *tortus*, meaning 'twisted' or 'crooked', and from the medieval Latin, *tortum*, meaning 'wrong' or 'injustice'.[1] Hence, the definition above aptly conveys that a great many causes of action fit under the Tort law 'umbrella'.

The corollary is that any shared or common characteristics among the torts – apart from the fact that all are claims for which damages are obtainable in a civil court – are nigh to impossible to identify. Indeed, it is a motley bunch of causes of action which fall within English Tort law!

The range of modern torts in English law

§1.2 There are at least 33 different torts which are recognised in English law.

The following Table provides an alphabetical list of those torts which, so far as the author's searches can ascertain, represent currently-recognised torts in the English jurisdiction. Each tort is either defined (with reference to a relatively recent authority in which the tort is discussed) or is referenced to detailed analysis elsewhere in this book:

[1] *Oxford Dictionary of English* (2nd edn, revised, 2006) 1862. See too *Oxford Dictionary of Law* (6th edn, 2006) 537; and J Penner, *The Law Student's Dictionary* (Oxford University Press, 2008) 292.

	The tort	Nutshell definition (or chapter treatment)
1	Abuse of judicial process	Originating in *Grainger v Hill* (1838), the tort requires that: D brings legal process principally for an improper, collateral, or ulterior purpose; and where the improper use to which the process was applied causes C damage (see, e.g., *Land Securities plc v Fladgate Fielder (a firm)*[a] and *Crawford Adjusters v Sagicor General Insurance (Cayman) Ltd*[b])
2	Assault	See Chapter 14, and the definition at §14.3 and §14.9
3	Battery	See Chapter 14, and the definition at §14.3 and §14.4
4	Breach of statutory duty	See 'Breach of statutory duty' (an online chapter), and the definition at §SD.1
5	Causing loss by unlawful means	The tort requires that: D interferes with the liberty of others; D's interference was intentional; D's interference was via unlawful means; and the interference with others (e.g., customers) causes C damage (see, e.g., *OBG Ltd v Allan; Douglas v Hello! Ltd*[c]). The unlawful means does not require any actual threat on D's part, thereby distinguishing the tort from that of Intimidation; and there is no need for a contract between C and the other party, thereby distinguishing the tort from Inducing Breach of Contract, and Interference with Contractual Relations
6	Champerty	The tort (now abolished as a tort in England, although it can still render a contract void as being contrary to public policy) requires that: D supports C's legal action in which D has no legitimate concern, without just cause or excuse; and contracts for a share of the proceeds of C's action or for some other pecuniary benefit if the action succeeds (see, e.g., *R (Factortame Ltd) v Sec of State for Transport, Local Govt and the Regions (No 8)*[d])
7	Conspiracy to injure	The tort requires: an agreement between two or more persons (Ds, the conspirators) to commit an act or omission with the intent of causing damage to C's trade or reputation; D's act or omission is *either* unlawful in nature (known as 'unlawful means conspiracy') *or* lawful in nature but where D had the sole or predominant purpose of injuring C (known as 'lawful means conspiracy'); and C suffers damage as a result of the conspirators' act or omission. The tort does not enable recovery for injury to C's reputation or injury to feelings, but is primarily directed to the recovery of financial loss (see, e.g., *Total Network SL v HMRC*[e] and *Aerostar Maintenance v Wilson*[f]). Conspirators can join the agreement at different times (per *QBE Management Services (UK) Ltd v Dymoke*[g])

[a] [2009] EWCA Civ 1402, [2010] 1 Ch 467. Although there was much debate as to whether such a tort existed in England ('the last reported successful action in this jurisdiction for the tort abuse of process was either about 140 or 170 years ago': at [41]), all CA members affirmed that it existed in limited form.

[b] [2013] UKPC 17, [2014] 1 AC 366.

[c] [2007] UKHL 21, [2008] 1 AC 1, [6]–[8], [45]–[64] (Lord Hoffmann).

[d] [2002] EWCA Civ 932, [2003] QB 381, [32] (Lord Phillips MR). See too: s 14(1), (2) of the Criminal Law Act 1967 (discussed in: Mulheron and Cashman, 'Third Party Funding of Litigation: A Changing Landscape' (2008) 27 *Civil Justice Quarterly* 312, 318–19; and *Code of Conduct for Litigation Funders* (Jan 2014).

[e] [2008] UKHL 19, [2008] 1 AC 1174.

[f] [2010] EWHC 2032 (Ch).

[g] [2012] EWHC 80 (QB) [198].

	The tort	Nutshell definition (or chapter treatment)
8	Conversion (aka trover, its ancient description[h])	The tort requires that: D's dealings with goods (e.g., depriving C of their possession) were inconsistent with C's rights, where C owned, possessed, or was entitled to immediate possession of the goods; D's conduct was intentional and not accidental; and D's conduct was sufficient to exclude C from being able to use and/or possess the goods (see, e.g., *Kuwait Airways Corp v Iraqi Airways Co (Nos 4 and 5)*[i] and *Glenbrook Capital LP v Hamilton*[j])
9	Defamation	See Chapter 15, and the definition at §15.1 and §15.2
10	Deceit (aka fraudulent misrepresentation)	The tort requires: a false (fraudulent) representation by D, which D either knows to be untrue or is recklessly indifferent as to whether it is true; D intended that C should act in reliance on the false representation; C, in fact, relied on the representation; and C suffered loss (see, e.g., *VTB Capital plc v Nutritek Intl Corp*[k] and *Derry v Peek*[l])
11	False imprisonment	See Chapter 14, and the definition at §14.13
12	Harassment	A statutory tort, created by the Protection from Harassment Act 1997. See 'The Statutory Tort of Harassment' (online), and the definition at §HA.1
13	Inducing (or procuring) breach of contract (aka the tort in *Lumley v Gye*[m])	The tort requires that: X commits an actionable breach of his contract with the other contracting party, C; D's conduct procured X to commit that breach of contract; D intended to induce X to breach his contract with C, or was recklessly indifferent (i.e., 'turned a blind eye') as to whether it was breached; D knew or foresaw that the conduct which was being induced would result in a breach of X and C's contract; and C suffered loss (see, e.g., *OBG Ltd v Allan; Douglas v Hello! Ltd*[n])
14	Interference with another's contractual relations	The tort requires that: D prevented or hindered X's performance of his contract with the other contracting party, C; D procured X to prevent/hinder the performance of his contract with C; D intended to induce X to hinder/prevent his contract with C, or was recklessly indifferent as to whether or not it was so; and C suffered loss (see, e.g., *OBG Ltd v Allan; Douglas v Hello! Ltd*[o]). D can be liable, even without the contracting party, X, actually committing an actionable breach of contract (distinguishing the tort from Inducing breach of contract)

[h] Also encompassed, statutorily, in the Torts (Interference with Goods) Act 1977, s 1(a).
[i] [2002] UKHL 19, [2002] 2 AC 883, especially [37]–[44] (Lord Nicholls).
[j] [2014] EWHC 2297 (Comm).
[k] [2012] EWCA Civ 808.
[l] (1889) LR 14 App Cas 337 (HL).
[m] (1853) 2 E&B 216.
[n] [2007] UKHL 21, [2008] 1 AC 1, [3]–[5], [39]–[44] (Lord Hoffmann).
[o] [2005] EWCA Civ 106, [2005] QB 762, and not discussed in detail on appeal, *ibid*.

	The tort	Nutshell definition (or chapter treatment)
15	Intentional infliction of mental distress or physical harm (aka the rule in *Wilkinson v Downton*)	See 'The Rule in *Wilkinson v Downton*' (online), and the definition at §WD.1
16	Intimidation	The tort requires: a threat made by D to do something unlawful or 'illegitimate'; which can take the form of *either* a threat to C that, unless C acts in a certain way, D will act impermissibly against C *or* a threat to X that, unless X acts in a certain way towards C, D will act impermissibly towards X; D's threat was intended to coerce C to take, or refrain from taking, some course of action; the threat did coerce C to take that action; and C suffered loss (see, e.g., *Berezovsky v Abramovich*[p])
17	Libel	See Chapter 15 (Defamation), and the definition at §15.2
18	Maintenance	The tort (now abolished as a tort in England, although it can still render a contract void as being contrary to public policy) requires that: D 'supports litigation, in which he has no legitimate concern, without just cause or excuse' (see, e.g., *R (Factortame Ltd) v Sec of State for Transport, Local Govt and the Regions (No 8)*,[q] and involves the notion of 'improperly stirring up litigation and strife by giving aid to one party to bring or defend a claim' (see, e.g., *Trepca Mines Ltd (No 2)*[r])
19	Malicious falsehood (aka injurious falsehood)	The tort requires that: D published false allegations about C; *either* knowing them to be false *or* being indifferent as to their truth or falsity; D published the information with malice; and C suffered loss (per *Friend v Civil Aviation Authy*,[s] and *Cornwall Gardens Ltd v RO Garrard & Co Ltd*[t]). It is not necessary that C suffers any loss of reputation; the tort is focused primarily upon C's economic or commercial interests (e.g., where D dishonestly tells C's customers that C has ceased trading (per *Gregory v Portsmouth CC*[u])). The tort may sometimes duplicate the tort of Defamation (per *Reachlocal UK Ltd v Bennett*[v])

[p] [2011] EWCA Civ 153, [2011] 1 WLR 2290, [5]; and earlier: [2010] EWHC 647 (Comm) [128].
[q] [2002] EWCA Civ 932, [2003] QB 381, [32] (Lord Phillips MR). See too: s 14(1), (2) of the Criminal Law Act 1967 (discussed in: Mulheron and Cashman, 'Third Party Funding of Litigation: A Changing Landscape' (2008) 27 *Civil Justice Quarterly* 312, 318–19.
[r] [1963] Ch 199 (CA) 219.
[s] [2005] EWHC 201 (QB) [235] (Eady J).
[t] [2001] EWCA Civ 699, [2002] 1 WLR 713.
[u] [2000] UKHL 3, [2000] AC 419.
[v] [2014] EWHC 3405 (QB) [65].

	The tort	Nutshell definition (or chapter treatment)
20	Malicious procurement of a search warrant	The tort requires: a successful application for a search warrant by D; a lack of reasonable and probable cause to make the application; *either* D knew that he had no power to apply for the warrant and that it would probably injure C, *or* D was recklessly indifferent as to whether that act would injure C; and C suffered loss or damage as a consequence of the issue or execution of the warrant (see, e.g., *Keegan v CC of Merseyside*[w] and *Crawford v Jenkins*[x]). The tort also extends to the malicious presentation of a bankruptcy petition or a winding-up petition
21	Malicious prosecution (aka injurious prosecution)	The tort requires: *either* a criminal *or* a civil claim was brought by D against C maliciously and in the absence of reasonable and probable cause; the proceedings ended in C's favour; D acted with malice in instituting the claim; C suffered loss or damage (e.g., damage to his reputation, if the matter is scandalous; damage to his person, if he is imprisoned; or damage to his property, if he is put to charges and expenses) (see, e.g., *Crawford Adjusters (Cayman) Ltd v Sagicor General Ins (Cayman) Ltd*,[y] and *Land Securities plc v Fladgate Fielder (a firm)*[z]). The prosecution is usually for a criminal charge, but the tort of maliciously bringing civil proceedings is also recognised
22	Misfeasance in public office	The tort requires that: D, a public officer, purported to exercise some power or authority; *either* D knew that his disregard of his duty would injure C *or* was recklessly indifferent to the consequences for C; D's exercise of power or authority was done with malice or dishonestly or 'in bad faith'; and C suffered loss (see, e.g., *Three Rivers DC v Governor of Bank of England*[aa] and *N v Sec of State for the Home Dept*[bb])
23	Misuse of private information (Privacy)	See 'Privacy' (online), and the definition at §PR.1
24	Negligence	See Chapter 2, and the nutshell analysis above at §2.1
25	Negligent misstatement	See Chapter 4, and the definition at §4.3

[w] [2003] EWCA Civ 936, [2003] 1 WLR 2187, [13], citing: *Gibbs v Rea* [1998] AC 786 (HL). Subsequently applied in: *Fitzpatrick v Commr of Police* [2012] EWHC 12.
[x] [2014] EWCA Civ 1035, [48].
[y] [2013] UKPC 17, [2014] AC 366.
[z] [2009] EWCA Civ 1402, [2010] 1 Ch 467, [67], [100], [110]. See earlier: *Gregory v Portsmouth CC* [2000] UKHL 3, [2000] AC 419 (especially Lord Steyn, 'The extension of the tort to civil proceedings').
[aa] [2000] UKHL 33, [2000] 2 WLR 1220.
[bb] [2014] EWHC 3304 (QB).

	The tort	Nutshell definition (or chapter treatment)
26	Passing-off	The tort requires that: D conducts his business on the basis that it misleads the public to believe that D's goods and/or services are those of C's business; at the time of the acts complained of, C had a significant reputation or goodwill; and D's acts gave rise to a false message which would be understood, by a not insignificant section of his market, that his goods have been endorsed, recommended or approved by C (see, e.g., *Irvine v Talksport Ltd*,[cc] and *Cranford Community College v Cranford College Ltd*[dd]). It is not necessary to prove that D intended to deceive; innocent passing-off is actionable as a tort
27	Private nuisance	See Chapter 16, and the definition at §16.1
28	Public nuisance	See 'Public Nuisance' (online), and the definition at §PU.1
29	*Rylands v Fletcher*, the rule in	See Chapter 17, and the definition at §17.1
30	*Scienter*, action for	This tort is now replaced as described in 'Liability for animals' (online), and the text under §AN.1
31	Slander	See Chapter 15 and the definition at §15.2
32	Trespass to chattels	The tort requires: a direct and immediate interference by D with goods; where those goods were in the possession of C at the time of the interference; and where the act of interference can constitute touching, handling, damaging or removing those goods; without C's permission or licence (see, e.g., *White v Withers LLP*[ee])
33	Trespass to land	The tort requires: D entered land without permission, or remained on that land which was entered into with permission following the withdrawal of that permission, and a reasonable opportunity to leave the land has passed; the land was owned by, or in the exclusive possession of, C; and D's entry, or remaining there, was intentional, negligent or innocent (see, e.g., *Monsanto plc v Tilly*[ff])

[cc] [2002] EWCA Civ 423.
[dd] [2014] EWHC 2999 (IPEC).
[ee] [2009] EWCA Civ 1122, [2009] 3 FCR 435, [44]–[50].
[ff] [1999] EWCA Civ 3044, [2000] Env LR 313.

There are some causes of action, ostensibly tortious,[2] which do **not** appear in the abovementioned Table, and the reasons for their exclusion are noted below:

[2] Not 'tortuous', even though the claims may feel to be just that by the litigants and their lawyers! This inaccuracy occasionally turns up even in law reports, e.g., *Watkins v Home Office* [2006] UKHL 17, [32].

	The 'non-tort'	Why it is excluded
a.	Breach of confidence	Although sometimes called a tort (e.g., in *Venables v NGN Ltd*[a]), this cause of action was developed by the Courts of Chancery during the 18th and 19th centuries, and modern appellate decisions have referred to it (correctly) as an *equitable* cause of action (see, e.g., *Tchenguiz v Imerman (Rev 4)*,[b] and *Wainwright v Home Office*[c])
b.	Detinue	This tort was abolished by the Torts (Interference with Goods) Act 1977. Detinue was proven where there was a wrongful detention of goods by the possessor of those goods, D, after C, their rightful owner, lawfully requested their return. The 1977 Act now governs that right of recovery[d]
c.	Wrongful interference with a body	English law does not currently recognise the tort of wrongful interference with a body (where D removes and retains organs from a child's body without knowledge or consent of the parent) (per *AB v Leeds Teaching Hosp NHS Trust*[e])
d.	Conversion of contractual rights	English law does not recognise a tort of conversion of contractual rights (e.g., where a receiver is invalidly appointed and wrongfully takes control of a company's, C's, contractual rights and business) – because there can be no conversion of intangible choses in action (per *OBG Ltd v Allan*[f])

[a] [2001] EWHC QB 32, [2001] 2 WLR 1038, [7] (President Elizabeth Butler-Sloss). Also, e.g.: *Campbell v MGN Ltd* [2002] EWCA Civ 1373, [2003] QB 633, [69] (Lord Phillips MR).
[b] [2010] EWCA Civ 908, [2011] 2 WLR 592, [74] ('A claim based on confidentiality is an equitable claim. Accordingly, the normal equitable rules apply': Lord Neuberger MR, writing for the court).
[c] [2003] UKHL 53, [2004] 2 AC 406, [18] (an 'equitable action for breach of confidence': per Lord Bingham).
[d] See s 2(1), subject to the following saving provision in s 2(2): 'An action lies in conversion for loss or destruction of goods which a bailee has allowed to happen in breach of his duty to his bailor (that is to say it lies in a case which is not otherwise conversion, but would have been detinue before detinue was abolished)'.
[e] [2004] EWHC 644 (QB), [2005] 2 WLR 358, [161] (Gage J).
[f] [2005] EWCA Civ 106, [2005] QB 762, [49]–[58].

Finally, as a matter of terminology, some so-called torts are merely generic, or compendious, terms for a 'bunch' of individual torts. To clarify:

This is not a tort *per se* ...	... but a generic term by which to describe other torts ...
Trespass to the person	... a series of common law torts whose purpose is to protect against violations of C's person, *viz*: assault; battery; and false imprisonment. See Chapter 14.
Wrongful interference with goods	... certain common law torts (*viz*, conversion, and trespass to chattels), and statutory torts (to the extent that the Torts (Interference with Goods) Act 1977 preserves a cause of action which would have operated in detinue).

Disparities among the torts

§1.3 There are numerous disparities across the torts, such that a common or shared characteristic among them is virtually impossible to identify.

This section highlights **ten (10)** disparities across the torts arising in English law:

i. Actionable *per se* versus proof of damage. For those torts which have, as their principal aim, the protection or vindication of C's rights, they are actionable without proof of damage. Trespasses to the person (assault, battery and false imprisonment), and wrongful interferences with goods (trespass to chattels, and conversion), fall into that category. However, for torts where compensation is the primary purpose, the tort will not be actionable unless there is some proof of compensable damage – negligence, the tort in *Wilkinson v Downton*, private nuisance, and the rule in *Rylands v Fletcher*, are examples of the latter category.

ii. Strict liability versus fault. For some torts, it is irrelevant if D was 'at fault', or whether D exercised reasonable (or even the utmost) care to avoid the harm to C. D will be strictly liable in tort, regardless. These torts include: the rule in *Rylands v Fletcher*, liability for defective products under the Consumer Protection Act 1987; defamation; and in some cases of breach of statutory duty. For the majority of torts, however (e.g., negligence; trespasses to the person such as assault, battery and false imprisonment; and private nuisance), some proof of fault or wrongdoing will be required.

iii. Intentional versus non-intentional conduct. Some torts require proof of intentional conduct, which may include a reckless indifference on D's part (e.g., the rule in *Wilkinson v Downton*, and trespasses to the persons, generally fall within this category, although, exceptionally, negligent conduct may be sufficient for battery). For other torts, intentional conduct is not required. For example, in negligence, and public or private nuisance, then careless, or even careful, conduct, respectively – which is not intended to harm C at all – is sufficient to make out the causes of action.

iv. The type of interests protected. The main purpose of the tort of negligence is to protect against damage to the person, property, or economic interests, of C. However, some causes of action protect different interests entirely. For example: defamation serves to protect the reputation of individuals or entities; trespasses to the person (assault, battery and false imprisonment), and the rule in *Wilkinson v Downton*, aim to protect personal bodily integrity; the torts such as passing-off, conspiracy to injure, intimidation; the rule in *Rylands v Fletcher*, and private nuisance primarily serve to protect C's economic or commercial, interests; and the protection of C's interest in personal property is addressed by torts such as conversion, and trespass to chattels.

v. C's personal culpability as a defence differs. For some torts, the careless or wrongful conduct of C constitutes a (partial) defence to the tort (e.g., the defence of contributory negligence is available in a claim for negligence as a matter of statutory law, via the Law Reform (Contributory Negligence) Act 1945). For other torts, however, any culpability on C's part is not a defence, or, at least, it is very doubtful, on current authority, whether a defence can be made out (as, e.g., for assault and battery).

vi. Availability of remedies differs. Remedies across the torts are not uniform either. For most torts, the appropriate remedy is that of damages (whether compensatory, aggravated, exemplary, or restitutionary – although the availability of these types of damages has not been confirmed across all torts). For limited torts, however (e.g., private nuisance, or trespass to land), self-help remedies are also available (i.e., abatement of the nuisance, or ejection of the trespasser, respectively), permitting C to protect his rights without recourse to judicial determination.

vii. Some torts are crimes, but most are not. Trespass to land is a tort, but is not usually a crime (unless exceptional circumstances apply, such as trespassing on diplomatic or consular premises), and hence, any sign, '*Trespassers will be prosecuted*', is commonly misleading, if no criminal prosecution is possible.[3] Some torts, however, are commonly crimes too (e.g., assault, battery, public nuisance and dangerous driving arising from negligent conduct), which can give rise to prosecution of D by the State.

viii. Standing to sue. Some torts restrict standing, by reference to C's proprietary or possessory rights. For example, for private nuisance, and the rule in *Rylands v Fletcher*, the claim is only capable of being brought if C has proprietary rights or exclusive occupation of the land upon which the interference occurred. For other torts, however (e.g., negligence, trespass to the person, the rule in *Wilkinson v Downton*), proprietary rights are irrelevant in establishing standing to sue.

ix. Source of the law. Some torts are vested in, or defined by, statute, and hence, are properly considered to be statutory torts. For example, the tort of harassment arises from the Protection from Harassment Act 1997; and the law of occupiers' liability, regarding liability towards lawful entrants or towards trespassers, is governed by the Occupiers' Liability Act 1957 and the Occupiers' Liability Act 1984, respectively. For most torts, however, they are sourced to judicial decision-making in case law.

x. Limitation periods. The period in which C may maintain an action in tort varies considerably. The general rule is that, by virtue of s 2 of the Limitation Act 1980, an action founded on a tort may not be brought after the expiration of six years from the date on which the cause of action accrued. However, that general rule is overridden by numerous other provisions, which impose different limitation periods for specific torts. Limitation periods are discussed in 'The beginning and end of liability' (an online chapter). For example, the variation can be briefly illustrated as follows: for an action for negligence, nuisance, or breach of statutory duty, which consists of, or includes, damages for personal injuries to C or to any person, the limitation period is three years; for defamation (whether libel or slander), the limitation period is only one year; and an action under the Protection from Harassment Act 1997 is permitted six years. Many law reform commissions have criticised the lack of uniformity of limitation periods in Tort law. The Alberta Law Reform Institute, for example, remarked that 'there is neither a sound theoretical nor practical foundation for the practice of assigning different fixed limitation periods to different categories of claim'.[4] Nevertheless, differing limitation periods remain the reality for the English landscape.

THE PURPOSES OF TORT LAW

§1.4 The are *seven* judicially-identified purposes of Tort law, the principal one of which is to provide compensation to C as a victim of the civil wrong committed by D against C, for the harm or damage suffered as a consequence of that civil wrong.

[3] Noted, e.g., in: *Oxford Dictionary of Law* (6th edn, Oxford University Press, 2006) 546.

[4] *Limitations* (DP 4, 1986) [2.63], and also cited in Irish LRC, *Limitation of Actions* (Rep 104, 2011) [2.02].

The purposes outlined below may be singly, or (sometimes) concurrently, evident in any one piece of Tort litigation. In other cases, the purposes may clash, and pull in different directions. However, in combination, they provide the basic reasoning as to why the subject has occupied an extremely important part of common law legal systems around the world.

i. Compensatory function. The compensatory function of Tort law has frequently been judicially acknowledged. For example, in *Devenish Nutrition Ltd v Sanofi-Aventis SA (France) (Rev 1)*, Arden LJ remarked, '[t]he aim of the law of tort is to compensate for loss suffered';[5] whilst in *Gregg v Scott*, Baroness Hale observed that, '[t]ort law is not criminal law. The criminal law is there to punish and deter those who do not behave as they should. Tort law is there to compensate those who have been wronged, [although] some wrongs are actionable whether or not the claimant has been damaged'.[6]

However, that cannot be its only function. Indeed, in *Smith New Court v Citibank*,[7] Lord Steyn observed that any view that the 'the sole purpose of the law of tort generally ... should be to compensate the victims of civil wrongs' was 'far too narrow'. In that particular case (which concerned the tort of deceit), the deterrent function also had an important role to play (as discussed below).

The 'compensatory' function of Tort law must be qualified in two respects. First, it is usually (but not always) met by an award of compensatory damages – assessed so as to put the victim, C, in the position in which he was placed before the tort was committed by the tortfeasor, D (insofar as money can do so). However, other awards of damages, where appropriate for the tort in issue, will also satisfy the 'compensatory' function. These include: ***restitutionary*** damages (where the purpose of the award is to strip D of his profit or to cause the reversal of a benefit conferred by C); ***user*** damages (where the purpose of the award is to assess the fair value of a right of which D's tortious conduct has wrongly deprived C, even if C would not have sought to use that right and so incurred no loss); ***aggravated*** damages (where the purpose of the award is to compensate C where the tortious conduct of D, or the circumstances surrounding the commission of the tort, subjected C to humiliation, distress or embarrassment); and even ***nominal*** damages (where C has not suffered any damage from the wrong committed by D, but nevertheless the award denotes that a legal right has been infringed).

Secondly, the victim of a tort is, invariably, **not** compensated for the entirety of his grievances. Some heads of damage are simply unavailable (e.g., damages for mere distress are not awardable in some Torts); some have been abolished altogether (e.g., damages for loss of consortium – the right of one spouse to the company, assistance and affection of the other – were abolished by the Administration of Justice Act 1982); and for some heads of general damage, the quantum may be either stipulated by pre-set awards or capped by statute (as discussed in Chapter 11). Hence, full compensation is not necessarily the aim of Tort law.

ii. Deterrent function. The fact that Tort law accommodates an award of exemplary damages – albeit in limited circumstances, and only where D's conduct deserves to be punished because it is egregious and worthy of condemnation – confirms that this strand of civil liability endorses a deterrent function.

[5] [2008] EWCA Civ 1086, [2009] Ch 390, [2]. [6] [2005] UKHL 2, [2005] 2 AC 176, [217].
[7] [1997] AC 254 (HL) 279–80.

That an award of compensatory damages may also fulfil a deterrent function accords with senior English judicial views, thereby acknowledging that deterrence is not exclusively the province of the criminal law. For example, in *Cassell & Co Ltd v Broome (No 1)*,[8] Lord Kilbrandon noted that compensatory damages, especially 'very large compensatory damages', carry an adequate deterrent function of themselves. Further, according to *Rookes v Barnard*, 'if, and only if, the amount [of compensatory damages] is inadequate to punish [D] for his outrageous conduct, to mark the disapproval of such conduct and to deter [D] from repeating it' can exemplary damages be awarded – thereby acknowledging that compensatory awards may have, themselves, some capacity to punish.[9]

Subsequently, in *Gleaner Co Ltd v Abrahams (Jamaica)*, the Privy Council approved of the 'orthodox view of the dual function of compensatory damages', so that 'compensatory damages may also have a punitive, deterrent or exemplary function', but that '[w]hat distinguishes exemplary damages ... is that they do not have a compensatory function'.[10]

iii. Striking a balance between competing rights. Another principal purpose of Tort law is to allocate responsibility for the obligations which one person owes to another; and to protect the rights that one person is permitted to assert against another – a disarmingly bland statement which belies the difficulties/conflicts which arise in practice and which is the role of Tort law to resolve. The problem was no better explained than by Lord Scott in *Ashley v CC of Sussex Police*:

> the civil law, in particular the law of tort, must strike a balance between conflicting rights. Thus, for instance, the right of freedom of expression may conflict with the right of others not to be defamed. The rules and principles of the tort of ***defamation*** must strike the balance. The right not to be physically harmed by the actions of another may conflict with the rights of other people to engage in activities involving the possibility of accidentally causing harm. The balance between these conflicting rights must be struck by the rules and principles of the tort of ***negligence***. As to ***assault and battery*** and self-defence, every person has the right in principle not to be subjected to physical harm by the intentional actions of another person. But every person has the right also to protect himself by using reasonable force to repel an attack or to prevent an imminent attack.[11]

iv. Public vindication. Public enquiries or investigations of what happened to C, at the hands of D, are typically undertaken via one of three means: criminal trials, coronial inquests and a formal public enquiry. Can a tortious cause of action fulfil that role too? Is that a legitimate purpose of Tort law?

In *Ashley v CC of Sussex Police*,[12] the House of Lords (by majority) held that it could. C was entitled to proceed with the claim for battery and assault, in that case, for 'vindicatory purposes', even if no damages could be awarded, due to a prior concession on damages by the police. Lord Scott commented that, '[a]lthough the principal aim of an award of compensatory damages is to compensate [C] for loss suffered, there is no reason in principle why an award of compensatory damages should not also fulfil a vindicatory purpose ... They want a finding of liability on their assault and battery claim in order to obtain a public vindication of the deceased's right not to have been subjected to a deadly assault ... They have pleaded a case that, if reasonably arguable on the facts, cannot be struck out as being unarguable in law. Why, therefore, should

[8] [1972] AC 1027 (HL) 1134. [9] [1964] AC 1129 (HL) 1228 (Lord Devlin).
[10] [2003] UKPC 55, [2004] AC 628, [41]. [11] [2008] UKHL 25, [2008] 1 AC 962, [18].
[12] *ibid*, with quotes at [22]–[23], [60].

they be denied the chance to establish liability at a trial?' The following statement in *Chester v Afshar* was also cited, in *Ashley*: '[t]he function of the law [of Tort] is to enable rights to be vindicated and to provide remedies when duties have been breached' – because unless an infringed right obtained an adequate remedy, the tortious obligation would become 'a hollow one, stripped of all practical force and devoid of all content'.[13]

In practice, the vindicatory purpose also manifests where the only damages awarded to C are nominal in nature. The very award proves that C's right was infringed by D's conduct.

v. A 'gap-filler' in the general common law. The law of tort also has the function of 'perform[ing] a gap-filling role to provide a needed remedy which otherwise would not be available' (as the Scottish Outer House commented in *Realstone Ltd v J&E Shepherd*[14]). That court noted that this function has been evident in negligently-inflicted pure economic loss (as discussed in Chapter 4). For example, in *White v Jones*,[15] Lord Goff explicitly noted that creating a tortious duty of care may be justified because of 'the simple filling of an unacceptable gap' in the common law (that gap was indeed 'filled' in *White v Jones*), while, in *Williams v Natural Life Health Foods Ltd*, Lord Steyn expressly acknowledged that 'the law of tort, as the general law, has to fulfil an essential gap-filling role'.[16]

vi. A vehicle for the apportionment of risk. In Contract law, the apportionment of risk between the contracting parties is a matter of negotiation and/or consent, and the loss falls where it is agreed (affirmed, e.g., in *Caledonia North Sea Ltd v British Telecommunications plc (Scotland)*[17]).

In Tort law, by contrast, the obligations falling upon C and D are imposed by law. In determining where the loss should fall, Tort pays particular regard to two factors (both of which were described, e.g., in *Re Deep Vein Thrombosis and Air Travel Group Litig*[18]):

- which, of C or D, is better equipped to insure against the risks associated with D's acts or omissions? If D is in a better position to distribute the loss (i.e., the liability to pay tortious damages) among its customers or clients, of what would otherwise be 'a crushing burden upon those few unfortunate enough to become accident victims', then doctrine may be construed accordingly; and
- which, of C or D, is better positioned to minimise or prevent C's injury or loss? When the event which caused the injury or loss is solely within D's capacity to control or to influence, then the risk apportionment theory of liability suggests that liability for that risk manifesting should be D's to bear.

Depending upon the outcome of this query, the compensatory purpose may be subjugated to the conclusion that C, the 'injured party', was better-placed to insure against the loss which he suffered (a verdict arrived at, e.g., in *West Bromwich Albion Football Club Ltd v El-Safty*,[19] a leading pure economic loss case discussed in Chapter 4).

vii. An alternative to statutory compensation. C may be entitled to statutory compensation when injured by D, and for which compensation derived in a tortious action can serve as a 'top-up'. There have also been various *proposed* statutory schemes for tortiously-caused injuries

[13] [2005] 1 AC 134, [87] (Lord Hope). [14] [2008] CSOH 31, [19] (Lord Hodge).

[15] [1995] UKHL 5, [1995] 2 AC 207, 268.

[16] [1998] UKHL 17, [1998] 1 WLR 830, 837, and cited with approval in: *Riyad Bank v Ahli Bank (UK) plc* [2006] EWCA Civ 780, [40]–[41].

[17] [2002] UKHL 4, [2002] 1 Lloyd's Rep 553, [13]. [18] [2002] EWHC 2825 (QB) [47], [106]–[108].

[19] [2007] PIQR P7 (CA) [63] (Rix LJ), [84] (Mummery LJ).

in England (e.g., as discussed in Chapter 17, brief consideration will be given to the suggested statutory scheme for damage caused by the escape of dangerous things in place of the tortious action under *Rylands v Fletcher*, which scheme has never been enacted). A snapshot of the principal and currently-available statutory compensation schemes is contained in the following Table:

Snapshot of some English statutory compensation schemes

- **the Criminal Injuries Compensation Scheme 2012**, 'a government funded scheme to compensate blameless victims of violent crime. Payment can never fully compensate for the injuries suffered, but it is a recognition of public sympathy';[a]
- **the compensation regime for road traffic accidents**, operated by the Motor Insurers' Bureau (MIB), per the Road Traffic Act 1988 (RTA). The MIB 'functions under two separate Agreements between Government and the motor insurance industry', and has responsibility for administering three separate regimes: (1) the Uninsured Drivers' Scheme, which requires the MIB to meet unsatisfied Civil Court Judgments against identified motorists who may not have been insured, as required by the RTA[b]; (2) the Untraced Drivers' Scheme, which requires the MIB to consider applications for compensation from victims of 'hit and run' motorists; and (3) the Green Card Scheme, which requires the MIB to act as the deemed insurer of visiting motorists, for the purpose of paying claims.[c] All insurers who offer compulsory motor insurance are required to belong to the MIB and to contribute to its funding;
- **the workers' compensation scheme**, governed by the Social Security Contributions and Benefits Act 1992. For example, under s 94(1) of that Act, 'industrial injuries benefit shall be payable where an employed earner suffers personal injury ... by accident arising out of and in the course of his employment'. Additionally, several diseases are stipulated by the Social Security (Industrial Injuries) (Prescribed Diseases) Regs 1985, as falling within the scheme, and include, say, diffuse mesothelioma, occupational asthma, and anthrax;[d]
- **compensation for designated diseases**, purportedly caused by the pertussis vaccination of either child or pregnant mother, under the Vaccine Damages Payments Act 1979 (providing for a fixed payment in circumstances of 80% disability, later amended to lower the level of minimum disability to 60% and raise the statutory sum to £100,000, per the Vaccine Damages Payments Act 1979 Statutory Sum Order 2000).[e]

[a] See: Criminal Injuries Compensation Authy, *A Guide to the Criminal Injuries Compensation Scheme 2012* (5 Mar 2013), Section 1, [1].
[b] Pursuant to s 143(1)(a).
[c] See: Motor Insurers' Bureau, 'Frequently Asked Questions', available at: http://www.mib.org.uk/making-a-claim/what-we-do/.
[d] See Regs 2, 43, and Sch 1 and 4.
[e] SI 2000/1983. Also: Regulatory Reform (Vaccine Damages Payments Act 1979) Order 2002, SI 2002/1592.

Occasionally, senior judicial figures have acknowledged that Tort law plays a crucial role in delivering compensation to **some** aggrieved parties, even if it fails to deliver to others – in circumstance where Parliament has not acted to facilitate statutory compensation, whether for political, economic, cultural or societal reasons. Compensation schemes require a political will which may be entirely lacking. As Lord Hoffmann observed in *Matthews v MOD*, whether a tort-based system of compensation should be supplanted or supplemented is 'a matter of national policy', and that whether a tort-based system 'is the most sensible way of providing compensation for accident victims is controversial ... the existing [Tort law] system is expensive and, in many respects, unfair'.[20]

Of course, sometimes Tort law may not provide **any** alternative to C at all, in the circumstances. Where C is injured by D's driving, then frequently that driving will have been negligent, giving rise to the right to court-ordered compensation, or the statutory and administrative arrangements governing road traffic accidents (as noted in the Table above) may enable C to recover compensation for his injuries. Nevertheless, there may still be those few who suffer from injuries arising from the driving of a vehicle by another, and who cannot recover anything at all, where negligence cannot be proven – e.g., where D, the driver, suffered from a hitherto-unknown hypoglacaemic state, as in the English case of *Mansfield v Weetabix Ltd*,[21] or a latent sick sinus condition, as in the Irish case of *Counihan v Bus Atha Cliath-Dublin Bus*,[22] which caused the respective drivers to black out whilst at the wheel, and cause serious injury and damage to C. Such cases inevitably attract judicial sympathy, as evident in *Snelling v Whitehead*,[23] where Lord Wilberforce noted:

> This case is one which is severely distressing ... [and] should attract automatic compensation, regardless of any question of fault. But no such system has yet been introduced in this country, and the courts, including this House, have no power to depart from the law as it stands. This requires that compensation may only be obtained in an action for damages and ... as a condition of the award of damages against the [driver], a finding of fault, or negligence, on his part.

Nevertheless, for all of the drawbacks, disadvantages, and vagaries which Tort jurisprudence may demonstrate, it must be reiterated that statutory compensation schemes can be afflicted with several difficulties too, both with their design and their application/outcomes. The following Table illustrates some of the conundrums, with reference to well-known statutory compensation schemes:

Statutory compensation schemes: a snapshot

Some examples:

New Zealand: originally, the Accident Compensation Act 1972, and subsequently replaced by: Injury Prevention, Rehabilitation and Compensation Act 2001[a]

Florida: the Birth-Related Neurological Injury Compensation Act (1988)[b]

Design features:

- **what range it covers** – comprehensive (NZ statute); or situation-specific (Florida statute)
- **what residual rights to pursue common law proceedings remain:** whether the regime entirely precludes a common law action; *or* precludes a common law action for personal injury only; *or* precludes a common law action for compensatory damages but permits an action for exemplary

[a] In force, 1 Apr 2002, and amended by: Injury Prevention, Rehabilitation and Compensation Amendment Act (No 2) 2005, mainly in force 1 Jul 2005.

[b] See subsequently: s 7666.302 of the Florida Statute.

[20] [2003] UKHL 4, [2003] 1 AC 1163, [2].

[21] [1998] 1 WLR 1263 (CA).

[22] [2005] IEHC 51, [2005] 2 IR 436.

[23] The Times (31 Jul 1975), [1998] RTR 385 (HL) 386.

damages; ***or*** precludes a common law action for statutorily-specified injuries, but allows a common law action for everything else; ***or*** precludes a common law action until C fails to establish that it is covered by the regime, whereupon a common law action is available; ***or*** precludes a common law action below a certain threshold of injury, but permits a common law action above that threshold; ***or*** puts C to an election, *viz*, either a common law action or a statutory action;

- **defining the triggers for compensatory awards** – e.g., note the triggers in the Florida statute: 'injury to the brain or spinal cord of a live infant [in excess of a minimum birth weight] caused by oxygen deprivation or mechanical injury occurring in the course of labor, delivery or resuscitation in the immediate post-delivery period in a hospital, which renders the infant permanently and substantially mentally and physically impaired. This definition shall apply to live births only, and shall not include disability or death caused by genetic or congenital abnormality'. Contrast the triggers in the NZ legislation: 'a personal injury suffered in New Zealand and [which] is caused by an accident, a medical misadventure, or a gradual process, disease or infection that is work-related, or [by] a medical misadventure, or as a result of a personal injury or its treatment';
- **what (if any) injury or disability thresholds apply** for eligibility for payment to arise;
- **whether any rights of appeal** are available (and if so, whether to court or to some other forum);
- **whether the regime is compulsory; opt-in; or opt-out,** in relation to either victim C, or the paying party D (and, if non-compulsory, what notice and consent requirements must be met, to ensure valid involvement);
- **what, and how, damages or expenses are compensated** (e.g., capped, indexed, or scaled); and **how those payments should be made** (whether lump-sum, periodical or other);
- **practically speaking,** how the claims should be processed, and how the claims facility should be funded.

Hence, there are considerable legal and policy conundrums vested in the exercise of drafting a statutory compensation scheme – as the somewhat problematical, and oft-litigated, regimes in Florida and New Zealand aptly demonstrate. (An analysis of that jurisprudence falls outside the scope of this book.)

TORTS IN CONTEXT

Obtaining monetary compensation

§1.5 More than one cause of action may be pleaded by C, in respect of the same grievance, from different legal avenues. However, C will recover the monetary redress to which he is entitled only once, regardless of how many causes of action are successfully instituted against D.

Tort law protects rights *in personam*, which amount to an injury to C's person or property, or economic well-being, or his reputation). Three other avenues of redress may protect the same type of rights:

Avenues, apart from Tort law

Contract law	The cause of action for breach of contract requires three matters to be proven: • formation of a contract; • breach of that contract; and • the absence of any factor that would vitiate the contract's formation.[a]
Equity	This avenue includes numerous causes of action, e.g.: • breach of confidential information; • breach of fiduciary relationship; • undue influence.[b]
Restitution	This avenue includes, e.g.: • an action for *quantum meruit*, for a reasonable value of goods or services obtained, following rescission (or, more rarely) termination of a contract • disgorgement of benefits conferred on D as a result of C's mistake of fact or of law.[c]

[a] See, e.g.: N Andrews, *Contract Law* (2nd edn, Cambridge University Press, 2015); M Chen-Wishart, *Contract Law* (4th edn, Oxford University Press, 2012).
[b] See, e.g.: A Hudson, *Equity and Trusts* (8th edn, Routledge, 2014); G Virgo, *The Principles of Equity and Trusts* (Oxford University Press, 2012).
[c] See, e.g.: A Burrows, E McKendrick and J Edelman, *Cases and Materials on the Law of Restitution* (2nd edn, Oxford University Press, 2007); R Goff and G Jones, *The Law of Restitution* (7th edn, Sweet & Maxwell, 2007).

Concurrently-prosecuted tortious wrongs are perfectly permissible, and indeed, are very common, albeit that pleading numerous causes of action does not guarantee success in any one of them:

> In *Keegan v CC of Merseyside*,[24] police officers, D, considered that there were reasonable grounds to arrest X on suspicion of involvement in armed robberies. However, the premises mistakenly targeted in the raid were those of the Keegan family, C, who pursued D for three causes of action: malicious procurement of a search warrant; trespass to land; and false imprisonment. **Held:** all three causes of action failed. D had a proper motive in deciding to seek a warrant and there was no malice involved; D's entry to the premises was lawful and not a trespass to land; and there was no false imprisonment.

Even where C may prove **all** concurrently-pleaded causes of action, C is only entitled to recover his damages **once**, if all claims are in respect of the same injury to C. In that respect, the causes of action are the doorways through which C must try to enter the room; and once in that room, C is entitled to monetary award, to redress the injury or damage which he has suffered. As Lord Rodger explained in *Ashley v CC of Sussex Police*,[25] double-recovery is **not** possible: 'as a general rule, the damages recoverable under both causes of action will be the same. Since the damages are intended to provide compensation for the injuries suffered by [C], he is entitled to the same damages, whether he succeeds on one cause of action or on both. The only material advantage to [C] in succeeding on both causes of action is that he will be entitled to retain his damages, even if an appeal court later holds that he should not have succeeded on one of them'.

[24] [2003] EWCA Civ 936, [2003] 1 WLR 2187. [25] [2008] UKHL 25, [2008] 1 AC 962, [58].

Indeed, the interaction between pleas for breach of contract and for negligence, arising out of the same grievance, have given rise to some controversy, and is discussed in the following section.

Concurrent liability in Contract and in Tort

In their contract, the parties, C and D, can freely allocate the risks and responsibilities between themselves as they see fit during negotiations (or lay off some of the risk to other parties involved in the project). Any risks and responsibilities in Tort, however, are imposed by law – the parties have no say in that allocation. Hence, in analysing the obligations and responsibilities which arise in Contract, the court is scrutinising the express terms (whether written or oral), and the implied terms (if any). In negligence, however, the obligations are determined by asking what duty of care arose between C and D, under one of the relevant tests governing duty (as discussed in Chapter 2).

Why it matters

The significance of plucking, and pleading, different causes of action from different avenues usually comes down to specific matters – and it is no different when choosing between Contract and Tort actions:

The measure of damages. There is a prospect of the measure of damages differing, depending upon which cause of action/s succeeds for C. The function of an award of damages in Contract is quite different from that of Tort. As Lord Scott stated, in *Rees v Darlington Memorial Hosp NHS Trust*,[26] for claims for breach of contract, C 'is entitled to the benefit of the contract and entitled, therefore, to be placed in the position, so far as money can do so, in which he would have been if the contractual obligation had been properly performed. But where the claim is in Tort, there being no contract to the benefit of which [C] is entitled, [C] is entitled to be placed in the position in which he would have been if the tortious act, the wrong, had not been committed'. Additionally, in Contract, the damages may be capped or circumscribed (e.g., liquidated) by the contract itself.

In addition, the rules of remoteness of damage differ between the actions. In Contract, the rule in *Hadley v Baxendale*[27] restricts the scope of damages recoverable to those for which a party assumed contractual responsibility as having been in the contemplation of the parties, or which arise normally in the course of things (per *Transfield Shipping Inc v Mercator Shipping Inc (The Achilleas*[28])). By contrast, in Tort, the remoteness rules are wider: provided that the type or kind of damage was reasonably foreseeable, and falls within the scope of the duty, then the damage is recoverable (per *Jolley v Sutton LBC*[29]).

The fact of damage. Proving damage **may** be necessary for the Tort action (e.g., in respect of negligence, '[i]t is trite law that damage is the gist of the action', per *Chester v Afshar*[30]), whereas it is **not** an element of the action, say, for breach of contract. Nominal damages can be awarded for a breach of contract, whereas substantive damage must be proven for an action in negligence. Hence, in the absence of any compensable damage, C will prefer a remedy in Contract, because it is the very defect, whether it be in the provision of a building, a chattel, or a service, which is actionable (see, e.g., the discussion by Stanley Burnton LJ in *Robinson v PE Jones (Contractors) Ltd*[31]).

[26] [2003] UKHL 52, [2004] 1 AC 309, [130]. [27] (1854) 9 Ex 341 (QB). [28] [2009] 1 AC 61 (HL).
[29] [2000] UKHL 31, [2000] WLR 1082. [30] [2004] UKHL 41, [2005] 1 AC 134, [9] (Lord Bingham).
[31] [2011] EWCA Civ 9, [2012] QB 44, [94].

Limitation periods. The limitation period for contract is generally more onerous, i.e., shorter, than for Tort, given that the limitation period starts running, in Contract, from the moment of the alleged breach; whereas the limitation period starts running, in Tort, from the moment that damage is allegedly incurred (a point which may occur much later than the breach itself, as discussed in 'The beginning and end of liability' (an online chapter). In *Henderson v Merrett Syndicates Ltd*, it was argued that the differences which may exist between the limitation periods in Contract and Tort should mean that no concurrent liability in Contract and in Tort should exist – for 'the temptation of elegance'.[32] However, this argument did not prevail (see below).

The standard of care. The standard of care expected of D may be quite different in Contract and in Tort – a point which is often seen in construction or in manufacturing contracts. In contract, D may undertake not to create a defective piece of workmanship, product or article. Any defect will thereby amount to a breach of contract on D's part (unless D has limited, excluded or off-loaded its liability for such defect by some other contractual clause). On the other hand, in the tort of negligence, D is under a duty to use reasonable care and skill to avoid causing damage to C as a result of any defective workmanship, but does not guarantee to produce something which is free of defects – otherwise, negligence would impose an obligation of perfection, or a warranty of a perfect outcome, which the law will not do. Hence, the duty in contract may be more onerous than, and not co-extensive with, the duty in tort – so that it is in C's interests to rely upon the contractual duty if possible (per *Payne v John Setchell Ltd*[33]).

The general principle

§1.6 As a general principle, the mere fact that C and D are in a contractual relationship does not preclude D from owing a tortious duty of care to C too, provided that D assumed a responsibility towards C to exercise reasonable care to avoid causing C loss or damage. C may, therefore, have concurrent remedies in contract and in tort against D, permitting C, if successful in both, to choose the most advantageous remedy.

The permissibility, in English law, of seeking concurrent remedies in contract and in tort was confirmed by Lord Goff in *Henderson v Merrett Syndicates Ltd*:[34]

> an assumption of responsibility, coupled with the concomitant reliance, may give rise to a tortious duty of care, irrespective of whether there is a contractual relationship between the parties, and in consequence, unless his contract precludes him from doing so, [C], who has available to him concurrent remedies in contract and tort, may choose that remedy which appears to him to be the most advantageous.

In *Henderson v Merrett Syndicates Ltd*, C were underwriting members at Lloyds (aka Names) who entered into underwriting agency agreements with Merrett, managing agents of the syndicate, D. In at least one group of actions (Gooda Walker), the Names alleged that D were contractually liable for their failure to exercise reasonable care and skill in relation to such underwriting. C's claims for pure economic loss were framed both in contract and tort. **Held:** C were entitled to pursue their remedies in contract and tort.

[32] [1995] 2 AC 145 (HL) 186. [33] [2001] EWHC 457 (TCC) [23].

[34] [1995] 2 AC 145 (HL) 194 (Lords Keith, Mustill, Nolan and Browne-Wilkinson agreeing).

Lord Goff considered the two options open to the House: that a contractual relationship should preclude any tortious action from arising (as applies in the French legal system); or that a tortious action could lie alongside a contractual action concurrently (as in the German legal system). Albeit recognising that the arguments favouring, or disfavouring, concurrent remedies, were finely-balanced, ultimately, *Henderson* permits C to choose, as between concurrent causes of action and concurrent remedies, that which best suits C's interests (indeed, this principle has been applied more widely – when C has a choice as between recovery under a statutory regime, and in restitution[35] – albeit that such discussion is beyond the scope of this book). Although *Henderson* itself concerned a claim by C to recover damages for pure economic loss, the principle applies where C is claiming for personal injury or physical damage to property too (per *Biffa Waste Services Ltd v Maschinenfabrik Ernst Hese GmbH*[36]).

Precondition for concurrent duties. A necessary condition for the imposition of a concurrent liability in contract and in negligence is that D must have *assumed a responsibility* to avoid the particular damage of which C complains (be it personal injury, property damage or, most controversially, economic damage sustained). Professional Ds, in particular, tend to give rise to the requisite assumption of responsibility, which will entail, for that D, that he owes a contractual duty to C, and a parallel (concurrent) duty in tort. Indeed, concurrent duties in contract and in tort have applied to the following:

- architects (per *Bellefield Computer Services v E Turner & Sons Ltd*[37]);
- builders who exercise design functions as well as workmanship (suggested obiter in an earlier decision in *Bellefield Computer Services Ltd v E Turner & Sons Ltd*[38]);
- insurance brokers (per *Punjab National Bank v DeBoinville*[39]);
- bankers to their customers to whom they provide, e.g., investment advisory services (per *Riyad Bank v AHLI United Bank (UK) plc*[40]), or creditworthiness references (as in *Hedley Byrne and Co Ltd v Heller and Partners Ltd*[41]);
- solicitors (per *Midland Bank Trust Co Ltd v Hett, Stubbs & Kemp*[42]);
- underwriting/managing agents (per *Henderson v Merrett Syndicates Ltd* itself);
- valuers and surveyors (per *Smith v Eric S Bush*[43]);
- accountants (per *Caparo Industries plc v Dickman*[44]); and
- engineers (per *Mirant-Asia Pacific Ltd v Oapil*[45]).

That will not always be the case – D may **not** have assumed responsibility to C, in tort, to avoid causing C damage, as Jackson LJ pointed out in *Robinson v PE Jones (Contractors) Ltd*:

> the conceptual basis, upon which the concurrent liability of professional persons in tort to their clients now rests, is assumption of responsibility ... [However], [w]hen one moves beyond the realm of professional retainers, it by no means follows that every contracting party assumes responsibilities ... to the other parties co-extensive with the contractual obligations. Such an analysis would be nonsensical. Contractual and tortious duties have different origins and different functions.

[35] *Deutsche Morgan Grenfell Group plc v Inland Revenue* [2006] UKHL 49, [2007] AC 558, [50]–[51], [136].
[36] [2008] EWHC 6 (TCC) [169(3)] (Akenhead J). [37] [2002] EWCA Civ 1823, [73] (May LJ).
[38] [2000] EWHC Admin 284 (Schiemann LJ). [39] [1992] 1 Lloyd's Rep 7 (CA).
[40] [2006] EWCA Civ 780, [36]–[47]. [41] [1964] AC 465 (HL).
[42] [1979] Ch 384. Approved in *Henderson v Merrett Syndicates Ltd* [1995] 2 AC 145 (HL) 184–94 (Lord Goff).
[43] [1990] 1 AC 831, and approved by Lord Goff in *Henderson, ibid.*
[44] [1990] 2 AC 605 (HL). [45] [2004] EWHC 1750 (TCC) [357], [395]–[396].

> Contractual obligations spring from the consent of the parties and the common law principle that contracts should be enforced. Tortious duties are imposed by law, as a matter of policy, in *specific situations*. Sometimes a particular set of facts may give rise to identical contractual and tortious duties, but self-evidently that is not always the case.[46]

For example, the current view is that builders do not owe concurrent duties of care in contract and in tort to protect their employers (developers) against any economic loss brought about by their defective workmanship (per Stanley Burnton LJ in *Robinson v PE Jones Ltd*, who stated that, to the extent that first-instance decisions had recognised concurrent obligations in contract and in tort, those decisions were wrongly decided[47]).

Disapproval of previous authority. A decade before *Henderson* was handed down, the Privy Council had taken quite the opposite view, in *Tai Hing Cotton Mill Ltd v Liu Chong Hing Bank Ltd*,[48] holding that a duty of care in tort should not co-exist with obligations arising under a contract. Lord Scarman (writing for the court) held, in dicta, that, in commercial relationships, 'it is correct in principle, and necessary for the avoidance of confusion in the law, to adhere to the contractual analysis: on principle, because it is a relationship in which the parties have, subject to a few exceptions, the right to determine their obligations to each other; and for the avoidance of confusion, because different consequences do follow according to whether liability arises from contract or tort, e.g. in the limitation of action'.

As it turned out, the approach of *Tai Hing* has been substantially 'reconsidered' in the light of *Henderson* (per *Biffa Waste Services Ltd v Maschinenfabrik Ernst Hese GmbH*[49]).

Query for the future. Recently, there has been some query, judicially, as to whether concurrent duties should apply, given the significant differences between contract and tort. In *Wellesley Partners LLP v Withers LLP*, Nugee J said this:[50]

> it has been established at the highest level that a professional retained by a client has (usually) a concurrent liability in tort as well as contract ... the well-known consequence of the client being able to sue in either contract or tort is to enable him to take advantage of the longer limitation period available in tort. Given that the test for remoteness of damage is different in tort from that which it is in contract, I do not think it is open to me to say ... that a client who chooses to sue in tort cannot equally take advantage of the more generous rules for remoteness of damage available in tort. If that step is to be taken, I think it must be by a higher court.

Whether that step is taken, and the Privy Council's views in *Tai Hing* reinstated, remains to be seen.

Exceptions

§1.7 The principle of concurrent liability will not apply in exceptional circumstances, where: (1) any tortious duty is so inconsistent with the contract so as to be excluded; and (2) a group of contracts governs the relevant obligations.

[46] [2011] EWCA Civ 9, [2012] QB 44, [74] (emphasis added), a theme to which Jackson LJ returned in a recent extra-curial lecture to the Technology and Construction Bar Assn and the Socy of Construction Law, 'Concurrent Liability: Where Have Things Gone Wrong?' (30 Oct 2014) [copy on file with the author].

[47] [2011] EWCA Civ 9, [2012] QB 44, [95]. [48] [1986] AC 80 (HL) 107.

[49] [2008] EWHC 6 (TCC) [74]. [50] [2014] EWHC 556 (Ch) [214].

Concurrent duties in contract and in tort may not be recognised, for the following reasons:

i. **The contract precludes concurrent duties between C and D.** As Lord Goff's classic statement in *Henderson* confirms, the contract between C and D may expressly preclude any tortious action from arising. There would be no room for concurrent liability in contract and tort (said Lord Goff) where the tortious duty was so inconsistent with the applicable contract that such tortious liability had to be taken as being excluded.[51] Of course, it all depends upon how the contract is worded.

As Akenhead J reiterated in *Biffa Waste Services Ltd v Maschinenfabrik Ernst Hese GmbH*, 'a duty of care should not be permitted to circumvent or escape a contractual exclusion or limitation of liability for the act or omission that would constitute the tort'.[52]

In *Robinson v PE Jones (Contractors) Ltd*,[53] James Robinson, C, bought his house from PE Jones, D, the builder, in April 1992, when the building work was completed. Then, in Oct 2004, C arranged to have the gas fires in the house serviced by British Gas, and the fires were declared unsafe, because of alleged defects in their construction and with the flues connected to them. The fires had to be uninstalled and rectified at great expense. C sued D in contract, and in tort, for those costs. **Held:** C's claim in contract was statute-barred. The claim in tort also failed, because it was precluded by cl 10 of the contract:

> The Vendor shall not be liable to the Purchaser ... under the Agreement or any document incorporated therein in respect of any defect, error or omission in the execution or the completion of the work, save to the extent, and for the period, that it is liable under the provisions of the NHBC Agreement on which alone his rights and remedies are founded.

That clause was reasonable under the Unfair Contract Terms Act 1977, and also excluded concurrent liability in tort: '[t]he parties expressly agreed that [D's] only liability to [C] should be that arising from the NHBC agreement ... the only sensible interpretation of cl 10 is that the parties are agreeing to exclude any liability in negligence'.

ii. **A group's contractual arrangements.** Where a *group of contracting parties* have entered into an arrangement, whereby they have each chosen the party/parties with whom to contract, but where one member of the group, C, then seeks to pursue a claim in tort against a party with whom that party has no contract (D), then C is using tort to circumvent the contractual arrangements formed among the group members. In such cases, the question (according to *Pacific Associates v Baxter*[54]) is whether, to permit C to pursue D in tort, would 'cut across and be inconsistent with the structure of relationships created by the contracts' (per Ralph Gibson LJ) – or, '[g]iven the contractual structure between the contractor and the employer, can it be fairly said that it was ever within the contemplation of the contractor [C] that, outside the contract, it could pursue a remedy against the engineer [D]' (per Russell LJ).

Actually, this is not strictly a *Henderson v Merrett Syndicates* scenario, because the court is not considering whether D owes C a parallel duty of care in negligence as well as an obligation in contract. Nevertheless, in such cases, the same principles have been broadly applied.

[51] [1995] 2 AC 146 (HL) 193–94. [52] [2008] EWHC 6 (TCC) [169(4)].
[53] [2011] EWCA Civ 9, [2012] QB 44, quote at [84]–[85] (Jackson LJ). [54] [1990] 1 QB 993 (CA) 1032, 1037.

In *BSkyB Ltd v HP Enterprise Services UK Ltd (Rev 1)*,[55] British Sky Broadcasting Ltd (BSkyB) and Sky Subscribers Services Ltd (SSSL), C, provided satellite broadcasting services. They had a dispute with those providing IT services to them, EDSC, D. The 'prime contract' was between SSSL and D, to which BskyB was not a contracting party. BSkyB sued D in tort, for alleged losses resulting from the unsuccessful IT systems (approx. £709m). **Held:** D did not owe a duty of care to BSkyB. Otherwise, if it did, that would circumvent the contractual arrangements which the parties had put in place. The parties had not included any provision within the prime contract which expressly referred to any liability of D towards BSkyB, when they could have done so. Hence, the contractual structure negated any possibility that such a duty of care should arise in these circumstances.

TORT LITIGATION

Sources of Tort law

§1.8 There are three principal sources of English Tort law: (1) domestic case law; (2) domestic legislation; and (3) the jurisprudence under the Human Rights Act 1998.

Dealing briefly with each in turn:

i. Domestic case law. As a 'black letter' common law subject, the vast majority of the law discussed in this book is derived from English judicial decisions. Courts from highest appellate level (whether Supreme Court or, previously, the House of Lords) to County Courts and Employment Tribunals, have pronounced on important points of Tort law which have been sufficiently noteworthy to include herein.

   Of course, in accordance the doctrine of authoritative precedent, great care must be taken, in the law of Tort, to distinguish, in a case, the *ratio decidendi* (Latin for 'the reason for deciding') from the *obiter dictum* (Latin for 'a remark in passing'). Only the ratio of a case – the reasoning of the court in reaching its decision on the facts of the case before it – is binding upon lower courts; dicta does not form part of the ratio of the case and creates no binding precedent, but is merely persuasive authority, no matter which court utters it.[56]

   Where appropriate, comparative vignettes of judicial viewpoint, sourced from other common law jurisdictions, have been cited throughout the book, if they provide a different perspective or varying case scenarios which shed light on the point of Tort law under consideration. These are, of course, of persuasive precedent only.

ii. Domestic legislation. As will be evident throughout the book (and from a cursory examination of the Legislation Table in the preliminaries), legislation has had a considerable impact upon substantive Tort law – e.g., from how tortious remedies can be sought in the event that the tortfeasor brings about the death of a victim (see below), to the allocation of damages between culpable Ds, all of whom have wrongfully exposed C to asbestos and where C suffers from mesothelioma as a result (see 'Multiple defendants', an online chapter).

There have been notable occasions, however, where the Law Commission of England and Wales has strongly recommended that an area of Tort law be clarified by the enactment of

[55] [2010] EWHC 86 (TCC) [538]–[543].

[56] See, e.g., the order of precedential authority in: *Oxford Dictionary of Law* (6th edn, Oxford University Press, 2006) 393, 404, 439.

legislation, but where Parliament has steadfastly refused to follow that recommendation (the area of negligently-inflicted psychiatric damage, examined in Chapter 5, readily springs to mind).

iii. The Human Rights Act 1998. The Human Rights Act 1998 (HRA), and the Convention rights to which it gives further effect,[57] has had a considerable impact upon the development of some areas of English Tort law. This has come about for two reasons.

First, the definition of a 'public authority' in the HRA includes a court or tribunal (per s 6(3)). Hence, courts must ensure that English Tort law is compatible with the Convention, when deciding disputes between purely private parties (the so-called 'horizontal effect' of the HRA). In that regard, it has been evident that, at times, domestic Tort law has been rendered incompatible with Convention rights and 'cannot survive the Human Rights Act' (as recognised by the Court of Appeal in *JD v East Berkshire Community Health NHS Trust*,[58] speaking of the decision in *X (Minors) v Bedfordshire CC*, as discussed in Chapter 13). On other occasions, however, it has not been necessary to develop (i.e., amend, reverse or supplement) English Tort law in order to ensure its compatibility with the Convention – the no-duty-to-rescue principle in 'Bad Samaritan' negligence law (see Chapter 2), and the lack of any *general* tort of privacy (see 'Privacy', an online chapter) being two notable examples where English courts have refused to re-write established doctrine.

The second impact of the HRA on English Tort law – of a more indirect nature – is that C may allege concurrent suits against D, one pleaded as a cause of action in Tort, and the other framed as a claim under the HRA against D, as a public authority which has allegedly acted in a way that was incompatible with C's Convention rights. For example, as discussed in Chapter 13, claims by the vulnerable and disadvantaged against public authorities which have obligations to provide social, housing or educational services are frequently brought in both negligence and under the HRA (as occurred, e.g., in the horrific abuse case of *X & Y v Hounslow LBC*[59]).

Costs rules in tort litigation

A general appreciation of how costs rules operate in English Tort law may be of value, in order to highlight the significant financial risks that both sides of the litigation run, and to canvass some recent and important changes to the costs rules that govern civil (including Tort) litigation.

§1.9 In English civil litigation, the general rule of costs-shifting applies. However, in respect of some areas of Tort litigation, exceptional scenarios have been legislatively-created, since the Jackson Costs Review.

The general rule of costs-shifting

The ramifications of C's losing his Torts suit against D may be very expensive, because of the general rule that 'costs follow the event' (also called the 'two-way' costs rule, the 'costs-shifting'

[57] Per the European Convention for the Protection of Human Rights and Fundamental Freedoms 1950 (in Sch 1 to the Human Rights Act 1998), in force Oct 2000.

[58] [2003] EWCA Civ 1151, [2004] QB 558, [83] (Lord Phillips MR, who delivered the judgment of the court).

[59] [2008] EWHC 1168 (QB) [84].

rule, the 'English rule', and the 'loser pays winner' rule – the terms are synonymous). Essentially, it means that the 'winner' of the litigation recovers the reasonable costs incurred in bringing, or defending, the litigation. English law follows the costs-shifting principle for contentious litigation[60] (which embraces all of the Tort litigation referenced in this book), although the court does retain a wide discretion to vary that order[61] (including a discretion not to award the winning party any costs at all).

Limits on recoverability. Costs-shifting does **not**, however, enable the recovery of all of the costs to which the successful party may be put. Broadly speaking, regardless of whether it is C or D who wins the litigation, there is likely to be a substantial discrepancy between the amount of the winner's actual costs in pursuing or defending the Tort action (termed the solicitor and client costs), and the amount that he will be entitled to recover from the unsuccessful opponent (termed the party and party costs).

The costs-shifting rule has been perceived to pose considerable barriers to bringing, or defending, civil litigation, given that each party faces two potential burdens: he must pay his own lawyers' fees and disbursements (of which he will receive only *a portion* of those total costs back, if successful), plus he faces the added burden of being liable for the opponent's party and party costs, if he loses the litigation. However, costs-shifting has the oft-cited benefit of deterring speculative, weak or blackmail claims – given that the party bringing the action has a 'skin in the game'.

The alternative costs rules. There are two other primary costs rules.

Under the **'no-way' costs rule** (also called the 'American rule', in recognition of the fact that a no-way costs rule frequently, but not always, operates in that jurisdiction[62]), the court does not award costs to the successful party. Rather, each party bears his own costs of the litigation, regardless of success or failure. The rule is perceived to give rise to the risk of abuse, for C may be more inclined to bring frivolous/blackmail actions, knowing that, if he loses, he will not have to pay D's costs.

The **one-way costs rule** entails that an award of costs can be made against a losing D, but not against a losing C. This means that D will generally be ordered to pay the costs of a winning C but, subject to certain exceptions, will not recover his own costs if he successfully defends the claim. It is perceived to be a means of removing the risk that C may become liable to pay D's costs in any litigation which C may wish to bring.

A changing costs landscape in Tort litigation

As a result of the ground-breaking costs review conducted by Sir Rupert Jackson, commencing in 2008,[63] progressing to a detailed preliminary report in 2009,[64] and culminating with a final report in 2010,[65] the application of the costs-shifting rule has undergone some significant changes in recent times, which directly impinge upon Tort litigation.

[60] Per: CPR 44.3(2)(a). [61] CPR 44.3(2)(b).

[62] A principle from an 1853 statute, subsequently codified as: 28 USC ¶1920, 1923(a), and see too: *Alyeska Pipeline Service Co v Wilderness Soc*, 421 US 240, 247 (1975) (as a general rule, 'the prevailing litigant is ordinarily not entitled to collect a reasonable attorney's fee from the loser'). See further: Mulheron, *The Class Action in Common Law Legal Systems: A Comparative Perspective* (Hart Publishing, 2004), ch 12.

[63] See: 'Lord Justice Jackson to Head Civil Costs Review' (2008) *Solicitors' Journal* (4 Nov 2008).

[64] *Review of Civil Litigation Costs: Preliminary Report* (May 2009).

[65] *Review of Civil Litigation Costs: Final Report* (Jan 2010).

The potential for radical changes to English law's traditional costs rule were flagged up quite early in the review, and the ultimate recommendations reflected that train of thought.

The law reform corner: Costs rules

Sir Rupert Jackson's Costs Review (2010) recommended that:[66]

- a regime of qualified one-way costs shifting (QOCS) be introduced for personal injury cases (qualified, in that costs-shifting could resume, depending upon the financial resources of C, and the conduct of C in bringing and conducting the suit);
- QOCS could be introduced for private nuisance claims in the future, if other changes in costs and funding showed that they were an obstacle to access to justice for those types of claims; and
- QOCS could be introduced for defamation and breach of privacy claims.

On 1 April 2013, QOCS was introduced for personal injury cases,[67] but at the time of writing, the recommendations for QOCS to be introduced in the other areas noted above has not occurred. These costs reforms are likely to have a large impact upon the commencement and conduct of a considerable amount of Tort-related litigation, and represent an important adjustment in the landscape (additional to the other innovative aspect of the Jackson reforms, *viz*, the introduction of percentage contingency fees, or 'damages-based agreements', for 'contentious' legal business for the first time in English law[68]).

In any event, a brief familiarity with the costs rules governing Torts litigation provides a sense of what is *at stake* (albeit that the rules do not impact whatsoever upon *substantive* Tort law).

Strike-out applications in Tort litigation

§1.10 Some of the most important Torts cases in English legal history have been determined as strike-out applications. However, these decisions should arguably not be regarded as being of any lesser precedential value, merely for that reason.

A court has the power to strike out C's claim, where it appears to the court that the claim discloses no reasonable grounds for bringing the claim.[69] A decision on a preliminary point of law[70] serves the same purpose; indeed, the two avenues are 'indistinguishable' for practical purposes (said the Court of Appeal in *Kent v Griffiths*[71]). Notably, although the hearing proceeds on a statement of agreed facts, a decision in a strike-out application is a decision on the merits.[72]

[66] *Review of Civil Litigation Costs: Final Report* (2010), chh 19, 31, 32. Earlier: 'Review of Civil Litigation Costs: Information that Would be Helpful for the Costs Review' (27 Nov 2008), published in: *Costs, Collective Redress, Contingency Fees ... The Way Forward?* (Practical Law, London, 26 Feb 2009), s 2.

[67] Per CPR 44.13–44.17.

[68] See the Damages-Based Agreements Regulations 2013, reviewed by an MOJ Working Group chaired by the author in: *The Damages-Based Agreements Reform Project: Drafting and Policy Issues* (Aug 2015).

[69] CPR 3.4(2)(a). [70] CPR 3.1(2)(i). [71] [2000] EWCA Civ 3017, [2001] QB 36, [38].

[72] See: A Zuckerman, *Zuckerman on Civil Procedure* (2nd edn, Thomson Sweet & Maxwell, 2006) 279–82.

The strike-out procedure has its limitations in English law too. In *Barrett v Enfield LBC*,[73] Lord Browne-Wilkinson pointed out that a court must not be too eager to strike out a tortious claim, especially where a novel area of law is taking shape. His Lordship referred to his previous judgment in *X (Minors) v Bedfordshire CC*,[74] that, 'in an area of the law which was uncertain and developing (such as the circumstances in which a person can be held liable in negligence for the exercise of a statutory duty or power), it is not normally appropriate to strike out ... it is of great importance that such development should be on the basis of actual facts found at trial, not on hypothetical facts assumed (possibly wrongly) to be true for the purpose of the strike out'. Lord Browne-Wilkinson summed up the position thus: there must be 'a clear and obvious case calling for striking out' – and several evolving areas of Tort law simply do not fall into that category. These judicial sentiments have been useful to various claimants in English Tort law, where the law has been unsettled and developing, enabling them to survive a strike-out application and resolutely carry on (either to settlement or trial).

As a corollary, the strike-out application has assumed an historical importance in Tort law. In *Vicario v Commr of Police for the Metropolis*,[75] Jacobs LJ noted that numerous important authorities governing whether D owed C a duty of care in negligence have been decided 'in strike-out or preliminary point circumstances'. By way of example:

Some notable strike-out cases in English negligence law

- *Donoghue v Stevenson* (1932)
- *Hedley Byrne & Co v Heller & Partners Ltd* (1964)
- *Dorset Yacht Co v Home Office* (1970)
- *Anns v Merton LBC* (1978)
- *Hill v CC of West Yorkshire Police* (1989)
- *Calveley v CC of Mersey* (1989)
- *Caparo Industries plc v Dickman* (1990)
- *X (Minors) v Bedfordshire CC* (1995)
- *Marc Rich & Co v Bishop Rock Marine Co* (1995)
- *Arthur JS Hall & Co v Simons* (2002)
- *JD v East Berkshire Community NHS Trust* (2005)
- *Brooks v Commr of Police of the Metropolis* (2005)

In addition (and not referred to in *Vicario*):

- *Sion v Hampstead HA* (1994)
- *W v Essex CC* (2001)
- *Michael v South Wales Police* (2014)
- *Kent v Griffiths* (1999)

Jacobs LJ added that, '[o]ne cannot imagine what our current law of negligence would look like without these cases, all decided without a trial. Standing above all is *Donoghue v Stevenson*. Not only was it decided on the Scottish equivalent of what the English used to call a demurrer [a strike-out], but no one knows whether there ever was a snail in the bottle'.[76] The view that strike-out applications have played an important role in English Tort law has drawn support in subsequent novel cases (e.g., in *Mitchell v Glasgow CC*[77]), in the evolving and difficult areas of Tort with which courts have had to grapple.

By contrast, some judicial suggestions that strike-out applications are of lesser weight, given their context, do occur from time to time – e.g., in *Taylor v A Novo (UK) Ltd*,[78] Lord

[73] [2001] 2 AC 550 (HL) 557. [74] [1995] 2 AC 633 (HL) 740–41.
[75] [2007] EWCA Civ 1361, with examples at [44].
[76] *ibid*, [45]. [77] 2008 SC 351, 2008 SLT 368 (IH) [134]. [78] [2013] EWCA Civ 194, [34].

Dyson MR remarked that a key case concerning negligently-inflicted psychiatric injury, *W v Essex CC*, was 'a strike-out case. All that the House of Lords decided was that the claim should not have been struck out because it raised an arguable case. For that reason alone, it is of limited value'.

However, and notwithstanding such sentiments, the strike-out applications which have guided, determined, and in some cases, revamped, English Tort law, are given the prominence in this book which, in the author's opinion, they so richly deserve. Some of their doctrines and influence have endured for decades, and 'good English law' would not be the same without them!

TORTS AND DEATH

§1.11 When a person dies as a result of D's tort, two potential actions are available: an action by the person's estate, under the Law Reform (Miscellaneous Provisions) Act 1934; and an action by the person's dependants, under the Fatal Accidents Act 1976.

Although it may seem somewhat odd to confront the subject of torts giving rise to death so early in this book, it will quickly become apparent from subsequent chapters that, unfortunately, whether through D's negligence, battery, breach of statutory duty, or some other tort, a person (the Deceased) may die as a result of D's acts or omissions. It is important to appreciate, from the outset, how claims may legally be brought in that event. In fact, two distinct claims are potentially available:

- a 'survival action', whereby the Deceased's estate (the Estate) may bring an action on behalf of the Deceased *for the Deceased's own losses*, pursuant to the Law Reform (Miscellaneous Provisions) Act 1934 ('the 1934 Act');[79] or
- a 'wrongful death action', whereby the Deceased's dependants (the Dependants) may sue, *on their own behalf*, for *their* loss of dependency, pursuant to the Fatal Accidents Act 1976 ('the FAA').[80] This is also called 'an FAA action', a 'dependency claim', or a 'Lord Campbell's Act action'.

The action against D is brought by either the Estate or by the Dependant (either of whom is C for these purposes, depending upon the Act being relied upon). Dealing with each in turn:

An action by/against the Estate

§1.12 Pursuant to s 1(1) of the 1934 Act, when the Deceased dies, all causes of action vested in him (or subsisting against him) survive for the benefit (or burden) of his Estate – subject to two exceptions: (1) claims for defamation, and (2) bereavement damages. When pursuing an action against wrongdoer D, the Deceased's Estate must prove that the Deceased had a 'cause of action', which was 'vested' in him at his death.

The key provision: Section 1(1) of the 1934 Act provides that, 'all causes of action subsisting against or vested in him shall survive against, or, as the case may be, for the benefit of, his

[79] In force 25 Jul 1934.

[80] In force 1 Sep 1976. It did not apply to any cause of action arising on a death before then (s 7(2)).

estate. Provided that this subsection shall not apply to causes of action for defamation'. This means that a tortious right of action by (or against) the Deceased may legally commence, following the Deceased's death. The action can be brought by, or against, the personal representatives of the Deceased's Estate.

On the one hand, where the Deceased's Estate makes a claim under the 1934 Act, then it is for the loss and damage *which the Deceased suffered* as a result of D's tort. On the other hand, where an action is brought *against the Deceased's Estate*, then any damages ordered to be paid by the estate (for the Deceased's wrong) becomes a liability which the Deceased's Estate must meet, because that liability is passed to the Deceased's Estate by virtue of the 1934 Act.

Where the Deceased's Estate is sued by C, the timing of events is important. In the usual case where D commits a tort (say, his negligent driving caused C's injury), and then D dies, C can continue his action against D's Estate, that death notwithstanding. However, under s 1(4), where the Deceased 'dies before, or at the same time as, the damage was suffered', then a cause of action is 'deemed' to have subsisted against that Deceased before his death. This covers circumstances where D dies instantaneously in the same car accident which injured C; or where C does not suffer his injury until some time after that car accident in which D died.

The previous common law: The 1934 Act reversed the harsh position which had prevailed at common law – in which, where a victim died as the result of D's tort, no cause of action either arose or could be continued. C's right of action in tort died with him, in that death extinguished the right to bring any action in tort. Similarly, at common law, where the wrongdoer D died as a result of the tort which he committed against C, then C (or, if C also died in the accident, his Dependant under the Fatal Accidents Act 1846, considered below) could not continue his action against D's Estate. This rule was known by the maxim, '*actio personalis moritur cum persona*' (a personal right of action dies with the person).

Exceptions: There are rare instances, however, where an action in tort does **not** survive the death of either C or of D. Where C complains that he was defamed by D, and then either C or D dies, that action is excluded by the 1934 Act, and does not survive the Deceased's death (per s 1(1)). Moreover, where C (whilst alive) had a claim against D for bereavement damages under the FAA, for the negligently-caused death of a spouse or child, but then either C or D dies, that claim for bereavement damages does not survive for the benefit of the Deceased's Estate either (per s 1(1A)[81]).

Two legal issues are particularly necessary to check, when the Deceased's estate is seeking to sue a tortious wrongdoer, D, under the 1934 Act:

Nutshell analysis: An action pursuant to the 1934 Act

Elements of the action:

1. A 'cause of action' had arisen, which the Deceased could either pursue or to which he was subject
2. That cause of action was 'vested' in or against the Deceased, at the time of death

Element #1: Cause of action. There is no statutory definition of what amounts to a 'cause of action' in the 1934 Act. Hence, the expression bears its ordinary meaning (per *Harris v*

[81] Inserted by the Administration of Justice Act 1982, s 4(1).

Lewisham and Guy's Mental Health Trust[82]), and was defined in *Letang v Cooper* to mean 'a factual situation, the existence of which entitles one person to obtain from the court a remedy against another person'.[83]

The effect of the 1934 Act is that it is **not** necessary to ask whether a Deceased's claim against D was a 'personal action' which could be assignable by operation of law. In *Ronex Properties Ltd v John Laing Construction Ltd*,[84] it was said that s 1(1) of the 1934 Act made 'comprehensive provision' for the survival of causes of action 'over the whole field'. Provided that the Deceased had a 'cause of action', then the benefit of it passed to his estate under the 1934 Act – whether it was a 'personal action' or not. However, not all benefits conferred by, or recoverable under, all statutes survive the victim's death. For example, in *D'Este v D'Este*,[85] an application for financial provision under the matrimonial causes legislation was not a cause of action.

Element #2: Vested in the Deceased. For a cause of action to be 'vested' in the Deceased at the time of his death, its elements must be complete. This means that if the tort is one which requires proof of damage, and if the Deceased had not suffered any relevant damage prior to his death, then there can be no cause of action 'vested' in the Deceased at his death. All the Deceased had was a potential cause of action, in the event that loss was to be suffered. In that case, s 1(1) has no effect, because there is nothing to 'survive' for the benefit of the Estate (per Carnwath LJ in *Daniels v Thompson*[86]).

As noted previously, s 1(4) is wider, in that it extends the survival of the action in tort *against* a Deceased's Estate, where the Deceased died *before* damage was incurred; but there is no similar extension for an Estate which is claiming on behalf of the Deceased.

Damages. As originally enacted, the 1934 Act permitted the recovery by the Estate of a wide array of damages on the Deceased's behalf. However, since s 1 of the Administration of Justice Act 1982 took effect on 1 January 1983, the damages recoverable in a survival action are limited to only certain types – loss of earnings, special damages, physical injury, pain and suffering and loss of amenity (PSLA), funeral expenses, and care and assistance for the Deceased. Conversely, certain heads of damage are not recoverable by the Estate in a survival action: damages for loss of expectation of life, or for fear of impending death; and bereavement damages. These issues are considered further in Chapter 11.

Contributory negligence. Some fault in causing the Deceased's death may rest with either the Deceased himself, or with someone in the Deceased's Estate (e.g., if the Deceased's wife's killed the Deceased due to her negligent driving). The effect of that contributory negligence is considered in Chapter 10.

The dependants' action

§1.13 Whereas, under the 1934 Act, the Estate seeks to recover damages accruing to the Deceased, a 'wrongful death' action under the FAA permits designated 'dependants' of the Deceased to recover specific damages for the deprivation of financial income or financially-measurable support caused to those dependants by the Deceased's death.

[82] [2000] EWCA Civ 87, [30] (also known as *Andrews v Lewisham and Guy's Mental Health Trust*).
[83] [1965] 1 QB 232 (CA) 242–43 (Diplock LJ). [84] [1983] QB 398 (CA) 405.
[85] [1973] Fam 55, 59, and cited in *Harris* [2000] EWCA Civ 87, [30(6)].
[86] [2004] EWCA Civ 307, [59]–[60].

Although both a survival action and an FAA action arise out of the Deceased's death, the types of damages, and for whom they are awarded, are entirely different. Note that any damages awarded under the 1934 Act do **not** fall to be deducted from damages awarded under the FAA.

The purpose of the FAA: The FAA confers a right upon the dependants of the Deceased, who died as a result of D's tort, to enable those dependants to recover the loss of financial support arising from the Deceased's wrongful death – provided that the Deceased would have been able to recover damages from D, but for his death. It was first introduced as the Fatal Accidents Act 1846 (known as Lord Campbell's Act). It has been judicially described as an action 'to recover the loss caused to those dependants by the death of the breadwinner' (per *Pickett v British Rail Engineering Ltd*[87]).

The Dependant's claim is both derivative from, and independent of, the Deceased's claim. It is derivative, because it will depend upon the validity of any claim which would have been open to the Deceased (i.e., if the claim was barred to the Deceased, it will be barred to the Dependant). However, the claim is independent, because the Dependant's claim is for damages in his own right, i.e. for damages sustained by him personally (per *Dick v Falkirk Burgh*[88]). As Denning LJ described in *Gray v Barr*, the Dependants 'stand in [the Deceased's] shoes in regard to *liability*, but not as to damages'.[89]

The previous common law: Until 1846, the common law applied, per *Baker v Bolton*,[90] whereby the death of another human being could not be complained of as an injury. Hence, where the Deceased died due to D's tort, then anyone who suffered financial loss as the result of that breadwinner's wrongful death was unable to recover damages for that loss (unless C had an independent cause of action arising from the Deceased's death, such as loss of consortium). This harsh result caused much disquiet among lawmakers. Indeed, the Law Commission has noted that the FAA 'was a response to fatalities on the railways',[91] whereby a lot of husbands/fathers were killed in railway accidents, due to faulty tracks and signalling equipment (if any), demolition works which went awry, and poor weather conditions.

The elements of an FAA action are as follows:

Nutshell analysis: The FAA action

Elements of the action:

1 The Deceased would have had a claim against D
2 The Dependant is an appropriate claimant under the Act
3 The Dependant has suffered loss of dependency
4 The action is not barred or excluded

Element #1: The Deceased would have had a claim against D. Under s 1(1) of the FAA, the death of the Deceased must have been 'caused by any wrongful act, neglect or default [of D]', and would have 'entitled the [Deceased] to maintain an action and recover damages in respect

[87] [1978] UKHL 4, [1980] AC 136, 146. [88] 1976 SC (HL) 1, 18–21 (Lord Wilberforce).

[89] [1971] 2 QB 554 (CA) 569 (original emphasis), quoted in EWLC, *Claims for Wrongful Death* (Rep 263, 1999) [2.2], fn 61.

[90] (1808) 170 ER 1033 (KB) (C was a publican, and his wife, who died in a stage coach accident because of D's negligence, had been useful in the business; C recovered £100 for his wife's loss of consortium).

[91] EWLC, *Claims for Wrongful Death* (1999) [2.1], fn 59, citing: *Hansard*, 21 Aug 1846, vol 88, col 926.

thereof'. Hence, it must be shown that, at the time of his death, the Deceased would have had a claim against D.

For example, insofar as a negligence action is concerned, the Deceased must have been able to prove that D's act or omission caused his injury and damage (i.e., death) – whether on the usual principle of 'but-for' causation or under one of the exceptional causal theorems (discussed in Chapter 8). In *Barker v Corus UK Ltd*,[92] which is authority for one of those exceptional theorems, the House of Lords noted that '[t]he approach to damages payable on a Fatal Accidents Act 1976 claim would be no different', whether it was C, or a Dependant under the FAA, bringing the claim. Similarly, where D's negligence caused some physical injury to the Deceased and the Deceased thereafter commits suicide, then for the Deceased's Dependant to claim damages under the FAA, the suicide must not be treated as an intervening act which breaks the chain or causation, and nor must it be too remote at law to be compensable (per *Corr v IBC Vehicles*,[93] where the Deceased's suicidal jump from a multi-storey carpark, after suffering horrendous facial injuries due to D's negligence, was neither an intervening act nor too remote, and hence, Mrs Corr and her two sons could recover under the FAA).

Element #2: The Dependant is an appropriate claimant. Any person who claims a loss of dependency resulting from the Deceased's death must be able to bring himself within the statutorily-prescribed categories of a Dependant. While s 1(2) provides that every such action shall be for the benefit of such Dependants of the Deceased, the term, 'dependant', is defined in s 1(3), to cover **only** the following:

(a) the spouse of the Deceased, including any former spouse who was financially supported by the Deceased (including one whose marriage to the Deceased was dissolved, annulled or declared void);

(b) a co-habitant of the Deceased – provided that the Dependant and the Deceased had been living in the same household as man and wife (or as same-sex partners)[94] for at least two years immediately before the Deceased's death. According to *Kotke v Saffarini*,[95] parties will be 'in the same household' if they are tied by their relationship – that tie being manifest, not by merely living under the same roof, but by 'the public and private acknowledgement of their mutual society, and the mutual protection and support which binds them together'.

> In *Kotke v Saffarini*, Trevor Snowdon and his partner, Ms Kotke, C, were hit by D's car while walking across a bridge in Bath. Hurled over the parapet wall into the River Avon below, Mr Snowdon was killed, and C was severely injured but survived. C sued D under the FAA. **Held:** her claim failed. She was not a suitable Dependant, not being Mr Snowdon's spouse, nor having lived with him in the same household for at least two years before his death. Their relationship 'did not cross the statutory threshold into the final stage'. Mr Snowdon kept a separate home in Doncaster with his wardrobe and possessions, and lived out of an overnight bag when staying with C in Bath. The splitting of shopping expenses 'was evidence of a sharing relationship, but one which fell short of the establishment of a joint household'.

(c) any parent or other ascendant (e.g., grandparent) of the Deceased;

(d) any person who was treated by the Deceased as his parent;

[92] [2006] UKHL 20, [2006] 2 AC 572, [63]. [93] [2008] UKHL 13, [2008] 1 AC 884.

[94] Pursuant to the Civil Partnership Act 2004, s 83.

[95] [2005] EWCA Civ 221, [23], with quote in case description at [59].

(e) any child or other descendant of the Deceased (including step-children, adopted and illegitimate children, and any unborn child conceived by the Deceased and born after the Deceased's death);
(f) any child (not the Deceased's own child) of any marriage to which the Deceased was a party and whom Deceased treated as a child of the family in relation to that marriage; and
(g) any person who is, or is the issue of, a brother, sister, uncle or aunt of the Deceased.

Element #3: The Dependant can prove loss of dependency. According to the 'reasonable expectation' test, each Dependant must separately prove that he reasonably expected to receive a pecuniary benefit arising from his relationship with the Deceased; and that he would have received it, but for the Deceased's death. That follows from s 3(1), which provides that damages under the FAA 'may be awarded as are proportioned to the injury resulting from the death to the dependants respectively'. Hence, individual amounts will generally be awarded to **each** Dependant named in the suit.

The 'reasonable expectation test' seems to have originated in 1858 in *Franklin v South Eastern Railway Co*,[96] where the correct question put to the jury was whether the Dependant, an old and infirm father, 'had any such reasonable expectation of benefit from the continuance of his son's life', where his son, 21, was negligently killed in a railway collision. More recently, in *Drake v Starkey*, it was said that '[t]his reasonable expectation test is a judicial interpretation of the archaic and somewhat diffuse wording of the [FAA Act]'.[97]

In *Drake v Starkey*, James Wilson died of mesothelioma which he contracted as a result of his exposure to asbestos when working for D as a boiler erector at Dartford power station. His two daughters, his grandson, his six other grandchildren, and four great-grandchildren, could each separately prove that they reasonably expected to receive a pecuniary benefit arising from the family relationship (e.g., birthday gifts, weekly shopping contributions, one-off purchases of white-goods), and that they would have received those benefits, but for Mr Wilson's death.

The date for assessing whether the claimant was a Dependant is assessed when the Deceased died. The dependancy cannot, say, reduce after the Deceased's death, because the Dependant happened to take over the Deceased's business, earning a good income in the process. As remarked by Smith LJ in *Welsh Ambulance Services v Williams*,[98] 'dependency is fixed at the moment of death; it is what the Dependants would probably have received as benefit from the Deceased, had the Deceased not died. What decisions people make afterwards is irrelevant'.

In *Welsh Ambulance v Williams*, Mr Williams was killed when negligently hit by D's ambulance. **Held**: Mr Williams' wife and children were his Dependants when he died. 'The fact that each of them was as well off after the death as before – because David and Sarah took over responsibility for managing the business, and did so successfully – is nothing to the point'.

Of course, where the claimants cannot prove dependancy upon the Deceased who died as a result of D's tort, then no FAA claim is possible (as, e.g., in *Hicks v CC of South Yorkshire*,[99] where the parental claimants were not dependent upon their two daughters killed in the Hillsborough disaster).

[96] (1858) 157 ER 448 (Exch Ct) 448. [97] [2010] EWHC 2004 (QB) [44].
[98] [2008] EWCA Civ 81, [49]–[50]. [99] [1991] UKHL 9.

Element #4: The FAA action is not barred or excluded. A number of factors may bar the Dependant from bringing an FAA action against D. These 'preclusive factors' – itemised both by the English Law Commission,[100] and in *Dick v Falkirk Burgh*[101] – consist of the following:

- where the Deceased had already obtained judgment against D in respect of the cause of action. Since the enactment of s 3 of the Damages Act 1996, an award of provisional damages to the Deceased (awarded where the victim of D's tort faces the prospect of a serious deterioration of his condition in the future, and where preferred to a lump sum damages award) does not bar an FAA claim, although it will be taken into account when assessing damages payable to the Dependant;
- where the Deceased had settled his claim prior to his death 'in full and final settlement of this claim' against D, thus precluding any further action by a Dependant (discussed in **'Multiple defendants'**, an online chapter);
- where defences such as *volenti*, or illegality, were available against the Deceased; or
- where a contract, or an expired limitation period which could not be extended by the exercise of judicial discretion, excludes a claim by the Deceased against D.

Damages. Although FAA damages are *principally* awarded for the Dependant's financial or pecuniary loss, certain non-pecuniary heads of damage are also recoverable, as discussed further in Chapter 11.

Contributory negligence. As under the 1934 Act, some fault in bringing about the Deceased's death may rest with either the Deceased himself, or with a Dependant of the Deceased who is claiming under the FAA. The effect of that contributory negligence is considered in Chapter 10.

[100] *Claims for Wrongful Death* (1999) [2.3]–[2.5]. [101] 1976 SC (HL) 1.

Part 1

Negligence

2

Duty I – General principles governing duty of care

INTRODUCTION

The framework for negligence

In order to prove the cause of action in negligence, C must establish **four** requirements, *viz*:

> **Nutshell analysis: The tort of negligence**
>
> 1 D owed C a duty of care to avoid causing C the type of injury of which he complains
> 2 D breached the duty of care, by falling below the standard of reasonable care which the law demands
> 3a D's breach caused the damage complained of by C
> 3b the damage complained of by C was not too remote (unforeseeable) at law to be recoverable

This, and the following three chapters, deal solely with the first element – the establishment of a duty of care – in a variety of scenarios. English courts have long drawn a distinction between the existence of a duty of care in the context of loss caused by *physical injury or property damage*, on the one hand (the subject of analysis in this chapter); and where *economic loss* or *psychiatric injury* is caused, on the other. In the latter scenarios, special rules apply for the establishment of a duty of care, which are the subject of consideration in Chapters 4 and 5, respectively.

In *JD v East Berkshire Community Health NHS Trust*,[1] Lord Rodger somewhat pessimistically remarked that, 'the world is full of harm for which the law furnishes no remedy'. That lack of remedy may be entirely attributable to the lack of any duty of care (as it was in *JD* itself). In that regard, this element is a very important control mechanism in restricting D's liability for the tort of negligence – and its use in restricting the ambit of liability has become a more

[1] [2005] UKHL 23, [2005] 2 AC 373, [100].

modern trend. A lack of duty can preclude D's liability in negligence, even where *every other element* of negligence is satisfied by C.

§2.1 A duty of care is a legal duty imposed on D, by law, to exercise reasonable care and/or skill to avoid the risk of injury to C. Whether a duty of care is owed by D, on a set of given facts, is a question of law.

This proposition (per Lord Thankerton in *Bourhill v Young*[2]) contains several points of significance:

- a duty is *imposed* upon D – it is not a legal obligation which D agrees to (or can contract out of);
- the duty is to exercise *reasonable* care, not to achieve perfection or a guaranteed perfect outcome;
- a duty of care is owed by D to either C, or a class of persons of whom C was one. It is not usually imposed upon D towards the *world-at-large*, in respect of any one act or omission of negligence (although there are exceptions, e.g., manufacturers to consumers of defective products).

Whether a duty of care arises on the facts is determined by one or more of **three** potential approaches. Before considering these, however, a brief canvass of the development of the duty of care concept is apposite.

A brief historical overview

The ease with which C has been able to establish a duty of care in English negligence law has waxed and waned over time. In fact, Lord Walker's description of negligence (in *Customs and Excise Commrs v Barclays Bank plc*[3]) as being, 'not one of steady advance along a broad front, [but] ... a much more confused series of engagements with salients and beachheads, and retreats as well as advances', is as appropriate to the element of duty of care as it is to the tort as a whole.

Recognition of the tort of negligence actually **preceded** the seminal case of *Donoghue v Stevenson* (1932),[4] but the treatment of the duty concept, before and after it, has frequently been in a state of evolution – noted in the Table below:

The duty of care over the years

Early 19th century	There were a few 'recognised cases' in which a duty of care was acknowledged to exist (outside of a contractual relationship) – per Lord Buckmaster's dissenting judgment in *Donoghue v Stevenson.*[a] These consisted of: road-users who injured others ('cases of collision and carriage'); manufacturers towards consumers where the product was dangerous (e.g., a gun, as in *Langridge v Levy,*[b] although that was probably a case of fraudulent misstatement, not of negligence); and occupiers who invited visitors onto their premises, where there was 'some hidden danger' on those premises. However, there was **no** general principle of law, as to when a duty of care would be owed by D to C.

[a] [1932] AC 562 (HL) 573 (Lord Buckmaster, citing Brett MR in *Heaven v Pender* (1883) 11 QBD 503, 509).
[b] (1837) 2 M&W 519, 150 ER 863.

[2] [1943] AC 92 (HL) 98 (Lord Thankerton), 104 (Lord Macmillan). [3] [2006] UKHL 28, [2007] 1 AC 181, [69].
[4] [1932] AC 562 (HL).

1842 In *Winterbottom v Wright*:[c]

a faulty mail carriage was hired by manufacturer, D, to the Postmaster-General (the other contracting party), and it collapsed, injuring the driver, C. As between manufacturer and a third party, there was no recognised category of a duty of care. **Held:** C could not recover against manufacturer D, as there was no cause of action by which to bring his claim (there was no contract between C and D, and to uphold a duty would undermine privity of contract).

Per Alderson B: 'The only safe rule is to confine the right to recover to those who enter into the contract. If we go one step beyond that, there is no reason why we should not go fifty'. Hence, the Postmaster-General could have sued in negligence, but not driver C. Liability in negligence was aligned with contractual, or quasi-contractual, relationships only.

1883 In *Heaven v Pender (t/as West India Graving Dock Co)*:[d]

a dockowner, D, supplied and put up scaffolding for a ship, under a contract with the shipowner. A painting firm contracted with the shipowner to paint the ship, and an employed painter, C, was injured when the scaffolding partly collapsed. **Held:** D was liable in damages to C, on the basis of an *implied invitation* by D to those painting the ship to use the scaffolding provided by him (i.e., there was a quasi-contractual, rather than any direct, relationship existing between C and D).

However, Brett MR (later to become Lord Esher) (dissenting) attempted to fashion a **general** principle upon which, apart from contract, the relationship between C and D could create a duty to take ordinary care: 'whenever one person [D] is, by circumstances, placed in such a position with regard to another [C] that everyone of ordinary sense ... would at once recognise that, if he did not use ordinary care and skill in his own conduct with regard to those circumstances, he would cause danger of injury to the person or property of [C], a duty arises to use ordinary care and skill to avoid such danger'. Hence, the suggestion was floated that a duty of care should be recognised in wider circumstances, independent of contractual relationships.

However, the majority members of the CA (Cotton and Bowen LJJ) declined to support that 'larger principle' put forward by Brett MR.

1893 In *Le Lievre v Gould*:[e]

a surveyor, D, provided completion certificates to lenders, C, who, on the faith of those certificates, advanced monies progressively to a builder. The certificates contained negligent statements. Surveyor D had not been appointed by lenders C, and hence, there was no contractual relationship between them. **Held:** D owed no duty to C to exercise care in giving his certificates.

Importantly, Lord Esher appeared to resile from his earlier statement in *Heaven v Pender*: 'But can [C] rely upon negligence, in the absence of fraud? ... What duty is there, when there is no relation between the parties by contract? A man is entitled to be as negligent as he pleases towards the whole world, if he owes no duty to them'.

---

[c] (1842) 10 M&W 109 (Ct Exch) 115, 152 ER 402.
[d] (1883) 11 QBD 503 (CA) 509–10.
[e] [1893] 1 QB 491 (CA) 497.

1906 In *Cavalier v Pope*:[f]

a landlord, D, let a house with a dangerous floor to a tenant, and he contracted to repair it. Before he did so, part of the floor gave way, and the tenant's wife, C, was injured. **Held**: D owed no duty of care to C to remedy the defect.

Lord James endorsed the requirement for privity of contract to substantiate a duty of care: 'there was but one contract, and that was made with the husband. The wife cannot sue upon it ... I regret this result, because [C] has been injured entirely through the failure of D's agent to fulfil the contract he made. But moral responsibility ... is not identical with legal liablity'.

1929 In *Mullen v AG Barr*:[g]

Mr Mullen bought a bottle of brewed ginger beer (manufactured by D) from a shop retailer, and poured the drink for his two children, C. After they had drunk some of it, Mr Mullen poured out the rest, and a decomposed mouse came out. The suggestion that the bottle was tampered with deliberately after it left D's factory as a practical joke or to damage its business was rejected. C sued manufacturer D in negligence (albeit that Lord Hunter noted that, 'the injury sustained was so slight that [C] might have been well advised to leave litigation alone'). **Held (3:1):** D owed no duty to C, with whom D had no contract.

Lord Anderson (for the majority): 'where the goods of [D] are widely distributed throughout Scotland, it would seem little short of outrageous to make the manufacturer responsible to members of the public for the condition of the contents of every bottle which issues from their works ... [D] might be called on to meet claims of damages which they could not possibly investigate or answer'.[h]

Lord Hunter (dissenting): 'To open the bottles would be prejudicial to the beer, and the tabs on the corks are intended to give the consumer confidence that the bottles have not been tampered with after they have left [D's] premises. The bottles are so dark in colour as to prevent the retail dealer or the consumer from detecting the presence of foreign or deleterious matter by any ordinarily careful examination of the bottle ... In these circumstances, ... there is such a relationship between the manufacturer and consumer as to impose a duty upon the former to exercise care that the latter does not suffer injury'.[i] It was this dissenting view which came to reflect the law, three years later.

1932 In *Donoghue (or M'Alister) v Stevenson*:[j]

Miss Donoghue's friend purchased a bottle of ginger beer in a café in Paisley, near Glasgow. The ginger beer was manufactured by Stevenson, D, manufacturer of 'aerated waters'. Some contents were poured into the glasses of C and her friend, and they drank some. The remainder was then poured into their glasses, and the bottle turned out to contain the decomposed remains of a snail. Being an opaque bottle, the snail could not be detected until the greater part of the contents had been drunk. C alleged that she suffered from shock and severe gastro-enteritis, and sued manufacturer D in negligence. **Held (3:2):** C could, as a preliminary point of law, recover damages in negligence. The case was remitted back to trial for proof (and, on that point, the allegation that a snail was in the bottle was never proved[k]).

[f] [1906] AC 428 (HL) 430.
[g] [1929] Sess Cas 461, 1929 SLT 341 (SCIH). This was joined with a similar case: *McGowan v Barr & Co*, also concerning a decomposed mouse in a bottle of ginger beer.
[h] *ibid*, 479.
[i] *ibid*, 477.
[j] [1932] AC 562 (HL) 580–81 (Lord Atkin, for the majority, with Lords Tomlin and Buckmaster dissenting).
[k] A point made in, e.g.: *Vicario v Commr of Police* [2007] EWCA Civ 1361, [45].

Per the majority, Lords Atkin, Macmillan, and Thankerton:

(1) a duty of care no longer depended on a contractual (or quasi-contractual, per *Heaven v Pender*) relationship between C and D. A duty could be imposed by law between C and D, nevertheless;

(2) a *new* category of duty of care was created (i.e., manufacturer–consumer, where no contractual relationship existed between them, and where there was no possibility of intermediate examination of the product in question, because of its presentation); and

(3) the 'neighbour principle' was proposed by Lord Atkin in these terms: a duty of care is owed by D to 'persons who are so closely and directly affected by my act that I ought reasonably to have them in contemplation as being so affected, when I am directing my mind to the acts or omissions called into question'; and where there is proximity, 'not confined to mere physical proximity; but be used ... to extend to such close and direct relations that the act complained of directly affects [C]'.

1964 In *Hedley Byrne & Co Ltd v Heller & Partners Ltd*:[l]

a bank, D, was asked about the creditworthiness and financial stability of one of the bank's customers, where it was made clear that the party on whose behalf the enquiry was being made, C, wished to know whether it could prudently lend a substantial sum of money to that customer. Bank D gave a favourable reference, but with a disclaimer of responsibility. C did extend credit to the customer, in reliance on the reference, but ultimately lost the money. **Held:** D was not liable, due to the disclaimer; but were it not for the disclaimer, a duty of care could arise in relation to negligent statements.

The basis of a duty of care could be predicated upon the so-called 'voluntary assumption of responsibility/reliance' test of duty of care (per Lord Morris). The case was notable, as the first occasion upon which negligence was (but for the disclaimer) available for economic loss resulting from C's reliance on a negligent misstatement (as discussed in Chapter 4).

1970 In *Home Office v Dorset Yacht Co*:[m]

Lord Reid described the difference between the 'categorisation approach' to a duty of care (i.e., that, when a new or novel scenario arises, it is necessary to ask whether it is covered by existing authority) and the 'principled approach' (i.e., that a single general principle, as espoused in *Donoghue v Stevenson*, should be applied in all new circumstances to determine the existence of a duty of care). Lord Reid favoured the latter approach: 'when a new point emerges, one should ask, not whether it is covered by authority, but whether recognised principles apply to it ... I think that the time has come when we should say that [the principled approach] ought to apply, unless there is some justification or valid explanation for its exclusion'. This view had the potential to expand the scope of a duty of care considerably.

1978 In *Anns v Merton LBC*:[n]

the question was whether a local authority, D, could be liable in negligence to long-term lessees, C, occupying maisonettes which were built on inadequate foundations, where the building had not complied with relevant statutory building regulations, and where D had not discovered by inspection the inadequacy of the foundations before they were covered over. **Held:** C had a cause of action against local authority D in negligence, for the cost of repairing cracks in the structure and of underpinning the foundations (i.e., physical damage).

[l] [1964] AC 465 (HL) 497, 502–3, 514.
[m] [1970] AC 1004 (HL) 1026–27.
[n] [1978] AC 728 (HL) 751–52.

(1) The 'principled approach' (advocated by Lord Reid in *Dorset Yacht*) was endorsed. Lord Wilberforce noted that: 'the position has now been reached that, in order to establish that a duty of care arises in a particular situation, it is **not** necessary to bring the facts of that situation within those of previous situations in which a duty of care has been held to exist';

(2) The principle posed by Lord Wilberforce, however, was **very wide** indeed: 'First, one has to ask whether, as between the alleged wrongdoer [D] and the person who has suffered damage [C], there is a sufficient relationship of proximity or neighbourhood such that, in the reasonable contemplation of [D], carelessness on his part may be likely to cause damage to [C] – in which case a *prima facie* duty of care arises. Secondly, if the first question is answered affirmatively, it is necessary to consider whether there are any considerations which ought to negative, or to reduce or limit, the scope of the duty, or the class of person to whom it is owed, or the damages to which a breach of it may give rise'.

This passage was subsequently interpreted, by several courts, to give rise to a 2-stage test: (1) whether the harm to C was foreseeable (so that proximity was established merely by a reasonable contemplation of likely harm – to all intents and purposes, they were treated as synonymous). (2) should a duty of care be excluded for public policy reasons?

1983 In *Junior Books Ltd v Veitchi Co Ltd*:[o]

Veitchi, D, were specialist subcontractors who laid flooring in a factory built for Junior Books, C, at Grangemouth. C alleged that the floor was defective, and would have to be replaced. C and D had no contractual relationship, because D's contract was with the builder. C, as owner, also had a contractual relationship with the builder, but declined to sue the builder for the defective flooring. Rather, C claimed damages from D, the subcontractor, in negligence, for the cost of replacing the floor. The defective flooring had not caused danger to the health or safety of any person, so C was only suing D for the loss caused to C by having to replace the floor. **Held (4:1):** C could recover in negligence from D. C's economic loss was reasonably foreseeable; and no policy reasons precluded a duty of care.

There was no similar case previously where C had recovered. But the question was no longer (post-*Anns*) whether any duty of care had been found in a similar previous case (i.e., the categorisation approach had been disapproved). Rather, the *Anns* 2-stage principled approach applied, which allowed the concept of duty to develop more expansively (held the House unanimously). However, Lord Brandon dissented in the result, holding that policy reasons negatived a duty.

1990 In *Caparo Industries plc v Dickman*,[p] the 2-stage *Anns* test was disapproved explicitly. First, that was because of 'the inability of any single general principle to provide a practical test which can be applied to every situation to determine whether a duty of care is owed and, if so, what is its scope' (per Lord Bridge). Also, to the extent that *Anns* dictated that a duty of care could be derived from reasonable foreseeability alone, and that foreseeability could be equated with proximity, that had resulted from a 'misinterpretation of the effect of the [*Anns*] decision' (per Lord Oliver). Instead, a more restrictive view was proposed (per Lord Bridge):

[o] [1983] 1 AC 520 (HL) 536.
[p] [1990] 2 AC 605 (HL) 606–7, 617–18 (Lord Bridge), 643 (Lord Oliver).

(1) There was no single or simple formula, touchstone or principle which would definitively state when a duty of care was, or was not, owed;
(2) In modern jurisprudence, 'the law has now moved in the direction of attaching greater significance to the more traditional categorisation of distinct and recognisable situations, as guides to the existence, the scope and the limits of the varied duties of care which the law imposes', i.e., the categorisation approach was reinstated; and
(3) English law should adhere to the view (expressed earlier by the High Court of Australia[q]) that 'the law should develop novel categories of negligence incrementally, and by analogy with established categories, rather than by a massive extension of a *prima facie* duty of care restrained only by indefinable [public policy] considerations' [to quote *Anns*].

1990 In *Murphy v Brentwood DC*,[r] the categorisation of damage in *Anns* was held to be wrong – future purchasers/lessees of the type in *Anns* had **no** interest in the property when the breach occurred, but would only realise that damage when it came time to sell the asset. Hence, the damage was pure economic loss to C. The actual decision in *Anns* was 'departed from' (and, in effect, overruled) as being wrongly-decided (thus invoking the *Practice Statement of 1966*[s]).

Also, the departure from the 2-stage *Anns* test, which had occurred five months earlier in *Caparo*, was endorsed. The categorisation approach, and an incremental approach to the development of a duty of care in novel scenarios, should be followed thereafter.

2006 In *Customs and Excise Commrs v Barclays Bank plc*,[t] the general approach in *Caparo* was thoroughly endorsed: 'there is no single common denominator ... by which liability may be determined. In my view, the threefold test of foreseeability, proximity and fairness, justice and reasonableness provides a convenient general framework, although it operates at a high level of abstraction' (per Lord Mance). Furthermore, the wide-ranging 'principled approach' from *Anns* was from a different era, and was **not** to be endorsed: 'the unhappy experience with the rule so elegantly formulated by Lord Wilberforce in *Anns* suggests that appellate judges should follow the philosopher's advice to "Seek simplicity, and distrust it"' (per Lord Rodger).

2009 In *Mitchell v Glasgow CC*,[u] Lord Hope reiterated that, just because *Caparo* was a pure economic loss case does not restrict the application of its test to that context, nor preclude it from operating in personal injury – a submission to that effect was specifically rejected.

---

[q] *Sutherland SC v Heyman* (1985) 60 ALR 1 (HCA) 43–44 (Brennan J).
[r] [1991] 1 AC 398 (HL).
[s] *Practice Statement (Judicial Precedent)* [1966] 1 WLR 1234.
[t] [2006] UKHL 28, [51] (Lord Rodger), [93] (Lord Mance).
[u] [2009] UKHL 11, [2009] 1 AC 874, [24] (Lord Hope).

2013 In *Woodland v Essex CC*,[v] the incremental approach to the development of the law, as espoused in *Caparo*, was again endorsed: '[t]he common law is a dynamic instrument. It develops and adapts to meet new situations as they arise. Therein lies its strength. But therein also lies a danger, the danger of unbridled and unprincipled growth to match what the court perceives to be the merits of the particular case. So it must proceed with caution, incrementally by analogy with existing categories, and consistently with some underlying principle' (Lady Hale). Further, even though the assumption of responsibility test in *Hedley Byrne* arose in the context of economic loss, it may incrementally apply, whether the potential loss is economic or physical (Lord Sumption).

[v] [2013] UKSC 66, [2014] 1 All ER 482, [28], [11].

This rather tortuous development of the concept of a duty of care aptly demonstrates the dynamic and evolving nature of the common law's development. Thankfully, the tests which govern the existence of a duty of care in English jurisprudence are far more settled now, and we now turn to those.

THE MODERN DUTY OF CARE TESTS

The three approaches: general

§2.2 As an overarching framework for analysis, three broad approaches have been adopted in English law, to assess whether a duty of care is owed by D to C: (1) the ***Caparo*** tri-partite test; (2) the ***Hedley Byrne*** 'voluntary assumption of responsibility/reliance' test; and (3) the incremental test.

In *Customs and Excise Commrs v Barclays Bank plc*,[5] the House of Lords outlined the 'conceptual basis' for deciding whether a duty of care exists in particular circumstances:

The three duty of care tests

The test	The definition	The source
The *Caparo* test	whether the '*Caparo* ingredients' are met: • harm to C was actually foreseen, or reasonably foreseeable, by D; • the requisite proximity (or 'neighbourhood') existed between C and D; and • it is fair, just and reasonable to impose a duty of care (or that no legal or public policy reasons preclude the imposition of a duty of care)	*Caparo Industries plc v Dickman* (per Lord Bridge)[a]

[a] [1990] 2 AC 605 (HL) 617–18 (Lord Bridge) ('*Caparo*').

[5] [2006] UKHL 28, [4] (Lord Bingham), [82] (Lord Mance).

The voluntary assumption of responsibility/ reliance test	applies where D, possessed of special skill, undertook to apply that skill for the assistance of C, who relied upon that skill. It requires: • an assumption of responsibility by D towards C to conduct himself with due care and/or skill; and • a reciprocal reliance by C upon D in so conducting himself	*Hedley Byrne & Co Ltd v Heller & Partners Ltd* (per Lord Morris)[b]
The incremental test	any new or novel duty of care scenarios should develop incrementally, by close analogy with established categories, 'rather than by a massive extension of a *prima facie* duty of care restrained only by indefinable considerations which ought to negative, or to reduce or limit the scope of the duty or the class of person to whom it is owed'. In other words, courts should 'hug the coastline' of established duties of care	*Caparo* (per Lord Bridge)[c]

[b] [1964] AC 465 (HL) 502–3.
[c] [1990] 2 AC 605 (HL) 618 (Lord Bridge).

In reality, these provide convenient reference points, or 'high-level' principles, of what a court will search for, in order to fix D with a duty of care – but to call them 'tests' is rather artificial. In truth, without teasing out the detailed factors which point in favour of, or away from, say, 'proximity', an 'assumption of responsibility', or public policy, the tests all verge upon meaningless phraseology. Several judgments make this point. The concepts are said to 'operate at a high level of abstraction', and that '[w]hat matters is how, and by reference to what lower-level factors, they are interpreted in practice' (per Lord Mance in *Customs & Excise Commrs v Barclays Bank plc*[6]). As Lord Hoffmann also said in *Customs and Excise*, '[t]here is a tendency ... for phrases like "proximate", "fair, just and reasonable", and "assumption of responsibility", to be used as slogans, rather than practical guides to whether a duty should exist or not. These phrases are often illuminating, but discrimination is needed to identify the factual situations in which they provide useful guidance'.[7] In *Caparo*,[8] Lord Bridge earlier held that the requirements of 'proximity', 'reasonable foreseeability' and 'policy', were labels only; were not definitive, or even capable of precise definition; but were all relevant in an appropriate case. Hence, when discussing these tests, close attention will inevitably have to be paid to the 'lower-level factors' which have been particularly important in assessing whether D owed C a duty of care.

[6] [2007] 1 AC 181, [83], citing: *Caparo* [1990] 2 AC 605 (HL) 617–18 (Lord Bridge), 633 (Lord Oliver).
[7] *ibid*, [35]. [8] [1990] 2 AC 605 (HL) 617–18.

The close interplay among the three elements of the *Caparo* test has been oft-cited. Indeed, it was said by Lord Oliver that they are 'merely facets of the same thing',[9] while Dyson LJ noted, in *Carty v Croydon LBC*, that 'these issues overlap, and it is not always possible to draw hard and fast lines between them'.[10]

§2.3 The *Caparo* tri-partite test is considered to be the primary test for novel negligence scenarios involving personal injury or property damage. However, the test of 'voluntary assumption of responsibility/reliance' may be used instead of, or in conjunction with, the *Caparo* test. The 'incremental test' serves primarily as a cross-check.

Inevitably, the fact that the House of Lords approved **all three** tests in *Customs and Excise*[11] gives rise to some degree of uncertainty and 'slipperiness' in the law of negligence.

That said, the *Caparo* test has been indicated, at the highest appellate level, to have the most prominent role of the three tests – whether in the area of pure economic loss out of which it arose (covered in Chapter 4) or in personal injury or property damage. In *Van Colle v CC of Hertfordshire Police*, Lord Bingham noted that *Caparo* was 'currently ... the most-favoured test' for imposing a duty of care in novel negligence scenarios,[12] an observation approved in *Mitchell v Glasgow CC*[13] – both of which were personal injury cases. That preference is partly because the *Caparo* test provides a structure which 'makes the analysis more easily intelligible' (per *Neil Martin Ltd v HMRC*[14]). Judges have certainly perceived the *Caparo* approach to be a distinct improvement on the liberalism that went before it, when the so-called 'generalist' approach was in vogue. In *Everett v Comojo (UK) Ltd (t/as the Metropolitan)*, Lady Justice Smith remarked, in 2011, that *Caparo* is 'the correct starting point' for the existence of a duty of care, and that it, 'provides some guide to the touchstone which eluded [previous courts]. If not a touchstone, the threefold test provides a process by which judges can determine whether a duty should exist and, if so, to determine its scope'.[15]

In any event, there are instances where the assumption of responsibility test really does not work well. The concept of whether D assumed any responsibility towards C is objectively-determined. Hence, 'the further this test is removed from the actions and intentions of the actual [D], and the more notional the assumption of responsibility becomes, the less difference there is between this test and the threefold [*Caparo*] test' (per Lord Bingham in *Customs and Excise*[16]). It follows that, where D did not **know** of the existence, let alone the identity, of C, at the time of the allegedly negligent act or omission, then to hold that D objectively assumed responsibility towards that unknown party, or that D knew, or should have known, that C was relying upon his skill, knowledge or expertise, tends to be a highly artificial analysis. The problem exists in reverse too. To say that C relied upon D, when he was never aware of D's existence or of his role in the arrangements for C's welfare, is very strained. That issue arose in *Marc Rich & Co v Bishop Rock Ltd*, where Lord Steyn refuted any application of the assumption of responsibility test: '[g]iven that the cargo owners [C] were not even aware of NKK's [D's] examination of the ship, and that the cargo owners simply relied on the undertakings

[9] [1990] 2 AC 605 (HL) 633 (Lord Oliver).

[10] [2005] 1 WLR 2312 (CA) 2318, citing: *A v Essex CC* [2004] 1 WLR 1881 (CA) (Hale LJ).

[11] [2006] UKHL 28, [2007] 1 AC 181, [4] (Lord Bingham).

[12] [2008] UKHL 50, [2009] 1 AC 225, [42].

[13] [2009] UKHL 11, [2009] 1 AC 874, [21] (Lord Hope).

[14] [2006] EWHC 2425 (Ch) [86].

[15] [2011] EWCA Civ 13, [2012] 1 WLR 150, [26]–[27], [29].

[16] [2006] UKHL 28, [5].

of the shipowners, it is ... impossible to force the present set of facts into even the most expansive view of the doctrine of voluntary assumption of responsibility'.[17] In those sorts of circumstances, the *Caparo* test will be the go-to test for the duty of care analysis.

To complicate matters, however, the tests have sometimes been used in conjunction together. The full 'battery' has been employed in some cases of serious personal injury (e.g., as in *Watson v British Boxing Board of Control*,[18] *Kent v Griffiths*,[19] and *Geary v JD Wetherspoon plc*[20]). The *Caparo* test is by no means the exclusive test for physical injury or property damage cases. In any event, in *Merrett v Babb*, May LJ stated that 'it is reaching for the moon – and not required by authority', to expect that one 'single short abstract formulation' of when a duty of care arises could be framed.[21] Some courts have noted that the various tests are 'mutually supportive, and likely to lead to the same conclusion' (per *Niru Battery Manufacturing Co v Milestone Trading Ltd*[22]). However, that conclusion has not always followed. One recent example of where a duty of care was proven under the *Caparo* test, but where it could not be proven under the assumption of responsibility/reliance test, occurred in *Biddick v Morcom*[23] (discussed later in this chapter).

Some decisions have also tended to conflate the proximity requirement of *Caparo* with the assumption of responsibility/reliance test – e.g., in *Geary v JD Wetherspoon plc*, that '[D] assumed no such responsibility towards [C], and there was no such reliance. In those circumstances, I do not consider that the necessary proximity has been demonstrated';[24] and *Watson v British Boxing Board of Control Ltd*, that, where there was no reliance or assumption of responsibility (re emergency services such as the police), then 'there is no close proximity between the services and the general public'.[25]

Hence, whilst three different approaches may provide desirable flexibility, it does create what appears, at times, to be a fluid and pragmatic (some would say, haphazard!) answer to the legal question: does D owe C a duty of care?

Assuming the existence of a duty of care

General rule

§2.4 Where C sustains personal injury or property damage, then if C can align his relationship with D with one of the recognised categories in which a duty of care has, traditionally, arisen as a matter of law, there is no need for C to prove the individual ingredients of the duty of care tests.

In some scenarios, a duty of care will be presumed, where C can align his scenario with one of the 'distinct and recognisable situations' in which a duty of care has been said to arise as a matter of law (per Lord Bridge in *Caparo*[26]). In 'real life' litigation, D will frequently *concede* a duty in such cases.

If, however, the scenario giving rise to C's grievance against D falls outside one of the traditional categories – or falls within an existing category, but arises out of a hitherto unconsidered or rarely-considered fact scenario – then a legal analysis of whether a duty of care should attach to D is always called for. It is in these scenarios that the three tests of duty of care essentially come into play.

The following Table outlines, by reference to a sample authority, the recognised categories of duty of care which arise in English law, where C suffers personal injury:

[17] [1996] AC 211 (HL) 242. [18] [2001] QB 1134 (CA) [35]–[45]. [19] [2001] QB 36 (CA) [37]–[52].
[20] [2011] EWHC 1506 (QB). [21] [2001] EWCA Civ 214, [2001] QB 1174, [41] (May LJ).
[22] [2003] EWCA Civ 1446, [2004] QB 985, [38]. [23] [2014] EWCA Civ 182. [24] [2011] EWHC 1506 (QB) [68].
[25] [2001] QB 1134 (CA) [77] (Lord Phillips). [26] [1990] 2 AC 605 (HL) 617–18 (Lord Phillips).

Relationships traditionally giving rise to a duty of care

School and teacher, D, to pupil, C, for his physical welfare and educational needs (except where TP does the harm to C – a duty is not 'assumed' there)	*Carmarthenshire CC v Lewis*[a] (a nursery school 'certainly owes a duty to the child to protect him from injury'); *X (Minors) v Bedfordshire CC*[b] (re older school pupils); except where third parties do the harm to the pupils, in which case the duty of care is a novel, not a recognised, scenario: *Webster v Ridgeway Foundation School*[c]
Road-user, D, towards other road-users (whether they be pedestrians, or bystanders nearby to the road, or passengers or drivers of other vehicles on or near the road)	*Mitchell v Glasgow CC* (per Lord Hope):[d] 'where a person is injured in the course of his employment, or in a road traffic accident ... then it can be taken for granted that the employer owes a duty of care to the person who is in his employment, or that a duty is owed to other road users by the driver of a vehicle which causes an accident. If commonplace situations of that kind had to be analysed, ... the duty is owed not simply because loss, injury or damage is reasonably foreseeable ... there is a relationship of proximity between the employer and his employees, and the driver and other road users. This is sufficient in law to give rise to a duty of care ... this is so obvious that there is no need to ask whether it is fair, or whether it is just and reasonable, that [C] should recover damages'. An illustrative authority, *Nettleship v Weston*,[e] held that a duty of care owed by one road-user to another was 'clear'
Employers, D, who cause physical injury to their employees, C	See Lord Hope's discussion in *Mitchell v Glasgow CC* above; and the discussion and authorities in 'Employers' liability', an online chapter
Transport operator (bus company, ferry operator, train operator, etc), D, towards passenger C	*Silverlink Trains Ltd v Collins-Williamson*[f] (a duty owed by the train company was uncontentious); *Fernquest v City of Swansea*[g] (bus companies owe a duty to their passengers, but not once they have alighted at their stop)
Healthcare practitioner (doctor, nurse, physiotherapist, midwife, etc), D, towards patient C	*Sidaway v Bethlem Royal Hosp Governors*[h] (a doctor owes a duty to his patients, which is 'a single comprehensive duty covering all the ways in which a doctor is called on to exercise his skill and judgment in the improvement of the physical or mental condition of the patient'); nurses (per *Barnett v Chelsea and Kensington HMC*[i]), and other health professionals

[a] [1955] AC 549 (HL) 563.
[b] [1995] 2 AC 633 (HL) 766.
[c] [2010] EWHC 157 (QB).
[d] [2009] UKHL 11, [2009] 1 AC 874, [16].
[e] [1971] 2 QB 691 (CA) 700.
[f] [2009] EWCA Civ 850.
[g] [2011] EWCA Civ 1712.
[h] [1985] 1 AC 871 (HL) 893 (Lord Diplock).
[i] [1969] 1 QB 428.

Jailers/custodian, D, towards prisoners C	*Ellis v Home Office*[j] ('[t]he duty on those responsible for one of Her Majesty's prisons is to take reasonable care for the safety of those within, and that includes those who are within against their wish'); *Home Office v Dorset Yacht Co Ltd*[k] ('a duty of care for their safety and welfare was owed by the Home Office to prisoners in a prison' (although D was not prepared to concede that such an automatic duty was owed to prison visitors)
Occupier of premises, D, who invites visitors, C, and C is injured from the state of the premises	This recognised duty of care relationship is now governed by statute, as discussed in Chapter 12

[j] [1953] 2 All ER 149 (CA) 154 (Singleton LJ).
[k] [1970] AC 1004 (HL) 1047 (Viscount Dilhorne).

Caveat

However, even in cases involving a relationship that traditionally gives rise to a duty of care, the common law may carve out, from that general duty, certain scenarios in which no duty is owed, or it may nominate certain classes of Cs to whom no duty is owed – regardless of the fact that C and D are in a recognised category of relationship that traditionally does give rise to a duty of care. For example:

- the doctor–patient relationship is one of the 'recognised categories' of a duty of care – yet not all scenarios in which a doctor carelessly causes physical injury to patient C give rise to a duty in C's favour. For example, case law has limited/precluded a doctor's duty to warn in some scenarios (as discussed in Chapter 3), and insofar as sterilisation operations are concerned, a doctor's duty is **not** to avoid or minimise **all** adverse consequences flowing from a failed sterilisation (as discussed later in this chapter);
- the employer–employee relationship is another 'recognised category', which applies to physical injury suffered by an employee, C. However, *psychiatric* injury incurred by an employee in the workplace does not automatically give rise to a duty on the employer D's part; rather, that is subject to special rules governing the existence of a duty of care (as discussed in Chapter 5).

The rest of this chapter considers the constituent elements of the relevant duty of care tests. As a result of the overlap of the *Caparo* elements noted previously, some of the factors identified in this chapter may be listed herein as going to proximity, whereas others may prefer the view that they are, more suitably, matters of legal and public policy. Regardless, it is worth noting Ouseley LJ's comment, in *Islington LBC v University College London Hosp NHS Trust*, that 'it may matter little under which particular heading the particular factors are posted. There is after all only one question: is there a duty of care?'[27] However, for the purposes of clarity of principle, the three elements of *Caparo*, and the two elements of the *Hedley Byrne* test, will be analysed separately.

[27] [2005] EWCA Civ 596, [49].

REASONABLE FORESEEABILITY OF HARM (*CAPARO* #1)

General principles

Different tests of foreseeability

D cannot be liable in negligence for the unforeseen or the unforeseeable. No reasonable D would take any precautionary steps or modify his conduct to avoid a risk that he does not know, or foresee, could occur, and the law does not expect that of him either.

Tests of foreseeability actually arise at recurrent stages of the negligence analysis – in the duty of care, breach of duty and remoteness of damage stages. The reality is that these may closely duplicate each other. Separate Courts of Appeal have made the point that the tests 'inevitably overlap' (per *Gabriel v Kirklees MC*[28]), that the different stages of negligence 'run continually into one another' (per *Roe v Minister of Health*[29]) and that '[t]his overlap between duty and remoteness of damage, and what constitutes negligent conduct in the circumstances of the case, means that [the analysis of foreseeability] can be telescoped into one issue of fact' in some cases (per *Billington v Maguire*[30]).

Clearly, how straightforward the test of foreseeability is to satisfy is a direct consequence of the specificity with which the question is framed in the first place. At duty stage, it is at its widest. The reality is that, where C suffers from physical injury or property damage, as a result of D's acts or omissions, then *some* injury of that nature is likely to have been a reasonably foreseeable occurrence. Many English cases show that a more specific, and factually focused, test of foreseeability is appropriately posed at the *breach-of-duty* stage, and then again at the *remoteness-of-damage* stage. This trend is particularly evident where C and D are already within a recognised or distinct category of relationship, discussed in the previous section, which traditionally points towards a duty of care; and where it is entirely foreseeable that C may suffer some harm from D's acts or omissions, but where subsequent enquiries of foreseeability cannot be met by C. Hence, the analysis adopted in several cases, and in this book, follows an inverted pyramid:

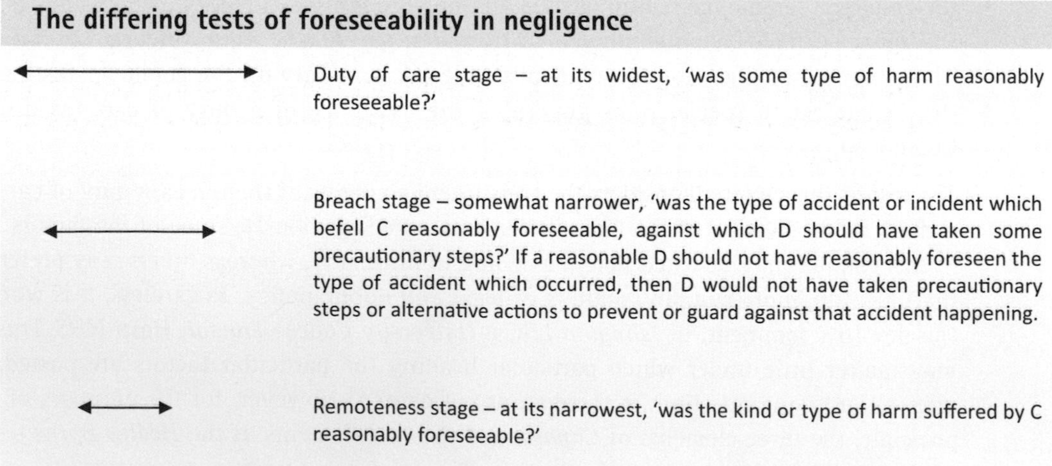

[28] [2004] EWCA Civ 345, [27] (Moses LJ). [29] [1954] 2 QB 66 (CA) 73.
[30] [2001] EWCA Civ 273, [21] (Sir Anthony Evans).

A few cases illustrate the distinction, and illustrate how easy the test is to satisfy at duty-of-care stage:

How the test of foreseeability becomes more focused, from duty of care to the latter stages

Road user to another road user: one road user owes a duty of care to another road user. The circumstances of the road accident may be so unusual or unpredictable so as to render the injury to C unforeseeable, but that is a question of breach. In *Billington v Maguire,*[a] D parked his van and trailer by the road and blocked the cycle lane; and cyclist C ran into the van and trailer, not having seen it ahead of her – 'it affronts common sense to say that [D] owed [C] no duty'. The trial judge held that the circumstances were so unusual that the risk of injury to C, by D's parking his van where he did, was not foreseeable, but that was overruled on appeal; a breach was proven (with 70% CN against C).

Hospitals/doctors and patients: where patient C attends hospital for surgical treatment by doctor/surgeon/ anaesthesist D, it is reasonably foreseeable that *some* physical injury may result, if reasonable skill is not exercised by D. The doctor–patient relationship is a recognised category of duty. However, if the accident suffered by C was so unusual, and hitherto unknown, so as to have been unforeseeable, then no precautionary steps should have been taken by D (e.g., as in *Roe v Minister of Health*[b] – where a duty was owed, but no 'act of negligence' was proven).

Employer and employees: employer D will owe a duty of care to its employee C in avoiding the risk of physical injury which the workplace (or work systems) pose to C. However, how the harm befalls C may be so unusual that it could not have been foreseeable, and no reasonable employer would have acted differently to prevent it (e.g., as in *Williams v Univ of Birmingham,*[c] where a duty of care was admitted by D, but breach towards C failed).

An accident victim and his rescuer: where D is negligent, and imperils himself or his property (or someone else), then it is reasonably foreseeable that people might attempt to rescue D (or that someone else), and that some accident may befall the rescuer, C, during the rescue. A duty will be owed (where C suffers physical injury); but if C's injury happens in a very unusual and unpredictable way, then that injury will be adjudged to be too remote, as in *Crossley v Rawlinson,*[d] where C saw D's lorry on fire beside the road, picked up a fire extinguisher and raced down a trodden path towards the lorry, stepped into a hidden rabbit-hole, and suffered a leg injury.

[a] [2001] EWCA Civ 273, [23] (Sir Anthony Evans).
[b] [1954] 2 QB 66 (CA) 83–85 (Denning LJ).
[c] [2011] EWCA Civ 1242.
[d] [1982] 1 WLR 369 (CA) 374–75. Cf: *Videan v British Transport Comm* [1963] 2 QB 650 (CA) 669 (rescuer stationmaster, killed whilst saving his son; negligence proven).

Foreseeability at duty of care stage

§2.5 D must have either actually foreseen (i.e., actually appreciated), or reasonably foreseenx (i.e., a reasonable person in D's position would have anticipated) the risk that his failure to exercise reasonable care and/or skill might cause harm of some type to C individually, or to a class of persons of whom C was one. A risk is reasonably foreseeable if it is a 'real risk', i.e., more than a mere possibility.

This principle brings two separate concepts into play.

Some general type of harm. Several leading House of Lords decisions have confirmed that the enquiry as to reasonable foreseeability is a very high-level one, at this early stage of the negligence action. In *Caparo v Dickman plc*,[31] Lord Bridge referred to a foreseeability test in the most general of terms – *viz*, 'the foreseeability of damage' – as 'an ingredient' of a duty of care. In this aspect of his judgment, he endorsed the very same wide test of foreseeability which was favoured at duty-of-care stage by Lord Wilberforce in *Anns v Merton LBC*.[32] Subsequently, in *Van Colle v CC of Hertfordshire Police*, Lord Bingham described the first limb of *Caparo* in the same very wide terms: 'it must be shown that harm to [C] was a reasonably foreseeable consequence of what [D] did or failed to do'.[33] The width with which this test of foreseeability has been enunciated explains why the 'unforeseeable claimant' is a rarely-sighted creature indeed!

Reasonable foreseeability is a rather ill-defined concept. Buxton LJ remarked, in *Islington LBC v UCL London Hosp NHS Trust*, that it was a matter of 'fluidity or flexibility', and that '[t]he level of certainty required for an outcome to be deemed, after the event, to have been foreseeable is, to a large extent, a matter of impression'.[34] However, its difficulty should not be overstated, because the threshold for establishing a reasonably foreseeable risk of injury to C has proven to be a very low one indeed. It must be a 'real risk, and not a mere possibility' – i.e., one which a reasonable person 'would not brush aside as far-fetched' (per *Overseas Tankship (UK) Ltd v Miller Steamship Co Pty*[35]). In *AG v Hartwell (British Virgin Islands)*,[36] Lord Nicholls said that it must not be 'fanciful'. It follows that merely possible (i.e., very small or far-fetched) risks may be foreseeable – after all, a person with a sufficiently vivid imagination or an obsessively worried disposition can probably foresee anything – but those risks are not *reasonably* foreseeable.

Certainly, the test of reasonable foreseeability does **not** require a balance of probabilities, or 'likelihood', that the risk of injury would happen. On several early occasions, the House of Lords did, unhelpfully, say that a reasonably foreseeable risk must be 'probable' or 'likely' to occur – e.g., in *Glasgow Corp v Muir* (D 'should have reasonably anticipated as a natural *and probable* consequence of neglect'[37]); and in *Dorset Yacht Co Ltd v Home Office* (one that was 'very likely' to occur[38]). However, later House of Lords' decisions have distanced the law from that view. As stated in *Smith v Littlewoods Organisation Ltd*, whenever the word, 'probable', is used in the context of reasonable foreseeability, it decidedly does not entail any proof on the balance of probabilities: '[i]t is not used in the sense that the consequence must be more probable than not to happen, before it can be reasonably foreseeable'.[39] In *Mitchell v Glasgow CC* too, it was said that, '[t]he concept of reasonable foreseeability embraced a wide range of degrees of possibility, from the highly probable to the possible but highly improbable'.[40] Hence, when asking whether a risk of injury was reasonably foreseeable, the use of terms such as 'probable' or 'likely' do not bear the same meaning as in an assessment of causation (as will be discussed in Chapter 8). The Scottish Outer House recently pointed out that, in the context of reasonable foreseeability, the 'balance of probabilities' meaning is completely inappropriate; rather, 'probable' is 'used in the sense of reasonably likely to occur'.[41]

[31] [1990] 2 AC 605 (HL) 618. [32] [1978] AC 728 (HL) 751–52. [33] [2009] 1 AC 225 (HL) [42].

[34] [2005] EWCA Civ 596, [14]. [35] [1967] 1 AC 617 (PC, on appeal from NSWSC) 642–43 (Lord Reid).

[36] [2004] UKPC 12, [2004] WLR 1273, [38]. [37] [1943] AC 448 (HL) 454 (Lord Thankerton) (emphasis added).

[38] [1970] AC 1004 (HL) 1018 (Lord Wilberforce). [39] [1987] AC 241 (HL) 269 (Lord Griffiths).

[40] [2009] UKHL 11, [2009] 2 WLR 481, [18] (Lord Hope), citing: *A-G (British Virgin Islands) v Hartwell* [2004] UKPC 12, [2004] 1 WLR 1273, [21] (Lord Nicholls).

[41] *French v Strathclyde Fire Board* [2013] Scot CS 3 (CSOH) [38].

All of this sets a very undemanding test – especially when combined with the fact that all that C has to prove, at the duty of care stage, is that *some physical injury or property damage* was reasonably foreseeable as a result of D's acts or omissions. As such, the first limb of *Caparo's* test has **not** acted as a stringent control mechanism in English negligence jurisprudence. The limb is, perhaps, slightly more likely to feature in cases involving pure omissions by D (see later below) and in failure-to-supervise-third-party cases (discussed in Chapter 3), although even there, reasonable foreseeability of physical injury or harm may be the **only** *Caparo* limb that C managed to prove (as, e.g., in *Hill v CC of West Yorkshire Police*[42] and *Palmer v Tees HA*,[43] where each C suffered the most extreme personal injury of all – murder – and yet reasonable foreseeability was the only *Caparo* limb which was met). Away from those contexts, it is difficult to identify **any** case since *Caparo* was handed down, in which the first limb of the *Caparo* test has failed. A couple of examples may demonstrate how unlikely is the 'unforeseeable claimant'.[44]

In the Manitoba case of *Urbanski v Patel*[45] (referenced by the author elsewhere[46]), where a doctor, D, operated on a patient, and mistook an out-of-place kidney for an ovarian cyst and removed it (with that turning out to be that patient's only kidney, due to a congenital accident never suspected), and where the patient's father, C, donated one of his kidneys, thereby suffering physical injury, could it be reasonably foreseeable, at the time that the doctor operated, that C (a person related to the patient) could suffer some physical injury? The answer in *Urbanski* was 'yes', but it is questionable whether an English court would follow suit. In the New York case of *Palsgraf v Long Island Rwy Co*,[47] C was standing on a train platform, when a man running for a train and carrying the package was pulled into the train by a train guard, D. The man dropped the package onto the railway line (unknown to D, it contained fireworks), and it exploded, whereupon scales at the other end of the platform got knocked over, hitting C. C was held to be an unforeseeable C. Under the *Caparo* test, however, C's injury was surely foreseeable, in that some physical injury to persons within a zone of danger from the explosion of fireworks would be a 'real possibility'. Twisting those facts as *a hypothetical example*, suppose that a person shopping at a supermarket drops his shopping bag, breaking some eggs. One of the eggs was rotten, and a passerby, C, suffered an allergic reaction from the sulphur dioxide emanating from the egg, when no physical injury resulting from that dropped shopping bag could be envisaged to anyone else. C's injury may plausibly be unforeseeable under the *Caparo* test.

C individually, or as one of a class. It is not necessary to prove that D ought to have reasonably foreseen harm *to C specifically* as a result of D's acts or omissions. Of course, where C is known to D personally, then C may be an actually *foreseen* victim – as a passenger will be to a negligent driver in whose car that passenger is travelling (per *Nettleship v Weston*[48]). However, where C and D never had any prior relationship before the allegedly negligent event happened and where C is unknown to D, then it is sufficient if C was foreseeable as one of a class of persons whose person or property might be harmed by D's activities (say, a class defined by its geographic location).

[42] [1989] AC 53 (HL). [43] [1999] EWCA Civ 1533, (1998) 39 BMLR 35.

[44] The author is grateful to her colleague, Mr Ian Yeats, for helpful discussions on this interesting point.

[45] (1978), 84 DLR (3d) 650 (Man QB).

[46] Mulheron, *Medical Negligence: Non-Patient and Third Party Claims* (Ashgate Publishing, 2010) 69–71.

[47] 248 NY 339 (NY Ct App, 1928). [48] [1971] 2 QB 691 (CA).

In *Bolton v Stone*,[49] Miss Stone, C, was one of a class of residents living nearby to Cheetham Cricket Club's cricket ground and whose property or persons could be hit by errant cricket balls hit out of D's cricket ground. A duty of care was owed to C; but there was no breach. The risk of C's being hit by an errant cricket ball was 'infinitesimal', so small that a reasonable cricket club in D's position was justified in disregarding it (considered in Chapter 7).

Exceptionally, in some contexts, even if the class of persons which is foreseeably at risk from D's act or omission *is the entire world* (of whom, of course, C is one), that does not necessarily preclude the test of foreseeability from being met. For example, where D drives negligently, then harm to any member of the public who is on or near the road is entirely foreseeable, but a duty of care is owed to the particular road user or pedestrian who is in fact injured. Where a manufacturer distributes defective products for widespread public consumption, then any member of the public may foreseeably be harmed by using/consuming the product, but a duty of care crystallises when a particular claimant suffers injury (discussed in 'Defective products', an online chapter).

Hence, because of the requirements of a 'limited class of whom C was one', and 'a duty attaches when the damage crystallises', there is no prospect of D being liable to the whole world, even where there is a foreseeable risk of injury to the general public as a result of D's negligence. Additionally, the other limbs of *Caparo* (considered below) provide better 'brakes' on liability. Hence, although, in *Jones v Wright*,[50] Stocker LJ noted that '[s]ome limitations must be put upon what is reasonably foreseeable, if a duty of care is not to be owed to the whole world at large', the reality is that the restraints imposed by the test of foreseeability are fairly non-existent at duty of care stage.

§2.6 Although reasonable foreseeability is an objective test, it is the ***particular D*** whose breach caused the injury to C to whom that test must be applied.

The test of foreseeability, whilst an objective test, is **not** to be applied to a completely-hypothetical D. Rather, it is a reasonable person *in that particular D's shoes* whose mindset is in issue. Should *that D* have reasonably foreseen that a lack of reasonable care and/or skill on his part might give rise to C's injury? The answer is that, if the particular D 'possesses a significant degree of knowledge' as to how some injury may manifest to C as a result of D's act or omission, then the test of reasonable foreseeability will, inevitably, be easier to satisfy.

In *Islington LBC v UCL Hosp NHS Trust*,[51] a cardiac surgeon's secretary informed patient C, Mrs J, that her operation was cancelled and that she should not recommence her Warfarin medication. C suffered a stroke, during the period when she was not taking Warfarin. With her lack of medical knowledge, the secretary could not have foreseen the ramifications of the care which C would require, should she suffer a stroke. Hence, it would not have been possible to sue the secretary in negligence, and to sue the NHS Trust, D, vicariously for that negligence. Rather, it was necessary to sue D directly for systemic (direct) negligence. **Held:** C's injury was reasonably foreseeable to D (and a duty was owed to her).

[49] [1951] AC 850 (HL), on appeal from: [1950] 1 KB 201 (CA). [50] [1991] 3 All ER 88 (CA) 114.

[51] [2005] EWCA Civ 596, quotes in text and case description at [15]–[16].

> 'The failure in this case was not that, or simply that, of the secretary. The failure was an institutional one, in that University College Hospital [operated by D] did not make proper arrangements for advising persons whose drug regime had been varied in anticipation of an operation and whose operation was then cancelled. The question is therefore what was foreseeable by the Trust ... the institutional body whose notional foresight has to be judged possesses a significant degree of medical knowledge.'

This case illustrates how important it is to select the relevant D carefully, when the test of foreseeability under *Caparo's* first limb is being considered.

§2.7 Reasonable foreseeability of injury to C is a necessary, but not sufficient, condition to prove a duty of care. *All* ingredients of the *Caparo* test must be met.

Given the liberal nature of the reasonable foreseeability test, the restraints on a duty of care are effectively set by a careful application of the proximity and policy tests. These are the *Caparo* limbs which **most effectively** act as factors which limit D's liability in negligence.

Occasionally, it has been judicially suggested that, where C suffers physical or personal injury, then 'reasonable foreseeability of harm is usually enough, in accordance with the principle in *Donoghue v Stevenson*, to generate a duty of care' (per Lord Hoffmann in *Customs & Excise Commrs v Barclays Bank plc*[52]). In *Perrett v Collins* too, the fact that C's claim was for a foreseeable physical injury was said to be, of itself, a 'potent factor' pointing to the existence of a duty.[53] However, such statements must be accorded real caution. Even in cases of foreseeable physical injury, proximity may be lacking, and public policy may preclude a duty of care. This has been particularly evident where C suffers personal injury or property damage in the failure-to-control-third-parties cases (per *Hill v CC of West Yorkshire Police*, where the House of Lords reiterated that, 'foreseeability of likely harm is not, in itself, a sufficient test of liability in negligence. Some further ingredient is invariably needed to establish the requisite proximity of relationship between [C] and [D] ... The nature of the ingredient will be found to vary in a number of different categories of decided cases'[54]). The paradigm example of the adage that reasonable foreseeability is never enough, on its own, to point to a duty is that of the blind man walking towards the cliff's edge – it is clearly foreseeable to bystander D, who says and does nothing, that the blind man will walk to severe injury or death, and yet, D owes no duty of care to him ('trite law', as Coulson J said in *Geary v JD Wetherspoon plc*[55]). The policy reasons which preclude a duty of care in that scenario are discussed below (under *Caparo* element #3).

Hence, any pre-*Caparo* cases which suggest that reasonable foreseeability was sufficient to prove a duty of care, in the context of C's suffering personal injury, must now be held to have been wrongly reasoned. Such cases resemble too closely the now-discredited *Anns* test (per *MacDonald v Aberdeenshire CC*[56]).

For some particular claimants – those susceptible to injury, and those unborn at the time of the alleged negligence – foreseeability of their injury is worth expansion.

Claimants susceptible to injury

§2.8 Where, unknown to D, C was particularly susceptible or vulnerable to the risk of the physical injury which befell him, as a result of D's acts or omissions (when no harm to an able-bodied

[52] [2006] UKHL 28, [2007] 1 AC 181, [31]. [53] [1998] PNLR 77, 114, 2 Lloyd's Rep 255 (CA).
[54] [1989] AC 53 (HL) 60. [55] [2011] EWHC 1506 (QB) [61]. [56] [2012] ScotCS 101 (OH) [47].

person would have been foreseeable whatsoever), that harm to C ***may*** nevertheless be reasonably foreseeable, C being within a class of persons to whom a duty is owed by D.

This principle applies, even where: (1) a duty would **not** have been owed to a person of ordinary physical robustness, because it could not have been foreseeable that an able-bodied person would have suffered any harm; (2) the harm to the physically-vulnerable C was, statistically speaking, very small; and (3) D was not personally aware of C's physical vulnerability, i.e., where C was one of a potential class of physically-vulnerable Cs. If any further evidence were needed, this aptly emphasises the wholly undemanding nature of the test of reasonable foreseeability at duty stage.

In *Haley v London Electricity Board*,[57] Mr Haley, C, had been blinded in an accident. He lived in Woolwich, London, and worked as a telephone operator for the London CC. Each day, he walked to the bus stop, and had learned to avoid ordinary obstacles with the aid of his white stick. However, unknown to C, the London Electricity Board, D, had been digging a trench, and put a long punner-hammer around it to warn pedestrians of the spot. C tripped over the punner-hammer, struck his head hard on the pavement, and was rendered deaf. **Held:** D, as electricity providers, owed a duty of care to blind persons affected by their servicing work. Some physical harm to C was reasonably foreseeable, even though the hammer would have warned a sighted person. Statistically, 1 in 500 people in London was blind, and many of them 'must walk pavements unaccompanied'. Hence, they were a foreseeable class to whom a duty was owed.

Note, however, that this is **not** an illustration of the so-called 'egg-shell skull' principle – the latter is a principle of remoteness of damage, and is considered in Chapter 9.

The unborn claimant

§2.9 Where C is born with a disease, deformity or abnormality which was due to the alleged negligence of D, whether caused whilst C was *in utero*, or pre-conception via parental treatment, the child, C, has the capacity to sue D for that ante-natal injury – provided that C was born alive.

The capacity for C to sue for injuries sustained as a result of acts or omissions committed whilst C was *in utero*, or because of treatment given to C's parent/s pre-conception, is statutorily-guaranteed, by virtue of s 1(1) of the Congenital Disabilities (Civil Liability) Act 1976 ('the 1976 Act'). The Act confers a right of action upon **a child** – born alive but disabled – because of 'an occurrence' which affected either parent's ability to have a normal, healthy child, or which affected the mother during pregnancy or affected her or the child during the child's birth, so that child C is born disabled (per s 1(2)(a) and (b), respectively). This is **not** a parental claim. The Act recognises a duty of care in favour of *the child*.

It follows that any of the following could fall within the scope of the Act, as an 'occurrence':

- something occurring pre-conception (e.g., where D negligently caused an injury to the mother's reproductive system before conception, condemning any child conceived thereafter, C, to disability);
- something which 'affected' C's mother during the mother's pregnancy (i.e., an act or omission which damaged C whilst *in utero*). The English Law Commission gave a number of examples in its 1973–74 study *Injuries to Unborn Children*.[58] (Notably, some of the scenarios postulated did

[57] [1965] AC 778 (HL) 791. [58] (CP 47, 1973) [6]–[14].

not involve the mother herself being 'injured', thus suggesting that the Act covers a wider array of circumstances than that, where C may suffer an ante-natal injury because of some act or omission by D which involved the mother but which did not injure her.) Just to mention a few examples of how C's claim could arise: where a trauma is inflicted upon C's mother by some car or train accident caused by D; or where harmful drugs were taken by the mother during pregnancy that cause injury to C *in utero* (the Commission's final report noted[59] the extraordinary statistic that '[t]here are known to be about 1,500 drugs having teratogenica effects (i.e., capable of causing damage to the foetus) with varying (usually slight) degrees of risk'); or where the mother's womb was irradiated whilst the foetus was *in utero* (e.g., where a pregnancy was actually misdiagnosed as a uterine tumour, leading to an X-ray that proved to be detrimental to C *in utero*); or where some diagnostic investigations or medical procedure performed on the mother damaged C *in utero*; or

- an event which affected C's mother during C's birth (e.g., where C's oxygen supply was cut off during birth, or shoulder dystocia affected C's delivery, either of which caused C hypoxia).

Additionally, disabled child, C, has an actionable claim where C's disability was caused by damage to the selection or handling of gametes (i.e., unfertilised human sperm and eggs) or embryo outside the mother's body during infertility treatment. This action was inserted in 1990, as s 1A(1)(b) of the 1976 Act.[60] There has not, to date, been any judicial decision turning on this provision – although in the Scottish case of *Holdich v Lothian Health Board*,[61] the court was somewhat quizzical of s 1A, noting that some of its wording was 'more immediately intelligible' in s 1 (the general provision providing C with a cause of action) than in s 1A. In particular, it is unclear whether s 1A actually sanctions a 'wrongful life' action (see Chapter 3).

Triggers for the Act to apply

The Act applies to any birth in England that occurred **after** 22 July 1976 (per s 4(5)), and displaces the common law. Given the time which has elapsed since the Act was passed; the 3-year limitation period that applies to personal injury cases; and the maximum suspension of limitation periods in English law, any litigation involving this type of C will be now covered by the Act, and not by the common law.

§2.10 Under the Act, there are several criteria for a duty of care to be owed to the unborn claimant, C. These do not replicate the common law requirements set by the *Caparo* (or any other) test, but are defined uniquely by the Congenital Disabilities (Civil Liability) Act 1976.

The Act sets **four** criteria for a duty of care, where a child is born disabled, allegedly due to D's negligence:

i. C is born alive. From a combined reading of s 1(1) and s 4(2), a cause of action is only vested in C, for ante-natal injury suffered, if C is born alive and viable. Section 4(2)(a) specifically provides that being 'born' means 'born alive (the moment of a child's birth being when it first has a life separate from its mother'), however brief that separation might be. Hence, if C dies

[59] EWLC, *Report on Injuries to Unborn Children* (Rep 60, 1974) [21].

[60] By virtue of the Human Fertilisation and Embryology Act 1990, s 44(1), and in force 1 Aug 1991.

[61] [2013] CSOH 197, [27]. The 1976 Act does not apply to Scotland; and this case concerned a parental claimant in any event. Hence, there was no requirement to consider s 1A.

prior to delivery/birth because of D's negligence and is still-born, C's estate has no capacity to sue under the Act. (Other suits may be possible, however – whether by the mother of that child, per *Grieve v Salford HA*,[62] or by one who may claim damages for psychiatric injury as a secondary victim, as discussed in Chapter 5.[63])

ii. C is born 'disabled', with disabilities which would not have been present, but for D's acts or omissions. 'Disability' is defined in s 4(1), and includes being born with 'any deformity, disease or abnormality'. The Act gives no cause of action for C with naturally-occurring or congenital disabilities, because the disability itself must result from the 'wrongful act' of D (per s 1(1)). Further, if C is born with some particular characteristic (e.g., skin colour) to which C objects, that will not constitute a 'disability' for the purposes of the Act.

In *A (a minor) v A Health and Social Services Trust*,[64] twins C were born as a result of IVF treatment provided by D's IVF facility. C's parents were white; and they were anxious that their child would have the same skin colour. D inseminated C's mother's eggs with sperm labelled, 'Caucasian (Cape coloured)'. The Cape coloured community in South Africa was derived from races of different skin colouring, including white, black and Malay, giving rise to C's being darker-skinned than their parents. **Held:** the 1976 Act could not apply, because C had suffered no 'disability' that would trigger its operation: 'these are healthy and normal children. In a modern civilised society the colour of their skin – no more than the colour of their eyes or their hair, or their intelligence, or their height – cannot and should not count as connoting some damage to them. To hold otherwise would not only be adverse to the self-esteem of the children themselves, but anathema to the contemporary views of right thinking people'.

iii. The disability was caused by an 'occurrence' attributable to D, which occurred before C's birth. The definition of an 'occurrence' has been noted above. Some aspects of an 'occurrence' necessary to trigger the 1976 Act have not been entirely clarified. For one thing, it is not entirely clear whether the event could be a drawn-out circumstance (e.g., the gradual accumulation of a drug in the mother's system), affecting the mother's ability to have a healthy child; or whether it must be something more singular and 'one-off'. In *Multiple Claimants v Sanifo-Synthelabo Ltd (the FAC Group Litigation)*,[65] Andrew Smith J noted that, in the insurance context, 'occurrence' signifies 'a degree of unity in relation of cause, locality, time, and, if initiated by human action, the circumstances and purposes of the persons responsible'. For another, defining the precise 'occurrence', when D's pharmaceutical product is in issue, can be very unclear.

In *The FAC Group Litigation*, a group of children, C, were born to mothers, each of whom suffered from epilepsy, and who took an anti-epileptic anti-convulsant drug, Epilim, manufactured by D, during their pregnancies. C argued that Epilim was a known teratogen, which crossed the placenta and which caused various deformities for foetuses exposed to it. It was likely that the risk to the foetus also depended upon the mother's genetic makeup. C argued that the 'occurrence' was 'the trans-placental spread' of the product to the embryo/foetus, which then affected embryonic and foetal development; whereas D argued that the only 'occurrence' that affected the mothers' ability

[62] [1991] 2 Med LR 295 (QB). [63] See pp 239–40.

[64] [2010] NIQB 108, with quotes at [10] and [18], and aff'd: [2011] NICA 28, [9].

[65] [2007] EWHC 1860 (QB) [55]–[57], citing: the award of Mr Michael Kerr QC in the Dawson's Airfield Arbitration dated 29 Mar 1972, re the meaning of 'occurrence' in the context of insurance policies.

to have a healthy baby was their epilepsy that required anti-epilepsy drugs, and that any transplacental spread of the drug could not constitute an 'occurrence'. This point could not be decided as a preliminary issue, but would require evidence at trial, as to whether the spread was caused by genetic make-up or the mothers' consumption of Epilim.

iv. C's claim is derivative upon a claim against C's parent/s. C's claim against D can only be maintained under the 1976 Act if D was under an actual or potential tort liability to either parent of C, for the act or omission which led to C's disability – except that it does not matter (per s 1(3)) if the parent has suffered no *actual injury*. Hence, if, say, C's mother takes a pharmaceutical drug during her pregnancy, and suffers no injury herself, but C does suffer injury whilst *in utero*, then C can still bring an action against the manufacturer of that drug, D. In that regard, C's claim under the 1976 Act is unusual for an action in tort, in that C's action is *derivative* upon D's tortious duty to the parent/s – but it is unnecessary to show that the parent suffered any actionable injury.

It also follows, from the derivative liability imposed by the 1976 Act and from the terminology of s 1(7), that any 'shared' negligence which may be pleaded by D as against the child's parent/s, will reduce the child's, C's, damages too. This is not contributory negligence as such (as it is not C's negligence which is at issue, but his parents' conduct). Furthermore, s 1(4) is worth noting: as a defence under the Act, D is not responsible to the child, if the child's parent/s knew, pre-conception, of the risk of C's disability.

What the Act does not do. The Act does **not** assist at all to prove whether D committed any breach of duty towards C, whether that breach (if any) caused C's harm, or whether C's harm was too remote at law to be compensable. These other aspects of the negligence action remain for determination solely according to common law principles – and indeed, they may be very difficult for C to prove.

In *McCoy v East Midlands Strategic HA*,[66] Brodie McCoy, C, was born severely brain-damaged, on 22 March, at 39 weeks. C sued her mother's treating doctors, D, for failing to carry out a cardiotocograph scan at 37 weeks. C argued that an earlier CTG trace had been 'suspicious'; a further scan would have shown a similarly-worrying fetal heart pattern indicating that the mother's placenta was failing; steps would have been taken to deliver C early by induced labour or by caesarean section; and if C had been delivered earlier, the brain injury would have been avoided. **Held:** C could bring a claim under the 1976 Act, but no negligence proven. Although D committed a breach in regarding the earlier CTG trace as satisfactory, that breach did not cause C's injury because, on the balance of probabilities, a further scan would not have led to an intervention to deliver C earlier than 22 March.

The other options

The 1976 Act was prompted by the recommendations of the EWLC (in *Injuries to Unborn Children*[67]), which endorsed the view that statutory standing be conferred on an unborn C, for injuries negligently-inflicted prior to that child's birth. At the time, English law was uncertain on this point, and the EWLC noted that, 'where a doubt exists as to what the law is on an important topic such as this, there is a strong case for resolving that doubt by legislation'.[68]

[66] [2011] EWHC 38 (QB). [67] See EWLC, *Injuries to Unborn Children* (CP 47, 1973), and (Rep 60, 1974).
[68] *ibid*, [4(c)], and see [4]–[15], for discussion and quotes in the Table.

The point of the Act is that, '[f]or there to be any cause of action there must be a live birth. The cause of action can be said to crystallise at birth',[69] because the damage was actually incurred at the point of a live birth. However, the EWLC had two other options to consider, on this point of standing.

The law reform corner: Standing to sue for the unborn claimant: three options

Option #1 (approved by the EWLC): according to the English Court of Appeal in *Burton v Islington HA*,[70] a child injured *in utero*, born alive, was owed a duty of care, because that risk of damage was reasonably foreseeable. Tina Burton, C, alleged negligence by medical staff when they carried out a dilation and curettage (D&C) procedure at a time when C's mother was about five weeks pregnant with C. D failed to carry out a pregnancy test before the procedure, where circumstances should have put experienced medical staff on enquiry. The common law applied (C was born on 26 April 1967, so being pre-22 Jul 1976, the Act did not apply). Earlier English authority supported that too. In *[an unnamed case cited by the EWLC]*,[71] a ladder fell upon a pregnant woman, caused by D's negligence. The child was born the next day and lived just one day. D paid $100 into court when the parents brought a claim for damages for loss of expectation of life, in settlement of the claim. The *Burton*/EWLC view was also endorsed in other jurisdictions. In *Watt v Rama*,[72] C suffered injury *in utero*, allegedly caused when D collided negligently with C's mother's vehicle. C's mother was rendered a paraplegic from the accident, and C, her son, was born with brain damage and epilepsy. In *Montreal Tramways Co v Léveillé*,[73] due to the negligence of the tram's motor man, C's mother fell from the tramcar and was injured. Two months later, she gave birth to C, who was born with club feet. Each C could pursue a negligence claim against D, provided that they were born alive and viable, in respect of their disabilities, even though the disabilities were caused *in utero*.

Option #2: was to recognise C, a damaged foetus, as a legal entity, separate from the mother, even if the foetus did not survive birth (permitted in some US jurisdictions in cases of still-birth[74]). That would enable C to recover heads of damage such as funeral expenses, and loss of expectation of life (albeit that damages for PSLA would be irrelevant). In *Burton*, Dillon LJ noted that earlier English authority[75] did not endorse the view that a foetus enjoyed an independent legal personality – 'a foetus cannot, while a foetus, sue and cannot be made a ward of court'. The EWLC[76] did not favour the proposition either, describing it as a 'fiction', and 'practically difficult'.

Option #3: was to deny any duty of care owed to C who was negligently injured *in utero*, even if the child was born alive. That view applied in the 1891 Irish decision in *Walker v Great Northern Rwy Co of Ireland*,[77] where C's mother, whilst pregnant with C, fell from D's

[69] See EWLC, *Report*, [32]. [70] [1992] EWCA Civ 2, [1993] QB 204.

[71] *Injuries to Unborn Children* (CP 47, 1973) fn 1, citing (1939) 83 Sol J 185 (Liverpool Assizes). The author's efforts to locate the name of this case have proven unsuccessful.

[72] [1972] VR 353 (CA) (Gillard J) 356.

[73] [1933] SCR 456 (SCC) 464 (a majority decision, re a Quebec statute: at 462–63).

[74] EWLC, *Injuries to Unborn Children* (CP 47, 1973) fn 3, citing: *White v Yup*, 458 P 2d 617 (1969).

[75] [1993] QB 204 (CA) 226, citing: *Paton v BPAS* [1979] QB 276; *Re F* [1988] Fam 122 (CA).

[76] (CP 47, 1973) [36]. [77] (1891) 28 LR (Ire) QB & Ex 69.

train because of D's alleged negligence. C was born crippled and deformed. C's statement of claim disclosed no cause of action. In *Burton*, the Court of Appeal considered *Walker* 'profoundly unsatisfactory'.[78] One of the reasons was that the *Walker* majority had 'attached weight to the fact that the Railway Company as a common carrier had sold the pregnant mother one ticket and not two – a conclusion which, if valid today, would carry the consequence that a child under three who can travel without a ticket on British Railways would have no remedy against British Railways if injured by the negligence of the British Rail employees'. The *Burton* court simply regarded *Walker* to be of 'no assistance today'.

PROXIMITY (*CAPARO* #2)

§2.11 The concept of proximity describes the degree of closeness or neighbourhood between C and D which must be proven to justify imposing a duty of care on D. It is traditionally proven via a combination of: geographical proximity; temporal proximity; relational proximity; and causal proximity. However, no particular proximity factor has a 'clinching' status.

The proximity enquiry requires the factual matrix to be examined, so as to show that C was a person 'so closely and directly affected by [D's] act that [D] ought reasonably to have [C] in contemplation as being so affected' (to revisit the words of Lord Atkin in *Donoghue v Stevenson*[79]). It was frankly acknowledged, in *Caparo Industries plc v Dickman*,[80] that 'proximity' is merely a label, and that, in novel cases, ascertaining whether the parties were sufficiently proximate could be viewed as the ultimate exercise in judicial pragmatism.

Four types were outlined by the High Court of Australia in *Sutherland SC v Heyman*,[81] and for the purposes of English law, were approved in *Stovin v Wise* as a 'valuable exposition' of proximity.[82]

The types of proximity – what they mean

geographical proximity	the physical closeness between C, when the damage was suffered, and D, when the breach occurred
temporal proximity	the closeness in time between when C suffered the damage, and when the breach by D occurred
relational proximity	an enquiry into several matters, e.g.: • was C in a vulnerable position vis-à-vis D? • was D exercising control over the circumstances in which C was harmed or injured? • did C and D have a pre-existing relationship, in which C obviously relied upon D to exercise reasonable care, or where D assumed responsibility to exercise care towards C?

[78] [1993] QB 204 (CA) 231 (Dillon LJ). [79] [1932] AC 562 (HL) 580 (Lord Atkin).
[80] [1990] 2 AC 606 (HL) 618 (Lord Bridge), 633 (Lord Oliver).
[81] (1985) 50 ALR 1 (HCA) 55. [82] [1996] AC 923 (HL) 932 (Lord Nicholls).

	• was C at 'special risk' as a result of D's breach, over and above the risk faced by the general public? If the same measure of risk was faced by all, or a large cross-section of the public, then the requisite proximity between D and C is unlikely
causal proximity	whether D precluded a step which, had it occurred, would have almost certainly protected C from the harm that eventuated – the availability of that intervening step (so that not taking it exacerbated C's vulnerability) can enhance a finding of proximity between D and C

Different weightings may be given to these various types of proximity, in different fact scenarios, and none of them is an absolute pre-requisite or unifying characteristic, for legal proximity between C and D to be found. It all depends upon a close scrutiny and analysis of the facts and circumstances of the case at hand. However, they have all proven to be of *some* relevance, under the *Caparo* test.

Although it has been judicially said that proximity has 'an uncertain status' (per *Islington LBC v University College London Hosp NHS Trust*[83]), and is a 'slippery word' (per *Stovin v Wise*[84]), it has certainly proven effective in circumscribing the number of Cs who have scrambled through the duty of care door in English jurisprudence. Of course, for the recognised categories of duty of care, proximity is a 'given'; but in novel cases, 'the nexus is not given, but has to be found' (per *K v Sec of State for the Home Dept*[85]). The application of proximity, as a control mechanism, has been particularly noticeable in failure-to-control-third-party cases (as discussed in Chapter 3).

Where D has physically injured C, or caused C property damage, by reason of his acts or omissions, then proximity is, generally speaking, a non-contentious matter. As Lord Hoffmann remarked in *Customs and Excise*, there will usually be geographical and temporal proximity wherever D has physically injured C's person or property. However, in some cases, relational proximity (especially control over C's safety) may be entirely absent, in which case proximity will fail, the physical proximity notwithstanding.

In *Harrison v Technical Sign Co Ltd*,[86] Cluttons, D, the landlord's agent of a shop in Putney, was asked by the lessee, Maison Blanc, to inspect a defective awning over the shop, to ascertain whether the landlord might pay for repairs. Following the inspection, the fascia of the shop became detached from the building and fell onto the pavement, causing serious injuries to passer-by, Gillian Harrison, C. **Held:** D did not owe C a duty of care. D's inspection had nothing to do with ensuring the safety of passers-by, but only to see whether the shop fixtures had sustained damage for which the landlord might be liable. If D had been asked by Maison Blanc to inspect the awning to ensure that it did not pose a danger to passers-by, the requisite proximity would probably have existed between C and D, because the very purpose of D's inspection would have been to ensure the public's safety. (Alternatively, by accepting such instructions, D would assume responsibility for the safety of passers-by, because then D would become involved in an activity which gave him a measure of control over, and responsibility for, their safety – per the assumption of responsibility/reliance test discussed later in the chapter.) But that was not the case here

[83] [2005] EWCA Civ 596, [20] (Buxton LJ). [84] [1996] AC 923 (HL) 932 (Lord Nicholls).
[85] [2002] EWCA Civ 775, [26]. [86] [2013] EWCA Civ 1569, [14].

and, hence, there was insufficient proximity between D and any passer-by injured by the awning. In *Stagecoach South Western Trains Ltd v Hind*,[87] Kathleen Hind owned Rose Cottage, situated adjacent to the railway in Staines. She arranged for an arborist, D, to cut out the dead wood in an ash tree. Subsequently, one of C's trains collided with a branch of the ash tree which had fallen onto the railway line. C sued D in negligence for the cost of repairing the damage to its train. **Held:** D did not owe a duty of care to C. D was engaged for the specific purpose of clearing dead wood, which had nothing to do with the safety of those using the railway. It was analogous to *Harrison*, above. D was not involved in an activity which gave him a measure of control over, and responsibility for, the safety of C's trains.

A school and its pupils provide a useful example of proximity in action. In this context, a school encompasses the school as an entity (in devising its systems), and the principal and teachers for their individual acts or omissions (for which the school may be vicariously liable). A school which accepts a pupil for tuition assumes responsibility for his physical well-being, as well as for his educational needs (per *X (Minors) v Bedfordshire CC*[88] and *Webster v Ridgeway Foundation School*[89]). There is also relational proximity, in that the principal and teachers bear the standard of a 'careful parent' (per *Gower v Bromley LBC*[90]). Temporally, a duty to exercise reasonable care towards pupils applies during school hours, and extends 'for a reasonable period after the end of the school day while [the pupil] was still on the school's premises' (per *Webster*[91]), as well as for a reasonable period before school actually begins (*Kearn-Price v Kent CC*,[92] where a duty applied to an incident at 8.40am). Geographically, the duty may also extend beyond the physical boundaries of the school grounds, if a student is being bullied frequently on the journey to and from school (per *Bradford-Smart v West Sussex CC*[93]). More controversially, the requisite proximity between school and pupil may also apply, where the pupil is attacked by outsiders (per *Webster*, where the attack took place after the end of the school day, on school premises, and where the requisite proximity was found) – an illustration of the difficult scenario where, by his omissions, D facilitates the opportunity for a third party to do harm to C, and where proximity is always at issue.

Even where C and D were geographically and relationally proximate, however, proximity may not be proven. It all depends upon the circumstances. In *Geary v JD Wetherspoon plc*,[94] C and D were entrant and occupier, yet no proximity was made out (there was nothing defective about the state of D's premises, and hence, the Occupiers' Liability Acts discussed in Chapter 12 did not apply, and the case had to proceed as a common law negligence claim).

In *Geary v JD Wetherspoon plc*, Ruth Geary, C, visited D's pub, which was situated at the Union Rooms in Newcastle, with some work colleagues. The premises (previously a gentlemen's club) retained the original feature of a grand open staircase in the centre of the building, with sweeping banisters on both sides. When leaving at the end of the night, C hoisted herself onto one of the banisters to slide down it 'like Mary Poppins', but she fell backwards, landed on her back on the marble floor four metres below, and broke her back, suffering tetraplegia. **Held:** D owed C no duty of care, as proximity was lacking. The mere relationship of occupier–entrant could not, of itself, give rise to sufficient proximity. Further, there was no third party involved, so no proximity could arise where the allegation was that D's duty was to protect C from her own foolish actions, as opposed to protecting her from the actions of third parties.

[87] [2014] EWHC 1891 (TCC) [95]–[96]. [88] [1995] 2 AC 633 (HL) 766. [89] [2010] EWHC 157 (QB).
[90] [2000] 2 LGLR 237 (CA) 240 (Auld LJ). [91] [2010] EWHC 157 (QB) [121]. [92] [2002] EWCA Civ 1539.
[93] [2002] EWCA Civ 7. [94] [2011] EWHC 1506 (QB) [58], [67]–[72].

§2.12 The gravity of harm to C, resulting from D's breach, has no impact upon the question of proximity.

Say that C dies as a result of D's negligence. Grievous injury to C, of itself, does **not** supply a nexus, or proximity of relationship, between C and D, sufficient to create a duty of care. This point was explicitly made in *K v Sec of State for the Home Dept*[95] (re an escapee awaiting deportation who raped C, a member of the public, while at large), and illustrated in *Geary* (where C suffered tetraplegia) and in *Palmer v Tees HA*[96] (where C was raped, murdered and mutilated). To hold otherwise would be to render D 'the world's insurer against grave danger' (per *K*[97]).

POLICY FACTORS (*CAPARO* #3)

General principles

§2.13 Both legal and public policy factors inform an assessment as to whether it is fair, just and reasonable to impose a duty of care on D. That judicial assessment of policy may change over time. The assessment of policy factors is a balancing exercise in novel fact scenarios, whereby some factors will support a duty of care, and others will disfavour it.

It is fair to say that there are distinctly contrasting perceptions of the role which policy plays in setting the existence of a duty of care under *Caparo*. At its most positive, an assessment of policy infuses a considerable degree of fluidity, which enables the court to come to the 'correct decision' on whether or not D **should** be liable in negligence. Lord Clyde put it this way, in *Phelps v Hillingdon LBC*:

> [policy considerations] have the advantage of flexibility, enabling the court to define the boundaries of claims for negligence, in the light of new situations and the recognition that incremental growth may require to be controlled, albeit at the risk of some uncertainty, at least in the prediction of the directions in which the law may develop.[98]

On the other hand, that very flexibility makes predicting the outcome of a duty of care in novel fact scenarios very uncertain. This was admitted a long time ago – back in 1824 – when Burrough J pithily stated, in *Richardson v Mellish*, that public policy was 'a very unruly horse, and when once you get astride of it, you never know where it will carry you'.[99]

In modern English law, it is hard to avoid the impression that the third limb of *Caparo* enables the court to dip into a 'bucket' of policy factors; extract from the bucket those which most suit the outcome which the court is seeking to achieve; return to the bucket those which do not 'suit' the desired outcome – and then 'dress the outcome' up as pragmatic judicial decision-making. At least Lord Pearson was honest in his assessment, in *Home Office v Dorset Yacht Co Ltd*,[100] that whether or not a duty of care was owed in that case 'must be a matter of impression and instinctive judgment as to what is fair and just'. In *Watson v British Boxing Board of*

[95] [2002] EWCA Civ 775, [24]–[30]. [96] (1998) 45 BMLR 88 (QB) 101 (Gage J). [97] [2002] EWCA Civ 775, [35].
[98] [2001] 2 AC 619 (HL) 671–72. [99] (1824) 2 Bing 229, 252. [100] [1970] AC 1004 (HL) 1054.

Control Ltd[101] too, Lord Phillips MR noted that, 'it is difficult, or perhaps impossible, to avoid a degree of subjectivity when considering what is fair, just and reasonable'.

This impression is surely enhanced by Buxton LJ's elliptical comment, in *Islington LBC v University College London Hosp NHS Trust*, that '"fair just and reasonable" is not to be read literally, nor is it to be read solely in the context of the relationship between the instant [C] and [D]. It still assumes ... that wider issues of policy may have to intervene'[102] (and, having duly 'intervened' in that case, a duty of care was 'a leap too far'). This passage emphasises a further important point – that while it may appear fair, just and reasonable for *that particular C* to recover for his injury or loss, his entitlement may be forsaken, because of other types of aggrieved Cs who could seek to press through the doorway over time.

To add to the uncertainty, policy has a tendency to change over time too. For example, no duty may be owed for public policy reasons by the police in 1989,[103] whereas in 2008, the House of Lords can admit that (although no duty remains the law) those reasons 'do not all stand up to critical examination today'.[104] That 'unruly horse' can change direction, responding to stimuli from its surroundings.

Lastly, an unfortunate terminological confusion has been introduced to this area, especially since 1999, by judicial references to 'public policy' and 'legal policy' factors under the third limb of *Caparo*. In *McFarlane v Tayside Health Board*,[105] Lord Millett remarked that '[l]egal policy, in this sense, is not the same as public policy, even though moral considerations may play a part in both. The court is engaged in a search for justice, and this demands that the dispute be resolved in a way which is fair and reasonable, and accords with ordinary notions of what is fit and proper'. Three years later, in *Rees v Darlington Memorial Hosp NHS Trust*,[106] Lord Steyn again distinguished the two types: '[t]he House did not rest its decision [in *McFarlane*] on public policy in a conventional sense ... Instead the Law Lords relied on legal policy'. However, neither of these judges explained precisely what was the difference between the types. Furthermore, other courts, before and since *McFarlane*, have used 'public policy' in precisely the sense in which Lord Millett described 'legal policy'. For example, in *Mitchell v Glasgow CC*,[107] Lord Hope used the terms interchangeably. As a result, it is not clear what the difference between legal and public policy factors actually is! Hence, the generic term, 'policy factors', will be used throughout this section, in the context of *Caparo's* third limb.

Under the now-overruled *Anns* two-stage test proposed by Lord Wilberforce, public policy was used to counter, or limit, the scenarios in which a duty of care could be owed. Under the *Caparo* line of authority, however, policy factors are used in a true balancing, or competing, exercise, whereby some factors will positively support a duty of care being owed.

A non-exhaustive sample of the most common policy arguments in novel fact scenarios involving personal injury or property damage to C, are summarised in the Table below:

[101] [2000] EWCA Civ 2116, [2001] QB 1134, [86].

[102] [2005] EWCA Civ 596, [34]; and also [53] (Ouseley LJ).

[103] *Hill v CC of West Yorkshire* [1989] AC 53 (HL) 63–64 (Lord Keith).

[104] *Smith v CC of Sussex Police; Van Colle v CC of Hertfordshire Police* [2008] UKHL 50, [2009] 1 AC 225, [73] (Lord Hope), referring to suits against the police for failing to prevent crime.

[105] [2000] 2 AC 59 (HL) 108.

[106] [2003] UKHL 52, [2004] AC 309, [29] (Lord Bingham drawing the same distinction at [6]).

[107] [2009] UKHL 11, [2009] 1 AC 874, [25]–[26].

Public policy factors: a deep 'bucket'

'corrective justice'	this rule of policy provides that, 'the first claim on the loyalty of the law [is] that wrongs should be remedied', or that 'every wrong should have a remedy' (per *X (Minors) v Bedfordshire CC*[a]). It has been described as 'the primary requirement of public policy' (per *Arthur JS Hall & Co v Simons*[b]) and 'the ideal of a system' (per *McFarlane v Tayside Health Board*[c]). Hence, if D has harmed C by his conduct without justification, then the balance between them should be restored by holding that a duty of care was owed
'distributive justice'	who would the 'commuters on the London Underground' consider should justly bear the burden of the loss suffered as a result of D's activities: C or D? (per *McFarlane v Tayside Health Board*[d]). This factor takes account of whether losses are being allocated in a way that gives the public confidence in the legal system (per *Arthur JS Hall & Co v Simons*) – albeit that '[j]udges do not have, and do not claim to have, any special insight into what contemporary society regards as fair and reasonable' (per *Rees v Darlington Memorial Hosp NHS Trust*[e]). Distributive justice 'is not a principle of English law recently adopted so as to allow free rein to ignore basic principles long established' (per *Tameside and Glossop NHS Trust v Thompstone*[f])
'floodgates concerns'	if to hold that D owed a duty of care would expose similarly-situated Ds to potential liability from many persons in C's position, and would likely increase the volume of litigation against similarly-situated Ds in the future, then that may preclude a duty of care (per *Hill v CC of West Yorkshire Police*[g])
'defensive practices'	if to impose a duty on D would promote overly cautious practices / assessments / treatments/etc, which could put third parties at risk, because D was not game to act for the protection of the public, for fear of ensuing litigation, then that may militate against a duty of care (per *Hill*[h])
'diversion of resources'	if to find a duty of care would divert D's manpower, money and staff resources away from frontline services into reviews of old cases or to defending litigation, that may preclude a duty (per *Hill*[i])

[a] [1995] 2 AC 633 (HL) 663 (Sir Thomas Bingham MR), and also 749 (Lord Browne-Wilkinson).
[b] [2002] 1 AC 615 (HL) 727 (Lord Hutton), citing: *Arenson v Arenson* [1977] AC 405 (HL) 419 (Lord Simon).
[c] [2000] 2 AC 59 (HL) 82 (Lord Steyn).
[d] [1999] UKHL 50, [2000] 2 AC 59, 82 (Lord Steyn).
[e] [2003] UKHL 52, [2004] AC 309, [14] (Lord Nicholls).
[f] [2008] EWCA Civ 5, [2008] 1 WLR 2207, [47] (Waller LJ).
[g] [1989] AC 53 (HL) 65 (Lord Templeman).
[h] *ibid*, 64 (Lord Keith).
[i] *ibid*.

'the no-need' policy reason	a duty of care may not be warranted, if it is unnecessary to afford C a remedy via negligence (i.e., if C has other forms of redress available, or there are other ways for making D accountable, e.g., public law remedies in respect of exercise of statutory powers; health departments subject to ministerial oversight; health workers subject to departmental disciplinary regimes; a criminal injuries compensation scheme; or complaints to an Ombudsman). Obversely, if D has other protections available to him, even where he is potentially liable in negligence, then that may favour a duty of care being imposed (per *Harris v Evans*[j])
'the insurability factor'	which of C or D could, and should, have insured himself against the loss suffered? Is the loss one against which C ought to have insured himself? If so, then the loss does (or should) fall upon the C's insurer, and not on D (*Marc Rich & Co AG v Bishop Rock Marine Co Ltd*[k]). The availability of insurance, both to C against the risk of injury, or to D against the risk of legal liability, is a divisive issue, as to whether or not it is potentially relevant (see text below)
'conflict of duties'	would D's duty to C require him to put C's interests above those of another party to whom he owes a duty of care? Any conflict of duties (actual or potential) will preclude a duty to C. On the other hand, if what is required of D to discharge any duty to C would *also* discharge his duty to the other party, then the duties are coincident, no conflict arises, and a duty may be upheld (*Capital and Counties plc v Hampshire CC*[l])
'the indeterminate liability problem'	if the losses sustained by C were very large, and if the time period over which losses were sustained was lengthy, and if the numbers of Cs could be very large, then the prospect of exposing D to indeterminate liability may preclude a duty of care (per *Ultramares Corp v Touche*,[m] who described the 'three indeterminates' as: 'a liability in an indeterminate amount for an indeterminate time to an indeterminate class', and was cited with approval in *Caparo Industries plc v Dickman*[n]). This tends to arise more frequently in cases of pure economic and pure psychiatric loss than in cases of personal injury or property damage. However, the mere prospect of indeterminate liability does not, of itself, preclude a duty of care from arising (as, e.g., in the context of consumers of a product, per *Wattleworth v Goodwood Road Racing Co Ltd*[o])

[j] [1998] EWCA Civ 709, [1998] 1 WLR 1285.
[k] [1996] 1 AC 211 (HL).
[l] [1997] QB 1004 (CA) 1036.
[m] 255 NY 170, 179 (1941) (Cardozo J).
[n] [1990] 2 AC 605 (HL) 621–22.
[o] [2004] EWHC 140 (QB) [122] (Davis J).

'the law's preference for personal injury'	if C is claiming only for economic loss, and not for personal injury, any duty to avoid such economic loss is more likely to be precluded by policy, personal injury being considered more worthy of compensation. Conversely, the law will more readily recognise a duty of care where physical harm has been inflicted upon C (per *Caparo*; and *Vowles v Evans*[p])
'a matter for the ballot box, or for Parliament'	if D's liability is better decided by elected parliamentarians, then the court should not usurp that democratic function (per *Hill*,[q] and *Home Office v Dorset Yacht Co Ltd*[r])
the 'what would it achieve?' factor	if to impose a duty of care on D would neither enhance the standard of care expected of D nor provide the general public with any greater confidence in D's activities, that may count against a duty (per *Hill*[s] – '[t]he court would have to decide whether an inspector is to be condemned for failing to display the acumen of Sherlock Holmes and whether a constable is to be condemned for being as obtuse as Dr Watson ... But that finding will not help anybody or punish anybody')
'the incalculables problem'	why should D be the subject of a duty of care, when C obtained benefits, resulting from D's breach, which are incalculable/unquantifiable/immeasurable? Those incalculables may count against a duty being imposed on D (per *McFarlane*[t])
'treating Ds alike'	if imposing a duty of care upon D would 'bring D into line' with other professions/similarly-situated Ds, that is a factor in favour of a duty (per *Arthur JS Hall & Co v Simons*[u])
'the-protection-of-the-public' argument	the purpose of negligence law is, in part, to set standards of D's behaviour for the public's benefit. Hence, if to impose a duty of care would 'weed out the bad eggs' amongst the profession/trade of which D is a member; or would otherwise fill a gap in redress for C, that may count in favour of a duty (per *Arthur JS Hall v Simons*[v])
'compromise of D's liberty/altruistic motives'	if to impose a duty of care on D would compromise D's individual liberty to act without positively hurting others; would seek to elevate an altruistic/moral motive to a legal duty; and/or would expose D to liability for acting/not acting, when others in the 'same boat' may not be sued in negligence, then that may militate against a duty (per *Stovin v Wise*[w])

[p] [2003] EWCA Civ 318.
[q] [1989] AC 53 (HL).
[r] [1970] AC 1004 (HL) 1026–27.
[s] [1989] AC 53 (HL) 64 (Lord Templeman).
[t] [2000] 2 AC 59 (HL) 111.
[u] [2002] 1 AC 615 (HL) 672.
[v] *ibid*, 729.
[w] [1996] AC 923 (HL).

'battle conditions'	where D must make difficult decisions with little or no time for considered thought, which decisions can expose C to physical injury, then it may be inappropriate to impose a duty of care, given that the fear of a negligence suit may compromise D's ability to make those critical decisions (per *Mulcahy v MOD*[x])
'subordination of the individual to the wider public good'	where C's ability to sue for compensation must be subordinated to a wider public or collective good, where D has acted as the executive arm of government (per *Bici v MOD*[y]) or in a quasi-state role (per *Marc Rich v Bishop Marine*[z]), that may count against a duty
'a lacuna in remedy'	if there is no lacuna in the law (i.e., no gap in compensation) that requires filling by imposing liability on D towards C, the courts will not fill it. But if there is a lacuna, in that C lacks a remedy against anyone other than D, then finding a duty in C's favour may be fair and just (per *Perrett v Collins*[aa])
'the disproportionate problem'	no duty will be imposed if it would have a punitive element, i.e., that to impose a duty 'might result in a burden of liability on [D] to so many people which was disproportionate to their tortious conduct' (per *McFarlane v Tayside Health Board*[bb])

[x] [1996] EWCA Civ 1323, [1996] QB 732.
[y] [2004] EWHC 786 (QB).
[z] [1996] AC 211 (HL).
[aa] [1999] PNLR 77 (CA) 90–91.
[bb] [2000] 2 AC 59 (HL) 96.

These various policy factors are considered, as and where appropriate, in the discussion which follows. Other 'one-off' policy factors have also arisen in specific scenarios, also discussed below.

Obviously, the **huge** array of factors gives an indication as to why the 'unruly horse' of policy has been hard to tether. It is 'an important but amorphous concept which the courts must keep within its proper limits' (per *Proactive Sports Management Ltd v Rooney*[108]). Certainly, English courts have had **ample** grounds upon which to say that any duty towards C would **not** be 'fair, just and reasonable'.

§2.14 Wherever policy reasons consistently dictate against a duty of care being imposed – with respect to a particular type of D, or a particular type of scenario – that effectively creates an immunity for D in negligence. That immunity must be justifiable, in light of C's right of access to the court, which is preserved both at common law and under Art 6(1) of the ECHR.

Immunities which D enjoys from suit in negligence have long caused concern at common law, because of the compromise of the access to justice which any such immunity entails.

Since the implementation of the Human Rights Act 1998, C's right of access to the court is enshrined in Art 6(1) of the ECHR. In *Golder v UK*, the European Court of Human Rights reiterated

[108] [2011] EWCA Civ 1444, [53].

that, '[t]he principle whereby a civil claim must be capable of being submitted to a judge ranks as one of the universally "recognised" fundamental principles of law; the same is true of the principle of international law which forbids the denial of justice. Article 6(1) must be read in the light of these principles'.[109] The Art 6 right is not absolute, but 'may be subject to limitations', brought about by either the state legislature or by the court (per *Fayed v UK*[110]). Any limitation, though, will only be justifiable if it is designed to pursue a legitimate aim, and is proportionate. If the restriction which the immunity imposes on C's right to access to justice is disproportionate to the public policy aims sought to be achieved by the immunity, then it will be incompatible with Art 6(1). Some categories of Ds, and scenarios, considered in this section, have inevitably entailed some very close judicial scrutiny, as to whether the policy reasons can withstand an Art 6 challenge.

Furthermore, as a matter of conceptual clarity – in some scenarios below, courts have consistently described D as having 'an immunity', whilst others have (more correctly) discussed the absence of liability as being attributable to no duty of care being owed by D. In *Jones v Kaney*[111] (which concerned the duty of care of an expert to the client who retained him), the Supreme Court internally divided. Lord Dyson suggested that reference to 'immunities' was outmoded, because the principle of immunity arose prior to the formation of the modern law of negligence – whilst Lord Collins remarked that it may not matter which terminology is used, '[b]ut it would be preferable to treat it as an immunity, to emphasise the strong element of policy involved'. In modern jurisprudence, however, an 'absence of a duty of care' is surely preferable. Any so-called 'immunity' conferred upon a particular type of D is only based on *policy grounds* which preclude a duty from arising, under *Caparo's* third limb. Furthermore, since the ECHR's implementation, appellate courts dislike speaking of 'blanket immunities', as they can tend to create an erroneous impression to the Strasbourg courts. Typical of this is Lord Steyn's comment, in *Brooks v MPC*,[112] that 'it would be best' for police duties of care to be 'reformulated in terms of the absence of a duty of care, rather than a blanket immunity'.

§2.15 English law is unsettled as to whether the (non)availability of insurance either to C (against the risk of injury) or to D (against the risk of legal liability) is a relevant policy factor governing a duty of care.

Pragmatically speaking, the law of negligence is about allocating losses among various parties – and if C suffers some injury as a result of D's negligence, then if a court considers that insurance for such liabilities 'naturally lie' with C rather than with D, that may be a policy reason for holding that it would not be fair, just and reasonable to impose a duty of care on D.

Some appellate authorities certainly take the view that, regardless of where the risk should lie, insofar as insurance availability or actual cover is concerned, that is **not** legally relevant. According to *Watson v British Boxing Board of Control Ltd*,[113] the argument that no duty of care should be imposed on a non-profit-making organisation (i.e., the British Boxing Board) because it did not carry insurance could not succeed, because '[c]onsiderations of insurance are not relevant [to the duty of care issue]'. Lord Phillips MR followed Buxton LJ's earlier view in *Perrett v Collins*[114] in that regard.

[109] (1975) 1 EHRR 524, 535–36, [35]. [110] (1994) 18 EHRR 393, 429–30, [65].
[111] [2011] UKSC 13, [2011] 2 AC 398, with quotes in text at, respectively, [111] and [73].
[112] [2005] UKHL 24, [2005] 1 WLR 1495, [27]. [113] [2001] QB 1134 (CA) [89]. [114] [1999] PNLR 77 (CA).

On the other hand, a differently-constituted Court of Appeal, in *Vowles v Evans*,[115] stated that the availability of insurance 'could bear on the policy question of whether it is fair, just and reasonable to impose a duty of care on referees'. It was also a key factor in *West Bromwich Albion Football Club Ltd v El-Safty*, so that where the medical mistreatment of employees (such as football player Michael Appleton in that case) caused the employer (the football club, WBA) financial loss, the Court of Appeal considered that insurance against that financial loss 'naturally lies with their employers'.[116] It was not reasonable to expect a surgeon to insure against additional loss of an economic kind, suffered by someone *other than his patient*, which was a factor against any duty of care being owed by the surgeon. Most crucially of all, however, the House of Lords has endorsed the relevance of insurance in a duty of care analysis in *Marc Rich & Co v Bishop Rock Ltd*.[117] A classification society owed no duty of care to a cargo owner (whose goods sank with an unseaworthy ship), partly because of the nature and function of a classification society such as NKK, and in the context of the complex arrangements for sharing, limiting and insuring the risks inherent in carriage of goods by sea.

The particular conundrum of whether an occupier should be liable for the acts or omissions of an independent contractor engaged by that occupier, where that contractor did not carry any public liability insurance, and whether the occupier's ignorance of that fact demonstrated that he had not taken sufficient care in selecting that contractor, is a separate issue which is discussed in Chapter 12.

The particular facts and reasoning of these disparate cases will be considered, as and where relevant, under the particular scenarios below (categories are arranged in roughly alphabetical order).

Children (young)

§2.16 Very young children do not owe a duty of care to those injured or killed by their acts or omissions.

So far as the author's searches can ascertain, there are no English authorities which expressly deal with whether a very young child, D, owes a duty of care to C to whom he causes injury or death, or at what precise age a duty of care does arise on the child's part. However, what case law there is, suggests that no duty of care is owed by very young children.

In *Carmarthenshire CC v Lewis*,[118] in which a very young child's actions caused C's death, Lord Reid said that 'the child was not old enough to be responsible' (albeit that the precise reason for that was not explained). None of the other members of the House explicitly addressed any discussion on the question of when a child would be an appropriate D, but all accepted that this child was not.

In *Carmarthenshire CC v Lewis*, 3-year-old David Morgan wandered out of his classroom at D1's nursery school, whilst the kindergarten teacher, D2, was attending to another child's cut knee. David was dressed up in coat and scarf and was waiting to go for a walk with the teacher and another nursery mate as a treat. Unexpectedly, he left the room, walked through a gate (that should have been locked), and out onto the adjacent main road, and into the path of Mr Lewis, C, who was driving his lorry. C swerved to avoid David, hit a lamppost, and was killed. His widow sued D1 (directly for

[115] [2003] EWCA Civ 318, [2003] WLR 1607, [12]. [116] [2007] PIQR P7 (CA) [63] (Rix LJ), [84] (Mummery LJ).
[117] [1996] AC 211 (HL) 239–41 (Lord Steyn, writing for the majority). [118] [1955] AC 549 (HL) 563 (Lord Reid).

negligence, and vicariously for D2's lack of supervision of David). **Held:** D2 was not negligent; but D1 was liable in systemic negligence for allowing David to 'escape' the confines of the kindergarten.

Moreover, since the 'rise' of the concept of distributive justice (in *McFarlane v Tayside Health Board*[119]), it is surely the case that to consider that a young child owes a duty of care in his conduct is inimical to what the commuter on the London underground would think fair and just. The child lacks judgment, maturity, voluntariness and, of course, insurance.

However, those same commuters would surely consider that, at some (hitherto judicially-unspecified) age, a child should be responsible for the harm inflicted by his acts or omissions. This is reflected in the findings of contributory negligence which have been held against children as young as 12 (e.g., in *Young v Kent CC*[120]). Of course, even if a duty were owed by a very young child, regardless of the points noted above, the standard of care expected of him would likely be suppressed to the point of negligibility (as discussed in Chapter 6).

The law reform corner: **Child defendants**

Irish LRC: As explained in *Liability in Tort of Minors and the Liability of Parents for Damage Caused by Minors*,[121] the allocation of responsibility in Tort depends upon the concept of voluntariness of D's conduct, which 'involves the direction and control over conduct by a conscious mind'. Canadian authority[122] has held that the actions of a 3-year-old child (in pulling an infant out of a pram and dragging her several metres) were not voluntary. Hence, it is against public policy to impose a duty of care upon a very young child who cannot act voluntarily; but older children, who can understand the consequences of their actions, can owe a duty of care.

Doctors: 'wrongful conception' claims

§2.17 'Wrongful conception' cases arise where a parent, C, seeks compensation for the consequences of a child which was born as a result of a negligently-caused conception. The negligence may occur because C's surgeon, D, failed to take reasonable care when performing a sterilisation operation, failed to advise C to use other contraceptive methods for a period thereafter, or failed to advise C on the risks of pregnancy.

When they arise. This area has been described, in *DN v Greenwich LBC*, as an 'exceptionally difficult area of the law of professional negligence'.[123] The leading authority is a House of Lords' Scottish case.

In *McFarlane v Tayside Health Board*,[124] Mr McFarlane underwent a vasectomy, as he and Mrs McFarlane (both Cs) wished to limit their family to four children. After negligent advice from his consultant surgeon, D, some six months later, that Mr McFarlane was now infertile and his sperm counts were negative, C ceased using other contraceptive measures. Mrs McFarlane then fell pregnant, giving birth to a healthy baby girl, Catherine. C sued jointly for the loss and damage incurred as a consequence of the birth of Catherine. **Held:** negligence proven, with certain damages recoverable.

119 [1999] UKHL 50, [2000] 2 AC 59, 82 (Lord Steyn). 120 [2005] EWHC 1342 (QB).
121 (Rep 17, 1985) 2–3. 122 *Tillander v Gosselin* [1967] 1 OR 203 (HC, Grant J), cited *ibid*, 3.
123 [2004] EWCA Civ 1659, [77]. 124 [2000] 2 AC 59 (HL), on appeal from CSIH.

It is notable, however, that 'wrongful conception' actions have been extended to encompass **any** situation where, had the parents been carefully advised not to conceive a child (because, say, the mother suffered from a particular condition), they would then have taken steps not to conceive.

In *Less v Hussain*,[125] Ms Less, C, had a complicated past medical and obstetric history, and together with her partner, sought advice before deciding whether or not to try to conceive and sustain a pregnancy. C consulted gynaecologist, D, who advised that there was 'no reason not to conceive, and that they could go ahead'. C's pregnancy was difficult, and the child (son Luis) was ultimately stillborn. To add to the tragedy, when Luis was taken away and photographs were taken of him at the hospital, he was wearing a dress, because that clothing was all that could be found. **Held:** C was owed a duty of care by D. However, negligence failed, because a causal link between D's breach (the advice) and C's damage (the conception of Luis) was not proven.

In wrongful conception cases, it is the actual conception, and not the birth, which is the injury or legal wrong suffered by C (per *Less v Hussain*[126]). Whatever happens after the point of conception merely goes to the question of damages. There are **three** possible outcomes for the parents, following a wrongful sterilisation (assuming that the mother, C, remains alive): the baby may be lost during pregnancy (i.e., stillborn, as in *Less*); the child may be born healthy; or the child may be born disabled.

Although healthcare practitioner D owes the parental C a duty of care to treat/sterilise/advise that parent carefully – wrongful conception is always a *parental* claim – the extent, or scope, of D's duty is limited, in that not **all** damages suffered by the parent/s will be recoverable. Although this question is perhaps more relevant to the 'scope of the duty', and hence, to the question of remoteness-of-damage (that was certainly Lord Hope's view in *McFarlane*), the majority in *McFarlane* held that it was not 'fair, just and reasonable' to impose a duty on D to avoid all the damages which the parental C may suffer in these circumstances. Hence, policy was invoked to limit the ambit of the undoubted duty of care which D owes to C in such a distinct and recognisable category as doctor–patient.

§2.18 D owes a duty of care to both his patient, C, who was negligently sterilised or who relied upon his negligent advice, and (according to dicta) to the ***existing*** sexual partner of C. However, C cannot recover damages for the costs of raising a child who was conceived and born subsequent to the failed sterilisation – except where the child is disabled, whereupon the costs associated specifically with the child's disability can be recovered.

A healthy child. In *McFarlane*, Lord Slynn framed the physical damage as 'the physical effects of the pregnancy and birth', and that the costs of raising and maintaining a healthy child were 'consequential [economic] responsibilities' resulting from that physical damage.[127] All members of the House of Lords unanimously held that the parental C is **unable** to recover those costs of raising and maintaining a healthy child, conceived and born following a failed sterilisation – as it is not fair, just or reasonable to impose liability for them on the negligent healthcare practitioner, D. Interestingly, prior to *McFarlane*, there was authority each way: in *Udale v*

[125] [2012] EWHC 3513 (QB). [126] [2012] EWHC 3513 (QB) [168]–[169].

[127] [2000] 2 AC 59 (HL) 67 (noting that, at first instance, the Lord Ordinary had held that C's pregnancy 'could not be equiparated with a physical injury').

Bloomsbury AHA,[128] Jupp J had rejected a claim for the cost of bringing up an unintended child, whereas in *Thake v Maurice*,[129] Peter Pain J had declined to follow *Udale* and allowed such a claim.

The amount for the costs of feeding, clothing and maintaining a healthy child, until such time as the child ceased to be dependent upon her parents, was put at £100,000 in *McFarlane* itself. In the Irish case of *Byrne v Ryan*,[130] the sum for raising two healthy children was estimated to be 350,000. Hence, the claim, if permitted, would be a high-value one. The policy reasons prohibiting the claim are drawn, collectively, from *McFarlane*[131] and from *Rees v Darlington Memorial Hosp NHS Trust*[132]:

Policy reasons re failed sterilisations: the costs of raising are *not* recoverable

- ***the incalculables problem***: it is unfair to allow the burdens of raising a child to be recovered, when the benefits brought to the family and to parenthood by a healthy child cannot be calculated and offset. This rendered the damages incalculable (Lords Steyn and Hope, *McFarlane*). In other words, 'the placing of a money value on the net detriment to a child's parents of having to rear the child would ... be inconsistent with the status of the child as a valued and loved member of the family' (Lord Scott, *Rees*);
- ***the disproportionate problem***: D's liability would be out of all proportion to his wrong, and should not be imposed upon his professional indemnity insurers (Lords Hope and Clyde, *McFarlane*). Plus, why should D be liable for the economic consequences of C's decision to keep the child – reasonable, praiseworthy and socially valuable though that be? (Lord Scott, *Rees*);
- ***distributive justice***: D's liability towards the parents of a healthy, but 'unwanted', child, for the costs of that child's upbringing, would not amount to a fair distribution of the limited 'insurance pot' available to remedy tortious wrongs (Lords Steyn, Slynn and Hope, *McFarlane*). As Lord Bingham put it in *Rees*, 'to award potentially very large sums of damages to the parents of a normal and healthy child against the NHS always in need of funds to meet pressing demands would rightly offend the community's sense of how public resources should be allocated'; and that it raised the 'spectre of well-to-do parents plundering the NHS'. It would not be 'fair just or reasonable, or consistent with the expectations of right thinking people in modern society', that the child could be regarded as a financial liability (Lord Nicholls, *Rees*);
- ***the 'no-need' argument***: the birth of a healthy child was 'always a blessing' (Lord Millett, *McFarlane*).

In *Byrne v Ryan*, Kelly J succinctly expressed the misgivings that many hold about the wrongful conception action – that, given express parental acknowledgement 'of the joy and satisfaction that the child [has] brought to her, there is a certain incongruity in the [mother, C] seeking to recover the costs of rearing from [doctor, D]'.[133] That incongruity simply cannot arise in English law, post-*McFarlane* (nor in Ireland, where *Byrne v Ryan* followed the reasoning in *McFarlane*).

[128] [1983] 1 WLR (QB). [129] [1986] QB 644. [130] [2007] IEHC 207, [2009] 4 IR 542.
[131] [2000] 2 AC 59 (HL), with quotes in Table at 82–3, 87, 106, 109, 114.
[132] [2003] UKHL 52, [2004] AC 309, and with quotes in Table at [6]–[8], and [137]–[138].
[133] [2007] IEHC 207, [2009] 4 IR 542, [143].

On the other hand, **three** heads of loss **are** recoverable in a wrongful conception action – and hence, it falls within the scope of D's duty of care to avoid causing C these types of damage. They are:

i. the mother's general damages for the pain, suffering and inconvenience of pregnancy and childbirth (by majority in *McFarlane*[134]);
ii. general damages for the parental C having the sterilisation repeated (conceded in *McFarlane*);
iii. the special damages for extra medical expenses, clothing, and loss of earnings associated with the pregnancy and birth (by majority in *McFarlane*[135]). As Lord Millett rather poetically said:

> A baby may come trailing clouds of glory, but it brings nothing else into the world. Today, he requires an astonishing amount of equipment, not merely the layette, but push-chair, car seat, carry cot, high chair, and so on. The expense of acquiring these is considerable ... If Mr and Mrs McFarlane disposed of them in the belief that they would have no more children, the cost of replacing them should be recoverable as a direct and foreseeable consequence of the information they were given being wrong.[136]

Although not permitted in *McFarlane* itself, a conventional award of loss of autonomy, because the parental C did not wish to have a child, and were now experiencing the 'mixed blessings' of parenthood, is now also allowed (by majority in *Rees*,[137] and adopting Lord Millett's dissenting view in *McFarlane*). The conventional award is discussed in detail in Chapter 11.

Notably, not every jurisdiction agrees that the costs of raising a healthy child should be irrecoverable, however. Although *McFarlane* (decided in 1999) was canvassed extensively in argument before the Australian High Court in 2003, a bare majority of the High Court, in *Melchior v Cattanach*,[138] refused to countenance the outcome in *McFarlane*, and permitted recovery of the full costs of raising a healthy child to the age of majority or independence, subject to the ordinary remoteness-of-damage limitations. Subsequently, in *Rees* (2003), the House of Lords considered whether it should reverse its policy reasoning in *McFarlane* by exercising the 1966 Practice Direction, given the decision in *Melchior*, but decided not to do so. However, as Lord Steyn remarked in *Rees*, the fact that the majority of the Australian High Court 'decided in favour of recovery merely underlines the controversy of the problem and the range of views on the subject'.[139]

The comparative corner: The contrary Australian view

At common law: damages for the costs of raising a healthy child **are** recoverable (*Cattanach v Melchior*, 4:3):

- that a child might be damaged by feeling 'unwanted' as a result of such litigation was overstated and speculative;
- there was no satisfactory reason as to why the law should shield the doctor from what otherwise constituted a claim in negligence, and to create a 'zone of immunity' around doctors would entail a legal error;

[134] Lord Millett dissented: [2000] 2 AC 59 (HL) 114.

[135] All members of the House of Lords, except for Lord Clyde, allowed this part of the claim.

[136] [2000] 2 AC 59 (HL) 114–15.

[137] [2003] UKHL 52, [2004] AC 309 (Lords Bingham, Millett, Nicholls, Hutton and Scott; with Lords Hope and Steyn dissenting).

[138] [2003] HCA 38, (2003) 215 CLR 1, with quotes in Table at [79], [90], [179]–[180], 301.

[139] [2003] UKHL 52, [32], and with Lord Bingham's quote in Box at [5].

- 'distributive justice' meant that the doctor/his insurer, having the 'deeper pocket', should pay for this damage;
- re the parents' damages, it was not correct to offset the 'benefits' received from the child's birth against the cost of the child's maintenance, so any difficulty in calculating the 'benefit' was irrelevant to damages assessment;
- a healthy child is not always a blessing, when parents have undergone a sterilisation precisely because they do not wish for any more children, and given the widespread use of contraception, including sterilisation procedures.

The HCA did **not** endorse the solution (reached in some US States) that the measure of damages for a healthy child should be the full costs of raising the child to majority, but with a deduction to take account of the joy and benefits, and economic income, brought to the parents by the child. Similarly, in *Rees*, Lord Bingham called the objections to that line of reasoning 'insuperable'. Most US States preclude recovery of the costs of raising altogether.

Statute: the decision in *Cattanach v Melchior* has been reversed by statute in some Australian state jurisdictions, e.g.: Civil Liability Act 2002 (NSW), s 71, provides that, 'the court cannot award damages for economic loss for: (a) the costs associated with rearing or maintaining the child that the claimant has incurred or will incur in the future, or (b) any loss of earnings by the claimant while the claimant rears or maintains the child'.

A disabled child. To what extent (if at all) D's duty to avoid causing the parental C damage should be modified where a *disabled* child is born as a result of negligently-performed sterilisation was left open in *McFarlane*. However, this 'factual variant' of the wrongful conception suit (as described in *Rees*[140]) arose two years later in the Court of Appeal.

In *Parkinson v St James and Seacroft Univ Hosp NHS Trust*,[141] Ms Parkinson, C, the mother of four children, underwent a sterilisation operation, which was performed negligently by surgeon D. A child was subsequently conceived, and C was warned, during the pregnancy, that the child might be born with a disability. C declined to have her pregnancy terminated. Thereafter, C's marriage broke down, and Mr Parkinson left the family home three months before C gave birth to baby Scott, who was severely disabled (including autistic spectrum disorder). Scott's disability was not caused by any breach of duty by D. C sought damages for the costs of Scott's upbringing. **Held (on a preliminary issue):** the ordinary costs of Scott's upbringing could not be recovered by C, but damages could be awarded for the additional costs of rearing the child that were attributable to his disabilities.

McFarlane was both distinguished, and followed, in part. In respect of a *disabled* child, the measure of damages obtainable from the negligent healthcare practitioner, D, could properly include:

- the additional costs attributable to the disability associated with bringing up a child with congenital or hereditary disabilities, i.e., any extra expenses to provide for the child's special needs and care, including modifications required to the family home, special educative needs, extra nursing care; and
- *all three* of the heads of damage which were permitted in *McFarlane* (see above). Indeed, the general damages awarded to the parental claimants, following the birth of a disabled child,

[140] [2004] 1 AC 309 (HL) [1] (Lord Bingham). [141] [2001] EWCA Civ 530, [2002] QB 266.

have been viewed very sympathetically in some cases, covering matters such as the mental distress of learning of the child's condition, and the disruption to family life caused by the disability (per *Ahern v Moore*[142]).

However, the *ordinary* costs of bringing up and caring for the child, which would have been incurred had the child been healthy, were not (held *Parkinson*) recoverable, in accordance with *McFarlane*. Again, policy reasons were invoked for the decision to allow the additional costs:[143]

Policy reasons re failed sterilisations: disabled children

- ***distributive justice***: on balance, 'ordinary people would consider that it would be fair for the law to make an award in such a case, provided that it is limited to extra expenses associated with the child's disability' (Brooke LJ). The solution 'treats a disabled child as having exactly the same worth as a non-disabled child. It affords him the same dignity and status. It simply acknowledges that he costs more' (Lady Justice Hale);
- ***corrective justice***: the main difference between a normal and disabled child (insofar as money can restore C to the position as if the tort had not been committed) 'is primarily in the *extra* care that they need, although this may bring with it *extra* expenditure. It is right therefore that the parent who bears those *extra* burdens should have a claim', noting that, '[a]t the heart of it all is the feeling that to compensate for the financial costs of bringing up a healthy child is a step too far' (Lady Justice Hale);
- ***no floodgates concerns***: the birth of a child with congenital abnormalities following a failed sterilisation, whilst foreseeable (between 1:200 and 1:400), was likely to be uncommon. Hence, there were a limited number of Cs who might suffer this type of damage, not leading to any floodgates concerns (Brooke LJ).

Two points arise from the *Parkinson* ratio, and both were dealt with by Lady Justice Hale.[144] First, how disabled must the child be, for the parental C to recover those additional costs? The answer was conveniently provided (said Hale LJ) by s 17(11) of the Children Act 1989, i.e., a child is taken to be 'in need' if, inter alia, 'he is disabled', meaning that 'he is blind, deaf, or dumb, or suffers from mental disorder of any kind, or is substantially and permanently handicapped by illness, injury or congenital deformity, or such other disability as may be prescribed'. Secondly, the disability, naturally-occurring, must arise from genetic causes or foreseeable events during pregnancy (e.g., rubella, spina bifida, or oxygen deprivation during pregnancy or childbirth) up until when the child is born alive. Hence, it would not encompass where an illness affected the child after birth or during his childhood.

A disabled mother. Where the mother brings a 'wrongful conception' case, and is disabled herself, the damages recoverable consist of the same three heads of damages as noted for the healthy child (above). In *Rees v Darlington Memorial Hosp*,[145] the approach to damages recovery for the healthy child adopted in *McFarlane* was re-examined – and affirmed.

[142] [2013] IEHC 72 (general damages of €100,000 awarded). [143] *ibid*, [50], [90], [94] (original emphasis).
[144] *ibid*, [91]–[92]. [145] [2003] UKHL 52, [2004] 1 AC 309.

In *Rees v Darlington*, Karina Rees, C, had been visually-impaired since she was 2 years old, due to a congenital condition. She feared that her lack of sight would prevent her from being able to care for a child, and underwent a sterilisation operation when aged 23. It was negligently performed by D, and she subsequently conceived, giving birth to Anthony, a healthy child. Anthony's father did not wish to be involved with his upbringing. C brought up Anthony with the help of her mother and relatives. However, C was severely limited with what she could do for Anthony. **Held:** D owed C a duty of care, and C was able to recover limited damages. By majority, a conventional award of £15,000 was awarded.

Although invited to depart from *McFarlane* (delivered four years previously[146]) and to allow the ordinary costs of raising a child, the seven-member House in *Rees* unanimously refused to do so:

> it would be wholly contrary to the practice of the House to disturb its unanimous decision in *McFarlane*, given as recently as 4 years ago, even if a differently constituted committee were to conclude that a different solution should have been adopted. It would reflect no credit on the administration of the law, if a line of English authority were to be disapproved in 1999, and reinstated in 2003, with no reason for the change, beyond a change in the balance of judicial opinion. I am not, in any event, persuaded that the arguments which the House rejected in 1999 should now be accepted, or that the policy considerations which drove the decision, have lost their potency.[147] [and] [a]ccepting that the subject is a highly controversial one, the decision [in *McFarlane*], rooted as it was in morality, justice and legal policy, represented the least bad choice ... the decision in *McFarlane* was a sound one.[148]

Hence, the measure of damages obtainable from the negligent healthcare practitioner, D, by the disabled mother, can lawfully include:

- a conventional award, signifying recognition of the loss of C's personal autonomy; and
- *all three* heads of damage permitted for the birth of a healthy child (see above).

In fact, *Rees* stands for two very controversial propositions, both of which were the subject of (differing) majority verdicts. First, the so-called '*Rees* award', or conventional award, emanated from this case, so as to recognise some nominal compensation awarded to C, for a denial of 'an important aspect of C's personal autonomy'. The infringed right, in *Rees*, was Karina Rees' right to live her life the way in which she had planned, i.e., without child, given her concerns about her disability and its effects upon her child-raising capacities.

Secondly, *Rees* confirmed that a disabled parent **cannot** recover any damages that may otherwise be referable to **her** disability. The Court of Appeal in *Rees* had held (by bare majority[149]) that C, as a disabled parent, was entitled to claim damages, for those 'extra' costs which were involved in discharging her responsibility to bring up a healthy child which were attributable to, and incurred as, a result of the fact of the parent's disability. However, the House of Lords overruled this (by bare majority[150]), solely for policy reasons.

[146] Per *Practice Statement (Judicial Precedent)* [1966] 1 WLR 1234 (but which did not permit 'an open sesame for a differently constituted committee to prefer their own views': *Rees*, Lord Steyn, [31]).

[147] [2003] UKHL 52, [7] (Lord Bingham). [148] *ibid*, [33] (Lord Steyn).

[149] [2003] QB 20 (CA) (Hale and Robert Walker LJJ; with Waller LJ dissenting).

[150] [2003] UKHL 52, with quotes in Table at [9], [114]–[120], [143] (Lords Bingham, Nicholls, Millett and Scott; with Lords Hope, Hutton and Steyn dissenting on this point).

Policy reasons disallowing extra costs for the mother's disability

- ***no corrective justice***: it is anomalous that D's liability should be related to a disability which the doctor's, D's, negligence did not cause. The causal link is broken, if it is the mother's disability which is being claimed for. Also, it is impossible to disentangle the costs attributable to the mother's disability and the child's birth (Lords Bingham and Millett);
- ***the 'no need' factor***: it is undesirable that parental Cs, in order to recover compensation, should be encouraged to portray themselves as disabled (Lord Bingham);
- ***the incalculables problem***: the State makes public provision for disabled persons, and to quantify additional costs attributable to parental disability is difficult (indeed, Mrs Rees could not manage it) (Lord Bingham);
- ***distributive justice***: the mother's circumstances can vary widely. What if a mother already has four children, and the birth of a 5th healthy child pushes her to a nervous breakdown? She cannot recover for the costs of caring for that 5th child (per *McFarlane*). So why should a disabled mother be able to recover for the extra costs associated with her disability, when the overburdened mother cannot? What if a disabled mother is very rich, should the law still compensate her at the expense of D's professional indemnity insurer? The law has never applied a 'means test' to recovery. All this precluded recovery for a disabled mother ('ordinary people would feel uncomfortable about the thought that it was simply the disability which made a difference') (Lords Bingham, Nicholls, Millett);
- ***the administration of justice***: *McFarlane's* ban on the recovery of the costs of raising the child is an exception to the usual principle that damages should put the parental C in the position as if the tort had not been committed (i.e., no child born). To permit a disabled mother to recover for her disability for the costs of raising, in any respect, would be an exception to an exception – 'apt to produce messy jurisprudence' (Lord Millett).

Interestingly, of the *Rees* majority who disallowed any damages referable to the disability of the mother, two of those judges – Lords Bingham and Nicholls – also considered that no damages should be payable which were referable to the disabilities *of a child*, in a wrongful conception suit. For example, and similarly to the 'no need' factor above, Lord Bingham held that it was undesirable that parental Cs, in order to recover extra compensation, should be encouraged to portray their own children as disabled. Hence, both Law Lords impliedly overruled the Court of Appeal decision in *Parkinson*. This point has occasionally been taken up by D since. For example, in *FP v Taunton and Somerset NHS Trust*,[151] D submitted that, in light of those observations in *Rees*, *Parkinson* may have been wrongly decided, but Blair J noted that he 'did not need to get into that debate', since *Parkinson*[152] was clearly binding on him. Certainly, notwithstanding the dissents in *Rees*, the ratio of *Parkinson* – that the extra costs referable to the disabilities of a child **may** be recovered in a wrongful conception suit – has never been overruled, and remains good law.

Who may claim, of the parents? Sometimes, in wrongful conception cases, only the parent who underwent the sterilisation operation brought the action as C (e.g., *Groom v Selby*[153] and *Greenfield v Irwin*[154]). This may have been a tactical litigation decision because all the damages

[151] [2009] EWHC 1965 (QB) [7]. [152] [2001] EWCA Civ 530, [2002] QB 266.
[153] [2001] EWCA Civ 1522. [154] [2001] EWCA Civ 113, [2001] 1 WLR 1279.

were attributed to that parent; or perhaps because the father had deliberately withdrawn from any involvement in the child's upbringing.

In other cases in which one or other of the parents has undergone a failed, negligently-performed, sterilisation, both parents have brought the action and recovered damages in a joint claim (e.g., *Thake v Maurice*[155] and *McFarlane*[156]). In *McFarlane*, none of the House discussed whether, and why, the surgeon owed Mrs McFarlane (the non-patient) a duty of care – this appears to have been assumed. Clearly the damages for the pain, suffering and inconvenience of pregnancy and childbirth were Mrs McFarlane's alone (and even as a non-patient, the majority held that she was entitled to recover these). Subsequently, the New South Wales Supreme Court remarked, in *McDonald v Sydney South West Area Health Service*, that the *McFarlane* decision 'does not assist on the issue of whether the duty of care of the doctor extends to the partner of his patient'.[157]

However, there is some English dicta support for the proposition that the biological parent of the child born of a failed sterilisation – but who was not the sterilised parent – can claim damages for economic injury from D who performed the operation. For example, in *Islington LBC v UCL London Hosp NHS Trust*, the Court of Appeal remarked, just because the surgeon's advisory letter was addressed to Mr McFarlane alone, did not mean that there was no duty to Mrs McFarlane.[158] Also, in *Parkinson*, where Mrs Parkinson was the patient, there was no claim for damages by Mr Parkinson against the surgeon, and the issue of his legal status did not arise on the facts, but Hale LJ commented that the proximity between D as surgeon, and his patient's sexual partner, was 'quite close', and that where any claim was made by a father 'who not only has, but meets, his parental responsibility to care for the child', then her 'tentative view' was that the father should have a potential claim against D too.[159] Interestingly, however, the Irish High Court was not prepared to award the father (who was the non-patient) any damages in *Ahern v Moore*, noting that Hale LJ's comment was 'obiter and conditional', and that there was 'no legal rule that would permit [the court] to award him damages'.[160]

In that light, the legal status of the biological parent of a child born of a wrongful conception to sue for damages against D, who performed the sterilisation operation on his or her partner, is not entirely settled.

§2.19 By contrast, no English authority supports a duty of care on D's part, to avoid *any* of the losses sustained by a future sexual partner of the patient in a wrongful conception action.

Where D negligently performs a sterilisation operation on a patient, and years later, that patient conceives a child with a partner, C, who, at the time of the operation, was not known to the patient, much less to D, then D will **not** be in a sufficiently proximate relationship with that future sexual partner, C. It follows that C will be unable to recover **any** costs associated with the birth (and the child-rearing costs would not be recoverable in any event, since *McFarlane*).

In *Goodwill v British Pregnancy Advisory Service*,[161] Mr MacKinlay, M, underwent a vasectomy operation, and was thereafter advised by the BPAS, D (a charity which arranged and provided for sterilisation operations, and counselling services) of 'permanent sterility'. The operation spontaneously

155 [1986] QB 644 (CA). 156 [2000] 2 AC 59 (HL). 157 [2005] NSWSC 924, [64].
158 [2004] EWHC 1754 (QB) [37]. 159 [2001] EWCA Civ 530, [2002] QB 266, [93].
160 [2013] IEHC 72, final para. 161 (1996) 31 BMLR 83 (CA), quote at 91.

reversed, without warning of this being given to M by D. Ms Goodwill, C, subsequently entered into a relationship with M, and relying on what M told her about his prior vasectomy, C stopped using other contraceptive measures. C conceived a child, 3 years after M's operation. C and M then separated, and given her lack of financial means, C sued D for the expenses associated with her daughter's birth, including the costs of raising her. **Held:** D owed no duty of care to C. It was 'manifestly unsustainable'.

Evidently, this verdict was the result of both policy factors under *Caparo's* third limb, and the lack of temporal and relational proximity between C and D which *Caparo's* second limb entails.

Doctors: 'wrongful birth' claims

§2.20 'Wrongful birth' claims arise where a healthcare practitioner, D, failed to exercise reasonable care to diagnose or to detect a condition which, had it been pointed out to the mother, C, would have resulted in C's electing to abort her child which was afflicted with that condition (and which ultimately caused, in her child, physical or mental disabilities, or both). The central tenet of the claim is that, because of the misdiagnosis, D permitted the pregnancy to continue, so that C was deprived of the opportunity to terminate lawfully her pregnancy.

When they arise. A parental C may seek to sue for wrongful birth, where the substance of the suit is that the healthcare practitioner, D, failed to detect an already-existing condition in their child *in utero*. These conditions could comprise, say: Down's Syndrome (as in *Rand v East Dorset HA*[162] and *McLelland v Greater Glasgow Health Board*[163]); spina bifida (as in *Lee v Taunton and Somerset NHS Trust*[164]); the congenital abnormality of Smith Magenis Syndrome which affects chromosome 17 (as in *Conway v Cardiff and Vale NHS Trust*[165]); foetal disabilities arising from the mother's contraction of rubella during pregnancy (as in *Hardman v Amin*[166]); and muscular dystrophy, which genetic testing of the X-linked recessive gene would have revealed (as in *Anderson v Forth Valley Health Board*[167]). C's claim is that, had these conditions been identified, they would have led to the mother's undertaking a lawful abortion of the foetus. This (hereafter, 'Type 1' wrongful birth) is the most common type of wrongful birth suit.

In *Rand v East Dorset HA*,[168] Mrs and Mr Rand, C, were the parents of K, a child born with Down's Syndrome. While Mrs Rand was pregnant with K, her treating doctors, D, failed to inform her of the results of a routine scan which indicated that C was likely to give birth to a child suffering from Down's Syndrome. Had C been informed of that, she would have elected to abort K. D conceded negligence, but disputed the heads of damages to which C was entitled. **Held:** C recovered £118,746 for the claim. Mr Rand recovered general damages of £5,000 separately, to reflect 'the true nature of the wrong done to the Rands, who have been deeply affected in their private lives by having to devote more time to the care and upbringing of K than the care and upbringing of a healthy child would have involved'. In *Lee v Taunton & Somerset NHS Trust*,[169] both Mr and Mrs Lee, C, suffered from epilepsy, for which they each had to take anti-convulsant medication, including

[162] [2000] Lloyd's Rep Med 181 (QB) [163] 2001 SLT 446 (SCIH).
[164] [2001] Fam Law 103, [2001] 1 FLR 419. [165] [2004] EWHC 1841.
[166] [2000] Lloyd's Rep Med 498 (QB). Also: *Salih v Enfield HA* [1991] 3 All ER 400 (CA) (congenital rubella).
[167] 1998 SLT 588 (CSOH). [168] (2000) 56 BMLR 39 (QB), quote at 69 (Newman J).
[169] [2001] 1 FLR 419 (QB).

sodium valproate, which gave rise to a risk of foetal abnormality. C wished to start a family, and sought medical advice. They were not concerned about their child being born with minor disabilities or operable conditions, but wished to terminate a foetus with any serious abnormalities. Mrs Lee fell pregnant, but unfortunately, the radiologist who examined a high-resolution ultrasound failed to report abnormalities diagnostic of spina bifida. C's child, George, was born severely handicapped, physically and mentally. **Held:** C was entitled to recover damages for the costs of meeting the child's special needs.

Alternatively, wrongful birth suits may arise from an allegation that D failed to carry out pre-natal DNA testing which would have identified a likely or certain foetal abnormality (e.g., the severe hereditary blood disease in *Farraj v King's Healthcare NHS Trust*[170]), which, had it been identified to the parents, they would have chosen **not** to conceive at all.

More unusually, a wrongful birth suit may arise where the mother's claim is that her pregnancy was missed by D when it ought to have been detected, and her child's disability developed due to some congenital disorder or from the processes of intra-uterine development (as in *Groom v Selby*[171]) ('type 2' wrongful birth). Again, it is hallmarked as a case of a wrongfully-continued pregnancy.

In *Groom v Selby*, Sarah Groom, C, had two children, and did not wish to have any more. She underwent a sterilisation operation by her gynaecologist D. D did not perform a pregnancy test before operating, and unknown to all, C was about six days pregnant at that time. C consulted D six weeks later, complaining of abdominal pain and discharge. Antibiotics were given, but no pregnancy test was done. The pregnancy was eventually diagnosed at 11 weeks. C was distraught, but felt unable to abort the child (the trial judge found that, if C had been told about the pregnancy at 6–7 weeks, she would have terminated the pregnancy). Baby Megan appeared to be well at birth, but suffered brain damage from salmonella meningitis (from bacteria in the birth canal), complicated by the fact that she was born very premature, and had very thin mucous membranes through which bacteria could easily spread. **Held:** this was treated as a wrongful birth claim, in that D's instances of negligence (at 6 days and at 6–7 weeks) allowed C's pregnancy to continue.

It was described[172] as a 'borderline case' of wrongful birth by Hale LJ, because in Type 1 wrongful birth suits, there was at least some connection between D's negligent failure to diagnose the disorder which leads to, or to screen properly for, the disability in question; whereas in *Groom*, the negligence consisted of allowing Ms Groom's pregnancy to continue, when she did not wish to be pregnant, and the disability then followed from a combination of prematurity and naturally-present bacteria.

Distinctions among the claims. In common with wrongful conception claims, a wrongful birth claim is a *parental* claim – but unlike for a wrongful conception claim (which can concern either a healthy or a disabled child), the wrongful birth claim will **always** concern a disabled child. Furthermore, a wrongful conception claim concerns the parental allegation that a child would not have been *conceived* but for the negligence complained of (per *Parkinson*, *Rees* and *McFarlane*); whereas a wrongful birth claim concerns a parental allegation that the pregnancy

170 [2009] EWCA Civ 1203, and earlier: [2006] EWHC 1228 (QB). The testing laboratory CSL was held to owe a duty of care to the parental Cs, re a misdiagnosis that their son did not suffer from beta-thalassaemia major, a severe hereditary blood disease. For later apportionment proceedings between hospital and CSL, see: [2008] EWHC 2468 (QB).

171 [2001] EWCA Civ 1522, [18].

172 *ibid*, [31]–[32].

would not have been *continued*, but for the negligence complained of (per *Groom v Selby*). Occasionally, however, this terminology is not adhered to (e.g., in *FP v Taunton and Somerset NHS Trust*,[173] Blair J called *Parkinson* a 'wrongful birth' claim).

The disabled child does not have a cause of action against the negligent doctor, D, for inflicting on the child an 'unfortunate life' by reason of his disability. That is a 'wrongful life' claim, which is disallowed, both under English common law[174] and, since 22 July 1976, by statute. A child cannot argue, 'I should have been aborted and destroyed' (as discussed in Chapter 3[175]). On the other hand, a wrongful birth claim is lawful, precisely because a pregnancy may be lawfully terminated by the mother. However, both wrongful birth and wrongful life claims (were the latter allowed) are predicated on the basis that, but for D's negligence, the disabled child would have been lawfully aborted.

Wrongful birth does not involve any allegation that, but for D's negligence, the child would have been born healthy, nor that D's negligence caused the disability in the first place. Where such an allegation is made by the child, that type of suit is entirely lawful at the child's instigation (that claim being governed by the Congenital Disabilities (Civil Liability) Act 1976, s 1(2), as discussed previously in this chapter[176]). By contrast, when a wrongful birth suit is in issue, the child was never going to be born otherwise than disabled, and that disability was not caused by D's negligence – it was naturally-occurring, but the child's birth should have been averted.

However, the main connecting factor between wrongful conception and wrongful birth claims – which render them the proper subject for consideration in this chapter – is that both arise out of a distinct and recognised relationship of doctor–patient, and yet, policy reasons circumscribe the scope of the doctor's duty, in that not all damage flowing from the doctor's breach is recoverable. Although this may sound like a remoteness-of-damage issue, it has been treated, in the case law, as a carve-out of the doctor's duty of care.

Pre-conditions for a wrongful birth claim to succeed. According to *Rance v Mid-Downs HA*,[177] where a wrongful birth claim arises, there are two matters upon which the court must be satisfied – that:

i. at the time of the negligent act or omission on D's part, the pregnancy could have been lawfully terminated by the mother, C. Under s 1(d) of the Abortion Act 1967,[178] a pregnancy may be lawfully terminated by the mother, where a foetal abnormality is identified *in utero*, at any time; and
ii. the mother would have agreed to undergo an abortion (and would not have persisted with the pregnancy, whether in accordance with her religious beliefs or for other reasons).

Damages recoverable. According to *Groom v Selby*,[179] *Hardman v Amin*,[180] and like cases, a claim for wrongful birth entitles the parental C to recover the following damages:

- the extra costs of caring for and raising the disabled child. This principle follows, analogously, from *Parkinson*, in which an award of compensation was made to the parental C, limited to the additional costs associated with rearing a child with a serious disability, because that was fair, just and reasonable. However, given that the child is disabled, damages awards will not necessarily cut off at the age of majority, but may extend for the term of the child's life expectancy.

173 [2009] EWHC 1965 (QB) [7]. 174 *McKay v Essex AHA* [1982] QB 1166 (CA). 175 See pp 127–30.
176 See pp 56–61. 177 [1991] 1 All ER 801 (CA).
178 As substituted by the Human Fertilisation and Embryology Act 1990, s 37(1).
179 [2001] EWCA Civ 1522. 180 [2000] Lloyd's Rep Med 498 (QB).

As in *McFarlane's* wrongful conception suit, the ordinary costs of raising the child cannot be recovered in a wrongful birth suit. This was made plain in *Groom v Selby*, where the Court of Appeal was clearly discussing *wrongful birth* when it analogised *Parkinson*, and said: 'as in *Parkinson*, an award of compensation which is limited to the special upbringing associated with rearing a child with a serious disability would be fair, just and reasonable'.[181] In that light, the views of Toulson J in *Lee v Taunton and Somerset NHS Trust* – although coming to the same 'bottom line' – were quite different, and must now be considered to have been overruled. Toulson J suggested that the **whole** costs of raising the disabled child should be recoverable ('I cannot see a barrier to Mrs Lee recovering the full costs of [George's] maintenance'), but subject to an off-setting exercise ('she was wanting to bear a healthy child. If, following a termination of her pregnancy with George, she had continued with her attempts and had been successful, she would have incurred the costs of bringing up a healthy child in any event'). *Lee* was referred to in *Groom v Selby*, but this reasoning was not referred to. In any event, *Groom* stands for the proposition that only the **extra** costs associated with the raising of the disabled child are recoverable in a wrongful birth suit.

- general damages – including for: pain and suffering relating to the pregnancy and birth – these would not have occurred, had an abortion been undertaken (per *Rand v East Dorset HA*[182]); for shock and distress upon discovering the birth of a disabled child (although *Hardman v Amin* indicated that the award of damages under this head 'would be modest'[183]); and for loss of amenity, *viz*, the additional strain resulting from the care of a disabled child, as compared with a healthy child (per *Rand*);
- special damages, of the type recoverable in wrongful conception (per *McFarlane*).

> In *FP v Taunton and Somerset NHS Trust*,[184] FP, C, brought a wrongful birth claim, for the birth of her very disabled son, RP. C sought an interim payment, plus a stay of a trial of the action whilst RP's prognosis (especially life expectancy) remained uncertain. **Held:** an interim payment of £1.2m was made. Damages were awardable to C for a period up to RP's life expectancy of 20–30 years, plus special damages including: therapies; education; mobility aids and equipment; specially-adapted seating and furniture, beds and accessories, bathing aids; adapted accommodation requirements; computers and electronic equipment; and extra burdens associated with travel, holidays, and leisure pursuits.

§2.21 English law is presently unsettled as to whether a father may bring a wrongful birth suit against D who did not detect the congenital disability or incompatibility, separately from the suit commenced by the mother.

Which parent/s may claim? Given that wrongful birth scenarios are associated with a misdiagnosis of the disabled foetus, the mother is the obvious claimant. It will be the mother who ought to have been advised of any disability *in utero* that would have prompted her election to abort.

At times, the mother has been the sole claimant (e.g., in *Hardman v Amin*, where the mother, C, was exposed to rubella during her pregnancy and which went undiagnosed, her husband

[181] [2001] EWCA Civ 1522, [24] (Brooke LJ). [182] (2000) 56 BMLR 39 (QB) 43, 58, 68.
[183] [2000] Lloyd's Rep Med 498 (QB) [10]. [184] [2011] EWHC 3380 (QB).

was closely involved in the care of their disabled son, but not a party to the litigation). In such cases, it may be that the damages incurred by the father have been recovered by the mother, who then held the sum recovered on trust for the father (a suggested explanation of such cases in *Schumann v Wasbrough*[185]).

Occasionally in wrongful birth claims, the father has brought a **joint** claim with the mother, in respect of the negligent failure to provide advice that would have resulted in the termination of the pregnancy, but with no judicial discussion as to the status of the father in the law suit (as in, e.g., *Salih v Enfield HA*,[186] and in the Scottish case of *Anderson v Forth Valley Health Board*,[187] where both parents were joint claimants). According to Laws LJ in *Whitehead v Searle*, '[i]n some of the wrongful birth cases, it seems to have been assumed, without argument, that the father as well as the mother may claim. The possibility is certainly not ruled out in the learning. It is clear ... that the law on the topic is still developing'.[188] In the Scottish case of *McLelland v Greater Glasgow Health Board*[189] too, the father recovered some damages in his own right in a wrongful birth suit – but without any detailed discussion of why D owed the father a duty of care.

Quite what status the father has, to bring a wrongful birth claim, is presently uncertain in English law – but the question of whether or not an independent claim for wrongful birth can be brought by the biological father of the disabled child may become very important where, *viz*, the financial burdens become the father's alone to bear. This may arise where the mother commits suicide and the father takes over the care of the disabled child (as in *Whitehead v Searle* itself); where the mother dies in childbirth and the father takes on the burden of raising the child (a hypothetical example given in *Whitehead*[190]); or where the father provided gratuitous care to the disabled child which would give rise to a claim for damages on the father's part (as in *Schumann v Wasbrough*). In *Whitehead*, Rix LJ said that there was a 'potentially difficult but realistically arguable claim by [the father] in his own right, once he had shouldered parental responsibility, for the extra costs of [the child's] care, over and above those costs which would have been involved in a normal birth'.[191] Unfortunately, the other two members of the Court of Appeal did not comment on the issue. Subsequently, in *Schumann v Wasbrough*, Dingemans J reiterated that whether the father had any personal action against a healthcare practitioner for the wrongful birth is 'not settled in English law'.[192]

Emergency services: fire brigade and coastal rescue services

§2.22 The emergency services of fire brigade and coastguard owe no duty of care to members of the general public to turn up to an emergency when summoned to do so. Exceptionally, a duty of care is owed where the rescue/protective services, through their own negligence, create the danger which caused C's injury or harm by some positive act of misfeasance (i.e., made the situation worse).

The distinction drawn in the principle above is entirely attributable to the different functions which the various emergency services perform. (For discussion about the legal principles applicable to the duty of care, if any, owed by the *police*, readers are referred to the separate section, 'Police', below.)

[185] [2013] EWHC 3730 (QB) [61]. [186] [1991] 3 All ER 400 (CA). [187] 1998 SLT 588 (CSOH).
[188] [2008] EWCA Civ 285, [50] (also known as *Whitehead v Hibbert Pownall & Newton (a firm)*).
[189] 2001 SLT 446 (SCIH). [190] [2008] EWCA Civ 285, [63].
[191] *ibid*, [67]. [192] [2013] EWHC 3730 (QB) [61].

The duty of the fire brigade and the coastal rescue service is owed to *the public at large* to prevent the spread of fire, and to save lives on the coast and at sea, respectively – both of which may involve a conflict between the interests of various parties who are at risk. Notwithstanding the fact that both these emergency services are providing 'rescue services' funded by, and for the benefit of, the public, English doctrine provides (re the fire brigade: *Capital and Counties plc v Hampshire CC*,[193] and re the coastguard: *OLL Ltd v Sec of State for Transport*[194]) for the following propositions:

Not turning up at all. Where a member of the public logs a 999 call, or activates an alarm which is received remotely, the fire brigade are **not** under a duty to answer that call for help, or to take all reasonable care to turn up. Hence, 'if they fail to turn up, or fail to turn up in time because they have carelessly misunderstood the message, got lost on the way, or run into a tree, they are not liable' (per *Capital and Counties*[195]). Although that case specifically concerned the fire brigade, the Court of Appeal held that the same position applies to the coastguard:

In *OLL v Sec of State*,[196] a tragedy occurred off Lyme Regis in Dorset on 22 Mar 1993, when a party of eight children and their teacher were taken on a canoeing trip with two instructors from the Lyme Regis Challenge Centre, C. They got into severe difficulties at sea. Four children died and the rest suffered severe hypothermia and shock. C claimed an indemnity from D, as employer of the coastguard, alleging that the coastguard took too long to launch a search, and despatched lifeboats and helicopters to the wrong place (inshore rather than offshore). **Held:** no duty of care was owed by D to the members of the party. This scenario was analogous to a fire brigade sending its fire engine to the wrong place. There was no obvious distinction between the two emergency services. D did nothing to make the situation worse.

Even though the role of these emergency services is to protect the community, in general, from foreseeable dangers (usually under statutory powers or duties), they do **not** bear a duty of care to reasonably protect *individual members of the community* from those dangers. There is no sufficient proximity (in *Caparo* terms), merely because an emergency call *is placed* to the fire brigade or the coastguard by that member of the public and a call operator answers it; and there is no assumption of responsibility towards that person merely by virtue of that call being answered.

Turning up and being ineffectual. Where the fire brigade or rescue services **do** respond to an emergency call, but deal with that emergency (e.g., fire, peril, accident) ineffectually, then those defendants do **not** enter into a sufficiently proximate relationship with any member of the public, merely by attending or dealing with the emergency. This principle applies, notwithstanding that a senior officer of those services may have assumed control of the emergency situation when he did turn up.

In *Capital & Counties plc v Hampshire CC*, there were **three** conjoined appeals, regarding: whether, and if so when, a fire brigade, D, owes a duty of care to the owner/occupier of premises which are damaged by fire. In the 'London fire brigade' case, a company specialising in creating special effects for film and TV caused a deliberate explosion on wasteland abutting C's industrial premises, where combustible materials were stored. Burning debris was scattered over a wide area, and some smoke was seen coming from a corner of C's yard. D attended and extinguished the visible fires on the wasteland, but left the scene without inspecting C's premises. A fire broke out that night on C's premises, causing extensive property damage. In the 'West Yorkshire' case, a fire was spotted in a

[193] [1997] QB 1004 (CA) 1030. [194] [1997] 3 All ER 897 (QB).
[195] [1997] QB 1004 (CA) 1030, [1997] 3 WLR 331 (CA). [196] [1997] 3 All ER 897 (QB) 905, 907.

classroom attached to a Church of Jesus Christ of Latter Day Saints chapel, and D attended. There were seven hydrants around the chapel, but either they were not working or could not be located. Water had to be obtained from a mill dam half a mile away. Given the delays and poor water supply, the classroom and chapel were destroyed. **Held:** no duty of care was owed by D in either case.

Both a lack of proximity between a general member of the public and the rescue services and fire brigade who respond to a summons, and various policy reasons, have dictated against any duty of care being owed in these situations – although, as to policy, the views have not been all the same way.

Policy reasons: mixed reasons re duty of care to the general public

- ***conflict of duties***: fire brigade officers could become involved in conflicts between the interests of various property owners whose properties are at risk from spread of fire (*Capital and Counties*[a] and *Kent v Griffiths*[b]);
- ***no floodgates***: given the 'paucity' of recorded cases against fire brigades, and given the difficulty in proving breach, given the split-second decisions that have to be made, floodgates were unlikely (*Capital and Counties*);
- ***no defensive practices***: any emergency services personnel will likely be distracted from their ordinary duties, but that should not be regarded as a valid ground for granting immunity. Also, it was 'not readily apparent why the imposition of a duty of care should divert the fire brigade resources from other fire-fighting duties' (*C&C*).

[a] [1997] QB 1004 (CA) 1036 (Stuart-Smith LJ).
[b] [2001] QB 36 (CA) [45] (Lord Woolf MR).

Hence, despite a close geographic proximity between them, and reliance by the person in peril upon the fire brigade or rescue services, English law has been unwilling to find a duty of care in these circumstances. The ambulance service, however, is treated quite differently in law (discussed below).

Creating the danger, or making it worse. Where the rescue services or fire brigade **creates** the danger which caused C's injury by some positive act of misfeasance, then C is owed a duty of care – albeit that it may be a very fine line between acts of misfeasance (creating a duty) and ineffectual non-feasance (examples above, where no duty is owed).

In *Capital & Counties plc v Hampshire CC*,[197] in the 'Hampshire' case, a fire broke out in a modern building equipped with a heat-activated sprinkler system where Capital & Counties, C, ran a computer-related business. It is a 'golden rule' in fire-fighting that the sprinklers are not turned off until absolutely sure that the fire is completely extinguished; 'there are no advantages in doing so which could possibly outweigh the adverse impact on the spread of the fire'. When the fire brigade, D, arrived, the sprinklers were working; 20 minutes later, the sprinkler system was shut down on the instructions of a fire officer, before the seat of the fire was located. This allowed the fire to spread rapidly, the sprinkler system itself was destroyed by the fire, and ultimately, the entire building complex was destroyed (with £16m damage). **Held:** D owed C a duty of care, because, by turning off the sprinklers when they attended the fire, they 'created or increased the danger. There is no ground for giving immunity in such a case'.

[197] [1997] EWCA Civ 3091, [1997] QB 1004, [83].

Further discussion of the 'making it worse' principle, giving rise to a duty of care, is contained in Chapter 13.

Emergency services: the ambulance service

§2.23 By contrast to the fire brigade and coastal rescue services, the ambulance service generally owes a duty of care to any specific individual who summons the ambulance, and where the ambulance accepts that request to attend.

The ambulance is in a different legal position from rescue services and fire brigade (and the police, discussed below). The ambulance's duty is to assist **specific individuals** who are in need of medical attention (per *Kent v Griffiths*[198]). Where the ambulance is called upon to render emergency services to C and agrees to assist, that agreement induces reliance on C's part, invoking a duty of care. With the ambulance, it is not a matter of 'general reliance' (as there is on the part of property owners and the fire brigade), but rather, of 'specific reliance' – the ambulance is 'dealing with a named individual upon whom the duty becomes focused'.[199]

In *Kent v Griffiths*, Mrs Griffiths, C, was pregnant, when she suffered a serious asthma attack at home. Her GP was summoned, and assessed that C urgently required hospital treatment. A 999 call was placed by her GP at 4.25 pm, and accepted by the ambulance, D, via its service operator. When no ambulance turned up, there were two follow-up calls made (at 4.38 pm and 4.54 pm), in which the operator again assured that an emergency ambulance was 'on its way'. The ambulance arrived at 5.05 pm, and C arrived at hospital at 5.17 pm. C suffered a respiratory arrest during the journey, and suffered a miscarriage and brain damage as a result of the delay in reaching hospital. The trial judge found that the record prepared by a member of the ambulance crew was deliberately falsified to indicate that the time of arrival at C's home was not 5.05 pm, but 4.47 pm. No satisfactory explanation for the ambulance taking 34 minutes to travel 6.5 miles from its base to C's home was ever given. **Held:** D owed C a duty of care, and negligence proven. No policy reasons precluded a duty of care on D's part here. As no explanation for the delay was given, conflicting resourcing issues was not a relevant consideration.

This case, and its reasoning, is also dealt with in Chapter 13 and later in this chapter, under the 'Assumption of responsibility/reliance' test, given that that is where the focus of the court's reasoning really lay. With respect to policy, however, *Kent v Griffiths* did suggest that, in a different set of circumstances, a duty **may** be precluded for policy reasons (but not in this case).

Policy reasons relevant to ambulance emergency services

- *conflicts of interest/resources:* Where the ambulance service, D, has undertaken to respond to a specific request by C to attend, there *could* feasibly be some conflict between the interests of one caller and the public-at-large (say, where the ambulance had to attend a large-scale incident which injured

[198] [2001] QB 36 (CA), with quotes in box locatable at [14], [27], [45]–[49], [51]–[52] (Lord Woolf MR).

[199] *ibid*, [9]. See too: *Aitken v Scottish Ambulance Service* [2011] CSOH 49 (duty of care arguable on ambulance's part where 999 call made).

numerous people), placing conflicting demands on D's resources. Any such conflicts of interest among different individuals would **either** render a duty of care infeasible, or a duty could still be owed when D gave the undertaking to assist, but no *breach* of duty would be found because D's conduct would be reasonable in the circumstances – either way, C's claim would fail. But in the absence of such facts, no policy reasons precluded a duty of care from arising on D's part;

- ***corrective justice***: expectations of 'common humanity' and 'a well-informed member of the public' would consider it to be the *right* outcome for a duty of care to be owed by the ambulance in a case like *Kent v Griffiths*;
- ***'Bad Samaritan' rule inapplicable:*** the policy reasons precluding D from having to assist someone in need did not apply to the ambulance service, as they were not 'volunteers', but rather, paid from the public purse.

Police

§2.24 Unless 'special and exceptional' circumstances apply, a police service, D, in the course of carrying out its functions of investigating, detecting and combatting crime, owes no duty of care to any individual member of the public, C, who suffers physical injury or property damage via the activities of criminals. Even where C is pre-identified to D, as a person in a vulnerable position with respect to actual or criminal activity, no duty of care is owed by D to C.

Known as the '*Hill* core principle', the source of this still-controversial proposition is to be found in the tragic case of Jacqueline Hill, who was the 13th and final murder victim of the 'Yorkshire Ripper'.

> In *Hill v CC of West Yorkshire*,[200] Jacqueline Hill, C, a 20-year-old law student at Leeds University, and the last victim of Peter Sutcliffe (PS), the 'Yorkshire Ripper', was murdered in Leeds in Nov 1980. PS was arrested in Sheffield in Jan 1981, confessed under interrogation, and was eventually convicted of 13 murders and 8 attempted murders from 1969–80, all bearing the same *modus operandi*. C's estate sued the West Yorkshire police service, D, claiming that D had been negligent in investigating the crimes committed by PS, and that if they had exercised reasonable care and followed reasonable lines of enquiry, D would have captured PS much earlier, thus preventing C's murder. (Ms Hill proposed to donate any damages awarded to a charity, but sought to establish that a police force owed a duty to members of the public, re the investigation of crime.) **Held (trial, CA, and HL):** C's claim was struck out. No duty of care was owed by D to C, as the victim of a crime. There was reasonable foreseeability of likely harm to persons such as Ms Hill, if PS were not identified and apprehended promptly – but the requisite proximity between D and C was lacking; plus several policy reasons precluded a duty of care.

The *Hill* principle was affirmed by two more 'milestone' House of Lords' decisions (to adopt the terminology in *An Informer v CC*[201]) – albeit that these further decisions do not lay down any wider principle of immunity from negligence suits than was suggested in *Hill* itself (per *Desmond v CC of Nottinghamshire Police*[202]). In both cases, C's claim was struck out as disclosing no cause of action:

[200] [1989] 1 AC 53 (HL). [201] [2012] EWCA Civ 197, [2013] 2 WLR 694, [87]. [202] [2009] EWHC 2362 (QB) [39].

In *Brooks v MPC*,[203] Duwayne Brooks, C, 18, was a friend of Stephen Lawrence (SL), also 18. On 22 Apr 1993, a gang of white men attacked them in a racially-motivated assault. SL died from stab wounds less than an hour later. C survived the attack, but was deeply traumatised, suffering PTSD. The way in which C was dealt with by the police, D, as a key witness, was severely criticised in the McPherson Enquiry into matters arising from SL's death. C sued D in negligence, alleging that, whilst the attackers remained at large and living in his locality, he was frightened for his own safety, and that D had not acted with reasonable care, support and assistance to ensure his safety as a witness, and to act more swiftly on his evidence to apprehend the attackers. C's claim failed. As the treatment of witnesses was part of, and inextricably bound up in, the investigation of a crime, the *Hill* core principle applied. In *Van Colle v CC of Hertfordshire Police; Smith v CC of Sussex Police*,[204] a threat was made against Stephen Smith, C, by his former partner, Gareth Jeffrey (GJ). On 21 Dec 2000, GJ assaulted C, after C had asked for a few days' break from their relationship. The assault was reported to Brighton police, D, who arrested GJ and detained him overnight. After the separation, GJ wanted to resume the relationship, but C did not. GJ sent C a stream of violent, abusive and threatening telephone, text and internet messages, including death threats (e.g., 'U are dead'; 'look out for yourself psycho is coming'; 'I was in the Bulldog last night with a carving knife. It's a shame I missed you'). C dialled 999 and reported the death threats to D. Two officers visited C, but declined to look at the messages which C offered to show them, and did not make entries in their notebooks, take C's statement, or complete a crime form. C filled in crime report forms the next day, including details of GJ's contact details and death threats. C told an inspector that he feared his life was in danger and asked about the investigation's progress. Again, the death threats were not looked at. Following further death threats by GJ, C was attacked by GJ at his home with a claw hammer, and suffered serious brain damage. C sued D in negligence, but again, no duty of care was owed to C.

The policy reasons precluding a duty on the police's part are extensive, and were stated principally by Lord Keith in *Hill*. Notably, at the time that *Hill* was decided, the *Anns* two-stage test[205] still had currency, and the immunity for barristers (per *Rondel v Worsley*[206]) was relied upon as being relevant as to why police also should not owe a duty of care. Of course, since *Hill*, both the *Anns* test, and the immunity in *Rondel v Worsley*, have (separately) been overruled (as discussed previously in this chapter). Further, in *Hill*, Lord Keith considered that, to uphold a duty of care on the part of the police would not be in the general public interest as promoting a higher standard of care, because the general sense of public duty which motivates police forces was unlikely to be appreciably reinforced by a duty of care being imposed. However, this factor was specifically discounted by Lord Steyn in *Brooks*, on the basis that the public had become more cynical of the police's conduct over the years. Hence, the judicial assertion in *Hill* that the police's 'best endeavours' could not be doubted was no longer necessarily a true reflection of public opinion. All of this is why, in *Brooks*, Lord Steyn said that, '[w]ith hindsight, not every observation in *Hill* can now be supported'.[207]

However, those various developments have not diminished the cogency of the numerous policy reasons which were articulated, primarily, in *Hill*.[208]

203 [2005] UKHL 24, [2005] 1 WLR 1495.

204 [2008] UKHL 50, [2009] AC 225, [23] (Lords Hope, Carswell, Brown, and Phillips; with Lord Bingham CJ dissenting). In *Van Colle*, C's estate's claim was limited to violations of Arts 2 and 8 of the ECHR (which failed), and negligence was not claimed.

205 *Anns v Merton LBC* [1978] AC 728 (HL) 751–52.

206 [1969] 1 AC 191 (HL), discussed online, in 'Barristers', earlier in this chapter.

207 [2005] UKHL 24, [2005] 1 WLR 1495, [28].

208 [1989] AC 53 (HL), with the points in the Table at: 59, 62–63 (Lord Keith), 64–65 (Lord Templeman).

Policy reasons precluding a duty on the part of the police, D

- *floodgates concerns*: Jacqueline Hill was 'one of a vast number of the female general public who might be at risk from [PS's] activities', and 'was at no special distinctive risk'. PS's identity was not known at the time when C was murdered, and no full or clear description of him was ever available to D. C could not be seen as a person 'at special risk', simply because she was young and female: 'all females [are potential victims] of an habitual rapist';
- *defensive practices*: if a duty was owed, then D would be likely to carry out their investigations in a 'detrimentally defensive frame of mind', e.g., more prone to making arrests with insufficient grounds;
- *diversion of resources*: if a duty was owed, then it would be commonly alleged that D failed to catch some criminal as soon as they might have done, with the result that the criminal went on to commit further crimes. To assess that, a trial would need to delve closely into the conduct of D's investigation, re decisions as to policy, discretion, what should have been done and when, which line of enquiry should have been adopted, etc. Elaborate factual investigations would be necessary. The preparation of D's defence, and calling police witnesses, would involve a great deal of time, trouble and expense, which would lead to a 'significant diversion of police manpower and attention from their most important function, that of the suppression of crime. Closed investigations would require to be reopened and re-traversed, not with the object of bringing any criminal to justice, but to ascertain whether or not they had been competently conducted';
- *subordination of the individual for the public good*: if a duty were imposed on D, then D's ability to perform their public function in the interests of the community, fearlessly and with dispatch, would be impeded. No doubt there will be some citizens aggrieved by D's negligence, without private law remedy, but 'domestic legal policy and the Human Rights Act 1998, sometimes compel this result' (*Brooks*);
- *the 'no-need' factor*: there were other torts for which D could be liable, at the suit of a victim in crime: e.g., assault and battery, false imprisonment, misfeasance in public office, malicious prosecution, or an ECHR breach;
- *the 'what would it achieve?' factor*: if a duty was owed, then retired police inspectors would have to be asked whether they would have been misled by the hoaxer who acted in the Yorkshire Ripper case, and whether they would have identified PS at an earlier stage; but 'finding that the police were closer to Watson than Sherlock Holmes would not, at the end of the day, help anybody or punish anybody';
- *potential conflict of duties*: if a duty was owed, then if a police officer were to concentrate on one crime, he might be accused of neglecting other crimes;
- *a matter for the ballot box*: Parliamentarians must ensure that the public 'get the police force they deserve'. Suits in negligence against police officers cannot achieve that aim, because the court cannot consider factors, e.g., whether rates of pay were sufficient to attract police recruits of good calibre, whether modern equipment and facilities were hampered by financial restrictions, whether the Yorkshire police force was 'clever enough' and if not, what could be done about it. Also, the threat of litigation would not make D more efficient or capable – that was truly suited to a public enquiry, and were matters of budgetary restrictions determined by parliamentarians.

The *Hill* core principle has manifested in a variety of scenarios, for the police's benefit. In each of the following,[209] the claim was struck out as disclosing no cause of action, as no duty of care was owed:

In *Michael v South Wales Police*,[210] Joanna Michael, C, made a 999 mobile phone call from her home east of Cardiff in the early hours of the morning. An operator with Gwent Police, D1, took the call. C said that her former partner, Cyron Williams (CW), had just found her with another man, had assaulted her, and had taken the man away in his car to drive him home, saying he would return to 'kill' or to 'hit' her (that bit of the 999 call was described as being inaudible). D1's call operator told C that her call would be passed on to South Wales Police, D2, who would want to call her back, and to keep the phone free; and she graded C's call as requiring 'immediate response' (response time: 5 mins). D1's operator passed the details to D2's emergency control room, but did not refer to CW's threat to kill C. The information was relayed to D2's police officers on mobile patrol, but the call was accidentally downgraded in priority (response time: 60 mins). C made a further 999 call 15 mins later, screaming, but that stopped suddenly during the call. D2's officers immediately attended C's premises, and found her stabbed to death. CW was convicted of C's murder. C's estate sued both D1 and D2 in negligence, but lost. Given that a 999 call had been logged, there was an 'investigation into criminal activity' already on foot, thus placing the case squarely within the *Hill* core principle. In *Alexandrou v Oxford*,[211] Socrates Alexandrou, C, occupied retail clothing store, Ziggys, in Birkenhead, in which he had installed a burglar alarm system. When activated, this raised an alarm at the local police station, with a recorded message re the alarm's location. One Sunday night, burglars entered C's store, stole a large quantity of clothing, and trashed the premises. The alarm sounded at 19.23. The police, D, attended, but because of their failure to properly inspect the rear of the shop when the alarm stopped at 21.26 (the burglars destroyed it), the burglary continued undetected. C sued D in negligence for failing to respond adequately to the alarm, but lost. If the police did owe a duty to an occupier of a property protected by a burglar alarm, then D would owe a similar duty to any person who informed them, whether by a 999 call or in some other way, that an actual or suspected crime was being committed against them/their property. This was unrealistic. It was 'unthinkable that the police should be exposed to potential actions for negligence at the suit of every disappointed or dissatisfied maker of a 999 call'. The *Hill* core principle also applied to emergency calls either not answered or answered ineffectually. In *Robinson v West Yorkshire Police*,[212] Mrs Robinson, C, was walking along a busy road in Huddersfield. Mr Williams was dealing in 'Class A' drugs on the opposite footpath. Plainsclothes police officers, D, arrested Mr Williams in the street, and in the ensuing struggle and melee, their momentum caused them to crash into C, who was injured. C sued D for arresting Mr Williams negligently, but lost. The act of arresting criminals was part of the 'core functions' of D and fell within the *Hill* core principle. It also had an 'obvious public interest', so that the risk of injury to passers-by like C was trumped by the risk to public as a whole if drug dealers were permitted to operate on the street. In *Osman v Ferguson*,[213] schoolteacher Paul Paget-Lewis (PL) formed an unhealthy attachment to a male pupil, Ahmet Osman, C, 15. PL made unfounded accusations of a sexual nature against C (accusing C of having a sexual relationship with a school friend). PL changed his name by deed poll to Osman; damaged and defaced the family's property and car, slashing tyres, spreading excrement over the Osman property, removing light bulbs and supergluing their locks, etc. PL also followed the

[209] See too: *CLG v CC of Merseyside Police* [2015] EWCA Civ 836, [22] (serving a witness summons, etc, part of the core functions of the police).

[210] [2015] UKSC 2, [2015] 2 WLR 343 (a 5:2 majority decision), affirming: [2012] EWCA Civ 981.

[211] [1993] 4 All ER 328 (CA) 334 (Slade LJ).

[212] [2014] EWCA Civ 15, [47].

[213] [1993] 4 All ER 344 (CA).

family when they were going about their daily business, causing serious traffic incidents. The police, D, were well aware of the harassment and interviewed PL, who said that the loss of his job was distressing, and he was concerned about doing something criminally insane. Almost a year after the campaign of harassment began, PL followed C and his family to their flat, shot and severely injured C, and killed C's father, Ali Osman. C's action against D for negligence was struck out.

Where C is a pre-identified victim. This scenario clearly did not arise in *Hill*, as Jacqueline Hill was not a pre-identified victim (or nor even a member of a small ascertainable class). However, in *Van Colle/Smith*, *Michael* and *Osman*, the dangerous predicament in which those Cs found themselves was clearly well known to the police – and yet, still no duty of care arose, for the reasons of policy articulated in *Hill*. Hence, even where C is a particular member of the public whose vulnerability or exposure to risk is well known to the police, the *Hill* principle will apply.

In *Osman*, there was an 'arguable case' (said the Court of Appeal[214]) that 'a very close degree of proximity amounting to a special relationship' between the Osman family and the police, D, was established, given the regular and long-standing dealings between the family and D. Yet, it was against policy to impose a duty of care because *Hill* applied, even in the case of these pre-identified victims.

However, whether the *Hill* principle **should** apply, in the case of a pre-identified victim who is at risk from criminal activity, has proven to be very controversial. In *Smith*, Lord Bingham CJ dissented,[215] and considered that a duty of care should be owed by the police to C in that case, pursuant to the so-called 'liability principle', defined as follows: 'where C, a member of the public, provides police officer D with credible evidence that a third party (whose identity and whereabouts are known) presents a specific and imminent threat to his life or physical safety, then D owes C a duty to take reasonable steps to assess such threat and, if appropriate, to take reasonable steps to prevent the threat from being carried out'. However, the *Smith* majority disagreed that any such principle should apply in English law.[216] More recently, the Supreme Court (by majority) again rejected Lord Bingham's liability principle, in *Michael v South Wales Police*,[217] in large part drawing upon the majority's reasoning in *Smith* (whereas Lord Kerr, dissenting in *Michael*,[218] endorsed a modified 'liability principle' which closely resembled Lord Bingham CJ's in *Smith*). Their contrasting views are set out in the Table below:

For and against: The 'liability principle'

Against (per the majorities in *Smith* and in *Michael*)	For (per the dissenters in *Smith* and in *Michael*)
• the liability principle may fit well with the facts of *Smith*, but in other cases it could be difficult to apply. The threat may not be so credible or as obvious, or the information may come to the police D via someone other than C (*Smith*);	• in *Smith*, C fulfilled the principle because his relationship with D was one of close proximity, based on direct, face-to-face meetings;

214 *ibid*, 350 (by majority, Beldam LJ reserving the question).

215 [2009] AC 225 (HL) [44], with quote in Table at [60].

216 *ibid*, [77] (Lord Hope), [100] (Lord Phillips), [109] (Lord Carswell), [129] (Lord Brown).

217 [2015] UKSC 2, [117]–[130] (Lord Toulson, with whom Lords Neuberger, Mance, Reed and Hodge, agreed).

218 *ibid*, [162]–[172], quote at [168]. Lady Hale agreed (at [197]–[198]).

- it is for D to judge whether the threat is credible and imminent. This would be difficult for a judge to decide, with all of the attendant difficulties and uncertainties of tracking back through an investigation which *Hill* articulated (*Smith*);
- the liability principle did not deal with several *Hill* policy reasons which apply, even if C was a pre-identified victim, e.g., defensive policing, the diversion of resources (*Smith*);
- why should the liability principle be limited to threats to life or to physical safety? Why not threats to property too? Where should its limits properly be set? (*Smith*);
- the court could not assume, 'on the basis of intuition', that the liability principle would either reduce domestic violence or improve police investigations (*Michael*);
- if there should be compensation of pre-identified victims of crime where D failed to prevent violence to C, then the criminal injuries compensation fund, and redress under Arts 2, 3 or 8 of the ECHR, may be available. Beyond that, it was for Parliament to legislate for such a scheme, and not for the common law to plug the gap (*Michael*).

- in *Smith*, D assumed responsibility to C by visiting him, assuring him that investigations were progressing, and inviting C to call 999 if concerned;
- C approached 'a professional force having a special skill in the assessment of criminal risk and the investigation of crime, [and] whose main public function is to maintain the Queen's peace, prevent crime and apprehend criminals' (*Smith*);
- public policy favoured a duty of care being owed by D to take reasonable steps to assess the threat to C and, if appropriate, take reasonable steps to prevent the harm from arising;
- the requisite proximity should not only arise where there was an assumption of responsibility (for that could depend upon the form of words used in the communications between C and the police, sometimes in a highly-stressful scenario). Rather, it should be determined by D's knowledge of 'an imminent threat to a particular individual, and that they have the means of preventing that threat and protecting the individual concerned' (Lord Kerr).

In various decisions since, victims of crime have attempted to distinguish *Hill*, but largely without success. In any circumstance where the police are investigating or combatting alleged criminal activity, and for any police activity which has, as its aim, the protection of the public, the case will fall within the *Hill* principle. Additionally, any attempt to invoke the 'liability principle' – as prevailing over the *Hill* principle – seems firmly closed to a victim of crime now, in light of *Michael* and *Smith*.

No blanket immunity. It is important to reiterate that the police do **not** enjoy a 'blanket immunity' from suits, whether in tort generally or in negligence specifically. In fact, in *Hill* itself, **none** of the Law Lords stated that they were proposing a blanket immunity for the police from suits in negligence.

Nevertheless, the decision in *Osman v Ferguson*[219] became the trigger for a marked dispute between the domestic courts and the European Court of Human Rights, on this very point. The Osman family – having failed in their suit against the police in the English Court of Appeal – took their case to the European Court of Human Rights, in *Osman v UK*,[220] alleging violations by the State of its obligations under Arts 2, 6, 8 and 13 of the ECHR. The European

[219] [1993] 4 All ER 344 (CA). [220] [1998] ECHR 101, (2000) 29 EHRR 245, [149]–[151].

Court disapproved of what it termed an 'exclusionary rule' which the House of Lords had laid down in *Hill*, and considered that the principle gave the police a 'blanket immunity' in respect of their policy and operational decisions. This type of reasoning – 'without further enquiry into the existence of competing public-interest considerations' – amounted to an 'unjustifiable restriction' on the Osmans' claims to have the merits of their claim against the police determined, as a 'deserving case'. Hence, to the extent that *Hill* represented an immunity upon any prosecution of the police in negligence, the European Court held that it could not withstand Art 6 of the ECHR.

However, that critique adopted by the European Court was later toned down in *Z v UK*[221] (which concerned the liability of local authorities for alleged failures in the performance of their functions regarding children in care, discussed in Chapter 13). In *Z*, the European Court admitted that it had misunderstood the precise ambit and source of the *Hill* immunity. Specifically, its reasoning in *Osman* 'was based on an understanding of the [English] law of negligence which has to be reviewed, in light of the clarifications subsequently made by the domestic courts, and notably the House of Lords ... the law of negligence, as developed in the domestic courts since the case of *Caparo* ... include fair, just and reasonable criterion as an intrinsic element of the duty of care, and that the ruling of law concerning that element in this case does not disclose the operation of an immunity'. Domestically, this somewhat embarrassing retreat by the European Court not only entrenched the *Hill* principle in English jurisprudence, but also led to statements of the type of Lord Steyn's in *Brooks*, that it 'would be best for the principle in *Hill* to be reformulated in terms of the absence of a duty of care, rather than a blanket immunity'.[222]

There was some indication, after *Z v UK*, that English courts might become more reluctant to strike out claims by C against the police, arising out investigations of alleged criminal activity (as, e.g., in *Commr of Police v Reilly*[223]). However, that reluctance has not manifested since. Appellate courts have not hesitated to strike out claims against the police (as in, e.g., *Smith*, *Michael*, and *Vicario v Commr of Police*[224]), if the *Hill* principle applied.

Exceptional circumstances where a duty will be owed. The House of Lords, in both *Brooks* and *Van Colle/Smith*, acknowledged that 'exceptional cases on the margins of the *Hill* principle' will entail a duty of care being owed by the police to C. But what are these exceptional categories, which fall outside the *Hill* core principle? Several judgments in *Brooks* and *Smith/Van Colle* unhelpfully make 'broad unspecified references to potential exceptions' (as the Northern Ireland Queen's Bench put it in *Rush v Police Service of Northern Ireland*[225]), without defining what they may be.[226]

However, a more explicit attempt to articulate the exceptional categories was usefully made by Arden LJ in *An Informer v CC*[227] and by Lord Brown in *Smith/Van Colle*.[228] Referring to these (and adding a couple of others which also emerge from an analysis of the case law):

i. **Where the police themselves created dangerous situations for C.** Rarely will the police proactively put members of the public in danger – but where that occurs, the activity will lie outside the *Hill* principle. In each of the following, a duty of care was owed, and negligence was proven

[221] (2002) 34 EHRR 3, [100]. [222] [2005] UKHL 24, [2005] 1 WLR 1495, [27]. [223] [2008] EWHC 2217 (QB).

[224] [2007] EWCA Civ 1361. [225] [2011] NIQB 28, [24].

[226] See, e.g. *Smith/Van Colle*: 'there might be exceptional cases where liability must be imposed. ... [but] I should prefer to leave the ambit of such exceptions undefined at present': [2008] UKHL 50, [109] (Lord Carswell).

[227] [2012] EWCA Civ 197, [2013] 2 WLR 694, [94]–[96] (Lady Justice Arden). [228] [2009] 1 AC 225 (HL) [135].

(although contrast *Robinson v West Yorkshire*,[229] considered previously, where a member of the public could not prove this exception):

In *Rigby v CC of Northamptonshire*,[230] C's gun shop was at risk from a lunatic, and the police, D, came to deal with the situation. D fired a canister of capsicum spray gas into the shop to flush out the suspect, knowing that it could cause a high risk of fire, but without ensuring that the fire engine which had previously been available was there to put out any fire that resulted. In *Gibson v Orr*,[231] the police left the scene of an unsafe bridge which had collapsed as a result of flooding, without leaving any cones or barriers or warning signs. C's car went onto the bridge and fell into the river, causing the death of two occupants and severely injuring the third.

ii. **Assuming a specific responsibility.** The police owe a duty of care to C where they have assumed specific responsibility for C's safety, and have knowledge of C's identity and vulnerability, and where there is a reciprocal reliance by C. This will occur rarely, but as the Supreme Court affirmed in *Michael v South Wales Police*,[232] such cases lie outside the ambit of the *Hill* principle altogether.

Examples include: where the police, D, assume a responsibility for the *physical* safety and well-being of police informants, particularly from threats by those being informed upon (per *Swinney v CC of Northumbria Police Force*,[233] and *An Informer v CC*,[234] although in the latter case, D owed C no duty to protect his *economic* interests); where C agreed with the CPS lawyer that his previous offences would be taken into account and that he would not have to appear on charges of theft, but that agreement was not honoured due to a negligent oversight by the CPS lawyer, and C was arrested when he did not appear on the theft charges (per *Welsh v CC of Merseyside Police*[235]); where D explicitly told a threatened person to do away with bodyguard protection because they would ensure his safety (an example by Lord Brown in *Smith/Van Colle*); and where D set up a sting to catch a criminal in a blackmail or abduction case, putting a participant in the sting at risk of physical injury (an example in *Commr of Police v Reilly*[236]).

Indeed, as the Northern Ireland Queen's Bench pointed out in *Rush*,[237] this exceptional category frequently carries with it public policy reasons in favour of a duty of care being imposed, which must be taken to outweigh the policy reasons in *Hill*. For example, in *Swinney*, the public interest in ensuring the protection of informants, thereby encouraging the solving of crimes, was to be regarded as outweighing the public interest in protecting the police from liability in negligence.

An assumption of responsibility towards those who are particularly vulnerable has also arisen by the police, D, to a prisoner, or to one who has suffered harm from another prisoner's actions.

In *Kirkham v CC of the Greater Manchester Police*,[238] D knew that prisoner C had self-harmed and had suicidal tendencies, but failed to pass on that information to prison authorities. C then hanged himself whilst on remand in custody. **Held:** a duty was owed to C, and it was breached. In *Orange v CC of West Yorkshire*,[239] D did not know that C presented a suicide risk, merely because he had been

[229] [2014] EWCA Civ 15. [230] [1985] 1 WLR 1242 (CA).
[231] 1999 SC 420 (CSOH), and approved in *Smith/Van Colle*, [53] (Lord Bingham CJ), [79] (Lord Hope).
[232] [2015] UKSC 2, [69]ff. [233] [1997] QB 464 (CA). [234] [2012] EWCA Civ 197, [2013] QB 579.
[235] [1993] 1 All ER 692 (CA). [236] [2008] EWHC 2217 (QB) [16]. [237] [2011] NIQB 28, [19].
[238] [1990] 2 QB 283 (CA). [239] [2001] EWCA Civ 611, [2002] QB 347, [47].

heavily drinking. C killed himself by hanging himself by his belt, and it was alleged that the belt should have been removed before he was placed into a cell. **Held:** no duty was owed: 'the special and unusual duty is one which is only owed where the [police] authorities know, or ought to know, of a suicide risk in an individual prisoner's case'.

However, in the latest word upon the subject by the Supreme Court majority in *Michael v South Wales Police*,[240] a pre-identified victim of crime is not able to assert that, where the police knew of an imminent threat to C's safety, an assumption of responsibility was undertaken towards him by the police. The decision also places the circumstances of a 999 call, and precisely what phrases were used by C and by a call operator in a highly-stressful and charged atmosphere, 'front and centre', as to whether an assumption of responsibility can be cast by that call (a proposition which Lord Kerr, dissenting, rightly called 'surely unacceptable'[241]).

In *Michael v South Wales Police*, the fact that the 999 operator of Gwent Police, D1, told C that South Wales Police, D2, would want to call C back, and to keep the line free, did not constitute any exceptional scenario in which the police assumed responsibility for C's safety. This was an 'expectation', and not an 'assurance'. By assuring C that the call would be passed onto D2, D1's call operator did not promise how quickly D2 would respond. The case was distinguished from *Kent v Griffiths*, because in the latter, the 999 operator assured the GP that an ambulance would be there 'shortly'. In *Vicario v Commr of Police*, the police, D, investigated allegations of indecent assault and cruelty made by C against her step-father. The step-father was arrested and interviewed, but D decided not to take further action. In conducting those investigations, D did not assume responsibility to C in deciding whether or not to proceed with a prosecution. Nor was there any specific reliance on D by C (in adjusting C's position on the strength of that reliance – that would be 'unpleadable').

iii. **Some other police function.** The police owe a duty of care where the activities under scrutiny are **not** done in the course of investigating or suppressing crime, but as part of some other police function.

In *Desmond v CC of Nottingshire Police*,[242] collating information for the Criminal Records Bureau, and for on-forwarding to C's employer, was arguably not an activity that fell within the *Hill* core principle.

iv. **System of work.** The police service, as an employer, owes a duty of care to a police employee, C, where the system of work established for police operations (whether for the investigation and suppression of crime, or for other operations) requires that the police assume substantial or total control of, and responsibility for, C's safety and well-being.

Examples include: *Costello v CC of Northumbria Police*,[243] in respect of a female police constable's, C's, injuries inflicted by a female prisoner, whilst another senior police officer was standing by and did not come to C's aid; and *Donachie v CC of the Greater Manchester Police*,[244] where an employed officer was put at grave risk during a tagging operation because of defective batteries in the device.

v. **Public safety at risk from known danger.** The police may owe a duty of care where the police knew that public safety was in extreme jeopardy because of a known danger, and yet the police stood by and did nothing to prevent it or to assist C.

[240] [2015] UKSC 2, [138], and earlier: [2012] EWCA Civ 981, [22] (Longmore LJ). [241] *ibid*, [167].
[242] [2009] EWHC 2362 (QB) [49]. [243] [1999] 1 All ER 550 (CA). [244] [2004] EWCA Civ 404.

In *Rush v Police Service of Northern Ireland*, the court refused to strike out a claim by the estate of Libby Rush, who was murdered by a bomb placed by the Real IRA in a car at Main Street, Omagh in 1998. The police, D, knew that a bomb had been placed in the street with date and time nominated, and despite the exactitude of information, arguably stood by and did not prevent the bomb from exploding.

Significantly, some 'outrageous negligence' on the police's part will **not** constitute an exception to the *Hill* core principle. In *Brooks*, Lord Steyn contemplated (in dicta) this as an exceptional category, but in *Smith/Van Colle*, the majority cast rejected that proposition. Indeed, Lord Phillips noted that, on the assumed facts of *Smith*, it came close to 'outrageous negligence' towards Mr Smith, but that was not sufficient to put the case outside the *Hill* core principle.[245]

Extension of the *Hill* principle. Although the *Hill* principle precludes a claim by a member of the general public who has been the victim of crime, it may also apply where C is a police employee, 'by analogy'. It applied in both of the following cases, involving aggrieved police employees:

In *Hughes v National Union of Mineworkers*,[246] PC Hughes, C, was injured during disturbances at a colliery in North Yorkshire in 1984 during the national miners' strike. C sued the Union, and also his police employer, D, for failing to provide him with adequate protection, and for inadequately coordinating the police forces available. Foreseeability and proximity were conceded. As a matter of public policy, no duty was owed. In *Calveley v CC of Merseyside Police*,[247] various police officers, C, sued their employer, D, in negligence, on the basis that disciplinary proceedings against them had been negligently conducted. C were eventually reinstated after the proceedings, and sued for loss of overtime payments which they would have received, had they not been suspended. D owed no duty of care to C.

Policy reasons precluding a duty of care

- ***defensive practices*:** if senior police officers were liable to individual officers under their command, where those employees were injured by attacks from rioters, that would be detrimental to the control of public order (*Hughes*);
- ***battle conditions*:** in arranging riot control, when employed officers could be in danger of physical injury, police must make critical decisions urgently, and to expose them to negligence claims would be likely to affect the decisions of those police, 'to the prejudice of the very tasks which the decisions are intended to advance' (*Hughes*);
- ***treating like cases alike:*** 'if no duty of care is owed by a police officer investigating a suspected crime to a civilian suspect, it is difficult to see any conceivable reason why a police officer who is subject to investigation under the Regulations of 1977 should be in any better position' (*Calveley*).

The ECHR tack. Given the *Hill* core principle, it may prove more fruitful for C to sue for infringement of the ECHR, alleging that the police failed to investigate properly. Whilst some cases have failed in that attempt (e.g., *Osman v UK*;[248] *Van Colle*[249]), some recent case law has demonstrated more success. For example, in *DSD v Commr of Police*,[250] the victims of the convicted London 'black cab rapist', successfully sued the police under Art 3, for their failure to

[245] [2008] UKHL 50, [2009] 1 AC 225, [101]. [246] [1991] ICR 669 (QB) 680. [247] [1989] AC 1228 (HL) 1238.
[248] (1998) 29 EHRR 245 (ECtHR). [249] [2009] AC 225 (HL).
[250] [2015] EWCA Civ 646, affirming: [2014] EWHC 436 (QB). No claim in negligence was instituted.

conduct an effective investigation into the allegations of serious sexual assault. In *Michael*,[251] the Supreme Court permitted Miss Michael's estate to proceed with an Art 2 claim that D failed to protect C's right to life, and that they should have appreciated that there was 'a real and immediate risk to the life of an identified individual/s from the criminal acts of a third party' (per the test laid down in *Osman*[252]).

The 'Bad Samaritan'

§2.25 Under English common law, there is no duty of care imposed upon D, a bystander, to intervene and to offer assistance to a stranger, C, who is endangered, imperilled or injured.

The general proposition. The 'Bad Samaritan' is one who does not help others in danger or distress. With reference to the 'Good Samaritan' parable,[253] and per *Home Office v Dorset Yacht Co Ltd*:[254]

> The very parable of the good Samaritan ... illustrates, in the conduct of the priest and of the Levite who passed by on the other side, an omission which was likely to have, as its reasonable and probable consequence, damage to the health of the victim of the thieves, but for which the priest and Levite would have incurred no civil liability in English law.

The proposition applies to lay persons **and** doctors, so that 'a doctor who happened to witness a road accident will very likely go to the assistance of anyone injured, but he is not under any legal obligation to do so, save in certain limited [statutorily-set] circumstances which are not relevant' (per *Capital and Counties plc v Hampshire CC*[255]).

Whilst, in *Kent v Griffiths*,[256] the Court of Appeal accepted as 'good sense' the general no-duty-to-assist rule in English common law, some judicial examples of lawful 'Bad Samaritan'-type activity may sound rather dreadful to a layman's ears. **None** of the following scenarios could give rise to liability in negligence, because a duty to exercise reasonable care to intervene/assist/rescue is not owed:

The unhelpful strangers

- failing to stop a blind stranger stepping out in front of busy traffic (cf. the positive act of carelessly propelling him into the traffic which may give rise to actionable negligence) (per *Gibson (AP) v Orr, Strathclyde Police*[a]);
- watching a person who is pre-occupied about to walk over a cliff (per *Yuen Kun-Yeu v A-G of Hong Kong*[b]);

[a] [1999] Scot CS 61, Scot SC 420 (OH) 435.
[b] [1988] AC 175 (PC) 192 (Lord Keith); and: *Mitchell v Glasgow CC* [2009] UKHL 11, [15] (Lord Hope).

251 [2015] UKSC 2, [139] (but trial would need to establish how D1's operator should have understood C's call).
252 (1998) 29 EHRR 245 (ECtHR) [116].
253 Gospel of Luke 10:25–37. See also: Mulheron, *Medical Negligence: Non-Patient and Third Party Claims* (Ashgate, 2010) ch 5 ('"Bad Samaritan" Liability'), from which some analysis herein is drawn.
254 [1970] AC 1004 (HL) 1060 (Lord Diplock), and approved in, e.g.: *Mitchell v Glasgow CC* [2009] UKHL 11, [39], and *Smith (or Maloco) v Littlewoods Org Ltd* [1987] AC 241 (HL) 261, 271.
255 [1997] QB 1004 (CA) 1035 (Stuart-Smith LJ).
256 [2001] QB 36 (CA), [18]–[19].

- eating lunch on a beach while watching another beach-goer drown in the sea (per *Horsley v MacLaren*[c]);
- watching a neighbour's goods destroyed by rain or fire, when minimal effort would have salvaged them (per *Home Office v Dorset Yacht Co Ltd*[d]);
- watching a child drown in shallow water, although he could have been easily saved (per *R v Evans*[e]);
- failing to stop a naval serviceman, with a known drink problem, from drinking himself to death on a remote military base in Norway (per dicta in *Barrett v MOD*[f]).

[c] (1970), 11 DLR (3d) 277 (CA) [34] (Jessup J), aff'd: [1972] SCR 441 (SCC), and cited in: EWLC, *Administrative Redress: Public Bodies and the Citizen* (CP 187, 2008) [3.161].
[d] [1970] AC 1004 (HL) 1060 (Lord Diplock).
[e] [2009] EWCA Crim 650, [17] (Lord Judge CJ).
[f] [1995] 1 WLR 1217 (CA) (dicta, because the deceased's colleagues eventually intervened to assist).

Notably, the ease with which D could have saved C; the resources or ability on D's part to provide assistance; and the degree of danger faced by C, have no apparent impact upon the principle under consideration. In *Smith v Littlewoods Organisation Ltd*,[257] Lord Goff spoke, no doubt for many reasonable thinkers, when he stated that, 'this proposition may be repugnant to modern thinking. It may therefore require one day to be reconsidered'. (However, to date, that has not occurred, except for certain exceptional circumstances, discussed shortly.) Two overall factors contribute to this rather sobering legal position in English law.

i. Various policy reasons. First, a number of policy reasons preclude a duty of care from arising (derived, principally, from *Stovin v Wise*[258] and *Mitchell v Glasgow CC*[259]), as shown in the Table below.

Policy reasons: no duty to rescue

- ***individual liberty***: to compel D to rescue would sit uncomfortably with the individual liberty of doing as one chooses – provided that D does not *do harm* to other people: '[i]n political terms, it is less of an invasion of an individual's freedom for the law to require him to consider the safety of others in his actions than to impose upon him a duty to rescue or protect' (*Stovin v Wise*). Besides, D would have to be constantly on the look-out to prevent all foreseeable harm, placing him under an 'intolerable burden' (*Mitchell v Glasgow CC*);
- ***indeterminate liability***: if D failed to intervene to help C, then many others may have 'looked the other way' too, meaning that any duty to rescue 'may apply to a large and indeterminate class of people who happen to be able to do something' (*Stovin*);
- ***the 'why pick on me?' argument***: obversely, if C only sues D, out of a large group of bystanders who did nothing to help (whether D is chosen at random, or has the 'deepest pocket', or is on unfriendly terms with C), then this gives rise to a 'moral' dilemma (*Stovin*);
- ***altruistic motive***: imposing a duty of care on D would elevate an altruistic/moral motive to a legal duty (*Stovin*);
- ***imposing expenditure or danger on D not justifiable***: the common law cannot justify a principle that requires bystander D, who is not involved with C's activities *and* who has not created the

[257] [1987] AC 241 (HL) 271. [258] [1996] AC 923 (HL), with quotes in Table locatable at 943–46 (Lord Hoffmann).
[259] [2009] UKHL 11, [2009] 1 AC 874, with quotes in Table locatable at [89] and [55].

danger himself, to spend money on behalf of, or put himself at risk during, C's rescue (*Stovin*). As the tragic facts of *Baker v TE Hopkins & Son Ltd*[a] showed, rescues can involve extreme danger to the rescuer (Dr Baker lost his life in that rescue attempt). Casting any burdens of this type on D deters recognising any duty to rescue at all;

- ***potential causation problems***: where an omission to act is at issue, causation problems arise, because D has, at best, created the opportunity for harm to occur. By failing to stop a blind man from walking over a cliff, has the bystander D's omission to shout out a warning caused the blind man's injury or death? Other, more immediate, causes of the tragedy are: (1) the blind man's own disability, and (2) the natural features of the land. In *Mitchell v Glasgow CC*, Lord Rodger noted that such a bystander 'plays no part in the events'. Also, if D's omission enables a third party's criminal act to harm C, that criminal act may be a *novus actus interveniens* (per *Smith v Littlewoods Organisation Ltd*[b]). While these issues are, strictly speaking, causally-related, Lord Goff noted that they 'throw back to the duty of care', and whether one should be owed at all.

[a] [1959] 1 WLR 966 (CA).
[b] [1987] AC 241 (HL) 271 (Lord Goff).

In response to this draconian position, some law reform commentary has queried whether, if no general duty to rescue exists, a duty of 'easy rescue' should be imposed. However, that notion has never gained any significant judicial support in England.

The law reform corner: 'Easy rescues'

Irish LRC:[260] the Commission defined an 'easy rescue' as one which did not impose expense, danger, or undue inconvenience upon the bystander. However, it recommended against any duty to perform an easy rescue, principally because of its 'uncertain nature'. What was 'easy' would be subjective, and dependent upon the particular onlooker concerned; requiring some 'least effort' standard may benefit the victim very little, if at all; and identifying the borderline between an 'easy' and a 'difficult' rescue 'would pose a virtually impossible task'.

ii. A pure omission. A second reason for the law's reluctance to impose a duty to assist on the Bad Samaritan – indeed, the 'fundamental reason', according to Lord Goff in *Smith v Littlewoods Org Ltd*[261] – is that his failure to intervene, rescue, etc, rings of an **omission** to do something. The common law does not, generally speaking, impose liability for what are considered to be 'pure omissions' or 'mere omissions' (a controversial topic discussed in Chapter 3[262]). Indeed, in *Bishara v Sheffield Teaching Hosp NHS Trust*,[263] arising from an alleged failure to intervene, Sedley LJ noted that, 'whether the case is one of simple omission, and therefore excluded as a matter of policy from the arena of tort liability, has to be decided in the light of the facts'.

260 *Civil Liability of Good Samaritans and Volunteers* (CP 47, 2007) [2.47]–[2.49], [2.88]–[2.89], citing: E Weinrib, 'The Case for a Duty to Rescue' (1980) 90Yale LJ247, 248.
261 [1987] AC 241 (HL) 271–72.
262 See pp 146–52.
263 [2007] EWCA Civ 353, [11], citing: *Stovin v Wise* [1996] AC 923 (HL).

The recent enactment of the Social Action, Responsibility and Heroism Act 2015[264] (the 'SARAH Act') does not appear to change the law in that respect, limited as it is to circumstances in which D 'was acting for the benefit of society',[265] or was 'carrying out an activity',[266] or when a person was 'acting heroically'.[267] Although the application of this controversial statute is yet to be tested in the courts, its wording seems, on its face, to preclude any application to the 'Bad Samaritan' scenario.[268]

Exceptions. However, there are some scenarios in which D will owe a duty of care to C to intervene, rescue, or assist, in an emergency scenario:

i. Doctors and hospitals in A&E departments: For hospital doctors, a duty of care at common law arises, whenever a person in need of medical assistance is 'accepted for treatment' (per *Cassidy v Ministry of Health*[269]), and hence applies, 'once a patient has been received or admitted into a NHS hospital, [so] the duty to provide (and thereafter to go on providing) treatment arises, whether the patient is competent or incompetent, conscious or unconscious' (per *R (on the application of Burke) v GMC*[270]). The point of 'acceptance' may occur (and a duty of care may arise) without a hospital doctor in A&E/casualty actually laying eyes, let alone hands, on the victim:

> In *Barnett v Chelsea and Kensington Hosp Management Committee*,[271] three night-watchmen attended D's casualty department, complaining to the nurse on duty that they had been vomiting for three hours after drinking tea at the Technical College where they worked. Mr Barnett, C, was so poorly that he lay down on the chairs. The on-duty A&E doctor was himself sick upstairs on the 2nd floor, and the nurse rang through to him, reporting the men's complaints. In a reference to the fact that it was New Year's Eve, the A&E doctor replied, 'Well, I am vomiting myself and I have not been drinking. Tell them to go home and go to bed and call in their own doctors' if the symptoms persisted. The men left the hospital (never having seen a doctor), and some five hours later, C died. An inquest held that arsenic had been introduced into the tea by person/s unknown, from which C died. An issue was whether the A&E officer owed any duty of care to C, when he had not actually sighted C. **Held:** D owed a duty of care to C (but C's estate ultimately failed because of the absence of a causal link, as discussed in Chapter 8).

The duty to assist/intervene was owed, because of a combination of factors: the casualty department was open and receiving patients; C presented himself complaining of illness or injury for the very purpose for which the A&E department offered its services; the symptoms of long-term vomiting warranted an examination of the watchmen by the A&E officer, rather than leaving any observation to the nurse on duty; and (in modern duty of care parlance), the advice which the A&E officer gave – to see their own GP's if their symptoms persisted (no matter how rudimentary) – demonstrated an assumption of responsibility for their care and treatment. In these circumstances, Nield J was satisfied that there was 'such a close and direct relationship between the hospital and the watchmen that there was imposed upon the hospital a duty of care which they owed to the watchmen'.[272]

[264] In force 13 April 2015, pursuant to the SARAH Act (Commencement and Transitional Provision) Regulations 2015, reg 2.

[265] SARAH Act 2015, s 2. [266] *ibid*, s 3. [267] *ibid*, s 4.

[268] The *Explanatory Notes* to the Act shed no light on the scope of the Act. See, generally, Mulheron, R, 'Legislating Dangerously: Bad Samaritans, Good Society, and the Heroism Act 2015' (2016) *Modern Law Review* [forthcoming].

[269] [1951] 2 KB 343 (CA) 360 (Denning LJ). [270] [2004] EWHC 1879 (Admin) [85].

[271] [1969] 1 QB 428. [272] *ibid*, 436.

There is no 'blanket duty' of care imposed on doctors who work in an A&E department, however. For example, in *Barnett*, Nield J noted that if a casualty department of a hospital closes its doors and says no patients can be received; or if a receptionist at A&E discovers that the person presenting there is already seeing his GP about a medical problem and only wants a second opinion; or if the victim has a small cut which an A&E nurse can easily treat without calling on the services of the A&E doctor on duty, then there would be no duty of care owed by an A&E doctor to the person attending, to either see or to examine him. 'Casualty departments are misused from time to time.'

ii. An emergency request, an affirmative undertaking and reliance: Wherever C *requests* medical or other assistance from D; and there is a reciprocal and affirmative *undertaking* given by D to provide that assistance; and C then *relies* on D, a duty of care will arise on D's part. This exception – whereby D cannot ignore the peril or difficulties in which C finds himself – arises by virtue of an application of the test of assumption of responsibility/reliance, discussed elsewhere in the chapter.[273] The scenario itself is best illustrated by *Kent v Griffiths*[274] (described above, under 'Emergency services').

Notably, *Kent v Griffiths* concerned a scenario where D undertook to assist C who was in medical need. However, where C requests assistance from D, and there is **no** undertaking by D to assist – indeed, quite the reverse, the request is refused – then there is no English authority to date which imposes a duty on D. Rather, the general rule would apply: that D is under **no** duty to go to C's rescue. There is certainly no decision that matches the pivotal Australian case of *Lowns v Woods*,[275] where the New South Wales Court of Appeal held (by majority) that a doctor who declined to attend an emergency did owe a duty of care to the patient in peril, and on whose behalf the request was made.

The comparative corner: An Australian perspective

In *Lowns v Woods*, Patrick Woods, C, 11, suffered an epileptic fit one morning in a flat where his family was holidaying, whilst his mother was out for a walk. Upon return, C's mother urgently sent her 18-year-old son to fetch an ambulance, and her 14-year-old daughter Joanna was dispatched to 'get a doctor'. Joanna ran to D's GP surgery about 300 metres away, and told him that her brother was 'having a bad fit', and requested him to come. D asked for C to be brought to his surgery. Joanna said, 'he's having a bad fit, we can't bring him down', to which D replied that an ambulance should be called for. Joanna said, 'we need a doctor. We have already got an ambulance', but D declined to attend. (D's case was that this conversation never occurred, but on that point, the evidence of Joanna was preferred by the trial judge.) C was treated by ambulance officers at the flat, but the fitting could not easily be brought under control, and C suffered serious and irreversible brain damage. Had D attended to C at the point of request, he would have used rectal Valium, which would have commenced 17–20 minutes earlier than it did, and C would not have suffered brain damage. **Held (CA, 2:1):** D owed a duty to attend/assist C in this emergency, and was negligent not to do so (C was awarded damages of approx A$3.2m).

[273] See pp 113–22. [274] [2001] QB 36 (CA). Lord Woolf MR delivered the judgment of the CA.
[275] [1996] Aust Torts R ¶81-376 (NSWCA, Kirby P and Cole JA, with Mahoney JA dissenting.

As the author has argued elsewhere,[276] it is very doubtful that *Lowns v Woods* would be followed in English law, were a similar fact scenario to come before this jurisdiction's courts. For one thing, England does not have any equivalent to the statutory provision that proved to be so important in *Lowns v Woods*, whereby the definition of 'misconduct' by D expressly covered non-attendance at an emergency without reasonable cause. For another, *Kent v Griffiths* is clearly distinguishable from *Lowns v Woods* on its facts, because an express undertaking to assist occurred in *Kent*, but not in *Lowns*. Indeed, in *Capital and Counties* (which was decided a year after *Lowns*), the Court of Appeal decided that there could be no assumption of responsibility, or duty of care, on the fire brigade's part towards any *one* property owner merely by taking control of the fire-fighting operations. Reliance there may have been, but an undertaking was not, and that was crucial to no duty of care being found.

Those who need rescuing

§2.26 Where D puts himself (or others) in a position of danger and peril, and rescuer C assists D (or others) and suffers physical injury in the course of the rescue, D owes C a duty of care, as a matter of policy. However, no duty will be owed by D, where rescuer C suffers from pure psychiatric injury as a result of carrying out the rescue.

In an oft-cited statement by American judge Cardozo J in *Wagner v Intl Rwy*:[277] '[d]anger invites rescue. The cry of distress is the summons to relief'. Closer to home, Morris LJ stated, in *Baker v TE Hopkins & Sons Ltd*,[278] that, '[t]here is, happily, in all men of goodwill, an urge to save those who are in peril'. However, those rescuers (i.e., Good Samaritans) may be seriously injured during the course of rescue. Does the rescued owe a duty of care to those brave souls who answer the cry?

In *Wagner*, Cardozo J remarked that, if D created the danger from which he then had to be rescued by C, then 'the wrongdoer may not have foreseen the coming of the deliverer [rescuer, C]. He is accountable as if he had'. However, the position in English law is that an attempt at rescue is *entirely* foreseeable. As canvassed earlier, where D imperils himself (or others), or someone else, then it is reasonably foreseeable that someone might attempt to rescue D or that someone else, and that some accident may befall rescuer C during the rescue (per *Crossley v Rawlinson*[279] and *Videan v British Transport Comm*,[280] respectively).

The rescuer C has not always been viewed so positively by English law, with some early cases holding that the rescuer voluntarily assumed the risk of his own injury by getting involved, where a dangerous situation was brought about by D's negligence, and that no liability towards C could arise (per *Dann v Hamilton*[281]).

However, some significant cases since undermined that view, and treated the 'Good Samaritan' rescuer far more kindly. As case examples: a policeman who intervened to stop bolting horses from trampling women and children in their path in Rotherhithe (*Haynes v Harwood*[282]); a bystander who pulled the dead and injured from the wrecked train carriages in the Lewisham train disaster (*Chadwick v British Rwys Board*[283]); and a doctor who went to the help of two men stuck down a well filled with carbon monoxide fumes and who died in the process of the

[276] Mulheron, *Medical Negligence: Non-Patient and Third Party Claims* (Ashgate, 2010) 173–82.

[277] 232 NY 176, 180–81 (1921), and cited in, e.g.: *Baker v TE Hopkins & Son Ltd* [1959] 1 WLR 966 (CA) 980 (Willmer LJ); *Frost (White) v CC of South Yorkshire Police* [1992] 1 AC 310 (HL) 408 (Lord Oliver).

[278] [1959] 1 WLR 966 (CA) 975. [279] [1982] 1 WLR 369 (CA) 374–75. [280] [1963] 2 QB 650 (CA) 669.

[281] [1939] 1 KB 509, 517. [282] [1935] 1 KB 146. [283] [1967] 1 WLR 912 (QB).

rescue (in *Baker v TE Hopkins & Son Ltd*[284]), all recovered in negligence for their injuries from those who put them in the situation of danger in the first place. The most recent authority on the issue – *Tolley v Carr* – reiterates that modern English law supports the imposition of a duty of care on D who imperils himself, and where C responds to the 'cry of distress' and suffers physical injury in the process.

In *Baker v TE Hopkins & Son Ltd*, TE Hopkins, D, a building company, was engaged to clear a deep well of water on a farm in Derby, by means of a petrol-driven pump. The operation of the pump created a haze of fumes, including carbon monoxide gas, in the well. Two workmen descended into the well, despite instructions from Mr Hopkins to wait for assistance to clear the well of dangerous fumes. The workmen were overcome by the poisonous gas, and fell unconscious. Dr Baker, C, was summoned, and was lowered into the well, with a rope tied to his body, to see whether he could rescue the workmen (even though C himself was also warned not to enter the well). Efforts to then pull C to the surface failed, because the rope which was tied to him became caught in a downpipe. By the time it was disentangled by the fire brigade (using suitable breathing apparatus), C and the two workmen had all died. **Held:** D owed a duty of care to rescuer C, and was liable in negligence for his death. It was foreseeable that, as a result of D's negligence towards its two workmen, they could be put in peril, that someone would attempt to rescue them, and that the rescue could have potentially dire consequences. In *Tolley v Carr*,[285] Claire Carr, D1, lost control of her vehicle on a high-speed motorway, and David Tolley, C, saw her predicament, stopped his car, and went to assist. Her car was partly in the outside fast lane, and C tried to move it further off the road, onto the central reservation. Whilst he was 'half in and half out' of the car, turning its hazard lights on, he was hit by two vehicles driven by D2 and D3. He suffered a broken spine, and almost total paralysis. **Held:** all Ds (including Ms Carr, D1) owed C a duty of care as rescuer, and negligence was proven, with 'very substantial damages' likely.

Policy reasons favouring a duty of care

- ***corrective justice***: the law should encourage altruistic and moral behaviour, where mishaps occur: '[i]t would indeed be regrettable if the message delivered by the law of Tort, to a member of the public faced with a cry for help, is that if they intervene, they do so at their own risk; and that it would be wiser to pass by on the other side ... neither the law nor morality has ever sought to encourage imitation of the Levite' (per *O'Neill v Dunnes Stores*[a]);
- ***distributive justice***: if D places C, his rescuer, in peril, then it is 'indeed ungracious' of D to suggest that C took on the risk of injury voluntarily. 'If C, actuated by an impulsive desire to save a life, acts bravely, and subjugates any timorous over-concern for his own well-being or comfort, I cannot think that it would be either rational or seemly to say that he freely and voluntarily agreed to incur the risks of the situation which had been created by D's negligence' (per *Baker v Hopkins*[b]). A duty of care owed to rescuers is a way for the common law 'to acknowledge the actions of such men, which often involve bravery as well as bare humanity' (per *Tolley v Carr*[c]).

[a] [2010] IESC 53, [2011] 1 IR 325, [51] (O'Donnell J).
[b] [1959] 1 WLR 966 (CA) 976.
[c] [2010] EWHC 2191 (QB) [21].

[284] [1959] 1 WLR 966 (CA). [285] [2010] EWHC 2191 (QB) (Chester District Registry).

The situation is different, however, where rescuer C does not suffer any physical injury at all, but suffers only from psychiatric injury as a result of what he witnessed during the rescue. In *Greatorex v Greatorex*,[286] the High Court confirmed that rescuer C who was never in the zone of danger himself, but who provided D with assistance after the danger had passed, cannot be owed any duty of care by D, whose own negligence placed himself in that position of peril (that C is to be regarded as 'a secondary victim having no special status'). The complex topic of negligently-inflicted psychiatric injury is discussed in Chapter 5.

Of course, the mere fact that D, who imperils himself, owes C, his rescuer, a duty of care, is not determinative of liability – e.g., the intervention of a third party may sever any proximate relationship between C and D (as discussed in Chapter 8). It is also possible that C's behaviour could reasonably be said to have constituted contributory negligence (contemplated, but rejected, in *Baker v TE Hopkins*, and described as 'particularly unattractive', and also rejected, in *Tolley v Carr*[287]).

The 'Good Samaritan'

§2.27 Once a 'Good Samaritan' D intervenes to assist C, then that 'Good Samaritan' owes a duty of care to C the subject of a rescue.

Once a 'Good Samaritan' voluntarily intervenes and renders assistance to C, a person in need, then a duty of care to avoid or to minimise injury and harm is owed to victim C. It is one of the great ironies of the common law that, '[w]hile there is no liability attached to a person who stands by while another is in peril in the absence of a special relationship, a duty of care does attach, once a person voluntarily undertakes to rescue another' (per the Ontario case of *Stevenson v Clearview Riverside Resort*[288]). Indeed, in one of the few 'Good Samaritan' cases in England, a duty of care was *conceded* by D (per *Cattley v St John Ambulance Brigade*[289]). That court affirmed that concession – noting that there was 'no doubt' that, in holding themselves out to attend events as they did, the ambulance volunteers owed a duty of care to victims to whom they had to render first-aid.

However (and as the result in *Cattley* itself demonstrated), 'the law is slow and cautious in finding negligence in those who imperil themselves to save persons from risks caused by the negligence of others' (per *Tolley v Carr*[290]). Indeed, whether (and in what circumstances) a Good Samaritan rescuer can be held liable for breach, where he has gone to the rescue of someone in peril and made things worse, is a separate legal conundrum which concerns the standard of care expected of that Good Samaritan (discussed in Chapter 6) and the relevant tests of breach (see Chapter 7).

Soldiers in combat

§2.28 The Ministry of Defence, D, owes a duty of care to its armed services employees, with the exception of those whose acts/omissions fall within the doctrine of 'combat immunity'. That is, it is against public policy for a duty of care to be owed by D (or by its armed service employees)

[286] [2000] 1 WLR 1970 (QB) 1976 (Cazalet J). [287] [2010] EWHC 2191 (QB) [24].
[288] Ont SCJ, 21 Dec 2000, [57] (Wilson J). [289] QB, 25 Nov 1988 (Judge Prosser QC).
[290] [2010] EWHC 2191 (QB) [21].

to D's armed service employees, or to affected civilians, where that party, C, is injured or killed as a result of acts or omissions during 'combat conditions'.

As with any other employer, the Ministry of Defence (MOD) owes a duty to take reasonable care to devise and operate a safe system of work for members of its armed forces (per *Hopps v Mott Macdonald Ltd*[291]). An employer's duty of care is discussed, in further detail, in 'Employers' liability', an online chapter.

However, this particular employer owes no duty where its employee is injured or killed during combat, solely for policy reasons. It is inevitable that, '[i]n the course of hostilities, service personnel will be exposed to the risk of death and of injury, both physical and psychological. That is the nature of warfare. But the welfare of the soldier, sailor or airman must be subordinated to their combat role. The military objective must override the interests of the individual' (as Owen J put it in *Multiple Claimants (Bell) v MOD*[292]). This is the province of the so-called 'combat immunity'.

The legal effect of combat immunity. Essentially, the immunity has two potential legal effects.

i. First, the immunity renders the question of breach non-justiciable – or, as the majority of the Supreme Court put it in *Smith v MOD*, it 'remove[s] the issue of liability for negligence from the jurisdiction of the court altogether',[293] so that the court is precluded from adjudicating upon the issue of whether a decision taken by D in the heat of battle fell below the standard of reasonable care. On the other hand, if combat immunity did not apply to D's activities, it meant that whether D was negligent was a justiciable issue. It will then be necessary to scrutinise the particular facts in order to determine whether, for reasons of public policy, D should not be under a duty of care to avoid C's death or injury, given that '[t]he circumstances in which active operations are undertaken by our armed services today vary greatly from theatre to theatre and from operation to operation'.[294]
ii. Alternatively, the occurrence of combat immunity defines a scenario in which it is not fair, just and reasonable that a duty be imposed on D (per *Caparo's* third policy limb), but should not be regarded as a separate principle *per se* (per *Multiple Claimants (Bell) v MOD*[295]).

Which of these two approaches should apply was the subject of notable disagreement in the Supreme Court's decision in *Smith v MOD*.[296] The majority favoured the view that the existence of the immunity should be a separate question from the 'fair, just and reasonable' limb of *Caparo*, whilst the minority considered the immunity to be simply the result of a conclusion that it would not be fair, just and reasonable to impose a duty of care.

In the author's view, it would be more consistent with the legal analysis of other novel areas of negligence (which are discussed in this chapter), concerning police, emergency services, local authorities, etc, if the question were framed as one of policy under *Caparo's* third limb, without the confusion of rendering allegations of negligence 'non-justiciable' via an immunity. The supposed immunity granted to police investigations, pursuant to the *Hill* principle,[297] prompted an

[291] [2009] EWHC 1881 (QB) [87].
[292] [2003] EWHC 1134 (QB) [2.C.12] (Owen J).
[293] [2013] UKSC 41, [2014] AC 52, [83].
[294] [2013] UKSC 41, [98].
[295] [2003] EWHC 1134 (QB), and aff'd in: *Smith v MOD, ibid,* [110].
[296] [2013] UKSC 41, [83] (Lords Hope, Walker and Kerr, and Lady Hale, in the majority); [114], [164] (Lords Mance, Wilson, and Carnwath in the minority on this point).
[297] Per *Hill v CC of West Yorkshire* [1989] AC 53 (HL).

unwelcome detour, via Strasbourg, because of the argument that any such immunity violated C's Art 6 right to a consideration of the merits of his claim. As discussed previously, this episode eventually culminated in the conclusion, in Strasbourg[298] and reiterated in the House of Lords,[299] that the *Hill* principle was best **not** expressed as a 'blanket immunity', but in any event, there was no violation of Art 6. Given this history alone, it is surprising that the *Smith* majority preferred the recognition of an immunity, separate from *Caparo's* third limb. In any event, the terms, 'combat doctrine' and 'combat immunity' will be employed interchangeably in this section.

Sometimes, the doctrine has been couched in terms of a defence – e.g., in *Bici v MOD*, Elias J noted that combat immunity is '[e]xceptionally a defence to the government, and indeed individuals, who take action in the course of actual or imminent armed conflict, and cause damage to property and injury (including possibly death) to fellow soldiers or civilians'.[300] However, the statement is **not** to be taken literally, for as with all scenarios which invoke the third limb of *Caparo*, it **cannot** operate as a defence which places the burden on D. The burden remains on C to prove that a duty is owed to him.

The effect of the doctrine is powerful, as Elias J also pointed out in *Bici* (where it did **not** apply): 'the court is being deprived of its historic and jealously-guarded role of determining a dispute where a citizen claims that his rights have been unlawfully infringed by an act of the executive'.[301] As a result, it is not to be widely-construed (a notion affirmed as correct in *Smith v MOD*[302]).

The role of policy. Although the doctrine was described in *Smith v MOD*[303] as being 'well-recognised', it is not one of long standing, at least in English law.

The decision of *Mulcahy v MOD*[304] (1996) was the **first** occasion upon which an English court decided that no duty of care in Tort could be owed by one soldier to another, when engaging the enemy in battle conditions. Until 1987, s 10 of the Crown Proceedings Act 1947 had precluded proceedings being brought in respect of the death of, or personal injury to, a member of the armed forces caused by the negligence of another member of the armed forces and attributable to service. However, s 2 of the Crown Proceedings (Armed Forces) Act 1987 removed the blanket protection of s 10, thereby raising for judicial consideration (in *Mulcahy*, *Smith*, etc) the existence and ambit of the duty of care owed to a combatant who is injured or killed whilst on active service, and the policy reasons that preclude a duty.

In fact, several policy reasons have militated against any duty of care being owed in circumstances of combat:

The policy reasons in play

- ***battle conditions:*** acts or omissions during wartime operations should not be subject to judicial control or interference which constitute 'battle conditions' (*Mulcahy*);
- ***subordination of the individual's interests to the wider public:*** the interests of armed service colleagues must necessarily be subordinated to attaining the objectives set out in military operations. A duty is not owed where C (whether employees or civilians) 'are the "innocent" victims of action which is taken out of pressing necessity in the wider public interest arising out of combat' (*Bici*);

[298] (2002) 34 EHRR 3 (ECtHR). [299] *Brooks v Commr of Police* [2005] UKHL 24, [2005] 1 WLR 1495.
[300] [2004] EWHC 786 (QB) [90] (Leeds District Registry). [301] *ibid*, [84], and for quote in the box, see [101].
[302] [2013] UKSC 41, [90]. [303] [2012] EWCA Civ 1365, [2013] 2 WLR 27, [55].
[304] [1996] EWCA Civ 1323, [1996] QB 772, quote in Box at [47]; leave to appeal: [1997] 1 WLR 294 (HL).

- ***the interplay with statute:*** although the immunity of the armed services from actions in tort was removed by s 2 of the Crown Proceedings (Armed Forces) Act 1987, the fact that there was no statutory protection available to D did not mean that all protection for D at common law should be removed (*Mulcahy*);
- ***the role of Parliament:*** the allocation of resources to the armed services, and as between the different branches of the services, and as to what equipment should be procured, is a political decision more appropriate for Parliament than by a court ('[i]t does not follow from the fact that decisions about procurement are taken remote from the battlefield that they will always be appropriate for review by the courts': *Smith*[a]).

[a] [2013] UKSC 41, [65].

What is 'combat', for the purposes of the immunity? It has become important for courts to carefully articulate and delimit the scope of D's 'combat immunity'.

Its availability does **not** depend solely upon C's being killed or injured in combat. Rather, D's act or omission must have occurred in the 'heat of battle', or during the terms of 'actual engagement', or in the 'course of hostilities', or as part of 'the full width of active operations'. What falls within this ambit, to which the doctrine attaches, is a question of fact (and depends upon 'the factual matrix for each case', per *Durrheim v MOD*[305]). Decisions as to training/equipment for future combats are not taken during 'active operations', and hence, cannot fall within the immunity (for, otherwise, 'it is difficult to see how anything done by the Ministry of Defence falls beyond it', according to Moses LJ in *Smith v MOD*,[306] a view affirmed by the majority of the Supreme Court in the same case[307]). However, the difficulties in assessing what falls within 'active operations' has troubled the judiciary. In *Shaw Savill and Albion Co Ltd v Cth*[308] (1940), and in a passage approved in *Mulcahy v MOD*,[309] Dixon J, of the High Court of Australia, remarked that:

> a real distinction does exist between actual operations against the enemy and other activities of the combatant services in time of war. For instance, a warship proceeding to her anchorage, or manoeuvring among other ships in a harbour, or acting as a patrol, or even as a convoy, must be navigated with due regard to the safety of other shipping, and no reason is apparent for treating her officers as under no civil duty of care ... It may not be easy under conditions of modern warfare to say, in a given case, upon which side of the line it falls. But, when ... the matters complained of formed part of, or an incident in, active naval or military operations against the enemy, then ... the action must fail on the ground that, while in the course of actually operating against the enemy, the forces of the Crown are under no duty of care to avoid causing loss or damage to private individuals.

For English purposes, in *Smith v MOD*,[310] Lord Hope accepted that the 'combat', necessary to trigger the immunity, could cover active operations against the enemy in which service personnel are exposed to attack/threat of attack when under actual or imminent armed conflict. However, the majority of the Supreme Court disagreed with the suggestion, in *Mulcahy v MOD*,[311] that the planning of, and preparation for, operations in which service personnel may come

[305] [2014] EWHC 1960 (QB) [63], [66]. [306] [2012] EWCA Civ 1365, [62]. [307] [2013] UKSC 41, [90].
[308] (1940) 66 CLR 75 (HCA) 361. [309] [1996] EWCA Civ 1323, [29]. [310] [2013] UKSC 41, [90].
[311] [2003] EWHC 1134 QB (Admin, Owen J) [2.C.20, 3b].

under attack or meet armed resistance and suffer injury, was also within the province of the doctrine. Such preparation could encompass activities 'taken far away in place and time from those operations themselves', which would extend the 'immunity' far too widely.

Notwithstanding this guidance, there is no doubt that, when considering this description of 'combat', English cases have, to date, shown how very finely-balanced that line is, in practice. On the one hand, the combat doctrine did **not** apply in the following cases:

> In *Smith v MOD*,[312] Private Hewett, C1 (and son of Susan Smith) was killed whilst travelling in a Snatch Land Rover when passing over an IED (improvised explosive device). His estate alleged that the vehicle was not fitted with electronic counter measures (ECMs) and other technology and equipment that would have prevented the incident. Corporal Allbutt, C2, was killed by 'friendly fire' during the offensive on Basra, whilst travelling in a Challenger II tank. His estate alleged that the MOD failed to provide available technology to protect against the risk of 'friendly fire' and adequate vehicle recognition training. Many of these acts or omissions being challenged as negligent (i.e., the choice and fitting out of the vehicles with technology and equipment, the recognition training given to soldiers) happened well before the active operations in which the soldiers were killed. Hence, the claims could not be struck out. In *Hopps v Mott Macdonald Ltd*,[313] Graham Hopps, C, was an electrical engineer, employed by MOD, working around Basra on projects designed to restore Iraq's shattered infrastructure. In Oct 2003, he was travelling in a vehicle, which was being escorted by a Land Rover following behind. C's vehicle drove over an explosive device, and C was badly injured, whilst soldiers also travelling in the vehicle were killed. The invasion of Iraq took place in March 2003, and by 30 April, the war phase was over, so no immunity applied in these circumstances. In *Bici v MOD*,[314] British soldiers, D, who were involved in a UN peacekeeping operation in Kosovo in 1999, shot at two Kosovar Albanians whilst they were passengers in a car travelling in Kosovo around midnight. Mohamet Bici, C1, was shot in the face but not killed, whilst his cousin, Skender Bici, C2, was not actually shot but suffered psychiatric injury. The shots were aimed at a third party on the roof of the car, Mr Fahri Bici, who was killed, but there was no intent on D's part to shoot either C1 or C2. The combat immunity did not apply, because D had not shot at the men in the car because of 'wider concerns which necessitated such draconian measures in the public interest, nor even that any such interest arose in the course of combat, however widely that concept is construed'. There was no concern that the men in the car were part of a wider group intending to attack buildings, civilians, or the soldiers, given that, 'the car was being driven away at increasing speed from that building'.

Combat immunity, which precluded a duty of care, **did** (or **could**) apply in the following cases, however, enabling the actions to be struck out as disclosing no cause of action:

> In *Smith v MOD*,[315] in a conjoined case, Private Ellis, C3, was killed by an IED detonated beside his vehicle, a Snatch Land Rover, whilst on duty in Iraq. His estate alleged that the MOD failed to provide suitable equipment, by re-introducing Snatch Land Rovers, having earlier withdrawn them from use following the deaths of soldiers. Some of the allegations in the Ellis claim (that D should have limited C's patrol to medium or heavily-armoured vehicles) did occur in a phase in which there was a constant threat of enemy action, in which case it was arguable that the combat doctrine applied; that part of the case was to be left to trial. In *Mulcahy v MOD*,[316] Richard Mulcahy, C, was part of the allied forces during the Gulf War in 1991. His battalion was in Saudi Arabia (firing into

[312] [2013] UKSC 41 (4:3), affirming: [2012] EWCA Civ 1365. [313] [2009] EWHC 1881 (QB).
[314] [2004] EWHC 786 (QB) [101]. [315] [2013] UKSC 41, [96]. [316] [1996] EWCA Civ 1323, [1996] QB 732, 737.

Iraqi territory). C was employed specifically to man a M110 8 inch Howitzer gun, and to swab out the breech of the gun after each firing. Only a colleague sergeant was allowed to fire the gun as gun commander. C was to the front of the gun when the gun commander negligently caused the gun to fire. The discharge knocked C off his feet, and caused hearing problems thereafter. When the incident happened, C was engaged as part of a gun crew, firing shells on enemy targets, although there was no return fire, nor had there been for several days before it. However, this constituted 'battle conditions' sufficient for combat immunity to apply. In *Multiple Claimants (Bell) v MOD*,[317] several former members of the armed forces, C, sued in negligence for psychiatric injury allegedly as a consequence of exposure to the stress and trauma of combat. Some Cs had been engaged in anti-terrorist policing and peacekeeping operations (e.g., as in Northern Ireland, Bosnia and Kosovo). Again, combat immunity applied to such operations, because those were operations 'in which service personnel come under attack or threat of attack'.

The type of C. The immunity applies to protect D, regardless of whether C is a member of the armed forces engaged in the heat of battle, or a civilian caught up in cross-fire. Either way, a duty of care is ruled out for policy reasons (per *Smith v MOD*[318]). Earlier, Sir Iain Glidewell had opined, in *Mulcahy v MOD*, that '[i]f, during the course of hostilities, no duty of care is owed by a member of the armed forces to civilians or their property, it must be even more apparent that no such duty is owed to another member of the armed forces.'[319]

The type of D. The immunity applies, whether D: is an armed services colleague of C, whose acts or omissions allegedly caused C's injury or death; is an employer (i.e., the MOD) who is being sued for a direct claim in systemic negligence; or is an employer being sued vicariously for the alleged breaches of an employed member of the armed forces. Whatever capacity D is being sued in, where injuries or death are sustained by C in active operations, the immunity applies (per *Mulcahy v MOD*[320]).

The type of damage. The immunity applies, whether C is claiming for death, personal injury (including psychiatric injury), or property destruction or damage.

In *Burmah Oil Co (Burma Trading) Ltd v Lord Advocate*,[321] Burma Oil Co's, C's, installations near Rangoon were destroyed by the British army, D, to prevent their falling into the hands of the Japanese army when Japan invaded Burma. They were destroyed the day before Japanese forces took control of Rangoon. The case was governed by English law. **Held (3:2):** compensation was payable to C, where D was exercising a prerogative power. However, all members of the House agreed that the destruction 'did not arise out of the military operations', so no question of combat immunity arose. Moreover, although the damage inflicted by D here was deliberate, the immunity could apply (said the court in dicta) in cases of accidental damage to C's property, where, say, a house 'had the misfortune to be in the centre of a battlefield', and was accidentally demolished during warfare; its owner 'can have no claim'.

Further, the territorial limits of combat immunity, for the purposes of negligence claims, were not necessary to explore in *Mulcahy*,[322] although it is clear, from the facts of that case (and affirmed in *Smith v MOD*), that the immunity applies to war zones well away from British shores.

[317] [2003] EWHC 1134. [318] [2012] EWCA Civ 1365, [57] (Moses LJ) and aff'd on appeal: [2013] UKSC 41, [90].
[319] [1996] EWCA Civ 1323, [1996] QB 732, [62]. [320] *ibid*, [65] (Sir Iain Glidewell).
[321] [1965] AC 75 (HL) 111. [322] [1996] EWCA Civ 1323, [1996] QB 732, [47].

Sporting contests: referees, participants and others

§2.29 Amateur referees owe a duty of care to participants of sporting contests, as a matter of policy.

Unfortunately, in sporting contests, matters can go very seriously wrong for participants, and the referees of those matches in which the participants are hurt can thereafter be sued in negligence. In many cases, the referee will be of amateur, and not professional, status.

The *Caparo* tripartite test[323] is again the relevant test in such cases (per *Vowles v Evans*[324]). The Court of Appeal adopted that test as the rightful premise, and held, further, that its first and second limbs would be met, as between participant C and referee D (i.e., it was reasonably foreseeable that, if D failed to exercise reasonable care in refereeing the match, injury to C might result; and the relationship between them was sufficiently proximate). The whole duty of care question revolved around whether it was 'fair, just and reasonable' to impose on an amateur referee a duty of care towards the players in the match.

In *Vowles v Evans*, Richard Vowles, C, was playing hooker for the Llanharan Rugby Football Club 2nd XV in a 'local Derby' in an amateur game. David Evans, D, was refereeing in an amateur capacity. During the game, C's team lost their loose-head prop when he dislocated his shoulder, and had no trained front row forward on the bench to replace him, nor anyone who had recent or significant experience of playing in the front row. D was aware that C's team did not have a suitable replacement on the bench, so he told their captain that they could provide a replacement from within the scrum, or opt for non-contestable scrummages. C's team mate, Christopher Jones, playing as a flanker, said that he would 'give it a go' as front row forward. D agreed to this without enquiring of Mr Jones, the captain, or anyone else, about Mr Jones's previous experience. During injury time, the opposing team aimed for a 'push-over' try from a scrum which, if converted, would enable them to snatch a victory. During that scrum, the scrum collapsed, and C was seriously injured, suffering tetraplegia. **Held:** D owed C a duty of care, and was liable in negligence.
In *Smoldon v Whitworth & Nolan*,[325] Mr Smoldon, C, 17, was playing hooker in an <19 colts game, and had his neck broken when a scrum collapsed. C claimed that the referee, D, owed him a duty of care to enforce the Laws of the Game and to 'effect control of the match so as to ensure that the players were not exposed to unnecessary risk of injury'. **Held:** a duty of care was conceded by D (and breach was proven, and *volenti* rejected).

The policy reasons in favour of a duty of care were multifarious, as described in *Vowles v Evans*:[326]

The policy reasons in play

- ***the availability of insurance:*** even if it was 'public knowledge' that the Welsh Rugby Union (the referee's employer) was heavily in debt (and insurance was expensive), and that public liability insurers were considering excluding cover for participants' sporting injuries, judicial notice could not be taken of the WRU's finances or the intentions of public liability insurers. It was possible for referees, or the WRU, to obtain insurance cover against legal liability, which helped to favour a duty of care;

[323] [1990] 2 AC 605 (HL). [324] [2003] EWCA Civ 318, [2003] WLR 1607. [325] [1997] PIQR P133 (CA) P137.
[326] [2003] EWCA Civ 318, with relevant discussion in the box at [11]–[25], quote at [24] (Lord Phillips MR).

- ***defensive practices:*** re arguments that the supply of amateur referees would 'be in danger of drying up' if they were liable in negligence, and that it was in the public interest that amateur referees should be available for amateur sports and offering their services for free without the risk of legal liability, that risk was covered by the availability of insurance and/or vicarious liability. Further, the very small risk of a player sustaining a serious injury and suing for it would not mean that it would 'discourage those who take their pleasure in the game by acting as referees';
- ***treating D's alike:*** policy considerations did not alter, whatever the age of C and whatever the type of game that D was refereeing: 'we do not consider that the distinction between a colts game and an adults game can affect the answer to the question of whether a referee owes any duty of care to the players';
- ***preference for personal injury:*** in a rugby match, which is an inherently-dangerous sport, some of the laws of the game are specifically designed to minimise the inherent dangers, and players are dependent for their safety on the enforcement of the rules by the referee. It is very unusual for the law to preclude a duty of care by D, whose acts or omissions are capable of causing physical harm to others in a structured relationship. There were no good reasons for treating rugby football as an exceptional case;
- ***no indeterminate liability:*** that there may be many participants in a sport, to whom a duty of care could be potentially owed, does not amount to indeterminate liability. A large but finite number of potential Cs is not the same as indeterminate liability.

Of course, as *Smoldon* demonstrated, whether a breach is proven – in circumstances where the game is fast-moving, and intentionally physical among the participants – is an entirely separate question.

THE VOLUNTARY ASSUMPTION OF RESPONSIBILITY TEST

§2.30 The second test by which to establish a duty of care in novel scenarios is to prove that D assumed responsibility to C in respect of his conduct towards C, and in turn, C relied on D to exercise due skill and care in that conduct.

The genesis of the test was the banking case of *Hedley Byrne & Co Ltd v Heller & Partners Ltd*,[327] where Lord Morris stated that 'if someone possessed of a special skill undertakes, quite irrespective of contract, to apply that skill for the assistance of another person who relies upon that skill, a duty of care will arise'. *Hedley Byrne* (discussed in detail in Chapter 4) was, of course, a world away from the personal injury and property damage suits being considered in this chapter – but the test has come to have a considerable application to these contexts too (albeit that economic loss cases are where it is *still* most significant). Its application to a wider ambit of scenarios than merely to *Hedley Byrne's* giving of information/advice was reiterated by the Supreme Court in *Michael v South Wales Police*.[328]

The analysis below draws out the key principles underpinning the two components of the test, in the context of both personal injury and property damage scenarios.

[327] [1964] AC 465 (HL) 502–3. [328] [2015] UKSC 2, [67].

Proving an assumption of responsibility

§2.31 An assumption of responsibility on D's part is, specifically, an undertaking to exercise reasonable care, judgment, expertise and skill in the provision of goods or services, and to apply any relevant special skills in a careful and reasonable manner.

D's undertaking is **not** to bring about a positive result or a perfect outcome for C, nor to promise a particular result for C. That sort of assumption of responsibility does not (indeed, cannot) arise in negligence – it can only result from a *contract*, in which D guarantees the outcome, but such a guarantee will only be upheld if it was given in clear and unequivocal terms.[329] The exercise of reasonable care by D may result in a terrible outcome for C, but that cannot give rise to negligence.

In *Wattleworth v Goodwood Road Racing Co Ltd*,[330] facts previously, **held:** no breach by the Motor Sports Assn (MSA), D, proven. It could not (and did not) give a guarantee as to track safety or safety barriers which would ensure the safety of drivers at the circuit, even though, 'on occasion at trial, [C's] case came close to saying that there must have been negligence on the part of someone, just because Mr Wattleworth was killed'.

When it arises

§2.32 The 'paradigm situation' in which D assumes legal responsibility to C is where their relationship is something akin to a contractual relationship – albeit that an assumption can legally arise even where such a relationship does not exist. Responsibility is not truly 'assumed' by D, however, but is imposed by operation of law. Any assumption of responsibility on D's part is to be determined objectively, from all the surrounding circumstances, and not by reference to what D thought or intended.

An assumption of responsibility is most likely, where the parties are in some relationship 'having all the indicia of contract, save consideration', according to Lord Bingham in *Customs and Excise Commrs v Barclays Bank plc*.[331] Some personal injury scenarios have involved situations which are contractual or 'close to contract', enhancing an assumption of responsibility, as noted below.

However, as Lord Slynn pointed out in *Phelps v Hillingdon LBC*, the phrase, 'assumed responsibility', can be misleading: 'it can suggest that the professional person [or other D] must knowingly and deliberately accept responsibility ... [but] the phrase means simply that the law recognises that there is a duty of care. It is not so much that responsibility is assumed, as that it is recognised or imposed by law'.[332] This seems counter-intuitive, because the test seems to imply that, subjectively speaking, D voluntarily *chose* to exercise some responsibility for the task undertaken for C. That, however, is not the legal position. Hence, D may be taken to have assumed responsibility for the performance of a task or service that affects C, even where he does not consciously *intend* to do so.

[329] *Thake v Maurice* [1986] QB 644 (CA) 688. See also: *Dow v Tayside Uni Hosp NHS Trust* 2006 SCLR 865 (Sheriff Ct). In neither case was a guaranteed successful outcome upheld.

[330] [2004] EWHC 140, [124].

[331] [2006] UKHL 28, [2007] 1 AC 18, [4].

[332] [2001] 2 AC 619 (HL) 654. See also: *Merrett v Babb* [2001] EWCA Civ 214, [2001] QB 1174, [41].

From an analysis of English case law, a number of factors have emerged, whether alone or in combination, to point to an assumption of responsibility on D's part. Many of these exhibit some degree of control or power by D or some vulnerability on C's part. Those circumstances in which the police may, exceptionally, assume a responsibility to victims, prisoners, etc, have been discussed earlier in this chapter.[333] Drawing upon other contexts (with illustrative authorities), this section highlights the key factors which will point to some legally-enforceable undertaking having been given:

i. Teaching or instruction: Where D instructed or taught C in something that he was unfamiliar with, where D made C aware of the dangers or risks of a certain activity – but where the instruction was not sufficient to prevent the harm that eventually befell C – an assumption of responsibility may arise:

In *Fowles v Bedfordshire CC*,[334] Mr Fowles, C, visited a gym owned/operated by D, and received some instruction on how to use the gym mats when doing a forward somersault, but he was not made aware of the dangers of practising these without supervision, or of how to use the crash mat properly. On his 2nd visit, when using the mats without supervision, C suffered serious injury. **Held:** D owed a duty of care to C, because, '[h]aving assumed the task of teaching [C] how to perform the forward somersault, [D] voluntarily assumed a responsibility to teach him properly and to make him aware of the dangers. They failed to do either.'

Such cases may occur (as with *Fowles* itself) where C is an entrant to D's premises, of which D is an occupier, but where it is not an 'Occupiers' Liability' case, because there was nothing wrong with the state of the premises, and hence, C's action must be brought in negligence.

Also, where D's relationship with C was one of superior rank, and where that relationship meant that D's teaching/instruction/authorisation were unquestioningly followed because of that rank, then D can be taken to have assumed responsibility to prevent C, a subordinate, from taking undue risks (of which he should have been aware), when knowing that C was very likely to follow the instructions or permissions. In such cases, assumption of responsibility is enhanced where C is not likely to question D's judgment. The military employment relationship, where 'authority derives from rank' (whether on- or off-duty), where 'following those more senior is fundamental', and where 'although the officers and men were relaxing off-duty [when the accident happened], rank and military discipline remained relevant', is a classic instance of this.

In *MOD v Radclyffe*,[335] officers and soldiers in an army unit in Germany were taking a break in between Adventure Training exercises. Captain Jones, D, was the officer-in-charge. Some army members wanted to jump from a bridge into a reservoir (about 20 metres below), and asked D for permission. He told them to check the bridge and the water depth, and authorised the guardsmen to do the jump. D and Mr Radclyffe, C, a junior army officer who had newly joined the unit, watched. D suggested that it would be 'bad form' if officers did not do the same. C did the jump without mishap. The next day, other guardsmen wished to jump from the same bridge, and C decided that he should demonstrate how to do it. He entered the water badly, and was severely injured. **Held:** D owed C a duty of care, based upon an assumption of responsibility.

[333] See pp 95–99. [334] [1995] PIQR P380 (CA) P390 (Millett LJ).

[335] [2009] EWCA Civ 635, quotes in text at [20]–[22].

ii. Creating circumstances that cause/contribute to C's vulnerability or incapacity, and then failing to supervise/assist C's conduct when D had complete control and responsibility to do so. Where C was unable to care for his own welfare (whether through his own actions, or for other reasons), then not supervising or sufficiently checking or arranging for treatment of C – when D permitted the very circumstances of that incapacity to occur in the first place and had complete control over and responsibility for the situation –may give rise to an assumption of responsibility. Oddly enough, the fact that C may render himself incapable does not refute an assumption of responsibility on D's part.

This scenario may arise where C and D are in an employee–employer relationship in circumstances where C's safety became *entirely* dependent upon D's acts or omissions, even outside the employment hours.

In *Barrett v MOD*,[336] navy serviceman Terence Barrett, 30, C, became drunk during his birthday night out with colleagues, at barracks at the royal naval air station in Norway, after some drinking games. C collapsed, in a coma and insensible, and was returned by stretcher to his cabin, where he was placed in his bunk in the recovery position. A senior naval officer visited him three times. At 2.30am, he was found dead in his bunk, having asphyxiated on his own vomit. C's widow sued his employer, the MOD, D, in negligence. **Held:** D owed C a duty of care, on the basis of an assumption of responsibility. Until he collapsed, C was solely responsible for his condition. Once he collapsed, D's senior naval officer assumed responsibility for his care.

In fact, in *Barrett*, the existence of a duty of care was actually conceded – which was 'understandable', said the Court of Appeal in *Capital and Counties plc v Hampshire CC*,[337] given the employment relationship; the fact that the MOD's senior officers had regularly not 'policed' its rules governing alcohol availability and consumption (thereby creating a 'perfectly deplorable situation' of a heavy drinking culture at the naval station, as the trial judge described it); and the strict chain of command and control that existed in the military.

The factor may also arise where C participated in an activity which D controlled, certified or regulated:

In *Wattleworth*,[338] facts previously, **held:** the MSA assumed responsibility to C, with regard to track and safety barriers and owed a duty (but negligence ultimately failed, because of failure to prove breach and causation). The MSA plainly gave advice to the occupier, Goodwood, both as to the circuit, and as to the safety and protective devices to be deployed around the track. It contemplated and expected that its advice would be acted upon by Goodwood, for MSA and for non-MSA events. Had the MSA made different recommendations with regard to the circuit or protective barriers, then Goodwood would have followed them, and MSA would have expected it to follow them. After C's fatal accident, the first person that Goodwood contacted was the representative for the MSA, indicating the MSA's close involvement and supervision of safety aspects at the circuit. In *Watson v British Boxing Board of Control Ltd*,[339] Michael Watson, C, was injured during the final round of his WBO super-middleweight title fight with Chris Eubank at Tottenham FC, when the referee stopped the fight. After returning to his corner, C became unconscious, having suffered a brain haemorrhage. It took seven minutes for C to be examined by a doctor at ringside, half an hour before he arrived at a nearby hospital (which had no neurological unit), and longer still before he was transferred to

336 [1995] 1 WLR 1217 (CA). 337 [1997] QB 1004 (CA) 1038. 338 [2004] EWHC 140 (QB) [117]–[121].
339 [2000] EWCA Civ 2116, [2001] QB 1134, [49] (Lord Phillips).

St Barts hospital for a brain operation. C sustained serious brain damage and left-side paralysis. The fight was conducted under the rules of the British Boxing Board, D, which set the requirements for medical assistance to be available ring-side. **Held:** D owed C a duty of care (and negligence also proven). D assumed responsibility for the reasonable care of C, because it had complete control over, and a responsibility for, a situation that involved inevitable physical injury to the participants (that was the very object of the boxing sport in which C was engaged). D also had access to specialist information about neurological hospitals, and the rapid assistance required for brain injuries. D's assumption of responsibility in relation to medical care probably relieved the promoter of such responsibility too.

iii. Where D's role is to enforce safety, rules or regulations designed for C's benefit. The rules are usually designed for the safety of a class of persons of whom C was one. In such cases, D will assume a responsibility to ensure that the rules or regulations are enforced, for the protection or safety of C, when D is in a position to control their enforceability. This facet was evident from *Barrett* (above). In addition, the feature has arisen in other contexts, re, e.g., sporting, building, and air safety, in each of which a duty was owed by D:

In *Vowles v Evans*,[340] facts previously, a duty of care was owed by the referee D to the participants of the rugby union game in which C was playing. The court principally applied the *Caparo* test. However, in a brief reference, it was noted that the referee had undertaken to perform the role of referee, where '[s]ome of the rules are specifically designed to minimise the inherent dangers. Players are dependent for their safety on the due enforcement of the rules. The role of the referee is to enforce the rules'. In *Clay v AJ Crump & Sons Ltd*,[341] D, an architect, was responsible for the safety of the site buildings. He was asked about the safety of a wall, but took no action and left it standing there. The wall then collapsed on C, a workman on the site. D owed a duty of care. In *Perrett v Collins*,[342] facts previously, both the inspector responsible for certifying airworthiness of the kit plane, and the PFA which employed him and which organised the certification of model airplanes, owed C a duty of care. Without D's certificate, C's aircraft could not have been flown, confirming the control exercised by D. In *Watson v British Boxing Board*, facts above, a duty of care was owed by the Boxing Board, D, to Mr Watson, C, because D had sole responsibility for regulating the safety of boxing, and for determining the medical care and facilities to be immediately available for boxers injured in the ring.

By contrast, where D has no 'enforcement' or regulatory role, then the requisite degree of control and responsibility on D's part, to safeguard C (or a class of persons of whom C was one), is likely to be absent, as it was in the following cases:

In *Sutradhar v Natural Environment Research Council (NERC)*,[343] the British Geological Survey (BGS, a Dept of the NERC), D, was commissioned by the Overseas Development Agency to undertake a hydro-geological study of a sample of artesian wells in a small area of Bangladesh, to test their efficiency in increasing food production. Mr Sutradhar, C, a villager living in that area, was affected by arsenic in his drinking water drawn from the well. He alleged that D's report about the well project did not flag up the presence of that arsenic, and gave the impression that testing for arsenic was unnecessary, whereas had that happened, the public health authorities in Bangladesh would have taken steps to ensure that the water was safe. **Held:** no duty of care owed, because D had

[340] [2003] EWCA Civ 318, [2003] WLR 1607, [25]. [341] [1964] 1 QB 533.

[342] [1998] 2 Lloyd's Law Rep 255 (CA). [343] [2006] UKHL 33, [27] (Lord Hoffmann), [41]–[42] (Lord Hutton).

no control over, or responsibility for, providing safe drinking water to the citizens of Bangladesh: D 'had no connection with the drinking water project, and no-one asked them to test the water for potability. They owed no duty to the government or people of Bangladesh to test the water for anything'. In *Yates v National Trust*,[344] Jamie Yates, C, was a member of a team of tree-fellers, independent contractors who were engaged by the National Trust, D, to take down a horse chestnut tree in Morden Hall Park, a property owned by D. C was working on the tree, about 50 feet up, when he fell to the ground, suffering permanent paraplegia. **Held:** D did not owe a duty of care to C. D was not his employer, and as hirer of the independent contractor, D did not owe any duty of care to that contractor's employees either. D did not exercise control over the tree-felling team so as to assume responsibility for C's welfare. The case was distinguishable from *Perrett* and *Watson*, and was analogous to *Sutradhar*. Further, the principle that an occupier owed a duty of care to C, for acts or omissions on the part of an independent contractor, if he did not take reasonable steps to satisfy himself that the contractor was competent and the work was properly done, applied only to ultra-hazardous activities – and whilst tree-felling was hazardous, it was not hazardous enough to fall within that principle (as discussed in Chapter 12).

A most unusual application of the assumption of responsibility principle – which falls broadly under this scenario of 'rules and regulations' – occurred in a religious context, where a caterer provided food for the bridal party and guests at a Sikh wedding. That food was not supposed to contain meat, fish or eggs, but in fact, a particular dish did contain egg. Bringing any such food into the Sikh temple was contrary to the rules of that temple.

In *Bhamra v Dubb (t/a Lucky Caterers)*,[345] Kuldip Singh Bhamra, C, attended as a wedding guest at a Sikh Temple at Forest Gate. Mr Dubb, D, provided the wedding feast, and served the dish, ras malai, which happened to contain some egg. C was allergic to eggs, and after eating the ras malai, suffered an anaphylactic reaction, and died. **Held:** D owed C a duty of care. Any person who provides food on a commercial basis for consumption by others owes a duty to take reasonable care to ensure that it does not contain harmful substances and is thus fit for human consumption. Eggs are not normally harmful, but D, himself a Sikh, understood that the food to be served at the wedding should not contain any ingredients of that kind. D also knew that some people are allergic to eggs; that any guests at this wedding would expect the food to be completely free of eggs and would feel confident that no harm would come from eating it; and C was entitled to rely on D to serve food which did not contain egg at a Sikh occasion.

iv. A request for emergency services, and an undertaking to provide same. Regardless of whether a healthcare practitioner (or an 'extension' of the medical services industry such as an ambulance service) had any antecedent relationship with a person in need of medical assistance, C, a duty of care will arise on D's part towards C where C specifically *requests* medical assistance from D, and there is a reciprocal and affirmative *undertaking* given by D to provide that assistance *to that* C. D acts in the capacity of a 'Good Samaritan' rescuer in such cases, and induces in C the expectation that 'the rescue' would be forthcoming.

In *Kent v Griffiths*,[346] facts previously, **held:** the ambulance service, D, owed a duty of care to assist C (the claim in negligence against C's GP was dismissed), because there was a legal assumption of responsibility on D's part. There was no pre-existing relationship between C and D before the 999

[344] [2014] EWHC 222 (QB) [47]–[48]. [345] [2010] EWCA Civ 13.

[346] [2001] QB 36 (CA), with quotes at [18]–[19], [45], [49] (emphasis added) (Lord Woolf MR).

call was placed, but a legal relationship between them 'crystallised' when the first 999 call was accepted: 'The *acceptance of the call* in this case established the duty of care'. The 'assumption of responsibility' was bolstered because the ambulance service should be treated as 'part of the health service ... providing services of the category provided by hospitals'. The ambulance service could not be considered as a 'volunteer' who did not have to assist (under the 'Bad Samaritan' rule above) either, because it undertook 'at least a public law duty', whereby '[t]he provision of ambulances is its statutory function. The London Ambulance Service and its crews are paid out of public moneys to provide their services. It is wholly inappropriate to regard the LAS and its employees as volunteers'.

It will be recalled (from previous discussion[347]) that the *undertaking* 'element of the equation' was precisely what could **not** be proven in the case of the fire brigade in *Capital and Counties*. The property owners, whose properties were destroyed by fire sought to argue that the fire brigade, D, had assumed responsibility to protect their property – but this failed, because there was no assumption of responsibility on the fire brigade's part towards any *one* property owner, but rather, to the public at large; and merely by taking control of the fire-fighting operations, the fire brigade was 'not to be seen as undertaking a voluntary assumption of responsibility to the owner of the premises on fire'.[348] (However, in the 'Hampshire case', the fire brigade created a *new or different danger* for the claimant property owners by a positive act of misfeasance – turning off the sprinkler system – which is why a duty of care was ultimately created.)

v. Where C engaged in inherently-risky and dangerous activity. It may seem counter-intuitive – indeed, downright odd – that, where C has voluntarily chosen to put himself into harm's way by engaging in a dangerous, even foolhardy enterprise, D could have legally assumed responsibility to exercise reasonable care to protect C from suffering injury. However, a legal assumption on D's part may still be held to apply (as evident in, e.g., *Barrett* and *Radclyffe*), although it will **not** be commonly-held. As Coulson J pointed out in *Geary v JD Wetherspoon plc*, 'only the existence of particular facts or specific reliance will lead to a finding that [D] assumed a responsibility to [C]. Generally, the cases show that [D] does not owe a duty to regulate [C's] activities for [C's] own benefit'.[349]

In *Geary v JD Wetherspoon plc*, facts previously, **held:** D owed C no duty of care, as there were no facts to support an assumption of responsibility by the pub owners towards C, nor any reliance by C either. (To reiterate, the case proceeded on common law negligence, and not under the Occupiers' Liability Acts, given that the premises were not defective.)

§2.33 Any disclaimer of D's assumption of responsibility must be made in very clear terms, and must comply with the Unfair Contract Terms Act 1977.

The terms and conditions under which D performs its activities may displace any assumption of responsibility towards C – although that exclusion must be in the clearest language.

In *Wattleworth v Goodwood Road Racing Co Ltd*,[350] facts previously, C was killed at a non-MSA event. **Held:** no disclaimer operated to exclude the MSA's liability: 'given the wide advisory role adopted by the MSA with regard to the Goodwood circuit, far clearer and more explicit wording was needed to bring home that no responsibility was to be taken as accepted by the MSA, save for the

[347] Cross cite pp 85–89. [348] [1997] QB 1004 (CA) 1036 (Stuart-Smith LJ).
[349] [2011] EWHC 1506 (QB) [57]–[58]. [350] [2004] EWHC 140 (QB) [124] (Davis J).

MSA event in question'. Further, had any disclaimer been given by the MSA in respect of non-MSA events, then the race track owner/occupier, Goodwood, probably would have sought safety advice from some other source for non-MSA events. They never considered doing so, indicating that MSA did not intend to disclaim responsibility to any user of the race circuit, such as C.

Proving reliance

The second component of the *Hedley Byrne* test is equally as important. As pointed out in *Vicario v Commr of Police*, 'reliance by [C] on that assumption of responsibility ... is a key part' of the test[351] (and it failed there). In the personal injury context, it means that D has placed himself in a relationship with C, whereby C's 'physical safety becomes dependent upon the acts or omissions' of D (per *Watson v British Boxing Board of Control Ltd*[352]).

Detrimental, versus non-detrimental, reliance

§2.34 Reliance is proven where C can show that he adjusted his position in reliance on D's exercising care, skill or expertise – such that C would have acted differently, if he had *not* relied upon D. However, this requirement may be applied fairly weakly, especially where C suffers personal injury.

A change of position. Lord Bingham observed, in *Customs and Excise*, that, 'reliance in the law is usually taken to mean that if A had not relied on B, A would have acted differently'.[353] The test is proved, if C adjusted his position, either by doing something or foregoing some opportunity, as a result of which he is worse off than he would have been, had he not relied on D.

In *Kent v Griffiths*,[354] C's reliance was proven because, but for operator D's acceptance of the 999 call, her husband would have driven C to casualty, precluding her respiratory arrest: 'if an ambulance service is called and agrees to attend the patient, those caring for the patient normally abandon any attempt to find an alternative means of transport to the hospital'. C had a choice open to her, which she forewent, when D promised that an ambulance was coming – a clear case of detrimental reliance.

If C cannot show some adjustment in his position because of the care, judgment or skill which he expected D to exercise, in doing or not doing something, then 'detrimental reliance' will be absent. However, that has not proven to be particularly crucial.

Some courts have fairly briefly stated that C reasonably relied on D to look after his safety, without articulating quite *how* C changed his position. In the sporting contests of *Vowles v Evans*[355] and *Watson v British Boxing Board*[356] – where a duty of care was owed – the participants were said to rely upon the referee to enforce the rules of the game, and the Board to provide adequate medical assistance to injured boxers, respectively. The option for the participants, presumably, was not to participate in the contests at all, although that was not expressly stated. It had been submitted, in *Watson*, that the boxer relied on the Board because, otherwise, he could have employed his own doctor to sit ringside (some boxers did), but Lord Phillips MR considered that to be an 'unrealistic' submission. Nevertheless, a duty was owed, because C's physical safety was 'dependent' upon the Board's arranging appropriate ringside medical

[351] [2007] EWCA Civ 1361, [27]. [352] [2001] QB 1134, 1149 (Lord Phillips MR). [353] [2006] UKHL 28, [14].
[354] [2001] QB 36 (CA) [9]. [355] [2003] EWCA Civ 318, [25] (Lord Phillips). [356] [2001] QB 1134 (CA) [84]–[85].

attention. Undoubtedly, though, that sort of argument – that C would have engaged his own assistance – is the clearest way of establishing detrimental reliance on C's part.

No change of position. Where C realistically had **no** alternative course of action open to him to protect himself in some other way, but to place his trust in D to act carefully and competently, then can this constitute legally-recognised 'reliance'? It is a more problematical scenario. Inevitably, it will be difficult to prove the 'direct and substantial reliance' on C's part which the law requires (per *Capital and Counties*[357]). The Irish Law Reform Commission[358] called this 'non-detrimental reliance', and gave the example of C who relies on a medically-qualified person to help him where no-one else can, due to the remote location in which C finds himself, but where that person drives on by – D's conduct simply 'speeds up the inevitable consequence, i.e., illness, injury or death' for C. As the Commission noted, whether non-detrimental reliance legally suffices may be doubtful.

A similar problem arises where D may have assumed responsibility for C's safety in some way, but C did not rely on D to do so (in fact, C may have thought the conduct of D unnecessary or uncritical to C's safety, and would have done nothing differently, whether or not D was involved). Proving reliance in such a scenario is perplexing.

In such cases, the better view is that, even if C cannot point to some change of position in reliance upon his expectation that D would conduct himself with reasonable care and skill, the *Caparo* test may still be met, in an appropriate scenario, if there were sufficient proximity and policy reasons to warrant the imposition of a duty of care on D. That approach has been adopted recently.

In *Biddick v Morcom*,[359] Mark Morcom, C, a DIY handyman, was engaged by Cyril Biddick, 80, D, to fix insulation material in the loft of D's house. The hatch cover in the loft ceiling could be locked by turning a long pole with a hook at the end in the lock. During the work, D offered to stand underneath the hatch and hold the lock in place with the pole, because of the danger of the lock working itself loose, and the hatch opening, from the vibration from C's drill. C agreed, but did not consider the measure to be critical to his safety or necessary to reduce the risk of his falling through the hatch. Whilst the insulation was being fitted, D's phone rang, and D answered it. Whilst away, the latch cover opened (probably because of the drilling vibrations), and C fell through to the floor below, suffering serious injuries. **Held:** D owed C a duty of care (subject to 67% CN). D involved himself to a limited, but important, extent in the potentially hazardous activity being carried out by C, *viz*, to keep the hatch door latched. There was no 'reasonable reliance' by C. However, it was entirely foreseeable that, if D did not keep the lock fixed, the hatch door might open, through vibration or pressure; there was requisite proximity, because once D took that task upon himself, he assumed a duty to perform it carefully, even if C did not see D's role as an element in his own safety; and it was fair, just and reasonable to impose a duty.

Other requirements

§2.35 Any reliance on C's part must have been both reasonable and limited. On D's part, he must have known, or should have known, that his undertaking to assume responsibility would be relied upon by C. On C's part, his reliance upon D's assumption of responsibility may be express or implied.

[357] [1997] QB 1004 (CA) 1034 (Stuart-Smith LJ).
[358] *Civil Liability of Good Samaritans and Volunteers* (Rep 93, 2009) [3.29]. [359] [2014] EWCA Civ 182.

i. Reasonable. C may fail to prove that he reasonably relied upon the care, skill or expertise of D, where C had feasible options to preserve his own interests (e.g., by seeking help from a source other than D), and neglected to do so. The reality is that, where D involves himself 'in an activity which gives him a measure of control over and responsibility for a situation which, if dangerous, will be liable to injure [C]', then reliance is likely to be reasonable (per *Perrett v Collins*[360]).

This has been exemplified where: D was in a position to control or regulate C's activities (as in *Perrett* itself); D entered the fray to assist C who was in peril or need (per *Kent v Griffiths*); C was trained or expected to follow D's instructions or permissions (per *MOD v Radclyffe*,[361] where the fact that C asked his superior-ranked officer whether he might jump from the bridge into the reservoir 'predicate[d] reliance sufficient for a duty of care'); or D undertook to assist C in a particular task that meant that C's physical safety became dependent on D's conduct (per *Biddick v Morcom*).

ii. Limited. C's reliance on D must be *limited*, not general. Essentially, this means that D's exercise of reasonable skill and care was relied upon by C, or by members of a class of whom C was one, rather than by the general public as a whole. It is, in some ways, a cross-check of the floodgates policy factor – too large a class which ostensibly relies upon D, and there will be no reliance at law.

The distinction especially arises in the case of emergency services. In *Kent v Griffiths*, Mrs Kent specifically relied upon the ambulance turning up, given that the service undertook to respond to the 999 calls placed to them by particular callers in need. By contrast, the police and fire brigade services have the role of protecting the public in general against risks which could spread quickly, affecting persons and property; and whilst there is a general reliance by the public on the fire service and the police to reduce those risks, there is no reliance necessary to make out the test. The distinction was pointed out in *Watson v British Boxing Board*, where the fact that Mr Watson was 'one of a defined number of boxing members of the Board' meant that those members, including Mr Watson, 'could reasonably rely upon the Board to look after their safety'.[362]

iii. Knowledge. In *Hedley Byrne & Co Ltd v Heller & Partners Ltd*[363] (arising in the context of pure economic loss, discussed in Chapter 4), D's actual or constructive knowledge that C, or a class of persons of whom C was one, was relying upon him, was essential. This requirement has not typically been an issue in personal injury litigation.

For C's part, he may rely upon D as a known entity (as occurred, e.g., in *Watson* and *Kent v Griffiths*, where the boxer and the expectant asthmatic mother were well aware of their respective D's activities, and relied upon D to perform those activities carefully and competently). However, there may be nothing on the facts to show that C specifically knew of, or relied upon, D's undertaking his activities responsibly, e.g., in the case of certifiers or inspectors, who have no contact with C at all. Nevertheless, reliance may still be proven by implication. In *Wattleworth v Goodwood Road Racing Co Ltd*,[364] Davis J remarked that there was no evidence that

[360] [1998] 2 Lloyd's Law Rep 255 (CA) 262. [361] [2009] EWCA Civ 635, [21] (Sir Anthony May).
[362] [2001] QB 1134 (CA) [87] (Lord Phillips MR).
[363] [1964] AC 465 (HL) 497, 503 (Lord Morris), 510 (Lord Hodson), 529 (Lord Devlin).
[364] [2004] EWHC 140 (QB) [118].

Mr Wattleworth, the deceased racing driver, 'relied on the existence of any MSA licence (even though ... he must have thought that the MSA would have had some involvement in regulatory terms with regard to the circuit) ... [but] in using the circuit, Mr Wattleworth was entitled to assume and would have assumed that all due care had been exercised by the persons – whoever they be – who had undertaken responsibility for safety matters'.

THE INCREMENTAL TEST

§2.36 The incremental test acts as a 'cross-check' on the circumstances in which a duty of care is imposed, albeit that it has been somewhat inconsistently applied in English negligence law.

As an analytical tool, the incremental test is not especially useful. Approved in *Caparo* itself (and derived from Brennan J's judgment in *Sutherland SC v Heyman*[365]), the incremental test occupies a fairly obscure status in English law. In novel or unusual cases of alleged negligence, D will customarily argue that the absence of any closely analogous cases or direct precedent indicates that no duty of care should be found – whilst C will contend that there 'has to be a first time', that the common law develops incrementally, and that there is at least one reasonably analogous case which satisfies the test.

Appellate courts do, however, continue to endorse its relevance. In *Customs and Excise*, Lord Bingham emphasised that the incremental test is not a stand-alone test in its own right, but must be used in combination with the other tests discussed earlier in this chapter: '[t]he closer the facts of the case in issue to those of a case in which a duty of care has been held to exist, the readier a court will be ... to find that there has been an assumption of responsibility, or that the proximity and policy considerations of the threefold test are satisfied. The converse is also true'.[366] In *Islington LBC v Univ College London Hosp NHS Trust*, Buxton LJ acknowledged that the status of the test 'is not easy to discern', but probably only means that if C 'could demonstrate that his case did no more than incrementally extend an already recognised head of liability, that was a good indication that his claim met the *Caparo* requirements'.[367] Both of these were pure economic loss cases, and it is apparent that the incremental test has been the subject of far more explicit consideration in that context (as discussed in Chapter 4).

Even so, where there have been no close analogies, courts have still been prepared to take a fairly significant incremental step to impose a duty in novel personal injury scenarios. *Watson v British Boxing Board of Control Ltd*[368] was one such example. Lord Phillips admitted that no case provided any close analogy to 'advance this case by a small incremental step' (the crashed kit aircraft case of *Perrett v Collins* was not a close analogy) – but the Court of Appeal was prepared to uphold a duty, although at pains to emphasise that the outcome in *Watson* did **not** mean that other sporting regulatory bodies for dangerous sports (e.g., for rugby, speedway, racing cars) owed duties of care to the participants in their sports ('[i]t does not follow that the decision in this case is the thin end of a wedge. The facts of this case are not common to other sports'[369]). However, the whole point of the incremental test is that the 'boundary rope' for sporting regulators was moved a little further towards liability, by virtue of *Watson*.

[365] (1985) 60 ALR 1 (HCA) 43–44.
[366] [2006] UKHL 28, [2007] 1 AC 181, [7].
[367] [2005] EWCA Civ 596, [25], [27].
[368] [2001] QB 1134 (CA) [86] (May and Laws LLJ concurring).
[369] *ibid*, [91].

No such incremental step was taken in *Michael*, however. Whilst Lord Toulson remarked that the 'established method of the court involves examining the decided cases to see how far the law has gone, and where it has refrained from going',[370] an incremental movement, from the 999 call in *Kent v Griffiths*, to the scenario that befell Joanna Michael, was not one which the majority was prepared to take. Similarly, in a recent case of alleged medical negligence, *ABC v St George's Healthcare NHS Trust*[371] (which is considered in detail in Chapter 3, under 'pure omissions'), Nicol J was confronted with an entirely novel claim in English law: that the medical Ds should have informed C, a non-patient, that her father, D's patient, had Huntington's Disease. C claimed that she would have terminated her pregnancy, had she known of her father's diagnosis, and that various economic and psychiatric consequences had followed from D's failure to inform C of the genetic condition to which she was at risk. The claim was struck out. To impose this duty would (said Nicol J) be a 'giant step' from established authority: 'this is not a case where [C] can show that a novel duty of care would be but an incremental development from some well established duty. It would, on the contrary, be a radical departure to impose liability in circumstances such as these'. Hence, these recent authorities confirm that the incremental test may still have a considerable impact in personal injury cases, in precluding a duty of care.

370 [2015] UKSC 2, [102]. 371 [2015] EWHC 1394 (QB), quote at [27].

3

Duty II – Particular duty scenarios

This chapter applies many of the principles discussed in Chapter 2, but considers four controversial and problematical scenarios involving a duty of care, *viz*, where:

- statute has precluded a duty of care, primarily for reasons of policy;
- D has failed to warn of material risks associated with a medical operation or treatment;
- D has committed a so-called 'pure omission'; and
- D has failed to manage, control or supervise third parties who injure or kill C.

Dealing with the four conundrums in turn:

STATUTORY PRECLUSIONS OF A DUTY OF CARE

There are two specific scenarios, arising under the Congenital Disabilities (Civil Liability) Act 1976 ('the 1976 Act'), in which a duty of care has been barred by statute. Both are entirely policy-driven.

A mother's immunity

§3.1 The 1976 Act confers an immunity upon C's mother, D, in respect of any of D's acts or omissions which occurred during D's pregnancy (i.e., *in utero*) or pre-conception which affected her ability to have a healthy child (per s 1(1)). However, D loses that immunity if her child, C, is injured *in utero* due to D's negligent driving (per s 2).

No negligence action is possible by a child, C, against his or her mother, D, for acts or omissions which cause damage to that child, such as the following, committed during or prior to the pregnancy:

i. if D participates voluntarily in sporting activity, and suffers an injury during that activity because of her own carelessness or lack of reasonable attention;
ii. if D smokes, drinks, takes drugs, or ingests something else, which affects the foetus adversely in some way and results in C's being born injured, disabled, drug-dependent or otherwise afflicted (in the recent case of *CP (A Child) v First-Tier Tribunal (Criminal Injuries*

Compensation),[1] where a child was born with Foetal Alcohol Spectrum Disorder as a direct consequence of her mother's excessive drinking while pregnant, the Court of Appeal confirmed, in dicta, that s 1 would preclude that child from being able to sue her mother in these circumstances);

iii. if D refuses medical intervention, and delivers a handicapped child (a hypothetical example suggested in *Re MB*,[2] where D refused blood samples, surgical procedures, etc, during her pregnancy, as she was frightened of needles). As Lady Justice Butler-Sloss noted in *MB*, the 1976 Act has a certain, perhaps illogical, ramification: '[a]lthough it might seem illogical that a child capable of being born alive is protected by the criminal law from intentional destruction; and by the Abortion Act from termination ..., [but that child] is not protected from the (irrational) decision of a competent mother not to allow medical intervention to avert the risk of death, this appears to be the present state of the law'.[3]

No equivalent immunity is available to the child's *father*, in respect of any acts or omissions which he may commit against his child, C, during the mother's pregnancy (e.g., the father's act of hitting the mother of his child in the stomach during her pregnancy) that may cause C to be born alive and disabled. In that event, the usual claim by a child may be brought under the 1976 Act (as discussed in Chapter 2).

An exception to the mother's immunity, per s 2 of the 1976 Act, applies where a mother is 'driving a motor vehicle', and in consequence of her failing to exercise reasonable care when driving, C 'is born with disabilities which would not otherwise have been present'. Note that the mother only loses her immunity if she knows, or should have known, that she was pregnant at the time of her negligent driving. However, a mother has immunity from her child's suit where she is not *driving* the motor vehicle, but is merely a passenger in it and has behaved negligently (e.g., failed to wear a seatbelt).

The mother's immunity, and the exception to it, adopted the recommendation of a 1974 English Law Commission report, *Injuries to Unborn Children*.[4] The reasons were complex, and policy-driven:

The law reform corner: The mother's immunity

Reasons for the mother's immunity:

- it reflected that such allegations could be difficult, unseemly, prone to create bitterness, and hard to prove, such that a child should not be able to sue his mother for pregnancy-related activities;
- if C could sue his mother for her negligence, that liability could 'easily' be used by the father as a 'weapon' in custody disputes;
- it is unlikely that the mother would be insured for any activities which caused harm to her child whilst *in utero* – in which case, any successful suit by C against his mother might result in a redistribution of family wealth and assets, in the child's favour (to be held on trust), and diverted away from the mother (who, herself, might be injured).

[1] [2014] EWCA Civ 1554, [2015] 1 QB 459, [47]. [2] [1997] EWCA Civ 3093, (1997) BMLR 175 (CA) [31].
[3] *ibid*, [50]. [4] (Rep 60, 1974) pp 21–6, 35.

Doesn't extend to the father:

The EWLC recommended that no immunity should extend to C's father, for any acts or omissions committed by the father against C, whilst *in utero* or pre-conception. The Pearson Committee thereafter recommended, in 1978, that C's father **should** have an immunity (because 'the danger of disrupting family life also applies to the father') and the 1976 Act be amended, but this has never occurred.[5]

Why abolish the immunity for driving?

This was for solely pragmatic reasons. The mother will be compulsorily insured for any negligent driving, and hence, any payout by the mother to her child will be paid by an insurer, and not by the mother herself. Hence, the suit will not result in a distasteful redistribution of the family's wealth in favour of the child. In fact, the Pearson Committee recommended that no immunity should apply to either parent in the case of negligent driving, or, where C's ante-natal injury arose from any other parental activity for which insurance was compulsory, but that has never been enacted.

Notably, however, a parental D does not enjoy any immunity from a child's action against him/her in negligence in other scenarios (as discussed in Chapter 2).

'Wrongful life' claims

§3.2 A wrongful life claim arises, when a child, C, who suffers from some naturally-occurring disability, alleges that it was D's legal obligation to bring about, or facilitate, the destruction of C's life prior to his birth. Such a claim is unlawful under English common law, as being contrary to public policy. Separately, by virtue of the Congenital Disabilities (Civil Liability) Act 1976, s 1(2)(b), it has been stated, in dicta, that wrongful life claims are abolished by that statute also.

Under a wrongful life claim, a disabled child, C, alleges that, in the absence of D's negligence, he would not have been conceived; or that the pregnancy would have been terminated – and, either way, C would not have been born in a disabled state.

The scenario entails that C's mother was under medical treatment during her pregnancy by her treating doctors, D; that D negligently failed to diagnose or detect the existence or likely prospect of C's naturally-occurring disability; at the time of D's negligent act or omission, an abortion would have been lawfully available to C's mother; C's mother would have aborted C, had she known of the existence or likelihood of the disability; and C's mother did not abort C, thus giving rise to C's disabled birth.

Note that D's acts or omissions do not **cause** C's disability, for a 'wrongful life' claim – if that scenario arises, and C argues that, but for D's negligence which injured the child, C would have been born healthy, then C's appropriate action is to sue under s 1(1) of the 1976 Act. That claim is perfectly permissible (as discussed in Chapter 2). By comparison, C's claim in a wrongful life claim is that, but for D's negligence, C *would not have been born at all.* D negligently failed to avert C's birth (e.g., by failing to inform C's mother that she was carrying a disabled child following a scan, or failing to competently conduct a test for rubella symptoms, or failing to advise C's parents, pre-conception, that they had a risk of chromosome incompatibility). This claim by the child is, in fact, the mirror version of the parent's 'wrongful birth' claim (also discussed in Chapter 2).

[5] Lord Pearson *et al.*, *Royal Comm on Civil Liability and Compensation for Personal Injury* (Cmnd 7054–1, 1978) 309.

At common law

In *McKay v Essex AHA*,[6] the child, C, was born on 15 August 1975, and hence, the common law applied to her claim, and not the 1976 Act (which only applies to births on or after 22 July 1976).

> In *McKay v Essex AHA*, Mary McKay, C, was born disabled as a result of an infection of rubella suffered by her mother in the third month of her pregnancy. Mrs McKay presented at her GP practice, D, with concerns that she had been exposed to a relative with rubella, and a blood test was taken, but the test result was mislaid. A second blood test was taken, and it is not entirely clear why the results of that test were mis-communicated to Mrs McKay. Mary was born in 1975, with very serious disabilities. She alleged that, but for the negligence of D, her mother would have had an abortion to terminate C's life. **Held (at trial):** C had a reasonable cause of action in negligence, and a strike-out application failed. **Held (CA, 3: 0):** C had no cause of action recognisable at law.

According to the English Court of Appeal, wrongful life claims are barred for **three** reasons of public policy:[7]

Why policy reasons preclude a wrongful life claim

- no duty can be owed by a healthcare practitioner D to the child, C, where the central argument was that D was under a duty to bring about C's destruction. That was contrary to public policy, 'as running wholly contrary to the concept of the sanctity of human life.' Plus, to uphold C's claim would endorse the view that a disabled child's life was of such lesser value than a normal child's life, that it was worth destroying – which the Court could not support (it might also have the effect of increasing the rate of abortion). Importantly, where would the line be appropriately drawn, to permit C to bring a claim against D for failing to advise C's mother, so as to provide her with an opportunity to abort – could C, a child with very minor disabilities (e.g., a squint), sue for wrongful life?
- the fact of birth is not an 'injury' to C that is recognisable at law. As the Irish LRC said, '[l]ife itself is said to be the injury' in such actions,[a] and it cannot be construed as such. (Cf: the birth of a disabled child can be construed as an injury for C's parent/s under a 'wrongful birth' action, because an abortion is lawfully available to them.)
- the assessment of C's harm or damage would be impossible, given that the court's task is to put C in the position as if the tort had not been committed – if the tort had not been committed, C's claim is that he would not exist at all. Hence, a court would have to compare the state of C's existence with his non-existence – of which the court can know nothing. Also, the court cannot compare 'the injured child's life in this world and determine that the child has lost anything, without knowing what, if anything the child has gained [from living]' (per Stephenson LJ). To assess damages would be to enter the realms of theology and speculation, leaving 'judges striving to solve the insoluble.'

[a] *Bioethics: Advance Care Directives* (CP 51, 2008) [5.29].

However, not all jurisdictions share the English court's abhorrence of the wrongful life claim, although many do. The contrary viewpoint is interesting to consider:

[6] [1982] QB 1166 (CA).

[7] *ibid*, with quotes in box locatable at: 1181 (Stephenson LJ), 1181, 1188 (Ackner LJ), 1193 (Griffiths LJ).

The comparative corner: Other jurisdictions on wrongful life claims

In some jurisdictions, the claim for wrongful life has been barred (e.g., in South Africa, per *Stewart v Botha*[8]; in Canada, per *Mickle v SA Grace Hosp*,[9] or abandoned, per *Arndt v Smith*;[10] in Scotland, per *P's Curator Bonis v Criminal Injuries Comp Bd*;[11] and in Singapore, per *Ju v See Tho Kai Yin*[12]).

Elsewhere, there has been some judicial support for the claim (e.g., in France, where the claim was permitted, per *Perruche*;[13] in Australia, where the claim was barred by the HCA in *Harriton v Stephens*,[14] but in the NSWCA below, Mason P dissented and would have allowed it;[15] and in US, a mix of judicial views and results have emerged (e.g., *Procanik v Cillo*,[16] *Harbeson v Parke-Davis Inc*,[17] *Speck v Finegold*[18] and *Turpin v Sortini*[19]).

Where wrongful life claims have been permitted in other jurisdictions, some salient points were that:

- the view that birth or life is deemed incapable of being a legal 'injury' was inconsistent with the principle of corrective justice (*Harriton*, Mason P);
- pragmatically, funds for the lifelong care of a profoundly-injured child are better protected in the hands of the Public Trustee, rather than treating damages as the parents' property in a wrongful birth claim (*Harriton*, Mason P);
- if wrongful life claims were permitted, then that would 'foster the societal objectives of genetic counselling and prenatal testing, and will discourage malpractice' (*Harbeson v Parke-Davis Inc*);
- a proper measure of damage (to counter the difficulty of assessment) is either: (1) by assessing the difference between the value of C's life as a healthy normal child, and the value of C's life as an injured child (*Harriton*, Mason P); or (2) restricting C's damages to medical/care expenses, excluding general damages (*Turpin v Sortini*);
- there are 'incalculables' in the parental wrongful conception claim too, where the 'benefits' of having the joys of a healthy child in the family are non-assessable – but that damages claim is assessable, the incalculable offset does not destroy the cause of action. Hence, why should courts be markedly more sympathetic to parental claims than to those of the children themselves? (*Harriton*, Mason P).

There has never been a wrongful life claim brought in England since *McKay*, so far as the author's searches can ascertain. Indeed, subsequent case law has approved of the *McKay* view that **no** wrongful life action exists in English common law: per *Hibbert Pownall & Newton v Whitehead*[20] (where the child, born with undiagnosed spina bifida, could not bring a personal action against his doctors). Nevertheless, it has occasionally been mentioned, judicially (see, e.g., Lord Steyn in *McFarlane v Tayside Health Board*[21]), that a parental claim for wrongful conception or wrongful birth also depends upon the court's assessing the parents' position with

[8] [2008] 1 LRC 370 ((HC (Cape of Good Hope Provincial Div). [9] (1998), 166 DLR (4th) 743.
[10] (1995), 126 DLR (4th) 487 (BCCA), rev'd [1997] 2 SCR 539, (1997), 148 DLR (4th) 48 (SCC).
[11] 1997 SLT 1180 (OH). [12] [2005] 4 SLR 96 (HC). [13] (Cass ass plén, 17 Nov 2000).
[14] [2006] HCA 15, (2006) 226 CLR 52 (HCA).
[15] [2004] NSWCA 93, with Mason P's observations in the Table at [130]–[162].
[16] 478 A 2d 755 (1984). [17] 656 P 2d 483, 496 (SC Wash, 1983) (Pearson J). [18] 408 A 2d 496 (1979).
[19] 643 P 2d 954 (SC Cal, 1982). [20] [2008] EWCA Civ 285, [2009] WLR 549, [3], [19]. [21] [2000] 2 AC 59 (HL).

a child, compared with the situation that would have prevailed if **no** child had existed at all – and yet, both parental claims are permitted in English law.

Under the Act

Under the 1976 Act, s 1(2)(b) allows actions to be brought by a disabled child, for negligently-caused injuries pre-conception, in the womb, and as an embryo – but all premised on the argument, 'but for the negligence, I would have been born healthy'. The section explicitly states that a suit is possible, where 'the child is born with disabilities which would not otherwise have been present'. However, in wrongful life claims, the child was **always** going to be born disabled, and the child's argument is that, 'but for D's negligence, I would not have been born at all, I would have been destroyed'. Hence, by virtue of its wording – and albeit that the statutory language has never been the subject of ratio discussion in England in this regard – it would appear that the 1976 Act does not facilitate wrongful life claims.

Certainly, by way of dicta, Ackner LJ opined, in *McKay v Essex AHA*, that the Act had achieved its aim of abolishing wrongful life claims (as noted, the Court of Appeal was considering the common law position of Mary McKay, born pre-22 July 1976). It was also the recommendation of the English Law Commission, in its 1974 report,[22] that English law should not recognise an action for wrongful life.

However, one query, in respect of the 1976 Act, arises from the insertion of s 1A, which deals with mishaps arising from fertility treatments. Suppose that the child, C, is born disabled, as a result of such treatment. C has a cause of action under s 1A, as a foreseeable claimant, where:

> s 1A(1)(b) the disability results from an act or omission in the course of the selection, or the keeping or use outside the body, of the embryo carried by [a woman] or of the gametes used to bring about the creation of the embryo

It is conceivable that mistreatment of embryo or gametes during the fertility treatment, before they are implanted in the woman who bears C, could result in C's being born disabled (e.g., a healthcare practitioner, D, could be negligent in the 'selection' in some physical respect, by crushing the embryo or maintaining inadequate temperature control during that selection). In such cases, the child, C, is entitled to bring an action against D under s 1A, and of course, is arguing that, 'but for the negligence, I would have been born healthy'. However, what if D negligently selects an embryo or gametes that contains some congenital defect (which D could have detected with reasonable care) and which gives rise to the birth of C as a disabled child? In that event, C is born disabled as a result of a naturally-occurring disability, and his claim, in that event, sounds more like a wrongful life claim, i.e., 'but for D's negligence, I would not have been born at all, I would never have come into existence', because, had his mother been informed of C's congenital disability, C would have been aborted. If that scenario were covered by s 1A(1)(b), then the provision may statutorily permit a wrongful life claim – despite the common law rejecting it so forcefully in *McKay*. Thus far, there has been no case law on this apparent conundrum, so far as the author's searches can ascertain.[23]

[22] *Injuries to Unborn Children* (Rep 60, 1974) 34.

[23] The author has benefited from very helpful discussions with her colleagues Mr Ian Yeats and Dr Noam Gur, on this point. See, for academic analysis: R Scott, 'Reconsidering "Wrongful Life" in England after Thirty Years: Legislative Mistakes and Unjustifiable Anomalies' (2013) 72 *Cambridge LJ* 115; and N Gur, 'Wrongful Life Claims and Negligent Selection of Gametes or Embryos in Infertility Treatments: A Quest for Coherence' (2015) 22 *Law and Medicine* 426.

FAILURE-TO-WARN LIABILITY

Introduction

The type of allegation

§3.3 A healthcare practitioner, D, has a duty to warn a patient, C, of the material or significant risks inherent in a medical treatment or procedure. An 'inherent risk' is one that cannot be eliminated by the exercise of reasonable care and skill.

Of the quadrant of most-commonly pleaded allegations against healthcare professionals – i.e., breaches of the duties to diagnose, to treat, to refer and to disclose (warn) – it is the last-mentioned type of litigation that probably irks that profession most. In such cases, the patient, C, often concedes that the medical or surgical treatment was skilful, competent and careful – and yet, substantial damages may be awarded, when C alleges that he pursued a particular form of treatment that he would not, if fully informed, have done.

The judiciary tends to give the failure-to-disclose allegation 'headline status', primarily because the legal obligation of disclosure promotes patient C's autonomy and human rights. As Lord Scarman remarked, in his minority judgment in *Sidaway v Board of Governors of the Bethlem Royal Hospital and the Maudsley Hospital*[24] (and in a passage cited subsequently in *Chester v Afshar*[25]), the duty to warn reflects 'the right of a patient to determine for himself whether he will or will not accept the doctor's advice ... the patient's right to make his own decision ... may be seen as a basic human right protected by the common law'.

Failure-to-disclose cases tend to turn upon any one of **four** issues, *viz*, (1) whether the relevant risk ought to have been disclosed by law (discussed in this section); (2) what precisely was said by D to C (which can give rise to credibility disputes); (3) if the risk ought to have been disclosed, whether D did so, in the required terms (a question of breach – either the correct warning was given, or it was not); and (4) if the disclosure of risks was inadequate, whether causation in negligence is made out, i.e., what would C have done, on the balance of probabilities, had an adequate warning been given (considered in Chapter 8).

What is not included

The mere fact that an inherent risk manifests for C cannot give rise to negligence. Indeed, there are a number of scenarios which do **not** fall within a failure-to-warn claim, e.g.:

- there can be no liability for D's not informing C of some automatic or inevitable consequence, that will follow surgery or treatment (e.g., pain). That is 'a given', not a risk;
- any failure to communicate what a procedure is about is not a failure-to-warn allegation, although it may still constitute a breach of the duty to treat – (per *Crouchman v Burke*,[26] where C alleged that she misunderstood the diagnostic nature of the procedure advocated);
- inherent risks do *not* include the risk that the treatment will be performed negligently or incompetently (the risk that a surgeon 'might have a bad day', as the court put it in *O'Sullivan v Little*[27]), because that would simply be dressing up a failure-to-warn claim as a failure-to-treat.

[24] [1985] AC 871 (HL) 882.

[25] [2004] UKHL 41, [2005] 1 AC 134, [18] (Lord Steyn), [57], [77] (Lord Hope), [92] (Lord Walker).

[26] (1997) 40 BMLR 163 (QB) (negligence proven). [27] [1995] ACTSC 92, [32].

The relevant cause of action

§3.4 Where non-disclosure of inherent risks is concerned, the relevant cause of action is negligence, and not assault and battery.

Provided that patient C knows, 'in broad terms', about the nature of the operation and consents to it, then the fact that C is not fully informed as to the risks associated with the operation does not vitiate his consent, so as to render the healthcare professional, D, liable in assault and/or battery. Negligence is the appropriate cause of action for most failure-to-warn cases; whereas an action in battery is appropriate where there was a lack of consent, whether express or implied, to the relevant procedure (and will require quite different matters to be dealt with at trial, as noted in *Border v Lewisham and Greenwich NHS Trust*[28]). That proposition, explicitly made in *Chatterton v Gerson*,[29] was later affirmed in *Sidaway*[30] and in *Hills v Potter*.[31]

For that reason, the phrase, 'informed consent', will be avoided in this chapter, for as May J noted in *The Creutzfeldt-Jakob Disease Litigation*, '[t]here is no English law doctrine of informed consent, and a person may succeed in a claim for failure to inform or warn only if the failure alleged amounts to negligence. To frame such a claim in battery is not only deplorable, but insupportable in law'.[32] Although the phrase, 'informed consent', continues to be used by the highest appellate courts in England (e.g., in *Chester v Afshar*[33]), it is potentially misleading. A lack of consent is certainly very relevant to torts of trespass to the person (see Chapter 14), but if there is a *general consent* to the procedure, then C cannot sue D in assault and battery. The action will have to be brought in negligence, for failure-to-warn.

Inherent risks

§3.5 Inherent risks which the law requires to be disclosed may be either objectively-significant, or subjectively-significant to C, or both.

The map of inherent risks is shown in the Diagram below:

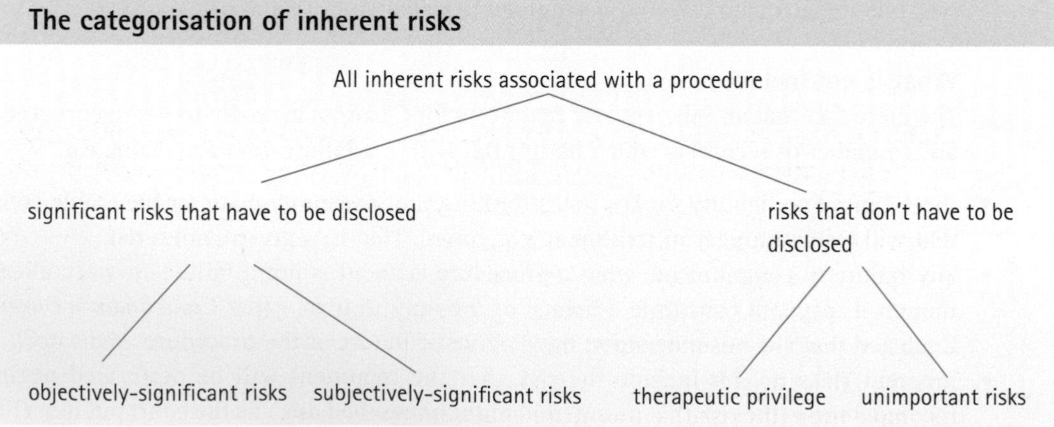

[28] [2015] EWCA Civ 8, [26]. [29] [1981] QB 432, 443 (Bristow J.)

[30] [1985] AC 871 (HL) 894–95 (Lord Diplock), 898–99 (Lord Bridge).

[31] [1984] 1 WLR 641 (QB) 647, (Hirst J).

[32] (1995) 54 BMLR 1 (QB) 7, citing the views in: *Sidaway* [1985] AC 871 (HL) 885 (Lord Scarman).

[33] [2004] UKHL 41, [2005] 1 AC 134, [14] (Lord Steyn).

Objectively-significant risks are those risks which are significant and important, having regard to objective factors; whereas subjectively-significant risks are those which are important to *that particular patient*, because of his particular needs, concerns or circumstances. When considering the question of 'objectively-significant risks', it is perhaps helpful to remember that it is the procedure rather than the patient which bears closest scrutiny; whilst the converse is true for subjectively-significant risks. Both types of risk must be disclosed at law.

Risks which are either unimportant, or subject to therapeutic privilege, do not have to be disclosed at law. The risks under therapeutic privilege are those which should be disclosed, but which can lawfully be held back from the patient where their disclosure could harm the patient's health and welfare (a defence discussed in Chapter 10). The unimportant risks fall into that residual basket of risks which are so trivial, so obvious, or so rare, that they can safely be ignored.

Objectively-significant risks

In English law, there used to be a real disparity as to how to assess an objectively-significant risk, due in no small part to the obscure language and divisions in opinion which occurred in what must rank as one of the most unenlightening House of Lords' judgments, in *Sidaway*.[34] Certainly, the judicial assertions in *Chester v Afshar* (Court of Appeal) that, '[t]he relevant law on the duty to warn is not controversial',[35] and in *Moy v Pettmann Smith (a firm)* that the principles 'are now relatively well understood',[36] were very doubtful – and difficult to reconcile with the (more accurate) remarks in *Birch v UCL Hospital NHS Foundation Trust* that, 'the matter is not as straightforward as it could be'![37]

Thankfully, this uncertainty has been swept aside by one of the most welcome Supreme Court decisions of recent times, *Montgomery v Lanarkshire Health Board*.[38]

§3.6 The test by which to determine whether an inherent risk is objectively significant is whether a reasonable patient would consider that the risk was significant enough that it ought to have been disclosed. An objectively-significant risk is not to be determined by what risks 'reasonable medical opinion' assesses should have been disclosed to the patient; the sole application of the *Bolam* test in this context has been rejected.

Under the 'reasonable patient' test, the court must put itself in the shoes of a reasonable person in the patient's position, and assess whether that patient would regard the risk as being significant. That significance is to be determined according to a range of objective factors, of which the magnitude of the risk is but one factor. Under a so-called *Bolam*[39]-type assessment, however, a risk is not relevant to disclose if D, in not disclosing it, acted in accordance with a practice accepted at the time as proper by a responsible body of medical opinion, even though other Ds might adopt a different practice about disclosure. Although the 'reasonable patient' and the *Bolam* tests will, frequently, give rise to the same answer to the question – should the risk have been disclosed? – that will not always be the case.

[34] [1985] AC 871 (HL). [35] [2002] EWCA Civ 724, [2002] 3 WLR 1195, 67 BMLR 66, [14] (Sir Dennis Henry).

[36] [2005] UKHL 7, [28] (albeit that '[i]t took the law some time to work out the principles governing what the patient is entitled to be told before deciding whether or not to agree to intrusive medical treatment: see *Sidaway*').

[37] [2008] EWHC 2237 (QB), (2008) 104 BMLR 168 (Cranston J) [73].

[38] [2015] UKSC 11, [2015] 2 WLR 768.

[39] Per *Bolam v Friern Hospital Management Committee* [1957] 1 WLR 582 (QB).

Until *Montgomery*, both tests had received strong appellate endorsement, and first-instance application, in English law – but it is the former which has, eventually, prevailed.

A brief history of the legal uncertainty which *Montgomery* has now removed is important, to obtain a fuller understanding as to how English law has arrived at its present endorsement of the 'reasonable patient' test.

The previous uncertainty in English law

In *Sidaway*,[40] the judgments were entirely at variance, and indeed some were patently unclear, as to which of the two tests should apply where a risk was not disclosed to a patient, but then manifested with disastrous results.

> In *Sidaway*, Mrs Sidaway, C, injured an elbow at work and suffered persistent pain in her right shoulder, which did not respond to conservative treatment. Scans showed that her 2nd and 3rd cervical vertebrae were congenitally fused. Dr Falconer, D, operated to remove the disc between the 5th and 6th vertebrae, and the pain disappeared. Subsequently, C complained of very persistent pain in the right arm, shoulder, and elbow, and getting gradually worse. D operated on C again, and C suffered paralysis, as a result of damage to the spinal column during the operation. That risk of injury was assessed at <1%, and was not disclosed to C beforehand. A 1–2% risk of damage to the nerve roots had been disclosed, but that did not occur. **Held (5:0):** no duty to warn was owed.

Lord Diplock favoured a strict *Bolam* test, pointing out that the *Bolam* case itself related to a 'failure to advise the patient of the risk involved in the electric shock treatment as one of the allegations of negligence against the surgeon as well as negligence in the actual carrying out of treatment ... To decide what risks the existence of which a patient should be voluntarily warned ... is as much an exercise of professional skill and judgment as any other part of the doctor's comprehensive duty of care to the individual patient, and expert medical evidence on this matter should be treated in just the same way. The *Bolam* test should be applied'.

> In *Sidaway*, it was the practice in 1974, by a responsible body of medical neurosurgery opinion, that C should have been informed of the risk involved in the operation in substantially the same terms as D had done, i.e., without specific reference to the risk of injuring the spinal cord. Hence, under the *Bolam* test, there was no liability on D's part.

Consequently, a strict *Bolam* assessment of what risks ought to have been disclosed by D received dicta approval at appellate level[41] – indeed, as recently as 2014 in *Meiklejohn v St George's Healthcare NHS Trust* ('[t]he duty to advise and warn about ... possible side-effects is to be assessed in accordance with the practice of a responsible body of such doctors'[42]); and earlier in *Gold v Haringey HA*[43] (where there was no duty to warn of the risk of the failure of a female sterilisation operation of 0.2–0.6%, which was a much higher failure rate than that of 0.05% for a vasectomy, because a responsible body of medical opinion in 1979 considered it unnecessary to warn of that risk). In several first-instance decisions too, no duty of care was owed, precisely because a responsible body of medical opinion considered that the risk was too

[40] [1985] AC 871 (HL) 895. [41] e.g., *Powell v Boldaz* [1998] Lloyd's Rep Med 116 (CA).
[42] [2014] EWCA Civ 120, [62]. [43] *Gold v Haringey HA* [1988] QB 481 (CA).

insignificant to disclose;[44] whereas, where the medical opinion dictated that the risk **ought** to have been disclosed, a duty to warn was upheld.[45]

However, in *Sidaway*,[46] Lord Bridge (with whom Lord Keith agreed) advocated this adjustment to the *Bolam* test of disclosure: that whilst the disclosure of risk 'must primarily be a matter of clinical judgment ... to be decided primarily on the basis of expert medical evidence, applying the *Bolam* test ... I do not see that this approach involves the necessity "to hand over to the medical profession the entire question of the scope of the duty of disclosure, including the question whether there has been a breach of that duty" ... the judge might in certain circumstances come to the conclusion that disclosure of a particular risk was so obviously necessary to an informed choice on the part of the patient that no reasonably prudent medical man would fail to make it.' Lord Bridge gave, as an example, that a duty to warn would arise, regardless of any *Bolam* evidence which approved non-disclosure, if there was 'a substantial risk of grave consequences such as a 10% risk of stroke' (referring to the Canadian case of *Reibl v Hughes*[47]) – because a reasonable patient would regard that as being significant. Lord Templeman (in what was possibly the most confusing judgment of them all[48]) also seemed to favour some form of 'reasonable patient' test in parts of his judgment, e.g.: 'the doctor is not entitled to make the final decision with regard to treatment which may have disadvantages or dangers. Where the patient's health and future are at stake, the patient must make the final decision'.[49]

Lord Scarman, in the minority, was the most explicit proponent of the 'reasonable patient' test, noting that a duty to disclose, 'is to be determined, not exclusively by reference to the current state of responsible and competent professional opinion and practice at the time ... but by the court's view as to whether the doctor, in advising his patient, gave the consideration which the law requires him to give to the right of the patient to make up her own mind, in the light of the relevant information whether or not she will accept the treatment which he proposes'.[50]

In *Sidaway*, the abovementioned judges agreed with the body of neurosurgery opinion as practised in 1974, i.e., the risk of damage to the spinal column would not have been disclosed. Per Lord Scarman, C had no prospect of proving a duty to warn because a 'lack of evidence was always her difficulty, and it remains so', whether the 'reasonable patient' or the *Bolam* test was applied – and he favoured the prudent patient test. (Hence, although Lord Scarman is often referred to as a dissenting judge, his was a **minority** opinion, as he was in agreement with the majority on the outcome, that no duty to warn arose.)

After *Sidaway*, the most significant English decision to endorse and apply the 'reasonable patient' test was that of *Pearce v United Bristol Healthcare NHS Trust*,[51] where Lord Woolf MR remarked: 'if there is a significant risk which would affect the judgment of a reasonable patient, then in the normal course, it is the responsibility of a doctor to inform the patient of

[44] e.g., *Smith v Eastern Health Board* (QB, 16 Dec 1988) (risk of femoral nerve irritation); *De Maynard v Streatham Hill Veterinary Surgery* 2001] EWCA Civ 1728 (risk of vaccination to C's prize-winning dog).

[45] e.g., *O'Keefe v Harvey-Kemble* [1998] EWCA Civ 701 (risk of breast enlargement surgery); *Deriche v Ealing Hospital NHS Trust* [2003] EWHC 3104 (QB) (risk of not aborting, where mother contracted chicken pox); *McAllister v Lewisham and North Southwark HA* (QB, 15 Dec 1993) (risk of hemiplegia from brain surgery).

[46] [1985] AC 871 (HL) 900. [47] (1980), 114 DLR (3d) 1, [1982] 2 SCR 880.

[48] See: *McAllister v Lewisham HA* (QB, 15 Dec 1993, Rougier J): 'having accepted that the *Bolam* test ... is the correct test to apply, it might be said that Lord Templeman came perilously close to propounding his own').

[49] [1985] AC 871 (HL) 903. [50] *ibid*, 876, and see too, 882, 884.

[51] (1998) 48 BMLR 118 (CA) 124 (Roch and Mummery LJJ agreed with Lord Woolf).

that significant risk, if the information is needed so that the patient can determine for him or herself as to what course he or she should adopt'.

In *Pearce*, Mrs Pearce, C, was expecting her sixth child. She consulted with her treating obstetrician, D, when she was 14 days over term in her pregnancy. She was very upset, and requested the birth to be induced or to have a caesarean section, but was advised that both courses presented risks, and that it would take her longer to recover from a caesarean, and that it was better that she should wait. C was not advised of any increased risk (0.1–0.2%) of the baby being stillborn if the pregnancy continued. The baby later died *in utero*, and was stillborn. **Held:** no duty to disclose the risk. The medical opinion was that it should not have been disclosed, and it was so low that a reasonable patient would not have attached significance to it.

Subsequently, the *Pearce* approach received some strong appellate endorsement. In *Wyatt v Curtis*, Sedley LJ confirmed that Lord Woolf's formulation in *Pearce* 'refine[d] Lord Bridge's test by recognising that what is substantial and what is grave are questions on which the doctor's and the patient's perception may differ, and in relation to which the doctor must therefore have regard to what may be the patient's perception.'[52] Further, in *Chester v Afshar*,[53] Lords Steyn and Hope (of the majority) approved Lord Woolf's view in *Pearce* (albeit that it was common ground that the risk *should* have been disclosed, and the appeal turned on the question of causation there,[54] as discussed in Chapter 8). Several first-instance decisions also adopted the 'reasonable patient' test.[55]

In *Poynter v Hillingdon HA*,[56] C, a child of 15 months, required heart transplant surgery. There was a 1% risk that, though he might survive the surgery, he might suffer permanent brain damage, but this was not disclosed to his parents. Unfortunately, brain damage occurred when C's heart stopped whilst C was under anaesthetic. **Held:** no duty to warn of brain damage. There was a reasonable body of medical opinion that the risk would not have been disclosed; and the court considered that view to be rational, given the low probability of risk and the gravity of the scenario in which the child was involved.

The *Montgomery* clarification

In *Montgomery v Lanarkshire Health Board*, the Supreme Court explicitly adopted the views of Lord Woolf MR in *Pearce* and of Lord Scarman in *Sidaway*. Lords Reed and Kerr put the position thus:[57]

The doctor is ... under a duty to take reasonable care to ensure that the patient is aware of any material risks involved in any recommended treatment, and of any reasonable alternative or variant treatments. The test of materiality is whether, in the circumstances of the particular case, a reasonable person in the patient's position would be likely to attach significance to the risk, or the doctor is or should reasonably be aware that the particular patient would be likely to attach significance to it.

That 'reasonable patient' test now represents the modern approach to the duty-to-warn issue in English law, and has usurped the *Bolam* 'peer professional medical opinion' test.

[52] [2003] EWCA Civ 1779, [16]. [53] [2004] UKHL 41, [2005] 1 AC 134, [15], [86], respectively.
[54] [2002] EWCA Civ 724, [2002] 3 WLR 1195, [15].
[55] e.g., *Jones v North West Strategic HA* [2010] EWHC 178 (QB) [24]; *Birch v UCL Hospital NHS Foundation Trust* [2008] EWHC 2237 (QB) [73].
[56] (1997) 37 BMLR 192 (QB). [57] [2015] UKSC 11, [87].

This switch from *Bolam* has occurred hand-in-hand with the greater importance of human rights jurisprudence. As Lord Walker stated in *Chester v Afshar*, 'during the 20 years which have elapsed since *Sidaway*, the importance of personal autonomy has been more and more widely recognised'.[58] In *Montgomery*, the Supreme Court agreed, noting the rights-based approach which now pervades patient care, 'under the stimulus of the Human Rights Act 1998' (which, of course, post-dated *Sidaway*).[59] As a result, 'patient autonomy' is frequently cited in this sort of litigation nowadays.[60] Further, as discussed in Chapter 7, a modified *Bolam* approach applies where patient C alleges medical *mistreatment or misdiagnosis*, per the decision in *Bolitho v City and Hackney HA*[61] – although the House of Lords expressly noted, in *Bolitho*, that it was *not* considering questions of disclosure of risk. Nevertheless, there is now a pleasing symmetry of legal attitude, across treatment, diagnosis *and disclosure*.

As well as these factors, the *Montgomery* Supreme Court pointed out that the decrease in 'medical paternalism'; the wider availability of public information about risks; the modern guidance given by the General Medical Council to doctors which reflected a 'reasonable patient' approach to risks-disclosure; the difficulties which English courts had experienced in applying (or departing from) *Sidaway*; and the successful adoption of a 'reasonable patient' test in other jurisdictions (e.g., in Australia, by virtue of the 1992 High Court of Australia decision in *Rogers v Whitaker*,[62] which was extensively cited in *Montgomery*, and whose test of materiality of risk was closely adopted in *Montgomery*), all contributed to a view that any continued application of the *Bolam* test in English law to risks-disclosure was 'unsatisfactory'.[63]

It is worth noting that the change of attitude in English law is not merely an academic nicety. *Bolam*, and the 'reasonable patient' test, may indeed give differing answers:

> In *Birch v UCL Hospital NHS Foundation Trust*,[64] Mrs Birch, C, was a Type-1 diabetic, with a long history of serious health problems. One morning, she woke up with a bad headache, blurred vision, a turned left eye, nausea and vomiting. At UCL Hospital, D, a cerebral catheter angiogram was performed, to rule out the possibility of an artery aneurysm. The angiogram involved inserting a catheter at the groin, and then working it up through the vascular system to the area of the brain to be scanned. It was a potentially life-threatening procedure, which carried a 1% risk of stroke. The risk of stroke from a cerebral angiogram **was** discussed with C and was properly disclosed. However, C was not informed that an investigation of her condition could have been undertaken by non-invasive magnetic resonance imaging (MRI), which did not entail any risk of stroke. **Held:** D should have discussed with C the different imaging methods – the catheter angiogram and the MRI – so as to provide C with comparable risks, even though the *Bolam* opinion had not considered that necessary. In *Montgomery v Lanarkshire Health Board*, Mrs Montgomery, C, gave birth to her first baby at D's hospital. The baby was born with severe disabilities, because of the condition of shoulder dystocia (where the baby's shoulders become stuck behind the mother's pelvis) which caused severe hypoxic injury. C was particularly at risk (a 9–10% risk), given that she was diabetic and small in stature, and that women with diabetes were more likely to have larger babies. **Held:** C ought to have been advised about the risk of shoulder dystocia associated

[58] [2004] UKHL 41, [2005] 1 AC 134, [92]. [59] [2015] UKSC 11, [75], [80].
[60] e.g., *A v East Kent Hospitals Univ NHS Foundation Trust* [2015] EWHC 1038 (QB) [20].
[61] [1997] 3 WLR 1151 (HL) 1160. [62] (1992) 175 CLR 479 (HCA) 490, and cited in *Montgomery* at [72].
[63] [2015] UKSC 11, [75–[86], quote at [86]. [64] [2008] EWHC 2237 (QB), (2008) 104 BMLR 168.

with a vaginal birth, and of the alternative of elective caesarean section. The *Bolam* evidence was that there was no duty on a obstetrician's part to disclose the risk of shoulder dystocia to C if the baby was born naturally, given that *the risks of permanent injury* to the baby were so small (approx. 0.2% or <0.1%), and that if such risk was customarily disclosed, then it would make most women 'simply request delivery by caesarean section.' However, the magnitude of that injury, plus the risk of injury to mother's own health from shoulder dystocia, meant that the risk should have been disclosed.

The *Bolam* test could clearly be more favourable to D, whilst the reasonable patient test favours patient autonomy over 'medical paternalism'.

The comparative corner: An Australian perspective

In *Rogers v Whitaker*[65] and confirmed later in *Rosenberg v Percival*,[66] the 'reasonable patient' test was adopted by the HCA, in preference to a *Bolam* assessment. In the latter, Kirby J helpfully set out the contrasting arguments for, and against, the reasonable patient test, many of which were cited in *Montgomery* too:

FOR the reasonable patient test:

- it endorses individual patient autonomy, in the wider context of an emerging human rights jurisprudence – and this requires an informed agreement to invasive treatment, except in emergency treatments;
- at the coalface, mis-communications will happen on the part of busy or reticent healthcare professionals, such that the reasonable patient test requires such Ds to pause and to provide warnings;
- it redresses somewhat the risks of conflicts between interest and duty which D may sometimes face in favouring one procedure or treatment over another, because a reasonable patient would wish to know the comparative risks;
- it helps to redress the inherent inequality and power between a healthcare practitioner and a vulnerable patient;
- the ultimate decision-making rests, and is seen to rest, on the patient, rather than on D, which may reduce the likelihood for recriminations and litigation following the disappointment that can follow unsuccessful treatment.

AGAINST the reasonable patient test:

- patients would fear being unsettled or made more anxious by a wide-ranging risks disclosure;
- many patients would understand risks imperfectly;
- it is impossible, within sensible time constraints, for D to communicate the detail of every slight, but material, complication/risk;
- the efficacy of warnings against slight risks had not been objectively-established, post-*Rogers*;
- where a wider test of disclosure applies, lawyers will seek to circumvent it via consent and waiver forms.

[65] (1992)175 CLR 479 (HCA) 490. [66] [2001] HCA 18, [143]–[145].

Notably, the *Montgomery* test of materiality (just as with the Australian *Rogers v Whitaker* test, upon which *Montgomery* heavily relied) embodies **both** an objective limb (i.e., what a reasonable patient would wish to have disclosed to him) **and** a subjective limb (i.e., whether that particular patient would wish to have any further risks information disclosed to him because of his particular circumstances, and which would not be considered by an otherwise reasonable patient to be material). The subjective limb will be discussed shortly. First, however, it is useful to have regard to the types of factors that, objectively speaking, tend to point to a material risk that ought to have been disclosed.

Factors identifying 'objective significance'

From a perusal of post-*Sidaway* case law, there are several factors which have proven to be relevant, as to whether a risk is 'significant', objectively-speaking.[67] These are set out below, with supporting authorities. None is conclusive, and some are not as legally weighty as others. It is a balancing exercise.

i. The probability of the injury occurring: if the risk of the injury occurring is extremely low (in the region of less than 0.5%), that indicates that the risk was not 'significant' in the legal sense; whereas risks that can be expressed in at least 'single digit' percentage terms (and sometimes less) have been considered high enough to have warranted disclosure. The factor is subject to an important caveat, however: probability must be considered *together with* other factors. A 'statistically insignificant' risk could be significant enough to be disclosed, if the harm to C would be catastrophic. As Lords Reed and Kerr stated in *Montgomery*, 'the assessment of whether a risk is material cannot be reduced to percentages', and 'is likely to reflect a variety of factors besides its magnitude'.[68] Similarly, in *Pearce v United Bristol Healthcare NHS Trust*,[69] Lord Woolf MR uttered the cautionary note that 'when one refers to a "significant risk", it is not possible to talk in precise percentages'.

   The following **were** significant, and hence disclosable, risks: the 1–2% risk of incomplete paralysis, following a fixation and fusion operation for shoulder and neck pain, in *Glancy v Southern General Hosp NHS Trust*; the 1–2% risk of damage to the spinal cord resulting in paralysis or *cauda equina* syndrome, from an operation to correct a large prolapsed disc, in *Chester v Afshar*; the <1–2% of cerebral palsy resulting from shoulder dystocia, in *Jones v North West Strategic HA*; the 9–10% risk of some shoulder dystocia (because of the health risks of that to the mother and baby), together with the 0.2% of serious and permanent injury to the baby, in *Montgomery*. **However**, the following were **not** significant disclosable risks: the 0.1–0.2% risk of stillbirth in *Pearce v United Bristol Healthcare NHS Trust*; the risk of paralysis of <1% in *Sidaway*; and the 0.2–0.6% risk of failure of female sterilisation in *Gold v Haringey HA*.

ii. The gravity of the injury, should the risk manifest: the more serious the injury to C if the risk manifests, the more likely that the risk will be 'significant'; whereas a risk of trivial, transient, temporary, or easily-resolvable, injury is not likely to be material in the legal sense. However, as noted above, the seriousness of the injury and the probability of occurrence are closely linked – some cases of very grievous injury (or death) were the unfortunate products of a very remote risk being realised, and were not 'significant' in the legal sense. The factor is, hence,

[67] See: Mulheron, 'Twelve Tests to Identify Whether a Medical Risk is "Material"' [2000] *National L Rev* 1. That article has been substantially reworked and expanded upon for this section.

[68] [2015] UKSC 11, [89]. [69] (1998) 48 BMLR 118, [1999] PIQR P53 (CA) P59.

not particularly helpful on its own. Serious harm may, arguably, not be only physical, but also emotional (brought about, e.g., from lifestyle changes forced upon C).

The following serious injuries **were** significant: disabling stroke in *Birch v UCL Hospital Foundation NHS Trust*; *cauda equina* syndrome in *Chester v Afshar*; cerebral palsy suffered as a result of shoulder dystocia during delivery in *Jones v North West Strategic HA*. **However**, the following were **not** significant risks, notwithstanding their great severity: brain damage in *Poynter v Hillingdon HA*; stillbirth in *Pearce v United Bristol Healthcare NHS Trust*; and permanent paralysis in *Sidaway*.

Injury to the mother, where C is her gravely-disabled baby who was damaged by D's negligence, may also 'count' towards the overall seriousness of the injury, should the undisclosed risk manifest. This was plain in *Montgomery*, where the major obstetric emergency which shoulder dystocia represented to the mother too, was significant.

iii. *Bolam* peer professional opinion: as discussed above, medical opinion as to what should be disclosed by way of risks is *no longer* determinative nor conclusive of what D ought to have disclosed by way of risks, under the 'reasonable patient' test. However, it is unlikely that *Bolam*-type evidence will entirely lose its relevance, in the post-*Montgomery* landscape. Interestingly, since *Rogers v Whitaker* was handed down by the High Court of Australia, the practice of other experts in D's field of expertise as to whether or not warnings should have been provided prior to C's medical treatment has been judicially regarded as being useful and of great assistance, regarding the question of materiality in that jurisdiction.[70] It is foreshadowed that, similarly in English law, evidence of professional practice or guidance will remain relevant to the objective test. Meanwhile, it is worth noting that, even pre-*Montgomery*, there were cases in which the 'reasonable patient' test and the *Bolam* test were perfectly aligned.

In *Jones v North West Strategic HA*, Jack Jones was born brain-damaged and severely disabled, due to the condition of shoulder dystocia, whereby Jack's shoulder got stuck behind his mother's pelvic bone during the course of delivery. It took 15 minutes to deliver Jack, by which time he was severely brain-damaged. Mrs Jones, C, claimed that she should have been advised, as part of her ante-natal care, of the risk of shoulder dystocia (assessed as being in the region of 1–2%), and that a caesarean section would avoid the risk associated with a natural birth. One of her previous two children, Rebecca, had suffered the same problem, but it had been resolved satisfactorily during the birth. **Held:** a duty to warn C of the risk of shoulder dystocia with a vaginal birth was owed. An expert witness accepted that he would have expected a consultation between D and C to have included a discussion of the advantages and disadvantages of doing a caesarean section rather than a vaginal birth, 'even if it was only to put it on one side'. The then-current Royal College of Obstetrician and Gynaecologist Guidelines also stated that, where there had been previous history of shoulder dystocia, then although a caesarean was not the routine course to be recommended, the option should be discussed between the mother and her doctors.

iv. Comparative risks: where C is proposing to undergo a medical treatment which carries a particular risk, and another avenue of treatment is available which does not, then the comparable risks may become significant, legally-speaking. Comparable procedures which entail different risks render those comparable risks legally significant. A reasonable patient would want to

[70] As discussed by the author in: 'Twelve Tests to Identify whether a Medical Risk is "Material"' (2000) 1 *National L Rev* 1, [64]–[67].

weigh up the pros and cons of the two treatments (one of which he will have to undergo) to make an informed choice about which of the two procedures was preferable, and that would require disclosure of the comparable risks.

In *Birch v UCL Hospital NHS Foundation Trust*, facts previously, **Held:** D should have discussed with C the different imaging methods – the catheter angiogram and the MRI – so as to provide C with comparable risks, and the lack of stroke risk with an MRI. In *Jones v North West Strategic HA*, facts previously, **Held:** not only was there was a duty to warn C of the risk of shoulder dystocia with a vaginal birth, but also mention should have been made of the comparative risks of a Caesarian, especially given C's previous history of shoulder dystocia. In *Montgomery*, the facts were notably similar to *Jones*, and the extremely small risk of a major obstetric emergency with a caesarean, should have been disclosed.

As affirmed subsequently in *Meiklejohn v St George's Healthcare NHS Trust*,[71] the problem in *Birch* was that the risk of one procedure (angiogram) was explained, but a less risky alternative procedure (the MRI) was not. *Jones* was a somewhat different case, because the risks of **both** alternatives (natural and Caesarian births) were not disclosed to C. However, these cases are as far as English law goes at this stage. The duty to warn of comparative risks does **not** extend to a scenario (as occurred in *Meiklejohn*) where D did not even contemplate the alternative diagnosis or treatment, and failed to give a risks assessment of the treatment. That is too onerous a position for the law to adopt.

v. Essential versus elective procedure: for elective surgery, it is easier to prove that a non-disclosure was a significant risk in the legal sense, because C will reasonably attach greater significance to risks that are purely a matter of his choice to undertake.

In *Chester v Afshar*, Miss Chester, C, a journalist, had suffered various episodes of back pain for several years, and had to have an epidural injection to tide her over on a work trip. On her return, she saw a specialist, and had an MRI scan, which showed a prolapsed disc high in the spine (the higher the prolapse, the riskier is surgery to correct it). The specialist referred C to Dr Afshar, a neurosurgeon, with instructions that C was 'anxious to avoid surgery if at all possible'. The surgery (which carried with it a 1–2% risk of damage to the spinal cord) was elective, rather than necessary. Three days after the consultation, C had a lumbar surgical operation, and suffered from *cauda equina* syndrome, leading to leg paralysis. **Held:** it was common ground that the risk should have been disclosed. At CA level,[72] Sir Deny Henry noted that C's surgery was elective, and not an emergency, which helped to render risk of this sort 'significant'.

vi. D's own experiences: where the risk was not one which had ever manifested in D's extensive personal experience, then it is justifiable that D would not have considered that C would attach significance to it, and hence, the risk is less likely to be legally significant. However, the converse view – that a risk could still be material, notwithstanding that D had never witnessed that risk in a long career of medical practice – prevailed at trial in *Chester v Afshar* (and thereafter, it was conceded that the risk should have been disclosed).

In *Chester v Afshar*, facts previously, C told neurosurgeon Dr Afshar, D, that she had heard a lot of horror stories about surgery, and that she wanted to know about the risks. She did not specifically mention paralysis as one of the risks that she wanted to be told about, and this

[71] [2014] EWCA Civ 120, [62].

was not mentioned as a risk of surgery by D – but D did say that he had performed about 300 similar operations per year, and that he 'had not crippled anybody yet'. D had never caused any nerve damages in the many hundreds of operations he had carried out over 20–25 years, and he considered the risk very small. **Held:** the risk should have been disclosed: 'however understandable such a response may have been in psychological terms, it was not an adequate response in legal terms'.

vii. The use of medical booklets/literature: any warnings about material risks contained within literature which is given by D to patient C forms part of the total evidentiary package. Whilst written material does not discharge the duty to warn of itself, it can assist D to defeat an allegation of failure-to-warn. Of course, handing to C voluminous lists of remote risks is hardly likely to impress an already-nervous patient, and the larger the volume of risks literature, the less likely the reasonable patient will read it. Lords Reed and Kerr emphasised this in *Montgomery*, noting that a doctor's duty to disclose material risks 'is not therefore fulfilled by bombarding the patient with technical information which she cannot reasonably be expected to grasp, let alone by routinely demanding her signature on a consent form'.[73]

In *Birch v UCL Hospital NHS Foundation Trust*,[74] facts previously, Mrs Birch, C, signed the standard consent form prior to the cerebral angiogram being performed. It read, 'I have explained the procedure to the patient/parent ... [under] 'Serious or frequently occurring risks': bleeding. renal damage. 1% stroke'. The form also stated that, 'I have also discussed what the procedure is likely to involve, the benefits and risks of any available alternative treatments and any particular concerns of those involved'. It was signed by both D and C. The risk of stroke was disclosed and manifested, but the alternative treatment of an MRI was not discussed, despite the form's content. **Held:** the alternative should have been discussed, under the duty to warn.

The problem of an undisclosed risk is more likely to arise where the literature does **not** contain any information about the risk that patient C alleges was significant. On one potential view, the fact a booklet omits mention of a risk that ultimately eventuates does not mean that it cannot be material in the legal sense. It may behove D to draw that omitted risk to C's attention, so that the omission imposes a *more* onerous duty on D. On the other possible view, the fact that the risk was not mentioned in a pamphlet may contribute to the finding that it must have been too remote and insignificant a possibility to be 'material' in the legal sense. There is yet to be any decisive authority on this point in English law (although the point has proven contentious in Australia, under *Rogers v Whitaker*[75]).

Subjectively-significant risks

§3.7 There are two indicators that a risk is subjectively-significant to ***that particular patient***, C: first, where C asks of D specific questions which highlight the particular significance of a risk ***for him***; and secondly, where C presents with a highly idiosyncratic medical history, set of needs, or unusual concerns.

[72] [2002] EWCA Civ 724, [2003] QB 356, [5], [17]. [73] [2015] UKSC 11, [90].

[74] [2008] EWHC 2237 (QB), (2008) 104 BMLR 168, [20]–[24].

[75] Mulheron, 'Twelve Tests to Identify Whether a Medical Risk is "Material"' [2000] *National L Rev* 1, Factor 9, [68]–[74].

The relevance of questions

When discussing the subjective limb of its newly-proposed test in *Montgomery*, the Supreme Court remarked that '[e]xpressions of concern by the patient, as well as specific questions, are plainly relevant'.[76] Earlier, in *Sidaway*,[77] Lord Diplock remarked that, 'if the patient manifested this attitude by means of questioning, the doctor would tell him whatever it was the patient wanted to know', while Lord Bridge noted that, 'when questioned specifically by a patient ... about risks involved in a particular treatment proposed, the doctor's duty must ... be to answer both truthfully and as fully as the questioner requires'. Subsequently, in *Poynter v Hillingdon HA*,[78] Sir Maurice Drake stated that the duty to disclose must be considered, 'in the context of what the particular patient wanted to know. That is to say, I would consider [the duty] subjectively'.

Hence, where the patient, C, incessantly and worriedly questions about an aspect of the operative procedure or medical treatment, the subjective limb will be triggered (evident in *Chester v Afshar*, where the patient was very nervous and anxious to avoid surgery). Asking questions is legally significant (albeit that the court must be satisfied that such questions were, *in fact*, asked).

But what if C asked **some** questions indicating concern, but did not ask the 'right questions', i.e., questions that would have elicited precisely the information about the risk that, ultimately, was not disclosed? Prior to *Montgomery*, there had been very little direct authority on this in English law, but what there was had tended to suggest that C **had** to ask the right question – failing which D would not be liable for failing to disclose. As Sedley LJ remarked in *Wyatt v Curtis*, that situation is unrealistic: 'there is arguably something unreal about placing the onus of asking upon a patient who may not know that there is anything to ask about'.[79]

> In *Wyatt v Curtis*, Miss Wyatt, C, presented to her locum GP, D1, with chickenpox in her 14th week of pregnancy. D1 did not advise C of the risk of serious abnormalities to her child. Four and a half weeks later, C went to Kings Mill Hospital for an ante-natal check-up, and the senior house officer, D2, learned that she had just had chickenpox, and likewise, did not advise C of the same risk. D2 had asked C whether she had been made aware of the rare problem of chickenpox in pregnancy, and had been told that she had been. C had already asked D1, 'Will the baby be all right?', and was told he would be. C did not put the same question to D2, probably because of the 'false sense of security' created by D1's answer. C's son Luke was ultimately born severely disabled. **Held:** D2 was not negligent, as the relevant question had not been asked by C. In *Poynter v Hillingdon HA*, facts previously, **Held:** no duty to warn. The parents did ask concerned questions about the transplant procedure, but did not ask any questions about the risk of permanent brain damage resulting from the operation.

However, in *Montgomery*, the Supreme Court took a more sympathetic line, noting that, 'courts should not be too quick to discard the second limb [i.e., that the risk was subjectively-significant] ... merely because it emerges that the patient did not ask certain kinds of questions'.[80]

> In *Montgomery*, facts previously, C was concerned about the size of the baby and whether she would be able to deliver the baby naturally. However, C did not ask her obstetrician, D, 'specifically about exact risks', otherwise D stated that she would have advised of the risk of shoulder dystocia. **Held:** even though C did not ask the right question, her personal circumstances of her own small

[76] [2015] UKSC 11, [73]. [77] [1985] AC 871 (HL) 890 (Lord Diplock), 898 (Lord Bridge).

[78] (1997) 37 BMLR 192 (QB), 193, 205–6 (where no particular questions were addressed to D).

[79] [2003] EWCA Civ 1779, [19]. [80] [2015] UKSC 11, [73].

size, her diabetes, the risk of a larger baby for a diabetic mother, a natural anxiety about a first-time birth, all contributed to this risk as being one that should have been disclosed.

Again, previous cases which indicated that, where C enquired about risk, D was only required to answer that question by reference to how a reasonable body of medical opinion would have answered it (i.e., a *Bolam*-type assessment), must now be taken to no longer apply. In *Blyth v Bloomsbury HA*,[81] Neill LJ remarked that, where questions are asked by a patient, then, 'as a general proposition it is governed by ... the *Bolam* test'. However, *Montgomery* confirmed that the duty to give full and honest answers to specific questioning is **no longer** to be assessed against *Bolam*-type evidence as to what medical practice deems sufficient to disclose, but goes beyond that.

The comparative corner: *Rogers v Whitaker*, and asking the 'right sort of question'

In *Rogers v Whitaker*,[82] Mrs Whitaker, C, had lost the sight in one eye, as a 9-year-old school girl in England, when she ruptured it in a collision with a paling fence which penetrated the eye socket. C emigrated to Australia, and lived a full life, and had a family. Several years later, advances in ophthalmic surgery meant that the restoration of sight in that eye was feasible. Dr Rogers, D, an ophthalmic surgeon, performed the surgery carefully, competently and without negligence. However, disaster befell C, because not only was sight not restored, but her good eye suffered a rare condition that can arise in this type of surgery – sympathetic ophthalmia – which rendered her blind in her good eye, and hence, totally blind. She was not warned of the risk of sympathetic opthalmia (which did not always lead to loss of vision in any case), and which occurred in approximately 1: 14,000 procedures, with a slightly higher risk where there had been an earlier penetrating injury to the eye operated upon. **Held:** there was a duty to warn of this remote complication in ophthalmic surgery, and a breach in not disclosing it. C has 'incessantly questioned [D] as to, amongst other things, possible complications. She was, to [D's] knowledge, keenly interested in the outcome of the suggested procedure, including the danger of unintended or accidental interference with her 'good', left eye. On the day before the operation, [C] asked [D] whether something could be put over her good eye to ensure that nothing happened to it ... [C] may not have asked the right question, yet she made clear her great concern that no injury should befall her one good eye'. Hence, whilst C did not ask D the specific query as to whether her good eye could be adversely affected, her questions clearly conveyed utmost concern that nothing bad happened to that eye.

Where patient C has idiosyncratic history/needs/circumstances

Any relevant physical or mental characteristics of patient C, of which D was (or should have been) aware, are also relevant, where it means that D ought to have reasonably been aware that, for that C, the risk information would matter. The scenario may arise where, say:

i. C's own historical experiences: Where a repeat of an event, unpleasant in the past, made C particularly anxious and concerned, that may render a risk significant.

[81] [1993] 4 Med LR 151 (CA).

[82] [1992] HCA 58, (1992) 175 CLR 479, with quote at 491. See also: *Johnson v Biggs* [2000] NSWCA 338.

In *Jones v North West Strategic HA*,[83] facts previously, 'Mrs Jones recalled her experience when Rebecca experienced shoulder dystocia as very traumatic, dramatic and scary. The risk of a repetition of that type of experience (even if ultimately the chances were good that the baby would be safely delivered) can ... properly be taken into account in deciding whether the risk was significant'.

ii. Any pre-existing medical condition on C's part: If C's particular medical history and/or health indicated that there was an elevated concern about the non-disclosed risk manifesting, then the risk is likely to be significant, legally-speaking (as illustrated, again, by the facts of *Jones v North West Strategic HA*, and in *Montgomery* itself, where the fact that C was small, and concerned about being able to deliver the baby naturally, were oft-expressed to D).

iii. C had an aversion to operative procedures: This was evident in *Chester v Afshar*, with medical notes confirming that C was 'anxious to avoid surgery, if at all possible'. Although a duty was conceded, this factor undoubtedly assisted to prompt that concession, as it demonstrated a subjectively-significant risk.

Other subjectively-significant factors have arisen in the extensive failure-to-warn jurisprudence in Australia (as part of *Rogers v Whitaker* jurisprudence), which is of comparative interest:

The comparative corner: **Additional factors of subjective risk**

- Special family needs. In *Burke v Humphrey*,[84] C underwent a laparoscopy, and sued for her gynaecologist's, D's, failure to disclose that, notwithstanding the tubal ligation, there was a risk of pregnancy (she fell pregnant 13 months later). **Held:** the risk was subjectively-significant, because D knew that C had a family of three boys <2 years due to an unplanned pregnancy: 'it was incumbent upon [D] to have alerted [C] to the possibility of the procedure failing, for he had ample reason to suppose that if warned of the risk she would be likely to attach significance to it'. On the facts, however, such a warning was indeed given.
- Irrational belief giving rise to extreme anxiety. In *Di Carlo v Dubois*,[85] barrister C had convinced himself that he had a brain tumour. His friend, a neurosurgeon, arranged for a scan to be done by another neurosurgeon, D. C was not warned of the risk involved in the administration of a scan enhanced with a non-ionic contrast agent, namely an allergic (anaphylactic) reaction, which is what he suffered. **Held:** the allergic reaction was a subjectively-significant risk, because D knew that C was 'particularly anxious' about the scan, in case it showed that he had a tumour, and that with an irrational anxiety, an adverse reaction was several times more likely.
- Religious/cultural concerns. In *Hassan v Minister for Health*,[86] C was admitted to hospital for a uterine evacuation following a foetal death *in utero*. Unfortunately, the placenta had adhered to the scar tissue from four prior caesareans, and removal of it caused abnormal blood loss, and C had to undergo a complete emergency hysterectomy to stop the ongoing blood loss. She was not warned of the risk of a hysterectomy prior to the

[83] [2010] EWHC 178 (QB). However, the claim ultimately failed on causation. [84] [2001] TASSC 133, [20].
[85] [2004] QCA 150 (Davies JA and McMurdo J, Williams JA dissenting), and especially [77].
[86] [2005] WADC 182, and especially [132]–[133], [149].

procedure being undertaken. C gave evidence that, due to the importance of retaining fertility in her Arabian culture, she would have 'preferred death' to a hysterectomy, that 'the womb for the woman was everything, and without it, she was nothing at all' and 'incomplete', and that it had rendered her marital relationship difficult and insecure. **Held:** D knew that C, if fully warned of the risk of hysterectomy, would have attached great significance to it in view of her culture. A failure-to-warn was proven.

Timings

§3.8 Whether D was under a duty to warn of material risk must be assessed at the time when D is giving the pre-operative advice, and not at a subsequent time (e.g., when the risk crystallises into injury, or even later at trial).

As one court pithily noted, in this context: '[a]ny fool can be wise after the event. That is not the test. The Court must be careful to judge the conduct of [D], where negligent failure to warn is asserted, by reference to what [D] reasonably knew at the relevant time'.[87] In *Jones v North West Strategic HA*,[88] the allegedly negligent failure-to-warn occurred 18 years prior to the trial – and the obstetrician D's disclosure had to be judged according to the standards of what ought to have been disclosed 18 years ago, a tricky task when medical research and knowledge about shoulder dystocia had moved on considerably since. This is an issue relevant to breach, rather than the duty itself, but is worth reiterating at this juncture.

As to when the warning of risk must be given, the timing must enable a reasonable patient to digest and evaluate the risks information. As the Irish Supreme Court remarked in *Fitzpatrick v White*, 'an invalid warning, i.e., one which [patient C] could neither assimilate nor act upon, would be equivalent to no warning' (albeit that C there could digest the warnings as to risks, a mere 30 minutes before his eye operation). Several matters would be relevant on this issue: was the surgery elective only? Was it major and perhaps life-threatening? Was C stressed, medicated, or in pain, and less likely to take on board the risks and make a calm and reasoned decision? Had C been evaluated pre-operatively, with many chances to discuss risks then?[88a]

PURE OMISSIONS

The general rule

§3.9 The law of negligence does not, as a general rule, impose a duty of care on D for 'pure omissions'. That is, D is not legally required to take positive steps to protect C's person or property from suffering foreseeable injury or harm. This general rule applies, regardless of whether C's injury emanates from the acts of third parties, or from natural causes.

Legal policy

Simply put, omissions are treated more leniently by English negligence law than positive acts are, as Lord Hoffmann explained in *Stovin v Wise*:

[87] *Capital Brake Service Pty Ltd v Meagher t/as Sparke Helmore* [2003] NSWCA 225, [30] (Ipp JA).
[88] [2010] EWHC 178 (QB), [2010] Med LR 90, [27]. [88a] [2007] IESC 51 (Kearns J).

> It is one thing for the law to say that a person who undertakes some activity shall take reasonable care not to cause damage to others. It is another thing for the law to require that a person who is doing nothing in particular shall take steps to prevent another from suffering harm from the acts of third parties ... or natural causes.[89]

The frequently-cited reference to 'mere' or 'pure' omissions, as used by the House of Lords in, e.g., *Smith (or Maloco) v Littlewoods Organisation Ltd*,[90] is a deliberately diminutive term, reducing their importance in the eyes of the law. The general principle has been approved by several appellate courts,[91] and ranks as one of the more immutable common law negligence principles. As Lord Reed said, in *Mitchell v Glasgow CC*, 'it is usually considered worse to do harm than to fail to help'.[92]

Various policy reasons which support the principle have already been canvassed, in the context of 'Bad Samaritans' who fail to intervene/rescue/assist C (discussed in Chapter 2). While it is in that sphere that these policy justifications have been most clearly stated, they apply to omissions more generally.

It is legally irrelevant that D's failure to assist is either contrary to what a reasonable body of peer professional opinion considered that D should have done (under the *Bolam* test of breach[93]), or otherwise plainly demonstrates a lack of reasonable care. In other words, it does not assist to prove a duty of care, that breach may be made out. Moreover, the mere fact that D's omission to take a step could foreseeably result in C's injury or even death does not create a legal duty either, for foreseeability of harm is only **one** element necessary to establish a duty on D's part under the three-fold *Caparo* test. The omissions principle is, as Sedley LJ noted in *Bishara v Sheffield Teaching Hosp NHS Trust*,[94] essentially a question of legal policy.

However, the general rule notwithstanding, there are recognised exceptional categories in which D owes a duty to C to take positive steps to protect C's person or property.

Acts versus omissions

Before considering those exceptions, it must be admitted that the line between an act (where a duty may arise) and an omission (where, generally speaking, it does not) can be very finely-drawn. Of course, where D watches a blind man walk over the edge of a cliff, that is clearly a complete failure to act and can easily be treated as an omission.

However, take an example from *Mitchell v Glasgow CC*[95] – where driver D hits C's car from the rear, while it is stopped at a red light, D having been distracted by something happening in the car, and C is injured in the collision. D's positive act of driving has brought about the harm; but D has clearly failed to keep a proper lookout, failed to pay due care and attention, and failed to brake in time. How should D's conduct be characterised? These omissions will be actionable, as part of a course of conduct or activity. In *Stovin v Wise*, Lord Hoffmann remarked that, 'the conditions necessary to bring about an event always consist of a combination of acts and omissions', but that the law of negligence 'distinguish[es] between regulating the way in which

[89] [1996] AC 923 (HL) 943–45 (Lord Hoffmann).

[90] [1987] AC 241 (HL) 261, 272 (Lord Goff).

[91] e.g.: *Gorringe v Calderdale MBC* [2004] 1 WLR 1057 (HL) [17] (Lord Hoffmann); *Customs and Excise Commrs v Barclays Bank plc* [2006] UKHL 28, [2007] 1 AC 181, [39]; *Mitchell v Glasgow CC* [2009] UKHL 11, [2009] 1 AC 874, [15] (Lord Hope), [39] (Lord Scott).

[92] [2008] CSIH 19, [89] (Lord Reed, dissenting), citing: *Yuen Kun-Yeu v A-G of Hong Kong* [1988] AC 175 (PC) 19.

[93] Per *Bolam v Friern Hospital Management Committee* [1957] 1 WLR 582 (QB).

[94] [2007] EWCA Civ 353, [11].

[95] [2009] UKHL 11, [76], and earlier: [2008] Scot CS 19 (CSIH) [88].

an activity may be conducted, and imposing a duty to act upon a person who is not carrying on any relevant activity [at all]'.[96] The reality is that the line can be distinctly blurred at times, because most omissions occur in a wider context, whereby D is engaging in some activity. A case of motor-racing, and a recent novel case of medical negligence, illustrate this well.

In *Wattleworth v Goodwood Road Racing Co Ltd*,[97] C was killed at a motor-racing circuit, when his vehicle collided with an earth bank. The motor-racing regulator, the FIA, submitted that it could not owe a duty of care because its FIA inspectors who visited the racing circuit never advised on the installation of the earth bank. The earth bank was installed by the owner/occupier of the track to meet local authority noise requirements, even before the FIA inspected the track. **Held:** this was not an example of a 'pure omission'. The FIA inspector had inspected and made recommendations on all parts of the circuit, including the earth bank. It was all part of the one activity which he carried out, for the purposes of making specific recommendations for improving racing safety (nevertheless, the FIA owed C no duty of care, for other reasons, discussed in Chapter 2). In *ABC v St George's Healthcare NHS Trust*,[98] ABC's father was diagnosed with Huntington's Disease in 2009, which is genetic in origin, and which a child has a 50% chance of inheriting if one of her parents has the disease. At the time of the diagnosis, ABC (C, in this case) was in fact pregnant. C's father was subject to hospital and restriction orders, having killed his wife and been convicted of manslaughter a couple of years prior to this diagnosis. He refused to allow his treating healthcare professionals, D, to inform C or his other daughter out of concern for their welfare. Although D questioned the wisdom of that decision, the wish for confidentiality expressed by their patient was respected. However, in 2010, the information about her father's medical condition was accidentally disclosed to C by one of his doctors, and a subsequent test confirmed that C also had the disease. C claimed that she would have terminated her pregnancy, had she known of her father's diagnosis, and that various economic and psychiatric consequences had followed from D's failure to inform C of the genetic condition to which she was at risk. **Held:** the claim was struck out as disclosing no cause of action. Nicol J classified D's failure to inform C of her father's genetic condition as a 'pure omission', arising in circumstances where there was no 'special relationship' or any assumption of responsibility towards C as a family member (daughter). There was no duty of care imposed upon D to inform C directly of information about her father's genetic condition that would have enabled her to test herself and terminate her pregnancy. An alternative claim in negligence, that D failed to counsel and advise C's father to persuade him that his daughters should be told, was not helpful to C either, as it was not alleged that, had her father received such counselling, he would have either told C directly, or permitted D to do so. Hence, in the absence of any consent from the patient himself, there was no overriding duty of care imposed on D to fix the omission and to inform C, as non-patient, of the genetic condition.

Some of the circumstances in the next section also demonstrate the difficulty.

Exceptional scenarios

§3.10 There are limited exceptions where English common law *does* recognise a duty on D's part to protect C's person or property, where there is some 'additional feature' which imposes a duty on D to take positive steps to prevent harm to C. Thus far, that additional feature has arisen

[96] [1996] AC 923 (HL) 945. [97] [2004] EWHC 140 (QB), [2004] PIQR P25.

[98] [2015] EWHC 1394 (QB) [27]–[28]. Cf: *Pate v Threlkel*, 661 So 2d 278 (Fla Sup Ct, 1995), and *Safer v Pack*, 677 A 2d 1188 (Super Ct App Div, 1996), and the analysis in: Mulheron, *Medical Negligence: Non-Patient and Third Party Claims* (Ashgate, 2010), ch 4.

where: (1) an occupier D owes positive duties to protect a lawful visitor; (2) D creates an inherent danger on or near a roadway; (3) D knows, or ought to know, that a third party has created, or interfered with, a hazard on D's property which could harm C's adjoining property; (4) D assumes responsibility to protect C's person or property by contract or by some closely proximate relationship between C and D; or (5) D owes a duty to C to supervise/control/detain a third party who harms C, by virtue of a 'special relationship' between D and the third party.

As Lord Goff pointed out in *Smith v Littlewoods Organisation Ltd*,[99] affirmative duties to step in and prevent harm to C are 'likely to be strictly limited'. Nevertheless, the exceptional circumstances have been described by Lord Goff in *Smith*, and endorsed by Lord Scott in *Mitchell v Glasgow CC*,[100] as, respectively, 'special cases' and as having an 'additional feature' which transforms an omission into a duty. Further, Lord Goff noted that a legal duty to perform positive acts may often be imposed on D by *Contract law*, but it is rarely done in Tort.

Each of the following instances represents an established, and exceptional, basis upon which D is under an obligation, in negligence law, to take reasonable and positive steps to protect C from harm to his person or property:

Exception #1. A duty to exercise reasonable care to protect or avert harm to C is imposed upon occupiers towards visitors and trespassers, by virtue of positive duties to protect entrants from dangers posed by the occupier's land which are imposed by statute[101] (as discussed in Chapter 12).

Exception #2. A duty to exercise reasonable care to protect C, a road user, is imposed upon D who is in control of a dangerous thing on or near the roadway, and which harms C. D must create the source of danger, and that danger must be *inherently* dangerous. On this point, two cases can usefully be contrasted:

In *Haynes v Harwood*,[102] a delivery person, Mr Bird, D, left a horse-drawn van unattended and untethered in a crowded street in Rotherhithe, to visit a wharf and collect his receipt. Whilst he was in the wharf, children threw stones at the two horses, which then bolted down the street. PC Harwood, C, a police officer, saw a woman and child in the path of the bolting horses, and suffered injury when he tried to stop the horses. **Held:** D owed C a duty of care. D had created a source of danger by leaving his horses unattended in a busy street. The noise and movement in the street, and the propensity to unnerve or spook inherently-dangerous animals such as horses, were all reasonably foreseeable. D, the driver, was well aware of the neighbourhood, as he frequently delivered there, and knew that there were three schools in the area. The accident happened between 4.00–5.00pm, when children were likely to frequent the streets, and the deliberate actions of mischievous boys were foreseeable.

But contrast:

In *Topp v London Country Bus (South West) Ltd*,[103] London Country Bus, D, had a system of leaving some of their buses parked in the public street, in a lay-by outside a pub, with the keys in the ignitions and unlocked, to facilitate the changeover of drivers. Normally, there was an 8–10 minute interval between shifts, but one night, a bus had been unlocked for over 9 hours, because a driver

[99] [1987] AC 241 (HL) 272–75; *Home Office v Dorset Yacht Co Ltd* [1970] AC 1004 (HL) 1060 (Lord Diplock).

[100] [2009] UKHL 11, [2009] 1 AC 874, [40], with Lord Goff's opinion also endorsed by Lord Rodger, [56].

[101] Contained in the Occupiers' Liability Act 1957 and Occupiers' Liability Act 1984, respectively.

[102] [1935] 1 KB 146 (CA). Also known as *Hynes v Harwood* in some case reports.

[103] [1993] 1 WLR 976 (CA).

called in sick. At 11.15pm, the bus was stolen, and five minutes later, it struck Mrs Topp, C, who was riding home from work. C was killed. The hit-and-run driver was never identified, and her husband and 9-year-old daughter brought actions under the FAA 1976 and on behalf of her estate. (The Motor Insurers' Bureau pays compensation for untraced drivers, but the amount was limited, and the MIB required Mr Topp to sue D, to seek to recoup some of that payment.) **Held:** D did not owe a duty of care to C. It was distinguishable from *Haynes v Harwood*, because there, horses were inherently dangerous to road users, given their unpredictable nature. However, a bus was not inherently dangerous – it required human intervention to be dangerous. Furthermore, to leave a vehicle unlocked with the keys in the ignition on a highway, near a pub, did not create a 'special risk' category necessary to give rise to a duty of care either.

The decision in *Topp* suggests that the exceptional scenarios are indeed of limited application, and will not easily be extended, such as to give rise to a duty on D for his failure to act. Furthermore, there were certain floodgates concerns, for if a duty were imposed on the bus company, then it could equally be imposed in 'very many different circumstances in which a private car, standing unlocked and with its ignition key in the switch, might be stolen, and then driven negligently so as to cause injury or damage ... Is it material or crucial if the vehicle is left outside a pub? And what if the car is left for several weeks in an airport long-term carpark?'[104]

The blurred line between acts and omissions is readily apparent in this exceptional scenario. For example, in *Mitchell v Glasgow CC*,[105] the Scottish Inner House remarked that *Haynes v Harwood* was not, strictly speaking, an 'omissions case' at all, but rather, one where D acted positively (leaving the horses untethered), in such a way as to create a risk of causing injury to the policeman as rescuer. By contrast, in *Chubb Fire Ltd v Vicar of Spalding*,[106] the Court of Appeal described *Haynes* as a case of omission, in that D failed to tie up the horses properly so that they did not run amok.

Exception #3. Where D knew, or should have known, that a third party was positively creating, or interfering with, a hazard on his property (especially by means of fire), D will be under a duty to take reasonable steps to abate that danger himself before it spreads to C's adjoining property. The principle especially arises wherever the danger is a 'natural nuisance' which has a 'known risk of [causing] damage or injury to one's neighbour or to his property' (per *Stagecoach South Western Trains Ltd v Hind*[107]).

Unlike under the previous exception, the source of the danger here does not need to be **inherently** dangerous (i.e., combustible – although the principle could certainly be invoked in that scenario, according to Lord Goff in *Smith v Littlewoods Organisation Ltd*,[108] giving the example of fireworks stored in a garden shed awaiting Guy Fawkes night which a third party interferes with). Again, two cases may be contrasted:

In *Goldman v Hargrave*,[109] Mr Goldman, D, the occupier of a West Australian wheat station, noticed that a 100 ft high redgum tree on the property was struck by lightning during an electrical storm on 25 Feb 1961. D arranged for a contractor to cut down the tree on 26 Feb. D left the tree to burn out, instead of watering it down. On 1 Mar, a strong hot wind blew up, and the fire spread out of control to the farm of his neighbour, Mr Hargrave, C, causing extensive damage. The natural windy

[104] *ibid*, [16], and citing the trial judge, May J, with approval.

[105] [2008] CSIH 19, 2008 SC 351, [97].

[106] [2010] EWCA Civ 981, [2010] 2 CLC 277, fn 35.

[107] [2014] EWHC 1891 (TCC) [65], citing: *Leakey v National Trust* [1980] 1 QB 485 (CA) 524.

[108] [1987] 1 AC 241 (HL) 273.

[109] [1967] 1 AC 645 (PC).

conditions and tinder-dry land were the most immediate causes of property damage suffered by C, but C sued D in negligence and in nuisance. **Held:** D was liable in both negligence and in nuisance. D owed C, his neighbour, a duty of care to make the tree safe, by watering the trunk down, which was easily and cheaply within the resources of D.

In *Smith v Littlewoods Organisation Ltd*,[110] the department store, Littlewoods, D, bought a disused cinema in Dunfermline, planning to demolish the cinema and build a supermarket. The cinema was left generally unattended for six weeks, except for some minor foundation work, and was set on fire by some teenage vandals. The fire spread to neighbouring buildings, seriously damaging C1's neighbouring church, and destroying C2's café. C1 and C2 alleged that D owed a duty to them, as neighbouring property owners, to take reasonable care against vandals gaining entry and setting fire in the old cinema. D were not on notice of any dangerous activity by trespassers, or that there had been any attempts to start fires in the past. It was commonly-accepted that only a 24-hour guard could have prevented the fires from being started. **Held:** no duty of care was owed by D to C. This case was distinguishable from *Goldman*, because here, D had no specific knowledge about the activities of trespassers and vandals on their property (the police, fire brigade and neighbours had passed on no information about previous vandalism). Also, the 'omission' here was the failure to install a 24-hour guard – substantially more onerous than watering down a tree.

Hence, both the level of knowledge which D possessed about the source of danger, and the expense or ease with which the omission could be corrected to secure the reasonable protection/rescue of C's person or property, are relevant to this exceptional scenario. As with the *Haynes* scenario, the possibility of floodgates of suits is also something to be guarded against. In *Smith*, Lord Goff pointed out that every house contains 'possible sources of fire if interfered with by third parties, ranging from matches and firelighters to electric irons and gas cookers and even oil-fired central heating systems'.[111] He did not regard it to be justifiable that those householders should be liable in negligence if a third party interfered with those implements.

Exception #4. A duty of care may be imposed on D to take reasonable care to protect C's person or property, where D is under a responsibility to protect C's person or property by virtue of a contract or other closely-proximate relationship between C and D.

In *Stansbie v Troman*,[112] Mr Stansbie, D, a decorator, was left alone on Mrs Troman's, C's, premises to undertake his work. He left the premises to buy some wallpaper, and went out leaving the door on the latch. Whilst he was absent, a thief entered the house and stole property (including a diamond bracelet. **Held:** D owed C, with whom he had a contract to decorate the place, a duty of care, and was liable for the lost property.

Exception #5. Where a special relationship exists between D and a third party, and that third party causes injury or harm to C because of D's omission to supervise or control that third party, then D may be under a duty of care to take positive steps to control, supervise or detain the third party (per *Home Office v Dorset Yacht Co Ltd*[113]). This complex area is the subject of discussion in the next section.

Do these exceptions still retain relevance? It was suggested by the Court of Appeal in *Selwood v Durham CC*[114] that these types of circumstances in which that 'additional something' could be established – and thereby transform an omission to act into a duty to protect/

[110] [1987] 1 AC 241 (HL). [111] *ibid*, 274. [112] [1948] 2 KB 48 (HL).
[113] [1970] AC 1004 (HL). [114] [2012] EWCA Civ 979, [2012] WLR(D) 231, [49]–[50].

supervise/control – no longer assumed the same importance, and that the establishment of any duty of care revolved around the tri-partite *Caparo* test.

However, given the continued relevance of the incremental test by virtue of *Caparo* and *Customs & Excise* (as discussed in Chapter 2), the exceptional categories listed above surely serve tangible ongoing importance, in demarcating the circumstances in which C can overcome the general rule that no duty attaches for pure omissions. Furthermore, these exceptional categories have been endorsed by the House of Lords in *Mitchell* (a post-*Caparo* case), including the *Haynes v Harwood* scenario.[115] Also, the Irish High Court recently noted, of the English cases, that the exceptions were justified, for 'it has been judicially recognised that the actions of troublesome children and delinquent juveniles often present a special case' (per *Ennis v HSE*[116]). For these reasons, the categories are still important precedents in negligence law.

THE FAILURE TO CONTROL, SUPERVISE OR DETAIN THIRD PARTIES

The area of negligence, in which liability is sought to be imposed on D for the consequences of the acts or omissions of a third party (TP), whom D did not control, supervise or detain, has been rightly described by the Court of Appeal, in *K v Sec of State for the Home Dept*, as a 'situation which has called for particular attention by the common law courts',[117] and in which, as the Supreme Court recently noted in *Michael v CC of South Wales Police*, liability is not imposed on D in English law 'as a general rule'.[118]

Introduction

A novel scenario

§3.11 Where a third party who is 'dangerous' does harm to C, and where D had some means of control or supervision over that third party, D may owe a duty of care to C to prevent that harm from occurring. In such cases, D does not directly harm C, but has created the opportunity for the third party to harm C.

It is a tragic reality that C may be harmed by the acts of the psychiatrically-disturbed, the murderously-inclined, the violently-disposed, or the youthfully-ignorant. In such cases, where some degree of control or supervision was being exercised over that third party (TP) by D, then a duty of care may be owed by D to C.

As a novel non-traditional duty of care scenario, it will be governed by the assumption of responsibility, and/or *Caparo*,[119] tests (as discussed in Chapter 2) – and it is the latter test which has been the principal one by which the modern cases have been analysed (and earlier authorities which eschewed such a detailed analysis may not be decided the same way now[120]). In the TP case of *Mitchell v Glasgow CC*, Lord Hope stated that *Caparo* 'was currently the most favoured test of liability'.[121] It has been applied, too, in several other TP cases, such as *Merthyr*

[115] [2009] UKHL 11, [2009] 1 AC 874, [23] (Lord Hope). [116] [2014] IEHC 440, [63].

[117] [2002] EWCA Civ 775, [13], [16] (Laws LJ). [118] [2015] UKSC 2, [97].

[119] [1990] 2 AC 605 (HL) 617–18 (Lord Bridge).

[120] e.g., *Holgate v Lancashire Mental Hosp Bd* [1937] 4 All ER 19 (Liverpool Summer Assizes), the correctness of which was doubted by Lord Diplock in *Home Office v Dorset Yacht* [1970] AC 1004 (HL) 1062–63.

[121] [2009] UKHL 11, [2009] 1 AC 874, [21].

Tydfil County BC v C,[122] *Webster v Ridgeway Foundation School*,[123] and *K v Sec of State for the Home Dept.*[124] The relevant questions under that test, of course, are whether it was reasonably foreseeable that C would suffer damage if D failed to control/supervise TP, whether there was a relationship of sufficient proximity between C and D, and whether it was fair, just and reasonable to impose a duty of care on D to avoid the damage of which C complains. The assumption of responsibility test has only been applied in the occasional TP case – e.g., it was relied upon in *Selwood v Durham CC*[125] (although the *Caparo* test figured largely in that case too).

It has become clear that establishing a duty of care in third party cases is problematical, and the decisions are, at times, difficult to reconcile. There are several legal difficulties with these cases. First, the allegation of breach levelled against D is frequently of an *omission* to act, and allegations of 'pure omission' are difficult to substantiate in English law (as considered earlier in this chapter[126]). Secondly, English courts have developed distinct policy reasons against a duty being held, for certain categories of D, such as the police who are investigating or seeking to suppress crime (discussed in Chapter 2). Thirdly, several of these TP cases involve public authorities (apart from the aforementioned police, the leading cases entail government departments, health authorities and local authorities), which may entail greater hesitation to impose a duty of care (a point acknowledged in *K*[127]). Fourthly, causation can be difficult to establish, given that it is the TP's intervention that has been the direct and immediate cause of C's harm (a point dealt with in Chapter 8). Fifthly, the problem of just how many exist in the class of whom C is one is an oft-recurring theme which gives rise to policy difficulties Sixthly, the scenario inevitably throws up a key question: how is the duty to be cast? Is it a duty to control, supervise or take some other step in relation to TP in order to protect C against harm, or is it a wider duty to take some direct step in relation to C (e.g., to warn C of the threat posed by TP)?

In combination, these factors mean that it is a challenging area of negligence liability. It is worth noting that these types of suits commonly arise because any action against TP would be futile, either legally or practically. Commonly, TP will be too young to owe C any duty of care, or TP will be 'shallow-pocketed' (i.e., uninsured), and hence, not worth suing, whereas D will be an insured party.

Not a derivative duty

§3.12 D's liability towards C is not derivative from, or dependent upon, any duty which D may owe to the third party. It is an entirely independent, or separate, duty of care which D may owe to C.

C's claim against D, where TP has wrought havoc against C's person or property, does not stand or fall upon whether D has any liability towards TP. It will certainly **not** assist C to prove that, just because D was negligent towards TP, then it would be 'fair, just and reasonable' that he should be found to owe a duty to C too – that argument was specifically put, and rejected, in *West Bromwich Albion Football Club Ltd v El-Safty*.[128] Conversely, even if D did not (indeed, could not) owe a duty of care to TP, a duty may still be owed by D to C (a possibility acknowledged in *Hill v CC of West Yorkshire Police*[129]).

122 [2010] EWHC 62 (QB) [12], [30]–[36]. 123 [2010] EWHC 157 (QB), [2010] ELR 694, [118]–[119].
124 [2002] EWCA Civ 775, [11]–[14], [30]–[36], with reference to *Caparo's* test at [12].
125 [2012] EWCA Civ 979, [2012] WLR(D) 231, [52]. 126 Cross cite pp 146–48
127 [2002] EWCA Civ 775, [20].
128 [2005] EWHC 2866 (QB) [67] (Royce J), and aff'd on appeal: [2007] PIQR P7 (CA).
129 [1989] AC 53 (HL) 62–63.

Hence, it follows that any duties owed by D to C and to TP are entirely independent of each other. The existence (or non-existence) of one does not influence a finding of the other. As will be seen in Chapter 5, this reflects the legal position where a secondary victim, C, brings a claim for negligently-inflicted pure psychiatric injury against D, for negligent acts visited upon the immediate victim. C's claim does not have to be derivative upon a successful claim being instituted by the immediate victim who was put in the 'zone of physical danger' by D's negligence – the House of Lords (per Lord Oliver) made this plain in *Alcock v CC of the South Yorkshire Police.*[130]

The leading cases

This section outlines the key scenarios, and leading cases, which illustrate the problem of suits against D for harm done by TP, whether they be violently-disposed, mentally-ill, or too young to know any better. Many of them conflict in outcome, for reasons which will be considered in the legal analysis which follows (albeit that a couple of them are difficult to reconcile, as noted below).

- Prison authorities – where D is a prison authority, TP a prisoner and C a person injured by TP:

In *Dorset Yacht Co Ltd v Home Office,*[131] prison officers employed by the Home Office, D, took a group of young boys from the Borstal youth detention centre to Brownsea Island in Poole Harbour, under the supervision and control of three Borstal officers. Due to inadequate supervision, seven of the youths escaped one night, and boarded a yacht, *Diligence of Marston*, and got that yacht moving. It collided with C's yacht, *Silver Mist*, which was moored off the island. The youths boarded C's yacht and wrecked much of it. C sued D in negligence for failing to adequately control, supervise and discipline the youths. **Held:** the Borstal officers, D, owed a duty of care to C, as they had created a potential situation of danger for C, the owner of a nearby yacht at risk of damage.

But contrast:

In *K v Sec of State for the Home Dept,*[132] Rashid Musa, a citizen of Kenya, was granted limited leave to remain in the UK. During his stay, he was arrested and charged with the buggery of a 15-year-old girl and was sentenced to 18 months jail. After release, Mr Musa was arrested and sentenced for burglary, and a court recommended his deportation. He was detained under the Immigration Act 1971 for that purpose. Due to lack of resources, Mr Musa was released from detention, by order of the Secretary of State, D. Mr Musa then raped Miss K, C, at knifepoint, and raped a boy on a train the following day. He was sentenced to life imprisonment. C sued D in negligence for the harm (including psychological harm) suffered as a result of the rape, on the basis that D released Mr Musa into the community when it knew, or should have known, that he was a very dangerous individual, liable to commit crimes of sexual violence; and that he ought to have been detained until he could be deported. **Held:** D did not owe C a duty of care. In *Thomson (AP) v Scottish Ministers,*[133] Ann Thomson, C, was the mother of Catherine Thomson, who was murdered by John Campbell, at C's house in Moodiesburn, while Mr Campbell was on a short period of 'home leave' from prison. Shortly after his arrest for the murder of Ms Thomson, Mr Campbell committed suicide. Ms Thomson had been a friend of the Campbell family – she had known Mr Campbell himself since childhood, had been his brother's girlfriend for five years, and knew his mother well too. C argued that Ms Thomson, the deceased, was within that group of persons that Mr Campbell was likely to 'have dealings with', during his weekend leave, should Mr Campbell become violent during his home release. **Held:** D did not owe C a duty of care.

[130] [1992] 1 AC 310 (HL) 412. [131] [1970] AC 1004 (HL).

[132] [2002] EWCA Civ 775. [133] [2013] CSIH 63.

- The police – where D are the police, TP a violently-inclined criminal and C the unfortunate victim of TP's violence. Of course, in leading cases in which the police were alleged to have failed to apprehend or adequately investigate/suppress the activities of those criminals who proceed to injure or kill C – e.g., the dreadful cases of *Hill v CC of West Yorkshire Police,*[134] *Osman v Ferguson,*[135] *Van Colle v CC of the Hertfordshire Police; Smith v CC of Sussex Police*[136] and *Michael v CC of South Wales Police*[137] – then (as examined in Chapter 2), many policy reasons preclude a duty of care on the part of police (under the so-called *Hill* principle). However, proximity was also at issue in each of those cases, and this aspect of the decisions is examined below.
- Educational authorities – where D is a school or kindergarten, TP a pupil, and C is injured by that pupil (whether C is another pupil, or a complete stranger to the school):

  In *Carmarthenshire CC v Lewis,*[138] 3-year-old David wandered out of his 'play pen' at a nursery school owned/operated by D, whilst the nursery teacher, Miss Morgan, was attending to another child from the play pen who had a cut knee. At the time, David was dressed up in coat and scarf and was waiting to go for a walk with Miss Morgan and another nursery mate, as a treat. Unexpectedly, David did not wait for his teacher, but left the room, went through a gate that was supposed to be locked, out into a main road. Mr Lewis, C, was driving his lorry down that street, saw David in the middle of the road, swerved his heavy vehicle to avoid David, and hit a lamppost. C was killed in the accident, and his widow sued the kindergarten for negligence (and vicariously), and the supervising teacher in negligence. **Held:** Miss Morgan was not negligent (in leaving the classroom for 10 minutes to bandage up the hurt child); but the nursery school did owe a duty of care to C, an adjacent road-user. In *Webster v Ridgeway Foundation School,*[139] Henry Webster, C, had arranged to have a 'one-on-one' fight with another student, MM, at his school, Ridgeway School, D. The fight was to be conducted at the school's tennis courts when the school day finished. Unbeknown to him, MM arranged for some older friends and relations to turn up too, and some of these (including Wasif Khan, a non-pupil, who wielded the most serious weapon) attacked C, using a claw hammer, and kicking and striking C whilst he lay on the ground. C sustained serious brain damage from the injuries inflicted in the fight, and sued the school in negligence, on three bases, that D: (1) failed to take reasonable care to keep the school premises secure, and should have fenced the site so as to keep intruders out, and had a staff member on duty at day's end; (2) failed to establish better discipline in the school and deal better with racial tensions there (C was white, and his attackers were Asians); and (3) should have done more to protect C, and failed to exercise management responsibilities for the safety and security of its pupils while on school premises, including during their departure at the end of the day. **Held:** D owed C a duty to take reasonable care to see that C was reasonably safe during school hours, and for a reasonable period after the end of the school day while he was still on the school's premises (however, both breach and causation failed).

- Health authorities (and healthcare practitioners who work there) – where D is a healthcare professional or a health authority, TP a mentally-ill patient who wreaks havoc, and C the unfortunate victim of that patient's harmful behaviour:

  In *Palmer v Tees HA,*[140] the patient, Shaun Armstrong, was released from a mental facility on an out-patient basis on 21 June 1993, having disclosed to a psychiatrist before his release that he

[134] [1989] AC 53 (HL). Subsequently: *R v Coonan (formerly Sutcliffe)* [2011] EWCA Crim 5.

[135] [1993] 4 All ER 344 (CA). Application for leave to appeal to HL was refused.

[136] [2008] UKHL 50, [2009] 1 AC 225 (HL). [137] [2015] UKSC 2.

[138] [1955] AC 549 (HL). [139] [2010] EWHC 157 (QB), [2010] ELR 694.

[140] [1999] EWCA Civ 1533. Mrs Palmer's claim for pure psychiatric illness is considered in Chapter 5.

harboured sexual feelings towards children. On 30 June 1994, he abducted, assaulted, killed and mutilated a 4-year-old neighbour, Rosie Palmer, C, who lived in the next street. C's estate sued the health authority, D, which operated the hospital at which Mr Armstrong was treated, for failing to provide him with adequate treatment, and for failing to diagnose that there was a real, substantial and foreseeable risk of his committing serious, sexual offences against children. **Held:** no duty of care was owed to C by the health authority; the claim was struck out as disclosing no cause of action.

But contrast:

In *Selwood v Durham CC*,[141] Claire Selwood, C, was a senior social worker employed by the Durham CC, D1, in their Children in Need team, and was the designated social worker for a daughter of Graham Burton, in family proceedings relating to Mr Burton's children. The Tees, Esk and Wear Valley NHS Trust, D2, operated a Community Mental Health Team and a Crisis Resolution Team, staffed by health workers and social workers employed by D1 and D2. Both signed a protocol, 'Working together in the delivery of services to adults and children', which applied to Mr Burton's circumstances, due to his mental health problems. D2 operated a mental health ward at Cherry Knowle Hospital, to which Mr Burton was admitted as a voluntary patient. During his stay, Mr Burton said that he was 'not pleased' with one of the social workers – the 'nastiest one' – but he did not name C specifically. At an assessment meeting by the CRT, Mr Burton again said that there was someone involved in the court case 'who I dislike and wish to harm, but I am trying to avoid her'. For a case review to be held at the hospital, the managing psychiatrist asked Mr Burton whether C could attend that meeting, but he refused, saying that he would 'kill her on the spot' if he saw her. None of these threats were passed on to C or to her employer, D1. C attended the case review, where Mr Burton attacked her, causing very serious injuries (for which he was sentenced to life imprisonment for attempted murder). D1 conceded that it owed C, its employee, a duty of care, but D2 denied that. **Held:** D2 owed C a duty of care.

- Social housing landlords – where D is a local authority/council, TP is ostensibly under the control of that local authority, and C is injured or killed by TP.

In *Mitchell v Glasgow CC*,[142] James Drummond (TP) and James Mitchell, C, lived in D's social housing, and the two got along very badly, due to TP's anti-social behaviour (e.g., playing loud music during the night, smashing C's windows with an iron bar), and TP was arrested and jailed for his behaviour. TP regularly threatened to kill C, and said that he would be 'dead meat'. Other tenants heard TP threaten C in this way. D warned TP that if he persisted, they would take action to recover possession of his house. However, TP's threats towards C and other neighbours continued at least once a month. D then invited TP to a meeting to discuss another violent incident involving TP, and about a notice of proceedings for recovery of possession that had been served on him. TP attended the meeting, lost his temper and became abusive. After it, he went straight home, and battered C with an iron bar or stick, causing serious injuries from which C died 10 days later in hospital. C's estate sued D, alleging that it did not warn C that it had summoned TP to the meeting nor of any possible risk of retaliation against C, and that if the warning had been given, C would have kept out of TP's way and would not have been attacked. **Held:** no duty was owed by D to prevent the risk of harm to C.

141 [2012] EWCA Civ 979. 142 [2009] UKHL 11, [2009] 2 WLR 481 (HL).

But contrast:

In *Merthyr Tydfil County BC v C*,[143] C and her two children, A and B, lived in social housing provided by Council, D. C reported to D that a young boy, X, in a neighbouring house had sexually abused her two children on two different occasions, in 2002 and in 2004. When C complained to D about the boy X's behaviour in 2002, she was told to keep her children indoors, but no further support was provided. C followed that advice but, over time, as X did not appear to be playing outdoors, C allowed A and B to play outside, but the sexual abuse again allegedly occurred in 2004. D allocated a social worker to C and her family, a person who was also the social worker allocated to X's family. X was later removed from his family by D, and placed with foster parents. C suffered psychiatric injury, allegedly arising from the way in which her complaints about X's abuse of her children had been dealt with. **Held:** it was arguable that D owed a duty to C; the claim could not be struck out.

Depicting the successful cases diagrammatically:

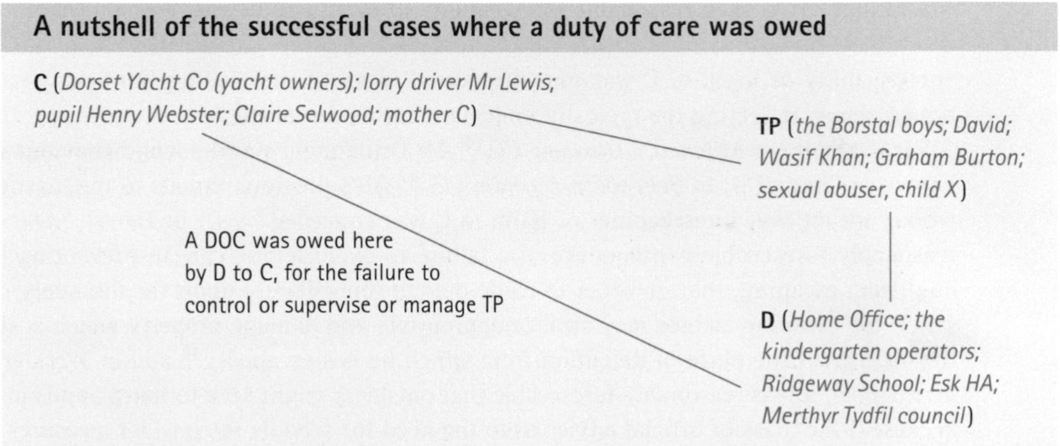

– and the unsuccessful cases:

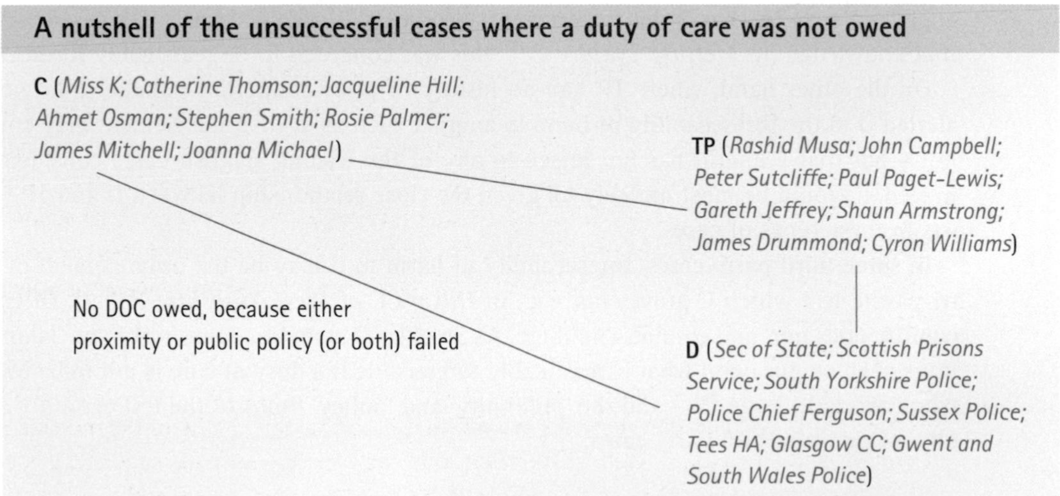

Notwithstanding that some of the leading cases are difficult to reconcile, the next section teases out the leading grounds on which these decisions have turned.

[143] [2010] EWHC 62 (QB) [30]–[36].

The legal analysis of the leading cases

As Laws LJ remarked in *K*, third party cases 'is the paradigm instance ... where issues of proximity and fairness are acute, and not merely given, in the law of negligence.'[144] As previously noted, the *Caparo* three-part test is customarily used in such cases. This is especially so where (as is frequently the case) C and D are not known to each other, for as Lord Bingham stated in *Customs & Excise Commr v Barclays Bank plc*,[145] to speak of an 'assumption of responsibility' where it does not actually reflect the actions and intentions of the actual D is to render the concept fairly 'notional', whereupon the *Caparo* test is more applicable.

Reasonable foreseeability of harm

§3.13 Where D knows, or should have known, of the 'dangerous' propensities of the third party who causes harm to C, then reasonable foreseeability of harm will be easily established.

Foreseeability of harm to C was uncontroversial in **all** of the leading third party cases mentioned above, reflecting the typically undemanding nature of the test.

For example, in *Mitchell v Glasgow CC*,[146] Mr Drummond's anti-social behaviour was well-known to Council D; in *Selwood v Durham CC*,[147] GB's previous threats to the 'nastiest' social worker meant that foreseeability of harm to C was conceded by D; in *Dorset Yacht*, it was 'a reasonably foreseeable consequence of a failure to exercise due care in preventing [a Borstal boy] from escaping, that, in order to elude pursuit immediately upon the discovery of his absence, the escaping trainee may steal or appropriate and damage property which is situated in the vicinity of the place of detention from which he has escaped';[148] and in *Webster v Ridgeway School*, it was reasonably foreseeable that outsiders might seek to harm pupils in a school, because '[t]he mass of official advice as to the need for schools to consider measures to secure their sites is premised on that reality.'[149]

Alternatively, even where D did not know beforehand of TP's propensities to do harm, the allegation may be that D did not respond adequately to risk of harm, once it was armed with that knowledge (in *Merthyr Tydfil v C*,[150] this was conceded to be reasonably foreseeable).

On the other hand, where TP had no history of prior dangerous conduct that would have alerted D to the foreseeability of harm to another such as C, then the element may conceivably fail – but that scenario has not arisen in any of the leading English cases considered above. Indeed, it would be most unlikely to, given the close relationship between D and TP which exists in these types of cases.

In some third party cases, foreseeability of harm to C may be the **only** element of *Caparo's* tri-partite test which C proves (as, e.g., in *Hill v CC of West Yorkshire Police*). Of course, the enquiry does not, and cannot, end there. As Stocker LJ stated in *Jones v Wright*, '[s]ome limitations must be put upon what is reasonably foreseeable if a duty of care is not to be owed to the whole world at large'[151] – and the 'proximity' and 'policy' limbs of the test certainly serve that vital purpose in third party cases.

144 [2002] EWCA Civ 775, [16]. 145 [2006] UKHL 28, [2007] 1 AC 181, [6]. 146 [2009] UKHL 11.
147 [2012] EWCA Civ 979, [2012] WLR(D) 231, [19]. 148 [1970] AC 1004 (HL) 1070.
149 [2010] EWHC 157 (QB), [2010] ELR 694, [118]. 150 [2010] EWHC 62 (QB).
151 [1991] 3 All ER 88 (CA) 114.

The requisite proximity

§3.14 When searching for the requisite nexus, or proximity, between C and D in third party cases, that may ultimately depend upon the circumstances as between C and the third party, and as between the third party and D, but it is the overall quality of the relationship between C and D which determines the issue.

To reiterate, it is the legal proximity *between C and D* of which the court must be satisfied – but in seeking to establish that, the relationship between the 'sides of the triangle', i.e., D's relationship with TP, and TP's closeness with C, will be relevant. The following proximity factors have been regarded in the leading cases as being relevant, although none of them is conclusive or definitive – it is a 'balancing act':

i. The degree of control. The control that D can feasibly exercise over TP's actions is highly relevant to the establishment of a duty of care.

On the one hand, where TP is *detained* or within D's physical control, and then harms C, that is more likely to give rise to a duty of care on D's part. In *Dorset Yacht*, the relationship of D and C was jailor–custodian, and entailed one of close supervision and control over TP, the Borstal boys.

On the other hand, if TP is living in the community, or was never within D's detention in the first place, then the degree of D's control over TP lessens considerably, and a duty of care is less likely. In *Palmer v Tees HA*, the involuntary detention of murderer Shaun Armstrong (TP) was not an option, given the 'considerable restrictions' which applied to the procedure – and it would have had 'doubtful effectiveness' in any event, given the time that elapsed between the confessions by TP of his violent fantasies and the murder of Rosie Palmer, C. This indicated that it would be 'unwise to hold that there is sufficient proximity'. In *Hill v CC of West Yorkshire Police*, it was a key factor, against a duty of care, that the control over TP that was evident in *Dorset Yacht* was 'lacking. Sutcliffe was never in the custody of the police force',[152] and a similar point was made, of Miss Michael's killer, in *Michael v South Wales Police*, that he was never in the police's control.[153] In *Thomson v Scottish Ministers*[154] too, Mr Campbell was on home leave from prison and not in custody at the time of C's murder, reducing the extent of D's control.

ii. The capacity to warn or protect C. If D could reasonably have warned C directly, to safeguard C against the resultant harm that befell him at the hands of a dangerous TP, but D failed to take any such steps, that will be highly relevant to the duty of care enquiry.

On the one hand, in some cases, the threat has been a long-standing one, and proximity is more likely then. In *Van Colle v CC of Hertfordshire Police; Smith v CC of Sussex Police*, the police were in a legally proximate relationship with Mr Smith, C, given that the police were aware of the repeated threats of serious violence which had been made by Gareth Jeffrey, TP, towards C. An arguable relationship of proximity was also present in *Osman v Ferguson*, on much the same basis. In both cases, however, no duty of care was upheld, for policy reasons. In *Michael v South Wales Police*, the threat to Miss Michael, C, was much more immediate, following the 999 call that was misdirected; but the majority was not prepared to accept that the police's capacity

152 [1989] AC 53 (HL) 62.
153 [2015] UKSC 2, [99], [131] (Lord Toulson, for the majority).
154 [2013] CSIH 63, [52].

to protect C generated a proximate relationship (although it must be said that the majority's core reasoning was based upon policy reasons, and a lack of an assumption of responsibility, both of which were considered in Chapter 2).

On the other hand, wherever C was a member of the public who happened to be in the wrong place at the wrong time, then the ability for D to provide warnings to C is likely to have been practically impossible, and this will militate against a duty of care being imposed. In *Mitchell*,[155] the Council had no duty to warn Mr Mitchell of the dangers posed by Mr Drummond, his co-tenant, for policy reasons (Lord Hope remarked that C 'very properly accepted that he could not present his argument on this basis'). The inability of the Tees HA's psychiatrists to warn C was also a significant factor that precluded a duty of care in *Palmer v Tees HA*: Stuart-Smith LJ asked,'what [could D] ... have done to avoid the danger?'.[156] They could not have warned the family of every child living in the vicinity of where Shaun Armstrong lived; and once released into community care, then any form of warning to potential victims ranged between 'doubtful effectiveness' and utterly infeasible: 'the most effective precaution cannot be undertaken as [D] does not know who to warn'.

The lack of any capacity on D's part to warn C will not automatically preclude a duty of care, however – e.g., in *Carmarthenshire CC v Lewis*, lorry driver Mr Lewis was the unlucky and courageous driver who took action to avoid hitting David in the street, and yet he was owed a duty of care by the kindergarten.

iii. The knowledge of TP's propensities. Where D has an information monopoly about TP, which C could not possibly know about, then that factor *may* render C 'vulnerable' – both because TP had that particular propensity, and D was aware of it and was in a position to do something about curtailing it. In *Dorset Yacht*, the Borstal officers' knowledge of the propensities of the Borstal boys to seek to escape, and of the damage that they might do to property during that escape, has already been adverted to.[157] A close knowledge of the various threats posed by TP also existed, on D's part, in *Selwood v Durham CC*, *Osman v Ferguson* and *Van Colle/Smith*. Proximity was made out in all three cases.

However, just because D did have some sort of information monopoly about TP – about which the unsuspecting C knows nothing, and simply cannot ascertain for himself from any other source – is not, by any means, conclusive. For example, the admission by Shaun Armstrong to his psychiatrist that he felt driven to sexually abuse a young child in an interview prior to his release was known only to D, yet no duty of care was owed in *Palmer*. The very nature of several of the relationships in third party cases – prison authority, healthcare, educational authority – will inevitably mean that D holds information about the propensities to violence or unpredictability of TP which were not known to external parties, including C. Hence, arguably D's monopoly on information about TP should not be a weighty factor in the matrix of proximity factors.

Where D knew nothing of TP's propensities at all, then most likely that will preclude any proximity arising – demonstrated, e.g., in *Hill v West Yorkshire Police*, where Lord Keith noted that, 'the identity of the wanted criminal [Peter Sutcliffe] was, at the material time, unknown, and it is not averred that any full or clear description of him was ever available'.[158]

155 [2009] UKHL 11, [29].

156 [1999] EWCA Civ 1533, [32], cf. the mechanic who fails to fix brakes, per Stuart-Smith LJ at [24]–[25].

157 See above, under 'reasonable foreseeability'.

158 [1989] AC 53 (HL) 62.

iv. **Temporal and geographic proximity.** A lack of temporal proximity between D's alleged breach, and the harm suffered by C, has proven to be a fairly significant factor against a duty of care – especially in those cases in which TP wreaks havoc and causes tragedy some considerable time after D's alleged breach. Moreover, the fact that the harm done by TP occurred at a place which was geographically remote from D's province of control has been specifically noted in some third party cases to militate against any duty of care being owed. For example, in *Palmer* (where the murder of Rosie Palmer occurred just over a year after D's release of Shaun Armstrong), Pill LJ observed that 'the passage of time and distance' between the two events meant that no duty of care could be owed.[159]

In *Lewis*, Mr Lewis's accident occurred on a road adjacent to the kindergarten, whose breach of perimeter security arrangements had allowed little David to 'escape' onto the road. In *Dorset Yacht*, too, the damage to C's yacht happened in close temporal proximity to the alleged breach (of failing to supervise adequately the Borstal boys), and in close geographical proximity too – albeit that Lord Pearson remarked, '[i]n other cases, a difficult problem may arise as to how widely the "neighbourhood" extends, but no such problem faces [C] in this case'.[160] The temporal and geographic proximity between attack and school hours was also significant in *Webster v Ridgeway Foundation School*, in upholding a duty of care: 'the attack on Henry took place after the end of the school day, but that is not necessarily decisive as to the end of a school's duty towards its pupils, particularly as [C] was still on school premises at the time'.[161]

Even so, in *Thomson v Scottish Ministers*,[162] John Campbell murdered C within three days of his release, but that close temporal proximity was not sufficient to fix D with a duty of care.

v. **Relational proximity.** In some third party cases, there is a close relational proximity between C and D – and where existing, this **may** assist to prove a duty of care.

In *Webster*, the relationship between pupil Henry Webster, C, and his school, D, justified that outcome in part – '[t]here is a relationship of proximity in the school/pupil relationship, at least while the pupils are on the school's premises'.[163] Similarly, in *Merthyr Tydfil County BC v C*,[164] the mother of children A and B had contacted the Council, D, twice, to report of the suspected abuse, and that report assisted to support an arguable duty of care on D's part. Even in *Mitchell v Glasgow CC*, the House of Lords accepted that there was a relationship of proximity between Mr Mitchell, the murdered Council tenant, and the Council itself, given that he was their tenant, and so too was Mr Drummond, who lived next door. D accepted that they had a responsibility for the situation that had arisen, being landlord to both C and TP, and that they had taken steps to address TP's anti-social behaviour. All of this gave rise to an arguable relational proximity between C and D – but policy reasons precluded a duty of care there, ultimately.

vi. **Knowledge of C's identity.** If D knows the identity of C who is at risk from TP's acts before the threat materialises, that is not sufficient, *of itself*, to fix the relationship between D and C with the requisite proximity to base a duty of care. It is not an automatic proposition of law that D owes a duty to a pre-identified victim.

This is clearly illustrated by several appellate decisions: by *Michael v South Wales Police*, where Miss Michael's identity could not have been plainer, given her 999 call; by *Mitchell v Glasgow*

[159] [1999] EWCA Civ 1533, [2000] PIQR P1, 19. [160] [1970] AC 1004 (HL) 1055.
[161] [2010] EWHC 157 (QB), [2010] ELR 694, [116]. [162] [2013] CSIH 63, [45]–[50].
[163] [2010] EWHC 157 (QB), [118]. [164] [2010] EWHC 62 (QB), [2010] PIQR P9, [36].

CC, where the public housing authority well knew of Mr Drummond's long-standing hatred for Mr Mitchell; by *Osman*, where the police knew of the deep resentment felt by Mr Paget-Lewis towards the Osman family; and by *Van Colle* too, where the police knew of the dangerous threats made by Gareth Jaffrey to Stephen Smith. In *Palmer v Tees HA* also,[165] Pill LJ posed the hypothetical example, that a psychotic patient says, 'after release from this mental facility, I will kill Y'. His Lordship 'saw force' in the argument that whether the identity of a victim 'is known *ought not* to determine whether the proximity test is passed' – and so subsequent decisions have demonstrated.

However, just because D does not know the identity of C, as a pre-identified individual, does not preclude a duty of care from being owed in third party cases. *Dorset Yacht* is a prime example: the Borstal officers did not know the identities of the yacht owners whose property the Borstal boys trashed, and yet, the officers owed a duty of care to them.

In any event, proximity is a nuanced enquiry. Even if TP were to say to D, 'I'm going to kill Y after I'm out of here', other factors – geographic and temporal proximity, the degree of control over TP, the ability to take precautions to prevent the harm to C, or to warn C – will also be highly relevant to the proximity enquiry. Some of these may well offset the fact that the identity of the unfortunate victim was known to D. In *Palmer*, Pill LJ's example may have been only hypothetical, but in each of *Osman*, *Van Colle/Smith* and *Mitchell*, the victims were killed by TPs whose propensities for violence were well known to relevant public authorities, and where the victims were also well known to D before the horrific events occurred. Ultimately, no duty of care was owed in any of them.

vii. **An identifiable class, or 'at special risk'.** Even where D did not know of C as a pre-identified victim, D may owe a duty of care, if C was one of an identifiable class *at special risk* from TP.

In *Osman v Ferguson*, the Osman family were exposed to a special risk from Mr Paget-Lewis, TP, over and above that of the public at large (said the court), thereby giving rise to 'an arguable case' that there was a 'very close degree of proximity, amounting to a special relationship', between the Osman family and the police investigating officers (albeit that policy reasons militated against a duty of care). In *Dorset Yacht*, the owners whose yachts were moored off Brownsea Island were in a class that was considered to be at special risk too. In *Selwood v Durham CC*,[166] the Court of Appeal was not prepared to hold that C, the stabbed social worker, was a member of the general public *per se*: she 'was not one of the world at large; she was one of a small group of social workers, working in close proximity and cooperation' with both local authority and health authority (plus she was the one who was the subject of TP's threats, and hence, was in a 'special position'). That also pointed (said the Court of Appeal) to an assumption of responsibility on the health authority's part towards C, because it had, via the joint protocol, assumed responsibility to do what was reasonable to reduce or avoid any foreseeable risk of harm to which an employee of those co-signatories was exposed, in the course of dealing with patients of the Crisis Resolution Team (such as Mr Burton). In some respects, C was almost treated as a 'quasi-employee', because of the joint protocol.

On the other hand, if C was merely one of the vast public who was at risk from TP, with no distinguishing feature separating C from the public (apart from the fact that C was the one

165 [1999] EWCA Civ 1533, [2000] PIQR P1 (CA) P19.

166 [2012] EWCA Civ 979, [54] (Dame Janet Smith).

harmed), then no requisite proximity will be found. Being in the wrong place at the wrong time does not put C at special risk. As admitted in *Hill v CC of West Yorkshire*, 'Miss Hill was one of a vast number of the female general public who might be at risk from TP's activities but was at no special distinctive risk in relation to them, unlike the owners of yachts moored off Brownsea Island'.[167] In modern case law, proving that C was at 'special risk' has become seemingly more difficult. In *Thomson v Scottish Ministers*,[168] C sought to argue that she was at special risk, precisely because she was within the group of persons that Mr Campbell was likely to 'have dealings with' during his home leave, given her close association with his family. However, she was not – and the Scottish Inner House was at pains to distinguish that other leading prisons case of *Dorset Yacht*, noting that it may have been from another era, and that 'the law has moved on' since that 1970 decision; that *Dorset Yacht* was a product of the wider 'foreseeability + no public policy reasons' test of *Anns v Merton London BC*;[169] and that it may be that the decision is limited to those persons 'having property in physical proximity to the place where the prisoners were confined'. Yet, however, neither the victims in *Hill* nor in *Palmer* knew their attackers; Catherine Thomson did, but that was not sufficient to fix proximity either, as she was treated as being a member of the general public. On the *Thomson* court reasoning, the only party likely to have been at special risk was Mr Campbell's mother, with whom he was residing. This grouping of cases does not favour a wide construction of 'at special risk'.

Certainly, it is *Palmer's* ongoing legacy that any 'special risk' that turns upon a targeted demographic is going to be difficult to establish. The class of children, of whom Rosie Palmer was one, did not constitute sufficient 'at special risk' status for that victim – notwithstanding that she lived in close geographic proximity to Shaun Armstrong and closely fitted the profile of those at risk from his violent sexual fantasies. In this regard, the hypothetical example provided by Cory J in the Canadian case of *Smith v Jones* ('it may be sufficient to engage the duty to warn if a class of victims, such as little girls under five living in a specific area, is clearly identified [rather than a specific individual]'[170]) is entirely distinguishable from, and does not represent, current English law. In fact, many other proximity factors counted against Rosie Palmer's claim too – the outpatient setting, the lack of temporal or physical proximity, the lack of control over TP Shaun Armstrong and the inability to warn the Palmers. Also, the class of whom the little girl was one was too large to sit comfortably with most other English jurisprudence concerning third party claims – *K* and *Hill* being other leading examples.

The notable exception – where a wider view was adopted – is the pre-*Caparo* decision of *Lewis v Carmarthenshire CC*.[171] Mr Lewis was a member of the public who was at no special risk from David's wanderings, and yet a duty of care was owed to him. That decision rested on the test of reasonable foreseeability, well before proximity and public policy were adopted as such strong 'control mechanisms' in *Caparo*. Nowadays, *Lewis* would probably be considered to be at the very limits of third party liability. However, the decision may be reconciled on the basis that Mr Lewis fell within an identifiable class of persons (nearby road-users to the kindergarten), and furthermore, he was within close temporal and physical proximity to TP *at the time of the kindergarten's breach*, and on that basis too, he was distinguishable from the general public because he was in heightened danger.

[167] [1989] AC 53 (HL) 62. [168] [2013] CSIH 63, [45]–[58]. [169] [1978] AC 728 (HL) 751.
[170] [1999] 1 SCR 455, [59]. [171] [1955] AC 549 (HL).

To summarise the proximity factors in some leading third party cases:

Factor	*Dorset*	*Lewis*	*Hill*	*Palmer*
degree of control which D exercised over TP	yes	yes	no	no
those Cs within geographical proximity to D	yes	yes	–	no
D's knowledge of TP's propensities	yes	yes	no	yes
temporal proximity	yes	yes	–	no
C at special risk	yes	?	no	no

Additionally, if C is harmed or killed by TP, a number of policy reasons may negate a duty of care too.

Whether policy favours, or disfavours, a duty of care

§3.15 Policy reasons may preclude any duty being cast on D, to avoid or to minimise injury to C caused by a dangerous or unpredictable third party.

In *Mitchell v Glasgow CC*,[172] Lord Brown noted that, 'there will be very few occasions on which a bare duty by A *to warn* B of possible impending violence by C will arise'. Even where *a failure to control* is the central allegation of breach, there have been many policy reasons raised against that type of duty too.

There are, of course, exceptional cases where a duty of care was held to be owed by D to C, for the criminal acts of TPs – *Dorset Yacht*[173] being one example. However, there were strong proximity factors in favour of imposing a duty (e.g., geographical and temporal proximity between Brownsea Island and the moored yachts, a close jailor–custodian relationship of control between D and TP), and in addition, it was another of the pre-*Caparo* decisions where the focus was on the requirement of reasonable foreseeability, rather than the other *Caparo* requirements which have become more prominent in third party cases since.

Notably, the many and varied policy reasons as to why no duty of care was imposed upon the Council in *Mitchell* are powerful indicators as to why English law is arguably becoming far more conservative (and pro-D), in respect of third party cases, than was the case pre-*Caparo*.

Before turning to these, however, it is worth noting one factor that is completely **irrelevant** to the duty of care analysis – and that is the gravity of injury that C suffers at the hands of TP. The very fact that C suffers death or some terrible personal injury does not assist to impose a duty on D. Both *K*[174] and *Palmer*[175] confirmed that proposition.

i. **An omission to act.** As discussed in Chapter 2, English law is notoriously hesitant to impose a duty, where the rubric of the allegation is that D failed to act to prevent harm befalling C. The alleged wrong on D's part in many of these third party cases is an omission – and some cases have made something of that, in denying that any duty of care was owed. For example, Lord

172 [2009] UKHL 11, [2009] 2 WLR 481, [81], [83] (emphasis added).

173 [1970] AC 1004 (HL).

174 [2002] EWCA Civ 775, [29]–[30].

175 [2000] PNLR 87 (CA) 108.

Brown remarked, in *Mitchell*,[176] that 'the contention that the Council was under a positive duty to warn [Mr Mitchell], and that the Council is liable for [Mr Mitchell's] death because of a mere omission to do so, appears to me plainly unsustainable'.

Obversely, D's positive acts are often referred to, to support a duty of care. For example, in *Merthyr Tydfil County BC v C*,[177] the court noted that C, the mother of the abused children A and B, 'relies upon failings by the Council of commission as well as omission', *viz*, that the Council assigned the same social worker to her family as to the abuser's family, and denied that any report was made following the 2002 complaint. These positive acts assisted to find a duty of care, sufficient to deny a strike-out application.

ii. The practical problems of imposing a duty to warn. In *Mitchell*, Lord Hope set out many policy grounds militating against a duty to warn being imposed upon the Council[178] (drawing on *Van Colle*[179] and others[180]).

The policy reasons against a duty to warn, in third party cases

- ***the beneficiaries of the duty?*** To whom would the duty to warn be owed? Others in the neighbourhood (other than Mr Mitchell) had complained to the Glasgow CC about D's behaviour too. Any duty would be owed to all of them – or none. The size of the class of threatened potential victims could be problematical;
- ***a burdensome duty:*** a duty to warn is not necessarily a one-off message – D, as landlords, would need to decide whether, and when, a warning should be given. Paradoxically, 'the more attentive they were to their ordinary duties [regarding the dangerous TP], the more onerous the duty to warn others would become' for D; as intervening would bring about awareness and control;
- ***defensive practices and delay:*** D might have to defer taking protective steps until the warning had been received by everyone, and an opportunity given for it to be acted on. Also, D 'would be likely to create a practice of giving warnings as a matter of routine. Many of them would be for no good purpose, while others would risk causing undue alarm'. They could also risk losing their effect, if given widely.

iii. Resource diversion. The problem of resources being diverted to deal with, prepare for, and defend litigious proceedings, was raised in the context of the *Hill* core principle concerning suits against the police (per *Hill v CC of West Yorkshire Police*) (as discussed in Chapter 2).

The same policy reason has arisen in third party cases too – re health practitioners who deal with mentally-ill and violently-inclined patients (per *Palmer v Tees HA*[181]), and re a Council's

[176] [2009] UKHL 11, [2009] 2 WLR 481, [83]. [177] [2010] EWHC 62 (QB), [2010] PIQR P9, [36].

[178] [2009] UKHL 11, [2009] 2 WLR 481, [27]–[28], with other members agreeing: [44] (Lord Scott), [72] (Lord Rodger), [73] (Baroness Hale), [83] (Lord Brown).

[179] [2008] UKHL 50, [2009] 1 AC 225.

[180] e.g., *Hill v CC of West Yorkshire* [1989] AC 53 (HL) 63, 65; *Phelps v Hillingdon LBC* [2001] 2 AC 619 (HL) 672–74; *McFarlane v Tayside Health Board* [2000] 2 AC 59 (HL) 83; *X (Minors) v Bedfordshire CC* [1995] 2 AC 633 (CA) 661–63, and on appeal: [1995] 2 AC 633 (HL) 749–51; *Alexandrou v Oxford* [1993] 4 All ER 328 (CA).

[181] (1998) 45 BMLR 88 (QB) 101–2 (Gage J) (aff'd: [1999] EWCA Civ 1533).

responsibility as a public housing authority: '[it is] desirable too that social landlords, social workers and others who seek to address the many behavioural problems that arise in local authority housing estates and elsewhere, often in very difficult circumstances, should be safeguarded from legal proceedings arising from an alleged failure-to-warn those who might be at risk of a criminal attack in response to their activities. Such proceedings, whether meritorious or otherwise, would involve them in a great deal of time, trouble and expense which would be more usefully devoted to their primary functions in their respective capacities' (per *Mitchell v Glasgow CC*).

iv. **Conflicts of duties.** If to owe a duty of care to C would actually or potentially conflict with D's existing duty to TP, then that conflict of duties will likely preclude a duty to C.

However, if whatever is required of D to discharge his duty to TP would **also** discharge any duty to C, the duties are coincident, and no conflict arises. The case of *Merthyr Tydfil County BC v C*[182] illustrates – Council, D, owed a concurrent duty of care to the mother, as well as to her children A and B; because 'her interests, and the interests of the children, are consonant. Whilst matters may conceivably have proceeded so that there could possibly have arisen a conflict of interest between mother and children – if, e.g., as a result of the alleged failings of the Council, C had been unable to cope with looking after her children, triggering the Council having to consider steps protective of the children – there was not in this case the same potential for conflict'. The court made the point that the mere existence of *potential* conflict 'is not a trump card' in determining whether a duty is owed; 'it is simply one factor which the court must take into account'.

The tactic of proving coincidental duties to C and to TP does not always work, however. The English Court of Appeal was invited to follow this line of reasoning in *Palmer v Tees HA* too[183] – but with a notable lack of success. Mrs Palmer argued that the duty imposed on Tees HA was, not to warn her and Rosie *per se* of the dangers posed by Mr Armstrong, but to provide adequate medical treatment for that TP to reduce the risk of his killing a child, and/or to stop him from being released whilst he posed a risk – which duty *coincided* with the Tees HA's duty to Rosie Palmer to prevent a mentally-ill person in TP's position from murdering her. However, the Court declined to accept this line of argument, and no such duty was owed.

Similarly, where a healthcare practitioner owes a duty of confidentiality to his patient (TP), then any duty to warn C of the potential threat posed by that patient would likely conflict with this duty of confidentiality. In some cases (*viz, W v Egdell*[184] and *R v Crozier*[185]), the scenarios have concerned psychiatrists who *voluntarily* acted to give information about a mentally-ill patient to another, in order to protect the public against that dangerous patient – quite a different context from any legally-imposed **duty** to give that information to protect C. The courts in both *Egdell* and *Crozier* did **not** suggest that a psychiatrist who was treating a violent patient was under *any duty* to inform or protect a potential victim. The issue arose again, however, in the recent case of *ABC v St George's Healthcare NHS Trust.*[186] One of the reasons for denying the existence of any duty of care owed by the medical Ds to ABC, the daughter of their patient who had been diagnosed with Huttington's Disease, was that there was a potential for conflicting

[182] [2010] EWHC 62 (QB), [2010] PIQR P9, [36].

[183] [1999] EWCA Civ 1533, (1998) 39 BMLR 35, [5], [32].

[184] [1990] 1 Ch 359 (CA).

[185] (1990) 8 BMLR 128 (CCA). Cf: *X (HA) v Y* [1988] 2 All ER 648 (QB).

[186] [2015] EWHC 1394 (QB) [26].

duties owed by doctors to patients and to non-patient claimants – for if a duty were upheld, then doctors could be sued by their patient if they disclosed information to aggrieved family members which should have remained confidential. As Nicol J put it,[187] the 'starting point' is that medical D are obliged to respect a patient's confidential information, albeit that this is 'a qualified duty' (given the statutory requirement to report notifiable diseases, e.g.[188]).

v. The size of the class. Where C was not 'at special risk', then by corollary, it is likely that the class of persons of whom C was one was too large for a duty of care to be owed to any member of that class. It raises the spectre of indeterminate liability – derived from Cardozo CJ's famous dicta, 'liability in an indeterminate amount for an indeterminate time to an indeterminate class', per *Ultramares Corporation v Touche.*[189]

Hence, wherever C was in the wrong place at the wrong time, and was genuinely a random member of the public, policy will generally preclude a duty of care – as illustrated, e.g., in *Hill*, *K v Sec of State*, and *Palmer.*[190] In *Dorset Yacht* too, Lord Diplock suggested, dicta, that a prison authority would not owe a duty of care to a member of the public who was the victim of crime from a 'habitual criminal' whom the Home Office had negligently permitted to escape and who caused damage to persons not in close proximity of the escape, but 'in further pursuance of his general criminal career'.

In that regard, in *Caparo*, Lord Oliver distinguished TP cases from cases of negligent driving or product liability: it is 'enough that [C] chances to be (out of the whole world) the person with whom [D] collided, or who purchased the offending ginger beer' – whereas, for TP cases, even where TP causes C physical harm, the requisite 'nexus' between C and D is not obvious.[191] Of course, the exception is the road user class in *Lewis*, which virtually equated to the general public, and yet the unlucky Mr Lewis was owed a duty by the kindergarten. However, *Lewis* was a pre-*Caparo* case which rested upon the principle of reasonable foreseeability – and C was in close temporal and geographic proximity with D at the time of breach.

Notably though, even where C was a pre-identified victim and, hence, within a tiny class of those at risk from TP's conduct, a duty may still be precluded for policy reasons (as, e.g., in *Van Colle* and *Osman*).

The comparative corner: The *Tarasoff* doctrine

In *Tarasoff v The Regents of the University of California,*[192] Prosenjit Poddar (P), a graduate student at University of California (Berkeley campus), had formed a friendly relationship with a fellow student which he took to be a serious romance, but which the young woman, Tatiana Tarasoff (T), did not. As a result, upon learning of T's true feelings, P underwent a severe emotional crisis. He eventually became a voluntary outpatient at the defendant hospital, and confided to the defendant psychotherapist Dr Moore that he intended to kill a friend 'when she returns from Brazil' (T spent the summer in Brazil). From the conversation, T was an unnamed but identifiable person. The therapist and his superiors decided that P should be confined by police. Later, the campus police at Berkeley interviewed P and were

[187] ibid, [17]. [188] e.g., Public Health (Control of Diseases) Act 1984, ss 10,11.
[189] 174 NE 441, 444 (1931). [190] [1999] EWCA Civ 1533.
[191] [1990] 2 AC 605 (HL) 632, citing the lower court: [1989] QB 653 (CA) 686 (Bingham LJ).
[192] 17 Cal 3d 425, 551 P 2d 334, 343, 131 Cal Rptr 14 (Cal 1976).

satisfied that P was rational, could not be involuntarily detained, and released him, on his promise to stay away from T. Neither T nor her parents were informed of the threat made by P. Two months later, P went to T's house and shot and fatally stabbed her. T's parents sued the hospital, doctors and police on behalf of their daughter's estate. **Held:** the actions in negligence could proceed, as a duty of care was arguable.

Comment: It is unlikely that English law would follow *Tarasoff*, where TP, who was known to D to present a threat to C, 'made good' that threat. Dicta in *Palmer*; the outcome of *Osman v Ferguson*; and the policy reasons put forward by the House of Lords in *Van Colle/Smith*, in *Mitchell* and in *Michael*, all strongly point to that outcome, even where the victim was an identified (or a clearly identifiable) individual. The fact that there may be a real risk, a foreseeable risk, of harm to [C] if [D] does not warn [C] is, of course, not conclusive – 'the question is one of fairness and public policy' (per *Mitchell*[193]). This difficulty in even casting the duty (to protect, to warn, or both), and the continuing influence of the 'mere omissions' rule in English law, add to the problem.[194]

vi. Compensation for C via other means. The point was made, in *Webster v Ridgeway Foundation School*, that the Criminal Compensation Fund is a state-provided financial source to provide compensation for those injured by TP's criminal acts – but that does not absolutely preclude a duty of care being owed to C. Otherwise, 'there would never be a duty of care to protect against possible criminally-caused personal injury'.[195]

However, the availability of other avenues of redress was certainly adverted to in *Michael* as one reason not to find a duty of care (the majority referred to the criminal injuries compensation scheme, and actions against the police under the Arts 2, 3 or 8 of the ECHR), with a suggestion that if further redress was required for C, it was up to Parliament, rather than the common law, to provide it.[196]

vii. The implications for other sectors. In *Mitchell v Glasgow CC*,[197] one of the reasons that a duty of care was denied was that the implication of a duty for other cases was 'complex and far reaching' – if a social landlord could be liable to warn a potential victim, then so could a social worker, or any person, who heard threats issued by D against C. Who would not be subject to the duty?

By contrast, in *Selwood v Durham CC*,[198] one of the reasons in favour of a duty towards social worker Mrs Shelwood, C, was that the proceedings in which social workers become involved is inevitably multi-disciplinary, and that 'it was important that social workers who undertook difficult and sometimes dangerous work should be protected, so far as was practicable'. However, the same sympathy is not extended to some vulnerably placed victims of crime whose paths unfortunately crossed with a violently disposed perpetrator – and for whom the *Hill* core principle remains firmly-entrenched. This aspect of *Selwood* is difficult to reconcile with other third party cases in which a duty of care was most assuredly denied.

193 [2009] UKHL 11, [26] (Lord Hope).
194 See further: Mulheron, *Medical Negligence: Non-Patient and Third Party Claims* (Ashgate Publishing, 2010) ch 3.
195 [2010] EWHC 157 (QB) [118]. 196 [2015] UKSC 2, [130].
197 [2009] UKHL 11, [27]. 198 [2012] EWCA Civ 979, [54].

The incremental test

§3.16 The fact that D has not previously been liable to that category of C for the acts or omissions of TP does not preclude a duty of care from arising, but it will invoke the incremental test.

In *Webster v Ridgeway Foundation School*,[199] the court acknowledged that there had not previously been a case in which a school, as D, had been liable to a pupil for personal injury caused by an attack by an outsider on the school premises, and that this 'does bring into operation the injunction that courts should take care to extend duties of care only incrementally'. The closest type of cases had occurred where D had been liable to pupils for harm caused by bullying co-pupils (per *Bradford-Smart v West Sussex CC*[200]), or where pupils were harmed by dangerous drivers outside the school premises. However, to hold that the school owed a duty of care to Henry Webster to protect him from attack by outsiders was sufficiently analogous to uphold a duty on the school's part to take reasonable care to see that Henry was reasonably safe during school hours, and for a reasonable period after the end of the school day, while he was still on the school's premises.

The ECHR angle

Some of the post-2000 cases explored in this section evidenced a multi-pronged type of claim – in negligence, and under the ECHR, for infringement by D of C's Convention rights (e.g., in *Thomson v Scottish Ministers*,[201] both negligence and a claim for infringement of Art 2, the right to life, were instituted – and both failed). Consideration of the ECHR Convention rights, where D is a public authority, is developed in Chapter 13.

Recent cases have shown a possible change of tack by C in third party cases, by eschewing a claim in negligence altogether, and pursuing a claim solely under the ECHR instead. For example, in *Bedford v Bedfordshire CC*,[202] C was brain-damaged by injuries inflicted by children who were in the care of Council D, under the 'looked after child' regime. In an interesting comment, Jay J noted that, '[t]his action is brought solely under the HRA; there is no claim at common law. [C] have taken the view that no duty of care is owed by the defendant local authority in these circumstances ... I should not be interpreted as disagreeing with him. I should add that, in any event, the Claimant would have been in no better position at common law, even had a duty of care been owed, because he would have had to demonstrate that the Defendant took decisions of a policy nature which were wholly unreasonable. The outcome would have been the same, although the route to it would have deviated slightly'. C brought his claim under Art 8 of the ECHR (right to private life), unsuccessfully, as it turned out. More recently, in *DSD v Commr of Police*,[203] C, two victims of the 'black cab rapist', successfully sued under Art 3 (the right not to be subject to inhuman or degrading treatment or punishment) of the ECHR, where the sole allegation was that the police failed to investigate the rape claims to the standard required by Art 3, given a vast array of systemic and operational failings during the long-running investigation of the case.

[199] [2010] EWHC 157 (QB) [118], [121]. [200] [2002] EWCA Civ 7.
[201] [2013] CSIH 63, [36]–[41]. [202] [2013] EWHC 1717 (QB) [12].
[203] [2014] EWHC 436 (QB), aff'd: *Commr of Police v DSD and NBV* [2015] EWCA Civ 646.

4

Duty III – Pure economic loss

INTRODUCTION

Liability for negligently-inflicted financial losses is both complex and challenging. This is due, in part, to the reluctance of English appellate courts to settle upon any **one** test by which to establish whether D owed C a duty of care to avoid the pure economic loss which C suffered.

It is also due, in part, to the sophisticated and 'broad network of economic links that exist in any developed society' (as the Court of Appeal put it in *Conarken Group Ltd v Network Rail Infrastructure Ltd (Rev 1)*[1]). The Scottish Inner House spoke for English law too, when it stated that, '[negligently-inflicted pure economic loss] is a difficult area of the law ... which continues to develop ... as a process of incrementalism' (per *Hines v King Sturge LLP*[2]).

Recovery for pure economic loss also tends to be an area of negligence which is governed to a large extent by policy – which calls to mind that 'unruly horse' of public policy that Burroughs J spoke of in *Richardson v Mellish*,[3] that 'once you get astride it, you never know where it will carry you'. Part of the challenge, in this chapter, is to provide some defined tracks upon which that horse may predictably pass! It should also be mentioned, at the outset, that English law has not adopted a sympathetic approach to pure economic loss claims. Just as with pure psychiatric injury claims (see Chapter 5), casting any duty of care on D's part to avoid such injury can be very challenging.

This chapter explores **four** principal categories of pure economic loss claims:

- negligent misstatements (also called the 'narrow principle in *Hedley Byrne*'[4]);
- the negligent provision of services (also known as the 'extended principle in *Hedley Byrne*');
- pure relational economic loss (also known as the 'exclusionary rule'); and
- pure economic loss arising from defective buildings (an online section).

Before turning to each in turn, it is important to reiterate a couple of preliminary points.

§4.1 Pure economic loss is financial loss which is *not* consequential upon either personal injury or property damage being suffered by C. The only loss suffered by C is the financial loss of which he complains.

Where C suffers some physical injury because of D's breach, then financial expenses may be incurred by C (e.g., loss of earnings in the future, out-of-pocket transport costs to attend

[1] [2011] EWCA Civ 644, [2011] BLR 462, [95]. [2] [2010] CSIH 86, 2011 SLT 2, [45], [50].
[3] (1824) 2 Bing 229, 252. [4] [1964] AC 465 (HL).

medical appointments), which are consequential economic losses. Similarly, where C's property (say, a car) is damaged by D's negligent driving, then repair costs and the hiring costs of another vehicle may be incurred by C – which, again, are consequential.

These types of economic losses are simply added to C's claim, as heads of damage flowing from the original physical or property damage suffered by C. They are not difficult or controversial to recover, provided that they are causally linked to the breach and are not too remote at law. Pure economic losses, however, are stand-alone losses, incurred by C as a result of D's breach.

§4.2 The duty of care owed by D to avoid pure economic losses on C's part is a duty to exercise *reasonable* care. D does not guarantee, nor give a warranty for either a perfect financial outcome for, or the avoidance of economic harm to, C.

In *Patchett v Swimming Pool and Allied Trades Assn*,[5] Lord Clarke MR reiterated that, even if a duty of care were owed by SPATA, D, to an aggrieved pool-owner, C (which was **not** held in that case), D did not make any warranties about the creditworthiness of that Association's members – '[n]o warranty was given. SPATA was saying that, before each member joined, checks were carried out on its financial record and on its experience in the trade, and there were inspections of its work'. Hence, even where a duty is owed, the standard of care is, as always in negligence, merely one of reasonableness, not perfection (per Chapter 6).

NEGLIGENT MISSTATEMENT

Introduction

§4.3 A negligent misstatement means either information or advice given by D, the statement maker, which (1) was inaccurate, (2) was made without a reasonable degree of skill and care about its accuracy, (3) caused C financial loss, (4) was within the province of D's special skill to provide and (5) D undertook to provide for C's benefit, who he knew, or ought to have reasonably foreseen, would be likely to rely upon D's exercising reasonable care in providing that information or advice.

This is known as the *Hedley Byrne* principle (or the 'narrow application of *Hedley Byrne*'[6]).

Elements (1) and (2) of the abovementioned principle pertain to breach (as discussed in Chapter 7), whilst element (3) pertains to causation (Chapter 8). Elements (4) and (5) pertain to the duty of care question, and will comprise the focus of this chapter.

Whether or not a duty of care arises on D's part to avoid economic loss being suffered by C, where C acted on information or advice conveyed by D, does **not** depend upon whether the parties shared a particular formalised relationship, such as solicitor–client, or banker–customer. A duty of care may not even arise in such a case; or conversely, it may arise in relation to a transaction which falls well outside those recognised relationships. Lord Devlin made that plain in *Hedley Byrne & Co Ltd v Heller & Partners Ltd*,[7] and many of the cases in this chapter bear out that sentiment. Indeed, Lord Mance's statement, in *Customs and Excise Commrs v Barclays Bank plc* – that *Hedley Byrne* is 'the fountain of most modern economic claims' in negligence[8] – sets the scene. Its importance in this area of negligence cannot be overstated.

The reference to 'skill', in the abovementioned principle, does **not** necessarily require that D possessed some particular *professional* qualification or expertise. The term is widely construed, and embraces circumstances where D had particular knowledge by virtue of his occupation

[5] [2009] EWCA Civ 717, [29]. [6] Per, e.g., *McLaughlan v Edwards* [2004] Scot SC 31, [7].
[7] [1964] AC 465 (HL). [8] [2006] UKHL 28, [2007] 1 AC 181, [85].

or position. As Lord Goff remarked in *Henderson v Merrett Syndicates Ltd*,[9] the term 'must be understood broadly, certainly broadly enough to include special knowledge'.

Ancillary causes of action

Several other causes of action may be pleaded, simultaneously with negligently-inflicted pure economic loss. For example, breach of contract may be sought, if the negligent provision of advice or information has occurred within the context of a contractual undertaking on D's part which was supported by consideration from C.

Alternatively, if a pre-contractual misstatement induced a contract between C and D, then an action under s 2(1) of the Misrepresentation Act 1967 may be more attractive than an action in negligence, given that there is no need for C to prove the intricacy of the duty of care analysis which follows in this chapter. This advantage was noted recently, by the Supreme Court, in *Cramaso LLP v Ogilvie-Grant, Earl of Seafield (Scotland)*,[10] that s 2(1) was 'a complex provision, which has the effect of dispensing with the need to establish a duty of care in English law'. The statutory misrepresentation only requires that C prove: the representation was made by D; it was intended to be relied upon; it was in fact relied upon; it was untrue; C entered into a contract in reliance upon the representation; and C suffered loss as a result. C does not need to prove that the representation was made negligently either – it is for D to prove that he had reasonable grounds for believing that the representation was true (per *Laws v Socy of Lloyd's*[11]), thus reversing the burden of proof. Damages awarded are likely to be better under the Act too, given that all actual loss directly flowing from the transaction induced by D is compensable (i.e., the measure of damages in deceit, rather than the measure of damages in negligence which is discussed in Chapter 11) (per *Pankhania v Hackney*[12]).

Rarely, and only where the evidence supports the allegation, false statements by D may give rise to a claim for fraudulent misrepresentation (i.e., deceit).

> In *Derry v Peek*,[13] C sued the directors of a company, D, in respect of false statements in a prospectus for fraudulent misrepresentation. **Held:** the action failed. D believed that their statements were true, although they had no reasonable grounds for their belief. That could not amount to fraud, as fraud requires dishonesty; mere credulity was not dishonesty.

Breach of fiduciary duty may also arise, where a negligent misstatement occurred (pleaded, but not proven, in the client's action against a solicitor in *Nocton v Lord Ashburton*[14]). However, it does not follow that, just because a fiduciary relationship exists, there necessarily would be a parallel tortious duty of care imposed on D (per *BP plc v AON Ltd*[15]). A fiduciary relationship does not import an assumption of responsibility on D's part sufficient to found a duty of care in tort.

Breaking new ground

The decision in *Hedley Byrne v Heller* in 1964 'broke new ground' for creating liability in negligence for pure economic loss (per *Spring v Guardian Assurance plc*[16]). There could be a 'duty to take care in word, as well as in deed', extending *beyond* scenarios in which C and D were in a contractual or a fiduciary relationship (per *Nocton v Ashburton*), or scenarios of fraud (per *Derry v Peek*).

In *Hedley Byrne*, a claim arose from an *innocent* negligent misrepresentation, involving no privity of contract at all.[17] Lord Devlin described the circumstances which could give rise to a duty of care as 'special relationships' – i.e., those which were 'equivalent to contract', and in which D assumed responsibility to avoid economic loss being suffered by C, as a result of negligent information or

[9] [1995] 2 AC 145 (HL) 180. [10] [2014] UKSC 9, [2014] 1 AC 1093, [37]. [11] [2003] EWCA Civ 1887, [86]–[87].
[12] [2004] EWHC 323 (Ch) [17]. [13] (1889) 14 App Cas 337 (HL). [14] [1914] AC 932 (HL).
[15] [2006] EWHC 424 (Comm). [16] [1994] UKHL 7, [1995] 2 AC 296, 317 (Lord Goff).
[17] [1964] AC 465 (HL) 528–29 (Lord Devlin), with quotes in Table at 488–89 (Lord Reid), 509 (Lord Hodson).

advice. It is clear, though, that this area of liability has since actually extended well **beyond** where C and D were in a relationship 'equivalent to contract' – i.e., where factors have indicated that the law recognises a duty of care, but where there are very little indicia of a contractual relationship at all.

Actually, prior to *Hedley Byrne*, English law had taken several twists and turns. The 1893 decision in *Le Lievre v Gould*[18] was called, about a century later in *Caparo Industries plc v Dickman*,[19] a 'wrong turn'. In *Hedley Byrne*, though, 'the law was once more set on the right path'.

The legal landmarks achieved in *Hedley Byrne*

1888 a requirement that a contractual or a fiduciary relationship was required, for a misstatement to give rise to an action by C, was **not** part of English law. In *Cann v Willson*[a] (where valuer, D, was engaged by the mortgagor to provide a valuation, and the mortgagee, C, relied upon it to his detriment), D was negligent – because D sent the valuation directly to C, to induce C to lend the money, and D 'knowingly had placed themselves in that position'. But twists followed:

1889 in *Derry v Peek*,[b] the court held that '[t]o found an action for damages [for misrepresentation], there must be a contract and breach, or fraud'

1893 in *Le Lievre v Gould*,[c] the court held that, 'in the absence of contract, an action for negligence cannot be maintained when there is no fraud'. However, both statements in *Derry v Peek* and *Le Lievre* were bad law, according to *Hedley Byrne* – as Lord Reid put it baldly, *Le Lievre* was 'wrong in limiting the duty of care with regard to statements to cases where there is a contract';

> Mr Gould, D, a surveyor, provided stage-of-completion certificates about a building project to lenders, C, who, relying on these, advanced monies to a builder, their mortgagor. The certificates contained negligent statements. D was not appointed by lenders C, so there was no contractual relationship between them. In fact, D knew nothing about the lenders or the terms of their mortgage with the builder. **Held:** D owed no duty to C to exercise care in giving his certificates. No liability arose for negligent misstatement, in the absence of a contract between them.

1914 in *Nocton v Ashburton*, Lord Haldane stated that 'a special duty [of care, re misstatements] may arise from ... an implied contract at law or a fiduciary obligation in equity'[d]

1916 in *Robinson v National Bank of Scotland*, Lord Haldane seemed to retreat from *Nocton*: 'I should be very sorry if any word fell from me which should suggest that courts are in any way hampered in recognising that a duty of care may be established when [special cases] really occur'[e]

1951 the majority decision in *Candler v Crane Christmas*[f] was also overruled in *Hedley Byrne*:

> C proposed to invest in a company, and asked to see the company accounts. The company's accountants, D, were requested by the company to prepare accounts, so that they could be shown to C. The accounts, which contained some negligent and misleading statements, were provided to C. **Held (majority):** no duty of care was owed by D to C (following *Le Lievre v Gould*). Given that the contract was between D and the company, and not with C, there could be no liability for the negligent misstatement. Nor was there any fiduciary relationship between them. **Denning LJ (dissenting):** *Le Lievre* was distinguishable, because here, D knew that C was relying on its skill and judgment, and why C wanted to see the accounts. In *Le Lievre*, the lender's existence/identity was not known to surveyor, Mr Gould. In *Hedley Byrne*, Lord Hodson noted that Denning LJ's dissenting judgment 'was to be preferred to that of the majority, although the opinion of the majority was undoubtedly supported by the ratio of*Le Lievre*, which they could not be criticised for following'.

[a] (1888) 39 Ch D 39, 42 (Chitty J). [b] (1889) 14 App Cas 337 (HL) 347 (Lord Bramwell).
[c] [1893] 1 QB 491 (CA) 498 (Lord Esher). [d] [1914] AC 932 (HL) 955. [e] 1916 SC (HL) 154, 157. [f] [1951] 2 KB 164.

[18] [1893] 1 QB 491 (CA). [19] [1990] 2 AC 605 (HL) 619.

Framework

A convenient framework for an analysis of this area of negligence law is as follows:

Nutshell analysis: Negligent misstatement

Identify whether C and D are in a bi-partite scenario, a tri-partite scenario, or a victim scenario

Proving a duty of care – a checklist:

1. Reasonable foreseeability of economic loss
2. An assumption of responsibility by D/a reciprocal reliance by C (the *Hedley Byrne* test); OR sufficient proximity and public policy to found a duty of care (the *Caparo* test)
3. The incremental test justified a duty of care being owed by D
4. Factors which do not preclude a duty of care

The rest of the negligence action, as per usual

Dealing with each in turn:

Reasonable foreseeability of economic loss

§4.4 D must have actually foreseen (i.e., appreciated) – or alternatively, should have reasonably foreseen – that his failure to exercise reasonable care and/or skill when giving information or advice could cause economic loss to C.

Proving reasonable foreseeability of the financial loss suffered by C is 'fundamental' to liability (per *McCullagh v Lane Fox & Partners*[20]), but it is **not** sufficient to establish a duty of care to avoid such damage. In *White v Jones*,[21] Lord Browne-Wilkinson stated that, '[t]he law of England does not impose any general duty of care to avoid negligent misstatements or to avoid causing pure economic loss, even if economic damage to [C] was foreseeable'.

In this context, the meaning of loss being 'reasonably foreseeable' is precisely the same as under the general principles of duty of care (see Chapter 2).

Indeed, it is difficult to identify a case in which the economic loss suffered by C was held to be unforeseeable (particularly given the importance of choosing the relevant D appropriately, as the facts of *Islington LBC v UCL Hosp NHS Trust*,[22] discussed in Chapter 2, demonstrated). Even in cases where proximity was doubtful, and policy dictated against a duty of care being owed, foreseeability was confidently proven (per, e.g., *Arrowhead Capital Finance Ltd v KPMG LLP*[23]). For example, in *Caparo Industries plc v Dickman*,[24] the House of Lords held that it may have been highly foreseeable that a potential bidder for a company might rely on audited accounts prepared by D – but that 'did not suffice to found a duty of care' (and indeed, both lack of proximity and policy precluded a duty of care there). Lord Oliver, in particular, thought the criterion almost useless, in economic loss cases, as placing any restrictions on a

[20] [1995] EWCA Civ 8, (1995) 49 Con LR 124, 225. [21] [1995] 2 AC 207 (HL) 274.
[22] [2005] EWCA Civ 596, [15]–[16]. [23] [2012] EWHC 1801 (Comm) [59].
[24] [1990] 2 AC 605 (HL), with quotes at 643.

duty of care from arising: 'it is almost always foreseeable that someone, somewhere and in some circumstances, may choose to alter his position upon the faith of the accuracy of a statement or report which comes to his attention and it is always foreseeable that a report – even a confidential report – may come to be communicated to persons other than the original or intended recipient'. It followed that, to rely only on a test of reasonable foreseeability of possible economic damage, 'without some further control, would be to create a liability wholly indefinite in area, duration and amount and would open up a limitless vista of uninsurable risk for the professional man'.

Hence, proximity, assumptions of responsibility, reliance, and policy reasons, all combine to circumscribe D's liability in this area of negligence.

The *Hedley Byrne*, *Caparo* and incremental tests

Inter-relationship between the three tests

§4.5 The same three broad approaches, or 'tests', as for personal injury or property damage, have been adopted, in order to assess whether a duty of care is owed by D in respect of negligent misstatement. They are generally assessed in the following order of analysis: (1) the *Hedley Byrne* test; (2) the *Caparo* test; and (3) the incremental 'cross-check' test.

Where negligent misstatement is concerned, the House of Lords has opined – in *Henderson v Merrett Syndicates Ltd*,[25] and subsequently in *Customs and Excise Commrs v Barclays Bank plc*[26] – that the *Hedley Byrne* assumption of responsibility/reliance test is the primary test, rather than the tri-partite *Caparo* test.[27] Where D assumed responsibility in providing advice or information to an identified (or identifiable) party who relied upon D's skill and expertise, it is generally unnecessary to consider the *Caparo* test, because the requisite relationship necessary to give rise to a duty of care will already exist between D and C. Lord Goff pointed out, in *Henderson*,[28] that satisfying the *Hedley Byrne* test will not expose D to liability to the whole world, or to an indeterminate (i.e., open-ended) class of Cs. Such policy reasons fall away. In *Customs and Excise*, Lord Hoffmann also noted that the assumption of responsibility test suited best where D provided the information or advice, knowing that it would be relied upon by someone else (whether the immediate contracting party or some identifiable third party).

However, where C is not an identified or identifiable party – and the *Hedley Byrne* test becomes more difficult to meet, other than in a 'deemed' or 'notional' fashion – then the *Caparo* test should be applied, including a detailed assessment of its third, policy-based, limb. To instance, the prospect of indeterminate liability will figure large, in precluding a duty of care, where D's statement or advice has been put into general circulation, and could be relied upon by numerous strangers to D and for many purposes, all of which D 'had no specific reason to anticipate' (per Lord Bridge in *Caparo*[29]). (In this chapter, 'indeterminate liability' will be used in circumstances where that one D could be exposed to an unknown number of Cs arising from D's act or omission, whereas the 'floodgates' problem will be used to denote the situation where, because of the 'precedential effect' of a finding of negligence against D, then so too could many others, in similarly-instituted suits in the future.)

Under this approach, the order is quite clear-cut: 'one may seek assumption of responsibility and, if it is not found, go back to the *Caparo* tripartite test'.[30] The most authoritative statement

[25] [1995] 2 AC 145 (HL). [26] [2006] UKHL 28, [2007] 1 AC 181. [27] [1990] 2 AC 605 (HL) 617–18 (Lord Bridge).
[28] [1995] 2 AC 145 (HL) 180–81. [29] [1990] 2 AC 605 (HL) 620–21.
[30] *Hines v King Sturge LLP* [2009] Scot CS (OH) 96, [44], but outcome overturned on appeal: [2010] CSIH 86.

of this analysis, whether for negligent misstatement or negligent provision of services, was set out in *Customs and Excise*.[31] To summarise:

Per Lords Bingham, Mance and Hoffmann in ***Customs and Excise v Barclays Bank*** (2007):

The test:	Comments about the test:
The **assumption of responsibility test** – has D (the statement maker) assumed responsibility for exercising care and skill in saying what he said, and did C (the loss sufferer) reasonably rely on D so assuming that responsibility?	• the *Hedley Byrne* test is the 'first port of call' – proof of assumption of responsibility, and corresponding reliance, is sufficient for a duty of care to arise (Lord Bingham); • the test is objective, not subjective – it is not what D intended in making the statement, but what the surrounding circumstances (e.g., a professional relationship) and D's conduct indicate, as to whether D assumed responsibility for its reasonable accuracy (Lord Hoffmann); • however, notions of 'deemed' assumption of responsibility stretch the test to 'breaking point' and render the test entirely artificial (Lord Bingham) – this will occur, e.g., where D has no knowledge or awareness of C's existence, let alone identity; and/or where C did not rely on D, because he did not know that D was rendering the service for his benefit; • the absence of any real and true assumption of responsibility does not necessarily disprove a duty of care, but it is then necessary to consider the *Caparo* test (Lords Bingham and Hoffmann).
The ***Caparo*** **test** – (a) Was economic loss to C a foreseeable consequence of D's statement? (b) Were C and D legally proximate? (c) Is it fair, just and reasonable to impose a duty on D?	• this test is to be used when there is no real and true assumption of responsibility on the facts; • in that event, the task is to analyse whether 'the features of different specific situations [is one] which, on a detailed examination of all the circumstances, the law recognises pragmatically as giving rise to a duty of care of a given scope' (per Lord Bridge[a]).
The **incremental test** – the law should develop novel categories of negligence by analogy with established categories/cases, rather than by massive extension of principle	• the test has little value as a 'stand-alone' test, but is to be used as 'an important cross-check', to verify whether the proposed result is fairly close to an already-decided scenario regarding pure economic loss (Lord Mance); • the closer the facts of the case are to one in which a duty of care has been already held to exist, the more likely a duty, and vice versa (Lord Bingham). Courts prefer to 'hug the coastline' of previously-decided cases.

[a] [1990] 2 AC 605 (HL) 618.

[31] [2006] UKHL 28, [2007] 1 AC 181, with points in the Table locatable at: [4]–[8] (Lord Bingham), [36]–[37], (Lord Hoffmann), [87]–[88], [93] (Lord Mance).

However, the three tests are not, strictly speaking, easily distinguishable from each other – and nor should they be. There can feasibly be a great deal of overlap. In earlier cases (e.g., in *Henderson v Merrett Syndicates Ltd*[32]), it was suggested that if the *Hedley Byrne* 'special relationship' was established, then 'there should be no need to embark upon any further enquiry whether it is "fair, just and reasonable" to impose liability for economic loss'. However, since then, and even in the intervening period since *Customs and Excise* was decided, the tests tend to be discussed, and applied, quite interchangeably by first-instance courts (per, e.g., *Khambay v Nijhar (t/a Gravitas Consulting)*[33]). What may show a strong degree of reliance by C under the *Hedley Byrne* test also assists to prove the requisite proximity between C and D under the second limb of *Caparo*. Lord Mance noted, in *Customs and Excise*, that '[t]he concept of assumption of responsibility ... may effectively subsume all aspects of the threefold [*Caparo*] approach', and that 'there is no single common denominator, even in cases of economic loss, by which liability may be determined'.[34] In *Merrett v Babb*,[35] May LJ also acknowledged that the two tests relevant to proving a duty to avoid causing foreseeable economic loss were not necessarily distinct:

> two strands of consideration emerged. These may for convenience be called the *Caparo* strand and the *Henderson [adopting the Hedley Byrne]* strand. The *Caparo* strand asks whether, in addition to foreseeability, there is a sufficient relationship of proximity and whether the imposition of a duty of care is fair, just and reasonable. The *Henderson* strand asks whether [D] is to be taken to have assumed responsibility to [C] to guard against the loss for which damages are claimed. The difficulty with the *Caparo* strand is that it is sometimes seen as being unhelpfully vague. The difficulty with the *Henderson* strand is that it was originally often expressed in terms of 'voluntary assumption of responsibility' which tended to import a degree of subjectivity. *Henderson* itself put paid to that ... that responsibility is recognised or imposed by the law. Thus, the *Caparo* strand and the *Henderson* strand, in reality, merge. In my view, it is very often a helpful guide to ask whether [D] is to be taken to have assumed responsibility to [C] to guard against the loss for which damages are claimed. But I also think that it is reaching for the moon – and not required by authority – to expect to accommodate every circumstance which may arise within a single short abstract formulation.

Very rarely will D give an **express** undertaking, written or oral, to C, to exercise reasonable care and skill to protect C against any economic loss arising from D's endeavours ('extremely unlikely in the ordinary course of events': said Lord Griffiths in *Smith v Eric S Bush*[36]). Of those cases, Lord Devlin noted, in *Hedley Byrne*, that 'there can be little difficulty. The difficulty arises in discerning those cases in which the undertaking is to be *implied*'.[37] The most important task, regardless of whether it is the *Caparo* or the *Hedley Byrne* test which is being applied, is to search for **facts and circumstances** which would show that such an undertaking (and concomitant reliance) were implied.

Notably, Lord Hoffmann reiterated in *Customs and Excise* that labels are often bandied about, when discussing whether an 'assumption of responsibility', 'reliance', or 'fair, just and reasonable', are proven. However, the **only** way to properly assess that question is to

32 [1995] 2 AC 145 (HL) 181 (Lord Goff).

33 [2015] EWHC 190 (QB) [96]–[99]. Also: *Barclays Bank v Grant Thornton UK LLP* [2015] EWHC 320 (Comm) [49]; *Sebry v Companies House (Rev 1)* [2015] EWHC 115 (QB) [110].

34 [2006] UKHL 28, [2007] 1 AC 181, [93].

35 [2001] EWCA Civ 214, [2001] QB 1174, [41].

36 [1990] 1 AC 831 (HL) 862.

37 [1964] AC 465 (HL) 528–29.

descend to a close examination of the facts, and to infuse the assessment with policy considerations too:

> There is a tendency ... for phrases like 'proximate', 'fair, just and reasonable' and 'assumption of responsibility', to be used as slogans rather than practical guides to whether a duty should exist or not. These phrases are often illuminating but discrimination is needed to identify the factual situations in which they provide useful guidance ... Because the question of whether D has assumed responsibility is a legal inference to be drawn from his conduct against the background of all the circumstances of the case, it is by no means a simple question of fact. Questions of fairness and policy will enter into the decision, and it may be more useful to try to identify these questions than simply to bandy terms like 'assumption of responsibility' and 'fair, just and reasonable'.[38]

Lord Bingham noted, similarly, that it requires 'attention on the detailed circumstances of the particular case, and the particular relationship between the parties in the context of their legal and factual situation as a whole'.[39]

In that regard, in the following section of scenarios, the leading cases are each accompanied by a 'factors box', which draws out the salient factors which were used to assess whether the *Hedley Byrne* and *Caparo* tests were proven, on the particular facts in question. The cases have been chosen to demonstrate a wide array of salient factors. As always, the court must undertake a balancing exercise of 'key competing factors' (as the court stated, and tackled recently, in *Barclays Bank plc v Grant Thornton UK LLP*[40]). In most difficult and novel scenarios giving rise to pure economic loss, not all of the relevant factors will point one way or the other; not all of them are to be given the same weight in every scenario; and none is necessarily conclusive.

As a final note on the incremental test, novel cases in pure economic loss still arise. In 2009, in *Patchett v SPATA Ltd*,[41] the Court of Appeal considered, for the first time, whether D could owe a duty of care, with respect to statements put up on a trade association website; while in 2012, a case was brought by a police informant for pure economic loss (*An Informer v Chief Constable*[42]) which had never been considered by an English court before, and where, as Toulson LJ reiterated, '[t]he fact that this is a novel claim is not necessarily fatal because the categories of negligence are never closed'. In neither case could C point to any case reasonably analogous in which a similar duty had been imposed on D (and, hence, no duty arose).

§4.6 An action for pure economic loss arising from negligent misstatement can come about via three different scenarios: (1) bi-partite relationships, where D provides the information or advice to C directly, and C relies on that information or advice to his detriment; (2) tri-partite relationships, where D provides the information or advice to X, and C relies upon that information or advice to his detriment; or (3) 'victim' scenarios, where D provides the information or advice to X, and X (and not C) relies upon that information or advice to C's detriment.

Notably, it is not necessarily easier to prove a duty of care in a bi-partite scenario, versus a tri-partite scenario – even where there is no third party intermediary X, the factors may comprehensively

[38] [2006] UKHL 28, [35]–[36]. [39] *ibid*, [8].

[40] [2015] EWHC 320 (Comm) [91] (no duty of care owed to Barclays Bank by auditors Grant Thornton).

[41] [2009] EWCA Civ 717, [2010] 2 All ER (Comm) 138.

[42] [2012] EWCA Civ 197, [2013] QB 579, [59], citing his own views in: *Glaister v Appleby-in-Westmoreland TC* [2009] EWCA Civ 1325, [55].

point away from the existence of a duty of care owed to C. Moreover, many of the same duty-of-care-factors arise across these categories; there is no mutual exclusivity about them.

Outlining each category in turn, and by reference to leading illustrative cases:

The bi-partite relationship

Most commonly, D makes some statement directly to C which is inaccurate, and upon which C relies, to his detriment. No other (third) party is involved; C and D deal directly with each other. There may be a contract between C and D, but not necessarily; a duty of care may arise, regardless.

The bi-partite relationship in negligent misstatement

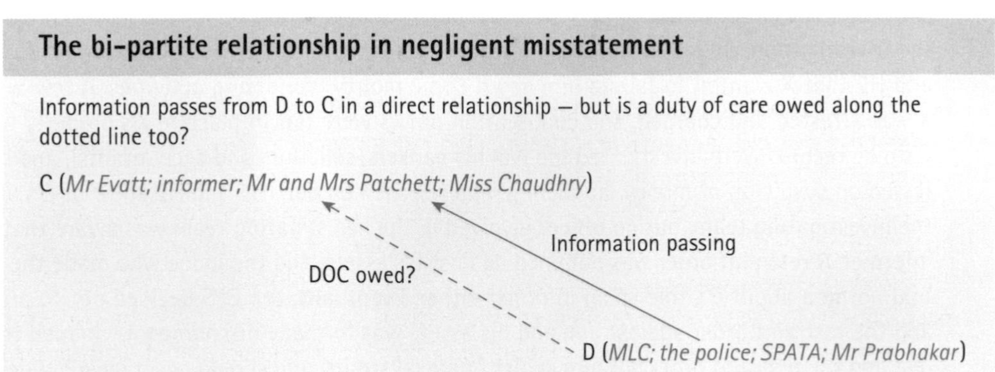

Dealing with the leading bi-partite cases:

> In *Mutual Life and Citizens' Ass Co Ltd (MLC) v Evatt*,[43] Mr Evatt, C, was a policy-holder of the insurance company, MLC, D. He sought advice from D's officer as to the financial stability of Palmer Ltd, one of D's related companies. C was told that Palmer Ltd was a safe vehicle for the investments which he had in mind. That advice turned out to be inaccurate, and C suffered a significant loss of value in his investments with Palmer Ltd. **Held (PC, 3:2):** no duty of care owed by D to C. D's officer's duty was merely to give C an honest answer to his enquiry (which he did).

The factors in play

- ***scope of expertise:*** D, as an insurance company, did not carry on the business of giving advice on investments, nor did it hold itself out as possessing the necessary skill and competence (any greater than C himself possessed) in assessing the safety of a company as an investment opportunity;
- ***payment:*** the fact that no fee was charged by D, or paid by C, did not preclude a duty of care from arising.

The decision in *MLC v Evatt* was strongly criticised by both the Court of Appeal in *Esso Petroleum Co Ltd v Mardon*,[44] and by the House of Lords in *Spring v Guardian Assurance*,[45] on the basis that the majority's decision meant that, to be actionable as a negligent misstatement, D's information or advice must have been provided in the course of a business or profession which involved D's giving information or advice of that kind. Both *Esso* and *Spring* considered that to be far too narrow a proposition, and preferred the dissenting view (of Lords Reid and Morris) in *Evatt*, that it was sufficient if the hallmarks of a 'special

[43] [1971] AC 793 (PC, on appeal from New South Wales). Lords Reid and Morris dissented.

[44] [1976] QB 801 (CA). [45] [1995] 2 AC 296 (HL) (Lord Goff).

relationship' between C and D were proven, no matter whether or not the information was given in the course of D's business or profession. However, this disagreement notwithstanding, the basic tenets of *Evatt* – that D's acting within his skill and expertise (and not outside that realm) is an important factor in assisting to prove a duty of care, and that a duty of care may attach, even to gratuitously-given information or advice – remain good law.

In *An Informer v Chief Constable*,[46] C, a police informer, supplied information about X to the police, D. C had two 'contact handlers', H1 and H2, who explained how they would protect C's identity, and that C had no authority to engage in any form of criminal activity, but there was no discussion about C's financial welfare. H1 and H2 were not part of the team who investigated X. During the investigation, police listened to X's conversations with other people, including C. C told H1 and H2 that X wanted to talk to him about some money laundering activities. A few weeks later, X was arrested and charged, and confiscation orders were put in place re X's property and assets. C's own records were investigated too (via his bankers, solicitors and accountants), and he was arrested on suspicion of money laundering, and released on bail. H1 and H2 knew of C's arrest from the investigating team, but no officer involved in the investigating team was aware that C was an informer. A restraint order was obtained against C's assets, and the judge who made the order was told nothing about C's role as an informer either. Eventually, the CPS decided not to prosecute C, and the restraint order against him and his assets was formally discharged. C claimed that his arrest and the restraint order put him in dire financial straits, and should never have happened, given that he was an informer. **Held (2:1):** no duty of care owed by D to C.

The factors in play

- ***conflict of duties:*** until the CPS decided not to prosecute C, there was a conflict between his financial interests and the public interest in preserving property reasonably suspected of being the proceeds of crime. It would not be just or reasonable to place the police, D, under a duty to give priority to supporting C's financial welfare, over the public interest in having crime, and the proceeds of crime, detected (Toulson LJ);
- ***parliamentary intent:*** the Regulation of Investigatory Powers Act 2000, s 29(2), refers to the police, D, having responsibility for an informer's 'security and welfare' or 'safety and welfare'. Those phrases are not defined, but would cover an informer's exposure to risks of death, injury, harassment and risks of a physical nature – but nothing in the statute indicated that Parliament intended an informer's financial well-being to be safeguarded, and hence, no duty of care of that scope could be owed to C (Toulson LJ);
- ***incremental test:*** the application of the *Hill* principle (see Chapter 2), which forbade a duty of care arising on the police's part re investigations into crime, applied to economic loss cases too. Each act complained of by C (his arrest and subsequent interview, obtaining restraint orders against him, and failing to apply for the restraint order to be lifted) was carried out in the course of investigating crime. The police had reasonable grounds to suspect that C had committed an offence, which was precisely when the *Hill* principle applied (Arden LJ). Moreover, C 'was not able to cite any case reasonably analogous to the facts of the present case in which a duty to prevent purely economic loss has been recognised' (Toulson LJ).

[46] [2012] EWCA Civ 197, [2013] QB 579, quote in Table at [57] (Pill LJ held that a duty of care to reasonably protect C's financial welfare was owed; but ('with some reluctance') that there had been no breach; hence, C's claim failed 3:0).

In *Patchett v Swimming Pool and Allied Trades Assn (SPATA) Ltd*,[47] Mr and Mrs Patchett, C, wished to have a swimming pool built in the garden of their home. They perused the website of SPATA, D, a trade association made up of most of the major swimming pool installers trading in the UK. C engaged a SPATA-advertised member company, Crown Pools Ltd, to build the pool, but Crown only half-finished the job due to financial difficulties. Although C paid instalments due under the contract, work stopped, and Crown ceased trading. C engaged other contractors to complete the job, and claimed £44,000 as their economic damage caused by the collapse of Crown. In fact, Crown was not a full member of D, but only an affiliate member, and hence, was not subject to D's bond and warranty scheme. C claimed that they were misled by D's website about that. **Held (2:1):** no duty of care owed by D to C.

The factors in play

- ***independent enquiry:*** D's website may not have given the impression to readers that there were different types of members (full and affiliate), and what the difference meant, but the website plainly urged C to make further enquiries, referring to an 'information pack': 'SPATA supplies an information pack and members lists which give details of suitably qualified and approved installers in the customer's area. The pack includes a Contract Check List which sets out the questions that the customer should ask a would-be tenderer, together with those which must be asked of the appointed installer, before work starts and prior to releasing the final payment'. D could expect that a potential customer would obtain the information pack (it might be different if a website was interactive, so that C could obtain all the information from the website, but this was not that type of website). Had C asked for the information pack, and the list of members referred to on the website, it would have become immediately apparent that Crown was not covered by the bond and warranty scheme;
- ***voluntarily given:*** the statements on D's website were put into general circulation, for those interested in having a pool built. It was not a case where C requested specific information which was duly provided in response. C was not entitled to rely on a bit 'here and there' on that website; it had to be taken as a whole. D could reasonably expect potential customers to have regard to all, not part, of the information on the website;
- ***incremental test:*** there was no closely analogous case to warrant a duty being upheld in this scenario.

In *Chaudhry v Prabhakar*,[48] Miss Chaudhry, C, 26, having just passed her driving test, asked her close friend, Mr Prabhakar, D, to find her a second-hand car that 'had not been in an accident'. C knew very little about cars, whereas D, whilst not a mechanic, 'knew something about cars'. He found C a 1-year-old Volkswagon, of low mileage, from a panel beater. C paid £4,500 for it, but then discovered that it had been in a serious accident, had been poorly repaired, and was unroadworthy. C sued D for the costs of replacing the car, hence the claim for pure economic loss. **Held:** D owed C a duty of care (the panel beating firm was also held liable, in contract, for breach of merchantible quality).

[47] [2009] EWCA Civ 717, (Lord Clarke, Scott Baker LJ; with Lady Justice Smith dissenting).
[48] [1989] 1 WLR 29 (CA).

The factors in play

- ***expressly requested:*** significantly, C expressly requested information as to a car of merchantible quality; it was not voluntarily given by D;
- ***social, but business:*** although the transaction was between friends, it was not merely a social occasion *per se*, there was a commercial context to it;
- ***no independent enquiry:*** D knew that C was relying on him solely, and was not going to obtain the benefit of other advice from elsewhere;
- ***payment:*** D's recommendation was given gratuitously, but that did not preclude a duty of care from arising.

It should be noted that a duty of care was conceded by counsel at first instance in *Chaudhry*, a concession which the Court of Appeal did not endorse with any great enthusiasm. For example, May LJ doubted whether the concession was properly made, and noted that, 'I do not find the conclusion that one must impose on a family friend looking out for a first car for a girl of 26 a *Donoghue v Stevenson* duty of care in and about his quest, enforceable with all the formalities of the law of tort, entirely attractive'. Indeed, the case does not appear to have been much-followed since.

The tri-partite relationship

Where C and D are 'remote to each other', with no direct dealings, or contract between them, many of the same factors arise – even though the relevant test to be applied is, more appropriately, *Caparo*'s tripartite test rather than the *Hedley Byrne* test (according to *Customs and Excise*). The second (proximity) limb of *Caparo* can certainly be met, the absence of any direct dealings notwithstanding. It is difficult to say, with any real conviction, that D assumes a responsibility towards C with whom he has had no direct dealings at all, or whom he did not know the existence of (whether specifically, or as a member of an identifiable class). Even on an objective basis, D is far more likely to have assumed a responsibility to those who paid him, employed him, or contracted with him. Hence, the relevant question becomes whether the law should deem D, as the provider of information or advice, to have assumed responsibility to C, as the person who acted on the information or advice. As Lord Bingham CJ explained in *Customs and Excise*, 'deemed' or 'notional' assumption of responsibility is a very artificial concept, and is analysed, preferably, under the *Caparo* test.

Nevertheless, as explained previously, it is the application of the salient factors which becomes all-important in the cases which follow (and which are described, diagrammatically, below):

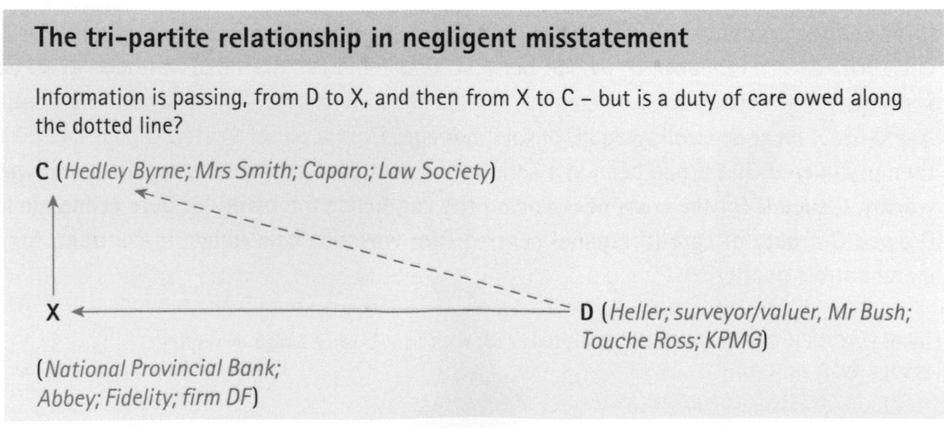

In the tri-partite scenario, it is feasible that D will not know the identity of C at all (i.e., C will be merely be one of a class of potential beneficiaries of D's information or advice). However, that lack of knowledge as to C's identity does not preclude D from owing a duty of care to C. *Hedley Byrne* itself confirmed that, and the point has been recently reiterated (e.g., in *Playboy Club London Ltd v Banca Nazionale Del Lavoro Spa*[49]).

One of the difficulties for D in this scenario is that, whilst D may have disclaimed or capped its liability in its contract with its own client X, it cannot do so in a tri-partite scenario, where it has no contract with C whatsoever. Recently, in *Barclays Bank plc v Grant Thornton LLP*,[50] the Commercial Court noted that it remained 'a vexed question' as to the extent to which D (an auditor in that case) could rely on a disclaimer or limitation clause in its contract with X, as a factor in the duty of care matrix of factors, to rebut any duty of care which may otherwise apply in C's favour. Cooke J opined that, whilst the question had been left open in several recent cases, it 'would be wholly unjust if [C, as the] non-contractual entity could rely on statements [by D] made primarily to a client [X] with a contractual limitation, and assert responsibility on behalf of [D] to it [C] without any such limitation.' The presence of the auditor D's disclaimer certainly assisted to negative any assumption of responsibility to Barclays Bank, C, in that case.

Dealing with the leading tri-partite cases:

The provision of advice on creditworthiness. This context gave rise to the leading case of misstatement.

> In *Hedley Byrne & Co Ltd v Heller & Partners Ltd*,[51] Hedley Byrne, C, advertising agents, placed substantial forward advertising orders to cost approximately £100,000, on TV and in newspapers, for a company, Easipower. Under the advertising terms, C were to be personally liable for those costs. Before placing the ads, C asked its bankers, National Provincial Bank (NPB), to enquire into Easipower's financial stability and whether Easipower 'would be good for an advertising contract of £8,000–£9,000'. NPB made enquiries of Heller & Partners Ltd, D, who were Easipower's bankers. D gave NPB favourable references about Easipower: 'Confidential. For your private use and without responsibility on the part of this bank or the manager. Respectably constituted company, considered good for its ordinary business engagements. Your figures are larger than we are accustomed to see'. Relying on that reference, C placed the ads. Easipower went into liquidation, and C was left with a loss of £17,000 for ads already placed on behalf of Easipower. **Held:** but for a disclaimer, a duty of care was owed.

The factors in play

- ***payment:*** the credit reference was given gratuitously by D, but that itself did not preclude a duty of care. A bank in D's position is not acting 'purely out of good nature', but was arguably getting some reward 'in indirect form'. Banks do not give credit references merely to assist commerce, but also to encourage their own custom, because if they would not testify to companies' credit, clients would be discouraged from approaching the banks;
- ***the intended recipient:*** Heller, D, knew that the enquiry about Easipower, made by NPB, was being made on behalf of a customer of NPB. Hedley Byrne, C, was unidentified to D, but was one of NPB's class of customers, and D knew that its advice would be passed on to, and relied upon by, a customer who was concerned about Easipower's ability to meet its debts;

[49] [2014] EWHC 2613 (QB) [39]. [50] [2015] EWHC 320 (Comm) [60].
[51] [1964] AC 465 (HL) 504 (Lord Morris's quote in the Table).

- ***no independent enquiry:*** Heller, D, knew, or should have realised, that the information about Easipower's creditworthiness was likely to be acted upon without independent enquiry being made by Hedley Byrne, C;
- ***the purpose test:*** the specific purpose for which the information was requested by D (a credit reference re Easipower) closely matched the purpose for which the information was used (D's extending credit to Easipower);
- ***an ascertainable class:*** Hedley Byrne, C, as one of NPB's customers, was one of a limited ascertainable class, which was sufficient, even though C was not specifically identified (it did not need to be);
- ***source of information:*** Heller, as Easipower's bankers, was almost the sole repository of information about Easipower's creditworthiness. It would have been almost impossible for C to obtain that information elsewhere;
- ***scope of expertise:*** assessing the creditworthiness of a business was within the scope of the bank's skill;
- ***disclaimer:*** Heller did effectively disclaim any assumption of a duty of care for the credit reference which it gave: '[i]f the enquirers chose to receive and act upon the reply, they cannot disregard the definite terms upon which it was given. They cannot accept a reply given with a stipulation, and then reject the stipulation': Lord Morris. (This case was decided in 1964, prior to the enactment of the Unfair Contract Terms Act 1977, and hence, the disclaimer did not have to satisfy any test of reasonableness.)

The provision of advice on valuation and structural soundness of a house. Two cases may be usefully contrasted on this type of alleged negligent misstatement – the key question being whether a valuer/surveyor can owe a duty of care to a prospective mortgagor–purchaser of a house/flat:

> In *Smith v Eric S Bush (a firm); Harris v Wyre Forest DC*,[52] Mrs Smith, C, applied to Abbey Building Socy for a mortgage to help her buy a house. She paid an inspection fee of £38.89. Abbey, as mortgagee, was under a statutory duty to obtain a written valuation on the house, and instructed a firm of surveyors and valuers, Eric S Bush, D, to inspect/value the house. The report contained a disclaimer that neither Abbey nor D warranted that the report and valuation would be accurate, and that it was supplied without any acceptance of responsibility. C received a copy of the report, which valued the house at £16,500, and which stated that no essential repairs were required. Without obtaining an independent survey, C purchased the house for £18,000. In fact, the first-floor chimney breasts had been removed, but D had not checked to see whether the chimneys above were adequately supported, and 18 months later, the chimney collapsed, and the house was much-devalued. **Held:** a duty of care was conceded on appeal (unless the disclaimer protected D from liability). In the other case, Mr and Mrs Harris, C, applied to the council, D1, for a mortgage to help them buy a house. They too paid an inspection fee. D1 instructed Mr Lee, D2, a valuer employed by the council, to carry out an inspection and to report. His report was not shown to C, but they were subsequently offered a mortgage by D1. The report was negligently prepared, failing to flag up possible settlement. The house subsequently needed structural repairs (£12,000) and its value fell considerably. **Held:** a duty of care was owed by D1 and D2 to C.

[52] [1990] 1 AC 831 (HL), with quotes in Table at 850, 865, 857–60, 870.

The factors in play

- ***payment:*** in both cases, C paid an 'inspection fee', which defrayed the valuers' fee (and which was billed to the mortgagee). Hence, C had some relationship 'akin to contract' with the valuer (Lord Templeman);
- ***no independent advice:*** valuer, D, was well aware that, if C were to buy a modest house, they would probably rely on D's valuation, without an independent survey. 90% of mortgagors relied on the valuation obtained by their mortgagees without obtaining their own valuation, and hence, the chances of C's obtaining independent advice was very low (and D knew that this was the norm for house purchases in English conveyancing). It was also unrealistic to expect purchasers of modest houses to pay for their own valuation (having already paid a fee to the valuer) (Lord Templeman). It might be different, if the transaction concerned a very large block of flats, industrial property, or a very expensive house, where a purchaser might be expected to obtain his own structural survey to 'guide him in his purchase' (Lord Griffiths);
- ***size of the transaction:*** although a 'modest house', the purchase was nevertheless a very significant purchase for these purchasers C, so that any loss in value was likely to cause significant hardship to them, and their reliance on D was likely to be all the more acute (Lord Griffiths);
- ***an identified C:*** in both cases, the valuers, D, knew of the mortgagors' identities, as they had signed the application forms for the valuations;
- ***the intended recipient:*** in the case of Mrs Smith, D knew that the valuation report would be passed on to her by Abbey (that was not the case for Mr and Mrs Harris, but other factors pointed to a duty owing);
- ***availability of insurance to D:*** the availability (and cost) of insurance was relevant when considering which of two parties should bear a financial loss, and in this case, the surveyor, D, will be insured against this loss;
- ***ineffective disclaimer:*** the disclaimers of liability by the valuers, D, did not satisfy the requirement of reasonableness provided by s 11(3) of UCTA 1977, and were ineffective. D was a professional person (whether acting independently as for Mrs Smith, or as an employee of the mortgagee as for Mr and Mrs Harris), and whose services were paid for by the mortgagor;
- ***scope of expertise:*** valuer, D, is typically a chartered surveyor who, by training and experience, will recognise defects and be able to assess value (Lord Templeman);
- ***no floodgates concerns:*** to hold that valuer D owed a duty of care to the prospective purchasers whose houses D valued, at the request of the purchaser's mortgagee, would not expose D to indeterminate liability – any repairs related to a modest house only; and duties would only arise where D knew that there was a *high degree of probability* that some other identifiable person, C, would act upon the advice.

However, not every purchaser who received an inaccurate valuation report and completed the purchase of a property in reliance upon it is owed a duty of care in negligent misstatement:

In *Scullion v Bank of Scotland plc (t/as Colleys)*,[53] Mr Scullion, C, decided to use some of his pension to participate in a buy-to-let scheme. Bank of Scotland, BOS, specialised in buy-to-let mortgages, and

[53] [2011] EWCA Civ 693, [2011] WLR 3212, with quotes in the Table at: [49], [57].

requested the valuation from Colleys, D, a group of property surveyors. D valued a flat for C's purchases, and its report was addressed to BOS, with a disclaimer of liability to any third party. Re Flat 17 (which is the one which C ultimately purchased), the valuation stated that the capital value was £353,000, and the achievable rental value was £2,000 pm. C did not see D's valuation until shortly prior to completion. C completed a mortgage application form, and returned it together with a cheque to pay for the valuation of the flat. C said that it did not occur to him to obtain his own valuation, because he thought that the purpose of the valuation was to satisfy the mortgagee of the value of the flat and that the rent would be sufficient to meet the payments on the mortgage. Thereafter, the flat could not be let for the foreshadowed £2,000 pm, and C found a tenant for £1,050 pm who vacated after a year. C had to sell the property, leaving a liability owing under the mortgage. **Held:** D did not owe C a duty of care.

The factors in play

- ***independent enquiry***: Colleys, D, did not know, nor ought to have appreciated, that their valuation report would be relied on by C when deciding to purchase the flat. This case was distinguishable from *Smith/Harris*, because there, the properties involved were relatively modest houses being acquired by C as their residences, and the valuers realised that no independent enquiry was likely in *Smith/Harris*. But it was different where valuer D knew that C was buying an investment property, for then, D could foreseeably have thought that C would obtain his own advice from an estate agent or valuer. The buy-to-let market was quite undeveloped, and nothing like 90% of those people who bought-to-let in 2002 relied only on valuations prepared by a valuer instructed by their mortgagees, rather than obtaining their own valuation. Buy-to-let purchasers were commercially astute people who were more likely to obtain their own valuation. Also, rental return was a very tricky issue, upon which independent advice by C should reasonably be sought on matters which were (deliberately) not covered in D's valuation (e.g., how easily could the flat be let, expected rental, rent-free periods, fees for finding tenants, etc);
- ***the purpose test:*** the valuation was directed primarily to the mortgagee by whom it was requested, and was mainly concerned with the capital value of the property – so that, if purchaser C defaulted, the flat would be adequate security. From C's point of view, the report only had a very small section, 'suitability for letting'; and it was not directed to buy-to-let purchasers' interest in rental values (as much as capital value). Hence, the reason why C relied upon the report, and the primary reason for which it was prepared, did not match;
- ***incremental test:*** the fact that the underlying transaction was a buy-to-let, rather than a purchase for owner-occupation, distinguished it from *Smith/Harris*. That case (especially Harris) was regarded as 'represent[ing] the high water mark in this field' in *Saddington v Colley Professional Services*.[a] To find in C's favour here would extend the boundaries of valuer liability in a way that should not be permitted;
- ***lack of fairness:*** the court noted the sentiments of the editors of *Jackson & Powell on Professional Liability*[b] that *Smith/Harris's* outcome should not be extended to other scenarios, 'because of the double jeopardy to which it exposes a valuer, namely to the mortgagee [via contract] and the purchaser [via a duty of care]'. However, the court disapproved of the notion of any unfairness. There was no reason at law why valuer D could not be liable to both mortgagee and prospective purchaser. This particular factor did not count against a duty of care;

[a] [1999] Lloyd's Rep PN 140, 143.
[b] (6th edn) [10-049]–[10-051].

- ***the type of transaction:*** for C, this transaction was 'essentially commercial in nature', which 'coloured the issue'. The 'class' of commercial purchasers of low-to-middle-value residential properties, such as buy-to-lets, were likely to be 'richer and more commercially astute than people who buy to occupy', and could 'properly be regarded as less deserving of protection by the common law against the risk of negligence than those buying to occupy as their residence'. That is, C was less deserving of the protection of tort, re the negligent misstatement;
- ***payment:*** C paid £35 for the valuation report (a small sum), but it was not significant one way or another, in deciding whether a duty was owed: 'one sees how it may be said that that is of a little additional assistance to [D's] case. However, I do not consider that it carries any significant weight', in the balancing scales.

As the court pointed out recently in *Freemont (Denbigh) Ltd v Knight Frank LLP*,[54] it was important in *Eric S Bush* that the property there was a modestly-valued residential property, whereas *Scullion* was an entirely different case, denying any duty by a valuer to an investor who relied on the valuer's report (prepared for the mortgagee) for his own purposes.

The provision of audited statements re a company's affairs. *Caparo Industries plc v Dickman*[55] was 'the case in which the threefold test was first stated', as acknowledged in *Arrowhead Capital Finance Ltd v KPMG LLP*[56] – and although it has proven to be relevant in personal injury and property damage cases too, it was in the province of negligent misstatement that the test first gained real cognisance.

In *Caparo Industries v Dickman*, Caparo Industries plc, C, a major company, owned shares in a public company, Fidelity plc. Touche Ross, D, accountants and auditors, prepared end-of-year (31 Mar 1984) accounts for Fidelity which showed a pre-tax profit, and a shortfall from what had been predicted, of £1.3m. C received the audited accounts in its capacity as shareholder, and relying upon those audited accounts, bought further shares in Fidelity, sufficient to amount to a takeover of Fidelity. Then, C discovered that Fidelity had actually made a loss of £400,000 for that year. C sued D (and Fidelity's directors, including Mr Dickman, which is not relevant for present purposes), alleging negligence in performing the audit. The audited accounts prepared by D were required by ss 236 and 237 of the Companies Act 1985. The issue was whether D owed C a duty of care for the financial losses suffered by C, either as a potential bidder for Fidelity because D ought to have foreseen that the accounts made Fidelity vulnerable to a takeover bid, or as an existing shareholder of Fidelity who was interested in buying more shares in Fidelity. **Held (5:0):** D did not owe C a duty of care.

The factors in play

- ***the purpose test:*** the statutory end-of-year accounts were prepared by D and distributed for certain purposes (*viz*, to enable shareholders to exercise their voting rights to supervise or oust directors at the AGM, or to influence future policy and management). Nothing in Part VII of the Companies Act 1985 suggested that the accounts were prepared and sent to members for any purpose other than to enable them to exercise class rights in general meeting. Their purpose was not to assist shareholders, such as C (or any other investor), in making decisions about their future investment in Fidelity. There was a clear mis-match of purpose here, pointing away from any duty of care;

[54] [2014] EWHC 3347 (Ch) [34]. [55] [1990] 2 AC 605 (HL) (Lord Bridge delivered the judgment on behalf of the House).
[56] [2012] EWHC 1801 (Comm) [55].

- ***independent advice:*** one of the key differences from *Smith v Eric S Bush* was that the purchaser there would probably rely on the valuation without independent advice, whereas for Caparo, a large company, to proceed with a takeover bid without 'independent verification' was unlikely, and put the case at odds with *Smith*;
- ***unascertainable class:*** if D was to be liable to Caparo, as a shareholder who was interested in launching a take-over bid, then so, too, a company could be vulnerable to such a bid from any investor of the public. D had no way of knowing of C's identity, or the terms of its likely takeover bid or intentions. The class of potential Cs was not only the current shareholders of Fidelity, but also *any other party* who could be interested in investing in Fidelity, on reading D's accounts. The class was too large and indeterminate to justifiy a duty of care;
- ***no gap in redress/lacuna in the law:*** where an auditor, D, negligently prepares end-of-year accounts, then it is not for individual shareholders, such as Caparo, to sue D. Rather, the company itself will bring a claim against D, and any loss suffered by an individual shareholder could be recouped in this way, rendering C's action unnecessary;
- ***no payment:*** in *Smith*, Mrs Smith paid a fee to defray the valuer's expenses in preparing the valuation, whereas Caparo, as a shareholder, was entitled to be given company accounts prior to the AGM. Hence, Caparo was a 'free-rider' (although Lord Bridge did not place much, if any, emphasis upon this point, other than to note it).

It is notable, however, that a takeover bidder **can** establish that he was owed a duty of care, by the auditors who prepared the company accounts, where the facts are distinguishable from *Caparo*.

In *Morgan Crucible Co plc v Hill Samuel Co Ltd*,[57] Morgan Crucible, C, who was not an existing shareholder, made a takeover bid for another company, First Castle Electronics plc, and initially made the bid in reliance on the audited company accounts prepared by Judkins & Co, D, First Castle's auditors. However, in seeking to defeat C's takeover bid, the directors of First Castle, and Judkins, made certain statements in 'defence documents', referring back to those company accounts. Ultimately, C increased its bid for First Castle, and achieved the takeover. C then alleged that both the audited company accounts and the post-bid statements were negligently-prepared, so that First Castle was worth much less than C had paid for its shares. **Held:** the claim could proceed; a duty of care was arguably owed.

The factors in play

- ***the purpose test:*** although the audited statements in *Caparo* were prepared for a different purpose (the supervisory function in the AGM) from the purpose which C relied upon (to launch a takeover), the facts were distinguishable here. When making their defence statements, both directors and auditors were fully aware that C, in particular, would rely on them for the purpose of deciding whether or not to make an increased takeover bid for First Castle, and in fact, made those statements for the purpose of C relying on them, as they were seeking to defeat C's bid;

[57] [1991] Ch 295 (CA).

- *source of the information:* although C had its own independent advisers, much of the information on which the accounts and profit forecast was based was information that only D could have possessed;
- *the intended recipient:* where auditor D approves a statement which confirms the accuracy of its previous audited accounts, or which contains a forecast of future profits, and D has been told that C, a bidder, will rely on the accounts and forecast for the purpose of deciding whether to make an increased bid, then C is an intended recipient.

However, undoubtedly the line between a *Caparo* and a *Morgan Crucible* scenario is not always easy to draw. Subsequently, in *Galoo Ltd v Bright Grahame Murray (a firm)*,[58] Glidewell LJ noted that the distinction 'is inevitably a fine one', while Evans LJ remarked that, while it would be 'tempting' to attribute the difference merely to the fact that Morgan Crucible's identity was known to the auditors as a takeover bidder, whereas Caparo's identity was not known to Touche Ross as a takeover bidder, that is perhaps too simplistic. What of the case of an existing shareholder who is known to auditor D as one who is interested in making a takeover bid – a scenario that falls somewhere between *Caparo* and *Morgan Crucible*? Evans LJ expressed the view, in dicta, that a duty of care would not automatically apply, just because C's identity was known. Rather, it would depend upon other factors too – as it was unlikely that D would have intended C to rely on the audited statements, without any independent enquiry being undertaken. This example demonstrates the nuanced enquiry that a duty of care ultimately requires in this area.

Of course, some cases will be at the other end of the spectrum from *Caparo*, where audited statements were intended for C alone, and where D must have intended for C to rely upon them:

In *Law Society v KPMG Peat Marwick*,[59] KPMG, D, were retained by a firm of solicitors, Durnford Ford, to prepare their annual reports for y/e 31 May 1990, as required by s 34 of the Solicitors Act 1974. DF paid D's auditing fees. Shortly afterwards, the Law Society, C, investigated DF for fraud and embezzlement of client trust funds, and the firm ceased practice. Eventually, £8.5m had to be paid out to about 300 defrauded clients from C's Compensation Fund. The Solicitors Act 1974, s 36, required C to maintain and administer that Fund, so as to make grants to relieve loss or hardship suffered in consequence of dishonesty on the part of a solicitor, in connection with that solicitor's practice. C argued that, when preparing DF's reports, D had missed signs of fraud, and that if D had qualified the reports as it should have done, then C would have exercised its statutory powers of intervention in DF's practice much earlier, and put an end to the activities, thereby reducing the amount which was paid out of the Compensation Fund. **Held:** D owed C a duty of care.

The factors in play

- *no indeterminate liability:* if a duty was found, the size of the class would be limited to DF's clients whose money had been wrongly misappropriated from their accounts; and time was limited too, because C requested a report every year, so any continued damage after C's receipt of an accurate report could not be attributed to D;

[58] [1993] EWCA Civ 3, [1994] 1 WLR 1360, 1382 (Glidewell LJ), 1388 (Evans LJ).

[59] [2000] EWCA Civ 5563, [2000] 1 WLR 1921.

- ***the intended recipient:*** the primary beneficiary of D's audit was not DF's clients, but the Law Society, C, as trustee of the Compensation Fund, because it was on the Law Society that the burden lay. C's function was to protect both the public and the Fund, and accurate audited reports were necessary for protective steps to be taken. KPMG knew that its report had to be passed to the Law Society, C, under s 34 of the Solicitors Act 1974, and that in some cases where the report was adverse on key points, C was the intended recipient;
- ***the purpose test:*** D's audited report was required under the Solicitors Act 1974, precisely to protect the Compensation Fund, if financial wrongdoing was detected. Hence, the purpose for which it was prepared, and the purpose for which C relied on it, were entirely coincidental;
- ***parliamentary intent:*** KPMG argued that, since the Fund was financed by the solicitors' profession (by virtue of premiums), then the policy of Parliament was that losses caused by dishonest members of the profession should be borne by the solicitors' profession as a whole, rather than for one accounting firm, D (or its professional indemnity insurer) to bear that loss. KPMG also argued that the sole purpose of suits such as this was, 'through the medium of expensive and time-consuming litigation, to move losses from the solicitors' profession to the accountants, and then back to the lawyers in costs'. However, that did not preclude a duty. It was for C to decide whether it wanted to take the risks of suing, and if so, then it was not for D to complain about the expense involved;
- ***no disclaimers:*** it was always open for auditors D to seek to disclaim responsibility for any lack of care in the preparation of the audit, which D had not done (and any disclaimer might have been disputed by C, on the basis of lack of reasonableness, anyway);
- ***no payment:*** if the fee for KPMG's, D's, report had been paid by the Law Society, C, there would have been a contract between C and D. The fact that the fee was paid by DF did not preclude a duty of care from arising.

This sample of cases gives a detailed indication of the factors which are legally relevant, as to whether or not a duty of care will be owed by D, in the case of negligent misstatement (whether bi-partite or tri-partite in nature). Similar factors may apply in the so-called 'victim' scenario.

The 'victim' scenario

It will be recalled that 'victim' scenarios occur where D provides information or advice to X, and X relies upon that, to C's detriment. These scenarios are characterised by the fact that it is another person, X, *and not C*, who has relied upon the information or advice – but it is C who ends up suffering the economic detriment from D's inaccurate statement.

This category is clearly not a *Hedley Byrne* situation, as the statement is not aimed at C who relied upon it – but it is a viable extension of the *Hedley Byrne* principle, as re-affirmed in *McKie v Swindon College.*[60] Further, D may not have exercised 'skill' in the narrow sense, but rather, applied his 'special knowledge' (i.e., his exclusive knowledge) about C, and to C's detriment – that is hardly the exercise of 'skill', but it does draw upon *Hedley Byrne* nevertheless (per *Paros plc v Worldlink Group plc*[61]). C's reliance on D is certainly indirect, in victim cases, but nevertheless, that can suffice for a duty of care to be owed to C.

[60] [2011] EWHC 469 (QB) [44]. [61] [2012] EWHC 394 (Comm) [103].

The same factors pointing in favour of, or against, a duty of care, as itemised in negligent misstatement scenarios above, are equally as relevant to the imposition of a duty of care in the 'victim' scenario. It involves, inevitably, a tri-partite relationship:

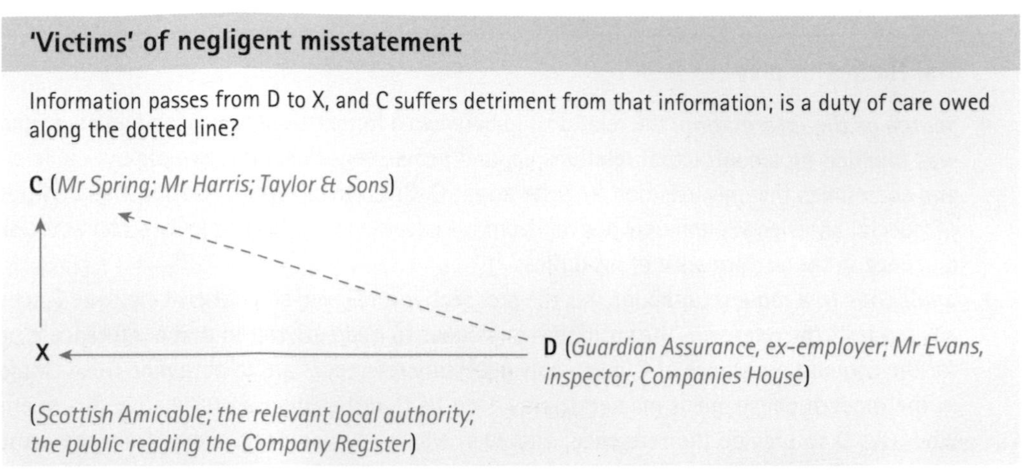

Dealing with the leading cases in this area:

The provision of references. Given that references are supplied to X, and are written about C, they are the paradigm 'victim-of-misstatement' scenario.

> In *Spring v Guardian Assurance plc*,[62] Mr Spring, C, was employed by Corinium, estate agents and sellers of insurance policies issued by Guardian Assurance, D, as sales director. Then, the major shareholder in Corinium sold the company to D, and C was dismissed by D without explanation. C sought a job selling insurance policies with Scottish Amicable Life Assurance Society. A positive reference was required, under the regulatory rules governing insurance selling. The reference provided by D was quite negative, including that C 'consistently kept the best leads for himself with little regard for the sales team that he supposedly was to manage', that 'we have found a serious case of mis-selling where the concept of "best advice" was ignored and the policies sold yielded the highest commissions', and that 'there have been other cases where there has been bad advice, but there is no current evidence to indicate whether it was deliberate or through ignorance'. Consequently, Scottish Amicable did not appoint C, nor did other prospective employers. C then sued D for a number of actions (e.g., malicious falsehood, breach of contract and negligence). **Held:** D owed C a duty of care in preparing the reference.

In *Customs and Excise*,[63] Lord Rodger noted that, in the circumstances of *Spring*, it was unrealistic to consider that D *assumed responsibility to C* for the preparation of the reference: the case 'does not readily yield to analysis in terms of a voluntary assumption of responsibility ... I see no reason to treat these cases as exceptions to some over-arching rule that there must be a voluntary assumption of responsibility before the law recognises a duty of care. Such a rule would inevitably lead to the concept of voluntary assumption of responsibility being stretched beyond its natural limits – which would, in the long run, undermine the very real value of the concept as a criterion of liability in the many cases where it is an appropriate guide'. Again, a

[62] [1994] UKHL 7, [1995] 2 AC 296 (Lords Lowry, Goff, Slynn and Woolf; Lord Keith dissenting).
[63] [2006] UKHL 28, [2007] 1 AC 181, [52].

descent into the particular factors that arose on the facts of *Spring*, rather than the application of mere labels, was necessary – and, in the House of Lords' view, a duty of care was owed for the following reasons:

The factors in play

- ***source of the information:*** the relationship between a former employer, D, and an ex-employee, C, was founded on a contractual relationship, and hence, very close. The ex-employer is in the best, and sometimes the only, position to write about C. Given their former relationship, D is possessed of 'special knowledge', uniquely derived from his experience of the employee's character, skill and diligence in the performance of his duties;
- ***analogous to a request:*** although it is the prospective employer, and not ex-employee C, who actually requests the reference, the position is analogous to *Hedley Byrne*, in that a reference is provided for the conjoint assistance of C, given how necessary references are to obtaining fresh employment in the modern employment market. It may even be C, rather than a prospective future employer, who asks D to provide the reference; and even where the approach comes from the prospective future employer, it will be made with either C's express or tacit authority;
- ***no conflict of duties:*** it did not necessarily follow that, because D owed a duty of care to his employee, C, in writing a careful reference, that there was any conflict in any duty of care owed to the recipient of the reference (and whether D owed a duty to the recipient of the reference was not necessary to decide here);
- ***scope of expertise:*** the skill of preparing a reference for an employee fell as much within the expertise of an employer as the skill of preparing a bank reference was within the expertise of Easipower's bank in *Hedley Byrne*;
- ***no defensive practices likely:*** just because a duty of care was owed, re the writing of references, did not mean that those asked to give them should be inhibited from speaking frankly or from writing what they thought, or writing one at all, lest they were liable in damages through not taking sufficient care in its preparation. It did not follow that bland and meaningless reference-writing would follow from this case;
- ***parliamentary intent:*** there were regulatory requirements to protect the public from exposure to the activities of company representatives selling insurance policies and who may be dishonest or incompetent, given many examples of mis-selling. Public interest required that suspicions be communicated.

The principle in *Spring v Guardian Assurance* has since been extended, where a bank provides a negative credit reference about a bank client, which damages the spouse of that client who was both a joint holder of the same account with her husband, and a co-director of the family business which largely depended on her husband's credit-rating (per *Gatt v Barclays Bank plc*[64]). That was considered to be an incremental development of the principle in *Spring* – albeit that no breach on the part of the bank was proven there.

Spring does not, however, impose a universally-applicable duty on D for all forms of reference of whatever kind, where public policy reasons dictated against any such duty arising, as

[64] [2013] EWHC 2 (QB).

in, e.g., the supply by the police of a clear criminal record certificate in *Desmond v Nottinghamshire Police*,[65] or in the supply of a reference for a teacher in *Camurat v Thurrock BC*.[66] In both cases, alternative remedies for the victim C were available, and the statutory frameworks under which the references were supplied also disinclined any duty of care from arising.

Certification or status of C's business. A business operator, C, may be a victim of a negligent misstatement, if inaccurate statements are made about that business upon which others rely.

In *Harris v Evans*,[67] Mr Harris, C, started a bungee jumping business, using a mobile telescopic crane, for public use, at various sites around south-west England, including Devon. C contacted the Health and Safety Executive (HSE) to obtain and comply with the safety requirements for using cranes that way. After the business started, Mr Evans, D, a HSE inspector, inspected C's business, and wrongly concluded that C's equipment required adjustment. C was told that he needed further certification before the cranes could be used for this business. Consequently, C's business was shut down by the relevant local authority, relying on that advice. This led to financial losses for C. Later, the Dept of the Environment concluded that D's advice was erroneous and was not in line with HSE policy. C claimed damages for his economic loss, flowing from the local authority's reliance on the inspector's, D's, negligent advice. **Held:** no duty of care was owed by D to C. In *Sebry v Companies House*, a winding-up order was made against the company, Taylor & Son Ltd, in Jan 2009. A copy of that order was received by the Companies House, D, where an employee accidentally noted the winding-up order against the wrong company, Taylor & Sons Ltd, C. As a result, C was described as a company being in liquidation, when it was not, and several suppliers and creditors found out the information by word-of-mouth. **Held:** a duty of care was owed by D to C.

The factors in play

- ***defensive practices:*** in *Harris*, any duty imposed on inspectors such as D, which rendered them liable for economic damage to the business enterprise they were inspecting, would be likely to cause utmost cautiousness and a desire to postpone making a decision until more concrete facts were found, which could place public safety at risk. However, in *Sebry*, this was a very unusual error, and would not create any undue defensive practices other than to cast a duty on D and its employees to exercise reasonable care to ensure that the information was accurately recorded on the Company Register; it was not the type of case where society should expect D to exercise a judgment without fear of litigation;
- ***parliamentary intent:*** in *Harris*, the statutory duties of an inspector under the Health and Safety at Work Act 1974 were designed to protect public safety, that was D's paramount consideration – so the freedom to act as D saw fit must prevail over C's individual economic losses. Hence, 'if steps which they think should be taken to improve safety would have an adverse economic effect on the business enterprise in question, so be it ... It would ... be seriously detrimental to the proper discharge by enforcing authorities of their responsibilities in respect of public health and safety if they were to be exposed to potential liability in negligence, at the suit of the owners of the businesses adversely affected by their decisions'. However, in *Sebry*, imposing a duty on Companies House, D, would only require D to do exactly what was required by the Companies Act 2006, i.e., that information about a company such as C was complete, accurate and easily retrievable;

[65] [2011] EWCA Civ 3, [2011] 1 FLR 1361. [66] [2014] EWHC 2482 (QB).
[67] [1998] EWCA Civ 709, [1998] 1 WLR 1285, with quotes in Table at 1298, 1301–2.

- ***other avenues of redress:*** the 1974 Act itself contemplated that economic losses could result to business proprietors, as a result of erroneous inspections, and provided remedies for such errors. 'It is implicit in the 1974 Act that Improvement Notices and Prohibition Notices may cause economic loss or damage to the business enterprise in question. [It] provides remedies against errors or excesses on the part of inspectors and enforcing authorities. I would decline to add the possibility of an action in negligence to the statutory remedies' (per Sir Richard Scott V-C). There was no lacuna in the law, given the remedies in the Act (*Harris*). However, in *Sebry*, C, a company damaged in that way, had no other remedy, unless it was provided by the tort of negligence;
- ***the incremental test:*** in *Sharp v Ministry of Housing and Local Govt*,[a] a clerk at the Land Registry produced a land certificate that omitted to mention a claim which the Ministry had against the vendor, and this mistake extinguished the right of the Ministry to pursue its claim against the purchaser. The clerk was liable to the Ministry for that error. Hence, there was a close analogy, whereby false information on an official register could give rise to a duty of care in favour of one who relied on the accuracy of that information;
- ***distributive justice:*** in *Sebry*, the effect of finding D liable was that the loss would be ultimately borne by either the business community (limited companies and users of the Register who paid fees) or by the public at large (via an increase in budgetary allocation to that government entity to cover the loss or via insurance). That result was fair and just, given that the compulsory registration system was designed to benefit the business community and the public.

[a] [1970] 2 QB 223 (CA).

Summary of salient factors

Having regard to the exhortations by the appellate courts in this area to avoid the use of labels and to descend to the particular facts and circumstances, the following list, together with supporting authorities derived from the aforementioned discussion, summarises those which the leading cases have demonstrated to be important, when upholding a duty of care:

	A duty of care is more likely (although not necessarily mandated) if ...	Relevant case, e.g. ...
1	the statement prepared by statement-maker D was in response to a **request for information or advice** from C who suffered the loss, rather than given voluntarily	*Chaudhry v Prabhaker*
2	the **purpose for which the statement was prepared** by statement-maker D, and the purpose for which C who suffered the loss relied on that statement, were the same, or very similar, rather than entirely mismatched	*Caparo Industries v Dickman*
3	the statement was passed on by X (the initial recipient of the information) to C who suffered the loss (the ultimate recipient), and D **knew that the information would be passed on** to that ultimate intended recipient	*Hedley Byrne v Heller*

	A duty of care is more likely (although not necessarily mandated) if ...	Relevant case, e.g. ...
4	C, who suffered the loss, was specifically known to statement-maker D, or was one of a **small or ascertainable class of persons** known to D, rather than one of a large and unascertainable class of persons who might rely on D's statement	*Caparo Industries v Dickman*
5	statement-maker D knew, or should have known, that the information prepared by him would be relied upon by C who suffered the loss, without any **independent enquiry** being made by C – and it was reasonable, in all the circumstances, that C would rely upon D's statement without independent enquiry being made by C (having regard to the type of transaction, and the type of C, etc)	*Smith v Eric S Bush*
6	statement-maker D was **likely to be insured** or **ought to have been insured** against the loss (as opposed to where C ought to have insured himself against the risk of economic loss), a relevant factor as to where, as between C and D, the loss should fall	*Smith v Eric S Bush*
7	the **transaction was a large and significant one**, where inaccurate information would have costly ramifications for C, and for which the law of tort might provide some protection (it was not a 'run of the mill' transaction, where C's reliance on the statement would not be quite as crucial or even likely)	*Smith v Eric S Bush; Caparo Industries v Dickman*
8	the information was **within the scope of D's skill and expertise** to give	*MLC v Evatt*
9	statement-maker D was the sole, or one of **the primary sources, of the information**, which increased C's reliance on the need for accuracy in the statement given by D	*Spring v Guardian Assurance*
10	C, who suffered the loss, **paid D for the statement**, or D had some other financial interest in C's acting on the statement	*Smith v Eric S Bush*
11	statement-maker D did not (or could not) effectively **disclaim any responsibility** for the accuracy of the statement (or service)	*Hedley Byrne v Heller*
12	the statement was provided by D in a **commercial or professional setting,** rather than in a social setting	*Chaudhry v Prabhaker*
13	C, who suffered the loss, had **no other avenue of redress** (by virtue of statute, self-help, common law rights, or otherwise), thus emphasising the need for a duty of care to be upheld in negligence, so as to preclude a **lacuna in the law**	*Harris v Evans; Caparo v Dickman*
14	statement-maker D had a **protective function re the public safety** which would conflict with any duty of care owed to C as an individual	*Harris v Evans*
15	the **parliamentary intent** was that a duty of care was not precluded by the statutory obligations cast on statement-maker D	*Caparo Industries v Dickman*

	A duty of care is more likely (although not necessarily mandated) if ...	Relevant case, e.g. ...
16	no **conflict of interest** between a duty to C and a duty to another (e.g., the public interest, or another party) would occur, if a duty of care was upheld	*An Informer v Chief Constable*
17	no **prospect of indeterminate liability** was likely to result from the imposition of a duty of care on statement-maker D (i.e., where D's exposure to liability, arising from that one statement, was limited)	*Law Society v KPMG*
18	no **prospect of floodgates** was likely to result from the imposition of a duty of care on statement-maker D (i.e., where the case could set a precedential effect for later Cs who were similarly-situated)	*Smith v Eric S Bush*
19	as a **matter of fairness**, a duty of care should be imposed on statement-maker D	*Scullion v Bank of Scotland*
20	**defensive practices** across an industry were not likely to flow from upholding a duty of care against statement-maker D	*Spring v Guardian Assurance*
21	according to **distributive justice**, liability should be imposed on D, rather than requiring an uncompensated C to bear the loss himself	*Sebry v Companies House*
22	there was a **close temporal proximity** (or, at least, not a long gap) between the making of D's statement and the damage suffered by C	*Goodwill v BPAS (discussed below)*

Matters which do *not* preclude a duty of care from arising

§4.7 The following matters do not preclude a duty of care from arising on D's part, in respect of pure economic loss suffered by C: the lack of detrimental reliance by C; either the presence, or absence, of a contractual relationship between C and D; and where information or advice is given by a managing director, shareholder or representative of a company, D (provided that D may only be liable where he assumed personal liability to C and where there was the requisite reliance by C on D *personally*).

Certain issues are worth stating, as they have tended to provoke much judicial discussion:

No detrimental reliance. In *Caparo*,[68] Lord Oliver, when describing the circumstances giving rise to the necessary relationship of proximity between C and D, noted that the information should have been 'acted upon by the advisee to his detriment'. However, in some cases in which a duty of care has been imposed on D, who has provided negligent information, advice or services, detrimental reliance on C's part has **not** been necessary to prove, i.e., C has not changed his position at all, in reliance on D's acting with reasonable care and skill, and yet, a duty has been upheld.

This feature is particularly apparent where, although D may have known that C's economic well-being depended upon his acting with careful skill and expertise, and D may have assumed a responsibility to act in C's best economic interests, C had no choice to place his affairs with

[68] [1990] 2 AC 605 (HL) 638, and cited, e.g., in *Law Society v KPMG* [2000] EWCA Civ 5563, [2000] WLR 1921, [13].

anyone else (*White v Jones*[69]). Consequently, C did nothing different in reliance on D's professional services being administered reasonably – there has been no change of position. Yet, a duty in C's favour has been found. This lack of detrimental reliance is one reason as to why the whole area is far from straightforward.

Similarly, whilst reliance may be possible where C and D had direct dealings with each other (where there was 'mutuality of dealing', as Lord Browne-Wilkinson described it in *White v Jones*[70]), tri-partite relationships are different. C and D may **never** have had any direct dealings at all, so that no express reliance by C can be proven. Yet that is not fatal to a duty to avoid pure economic loss either (as *Hedley Byrne* itself showed). Plainly, D can be liable to C for negligent misstatement under the *Caparo* test, where proximity of relationship, rather than reliance *per se*, characterised their relationship.

The presence, or absence, of a contractual relationship. As discussed in Chapter 1, concurrent duties in Contract and in Tort are permissible at law. In *Henderson v Merrett Syndicates Ltd*,[71] Lord Goff said that 'an assumption of responsibility [by D], coupled with the concomitant reliance [by C], may give rise to a tortious duty of care, irrespective of whether there is a contractual relationship between the parties'. A contractual duty of care between C and D does not preclude a concurrent tortious duty of care. Further, the fact that D owes a contractual duty to X, and a tortious duty of care to C, is perfectly permissible at law – the first duty is defined by the terms of the contract, and the second duty by the general law (as Lord Nolan noted in *White v Jones*[72]).

However, merely because C and D are in a contractual relationship does not **automatically** mean that there is an assumption of responsibility by D, and reliance on C's part, necessary to give rise to a duty of care on D's part to avoid C's financial losses. The court must ask what, precisely, D has contracted to do. According to Lord Goff in *Henderson*,[73] that is a two-stage process: (1) has D undertaken to provide relevant advice, information or services, and if so, did the contract expressly or impliedly provide that D was to exercise reasonable skill and care in so doing? If so, then a duty of care in tort is potentially owed; (2) do the terms of the contract exclude or limit D's liability for failure to perform such obligations, either carefully or at all?

Obversely, the fact that, as between C and D, there is no direct contract, does not necessarily preclude a duty of care from being imposed on D. That argument was raised, and rebutted, in *Henderson*, where D (the managing agents) sought to deny any duty of care in tort to C (the indirect Names in an insurance syndicate), by arguing that they had direct contracts with some Names, but not with the indirect Names, depending upon which contractual chain governed the relationship. Hence, D argued that, by structuring their contractual relationship in that way, C and D had deliberately excluded any assumption of responsibility arising towards the indirect Names. However, a duty of care was nevertheless upheld.

The appropriate D. This issue will become particularly important, if a company has been wound up, and the director, shareholder or employee, D, carried professional indemnity insurance. It must be D who assumed responsibility in law, for the task at hand. Otherwise, the undertaking of responsibility may be attributed to the corporate entity – or to no party at all. In *Williams v Natural Life Health Foods Ltd*,[74] where that precise scenario occurred, Lord Steyn

[69] [1995] 2 AC 207 (HL). [70] *ibid*, 272. [71] [1995] 2 AC 145 (HL) 194. [72] [1995] 2 AC 207 (HL) 293.
[73] [1995] 2 AC 145 (HL) 197, and also 206 (Lord Browne-Wilkinson). [74] [1998] 1 WLR 830 (HL) 837.

noted that the relevant test is whether C, 'could reasonably rely on an assumption of personal responsibility by the individual who performed the services on behalf of the company' (and, in that case, C could not). His Lordship also approved of the reasoning of the Supreme Court of Canada, in *Edgeworth Construction Ltd v MD Lea & Ass Ltd*,[75] that to successfully sue an employee, D, C 'would have to show that it was relying on the particular expertise of an individual engineer, without regard to the corporate character of the engineering firm'.

In *Williams v Natural Life Health Foods Ltd*,[76] Mr Mistlin, D1, was managing director and controlling shareholder of Natural Life Health Foods, D2. Mr Williams and Mrs Reid, C, entered into a franchise contract with D2 to open a health food shop in Rugby, relying on D1's financial projections for the health food business. The turnover from C's shop was substantially less than predicted, and after 18 months, it ceased trading. D1 had no direct dealings with C, but he played a prominent role in preparing the financial projections, and D2's brochure advertised D1's experience in the health food trade. The franchisor company D2 was wound up, and as a result, C's action proceeded against D1 alone, alleging that C had been given negligent advice. **Held:** D1 did not owe a duty of care to C. D1 did not objectively assume personal responsibility for the accuracy of the statements in the brochure, nor had C relied upon D1 so as to create a special relationship between D1 and C: (1) while the brochure claimed that D1 had expertise in the retail health foods industry (via personal experience in operating a shop at Salisbury), his earlier experience fell a long way short of amounting to an assumption of responsibility to franchisees as to the accuracy of the projections contained in the brochure; (2) a managing director cannot be personally liable to the franchisees, simply because, in a small one-man company, he is the one who will possess the qualities essential to the running of the business; (3) there were no personal dealings between D1 and C – no exchanges, personal dealings, requests for information, conversations, oral assurances, etc – which could have conveyed to C that D1 assumed personal responsibility to them. In *Riyad Bank v Ahli United Bank (UK) plc*,[77] the Fund, C, had a contract with an investment bank, and claimed that it sought technical advice as to its investments from an adviser, D, who was a subcontracted technical adviser to the bank. C suffered loss when those investments failed. There was no direct contractual relationship between C and D, C's contract was with the investment bank. **Held:** D owed a duty of care to the Fund, C: (1) there were close dealings, in that, to provide specialist advice, D regularly attended board meetings of the Fund; and (2) the technical advice was given directly to the Fund by D, and was intended to be relied and acted upon by C, all parties had that expectation.

NEGLIGENT PROVISION OF SERVICES

Introduction

§4.8 According to the 'extended *Hedley Byrne* principle', D who provides professional services within the scope of his skill and expertise, and who causes economic loss to C who relied on the reasonably careful performance of those services, owes a duty of care to C to avoid that economic loss.

The very reason that it is called the 'extended *Hedley Byrne* principle' is because the assumption of responsibility principle has been extended to the provision of professional services, and is

[75] [1993] 3 SCR 206 (SCC) 212 (La Forest J). [76] [1998] 1 WLR 830 (HL) 830.
[77] [2006] EWCA Civ 780, [2006] 2 Lloyd's Rep 292.

no longer confined to information or advice (per Lord Goff in *Henderson v Merrett Syndicates Ltd*[78]). *Hedley Byrne* concerned advice about creditworthiness – and anything which sought to extend it wider than that (as Lord Devlin foreshadowed in *Hedley Byrne* itself, referring to solicitors' professional services[79]) was dicta only. However, the extended *Hedley Byrne* principle was 'the rationalisation, or technique, adopted by English law, to provide a remedy for the recovery of damages in respect of economic loss caused by the negligent performance *of services*' (per Lord Steyn in *Williams v Natural Life Health Foods*[80]).

Of course, many scenarios involve D's providing **both** statements and services, within the one transaction. Not a great deal turns on that, as the extended *Hedley Byrne* principle enables liability to be imposed in respect of any negligence which can be proven in respect of the service too. The categorisation of economic loss claims is much more difficult, however, in cases such as *Smith v Eric S Bush*, where C ended up with a defective structure, but was able to bring the claim in negligent misstatement (with all the assistance which the *Hedley Byrne/Caparo* tests provided). C would not have been nearly so fortunate, had that case been considered as a defective structure, against which English law has rather turned its face (as discussed in 'Defective buildings', online).

The two cases commonly attributed with the development of this area are *Henderson v Merrett Syndicates Ltd*[81] and *White v Jones.*[82] By coincidence, both were heard by an identically-constituted House of Lords. Although *Henderson* was heard subsequent to the case of *White v Jones*, the latter was delayed some six months after *Henderson* was handed down. As Lord Goff admitted in *White v Jones*, a **strict** application of *Hedley Bryne* could **not** give rise to any liability for pure economic loss in that case. Of course, at a very elementary level, *Hedley Byrne* concerned statements, whereas *White v Jones* concerned a solicitor's professional services. However, and significantly, there was detrimental reliance on D's part in *Hedley Byrne* (i.e., the advertising agency could have withheld placing the advertisements on Easipower's part), whereas there was no detrimental reliance in *White v Jones* (as noted above, C had no choice but to rely on D's professional services) and yet, a duty of care was upheld in *White*, because the court was prepared to 'fashion a remedy to fill a lacuna in the law' (per Lord Goff[83]), and because 'the law in this area has not ossified' (as Lord Browne-Wilkinson put it[84]).

Hence, the goal-posts moved considerably, in light of both decisions. That has subsequently been judicially admitted – e.g., in *BP plc v AON Ltd*,[85] Colman J remarked that it was clear from *White v Jones* that the majority, 'appreciated that they were recognising a **new** set of circumstances in which there could be an undertaking of responsibility which gave rise to liability for pure economic loss'.

Any duty of care requires that C and D be in a 'special relationship', according to Lord Browne-Wilkinson in *White v Jones*[86] – a label that, with respect, means very little, without descending into a close analysis of the facts and circumstances (a point emphasised by Lord Hoffmann in *Customs and Excise*, a case regarding the negligent provision of banking services). Notably, that 'special relationship' can exist, even where D assumes responsibility for C's affairs **but** where there was no contractual relationship between C and D at all (i.e., where D was acting pursuant to a contract with another party, X).

[78] [1995] 2 AC 145 (HL) 180 (Lord Goff). [79] [1964] AC 465 (HL) 530–32, cited *ibid.*
[80] [1998] 1 WLR 830 (HL) 834 (emphasis added). [81] [1995] 2 AC 145 (HL). [82] [1995] 2 AC 207 (HL).
[83] *ibid*, 268, and 275 (Lord Browne-Wilkinson). [84] *ibid*, 276.
[85] [2006] EWHC 424 (Comm) [75] (emphasis added). [86] [1995] 2 AC 207 (HL) 275–76.

Relevant scenarios and legal reasoning

§4.9 Under the extended *Hedley Byrne* principle, the same tests apply to negligent provision of services as applied to negligent misstatement – the *Hedley Byrne* voluntary assumption/reliance test; the *Caparo* test; and the incremental test. The extended *Hedley Byrne* principle has been applied to the provision of services relating to, e.g.: insurance underwriting; legal; building security; banking; and medical.

The same tests as applied in the case of the narrow *Hedley Byrne* negligent misstatement principle, and all of the salient factors outlined above, apply to the establishment of a duty of care under the extended *Hedley Byrne* principle too. Just as with the narrow *Hedley Byrne* principle, in very few cases will the factors all point unambiguously in one direction (and dissenting judgments are fairly frequent too!).

The tri-partite relationship in negligent provision of services

Is a duty of care owed along the dotted line?

C (*two daughters; Commr of Customs and Excise; the indirect Names; the franchisee; Islington LBC; West Bromwich Albion Football Club*)

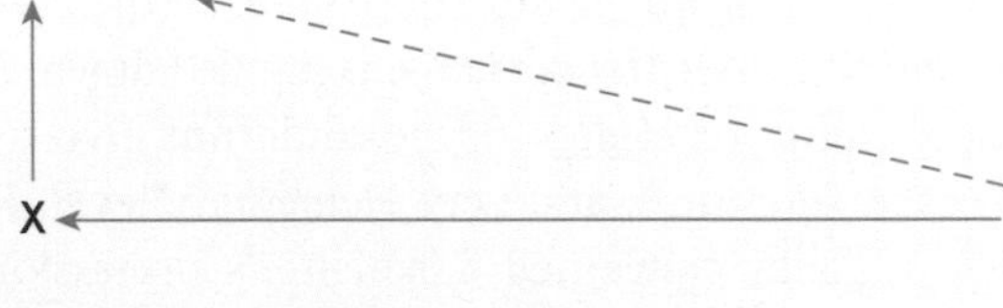

D (*solicitor Mr Jones; Barclays Bank; the managing agents; Mr Mistlin, director; UCL NHS Trust; surgeon Dr El-Safty*)

X

(*testator, Mr Barrett;*
the two companies, Brightstar and Doveblue;
the intermediary agent; the company, Natural Health Foods;
Mrs J; Michael Appleton)

Leading cases

- Insurance underwriting services:

In *Henderson v Merrett Syndicates Ltd*,[87] D was a managing agent at Lloyd's Insurance, and offered underwriting services to a syndicate of, first, direct names (i.e., those who entered into an underwriting agency agreement with the managing agent), and secondly, indirect names (i.e., those who entered into an underwriting agency agreement with a 'names agent', who had, in turn, entered into a managing agency agreement on behalf of those names with the managing agent, D). Hence, there was no privity of contract between the indirect names and D, and the underwriting services were delegated by the indirect names, via their names agent, to D. Both direct names and indirect names, C, suffered financial losses, when unprecedented claims were made on Lloyd's underwriters because of expensive natural disasters, especially in the US. The forms of agreement used by C and D were pro forma standard agreements which could not be negotiated. **Held:** a duty of care was owed by D to both sets of names, direct and indirect. D assumed a responsibility to take reasonable care of their choice of insurance risk, and their reliance was an 'inseparable facet' of their relationship with D, as they entrusted D with the conduct of their underwriting business.

[87] [1995] 2 AC 145 (HL).

The factors in play

- ***the incremental test:*** in *Punjab National Bank v de Boinville*,[a] a duty of care was owed by an insurance broker, D, not only to his client, but also to a specific person whom he knew was to become an assignee of the insurance policy. By analogy, a duty of care could likewise be owed by managing agents at Lloyd's to a name who was a member of a syndicate under the management of agents;
- ***scope of expertise:*** managing agents, D, held themselves out as possessing a special expertise to advise C on the suitability of risks to be underwritten;
- ***significance of the transaction:*** C was giving authority to D to bind them to sometimes large contracts of insurance and reinsurance, and to the settlement of claims.

[a] [1992] 1 Lloyd's Rep 7 (CA).

- Legal services:

In *White v Jones*,[88] Mr Barrett, 78, quarrelled with his two daughters, C, and he executed a new will, cutting them out of his estate. In June, they made up, so Mr Barrett instructed his solicitor, Mr Jones, D, to draft a new will, giving each daughter a legacy of £9,000. Those instructions were received by D in July, but due to holidays, workload, etc, the next available appointment to meet with Mr Barrett was for 17 September. Mr Barrett went on holiday in the meantime, and he fell and hit his head, from which he died on 14 September, before the new will was executed. C were 'disappointed beneficiaries', and sued D for negligence. **Held (3:2):** a duty of care was owed by D to C, to act with expedition and care in relation to drawing up the new will and having it executed. In *Carr-Glynn v Frearsons (a firm)*,[89] another disappointed beneficiary case, Mrs Larder, the testator, was joint tenant with her brother, in the property, 'Homelands'. That joint tenancy was not effectively severed by the solicitor acting for the testator, D, and converted to a tenancy in common. Hence, the testator's share in the property passed to her joint tenant on her death, and not to her financially hard-up niece, Helen, C, via her will, for whom the testator wanted to make specific provision. **Held:** a duty of care was owed by D to C, and C recovered the loss.

The factors in play

- ***a lacuna in the law:*** there was a gap (of 'cardinal importance', per Lord Goff), because if D was negligent in carrying out the instructions, and that did not come to light until after the testator's death, then the disappointed beneficiaries, C, would have no remedy for obtaining their legacies, unless D owed them a duty of care. Once the testator had died, any alleged negligence could not be fixed for C's benefit – whereas if the mistake was evident before the testator died, then he could insist to D that his instructions were carried out or sue if he did not. Also, the Contracts (Rights of Third Parties) Act 1999 did not apply here, so C could not take advantage of its provisions either. The testator's estate could sue D for failing to carry out his instructions in a timely manner – but

[88] [1995] 2 AC 207 (HL) (Lords Goff, Browne-Wilkinson and Nolan; with Lords Keith and Mustill dissenting), and with quotes in the Table at: 254, 275–76.

[89] [1998] EWCA Civ 1325.

the testator did not suffer any loss from D's failing to put his instructions into effect. Hence, the persons who suffered the loss (the daughters, C) had no claim, and the person who had the claim (the testator) suffered no loss;

- ***no conflict of duties:*** D owed a duty to the testator, when asked by him to draft the will, and D also owed a simultaneous duty to the intended beneficiaries, C. That co-existence of duties was recognised in New Zealand for 15 years in *Ross v Caunters*,[a] and 'we can say, with some confidence, that a direct remedy by the intended beneficiary against the solicitor appears to create no problems in practice'. Besides, where the testator gave D instructions to convey legacies to C, then there could be no realistic conflict of interest between the testator and C: 'the duties owed by the solicitors to the testator and to the specific legatee are not inconsistent. They are complementary' (per Chadwick LJ in *Carr-Glynn*);
- ***the intended recipient:*** D's assumption of responsibility to the testator was to be treated, legally, as if it were an assumption of responsibility to C – '[i]t is not to the point that the solicitor only entered on the task pursuant to a contract with the third party (i.e. the testator)';
- ***sole repository:*** where the testator gave instructions to D about changing his will, D knew that Cs' economic well-being was wholly dependent upon his carefully carrying out his function. No-one else could do that: D was the sole repository of the responsibility for performing the professional services for the testator;
- ***scope of expertise:*** D had the skill and expertise to carry out the testator's task of drafting the will;
- ***the incremental test:*** in cases in which *a fiduciary*, D, is liable to a beneficiary, C, any liability arising from that relationship is not dependent upon actual reliance by C on D's actions, but rather, on the fact that the fiduciary, D, 'is well aware [that C's] economic well-being is dependent upon the proper discharge by the fiduciary of his duty'. Incrementally, then, D could be liable to the disappointed beneficiaries here;
- ***no indeterminate liability:*** given the limited number of designated beneficiaries in the will (i.e., two here), there could be no prospect of any duty of care being owed to the whole world. Plus the principle would be applied very narrowly – there would be very few cases where a testator died prior to his instructions being given effect to, meaning that the mistake could not be rectified, and thus requiring a duty of care to be imposed on D.

[a] [1980] Ch 297.

In *Vinton v Fladgate Fielders (a firm)*,[90] the court acknowledged that *Carr-Glynn* was an extension of the principle in *White v Jones*, because it did not concern 'pure will-making', but extended to the solicitor D's failure to advise the testator of the need to serve a notice of severance to her joint tenant, to ensure that her share actually could be passed on by her will. It concerned legal services, in a wider context than in *White v Jones*, but in a similar scenario where D's error could not be fixed.

- **Building security systems (e.g., fire alarm):**

  In *Hines v King Sturge LLP*,[91] Vancouver Muffin Co, C, a tenant, sued King Sturge, D, a commercial property management company, for a fire at a Glasgow property where D was property manager. By

[90] [2010] EWHC 904 (Ch) [24].
[91] [2010] CSIH 86, 2011 SLT 2 (Lords Osborne and Emslie; Lord Carloway dissenting).

the time that the fire was brought under control, much of the building had been destroyed. It had a fire alarm system fitted, which relied upon an alarm signal being transmitted, by way of a dedicated telephone line, to the Strathclyde Fire & Rescue Service; but the telephone line linking the alarm system to the monitoring control room had been disconnected. D was aware that this was because the building owners had not paid their British Telecom accounts. D (although not responsible for that non-payment) knew of that position, and suggested to the fire authorities that they (D) would attend to the reconnection of the telephone line. That never happened, and at the time of the fire, the monitoring element of the system was not operational. C alleged that D, as managing agents, owed a duty of care to all tenants of the building to exercise reasonable care in the maintenance of the fire alarm system (although C's losses were not specified, the case proceeded on the basis that they were 'financial losses'). **Held (2:1):** a duty of care by D to C was arguable, and the claim could not be struck out.

The factors in play

- ***sole repository:*** the building's tenants, including C, had no way of knowing that the dedicated telephone line had been disconnected on account of unpaid British Telecom accounts. They assumed that they were paying a service charge which met the costs of the fire alarm system. They could not know of the disconnection via any source other than D, which helped to prove a degree of reliance by C upon D to perform their duties with reasonable care;
- ***incremental test:*** the Occupiers Liability (Scotland) Act 1960 recognised the potential for landlords to owe tortious duties of care to tenants – and a landlord's agent could owe duties of care to those tenants by analogy;
- ***identified C:*** C was one of a finite class of tenants of that building, whose properties and businesses were at risk if the alarm monitoring device was not working properly.

- Banking services:

In *Customs and Excise Commr v Barclays Bank plc*,[92] two companies, Brightstar Systems Ltd and Doveblue Ltd, held accounts with Barclays Bank, D. Both owed the Commr, C, large sums of unpaid VAT. The Commr obtained freezing (Mareva) injunctions[93] against each company, to stop them transferring £1.8m for Brightstar, and almost £4m for Doveblue, from specified accounts out of the jurisdiction, to defeat any judgments that the Commr might obtain against them. The injunctions were served on D by fax, but two to three hours later, D authorised payments out of these accounts at the companies' requests. There was no prospect of the VAT sums ever being recovered by C. It was assumed that D negligently permitted the payments. **Held:** D did not owe C a duty of care. The *Hedley Byrne* test could not be met – and neither could the *Caparo* test (foreseeability and proximity were met, but the third limb, *viz* policy, was not).

[92] [2006] UKHL 28, [2007] 1 AC 181, with quotes in the Table at: [17]–[18], [21], [23], [39], [61], [74], [102].
[93] Per CPR 25.1(f).

The factors in play

- ***no assumption of responsibility by D:*** when this Mareva injunction was granted, Barclays Bank, D, was restrained from disposing of, or dealing with, the bank accounts. However, this did not equate to D's assuming any responsibility towards C. D was legally obliged to comply with the injunction, it had no choice about the matter, and if it did not, it was exposed to a contempt of court order (the bank 'has not, in any meaningful sense, made a voluntary assumption of responsibility. It has, by the freezing order, had responsibility thrust upon it': per Lord Walker). D did not assume responsibility, as the Bank assumed responsibility to the advertising agency in *Hedley Byrne*, or the reference-writer assumed responsibility to Mr Spring in *Spring v Guardian Assurance*, or the valuers assumed responsibility towards the mortgagor–prospective purchaser in *Smith/Harris* (Lord Bingham CJ);
- ***no reliance:*** there was no detrimental reliance either. Reliance at law usually meant that, if A had not relied on B, he would have acted differently. However, C could not have acted any differently, since it had sought a Mareva injunction and availed itself of the only remedy which the law provided;
- ***lack of fairness:*** Mareva injunctions were relatively common – and although banks were the usual recipients of the orders, sometimes a garage which is looking after X's car might be 'startled to receive notification of a freezing order. This puts him in essentially the same position as a bank which is notified of an order. Usually, he will do his best to respect the order and to hold on to the car. Should the law add to his burdens, however, by exposing him to an uninsured liability in damages, if he fails to take the care which is ultimately considered to be reasonable and the addressee makes off with the car?' (Lord Rodger);
- ***the intended recipient:*** once ordered, the intended recipient of D's compliance with a Mareva injunction could only be the court, not C. The Mareva jurisdiction was judicially developed in the 1970s, enforceable only by the court's power to punish those who broke the injunction via contempt of court. There had never been any suggestion of another remedy being available to C, for whose benefit the injunction was granted: '[t]his regime makes perfect sense on the assumption that the only duty owed by a notified party [D] is to the court' (Lord Bingham CJ);
- ***an omission:*** this failure to comply with a court order is analogous to a failure to comply with a statutory duty imposed upon D. In neither case can the mere failure to comply give rise to an actionable duty of care in negligence (absent some assumption of responsibility on D's part, which was missing here). 'The question of whether the order can have generated a duty of care is comparable with the question of whether a statutory duty can generate a common law duty of care. The answer is that it cannot (per *Gorringe v Calderdale MBC*[a]). The statute either creates a statutory duty or it does not ... you cannot derive a common law duty of care directly from a statutory duty. Likewise, ... you cannot derive one from an order of court. The order carries its own remedies, and its reach does not extend any further' (Lord Hoffmann);
- ***the prospect of indeterminate liability:*** it would be unjust and unreasonable for the bank D to be notified of an order that it had no opportunity to resist, and that it could then be liable for a judgment like this – in this case, 'for a few million pounds only, but might, in another case, be for very much more' (Lord Bingham CJ);
- ***the incremental test:*** C could not show any analogous case to support their argument that a duty was owed to them; no case 'on examination, reveal[ed] any real similarity' (Lord Bingham CJ);
- ***the availability of insurance:*** it was likely that this D would be covered under D's blanket insurance policy, 'the terms of which are typically of extreme width' – but if third parties (other than banks) breached a Mareva injunction, it was 'not so obvious that they will have, or could obtain, insurance to cover the risk of negligent release' of assets or monies (Lord Mance).

[a] [2004] 1 WLR 1057 (CA).

- **Medical services:** In most cases, medical services negligently undertaken by D will cause personal injury to the patient, but in less common cases, that negligence will visit pure economic losses on a connected third party, C.[94] The three cases below demonstrate different ways that such loss can come about, *viz*, where employer C is financially affected by D's medical treatment of D's employee; where institutional carer D is put to the costs of caring for D's negligently-treated patient; or in cases of failed sterilisation affecting the patient's partner, and not the patient himself.

In *West Bromwich Albion FC Ltd v El-Safty*,[95] professional footballer Michael Appleton signed a 3.5-year contract with football club, WBA, C, in Jan 2001. In Nov 2001, the player suffered a serious injury to his right posterior cruciate ligament in training, and he was referred to Dr El-Safty, D, for surgery. Reconstruction of the player's knee was unsuccessful, and he was forced to retire. It was conceded that D's advice to the player was negligent, and that had he been treated conservatively, he would have recovered within four months, and returned to professional football. C suffered economic loss, because the player's value in the transfer market was considerably reduced, and C was put to the cost of replacing him ('potentially several million pounds'). D had treated over 30 players for C. **Held:** D did not owe C a duty of care. In *Islington LBC v Univ College London NHS Trust*,[96] Mrs J, the patient, was advised by a receptionist employed by the NHS Trust, D, not to recommence taking Warfarin, after her heart operation was postponed. Ten days later, Mrs J suffered a serious and disabling stroke. Thereafter, Mrs J required institutional care, funded by her local authority, Islington LBC, C, who was under a statutory duty to provide care accommodation for Mrs J. That care was provided for five years, but because of relevant legislation governing the NHS, D could not recover the costs of care from Mrs J, who was unable to pay due to lack of personal resources. Hence, C sought to recover those costs from D, whose employee's negligence had caused the stroke. **Held:** no duty of care was owed by D to C. In *Goodwill v British Pregnancy Advisory Service*,[97] Mr McKinlay, the patient, underwent a vasectomy, and was then advised by the BPAS, D (a charity which arranged the operation and counselling) of 'permanent sterility'. He was not warned of the risk of spontaneous reversal which occurred. Ms Goodwill, C, entered into a relationship with Mr McKinlay, and ceased other forms of contraception, in reliance on the vasectomy, but conceived a child three years after her partner's vasectomy operation. C sued D for expenses re her daughter's birth, and for the costs of raising her. **Held:** no duty of care was owed.

The factors in play

- ***lack of temporal proximity:*** C's forming a relationship with Mr McKinlay and conceiving three years after the negligence in not warning about the spontaneous reversal (*Goodwill*), and any costs of care incurred for a negligently-treated patient 'some substantial time' later (*Islington*), were significant in precluding proximity;
- ***no knowledge of C's identity:*** Ms Goodwill was not in a 'known or identifiable' category of partners, except for the class of 'future sexual partners' when the vasectomy was performed (*Goodwill*), while the Islington LBC was in the class of 'potential carers' of Mrs J (*Islington*), creating

[94] See: Mulheron, *Medical Negligence: Non-Patient and Third Party Claims* (Ashgate, 2010), ch 7.
[95] [2006] EWCA Civ 1299, affirming: [2005] EWHC 2866. The player himself recovered £1.5m in damages in his personal action against D: *Appleton v El-Safty* [2007] EWHC 631 (QB).
[96] [2005] EWCA Civ 596, [2006] LGR 50. [97] (1996) 31 BMLR 83 (CA) 91.

insufficient proximity (whereas WBA was known, as a specific entity, to Dr El-Safty, but that was insufficient to establish a duty of care in *WBA*);

- ***lack of independent enquiry:*** in *Goodwill*, C should not have been content with 'receiving [BPAS's] advice at second hand', but should have made some independent enquiry about contraceptive measures;
- ***absence of reliance:*** in *WBA v El-Safty*, WBA's reliance on D was not financial (i.e., to protect their financial well-being), but rather, was medical (i.e., to look after the health of their employee, Michael Appleton). The Court of Appeal did not explore the proposition that these interests could be entirely coincident, from WBA's perspective, i.e., whilst interested in his medical welfare, it was also vitally interested in its investment!
- ***conflicts of interest:*** any risk that surgeon D would place a duty to avoid causing financial loss to C above his already-existing duty towards his own patient, had to be precluded, by not finding a duty of care (*WBA v El-Safty*) – although it was difficult to see how those duties could have been at odds here (e.g., there was no suggestion that D's medical treatment of Michael Appleton would be compromised by a short-term gain to C in getting him back onto the field more quickly);
- ***floodgates concerns:*** if medical staff, D, were liable to Islington, as an institutional carer, for the costs of caring for a negligently-treated patient, then so too, many others in the same boat of outlaying costs for patient care could claim similarly (*Islington*), and if WBA was entitled to a claim against D, then other employers would similarly be able to sue doctors who negligently-treated their employees and caused the employer financial loss (*WBA*);
- ***parliamentary intent:*** in *Islington*, it was two public authorities in dispute (an NHS Trust and a local authority), both with different sources of public funding, and it was wrong to use the law of negligence to shift the loss away from where it lay (i.e., on the local authority): 'the sorting out of the present position, accidental or not, would seem to be essentially a matter for Parliament, or at least for political decision, rather than for a court deciding a particular case';
- ***insurance availability:*** in *WBA*, it was unreasonable to expect a surgeon to insure against additional loss of an economic kind, suffered by someone other than his patient; that insurance against financial loss 'naturally lies with the employers'. This helped to preclude any duty of care being owed to employer C;
- ***disclaimer of liability:*** in *WBA*, Dr El-Safty had no contract with WBA, C, and could not disclaim liability; had WBA indicated that it wanted D's advice for the purposes of looking after its own interests, then D would have been in a position where he could charge for that advice and disclaim liability;
- ***lack of fairness:*** under the 'artificial' principle in *Hunt v Severs*, D does not owe a duty of care to a private carer. Rather, D owes a duty of care to the injured party, and the law imposes a 'notional payment in respect of that liability by the injured party to that carer'. Hence, if institutional carers were owed a duty of care by D, then it would create a different entitlement as between institutional carer and private carer (*Islington*).

White v Jones: testamentary versus *inter vivos* transactions, and other extensions

§4.10 The extended *Hedley Byrne* principle is being cautiously extended on a case-by-case basis. For example: *White v Jones* concerned a testamentary disposition, i.e., a transaction (will) which was to take effect upon death. However, its principle has since been extended to include *inter-vivos* transactions (i.e., those intended to take effect during the life of the contracting parties).

The fact that *White v Jones*[98] concerned a will was very important, in upholding the duty of care to the disappointed beneficiaries – the 'lacuna in the law', in that the testator could not fix any negligence on D's part so as to rectify the disappointment of his daughters, was clearly evident. It was Mr Barrett's incapacity to remedy matters which brought the daughters and Mr Jones, the solicitor, within the realms of a 'special relationship'. For *inter vivos* transactions, however, any mistakes on D's part can, arguably, be fixed during the client's lifetime (should the client wish to fix the mistake). Lord Browne-Wilkinson drew this distinction:

> in transactions *inter vivos*, the transaction takes immediate effect, and the consequences of solicitors' negligence are immediately apparent. When discovered, they can either be rectified (by the parties) or damages recovered by the client. But in the case of a negligently drawn will, the will has no effect at all until the [testator's] death. It will have been put away in the deed box, not to surface again until the testator either wishes to vary it, or dies ... the negligence will lie hidden until it takes effect on the death of the testator, i.e. at the very point in time when normally the error will become incapable of remedy.

– as did Lord Goff:

> take the example of an *inter vivos* gift where, as a result of the solicitor's negligence, the instrument in question is for some reason not effective for its purpose ... I do not think that the intended donee could, in these circumstances, have any claim against the solicitor. It is enough, as I see it, that the donor is able to do what he wishes to put matters right.

However, in *Richards v Hughes*,[99] the court noted that anything said on that point in *White v Jones* was dicta only, and the remarks had never been applied directly to a case. Since *White v Jones*, there have been several attempts to extend the principle to other contexts too (such as the provision of tax advice) – strongly resisted by D, on the basis that they constitute unwarranted extensions of what was a novel development of the law in any event. However, some courts have been prepared to extend the boundaries of the *White v Jones* principle, by denying D's strike-out application.

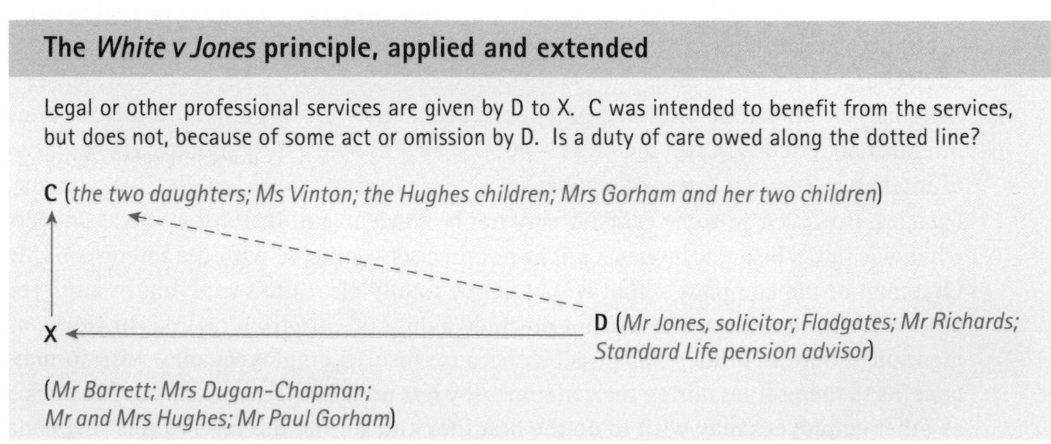

Summarising the leading cases, with reference to their illustration in the diagram above:

[98] [1995] 2 AC 207 (HL), with quotes respectively at 276 and 262. [99] [2004] EWCA Civ 266, [27].

In *Vinton v Fladgate Fielder (a firm)*,[100] the law firm, Fladgates, D, provided tax advice to Mrs Dugan-Chapman. She was shareholder in a family company, Wilton, and at a time when she became seriously ill, the company needed an injection of funds. D advised Mrs Dugan-Chapman to reorganise her shareholdings so that her residuary beneficiaries (including Ms Vinton, C) would not have to pay inheritance tax upon her death. However, the advice turned out to be inaccurate because of how the shares had been acquired. According to HMRC, the residuary beneficiaries had to pay significant sums (approx. £360,000). **Held:** a duty of care was arguably owed by D to C; the strike-out application failed. In *Richards v Hughes*,[101] Mr and Mrs Hughes asked Mr Richards, D, a chartered accountant, to set up a trust fund for the benefit of their children's future education expenses. The trust fund ended up having little capital value. The children, C, sued D in negligence, alleging that he had failed to monitor the performance of the trust fund, and had failed to inform their parents of the erosion of capital value by charges and other outgoings. **Held:** a duty of care was arguably owed by D to C; the strike-out application failed. In *Gorham v British Telecom plc*,[102] Mr Gorham, as an employee of BT, was eligible to join the BT occupational pension scheme, but he did not join it, nor did he send back the opting-out form either (nor were any deductions being made from his payslips). He also had pension rights with his ex-employee, Cable & Wireless, with Standard Life. Mr Gorham ceased making contributions to the Standard Life scheme that would have entitled his wife and two children, C, to extra benefits when he died (Mr Gorham died at just 35). C sued Standard Life, alleging that Standard Life owed them a duty of care, as potential beneficiaries of the arrangements for insurance cover which had been advised to Mr Gorham by Standard Life, and they also sued BT for failing to make the situation about pension entitlement plainer to Mr Gorham. **Held (first instance):** both Ds owed C a duty of care, but causation failed, because of the inactivity of Mr Gorham to follow advice and to follow up gaps in information. **Held (CA, 3:0):** both D's owed C a duty, per *White v Jones* (but causation again failed, by majority).

In *Vinton v Fladgate Fielder*,[103] Norris J stated that, 'the implications of *White v Jones* are being explored case by case' (citing *Richards v Hughes*[104] in that regard). Clearly, the above-mentioned body of case law supports an extension of the ratio in *White v Jones*, notwithstanding that:

i. the transaction extends beyond legal services, and may concern professional tax, pensions or insurance advice, and where D is someone other than a solicitor (e.g., accountants, pension advisers);
ii. there may be an actual, or even a potential, conflict between D's client on the one hand, and the intended beneficiary, C, on the other – but D may still owe a duty of care. There was no conflict of interest in *White v Jones*, of course, because Mr Barrett wanted to give his two daughters the legacies. However, in some cases, it may not be so clear-cut. In *Vinton*, it was conceivable that what was in C's best tax interests might not precisely coincide with the interests of Mrs Dugan-Chapman or the company – that would not be totally clear until trial, but in any event, even a potential conflict of interest did not preclude a duty of care from arising. In *Gorham*,[105] it was mentioned that a conflict was possible, because insured employees may wish to maximise the benefits to themselves during their lifetimes (by less premium deductions per pay packet), whereas other employees may wish to do the best they can for the interests to their dependants – but

[100] [2010] EWHC 904 (Ch). [101] [2004] EWCA Civ 266. [102] [2000] EWCA Civ 234.
[103] [2010] EWHC 904 (Ch) [24]. [104] [2004] EWCA Civ 266, [25] (Peter Gibson LJ).
[105] [2000] EWCA Civ 234, [2000] 1 WLR 2129, 2141–42.

even so, a potential conflict of interest was no obstacle to the recognition of a potential duty of care in C's favour. If there is a conflict of duties on the facts, though, then it may be more difficult to say that D assumed any responsibility to the intended beneficiary, and on that point, no duty to C may be feasible (per *Steven v Hewats*[106]);

iii. the intended beneficiary may have been **both** the giver and receiver of information. The beneficiaries in *White v Jones* were entirely 'passive recipients' of the transaction (the solicitor D was given the names by the testator and needed to make no further enquiry) – but not all intended beneficiaries will be entirely passive, some instructions may be needed from them. In *Vinton*, Mrs Dugan-Chapman and the residuary beneficiaries were all interested in raising capital in an 'inheritance tax efficient way', and gave instructions to that effect; and in *Gorham*, Mrs Gorham had received personal correspondence from D and was asked to confirm that recommendations made by D had been received and understood;

iv. the intended beneficiary, C, may have been advised by solicitor D to obtain separate legal advice for the transaction for which D was advising his client (as noted, e.g., in *Steven v Hewats*[107]);

v. the error on D's part may be discovered during the client's lifetime, enabling that client to instruct D to fix the problem, or to sue D himself for at least some of the loss – all of which was impossible in *White v Jones* itself. However, wherever the mistake cannot be rectified, that leaves a gap in redress, for which the *White v Jones* principle can apply. For example, in *Richards*, the problem was that 'the consequences were not immediately apparent, but only emerged several years after the scheme which the parents intended to enter into was implemented; only then was the loss of the investment discovered'.[108]

Hence, given the numerous features which distinguish these cases from the *White v Jones* scenario (1995), it is evident that the 'extended *Hedley Byrne* principle' is constantly evolving. As commented by the Court of Appeal in *Richards v Hughes*, the area is one which is 'still subject to some uncertainty and developing', and hence, it is more difficult to strike out a claim in that circumstance, where 'any development of the law should be on the basis of actual, and not hypothetical, facts'.[109] Notwithstanding, however, a recent attempt to extend *White v Jones*, and to bring a novel case of alleged negligence within the extended principle of *Hedley Byrne*, failed, with a categorical finding that the third limb of *Caparo* had failed, and that no useful purpose would be served by the continuation of the litigation (per *James-Bowen v Commr of Police*[110]). Even so, claimants are constantly pushing at the boundaries of *White v Jones's* principle, and for every strike-out application which fails, the door is opened just a little further ajar, in the field of professional negligence liability.

PURE RELATIONAL ECONOMIC LOSS

The scenario

§4.11 Under the exclusionary rule, where D negligently causes damage to property owned by a third party (TP), C cannot recover any pure economic loss (i.e., lost profits) which he suffers as a result of that damage to TP's property, where C possesses (at most) a contractual right to use that property, falling short of a proprietary or possessory interest in that property. For policy reasons, English law does not regard C's pure economic loss as being recoverable damage.

[106] [2013] CSOH 61, [13]. [107] [2013] CSOH 61, [6]. [108] [2004] EWCA Civ 266, [27].
[109] *ibid*, [30]. [110] [2015] EWHC 1249 (QB).

The exclusionary rule actually originated in the negligence/*Rylands v Fletcher* case of *Cattle v Stockton Waterworks Co*[111] (as described in Chapter 17). It has been applied consistently since then, in the context of both of these torts (and in private nuisance, of which *Rylands v Fletcher* is a subspecies, discussed in Chapter 16). This chapter will concentrate upon the manifestation of the principle in negligence.

What C is seeking to claim here is a form of pure economic loss (also called 'relational economic loss'), but it cannot be recovered in English law for policy reasons. To clarify, it is properly classified as 'pure economic loss', because C himself has suffered no property damage. Significantly, C possesses no proprietary or possessory interest in TP's property (per *The Aliakmon*[112]). It is TP's property which was damaged, and hence, any economic losses claimed by C must be 'pure', and not consequential. C's economic losses may be caused because he had contractual relations with TP which entitled C to use TP's property to earn income; or C's economic losses may arise regardless of any contractual relations with TP. Either way, C cannot recover those losses.

The scenario is summarised in the Diagram below (with key cases italicised for convenience):

The exclusionary rule (*aka* relational economic loss) in negligence

Imagine that an essential facility (e.g., an electricity cable, bridge, telephone line, oil supply line, seawater farms) is owned by **TP** (*Midlands Elec Board; oil pipeline owned by WLPS/UKOP; Public Works Canada; AOR; various salmon farmers; livestock farmers affected by FMD*) –

D negligently damages/destroys that essential facility (*Martin; Total, the owners of the Buncefield oil depot at Hemel Hempstead; the tug operators Norsk; the dredge operators; Braer Corp; DEFRA*)

C uses the facility owned by TP (*Spartan Steel; fuel company Shell; Canadian National Rwy; Caltex Oil; Landcatch, the grower of salmon smolt; livestock farmers*)

- C usually has a contract with TP for use of TP's facility or property, for C's business or profit-making endeavours. C relies upon that facility or property to be undamaged, for his economic welfare, and his economic welfare suffers a downturn because the essential facility is out of action or the property is damaged;
- TP can sue D for his *own* property damage. But TP won't be either able or willing to sue D for C's economic losses (claiming them as his own consequential losses)
- hence, for C, the financial loss which he suffers is *pure* (and not consequential) economic loss;
- C cannot sue D in contract for the financial losses suffered, because there is no contract between them. Hence, there is a 'lacuna in the law' – TP, as owner of the facility or property, has the potential to claim, but has not suffered the particular economic loss suffered by C; whereas C has suffered the economic loss, but does not have any claim (unless the law of tort steps in to impose a duty of care on D in C's favour);
- for this particular lacuna, English law has not created a right of remedy for C. Tort law will not assist C.

[111] (1874–75) LR 10 QB 453 (Div Ct).

[112] *Leigh & Sillivan Ltd v Aliakmon Shipping Co Ltd* [1986] AC 785 (HL) 809 (Lord Brandon).

The governing policy reasons

The *Spartan Steel* analysis

C's problem, in this scenario, is that he has suffered a type of loss which falls outside the boundaries of what English law regards as being recoverable damages – strictly for policy reasons. Indeed, in *Spartan Steel and Alloys Ltd v Martin & Co (Contractors) Ltd*, Lord Denning MR candidly admitted that, 'the question of recovering economic loss is one of policy. Whenever the Courts draw a line to mark out the bounds of duty, they do it as matter of policy, so as to limit the responsibility of [D]'.[113]

> In *Spartan Steel v Martin & Co*, Spartan Steel, C, manufactured stainless steel in a Birmingham factory which was powered via an electricity cable from a power station of the Midlands Electricity Board. Martins, D, roadworking contractors, were doing roadworks about 0.25 miles away from C's factory, digging up the road with a power-driven excavating shovel. D enquired about where the cables, mains, etc were under the road, and were given plans showing their location. Unfortunately, D damaged the cable which supplied electricity to C's factory. The Electricity Board shut down the power for the 14.5 hours during C's nightshift, whilst they repaired the cable. At that time, metal was in an arc furnace, being melted in order to be converted into ingots. Electric power was needed throughout, to maintain the temperature and melt the metal. When the power failed, and to avoid the metal solidifying in the furnace and damaging the lining of the furnace, C used oxygen to melt the material and pour it out of the furnace. The loss of the melted material was £368 (loss #1, property damage). The profit that would have been made on that particular melt was £400 (loss #2, consequential economic loss on the property damage). However, during the hours when the power was cut off, C would have been able to put four more melts through, and being unable to do so, they lost a profit of £1,767 (loss #3, pure economic loss). D admitted breach. **Held (2:1):** C could recover losses #1 and #2 (i.e., damages of £768), but D owed C no duty of care to avoid loss #3.

In *Conarken Group Ltd v Network Rail Infrastructure*, Moore-Bick LJ remarked that the fact that the exclusionary rule still applies in English law, more than a century after *Cattle v Stockton*, owes everything to 'reasons of policy rather than principle'.[114] The Table below summarises those reasons, as derived from Lord Denning MR's judgment in *Spartan Steel*:[115]

The factors in play

- ***parliamentary intent:*** if the Midlands Electricity Board did not maintain the cable or shut it down for repairs, then under the governing legislation, Parliament did not intend to expose the Board to liability for damages to the citizens whose lives could be disrupted by the interruption to electricity supply and who suffered financial losses as a result. If the Electricity Board could not be sued for financial losses, then by analogy, 'it would seem right for the common law to adopt a similar policy in regard to contractors [who cause economic loss]';
- ***no lacuna in the law/insurability:*** interruptions to electricity supply could arise from a number of sources, apart from an excavating shovel severing a cable: a short circuit, a flash of lightning, a tree falling on the wires. Supply is usually restored within hours, so that inconvenience and economic losses to C may not be very large. There are three options available to C: either put up with it and

[113] [1973] QB 27 (CA) 36 (Lord Denning MR and Lawton LJ; Edmund Davies LJ dissenting).
[114] [2011] EWCA Civ 644, [95]. [115] [1973] QB 27 (CA), with quotes in Table at 38.

work harder to make up the losses ('they do not go running around to their solicitor'); or install a back-up generator; or take out insurance against the interruption of supply. Consumers and businesses should anticipate, and take on, the risk themselves, rather than seek to place full liability on the contractor, D;

- ***the prospect of indeterminate liability/'floodgates':*** an interruption to electricity supply could give rise to 'no end of claims' – some genuine, some inflated and some made-up. It would be difficult to check the validity and quantum of claims made;
- ***distributive justice:*** where electricity supply is cut, then it is fairer that the consequences are sustained by the whole community who suffer small individual losses, rather than casting the entire loss onto contractor, D;
- ***physical damage is deemed more 'deserving' of compensation:*** where the severance of electricity supply causes actual physical damage to person or property, that physical damage can be recovered at law (and any consequential economic losses, as per, e.g., *British Celanese Ltd v Hunt*[a]). Not only will there be fewer of them, but they are 'readily capable of proof and will be easily checked'.

[a] (1969) 1 WLR 959 (CA).

The last policy reason was aptly demonstrated in a case which was almost identical to *Spartan Steel*, but for one important difference: **all** of C's damages were judicially treated as either property damage or consequential economic loss, and that was recoverable:

> In *SCM (UK) Ltd v WJ Whittall and Son Ltd*,[116] D's employees damaged an electric cable which serviced C's typewriter factory, and the electricity was cut off for several hours. The molten material in C's machines solidified, and the machines were extensively damaged. C lost one day's production. **Held:** D was liable for the costs of repairing the machines, and also for the loss of production on the day of the power failure. This was treated as physical damage to C's property, and the day's lost production as 'economic loss consequent on it'.

As clarified by Jackson LJ in *Conarken Group v Network Rail*, the decision in *SCM* is only explicable on the basis that C could recover damages for loss of production if it were treated as being consequential on damage to the machinery, and not consequential upon the power cut.[117]

One factor which did **not** particularly feature in *Spartan Steel* (because the governing statute ruled out any compensation payable by the electricity supplier TP to Spartan Steel C) – but which **has** been mentioned in other cases, e.g., in the Canadian case of *Canadian National Rwys v Norsk Pacific Steamship Co*[118] – is the so-called 'contractual allocation of risk'. The argument goes that C, the entity using the essential facility owned by TP, will usually (but not always) have a contractual relationship with TP for the use of that essential facility. In that case, C has an opportunity to negotiate with TP the terms of compensation, if C's business is damaged because the essential facility is not available. La Forest J (dissenting) remarked that C and D ought to have considered (or perhaps did consider, as in that case) the issue of allocating the risk of the essential facility's closing or being rendered useless, as a result of D's negligence. In that event, it is unnecessary for tort to step in, to uphold a duty of care in C's favour, because C had a prior opportunity to define where the loss should lie, if D did put the essential facility 'out of action'.

[116] [1971] 1 QB 337 (CA). [117] [2011] EWCA Civ 644, [132]–[134].
[118] (1992), 91 DLR (4th) 289, with quotes at 336–37, and 343, respectively.

Hence, there was no gap in redress, for the opportunity for redress lay entirely in C's control. However, the majority in *Norsk Pacific* (per McLachlin J) considered that the opportunity (or even achievement) of a contractual allocation of loss as between C and D should not deny a duty of care in C's favour. This was because, e.g., 'the parties who control the situation (e.g., the owners of the [essential facility, a bridge in that case]', may have superior bargaining power compared with C; and the argument also tended to ignore the essential concept of negligence, *viz*, to curb negligent conduct by placing liability on the wrongdoer, D. These diverse lines of reasoning have not, as yet, particularly featured in English law, perhaps because of the sparse regard which has been given to this type of pure economic loss since *Spartan Steel.*

The exclusionary rule has been an immutable rule in the context of negligence (as well as for both private nuisance and *Rylands v Fletcher*). In *Shell UK Ltd v Total UK Ltd*, the Court of Appeal noted that it was plain that, in *Cattle v Stockton*, 'the judges were not particularly enamoured of the law that they were laying down', and that, even in 2010, '[d]iffering views about the wisdom of the exclusionary rule are widely held'.[119] Nevertheless, the rule has been frequently applied/upheld in a number of contexts, e.g.:

- the exclusionary rule applies, even where C's pure economic loss was suffered because of damage to TP's property, but where C had **no** contractual relations with TP at all – in such a scenario, C's claim appears even weaker than where C had a contract with TP by which to make a profit or run a business:

  In *D Pride & Partners v Institute for Animal Health*,[120] 14 owners and/or occupiers of livestock farms, C, alleged that DEFRA, D, caused, or failed to prevent, the escape of the foot and mouth disease from its animal research facility at Pirbright in 2007. C's properties were not affected by the virus, but TP's farms were. A prohibition on any livestock movement was imposed, and C lost the chance to take their livestock to market at the most profitable time, had to feed and maintain livestock when otherwise they would have been sold; and some of the stock that would have been sold for breeding had to be sold for meat at a lower price. **Held:** C's claim in negligence failed, as it concerned relational economic loss. Tugendhat J noted that it was a weaker type of claim than usual, because farmers C had no contractual relations with TP, the affected farmers, nor expected to make any profits from their dealings with TP. The relation between C and TP was very slight indeed.

- however, C's scenario will fall outside of the exclusionary rule, if C actually owns the essential facility itself (in a beneficial capacity) – which means that C's claim is not pure economic loss at all, but can be considered to be consequential upon the damage to C's property which D inflicted on the essential facility:

  In *Shell UK Ltd v Total UK Ltd (formerly, Colour Quest Ltd v Total Downstream UK plc)*,[121] explosions at the Buncefield Oil Storage Depot at Hemel Hempstead were caused by an enormous vapour cloud igniting, which had developed from 300 tons of petrol spilling from a storage tank. From the consequent fire, which burned for a long period, there was a substantial impact on the adjacent industrial estate. Total, D, was the joint venturer which owned the Buncefield site. Shell, C, a major fuel company, claimed that significant damage was done to the West London Pipeline System as a result of the explosion, which C did not own, but which C was unable to use, to supply both aviation and ground fuels to customers, except in reduced volumes and/or at increased costs to

[119] [2010] EWCA Civ 180, [2011] QB 86, [134], [143]. [120] [2009] EWHC 685 (QB).
[121] [2010] EWCA Civ 180, [2011] QB 86, overruling: [2009] EWHC 540 (QB (Comm) [409], [471]–[472].

itself. **Held (first instance):** C failed on the basis of the exclusionary rule. **Held (CA):** although the exclusionary rule was recognised, this case fell outside it, as C had a (shared) equitable ownership of the pipelines, which was enough to give C title to claim for property damage and consequential economic loss.

- the exclusionary rule applies in English law, even where the class of potential Cs is a small and finite class. The prospect of indeterminate liability (or 'floodgates') – which was given as an important policy reason in *Spartan Steel* – cannot arise in such a scenario, but nevertheless, the rule applies. This was confirmed in two shipping cases decided in 1986, and in a Scottish case (specifically approved in *D Pride & Partners*[122]), in all of which the affected class comprised just a single C, but where C could not recover, because of the rule:

In *Landcatch Ltd v Intl Oil Pollution Compensation Fund*,[123] Landcatch, C, ran a farm, on which it reared salmon eggs to smolt (juveniles up to two years of age) in freshwater conditions, and then sold them to other farmers, TP, who grew the salmon to maturity in seawater conditions, mostly around Shetland. As a result of an oil spill in the sea off Shetland, caused by the grounding of a vessel by D, the Secretary of State for Scotland designated the affected area an exclusion zone, which included TP's farms to which C contracted to sell their smolt. C suffered economic loss, but this entailed 'nothing more than relational economic loss', notwithstanding that there could only be one C affected in this scenario. In *Candlewood Navigation Corp Ltd v Mitsui Lines Ltd*,[124] D collided with TP's ship, causing it to undergo repairs in dock. C was a time charterer of the vessel, and sued for the profit that it would have made, during that period that TP's vessel was out of operation. No recovery was possible.

The rejection of the principle of 'transferred loss'

§4.12 The principle of 'transferred loss' has not been accepted as part of English law, by which to provide C, who suffers pure economic loss, an avenue of redress by which to avoid the operation of the exclusionary rule.

In *Leigh & Sullivan Ltd v Aliakmon Shipping Co Ltd (The Aliakmon)*,[125] Goff LJ (as he then was, of the Court of Appeal), proposed what he called 'the principle of transferred loss', as an exception to the exclusionary rule, drafted in 'deliberately narrow terms' (D, C and TP are inserted in the following passage as appropriate):

> Where D owes a duty of care in tort not to cause physical damage to TP's property, and D commits a breach of that duty in circumstances in which the loss of or physical damage to the property will ordinarily fall on TP but (as is reasonably foreseeable by D), such loss or damage, by reason of a contractual relationship between TP and C, falls on C, then C will be entitled, subject to the terms of any contract restricting D's liability to TP, to bring an action in tort against D in respect of such loss or damage to the extent that it falls on him, C.

However, that proposal was rejected by the House of Lords. In the view of Lord Brandon,[126] the exclusionary rule was 'simple to understand and easy to apply, [and] has been established by a long line of authority over many years'. No exception could be created for commercial

122 [2009] EWHC 685 (QB) [95].

123 [1998] 2 Lloyd's LR 552 (OH) (Lord Gill), aff'd: [1999] 2 Lloyd's LR 316 (IH).

124 [1986] 1 AC 1 (PC). 125 [1985] 2 WLR 289 (CA) 330. 126 [1986] AC 785 (HL) 816–17.

contracts of sea carriage, as otherwise the certainty of the exclusionary rule 'would be seriously undermined'.

As Lord Goff himself later pointed out in *White v Jones*,[127] this principle of transferred loss did not apply to that case, given that the lost expectation of the two legacies, due to D's negligence, could **never** have been suffered by the testator, but only by C, the disappointed legatees, albeit that there was a 'close analogy'. In any event, the principle has not achieved recognition at the senior appellate level (as noted, e.g., in *Smith v Littlewoods Organisation Ltd*[128]).

Exceptions to the exclusionary rule

§4.13 There are some recognised exceptions to the exclusionary rule, where D negligently causes damage to property owned by a third party (TP), and C can recover pure economic loss which he suffers as a result of that damage to TP's property, because in those particular instances, C and D have sufficient proximity, and policy reasons favour a duty of care.

There are some limited exceptions to the exclusionary rule in negligence, which Tugendhat J noted, in *D Pride & Partners v Institute for Animal Health*, to be case-specific, and not standing for any particular general principle of, say, C's loss being 'analogous to physical damage'.[129] They turn on their own facts.

For example, in *Morrison Steamship Co Ltd v Greystoke Castle (Cargo Owners)*,[130] Lord Roche gave the example of C's goods being loaded onto the back of TP's lorry; and due to D's negligent driving, TP's lorry runs off the road and is damaged; C's goods are not damaged, but the lorry is so badly damaged that the goods have to be unloaded, reloaded and carried on, which may cause C economic loss, if he has to pay for the costs of unloading and reloading. Inevitably, it must be pure economic loss, because the goods themselves were not damaged and, as with the exclusionary rule, it was TP's property that was damaged, and which caused C's loss. But C could recover those losses in that scenario (said Lord Roche). Similarly, in *Greystoke* itself, it was held that, where cargo owners, C, had their goods loaded for transport at sea in TP's ship, and those cargo owners paid in advance a proportion of any damage done to the goods during transit (a form of pooled insurance), and D damaged TP's ship (but not C's own cargo), then each C could recover any pure economic loss arising from unloading, reloading and relating to that undamaged cargo.

The reasoning in *Greystoke* was that, under this arrangement of a 'general average contribution', TP and C were engaged in a relationship of 'joint adventurers at sea'. In *Murphy v Brentwood DC*,[131] the House of Lords reiterated that *Greystoke* turned on the 'specialties of maritime law', and that it was not an assumption of responsibility/reliance scenario as between C and D (hence the reference to proximity and policy, a *Caparo*-type analysis, in the principle above).

Conclusion

The stark refusal of English law to depart from the exclusionary rule is particularly difficult to countenance, when the House of Lords was prepared to step in on behalf of the disappointed beneficiaries in *White v Jones*, so as to recognise a newly-constructed duty of care, precisely to fill a 'lacuna in the law'. The problem was that the only persons who might have a valid claim

[127] [1995] 2 AC 207 (HL) 216. [128] [1987] 2 AC 241 (HL) 280 (Lord Goff).
[129] [2009] EWHC 685 (QB) [83], [120]. [130] [1947] AC 265 (HL) (decided by a narrow majority).
[131] [1991] 1 AC 398 (HL) 406.

(the testator, Mr Barrett, and his estate) had suffered no loss, and the only persons who had suffered a loss (the two daughters, as 'disappointed beneficiaries') had no claim, but for the law stepping in to create a tortious duty of care. The same lacuna is evident under the exclusionary rule, but for which the law will offer C no assistance. Some types of Cs are seemingly more deserving of compensation than others!

A comparative perspective

In other key Commonwealth jurisdictions, the exclusionary rule in English law has been departed from, at the highest appellate level.

The comparative corner: Canada and Australia

Canada: In *Canadian National Rwy v Norsk Pacific Steamship Co*,[132] a barge was being towed down the Fraser River by a tug owned by Norsk, D. The barge collided in heavy fog with the New Westminster railway bridge, which caused extensive damage to the bridge. That bridge, owned by Public Works Canada (PWC), was closed for several weeks. It was used by four railway companies, including CNR, C, who was the bridge's main user. PWC recovered compensation for the property damage from D, but PWC could not sue for C's lost profits during the period that the bridge was closed. Hence, C sued D in negligence for those losses. **Held (4:3):** C was owed a duty of care by D, and was able to recover its pure economic loss.

- ***physical proximity:*** by damaging the bridge, D caused the risk of physical injury to CNR's property, because its trains were frequently on the bridge and could have been damaged during a bridge accident. That danger indicated the closeness between C and D, which was not determinative, but relevant;
- ***vulnerability and reliance:*** CNR's property could not be enjoyed without the link of the bridge because it was an integral part of its railway system; CNR supplied materials, inspection and consulting services for the bridge; and CNR was included in the periodic negotiations surrounding the closing of the bridge;
- ***a common venture (relational proximity):*** PWC and CNR were so closely assimilated that they were in a joint or common venture to use the bridge. CNR could be considered as a joint venturer with PWC as the owner of the property. To deny recovery for CNR would be to deny it to a party who, for practical purposes, was in the same position as if it owned the bridge;
- ***no floodgates possible:*** only four possible Cs existed here. To allow C to recover would not open up the prospect of floodgates to 'casual users of the property'. Also, where contractual relations were in place between TP and C, then potential tortfeasors such as D could gauge in advance the scope of their liability, and insure for it.

Australia: In *Caltex Oil (Aust) Pty Ltd v The Dredge, 'Willemstad'*,[133] an underwater pipeline (four pipes) owned by Australian Oil Refining Ltd carried oil from AOR's refinery on

[132] [1992] 1 SCR 1021 (SCC) (L'Heureux-Dube, Cory, McLachlin, and Stevenson JJ; La Forest, Sopinka and Iacobucci JJ dissenting).

[133] (1975) 136 CLR 529 (HCA).

the southern shore of Botany Bay to Caltex Oil's Banksmeadow oil terminal on the northern shore. That pipeline was negligently severed by the dredge Willemstad, D, while it was deepening a shipping channel in the bay. There were errors recorded on Decca's track plotter chart of D's proposed route in the bay, but D's navigators did not notice the error, which constituted negligence on their part. Caltex Oil, C, had to arrange alternative methods of transporting the oil to its terminal while the pipeline was being repaired. **Held (5:0):** C was owed a duty of care by D, and was able to recover those losses.

- *no floodgates possible:* D's navigators knew that the pipeline led directly from the refinery to C's terminal, and that it was not like a water main or electric cable serving the public generally – C was foreseeable as the entity which would probably suffer economic loss if the pipes were broken, hence, a class of one;
- *close proximity:* D's navigators were obliged to take care to avoid damage to the pipeline, which was shown on the drawing supplied to them for the very purpose of enabling them to avoid it whilst dredging. Hence, they had a close relationship with C;
- *vulnerability:* C could not readily avoid the risk of incurring alternative costs of transportation of the oil awaiting transfer to its terminal;
- *fairness:* to uphold a duty of care by D to C would not curb D's freedom of action, because it already owed a duty of care to AOR, the TP, as the owner of the relevant property (the pipelines).

5

Duty IV – Pure psychiatric injury

INTRODUCTION

Uncertainties and problems

Judicial consternation

It is an unfortunate truism that the topic of negligently-inflicted pure psychiatric illness is afflicted with many vagaries and complexities.[1]

That has been openly admitted, judicially. In *Tredget and Tredget v Bexley HA*,[2] the court described the law, in something of an understatement, as 'by no means straightforward', and that 'the arguments must have seemed to the parents as they listened, to have an air of unreality, but unsatisfactory as the legal frame-work has ... been shown to be, the court can only act within its constraints' – while, in *Taylorson v Shieldness Produce Ltd*, Ralph Gibson LJ remarked that the relevant principles are 'as unconvincing as they are surprising'.[3] Soberingly, even the House of Lords has admitted, in *White v CC of South Yorkshire Police*,[4] that, in this area of law, 'the search for principle has been called off' (per Lord Hoffmann), while in the same case, Lord Steyn despaired that the law 'is [neither] coherent [n]or morally defensible'. Earlier, in *Alcock v CC of South Yorkshire Police*, Lord Oliver stated that the law 'is not wholly logical'.[5]

All of this is, indeed, an unpromising start. The special rules governing whether D owes C a duty of care in this area are among the most judicially-criticised of any area of Tort law.

Law reform consideration

As a hallmark of its controversy, the issue has been the subject of frequent law reform consideration, e.g., by the English Law Commission in 1998,[6] the Australian Ipp Commit-

[1] The author has discussed several of the issues in this chapter elsewhere, from which some of this chapter is drawn, *viz*: 'Rewriting the Requirement for a "Recognized Psychiatric Injury" in Negligence Claims' (2012) 33 *OJLS* 1; *Non-Patient and Third Party Claims* (Ashgate, 2010), ch 5; 'The "Primary Victim" in Psychiatric Illness Claims: Reworking the "Patchwork Quilt"' (2008) 19 *KCLJ* 81; 'Medical Negligence, Secondary Victims and Psychiatric Illness: Family Tragedies and Legal Headaches' in R Probert (ed), *Family Life and the Law* (Ashgate, London, 2007), ch 5; 'Secondary Victim Psychiatric Illness Claims' (2003) 14 *KCLJ* 213.

[2] [1994] 5 Med LR 178 (Central London CC) 179.

[3] [1994] PIQR P329 (CA) 336.

[4] [1999] 2 AC 455 (HL) 511, and with Lord Steyn's quote at 500.

[5] [1992] 1 AC 310 (HL) 417.

[6] *Liability for Psychiatric Illness* (Rep 249, 1998) ('*English Report*'), and the draft Negligence (Psychiatric Illness) Bill.

tee in 2003,[7] the British Columbia Commission in 1992,[8] and the Scottish Law Commission in 2004.[9]

Close to home, both the English and Scottish Commissions recommended statutory reform, such is the disarray in which the case law finds itself, but both remain unenacted. The Department for Constitutional Affairs stated, in 2007, that it rejected the English Law Commission's recommendation to legislate: 'the Government considers it preferable to allow the courts to continue to develop the law in this area'.[10] More recently, the Scottish Government has also rejected the Scottish Law Commission's recommendations for legislative reform.[11] Hence, both the English and Scottish attempts to clarify the law have, so far, fallen upon deaf legislative ears, and that position is unlikely to change.

Nevertheless, some judges have been adamant that Parliament **should** get involved to legislate in this area. In *Walters v North Glamorgan NHS Trust*,[12] the Court of Appeal remarked that if the law needed to be changed to narrow the scope for recovery, then 'Parliament must do it' – a notion that has been repeated by the House of Lords, in *White (Frost) v CC of South Yorkshire Police*,[13] and in *Rothwell v Chemical and Insulating Co Ltd*.[14] More recently, in *Taylor v A Novo (UK) Ltd*,[15] the Court of Appeal also called for legislative intervention – albeit that 'the case law shows that some modest development by the courts may be possible'.

Where appropriate, some law reform insights will be referred to throughout this chapter, to indicate how some of these Commissions considered that the law *could* be clarified and improved.

Practical considerations

In the scenario of negligently-inflicted psychiatric injury, there is the potential, of course, for numerous claims of large amounts, or 'indeterminate liability',[16] arising out of D's negligence. Not only may C himself suffer some pure psychiatric illness as a result of D's act or omission, but also, C's *relatives and friends* may bring claims for pure psychiatric injury, thereby comprising a class of Cs, the identities of whom D may have no knowledge at all. Hence, this is an area rife with 'third party' claims, and is certainly a well-established one in which healthcare professionals can owe a duty of care to persons who are not their patients.[17] The House of Lords acknowledged this explicitly in *JD v East Berkshire Community Health NHS Trust*:[18]

> [D] may owe a duty of care, not only to the person whom he injures [the immediate victim], but also to that person's parents or spouse who suffer nervous shock through seeing or hearing the event or its immediate aftermath. Medical mishaps can give rise to such a duty.

[7] 'Mental Harm' in *Review of the Law of Negligence: Final Report* (2002) ('*Ipp Report*') ch 9.

[8] *Pecuniary Loss and the Family Compensation Act* (WP 69, 1992).

[9] *Damages for Psychiatric Injury* (Rep 196, 2004) ('*Scottish Report*'), and the draft Reparation for Mental Harm (Scotland) Bill.

[10] *Law on Damages* (CP 9, 4 May 2007), ch 3, [97].

[11] *Civil Law of Damages: Personal Injury* (2013) 21, cited in: *Young v MacVean* [2014] CSOH 133, [40].

[12] [2002] EWCA Civ 1792, [2003] PIQR P16, 250.

[13] [1999] 2 AC 455 (HL) 500 (Lord Steyn), 504 (Lord Hoffmann).

[14] [2007] UKHL 39, [54].

[15] [2013] EWCA Civ 194, [2014] QB 150, [24].

[16] A phrase derived from Cardozo CJ in *Ultramares Corp v Touche*, 174 NE 441, 444 (1931): 'liability in an indeterminate amount for an indeterminate time to an indeterminate class'.

[17] As discussed in: Mulheron, *Non-Patient and Third Party Claims* (Ashgate, 2010), ch 5.

[18] [2005] UKHL 23, 2 AC 373, [107].

The number of claims for negligently-inflicted psychiatric illness has markedly increased over the last decade – a point noted by the Court of Appeal in *Leach v Gloucestershire Constabulary*.[19] Hence, this type of lawsuit presents particularly topical concerns for Ds and their insurers. Sensible limits need to be imposed.

As a further problem, many claims brought for negligently-inflicted psychiatric injury do not bear much resemblance to those brought by victims of the Hillsborough stadium disaster out of which the modern framework for 'nervous shock' law in England arose. At an FA Cup semi-final on 15 April 1989, at the Hillsborough Stadium in Sheffield, between Liverpool and Nottingham Forest, overcrowding and crushing in two spectator pens resulted in 96 dead, 400 injured, and numerous psychiatric illness claims brought by relatives, friends, and police officers, who witnessed the horrific crushing and the aftermath. The disaster spawned significant psychiatric illness claims against the Chief Constable, e.g.: *Alcock*,[20] *Hicks*,[21] *McCarthy*,[22] *White (Frost)*[23] and *Hugh v Gray*.[24] English law has struggled, at times, to apply the relevant principles to more drawn-out scenarios.

Pure versus consequential mental injury

§5.1 'Pure' psychiatric injury is a mental injury that is *not* consequential upon personal injury of any type to C. However, where C's property is damaged and C suffers consequential mental injury, then that has been judicially regarded as being a 'pure' mental injury.

Personal injury

'Pure' psychiatric injury occurs where that is the **all and only** personal injury that C suffers as a result of D's negligence. Those sorts of cases raise 'unusual difficulty for the court'; whereas consequential mental distress claims are reasonably 'commonplace in personal injury cases', and do not raise the same types of difficulty (per *McCafferty v Scott's Caravans*[25]).

Where psychiatric injury is negligently-inflicted and consequential upon physical injury, then it is much easier for C to recover damages by way of compensation. That is because the cause of action is complete upon proof of the immediate physical damage, and damages are then recoverable for any consequential mental injury, anxiety, worry, etc, associated with that physical damage. That mental harm forms one of the heads of non-pecuniary loss (i.e., pain, suffering and loss of amenity, or PSLA). By contrast, the cause of action is only complete, for negligently-inflicted pure psychiatric injury, when C has suffered a recognised psychiatric injury. Damages for a lesser form of mental harm, such as worry, anxiety, etc, can be recovered by C if the claim is for consequential mental harm, but that lesser form of harm will not do, for claims of negligently-inflicted pure psychiatric injury. Hence, the distinction between consequential and pure mental harm is very important in English common law.

To give a couple of examples of consequential mental injury: in the *Guidelines for the Assessment of General Damages in Personal Injury Cases*, it is noted that, if C suffers from a negligently-inflicted physical injury or disease which will lead to death, then a component will be permitted for mental suffering, if C knows that death is approaching and is suffering during

[19] [1998] EWCA Civ 1368, [1999] 1 WLR 1421, 1433. [20] [1992] 1 AC 310 (HL). [21] [1992] 2 All ER 65 (HL). [22] (QB, 11 Dec 1996). [23] [1999] 2 AC 455 (HL). [24] [2006] EWHC 1968 (QB). [25] [2011] CSOH 16, [30].

the course of it.[26] Negligently-caused disfigurement can also entail consequential psychological damage:

In *Johnson v Le Roux Fourie*,[27] Penny Johnson, C, 42, a successful businesswoman with family and active social life, consulted a plastic surgeon, D, for advice as to minor plastic surgery to her nose and dark circles under her eyes. D proposed (and C agreed to) more radical plastic surgery, including replacement of pre-existing breast implants, and a type of facelift. The surgery had serious consequences, e.g., C's right facial nerve was permanently damaged, causing an abnormal grimace and twitching; her right eye had to be taped shut as she could not shut it herself; her breast was left lopsided, oddly-shaped, excreting blood and pus, and with unsightly lumpy scarring; and C suffered from depression. **Held:** the psychiatric consequences of C's physical injuries were taken account of, in assessing PSLA at £80,000.

However, some cases appear to treat psychiatric injury as 'pure', when it actually appeared to be consequential upon personal injury (e.g., a mother's pain and suffering during a difficult birth).

In *Farrell v Merton, Sutton and Wandsworth HA*,[28] Mrs Farrell, C, gave birth to her son Karol at D's hospital, but due to D's negligence, Karol was born with severe and irreversible brain damage, and suffered from cerebral palsy. C was not allowed to see Karol until he was one day old, and was not told about his grievous injuries. Instead, C was shown a photograph of Karol lying on a mattress shortly after he was born, and was told that he 'had had a hard time with the caesarian'. **Held:** C recovered £75,000.

The principles governing recovery of pure psychiatric injury (e.g., the 'immediate aftermath' doctrine) were applied in *Farrell*; whereas in other cases, the death *in utero* and stillbirth of a baby has been regarded as an injury to the mother to which additional physical or psychological damage could be appended, i.e., treating her claim for 'psychological injury' as a consequential claim (as in, e.g., *Wild v Southend Univ Hosp NHS Foundation Trust*,[29] in which *Farrell* was not cited). Such inconsistencies do not aid the clarity of the law.

Property damage

Where C's cherished property is damaged or destroyed, and from which C suffers mental injury as a result of witnessing it, then somewhat confusingly, that does **not** appear to have been treated as a consequential mental injury, but instead, invokes the principles of pure psychiatric injury (per *Attia v British Gas plc*[30]). In fact, the treatment of psychiatric injury arising from property damage has become more acute, as a result of recent cases involving the destruction of sperm in fertility banks (e.g., *Yearworth v North Bristol NHS Trust*,[31] and *Holdich v Lothian Health Board*[32]), and is discussed later in the chapter. Indeed, in *Holdich*, the Scottish Outer House aptly described the type of psychiatric injury claim arising from property damage as being 'less pure' than the traditional type of case where C suffers no damage at all, other than psychiatric injury.[33]

[26] Judicial College (12th edn, 2013) 1. [27] [2011] EWHC 1062 (QB).
[28] (2001) 57 BMLR 158 (QB), quotes at 158, 164. [29] [2014] EWHC 4053 (QB) [1].
[30] [1987] EWCA Civ 8, [1988] QB 304, especially 320. [31] [2009] EWCA Civ 37, [2010] 1 QB 1, [55].
[32] [2013] CSOH 197, 2014 SLT 495. [33] *ibid*, [89].

The framework

A convenient framework for an analysis of this rather complicated area of the law is as follows:

Nutshell analysis: **Pure psychiatric injury**

Pre-conditions:

#1 proof of a recognised psychiatric injury

#2 the type of C must be identified – whether C is a primary victim; a secondary victim; an elevated primary victim; a fear-of-the-future C; a residuary C; or a stress-at-work C

Proving duty of care (for *that particular* category of C) – a checklist:

the 'primary victim' claimant

- for *Page v Smith*-type Cs, reasonable foreseeability of psychiatric *or* physical injury; for other primary victims, reasonable foreseeability of psychiatric injury
- legal proximity, according to the usual proximity factors
- the 'normal fortitude' rule does not apply
- whether shock is required is unclear
- public policy considerations may apply to preclude a duty from being owed

the 'secondary victim' claimant

- reasonable foreseeability of psychiatric harm
- relational proximity: close ties of love and affection
- spatial and temporal proximity
- direct perception of events
- the 'normal fortitude' rule applies
- proof of 'shock', in the legal sense, *is* required
- public policy considerations may apply to preclude a duty from being owed

the 'elevated primary victim' claimant

- not a *Page v Smith*-type claimant
- the 'normal fortitude' rule does not apply
- otherwise, refer to the 'primary victim', above

the fear-of-the-future claimant

- not a *Page v Smith*-type claimant
- the 'normal fortitude' rule applies
- otherwise, refer to the 'primary victim', above

the residuary category of claimant

- reasonable foreseeability of psychiatric harm
- legal proximity (depending on an assumption of responsibility by D to avoid psychiatric harm to C, and reliance by C upon D's exercising that responsibility)
- public policy considerations may apply

the stressed-at-work claimant

- reasonable foreseeability of psychiatric harm
- legal proximity, by virtue of employment relationship (but not every employer will be liable for an employee's psychiatric injury)
- the normal fortitude rule applies to the psychiatrically-vulnerable employee

The rest of the negligence action, as per usual

Occasionally, other aspects of the negligence action can also be in issue, when C is pursuing a negligently-inflicted psychiatric injury claim. For example, fixing the relevant standard of care, and proving breach on the part of D, must be undertaken in the usual way (per Chapters 6 and 7). The usual principles of causation (per Chapter 8) apply – and notably, whether D's breach caused C's psychiatric injury may be just as much at issue as in the case of physical injuries to C (e.g., in the leading case of *Page v Smith (No 2)*,[34] the causal connection between D's breach and C's psychiatric injury was ultimately upheld, having been referred back to the Court of Appeal for decision). The principles of remoteness of damage, as discussed in Chapter 9, also apply – with the noteworthy exception that, in *Page v Smith*, physical injury to C was foreseeable, but the psychiatric injury that actually occurred, whilst unforeseeable, was compensable. This exceptional scenario to the *Wagon Mound* principle,[35] which states the damage suffered must have been of a foreseeable type, is the only instance in English law where C can recover, in negligence, for a type of damage that was unforeseeable. However, in respect of all other types of victims and scenarios described in this chapter, the ordinary *Wagon Mound* principle applies – C, who has suffered psychiatric injury, must show that such injury was reasonably foreseeable.

However, it is in proving a duty of care that most problems arise in negligently-inflicted psychiatric injury suits, and is where this chapter will be focused.

Dealing with each aspect of the abovementioned framework in turn:

PRECONDITION #1: A RECOGNISED PSYCHIATRIC INJURY

The threshold principle

§5.2 As a threshold principle, D cannot be liable to C for negligently-inflicted pure psychiatric injury, unless C suffered a recognisable psychiatric injury. Three different reasons have been judicially given for this principle: legal policy; remoteness of damage; and *de minimis* damage.

Some judges may have differed in the labelling – i.e., a 'genuine psychiatric injury' (per the *Creutzfeldt-Jakob Disease (CJD) Litig, Andrews v Sec of State for Health (Damages Assessments)*[36]); a 'recognised psychiatric injury' (per *White (Frost) v CC of South Yorkshire Police*[37]);

[34] [1996] 1 WLR 855 (CA). Note, too, the unsuccessful '*novus actus interveniens*' argument by D in *Farrell v Merton, Sutton and Wandsworth HA* (2000) 57 BMLR 158 (QB).

[35] *Overseas Tankship (UK) Ltd v Morts Dock & Eng Co Ltd (Wagon Mound (No 1))* [1961] AC 388 (PC) 426.

[36] (1998) 54 BMLR 111 (QB) 113.

[37] [1999] 2 AC 455 (HL) 500. Also: *North Glamorgan NHS Trust v Walters* [2002] EWCA Civ 1792, [12], [20]; *Page v Smith* [1996] AC 155 (HL) 167, 190.

or even a 'recognizable psychiatric injury' (per the EWLC, to take account of future psychiatric diagnoses[38]) – but it all represents the same threshold requirement for the level of injury which is compensable.

The principle was established by Lord Bridge in *McLoughlin v O'Brian*,[39] who said that 'the first hurdle which [C] claiming damages of the kind in question must surmount is to establish that he is suffering, not merely grief, distress or any other normal emotion, but a positive psychiatric illness'.

In *McLoughlin v O'Brian*, Mrs McLoughlin's, C's, husband and three of her children were seriously injured in a car accident, shortly after leaving home. C was at home when the accident happened, about 2 miles away. C was told about the accident by a friend, about an hour after it happened, and she rushed to hospital. C saw her husband and children about two hours after the accident, in a bloodied and badly-injured state. C's daughter later died in hospital. C suffered from depression and personality changes after the accident. **Held:** C suffered a compensable recognised psychiatric injury.

The requirement of a recognised psychiatric injury, as opposed to something less, has been confirmed at the highest English appellate level several times since,[40] and currently represents an incontrovertible dogma of negligence law in this jurisdiction. The position is different, if proof of damage is **not** an ingredient of the tort, such as in assault. In that scenario, mental distress, anger and upset is sufficient to constitute compensable damage (per *RT v CC of the Police Service of Northern Ireland*[41]).

Undoubtedly, the threshold principle acts as an important ring-fence (a 'powerful control mechanism', per *CJD Litigation; Group B Plaintiffs v UKMRC*[42]) for these types of claims. Three reasons have been given for the principle.

i. **Policy reasons.** The requirement is directly attributable to policy (indeed, 'reasons more to do with policy than logic', admitted the Court of Appeal in *White v London Fire & Civil Defence Athy*[43]).

The main policy reason is 'floodgates' concerns, for as Lord Wilberforce remarked in *McLoughlin v O'Brian*: '"shock", in its nature, is capable of affecting so wide a range of people, [so there remains] a real need for the law to place some limitation upon the extent of admissible claims'.[44] That is, the principle ring-fences the potential number of Cs (arising, say, out of a large group of spectators who witness an horrific accident). A number of other policy reasons have been put forward in relevant case law:[45]

[38] *English Report*, [2.3]. [39] [1983] 1 AC 410 (HL) 431.

[40] *Calveley v CC of Merseyside Police* [1989] AC 1228 (HL) 1029; *Alcock v CC of South Yorkshire Police* [1992] 1 AC 310 (HL) 422; *Page v Smith* [1996] AC 155 (HL) 167, 171, 181, 189, 197; *White (Frost) v CC of South Yorkshire Police* [1999] 2 AC 455, (HL) 469, 491, 501; *Barber v Somerset CC* [2004] UKHL 13, [2004] 1 WLR 1089 [6]–[7]; *Hicks v CC of South Yorkshire Police* [1992] PIQR P433 (HL) P436; *R v Ireland* [1998] AC 147 (HL) 156; *Wainwright v Home Office* [2003] UKHL 53, [2003] 2 AC 406 [45]–[47], [62].

[41] [2011] NIQB 13, [22]. [42] [2000] Lloyd's Rep Med 161 (QB) 163 (Morland J). [43] [1999] PIQR P314 (CA) P316.

[44] [1983] 1 AC 410 (HL) 421. Also: *White v CC of South Yorkshire Police* [1992] 2 AC 455 (HL) 493–94; *Page v Smith* [1996] AC 155 (HL) 197; *JD v East Berkshire NHS Trust* [2005] 2 AC 373 (HL) [133] (Lord Brown).

[45] Derived, variously, from: *McLoughlin v O'Brian* [1983] 1 AC 410 (HL); *White (Frost)* [1999] 2 AC 455 (HL) 493–94; *Creutzfeldt-Jakob Disease (CJD) Litig, Andrews v Sec of State for Health (Damages Assessments)* (1998) 54 BMLR 111 (QB); *Hinz v Berry* [1970] 2 QB 40 (CA); and cited also in Mulheron (*OJLS*) 6–7.

- the prospect of disproportionate burdens being imposed on D are correspondingly reduced;
- mental injury is easier to 'fake' or to exaggerate than physical injury, and hence, more deserving of a higher threshold of injury;
- conflicting witness and expert evidence as to the nature, or existence, of mental harm is more likely than in the case of physical injury, so that a reference point based upon external classifications of disorders is more objectively verifiable for a court;
- permitting C to recover for mere mental injury may either act as a disincentive to rehabilitation, or may actually create/prolong that type of mental harm;
- it is not in the best societal interests to permit claims for distress only, given that a certain level of mental fortitude is expected and required;
- from a distributive justice view, physical harm is more important than psychological injury; and
- abusive or vexatious claims are less likely, if the law insists upon C's proving that he has suffered a genuine psychiatric illness.

ii. Damages too remote. Alternatively, it was suggested, by Evans LJ in *Vernon v Bosley (No 1)*,[46] that damages for feelings of grief, anxiety, bereavement, etc, are too remote to be compensable in law, and that the principle is 'not [a] policy-induced rule ... but rather, a restriction on the heads of damage which may be recovered by a successful [C].'

However, this observation does not sit comfortably with other judicial observations that mental harm of whatever description is of a 'type' or 'kind' of injury that is foreseeable under the ordinary *Wagon Mound* principle. For example, even in the odd case of *Attia v British Gas plc*,[47] where C suffered an anxiety-based disorder from witnessing the destruction of her home, Bingham LJ was satisfied that when 'applying the ordinary test of remoteness in tort, ... [D] should reasonably have contemplated psychiatric damage to [C] as a real, even if unlikely, result of careless conduct on his part'. In *Alcock* too, Lord Ackner expressly acknowledged that '[m]ere mental suffering' was reasonably foreseeable.[48] Hence, it is submitted that the better view is that grief, anxiety, etc, is not a type of injury that is too remote in law to be recoverable.

iii. The *de minimis* principle. It was suggested by Lord Bingham, in *Watkins v Home Secretary*,[49] that distress, anxiety, etc, do not meet the *de minimis* threshold of damage which the law will compensate in negligence (per the principle of '*de minimis non curat lex* – the law does not take account of trifles). *Watkins* was an alleged misfeasance in public office case, but any torts which are not actionable *per se* will require some 'material damage' to be proven: 'an expression understood to include recognised psychiatric illness, but not distress, injured feelings, indignation or annoyance'.

Of the three, the policy justification is by far the most judicially-cited and accepted.

The diagnostic classifications

§5.3 To determine the threshold requirement of a recognised psychiatric injury, English courts typically have regard to two international classifications for psychiatric injury, DSM-V and ICD-10.

46 [1997] PIQR 255 (CA) 313.
47 [1987] EWCA Civ 8, [1988] QB 304 (CA) 319.
48 [1992] 1 AC 310 (HL) 401.
49 [2006] UKHL 17, [2006] 2 AC 395, [7].

The Court of Appeal observed, in *Sutherland v Hatton*,[50] that there was a 'considerable degree of international agreement on the classification of mental disorders and their diagnostic criteria' in English law, by reference to the following two classifications:

- the American Diagnostic and Statistical Manual of Mental Disorders (DSM-V), i.e., the 5th edition of the Manual, produced by the American Psychiatric Assn;[51] and
- the International Statistical Classification of Mental and Behavioural Disorders (ICD-10), i.e., the 10th revision of the classification by the World Health Organisation.[52]

Under each classification, each recognised mental disorder is given a unique reference code. It was said, in *Dickie v Flexcon Glenrothes Ltd*, that there was 'no suggestion that one was better than the other, although DSM-IV covers a wider range of symptoms and is more prescriptive than its ICD counterpart'.[53] Certainly, from a psychiatrist's perspective, DSM-V is more-developed than ICD-10, given its exclusive focus on mental health.

The use of these diagnostic classifications in the medico-legal context has given rise to four particular dilemmas, *viz*, (1) the classifications were never designed or intended for legal use, and hence, the several caveats and qualifications that exist in both DSM-IV and ICD-10 for diagnostic purposes are routinely overlooked, and are rarely mentioned in judgments; (2) there is continuing uncertainty as to whether the classifications are *a*, or *the*, reference point for a recognised psychiatric illness at law;[54] (3) whether judges, and not expert psychiatric witnesses, should (or can) decide whether the criteria in the classifications are satisfied, or whether deference to the psychiatrist experts is always required, remains uncertain;[55] and (4) a court's reliance on the classifications can be problematical, where changing diagnostic criteria have not been incorporated.[56] These difficulties have been analysed by the author in further detail elsewhere.[57]

What is excluded

§5.4 A number of emotional manifestations or reactions are not compensable injuries, where pure mental injury is claimed. These include: grief, distress, apprehension, annoyance, worry, sorrow, fear, anxiety, outrage, shame, horror or despondency.

For a claim for pure psychiatric injury, '[e]motional responses to unpleasant experiences of even the most serious type do not found a claim for damages' (as the court put it in *RK v Oldham NHS Trust*[58]). It follows that a number of Cs have been unable to advance their claims, as this sample shows:

[50] [2002] EWCA Civ 76, [5] (Hale LJ), aff'd on appeal: *Barber v Somerset CC* [2004] UKHL 13.

[51] Published in May 2013 (see: http://www.dsm5.org/Pages/Default.aspx). DSM-IV-TR, was published in 1994, and revised in 2000.

[52] Published 1992. The 11th revision is due by 2017 (see: http://www.who.int/classifications/icd/revision/en/).

[53] [2009] Scot (D) 3/11 (Sheriff Court, Kircaldy, 4 Sep 2009) [129].

[54] Contrast: *CJD Litigation; Andrews v Sec of State for Health (Damages Assessment)* (1998) 54 BMLR 111 (QB) 113, with *Hussain v CC of West Mercia Police* [2008] EWCA Civ 1205, [16], and see too: *Wild v Southend Univ Hosp NHS Foundation Trust* [2014] EWHC 4053 (QB) [3].

[55] See, e.g.: *Calvert v William Hill Credit Ltd* [2008] EWHC 454 (Ch) [134], point not considered on appeal: [2008] EWCA Cvi 1427.

[56] See, e.g.: *Murtagh v MOD (Ireland)* [2008] IEHC 292 (re PTSD).

[57] 'Rewriting the Requirement for a "Recognized Psychiatric Injury" in Negligence Claims' (2012) 33 *OJLS* 1, 10–19 (sources and citations mostly omitted).

[58] [2003] Lloyd's Rep Med 1 (QB) [20].

In *Reilly v Merseyside HA*,[59] Mr Reilly, C, a hospital visitor, was trapped in a jammed hospital lift for a considerable time, and suffered an anxiety disorder; 'here there was no recognisable psychiatric injury, but only normal emotion in the face of a most unpleasant experience'. The temporary physical manifestations of vomiting and sweating were not sufficient to constitute physical damage either. In *RK v Oldham NHS Trust*,[60] baby MK, C, suffered a spiral fracture of her leg when two months old, and a paediatrician, D, wrongly diagnosed the injury as 'non-accidental'. MK was removed from her parents' home. After brittle bone disease was correctly diagnosed, MK was returned to her parents' care, after a separation of eight months. MK displayed behavioural disturbances and reduced development of 'the attachment dynamic' between parents/child. The medical evidence was that MK had suffered a psychological injury, but not a genuine psychiatric illness (the extreme youth of MK making a diagnosis of the latter very difficult).

In neither of the above did C meet the threshold pre-requisite of a genuine psychiatric disorder.

One exceptional case in which damages were awarded for 'ordinary shock' (*Whitmore v Euroways Express Coaches Ltd*[61]) was described by the EWLC as 'an aberration';[62] and the author's searches have not revealed any case in which *Whitmore* has been either cited or followed since, apart from a very brief reference in *Ravenscroft v Rederiaktiebølaget Transatlantic*.[63]

Perhaps more significantly, though, it was suggested by Maurice Kay LJ, in the misfeasance case of *Hussain v CC of West Mercia Constabulary*,[64] that English law may have set the bar too high, in requiring proof of a recognised psychiatric injury for negligently-inflicted mental harm. Rather, his Lordship used the terminology of 'a grievous non-physical reaction' to describe the threshold which could give rise to a claim for pure mental injury arising from misfeasance. Additionally, he said (dicta) that: 'what Lord Bridge was concerned to discount in *McLoughlin v O'Brian* was "normal human emotions", not significantly abnormal manifestations of non-physical sequelae. If my approach does not live easily with the established approach in cases of negligence resulting in personal injury, I would strive to treat misfeasance in public office exceptionally'.[65] However, this view that something lesser will (and should) constitute compensable harm has not received other English judicial support – although it does enjoy considerable support in some other jurisdictions.

The comparative corner: Something lesser will do

New Zealand: in *J&P Van Soest v Residual Health Management Unit*[66] (a case concerning fatal medical mistreatment of patients by a cardiac surgeon at the Christchurch Public Hospital), Thomas J (in the minority of the NZCA) held that 'mental suffering ... of the order, or approaching the order, of a psychiatric illness and therefore plainly outside the range of ordinary human experience' should be compensable. The majority disagreed, as assessing what suffering fell outside 'ordinary human experience' would make the test unworkable, and floodgates problems may arise, 'to throw the courts open to everyone caused distress by the negligent injuring of a loved one'.

[59] (1994) 23 BMLR 26 (CA) 30. See, for similar facts: *AD v Bury MBC* [2006] EWCA Civ 1.
[60] [2003] Lloyd's Rep Med 1 (QB) [20].
[61] *The Times*, 4 May 1984.
[62] *English Report*, [2.3], fn 15.
[63] [1991] 3 All ER 73 (QB) 80.
[64] [2008] EWCA Civ 1205. Sir Anthony Clarke MR preferred to leave the issue on another occasion.
[65] *ibid*, [19] and [20].
[66] [1999] NZCA 206, [2000] 1 NZLR 179, [83] (Thomas J), [69] (Blanchard J, giving the majority judgment).

Canada: in *Mustapha v Culligan of Canada Ltd*[67] (a case concerning dead flies in an unopened bottle of drinking water), McLachlin CJ (writing for the court) suggested that something less than a recognised psychiatric injury could suffice for negligently-inflicted mental harm: '[t]he law does not recognize upset, disgust, anxiety, agitation, or other mental states that fall short of injury. I would not purport to define compensable injury exhaustively, except to say that it must be *serious and prolonged and rise above the ordinary annoyances, anxieties and fears that people living in society routinely, if sometimes reluctantly, accept* ... minor and transient upsets do not constitute personal injury, and hence do not amount to damage.' In *Healey v Lakeridge Health Corp*,[68] the Ontario CA said that, '[t]he precise manner in which the threshold is defined or identified is a matter of legitimate debate'.

United States: the tort of negligent infliction of emotional distress requires 'mental anguish', which can comprise a spectrum of emotional disturbances, from a recognisable psychiatric injury, to lesser emotions of, say, grief, embarrassment or anger (per *Renville v Fredrickson*[69]).

Hence, clearly there is some level of judicial unease – both with the English and overseas judiciary – about the delineation between **degrees** of compensable mental damage.

Subtle distinctions abound

Much will depend upon the psychiatric evidence adduced – and the delineations between compensable and non-compensable injuries can appear, at least to the lay-person, to be very fine indeed.

In *Ward v Leeds Teaching Hosp NHS Trust*,[70] Mrs Ward's, C's, daughter, Katherine, entered hospital to have her wisdom teeth removed, but failed to regain consciousness after the operation, and died two days later. The NHS Trust, D, denied that any duty of care was owed to C in respect of her claim for PTSD. **Held:** C failed, because (inter alia) C suffered 'a severe and prolonged bereavement reaction', described by the court in terms that cast doubt on whether it was a recognised psychiatric illness worthy of compensation. In *Tredget and Tredget v Bexley HA*,[71] Mrs Tredget, C1, gave birth to her son amid chaos and pandemonium in the delivery theatre. Mr Tredget, C2, was present at the delivery, and was asked to encourage his wife during the delivery. The baby, severely asphyxiated, died of his injuries when 48 hours old. Both Cs sued for pathological unresolved mourning caused by their child's death. **Held:** C could recover for pure psychiatric injury (£32,500 for C2, and £17,500 for C1).

So, in legal terms, pathological unresolved mourning was deserving of compensation, but a severe bereavement reaction was not. On such fine delineations turn the success of C's claim.

Another subtle distinction is that C may try to circumvent the need to prove a recognised psychiatric injury, by establishing some actionable physical injury which would enable C to

[67] [2008] SCC 27, (2008), 293 DLR (4th) [9]. [68] [2011] ONCA 55, (2011), 328 DLR (4th) [43], [66] (Sharpe JA).
[69] 324 Mont 86, 89 (Mont SC 2004). [70] [2004] EWHC 2106 (QB) [18].
[71] [1994] 5 Med LR 178 (Central London CC) 181.

recover some lesser psychological injury as being consequential upon that physical injury. Not only does this tactic obviate the need to bring a claim for **pure** psychiatric injury, but it would also render engagement with the arbitrary rules governing primary-versus-secondary-victim recovery unnecessary. There are **three** possible ways in which proof of some physical injury may permit a route to the recovery of a lesser type of mental harm, such as distress, worry, etc:

i. the psychological disturbance may, medically-speaking, arise directly from a physical impairment that is, itself, non-observable (e.g., a disturbance in C's central nervous system), but which constitutes a physical impairment, in itself, that is compensable;
ii. in reverse, C's psychological damage may have translated into some actionable physical damage. In *Morris v KLM Royal Dutch Airlines*,[72] C's peptic ulcer disorder was brought about by a psychological disturbance, and he could recover for that ulcer. By contrast, in *Hussain*,[73] C argued that he had physical symptoms of anxiety (*viz*, discomfort and numbness in his left arm and leg when 'under stress') which amounted to physical injury, but it was held that these physical manifestations were simply not significant enough to cross the *de minimis* threshold to be recoverable at law; and
iii. if D's act or omission causes C some physical injury, then the cause of action is complete upon proof of immediate physical damage, and damages are then recoverable for any consequential anxiety, worry, etc, associated with that physical damage, as PSLA heads of damage. As Lord Steyn stated in *White (Frost) v CC of South Yorkshire Police*, '[t]here are those whose mental suffering was a concomitant of physical injury. This type of mental suffering is routinely recovered as "pain and suffering", where "mental suffering" was said to include either a recognised psychiatric illness or something lesser such as "extreme grief"'.[74] For this reason, it would be helpful for C to construe physiological changes as 'physical damage', to which anxiety-based damages can 'tag' or attach. To date, English authority does not support either symptomless physiological change to the human body, or the inhalation, ingestion or absorption of chemical compounds, as constituting 'physical injury' upon which anxiety-based damages could be grafted.

In the *Pleural Plaques Litig*,[75] arising from wrongful asbestos exposure in the workplace, 9 of the 10 test Cs had not suffered any recognised psychiatric illness as a result of their developing pleural plaques from that wrongful exposure. (The 10th victim, Mr Grieves, was the only C to suffer a recognised psychiatric injury, *viz* depression, and hence, his claim was legally treated differently, discussed later.) All nine test Cs had each suffered anxiety and a physiological change, caused by the presence of symptomless pleural plaques in their lungs. The crucial question for these Cs was whether that physiological change amounted to physical *damage*. **Held (CA, 2:1, HL, 5:0):** the pleural plaques were not physical damage, and hence, any claims for 'tagged-on' anxiety-based damages could not succeed. An earlier line of authority,[76] upholding that pleural plaques were actionable physical damage, was overruled.

[72] [2001] EWCA Civ 790. [73] [2008] EWCA Civ 1205. [74] [1999] 2 AC 455 (HL) 491.
[75] *Grieves v Everard & Sons* [2006] EWCA Civ, aff'd: *Johnston v NEI Intl Combustion Ltd* [2007] UKHL 39.
[76] i.e., cases against the MOD: *Church* (1984) 134 NLJ 623 (QB); *Sykes* (1984) 134 NLJ 783 (QB); *Patterson* [1987] CLY 1194, all noted in *Pleural Plaques*, [3]–[6].

The law reform corner: The threshold damage

The English Comm:[77] the Negligence (Psychiatric Illness) Bill required a 'recognizable psychiatric illness'.

The Scottish Comm:[78] although the law was right to impose the threshold principle, there will be cases 'in which drawing the line between a recognised psychiatric injury or disorder, and mere stress or anxiety, may not be easy.'

The Ipp Committee:[79] despite the widespread reliance of C's experts on DSM-IV in seeking to prove a recognisable psychiatric illness, such reliance may be misplaced, given that the Manual warns against its use in legal contexts, and that it was developed as a tool for clinical, not legal, purposes. It recommended, instead, that a panel of experts develop guidelines for compensable psychiatric illnesses for use in litigious contexts.

PRECONDITION #2: THE TYPE OF CLAIMANT

§5.5 The requirements for establishing that D owed C a duty of care to avoid C's psychiatric injury differ, depending upon the type of C.

The establishment of a duty of care in this area of negligence depends very much upon the type of claimant – some types have a far easier job of proving the criteria than others. There are *six* possible categories of C who may suffer from pure psychiatric injury, which categories are not mutually exclusive. To summarise:

the 'primary victim' C	EITHER a person who is directly involved in a traumatic or dangerous event as a participant, and in the zone of physical danger, but who, although not physically harmed, suffers from a psychiatric injury, OR a guilt-ridden person
the 'secondary victim' C	a person who is a spectator to a traumatic or dangerous event which injures or kills a loved one, and who suffers from a psychiatric injury as a result of what he witnessed
the 'elevated primary victim' C	a person who appears to be a secondary victim, but who is 'elevated' to fulfil the role of primary victim, given that there is no-one who is ultimately killed or injured
the stressed-at-work C	a person who suffers from a psychiatric injury in the workplace, from undertaking the ordinary tasks which form part of that employee's job description
the fear-of-the-future C	a person who is exposed to a disease-causing agent, and who suffers no immediate physical injury, but who develops a psychiatric injury from the despair and worry that the disease will manifest in the future ('the worried well')
the residuary category of C	the person who develops a psychiatric injury as a result of the negligent act or omission of D, and who does not fit within any of the abovementioned categories, but obtains compensation nevertheless

[77] *English Report*, [5.3], [5.5]–[5.6]. [78] *Scottish Report*, [2.3]. [79] *Ipp Report*, [9.6], and Rec #33.

The law's recognition of an entitlement to recovery for pure psychiatric injury is usually traced to *Dulieu v White & Sons*,[80] and *Bourhill v Young*,[81] for primary and secondary victims, respectively. However, the differing duty of care criteria, depending upon the type of victim – and the expansion of the categories beyond the primary/secondary victim dichotomy – is primarily why the category of C must be correctly identified at the outset. The existence of a duty of care is the *principal* battleground for C's alleging pure psychiatric injury.

Dealing with each category in more detail:

Primary victims

The changing definition

§5.6 The *main* type of primary victim is where C is in the range of foreseeable physical injury from D's act or omission, as a participant who was in the 'zone of danger', and who suffers no physical injury as a participant, but who suffers psychiatric injury instead. The 'zone of danger' may constitute either physical injury/death or a loss of bodily integrity (e.g., imprisonment). Alternatively, a primary victim is one who genuinely believes that he has been the unwitting cause of, or a contributing factor in, another's injury, death or imperilment.

In *North Glamorgan NHS Trust v Walters*, a primary victim was defined as 'one who was *involved, either mediately or immediately as a participant*, as opposed to one who was no more than a passive or unwilling witness or spectator to the injury caused to another'.[82] This was a paraphrase of the House of Lords definition in *Alcock v CC of Yorkshire Police* (the relatives' claim in Hillsborough).[83]

However, and to contribute some considerable confusion to the issue, the House of Lords has subtly varied the definition of the primary victim since *Alcock*, as the following Table shows:

The changing primary victim definition

Case	about ...	The evolving PV definition ...
Alcock v CC of South Yorkshire Police (1992)	Hillsborough stadium disaster (relatives' claims)	someone 'involved, either mediately or immediately, as a participant' in the event which gave rise to his psychiatric illness – such 'participants' would include (a) those who feared for their own safety; (b) rescuers who go to the assistance of others; and (c) 'unwilling participants in the event', including guilt-ridden parties (Lord Oliver)
Page v Smith (1996)	car accident	someone who was 'a participant' – i.e., someone 'directly involved in the accident' and 'well within the range of foreseeable physical injury' – 'someone who is in the range of foreseeable physical injury flowing from an event, even though he suffers no actual physical injury, provided that he was in fact exposed to a risk of physical injury, or reasonably believed that he was so exposed' – i.e., within the 'zone of danger' (Lord Lloyd)[a]

[a] [1996] AC 155 (HL) 184. The expression, 'zone of danger', was used by Henry LJ in *Frost* (CA) to describe the *Page* test. It was sourced to US authority in *Grieves* [2006] EWCA Civ, [88].

[80] [1901] 2 KB 669 (KB). [81] [1943] AC 92 (HL) 103. [82] [2002] EWCA Civ 1792, [12] (emphasis added).
[83] [1992] 2 AC 310 (HL) 407–8 (Lord Oliver).

White (Frost) v CC of South Yorkshire Police (1999)	Hillsborough stadium disaster (police claims)	someone within the range of foreseeable risk of injury (i.e., within the 'zone of physical danger') – as a 'threshold requirement', he must have objectively been exposed to danger and a risk of physical injury, or reasonably believed that he was so exposed (Lord Steyn)[b]
W v Essex CC (2001)	child abuse by foster child	someone who (a) is himself in the range of foreseeable physical injury/zone of physical danger; or (b) believes that he has been the unwitting cause of, or a contributing factor in, another's injury, death or imperilment – the primary victim is an 'unwilling participant in the event' (Lord Slynn)[c]
Rothwell v Chemical and Insulating Co (Pleural plaques litigation (2007)	asbestos exposure causing pleural plaques	someone who was himself in the range of foreseeable physical injury/zone of physical danger ('who suffers psychiatric injury caused by fear or distress resulting from involvement in an accident caused by [D's] negligence or its immediate aftermath') (and *W v Essex CC* was not referred to) (Lord Hope)[d]

[b] 1999] 2 AC 455 (HL) 499 (Lord Steyn).
[c] [2001] 2 AC 592 (HL) 601 (Lord Slynn, with whom the other members of the House agreed).
[d] [2007] UKHL 39 (a conjoined appeal from: *Grieves v FT Everard & Sons* [2006] EWCA Civ 27).

It is evident that *Alcock's* definition of 'primary victim' – which has never been explicitly overruled – was much wider than **any** of the definitions that followed it. The definition of primary victim in *Page v Smith*, *White (Frost)*, and *Pleural Plaques*, all closely resemble each other, and posit the primary victim as one in the zone of physical danger. *W v Essex CC* was significant, because it drew the 'guilt-ridden' participant back into the primary victim definition, as an 'involuntary participant', **and** it circumvented the requirement that the primary victim must have been within the range of foreseeable physical injury: that is a sufficient, but not a necessary, pre-requisite for a primary victim. The *W v Essex* line of authority has been approved by the House of Lords since (in *JD v East Berkshire Community Health NHS Trust*[84]). In *Pleural Plaques*, however, the House of Lords did not refer to *W v Essex* at all, citing only the 'zone of physical danger' definition. Indeed, *Pleural Plaques* (2007) was itself a difficult decision, given that (as the author has noted elsewhere):

> the five speeches created a myriad of difficulties for primary victim analysis: Lord Hope and Lord Mance thought it doubtful whether the leading case on primary victims, *Page v Smith*, had been correctly decided, and said that it should be reviewed on another occasion; in contrast, the other three members of the court either stated or assumed that *Page* was correct. Only Lord Hope offered any definition of the primary victim, and none of their Lordships made any reference to the various (and differing) primary victim definitions that have been given by the House of Lords since *Page*.[85]

[84] [2005] UKHL 23, [2005] 2 AC 373, [27].
[85] 'The "Primary Victim" in Psychiatric Illness Claims, etc' (2008) 19 *KCLJ* 81, 83 (footnotes omitted).

Hence, the whole landscape of just who is a primary victim remains somewhat murky and confused.

Furthermore, the policy of the House of Lords in the area of negligently-inflicted psychiatric injury has been difficult to discern. On the one hand, it contemplated, in *W v Essex*, the ongoing development of rather loose boundaries for those who may constitute a primary victim C, with Lord Slynn remarking that the categorisation of primary/secondary victims was not 'finally closed. It is a concept still to be developed in different factual situations'.[86] On the other hand, in *White*, Lord Steyn said that the *Alcock* definition was deliberately couched to limit the 'ever widening circle of plaintiffs'. Yet it seems that the courts' desire to limit the number of potential primary victim claims has wavered, for *Essex* clearly contemplates a larger number of potential primary victims than *White* did. Given all this development post-*Alcock*, it is somewhat surprising that the Court of Appeal in *Walters*, in 2003, chose to paraphrase *Alcock's* relatively distant definition of primary/secondary victims delivered back in 1992, and omit the developments in between!

Those included within primary victim status

The abovementioned refinements and adjustments in legal position mean that, essentially, a primary victim can take two forms: the 'zone-of-danger' primary victim, and the 'guilt-ridden' primary victim. Expanding upon each category in turn:

'Zone-of-danger' primary victims. This type of victim has featured in the following scenarios:

- where C was involved in a car accident, due to D's negligent driving:

  In *Page v Smith*,[87] Mr Page, C, was involved in a relatively minor car accident, due to the negligent driving of Mr Smith, D, who turned right immediately into C's path. C's previous myalgic encephalomyelitis (ME) (or CFS), which he had suffered for some 20 years, became chronic and permanent. That type of injury was deemed to be unforeseeable, arising from a minor car accident. **Held (3:2):** C was a primary victim, and could recover for his pure psychiatric injury. He was in the zone of physical danger, as the victim of a car accident. In *Boumedien v Delta Display Ltd*,[88] Mr Boumedien, C, was in bed asleep in his ground floor bedroom in the middle of the night, when D's car crashed into the front garden wall of his property. C was not physically injured, but was very shocked and frightened, and thought that his house was falling down or that there had been an earthquake. C suffered a psychiatric illness. **Held:** C was a potential primary victim, being within the range of foreseeable physical injury.

- where C was involved in a workplace accident or incident, due to employer D's negligence:

  In *Donachie v CC of the Greater Manchester Police*,[89] Mr Donachie, C, a police officer with the Crime Squad, had to undertake nine separate and highly-risky trips by foot to tag the underside of a criminal gang's car, due to a faulty battery in the tagging device. C was subjected to the fear of serious injury or death if observed by the gang during a tagging operation. C had a particular vulnerability to stress because of a pre-existing hypertension condition, and this eventually led to a stroke. **Held (trial):** C lost his claim, given his pre-existing vulnerability to psychiatric injury. **Held (CA):** C could recover for his psychiatric injury, as he was a *Page*-type primary victim, in the zone of

[86] [2000] UKHL 17, [2001] 2 AC 592, 601.
[87] [1996] AC 155 (HL) (Lord Lloyd gave the majority speech, Lords Ackner and Browne-Wilkinson agreeing).
[88] [2008] EWCA Civ 368, [6]. [89] [2004] EWCA Civ 405.

danger. In *Young v Charles Church (Southern) Ltd*,[90] Mr Young, C, a construction worker, handed a scaffold pole to his co-employee, who accidentally brought it into contact with live overhead power lines. The co-employee was killed instantly, and another employee nearby suffered burns. C was not physically injured, but suffered psychiatric illness. **Held (trial):** C lost his claim, because he was not a 'participant in the accident', but merely very close to it. **Held (CA):** C was a primary victim, as he was in the area of physical danger created by D's negligent system of work in allowing scaffolding to be erected near 'live' powerlines.

- where C was the victim of medical misdiagnosis or mistreatment by D:

In *RK v Oldham NHS Trust*,[91] facts previously, baby MK was in the zone of physical danger, because she was a sufferer of undiagnosed brittle bone disease, but did not suffer the requisite psychiatric injury.

- where C was in the vicinity of a violent person or a violent act, because of D's negligence:

In *A v Essex CC*,[92] adoptive parents, Mr and Mrs A, C, were not told by the council, D, that their adopted son, William, was extremely disturbed and violent. D was aware, before the placement, that William had a history of aggression towards family members, and that Mr A was mentally fragile. William caused psychiatric injuries to both parents, as a result of his bad behaviour (which included throwing an iron at their natural child). **Held:** D owed C a duty of care to avoid psychiatric injury, as C were within the range of foreseeable physical injury (the 'zone of danger') from William's behaviour. In *Burns v Boots UK Ltd*,[93] Margaret Howieson, C, went shopping in Dundee with her family, including Alyssa, 20 months, who was in a child buggy. Whilst other family members went into a Boots (D's) store, C stayed with the children outside. A rolling pin fell from a third floor window of D's store, striking Alyssa on the head as she sat in her buggy, fracturing her skull. C took the screaming infant into her arms, and suffered psychiatric injury. **Held:** C was a primary victim, for standing right beside Alyssa, she was also within the range of foreseeable physical injury.

However, in *McLoughlin v Jones*,[94] Hale LJ took a different tack regarding 'physical injury', holding that 'loss of liberty is just as much an interference in bodily integrity as is loss of a limb' (Brooke LJ considered that it was an 'interesting point ... clearly worthy of full argument on some other occasion'). Clearly, that concept of what amounts to 'physical injury' goes well beyond the *Page v Smith* scenario of potential broken bones, etc, in the eyes of some judicial opinion.

In *McLoughlin v Jones*, Mr McLoughlin, C, was charged with grievous bodily harm and robbery. At his trial, he was represented by a firm of solicitors, D. C was convicted and sentenced to four years' imprisonment. After serving three months, C was acquitted at a retrial, because of new witness evidence which had not previously been available. C alleged that D had conducted his defence negligently, and that he suffered serious depression as a result of his wrongful imprisonment. **Held**: D owed C a duty of care to avoid the psychiatric injury. C was a primary victim, arguably 'the same sort of primary victim as in *Page v Smith*', because conviction and imprisonment was an interference with his bodily integrity.

[90] (1997) 39 BMLR 146 (CA) (C was not a secondary victim either). [91] [2003] Lloyd's Rep Med 1 (QB) [20].
[92] [2003] EWCA Civ 1848, [2004] 1 WLR 1881. [93] [2011] CSOH 182.
[94] [2001] EWCA Civ 1743, with quotes in text and case description at [49] (Brooke LJ) and [57] (Hale LJ).

'Guilt-ridden' primary victims. This was clearly an additional category to the 'zone of danger' primary victim, given that, in *W v Essex CC*,[95] Lord Slynn expressly acknowledged that, 'it is beyond doubt that [C] were not physically injured by the abuse and ... it does not seem reasonably foreseeable that there was a risk of sexual abuse of the parents [by G]'.

Although the 'guilt-ridden' C was approved as a potential primary victim in *W v Essex CC* (as discussed above), the 'survivor guilt' victims have actually had a very chequered history, insofar as recovery for psychiatric injury is concerned. That a person who is the unwitting cause of another's peril could be a primary victim has some early precedence (in *Dooley v Cammell Laird & Co Ltd*[96]), but this was described in less-than-endorsing terms by Lord Jauncey in *Alcock* as a 'very special case'.[97] The category, however, certainly was encompassed within Lord Oliver's description, in *Alcock*, of an 'involuntary participant'. The possibility was then directly canvassed, but *failed*, in *Hunter v British Coal Corp*[98] – which was decided in 1999, post *Page v Smith* in 1996, and pre-*W v Essex* in 2001. Subsequently, of course, the guilt-ridden primary victim was approved in *W v Essex CC*[99] – without the inconsistency with *Page v Smith* being explained or reconciled. Additionally, *Hunter* was only briefly referred to in *Essex*, but without any detailed discussion. Then, in the *Pleural Plaques* litigation, the primary victim was again expressed solely in *Page v Smith*-type terms, and *W v Essex*, and the guilt-ridden victims, were (confusingly) not referred to at all.

Hence, whilst the guilt-ridden victim is endorsed as a primary victim at the highest appellate level in English law, all of this represents a chequered and unsatisfactory history. Be that as it may, the 'guilt-ridden' primary victim scenarios have included (but with very mixed success):

- parents whose children were sexually abused:

  In *W v Essex CC*,[100] Mr and Mrs W, C, were approved adolescent foster carers. They accepted G, 15, into their home as a foster-child. C had taken steps to ensure that the council, D, would not place any sexual abuser with them, given that they had four children (aged 8–12) of their own. Unknown to C, but known to D's social worker, G had a history of serious sexual misconduct. G had been cautioned by the police for an indecent assault on his own sister, and was being investigated for an alleged rape. During the month that G stayed with the family, it was alleged that he systematically abused each of C's children. C suffered psychiatric injuries, their marriage broke down, and Mr W was unable to work for long periods. **Held:** the claim could not be struck out; C could proceed to trial as potential primary victims. C were 'unwilling participants', having brought their children and G together under the one roof, and feeling responsible for failing to recognise the seriousness of their children's plight more quickly. In *Merthyr Tydfil County BC v C*,[101] C lived in an area in which the Council, D, was obliged to provide social services. C became aware that her two children had been subjected to inappropriate sexual behaviour by a neighbour's child, X, and C reported the abuse to authorities, who passed on the complaint to D. D advised C to keep her children indoors, but over time, given that X did not appear to be playing outdoors, C allowed her children to play outside again. Two years later, X abused the children again, which C reported to D. D denied that C had ever reported a previous incident; and then allocated the same social worker to both C's and X's families. C suffered psychiatric injury, due to suffering 'irrational guilt feelings that she has been unable to protect her children, and that she felt tormented by uncertainty about how she could protect them

[95] [2001] 2 AC 592 (HL) 600–1. [96] [1951] 1 Lloyd's Rep 271 (Liverpool Assizes).
[97] [1992] 1 AC 310 (HL) 420. [98] [1999] QB 140 (CA). [99] [2001] 2 AC 592 (HL).
[100] [2001] 2 AC 592 (HL). [101] [2010] EWHC 62 (QB) [5].

in the future'. Later, X was removed from her family by D, and placed in foster care. **Held:** C's claim could proceed, given her potential primary victim status as a guilt-ridden C.

- employees who are involved in mishaps and accidents with fellow employees in the workplace:

  In *Hunter v British Coal Corp*,[102] Mr Hunter, C, suffered from depression stemming from his (incorrect) belief that he brought about the death of a work colleague who was killed by an exploding water hydrant. C had accidentally backed into the hydrant when operating a forklift, and as he drove away, it exploded. C was at least 30 metres away when the hydrant exploded, and never saw the body of his dead colleague. **Held:** C's claim failed. C was not 'an actor' in the tragic incident, and was not in the zone of physical danger himself: 'the law requires a greater degree of physical and temporal proximity than was present in this case before Mr Hunter could properly be treated as a direct, or primary, victim'. In *Monk v PC Harrington Ltd*,[103] Mr Monk, C, was working at Wembley Stadium, when a temporary platform fell about 20 metres onto two fellow construction workers. C did not observe the accident, but heard about it on his portable radio. C rushed over to both men to assist them. One was very seriously injured and non-responsive and died at the scene, and the other suffered a badly broken leg. C suffered PTSD, and sued his employer in negligence for an unsafe system of work. **Held:** C could not be a primary victim founded on being a guilt-ridden victim because he was unable to save his injured co-employee, because C's psychiatric injury was not induced by a genuine belief that he had caused his co-employee's death.

Those excluded from primary victim status

i. Rescuers. Rescuers (i.e., those who provide medical or other assistance of a type that is neither trivial nor peripheral, per *Monk v PC Harrington Ltd*[104]) are in a much worse position now, post-*White/Frost*, than was the position under Lord Oliver's definition in *Alcock*.

§5.7 Where C rescues X, where the rescue was necessary because of D's negligent act or omission, and where C was in danger during that rescue attempt, then that rescuer qualifies as a primary victim. However, if C as rescuer is *never* in the zone of danger when effecting the rescue, then C is not a primary victim.

Rescuers were expressly classified as primary victims under the *Alcock* definition, but the subsequent *Page v Smith* definition was much narrower. Subsequently, in *White (Frost)*, a bare majority of the House of Lords[105] considered that rescuers should **not** be in a 'special category', for the purposes of recovering for psychiatric injury. The dissenters[106] had considered that rescuers **should** remain in the 'special category' that previous decisions such as *Alcock* had placed them, but this view did not prevail.

Rescuers will not always be at risk of physical injury when involved in, or attending to, an accident or its aftermath – and if they are not, then they will not be primary victims. Hence, where C provides rescue services in a particularly grievous accident, and where 'justice may cry out for compensation for the psychiatric harm he suffers in consequence' (to quote a

[102] [1999] QB 140 (CA) 149 (Brooke LJ) 154. [103] [2008] EWHC 1879 (QB), [2009] PIQR P3.

[104] [2008] EWHC 1879 (QB).

[105] [1999] 2 AC 455 (HL) 497, 499 (Lord Steyn), 509–11 (Lord Hoffmann), Lord Browne-Wilkinson agreeing with both.

[106] Lords Goff and Griffiths.

submission in *Greatorex v Greatorex*[107]), C cannot recover, unless he, himself, *was exposed to physical danger*. On that basis, the following did **not** fall into that category:

In *White (Frost) v CC of South Yorkshire Police*,[108] six police officers, C, who were involved in various forms of post-accident rescue and assistance at the Hillsborough disaster, brought a test case against their employer, D, in negligence, alleging inadequate training. All Cs suffered PTSD, having witnessed gruelling and horrible scenes; one had set up a makeshift morgue; and others had helped the injured and carried the dead from the spectator pens to the middle of the ground. **Held (3:2):** no C could recover damages for psychiatric injury. They were never actually in the zone of physical danger themselves or 'personally threatened'; all danger had passed by the time they arrived. In *Monk v PC Harrington Ltd*,[109] facts previously, **held:** C was not in the zone of danger during/after the scaffolding collapse, and nor was it reasonable for C to think that he was risking his own physical safety in assisting his colleagues.

However, where the rescuers were in the zone of danger, they can be classified as primary victims in modern law, post *White/Frost*:

In *Chadwick v British Transport Comm*,[110] in the Lewisham train disaster of 1957, two trains collided in bad weather, and 90 people were killed. Mr Chadwick, C, lived about 200 yards from the scene, and went to offer assistance. He spent over 7 hours continuously pulling the dead and injured from the train wreckage, and returned to his house covered in mud and blood. Following the accident, C changed from a productive worker, and cheerful man, to a depressed person, unable to work. C died before trial, and his estate sued for C's psychiatric injuries. **Held:** C's estate could recover. The case was explained *ex post facto*, in *White*, on the basis that C, as rescuer, was a primary victim, because he was in danger of the roof collapsing throughout the long night in which he helped pull the dead and injured from the wreckage.

§5.8 However, where rescuer C assists victim D who *self-inflicted* his injuries due to his own negligent or deliberate act, and C suffers a psychiatric injury in effecting that rescue, D does not owe C a duty of care to avoid that psychiatric injury for policy reasons.

This principle stems from *Greatorex v Greatorex*,[111] for two policy reasons:

In *Greatorex v Greatorex*, Mr Greatorex Jnr was involved in a car accident, after he had been drinking. He was trapped in the car with grievous injuries, and emergency services were called. Coincidentally, the Leading Fire Officer who attended was Mr Greatorex Snr, C, who was the father of the driver. C was nowhere near the scene of the accident when it happened; he attended the accident solely in the course of his employment. C suffered severe PTSD afterwards. **Held:** C could not recover damages as a primary victim, as he was never in any physical danger, nor in fear of any danger, from the car accident.

As a first policy reason, this scenario, whereby a rescuer assists a victim who brought about his own peril, will often (but not always) occur in a family situation. 'Home life may involve many instances of a family member causing himself injury through his own fault'[112] – and it would be contrary to public policy for one family member, who had injured himself, to owe a duty of care to another family member who sought to help and rescue him, and suffered psychiatric injury from what he witnessed. The following examples were provided in *Greatorex*: a father commits suicide and his body is found by his son; or a husband negligently wounds himself

[107] [2000] 1 WLR 1970 (QB) 1976. [108] [1999] 2 AC 455 (HL). [109] [2008] EWHC 1879 (QB).
[110] [1967] 1 WLR 912 (CA). [111] [2000] EWHC 223 (QB), [2000] 1 WLR 1970, [66]–[81]. [112] *ibid*, [72].

with a kitchen knife in front of his wife; or a son has extensive loss of blood from a fall caused by his own negligence and is found by his mother. Should the son, the wife and the mother, C, respectively, suffer psychiatric injury, public policy should prevent that psychiatrically-injured relative from suing their injured relative, or the relative's estate, D.

Secondly, for D who self-inflicts an injury to owe a duty of care to his rescuer C would be a serious imposition upon D's right of self-determination. D injures himself – whether negligently or deliberately – but he should not owe a duty to someone who then comes to rescue him. Any such duty should be for Parliament to impose, via legislation (which has never occurred). It is a difficult field of law, and 'Parliament is the best arbiter of what the public interest requires'.[113]

ii. Fear-of-the-future victims. The fear-of-the-future victim is distinguishable from the *Page v Smith*, zone-of-physical-danger primary victim.

§5.9 Those who have been exposed to a disease-causing agent, and worry about contracting a disease in the future, are not primary victims under the *Page v Smith* category, notwithstanding that the very fact that C has been exposed to that dangerous agent has put C in the 'zone of danger'.

The leading case sets this principle:

> In *Creutzfeldt-Jakob Disease Litig; Group B Plaintiffs v UKMRC*,[114] several young children, C, who had shown signs of stunted growth, were injected with human growth hormone (HGH) as part of a clinical trial. Studies then suggested that this type of HGH was capable of infecting injectees with Creutzfeldt-Jakob disease, a brain-wasting and untreatable condition that consigned its sufferers to 'unimaginable suffering and certain death'. By 1 Jul 1977, information received by the Dept of Health, D, was that it would be unsafe to continue with the HGH clinical trials. That was forwarded to key Committees with advice to immediately withdraw HGH supplies for clinical use. This was not done. Later, C (the Group B claimants) were informed of the risk of their developing the horrible and incurable CJD, and developed psychiatric injuries. **Held:** Cs were not primary victims. (However, they could recover for their psychiatric injuries, on a separate basis.)

There were two principal distinguishing features, according to Morland J, which meant that fear-of-the-future victims were not primary victims:

i. The triggering event for Mr Page's shock was the involvement in the car accident. There was a close temporal proximity between D's breach and C's onset of injury. By contrast, the triggering event for the HGH recipients' distress was from learning, *several years after the treatment*, through medical advisers, friends, family and the media, that they were at risk of developing the disease. Their realisation was also exacerbated by sensationalist media coverage. Hence, the breach in administering the injections when they ought not to have been given was not at all contemporaneous with the onset of C's psychiatric injury. Hence, for primary victims in the zone of danger, they must be within the zone of *immediate* physical danger (i.e., with close temporal proximity to D's act or omission), in order to claim primary victim status. A long gap between D's negligence, and C's psychiatric injury, will not give the immediacy and proximity that a primary victim needs. C's psychiatric injury must be an immediate response to physical danger or to some traumatic event, to constitute a primary victim.
ii. For Mr Page, all the physical danger had passed by the time that his psychiatric injury manifested. However, for the HGH recipients, the physical dangers that they faced were entirely in the future.

[113] *ibid*, [77]. [114] (1997) 41 BMLR 157 (QB) 164.

The injection itself was no physical danger – but the contracting of a ghastly terminal disease in the future certainly was. Hence, the *CJD Litigation* was not the same type of case as was *Page v Smith.*

Hence, even though those who are exposed to a disease-causing agent are ostensibly in the zone-of-physical-danger, they are **not** primary victims in the *Page v Smith* sense, in English law. However, whilst they were not treated as primary victims *per se*, they are treated, in English law, as a residuary category of Cs who may prove a duty of care under the *Caparo* test. This avenue is considered later in the chapter.

Secondary victims

Physical injury

§5.10 A secondary victim, C, is a spectator or bystander to the death or injury of an immediate victim which was caused by D's negligence, and who suffers psychiatric injury as a result.

This description was posed by Lord Lloyd in *Page v Smith*;[115] alternatively, it is someone who was a 'passive and unwilling witness of injury caused to others' (per Lord Oliver in *Alcock*[116]).

> In *Alcock v CC of South Yorkshire*, a test case was brought by a range of relatives and friends of the dead and injured in the Hillsborough disaster – brothers, sisters, fiancés, parents, children of the injured and dead, and in a variety of locations – in the ground itself, outside the ground, some at home watching the game on TV in Liverpool. Some had seen the dead bodies at the ground and the makeshift morgue approximately 8 hours after the disaster happened; some saw TV broadcasts; and some saw the events unfold from within the stadium itself from another stand. **Held:** all test Cs failed to recover as secondary victims, because all failed one or more of the criteria for secondary victim recovery.

There is inevitably a tri-partite relationship arising in secondary victim scenarios, as the diagram below shows (with reference to some of the leading cases, discussed in this chapter):

The secondary victim scenario

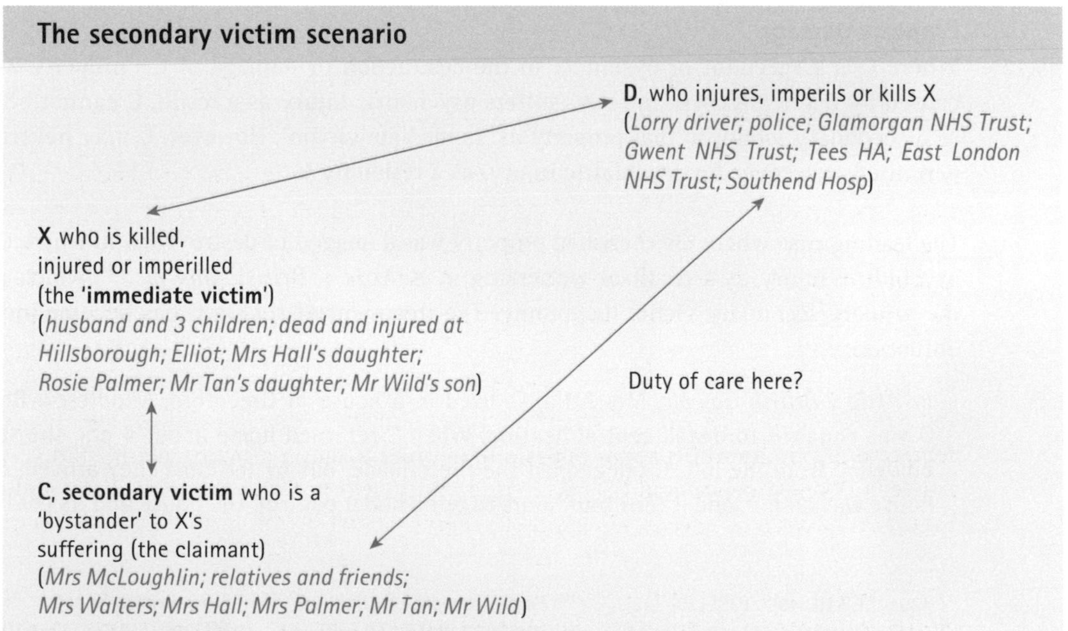

115 [1996] AC 155 (HL) 184. 116 [1992] 1 AC 310 (HL) 407.

Two of these cases concerned fathers, each of whom was present when his child, who died *in utero* due to D's medical negligence, was delivered as a stillbirth. The foetus itself does not have a separate legal personality (unless born alive, as per Chapter 2), and neither father witnessed the actual or threatened death or injury of the child's mother prior to, or at, the stillbirth. Hence, in order to avoid a type of 'legal black-hole', the Court of Appeal confirmed recently, in *Wild v Southend Univ Hosp NHS Foundation Trust*,[117] that *the mother* is to be considered as the immediate victim, to whom the father is a potential secondary victim.

§5.11 The duty of care which D owes to a secondary victim, C, is not derivative from, or reliant upon, legal liability being owed by D to the immediate victim whose peril C witnessed. A duty may be owed to C, even if no liability arises from D to the immediate victim.

D may not be liable to the immediate victim for a number of reasons (e.g., because of some defence), or because there was **no** breach of duty by D towards the immediate victim, or because no damage was proven (e.g., because the immediate victim is not **actually** harmed). Legally-speaking, D may be found to have been negligent towards secondary victim C, without the immediate victim having any cause of action against D at all. Hence, any duty owed to the secondary victim is independent, distinct and separate.

The English Law Commission,[118] together with other law reform bodies,[119] have reiterated this point. The House of Lords has approved of that proposition too. For example, suppose that a parent sees his child in peril, but the child skips away from the incident unharmed – in *Alcock*,[120] Lord Oliver remarked that the parent could be a secondary victim, even though there was no immediate victim existing. Although some courts since have suggested, in dicta, that any duty to the secondary victim is derivative (per *Farrell v Merton, Sutton and Wandsworth HA*,[121] *Hall v Gwent Healthcare NHS Trust*,[122] and in *Storey v Charles Church Developments plc*[123]), both precedent and logic suggest that this is incorrect. There **can** be a secondary victim, without any immediate victim existing.

Property damage

§5.12 Where C is a spectator or bystander to the destruction or damage of C's property which was caused by D's negligence, and who suffers psychiatric injury as a result, C cannot be regarded as a secondary victim to that property as 'immediate victim'. However, C may nevertheless be permitted to recover for psychiatric injury, as a residuary C.

The leading case where C's cherished property was damaged or destroyed, and where C suffered psychiatric injury as a result of witnessing it, is *Attia v British Gas plc*,[124] which pre-dated the primary/secondary victim dichotomy. The treatment of such a C has become increasingly obfuscatory.

In *Attia v British Gas plc*, Mrs Attia, C, lived in a house in Greenford, Middlesex. British Gas, D was engaged to install central heating. When C returned home about 4 pm, she saw smoke billowing from the loft. C telephoned the fire brigade, but by the time they arrived, the whole house was on fire, and it took four hours to bring under control. The house and its contents were

[117] [2014] EWHC 4053 (QB) [20]–[22]. [118] *English Report*, [2.22]–[2.24]. [119] *Ipp Report*, [9.31].
[120] *Alcock* [1992] 1 AC 310 (HL) 412. [121] (2000) 57 BMLR 158 (QB) 161. [122] [2004] EWHC 2748 (QB) [16].
[123] (1995) 73 Con LR 1, 19. [124] [1987] EWCA Civ 8, [1988] QB 304.

extensively damaged whilst C watched. D conceded negligence, and settled the property damage aspect of C's claim. However, C also claimed for psychiatric/mental injury, from the shock of seeing her home and its contents ablaze. **Held:** C's claim was permitted to proceed to trial; D owed C a duty to avoid causing psychiatric damage from witnessing the destruction of cherished property.

Bingham LJ gave an example, in *Attia*, of where C may have a similar claim, i.e., where 'a scholar's life work of research or composition was destroyed before his eyes as a result of [D's] careless conduct'.[125] In any event, the injury flowing from property damage was regarded, in *Attia*, as needing to be a recognised psychiatric injury.

In both of these examples, C sustained psychiatric injury, as a result of *witnessing* damage to cherished property. Would the situation be the same, if C did not witness it, but merely was told about the damaged/destroyed property and suffered psychiatric injury as a result? That distinction, between what is and is not directly perceived, is crucial in the law governing recovery by secondary victims of damages for psychiatric injury arising from physical injury, whereby direct perception is a necessary pre-requisite to recovery (as discussed later in the chapter). In *Yearworth v North Bristol NHS Trust*,[126] the English Court of Appeal did not need to decide this issue and left the question open for another day.

In *Yearworth*, six men, Cs, underwent chemotherapy for cancer. Due to the risk that such treatment could damage or remove Cs' fertility, they elected to produce samples of their semen for storage at D's hospital's fertility unit. Prior to the sperm being used, the amount of liquid nitrogen in the storage tanks fell below the requisite level, the automated system for topping up the levels did not work, and they were not manually topped up either. The semen samples thawed and perished. Five Cs suffered psychiatric injuries upon being told that news (the other suffered mental distress). **Held:** the sperm was Cs' property for the purposes of their tort claims; but these Cs were only told of the destruction of their property, they did not witness it. However, they were permitted to proceed with their claims under the law of contract (bailment), which enabled them to recover damages for mere mental distress,[127] as well as for psychiatric injury. In *Holdich v Lothian Health Board*,[128] Mr Holdich, C, elected to have sperm samples stored at D's cryogenic storage facility, prior to receiving treatment for testicular cancer. The liquid nitrogen in the storage vessel in which the sperm was stored leaked, and the temperatures in the vessel raised, rendering the samples unusable. C claimed damages for depression, as a result of the loss of a chance of fatherhood. **Held:** C's claim could proceed in tort.

The Scottish Outer House recently stated, in *Holdich*, that the *Yearworth* Court of Appeal assumed, without deciding, that the primary/secondary classification applied to such cases, that Mrs Attia was considered as a 'primary victim', and that the cancer victims in *Yearworth* were analysed as secondary victims.[129] (However, rather than categorising those Cs as secondary victims, arguably all that the *Yearworth* court was doing was to point out that *direct perception* of the property's destruction may be required for policy reasons, to circumvent the number of potential claims, just as the requirement applies to secondary victims.)

However, in this author's view,[130] these cases of property damage giving rise to psychiatric injury are 'special cases' which fall into the residuary basket, and which do not involve any

[125] *ibid*, 320. [126] [2009] EWCA Civ 37, [2010] 1 QB 1, [55].

[127] Per: *Jarvis v Swans Tours Ltd* [1973] 1 QB 233 (CA). [128] [2013] CSOH 197, 2014 SLT 495.

[129] *ibid*, [87]. [130] Mulheron, 'The "Primary Victim" in Psychiatric Illness Claims, etc' (2008) 19 *KCLJ* 81, 99–105.

necessity to descend to the primary/secondary victim classification at all. That view is supported by the Court of Appeal in *Boumedien v Delta Display Ltd*,[131] where D negligently crashed his car into C's front garden wall. Smith LJ noted that, 'if this [C] was a victim of [D's] negligence, it was as a primary or ordinary victim; no question arose of his being a secondary victim. He could not claim to be a secondary victim caused by seeing or hearing damage to a wall'. In *Holdich* itself, the Outer House also preferred the view that the primary/secondary classification 'should not arise in sole victim cases, where the allegation is of wrong done directly to [C's] interests, where [C's] identity, as an individual or possibly as a member of a class, is known in advance to [D], and where [D] has a duty of care by virtue of pre-existing legal proximity to safeguard the interest in question'.[132]

To conclude, whether the property is a house, a wall, or sperm, C **may** potentially recover damages for psychiatric injury arising from the destruction of that property, but that will be analysed under the ordinary principles of negligence as residuary Cs (per the *Caparo* and *Hedley Byrne* tests). The better view is that there is **no** question of C's constituting a 'secondary victim', where the property was the 'immediate victim'.

The elevated primary victim

§5.13 Elevated primary victims occur where a would-be secondary victim, C, is not a bystander to any immediate victim (because there is no immediate victim of D's act or omission), and hence, C is treated as a primary victim.

In the typical secondary victim scenario, C is a bystander, and D imperils the immediate victim by his act or omission, which C witnesses and suffers psychiatric injury as a result. However, what if there is no immediate victim at all? Legally speaking, how should C be legally treated then – as a secondary victim for whom there is no immediate victim? Or as a primary victim, because there is no immediate victim to whom he could be a secondary victim?[133]

Controversially, it is the **second** of these options which has been adopted in the key English cases to date. English courts have been reluctant to designate C as a secondary victim, where there is no immediate victim existing. In effect, C has been 'promoted' to the status of primary victim, even though C does not satisfy the definition of primary victim (i.e., C was not in the 'zone of danger', and was not 'guilt-ridden' either). Two cases are illustrative:

In *AB v Leeds Teaching Hosp NHS Trust*,[134] this group litigation[135] arose out of an enquiry into paediatric cardiac surgery at the Bristol Royal Infirmary, which revealed that various babies who had died at, or soon after, birth had had their organs (e.g., brains, lungs, spinal cords and hearts) removed and retained for histopathological examinations, without their parents' consent. The parents, C, alleged that learning of this unauthorised organ retention caused them psychiatric injuries. Lead Cs, Mrs Shorter, Mrs Carpenter, and Mr and Mrs Harris, C, claimed damages for psychiatric injury. **Held:** Cs were classified as primary victims, principally because their children were not immediate victims to whom a duty could

[131] [2008] EWCA Civ 368, [6]. [132] [2013] CSOH 197, [88].

[133] This section is partly derived from the analysis in Mulheron, 'The "Primary Victim" in Psychiatric Illness Claims, etc' (2008) 19 *KCLJ* 81, 93–94.

[134] [2004] EWHC 644, [2005] QB 506, especially at [252]–[253], [279].

[135] Certified as a Group Litigation Order under Pt 19.III of the Civil Procedure Rules, and entitled, *Nationwide Organ Retention Group Litigation.*

have been owed post-mortem. However, two of the three Cs failed, because they failed one or more of the duty of care criteria. In *Farrell v Avon HA*,[136] Mr Farrell, C, excitedly attended D's hospital to see his newborn son Jordan (J), who was born of a brief relationship with J's mother (C and the mother were not a couple at the time of J's birth). Upon arriving, C was told that the baby had died, and he was given a corpse to cradle. Twenty minutes later, C was then told that there had been a terrible mistake, and that this was someone else's baby who had died, and that J was alive. C suffered PTSD, and relapsed into previous alcohol and drug dependency. **Held:** C was a primary victim, and recovered £10,000.

These parental Cs were not participants in these incidents; they were not guilt-ridden in the *W v Essex* sense, because they did not cause or contribute to the decision to harvest the organs or imperil their children; and they were not in the zone of physical danger from the hospitals' activities. However, in *AB*, Gage J said that, if there was no immediate victim in respect of whom the parents could be secondary victims, then if they 'are victims at all, they must be primary victims'.[137] One of the most interesting aspects of *Farrell* (and there were many!) was that Mr Farrell would not have satisfied the various secondary victim pre-conditions for recovery. It was fortunate, then, that he was decreed to be a primary victim, as there was no other primary victim – 'the only victim of the incident was [C] himself'; no other person was 'physically involved in the incident as a potential victim'; and '[h]ow can there be a secondary victim if there is no other person who was physically involved in the incident as a potential victim?'[138] However, Mr Farrell clearly did not fit any of the definitions of primary victim.

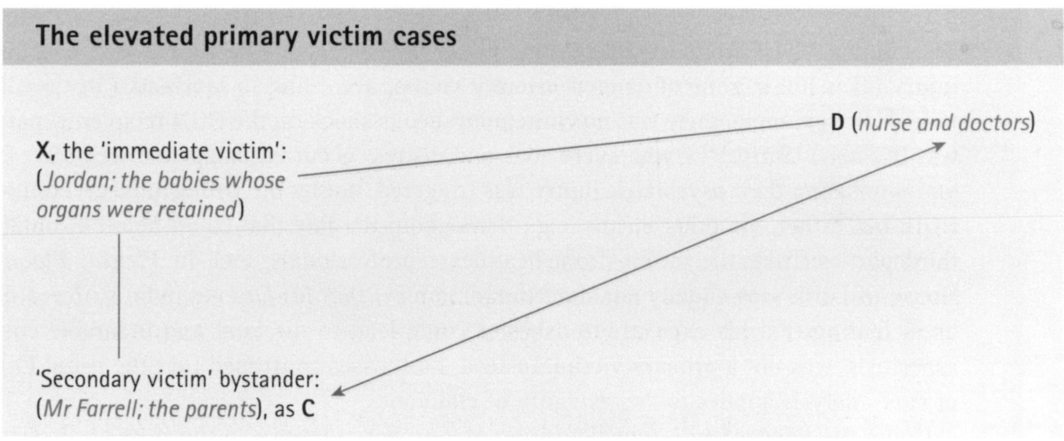

There is a certain logic in *AB's* and *Farrell's* outcomes. A secondary victim imputes, 'secondary to someone' – and without an immediate victim, the secondary victim should be elevated. Otherwise, the definition of Lord Lloyd in *Page v Smith*, of a secondary victim 'in the position of a spectator or bystander', is impossible to apply, in these rather odd cases. In addition, in *AB* and *Farrell*, the secondary victim is the **only** (i.e., the primary) victim of D's negligence. Hence, the case for applying the various control mechanisms that are pertinent to secondary victims do not apply with nearly the same force, in that there will be very few Cs who are psychiatrically injured in a scenario where their immediate victim was not injured or killed.

136 [2001] Lloyd's Rep Med 458 (QB). 137 [2004] EWHC 644, [2005] QB 506, [199].
138 [2001] Lloyd's Rep Med 458 (QB) 466, 471.

However, instead of elevating the parents and Mr Farrell to primary victim status, it is strongly arguable that they **ought** to have been treated as secondary victims, with no immediate victim existing. This would enable the primary victim definitions couched by the House of Lords to be applied consistently and meaningfully, rather than departing from those definitions because of the coincidental matter that *the immediate victim* did not happen to be the subject of any actual negligence. Also, given the easier task which primary victims face in establishing a duty of care, a bright-line division between the categories is all the more important to maintain. Finally, to hold that the parents and Mr Farrell must have been primary victims suggests that any duty to a secondary victim must be *derivative* (i.e., that it can only be established if there was some negligence towards the immediate victim) – but as discussed above, the duty to the secondary victim is entirely separate from, and independent of, any duty of care owed to/negligence toward/harm suffered by the immediate victim. The parents and Mr Farrell would equate to Lord Oliver's example, in *Alcock*, of the child who walked away unharmed from the situation of peril, leaving his psychiatrically-injured parents to claim as secondary victims.

Notably, the decision in *Farrell* has been doubted (in *Walters v North Glamorgan NHS Trust*[139]), but never overruled.

Fear-of-the-future claimants

§5.14 A fear-of-the-future victim of psychiatric injury is not a 'zone of danger' primary victim, despite having been in the zone of danger in contracting a disease later in life. For that C who suffers pure psychiatric injury, the analysis of a duty of care adheres to the tri-partite *Caparo* test.

To reiterate, there were several reasons as to why a fear-of-the-future victim of psychiatric injury (C) is not a 'zone of danger' primary victim, according to Morland J in the *CJD Litigation.*[140] For example, there was no contemporaneous shock on the HGH recipients' part, as there was in *Page v Smith*[141] – whatever shock and distress occurred, happened well after D's acts or omissions; and their psychiatric injury was triggered, not by the wrongfully-given injections of HGH, but rather, via other means (e.g., news about the fate that could befall C, obtained from third parties, from the media, from healthcare professionals, etc). In *Pleural Plaques,*[142] the House of Lords was equally adamant (unanimously) that Mr Grieves, who suffered depression upon fearing that his exposure to asbestos could lead to the fatal and incurable condition of asbestosis, was not a primary victim. Instead, both cases confirmed that the usual *Caparo* duty of care analysis applies to this category of claimant.

Under the *Page v Smith*-type definition of a primary victim – in the zone of physical danger, a participant in the event and not a bystander, someone who did not develop physical injury as a result of D's breach, but who suffered psychiatric injury instead – it is difficult to conceive of how these HGH recipients were not primary victims. The lack of temporal immediacy between their injury and the breach is the only important aspect in which they differed from Mr Page's situation, and on this point, *W v Essex CC*[143] did not require a close contemporaneous link between the Council's breach and the parents' psychiatric injury either.

139 [2002] EWHC 321 (QB) [23].

140 [2000] Lloyd's Rep Med 161 (QB), (1998) 41 BMLR 157, 163–64.

141 [1996] AC 155 (HL).

142 *Johnston v NEI* [2007] UKHL 39, [33] (Lord Hoffmann), [54] (Lord Hope), [77] (Lord Scott), [95] (Lord Rodger), and [104] (Lord Mance). The CA, by majority, had earlier reached the same view: *Grieves* [2006] EWCA Civ 27, [89]–[91] (Lord Phillips (CJ)).

143 [2001] 2 AC 592 (HL).

Residuary claimants

§5.15 In limited circumstances, C can recover damages for negligently-inflicted psychiatric injury, without establishing primary or secondary victim status at all. Nor is there any question of C's being a stress-at-work or a fear-of-the-future victim. Nevertheless, C is permitted to recover, as a residuary C.

It was suggested by Gage J, in the organ-retention case of *AB v Leeds Teaching Hosp NHS Trust*,[144] that those claiming for pure psychiatric injury must be placed in **either** primary **or** secondary victim categories – 'the House of Lords has made it clear that those claiming solely for psychiatric injury must be placed in one or other category'. The majority of English cases have made an earnest attempt to adhere to this viewpoint.

However, the House of Lords has not limited itself in this way. In *Barber v Somerset CC*, the employees' claims for free-standing psychiatric injury, brought about by excessive workloads, were permitted. Not one of their Lordships mentioned *Alcock*, *Page v Smith*, *White*, or *Essex*; and the terminology of primary and secondary victims was not used at all. Fear-of-the-future victims, whilst permitted, have not been treated under the primary/secondary victim framework either. This class of residuary claimant imbues the area with even further uncertainty. The limited circumstances giving rise to the basket of residuary claimants are outlined later in the chapter.

Stress-at-work claimants

§5.16 Workplace stress claims, by employee against employer, have been treated separately from, and outside of, the primary victim/secondary victim classification.

Even though the 'stressed-at-work' employee C has been described as a 'primary victim' in some cases (per *White v CC of South Yorkshire Police*[145]) clearly they are not within the zone of physical danger, nor feel the type of guilt that the primary victim definition requires. No attempt has been made, judicially, to fit them within a *Page v Smith*-type analysis. Also, there is no question of secondary victim status for these employees.

In fact, entirely different principles have been developed by English courts to permit recovery in these types of cases.[146] The 'stressed-at-work' C, for whom the employer has assumed a responsibility to avoid or minimise psychiatric injury, has been able to recover, but only in certain defined circumstances.

In *Johnstone v Bloomsbury HA*,[147] a junior doctor, C, had a breakdown after being required to work at D's hospital, the University College Hospital, as a senior house officer, for excessive hours without rest. His contract of employment provided that he had a standard 40-hour working week, and that, in addition, he would be available on call for a further 48 hours a week on average. On some weeks, C was required to work >100 hours, with inadequate periods of sleep. As a result, C suffered from depression, lethargy, diminished appetite and suicidal feelings. **Held:** C was owed a duty of care to avoid his foreseeable psychiatric injury. This duty was owed, irrespective of the

[144] [2004] EWHC 644 (QB), [2005] QB 506, [197].

[145] [1999] 2 AC 455 (HL) 506. Also: *Hatton v Sutherland* [2002] EWCA Civ 76, [21]; *McLoughlin v Jones* [2001] EWCA Civ 1743, [55].

[146] Especially: *Hatton* (*ibid*); *Barber v Somerset CC* [2004] UKHL 13, [2004] 1 WLR 1089.

[147] [1991] IRLR 118.

contractual terms in the employment contract which required him to work overtime. In *Walker v Northumberland CC*,[148] Mr Walker, C, a social worker employed by D, was under an excessive workload, and had a mental breakdown in 1986, for which he had four months of leave. The nature of the work (especially child abuse cases) was inherently very stressful. C was reassured by his superiors that he would receive an assistant and a lower case load when he returned. However, when C returned, he had to deal with the case backlog created whilst he was away, plus a considerable new case load, and had a second breakdown. C was dismissed. C sued D, for failing to take reasonable steps to avoid exposing him to a health-endangering workload. **Held:** C was owed a duty of care. By 1985/86, there was no evidence that those in C's position were particularly vulnerable to stress-induced mental illness, and it was not reasonably foreseeable to D that the workload to which C was exposed gave rise to a material risk of mental illness. However, when C returned to work after his first breakdown, a repetition of illness was reasonably foreseeable, if C was again exposed to the same workload, and C's duties were not alleviated by effective additional assistance.

Conclusion

The categorisation outlined above matters enormously to the legal analysis required to establish a duty of care. As discussed below, primary victims who fall within the *Page v Smith* category possess certain legal advantages over secondary victims. For example, the secondary victim is subject to the 'normal fortitude' rule, whereas a primary victim does not have to cope with the restrictions of that rule. Also, the test of 'reasonable foreseeability' for a primary victim is wider (i.e., **either** physical or psychiatric injury to C must have been foreseen or reasonably foreseeable) than it is for a secondary victim (i.e., it must have been reasonably foreseeable that C would suffer psychiatric injury). Moreover, secondary victims must prove that their psychiatric injuries were induced by 'shock', probably unlike other Cs.

Turning now to the criteria governing the duty of care which each category of C requires:

PRIMARY VICTIM CLAIMANTS

A primary victim C must prove the relevant test of reasonable foreseeability (albeit that the type of test depends upon the type of primary victim at issue); that there was a sufficient legal proximity between wrongdoer D and C who suffered the psychiatric injury (either established by the usual factors of spatial and temporal proximity, or by the proof of an assumption of responsibility by D towards C to avoid causing psychiatric injury); and that public policy favoured the imposition of a duty of care.

Duty of care requirements

Reasonable foreseeability

§5.17 For the 'zone of danger' primary victim who was within the range of foreseeable physical injury, C's psychiatric injury does not have to be foreseeable. As an exception to the usual *Wagon Mound* principle of foreseeability, it is sufficient if there is some foreseeable *physical* injury to C (or to a class of persons of whom C is one) as a result of D's negligence.

[148] [1995] 1 All ER 737 (QB).

The *Page v Smith* anomaly. For the 'zone-of-danger' primary victim, *physical* injury will be foreseeable, given that C was in the zone of physical danger – but psychiatric injury may be so unlikely and far-fetched as to be unforeseeable. Nevertheless, the zone-of-danger C can prove the requisite test of foreseeability, according to *Page v Smith*.[149] This is the sole instance, in English law, where C can recover for a type of injury (i.e., psychiatric injury) which was not reasonably foreseeable. This category of C thereby represents a rare exception to the general *Wagon Mound* principle[150] of remoteness, which provides that the damage suffered must have been of a reasonably foreseeable type in order to be compensable.

In *Page v Smith*, Mr Page's chronic and permanent CFS, arising from his involvement in a minor car accident, was a type of injury which was unforeseeable, but physical injury in a car accident was entirely foreseeable. In *A v Essex CC*,[151] it was 'difficult to accept' that the parents could foreseeably suffer from psychiatric injury as a result of D's placing William, the violent child, with them – but it was certainly foreseeable that William might assault them and damage their property, hence, *Page v Smith* applied.

The justifications for this wide test of foreseeability were put by Lord Lloyd in *Page v Smith*[152] on two bases – first, as a matter of medical diagnosis ('[i]n an age when medical knowledge is expanding fast, and psychiatric knowledge with it, it would not be sensible to commit the law to a distinction between physical and psychiatric injury, which may already seem somewhat artificial, and may soon be altogether outmoded. Nothing will be gained by treating them as different "kinds" of personal injury, so as to require the application of different tests in law'); and secondly, there was no prospect of floodgates of claims, even if a wide test of foreseeability was applied. Lord Lloyd described the foreseeability of physical injury in *Page v Smith* as a 'limiting factor', so that there could be 'no question' of D being liable to the whole world. Merely 'bumping the neighbour's car while parking in the street', where no physical injury to the neighbour was remotely foreseeable, would not render D liable, should the neighbour develop (unforeseeable) psychiatric injury.

In fact, the test of foreseeability is even more claimant-friendly, given that (as discussed in Chapter 2) the correct legal question to ask is, not whether injury to that particular C was foreseeable, but whether injury to *a class of persons of whom C was one*, was foreseeable. Hence, if C's injury arises out of road accident, then the correct question is – should D have reasonably foreseen injury to another road user of any kind. It is **not** correct to ask whether D should have foreseen physical injury to that particular road-user C.

In *Smith v Co-op Group Ltd*,[153] Joshua Smith, D, 13, was a paper-boy employed by the Co-op, D. He was riding his bike and delivering newspapers to houses in a relatively quiet street, when he rode straight out into the street without looking, and into the path of a lorry being driven by Mr Hammond, C. D was very seriously-injured, and C suffered psychiatric injury as a result of hitting the boy. **Held (trial):** C could not recover: 'I just cannot see that someone of that age [13] would foresee that if he cycles into the road, and is hit by a lorry, that he could foresee physical injury to the lorry driver'. **Held (CA):** C could recover for his psychiatric injury because the correct test was wider: 'it would have been obvious to a boy of 13 that the risk of causing personal injury to another road

[149] [1996] AC 155 (HL). Lord Lloyd gave the majority's speech (Lord Ackner and Lord Browne-Wilkinson agreeing).

[150] *Overseas Tankship (UK) Ltd v Morts Dock and Engineering Co Ltd (Wagon Mound (No 1))* [1961] AC 388 (PC) 426.

[151] [2003] EWCA Civ 1848, [2004] 1 WLR 1881, [71].

[152] [1996] 1 AC 155 (HL), with quotes at 188, and 189–90, respectively.

[153] [2010] EWCA 725, [20] (Moore-Bick LJ).

user by cycling across the road without warning would have been great ... he would have realised that the driver (even of a car) might brake violently, swerve or skid, collide with other vehicles or a stationary object and suffer injury as a result'.

Judicial uncertainty about *Page v Smith*. Some senior appellate judges have openly questioned whether the wide test of foreseeability in *Page v Smith* should be reviewed for zone-of-danger primary victims. In *Johnston v NEI Intl Combustion Ltd*,[154] Lords Hope and Mance thought it doubtful whether *Page v Smith* had been correctly decided, and stated that it should be reviewed on another occasion. In *White (Frost)*, Lord Goff also questioned the correctness of *Page v Smith*.[155] In *Corr v IBC Vehicles Ltd*,[156] Lord Neuberger called *Page v Smith* 'somewhat controversial', and foreshadowed that it may come up for challenge before the Supreme Court at some point.

However, as Lord Walker noted in *Corr*, whilst *Page v Smith* 'has attracted adverse comment from some legal scholars', it serves as 'a much simpler test for judges trying personal injury cases, even if it sometimes results in compensation for damage in the form of psychiatric sequelae which might not, on their own, have been reasonably foreseeable by [D]'.[157] In *Johnston*, Lord Hoffmann also supported the principle in *Page v Smith*, opining that it had not given rise to any difficulties in application.[158]

In any event, the ratio of *Page v Smith* remains in place for now.

The law reform corner: Reasonable foreseeability

The Scottish Comm:[159] recommended that the law would be more coherent and principled if there was only liability for negligently-inflicted psychiatric injury when that injury was a reasonably foreseeable consequence of D's actions, so as not to depart from the *Wagon Mound* principle.

§5.18 For the 'guilt-ridden' primary victim, however, the *Wagon Mound* principle applies, i.e., C's psychiatric injury must have been reasonably foreseeable.

For the guilt-ridden primary victim, C **must** prove foreseeability of psychiatric injury, in order to recover for precisely that type of injury, thus complying with the *Wagon Mound* principle (per Lord Slynn in *W v Essex CC*, who considered the parents' psychiatric injury as a result of bringing their children and boy G under the one roof was reasonably foreseeable – it was certainly not foreseeable that the parents would suffer any physical injury, i.e., sexual assault, from G, but the key point was that the type of injury for which the parents were claiming had to be foreseeable, *viz*, psychiatric injury).

Proximity

§5.19 If D has placed C in a zone of physical danger via his acts or omissions, then proximity will customarily be established by the parties' physical and temporal closeness. However, C must have been, in fact, exposed to a risk of physical injury, or reasonably believed that he was so exposed.

Where psychiatric injury occurs from C being placed by D in the zone of physical danger, that is *prima facie* sufficient to fix proximity, as it follows from the immediacy of the physical danger to C.

[154] [2007] UKHL 39, [52] and [104], respectively. [155] [1999] 2 AC 455 (HL) 473–76.
[156] [2008] UKHL 13, [2008] 1 AC 884, [54]. [157] *ibid*, [40].
[158] [2007] UKHL 39, [32]. [159] *Scottish Report*, [1.10], [3.32].

However, if C cannot prove that he was, in fact, exposed to a risk of physical injury, or reasonably believed that he was exposed to that risk, then the requisite proximity will be lacking, and no recovery will be permitted. In *McFarlane v EE Caledonia Ltd*,[160] Stuart-Smith LJ considered that the notion of a primary victim could be expanded somewhat, to include not only a C who is in the actual area of danger created by the event, but also a C who is never in danger, but who reasonably thinks that he is, 'because of the sudden and unexpected nature of the event'. Any belief by C, that he was within the danger zone, must not be 'genuine but irrational': it must be reasonable in all the circumstances – and this is harder to prove, if C was never actually in physical danger. To contrast some cases:

In *Young v Charles Church (Southern) Ltd*,[161] facts previously, **held (CA):** Mr Young, C, was a primary victim, because he was in the area of physical danger created by D's negligent system of work in allowing scaffolding to be erected near 'live' powerlines. In *McFarlane v EE Caledonia Ltd*, Mr McFarlane, C, a painter on an Alpha Piper oil rig, was near to the rig when it exploded in 1988, and 164 men died. C was on a support vessel, 550 metres away, at the time of the explosion. The closest that he got to the flames was 100 metres, when the support vessel sought to render assistance to fight the fire, but C could still hear the screams of the men who were in the midst of the fire. **Held:** C could not recover for his psychiatric injury, as he was not genuinely in fear of his own safety, nor objectively was he endangered whilst on the support vessel. In *Fagan v Goodman*,[162] Ms Fagan, C, witnessed an accident whilst driving on a motorway. Another car driver, Mr Goodman, D, changed lanes, without seeing a police motorcyclist in his 'blind spot'. The policeman swerved and crashed into the central road barrier, and died at the scene. C saw the horrific fatal injuries that the policeman sustained, including a severed arm, and suffered psychiatric injury. **Held:** C could not recover, as she did not need to take emergency action to avoid being caught up in the accident, nor was she at any risk of colliding with the policeman, his out-of-control motorcycle, or D's car. 'The fact that a (near) collision involving vehicles in another lane of a major road may have led to one of the vehicles losing control and thus immediately ... in an accident does not give rise to a foreseeable risk that a person in the general vicinity of where the negligence takes place is ... involved in that accident ... The result for [C] would have been otherwise if she had been forced to take emergency action to avoid the results of [D's] negligence'.

Undoubtedly, fine factual distinctions are raised by the 'close-to-physical-danger-but-not-in-fact-injured' type of case. Arguably, Mrs Fagan was as much in the zone of danger created by D's negligent driving, as was Mr Young by his employer's negligent system of scaffolding; and Mr Young did not need to take 'emergency action' to avoid the electrocution that struck his workmate dead. Yet Mr Young could recover as a primary victim, and Mrs Fagan could not. Thus, much depends upon how the court chooses to define the 'zone'. Obviously, the wider that 'zone', the better for the primary victim C.

§5.20 If C is a guilt-ridden primary victim, proximity may be established where there was a sufficient closeness in time and space with the immediate victim, or where D legally assumed a responsibility for C's well-being. Additionally, C must have a genuine belief that he caused the immediate victim's injury or death.

Again, the borderline between the recoverable scenarios, and those which do not suffice for primary victim status, can be very finely-drawn, as the two contrasting cases below demonstrate:

[160] [1994] PIQR 154 (CA) 162, citing the lower court: [1993] PIQR 241 (QB) 249 (Smith J).
[161] (1997) 39 BMLR 146 (CA). [162] QBD, 30 November 2001, quotes at [25]–[26].

In *Hunter v British Coal Corp*,[163] facts previously (re the exploding fire hydrant), C suffered from guilt-induced depression after the death of his colleague. **Held:** C was not a primary victim, because of a lack of proximity: 'the law requires a greater degree of physical and temporal proximity than was present in this case before Mr Hunter could properly be treated as a direct, or primary, victim'. In *W v Essex CC*,[164] parents Mr and Mrs W, C, suffered from guilt, for bringing boy G and their children under the one roof. **Held:** C could proceed as potential primary victims. D knew that G was known to be or suspected of being a sexual abuser; and it was impossible for C to verify that from any other source. Hence, C were in a very vulnerable position, once D chose not to disclose that information.

While *Hunter* was only briefly cited in *Essex*, the cases are difficult to reconcile. *Hunter* did not have sufficient physical proximity, whereas, in *Essex*, no such physical proximity to danger *for parents* C was present on the facts, for all the parents did was to 'bring the abused and the abuser together'. Hence, the reasoning in *Hunter* (where guilt was not sufficient) and *Essex* (where it was) is distinctly at odds. However, the parents in *Essex* could point to another proximity factor, *viz*, that D withheld information which could not be ascertained or verified elsewhere, and knew that supplying the information to C would have prompted C to act differently.

§5.21 Where C is temporally and physically proximate to horrifying events caused by D's negligence, and suffers psychiatric injury from what C witnessed, that is not sufficient, of itself, to establish C as a primary victim.

The wider *Alcock* definition of the primary victim[165] – i.e., 'one who was involved, either mediately or immediately as a participant' in events – has *not* been literally applied, in circumstances where C was closely proximate to and involved in very upsetting events, but was not in the zone of physical danger himself. That close proximity is simply insufficient to prove primary victim status.

In a trio of cases involving three mothers – who brought claims for pure psychiatric illness arising out of the death of their children, allegedly as a result of the acts or omissions of the relevant health authorities – each mother was closely exposed to the events surrounding her child's death; and each **lost** her primary victim claim.

In *North Glamorgan NHS Trust v Walters*,[166] Ms Walters', C's, son, Elliot, developed acute hepatitis and liver failure which treating doctors, D, failed to diagnose. Elliot suffered a seizure in front of C in hospital, and also lost the opportunity to undergo a liver transplant because of the misdiagnosis. He was then transferred to another hospital, where C was told that Elliot had been severely brain-damaged by the seizure, would never recognise her, and would have practically no quality of life. C stayed with her son, or close by, for the 36 hours of his medical treatment, witnessing the events first-hand, and turned off Elliot's life support machine at the end. **Held (trial,[167] and CA)**: C was not an 'unwilling participant' in the events which brought about Elliot's death, because she was not within the range of foreseeable physical injury herself, nor did she play any causative role in Elliot's death for which she could feel guilty. In *Hall v Gwent Healthcare NHS Trust*,[168] Karen Hall's, C's, mentally disturbed husband, Andrew Hall, had been under the care of health authority, D, for serious mental illness since 1992. For his family, certain care orders were in place (e.g., all sharp knives had to be removed from the home). In 2000, Mr Hall was the target of a cruel hoax played

[163] [1999] QB 140 (CA) 149 (Brooke LJ) 154. [164] [2001] 2 AC 592 (HL) 601 (Lord Slynn).
[165] [1992] 1 AC 310 (HL) 407. [166] [2002] EWCA Civ 1792, [12].
[167] [2002] EWHC 321 (QB), [21]–[22]. [168] [2004] EWHC 2748 (QB) [16]–[17].

by his work colleagues, in which he went to India for a 'business trip' which was non-genuine. The hoax mentally destabilised C, and he showed disturbed behaviour on the return flight to England, suffering a 'florid psychotic state' in which he developed the belief that 15 Christian families were going to be killed because of him, and to avoid this, he would have to kill his 12-year-old daughter, Emma. He acted upon this belief soon after (having purloined a knife from his sister's house during a brief visit there on his return to England). C was in the house at the time of the fatal attack on Emma, and took the knife from her husband after the stabbing. Mr Hall was confined to Broadmoor, following trial. **Held:** C was not a primary victim, as she was not herself at risk of physical injury, nor had she unwittingly contributed to her daughter's peril (quite the opposite, she had ensured that no knives were kept in the home). In *Palmer v Tees HA*,[169] Sean Armstrong was released from D's mental facility, having disclosed to a psychiatrist before his release that he harboured sexual feelings towards children. About a year later, he abducted, assaulted, killed and mutilated a 4-year-old girl, Rosie Palmer, who lived nearby. Rosie's mother, Ms Palmer, C, suffered psychiatric illness, and alleged that D failed to provide adequate treatment for Mr Armstrong, failed to prevent his release, and failed to diagnose that there was a substantial risk of his committing serious sexual offences against children. **Held:** C was not a primary victim – for the same reasons as Ms Hall and Ms Walters after her. 'Although at one stage [counsel] suggested that [C] was a primary victim, he did not seriously argue the point; in my judgment, she clearly was not.'

Of the trio, only Ms Walters managed to prove that she was, in the alternative, a secondary victim (but for reasons that have attracted controversy). Both Mrs Hall and Ms Palmer also failed in their secondary victim claims, for reasons considered in the next section.

These cases give rise to an odd anomaly. Where parents (such as Mr and Mrs W) are 'guilt-ridden' victims, they are candidates to be treated as potential primary victims, whereas the law treats parents whose children are imperiled or killed by D's negligence far less sympathetically, where those latter parents do nothing for which they subsequently experience feelings of guilt or responsibility – even though they may have been closer in space and time to the tragedies that enveloped their children. This is one reason why *W v Essex CC* represents (in the author's opinion) a 'legal wrong-turn'.[170]

Public policy considerations

§5.22 Policy reasons such as 'floodgates concerns' and 'distributive justice' may preclude any finding of primary victim status.

The Group B victims in the *CJD Litigation* were distinguished from the 'zone of danger' primary victims for various reasons, one of which was 'floodgates' public policy concerns:

> if they were [primary victims], the ramifications would be incalculable. If they were primary victims, so would be those exposed to asbestos or radiation where primary liability may depend not upon common law negligence but on statutory duty or even strict liability, even if they became aware of the risk of physical injury years later and consequently developed psychiatric injury. The potentiality of a huge number of claims in similar situations would arise, making insurance difficult or impossible. It could involve all manner of products and a huge range of potential tortfeasors. It could inhibit the producers, prescribers and suppliers of a product from warning the public of the danger of a product. For example, if a potentially lethal substance had been negligently

[169] [1999] Lloyd's Rep Med 351 (CA), [35]–[37], quote at [35] (Stuart-Smith LJ).

[170] 'The "Primary Victim" in Psychiatric Illness Claims, etc' (2008) 19 *KCLJ* 81, 90.

introduced into a production batch of canned food, it would be disastrous if a supplier or producer were inhibited from warning the public of danger for fear that, among those who had already eaten the canned food, some might bring a claim as a primary victim for psychiatric injury triggered by the warning.[171]

Further, whereas the number of potential secondary victims is circumscribed by a number of 'control mechanisms' and by the normal fortitude rule (described in principle §5.33), those factors do not operate in primary victim claims. Hence, floodgates concerns were real, and not fanciful, in Morland J's view, if the CJD claimants were to be treated as zone-of-physical-danger primary victims.

The policy factor, 'distributive justice', has also figured in the primary victim context. It will be recalled (from Chapter 2) that this factor requires judges to determine whether they reasonably believe that ordinary people in the community ('commuters on the Underground', per *McFarlane v Tayside Health Board*[172]) would consider it just and fair to compensate C, in light of what those people would consider to be a just distribution of burdens and losses among members of a society.

In *White (Frost) v CC of South Yorkshire*,[173] facts previously, the police officers who performed rescue and other services during the Hillsborough stadium disaster were unable to recover damages as primary (or secondary) victims – partly because ordinary citizens would think it unfair if the police received damages, after the relatives had received nothing in *Alcock* seven years earlier. The ordinary citizen would think that this was, at best, not treating like cases alike, and at worst, favouring the less deserving against the more deserving.

Other features of note

The 'normal fortitude' rule is inapplicable

§5.23 As a primary victim, C can recover for his psychiatric injury, even if it was sustained because C lacked the mental fortitude or 'natural phlegm' of an ordinary person. That is, a pre-existing vulnerability may render C's psychiatric injury unlikely, but nevertheless, it may be foreseeable, given that the 'normal fortitude' rule does not apply to C.

The source of the principle. According to Lord Lloyd in *Page v Smith*,[174] a primary victim is **not** subject to the 'normal fortitude' rule. Hence, for a primary victim with a so-called 'egg-shell skull personality', he can establish that D owed him a duty of care to avoid his psychiatric injury, even if that injury would only have been foreseeable in a person of vulnerability.

This principle means that C's past history of mental illness or instability is no bar to his recovering for psychiatric injury which a negligent D may inflict upon him.

In *Page v Smith*, facts previously, Mr Page, C, had suffered from CFS in the past, and was vulnerable to a relapse – but could still recover damages for psychiatric injury, even if it was sustained because C lacked the fortitude of an ordinary person to withstand the tribulations of a minor car accident. In *Donachie v CC of Greater Manchester Police*, facts previously, police officer Mr Donachie, C, had a particular vulnerability to stress by reason of his pre-existing hypertension, but that pre-existing susceptibility could be taken into account when assessing whether his psychiatric injury was

[171] [2000] Lloyd's Rep Med 161 (QB) 165. [172] [2000] 2 AC 59 (HL) 82 (Lord Steyn).
[173] [1999] 2 AC 455 (HL) 510 (Lord Hoffmann). [174] [1996] AC 155 (HL) 197.

foreseeable, as he was a *Page*-type victim. Had C been a secondary victim, any pre-existing vulnerability could **not** have been taken into account, when assessing whether his psychiatric injury was reasonably foreseeable.

In *Page*, Lord Lloyd remarked that the lack of a normal fortitude requirement for a primary victim was defensible in that, 'liability depends on foreseeability of physical injury, [and so] there could be no question of [D] finding himself liable to all the world'.[175] However, as demonstrated in this chapter, primary victims can seemingly also encompass Cs who were not in the zone of physical danger at all (but were 'guilt-ridden'), and hence, the field of potential Cs is not as ring-fenced as Lord Lloyd perhaps envisaged. Whatever its justification, the Court of Appeal remarked, in *Greatorex v Greatorex*, that the consequence of the distinction between primary and secondary victims is that a primary victim does have that advantage, of recovering damages, notwithstanding that he could not have met the normal fortitude rule.[176]

Contrasts with other areas. By contrast, for a secondary victim, it is assumed, at law, that a person of normal fortitude should be able to withstand the ordinary jolts and jogs of life without succumbing to psychiatric injury. In *Page v Smith*,[177] Lord Lloyd remarked that this is one of the advantages that primary victims enjoy over secondary victims – D has to take a primary victim exactly as D finds him. By contrast, a secondary victim must prove that D should have reasonably foreseen psychiatric injury to *a person of normal fortitude* before he can recover. As Otton LJ reiterated in *Bridges v P&NE Murray Ltd*, in the case of a primary victim:

> D must take C as he finds him, it will avail D nothing that C has a psychologically vulnerable egg-shell personality. This is in contrast to those cases involving secondary victims, where it must be established that the defendant should have foreseen injury by shock to a person of normal fortitude.[178]

In this respect, primary victims claiming for pure psychiatric injury **also** have a distinct advantage over victims who are claiming damages for *physical* injury, because in physical injury cases, D is entitled to require foreseeability of harm in a person of normal physical robustness, and the test of foreseeability of harm (at the remoteness of damage stage) is based upon that assumption. Once an egg-shell claimant proves that some physical harm, even for a person of normal physical vulnerability, was foreseeable, then D must take C as he finds him and compensate him for *all* his losses, even if his injury was particularly grave because of some pre-existing vulnerability (see Chapter 9).

Hence, the law associated with primary victim recovery on this point is an oddity, in comparison with other areas of negligently-inflicted injury.

A change in the law needed? As pointed out in *White*,[179] it was the assumption that the normal fortitude rule applied to both primary victims and secondary victims, up until *Page v Smith* in 1996. The requirement for primary victims was dropped in that case – to Mr Page's great advantage, for he did not have to prove that it was reasonably foreseeable that a person of ordinary fortitude would have suffered chronic fatigue syndrome as a result of the minor car accident in which he was involved.

This case effected a turnaround in the law, as prior to that, any C, whether primary or secondary victim (i.e., 'the ordinary frequenter of the streets'), could only recover for psychiatric

175 [1996] AC 155 (HL) 189. 176 [2000] 4 All ER 769 (QB) 773.

177 [1996] AC 155 (HL) 189, 197. Also: *AB v Leeds Teaching Hosp NHS Trust* [2004] EWHC 644, [190]; *McLoughlin v O'Brian* [1983] 1 AC 410 (HL) 429; *Bourhill v Young* [1943] AC 92 (HL) 110, 117.

178 (CA, 21 May 1999). 179 [1999] 2 AC 455 (HL) 476.

injury if it was reasonably foreseeable that a person of ordinary fortitude or robustness would have suffered the same injury as a result of D's breach (per *Bourhill (or Hay) v Young*[180]).

There is a strong case for returning the law to the pre-*Page v Smith* position, so as to ensure that the normal fortitude requirement is re-established for primary victims. For one thing, the reason given by Lord Lloyd for dropping the normal fortitude requirement has fallen away as this area of the law has developed (the inclusion of the 'guilt-ridden primary victims' has already been noted above, not to mention the elevated primary victim). Hence, D can be liable to a larger cohort of potential Cs than the zone-of-danger primary victims which Lord Lloyd envisaged. Hence, the restriction on liability provided by the normal fortitude requirement may be worth reinstating, to 'ring-fence' D's liability to psychiatrically-vulnerable Cs.

Moreover, the law would certainly be simplified if this distinction between the primary and secondary victim was eliminated. Notably, Lord Ackner remarked, in *Page v Smith*, that 'normal fortitude' is an 'imprecise phrase'.[181] Also, for the elevated primary victim cases, it appears that the normal fortitude requirement is also disapplied, although the requirement certainly applies to the secondary victim before he is 'elevated' (a point that was evident, e.g., in *AB v Leeds*[182]).

The law reform corner: **Commentary on this requirement**

Scottish Law Comm:[183] that a primary victim is not assumed to be a person of normal fortitude is asymmetrical with both secondary victim, and physical victim, recovery. The rule of normal fortitude 'stalks the current law' on recovery for pure psychiatric injury. It should be revised, so that D could assume ordinary mental robustness on the part of all primary or secondary victims.

English Law Comm:[184] described the normal fortitude rule as a 'deceptively difficult issue', and a 'blunt and arbitrary control device', so that the rule should be 'best interpreted as meaning nothing more than that ... in deciding whether psychiatric illness was reasonably foreseeable (and analogously to reasonable foreseeability in physical injury cases), one can take into account the robustness of the population at large to psychiatric illness'.

Ipp Committee:[185] the normal fortitude rule should be abolished for *all* Cs seeking damages for pure psychiatric harm. Such revision would bring the law on psychiatric and physical harm into parallel.

Requirement of shock

§5.24 It is unsettled as to whether the psychiatric injury incurred by the primary victim must have been induced by a 'shock', in the legal sense, in order to be compensable.

The term, 'shock', means (per *Alcock*[186]), 'a sudden assault on the nervous system' (Lord Keith), 'the sudden appreciation of a horrifying event, which violently agitates the mind, [as opposed to] the accumulation over a period in time of more gradual assaults on the nervous system'

[180] [1943] AC 92 (HL) 110, 117. [181] [1996] AC 155 (HL) 170.
[182] [2004] EWHC 644 (QB), [2005] QB 506, [259], [268], [279] (Gage J).
[183] *Scottish Report*, [2.16]–[2.20], [3.19]. [184] *English Report*, [5.21], [5.26].
[185] *Ipp Report*, [9.16] and [9.19]. [186] [1992] 2 AC 310 (HL), with quotes at, respectively, 396–98, 401, 411.

(Lord Ackner), and 'a sudden and unexpected shock to [C's] nervous system' (Lord Oliver). Lord Ackner's has been particularly endorsed as being 'generally accepted as the correct formulation' of the requisite shock (per *Wild v Southend Univ Hosp*[187]).

For secondary victims, it is a limiting criterion. However, there is uncertainty as to whether shock is a requirement for primary victims, which arises for various reasons:

- undoubtedly, in *Page v Smith*, Mr Page **did** suffer a shock when colliding with Mr Smith's car – but none of the Lords stated shock to be a criterion for a primary victim who was in the zone of danger;
- in *W v Essex CC*, the parental C's were potential primary victims, albeit that they suffered no shock which was contemporaneous with G's abuse of their children;
- in the employment context, English (and Scottish[188]) case law has doubted whether shock is a requirement beyond the secondary victim scenario. Indeed, in *Alexander v Midland Bank plc*,[189] the Court of Appeal was adamant that shock did **not** apply, because *Alcock* was 'concerned with secondary victims, where the law has restricted liability to those who were closely related to the primary victim and who witness through sight and sound an horrific event which causes shock. The rule has nothing to do with primary victims'. However, that was dicta only, given that 'stress-at-work' cases have always been governed by different rules;
- in the fear-of-the-future *CJD Litigation*,[190] the lack of contemporaneous shock was also problematical for the HGH recipients – and partly for this reason, they were not *Page v Smith*-type primary victims.

Given these precedents in combination, the better view seems to be that the primary victim does **not** need to prove psychiatric injury by shock.

The law reform corner: Commentary on this requirement

English Law Comm:[191] whether shock applies to primary victims was, at the time of the report, an open question – but in any event, the requirement should be abolished for all victims. The full extent of any injury might only become obvious to C over a period of time, so that rather than becoming 'suddenly aware of the full horror, [C] learns of the severity of the injuries after a number of ... years'. Moreover, 'the fixing of any cut-off point for "suddenness" will be essentially arbitrary'. It would be better to exclude the requirement altogether.

Scottish Law Comm:[192] it is not a pre-requisite for some so-called primary victims, such as work stress claims. In any event, the shock requirement should be entirely done away with.

Hence, to conclude: although the law associated with secondary victims is frequently perceived to create the most difficulties in negligently-inflicted psychiatric injury law, in many respects the primary victim is the more troublesome twin. All too frequently, the courts have chosen to sacrifice doctrinal clarity to help an unfortunate C, acknowledging that C is not in the 'secondary victim' category, and yet finding for C nevertheless, by 'finessing' the primary victim definition.

[187] [2014] EWHC 4053 (QB) [26]. [188] *Cross v Highlands & Islands Enterprise* 2001 SLT 1060 (OH) [61].
[189] [1999] IRLR 723 [50]. [190] [2000] Lloyd's Rep Med 161 (QB) 165.
[191] *English Report*, [2.62], [5.29(4)]. [192] *Scottish Report*, [2.5].

Contrary to the primary victim scenario, thankfully the definition of a secondary victim has remained fairly static over the years. It is the application of the duty of care criteria to different scenarios which has proven problematical.

SECONDARY VICTIM CLAIMANTS

Duty of care requirements

The secondary victim C has a number of hurdles to overcome, if he is to prove that D owed him a duty to avoid his psychiatric injury. Amongst other pre-requisites, secondary victims have to satisfy the legal loopholes known as the '*Alcock* control mechanisms' (named after the case in which they were most notably couched by the House of Lords[193] – although their actual origin was earlier, in *McLoughlin v O'Brian*[194]). They are known colloquially[195] as 'dearness, nearness and hearness', respectively, and will be considered shortly.

These control mechanisms provide a considerable bulwark against the prospect of indeterminate liability on D's part. This is important, where one highly-distressing event may be witnessed by many – precisely the context of *Alcock* itself.

Of course, even where one traumatic incident afflicts only one or two people with psychiatric injury, the *Alcock* control mechanisms have posed significant barriers to that secondary victim recovery too.

Dealing with each duty of care requirement in turn:

Reasonable foreseeability

§5.25 A secondary victim, C, must prove that his psychiatric injury was a reasonably foreseeable consequence of D's acts or omissions.

Whereas, for the *Page v Smith*-type primary victim, **either** physical **or** psychiatric harm must have been foreseeable, the position for secondary victims is more onerous. According to Lord Lloyd in *Page v Smith*, as a control device, '[f]oreseeability of psychiatric injury remains a crucial ingredient when [C] is the secondary victim, for the very reason that the secondary victim is almost always outside the area of physical impact, and therefore outside the range of foreseeable physical injury'.[196] More recently, in *Taylor v A Novo (UK) Ltd*,[197] Lord Dyson MR reiterated that, as the 'starting point' for secondary victims, C's psychiatric injury must have been a reasonably foreseeable consequence of D's negligence.

Typically, it has not been particularly difficult for a secondary victim to prove that test of foreseeability, where a traumatic event has occurred. Psychiatric evidence is frequently called in aid.

In *Tredget v Bexley HA*,[198] facts previously, psychiatric harm on C's part (the parents involved in the chaotic birth of their deceased child), was reasonably foreseeable, because the psychiatric evidence was that neonatal death is more difficult to bear, where birth and death are wrapped up in the same moment.

[193] *Alcock v CC of Yorkshire Police* [1992] 2 AC 310 (HL). [194] [1983] 1 AC 410 (HL) 421–23 (Lord Wilberforce).

[195] See, e.g., the reference to American commentary's use of these terms, noted in: *Frost v CC of South Yorkshire Police* [1996] EWHC Admin 173 (CA) [70] (Henry LJ).

[196] [1996] AC 155 (HL) 184 (Lord Lloyd). [197] [2013] EWCA Civ 194, [5].

[198] [1994] 5 Med LR 178 (Central London CC) 183.

However, if the secondary victim's psychiatric injury is extreme and idiosyncratic, then the law of negligence will not require a reasonable D to avoid it. That scenario has occurred, but rarely.

In *Powell v Boldaz*,[199] Mr and Mrs Powell, C, were the parents of Robert, 10, who died of un-diagnosed Addison's disease. Robert's treating GPs, D, admitted negligence. C brought a disciplinary complaint against D, and learnt, during these proceedings, that false documents (a clinical summary sheet and letter) had been substituted for the originals. Mr Powell claimed that he suffered psychiatric injury as a result of learning of the substitution of the documents ('my head exploded'), and Mrs Powell also claimed for psychiatric injury arising from both Robert's death, and then the substitution. **Held:** neither C recovered. It was not reasonably foreseeable that a parent in this position would suffer such injury because of the substitution, or that this could invoke in both Cs such a reaction, when it was 'far from clear that the substitution ... made any material difference to the medical history'.

Relationship proximity: close tie of love and affection

§5.26 As a secondary victim, C must prove that he shared a 'close tie of love and affection' with the immediate victim of D's negligent act or omission (i.e., the first *Alcock* control mechanism). Close ties may be rebuttably presumed in some types of relationship between C and the immediate victim, but in other cases, that tie must be established by evidence.

In *Alcock*, Lord Keith stated that close ties between the secondary victim, C, and the immediate victim were essential for the secondary victim's recovery, precisely because it was 'the existence of such ties which leads to mental disturbance when the loved one suffers a catastrophe'.[200] This is the first *Alcock* control mechanism.

In some types of relationship, close ties may be presumed – in *Frost (White) v CC of South Yorkshire Police*, Lord Hoffmann put husband and wife, parent and child, and engaged couples, into this category; 'otherwise, they must otherwise be established by evidence'.[201] All of this constitutes a distasteful exercise in 'proving (and disproving) the love', according to some.[202] Even where a close tie of love and affection was presumed, that can be rebutted on the evidence. Indeed, sometimes, a close tie cannot be established at all, e.g.:

- long-standing workmates and friends were not close enough in *Gregg v Ashbrae Ltd*;[203]
- cousins employed as army officers in a war-zone were not close enough in *Bici v MOD*;[204]
- strangers involved in a car accident will always fail the criterion, per *Fagan v Goodman*.[205]

On the other hand, even a mother and child relationship of only a few hours can suffice (per *Farrell v Merton, Sutton and Wandsworth HA*[206] – in circumstances where a birth went badly, and baby Karol was born with severe and irreversible brain damage, his mother could recover damages for depression and anxiety as a secondary victim, because the fact that the child was 'only hours old' did not diminish the close emotional tie which existed between Mrs Farrell and her child as the immediate victim).

199 [1998] Lloyd's Rep Med 116 (CA), with quotes at 124 and 122 (the case is also reported as *Powell v Boladz*).

200 [1992] 1 AC 310 (HL) 397. Also, 411 (Lord Oliver).

201 [1999] 2 AC 455 (HL) 502 (Lord Hoffmann).

202 Most oft-cited is the criticism of J Stapleton, 'Restraint of Tort' in P Birks (ed), *Frontiers of Liability* (1994) 95 ('Is it not a disreputable sight to see brothers of Hillsborough victims turned away because they had no more than brotherly love towards the victim?'), cited, e.g., in: *Van Soest* [1999] NZCA 206, [118] (Thomas J).

203 [2005] NIQB 37.

204 [2004] EWHC 786 (QB).

205 (QB, 30 Nov 2001).

206 (2000) 57 BMLR 158 (QB) 163.

It is the lack of these ties between rescuer C and the immediate victim being rescued that precludes C from claiming secondary victim status. None of the police officers in *White* had any such ties with the victims of the Hillsborough disaster; nor did the rescuer co-employee in *Monk v PC Harrington Ltd*. Hence, if the rescuer is not in the zone of danger himself, and suffers psychiatric injury from what he witnesses or endures during the rescue operation, then that injury will go uncompensated.

The criterion becomes particularly acute where C, as secondary victim, and the immediate victim, do fall within one of the presumed relationships of close love – but all the evidence points to the fact that no such close tie was ever maintained. That will harm a secondary victim's prospects of recovery, but not an elevated primary victim's, as demonstrated by the following leading case:

> In *Farrell v Avon HA*,[207] facts previously, Mr Farrell, C, did not maintain any close tie of love and affection with the mother of his child before Jordan's birth, or with Jordan following his birth. D sued for PTSD and for subsequent alcohol and drug dependency. **Held:** C recovered £10,000 for the injury.

Had Mr Farrell been legally treated as a secondary victim, it is questionable whether he would have recovered any damages, as he maintained no close tie of love or affection with the mother or the child, either before or after the birth of Jordan. Mr Farrell's lack of close ties surely would have rendered that criterion very difficult to satisfy, *ex post facto*.

The law reform corner: Commentary on this requirement

English Law Comm:[208] 'relational proximity' was the one *Alcock* control mechanism that the Commission thought should be retained, and this requirement for a close tie between C and the immediate victim could be satisfied either at the time of D's act or omission or at the onset of C's psychiatric illness. It also recommended that the legislation stipulate a fixed list of relationships where a close tie would be presumed, i.e., spouse; parent; child; brother or sister; a partner who had lived with the immediate victim for at least two years. In other cases, C would need to prove the close tie of love and affection by evidence.

Ipp Committee:[209] re a close tie of love and affection, it 'necessitate[s] the forensic examination and assessment of the nature and quality of intimate human relationships in a way that may bring the law into disrepute'. If (1) C was assumed to be a person of normal fortitude, and (2) the test of reasonable foreseeability of mental harm were properly applied, then sufficient restrictions on recovery would exist, without need to resort to this *Alcock* criterion.

Scottish Law Comm:[210] a list of relationships in which persons were presumed to have a close relationship should be stated – plus it favoured the use of the slightly wider term, 'close relationship', in order to give those with feelings of 'personal responsibility' (say, a nanny toward a child) or loyalty (say, employees or neighbours towards each other) an opportunity to prove that sufficient ties existed to justify secondary victim status.

[207] [2001] Lloyd's Rep Med 458 (QB).

[208] *English Report*, [6.10], [6.26]–[6.34]; and cll 1(3)(b), 3 of the Draft Negligence (Psychiatric Illness) Bill.

[209] *Ipp Report*, [9.25]–[9.26].

[210] *Scottish Report*, [3.54]–[3.55], and cl 5.

Spatial and temporal proximity

§5.27 A secondary victim, C, must have been present at the accident involving the immediate victim, or at the immediate aftermath of the accident. With respect to temporal proximity, it is apparent that the immediate aftermath is approximately two hours only.

The event, or the immediate aftermath. This is the second *Alcock* control mechanism. The requirement for spatial and temporal proximity has been articulated in several House of Lords' decisions; and in *Alcock* itself, Lord Oliver noted that Cs in earlier successful cases were:

> either personally present at the scene of the accident, or [were] in the more or less immediate vicinity and witnessed the aftermath shortly afterwards; ... there was not only an element of physical proximity to the event but a close temporal connection between the event and [C's] perception of it.[211]

Similarly, in *AB v Leeds Teaching Hosp NHS Trust*, Gage J reiterated that, as a control mechanism, secondary victim C 'must be close in time and space to the event caused by [D's] breach'.[212]

Even if C is not present at the accident itself which was brought about by D's negligence, the immediate aftermath is sufficient to render C in close proximity in time and space to the accident. The period is rather artificially and arbitrarily construed. Two hours after the negligence/injury was acceptable in *McLoughlin v O'Brian*, although it was right 'on the margin of what the process of logical progression would allow' (said Lord Wilberforce[213]). Two hours and 10 minutes was also within it:

> In *Galli-Atkinson v Seghal*,[214] C's daughter, Livia, 16, was killed at 7.05pm, when D's car mounted a footpath and hit her. Livia died at the scene. C saw the accident site, not aware that anything was wrong, but then attempted to cross the police cordon to look for Livia, who was late returning from a ballet lesson. At that point, one hour after the accident, C learnt that her daughter had been killed (a police officer described her screaming as 'unforgettable'). C and her husband then went to the mortuary and viewed Livia's body at 9.15 pm. C suffered psychiatric illness. **Held:** C could recover, as the mortuary visit was within the requisite immediate aftermath. That period 'extended from the moment of the accident until [C] left the mortuary: there was an uninterrupted sequence of events'.

On the other hand, 8–9 hours after the negligence/injury was outside the 'immediate aftermath' in *Alcock* (re the Hillsborough accident),[215] and three hours was also too long in *Hevican v Ruane*[216] (another car accident).

Hence, although different Courts of Appeal have stated that the 'immediate aftermath' is a 'flexible idea ... not confined to what happens "immediately" upon the termination of the relevant physical acts' (per *RS v Criminal Injuries Compensation Authy*[217]), and that 'a somewhat more relaxed approach to what constitutes the immediate aftermath' has been adopted in case law (per *Taylor v Novo*[218]), the reality is that the dividing line is entirely arbitrary.

[211] [1992] AC 310 (HL) 411. See too, 402, 404 (Lord Ackner), 422 (Lord Jauncey); *Page v Smith* [1996] AC 155 (HL) 189 (Lord Lloyd); *Frost/White* [1999] 2 AC 455 (HL) 502 (Lord Hoffmann), 477 (Lord Goff).

[212] [2004] EWHC 644 (QB) [190]. [213] [1983] 1 AC 410 (HL) 419. [214] [2003] EWCA Civ 679.

[215] [1992] 1 AC 310 (HL). [216] [1991] 3 All ER 65 (QB).

[217] [2013] EWCA Civ 1040, [11]. [218] [2013] EWCA Civ 194, [34].

§5.28 C must be physically and temporally proximate to either D's act or omission which gave rise to the accident or to the immediate aftermath. It is ***not*** sufficient if C is proximate *only* to the immediate victim's death, where that death occurred some time after D's act/omission and injury to the immediate victim, and outside the immediate aftermath of the accident.

In the paradigm scenario, D's negligent act or omission may cause the almost simultaneous death or injury of the immediate victim. The whole event is the accident. But what if C did not witness the negligently-caused accident itself, but was only present at the death of the immediate victim, some time later, and well outside the immediate aftermath? That is not sufficient proximity, according to the Court of Appeal in *Taylor v A Novo (UK) Ltd*[219] – a case which was not the usual kind of secondary victim dispute (said that court).

> In *Taylor v Novo*, Cindy Taylor was injured in a work accident, when a fellow employee caused a stack of racking boards to tip over on top of her. Her employer, D, admitted breach. She suffered injuries to her head and left foot, and seemed to be making a good recovery when, 21 days later, she suddenly collapsed and died at home, due to deep vein thrombosis and consequent pulmonary emboli from her injuries. Her daughter, Crystal Taylor, C, had not witnessed the accident, but did witness her mother's death at home, and suffered PTSD. **Held:** C was not sufficiently proximate, because she was not present at the scene of the accident, nor involved in its immediate aftermath. Witnessing the death 21 days later was not sufficient to prove this criterion.

The death of the immediate victim was not a part of the 'event' to which secondary victim C had to be proximate. After all, if a death (witnessed by C) which occurred some 21 days after D's negligence was to be regarded as part of the event, then why not a death months or even years later? The Court of Appeal considered that the *Alcock* control mechanisms had to be applied with rigour and restriction. As Lord Dyson MR stated, if the death were part of the 'event', then that would 'potentially extend the scope of liability to secondary victims considerably further than has been done hitherto ... these same policy reasons militate against any further substantial extension. That should only be done by Parliament.'[220] Clearly, the necessary ring-fencing of secondary victim claims (as rightly occurred in this case) is continuing to drive legal analysis in this unsatisfactory area of negligence.

However, the fact that, in *Taylor v Novo*, C did not witness the negligence itself – but was removed from the scene and only witnessed the **effects** of D's negligence – aligns the situation with many medical negligence scenarios. The problem is that secondary victim C is often physically or temporally remote from the medical negligence 'event' – the medical mistreatment or misdiagnosis occurred behind closed doors, in operating theatres, recovery rooms, or in doctors' surgeries. Often, all that the secondary victim witnesses is the effects of the negligence on the immediate victim afterwards, in the hospital ward or later at home. Although the House of Lords stated, in *JD v East Berkshire Community Health NHS Trust*, that medical mishaps can give rise to a duty of care owed by a healthcare professional/hospital towards one who 'suffer[ed] nervous shock through seeing or hearing the event or its immediate aftermath',[221] that does not apply in medical negligence scenarios, as a general rule, where the effects of the negligence take hours, days, weeks, or even months, to manifest (and which secondary victim

[219] [2013] EWCA Civ 194. [220] *ibid*, [31]. [221] [2005] UKHL 23, [10].

C witnesses). That delay will result in C **not** having the requisite proximity with D's breach to satisfy the *Alcock* requirement of spatial and temporal proximity.

In *Taylor v Somerset HA*,[222] Mr Taylor's heart disease went misdiagnosed by treating doctors, D, for many months. Mr Taylor then suffered a fatal heart attack at work. Mrs Taylor, C, was told her husband was ill at hospital, and she visited within the hour. Twenty minutes later, C was told of her husband's death. She could not believe the fact of Mr Taylor's death, and viewed his body as 'proof'. C sued D for the shock and distress caused by her husband's death. **Held:** C failed, as the news of her husband's death was not within the 'immediate aftermath' of D's original medical negligence of failing to diagnose and treat. Mr Taylor's death at work, and the transfer of his body to hospital where Mrs Taylor saw him, was not part of the relevant 'event' – it was far too removed in time. In *Palmer v Tees HA*,[223] facts previously, **held:** Mrs Palmer, C, was never within the aftermath doctrine in respect of the alleged negligence of the treating psychiatrist, D, who released Sean Armstrong into the community, despite his confessions beforehand of his evil intentions towards young children, and of the ongoing lack of supervision. The effects of that negligence – Rosie Palmer's murder, almost a year after Mr Armstrong's release – was far too removed in time from the alleged negligence.

Taylor v Novo sits comfortably with this general rule, i.e., witnessing *the effects* of negligence is not 'good enough'. However, it does not necessarily sit well with the exceptions that have been judicially crafted in that area. This rather messy scenario is described below.

Exceptions to the immediate aftermath. In medical negligence scenarios, English courts have compromised (softened) the spatial and temporal proximity requirement in **two** respects:

§5.29 As exceptions to the immediate aftermath doctrine: (1) if the failure of secondary victim C to fit within the immediate aftermath was brought about, in part, by D's *own preventative actions*, then the doctrine will be more sympathetically construed in favour of C; and (2) witnessing the *effects* of the negligence can, exceptionally, be held to be within the aftermath doctrine, even if outside the immediate aftermath.

Alcock was a disaster scenario – an accident, quickly followed by the immediate victim's injury or death, and where an immediate aftermath could feasibly (albeit artificially) apply. However, the corollary of more drawn-out affairs which do not neatly fit the *Alcock* pattern is a real inconsistency in the manner in which claims for pure psychiatric illness are treated at law.

Any deliberate attempts by D to prevent the secondary victim from witnessing the effects of D's negligent act or omission may assist the prospects of the secondary victim's recovery.

In *Farrell v Merton, Sutton and Wandsworth HA*,[224] facts previously, where Mrs Farrell, C, gave birth to a son, Karol, who suffered severe and irreversible brain damage, **held:** C recovered. What C witnessed was within the 'immediate aftermath' of the trauma of the birth, because 'the unusual delay of just over a day between [C] giving birth and first seeing her son was wholly attributable to [D], who had chosen not to take her to the hospital to which her baby had been sent and not to tell her of the injury and difficulties which had occurred'. C's ignorance of Karol's condition was solely due to the hospital staff's conduct.

Additionally (and somewhat inconsistently with *Taylor v Novo*, where the collapse and death of Mrs Taylor was not within the immediate aftermath), there have been cases in which all that C witnessed was the effects of D's negligence, well outside the immediate aftermath of the

[222] [1993] 4 Med LR 34 (QB). [223] [1999] EWCA Civ 1533. [224] (2001) 57 BMLR 158 (QB), quotes at 158, 164.

negligence itself, or of the injury inflicted on the immediate victim – and yet, the second *Alcock* control mechanism was met.

In *Froggatt v Chesterfield and North Derbyshire Royal Hosp NHS Trust*,[225] Mrs Froggatt, 28, underwent a mastectomy, following D's misdiagnosis that she was suffering from cancer. Three weeks later, she was informed of the misdiagnosis. When Mr Froggatt, C1, saw his wife undressed for the first time, 12 days after the operation, he suffered a shock; as did her son, C2, when he overheard his mother telling her friend on the phone that she had been diagnosed with cancer. **Held:** C1 recovered £5,000 for his psychiatric injury, and C2 recovered £1,000. There was 'closeness in time' between the misdiagnosis and the shock which C1 and C2 received (although the term, 'aftermath doctrine', was not referred to). They suffered an 'affront to the senses'. In *W v Essex CC*,[226] facts previously, Mr and Mrs W, C, did not witness any sexual assaults perpetrated by G upon their children, and had not come across the children or G in their 'immediate aftermath'. Rather, C were told about the abuse some time after the final abuse, and four weeks after the abuse started. **Held:** C could proceed to trial as potential secondary victims: '[w]hilst there has to be some temporal and spatial limitation on [C] who can claim to be secondary victims, ... it seems to me that the concept of "the immediate aftermath" of the incident has to be assessed in the particular factual situation. I am not persuaded that, in a situation like the present, the parents must come across the abuser or the abused "immediately" after the sexual incident has terminated'.

This exceptional line of authority has received endorsement in some Commonwealth jurisprudence:

The comparative corner: Spatial and temporal proximity

Singapore: in *Pang Koi Fa v Lim Djoe Phing*,[227] secondary victim C was the mother of a patient for whom a medical operation went wrong. C was told of the need for her daughter to have an operation to remove a tumour from her pituitary gland. She recommended that course to her daughter; was at her daughter's bedside in intensive care after the operation, was present when her daughter was negligently discharged whilst still sickly, brought her daughter back to hospital as her condition worsened, and was there when her daughter died. **Held:** C could recover for psychiatric injury. Amarjeet JC noted that medical negligence is far removed from the accident which plays out over a few minutes only, and causes calamitous shock as it unfolds – operative procedures, by contrast, will occur behind closed doors, and the results of negligently-administered medicine may take some time to manifest.

These exceptions vest the law of secondary victim recovery with inconsistency. Plenty of secondary victims have witnessed the 'effects' of D's alleged negligence, and that has simply not been sufficient to base recovery for pure psychiatric illness (e.g., Mrs Palmer, Mrs Hall, Mr Tan, Mrs Taylor and Mr Sion, to name a few who are considered in this and the following section), as they have not been able to take advantage of the exceptional scenarios. Also, the exceptional cases do not sit well with the *Alcock* authority on what constitutes the 'immediate aftermath',

225 [2002] All ER (D) 218 (QB) [78]. 226 [2001] 2 AC 592 (HL) 601.

227 [1993] 3 SLR 317 (HC, Amarjeet JC), quote at 329.

nor do they sit easily with the Court of Appeal's view in *Taylor v Novo* that a restrictive attitude towards secondary victim recovery is warranted for policy reasons. Further, the correctness of *Froggatt* was doubted in *Wild v Southend Univ Hospital*,[228] while *W v Essex CC* was a strike-out application, and as such, the weight of its authority was questioned ('or limited value') by Lord Dyson in *Novo*.[229] All of this vests the law with a messy appearance.

Clearly, the immediate aftermath/spatial and temporal proximity criterion has been watered-down, both by exceptions and by its inconsistent application. Unsurprisingly, some law reform opinion is to the effect that secondary victim recovery would be better off without the criterion altogether.

The law reform corner: Commentary on this requirement

English Law Comm:[230] this second *Alcock* control mechanism should be abolished. In addition to the unsatisfactory tensions in case law as to what constituted a compensable 'immediate aftermath', the most important factor both to ring-fence the number of secondary victims, and to explain the aetiology of psychiatric injury, is a close tie of love and affection, and not the fact of how close to the event was the secondary victim.

Scottish Law Comm:[231] the 'immediate aftermath' requirement was a blunt instrument which discriminated against those who were simply too far away from the scene to make it in time to obtain compensation for their psychiatric injuries. Also, the 'immediate aftermath' varied, from 20 minutes, to a few hours, to several days.

Direct perception

§5.30 As a secondary victim, C's psychiatric injury must have been caused by direct perception of the accident or of its immediate aftermath, with C's own eyes and ears, and not by hearing about it from a third party.

This third and final *Alcock* control mechanism, reiterated by Lord Hoffmann in *Frost (White)*,[232] was affirmed earlier in *Alcock*, by several of the Law Lords,[233] and even earlier in *McLoughlin v O'Brian*.

In *McLoughlin v O'Brian*,[234] facts previously, it was not Mrs McLoughlin's friend telling her the bad news about her family's car accident that C was entitled to recover for. It was the sight and sound of her loved ones in pain and distress which C witnessed at the hospital. In *Tredget and Tredget v Bexley HA*,[235] facts previously, the 'chaos' and 'pandemonium' of the birth in the delivery theatre happened 'in full sight' of Mr Tredget, C1. Mrs Tredget, C2, was sedated and suffering from exhaustion and not fully conscious of what was happening around her, but had sufficient senses and instinct during the course of labour and birth to know that something was terribly wrong. Direct perception was made out for both Cs.

228 [2014] EWHC 4053 (QB) [51]. 229 [2013] EWCA Civ 194, [2014] QB 150, [34].
230 *English Report*, [6.10]–[6.16], and citing: *Jaensch v Coffey* (1984) 155 CLR 549 (HCA) 600.
231 *Scottish Report*, [2.23]. 232 [1999] 2 AC 455 (HL) 502 (Lord Hoffmann).
233 [1992] 2 AC 310 (HL) 398 (Lord Keith), 405 (Lord Ackner), 411 (Lord Oliver).
234 [1983] 1 AC 410 (HL) 422–23. 235 [1994] 5 Med LR 178 (Central London CC) 183.

The requirement, however, does not square with medical science. The medical testimony in *Ravenscroft v Rederiaktiebolaget Transatlantic*[236] was that there is no diagnostic or medical difference in the triggers for psychiatric injury for a person who has witnessed an accident, or a person who was present at the aftermath, or a person who simply is told about the accident from another person. Furthermore, it is difficult to reconcile that recovery should be denied to a wife who is told on the phone that her husband has been killed in a negligently-caused accident, whereas a wife who sees her husband with serious but not fatal injuries can recover, merely due to a rule based on public policy (per *Ravenscroft*[237]). Nevertheless, current English law does not reflect that medical or policy view.

Again, secondary victims may find this criterion difficult-to-impossible, where much of what happened was behind closed doors, out of sight, or at some place geographically removed from C.

§5.31 If C receives bad news about the immediate victim orally in person, by phone or in writing, then as a general rule, the direct perception requirement will not be satisfied (even where C witnesses that victim's dead body). However, recovery of damages for pure psychiatric injury may exceptionally be achieved by C by some other legal avenues.

Receiving bad news – no recovery. Direct perception is very difficult to establish, where C was merely told of the effects of D's negligence towards the immediate victim, without witnessing those acts or omissions first-hand. As the Court of Appeal recently put it, in *Brock v Northampton General Hosp NHS Trust*, '[i]t is one of the fine distinctions which have been made in the cases, that a telephone call giving bad news cannot found liability to secondary victims, whereas seeing someone can in appropriate cases'.[238] The problem is particularly acute in medical negligence cases. **None** of the following could meet 'direct perception':

> In *Tan v East London and the City HA*,[239] Mrs Tan attended D's hospital to give birth, but due to D's negligent treatment, the baby girl died *in utero*. Mr Tan, C, who had been eagerly looking forward to the birth, was told of the death by D's staff by phone, about 20 minutes after it occurred. C immediately visited the hospital, was present during the stillbirth, held his dead daughter after delivery and during the night, and saw her placed in a metal coffin box the following day. C suffered severe depression, contributing to his loss of employment. C was unable to directly perceive of the negligence that occurred, even though he was intimately involved in events thereafter. That involvement was insufficient for direct perception. In *Wild v Southend Univ Hosp*,[240] Mr and Mrs Wild were expecting the birth of their child, when Mrs Wild had a show of blood, and attended hospital. No foetal heartbeat could be detected, and the death *in utero* of the baby was diagnosed. Mr Wild, C, was devastated and horrified. C and his wife went home overnight, and attended next day for the stillbirth. Thereafter, C suffered PTSD. However, C was held to suffer from a 'growing and acute anxiety' that successive medical staff could not find a heartbeat, and looked and sounded as if something was terribly wrong, after which point C realised that his baby had died. 'But none of that ... equates to actually witnessing horrific events leading to a death or serious injury'. In *Taylor v Somerset HA*,[241] facts previously, Mrs Taylor, C, received the phone call with the

236 [1991] 3 All ER 73 (CA) 79.
237 *ibid*, and see too: *Jaensch v Coffey* (1984) 155 CLR 549 (HCA) 608 (Deane J).
238 [2014] EWHC 4244 (QB) [84].
239 [1999] Lloyd's Rep Med 389 (Chelmsford CC).
240 [2014] EWHC 4053 (QB) [47].
241 [1993] 4 Med LR 34 (QB) 37.

bad news that her husband had become ill at work and had been taken to hospital, and she thereafter saw his body at the mortuary. Direct perception was absent, as the law could not compensate for shock brought about by communication of the bad news by the doctor. In *Palmer v Tees HA*,[242] facts previously, the dreadful news communicated to Mrs Palmer, C, that they had found Rosie's mutilated body, and her observance of that body a few days later, was not sufficient to constitute 'direct perception'. In *Brock v Northampton General Hosp NHS Trust*, Rachel Brock took an overdose of paracetomal and required urgent hospital treatment. To relieve intra-cranial pressure, a bolt was inserted into Rachel's head, but it was inserted too deep into her brain, causing a brain haemorrhage, and she died two days later. Her parents, Mr and Mrs Brock, C, were with their daughter often during the medical treatment, and saw the bolt (but did not know, at that time, that it had been inserted negligently). C were living close-by on-site at the hospital, and received a call that their daughter's condition had greatly deteriorated. They realised, from that call, that Rachel was going to die. Following a further brain scan showing irretrievable bleeding on the brain, the life support machine was turned off. The news conveyed by the call could not found liability in these circumstances.

It follows that C's viewing the dead body of a loved one, however traumatic, is not sufficient for direct perception. Furthermore, earnest efforts by D to minimise the trauma of the events surrounding a relative's extremely grave situation may reduce the 'direct perception' of events. It seems that it is within D's power to reduce the opportunities for C, the distressed relative, to claim as a secondary victim, by instigating suitable systems by which to reduce the causes of distress – a point which is presumably well-practised by hospital administrative and clinical staff.

In *Ward v Leeds Teaching Hosp NHS Trust*,[243] facts previously, Mrs Ward, C, observed her daughter, Katherine's, poor health following the wisdom teeth extraction, but lacked sufficient direct perception of the distressing events. D's nurses and medical staff 'were careful to keep [C] informed of the gravity of Katherine's condition, without alarming her unduly or exposing her to any sights or sounds which might cause her distress. Even the viewing of Katherine's body at the mortuary, assuming for these purposes it was sufficiently proximate in time, did not take place without [C's] nephew first taking the trouble to view the body, to ensure that nothing untoward would be seen'. Hence, the 'overwhelming factor' in C's psychiatric injury was that her cherished daughter had died, rather than the events at the hospital.

Receiving bad news – allowing recovery. Exceptionally, where bad information about D's negligence has been conveyed to C orally in person, or by phone, or in writing, at some point thereafter, on only rare occasions has C been owed a duty of care:

- that duty was conceded:

In *AB v Tameside and Glossop HA*,[244] a former healthcare professional involved in obstetric treatment tested HIV-positive. His employer, D, had to inform women, C, who were under treatment from that health worker, of the very slight risk of HIV infection, and letters were sent advising C of the availability of 'further advice, counselling, and possibly a test'. **Held:** a duty to take care when conveying accurate, but distressing, news was *conceded* by D (but D successfully defended the negligence claim on the basis that breaking the news to C in that way was not negligently done).

242 [1999] EWCA Civ 1533.

243 [2004] EWHC 2106 (QB) [20], [2004] Lloyd's Rep Med 530, 535.

244 [1997] 8 Med LR 91 (CA), quote at 92, and also: 94 (Brooke LJ), 101 (Kennedy LJ), with Nourse LJ agreeing with both judgments (the CA overturned the trial judge who had permitted recovery: French J, 31 Jan 1995).

- C sued in negligent misstatement:

  In *Allin v City and Hackney HA*,[245] Mrs Allin, C, gave birth to a baby, but was told that the baby had died. About six hours later, Mrs Allin discovered that the baby was alive. Mrs Allin sued for PTSD, as a result of receiving this inaccurate information, and for D's failure to refer her for psychological treatment afterwards. **Held:** C recovered £10,000 for psychiatric injury.

- C was treated as an elevated primary victim, and not a secondary victim. Communication of bad news (inaccurate information that Mr Farrell's baby son had died, **plus** the sight of the 'dead' body of his son) grounded recovery for Mr Farrell in *Farrell v Avon HA*[246] (facts previously). However, Mr Farrell was ultimately treated as a **primary** victim, and that allowed him to tiptoe around this common law rule of 'direct perception' governing secondary victim recovery which Mrs Taylor, Mrs Ward, Mr Tan and Mrs Palmer were unable to surmount;
- C was told the information (about the death of a close relative, say) at the scene of the accident, within the immediate aftermath of D's negligence, and when experiencing the sights and sounds associated with a very serious accident.

  In *Galli-Atkinson v Seghal*,[247] facts previously, the combination of the limited scenes which C saw at the accident site, together with the mortuary visit (also within the immediate aftermath), was sufficient to amount to direct perception. In *Young v MacVean*,[248] Martha Young's, C's, son David was hit whilst walking on the footpath, due to D's negligent driving. C came across the crash scene on her way to a gym visit without knowing that David was involved, but it brought back memories of her husband's death in a North Sea helicopter crash. C saw the car wreck, knew that David was in the vicinity, started to be very concerned that David was involved, and was frantic even before the police attended the gym to inform her of her son's death. C's psychiatric injury was caused by the shock of coming upon the aftermath of the crash scene, rather than as a result of the shock of being told that David had been killed.

- C was treated outside the primary victim/secondary victim classification altogether, so as to recover under the *Caparo* test (per *Creutzfeldt-Jakob Disease Litig; Group B Plaintiffs v UKMRC*[249]).

Hence, there are legal avenues open to the recipient of bad news which causes psychiatric injury, by which that C can recover compensation – but they have been fairly sporadic, and **not** via the secondary victim route.

§5.32 Where secondary victim C directly perceives the *effects* of D's negligence, the better view appears to be that English law will not consider that C has satisfied the direct perception requirement, although exceptions to the contrary do exist.

Quite apart from the other avenues for recovery referred to above, some authority has (confusingly) supported the notion that C's direct perception, by sight or by ear, of the *consequences or effects* of D's negligence upon a loved one, can adequately satisfy this pre-requisite for a secondary victim.

[245] [1996] 7 Med LR 167 (Mayor's and City of London Court). [246] [2001] Lloyd's Rep Med 458 (QB).
[247] [2003] EWCA Civ 679. [248] [2014] CSOH 133. [249] [2000] Lloyd's Rep Med 161 (QB).

> In *Froggatt v Chesterfield and North Derbyshire NHS Trust*,[250] facts previously, both Mr Froggatt and his son, C, had directly perceived the effects of the medical negligence perpetrated by D upon Mrs Froggatt, seeing the disfigurement of the mastectomy, and overhearing the news being discussed on the phone, respectively. In *North Glamorgan NHS Trust v Walters*,[251] facts previously, Ms Walters, C, witnessed, not the medical acts or omissions perpetrated on her son Elliot *per se*, but the *effects* of that negligence. However, being told information about Elliot's condition as events were unfolding in, and between, hospitals, together with her own observations, were sufficient for direct perception. In *Galli-Atkinson v Seghal*,[252] facts previously, Mrs Galli-Atkinson, C, viewed Livia's body at the mortuary, but was kept away from the actual scene of the accident by police cordon. Nevertheless, she could recover, as her psychiatric injury was not only sustained by what she had been told about the accident; she was around the scene, which was obviously a very serious accident, where she experienced mounting panic; and the injuries to Livia's body, which C saw at the mortuary, were horrific.

In *Froggatt*, a passage from *Sion v Hampstead HA*,[253] by Peter Gibson LJ, was quoted with approval (and had more impact on the result in *Froggatt* than it did in *Sion* itself!):

> I can see no reason in logic why breach of duty causing an incident involving no violence and suddenness, such as where the wrong medicine is negligently given to a hospital patient, could not lead to a claim for damages for nervous shock, e.g., where the negligence has fatal results and the visiting close relative, wholly unprepared for what has occurred, finds the body and thereby sustains a sudden and unexpected shock to the nervous system.[254]

That legal view would go some way to reducing the importance of the direct perception requirement for secondary victims (although the 'immediate aftermath' doctrine could still prevent such actions).

However, this strand of reasoning has neither been developed nor applied consistently, rendering the criterion uncertain. It certainly sits uncomfortably with cases such as *Taylor v Somerset HA* and *Ward v Leeds Teaching Hospital*. Even more recently, in *Brock v Northampton General Hosp NHS Trust*,[255] parents who witnessed the effects of a bolt being inserted too far into their daughter's brain was insufficient to base recovery (it may have been different, said the court, if their daughter had collapsed in front of them, after undergoing such a procedure). Moreover, the passage of Peter Gibson LJ was dicta (the ratio of *Sion* being that C, the secondary victim, had not suffered from a shock-induced psychiatric injury, discussed below) – and in *Taylor v Novo*,[256] Lord Dyson MR disapproved of the passage in *Sion*, and regarded it as not binding on the Court of Appeal.

The law reform corner: **Commentary on this requirement**

English Law Comm[257] and Ipp Committee:[258] both regarded the requirement of direct perception as giving rise to distinctions which were arbitrary and artificial, and that it should be abolished. The secondary victim's proximity to the event or its aftermath was not always a relevant factor in determining how the person would react.

[250] [2002] All ER (D) 218 (QB) [78]–[80]. [251] [2002] EWCA Civ 1792, [35], [40] (Ward LJ).
[252] [2003] EWCA Civ 679. [253] (1994) 5 Med LR 170 (QB) 174, 176, appeal dismissed: [1994] 4 Med LR 170 (CA).
[254] [2002] All ER (D) 218 (QB) [78]. [255] [2014] EWHC 4244 (QB) [93].
[256] [2013] EWCA Civ 194 [33]. [257] *English Report*, [6.10]–[6.16]. [258] *Ipp Report*, [9.24].

Scottish Law Comm:[259] was critical of the ungenerous attitude which the law took towards those who were told of the death of a loved one but who were too distraught, or coincidentally too far away, to directly perceive of the negligence or of its immediate aftermath. It also recommended that the rule be abolished.

'Normal fortitude'

§5.33 D is not liable for a psychiatric injury that a secondary victim, C, has suffered only because C is abnormally susceptible or vulnerable to such injury. D is only liable to C if a person of ordinary fortitude would foreseeably have suffered some psychiatric injury. Once that is proven, then C can recover for the full extent of his psychiatric injury.

The requirement of normal fortitude appears to emanate from the early (1942) case of *Bourhill (or Hay) v Young*,[260] and was confirmed by Lord Lloyd, in *Page v Smith*, as being one of the important control mechanisms applicable to secondary victim recovery.[261]

In *Bourhill v Young*, C, a pregnant lady, heard a motor accident in which a motorcyclist was killed, saw the scene afterwards (but not the accident itself), and the bloodstains on the road from where the motorcyclist had eventually come to rest. She suffered a psychiatric illness from what she had seen and heard, and also gave birth to a stillborn child. **Held:** C was not permitted to recover compensation.

The following statement explained, in part, the reasons for the decision:

> The driver of a car or vehicle, even though careless, is entitled to assume that the ordinary frequenter of the streets has sufficient fortitude to endure such incidents as may from time to time be expected to occur in them, including the noise of a collision and the sight of injury to others, and is not considered negligent to one who does not possess the customary phlegm.[262]

It is important to note that the principle does not require the secondary victim himself to be a person of normal fortitude. As the Ipp Committee noted, 'being a person of normal fortitude is not a precondition of being owed a duty of care' as a secondary victim.[263] Rather, it must be foreseeable that a person of normal fortitude or 'customary phlegm' would have suffered some psychiatric injury. If that is proven, then an emotionally fragile secondary victim can recover for the full extent of his psychiatric injury (an application of the 'egg-shell skull' rule). On the other hand, if the secondary victim is an 'egg-shell skull personality', and the psychiatric injury sustained was *only* foreseeable in a person of vulnerable tendencies, the secondary victim will not recover.

In that respect, the principle of normal fortitude operates, for secondary victims, much the same as for C's recovery for physical injury – a vulnerable C can recover for the full extent of his injuries, but only if some physical injury would have been sustained by the notional person of normal fortitude. D is not expected to foresee injury to 'egg-shell psyche' persons, when no injury would have been suffered by anyone else.

In *Powell v Boldaz*,[264] facts previously (re the substitution of one page for another), the normal fortitude rule was an insurmountable barrier for both secondary victim parental Cs. Mrs Powell had 'an

[259] *Scottish Report*, [2.23]–[2.24]. [260] 1942 SC (HL) 78. [261] [1996] AC 155 (HL) 197.
[262] [1943] AC 92 (HL) 117 (Lord Porter). [263] *Ipp Report*, [9.13].
[264] [1998] Lloyd's Rep Med 116 (QB) 123–24.

innate pre-disposition to develop an anxiety disorder', while Mr Powell was 'still grieving' about son Robert's death at the time when the substitution occurred. It seemed likely that normally robust Cs would have withstood news of the alleged substitution without succumbing to psychiatric illness; or, in other words, it was most unlikely that the same injury would have been sustained by persons of normal fortitude. In *Farrell v Avon HA*,[265] Mr Farrell, C, had a pre-existing psychological problem which rendered him more at risk than others of developing PTSD. As a primary victim, this did not preclude C's recovery for psychiatric injury. However, even had C been considered a secondary victim (with no immediate victim existing, as discussed previously), being given a corpse to hold in the mistaken belief that it was his son was surely the type of exceptionally catastrophic event that could foreseeably cause psychiatric injury in a person of normal fortitude. However, C would likely have failed the 'close tie' requirement (above). In *Tredget and Tredget v Bexley HA*,[266] Mr and Mrs Tredget, C, could recover for their 'pathological unresolved mourning', following the death of their son Callum at two days old. The medical opinion was that each parent 'had a prior susceptibility towards an aggravated reaction to Callum's birth and death. There had been the prior loss or termination of pregnancies'. However, presumably a person of normal fortitude would foreseeably have suffered some psychiatric injury as a result of the circumstances of this tragic birth.

The law reform corner: Commentary on this requirement

English Law Comm:[267] the normal fortitude rule should be implemented as part of the usual test of foreseeability – i.e., the rule is 'best interpreted as meaning nothing more than that ... in deciding whether psychiatric illness was reasonably foreseeable (and analogously to reasonable foreseeability in physical injury cases), one can take into account the robustness of the population at large to psychiatric illness'.

Scottish Law Comm:[268] the normal fortitude rule, which 'stalks the current law', as it applies to secondary victims, has distinct problems in the way in which it seeks to limit liability – partly because 'there is a wide range of susceptibility to mental harm among the general population. Thus, *ordinary* fortitude is difficult to assess'. Also, the rule can hardly mean, 'average fortitude', because most people do not suffer psychiatric injury at all, as a result of witnessing negligence to loved ones. Overall, the Commission called the rule 'a legal construct which is difficult to evaluate'. Instead, it favoured a rule that, for both primary and secondary victims, there should be no recovery if the injury was of the type that C could reasonably be expected to endure without seeking compensation, because it either represented one of the vicissitudes of life or a normal bereavement.

Shock

§5.34 For secondary victims, the psychiatric injury must be induced by shock – a concept which constitutes 'a sudden assault on the nervous system'. Whether C suffered a shock is to be judged objectively.

Alcock was the first occasion in English law in which 'shock' emerged as an independent criterion for liability governing secondary victim recovery (the meaning of 'shock', in the legal

265 [2001] Lloyd's Rep Med 458 (QB) 462. 266 [1994] 5 Med LR 178 (London CC) 181.
267 *English Report*, [5.21], [5.26]. 268 *Scottish Report*, [1.5], [3.18]–[3,19], [2.20], [3,30].

sense, has been described previously in this chapter[269]). Without an 'assault on the senses' or a 'violent agitation of the mind', C will be vulnerable to the finding that his injury should be borne without compensation.

When deciding whether the event was 'horrifying' or capable of constituting a 'violent agitation of the mind' is to be determined 'by objective standards, and by reference to persons of ordinary susceptibility', and not by reference to how much medical knowledge that particular C may have possessed (per *Liverpool Women's Hospital NHS Foundation Trust v Ronayne*[270]).

Several would-be secondary claimants have had difficulty in proving the requisite shock – and this is especially so, if they have also failed the 'direct perception' requirement. The shock criterion **precludes** secondary victim recovery in a number of scenarios:

- where C suffers a psychiatric injury caused by a gradual wearing-down by giving long-term care to the immediate victim:

  In *Alcock*,[271] Lord Oliver ruled out a secondary victim recovering because of caring for loved ones who had suffered injury or misfortune – that had to 'be considered as ordinary and inevitable incidents of life which, regardless of individual susceptibilities, must be sustained without compensation';

- where C has a dawning or gradual realisation that things are not going to turn out well for the immediate victim (as all of the following cases demonstrated, in none of which could C recover):

  In *Sion v Hampstead HA*,[272] Mr Sion Snr's, C's, son was injured in a motorcycle accident and taken to D's hospital. D's staff failed to diagnose substantial and continuing bleeding from Mr Sion Jnr's left kidney, and he fell into a coma from which he never recovered, dying 14 days after admittance. C maintained a bedside vigil throughout this time, witnessing his son's deterioration and eventual death, and suffered psychiatric injury. C could not recover. Whilst it was not necessary that medical negligence be sudden and violent, it was still necessary that C sustained a 'sudden and unexpected shock to the nervous system'. Within a week of hospitalisation, C realised that it was almost certain that his son would not survive, and when death came, 'he was not surprised, and felt that, in a way, he had been preparing himself for this to happen'. That did not satisfy the 'shock' requirement. In *Ward v Leeds Teaching Hosp NHS Trust*,[273] facts previously, Mrs Ward, C, had not suffered a sudden shock with the death of her daughter Katherine after the wisdom teeth operation. C suffered '[a]n event outside the range of human experience, [which] sadly, does not ... encompass the death of a loved one in hospital unless also accompanied by circumstances which were wholly exceptional in some way so as to shock or horrify'. In *Brock v Northampton General Hosp NHS Trust*,[274] facts previously, there was nothing 'wholly exceptional' to shock or horrify Mr and Mrs Brock, C, 'dreadful as it may have been'. A nurse's call made them realise that daughter Rachel was going to die, and their sight of her, when told that she was brain-dead, was not a shocking event, but rather, a confirmation of the terrible realisation.

[269] See pp 254–55.

[270] [2015] EWCA Civ 588, [13] (Tomlinson LJ), citing with approval: *Shorter v Surrey & Sussex NHS Trust* [2015] EWHC 614 QB, [214] (Swift J).

[271] [1992] 1 AC 310 (HL) 416 (Lord Oliver).

[272] (1994) 5 Med LR 170 (QB) 174, 176, appeal dismissed: [1994] 4 Med LR 170 (CA).

[273] [2004] EWHC 2106 (QB) [21] (HHJ Hawkesworth QC).

[274] [2014] EWHC 4244 (QB) [95]–[96].

- where C has already received notice of bad news about the immediate victim, and hence, seeing the immediate victim later on does not involve shock (in neither of the following could C recover):

In *Tan v East London and City HA*,[275] Mr Tan, C, was told of the death of his unborn daughter over the phone, and he travelled straight to the hospital, and was present during the operation. His visit to the hospital was made in the full knowledge that his baby had died, and hence, he did not suffer a shock in the legal sense. In *Taylor v Somerset HA*,[276] Mrs Taylor, C, insisted upon seeing her husband's body in the mortuary after being informed of his death, but that did not constitute a 'shocking event', because the purpose of the mortuary visit was only to 'settle her disbelief'. Plus the body 'bore no marks or signs to her of the sort that would have conjured up for her the circumstances of his fatal attack'.

- where C may have been present at a shocking and horrifying event, and suffered psychiatric injury as a result of grief and bereavement, but not as a result of an 'assault' in the *Alcock* sense. Naturally, these cases are very much 'at the borderline' of what is, and is not, permissible by way of recovery:

In *Less v Hussain*,[277] on 4 May, Ms Less, who was pregnant, realised that she could not feel foetal movement, and went to the hospital, accompanied by her partner, Mr Carter, C. Death *in utero* was diagnosed. Ms Less was given tablets to induce labour, and C stayed with her. On 6 May, baby Luis was delivered stillborn, C held him, and Luis' body was taken away and brought back dressed in a dress ('because, despite his sex, that was all that could be found'). C suffered a bereavement reaction. **Held:** C could not recover, as his injury did not arise from shock, i.e., the sudden appreciation by sight or sound of the hugely distressing events he witnessed.

However, the criterion of 'shock' has suffered from two grave inconsistencies, since *Alcock* made the requirement mandatory for secondary victims.[278]

Problem #1: A drawn-out and 'seamless' shock

§5.35 The shock requirement has been held, on occasion, to constitute a series of events and assaults on C's nervous system which, although separate, can comprise ***one*** shocking and seamless event.

This interpretation, where it applies, enables the scenario to play out over several hours – and, clearly, what one judge may consider to be a 'dawning realisation' of the fate to befall an immediate victim may comprise a drawn-out, yet sudden and violent agitation of the mind, to another.

In *North Glamorgan NHS Trust v Walters*,[279] facts previously, Mrs Walters, C, succeeded in proving one shocking event. It was 'an inexorable progression from the moment when the fit occurred as a result of the failure of the hospital properly to diagnose and then to treat the baby, the fit causing the brain damage which shortly thereafter made termination of this child's life inevitable and the dreadful climax when the child died in her arms. It is a seamless tale with an obvious beginning

[275] [1999] Lloyd's Rep Med 389 (Chelmsford CC). [276] [1993] 4 Med LR 34 (QB) 37–38.
[277] [2012] EWHC 3513 (QB).
[278] Some of this analysis is drawn from Mulheron, 'Secondary Victim Psychiatric Illness Claims' (2003) 14 *KCLJ* 213.
[279] [2002] EWCA Civ 1792, [2003] Lloyd's Rep Med 49, with quotes at [34], [40] (Ward LJ).

and an equally obvious end. It was played out over a period of 36 hours, which for her both at the time and as subsequently recollected was undoubtedly one drawn-out experience'; and 'the assault on [C's] nervous system had begun and she reeled under successive blows as each was delivered'. In *Tredget and Tredget v Bexley HA*,[280] Mr and Mrs Tredget, C, recovered, because their full appreciation of their newborn's condition after the pandemonium birth 'only came with time', and it was 'unrealistic to separate out and isolate the delivery as an event, from the other sequence of happenings from the onset of labour to Callum's death two days later ... although lasting for over 48 hours from the onset of labour to the death, this effectively was one event'. In *Galli-Atkinson v Seghal*,[281] facts previously, *Walters* was expressly relied upon, such that the events following Livia's accident were an uninterrupted sequence that constituted the aftermath of D's negligent driving which killed Livia, and which retained sufficient proximity to that initial event.

In *Walters*,[282] Ward LJ considered that the verdict for Mrs Walters had not achieved any change in the law; Clarke LJ expressly observed that, *if* the Court of Appeal's finding in favour of Ms Walters did mean that an incremental step in the law needed to be taken, 'I for my part would take that step on the facts of this case'; and Sir Anthony Evans agreed with both judgments.

Walters has received some judicial endorsement since. In *Galli-Atkinson v Seghal*, the court noted that the law is not 'restricted by what Lord Ackner said in *Alcock* to a frozen moment in time ... an event itself may be made up of a number of components; this was accepted by this court in *Walters*'.[283] Even more significantly, in *JD v East Berkshire Community Health NHS Trust*, the House of Lords described the *Walters/Tredget* decisions as a 'distinct line of authority'[284] in the field of pure psychiatric injury and secondary victim recovery.

It comes as no surprise that Cs, in drawn-out negligence scenarios, have sought to expand the 'seamless tale' to something longer than 36 hours, and that courts have had to draw arbitrary lines in the sand, where that has been attempted. However, the *Walters* line of authority has not enjoyed much success in recent English case law; it has been distinguished, or restricted to its facts. Indeed, in a quartet of cases over the course of 2014–15, none of the following Cs could recover as secondary victims (with *Walters* being cited, but distinguished, in each of them[285]):

In *Taylor v Novo*,[286] facts previously, the death of Mrs Taylor, some 21 days after she was injured at work, was 'certainly not part of a single event or seamless tale'. Her injury at work, and her death at home, were 'distinct events'. In *Wild v Southend Univ Hosp*,[287] facts previously, the court noted that, in *Walters*, the sequence started with the very serious illness of Elliot, and with various good and bad news and diagnoses, until he died 36 hours later in his mother's, C's, arms, whereas in *Wild*, the sequence started with C's realisation that his child had died *in utero*, and then C and his wife had to endure the agony of waiting until the next day until the stillbirth: 'this case is materially different from the facts in *Walters*, being based on an "event" which starts with the realisation that Matthew has already died'. In *Liverpool Women's Hosp NHS Foundation Trust v Ronayne*,[288] Mrs Ronayne entered D's hospital to undergo a hysterectomy, but suffered septicaemia when a suture was inadvertently misplaced in her colon. She was re-admitted to hospital, and her husband,

280 (1994) 5 Med LR 178, with quote at 183–84. 281 [2003] EWCA Civ 697.

282 [2002] EWCA Civ 1792, with quotes at [43], and [51]. 283 [2003] EWCA Civ 697, [25].

284 [2005] UKHL 23, [2006] 2 AC 373, [107] (Lord Rodger).

285 To this quartet must be added a very recent decision: *Owers v Medway NHS Foundation Trust* [2015] EWHC 2363 (QB), where again, *Walters* was distinguished, and the husband's claim for pure psychiatric injury failed.

286 [2013] EWCA Civ 194, [2014] QB 150, [35]. 287 [2014] EWHC 4053 (QB) [48], [53].

288 [2015] EWCA Civ 588, [35]–[41] (Tomlinson LJ).

Edward Ronayne, C, suffered PTSD upon seeing the deterioration in his wife's condition and appearance over two days following her re-admittance, which he described as like 'the Michelin Man'. Mrs Ronayne eventually recovered, after a lengthy hospital stay. The claim failed, as there was no 'inexorable progression', and nor was it 'seamless'. Rather, it was 'a series of events over a period of time', and a 'dawning realisation' that his wife's life was in danger, plus this was told to C orally by the treating doctors before C saw his wife in a swollen condition; there was no 'sudden appreciation of an event'. In *Shorter v Surrey & Sussex HC NHS Trust*,[289] Mrs Sharma had a brain aneurysm on 5 May, which went undetected from a CT scan. She was re-admitted to hospital a week later, after the CT scan was interpreted correctly, but suffered a fatal re-bleed that night, and died the following day (negligence towards Mrs Sharma was conceded). Julie Shorter, C, was Mrs Sharma's sister, and thereafter suffered depression. C submitted that there was a seamless tale of events, from when the incorrect diagnosis was conveyed to her on 12 May, to when Mrs Sharma passed away on 13 May. C's claim failed, as she lacked physical proximity to her sister throughout these events. C received four phone conversations which increased her fears as to her sister's welfare; and her sight of her sister was not of the same category of unpleasantness as Mrs Walter's view of her baby suffering from an epileptic fit, rigid and convulsing and with blood pouring from his mouth. The facts of *Walters* were distinguishable.

This cadre of recent cases precluding family members as secondary victims is undoubtedly a welcome trend by the NHS Litigation Authority, and serves notice that *Walters* will be very strictly construed.

The comparative corner: The treatment of *Walters* elsewhere

Hong Kong: In *Wong Fung Sze v Tuen Mun Hosp*,[290] Mr Sze was operated on by the treating doctors, D, for oesophageal cancer. Mr Sze and his wife, C, were told in May 2001 that relevant CAT and MRI tests were negative. They were then told, on 21 July, that the cancer had spread to Mr Sze's skull, brain and upper neck. C claimed that she suffered shock on receiving that news; or alternatively, that she received a series of shocks between when she thought that her husband was clear of cancer, to the point at which he died on 22 Sep. C argued that her husband was destined to die of cancer, but that the quality of his end-of-life would have been better, and her psychiatric injury would have been prevented, if D had not negligently misdiagnosed his cancer. **Held:** C could not recover. The series of events, May–Sep, could not constitute one horrifying event; and C did not suffer the requisite shock. Whilst acknowledging that *Walters* represented a 'very realistic approach' in medical negligence cases, there were three key points of distinction between this case and *Walters* (said the court):

(1) it would be a 'quantum leap' from a 36-hour horrifying event to one lasting four months;
(2) Mrs Walters was given high hopes of baby Elliot's likely recovery by the hospital, whereas Mrs Sze realistically must have harboured doubts about her husband's prospects of survival; and

[289] [2015] EWHC 614 QB.
[290] [2004] HKDC 154, quotes at [25]–[29], leave to appeal denied: Judge To in Chambers, 11 Oct 2004.

(3) in *Walters*, D initially gave a very positive assurance that Elliot had suffered no brain damage, whereas no such positive statement was made by D here, meaning that, '[t]he psychiatric illness of [C] was therefore the result of gradual assaults on her mind during this period of four months', because of her worry and gradual realisation of her husband's true condition.

Singapore: In *Pang Koi Fa v Lim Djoe Phing*,[291] facts previously, **held:** C could recover. C witnessed gradual deterioration of her daughter's condition for about three months, compounded by D's neglect or refusal during that time to attend to her daughter: 'the dicta of Lord Ackner no doubt left open the inclusion of situations of psychiatric illness in the appropriate and abnormal case where the elements of suddenness may not be present, and where psychiatric illness assaults the nervous system, builds up, and manifests itself over some short period of time'.

The author has criticised the lack of consistency displayed by the decision in *Walters* elsewhere (and some other academic commentary since has not been particularly kind to it either[292]):

> Mrs Ward and Mr Sion would no doubt argue that their experiences in hospital were equally as seamless as Mrs Walters', with an initial expectation that their children were ill, but then gaining the realisation that their lives were ending. Furthermore, the psychiatric evidence given in *Walters* suggested that it was the *longer* duration of events surrounding Elliot's death, rather than his sudden death, which resulted in Ms Walters' shock: 'the psychiatric impact is more severe than if the child had died suddenly, as it was compounded by uncertainties over the diagnosis and re-admission to various hospitals'.[293] Surely the protracted experiences of Mr Sion and Mrs Ward were just as capable of producing that type of shock? The inconsistencies in outcome are obvious, despite Ward LJ's assertion in *Walters* that *Sion* was 'a very different case'.[294] The Scottish Commission's semantic discussion[295] of how the cases differ – that *Walters* demonstrates that the 'sudden realisation of danger within a continuing process' is compensable whereas *Sion's* 'continuing process [of realisation]' is not – only serves to emphasise the difficulties inherent in the reasoning of the two decisions … In that respect, the law may well have moved on to embrace what Lord Ackner envisaged in *Alcock* – that shock 'has yet to include psychiatric illness caused by the accumulation over a period of time of more gradual assaults on the nervous system'.[296] That position, it seems, *has* been reached in English law, and an explicit acknowledgment of that fact should have been made in *Walters*.[297]

Problem #2: Witnessing a body

§5.36 Whether viewing an immediate victim's body in order to fully comprehend the consequences of D's negligence can give rise to a shock has not been treated entirely consistently either.

[291] [1993] 3 SLR 317 (HC) 334.

[292] e.g.: V Chico, 'Saviour Siblings: Trauma and Tort Law' (2006) 14 *Med L Rev* 180, 211; Editorial, 'Clinical Negligence: Secondary Victims and Recovery for Nervous Shock' (2003) 11 *Med L Rev* 121, 124; M Puxon, 'Comment' on *Tredget* [1994] 5 Med LR 184, and a similar observation at: [1994] 5 *Med LR* 177; S Allen, 'Post-traumatic Stress Disorder: The Claims of Primary and Secondary Victims' (2000) 2 *JPIL* 108, 109.

[293] [2002] EWCA Civ 1792, [10]. [294] [2002] EWCA Civ 1792, [29].

[295] *Scottish Report*, [2.4]. [296] [1992] 2 AC 310 (HL) 400.

[297] Mulheron, 'Pure Psychiatric Injury Claims by Third Parties Associated with the Patient' in *Medical Negligence: Non-Patient and Third Party Claims* (Ashgate Publishing, 2010) 291.

In *Taylor v Somerset* and *Tan v East London*, C's viewing of the immediate victims' dead bodies was merely for confirmation, and did not constitute a 'shocking event' in either case. The purpose was to grieve, to settle disbelief, and the like.

However, against these decisions must be contrasted the husband's recovery of £5,000 for psychiatric damage in *Froggatt v Chesterfield and North Derbyshire Royal Hosp NHS Trust.*[298] Mr Froggatt knew that his wife had undergone a (needless, as it turned out) mastectomy. Yet, the court was willing to hold that, 'when he saw [his wife] undressed for the first time after the mastectomy, he was quite unprepared for what he saw and he was profoundly and lastingly shocked by it.'[299] Mrs Taylor witnessed her dead husband; Mr Froggatt witnessed his disfigured wife; and yet only the latter could recover at law.

It will be recalled that the direct perception requirement was 'watered down' in *Froggatt* – as was the shock requirement. All of this renders the application of the shock requirement very uncertain.

Conclusion. More than for any other secondary victim criterion, the requirement for a 'sudden shock' is the most problematical. It tends to be applied either strictly or in a distinctly watered-down version, with little consistency demonstrated in the case law. The concept is artificial, for something that 'violently agitates the mind' may occur over a fairly lengthy period.

The expert medical report given in *White (Frost) v CC of South Yorkshire Police*, cited in the Court of Appeal, was that, '[i]n fiction, and perhaps in a layman's view of shock as a psychological event, the individual experiences a grossly untoward event or situation with one or more sensory modalities but almost always vision, and is instantaneously "shocked" or traumatised. In practice, this almost never occurs'.[300] Indeed, as a psychiatric expert pointed out in *North Glamorgan v Walters*, the protracted nature of the immediate victim's decline may be the very reason that the secondary victim sustained 'shock'.[301] It also leads to factual lotteries, for if C happens to have been told something that raises his hopes but those hopes prove false (as in *Walters*), it may be easier to prove the requisite shock. Moreover, the Court of Appeal was invited to take a 'small incremental step ... to replace the shock requirement and substitute a requirement that the psychiatric illness need only be caused by directly witnessing or experiencing some trauma'.[302] Ultimately, this step was not directly taken – but C could prove a 'series of assaults' equating to shock in any event.

The law reform corner: Commentary on this requirement

English Law Comm:[303] given all of its problems, the requirement of shock for secondary victims should be abolished by statute. As a control mechanism, it was blunt and crude. It excluded those worn down by a lifetime of caring for the immediate victim, whom society may feel most worthy of compensation. Also, to retain the shock criterion emphasised the requirement of proximity of time and space, itself a problematical control mechanism. The ***only*** control mechanisms that ought to be retained for secondary victims of any type were proof of a recognisable psychiatric illness, reasonable foreseeability of pyschiatric harm to a person of normal fortitude, and a close tie of love and affection between C and the immediate victim.

[298] [2002] All ER (D) 218 (QB). [299] *ibid*, [79]. [300] [1997] 3 WLR 1194 (CA) 1207.
[301] [2002] EWCA Civ 1792, [10]. [302] *ibid*, [19(iv)].
[303] *English Report*, [5.29], and expressly abolished in: Draft Negligence (Psychiatric Illness) Bill, cl 5(2); and [5.6], [5.10], [5.27], [6.16].

Scottish Law Comm:[304] the shock requirement should be abolished, as it represented an outdated mode of medical and judicial understanding as to how mental injury was incurred. Some psychiatric injury for which shock is a precursor to diagnosis, such as PTSD, are inherently more compensable, in comparison to depression, for which shock is not necessarily a precursor. Plus, shock has not been applied to work-related stress claims.

Can C be *both* 'primary' and 'secondary' victim?

§5.37 English case law demonstrates that, despite the different duty of care requirements which attach to each type, C can indeed be *both* a primary victim and a secondary victim.

The House of Lords has appeared to vacillate as to whether C had to be either/or, or whether he could be both, primary victim and secondary victim.

In *Alcock*,[305] Lord Oliver described primary victims, and 'on the other hand', secondary victims. It seemed to be a definition of two halves. In *White*,[306] Lord Steyn described primary victims, and said that 'all other victims, who suffer pure psychiatric harm, are secondary victims.'

However, in *Page v Smith*,[307] Lord Lloyd rationalised some earlier cases as examples of where C was 'both primary and secondary victim of the same accident'. In *W v Essex CC*[308] too, Lord Slynn allowed the parental Cs to take both primary **and** secondary victim claims to trial.

Lower level cases have also adhered to this view that C can be both primary and secondary victim, with a lack of clear demarcation. For example, in *Farrell v Merton, Sutton and Wandsworth HA*,[309] (where C's son, Karol, was born with irreversible brain damage), the court made no bold statement as to what type of victim Mrs Farrell was, but hedged its bets. It held that Mrs Farrell was either a primary victim, directly involved in the events (the trauma of the birth), or a secondary victim, who witnessed the aftermath of the medically-caused injury suffered by Karol. In *Tredget v Bexley HA*,[310] Judge White was not conclusive as to whether the parents were primary or secondary victims either. At one point, the parents were described as 'directly involved in and with the event of the delivery' ... and 'each principals rather than passive witnesses'; whereas earlier, the legal criteria for the parents to fulfill were described in secondary victim-type terms.

The lack of a clear-cut distinction between the two categories has been confusing and problematical, given that different rules apply to each category, which the author has criticised elsewhere:

> no clear-cut distinction between [primary and secondary victim definition] has been maintained. Yet surely how we define a primary victim is a matter of law. Once a definition has been laid down, it is then a question of fact whether [C] falls within it. To treat secondary victim status as a 'fallback position' into which [C] might fall if he does not 'make it as a primary victim', is symptomatic of the courts' inability to produce a stable definition of the primary victim.[311]

To summarise, the following Table sets out why the secondary victim has a 'harder job' of proving a duty of care was owed to him than the primary victim does:

304 *Scottish Report*, [2.4]–[2.5]. 305 [1992] 1 AC 310 (HL) 407–8. 306 [1999] 2 AC 455 (HL) 496–9.
307 [1996] AC 155 (HL) 190. 308 [2001] 2 AC 592 (HL). 309 (2001) 57 BMLR 158 (QB) 164.
310 [1994] 5 Med LR 178 (Central London CC), with quotes at 183 and 182 respectively.
311 'The "Primary Victim" in Psychiatric Illness Claims, etc' (2008) 19 *KCLJ* 81, 87.

A comparison of primary and secondary victims

Primary victim	Secondary victim
The *Page v Smith* primary victim may recover for either a foreseeable psychiatric injury, or for an unforeseeable psychiatric injury if some *physical* injury was foreseeable but did not actually occur	A secondary victim must prove that his *psychiatric* injury was reasonably foreseeable
Primary victims are not subject to the control mechanisms emanating from *Alcock*	Secondary victims must satisfy the three '*Alcock* control mechanisms' (however interpreted)
Some types of primary victim are definitely not subject to the shock requirement; and whether a *Page v Smith* primary victim is subject to the requirement is unclear	Secondary victims must prove that they suffered a 'sudden shock', a sudden appreciation of a horrifying event, as opposed to a dawning and gradual realisation of pending tragedy or misfortune
D must take a primary victim just as he finds him	Secondary victims must prove that pure psychiatric injury was foreseeable in a person of 'normal fortitude'

Primary victims have access to several advantages over their secondary victim counterparts – but neither type of C enjoys an easy time of proving that a duty of care was owed. The definition of the primary victim has changed over time; and the rules governing the imposition of a duty of care towards secondary victims are littered with inconsistencies. Certainly, it is useless to base any outcome upon whether C is 'deserving' of compensation. In *Walters*, Elliot's fit occurred before Mrs Walters' eyes because she happened to be in the same hospital room as he was; whereas in *Taylor*, Mr Taylor died of his undiagnosed heart condition at work, and so Mrs Taylor lost her claim. In *Farrell v Merton*, Mrs Farrell was only vaguely aware of son Karol's damaged condition following his birth (due, in part, to the hospital's removal of Karol to another treatment site), and she could recover; whereas Mr Sion, who maintained a vigil beside his dying son's bedside in hospital for two weeks, failed in his claim. *Walters* states that the *Alcock* control mechanisms should not be applied 'too rigidly or mechanistically',[312] whereas in *White*, Lord Steyn conceded that 'the only sensible general strategy for the courts is to say thus far and no further'.[313] And many unsuccessful secondary victims, including Mrs Ward, Mrs Taylor, Mrs Palmer, Mrs Hall, Mr Tan and Mr Sion, would no doubt say that an overly-mechanistic application of the legal criteria was exactly why they lost their claims.

Given the disarray in secondary victim law, it is unfortunate that EWLC's recommendations by which to simplify this area of the law have not been adopted in England, nor has their draft Bill been enacted. The area will inevitably have to develop incrementally, on a case-by-case basis.

ELEVATED PRIMARY VICTIM CLAIMANTS

Whether D owes an elevated primary victim, C, a duty of care, has followed a fairly abbreviated pattern of primary victim analysis. As dealt with in the leading cases of *AB v Leeds* and in *Farrell v Avon HA*:

[312] [2002] EWCA Civ 1792, [48] (Clarke LJ). [313] [1998] UKHL 45, [1999] 2 AC 455 (HL) 500.

Reasonable foreseeability of psychiatric injury

§5.38 For the elevated primary victim, the wide test of reasonable foreseeability, relevant to the 'zone of danger' primary victim, is not applicable. Rather, C must prove that the risk of psychiatric injury was foreseen or reasonably foreseeable.

Occasionally, an elevated primary victim will *not* be able to prove that his psychiatric injury was a foreseen or reasonably foreseeable consequence of D's wrongdoing. The claim will fail at that point.

In *AB v Leeds Teaching Hosp NHS Trust*,[314] facts previously, the parents of the babies whose organs were harvested and retained post-mortem were treated by Gage J as primary victims, but two out of the three Cs (Mrs Harris and Mrs Carpenter) failed to prove that it was either foreseen or reasonably foreseeable that they would suffer psychiatric injury when they discovered that their dead children's organs had been retained. Mrs Harris 'was a robust person and someone whom Dr Clifford would have regarded as unlikely to collapse under the strain'. Mrs Carpenter 'was a well-adjusted, practical and sensible woman. It was foreseeable that she would be angry and distressed by the knowledge of organ retention, but not that she would suffer psychiatric injury'.

Proximity

§5.39 In the case of an elevated primary victim, the usual proximity factors (i.e., geographic, temporal and relational) have, to date, been assumed.

Given that, in both *AB v Leeds* and *Farrell v Avon HA*, the mishaps occurred in a hospital setting, and by healthcare professionals who were operating in that environment in their professional capacity, some degree of relational proximity towards the more vulnerable C was inevitable. There was no discussion of proximity in either case, indicating how obvious the proposition was in those scenarios.

The 'normal fortitude' rule

§5.40 An elevated primary victim C can recover for his psychiatric injury, even if it was sustained because C lacked the mental fortitude or 'natural phlegm' of a person of normal fortitude.

This is a significant advantage which an elevated primary victim enjoys over secondary victims – and a prime reason for the importance of the *AB v Leeds/Farrell v Avon* line of authority.

In *AB v Leeds Teaching Hosp NHS Trust*,[315] it was not fatal to Mrs Shorter's claim that she was an 'emotionally fragile person' who was in a very distressed state following the birth of her daughter, and then her death at a very early stage. Gage J concluded that 'the reasonable consultant obstetrician would have reasonably foreseen that this event would result in some psychiatric injury in Mrs Shorter'. C recovered £2,750 for her psychiatric injury. In *Farrell v Avon HA*,[316] Mr Farrell, C, was not a person of normal fortitude; according to the psychiatric evidence, C 'was probably always going to react badly to death', given his previous psychological history, treatment of his heroin addiction with a methadone programme, and alcohol dependency. Hence, C was more at risk of developing

[314] [2004] EWHC 644 (QB), [2005] QB 506, [253] (Mrs Harris), [279] (Mrs Carpenter), [268] (Mrs Shorter).
[315] [2004] EWHC 644, [2005] QB 506, [268]. [316] [2001] Lloyd's Rep Med 458 (QB) 464.

PTSD than the general population. Perhaps a father of normal fortitude may have withstood the shock of what was undeniably a terrible incident without suffering psychiatric injury, but this question was legally irrelevant. As a primary victim, D had to take Mr Farrell, C, exactly as they found him.

Shock

§5.41 It is unclear whether an elevated primary victim needs to prove that his psychiatric injury was caused by a 'shock' in the legal sense.

The criterion is not explicitly discussed in either *AB* or in *Farrell*. Undoubtedly, both sets of parental Cs did suffer trauma upon learning bad news about their children (false bad news, in Mr Farrell's case), but the relevant courts did not clarify whether a shock-induced injury was a pre-requisite to recovery.

FEAR-OF-THE-FUTURE CLAIMANTS

It will be recalled that 'fear-of-the-future' claimants are **not** primary victims *per se* (per the *CJD Litigation*), but have nevertheless been permitted to recover for psychiatric injury under the tri-partite *Caparo* test.

Reasonable foreseeability, and the normal fortitude rule

§5.42 For a fear-of-the-future C, his psychiatric injury must have been reasonably foreseeable. C must prove that a person of 'normal fortitude' would foreseeably suffer from some psychiatric injury, in which event C can recover for the full extent of his injury.

Notwithstanding that fear-of-the-future victims were in the zone of physical danger by being exposed to a disease-causing agent, they are not primary victims in the *Page v Smith* sense. Hence, they cannot take advantage of the wider test of foreseeability which applies to *Page v Smith*-type claimants – instead, their *psychiatric* injury must be foreseeable. This may be difficult to prove. On this point, the two leading English fear-of-the-future cases can be usefully contrasted.

In the *CJD Litigation*,[317] facts previously, **held:** the illnesses suffered by the various HGH recipients, C, were reasonably foreseeable to the treating doctors, D, especially when there was a real prospect that C would learn of the dire consequences possibly awaiting them, not only from doctors and counsellors, but from angry, ill-informed, relatives and from sensational media reports which would tend to highlight or sensationalise the risk of the potential terrible outcome. In the *Pleural Plaques Litig*,[318] facts previously, **held:** Mr Grieves', C's, psychiatric injury was not reasonably foreseeable. C had a long-standing fear of developing asbestos-related illness. Medical evidence described C's condition as 'relatively unique' among those workmen who had been exposed to asbestos dust. Also, C was not alarmed by the actual inhalation of asbestos fibres or by anything else done by the employer D, but by information given to him some 20 years later, following an X-ray. All of this rendered his psychiatric injury unforeseeable.

317 [2000] Lloyd's Rep Med 161 (QB).

318 [2007] UKHL 39, [2008] 1 AC 281, [30] (Lord Hoffmann), [57]–[58] (Lord Hope), [77] (Lord Scott), [100] (Lord Rodger), and [104] (Lord Mance). In the CA: *Grieves* [2006] EWCA Civ 27, [76] and [94] (Lord Phillips CJ).

Just as with secondary victims, the normal fortitude rule applies, in that C must establish that a person of reasonable fortitude and 'customary phlegm' would foreseeably suffer from some psychiatric injury. This proposition was confirmed in the *CJD Litigation*, where Morland J stated that, '[i]t was reasonably foreseeable that, if the worst fears were realised and deaths from CJD occurred, Hartree HGH recipients, both *those of normal fortitude* and those more vulnerable, might suffer psychiatric injury'.[319]

The same proposition was applied in *Pleural Plaques*. Mr Grieves was not a person of normal fortitude – he suffered from an irrational fear of developing a terminal illness resulting from asbestos exposure. However, Lord Hoffmann stated that he must nevertheless be taken to be subject to the rule of normal fortitude, given that 'the employer would be unlikely to have any specific knowledge of how a particular employee was likely to react to the risk of asbestos-related illness more than 30 years after he had left his employment. An assumption of ordinary fortitude is therefore inevitable'.[320]

Proximity

§5.43 Given that temporal proximity between C's psychiatric injury and D's acts or omissions may be absent (if the injury manifests well after the breach occurred), legal proximity will usually depend upon whether D assumed a legal responsibility toward C to avoid his psychiatric injury.

Proximity requires, as always, a close examination of the circumstances and relationship between C and D. On this point, the two leading cases were in sympathy.

In the *CJD Litigation*,[321] an assumption of responsibility was proven, from the following factors: D treated, diagnosed or otherwise cared for the HGH recipients of the clinical trial, as identifiable Cs; D's clinical trial entailed highly skilled and specialist treatment, rendering the recipients of the clinical trial vulnerable, and reliant upon D; in arranging the clinical trial, D constituted monopolistic providers of the medical services or were otherwise in a powerful position vis-a-vis the recipients, such that the recipients were vulnerable; the relationship between the clinicians, D, and the recipients was 'akin to that of doctor and patient, one of close proximity. But they were all children. They themselves did not choose to receive the treatment. They were selected for the treatment by clinicians at growth centres', i.e., relational proximity; D withheld information which could not be ascertained or verified elsewhere, and knew that supplying the information to the recipients would have prompted them to act differently. These factors, in combination, established that D assumed a responsibility toward the recipients to avoid causing them psychiatric harm in the conduct of the trial. In *Pleural Plaques*, Mr Grieves, C, was in a sufficiently-proximate relationship with D, his ex-employer. There was no debate about that point in the case.

Public policy

§5.44 No policy reasons have precluded recovery for psychiatric injury by a fear-of-the-future C to date.

In *Pleural Plaques*, there was no public policy reason precluding an ex-employee's recovery; and in the *CJD Litigation*,[322] Morland J noted that D 'committed a wrong upon the Group B

[319] [2000] Lloyd's Rep Med 161 (QB) 168 (emphasis added). [320] [2007] UKHL 39, [2008] 1 AC 281, [25]–[26].
[321] [2000] Lloyd's Rep Med 161 (QB) 165. [322] [2000] Lloyd's Rep Med 161 (QB) 168–69.

[Cs], by imperilling their lives from a terrible fatal disease', but that there was nothing 'in the facts and circumstances of this litigation why public policy, including social and economic policy considerations, should exclude them from compensation'. Policy reasons may preclude these types of Cs from being *primary victims*, but those reasons have not been transposed into an analysis under the *Caparo* test.

RESIDUARY CLAIMANTS

§5.45 The primary victim/secondary victim classification has been departed from in limited circumstances, *viz*, where: (1) inaccurate medical advice was given by D which gave rise to psychiatric injury on C's part, and where negligent misstatement was relied upon; or (2) C was not in the zone-of-danger by reason of the acts or omissions of D, but for whom psychiatric injury was reasonably foreseeable, and towards whom D assumed responsibility to avoid causing such psychiatric injury.

i. **Negligent misstatement.** Framing the cause of action in this way has been (rarely) employed, to enable C to avoid classification as either primary or secondary victim (as discussed previously under the heading, 'Receiving bad news').
ii. **Assumption of responsibility/reliance.** Alternatively, courts have found for C by invoking the 2-part *Hedley Byrne*-type assumption of responsibility/reliance test and/or the 3-part *Caparo* test, which govern novel duty of care scenarios. This type of residuary C, whilst infrequently-occurring, has featured in some quite differing scenarios:

The residuary C category: examples

- a claim against the Home Office:
  In *Butchart v Home Office*,[a] Mr Butchart, C, was a prisoner on remand at Winchester Prison. C was earlier in a mental health facility; had self-harmed whilst in police custody; and once in prison, was put under supervision and regular watch because his legal representatives were concerned about his suicide risk. C was placed with a cellmate who also had suicidal tendencies. C woke up early one morning to discover that his cellmate had strangled himself, and C suffered a severe shock. Later, C was told that 'if the suicide was anyone's fault, it was his', and was allocated a cell with another suicidal prisoner. **Held:** C could recover, as he was psychiatrically injured by breach of a 'primary duty of care owed to him'.
- a claim against a utilities supplier:
  In *Attia v British Gas plc*,[b] facts previously, Ms Attia, C, could recover for her psychiatric injury, for the destruction of her home, albeit that she was neither a primary nor a secondary victim.
- a claim against the police (and two cases can be usefully contrasted):
  In *Swinney v CC of Northumbria Police*,[c] Mrs Swinney, C, a pub landlady, supplied information to police about the identity of driver X, a hit-and-run driver who had killed an off-duty police officer, which she had overheard in pub conversation. The information, along with C's contact details, was then stolen from a police vehicle, due to the police, D's, negligence, and fell into X's hands. Subsequently, C was threatened with violence and arson, and suffered psychiatric injury. C alleged that

[a] [2006] EWCA Civ 239.
[b] [1988] QB 304 (CA).
[c] [1997] QB 464 (CA).

D owed her a duty of care with respect to the storage and safe keeping of the information, given that the police knew of X's violent character and that any informant's information was given in the strictest confidence. **Held:** C's claim was permitted to proceed. In *Leach v CC of Gloucestershire Constabulary*,[d] Mrs Leach, C, a voluntary worker on the Young Homeless Project at Cheltenham, was appointed to assist the notorious serial murderer Frederick West in his police interviews, in her capacity as an 'appropriate adult'.[e] C had to listen to harrowing and traumatic accounts in approximately 40 interviews, to accompany Mr West to the murder scenes, and to remain alone with him in a locked cell. During the interviews, Mr West admitted to 30 murders, and was charged with 11, and hanged himself while in remand in 1995. Mrs West was tried a few months later, and found guilty of 10 murders. C suffered PTSD, and sued the police, D, in negligence for failing to provide her with counselling. **Held:** C's action was struck out.

[d] [1998] 1 WLR 1421 (CA).
[e] Pursuant to the Police and Criminal Evidence Act 1984.

These cases proceeded upon a duty of care analysis of foreseeability; an assumption of responsibility/reliance; and no public policy precluding a duty of care (below).

The treatment of cases in which C suffers damage to his 'cherished property', and from which C suffers mental injury, has already been adverted to in this chapter.[323] It is not treated as a consequential mental injury, but instead, invokes the principles of pure psychiatric injury (per *Attia v British Gas plc*[324]). Notably, if these property damage cases are treated according to the residuary category of C, then the 'direct perception' requirement does not apply – which is significant, where C's property is destroyed, but C does not witness that destruction. In *Attia*, C did witness her house burning. However, in the sperm wastage cases of *Yearworth* and *Holdich*, no such direct perception occurred. As noted previously,[325] the *Yearworth* Court of Appeal queried whether recovery of psychiatric injury should only arise where C's property is destroyed and is observed by C, as a policy ring-fencing upon the number of potential claims, but without deciding the question. In *Holdich*, the Scottish Outer House permitted the claim in tort to proceed, without addressing that issue explicitly.

Expanding upon each duty of care limb in turn:

Reasonable foreseeability

§5.46 For a residuary C, his psychiatric injury must have been reasonably foreseeable (reflecting the *Wagon Mound* principle). The normal fortitude rule applies.

In *McLoughlin v Jones*,[326] the court remarked that, if it were wrong in holding that C was a *Page v Smith*-type primary victim (discussed previously[327]), then in the alternative, the 'ordinary [*Wagon Mound*] principle should apply: psychiatric injury to C should be the reasonably foreseeable result of [D's] negligence' (and, in that case, psychiatric injury resulting from a wrongful imprisonment was foreseeable). The important point is that foreseeability of psychiatric injury is necessary to give rise to a duty of care, in these types of residuary cases. For example:

[323] See pp 240–42. [324] [1987] EWCA Civ 8, [1988] QB 304, 320. [325] See pp 241–42.
[326] [2001] EWCA Civ 1743, [59] (Hale LJ). [327] See pp 231–33.

In *Butchart v Home Office*,[328] Mr Butchart, C, was known to the Home Office, D, to have been psychiatrically vulnerable before the suicide of his cellmate occurred, self-harming, and on suicide watch; it 'knew, or ought to have known, that [C] was a prisoner vulnerable to psychiatric harm'. In *Swinney v CC of Northumbria Police*, C's psychiatric injury was held to be foreseeable, given the campaign of terror from a criminal gang.

The comparative corner: **A Canadian example**

In *Mustapha v Culligan of Canada Ltd*,[329] Mr Mustapha, C, sued for psychiatric injury sustained as a result of seeing the dead flies in a bottle of water supplied by Culligan of Canada, D. C was replacing an empty bottle of drinking water with a full one when he saw a dead fly and part of another dead fly in the unopened replacement bottle. He became obsessed with the event, considered that it had 'revolting implications' for the health of his family, which had been consuming water supplied by D for the previous 15 years, and developed a major depressive disorder with associated phobia and anxiety. **Held:** C's damage was too remote to be compensable. Such a psychiatric reaction would not have been reasonably foreseeable in a person of ordinary fortitude (and there was no evidence that D had special knowledge of C's peculiar sensibilities). The medical evidence was that C's reaction was 'highly unusual' and 'very individual', and flowed in part from 'cultural factors' such as C's unusual concern over cleanliness, and the health and well-being of his family.

Assumption of responsibility/reliance

§5.47 A number of factors have indicated that D must have assumed a responsibility to minimise the risk of C's suffering psychiatric injury, and that C exercised a reciprocal reliance upon D.

If the primary victim/secondary victim categorisation is not to apply (nor the elevated primary victim, nor the stress-at-work categories), and if C is nevertheless permitted to recover for negligently-inflicted psychiatric injury, then C's claim has generally been analysed under an 'assumption of responsibility' test. The following factors have been used to separate the deserving cases from those that should fail:

- if D could identify C before the event, then a special relationship between them is easier to establish:

  In *Swinney*, the police, D, assumed responsibility for preserving the confidentiality of information about illegal activities which C supplied. D was the only recipient to whom C could have given that information. If disclosed, then that was likely to expose C to a greater risk than the ordinary risk to the general public. She was in an entirely different category from the vast class of potential female victims of the 'Yorkshire Ripper', distinguishing the case from *Hill v CC of West Yorkshire Police* (per Chapter 2).

- if D performed professional services entailing highly-skilled and specialist work on C's behalf (albeit that a mere contract of engagement, without more, could not give rise to a duty of care):

[328] [2006] EWCA Civ 239, [20] (Latham LJ). [329] [2008] SCC 27, quote at [18].

In *McLoughlin v Jones*, solicitors, D, were engaged by client, C, to exercise reasonable skill and care in preparing his case for trial in such a way as to minimise the risks of a wrongful conviction, and of his suffering false imprisonment and psychiatric injury, should he be convicted. On that basis, D 'should be deemed to have assumed responsibility for those consequences' (by contrast, where solicitors D, were not engaged by C at all, but the outcome of the litigation turned out to be detrimental for C, *McLoughlin* will be distinguished, as in *James-Bowen v Commr of Police*[330]). In *Attia v British Gas*, British Gas, D, assumed responsibility to C to perform the specialist hazardous activity of installing central gas heating with skill and care, a task for which she had to rely upon their professional competence.

- if D is in a powerful position vis-à-vis C, so that C is vulnerable and exposed:

In *Butchart*, the custodial relationship placed Mr Butchart, C, in a vulnerable position; and the assumption of responsibility which D undertook towards C was heightened by the fact that C was known to have been psychiatrically vulnerable before the suicide of his cellmate occurred. 'The [Home Office] knew or ought to have known that [C] was a prisoner vulnerable to psychiatric harm. In those circumstances it [is] ... inevitable that the duty of care ... included a duty to take reasonable steps to minimise the risk of psychiatric harm'. In *Swinney*, the police, D, were the repositories of information about X's illegal activities, and the only recipients to whom Mrs Swinney, C, could give such information. Hence, they wielded considerable power *vis-à-vis* the Swinneys, and assumed a responsibility toward them to keep the informant's information safe. In *McLoughlin*, the fact that C's liberty could be lost, if D's conduct was negligent, put C in a position of real vulnerability, and helped to contribute to an assumption of responsibility.

- if D has not assumed legal responsibility towards a third party that would conflict with a legal responsibility towards C (any such conflict will rule out an assumption of responsibility):

In *Leach*, this factor was significant in striking out Ms Leach's, C's, claim against the police, D: 'the whole essence of [C's] relationship to the police is that they did not assume responsibility towards her in relation to her duties as appropriate adult. She was there at the police station to be of assistance to Mr West, and the police might not be able to do their job of interviewing Mr West effectively if they were under a concurrent legal duty to be protective of [C's] psychological well-being'.

STRESS-AT-WORK CLAIMANTS

The employment relationship, of itself, does **not** entail an automatic duty on the employer's part to avoid psychiatric injury on the employee's part (otherwise, the police officers in *White* should have established a duty owed to them by their employer, the Chief Constable, for their psychiatric injuries, which they certainly could not). English precedent clearly demonstrates that the employment contract gives rise to an automatic duty of care to avoid *physical* injury to an employee – but it does **not** prescribe that the employer is liable for **all** types of injuries suffered by the employee.

To reiterate, employees may have **other** avenues for recovering damages for psychiatric injuries sustained in the workplace. For the employee who is in the zone-of-danger himself (per *Page v Smith*), or who is guilt-ridden at a co-employee's injury or death (per *Monk v*

[330] [2015] EWHC 1249 (QB) [60]–[62].

Harrington), the relevant principles discussed earlier in the chapter apply.[331] However, secondary victim claims are most unlikely for an employee who witnesses a work accident, as rarely will work colleagues have shared the requisite ties of love and affection required.

For the stress-at-work employees, important guidance was provided by Lady Justice Hale in the leading case of *Hatton v Sutherland*[332] (reversed on another point, but the guidance was affirmed on appeal to the House of Lords, where the case is known as *Barber v Somerset CC*[333]). Employees who are overworked to the point of mental illness have been permitted to recover damages for their injury, on the basis that responsibility for causing the psychological risks faced by an employee must be borne, at least in part, by the employer. However, it is **not** an all-encompassing duty to avoid an employee's mental injury, whatever the circumstances, as Hale LJ's propositions demonstrate:

> [*Principles relevant to duty of care*]:
>
> (2) The threshold question is whether this kind of harm to this particular employee was reasonably foreseeable: this has two components (a) an injury to health (as distinct from occupational stress) which (b) is attributable to stress at work (as distinct from other factors).
>
> (3) Foreseeability depends upon what the employer knows (or ought reasonably to know) about the individual employee. Because of the nature of mental disorder, it is harder to foresee than physical injury, but may be easier to foresee in a known individual than in the population at large. An employer is usually entitled to assume that the employee can withstand the normal pressures of the job unless he knows of some particular problem or vulnerability.
>
> (4) The test is the same whatever the employment: there are no occupations which should be regarded as intrinsically dangerous to mental health.
>
> (5) Factors likely to be relevant in answering the threshold question include:
>
> (a) The nature and extent of the work done by the employee. Is the workload much more than is normal for the particular job? Is the work particularly intellectually or emotionally demanding for this employee? Are demands being made of this employee unreasonable when compared with the demands made of others in the same or comparable jobs? Or are there signs that others doing this job are suffering harmful levels of stress? Is there an abnormal level of sickness or absenteeism in the same job or the same department?
>
> (b) Signs from the employee of impending harm to health. Has he a particular problem or vulnerability? Has he already suffered from illness attributable to stress at work? Have there recently been frequent or prolonged absences which are uncharacteristic of him? Is there reason to think that these are attributable to stress at work, for example because of complaints or warnings from him or others?
>
> (6) The employer is generally entitled to take what he is told by his employee at face value, unless he has good reason to think to the contrary. He does not generally have to make searching enquiries of the employee or seek permission to make further enquiries of his medical advisers.

[331] See pp 233–36 [332] [2002] EWCA Civ 76, [43]. Hale LJ wrote the judgment for the court.

[333] [2004] UKHL 13, [2004] 1 WLR 1089, [5] (Lord Scott) (one of the conjoined appeals). Hale LJ's 16 propositions have been much-cited since.

[*Principles relevant to proving breach*]:

(8) The employer is only in breach of duty if he has failed to take the steps which are reasonable in the circumstances, bearing in mind the magnitude of the risk of harm occurring, the gravity of the harm which may occur, the costs and practicability of preventing it, and the justifications for running the risk.

(9) The size and scope of the employer's operation, its resources and the demands it faces are relevant in deciding what is reasonable; these include the interests of other employees and the need to treat them fairly, for example, in any redistribution of duties.

(10) An employer can only reasonably be expected to take steps which are likely to do some good: the court is likely to need expert evidence on this.

(11) An employer who offers a confidential advice service, with referral to appropriate counselling or treatment services, is unlikely to be found in breach of duty.

(12) If the only reasonable and effective step would have been to dismiss or demote the employee, the employer will not be in breach of duty in allowing a willing employee to continue in the job.

This section sets out some summary propositions pertinent to the establishment of a duty of care (readers are referred to detailed works for further analysis regarding stress-at-work claims[334]).

Reasonable foreseeability

§5.48 An employer D's duty to avoid psychiatric injury on the employee's, C's, part arises where either (1) D *knew* that a particular employee was vulnerable to stress-induced illness; or (2) it was objectively foreseeable, to a reasonable employer, that psychiatric injury could foreseeably result from a particular task or tasks.

The abovementioned test of foreseeability, derived from *Hatton v Sutherland* (CA) and also from Brown LJ in *Bonser v UK Coal Mining*,[335] reflects the fact that, in most cases, employer D will know his employee C.

Employer D must have foreseen that its employee would suffer *illness*; foreseeability that C would suffer stress in his work environment is **not** sufficient. As Brown LJ stated, '[o]verwork, of itself, is likely to lead to stress. It is altogether less likely to lead to the breakdown of the stressed employee's health. For that to be foreseen, [C] will generally need to establish, not only that the employer knew that he or she was being overworked, but, in addition ... either (i) that the employer knew that the individual employee was, for some reason, particularly vulnerable to stress-induced illness; or (ii) that the [employee] was manifesting clear signs of some impending harm to health before eventually illness followed'.[336]

Stress-at-work claims must arise from circumstances in which 'the stresses inherent in [the] employment' have put the employee at risk of psychiatric illness, and where he has done precisely the work which the employer required him to do. In other words, the employer's assumption of responsibility arises from the employee performing the very tasks required of his employment.

334 e.g., I Smith and A Baker, *Employment Law* (11th edn, Oxford University Press, 2013); S Honeyball, *Honeyball and Bowers' Textbook on Employment Law* (13th edn, Oxford University Press, 2014).

335 [2003] EWCA Civ 296, [30].

336 *ibid.*

These cases are very fact-specific, but a couple of examples will suffice to illustrate:

In *Melville v Home Office*,[337] Mr Melville, C, was employed by the Home Office, D, as a health care officer at HMP Exeter. His duties included recovering the bodies of prisoners who had committed suicide. He attended eight suicides between 1981 and 1988. In the last, he helped to cut down the body, remove a ligature, and attempt revival. C subsequently suffered from nightmares and flashbacks, developed a stress-related illness, and retired on grounds of ill-health early the following year. Before he stopped work, C gave no indication that he was developing a stress-related illness; but D's documents recognised that persons who were called on to deal with traumatic incidents in prisons (e.g., suicides), might suffer health problems, and that they should receive support from the prison care team. **Held:** C could recover. Even though C had not shown troubles in his health, D foresaw that employees who were exposed to particular traumatic incidents might suffer psychiatric injury.

But contrast:

In *Pratley v Surrey CC*,[338] Miss Pratley, C, was employed by Surrey CC, D, as a care manager. The demands of the work and a lack of funding made it a pressurised job (which D knew). However, C gave no indication that she felt pressurised, and deliberately withheld information about the fact that she took time off for stress (the doctor's certificate indicated 'neuralgia'), nor did she use the occupational health and counselling services which were available to D's employees. C spoke to her line manager prior to going on holiday, in which it was 'promised' that a new stacking system would be introduced to ease her workload – but when C returned from holidays and found that it had not been implemented, she suffered psychiatric illness, and was subsequently dismissed. The line manager had not taken immediate steps to implement that system, deciding rather to wait to see how things were and how C felt when she returned from holiday. **Held:** C could not recover. Her psychiatric injury (immediate collapse, following the disappointment of a 'cherished idea' about the stacking system, arising from the conversation about workload) was not a reasonably foreseeable psychiatric injury. In *Yapp v Foreign and Cth Office*,[339] the FCO, D, withdrew Mr Yapp, C, from his post without his having had the opportunity to state his case, and C suffered a psychiatric illness. **Held:** C could not recover. C was an 'apparently robust employee, with no history of any psychiatric ill-health'. A major setback to his career was foreseeably likely to cause C distress and anger, but it was not a dismissal, a disciplinary sanction, or based on any established misconduct. D could not have reasonably foreseen, in the absence of any sign of special vulnerability, that C might develop a psychiatric illness as a result of its decision.

In *Yapp*, Davis LJ pointed out that the second limb of the principle – whereby psychiatric injury resulting from a breach of duty by an employer will be assessed as reasonably foreseeable, even if there was no awareness of a prior relevant susceptibility or vulnerability on the part of that employee – will 'likely be very unusual', and will probably require 'appropriately special facts' of the type in *Melville*. Hence, the legal principles in this area are not particularly sympathetic towards the C employee.

The normal fortitude rule

§5.49 For employee C whom employer D knows to be particularly vulnerable to stress-related illness, D must take C as he finds him. Otherwise, D is entitled to rely on the normal fortitude rule.

[337] [2005] EWCA Civ 6, [133]–[134]. [338] [2003] EWCA Civ 1067. [339] [2014] EWCA Civ 1512, [155]–[156].

The interplay of the normal fortitude rule and stress-at-work claims has been somewhat controversial. It will be noted that, in proposition (3), Hale LJ opined that an employer was usually entitled to assume the employee could withstand the normal pressures of the job, unless he knew of some particular problem or vulnerability. In other words, any pre-existing disposition to mental injury may be taken into account. Hale LJ justified that view thus: '[t]he question is not whether psychiatric injury is foreseeable in a person of "ordinary fortitude". The employer's duty is owed to each individual employee, not to some as yet unidentified outsider ... The employer knows who his employee is [and whether he has a pre-existing vulnerability to stress]'.[340]

> In *Daniel v Dept of Health*,[341] Patricia Daniel, C, a cancer research network manager employed by D, alleged that she suffered psychiatric injury, arising from bullying by a senior colleague and serious overwork. C had a history of bipolar disorder (which has a very high rate of recurrence), but C's condition was unknown to D, and C did not mention it in her liaisons with work colleagues. **Held:** C could not recover, as no duty of care owed. D did not know that a risk of occupational stress and subsequent mental injury existed for those in C's position; and there were no signs that others doing the same work, in a pressured job, had suffered injury to their health. The focus must then turn to the individual employee, but there were no individual indications or signs from C herself of impending mental injury (C mentioned stress, insomnia and losing weight to a senior colleague, but he was unable to observe those changes himself). C was reticent about her health problems, 'consistent not only with her desire not to appear weak to her employer, but also her desire to remain at all times professional in her conduct and approach'.
> In *Croft v Broadstairs Town Council*,[342] Mrs Croft, C, was D's town clerk. C received a warning letter about her conduct, and there were follow-up meetings and correspondence. The letter was unexpected, and C was shocked and distressed to receive it. She then suffered depression as a result of the letter, rendering her unfit for work. Two town councillors knew that C had been undergoing counselling when the letter was received. **Held:** C could not recover, as no duty was owed. D did not know of C's psychiatric vulnerability to depression (despite the knowledge about the counselling). Absent actual knowledge, D was entitled to expect C to be a person of ordinary robustness, including in dealing with disciplinary matters. Her breakdown was not reasonably foreseeable.

However, although that notion was approved by Lord Hoffmann in the *Pleural Plaques Litig*,[343] it was with the caveat that an assumption of ordinary fortitude on the employee's part was necessary, where employee C was long-departed from employer D's workplace. Although Mr Grieves was not a person of normal fortitude (he suffered from an irrational fear of developing a terminal illness resulting from asbestos exposure), Lord Hoffmann stated that the rule must apply to him, given that 'the employer would be unlikely to have any specific knowledge of how a particular employee was likely to react to the risk of asbestos-related illness more than 30 years after he had left his employment. An assumption of ordinary fortitude is therefore inevitable'.[344] Presumably, where the workforce is very large, an assumption of ordinary fortitude may also be appropriate.

[340] [2002] EWCA Civ 76, [23]. [341] [2014] EWHC 2578 (QB) [177]–[186]. [342] [2003] EWCA Civ 676.
[343] *Grieves v FT Everard & Sons Ltd* [2007] UKHL 39, [25]–[26]. [344] *ibid*, [25]–[26].

The law reform corner: The 'normal fortitude' rule

Scottish Law Comm:[345] the normal fortitude rule should be applied to all occupational stress claims: '[p]ersons who have responsible jobs are expected to accommodate the stress inherent in their work and can reasonably be expected to endure any resultant mental harm without seeking reparation. Similarly, there are professions, the armed forces, firemen and the police for example, which involve exposure to personal danger and participation in horrifying situations'. However, that should not rule out occupational stress claims altogether (said the Commission), as such professionals, 'will be able to do so when the mental harm is a consequence of an event that goes well beyond what can usually be expected to occur in the ordinary course of their jobs.'

Proximity

§5.50 The relationship of employment gives rise to the requisite proximity.

Where an employer, D, employs an employee, C, who sustains a psychiatric injury as a result of D's acts or omissions at the workplace, the question of proximity tends to be enmeshed with that of reasonable foreseeability (as Lady Justice Hale's propositions demonstrate). Hence, this element has not attracted much discussion in the context of 'stress-at-work' claims.

The rest of the cause of action

Breach of duty must be proven in the usual way, as noted in *Hatton*. Hence, the principles in Chapter 7 are pertinent. For example, in *Daw v Intel Corp*,[346] Pill LJ remarked that the provision of counselling services would not automatically preclude a finding of breach (although such a step will always be relevant, per *Hartmann v South Essex Mental Health NHS Trust*[347]). The usual principles of causation (per Chapter 8) and remoteness (per Chapter 9) will also apply.

[345] *Scottish Report*, [3.25]; also [3.30] and Recommendation 5(b), Draft Bill, s 3(2).
[346] [2007] ICR 1318 (CA) [45]. [347] [2005] EWCA Civ 6.

6

Breach I – The standard of care

Under the second element of the tort of negligence, the relevant question is whether the conduct of D fell below the standard of care which the law expects of D, and so constitutes negligent behaviour. This enquiry necessarily involves a two-stage analysis: (1) setting the standard of care against which D's behaviour should be judged (a question of law); and (2) deciding whether D's conduct met, or fell below, that standard (a question of fact). This chapter considers the first enquiry, while Chapter 7 considers the second.

INTRODUCTION

Reasonableness, not perfection

The requisite legal standard

§6.1 The law of negligence imposes a reasonable standard of care on D, and not a standard of perfection (the latter would, if permitted, impose a form of strict liability). Fixing the requisite reasonable standard of care in any given case is a question of law.

That proposition was espoused in the seminal judgment of Lord Atkin in *Donoghue v Stevenson*: '[y]ou must take *reasonable care* to avoid acts or omissions which you can reasonably foresee would be likely to injure your neighbour'.[1] In *Bolton v Stone* too,[2] the House of Lords remarked that, '[t]he standard of care in the law of negligence is the standard of an ordinarily careful man' – or an ordinarily careful cricket club, in that case. The synonymous phrases of 'ordinary care', 'proper care', or 'prudent care', were all used in *Bolton v Stone* to describe the standard which the law expects of D. That ordinary careful adult has traditionally been equated to the person 'on the top of the Clapham omnibus' (per *Bolam v Friern Hosp Management Committee*[3]).

What the law of negligence does **not** impose upon D is a requirement that he meet a standard of perfection, i.e., a level of conduct which is so unattainably high that breach is inevitable, because even reasonable conduct could not satisfy such a standard. The reality is that mistakes, errors of judgment, and acts and omissions falling short of perfection, commonly **do** occur in

[1] [1932] AC 562 (HL) 580 (emphasis added).

[2] [1951] AC 850 (HL), with quotes respectively at: 863 (Lord Oaksey), 865 (Lord Reid), and 868 (Lord Radcliffe).

[3] [1957] 1 WLR 582 (QB) 586 (McNair J).

any endeavour of life – but they do not represent breach, and negligence, **unless** they fall below what would be expected of a reasonable person in D's position. As the Privy Council endorsed, in *Hamilton v Papakura DC (NZ)*,[4] the law does not impose 'an unattainable standard that guarantees against all harm and all circumstances'.

There is an important distinction to be drawn here, as the Court of Appeal noted in *Barrie v Cardiff CC*: '[t]he standard of care is a question of law; but whether or not, in any given case, that standard has been attained is a question of fact for the judge to decide, having regard to all the circumstances of the case'.[5] It follows that any error in setting the standard of care too high (or too low) will be an appealable error of law – and, in that regard, first-instance courts must resist the temptation to set the bar *too high*. Additionally, if a first-instance court takes into account a characteristic or circumstance which is legally irrelevant to the question of standard, that will be an error of law too. Appellate courts can readily interfere with an assessment of the standard of care, given that it is a question of law.

In *Barrie v Cardiff CC*,[6] Sam Barrie, C, aged 6, tripped over protruding concrete edging at her school playground in Cardiff. The edging was about 15 mm higher than the surrounding area of tarmac. The Cardiff Council, D, as the local education authority, owed a duty of care to C; but setting the standard, and whether D was in breach of that standard, were at issue, because of the playground's condition. C had brittle bone disease, but that did not play any role in her tripping. The playground was commonly used by children 4–7 years old. **Held:** the requisite standard of care was a school playground which was reasonably (not perfectly) safe for a school for ordinary infants of 4–7 years: 'a playground is ... not to be criticised by the standards of a bowling green'. The standard was not to be elevated because of C's brittle bone disease. The standard set by the trial judge was too high. No breach occurred here, as D had met the reasonable standard of care.

In *Penney, Palmer and Cannon v East Kent HA*,[7] cytoscreeners employed by health authority D reported four cervical smears taken from various patients, C, as being negative, which meant that there was no timely follow-up or diagnostic or therapeutic interventions. Each C went on to develop invasive adenocarcinoma of the cervix. **Held (trial):** D was negligent. However, D appealed on the basis that the case set a dangerous precedent 'by requiring inappropriately high standards of care by those responsible for primary screening' under the national cervical screening programme. **Held (CA):** the standard was properly set (i.e., 'a reasonably competent screener exercising reasonable care at the time when the screening took place'). Breach was also proven, given that, on each slide, there was a small number of inflamed groups of endocervical cells showing changes in nuclear and cytoplasmic morphology, such that the smears should have been classified as at least 'borderline'.

§6.2 An unattainable standard of care – i.e., one which D *cannot* achieve because of D's particular characteristics or circumstances – is nevertheless lawful.

Albeit that the standard of care is to be set at a reasonable, rather than a perfect, level of care and/or skill, there will still be some circumstances (discussed below) in which it may be impossible for D to meet even that reasonable standard of care – because of D's own frailties, inexperience,

[4] [2002] 3 NZLR 308, [2002] UKPC 9, [31], endorsing the comments of the NZCA in the court below.

[5] [2001] EWCA Civ 703, [19]. Although this quote is commonly attributed to Lord Wilberforce in *Goldman v Hargrave* [1967] 1 AC 645 (PC) 663, it does not seem to appear anywhere in Lord Wilberforce's judgment.

[6] [2001] EWCA Civ 703, [2002] ELR 1, quote at [23].

[7] (2000) 55 BMLR 63 (CA), quotes at [3], [22] and [34].

or circumstances. Nevertheless, an unattainable standard of care is not unlawful, merely by virtue of the fact that it is out of reach for D. English law is content to set artificially high standards of care for some categories of D, for policy reasons, as discussed later in the chapter. Principally, in such cases, D is an insured party, such that if D falls below that unattainable standard of care, then C is enabled to obtain compensation for his injury – a 'better' result, concludes the law of negligence, than suppressing the standard and thereby perhaps precluding any finding of breach.

No average or team standard

§6.3 There is no concept of an '*average* standard of care' in English law; every single act or omission by D is assessed against the reasonable standard. There is no concept of a '*team* standard of care' either; the acts/omissions of each member of a team will be assessed separately, against the level of skill expected of a reasonable person in that team member's position.

Importantly, *every single act or omission* by D is to be judged against the reasonable standard of care. There is no legal recognition of D's achieving an average – or even a higher-than-average – standard of care on a regular basis (whether as a driver, a doctor, or otherwise), so as to compensate for one momentary lapse of care, amounting to negligence. In other words, it is **not** possible for D to allege that, 'so long as he had provided an adequate service on average, he should not be held liable for the very odd occasion when his performance fell below the norm' (per *Wilsher v Essex AHA*[8]). All that matters is whether, *at any particular instance* when dealing with a specific activity, D's conduct dropped below the reasonable standard.

Additionally, there is **no** concept of 'a *team* standard of care', whereby the standard of care which the law requires of each person operating within a team, is set at the standard which an ordinarily competent team, as a whole, has provided to C. A 'team standard of care' – whether that team consists of professional or non-professional members – is not a tenable proposition in English law. That was also made plain by *Wilsher v Essex AHA*,[9] in which the Court of Appeal held that it would not be right to expose a nurse to an action in negligence for failing to possess the skill and experience of a specialist consultant who worked in such a unit, by applying some artificial and over-arching 'team standard of care' (although it must be emphasised that the early mistakes made in treatment of this baby were not made by the nurses involved in his care).

In *Wilsher v Essex AHA*, Martin Wilsher, C, was born very prematurely, and was cared for in a special care baby unit at Princess Alexandra Hospital, Harlow, by a team of senior and junior doctors and nurses. The trial judge accepted that the fact that C survived at all and without brain damage 'is due both to the remarkable advances of medical science ... and to the treatment he received in the [hospital]'. However, within the first 36 hours of his life, C was super-saturated with oxygen, due to a mistake by two members of the team. **Held:** breach proven. Just because the unit was a very specialised one did not necessarily mean that all members working in the unit held themselves out as capable of undertaking the specialised procedures which that unit set out to perform. Furthermore, the fact that C only survived his very premature birth because of the extremely high and dedicated level of care that he received throughout his 6 month stay at the hospital did not preclude a finding of breach, regarding what occurred during the first 36 hours. (Ultimately, though, causation failed.)

[8] [1987] QB 730 (CA) 747 (Mustill LJ) (the case went to the HL only on causation; statements by the CA regarding standard and breach were not the subject of appeal).

[9] [1987] QB 730 (CA) 749–50 (Mustill LJ), 775 (Glidewell LJ), quote in text by Lord Bridge (on appeal to HL).

An objective standard, subject to exceptions

§6.4 The standard of care set by the law is, with limited exceptions, an objective standard, i.e., the standard is not ordinarily dependent upon the particular characteristics of, or circumstances affecting, D.

An objective standard – assessed according to the conduct expected of an ordinary reasonable adult – 'eliminate[s] the personal equation ... [and is] independent of the idiosyncrasies of the particular person whose conduct is in question' (per *Glasgow Corp v Muir*[10]).

This approach has two advantages. First, it standardises how citizens of society are expected to behave (i.e., to act as a person of ordinary prudence would behave) and omits any enquiry as to how reasonable D, himself, believed his conduct to be; and secondly, it more easily permits the court to adjudge D's acts or omissions as negligent or not – 'the spokesman of the fair and reasonable man, who represents after all no more than the anthropomorphic conception of justice, is and must be the court itself' (per Lord Radcliffe in *Davis Contractors Ltd v Farnham UDC*[11]). The court has a far more successful prospect of setting the reasonable standard, if the law eliminates the personal angle.

However, as with most matters in law, the general rule is proven by the exceptions thereto. Sometimes the 'personal equation' **does** matter, in that there are several factors which **do** impinge upon the reasonable standard of care, whereby the court must set the standard according to the particular idiosyncracies of D, or according to the particular circumstances in which D operates. In other words, the law does not always insist upon a purely objective standard. However – and the law is not entirely consistent on this point – there are several idiosyncracies or circumstances, about which D can do nothing, of which the law takes **no** account at all. These various factors and disparities are explained in the following sections. By way of summary of this chapter's content, the following nutshell analysis may assist (where ↑ denotes an elevated standard; ↓ denotes a suppressed standard; and ↔ denotes that the standard does not change at law):

Nutshell analysis: **Fixing the standard of care**

Check for any of the following, and assess its impact on the reasonable standard of an ordinary adult:

CHARACTERISTICS:

Specialism ↑
Age ↓
Disability depends: ↔ (where known) or ↓ (where unknown)
Inexperience ↔
Parents ↑
Gender ↔

[10] [1943] AC 448 (HL) 457 (Lord Macmillan).

[11] [1956] AC 696 (HL) 729, noted in the context of frustrated contracts, not negligence, but the sentiment is equally applicable. See too: *Badger v MOD* [2005] EWHC 2941 (QB), [9].

CIRCUMSTANCES:

'Agony of the moment' or 'battle conditions' ↓
'Diagnosis with a focus' ↑
Locality perhaps ↓, but scant authority
Dangerous or fast-moving recreational or sporting contests ↓ to some extent (except for promoters and organisers, for which ↔)
Available resources and facilities perhaps ↓, but divided views
Local practices ↔

It is important to appreciate that, should the law elevate the standard of care for any reason, breach is more likely, because the mistake/error complained of is more likely to fall below that elevated standard. Obversely, if the standard of care is suppressed because of some characteristic or circumstance, then breach is less likely, as whatever happened is less likely to fall below such a suppressed standard of care. It may be useful to consider the standard of care as a 'floating level' – whatever the conduct of D, it cannot be changed, but the standard of care at law can vary, up or down, depending upon either D's characteristics or the surrounding circumstances.

THE IMPACT (IF ANY) OF D'S CHARACTERISTICS

Specialism

§6.5 For D who has a particular profession or specialism, the requisite standard is 'the ordinary skill of an ordinary competent man exercising that particular art'.

This so-called *Bolam*-standard of care – named after the seminal case of *Bolam v Friern Hospital Management Committee*[12] – is set neither by the unskilled person (i.e., the 'ordinary person on the London underground'), nor by reference to the person holding the highest degree of skill. As McNair J said, when instructing the jury in this medical negligence action brought by Mr Bolam against his psychiatrist (in respect of electro-convulsive therapy which went badly), where D exercises some special skill or competence, the test:

> is not the test of the man on the top of the Clapham omnibus, because he has not got this special skill. The test is the standard of the ordinary skilled man exercising and professing to have that special skill. A man need not possess the highest expert skill; it is well-established law that it is sufficient if he exercises the ordinary skill of an ordinary competent man exercising that particular art.

Hence, if D, who is exercising a professional or specialist calling, makes an error which any similar professional, 'acting with ordinary care, might have made too', then no breach will lie, for the legal standard of care will have been met (per *Whitehouse v Jordan*[13]).

Graduated specialisms

§6.6 Within one type of profession (say, legal, medical, engineering, etc), the degree of specialism possessed by D determines the requisite standard of care. However, even at a lower specialism,

[12] [1957] 1 WLR 582 (QB) 586 (McNair J). [13] [1981] 1 WLR 246 (HL) 263 (Lord Fraser).

D may fail to meet the relevant standard of care, by failing to refer C to a more specialist or expert environment, which could have provided better resources and expertise for C.

Given the graduated levels of knowledge, skill and expertise within a profession, the standard of care necessarily will vary across those levels. The Table below illustrates, by reference to the *medical* profession. As Lord Scarman stated, in *Maynard v West Midlands Regional HA*, 'a doctor who professes to exercise a special skill must exercise the ordinary skill *of his specialty*'.[14]

Graduated specialisms within the medical profession

The type of specialist	Illustrative case
A ***tertiary specialist***, who accepts referrals from other specialists, will be judged against the ordinary standard of care and skill in that tertiary specialism.	In *De Freitas v O'Brien*,[a] D was a spinal specialist who took referrals from orthopaedic and neuro-surgeons who were engaged in a wider field of surgical practice. **Held:** D was judged against (the limited number of) tertiary specialists in his field (no breach proven).
A ***specialist doctor*** must meet the ordinary skill of his speciality.	In *Lillywhite v University College London Hosp NHS Trust*,[b] D was a professor of obstetrics and gynaecology who was experienced at reading and interpreting foetal ultrasound scans. His conduct, in examining a foetal scan, was examined against 'the ordinary skill of his speciality, i.e., a consultant sonologist at a tertiary referral centre' (breach proven).
A ***general practitioner (GP)*** must meet the standard of general practice, but nothing higher than that.	In *Holt v Edge*,[c] the patient, C, slipped and fell in the shower, and complained of neck cramp, breathing difficulties, and pins and needles in her arms. Her husband phoned D, a GP at the local medical centre, and C was told to rest; a night doctor visited and detected high blood pressure and recommended further rest; but feeling no better three days later, C was admitted to A&E, where she was diagnosed with an atypical brain haemorrhage. She was operated on, suffered a stroke, and was left disabled. **Held:** the standard expected of a conscientious and competent GP, who was not expected to know of these unusual symptoms of a brain haemorrhage, was met. The usual symptoms of pounding headaches and vomiting were entirely absent in C's case. In *Stockdale v Nicholls*,[d] a GP sent a practice nurse to check on an ill baby at the baby's home. The nurse diagnosed 'nose infection and snuffles'. The baby later suffered septicaemia. **Held:** the GP met the standard of a reasonably competent GP in sending the practice nurse, rather than attending himself.

[a] (1995) 25 BMLR 51 (CA).
[b] [2005] EWCA Civ 1466, [22], [84] (condition of holoprosencephaly).
[c] [2006] EWHC 1932 (QB) [75], aff'd: [2007] EWCA Civ 602. Also: *Hardman v Riddell* [2004] EWHC 1691 (QB).
[d] [1993] 4 Med LR 191 (QB) 199.

[14] [1985] 1 WLR 634 (HL) 648 (emphasis added).

A ***medical practitioner working in a prison hospital*** has been the subject of somewhat contrary authority. On the one hand, the medical practitioner is not required to meet as high a standard of care as that which must be provided in a civilian hospital – given the different functions that these hospitals perform (lawful detention versus seeking a cure) (per *Knight v HO*[e]). On the other hand, a prisoner, while detained in prison, is legally entitled to expect the same level of medical care, as if she was at liberty, subject to the constraints of having to be escorted to a general hospital (per *Brooks v HO*[f]).

In *Knight v Home Office*, medical staff working in the hospital psychiatric wing of Brixton prison were caring for C, a prisoner at suicide risk. Only 15-minute inspections were possible, rather than continuous observation of C, and C committed suicide in between two inspections. **Held:** no breach proven. The higher patient/staff ratio at Brixton was appropriate for the different function which the prison hospital served. D's hospital met the standard of a reasonable institution whose primary function was detention.

In *Brooks v Home Office*, C, a female prisoner on remand, and in the stages of a high-risk pregnancy, had a scan which indicated potential difficulties with both twins (one was eventually stillborn, and the other suffered from considerable disabilities). C was not immediately referred from the mother-and-baby unit at Holloway Prison to a maternity hospital. **Held:** breach proven. C, while detained, was entitled to expect the same level of ante-natal care, for herself and her children, as if at liberty, subject to the constraint of having to be escorted to hospital.

A ***medical practitioner in a military environment*** will be judged according to the standard accepted by a reasonable and responsible body of military psychiatrists or nurses (which takes account of any additional training or instruction given to doctors or nurses practising in the military environment).

In *Multiple Claimants v MOD (Pt I)*,[g] Cs were former members of the Armed Forces who allegedly suffered psychiatric injury as a result of combat exposure during service for their country. The case was not about exposure to the stress and trauma of combat, but rather, that the MOD were negligent in failing to take any adequate steps to prevent the development of psychiatric illness, and in failing to detect, diagnose or treat such illness. **Held:** the MOD had committed systemic breach in three limited respects.

A ***practitioner of alternative medicine*** will be judged against two standards: (1) the reasonable standard of skill and care appropriate to traditional Chinese herbal medicine, which had a long and distinguished history; and (2) given that D operated alongside orthodox medicine, D had reasonably to satisfy himself that the remedy was not actually or potentially harmful; and that there was no adverse report in orthodox medical journals re the remedy.

In *Shakoor v Situ*,[h] Mr Situ, D, a practitioner of Chinese herbal medicine, treated Mr Shakoor, C, for fatty lumps of tissue beneath the skin, by prescribing a herbal remedy containing 12 different herbs. After taking 9 doses, C fell ill with nausea, yellowing of the eyes and skin, and heartburn. C's liver turned necrotic, and despite an urgent liver transplant, C died. The treatment was considered safe in Chinese medicine, although some letters and articles in *The Lancet* had queried the safety of one particular herb in the medicine. D had not read those articles. **Held:** no breach proven. D met both standards.

---

[e] [1990] 3 All ER 237 (QB) 243.
[f] (1999) 48 BMLR 109 (QB) 114–15.
[g] [2003] EWHC 1134 (QB) [2.D].
[h] (2000) 57 BMLR 178 (QB) 185–86.

Those who offer ***voluntary first-aid services*** must meet the standard of the ordinary skilled first-aider exercising and professing to have the skill of a first-aider trained in accordance with the First Aid Manual.	In *Cattley v St John Ambulance Brigade*,[i] Sean Cattley, C, a young motorcross rider participating in a motor scrambling event at Bedford, was injured when he was thrown off his bike and hit his head directly on the trackside bank and came to rest on his back. He lost consciousness, could not move his legs, was treated trackside by voluntary St John Ambulance officers, D, and taken to hospital. Although C recovered the ability to walk, he suffered permanent spinal damage and residual disabilities. C alleged that D treated him negligently at the scene. **Held:** the standard of care was set by the First Aid Manual, and was met.
A ***midwife*** must meet the standard of a reasonably competent midwife carrying out the functions expected of the post-natal ward of a district general hospital.	In *Spencer v NHS North West*,[j] C alleged that the midwifery staff at the hospital where she was born failed to suspect that she was developing a streptococcal infection on her first night. Her condition was picked up too late to avoid very serious long-term disability. **Held:** the standard of care was met. The fact that C was unsettled and crying, when less than a day old, was not a reason to suspect serious infection.
A person who ***undertakes medically-related tasks, but who does not hold himself out as having any medical qualifications or expertise***, will be judged according to the standard of a reasonable person without medical qualifications or expertise who undertakes such a task.	In *Philips v William Whiteley Ltd*,[k] a jeweller, D, conducted an ear-piercing operation for Ms Philips, C, at a department store's jewellery department. A septic abscess formed on C's ear. D had cleaned his instruments before he arrived, and then passed them through a flame to disinfect. His instruments were found to be in a septic condition. **Held:** D met the standard of a reasonable jeweller undertaking a minor surgical operation within the limitations of what antiseptic measures could be taken in a department store, and was not required to meet the standard of a doctor or surgeon. Goddard J said: '[i]f a person wants to ensure that the operation of piercing her ears is going to be carried out with that proportion of skill that a Fellow of the Royal College of Surgeons would use, *she must go to a surgeon*'.

[i] (QB, 25 Nov 1988, Judge Prosser QC).
[j] [2012] EWHC 2142 (QB) [17]. See too: *Croft v Heart of England NHS Fndn Trust* [2012] EWHC 1470 (QB) [22].
[k] [1938] 1 All ER 566 (KB), quote at 569 (emphasis added).

The notion of graduated specialisms applies equally in other professional contexts. For example, in *Fraser v Bolt Burdon Claims*, the court noted that, 'in the legal context, it is no proper criticism of a solicitor in general practice that he has not the advocacy skills or specialist experience of a barrister', and that '[e]ach professional person falls to be judged by the standards of his fellows in his particular profession, not by the standards of … a more specialised branch of his profession than that of which he is part'.[15]

[15] [2009] EWHC 2906 (QB) [52].

A caveat

The fact that D does not need to attain the standard of care expected of a more skilled part of his profession may be offset by the fact that those of more limited expertise may be required to refer C to one with greater expertise, in order to attain the requisite standard of care (per *Hardman v Riddell*[16]).

> In *Brooks v Home Office*,[17] facts previously, **held:** breach proven. Given that the consultant in charge of the obstetric unit at Holloway was away at the time that the pregnancy scan was done, and given that the doctor left in charge had limited expertise in reading scans, 'the only prudent course ... was to refer [C] to a specialist so as to provide the obstetrical expertise which should have been available to her'. A civilian hospital would have had greater resources to deal with the problem. (However, causation failed, and so negligence ultimately failed.)

Whilst the medical environment in which D's conduct is being performed has, occasionally, given rise to a lower standard of care than would apply in a 'superior' environment, that variation in the standard can also be overcome by C, by relying upon a duty-to-refer, under the so-called 'locality rule' (discussed below).

A tension between judicial viewpoints?

Several English judges have exhorted that a check **must** be kept on the standard of care in the professional context, so as not to move the law of negligence towards strict liability, by treating any less-than-perfect conduct by a professional D as a breach.

For example, as Bingham LJ reiterated in the auditing case of *Eckersley v Binnie & Partners*, '[t]he law does not require of a professional man that he be a paragon, combining the qualities of polymath and prophet'.[18] In general terms, the classic statement by Taschereau J from the Supreme Court of Canada continues to resonate: '[c]ases necessarily occur in which, in spite of exercising the greatest caution, accidents supervene and for which nobody can be held responsible ... Perfection is a standard required by law no more for a doctor than for other professional men, lawyers, engineers, architects, etc' (per *Cardin v La Cité de Montréal*[19]). Professional Ds 'are not insurers' of a good outcome (per *Bull v Devon AHA*[20]), and they do not 'warrant a perfect result' (*Wilsher v Essex AHA*[21]). In *Phelps v Hillingdon LBC*, the House of Lords too recognised the care that should be taken, when adjudging whether a standard of care was breached: '[t]he recognition of the duty of care does not of itself impose unreasonably high standards ... The difficulties of the tasks involved, and of the circumstances under which people have to work in this area, must also be borne fully in mind. The professionalism, dedication and standards of those engaged in the provision of educational services are such that cases of liability for negligence will be exceptional'.[22]

Nevertheless, some judicial statements, especially in other jurisdictions, have cast the standard imposed upon a professional D very highly indeed.

[16] [2004] EWHC 1691 (QB) [64] (no breach). [17] (1999) 48 BMLR 109 (QB) 114–15.

[18] (1988) 18 Con LR 1 (CA) 80 (Bingham LJ). Applied since, to hold a professional D not negligent, e.g.: *Barings plc (in liq) v Coopers & Lybrand (a firm)* [2003] EWHC 1319 (Ch) [578]–[579].

[19] [1961] SCR 655 (SCC), 29 DLR (2d) 492 (SCC) 494 (Taschereau J).

[20] (1989) 22 BMLR 79, 113, [1993] 4 Med LR 117 (CA) (Dillon LJ).

[21] [1987] QB 730 (CA) 747 (Mustill LJ). [22] [2001] 2 AC 619 (HL) 655 (Lord Slynn).

The comparative corner: Vignettes from other jurisdictions

Ireland: in *Dunne v National Maternity Hosp*,[23] the standard of care applying to doctors was said to be very high, for two reasons: '[t]he complete dependence of patients on the skill and care of medical attendants, and the gravity from their point of view of a failure in such care, makes it undesirable and unjustifiable to accept as a matter of law a lax or permissive standard of care for the purpose of assessing what is and is not medical negligence'.

Australia: in *Bankstown Foundry Pty Ltd v Braistina*,[24] McHugh JA remarked that, '[t]hroughout the common law of negligence ... the standard of care required of a defendant has moved close to the border of strict liability'. This statement drew criticism from the High Court of Australia, on appeal, for its 'tendency to mislead',[25] but it was subsequently approved by a differently-constituted NSWCA (in *Inverell MC v Pennington*[26]).

The limits of the *Bolam* standard of care

§6.7 The *Bolam* standard of care does not apply where a professional D commits an act or omission in circumstances where he is exercising *no* professional judgment and skill whatsoever. The concept of the 'professional D' extends beyond 'the learned professions'.

Where D's task is not one which requires some special skill, then the standard required of D must accord with that which would be reasonably expected of 'the person on the Clapham bus'. However, the line between professional and non-professional judgment can be quite blurred.

> In *Kelly v Board of Governors of St Laurence's Hospital*,[27] nurses employed at the hospital, D, failed to accompany an epileptic in-patient, C, to the toilet, at a time when C was taken off all medication preparatory to tests. The question arose as to whether that decision not to accompany C was a matter of professional judgment, or a custodial matter 'where the standard of care is much more the standard of the ordinary individual than such as might be dictated by medical practice'. **Held (2:1):** the *Bolam* medical standard was applicable.

The application of the *Bolam* standard depends upon D's exercising a 'special skill', albeit that just who possesses special skill has been the subject of some division of judicial opinion. According to *Carty v Croydon BC*, '[t]he phrase "professional person" is not a term of art'.[28] To fall within that phrase, the guidance in *M v Newham LBC*[29] was cited in *Carty* as relevant: '[t]hose who engage professionally ... bring to their task skill and expertise, the product partly of training and partly of experience, which ordinary uninstructed members of the public are bound to lack'.[30] Apart from medical Ds (the subject of *Bolam* itself), some callings in life comfortably fit within that phrase, for example:

[23] As observed in: [1989] IR 91 (SC) 110 (Finlay CJ). [24] [1985] Aust Torts Reports ¶80–713 (NSWCA) 69,127.
[25] *Bankstown Foundry Pty Ltd v Braistina* (1986) 160 CLR 301 (HCA) 307 (Mason, Wilson and Dawson JJ).
[26] [1993] Aust Torts Rep ¶81–234 (NSWCA) 62 406 (Clarke JA). [27] [1988] IR 402 (SC).
[28] [2005] EWCA Civ 19, [2005] 1 WLR 2312, [45].
[29] Reported as part of the litigation: *X (Minors) v Bedfordshire CC* [1995] 2 AC 633.
[30] [1995] 2 AC 633 (HL) 666 (Sir Thomas Bingham MR).

- architects (*Nye Saunders & Partners (a firm) v Alan E Bristow*[31]);
- chartered surveyors and property consultants who perform valuations and give property investment advice (*Capita Alternative Fund Services (Guernsey) Ltd v Drivers Jonas (a firm)*[32]);
- project managers of a construction project (*Royal Brompton Hosp NHS Trust v Frederick A Hammond*[33]);
- educational psychologists, teachers and those who provide special educational needs for vulnerable children (*Barrett v Enfield BC*[34]);
- social workers (per *M v Newham LBC*[35]);
- education officers who decide whether a child is to be kept at a school or moved to another educational environment (*Carty v Croydon BC*[36]).

However, the *Bolam* standard applies more widely than just to the 'learned professions', for example:

- tree inspectors who inspect premises to ensure that trees are reasonably safe for visitors (*Bowen v National Trust*[37]);
- football referees (*Vowles v Evans*[38]);
- window lock installers and technicians (*Adams v Rhymney Valley DC*[39]).

In *Adams*, this issue split the members of the Court of Appeal. The key question was whether it was negligent to provide a tenanted property with lockable windows with removable keys, rather than with push-button locks which could be opened by a child. Question – was that issue to be determined in accordance with what 'the person on the Clapham bus' would regard as reasonable, or by what a window lock designer would regard as reasonable? In other words, were the characteristics of the particular D to be taken into account? According to the majority, the *Bolam* standard of care applied. Morritt LJ said that the *Bolam* standard 'does not depend on the actual possession of the relevant qualification. Emergencies apart, if the act in question can only safely be done by a person with the necessary skill to do it, then the standard of care to be shown is that appropriate to one possessing that skill'; whilst Sir Christopher Staughton agreed that: '[t]he key question is whether the *Bolam* test still applies, although the particular D did not in fact have the qualifications of a professional in the relevant field of activity ... [however] the *Bolam* test is not the monopoly of the expert'.[40]

However, Sedley LJ dissented, and considered that the *Bolam* standard had no application in the case: 'no design skills at all were applied to the choice of window lock ... The reason why the test [and *Bolam* standard] has no relevance to this case is that its purpose is to enable the court to determine whether a person professing and purporting to exercise a particular skill has exercised it with sufficient competence to escape a charge of negligence. In the present case, the problem is that nobody in the council purported to exercise the relevant design skill ... [D], which has failed altogether to set about exercising a professional skill, cannot expect to be judged by the court as if it had exercised it: the court cannot proceed as if an educated choice was made, when it knows that it was not'.[41]

[31] (1987) 37 BLR 97 (CA) 103 (Stephen Brown LJ). [32] [2011] EWHC 2336 (Comm).
[33] [2000] EWHC Technology 39. [34] [2001] 2 AC 550, [1999] 3 WLR 79 (HL).
[35] See: *X (Minors) v Bedfordshire CC* [1995] 2 AC 633 (HL) 666 (Sir Thomas Bingham MR).
[36] [2005] EWCA Civ 19, [2005] 1 WLR 2312. [37] [2011] EWHC 1992 (QB). [38] [2003] EWCA Civ 318.
[39] [2001] PNLR 4 (CA). [40] *ibid*, [42] and [57]. [41] *ibid*, [15]–[16].

Although the *Adams* principle has not been widely applied since, and the division in the Court of Appeal's reasoning notwithstanding, Mackay J noted, in the tree inspector case (*Bowen v National Trust*), that the principle 'is now well established'.[42] The issue is equally significant when the *Bolam* test of proving breach is called upon – as discussion in Chapter 7 will demonstrate.

Age

§6.8 The standard of care which the law imposes upon a child, D, is suppressed to the standard expected of a reasonable or 'ordinary' child of the same age as D.

The relevant standard, where a child's behaviour is under scrutiny for negligence, is that of 'an ordinarily prudent and reasonable child' of the same age (per *Mullin v Richards*[43]). The relevant standard is not that of either a 'paragon of prudence' or a 'scatterbrained child' (per Salmon LJ in *Gough v Thorne*[44]).

A child, for this purpose, is anyone below the age of majority – in *Mullin* itself, the child was 15 years old; and in *Foskett v Mistry*,[45] the child was 16.5; and a somewhat suppressed standard of care was still applied in both cases.

It will be recalled from Chapter 2 that very young children do not owe any duty of care to D (per *Carmarthenshire CC v Lewis*[46]), nor to themselves where contributory negligence is at stake ('a judge should only find a child guilty of contributory negligence if he or she is of such an age as to be expected to take precautions for his or her own safety': per *Gough v Thorne*[47]). Hence, the principle under discussion in this section is only pertinent to those children who are of sufficient age to be found liable in negligence.

It follows that, for a child to fall below the suppressed standard of care and to be found negligent, that child's conduct 'must be careless to a very high degree' (per *Mullin*). That degree of carelessness might be shown by the child's breaking the rules or acting beyond the norms of a game; or acting quite recklessly towards C (in the sense of showing a very high degree of carelessness) (per *Orchard v Lee*[48]). However, in these leading cases, there was **no** breach of duty in either, given where the standard of care was set.

In *Mullin v Richards*,[49] two 15-year-old school friends, Teresa Mullin (C) and Heidi Richards (D), were sitting side by side at a desk at their school in Birmingham, and were playing around at the end of their maths class, hitting each other's white plastic 30 cm rulers as though in a play sword fight. One of the rulers snapped, a sharp piece of plastic went into C's eye, and she lost all sight in that eye. C sued D and the Birmingham CC (as the relevant education authority) in negligence. The maths teacher was held not liable in negligence for any failure to supervise. Re the claim against D, the standard against which D's behaviour should be judged was that of an ordinary, reasonable 15-year-old schoolgirl, who would have appreciated that there was some risk of injury involved in using plastic rulers as though they were swords – and Heidi met that standard. In *Orchard v Lee*,[50]

[42] [2011] EWHC 1992 (QB) [7].

[43] [1997] EWCA Civ 2662, [1998] 1 WLR 1304, 1308–9, and affirmed in: *Dunnage v Randall* [2015] EWCA Crim 673, [123].

[44] [1966] 1 WLR 1387 (CA) 1391. [45] [1984] RTR 1 (CA). [46] [1955] AC 549 (HL).

[47] [1966] 1 WLR 1387 (CA) 1390 (Lord Denning MR). [48] [2009] EWCA Civ 295, [2009] PIQR P16, [10]–[11].

[49] At first instance, the trial judge held Heidi, D, liable in negligence, but that Teresa, C, was liable for 50% CN.

[50] [2009] EWCA Civ 295, quote at [19].

Mr Lee, 13, D, and his friend, 13, were playing a game of tag in a courtyard and in part of a walkway reserved for a playing area, when D, running back and taunting his friend, collided with Miss Orchard, C, a lunchtime assistant supervisor at the school, causing C injury. D was playing a game of tag within a designated play area; he was not breaking any rules in playing the game, because running in those areas was not prohibited; and he was not acting to any significant degree beyond the norms of that game. Hence, D met the standard of care required: '13-year-old boys will be 13-year-old boys who will play tag. They will run backwards and they will taunt each other. If that is what they are doing and they are not breaking any rules, they should not be held liable in negligence. Parents and schools are there to control children, and it would be a retrograde step to visit liability on a 13-year-old for simply playing a game in the area where he was allowed to do so'. It might have been different if D had been 'playing tag close to traffic in the street'.

Reasons for, and ramifications of, the legal approach

In *Mullin*,[51] the justifications for a suppressed standard for children were derived from the High Court of Australia's majority decision in *McHale v Watson*:[52]

i. children often behave in unpremeditated and impulsive ways, and are not yet of an age to have an adult's realisation of danger or wariness – that requires 'a degree of sense and circumspection which nature ordinarily withholds till life has become less rosy';
ii. children may consider something to be an interesting and exciting activity, but which is in fact dangerous (in *McHale*, e.g., the court took judicial notice 'that the ordinary boy of 12 suffers from a feeling that a piece of wood and a sharp instrument have a special affinity');
iii. it is always open to Parliament to overrule the common law on this point, and raise the standard of care expected of children – but unless it does, children (and adults) 'must accept, as they go about in society, the risks from which ordinary care on the part of others will not suffice to save them. One such risk is that boys of 12 may behave as boys of 12; and that, sometimes, is a risk indeed'.

In *McHale v Watson*, D was a 12-year-old boy who sharpened a metal instrument, and then later threw it at a post, expecting it to embed in the post. The metal shard glanced off the post, or else missed it altogether, and hit C, a young girl, in the eye. C lost her eye as a result. **Held (3:1):** no breach occurred.

In addition, the lower standard of care to be applied to a child accords with the lower standard which also applies to recreational endeavours involving horseplay between participants (discussed shortly) – and, in that regard, the law achieves a welcome consistency. This was pointed out in *Orchard v Lee*,[53] where Waller LJ discussed the case of *Blake v Galloway*,[54] in which two 15-year-olds, C and D, engaged in some 'mucking around', eventually causing injury to C's eye. The standard of care imposed in such cases is suppressed, such that only conduct that amounts to 'recklessness, or a very high degree of carelessness' will amount to a breach. Whilst the child cases of *McHale* and *Mullin* were (somewhat surprisingly) not cited in *Blake v Galloway*, it was entirely coincidental with *Blake* that a lower standard of care should be applied to children's acts or omissions – because those cases 'demonstrate consistently with *Blake* that, for a child to be held culpable, the conduct must be careless to a very high degree' (according to *Orchard v Lee*[55]).

[51] [1997] EWCA Civ 2662, [1998] 1 WLR 1304 (CA). [52] [1996] HCA 13, (1996) 115 CLR 199, [9]–[10].
[53] [2009] EWCA Civ 295, [10]. [54] [2004] EWCA Civ 814. [55] [2009] EWCA Civ 295, [2009] ELR 178, [11].

The legal ramification, of course, is to render it less likely that C, the person injured by the child's acts or omissions, will recover compensation. The young girl who lost her eye in *McHale* could not recover damages for her injury, and nor could the teaching supervisor in *Orchard* – despite the courts' expressed 'sympathy' for their predicaments. Should the law change, in that regard?

The law reform corner: A vignette from Ireland

Recognition that children may escape liability: The Irish LRC[56] considered that the suppressed standard of care that applied to children would make a difference to the legal outcome (i.e., child D would not be negligent, whereas an adult D would be) in limited cases – and asked whether the lower standard of care should be changed by statute:

> 'Our [common] law could, of course, impose an adult standard of care in such instances and hold the child liable. But it may be argued that to do so would offend against the principle of justice, since the law would thus require the child to act according to a standard beyond his or her capacities. However attractive this may be as a pragmatic solution, we consider that it should not be accepted because of its injustice.'

Redress by statute? The Irish LRC considered that Parliament should intervene, and create a legislative remedy for the unfortunate road-user C who is injured by a child D, in the case of that child's *negligent driving*:

> 'society as a whole should bear the responsibility of compensating victims of injury involving motor vehicles on the roads where the driver of the car causing the injury is a child, and by reason only of his or her particular age, mental development and experience is free from liability which would otherwise attach if the adult standard of care were to apply. For this very small band of cases, we recommend that there be established a fund for compensation to be paid for by the State'.

Conditions for liability: The Fund would apply to provide compensation to C where three conditions were met:

(a) The Fund would relate only to injuries on the road where the driver of a motor vehicle was < 16;

(b) Recourse to the Fund would not be possible where the child was found liable in negligence or, conversely, where the child was found not to have been liable in negligence in cases where, applying the adult standard of care, no liability would have been involved;

(c) If someone other than child D is liable for C's injury, that party, and not the Fund, should compensate C.

Outcome: This legislative proposal was never enacted by the Irish Parliament.

Objective or subjective?

§6.9 English law is presently unsettled as to whether child D's behaviour is to be compared with that of an ordinary child of similar age – or with a child who has a similar experience, development and intelligence to that child D.

[56] *Liability in Tort of Minors and the Liability of Parents for Damage Caused by Minors* (Rep 17, 1985) 58.

Of course, the latter option would render the enquiry a subjective, rather than an objective, test – and indeed, the subjective approach was suggested by the Australian case of *McHale v Watson*.[57] Owen J stated that, 'the standard by which [the child's] conduct is to be measured is ... that reasonably to be expected of a child of the same age, intelligence and experience' – which certainly imputed a subjective component.

However, that notion has seemingly been dismissed in English law. In *Mullin v Richards*,[58] Waller LJ specifically 'questioned' (i.e., doubted) the use of the term, 'intelligence', in Owen J's statement in *McHale*, and thereafter referred to the requisite standard as being that of 'an ordinary, reasonable 15-year-old schoolgirl' – with no reference to D's intelligence or experience at all. This construction in *Mullin* of the relevant standard applicable to child D was consistent with earlier English authority, which had appeared to endorse the objective approach too. As the Irish LRC explained,[59] in *Yachuk v Oliver Blais Co Ltd*, the Privy Council (on appeal from Canada) favoured 'the objective view of the child's age alone (rather than his intelligence and experience as well)', and that objective approach was favoured in other cases such as *Gough v Thorne* ('the court, in exempting [the child] from any fault under this test, had no need to consider the subjective approach').

Hence, the subjective approach towards the standard of care expected of a child appears to have no modern support in English case law. However, the Commonwealth position is mixed, or to the contrary.

The comparative corner: **Relevant Commonwealth vignettes**

Australia: subsequent to *McHale v Watson*[60] (where a subjective approach appeared to be contemplated), there was division of opinion in some lower courts, as to the appropriate standard which the majority's judgment represented. In judicial consideration of the subject in 2012, the Western Australian Court of Appeal said somewhat confusingly, in *Town of Port Hedland v Hodder*,[61] that, '[t]he decision of the majority in *McHale v Watson* might be summarised (with some risk of generalisation) in the proposition that the standard of care expected of children ... is subjective in the sense that it takes account of their age and development, and the degree of foresight and prudence that might be expected of a child of like age, but objective in the sense that the child is expected to conform to the standards of behaviour reasonably expected of children of that age and development generally'.

Canada: the subjective approach appears to have been favoured in Canada. In *McEllistrum v Etches* (SCC),[62] Kerwin CJ stated that, 'it is a question for the jury in each case whether the infant exercised the care to be expected from a child of like age, intelligence and experience'. In *Ottosen v Kasper*,[63] this was described as a 'foundation case' for the principles for assessing the negligence of a child. More recently, in *Hixon-Gause v Roberts*,[64] the subjective approach was again preferred, endorsing the comments in *Bourne v Anderson*:[65] 'in referring to the care to be expected "from a child of like age, intelligence

[57] [1996] HCA 13, (1996) 115 CLR 199 (HCA) [6]. [58] [1997] EWCA Civ 2662, [1998] 1 WLR 1304 (CA) 1309.
[59] *Liability in Tort of Minors and the Liability of Parents for Damage Caused by Minors* (Rep 17, 1985) fn 61.
[60] [1996] HCA 13, (1996) 115 CLR 199 (HCA). [61] [2012] WASCA 212, [193]. [62] [1956] 5 SCR 787 (SCC) 793.
[63] [1986] BCJ No 139, [4]. [64] [2003] BCSC 874, [40]. [65] [1997] BCJ No 915, [59]–[60].

and experience", *McEllistrum* was referring to the reasonable or prudent child, and to an objective standard of care. The subjective factors, of the particular child's age, intelligence, and experience, are only relevant to the fixing of that standard of care [which is] the conduct to be expected of a 7 year and 4 month old child having the same intelligence and experience as Geordie'.

The standard, whether C or D

§6.10 Whether the child's behaviour is being judged as one who has been contributorily negligent, or as one who has negligently inflicted injury upon C, the same suppressed standard of care applies.

Very frequently, it is the child's behaviour as *claimant*, where the standard of care is most relevant, i.e., where an allegation of the defence of contributory negligence has been made against that child, for being careless of his own well-being, and for bringing about his own injuries in some way (per Chapter 10). The same suppressed standard of care continues to apply. In determining whether the child was contributorily negligent, it was necessary to judge what he did against the standards to be expected of a similarly-aged child.

In *Toropdar v D*,[66] a child, 10, C, was playing a game with friends in which they tried to find a hidden object. He found the object and ran excitedly out into the road, from behind a bus, and collided with Mr Toropdar's, D's, car, which was being driven within the speed limit down the street. C suffered serious injuries when flung onto the bonnet and then onto the road. C had not stopped or looked in D's direction from his concealed position behind the bus. **Held:** C was contributorily negligent (33%). Being 10, C was of an age where he could be reasonably be expected to take precautions for his own safety; and to appreciate the dangers involved in running from behind a bus into a city street, in contravention of road rules – but, '[a]t the same time he could not be expected to have the same ingrained approach to safety and self-preservation as an adult or even a teenager'.

Of course, anything said about a suppressed standard of care, in relation to a child who is contributorily negligent, is dicta only, where the standard of care expected of *a child D* is concerned. Nevertheless, there is a clear alignment in English law between the standard of care expected of a child, whether C or D.

Disability (physical or mental)

The standard of care expected of D at law depends upon whether or not D was aware of his disability.

Non-awareness of the condition

§6.11 Where D suffers from a disability (e.g., a medical condition) of which he was unaware, and of which he could not reasonably have been aware, the standard of care is suppressed to that of a reasonable D who is unaware that he was suffering from that condition.

[66] [2009] EWHC 2997 (QB), quote at [13] (Clarke J).

This proposition has been set, in English law, by *Mansfield v Weetabix Ltd.*[67] The justification is that to apply a purely objective standard (e.g., the ordinary reasonable driver) that does not take account of a medical condition of which D was unaware, would render D strictly liable. That was not a fair or just outcome. In such cases, given the suppression of the standard of care, D is unlikely to be found liable for breach.

Hence, what matters is whether D knew, or ought to have known, of his disability. If not, the standard is reduced. If so, the standard is the usual objective standard of a reasonable driver, etc. The infirmity that gives rise to D's loss of control or incapacity may be sudden, or it may be gradual – either condition suffices to invoke the *Mansfield* principle, provided that D is unaware of it, and should not reasonably have been aware of it.

In *Mansfield v Weetabix*, Mr Tarleton, D, was a lorry driver for Weetabix. On the day of the accident, he was driving a 38-ton lorry, and failed to take a sharp bend in the village near Stoke-on-Trent, and crashed into a shop belonging to Mr and Mrs Mansfield, C, causing extensive damage. D did not know that he suffered from the condition, but he had malignant insulinoma which resulted in a hypoglycaemic state in which the brain is starved of glucose and unable to function properly. D had a propensity to suffer from blackouts; he would recover from the blackouts but was completely unaware of anything having happened; D's wife knew of his condition, but had concealed it from her husband because she did not wish to worry him. D did not have much to eat on the day, which probably helped to induce that state by lowering his blood sugar level. D had been driving erratically before the accident happened, and he could not remember anything of the journey between 1.00pm when he started off, and at 3.40pm when the accident happened. D had died prior to trial. **Held:** no breach proven. A person with D's condition commonly did not appreciate that his ability was impaired, and D was no exception. The standard of care which D was obliged to show was that of a reasonably competent driver unaware that he was or might be suffering from a condition that impaired his ability to drive.

Prior to *Mansfeld*, there had been another example of the standard of care being suppressed where D was not aware of his infirmity, and nor could he reasonably have suspected that he was afflicted with that infirmity (*Jones v Dennison*[68]), where negligence was not proven either.

The reasoning, and the ramifications. To apply the objective standard of the ordinary reasonable driver to Mr Tarleton's grave situation, of which he had no knowledge, 'would be to impose strict liability. But that is not the law' (held Leggatt LJ in *Mansfield v Weetabix*).[69]

Of course, if 'strict liability' means that D should not be liable for a condition of which he is unaware, then that is a supportable proposition. On the other hand, if 'strict liability' means to impose a standard of care upon D which is impossible for him to achieve, and which is unattainable in all the circumstances, then the law regularly imposes such a form of strict liability – inexperienced Ds may often find themselves in that position (discussed below). Yet, in *Mansfield*, the Court of Appeal firmly approved of the proposition that an inexperienced D should not benefit from a suppressed standard, because there, an inexperienced D is aware of his limitations. Mr Tarleton was not.

The suppression of the standard of care, per the *Mansfield* principle, means that C will likely not recover. Hence, unless C is insured for the damage or injury that he suffers at D's hands, C will go uncompensated. As in other instances in which the standard of care has been suppressed (see discussion of D's age, above), the idea was floated by Leggatt LJ that it was always open

[67] [1998] 1 WLR 1263 (CA) 1267–68. [68] [1971] RTR 174 (CA). [69] [1998] 1 WLR 1263 (CA) 1268.

to Parliament to reverse the law and hold D to a reasonable standard of care. In the meantime, however, D 'was in no way to blame, he was not negligent'.[70] The Irish High Court agreed with this view, in *Counihan v Bus Atha Cliath-Dublin Bus*. It noted that most drivers are insured, and a state compensation fund is available for harm done by the uninsured driver, so that 'it is, perhaps, somewhat surprising that a category of persons [C, in a *Mansfield* scenario] who are injured due to no fault of their own are, as a result of the state of the law, deprived of appropriate compensation ... [but] a change in that law is a policy decision which is a matter for the Oireachtas'.[71]

Awareness of the condition

§6.12 Where D suffers from a disability (physical or mental), of which he is aware, then the standard of care expected of D is not suppressed at law.

Although this proposition has been stated in the context of D as a road-user, there is no reason that it should be restricted to that scenario.

Essentially, if D was indeed alert to the fact that his ability was impaired, or if he ought to have known of his infirmity, but continued to act anyway, then the *Mansfield* principle has no application to D at all. Just because D may have been impaired mentally or physically, or have lost some partial control of his movements and/or judgment at the time of the accident, is not enough to bring D within the protection of that principle.

In *Das Intl Ltd v Manley*,[72] D suffered a serious car accident, in which he suffered a mild concussion. D could not remember much of what happened after his accident (including his own subsequent actions towards C, another road-user). That scenario was expressly distinguished from *Mansfield*, and D's actions towards C were negligent because they fell below the standard of a reasonable road-user (albeit, a road-user acting in emergency conditions). In *Roberts v Ramsbottom*,[73] D was involved in a car accident when he suffered a cerebral haemorrhage/stroke. D had awareness of his surroundings and of the traffic conditions during the episode, and tried to manipulate the car's controls, but collided with a stationary van. D drove off and then crashed into C's vehicle, causing injury. The Court of Appeal in *Mansfield* endorsed the outcome in *Roberts* that D was negligent, noting that the standard of a reasonable driver should apply, if D continued to drive when he was unfit to, and when he should have appreciated his unfitness to drive, but deliberately decided to continue. D's actions fell below that standard.

If a driver injures a pedestrian or passenger, because he lacks good eyesight or hearing, or has some other physical infirmity that affects his capacity to drive, the law still insists that D meet the standard of a reasonable driver. The infirmities do not suppress the standard expected of D in any respect. That much was made plain, in dicta, in *Nettleship v Weston*,[74] and has been applied in tragic case law since.

In *C v Burcombe*,[75] Mr Burcombe, D, aged 70, had stopped his car at a layby to fix a flat tyre. At the time, D was under medication for heart disease, and though declared fit to drive, he had been warned by his GP not to attempt strenuous activity. In changing the wheel on his car, this degree

[70] *ibid*, 1268. [71] [2005] IEHC 51, [2005] 2 IR 436. The Oireachtas is the legislature of the Irish Republic.
[72] [2002] EWCA Civ 1638. [73] [1980] 1 WLR 823 (QB).
[74] [1971] 2 QB 691 (CA) 699, citing: *Richley v Faull* [1965] 1 WLR 1454 (QB) and *Watson v Whitney* [1966] 1 WLR 37 (CA).
[75] [2003] CLY 3030 (CC Watford, 27 May 2002).

of activity brought on a severe heart attack. Nevertheless, he got back into the car and drove off, pulling away from the layby very slowly in first gear, with his hazard lights flashing and wearing no seatbelt. D then lost control, and veered onto the opposite side of the road, and collided with two vehicles in succession, killing both drivers and one passenger, C. D also died of the heart attack. His estate denied liability. **Held:** breach proven. Having driven off with at least some awareness that he was very unwell and unfit to drive, that meant that D was aware of his condition, and could not rely on *Mansfield*. D also failed to heed his GP's advice, another instance of not meeting the standard of reasonable care.

Inexperience

Professional and non-professional Ds treated alike

§6.13 The inexperience of D, who is undertaking a *non-professional* activity, does not suppress the standard of care which the law expects of D ('the *Nettleship* rule'). The inexperience of D, who is undertaking a *professional* activity, does not suppress the standard of care either; D's conduct is to be compared with the standard of an ordinary skilled and experienced D who is professing to exercise that professional skill ('the *Wilsher* rule').

The '*Nettleship* rule' stems from *Nettleship v Weston*,[76] where it was held that a learner driver was held to the same standard of care as that of a reasonably competent driver.

In *Nettleship v Weston*, Mr Nettleship, C, agreed to give a friend's wife, Mrs Weston, D, some driving lessons. Before taking on the responsibility, C satisfied himself that the car was insured against risk of injury to a passenger. They negotiated two lessons successfully. However, during the third, D was holding the steering wheel and controlling the pedals, whilst C was moving the gear lever. D failed to straighten up after turning left, and panicked. The car mounted the kerb and collided with a lamp post. D was convicted of driving without due care and attention. C was injured in the collision. **Held (at trial):** D not negligent, on the basis that the defence of *volenti* applied. **Held (CA, 2:1):** breach/negligence proven. *Volenti* could not apply, given the check that C carried out before doing the lessons, that showed expressly that he did not consent to run the risk of injury which might occur through D's lack of skill. Further, D did not meet the standard of a reasonable driver.

As Lord Denning MR, of the majority, memorably put it, '[t]he learner-driver may be doing his best, but his incompetent best is not good enough'. (Salmon LJ dissented, preferring the view that a learner driver should be judged by the standard of a reasonable learner driver.) Although subsequent cases (such as *Das Intl Ltd v Manley*[77]) have noted that the *Nettleship* rule applies '[i]n the context of driving', there is no rational basis for limiting the rule to inexperienced drivers alone. Essentially, this is an instance where the law imposes a standard of care which the inexperienced D may not possibly be able to achieve.

The professional D is in the same position. Although stated much earlier (in 1952, per *Jones v Manchester Corp*),[78] the principal authority for that proposition is the 1987 Court of Appeal decision in *Wilsher v Essex AHA*.[79] Both cases concerned medical Ds, but again, as with the inexperienced D, the principle appropriately extends to all professional Ds.

[76] [1971] 2 QB 691 (CA) 699. [77] [2002] EWCA Civ 1638, [15].
[78] [1952] 2 QB 852 (CA), with quotes in the following case description at 871 and 867 (Denning LJ).
[79] [1987] QB 730 (CA), with quotes in the following case description at 773–74 (Glidewell LJ).

In *Wilsher v Essex AHA*, a doctor, D, 'a fairly junior doctor of limited experience',[80] mistakenly inserted a catheter into a vein, instead of in the umbilical artery, of Martin Wilsher, C, who was born a very premature baby. The aim had been to measure arterial blood oxygen levels. The mistake meant that the monitor gave a lower reading of blood oxygen levels (reading venal blood), so that, as a result, C was 'supersaturated' with oxygen for up to 8–12 hours. It was not actually the insertion of the catheter into a vein instead of an artery which was alleged to be negligent ('it was an error which competent doctors could and from time to time did commit'), but rather, the failure to pick up, from an examination of an X-ray, that the catheter was in the wrong place. C ultimately developed the incurable eye condition, retrolental fibroplasia (RLF), which resulted in blindness, for which supersaturation of oxygen was a possible cause. After inserting the catheter, the junior doctor asked the senior registrar to check what he had done. The registrar did so and failed to see the mistake, he inspected the X-ray with the junior doctor and failed to detect that it was misplaced, and some hours later, when replacing the catheter, did exactly the same thing. **Held:** the junior doctor committed a breach of duty, in mis-reading the X-ray, but not in placing the catheter.

Wilsher went up to House of Lords,[81] but only on the question as to whether the super-saturation of oxygen in the first 30 hours of the patient's life caused or materially contributed to his injury, i.e., blindness (ultimately, it did not). The standard of care expected of the junior inexperienced doctor was not revisited on appeal, and hence, the Court of Appeal approach governs the legal position on this issue.

The justifications for the *Nettleship/Wilsher* rules

Several reasons underpin the view that inexperienced Ds should be held to an often unachievable standard of care, according to judicial reasoning:

i. the rule avoids the haphazardness that could arise if courts had to take the particular experience of D into account. One standard is legally more convenient. In *Nettleship*, Megaw LJ remarked that '[t]he disadvantages of the resulting unpredictability, uncertainty and, indeed, impossibility of arriving at fair and consistent decisions outweigh the advantages [of a variable standard]. The certainty of a general standard is preferable to the vagaries of a fluctuating standard';[82]
ii. as the Singapore High Court has since observed in *Ng Keng Yong v Public Prosecutor*,[83] if the 'indulgence' of a lower standard of care is to be extended to trainees in one area of life, then how can those limits properly be circumscribed? If extended to learner drivers (or a trainee navy officer in that case), why not to every other field of endeavour where trainees operate? Also, why should the standard not also be variable, depending upon 10-years' post-qualification experience, 20-years' experience, etc? The High Court refused to countenance such a variable standard of care, as a matter of policy;

In *Ng Keng Yong v Public Prosecutor*, the acts and omissions of a trainee navy ship officer, D, resulted in a collision and the death of four crew members. The inexperienced navigator had taken control

[80] The trial judge's description, cited at: [1987] QB 730 (CA) 748.

[81] [1988] AC 1074 (HL).

[82] [1971] 2 QB 691 (CA) 707. His Lordship dissented on the issue of quantum, but not on this point of law. More recently, see: *Das Intl Ltd v Manley* [2002] EWCA Civ 1638, [15].

[83] [2004] SGHC 171, [2004] 4 SLR 89, [78]–[79]. The court was certainly not attracted to D's argument that the standard to which she should be held was that she 'took her training seriously'.

of a vessel that was plying in open waters with heavy merchant traffic. Furthermore, once she took the control of the Courageous, she was responsible for the lives and safety of the crew on board. **Held:** breach proven. The court expressly approved of the *Wilsher* rule. D had to be held to the same standard as a reasonably competent and qualified Officer-On-Watch. 'This may seem harsh, but to subject her to a lower standard of care would unfairly place the safety of everyone else around her at risk [of not recovering compensation]'.

iii. all young professionals needed to be treated alike, with a uniform standard of care applying to all of them – Mustill LJ made the point, in *Wilsher*, that doctors are not the only professionals who learn their craft, 'not only from lectures or from watching others perform, but from tackling live clients or customers, and no case was cited to us which suggested that any such variable duty of care was imposed on others in a similar position'.[84] Trainees are similarly held to the standard of a reasonable and experienced solicitor;

iv. the rule assists C, who is damaged by an inexperienced D's conduct, to recover compensation. Suppressing the standard of care, in any scenario, compromises the compensatory function, because breach is less likely to be found. This is even more marked where D is compulsorily insured for the harm which C suffers – as in the case of negligent drivers (per Lord Denning MR in *Nettleship v Weston*). For those, like Fleming, who hold the view that the 'paramount social need for compensating accident victims ... clearly outweighs all competing considerations',[85] this is the strongest argument for a fixed standard that disregards inexperience. A similar point was made by Mustill LJ in *Wilsher*, that to depart from a uniform standard of care would mean that the standard of care which a patient was legally entitled to demand would depend upon the fortunes of 'rostering', and that C's chances of recovery would be far more limited if he was entrusted to the care of a 'complete novice ... (unless perhaps he can point to some fault of supervision in a person further up the hierarchy) than if he has been in the hands of a doctor who has already spent months on the same ward';[86]

v. the *Nettleship/Wilsher* rule, insisting upon the standard of the experienced D, certainly does not condemn junior or inexperienced Ds to a finding of negligence. Some inexperienced Ds *will* be able to clamber over the reasonable threshold of care which the law requires of them. It is not always unattainable.

In *Colwill v Oxford Radcliffe Hosp NHS Trust*,[87] a junior doctor, D, placed an intravenous cannula in the forearm of a patient, C. Unfortunately, a staph infection developed at the site of the cannula, and despite antibiotics, C developed staphylococcal septicaemia and other illnesses which left her hemiplegic, almost blind, and with severe cognitive impairment. The trial judge remarked that this was a case of a junior doctor, 'unschooled in the hospital policy, carrying out a practice to which she had become accustomed on another ward, without any consideration of the discomfort to the patient', a 'poor practice' which a senior doctor at the hospital admitted he was 'not proud' of. **Held:** D's insertion of the cannula at that site, whilst 'undesirable', was not negligent (but breach on the part of another doctor, for failing to administer anti-biotics in a timely manner, was proven). In *Jones v Manchester Corp*,[88] a young and inexperienced house doctor of 5 months post-qualification experience allowed only 10 seconds between injections rather than 30. **Held:** this was 'negligent to a degree which was inexcusable even in an inexperienced person'.

[84] [1987] QB 730 (CA) 750–51.

[85] *Law of Torts* (8th edn, Law Book Co, London, 1992) 111, cited in: *Lindahl Estate v Olsen* [2004] ABQB 639, fn 100.

[86] [1987] QB 730 (CA) 750.

[87] [2007] EWHC 2881 (QB), especially, [40] and [60]–[79].

[88] [1952] 2 QB 852 (CA).

The impact of the *Wilsher* rule

§6.14 As a result of the *Wilsher* rule, an inexperienced professional D must seek guidance from a more senior colleague, if he is 'out of his depth'.

In *Wilsher* itself, both Glidewell LJ and Lord Browne-Wilkinson VC held that, had the junior doctor D not summoned the senior registrar to check the position of the catheter and to check the X-ray, but carried on regardless in administering oxygen to the premature baby C, then D would have fallen below the standard. The Court of Appeal has since noted, in *Marwan v Hillingdon HA*,[89] that for a 'senior house officer of limited experience', there are practical and legal protections available: '[i]f [he] had felt himself out of his depth, he had access to the Registrar on duty or by telephone ... The safeguard against the dangers of his inexperience lay in his own commonsense appreciation of when he was out of his depth and needed more experienced guidance'. If a junior professional fails to take advantage of those steps, he will be negligent.

Furthermore, decisions from elsewhere demonstrate that it is not open for D to argue that the operation or transaction for C was particularly difficult for one who was inexperienced *in that particular procedure*.

The comparative corner: **Inexperienced surgeons**

Scotland: in *Greenhorn v South Glasgow Univ Hosp NHS Trust*,[90] C, a patient, underwent a hysterectomy, and suffered incontinence, due to over-activity of the bladder muscle. C did not respond to physiotherapy, so had a further operation, during which her iliac artery was ruptured by D, a surgeon-in-training, resulting in serious blood loss and neurological injury for C. The evidence was that for obese patients (such as C), the operation was more difficult and hazardous for inexperienced surgeons. **Held:** breach proven. That D was a surgeon-in-training and lacked relevant recent experience did not alter the standard of care; the standard expected of an inexperienced doctor learning a surgical procedure 'was the same as that of an experienced doctor of her grade'.

Canada: in *Miles v Judges*,[91] D, a fully-qualified and experienced surgeon, had performed numerous (about 20) laparoscopic cholecystectomies, mostly by one procedure. D then changed to another procedure for which he was on a 'learning curve'. The operation for patient C went horribly wrong, resulting in C's common iliac artery and iliac vein being pierced. This led to serious irreversible brain damage. **Held:** breach proven. That D was an experienced surgeon who was 'on a learning curve' for this procedure did not reduce the standard of care.

The difficulties with the *Wilsher* rule

Wilsher is a difficult decision. It was a majority decision, in which the two majority members, Mustill and Glidewell LJJ, did not precisely agree what the correct legal effect of inexperience should be, nor did they agree on the outcome of the legal analysis – and where the Vice-Chancellor, Sir Nicolas Browne-Wilkinson, strongly dissented on the legal effect of inexperience altogether. Given these disparities, it is, in hindsight, perhaps a pity that the question of standard of care did not also proceed on appeal to the House of Lords.

89 (CA, 23 May 1996, Waite LJ).

90 [2008] CSOH 128, [109].

91 (1997), 72 ACWS (3d) 378 (Ont Gen Div) [62].

	Mustill LJ	Glidewell LJ	Browne-Wilkinson VC
The relevant standard of care applied to the junior doctor	The standard was that expected of a doctor holding *that particular post* at the hospital – 'different posts make different demands. If ... the structure of hospital medicine envisages that the lower ranks will be occupied by those of whom it would be wrong to expect too much, the risk of abuse by litigious patients can be mitigated, if not entirely eliminated'.[a]	The junior doctor must be judged by the same standard as his more experienced colleagues. If a lower standard applied, then inexperience would frequently be urged as a defence to an action for professional negligence.	A chief hazard of inexperience is that one does not always know the risks which exist. A doctor who has properly accepted a post in a hospital in order to gain necessary experience should only be held liable for acts or omissions which a careful doctor *with his qualifications and experience* would not have done or omitted.
Applying the standard to the facts, was there a breach by the junior doctor, D?	Yes. In spite of his inexperience, D knew that it was possible for a catheter to be accidentally inserted in a vein, for he himself had diagnosed just such an occurrence about a month previously. D did not do enough to guard against that possibility occurring.	No. D sought the advice and help of his superiors when he considered that he needed it, and that met the standard of care expected, even though he may himself have made a mistake. D was not negligent (by contrast, the senior registrar who checked the X-ray and who failed to notice the mistake was negligent).	No. D failed to identify the wrongly inserted catheter, despite the absence of a 'loop' disclosed on the X-rays, because he lacked the experience to look for such loop. Junior doctors of his experience in special care baby units were, in general, unaware of the significance of such loop. Also, he called in his superior doctor to check what he had done, which met the standard of care expected of D.

[a] [1987] QB 730 (CA) 751, 756 (Mustill LJ); 774 (Glidewell LJ); 777 (Browne-Wilkinson VC).

Mustill and Glidewell LJJ formed the majority in *Wilsher*, because on the question of law posed, neither considered that inexperience should reduce the standard of care expected of a junior physician. Since then, English cases have affirmed that the *Wilsher* rule, denying inexperience as a defence in medical negligence claims, is 'well established' (per *E v Castro*[92]); and it has been oft-cited.[93]

[92] [2003] EWHC 2066 (QB) [100].

[93] e.g., *Ryan v East London and City HA* (QB, 2 Feb 2001) [24]; *Skelton v Lewisham and North Southwark HA* [1998] Lloyd's Rep Med 324 (QB); *Dowdie v Camberwell HA* (QB, 1 Jul 1997).

However, the subtle difference between the majority opinions should not be ignored. Glidewell LJ's view was the most draconian, holding an inexperienced doctor to the standards of his experienced colleagues, whereas Mustill LJ held that the standard of care was to be fixed, not by the level of experience, but by *the post held*. This distinction between the two majority views has, occasionally, been glossed over – in *Djemal v Bexley HA*,[94] the court endorsed the view of Mustill LJ that the standard of care depends upon the particular post held, and stated that 'Glidewell LJ was of the same opinion' (which clearly he was not).

In *Djemal v Bexley HA*, a senior houseman, D, was acting as an A&E casualty officer, and had four months' experience in that position. C presented in A&E at 9.00pm with a sore throat and swallowing difficulties. A viral upper respiratory tract infection was diagnosed, whereas C had, in fact, an infection of the epiglottis and obstruction of the airway. C's condition later that night deteriorated, which led to an emergency, and subsequently, hypoxic brain damage and a persistent vegetative state. **Held:** breach proven. D had to meet the standard of an experienced A&E physician, and that was not met in the conduct of the initial A&E diagnosis.

Finally, a brief mention should be made of Browne-Wilkinson VC's dissenting judgment in *Wilsher*. To reiterate, his view was that inexperience **should** suppress the standard of care expected of a professional D. If adopted, that would not necessarily preclude an action by C because of that suppressed standard. Rather, C's recourse in negligence would, instead, be two-fold: (1) a systemic claim in negligence against the hospital which permitted or arranged that staffing in the first place; and/or (2) a negligence claim against the inexperienced D's supervisor/superior, for which negligence the hospital would be vicariously liable. That view has been reflected, for example, in some Canadian decisions. Also, there was earlier English authority that suggested that inexperience on the part of a house officer (a newly qualified hospital resident) **would** reduce the standard of care that could legally be expected, because 'such a position was held by a comparative beginner' (per *Junor v McNicol*[95]). The *Wilsher* dissenting view would also recognise the inherent unfairness of the law's setting an artificial standard which it knows may be utterly out of the reach of junior or inexperienced professionals.

The dissenting view re the *Wilsher* rule

- doctors and other young professionals require 'on-the-job training' – for how else are they to acquire the necessary skills, other than by 'practising' their craft upon 'real patients' and 'real clients'? Per Lord Browne-Wilkinson V-C: 'anyone who ... wishes to obtain specialist skills has to learn those skills by taking a post in a specialist unit ... such doctors cannot in fairness be said to be at fault if, at the start of their time, they lack the very skills which they are seeking to acquire';[a]
- it would be fair to suppress the standard for the inexperienced professional D, when C has alternative legal avenues available by which to recover compensation, *viz*, either (1) C may sue D's employer directly for systemic negligence, because that employer failed to provide sufficiently-qualified and competent staff (per Glidewell LJ), or failed to ensure staff of sufficient skill and experience were on hand to treat C (per Browne-Wilkinson V-C), or failed to provide proper supervision for junior staff (per *Jones v Manchester Corp*[b]). As Mustill LJ explained in *Wilsher*,

[a] [1987] QB 730 (CA) 777.
[b] [1952] 2 QB 852 (CA) 871 (Denning LJ).

[94] [1995] 6 Med LR 269 (QB), quote at 271.
[95] (*The Times*, 26 Mar 1959, HL, Lord Kilmuir LC).

this allegation would 'not require any consideration of the extent to which the individual doctors measured up to the standards demanded of them as individuals, but would focus attention on the performance of the [hospital] as a whole';[c] or (2) C may sue the senior professional employee under whose supervision D, the junior professional, was acting, in negligence; and pursue the employer for vicarious liability;

- setting a lower standard for inexperience did *not* entail any knowledge or consent of the patient, in acknowledging that a lower standard of care would apply. Instead, that C would be left to his alternative avenues, noted above (per Lord Browne-Wilkinson V-C).

[c] [1987] QB 730 (CA) 747.

As mentioned above, Canadian medico-legal jurisprudence has variously supported a departure from the *Wilsher* rule – for reasons that reflect Lord Browne-Wilkinson V-C's concerns – although more recent Canadian case law supports the uniform standard of care:

The comparative corner: Some vignettes of inexperienced doctors in Canada

There were early dicta, from the Supreme Court of Canada, in *Fraser Estate v Vancouver General Hosp*,[96] that junior doctors learning their craft should be held to a lower, more realistic, standard of care. A lower standard of care was set for two inexperienced interns – but even that lower standard of care was not met. They treated a car accident casualty, C, in hospital, took X-rays, inspected them without realising that C had a dislocated neck, and discharged C. C went home and died of his injuries. The interns' conduct fell below even a low standard of care, for they had failed to consult a skilled radiologist in the reading of X-rays. In Ontario, in *Crits & Crits v Sylvester*, the Ontario CA described the standard for doctors as 'that degree of care and skill which could reasonably be expected of a normal, prudent practitioner of the *same experience* and standing'.[97] However, in her leading treatise, *Legal Liability of Doctors and Hospitals in Canada*, Justice Picard noted that 'there is no authority for the use of this comment to support a lower standard for the inexperienced'; and subsequent Ontario judgments have since held the same (per *Dale v Munthali*: 'the reference to a practitioner "of the same experience" does not appear to be supported by the authorities. The standard to be applied to Dr Munthali should not be lower by reason of his inexperience. The standard which could reasonably be expected of a normal, prudent practitioner must be applied'[98]).

To conclude, English jurisprudence shows no signs of departing from the *Wilsher* rule, which prescribes one uniform standard of care for all professional Ds. The rule is supportable, as a matter of policy, because of the consistency and certainty that it provides to C.

[96] [1952] 2 SCR 36 (SCC) 46.

[97] [1956], 1 DLR 502 (CA) 508, affd: [1956] SCR 991, (SCC) (emphasis added), and cited in, e.g.: *Lindahl Estate v Olsen* [2004] ABQB 639, [100].

[98] (1977), 16 OR (2d) 532 (HC) 538.

THE IMPACT (IF ANY) OF THE CIRCUMSTANCES IN WHICH D IS OPERATING

Back in 1946, Asquith LJ remarked, in *Daborn v Bath Tramways Motor Co Ltd*, '[i]n determining whether a party is negligent, the standard of reasonable care is that which is reasonably to be demanded in the circumstances'.[99] In most cases, the circumstances do not, in fact, impact upon the standard of care expected of D; but exceptionally, some do. This section sets out those exceptions.

Before doing so, it is useful to have brief regard to the recent enactment of the Social Action, Responsibility and Heroism Act 2015 (the 'SARAH Act'),[100] which appears to do no more than to reflect the existing common law (at best), or to infuse that common law with unnecessary confusion (at worst). The Act provides as follows:

s 2 The court must have regard to whether the alleged negligence or breach of statutory duty occurred when the person was acting for the benefit of society or any of its members.

s 3 The court must have regard to whether the person, in carrying out the activity in the course of which the alleged negligence or breach of statutory duty occurred, demonstrated a predominantly responsible approach towards protecting the safety or other interests of others.

s 4 The court must have regard to whether the alleged negligence or breach of statutory duty occurred when the person was acting heroically by intervening in an emergency to assist an individual in danger.

As evident from the discussion below, the common law already provides considerable protection to those acting beneficially for society, or who act 'heroically'. To what extent this statute amends these common law principles remains to be seen – but as with the (equally unnecessary) enactment of s 1 of the Compensation Act 2006 (discussed in Chapter 7), it is likely to prompt some quizzical discussion from the judges tasked with deciding negligence cases which feature Ds who fit within the parameters of the statute.

'Agony of the moment' scenarios

§6.15 Where D is conducting himself in emergency, or 'agony of the moment', scenarios (i.e., in 'battle conditions'), the standard of care is suppressed (but is never rendered negligible).

The relevant principles

Emergency or 'agony of the moment' scenarios involve a 'sudden and serious difficulty' for D to cope with, hence the sympathetic standard of care (per *The Ariguani*[101]). Typically, resources (whether human or equipment) may be stretched; and/or hasty judgments necessary on D's part; and/or appropriate resources with which to treat the emergency may be entirely lacking.

A suppressed standard of care in such circumstances has extensive English judicial support. As the Court of Appeal noted in *Das Intl Ltd v Manley*: 'the same standard of care is not expected of persons faced with emergency situations. Such people should behave in a way which is not unreasonable, taking into account the exigencies of their situation. Even where the

99 [1946] 2 All ER 333 (CA) 336. 100 In force on 13 Apr 2015. 101 [1940] 66 Lloyds' List L Rep 244.

situation allows some time for reflection, but still presents a person with a dilemma, the courts will be prepared to make allowances'.[102] The term, 'battle conditions', was coined by Mustill LJ in *Wilsher v Essex AHA*[103] to describe where a medical emergency may overburden the available resources, where the healthcare practitioners are being forced, by circumstances, to do too many things at once, or where they have to take a difficult decision on the spur of the moment. In these scenarios, mistakes 'should not lightly be taken as negligence', according to the Court of Appeal. The statement was actually dicta (i.e., no 'battle conditions' applied during the treatment of a premature baby there). In *Kent v Griffiths*,[104] Lord Woolf also confirmed that, in battle conditions, a court may be more inclined to find that an 'error of judgment' was made, i.e., a mistake which nevertheless satisfied the reasonable standard of care; whilst in *In Re F*, Lord Donaldson stated that, '[i]n an emergency, a doctor has little time to ponder the choices available. He must act in the best interests of his patient, as he sees them, but he can be more readily forgiven if he errs in his judgment'.[105]

It follows that, the more time there is for considered reflection by D, the less likely that the standard will be suppressed, as it will not be a true emergency or 'agony of the moment' scenario at all.

In *Davis v Stena Line Ltd*,[106] Stena, D, owned and operated the 'Koningin Beatrix', a roll-on roll-off ferry that plied the southern Irish Sea route. Mr Davis, C, fell overboard from the ferry due to an accident, and through no fault of anyone. The captain employed by D was not aware of a rescue boat's readiness to launch, and so proceeded with his plan to manoeuvre the ferry close to C, who had spent up to 50 minutes in the water at that point, in order to try and retrieve him through the vessel's bunker door. C drowned. **Held:** The captain was negligent in his attempts to save C. No suppressed standard of care, due to 'agony of the moment', could apply, as the captain's decision to rescue C 'was a calculated decision, reached after discussion with another bridge officer ... although [the captain] was faced with an emergency (i.e. a man overboard), he had plenty of time between the commencement of the emergency and the time that Mr Davis was located, in which to decide on his course of action in effecting the actual rescue ... therefore, the decisions that Captain Williams had to and did make in order to rescue Mr Davis were not 'agony of the moment' decisions'.

Relevant scenarios

Emergency, or 'agony of the moment', scenarios – and the ancillary 'tolerance' for a suppressed standard of care – has been particularly evident in **four** scenarios: 'Good Samaritan' interventions; road-users; emergency services; and in fast-moving recreational endeavours. (The principle also applies, where C is put in peril by D, and contributory negligence against C is being assessed, as discussed separately in Chapter 10.)

Dealing with each in turn:

i. **Good Samaritan interventions.** A 'Good Samaritan' D is one who provides assistance voluntarily to C, who is ill, injured or unconscious as a result of an accident or other emergency, where D has no reasonable expectation of compensation or reward, and has no pre-existing relationship with C. Not only will 'battle conditions' suppress the standard of care, but also, D may be operating in circumstances where he does not profess to have the particular skills and expertise which would best suit the emergency.

[102] [2002] EWCA Civ 1638, [18]. [103] [1987] QB 730 (CA) 749. [104] [2000] EWCA Civ 25, [2001] QB 36 (CA) [46].
[105] [1990] 2 AC 1 (HL) 17. [106] [2005] EWHC 420 (QB), quote at [74].

In *Cattley v St John Ambulance Brigade*,[107] facts previously, **held:** no breach proven. It was conceded that a duty of care was owed to C; but D had acted according to the procedures outlined in the St John First Aid Manual.

Judge Prosser concluded that, although varied, the standard is not negligible: '[a]nyone confronted with an emergency situation is not to be held to the standard of conduct normally applied to one who is not in that situation [although] ... the conduct required is still that of a reasonable person under the circumstances as they would appear to one who was using proper care, and the emergency is to be considered only as one of the circumstances'.

Notably, the standard of care expected of a 'Good Samaritan' was **not** suppressed, in *Cattley*, by either of the following: (1) that D acted voluntarily and without reward, or (2) that D was motivated by altruism and by the best of intentions in seeking to assist C.

ii. **Emergencies for road users.** If D, a road-user, has been placed in an emergency situation because of the actions of another road-user, then D's actions may be hurried, and done without time for the thought or judgment that a reasonable road-user, not afflicted with that emergency, would have shown. However, even then, D may not have done enough to meet the suppressed standard of care. It will depend upon all the circumstances. Two cases may be usefully contrasted.

In *Ng v Lee*,[108] Mr Lee, a coach driver, D, saw a blue car cut suddenly in front of his coach, causing D to brake and swerve suddenly, skidding across the road and colliding with a small bus. Two passengers in the small bus, C, were killed, and many others were injured. The owner/driver of the blue car was never traced. **Held (PC):** no breach proven. D's driving had to be judged in light of the emergency in which he had been placed by the driver of the untraced car: D was 'attempting to extricate himself, his coach and his passengers from a situation ... of extreme danger. The consequences of his action were in fact unfortunate, but that should not be laid at his door. He did what any careful driver would instinctively have done in the circumstances, and we are satisfied that he acted with the alertness, skill and judgment which could reasonably have been expected.'

In *Das Intl Ltd v Manley*,[109] Mr Manley, D, was driving along a motorway at 5 am, in darkness, when he swerved to avoid a pedestrian at the side of the road. He crashed into the central reservation barrier, rebounded back across the carriageway and eventually came to rest in a field. He suffered whiplash and shock, got out of his car, and headed towards the motorway, to get help. Shortly after, Mr Parker, C, driving along the same motorway, suddenly saw D in the cycle lane, waving his arms. C also crashed off the motorway. He was not seriously injured, but his vehicle was written off. Witnesses described D as being shocked and confused in the aftermath of both accidents. D suffered from mild concussion and found it difficult to remember what had happened after his own accident. **Held:** breach proven. Notwithstanding the 'very great sympathy for [D] in the situation in which he found himself, it was an unhappy one indeed', he did not meet the standard of care of a reasonable road user. Even though D had been involved in a serious accident, and needed to attract the attention of other motorists for help, 'it cannot be reasonable to move suddenly from the side of the road straight into the path of a fast moving vehicle when it is pitch dark and one is wearing dark clothing, which makes it even more difficult to be seen'.

[107] QB, 25 Nov 1988, Judge Prosser QC.
[108] [1988] RTR 298 (PC, on appeal from the HKCA) 302.
[109] [2002] EWCA Civ 1638, quote at [18].

Notably, in *Das*, Hale LJ commented that, '[t]here are accidents for which no-one can be blamed. That is correct. But I would accept that such situations are comparatively rare'.[110] This observation reiterates that a suppressed standard of care will still not exculpate most D road-users from breach.

iii. Emergency services scenarios. Emergency services frequently confront 'agony of the moment' or emergency conditions – and that has judicially been taken into account in leading cases, albeit that professional rescuers, and those professionally trained to cope with emergency situations, will be held to a standard of care higher than that of mere volunteers. Nevertheless, courts have constantly cautioned against setting the bar too high for this class of defendant:

- re ambulances, per *Kent v Griffiths*[111] – Kennedy LJ said that, 'the standard of care owed by the ambulance service was not to be set too high, given that the ambulance service operates in a difficult area, with cash limits, competing claims on limited sources, difficulty in deciding between competing calls for assistance from different locations, and the ever present problems of traffic hazards'; and earlier, the trial judge Turner J had also stated that '[in] a situation of emergency the consequent duty will not be set at an unrealistically or unattainably high level';[112]
- re police, per *Macleod v Commr of Police*[113] – unfortunately, road and other accidents do arise when the police are attempting to apprehend a criminal, or to respond to an emergency summons for help. As noted in *Macleod* (where breach was proven), 'the duty on the driver of the police car is to drive with such care and skill as is reasonable in all the circumstances. He owes C a duty of care, notwithstanding the fact that this was an emergency'. The flashing of the emergency lights by D, so as to give 'conspicuous warning of their presence or approach', must be taken into account too: 'it would inhibit the valuable work done for the community as a whole, if drivers in the emergency services were not allowed to drive their vehicles on the basis that pedestrians [and other road-users] would recognise their warning lights and sirens and give them proper priority by keeping out of their paths'. That standard expected of D would be lower than for a civilian who was driving his child to hospital in an emergency, which emergency was not apparent to any other road user (per *Keyse v Commr of Police*,[114] where no breach was proven). However, just what constitutes police driving sufficient to exceed that requisite standard of care can divide judicial opinion, as aptly demonstrated in *Henry v Thames Valley Police*.[115] The majority of the Court of Appeal held that the police constable, D, had left insufficient room for a suspect, C, to dismount safely from his motorcycle, thereby running over C's leg; whereas the dissenter agreed with the trial judge that C's conduct had 'put the police officers into a very tricky situation in which they had to make judgments in seconds about what he was going to do' and that it was a 'stressful situation' for D, where C had driven at grossly excessive speeds and had sought to evade capture. These are frequently borderline assessments;

[110] *ibid*, [16].
[111] [1998] EWCA Civ 1941, (1998) 47 BMLR 125, 134; and later: [2000] EWCA Civ 25, [2001] QB 36, [46].
[112] [1999] Lloyd's Rep Med 424 (QB).
[113] [2014] EWHC 977 (QB) [16], citing: *Marshall v Osmond* [1983] QB 1074 (CA).
[114] [2001] EWCA (Civ) 715, [29], [31] (Judge LJ).
[115] [2010] EWCA Civ 5, [2010] RTR 14 (Smith and Arden LJJ; with Pill LJ dissenting).

- re fire brigades, per *Capital & Counties plc v Hampshire CC*[116] – Stuart-Smith LJ remarked that, '[i]t seems hardly realistic that a fire officer, who has to make a split second decision as to the manner in which fire-fighting operations are to be conducted, will be looking over his shoulder at the possibility of his employers being made vicariously liable for his negligence. If there can be liability for negligence, it is better to have a high threshold of negligence established in the *Bolam* test, and for judges to remind themselves that fire officers, who make difficult decisions in difficult circumstances, should be given considerable latitude before being held guilty of negligence'; and
- re GP's who confront urgent scenarios in medical surgeries, per *Knight v Home Office*[117] – as Pill LJ said, '[t]he facilities available to deal with an emergency in a general practitioner's surgery cannot be expected to be as ample as those available in the casualty department of a general hospital', so that, 'the standard of care required will vary with the context'.

iv. Recreational endeavours. For those involved in hurly-burly sporting or recreational contests, the standard of care will be suppressed, primarily because of the 'agony of the moment' scenarios which often arise in such contests, and which are often an inherent part of the game or competition. This is discussed separately below.

Hence, English courts have endorsed the principle that the standard of reasonable care is suppressed in 'agony of the moment' scenarios; so that the temptation to set the bar too high, when so-called 'battle conditions' are confronted, must be strenuously resisted.

'Diagnosis with a focus' scenarios

§6.16 Where the need for a particular diagnosis is flagged up to D, then that 'diagnosis with a focus' may elevate the standard of care; it must certainly be taken into account when assessing the standard required.

If patient C has been referred by one health care professional to another, D, with concerns noted about the patient's presentation, then a higher standard of care will be required, because D must conduct 'a scan with a focus', as the court put it in *Pithers v Leeds Teaching Hosp NHS Trust.*[118] In both of the following cases, breach was proven on this basis:

In *Pithers v Leeds Teaching Hosp*, a sonographer at a local hospital was unable to visualise the foetal bladder in a routine abdominal ultra-sound scan, and C, the patient, was referred to Leeds General Infirmary for a further opinion by D, a specialist registrar. D's diagnosis of a further scan noted the bladder to be 'well visualised and appear[ing] normal'. In fact, C was born with a condition, cloacal-exstrophy, in which substantial parts of the abdominal content develop outside the abdominal wall, and for which no bladder can be visualised. The law demanded of D, as a senior physician at a major hospital, 'a high standard of care and skill specifically when focusing on the issue thus raised: "cloacal exstrophy or not"'. It was 'a scan with a focus', so that 'there is a heavy burden on Leeds, when seeking to reconcile its incorrect visualisations, with the exercise of all reasonable care and skill'. In *Lillywhite v University College London Hosp NHS Trust*,[119] Alice Lillywhite, C, suffered from the condition of holoprosencephaly, in which her forebrain failed to divide into two early in her foetal

[116] [1997] QB 1004 (CA) [87]. [117] [1990] 3 All ER 237 (QB) 243.
[118] [2004] EWHC 1392 (QB), with quote in following case description at [13].
[119] [2005] EWCA Civ 1466, [30] (Latham LJ, with whom Buxton LJ agreed).

development, and no falx was formed by which to divide the forebrain. C was born with quadraplegia, and profoundly mentally-disabled. The radiographer who initially studied the foetal scan could not detect the falx, and referred the scan, with a note, 'falx?', to D, a professor of obstetrics and gynaecology at D's university hospital, and who was experienced at reading and interpreting foetal ultrasound scans. D diagnosed that the falx was present, and that C's brain development showed no abnormalities. Ultimately, it was concluded that D must have seen 'shadows' on the ultrasound which resembled a falx. In any event, the referral had constituted a diagnosis with a focus, and that scenario 'demanded a high standard of care and skill in the context of a focused referral based upon the concerns of [the radiographer]'.

Although this elevated standard has only arisen for consideration in the medical context (so far as can be ascertained), there is no reason in principle as to why it could not be applied in any other context.

Locality

§6.17 If D is operating in a rural/country environment without access to the resources, equipment or collegiate expertise which would be available to a counterpart in a city/urban environment, then there is a *very limited* recognition in English law that the standard of care may be suppressed. As a corollary, D may fail to meet the standard of care if C should have been referred elsewhere, and was not.

The relevant principles

A so-called 'locality' rule – whereby a lower standard of care is legally tolerated of the rural/country D than of the urban/city D – has very limited recognition in English jurisprudence (and it does not go by that name, in any event). The highest that can be said is that, in some rare cases, the court has taken into account the fact that D was operating in a rural environment.

For example, in *Hickey v Marks*,[120] the Court of Appeal approved of the trial judge's decision that D doctor's treatment of his patients 'was to be judged by the standards of a general practitioner working single-handed in a rural area' (and, even so, negligence was held there – although that was actually a libel action brought by the doctor, regarding a TV programme concerning the doctor's treatment of a young drug addict). Similarly, in the employment negligence case of *Yorkshire Traction Co Ltd v Searby*,[121] the locality of where the incident happened had some impact upon the standard of care, and what precautionary steps a reasonable employer needed to have taken.

In *Yorkshire Traction Co Ltd v Searby*, Walter Searby, C, a bus driver, was assaulted by a passenger one night, about 10:50pm. He suffered both physical injury and PTSD. His assailant was never identified. C alleged that there should have been a screen installed by his employer, D, to separate the driver from his passengers. There was evidence of prior assaults by passengers on bus drivers, but these were more prevalent in urban than in rural areas. C had, himself, twice been assaulted; and in the preceding 14 years, an average of 8 assaults a year were of sufficient gravity to require D's drivers to take time off work. In some urban areas, buses had been fitted with screens (as in Cleveland, as a trial), but in other areas, such as in South Yorkshire, they had not. **Held:** no breach proven. The risk of injury to a bus driver in South Yorkshire was very low, which was relevant when

[120] (CA, 6 Jul 2000) [31], [53]. [121] [2003] EWCA Civ 1856.

determining what was expected of a reasonable employer. Just because screens had been installed in Cleveland conditions did not mean that it was negligent of D not to have installed them in South Yorkshire conditions.

However, even if the so-called 'locality rule' reduces the standard of reasonable care against which the acts or omissions of D are judged, then C is not necessarily without remedy.

Failure to refer

Even where locality may suppress the standard of care, D may not meet it, if D failed to refer C to another location/venue where more specialist facilities, expertise or more experienced staff existed. If facilities or staffing levels were not adequate to cope with C's problem, then a duty to refer has commonly been upheld.

> In *Gouldsmith v Mid-Staffordshire General Hosp NHS Trust*,[122] Mrs Gouldsmith, C, presented at hospital with a lesion on her left (dominant) hand which caused blockages in arteries. C had previously suffered from arterial thrombosis (blood clotting) and antiphospholipid syndrome (where vessels become narrowed or blocked by blood clots). Within six weeks, all digits on C's left hand had to be amputated. **Held:** breach proven. If the hospital did not have the medical staff qualified to carry out what would have been a complicated and difficult treatment, C should have been 'seen and treated in a tertiary centre of excellence (on the evidence, and for reasons of geography, either Birmingham or Manchester)'.

Thus, on balance, any differential standard of care brought about by locality, and a consequent lack of facilities, equipment and medical staffing expertise, may be 'evened out' by a duty to refer – rendering any so-called 'locality rule' otiose. The fact that D should have referred C on does **not** automatically mean liability in negligence, however, for three reasons:

i. just because D did not refer does not automatically mean that D fell below the standard of reasonable care. The level of performance undertaken by D, in the less-than-ideal circumstances, may have reached the reasonable standard of care in any event, given that perfection is not the touchstone;
ii. any inherent risks to C that were likely to be encountered during C's transfer elsewhere may outweigh the benefits of the treatment which C would have received at the other venue:

> In *Macey v Warwickshire HA*,[123] baby Macey, C, suffered cerebral palsy. He alleged that this was due to his post-natal care, when his mother, presenting with a premature labour at 34 weeks, ought to have been transferred from the local hospital, St Mary's, where there was no special care baby unit, to Walsgrave Hospital, the principal regional maternity hospital, where facilities and staff could have dealt with C's severe respiratory distress, which started 7 minutes after his birth, and carried on for two hours until after C's emergency transferral to Walsgrave. C also alleged that he should have been intubated and ventilated before being transferred. **Held:** breach not proven on these grounds. Although the facilities at St Mary's were 'limited', the standard of care which could be provided there was reasonable for the time (1981). Also, C should not have been intubated and ventilated at St Mary's prior to his transfer, because no-one at St Mary's had expertise to carry out intubation on a newborn infant; it was not a specialist maternity hospital equipped with suitable

122 [2007] EWCA Civ 397, quote at [41] (per Kay LJ, dissenting on causation, but not on breach).

123 [2004] EWHC 1198 (QB), with quotes at [44]–[51], and [63]–[65] .

staff. Also, there were real risks to C, if intubated and hand-ventilated during an ambulance journey of 20 minutes. (However, breach was proven because of the 45 minute delay following C's birth, before medical attention was drawn to C's respiratory distress.)

iii. if referring C elsewhere to superior equipment, expertise, etc, would probably have made no difference to the ultimate result for C, then there is no causal link between the breach (the failure to refer) and C's damage (per Chapter 8, and illustrated in *Gouldsmith*,[124] where causation was proven).

Thus, to summarise, there is some limited judicial support in England for a suppressed standard of care, depending upon the locality in which D is operating, but any variations in the standard of care are generally 'smoothed out' by a duty to refer in such cases. Even then, failing to refer will not automatically entail a finding of negligence, if a referral probably would not have derived a better outcome for C, or if the failure to refer is supported by a reasonable body of respected medical opinion.

The comparative corner: A snapshot of the locality rule in Canada

The locality rule is particularly rooted in Canadian jurisprudence, in a geographically large country with a dispersed population, albeit that the locality rule has come in for some strident criticism in Canadian case law.

The locality rule: derived from *Wilson v Swanson* (SCC), 'the medical man must possess and use that reasonable degree of learning and skill ordinarily possessed by practitioners *in similar communities* in similar cases.'[125] The rule has been applied to the standard of care expected in the provision of care, diagnosis and treatment, but *not* in respect of the provision of advice and information.[126] The rule has been supported in several provinces in Canada – e.g., in *Challand v Bell*[127] ('From a GP at a rural point, a different standard is exacted than from a specialist at an urban point'); and *Kivisalu v Brown*[128] ('[a]lthough I hesitate to use the word "geographical" when employing this test [for standard of care], there is a measure of geography that enters into the assessment');

Reasons for the rule: rural doctors regularly faced difficulties such as a lack of specialists to refer to, lack of facilities, lack of support staff, long periods of being on-call, and with a general overload of patients to cope with (per *Sunnucks v Tobique Valley Hosp*[129]); as a matter of fairness, a court should not hold a family GP conducting a medical practice in a rural area of Vancouver Island to the same standard as an obstetrician practising in the city of Vancouver (a statement that had as much to do with locality as with specialisation) (per *St Jules v Chen*[130]).

Departures from the rule: more recently in 2007, in *Smith v Liwanpo*[131] (where a CT scan was not performed on a patient, following a difficult colonoscopy), the locality rule was considered not to be a valid reason to suppress the standard of care, for two reasons:

[124] [2007] EWCA Civ 397.
[125] (1956), 5 DLR (2d) 113 (SCC) [43] (emphasis added); *McCormick v Marcotte* (1971), 20 DLR (3d) 345 (SCC) 346.
[126] Noted in the introductory annotations to: *Hopp v Lepp* (1979), 98 DLR (3d) 464 (Alta SC App Div).
[127] (1959), 18 DLR (2d) 150 (Alta TD) 154.
[128] [2002] BCSC 1901, [34].
[129] (1999), 216 NBR (2d) 201 (QB) [179] (Clendening J).
[130] [1990] BCJ No 23 (Gow J).
[131] (SCJ, 23 Apr 2007, Morissette J) [114]–[116], citing: *Crawford v Penney* [2003] OJ No 89 (SCJ).

(1) the community hospital had an arrangement with a nearby major hospital whereby an urgent referral of the patient could have been done; and (2) '[t]he courts have long ago settled the issue of locality. It should be abandoned'. Other provincial Canadian decisions have also expressly refused to follow the locality rule.[132] In their leading medical text, Picard and Robertson considered the rule 'ripe to be buried'.[133]

Reasons given for departing from the rule, and imposing one uniform standard of care: the rule creates a geographic lottery; it defies the national standards of competence set by professional examinations and continuing medical education; rural doctors themselves felt uncomfortable about the rule; so much medical practice was conducted in areas that could be described as 'rural' that a differentiation would be a 'sad comment indeed'; due to technological advances, particularly in communication, consultive help was always relatively near; and the duty of D to refer the patient, if the situation called for it, reduced the significance, and justification, of a locality rule.

Dangerous recreational/sporting pursuits

Participants towards spectators

§6.18 The standard of care expected of a participant in a sporting or recreational activity, D, vis-à-vis a spectator, C, is suppressed, in that D must not act with either a reckless disregard of C's safety or a deliberate intent to cause C harm.

The law clearly sets a suppressed standard of care for the participant in a sporting or recreational activity, where injuries are caused to spectators. It has been called a 'special' relationship, so that this 'different relationship involves its own standard of care' (per *Wooldridge v Sumner*[134]).

The participant, D, must meet the standard of not acting recklessly towards spectators (i.e., acting in disregard of the safety of others); of not acting with deliberate intent to cause them harm; and of complying with the rules of the game. It follows that mere lapses of skill by D, or errors of judgment, may well meet the expected standard of care. In this context, D would act recklessly if he participated in a game or a competition, 'when he knew, or ought to have known, that his lack of skill was such that, even if he exerted it to the utmost, he was likely to cause injury to a spectator watching him' (per Diplock LJ in *Wooldridge v Sumner*[135]). That observation was dicta, because D was an 'exceptionally skilful and experienced' horse-rider there. Nevertheless, the proposition is important – D does not have to be incredibly skilful, but must have adequate competence to take part in the competition without posing a threat to the safety of spectators.

In *Wooldridge v Sumner*, during the 1959 National Horse Show at White City Stadium, London. Mr Wooldridge, C, a professional photographer, attended a competition for heavy-weight hunters (involving the horses demonstrating a walk, a trot, a canter and a gallop). A horse called 'Work of Art', owned by Mr Sumner and ridden by Mr Holladay, D1, collided with C, during the gallop. At the time of the accident, C was not taking any pictures because he had run out of film, but was sitting on a bench seat just beside the racing track, between two planter boxes/tubs. C was not

[132] e.g., *Sunnucks v Tobique Valley Hosp* (1999), 216 NBR (2d) 201, [180]; *Skeels v Iwashkiw* [2006] ABQB 335, [76].
[133] *Legal Liability of Doctor and Hospitals in Canada* (4th edn, Carswell, Toronto, 2007) 251.
[134] [1963] 2 QB 43 (CA) 57. [135] *ibid*, 68.

experienced in regard to horses (and was described as 'unfamiliar with and wholly uninterested in them'). The steward of the course had told C to move off the side of the running track, but C did not heed the warning. C then 'took fright', and stepped or fell into the path of the galloping Work of Art, and was knocked down and severely injured. **Held:** no breach proven. D1, as rider, may have shown 'some errors of judgment' or 'a lapse of skill', in the way that he rode Work of Art around that corner of the track, but he had shown no reckless disregard for C's safety. He was 'riding within the rules [when] he won'. (D2, the British Horse Society, as the promoters of the show, also met the standard of care expected of an occupier, in taking reasonable care to provide a suitable arena for the event.)

It follows that mere 'misfortunes' which spectator C suffered in the 'best tradition of sporting competitive endeavour' (to cite an expression of Sellers LJ in *Wooldridge*[136]) would **not** expose D to any finding of breach, e.g., where at a cricket match, D hits a six, and the ball hits C in the crowd; or a tennis player hits a ball or throws a racket accidentally into the crowd; or at a rugby match, a player dives into a tackle and comes into heavy contact with the surrounding barrier, injuring an adjacent spectator C (hypothetical examples in *Wooldridge*); or at a car rally, a driver collides with another rally car, causing D's car to deviate, jump the barriers, plough into the crowd, and injure C (dicta in *Hall v Brooklands Auto Racing Club*[137]); or D skids on 'black ice' that was unknown to exist on a road during the Monte Carlo Rally, crashes into a tree, badly injuring a spectator crew (an unreported case cited in *Wooldridge v Sumner* – '[i]f the road had been known to be icy, then it would clearly have been reckless or foolhardy for even a skilled driver in the rally to travel so fast; then the decision would, and I think should, have been [negligence]'[138]); or driver D in a Jersey road race crashes at speed due to brake-failure, killing spectator C (per *O'Dowd v Frazer-Nash*[139]).

On the other hand, if participants in a game 'divert clearly from the rules [of the game], there may well be room for liability' towards spectators, precisely because recklessness or a deliberate intent to cause spectator C harm will be easier to prove (per *Wooldridge v Sumner*[140]). To provide some examples cited therein: if ice-hockey players fight off the play well away from the game and injure spectator C during their fight (per *Payne and Payne v Maple Leaf Gardens Ltd*[141]); or a golfer, not in the course of play, swings a club and injures spectator C standing by (per *Cleghorn v Oldham*[142]), or loses his ball, and then plays it against the rules of the game and in disregard for the safety of those in the 'line of danger', and hits a spectator in the eye; or a tennis player hits a ball or throws a racket into the stands in temper or annoyance, when play was not in progress, thereby injuring spectator C (dicta examples in *Wooldridge*).

An alternative test? In a curious twist, the *Wooldridge* test was judicially modified several years later, in *Wilks v Cheltenham Homeguard Motor Cycle and Light Car Club.*[143] That was another suit by injured spectators against a participant (this time a motor-cycle rider). The Court of Appeal cited with approval an academic view[144] that the correct standard to apply was that

[136] *ibid*, 54.

[137] [1933] 1 KB 205 (CA). This case concerned the liability of the promotor of the event, not that of the rally car driver.

[138] [1963] 2 QB 43 (CA) 56.

[139] [1951] WN 172 (McNair J), and cited in: *Wooldridge v Sumner*, *ibid*, 49–50, 56 (Sellers LJ).

[140] [1963] 2 QB 43 (CA) 55–57.

[141] [1949] 1 DLR 369.

[142] (1927) 43 TLR 465, and cited in *Woodridge v Sumner* [1963] 2 QB 43 (CA) 55–56 (Sellers LJ).

[143] [1971] 1 WLR 668 (CA).

[144] A Goodhart, 'The Sportsman's Charter' (1962) 78 *LQR* 490, 496.

D, the participant, must not commit an 'error of judgment that a reasonable competitor, being the reasonable man of the sporting world, would not have made'.

This *Wilks* test imposes a potentially higher standard than not acting with reckless disregard of a spectator's safety. It was admitted by the Scottish Inner House (in *Sharpe v Highland and Islands Fireboard*[145]) that the *Wooldridge* and *Wilks* tests were not precisely the same. Indeed, most recently, in *McMahon v Dear* (where a ball spotter was struck and injured by a golf ball hit by a competitor), the Scottish Outer House refused to follow *Wooldridge's* recklessness test, preferring *Wilks'* test (ultimately, no breach was found, on the basis of that test).[146]

However, insofar as English case law is concerned, the *Wooldridge* and *Wilks* standards of care appear to have been equated as being the same test. In *Smoldon v Whitworth*,[147] Lord Bingham CJ treated them equivalently, but in doing so, plainly reiterated the *Wooldridge* standard, for participants towards spectators, where he said that *Wooldridge* and *Wilks* 'recognised that a sporting competitor, properly intent on winning the contest, was (and was entitled to be) all but oblivious of spectators. It therefore followed that he would have to be shown to have very blatantly disregarded the safety of spectators before he could be held to have failed to exercise such care as was reasonable in all the circumstances'. Hence, whatever difference in view may have been cast by *Wilks*, the *Wooldridge* standard is the prevailing standard, insofar as modern English law is concerned.

Reasons for the suppressed standard. Why is the standard set so low, for participants towards spectators? There are four reasons, according to the case law:

i. a reasonable spectator would expect, and would be entitled to expect, no different, because they are there to watch a sporting spectacle, in which D is a competitor/player who is 'merely seeking to excel and to win, it being the very purpose on which he is engaged, and the very endeavour which people have assembled to witness and applaud' (per *Wooldridge v Sumner*[148]);
ii. even with a suppressed standard of care, it is not a negligible standard, and provides *some* protection for spectator C. The game or tournament must be performed 'within the rules and the requirement of the sport, and by a person of adequate skill and competence' – albeit that C, 'the spectator, does not expect his safety to be regarded by the participant [D]' (per *O'Dowd v Frazer-Nash*[149]);
iii. there is often an element of 'agony of the moment' in these scenarios, which suppresses the standard of care expected at law (discussed above). For example, in *Wooldridge*,[150] Danckwerts LJ pointed out that the rider's duty to his employer, who owned the horse, 'was to utilise the qualities of the horse so as to show it to the best advantage. This involved the horse going at a fast gallop. Decisions have to be taken in a split second'. Diplock LJ agreed: 'a participant in a game or competition gets into the circumstances in which he has no time, or very little time, to think ... If, therefore, in the course of the game or competition, at a moment when he really has not time to think, a participant by mistake takes a wrong measure, he is not, in my view, to be held guilty of any negligence', and that D's decison-making 'had to be made in circumstances in which he had no time to exercise an unhurried judgment';
iv. a suppressed standard of care reflects that it is expected, at some level, that spectators will be versed in the art of self-preservation. In *Wooldridge v Sumner*, Diplock LJ noted that any reasonable competitor 'would be entitled to assume that spectators actually in the arena would be paying attention

[145] [2007] CSIH 34, [10]. [146] [2014] CSOH 100, 2014 SLT 823, [209].
[147] [1997] PIQR P133 (CA), quote at P138–P139. [148] [1963] 2 QB 43 (CA) 52 (Sellers LJ).
[149] [1951] WN 172 (QB, McNair J), cited *ibid*, 156.
[150] [1963] 2 QB 43 (CA) 60 (Danckwerts LJ), 67–68, 70 (Diplock LJ).

to what was happening, would be knowledgeable about horses, and would take such steps for their own safety as any reasonably attentive and knowledgeable spectator might be expected to take'.[151] That assumption can be translated to other stadiums and arenas where other sports are played. A suppressed standard on the competitor's part is an apt recognition that, in dangerous or heated sporting spectacles, the law expects a level of conduct on **both** C's and D's part.

Participants towards participants

§6.19 The standard of care expected of one participant in a sporting contest, D, towards another participant, C, is suppressed somewhat differently, in that D must not act recklessly nor show a high degree of carelessness towards C, where D is conducting himself in the 'hurly-burly' and fast-moving, vigorous contest.

In *Caldwell v Fitzgerald and Maguire*,[152] Tuckey LJ affirmed that, 'there will be no liability for errors of judgment, oversights or lapses of which any participant might be guilty in the context of a fast-moving contest. Something more serious is required'. The Court of Appeal, noting the proposition above, also approved of the trial judge's view that, practically-speaking, 'it may ... be difficult to prove any breach of duty, absent proof of conduct [by D] that ... amounts to reckless disregard for the fellow contestant's safety'. In *Collet v Smith*,[153] the court explained the requisite degree of wrongdoing in these terms, i.e., that participant D knew that there was 'a significant risk of serious injury' to another participant C, if D behaved as he did. The standard expected of a participant towards another probably represents a higher standard than the *Wooldridge* standard, because D can fail to meet the requisite standard, even if he has **not** acted recklessly. None of these cases supports any notion, however, that D's breach of the rules of the game or contest establishes negligence.

Notwithstanding the suppressed standard which operates in these circumstances, breach may nevertheless be proven, in that participant D's conduct fell below that standard – as occurred in the following:

> In *Condon v Basi*,[154] C and D were playing for opposing teams in a non-professional football match, when C suffered serious injury (a broken leg) as a result of a dangerous tackle by D. In effecting that tackle, D showed a reckless disregard of C's safety, and his conduct fell far below the standard reasonably expected of any participant in an amateur game. In *Caldwell v Fitzgerald and Maguire*, Mr Caldwell, C, a professional jockey, was injured when he was unseated from his horse, as a result of dangerous manoeuvres by two fellow jockeys, D, for which D were liable in negligence.

Alternatively, the scenario may be mere horseplay between friends – and even that (whilst not an organised regulated sporting contest which is governed by explicit rules) is conducted in accordance with certain tacitly-agreed understandings or conventions. There will be no expectation, in such circumstances, that either skill or judgment will be exercised by D. Among those participants, Lord Dyson MR commented, in *Blake v Galloway*,[155] that they will be required to meet the standard of not acting 'either recklessly or with a very high degree of carelessness'.

[151] *ibid*, 71. [152] [2001] EWCA Civ 1054, [2002] PIQR P6, [5], [11], [22].

[153] [2011] EWHC 90208 (Costs) [42]–[43], citing: *Watson and Bradford City AFC v Gray and Huddersfield Town FC* (*The Times*, 26 Nov 1998, Hooper J).

[154] [1985] 1 WLR 866 (CA). [155] [2004] EWCA Civ 814, [2004] 1 WLR 2844, [8], with reasoning at [13], [15]–[16].

In *Blake v Galloway*, Master Blake, C, was practising with a jazz quintet with four friends at a venue in South Devon, when they adjourned for a lunchtime break in the grounds. They all engaged in some high-spirited, good-natured and friendly horseplay, throwing twigs, pieces of bark chipping, and mulch, at each other. C picked up a piece of bark chipping, approximately 4 cm in diameter, and threw it towards the lower part of Master Galloway's, D's, body; and D picked up the same piece of bark and threw it back at C, striking him in the right eye. C lost sight in the eye from the injury. No participant was throwing items towards anybody's head, or picking on another. C was not looking in D's direction when the bark was thrown, otherwise he probably would have taken evasive action. **Held:** no breach proven. There was no reckless disregard or a high degree of carelessness here. D did not depart from the tacit understandings or conventions of horseplay; did not deliberately aim the piece of bark at C's head; and the game was conducted at speed and fairly vigorously.

Reasons for the suppressed standard. In *Blake v Galloway*, Lord Dyson MR drew a close analogy between organised formal sports, and informal horseplay, and considered that the suppressed standard of care applied in both scenarios, for three reasons:

i. the contests or games both involved participation in an activity which involved physical contact, or at least the risk of it, on a consensual basis;
ii. in such contests, decisions are usually expected to be made quickly, and often as an instinctive or urgent response to the acts of other participants – hence, an 'agony of the moment' scenario; and
iii. the very nature of the activity makes it difficult to avoid the risk of physical harm.

Variations in standard? In *Condon v Basi*,[156] which concerned the action between footballers over a dangerous tackle by D against C, the Court of Appeal opined that the standard of care from one participant to another depended upon the level of competence and seniority of the game being played. According to Sir John Donaldson MR, '[t]he standard is objective, but ... there will of course be a higher degree of care required of a player in a First Division football match than of a player in a local league football match.'

The correctness of this proposition was doubted in the Scottish case of *Sharpe v Highland and Islands Fire Board*,[157] but has not, as yet, been considered further in English case law.

Referees towards participants

§6.20 The standard of care expected of a referee, D, towards a player/participant in a game or competition, C, is similarly suppressed, in that D must not act recklessly nor show a high degree of carelessness towards C, where D is conducting himself in the 'hurly-burly' and fast-moving, vigorous contest.

This proposition was enunciated in *Smoldon v Whitworth*,[158] and was confirmed in *Vowles v Evans*.[159] (In both of these tragic cases, C were young men playing games of rugby, who packed into a scrum in the position of hooker, and whose necks were broken when the scrums collapsed.)

In *Smoldon*,[160] the Court specifically rejected the *Wooldridge* standard of care, as being inapplicable to referees. The proposition – that the standard that a referee must meet is that

[156] [1985] 1 WLR 866 (CA) 868. [157] [2005] CSOH 111, 2005 SLT 855, [23].
[158] [1997] PIQR P133, [1997] ELR 249, 256. [159] [2003] EWCA Civ 318, [2003] 1 WLR 1607, [26].
[160] [1997] PIQR P133 (CA) P139.

he cannot act with **either** a deliberate intention of causing injury to the participant **or** a reckless disregard for the safety of the participant – was unpalatable because (according to Lord Bingham CJ, who gave the judgment of the court) '[t]he position of a referee *vis-à-vis* the players is not the same as that of a participant in a contest *vis-à-vis* a spectator. One of his responsibilities is to safeguard the safety of the players'. For that reason, a **higher** standard of care is imposed on a referee than on a participant.

Nevertheless, referee D operates under a suppressed standard of care at law, in that the circumstances in which D is operating can lawfully and properly be taken into account, when determining the standard of behaviour which the law imposes on him. Those circumstances properly include whether D was required to act in a heated, fast-moving, or rushed context, or whether he had time to come to a considered decision. Two reasons were given by the Court of Appeal in *Smoldon*:[161]

i. 'The threshold of liability is a high one. It will not easily be crossed' (said Lord Bingham CJ). In other words, the lower the standard of care, the more difficult it is to prove D negligent. That lower standard is defensible, because the standard should not be set so high that referees should be fearful of being held negligent for not meeting that standard; and
ii. referees 'could not be properly held liable for errors of judgment, oversights or lapses of which any referee might be guilty in the context of a fast-moving and vigorous contest'. In other words, the 'agony of the moment' scenario can serve to suppress the standard of care expected of referee D.

Naturally, there will be no suppression of the standard of care where, rather than decisions being taken during the heat of play, a referee acted while play was stopped and there was time for considered thought.

In *Vowles v Evans*,[162] Richard Vowles, C, suffered permanent incomplete tetraplegia, when he was injured in a collapsed scrum during an amateur rugby game, which was being refereed by David Evans, D. C was playing as hooker, when his team's loose head prop dislocated his shoulder and had to leave the field. The team did not have a trained front row forward on the bench to replace him (nor anyone else who had that training or experience of playing in the front row). D was aware of this problem, and told the team captain that they could provide a replacement from within the scrum, or opt for non-contestable scrummages – the choice was theirs – adding that, if the team opted for non-contestable scrummages and won the match, they would not be entitled to an award of points in the League competition. Hence, one of the team, CJ, said that he would 'give it a go', and things proceeded uneventfully until injury time, when the other team was aiming for a 'pushover' try. The two sets of forwards scrummaged, and C collapsed, breaking his neck. Rule 3(12) of the Laws of the Game provided:

> In the event of a front row forward being ordered off, the referee, in the interests of safety, will confer with the captain of his team to determine whether another player is suitably trained/experienced to take his position; if not, the captain shall nominate one other forward to leave the playing area and the referee will permit a substitute front row forward to replace him ... When there is no other front row forward available, ...then the game will continue with non-contestable scrummages ...

[161] *ibid*, P139. [162] [2003] EWCA Civ 318, [2003] WLR 1607, [37]–[38].

Held: breach proven. D did not satisfy himself that CJ was suitably trained/experienced for the front row, but left the decision to the team captain. Under the Law, it was not proper to offer the captain that option. D abdicated the responsibility, which was his, of deciding whether the situation had been reached where it was mandatory to insist upon non-contestable scrummages. Hence, D breached his duty to exercise reasonable care for the safety of the players. Also, D's decision was taken while play was stopped, and there was time to give considered thought to it.

Cross-fertilisation. There has been cross-fertilisation of relevant jurisprudence in this context, in that *Caldwell*[163] referred to judicial statements in *Wilks* (re participants towards spectators) and *Smoldon* (re referees towards participants). Indeed, Judge LJ aligned the referee's standard with the participant's standard of care toward other participants, in that both were entitled to a suppressed standard of care, depending upon the circumstances. In *Blake v Galloway*, reference was made to the *Wooldridge* standard, but 'in a slightly expanded form' (per Lord Dyson MR) – a fact that is clear when the principles governing participants to spectators, and participants to participants, are compared; they are not quite the same principle.

Does the grading of the referee matter? Could the 'circumstances', by which the standard is set, include the grade of certificate which D possessed as referee? That notion appeared to gain some support in *Vowles v Evans*,[164] where the Court of Appeal referred to the scenario where, in a low-level amateur game or contest, the designated referee may not turn up, or may be injured, and from the crowd of spectators, a volunteer referee is recruited. Lord Phillips MR stated that 'the volunteer cannot reasonably be expected to show the skill of one who holds himself out as referee, or perhaps even to be fully conversant with the laws of the Game'.

Alternatively, could the 'circumstances' include the grade of match that D was refereeing? In *Smoldon*, this view gained support from Bingham CJ, who preferred that D, as referee, had to reach the level of skill appropriate to that expected of a referee who was refereeing a match of a certain seniority/standard; and that the requisite standard was **not** set by his grade of certified refereeing.

In neither case did the issue require deciding, because both referees were graded appropriately for the level of game that they were refereeing. However, the law is not entirely resolved on these points.

Furthermore, it is unclear as to how the remark (albeit dicta) of Lord Phillips MR in *Vowles v Evans* is to be reconciled with the *Nettleship* rule. According to the latter, any inexperience does not suppress the standard of care expected of D. Yet, a referee plucked from the crowd may be vastly inexperienced, and still can take the benefit of a suppressed standard of care under the *Vowles* dicta. No attempt has been made to reconcile those points of view since.

Promoters towards spectators/participants

§6.21 The promoter or organiser of a sporting event, as occupier of the premises at which the event is held, owes a reasonable standard of care towards spectators and participants, with no suppression of the standard applicable.

The occupier's duty to lawful visitors to his premises is covered in Chapter 12, and readers are referred to that analysis for further detail. For present purposes, it is sufficient to note that, even in the case of dangerous sporting contests or competitions, spectators enjoy seeing competitors taking risks, but 'they expect, and rightly expect, the organisers to erect proper enclosures, and to do all that is reasonable to ensure their safety' (per Lord Denning MR in *White v Blackmore*[165]).

[163] [2001] EWCA Civ 1054, [2002] PIQR P6, [17], [20].
[164] [2003] EWCA Civ 318, [2003] WLR 1607, [28].
[165] [1972] 2 QB 651 (CA) 663.

Those who promote sporting events have to be 'mindful' of the dangers presented by the competitors (e.g., of the 'unpredictable conduct of horses, however well-trained and however skilfully ridden, especially in the excitement of competition or when confronted with some unexpected movement on or about their course', per *Wooldridge v Sumner*[166]). But provided that the promoter managed and planned the event with sufficient care, there will be no negligence.

In *White v Blackmore*,[167] Mr White, C, was an experienced 'jalopy' racing driver, and Mr Blackmore, D, organised jalopy races. During one race, C was 'sitting out', and stood next to the spectators' enclosure rope. The rope became entangled in the rear wheel of a racing car, and the stakes attached to the rope were pulled out. C was catapulted into the air, and suffered serious injuries, from which he died. **Held (at trial):** D was negligent, as occupier, in tying all the ropes to one stake, but D prevailed because of the defence of *volenti*. **Held (CA):** negligence was upheld, but *volenti* did not apply where the risk of injury arose, not from participation in the dangerous sport of motor-racing, but from the organisers' failure to take reasonable precautions for the safety of visitors to the meeting. A visitor to a motor race meeting did not willingly accept the risk of injury due to the organisers' defaults in ensuring his safety.

It is also significant that promoters customarily are not acting in the 'agony of the moment' – their safety systems and arena designs are established well before the competition or contest commences. The point was made by the Northern Ireland Queen's Bench recently, in *Browning v Odyssey Trust Co Ltd*,[168] that '[p]romoters and organisers ... are not taking decisions in the excitement of the competition. Their assessments [of appropriate safety precautions for spectators and competitors] should be measured and proportionate to the risk involved'. The legal effect, of course, is that the standard of care applying to this D is not suppressed, by virtue of any 'heat of battle' during which a competitor or a spectator is injured.

In *Browning v Odyssey Trust*, Courtney Browning, 12, C, was hit on the forehead by a puck which left the ice-rink, whilst she was sitting as a spectator at an ice hockey game in Belfast during the warm-up. C claimed that the owners/occupiers of the Odyssey Arena, where the accident happened, breached its duty to her, in failing to provide barriers and netting which would afford sufficient protection for spectators. **Held:** no breach proven, the standard of reasonable care was met by D, in taking the safety precautions (e.g., netting, perspex glass) that were provided at the arena.

In summary

The variable standards of care operating in the context of dangerous sporting or recreational pursuits are illustrated in the following Diagram:

Variable standards of care

- the reasonable standard, expected of **promotors/organisers towards spectators** – to act with reasonable care in ensuring their safety
- the suppressed standard, expected of **participants towards participants**, and of **referees towards participants** – to act with such degree of care as is appropriate in all the circumstances, including that of the 'hurly-burly' and swift-moving nature of the game/contest
- the further suppressed standard, expected of **participants towards spectators** – to not act recklessly or with deliberate intent to do harm and to not breach the rules of the game/contest

[166] [1963] 2 QB 43 (CA) 55. [167] [1972] 3 All ER 158 (CA). [168] [2014] NIQB 39, [24].

Available resources and facilities

§6.22 Where D has to contend with limited resources and facilities, then 'resource allocation' difficulties may be taken into account when setting the standard of care required of D, only in *very limited* circumstances, *viz*, for occupiers towards neighbouring landowners, and (more controversially) for healthcare authorities.

In an ideal world of 'deep-pocket' monetary resources, D could have implemented a system to prevent C's injury – but the ideal world is too expensive, and unrealistic, to countenance. Where D proves that it has available only limited resources (whether human, monetary or equipment), then – apart from the controversial 'locality rule' which has already been considered – there are two areas in which those scarce resources have been taken into account in setting the standard of care at law: occupiers from whose land something dangerous emanates or from which danger is created to an adjoining landowner; and health authorities.

Notably, this issue is not to be confused with a discretion as to how to deploy resources, which may preclude D from owing C any duty of care whatsoever, either because the issue is non-justiciable or because the third limb of the *Caparo* test fails (as discussed in Chapter 2). The analysis in this section assumes that a duty of care is owed – the only question here is what, if any, effect the scarcity of resources has upon the standard of care which must be achieved by D.

Apart from the two areas noted above, basing a decision in negligence on resource issues has sometimes led to appellate judicial discomfort.

In *Carty v Croydon LBC*,[169] C suffered a number of physical and developmental problems from a young age, and brought a claim for educational negligence. **Held:** no breach proven. C argued that the trial judge was wrong to take into account a lack of resources available to D, the educational authority, when deciding whether there had been a breach of duty. The trial judge stated that it would be wrong to characterise as negligent a decision 'which, whilst not ideal, was reasonable in the light of available resources', and also that any alternative placement of C would have to be at a specialist school within the borough 'or (subject to ... funding ...) outside the borough'. However, the Court of Appeal held that, on a fair reading of the judgment, 'the judge did not base his conclusion, that the failure to remove [C] from [a school] was not negligent, on the fact that there were no resources available to fund a placement outside the borough'.

Occupiers, and damage to adjoining landowners

§6.23 An occupier of land, D, owes a duty of care to a neighbouring occupier, C, to prevent the spread of a hazard (whether natural or man-made) from his land. The standard of care required of D is to take such steps *as are reasonable in all the circumstances* to prevent or minimise the risk of injury or damage to C caused by that hazard. Hence, the standard is subjectively-assessed, having regard to D's resources.

This section does **not** concern the standard of care which an occupier, D, must meet, when considering his conduct towards either visitors or trespassers to his land. That topic (which

[169] [2005] EWCA Civ 19, [2005] 1 WLR 2312, [77].

is governed to large extent by the Occupiers' Liability Act 1957 and the Occupiers' Liability Act 1984, respectively) is considered separately, in Chapter 12. Rather, this section concerns D's conduct towards neighbouring landowners, which is governed entirely by the common law.

D's relevant 'circumstances'. In *Goldman v Hargrave*,[170] Lord Wilberforce referred to D's duty towards neighbouring landowners as being a 'measured duty of care'. To meet that duty, 'if the small owner does what he can, and promptly calls on his neighbour to provide additional resources, he may be held to have done his duty: he should not be liable, unless it is clearly proved that he could, and *reasonably in his individual circumstances should*, have done more'. In *LMS Intl Ltd v Styrene Packaging and Insulation Ltd* too, the court grouped a number of cases together, in which C's injury was caused by a hazard emanating from D's land, and stated three principles:

i. D, the occupier, has a positive duty to take reasonable steps to prevent or minimise the risk of injury or danger emanating from his land, howsoever caused (i.e., whether natural or man-made, and whether made by a lawful entrant or by a trespasser);
ii. D cannot discharge that duty simply by not creating or adding to the source of danger or hazard, the liability can arise from not abating it; and
iii. importantly for the standard of care expected, D is assessed according to the personal resources *of that particular D*, such that 'it will be a matter of fact and degree as to whether what the occupier does in purported compliance with that duty *was reasonable in all the circumstances*.'[171]

The court may take into account the following, regarding D's circumstances:

i. the personal resources of D (whether they are plentiful or modest);
ii. the type (or magnitude) of danger on D's land and how expensive it is for D to abate or remove it;
iii. the time that would be required to abate or remove the hazard;
iv. the physical abilities of D (whether he was able-bodied or infirm); and
v. the comparative means of C and D (the owner of a small property where a hazard arises should not have to do as much as D who owns a larger property and who has greater resources to protect it).

Why does the law take account of D's resources in this type of case? In *Goldman*, it was said to be because D, the occupier, 'has had this hazard thrust upon him through no seeking or fault of his own ... A rule which required of him in such unsought circumstances, in his neighbour's interest, a physical effort of which he is not capable, or an excessive expenditure of money, would be unenforceable or unjust.'[172] That is, fairness requires a modification of the standard of care, so as to be more subjectively-assessed than usually applies.

Applications. The principle has applied, whatever natural nuisances emanate which affect D's neighbour, C (per *Stagecoach South Western Trains Ltd v Hind*[173]). Notably, where D is a public (local) authority, then the reality is that D will have substantial financial resources – and yet, the court must still take into account the competing demands on those resources and

[170] [1967] 1 AC 645 (PC, on appeal from the HCA) 663 (emphasis added).
[171] [2005] EWHC 2065 (TCC), [2006] TCLR 6, [46] (emphasis added).
[172] [1967] 1 AC 645 (PC, on appeal from the HCA) 663–64. [173] [2014] EWHC 1891 (TCC) [65].

the public purposes for which they are held. In other words, it may not be fair to require D to expend those resources on infrastructure works in order to protect a few individuals against a modest risk of property damage (per *Vernon Knight Associates v Cornwall CC*[174]).

- ***escape of fire*** – occupier D has a continuing duty to abate a fire from spreading from his property to the property of adjoining landowner, C, according to the leading authority of *Goldman v Hargrave*.[175]

  In *Goldman v Hargrave*, a farmer, D, failed to put out a fire in a tall redgum tree which had been struck by lightning in an upper fork, 100 ft above ground. D dealt with the problem by clearing and dampening the area round the tree, and cutting it down. However, D then took no further steps to prevent the spread of fire, which he could readily have done by dousing the burning tree with water. Instead, he let the fire burn itself out. However, a hot dry wind sprang up, revived the fire, caused it to spread rapidly, resulting in extensive damage to C's neighbouring farm. **Held:** breach proven. Although the fire had started by natural causes, D did not meet the standard of care expected. The resources required to extinguish the fire were not excessive – some water and some time on D's part. The fire could be removed with little effort and no expenditure.

  The principle has since been affirmed. As the court put it in *LMS v Styrene Packaging*, 'in any such case, it is always necessary to decide how far the occupier needs to go to discharge that duty'.[176]

  In *LMS*, fire broke out in Styrene Packaging's, D's, factory premises in Bradford. The factory was used to make polystyrene blocks for insulation purposes and polystyrene mouldings for use in packaging. The fire started when D's employee cut expanded polystyrene blocks with a hot wire machine – a practice which was liable to cause explosion of the flammable materials. The fire spread to two adjoining factory premises which were leased and occupied by LMS, C. Over £3m worth of damage was caused to C's property, machinery, plant and contents. **Held:** breach proven. D fell below the standard of care required, because prevention measures were possible, *viz*: D should have implemented adequate training and safety systems; following correspondence with the Fire Authority and the Health and Safety Executive, D should have compartmentalised the stored blocks or put in an automatic fire detection system; D should have installed interlocks on the hot wire cutting machine; and D also failed to put out the fire around the hot wire cutting machine, when it was within its capabilities to do so.

- ***escape of mosquitoes*** – where a public authority, D (Thames Water Utilities) allegedly expended insufficient effort to stop the breeding and escape of mosquitoes from its Mogden Sewerage Treatment Works, D owed the surrounding residents 'a measured duty of care in respect of mosquitoes', whereby 'the standard of care is to be shaped by the personal capabilities and circumstances of Thames Water' (per *Dobson v Thames Water Utilities Ltd (No 2)*[177]). No negligence was proven.

- ***loss of support for C's land*** – in *Holbeck Hall Hotel Ltd v Scarborough BC*,[178] there was no distinction (said the Court of Appeal) between a hazard caused by loss of support, and a danger on D's land which spread or encroached onto C's land. There did not need to be an encroachment as such – only a danger or hazard to C's land. This has become known as the *Leakey* principle, named after the leading case. Again, in such cases, the standard of care is set, according to the circumstances and resources of D.

[174] [2013] EWCA Civ 950, [49(iii)]. [175] [1967] 1 AC 645 (PC). [176] [2005] EWHC 2065 (TCC), [2006] TCLR 6, [41].
[177] [2011] EWHC 3253 (TCC), 140 Con LR 135, [946]. [178] [2000] 2 All ER 705 (CA).

In *Leakey v National Trust*,[179] the homes of a group of people, C, had been built at the foot of a large mound situated on D's land. Over the years, soil and rubble had fallen from the National Trusts', D's, land onto C's land, due to natural weathering and the nature of the soil. By 1968, D knew that this weathering was a threat to C's properties. After a very dry summer and wet autumn, a large crack opened in the mound above C's house, and C notified D of the danger to their houses, but D denied responsibility. A few weeks later, a large quantity of earth, and some stumps, fell onto C's land. C brought an interlocutory application to seek an order that D urgently carry out the work required to abate the danger. **Held:** D was liable in negligence (and in nuisance, see Chapter 16). The danger resulted from the forces of nature, which constituted a hazard that D was legally required to abate, and it was within its resources to do so. Hence, in this particular case, C did not need to contribute to the repair bill.

- ***escape of floodwaters onto C's land*** – a public authority may not be required to install very expensive infrastructure works to prevent flooding, where those works were expensive, and its resources did not warrant it. It will all depend upon the circumstances, and the resources available to D.

In *Lambert v Barratt Homes Ltd*,[180] Mr Lambert, C, was one of several householders whose properties were flooded by surface water flowing from land belonging to Rochdale MBC, D. **Held:** D was not in breach of its 'measured duty,' because D's duty did not extend to constructing drainage ditches and a catchpit at their own expense. Although D had funds far in excess of those available to householders, C, D was under financial pressure too, especially where its resources were held for public purposes and were not generally available for the benefit of private persons. However, in *Vernon Knight Associates v Cornwall CC*,[181] floodwater escaped from one of D's roads in the county, which flooded C's holiday village in Cornwall, twice. **Held:** breach proven: 'even after making due allowance for the pressures on local authorities, the measured duty on the council did require it to take reasonable steps to keep that drainage installation functioning properly.' D had decided that the risk of flooding from the road was serious enough to justify building special infrastructure works (e.g., installing drains, gullies and a catchpit), but ultimately, these were not maintained as they should have been.

Health authorities

§6.24 English law is presently unsettled as to whether the standard of care required of a health authority *may* be suppressed because of limited or scarce resources, albeit that the standard will never be reduced, at law, to a negligible level of care.

For a Health Authority or hospital, D, English courts have dealt with the application of resources (or the lack of them) to the relevant standard of care in a somewhat inconsistent fashion to date.

This principle is only relevant where systemic negligence on the Health Authority's part is alleged (quite separately from alleged negligent acts or omissions on the part of a healthcare practitioner, for whom the Health Authority is allegedly vicariously liable). 'systemic negligence' – arising from an 'institutional duty of care', or a 'non-delegable duty on the hospital authority toward the patient', as it is otherwise termed – means the failure by the Health Authority to put in place the requisite managerial or operational procedures that reasonably

[179] [1980] 1 QB 485 (CA), and applied recently in: *Coope v Ward* [2015] EWCA Civ 30.
[180] [2010] EWCA Civ 681. [181] [2013] EWCA Civ 950, [58].

would have prevented patient C's harm from occurring. It is an allegation of direct wrongdoing against the governing Health Authority (as discussed in Chapter 7).

Of course, the standard of care must not be set too high – a Health Authority is only required to implement a system 'framed to deal with that which is reasonably foreseeable, [but not a system] framed to deal with the possibility that a rare occurrence will happen' (per *Garcia v St Mary's Trust*[182]). Hence, Health Authorities do not have to meet the very high standard of 'ensur[ing] that proper assistance was readily available' to prevent C's harm – that had been the view of the trial judge in *Bull v Devon HA*, but it was disapproved on appeal, because it:

> implies an absolute and unqualified obligation [and] overstated the duty falling on the authority, again having regard to the number of suitably qualified obstetricians available to the hospital on the particular Saturday afternoon ... With that limited manpower available, it might have been quite impossible, however diligent the attempt, to secure the attendance of either [obstetrician] within 10–15 minutes, because both of them might have had inescapable other commitments.[183]

However, English case law is somewhat divided, as to whether a Health Authority's resources are legitimately to be taken account of, in reducing the standard required, if resources are scarce and limited.

View #1. On one view, the standard of care should be suppressed, because of the 'logistical constraints' (as the court put it in *Richards v Swansea NHS Trust*[184]) under which a Health Authority operates. The 'limited resources' argument is one factor that a court **can** legitimately take into account, when pitching the standard of care required to be met by the Health Authority. Its relevance is judicially supported for several reasons:

i. a Health Authority owes co-duties to other patients, which may prevent it from giving one patient the treatment or resources that it 'would ideally prefer' (per *Arthur JS Hall & Co v Simons*[185]);
ii. moreover, a Health Authority must manage and provide an effective and careful workplace for its own staff (per *Garcia v St Mary's Trust*[186]);
iii. whether a public authority has 'got its resource allocation right' is not a matter for a judge to adjudicate – rather, it is a parliamentary decision (an argument also made, in the police context, in *Hill v CC of West Yorkshire*[187]).

As always, where a standard is suppressed due to circumstances, then the *practical* effect is that it will be harder – although not impossible – to prove breach.

> In *Hardaker v Newcastle HA*, Mr Hardaker, C, a diver, suffered from symptoms of serious decompression illness ('the bends'), which required treatment in a decompression chamber. C alleged that a decompression chamber available at Newcastle University, adjacent to the hospital there (the Royal Victoria Infirmary, RVI), ought to have been open at all hours. It was closed on the weekends, the time at which C suffered the bends, meaning that he had to be transferred to the police diving school's decompression chamber in Sunderland). The decompression chamber at Newcastle University was under the control of the Newcastle HA, D. **Held:** no breach proven.

182 [2006] EWHC 2314 (QB) [96]. 183 (1989) 22 BMLR 79 (CA) 83 (Slade LJ).
184 [2007] EWHC 487 (QB) [31] (no breach proven).
185 [2002] 1 AC 615 (HL) 690 (Lord Hoffmann, referring to doctors, but of equal application to Health Authorities).
186 [2006] EWHC 2314 (QB) [95]. 187 [1989] AC 53 (HL) 63–64 (Lord Keith).

[D's duty of care to C] was qualified by the resources available to them ... They cannot be held to have been negligent for failing to apply sufficient resources to the [Newcastle University] chamber to keep it available at all hours: such an allegation involves an assessment of the priority of allocation of resources which a Court cannot perform ... The suggestion that the RVI should have secured the attendance of a doctor at Sunderland assumes the availability of a suitable doctor who was not otherwise required and the resources to pay him. The evidence came nowhere near to establishing that [D] had been negligent in this regard, quite apart from the fact that issues of resource allocation are not for the Court. On the day in question, Dr Dorani said he could not have left the A&E Department, even to go to the helicopter landing site, without significantly depleting the staff. He was on duty with two junior doctors, and would not have wanted to send either of them to accompany the helicopter. It was reasonably the practice at the RVI to send out medical staff only in the event of a major medical disaster, such as a rail crash or major road crash. Mr Hardaker's case did not come into this category.[188]

Hence, the court was prepared to accept that the Royal Victoria met the standard of care required of it by law, as 'qualified' by its limited resources.

Nevertheless, any suppressed standard of medical care expected of Health Authority D, due to its resource limitations, cannot be reduced to a standard that is manifestly inadequate or absent altogether. Nor can the non-availability of resources, due to governmental budgetary constraints, be used by D as a defence to a negligence claim. In *Knight v Home Office*[189] (the suicide-at-Brixon-prison-case), Pill J provided the following hypothetical example: what if Parliament did not provide any funds to a prison to operate a hospital wing, so that prisoners did not receive any on-site medical care? An ordinary reasonable standard of medical care to those housed in the prison would **still** be operative, and a breach would thus be found if no medical treatment was provided at all. The criticism by Pill J, that any suggestion that a lack of resources could not possibly be a defence, has been endorsed at appellate level (per *Sussex Ambulance NHS Trust v King*[190]). Nevertheless, Pill J confirmed that the allocation of resources by Parliament is 'one factor' which the court must consider when deciding what standard of care the law should demand.

View #2. On the other hand, some cases suggest a harder-line approach, whereby no reduction in the standard of care is appropriate where resources are scant/limited. Two reasons have been cited:

i. many potential Ds face resource problems, and do not benefit from a suppressed standard of care.

In *Bull v Devon HA*[191] Mrs Bull gave birth to twins at a campus of a hospital which was operated by the Devon HA, D. It was a 'split-site' hospital, constructed over three campuses. First twin, Darryl, was delivered without incident, but an obstetric emergency developed with the birth of the second twin, Stuart, C, who was born 68 minutes later. C suffered brain damage due to hypoxia, causing profound mental disability and spastic quadriplegia. C alleged that D failed to have an adequate system for summonsing an obstetrician, so that all attempts made to summon the registrar between births were unsuccessful, and the pager went unanswered. **Held:** breach proven. The system of summoning the obstetricians on call between campuses was 'precarious', 'unreliable and essentially unsatisfactory', and 'operating on a knife-edge', with no reasonable explanation as to why the system had broken down.

[188] QB, 15 Jun 2001, [54]–[56].
[189] [1990] 3 All ER 237 (QB), with example and quote at 243.
[190] [2002] EWCA Civ 953, [45].
[191] (1989) 22 BMLR 79 (CA).

It had been suggested in argument that 'since the small number of consultants and registrars had to deal with three different sites, [t]hey could not be expected to do more than their best, allocating their limited resources as favourably as possible'. Mustill LJ replied that he had 'some reservations' about the argument, and that 'there are other public services in respect of which it is not necessarily an answer to allegations of unsafety that there were insufficient resources to enable the administrators to do everything which they would like to do'. The statement was dicta: because C had not argued that the hospital had been negligent in providing insufficient resources, the court would leave this 'important issue of social policy' to another day.

ii. in *Wilsher v Essex AHA*, Sir Browne-Wilkinson V-C supported the notion that the Health Authority's standard of care should not be reduced (so that it could more easily escape liability) if resources available to it were limited – rather, holding up the standard, and finding direct liability against an under-resourced Health Authority, was preferable to deciding that a doctor was in breach, when he could do nothing about the under-resourced system in which he had to operate:

> Claims against a health authority that it has itself been directly negligent, as opposed to vicariously liable for the negligence of its doctors, will, of course, raise awkward problems ... But the law should not be distorted by making findings of personal fault against individual doctors who are, in truth, not at fault in order to avoid such questions. To do so would be to cloud the real issues which arise.[192]

Although Sir Browne-Wilkinson VC dissented on the issue of the effect of inexperience, his views on resource allocation and its impact on standard of care were not subject to any criticism by the majority in *Wilsher* (and the issue was not dealt with on further appeal to the House of Lords).

Resource allocation is, at the end of the day, a political decision upon which Health Authorities who are sued – and the courts which must determine those suits – have no control. In *Hardaker v Newcastle HA*,[193] it was pointed out that, how Royal Victoria Infirmary spent its not overly-indulgent budget allocation was a question for the NHS Trust, and not for the court to examine and overrule. In *Kent v Griffiths* too,[194] the Court of Appeal concurred that, 'where what is being attacked is the allocation of resources, whether in the provision of sufficient ambulances or sufficient drivers or attendants, different considerations could apply. There then could be issues which are not suited for resolution by the courts'.

Hence, judicially speaking, opinion as to the relevance of the resources available to a Health Authority on the standard of care expected of it, is somewhat divided. However, the better view (on the basis of the abovementioned authorities) is that the standard of care required of a Health Authority *will* be suppressed, where D can show that the harm to C was brought about due to D's limited resources – but having said that, the standard will never be reduced, at law, to a negligible standard.

[192] [1987] QB 730 (CA) 778. [193] QB, 15 Jun 2001, [54]. [194] [2000] EWCA Civ 25, [47].

7

Breach II – Proving negligence

INTRODUCTION

§7.1 Breach is doing something which a prudent and reasonable person would not do, or failing to do something which a prudent and reasonable person would do.

This definition of breach, adapted from Alderson B's 'classic statement'[1] in *Blyth v Birmingham Waterworks Co*[2] back in 1856, highlights the key question: what would a reasonable person have done differently, to avoid the risk of harm or injury occurring to C? If the answer to that is, 'nothing', then breach will fail.

That something has gone wrong is, of itself, absolutely no evidence of breach. Injuries, damage, adverse outcomes, and less-than-desirable results, may all arise from an exercise of reasonable care. Courts have, on occasion, addressed remarks to Cs for whom they obviously felt a great deal of sympathy for their misfortunes, but for whom they could not find in favour, because there was no lack of reasonable care. For example, motor vehicle accidents, and medical mishaps, may ruin young lives, e.g., in *Arnot v Sprake*, where the Court of Appeal held against car accident victim C, concluding that it was 'highly regrettable that unfortunately [C] has suffered serious injury as a result of the impact he sustained'[3]; and in *Nawoor v Barking Havering and Brentwood HA*, where a birth went very badly:

> the family of this child must feel that an injury so severe, with such obvious long-term consequences, could only be the product of something going wrong, and negligently wrong. Understandable that may be, but it is not the appropriate conclusion in this case. I regret to have reached the conclusion I have, because this child is clearly going to be affected in the longer term as a teenager and an adult, but regret it though I do, it is the conclusion I firmly reach.[4]

[1] As recently described in: *Dunnage v Randall* [2015] EWCA Crim 673, [123].

[2] (1856) 11 Ct Exch 781, 156 ER 1047–1049.

[3] [2001] EWCA Civ 341, [54].

[4] [1998] Lloyd's Rep Med 313 (QB) [last paragraph].

The framework

The framework of analysis for breach is set out in the following Table:

Breach in a nutshell

Preliminary matters:

i Proving the requisite foreseeability
ii Assessing the date of breach
iii Ruling out 'inevitable accident'
iv Potential dual bases of liability: vicarious liability and systemic breach

Modes of proving breach – where applicable on the facts:

1 Testing the precautionary steps against *Bolton v Stone's* 'breach factors'
2 Applying the *Bolam* test (as qualified by '*Bolitho's* gloss')
3 Other potential tests of breach:
- Contravening specific duties of care
- Contravening relevant rules/standards
- Contravening the 'making it worse' rule

4 The doctrine of *res ipsa loquitur*

What does not prove breach:

- D's view, pre-event or pre-accident
- An expert organisation's opinion
- Changing the system, post-accident
- Failing to remove an inherent risk in D's conduct
- And finally, the (ir)relevance of proving 'gross negligence'

A matter of terminology

§7.2 Any distinction between mere 'errors of judgment', and breaches of duty, has proven unhelpful, and is not determinative of the question of breach.

In *Barrett v Enfield LBC*,[5] Lord Hutton stated that 'the court must be satisfied that the conduct complained of went beyond mere errors of judgment in the exercise of a discretion and constituted conduct which can be regarded as negligent'; and, in *Arthur JS Hall & Co v Simons*,[6] Lord Hope noted that, 'a mere error of judgment on [a barrister's] part will not expose him to liability for negligence'.

However, this terminology has proven unhelpful in English cases. An error of judgment, as with any other mistake, **can** constitute negligence. As Lord Fraser said in *Whitehouse v Jordan*,[7] any statement that 'in a professional man, an error of judgment is not negligent' is an inaccurate statement of the law – correctly, it must say that an error of judgment 'is not *necessarily*

[5] [1999] UKHL 25, [2001] 2 AC 550 (HL) 591. [6] [2000] UKHL 38, [2002] 1 AC 615 (HL) 726.
[7] [1981] 1 WLR 246 (HL) 263 (emphasis added).

negligent' – because '[m]erely to describe something as an error of judgment tells us nothing about whether it is negligent or not. The true position is that an error of judgment may, or may not, be negligent; it depends on the nature of the error'. This position was emphasised later in *Davis v Stena Line Ltd*,[8] where Forbes J described an 'error of judgment' as 'ambiguous and not very helpful', and in *Henry v Thames Valley Police*,[9] where Smith LJ remarked that, '[w]hat matters, in a civil action, is whether [D's] actions were negligent, in that they fell below the expected standard of reasonable skill or care. It may be wise to avoid any argument about whether there has been an error of judgment'.

Given this judicial admonishment, the terminology, 'error of judgment', is avoided in this chapter.

PRELIMINARY MATTERS

The test of foreseeability

The general principles, and leading authorities, governing the test of foreseeability of damage were examined in Chapter 2. To reiterate, negligence is concerned with a *reasonable* D, not a highly-anxious, or highly-perceptive or visionary, perfectionist.

In *Jolley v Sutton LBC*,[10] Lord Hoffmann stated that the concept of reasonable foreseeability 'does not denote a fixed point on the scale of probability'. Merely possible (i.e., very small or far-fetched) risks may be foreseeable, but they are not *reasonably* foreseeable; a risk must be likely enough that a reasonable D, careful of the safety of his neighbour, would not think it right to neglect or ignore that risk (per *Overseas Tankship (UK) Ltd v Miller Steamship Co Pty Ltd (Wagon Mound No 2)*[11]). It must be a 'real risk, and not just a mere possibility' (per *Khan v Harrow CC*[12]). To reiterate, and as clarified in *Smith v Littlewoods Organisation Ltd*,[13] whenever the word, 'probable', is used in the context of reasonable foreseeability, it decidedly does **not** entail any proof on the balance of probabilities. Rather, 'it is used as indicating a real risk, as distinct from a mere possibility of danger. It is **not** used in the sense that the consequence must be more probable than not, before it can be reasonably foreseeable.'

A narrower foreseeability test

§7.3 The reasonable foreseeability test, under breach, is a narrower test than that which is applied at duty of care stage. At breach stage, the court is required to assess whether the event or accident was so unlikely (i.e., unforeseeable) as not to require any precautionary steps or alternative course of action to be taken by D.

The enquiry, at breach stage, is quite specific – was the event or accident foreseeable, so that D acted unreasonably in not taking steps to forestall its occurrence? After all, if the event was so remote and so unlikely as to be unforeseeable, then no reasonable D would have taken precautionary steps to guard against the risk of that danger or harm manifesting (even if some steps or alternative course of conduct can be identified, which probably would have precluded the harm from occurring).

[8] [2005] EWHC 420 (QB) [11]. [9] [2010] EWCA Civ 5, [2010] RTR 14, [43].
[10] [2000] 1 WLR 1082 (HL) 1091. [11] [1967] 1 AC 617 (PC) 642–43.
[12] [2013] EWHC 2687 (TCC) [59]–[62] (Ramsey J). [13] [1987] AC 241 (HL) 269.

However, there is an 'inevitable overlap' between the establishment of a duty of care and the proof of breach, insofar as proving a foreseeable risk of injury is concerned – that was acknowledged, e.g., in *Gabriel v Kirklees MC*.[14] Indeed, in the following, a duty of care was owed to C (hence, that test of foreseeability was upheld), but no breach ensued because the event or accident was unforeseeable, although judicial opinion differed as each case proceeded to appeal, highlighting the difficulty of assessing the issue:

In *Bolton v Stone*,[15] C, Miss Stone, was hit by a cricket ball while standing on the footpath outside her house at Cheetham Hill. The Cheetham Cricket Ground, owned by the Club, D, was adjacent to the road, and matches had been regularly played there since about 1864. The residential area where C lived was constructed in 1910. The ball had travelled a distance of about 100 yards, over a 7-foot high fence (but, with the upward slope of the ground, about 17 feet above the cricket pitch where the ball exited the ground). The evidence was that hitting a ball onto the road was altogether exceptional, and had occurred about 6 times in 38 years. **Held (CA):** D was not liable in nuisance, but was liable in negligence. **Held (HL):** D was not liable in negligence or in nuisance. Re negligence, the risk of C's injury was too small to be reasonably foreseeable, although it was variously assessed as 'infinitesimal', or 'not far from the borderline'. In *Whippey v Jones*,[16] Mr Jones, 42, C, was jogging along a footpath at Riverside Walk in Leeds when he was accosted by Hector, a fully-grown 2-year-old Great Dane, owned by Christopher Whippey, D, an RSPCA Inspector. After colliding with Hector, C fell down a slope to the river and badly broke his ankle. **Held (trial):** breach proven, because D failed to take sufficient care to ensure that there were no other people about before he let Hector off the lead. **Held (CA):** no breach proven, because the test of foreseeability necessary for proof of breach failed. Hector had no tendency to jump up at other people; at the most, he stopped and barked at people 5–10 feet away. There was no reason why D, as a reasonable dog handler in the park, should have anticipated that if Hector was let off the lead when some other adult was about, that person would be physically harmed from Hector bounding up and colliding with him.

Previous occurrences

§7.4 Where C suffered an injury or harm from an event or accident which had *never* happened previously, that does not, of itself, render the risk unforeseeable. Obversely, if the risk had eventuated prior to C's accident, it does not automatically render the risk *reasonably* foreseeable. In all cases, the question is whether that risk was sufficiently foreseeable to require a reasonable D to take precautionary steps to avert the risk of injury.

It is impossible to draw any clear conclusions, where there is an absence of any previous similar accident. That very fact 'is not conclusive, but it is helpful', in disproving foreseeability (per Swinton Thomas LJ in *McGivney v Golderslea Ltd*[17]) – or, as Waller LJ put it in *Simkiss v Rhondda BC*,[18] no previous incident tends to offset 'to a great extent' an argument that the risk of injury was foreseeable.

In *Abouzaid v Mothercare (UK) Ltd*,[19] Iman Abouzaid, C, 12, was helping his mother to attach a 'Cosytoes' sleeping bag to a pushchair, manufactured by D, when its elasticised strap slipped from

[14] [2004] EWCA Civ 345, [27].

[15] [1951] AC 850 (HL) 860 (Lord Normand), 863 (Lord Oaksey), 867 (Lord Reid), 869 (Lord Radcliffe), on appeal from: [1950] 1 KB 201 (CA).

[16] [2009] EWCA Civ 452.

[17] [1997] EWCA Civ 2656, (2001) 17 Const LJ 454.

[18] (1983) 81 LGR 460 (CA).

[19] [2000] EWCA Civ 348.

his grasp and the buckle hit him in the left eye, causing a detached retina injury. **Held:** no breach in negligence. There had never been any comparable accidents; elastic was a commonly used fabric; and long experience had not shown that its use in children's products was likely to cause injury.

However, it can never be said that, just because something has not occurred before, it is unforeseeable. It may be a matter of sheer good fortune and coincidence that the accident had not happened previously.

In *Bunker v Charles Brand & Son Ltd*,[20] Mr Bunker, C, was an employee of a construction and engineering firm engaged in work in a tube tunnel. It was being drilled out by a machine being used by Charles Brand, D. The normal way to reach the front of the machine was by walking along the angle irons, using a girder as a handhold. As C was doing so, his foot slipped off onto the rollers, which moved, and C fell, suffering serious injury. **Held**: D was liable for breach, under the OLA 1957: '[t]he mere fact that no accident had happened in the past does not absolve [D] from taking further precautions'. D should have put down planks beside or on top of the rollers, to enable a firm walkway for getting up to the front of the machine.

Obversely, just because the incident had occurred previously (without injury) does not, of itself, indicate that the test of foreseeability will automatically be proven. The latest manifestation of the incident may still be reasonably unforeseeable, especially if its past occurrences have been rare (of course, it cannot be totally unforeseeable, as it has happened before!). Two sporting cases provide good illustrations, in which there was no breach:

In *Bolton v Stone*,[21] facts previously, there was no breach, even where the cricket ball had been hit out of the ground on a few occasions previously. In *Horton v Jackson*,[22] a golfer's drive shot hit another golfer, Mr Horton, C, the shot being executed without looking up to see where the injured golfer was located and in plain view. There had been only two proven incidents before this accident at this part of D's golf course in the previous 16 years, with upwards of 800,000 rounds of golf played from this tee. This eventuality was foreseeable – but was not *reasonably* foreseeable, so there was no need for the golf club to institute further precautions. In any event, the golfer 'was so intent on playing his shot and, for some reason, playing it quickly, that he simply did not look, and on his own evidence was not aware of the presence of [C] until after his ball had struck him. No steps could have been taken by the golf club to prevent folly of this kind'.

On the other hand, foreseeability is likely to be proven if previous complaints had been made to D about the very same event/incident – or if the very incident which gave rise to C's injury or harm happened shortly after a similar incident. In the following, breach was proven:

In *Stimpson v Wolverhampton MBC*,[23] Mr Stimpson, C, a member of the public, was hit in the mouth by a golf ball which was played in Council D's public park. The accident was foreseeable, given evidence from a park attendant that people regularly played golf, in spite of being told not to; sometimes by repeat offenders; and some complaints had been made by the public who had been physically struck by golf balls. In *Cunningham v Reading FC*,[24] Mr Cunningham, C, was an on-duty police officer at a football match at D's Reading Football Stadium, when, during a match, there was an outbreak of horrible and terrifying violence, with Bristol City fans attacking Reading fans and invading the pitch. Dangerous missiles were thrown, including lumps of concrete torn up from the

[20] [1969] 2 QB 480, 489. [21] [1951] AC 850 (HL). [22] [1996] CLY 4475 (CA) (Douglas Brown J).
[23] CA, 22 May 1990. [24] [1992] PIQR P141 (QB) P153.

dilapidated terraces, and one of these struck C, injuring him. Concrete had been broken and used as missiles less than four months previously, and hence, D 'had been put on full notice of the potential danger from this state of affairs, and had done nothing whatsoever to remedy it'.

Occasionally, the lack of previous occurrence of the accident is because C's behaviour in the instant case was unusual, almost unprecedented. In that event, it will be difficult to prove that C's injury was reasonably foreseeable.

In *Cornish Glennroy Blair-Ford v CRS Adventures Ltd*,[25] Glenn Blair-Ford, C, suffered permanent tetraplegia when he threw a wellington boot backwards through his legs at D's outdoor pursuits centre at the River Dart Country Park in Devon. C's head was low down by his legs, his hands went through his legs with a lot of force, throwing the welly high into the air, not what was intended; and then C toppled over and fell onto his head and neck, rather than toppling forwards onto his face and chest. **Held:** C's injury was not reasonably foreseeable. The execution of his throw 'could not have been foreseen, namely, considerable force, bending very low, positioning the head almost between the knees, falling forwards when the hands were still between the knees, and striking the ground with his head and neck at such an angle as to cause the catastrophic injury sustained by him. His was no ordinary throw. The fact that the welly went almost straight up in the air rather than being thrown a long distance is powerful evidence that he threw it and fell in an unusual way that was not and could not have been foreseen'.

Known susceptibilities

§7.5 Where D *knows* that C is particularly susceptible to injury, then the test of foreseeability will be proven, as that particular D has *foreseen* the risk.

Where the susceptibility of C to injury is actually known to D, then the risk is foreseen; and the question of breach will then be assessed by reference to what (if any) precautions a reasonable D should have taken to protect **that particular** C. D's knowledge may relate to its systems' or its employees' vulnerabilities, either of which pose a potential risk. For example:[26]

In *Paris v Stepney BC*,[27] Mr Paris, C, was a garage hand employed in D's garage. He had only one functioning eye, due to a war-time injury. C was hammering at a wheel to remove a bolt, when a chip of metal flew up and entered his good (right) eye, blinding him. Goggles were not supplied to the employees in this garage; indeed, there was no evidence that it was customary for employers of garage employees to supply goggles. **Held (3:2):** breach proven. In *AG (British Virgin Islands) v Hartwell*,[28] PC Kelvin Laurent was the sole police officer in charge on the island of Jost Van Dyke in the BVI. He was entrusted with guns and ammunition. One evening, PC Laurent abandoned his post, left the island, taking a gun with him, visited a restaurant at another island where his former partner (Ms Lafond) waitressed, and fired four shots at her and her current partner. Craig Hartwell, C, a pub customer, was caught up in the shooting and suffered serious injuries. C sued the police employer, D, for entrusting PC Laurent with a gun, when he was known to have 'personal troubles', and had

[25] [2012] EWHC 2360 (QB) [66].

[26] Also: *Hicks v Young* [2015] EWHC 1144 (QB) (a blind guest fell out of a second-floor open window of a guest-house, suffering grievous injuries), discussed further in Chapter 12, 'Occupiers' Liability'.

[27] [1951] AC 367 (HL) 376. Also: *McDonald v Highlands & Islands Enterprise* 2001 SCLR 547, [2001] IRLR 336, [68].

[28] [2004] UKPC 12, [2004] WLR 1273 (on appeal from the British Virgin Islands).

threatened another companion of Ms Lafond's with a long-bladed knife shortly before this incident. PC Laurent had been visited by a supervisor; that colleague accepted his explanation of events (he was using the knife to peel an orange) and did not question the threatened party; and merely told PC Laurent to sort out his personal problems in a more professional way. **Held:** breach proven. This particular employee posed a real risk to members of the public such as C, with his volatility, access to guns, and past threatening behaviour, i.e., that he would 'lose control of himself over his family problems and find the lure of a gun irresistible'.

The English Court of Appeal has since acknowledged, in *Armstrong v British Coal Corp*,[29] that the 'essence' of *Paris* was that C succeeded, 'because he was known by his employers to have only one sound eye, and they failed to provide him with appropriate goggles. The claim did not succeed on the basis that goggles should have been provided for *anyone* working in the same process as [C], although, obviously, being rendered blind in one eye is a very serious injury even for a man with two sound eyes'.

Hence, it is always relevant to ask: what **actual** knowledge did D have of any particular susceptibility of C to harm? The point is particularly important in the employment context, for as *Paris* and *Hartwell* demonstrate, employers will typically know of the physical infirmities afflicting their employees. The rationale was explained by Lady Justice Hale in *Sutherland v Hatton*:[30] an employer's duty is owed *to each individual employee*, and not to some 'unidentified outsider' – the latter being the usual case where D injures C, and has no knowledge of C's particular susceptibilities to grave injury at all. In an employer's case, C's susceptibilities are typically **known** to D, because '[t]he employer knows who his employee is', and hence, may know of C's 'particular vulnerability' – in which case, both foreseeability, and the precautionary steps that D should have taken as a reasonable employer, may be even more starkly realised.

The date for assessing breach

§7.6 Whether D's conduct met the standard of reasonable care must be assessed at the date that the alleged negligence occurred.

D is not to be judged by the wisdom of hindsight. One Canadian judge aptly stated the challenge thus:

> Hindsight has no role to play in evaluating conduct that is said to fall below a reasonable standard of care. Practices change and standards evolve. As much as possible, one must try to go back and experience the event as it was then.[31]

In *Roe v Ministry of Health*,[32] Denning LJ put it more artistically: that 'we must not look at what happened in 1949 through 1954 spectacles'.

The principle has some very practical consequences. First, it can adversely affect C, where some accident has befallen him, ahead of advances in scientific knowledge – because whatever happened to him may well have been unforeseeable. Scientific knowledge itself may have

[29] [1998] EWCA Civ 1359, [1998] CLY 975 (emphasis added).

[30] [2002] EWCA Civ 76, [2002] IRLR 263, [23].

[31] *Latin v Hosp for Sick Children* [2007] OJ No 13 (SCJ) [30] (Lax J). Also: *Hardman v Riddell* [2004] EWHC 1691 (QB) [61].

[32] [1954] 2 QB 66 (CA) 72.

advanced and later shown up, as disastrous, a practice that could not have been known to be faulty when C's injury or damage happened. The problem has arisen particularly in the engineering, product liability and medical contexts:

In *Williams v Univ of Birmingham*,[33] Michael Williams, C, studied physics at D's university, as an undergraduate, between 1970–74. He died of malignant mesothelioma, aged 54. His estate claimed that C undertook speed-of-light experiments in a 90-foot-long service tunnel, which was not ventilated, and had central heating pipes running through it, which were lagged with asbestos installed in the 1930s or 1940s. D's asbestos dust tests in 2004, 2006 and 2007 on dust residues taken from the tunnel showed all forms of blue, brown and white asbestos present. D argued that C's exposure to asbestos during those tunnel experiments was minimal, and that it was not liable for causing C's fatal mesothelioma. **Held:** no breach. As to what D should reasonably have foreseen about the dangers of asbestos exposure in 1974, the acceptable levels of exposure were contained in the Factory Inspectorate's 'Technical Data Note 13' (1970), which D was entitled to rely on, as recognised and established guidelines. Given the level of exposure to asbestos fibres actually found, D could not have reasonably foreseen that C would be exposed to an unacceptable risk of asbestos-related injury. In *Abouzaid v Mothercare (UK) Ltd*,[34] facts previously, **held (CA)**: no breach proven. Manufacturer D had not equipped his product with a securing device, but in 1990, no manufacturer of childcare products could reasonably have recognised that the elastic attachment straps for a Cosytoes could pose a hazard to the eyes of children or adults. 'We must not look at the 1990 accident with 2000 spectacles.' The fact that D should either give a warning or take steps to eliminate the risk of eye injuries at the time of trial (2000) was irrelevant, when determining negligence against D in 1990. In *Roe v Ministry of Health*, nupercaine, a spinal anaesthetic, was stored in sealed glass ampoules, themselves stored in a phenol solution. Phenol percolated through tiny invisible cracks in the glass contaminating the nupercaine. When injected, it caused paralysis from the waist down for two young labourers, C, who had minor surgery for back pain. Knowledge of cracks in glass was known in 1951, but not in 1947 when the operations on C occurred. **Held:** no breach. The possibility of cracks in glass was not known or foreseeable at the time of the operation, and hence, dyeing the phenol with a colourant, which would have shown any infusion of phenol into the nupercaine, was not required.

Even if D's breach is alleged to have occurred over a lengthy time interval, the court will need to take account of developing knowledge about the particular risk concerned over that **same** time period, but not later.

In *Baker v Quantum Clothing Group Ltd*,[35] employers were sued in negligence and under the Factories Act 1961, s29(1), for hearing loss experienced by employees in the knitting industry of Derbyshire and Nottingham prior to 1990, who suffered noise-induced hearing loss resulting from exposure to noise levels between 85–90dB. **Held (3:2):** no breach proven. The 1972 Code of Practice provided official guidance re the maximum acceptable levels of noise; to comply with 90dB, as the highest acceptable level, met the standard of the reasonable and prudent employer during the 1970s and 1980s, at least until the 1986 Directive became generally known in the industry.

As Lord Saville said, to hold D liable for breach in this case would have been to 'depend, to a significant degree, on hindsight, and consequently place an undue burden on employers'.[36]

[33] [2011] EWCA Civ 1242, [2012] PIQR P4, [61]. [34] [2000] EWCA Civ 348, [51]–[52].
[35] [2011] UKSC 17, [2011] 1 WLR 1003. [36] *ibid*, [136].

Secondly, delay in achieving trial can render the proof of liability very challenging – particularly in professional negligence cases, as pointed out in *Mortgage Express Ltd v Joliffe & Flint (a firm)*:

> to make good a charge of professional incompetence will often involve a fellow professional in the same area of practice, indulging in an attempt to second-guess the judgment of [D], sometimes many years after [D] was called on to express his professional opinion, and in circumstances where neither party is able, with confidence, to replicate the precise circumstances in which the opinion under attack came to be expressed, and where [D] thereby may well find himself seriously disadvantaged. It is for reasons such as these that an allegation of professional negligence should not be lightly made, and that the law requires that such an allegation should be distinctly proved.[37]

The problem manifests acutely where C was injured during birth, because given the suspension of limitation periods until C reaches the age of majority,[38] the court may be asked to determine whether a breach of the reasonable standard occurred, at some point a quarter of a century or more before the trial itself occurs (e.g., there was a 25-year gap between alleged negligence and trial in *Macey v Warwickshire HA*,[39] and an even longer 28-year gap in *C v Cairns*[40]). As one court despaired, the trial was 'long after the facts have faded from recollection' (per *Bull v Devon AHA*[41]). Frequently, D (or D's staff) who was involved in an allegedly negligent event will genuinely have no recollection of the event, and contemporaneous notes, even where they have survived, may be incomplete (per *Macey*[42]). Other documentary evidence may be missing too (e.g., scan photographs, as occurred in *Lillywhite v UCL Hosp NHS Trust*[43]). Key medical witnesses, including D, may have moved jurisdiction (as in *Wisniewski v Central Manchester HA*, where D had moved to work in Australia and did not return for the trial, leading to certain adverse inferences being drawn against him[44]). Also, practices within the medical profession may have significantly changed since the alleged breach – but such advances must be ignored by the trial judge, *viz*: in the provision of ante-natal and neo-natal care (*Macey*), or in cervical screening practices (*Penney, Palmer and Cannon v East Kent HA*[45]), or in the drug treatment available for a medical condition (*Bellarby v Worthing and Southlands Hosp NHS Trust*[46]), or in a hospital's procedures for managing staff (*Bull v Devon AHA*).

The degree of speculation may be just too great for a court, given the gaps in evidence, to find that breach occurred. That is a direct consequence of the difficulty in reconstructing the evidence as to what happened on a fateful day. As the court stated in *Leggett v Norfolk, Suffolk and Cambridgeshire Strategic HA*: '[i]t is ... my sad conclusion that the evidence of what happened on 19 March 1990 to cause kernicterus contains so many gaps, and is now so difficult to reconstruct with confidence, and the degree of speculation has become so great, that I am quite unable to find that there was, on the balance of probabilities, a lack of reasonable care [by doctor D]'[47]). There is also the temptation to adduce evidence, of what competent practice amounted to, from secondary literature published and/or available at some point

[37] (QB, 20 Dec 1995). [38] Per the Limitation Act 1980, s 38(2).
[39] [2004] EWHC 1198 (QB). See too: *Mirza v Birmingham HA* (QB, 31 Jul 2001).
[40] [2003] EWHC 437 (QB).
[41] (1989) 22 BMLR 79 (CA) 116 (Mustill LJ). (The trial judge Tucker J described the 17-year gap there as 'deplorable'.)
[42] [2004] EWHC 1198 (QB) [2]–[3]. [43] [2005] EWCA Civ 1466, [9].
[44] [1998] EWCA Civ 596. [45] (2000) 55 BMLR 63 (CA) [22].
[46] [2005] EWHC 2089 (QB) [106] (advances in available drugs had occurred since the alleged negligence in 1999).
[47] [2006] EWHC 1238 (QB) [114].

after the alleged negligence occurred, which must be sternly resisted. The court noted in *French v Thames Valley Strategic HA* that, '[i]n determining the state of medical knowledge and practice in 1991, both parties, but in particular [C], referred to and sought to rely on literature significantly later than 1991 ... The use of such literature significantly increases the risk of inappropriate hindsight ... where the conflicts between the experts should be resolved by reference to the literature, I have relied on that which is the most contemporary to [C's] delivery'.[48]

Ruling out 'inevitable accidents'

§7.7 Inevitable accidents occur where a reasonable D could not have taken any precautionary steps to avoid the risk of injury to C; and hence, these accidents cannot constitute negligence.

What it means

An inevitable accident is one which D could not avoid by any reasonable measures (per *The Merchant Prince*[49]). The doctrine has been difficult to prove, in reality. The cases in which D has sought to plead this include the following circumstances:

i. a natural external event, constituting an Act of God (per *Baldwin v Foy*,[50] due to a hailstorm – but no inevitable accident was proven);

ii. an unexpected medical condition suffered by D, which brought about the injury to C.

In *Stotardt v Selkent Bus Co*,[51] Michelle Stotardt, C, was seriously injured when a single-decker bus owned by Selkent, D, drove into shop premises in Eltham. The bus stopped at traffic lights, then turned into a road and crossed onto the southbound carriageway, struck a car, demolished three bollards on the pavement, and ended up ploughing into the shop where C was trapped between the bus and the shop wall. The bus driver, Mr Benjamin, claimed that he had post-traumatic amnesia following a blow to the head in the crash, and only recalled what happened when he heard people shouting at him after the collision. **Held:** no inevitable accident proven. MRI scans showed no brain abnormalities; and passengers stated that D's driver was perfectly conscious (and swearing) whilst driving on the wrong side of the road.

iii. a series of circumstances so unexpected that D could not have avoided the outcome (i.e., the harm to C) by any reasonable measures, in 'agony-of-the-moment' scenarios. Provided that there were **some** precautionary measures that D could have undertaken (e.g., changing lanes to avoid a collision, per *Whitehead v Bruce*[52]), then an inevitable accident will be ruled out, as a matter of law. However, even so, C may fail to prove negligence, precisely because a reasonable D would not have taken those precautionary steps which were at least theoretically available – that, however, is a different point, whereby the reasonable standard of care was not met. In cases of inevitable accident, there is nothing that D reasonably *could* have done to avoid C's accident.

In *Knightley v Johns*,[53] an accident occurred in a one-way tunnel in Birmingham, when Mr Johns, D1, overturned his car, close to a tunnel entrance. Inspector Sommerville, D2, forgot to

[48] [2005] EWHC 459 (QB) [12]. [49] [1892] P 179 (CA) 187 (Lord Esher MR). [50] [1997] IEHC 111.
[51] [2003] EWHC 2135 (QB). [52] [2013] EWCA Civ 229, [32]. [53] [1982] 1 WLR 349 (CA) 367–68.

close the tunnel immediately, and hence, instructed PC Knightley, C, to ride his motor-cycle the wrong way down the tunnel to close it. C collided with Mr Cotton's, D3's, oncoming car, which Mr Cotton was driving in the correct manner, and C suffered serious injuries. C sued Mr Cotton in negligence, as well as Inspector Sommerville, for instructing him to ride the wrong way, and he sued Mr Johns, because it was his negligent driving in the tunnel 'which was the cause of all the trouble'. **Held:** an inevitable accident proven so that Mr Cotton, D3, was not negligent, for there was nothing that he could reasonably have done to avoid the accident with PC Knightley, riding the wrong way down a one-way tunnel. In *Arnot v Sprake*,[54] Lindsey Arnot, C, was riding his motorcycle in Countryman Lane, a small unclassified rural road in Sussex, when he rounded a bend at 45 mph and collided with a crop sprayer pulling a trailer, driven by D. C suffered very severe injuries. **Held:** no inevitable accident proven. D could have taken a number of precautionary steps, *viz*: stopped at the give way sign at the junction; left his vehicle with its hazard warning lights on and walked up the road and placed a red-coloured warning triangle in the road; switched on the flashing light on his cab; sounded the horn on his vehicle; and flashed the headlights of the vehicle as it pulled out of the junction. (However, D did not need to take any of these steps; he had met the standard of reasonable driving; the sole cause of this accident was C's taking the bend too fast.)

Burden of proof

In *The Merchant Prince*,[55] it was held that, if D was claiming that what happened was an inevitable accident, then D had to show that the accident was inevitable, such that the result (i.e., the accident) could not have been avoided. That is, the burden of proof shifted to D to prove that he was not negligent, on the balance of probabilities.

This shift was confirmed, more recently, in *Stotardt v Selkent Bus Co*, where Brown J noted that it was 'common ground' between C and D that it was for D to displace negligence, and to show on the balance of probabilities that the accident was caused without fault on the part of D.[56]

Potential dual bases of liability: vicarious liability and systemic breach

§7.8 D may be liable to C for direct wrongdoing because of some systemic fault on D's part. Direct liability arises where D owes a personal, non-delegable duty of care to C which D breaches. Additionally, where D's employee injures C, then D may be vicariously liable to C for that wrongdoing. Claims by C against D for vicarious liability and for systemic negligence may be brought concurrently, notwithstanding that the bases for the claims are entirely different.

The distinction

Where C is injured because of some act or omission by D's employee, then D may be vicariously liable to C for that employee's wrongdoing, if the employee's tort was committed in the course of his employment with D. That type of claim entails no corporate failure on D's part, but is a form of strict liability. By contrast, 'systemic negligence' (also called an 'institutional

[54] [2001] EWCA Civ 341. [55] (1892) P 179 (CA) 189–90 (Fry LJ). [56] [2003] EWHC 2135 (QB) [5].

duty of care', and a 'non-delegable duty' on D's part) means that D failed to have in place management and operational procedures that would reasonably have prevented the injury to C.

This dual basis of liability may be evident where C is *an employee of D*, and is injured in the workplace by a work colleague – as discussed in 'Employers' liability' (an online chapter), employee C may sue his employer both for vicarious liability, and for systemic negligence. This dual basis of liability is reflected more broadly too, where C is **not** an employee injured in the workplace, but an 'outsider' who is injured by D's systemic wrongdoing, and/or by D's employee. Vicarious liability is discussed in detail in Chapter 18. This section deals only with the systemic negligence allegation.

It was noted, in *EL v Children's Socy*,[57] that systemic negligence can entail a much more extensive inquiry than vicarious liability, because it will be the entire systems and organisation which will be under scrutiny. By contrast, vicarious liability for an employee's alleged wrongdoings (e.g., his sexual assaults against C), rather than for systemic negligence in failing to prevent them, will probably involve 'narrower factual disputes' (per *AB v Nugent Care Socy*[58] and *A v Hoare*[59]); and be 'generally more straightforward' (per *NXS v Camden LBC*[60]), rendering vicarious liability easier to prove.

One advantage of systemic negligence (for C) is that an extension to the 3-year limitation period that would apply to systemic negligence claims for personal injuries is possible, under s 11 of the Limitation Act 1980; whereas claims for personal injuries in respect of *deliberate conduct* by an employee are not subject to an extendable limitation period under s 11, but rather, are subject to a non-extendable 6-year limitation period, which can rule out C's claim altogether (per *KR v Bryn Alyn Community (Holdings) Ltd*).[61]

Systemic negligence for medical wrongdoing

A claim of systemic negligence by a patient against the owner/operator of the hospital at which the patient was treated was raised in a line of English cases more than half a century ago, but the authorities were 'weak', in that the judgments were minority opinions in appellate courts. In the modern era, the claim is more viably asserted, but frequently without success.

In *Cassidy v Ministry of Health*,[62] the Court of Appeal unanimously found in favour of the patient – but whilst the majority relied upon vicarious liability, Denning LJ based his view on the proposition that 'the hospital authorities are themselves under a duty to use care in treating the patient'. A year later, in *Jones v Manchester Corp*,[63] Denning LJ followed his earlier decision and held a hospital board *directly* responsible for a man's death under anaesthetic (the other two members of the Court of Appeal again did not support this view). Two years later, in *Roe v Minister of Health*,[64] again one member of the Court of Appeal (Morris LJ) was prepared to at least find a direct breach on the part of the hospital, but none was proven:

[57] [2012] EWHC 365 (QB) [72]. [58] [2009] EWCA Civ 827, [2010] 1 WLR 516, [18].
[59] [2008] AC 844 (HL) [85]. [60] [2009] EWHC 1786 (QB) [191]. For the same observation: *Raggett v Soc of Jesus Trust 1929 for Roman Catholic Purposes* [2009] EWHC 909 (QB) [121].
[61] [2003] EWCA Civ 85, [2003] QB 1441, [108]. [62] [1951] 2 KB 343 (CA) 362 (Denning LJ).
[63] [1952] 2 All ER 125 (CA) 133. [64] [1954] 2 QB 66 (CA) 90.

> a hospital might have undertaken to provide all the necessary facilities and equipment for the operation, and the obligation of nursing, and also the obligation of anaesthetizing a patient for his operation. The question ... is whether the hospital undertook these obligations. In my judgment, they did.

The Irish High Court noted, in *Byrne v Ryan*, that these views about a hospital's direct liability were 'somewhat ahead of their time'.[65]

Since then, however, there have been several English medico-legal cases in which the *possibility* of systemic negligence, on the part of a governing Health Authority in conducting a hospital, has been judicially recognised. For example, in *A (a child) v MOD*: '[t]hose responsible for the operation of a hospital offer a medical service to those whom they accept for treatment ... this acceptance for treatment carries with it personal positive duties to the patient which cannot be discharged by delegation ... [including a] duty to use reasonable care to ensure that the hospital staff, facilities and organisation provided are those appropriate to provide a safe and satisfactory medical service for the patient. This is an organisational duty';[66] in *X (Minors) v Bedfordshire CC*: 'those conducting a hospital are under a direct duty of care to those admitted as patients to the hospital';[67] and in *Robertson v Nottingham HA*, a hospital 'has a non-delegable duty to provide a proper system of care, just as much as it has a duty to engage competent staff and proper and safe equipment'.[68]

Nevertheless, the allegation has been rarely upheld. The following Table provides a sample of illustrative cases in the medical context (where C is the patient):

The systemic breach alleged	An illustrative case	The result
Failing to provide adequate staff for posts in a hospital – if doctors did not have sufficient skill or experience to provide the special care demanded by particular patients, then the Health Authority would be at fault in appointing them to the posts which they held	In *Wilsher v Essex AHA*,[a] this claim was not put by C who was a very premature baby being treated in the Special Care Baby Unit, but it was canvassed as a potential allegation of negligence, *against the hospital itself*, by all three members of the Court of Appeal	No breach proven. However, in *Knight v Home Office*,[b] the court said that *Wilsher* 'clearly contemplated that a hospital authority could be held liable if it failed to provide staff of sufficient skill and experience to give the treatment offered at the hospital'
Failing to provide adequate staff training and supervision, particularly for junior doctors	In *Jones v Manchester Corp*,[c] the doctor employee administered anaesthetic to C, who subsequently died	This systemic breach was upheld by Denning LJ

[a] [1987] QB 730 (CA) 747 (Mustill LJ), 778 Browne-Wilkinson V-C), 775 (Glidewell LJ).
[b] [1990] 3 All ER 237 (QB) 242.
[c] [1952] 2 All ER 125 (CA) 133.

[65] [2007] IEHC 207 [no pp]. [66] [2004] EWCA Civ 641, [32].
[67] [1995] UKHL 9, [15]. [68] (1996) 33 BMLR 178 (CA) 197.

The systemic breach alleged	An illustrative case	The result
Failing to provide adequate staffing levels, or to implement a reasonably safe system for summonsing staff in the event of hospital emergencies	This was the allegation of systemic breach in *Garcia v St Mary's NHS Trust*,[d] where C had heart by-pass surgery, and a post-operative bleed several hours later led to brain damage. C claimed that the hospital had a 'crash call' procedure which was deficient in that, even with the speediest arrival from the doctor's home to the operating theatre (here, the response time was 31 minutes), that would *condemn* C to significant brain damage	These systemic negligence allegations failed
The arrangements for the hospital set-up – e.g., if a 'split-site' hospital is constructed over two campuses, and the hospital failed to ensure that an adequate or efficient system was in place for summonsing doctors from one site to the other	In *Bull v Devon AHA*,[e] a mother gave birth at one campus of the hospital, where the second twin, C, was not delivered until 68 minutes after the first twin and as a result suffered brain damage from hypoxia. Urgent attempts were made to summon the registrar from the other campus between births, but he could not be found, and the pager went unanswered	Direct liability on the part of the Health Authority succeeded. This 1970 system was judicially described as 'precarious', 'unreliable and essentially unsatisfactory', 'operating on a knife-edge'
Failing to establish adequate communications systems between hospital staff, e.g., in between change of shifts	In *Robertson v Nottingham HA*,[f] C claimed that the hospital failed to have sufficient systems in place for reliable communication of information between medical staff working on different shifts and, more generally, between medical staff and nursing staff	Systemic negligence proven

[d] [2006] EWHC 2314 (QB) [82], [95].
[e] (1989) 22 BMLR 79 (CA).
[f] (1996) 33 BMLR 178 (CA) 198 (also known as: *Re R (A minor) (No 2)*).

The systemic breach alleged	An illustrative case	The result
Failing to have adequately sufficient or timely assessment procedures for patients in place, or to provide adequate and sufficient opening hours during which specialist medical equipment was available	In *Hardaker v Newcastle HA*,[g] C alleged that the hospital was required to pre-assess a diver for numbness, paralysis, and other symptoms of 'the bends', before invoking treatment in a decompression chamber, which method of pre-assessment meant an in-built delay to treatment; and that the decompression chamber at Newcastle University, next to the hospital, should not have been closed on the weekends, meaning that C had to be transferred to the police diving school's decompression chamber in Sunderland	These allegations of systemic negligence failed

[g] QB, 15 Jun 2001.

Hence, systemic negligence allegations against health authorities are certainly permitted, but breach of that non-delegable duty to the patient has been difficult to prove.

TESTING PRECAUTIONARY STEPS AGAINST THE QUADRANT

§7.9 When assessing breach, a court will consider what precautionary steps D *could* have taken, in order to avoid the injury or harm to C. Whether a reasonable D *ought* to have taken those precautionary steps depends upon an analysis of: the magnitude of the risk; the gravity of the injury, should the risk manifest; the cost of taking those precautionary steps; and the social or economic utility which could be compromised if the precautionary steps were taken ('the *Bolton v Stone* factors'). Although every possible precautionary step, if taken, would have prevented C's injury, the purpose of the law of negligence is not to obliterate all risk of injury arising from D's activities, or to guard C against obvious risks.

Successful negligence suits can only arise in circumstances where some precautionary step was possible. Unavoidable or inevitable accidents cannot, by definition, be instances of negligence, as no reasonable D could have acted differently in avoiding them. Agony-of-the-moment, or emergency, scenarios (as described in Chapter 6) will result in a suppressed standard of care (as in, e.g., *Wooldridge v Sumner*[69]) – but, in addition, it will be difficult to point to a reasonable D as having done anything differently.

The list of precautionary steps represents the acts or omissions which C hopes to prove as being D's breaches. They represent what D *could* have done to avoid the accident. However, whether breach succeeds depends upon whether a reasonable D *should* have undertaken them, which is quite a different question.

[69] [1963] 2 QB 43 (CA).

Take the example of C, who enters an occupier's premises, and suffers some injury due to the state of the premises (per Chapter 12). The precautionary steps commonly alleged in these cases include:

- erecting further and better warning signs;
- removing the danger altogether by taking down the structure which posed the danger to C;
- concealing the source of the danger with a cover of some description;
- making it more difficult (or impossible) for C to gain access, by erecting more physical barriers;
- refusing C permission to enter the premises at all;
- organising security patrols of the premises; or
- providing better education about the dangers to a class of persons of whom C was one.

If every possible precautionary step were taken, then the injury would not have happened. However, as remarked in *Scout Assn v Barnes*,[70] 'it is not the function of the law of tort to eliminate every iota of risk' (per Jackson LJ) and that 'the law of tort must not interfere with activities just because they carry some risk' (per Smith LJ). Unfortunately accidents happen, for which no compensation may be awarded, if the quadrant of factors, discussed in the following section, does not point towards breach.

The quadrant of factors

The four factors derived from the seminal House of Lords' decision in *Bolton v Stone*,[71] and identified in the Table below, govern the breach assessment. This is the primary test of breach.

Quadrant of factors re breach

Magnitude/probability:	*Gravity/seriousness:*
What was the probability of injury or harm being suffered by C, if the precautionary steps were not taken? The higher the probability, the more arguable it is that a reasonable D would have taken one or more of those steps, and vice versa. *The relevant probability relates to that particular injury suffered by C and the way that it happened, and not of accidents generally (per* Uren v Corporate Leisure (UK) Ltd[a]*). Historical data of accidents can be useful in establishing whether the probability was sufficient to warrant the precautionary steps being taken (per* Tomlinson v Congleton BC[b]).	What was the gravity of the injury or harm that could have occurred to C, if the precautionary steps were not taken? The graver the potential injury or harm, the more arguable it is that a reasonable D would have taken one or more of those steps, and vice versa. *The gravity of injury has been assessed in various ways: (1) by reference to historical evidence of injuries suffered in similar cases (per* Bolton v Stone[c]*); (2) by reference to the actual harm suffered by C (per* Stimpson v Wolverhampton MBC[d]*); and (3) by reference to the probability of potential serious harm to C (per* Abouzaid v Mothercare (UK) Ltd[e]*). The gravity of injury may be quite differently-assessed, under each of these.*

[a] [2011] EWCA Civ 66, [76], and later: [2013] EWHC 353 (QB).
[b] [2004] 1 AC 46 (HL) [22]–[25].
[c] [1951] AC 850 (HL) 862.
[d] CA, 22 May 1990.
[e] [2000] EWCA Civ 348, [33].

[70] [2010] EWCA Civ 1476, [34] and [49], respectively.
[71] [1951] AC 850 (HL).

Cost and practicability of precautionary steps:	*Social (including economic) value/utility considerations:*
What were the costs, difficulties and inconvenience to D of taking those precautionary steps? The cheaper the cost and less burdensome the task, the more arguable it is that a reasonable D would have taken one or more of those steps, and vice versa. *The costs may be of three types: (1) the monetary expense necessary to undertake the precautionary steps (per* Overseas Tankship (UK) Ltd v The Miller Steamship Co Ltd[f]*); (2) the time required to undertake those steps; and (3) the resources, facilities, and staffing available to undertake the steps (per* Walker v Northumberland CC[g]*).*	To what extent (if any) would taking those precautionary steps have affected the social utility of D's activities for third parties, other than C? If the social value would not have been affected, or if no third parties would be inconvenienced by those precautionary steps being adopted, then it is arguable that a reasonable D would have taken those precautionary steps, and vice versa. *The social utility of D's activities can be assessed in a variety of ways: (1) re the recreational enjoyment which third parties derive from sporting endeavours, organised games, etc (per* Tomlinson*); (2) re the benefits of the activity to the young, or to some other deserving sector of society (per* Wilkin-Shaw v Fuller[h]*); (3) re the economic benefit to the community (per* Latimer v AEC[i]*); and (4) re the value which emergency services provide to society (per* Watt v Hertfordshire CC[j]*).*

[f] [1967] 1 AC 617 (PC, on appeal from Australia) 642 (Lord Reid).
[g] [1995] 1 All ER 737, [1995] PIQR P521 (CA) P534.
[h] [2012] EWHC 1777 (QB) [98], aff'd: [2013] EWCA Civ 410.
[i] [1953] AC 643 (HL).
[j] [1954] 1 WLR 835 (CA).

The most notable subsequent application of the *Bolton v Stone* quadrant occurred in the tragic case of *Tomlinson v Congleton BC*,[72] but the four factors have been explicitly referred to in a number of other cases too. For example, in *Wilkin-Shaw v Fuller*,[73] the first-instance court referred to the 'balance of risk, gravity of injury, costs and social value'; while recently, when the Scottish Outer House was discussing the English case law on breach, it summarised the balancing act in these terms: 'the likelihood of injury, the seriousness of the injury which might occur, and the social value of the activity giving rise to the risk, and cost of preventative measures must all be balanced' (per *French v Strathclyde Fire Board*[74]).

It is a genuine 'balancing exercise' (per Jackson LJ in *Scouts Assn v Barnes*[75]), because rarely will all the factors either point towards breach, or refute it. It will depend upon **all** the facts and circumstances. The Court of Appeal spoke for all such cases by stating, in *Allen v Stoke-on-Trent CC*,[76] that '[t]here is clearly a balance which has to be struck between placing burdens on [Ds] which they find it impracticable to fulfil, and allowing [Ds] to ignore their responsibilities'.

[72] [2003] UKHL 47, [2004] 1 AC 46 (HL).
[73] [2012] EWHC 1777 (QB) [44] (Owen J), aff'd: [2013] EWCA Civ 410.
[74] [2013] ScotCS 3 (CSOH) [43]. [75] [2010] EWCA Civ 1476, [30]. [76] CA, 14 Feb 1989, Woolf LJ.

After all, the cost of taking a precaution may be very small – but so may the risk be, and a reasonable person may validly decide to take no steps to eliminate that risk at all (per *Gabriel v Kirklees MC*[77]). The tension among the quadrants was well-illustrated in *Tomlinson*:

> In *Tomlinson v Congleton BC*,[78] Mr Tomlinson, C, injured himself when he went swimming in a lake in a disused quarry in a country park owned and occupied by two local authorities, D. Swimming in the lake was prohibited, and there were prominent notices stating, 'Dangerous water: no swimming'. D was aware that the notices were frequently ignored, that they did not prevent visitors to the park from entering the water, and that several accidents had resulted from swimming in the lake. T stood in shallow water (up to his knees), and from that standing position, dived and struck his head on the sandy bottom, breaking his neck. **Held (by the CA, upheld by HL):** no breach proven. A reasonable occupier would not have done anything different to avoid the risk of injury to C.

The quadrant pulled in entirely different directions. The gravity of harm, should it occur, was immense (death by drowning, or very serious personal injury), whereas the risk of injury was low; some of precautionary steps would have been expensive to implement (at least for these local authorities); and most crucially of all, the social value derived from using the beaches of the lake for purposes of sunbathing, paddling, playing with children ('the harmless recreation of responsible parents and children with buckets and spades on the beaches', said Lord Hoffmann) would have to be prohibited if the beaches were planted up with bushes and shrubs to prevent access to the lake, i.e., 'there is an important question of freedom at stake', in that it was unjust for the 'harmless' activities of responsible third parties to be prohibited by some so-called duty on the occupier's part to safeguard 'irresponsible visitors against dangers which are perfectly obvious'.[79] Indeed, *Tomlinson* (and other cases like it before[80] and since[81]) reflect the modern reality that D does not have to show unreasonably risk-averse behaviour to avoid a finding of breach. Lord Hobhouse put it this way:

> Does the law require that all trees be cut down because some youths may climb them and fall? Does the law require the coastline and other beauty spots to be lined with warning notices? Does the law require that attractive waterside picnic spots be destroyed because of a few foolhardy individuals who choose to ignore warning notices and indulge in activities dangerous only to themselves? The answer to all these questions is, of course, no. But this is the road down which your Lordships, like other courts before, have been invited to travel ... In truth, the arguments for C have involved an attack upon the liberties of the citizen which should not be countenanced. They attack the liberty of the individual to engage in dangerous, but otherwise harmless, pastimes at his own risk, and the liberty of citizens as a whole fully to enjoy the variety and quality of the landscape of this country.

Lord Scott was equally as forceful:

> why should the council be discouraged, by the law of tort, from providing facilities for young men and young women to enjoy themselves in this way? Of course there is some risk of accidents arising

[77] [2004] EWCA Civ 345, [25].

[78] [2003] UKHL 47, [2004] 1 AC 46 (HL) [39]–[43] (Lord Hoffmann), [81] (Lord Hobhouse), [94] (Lord Scott), and affirming: [2002] EWCA Civ 309, [2003] 2 WLR 1120.

[79] *ibid*, [27], [46].

[80] e.g., *Simkiss v Rhondda BC* (CA, 22 Feb 1983) ('If the exercise of reasonable care required [D] to fence off this bluff, ... it would also require them to fence every natural hazard in the Rhondda Valley adjacent to housing estates').

[81] e.g., *Evans v Kosmar Villa Holidays* [2007] EWCA Civ 1003, [2008] 1 WLR 297, [41].

out of the joie-de-vivre of the young. But that is no reason for imposing a grey and dull safety regime on everyone.

Indeed, *Tomlinson*, and other cases like it, illustrate that a reasonable D does **not** need to take precautionary steps against obvious risks.

In *Vaughan v MOD*,[82] Spencer Vaughan, C, 22, was a member of the Royal Marines. He participated in a week's Adventure Training Exercise in Gran Canaria, as an opportunity to crew a yacht during off-shore sailing exercises. During a lunch break, C made a shallow dive into the sea, when he was in waist-deep water, hit his head on a concealed object beneath the surface of the water (which may, or may not, have been a sandbank), and suffered tetraplegia. There had been no recorded incident of any injury caused to any Marine by his diving into shallow water, over a 5-year period prior to this accident. **Held:** breach failed against D. Reasonable foreseeability of the accident was proven; but the risk of diving into shallow water was so obvious that D did not need to warn C of those dangers.

The following Table has regard to instructive negligence cases[83] which show the various factors straining in different directions – with those factors which most significantly contributed to the outcome bolded:

Breach: Application of the quadrant test

Case	Nutshell facts	Precautionary steps?	Probability / cost	Gravity / compromise	Held:
Bolton v Stone (1951)	cricket ball hit Miss Stone, C – it was hit 100 yds, and cleared the fence of cricket club – a similar 'six' had been hit approx. only 6 times in 30 yrs	– erect a higher fence – close cricket club down altogether, to protect surrounding houses	**Very low** **Very costly**	Medium to high **Highly compromised**	No breach
Tomlinson v Congleton BC (2003)	C broke his neck in a swimming accident at a lake – disregarded signage forbidding swimming	– plant up beaches with prickly bushes, to stop access – more warning signs – employing full-time lifeguards	**Very low** Variable, from cheap to very expensive	Very grave **Highly compromised**	No breach
Paris v Stepney BC (1951)	C, a partially-sighted mechanic employee, was hammering at a wheel at D's garage – a chip of metal flew up and entered his good eye, blinding him	– supply goggles to mechanics during work tasks	Low **Very cheap**	**Very high** –	Breach

[82] [2015] EWHC 1404 (QB) [33].

[83] The citations for these cases are located elsewhere in the chapter, and will not be reproduced here.

Case	Nutshell facts	Precautionary steps?	Probability	Gravity	Held:
			cost	compromise	
Latimer v AEC Ltd (1953)	employee C slipped on factory floor during night-shift – factory engaged in post-war construction work – floor flooded during heavy rain storm – some oily coolant was spread from its usual channel to coat the floor – sawdust had been spread, but some areas left untreated	– close down factory, and send night-shift home, until floor was properly cleaned – spread more saw-dust than had been spread, to cover it properly	Very low (no previous accidents)	Medium	No breach
			Varied between low cost and very heavy cost	**Very highly compromised (D doing vital post-war manufacturing work)**	
Watt v Hertfordshire CC (1954)	car accident in which a woman was pinned under the car; fire brigade was asked to respond – a lifting jack in fire brigade vehicle shifted when braking suddenly, 100 m from the depot – it hit one fireman, C, injuring him	– wait until the correct vehicle arrived back at depot, to which the jack could be fitted properly – further efforts made to restrain jack used, before the vehicle set out to save the victim	Medium to high	Medium to high	No breach
			Cheap (to fire brigade)	**Very highly compromised (when life and limb are at stake, more risk justified)**	
Stimpson v Wolverhampton MBC (1990)	C, a visitor to a public park, was hit in the mouth by a golf ball while walking through the park – golf was prohibited in the park	– instruct Council staff to admonish offenders – strictly enforce on-the-spot fines – erect further and more visible notices prohibiting golf	**High (people regularly played golf in the park)**	Previous injuries had been slight	Breach
			Relatively cheap	–	
Cunningham v Reading FC (1992)	C, an off-duty policeman was injured when football hooligans threw concrete missiles from the delapidated terraces	– repair the concrete on the terraces – fix major cracking and portions of the crumbling concrete	**Very high**	Very serious	Breach
			Cheap (<£3,000)	–	

Case	Nutshell facts	Precautionary steps?	Probability / cost	Gravity / compromise	Held:
Collins-Williamson v Silver-link Train Services (2009)[a]	C, a passenger, was mucking around on a train platform late at night, drunk – as train left platform, C was too close, fell between train and platform, and his leg was partially amputated	– employ more staff to see trains off, especially late night trains – CCTV at stations, which are constantly supervised	Extremely low	Very high	No systemic breach
			Very costly	Some compromise	
Uren v Corporate Leisure (UK) Ltd (2011, 2013)	C participated in a 'Health and Fun Day' at MOD, his employer – including games of a kind played in, 'It's a Knockout' – C dived headfirst into a pool, and was rendered a tetraplegic, at 21	– give instructions to avoid a head-first entry into the pool, which would have still preserved the 'fun' for the participants – undertake a risk assessment associated with headfirst entry into the pool, and take reasonable steps to eradicate the risks of serious injury	High (trial judge had held, in error, that the risk of spinal injury was low)	Very high	No breach – but remitted back for trial because of error;on retrial, breach proven
			Very cheap	High – 'some social value' in the game and in the whole afternoon	

[a] [2009] EWCA Civ 850.

Clearly, the outcome of these cases will sometimes turn on very finely-balanced, intuitive, and difficult-to-predict judgments by the court.

The public employee's dilemma

Undoubtedly, the assessment of *Bolton v Stone* factors sometimes produces 'winners' and 'losers', which may seem to be unjust. For example, private sector employees are arguably better off in seeking to prove breach than their counterparts in emergency services, if injured in the course of their employment – because their employer is predominantly engaged in profit-making activities, and hence, the fourth quadrant is not significant (or as significant) in the balancing exercise, as it is when the employer is an emergency services provider. In other words, private sector employers are not engaged in 'social utility' of the sort that emergency service providers are, and hence, the private employee has a better chance of proving negligence.

In *Sussex Ambulance NHS Trust v King*,[84] Buxton LJ suggested that the reasoning in *Watt v Hertfordshire CC*, which gives rise to this result, should be revisited on appeal, for several reasons:

i. if employees of emergency service providers were exposed to the risk of injury, and were less well-protected by the law of negligence, then that would 'raise considerations of distributive justice ... [because] if employees required to run risks to advance private interests can recover if doing their employer's bidding leads to injury, so employees required to run risks to advance public interests should, by the same token, be able to recover';
ii. in *Ogwo v Taylor*,[85] the House of Lords rejected the 'fireman's rule', under which a public employee could not complain in negligence if that employee is injured whilst engaged in the very hazard (e.g., fire-fighting) that he was employed to deal with. *Watt* is difficult to reconcile with 'the spirit of *Ogwo v Taylor*';
iii. the public interest of emergency service providers helping the community that they serve is treated, under *Watt*, as a matter to do with breach; whereas it should properly be dealt with under the third limb of the *Caparo v Dickman* test, i.e., that it must be fair, just and reasonable to impose a duty of care.

However, to date, the decision and reasoning in *Watt* remains good law, despite these misgivings. As an aside, further discussion of the requirement of employer D to undertake risk assessment of the dangers posed to employee C in the workplace, especially in light of *Uren v Corporate Leisure (UK) Ltd*,[86] is contained in 'Employers' liability' (an online chapter).

The impact of the Compensation Act 2006, s 1

§7.10 According to s 1 of the Compensation Act 2006, the court must take into account whether D was conducting a 'desirable activity', when assessing whether D ought to have taken a precautionary step. However, judicial commentary since the enactment of s 1 suggests that the section adds nothing to the common law.

The purpose of the provision

The Compensation Act 2006, s 1,[87] is a curious provision. It states as follows:

s 1 Deterrent effect of potential liability

A court considering a claim in negligence ... may, in determining whether the defendant should have taken particular steps to meet a standard of care (whether by taking precautions against a risk or otherwise), have regard to whether a requirement to take those steps might:

(a) prevent a desirable activity from being undertaken at all, to a particular extent or in a particular way, or
(b) discourage persons from undertaking functions in connection with a desirable activity.

[84] [2002] EWCA Civ 953, [2002] ICR 1413, especially [47]. [85] [1988] 1 AC 431 (HL) 438–39 (Lord Bridge).
[86] [2013] EWHC 353 (QB). [87] In force on date of Royal assent, 25 Jul 2006.

The main concern about this provision is – why enact it at all? The fact that 'desirable activities' by D or by others similarly-situated may be compromised was already 'part and parcel' of the fourth *Bolton v Stone* quadrant (especially in light of the decision in *Tomlinson v Congleton BC*). Perhaps some cases did not always emphasise that fourth quadrant – e.g., in *Stimpson v Wolverhampton MBC*,[88] the Court of Appeal noted that the duty on D 'has to be considered in the light of the frequency and seriousness of the risk in the context of the burden imposed on [D], when considering the measures which should be taken to reduce or prevent the incidence and frequency of the risk', with no reference to the social values that could be compromised – but that fourth quadrant certainly has plenty of judicial authority to support it.

The drafters of the Explanatory Memorandum[89] professed to state that the section did not amend the common law at all, but merely sought to 'clarify' it, and that s 1:

i. had a community education aspect, i.e., it was 'intended to contribute to improving awareness of this aspect of the law; providing reassurance to the people and organisations who are concerned about possible litigation; and to ensuring that normal activities are not prevented because of the fear of litigation and excessively risk-averse behaviour';
ii. was 'not concerned with, and does not alter, the standard of care ... It is solely concerned with the court's assessment of what constitutes reasonable care in the case before it'; and
iii. provides that a court may, when assessing precautionary steps, 'have regard to whether a requirement to take those steps might prevent an activity which is desirable from taking place (either at all, to a particular extent, or in a particular way), or might discourage persons from undertaking functions in connection with the activity'.

As the Explanatory Notes suggest,[90] taking account of D's desirable activities, when determining whether D complied with the 'standard of reasonable care', was **already** a long-standing part of English law. Indeed, many cases (apart from *Tomlinson*) illustrate that proposition, where D's conduct was held to be reasonable – in part because of the socially useful activity which D performed. In none of the following was breach proven:

> In *Bolton v Stone*,[91] the cricket club, D, was not negligent in permitting a cricket ball to be hit out of the ground into C's adjoining property, because any further preventative measures could have meant the socially useful activity of cricket ceased at the ground. In *King v Sussex Ambulance NHS Trust*,[92] Anthony King, C, an ambulance officer, suffered injuries when a patient-and-stretcher chair slipped onto him as he and his colleague were negotiating a narrow winding stairway in the patient's cottage. His colleague had to let go of the chair because of sudden pain, and the whole load fell onto C, causing him injury. However, the ambulance service, D, did not have a choice but to respond to the patient's urgent needs. D had limited resources, and there was no other equipment that D could have given its employees to manage patients in houses; and calling upon the fire brigade to do the job for them was not an option. There was simply no alternative equipment for speedy use in this sort of situation, given the 'reasonable despatch' that care for the patient entailed. In *Daborn v Bath Tramways*,[93] D, the driver of a left-hand-drive ambulance during war-time, collided with C

[88] CA, 22 May 1990 (Sir Roualeyn Cumming-Bruce).

[89] See: cl 10–13, especially, 'Background and useful information' by the Dept for Constitutional Affairs, available at: <http://www.dca.gov.uk/legist/compensation.htm#c>.

[90] Cl 13 (s 1 'reflects the existing law and approach of the courts as expressed in recent judgments of the higher courts').

[91] [1951] AC 850 (HL). [92] [2002] EWCA Civ 953, (2002) 68 BMLR 177. [93] [1946] 2 All ER 333 (CA).

whilst turning, not being used to the left-hand-drive. Driving such a vehicle was a socially necessary duty to assist the injured during a national emergency.

Hence, the social value of D's activities has **long** been a factor in determining what amounts to taking reasonable care, so as to attain the legal standard of care. However, it was felt to be beneficial to non-lawyers, especially, to restate the law in s 1 (assuming that non-lawyers devote time to reading such legislation!).

Political opinion was, however, less-than-convinced about s 1's utility.

The political corner

The House of Commons Select Committee on Constitutional Affairs:[a] the Committee disagreed with s 1, noting that 'it would undoubtedly, at least in the short term, lead to an increase in costly satellite litigation to define what is a "desirable activity". Moreover, the wide breadth of that term (or any alternative, such as "social value" or "utility") ... is not to change the law, [D] would likely ... seek to rely upon [s 1, to obtain] a shield against liability. This could result in possibly inconsistent decisions'.

[a] *Compensation Culture: Third Report* (HC 754-I) (1 Mar 2006) [68].

Judicial consideration

Courts have not been enamoured of s 1 since its introduction either.

In *Wilkin-Shaw v Fuller*,[94] the court stated that, 'it does not seem to me that section 1 adds anything to the common law. Some risk is inherent in many socially desirable activities ... the question in any individual case is whether the social benefit of any activity is such that the degree of risk that it entails is acceptable'. Indeed, Owen J disparaged its enactment, noting that s 1 'appears to have been introduced as a response to the perception of the growth of a "compensation culture". The draft bill was ... accompanied by explanatory notes that asserted that section 1 did no more than "reflect the existing law". In that case, it is somewhat difficult to see why it was felt necessary to enact it, and why, as enacted, it was couched in discretionary terms'. In *Scout Assn v Barnes*[95] too, Jackson LJ reiterated that s 1 merely 'enshrined' the common law principle that it was not negligence's function 'to stamp out socially desirable activities'. Further, in *Uren v Corporate Leisure (UK) Ltd*,[96] Smith LJ noted that it was 'common ground' that s 1 'did not add anything to the common law position ... At least since *Tomlinson*, if not before, the common law has required the court to take such matters into account'. Indeed, in the retrial in *Uren*, Foskett J seemed to question whether the provision was perhaps out-of-step with modern attitudes, noting that, 'rightly or wrongly, and despite the influence of a case such as *Tomlinson* and s 1, we live in a more "risk averse" age now than when those earlier cases were decided'.[97]

The problem is that, far from the provision not adding anything to the common law, its enactment may give **greater** weight to that 'fourth quadrant' than the common law envisaged.

[94] [2012] EWHC 1777 (QB) [42], [46], aff'd: [2013] EWCA Civ 410.

[95] [2010] EWCA Civ 1476, [34], citing: D Owen (ed), *The Philosophical Foundations of the Law of Tort* (Clarendon Press, 1995), ch 11.

[96] [2011] EWCA Civ 66, [13].

[97] [2013] EWHC 353 (QB) [75].

Indeed, *Scout Assn v Barnes*[98] illustrates this uncertainty at judicial level. In Jackson LJ's (dissenting) view, the social utility of scouts' training, recreation and health benefits for young people counted for sufficient, in the overall balancing exercise, to negate negligence.[99] However, the majority held that, while the scouts' game in which C was injured 'had some social value; it was a good active competitive game to keep boys occupied on long winter evenings', playing it in the dark did not add to its value but only to its excitement. Yet, it significantly increased the risk of injury to C, and the game was negligently-conducted. Clearly, Ward LJ also had some serious reservations, characteristic of many of the finely-balanced outcomes of the quadrant's application:

> Here was a big strong 13-year-old lad, well-used to rough and tumble, playing rugby with distinction for his county, ever ready to take the bumps and the bruises, ever willingly to put his body on the line for the thrill of his sport. For him, you get hurt, you get up, and you get on with it. He brought the same enthusiasm and competitive instincts to his participation in his local Scout troop. He was the least likely boy to need wrapping in cotton wool. So, is awarding him damages for an injury suffered playing the game, 'Objects in the Dark', not an example of an overprotective nanny state robbing youth of fun simply because there was some risk involved in the exercise? Is this a decision which emasculates those responsible for caring for our children and in so doing, enfeebles the children themselves? Where do you draw the line? I have found that hard to answer.[100]

The answer was (somewhat surprisingly), 'negligence'. In other cases too, the provision, whilst cited, did not save D from a finding of breach.

> In *Sutton v Syston Rugby Football Club Ltd*,[101] a rugby colt player suffered a serious knee injury when he fell and gashed his knee on the broken stub of a cricket boundary marker which (he claimed) a pitch inspection would have detected. The law did not require steps that were too difficult for ordinary coaches and match organisers to meet. 'Games of rugby are, after all, no more than games and, as such are obviously desirable activities within the meaning of s 1 of the Compensation Act 2006', but even so, 'before a game or training session, a pitch should be walked over at a reasonable walking pace by a coach or match organiser, and if that is done, that will satisfy a Club's common law duty of care in relation to such inspection'. However, ultimately causation failed. In *Reynolds v Strutt & Parker LLP*,[102] C, an employee of a real estate firm, D, suffered a very severe head injury when involved in a bike accident, during a 'team building day' organised by D. The 'reward of employees by employers in ways such as that chosen in this case is a desirable activity', but still, D committed a breach, in failing to carry out a risk assessment and communicate better about safety equipment (e.g., helmets).

Nevertheless, in other cases in which D's activities obviously carried a 'social value', there was no breach:

> In *Wilkin-Shaw v Fuller*,[103] Charlotte Shaw, 14, C, drowned whilst on a training exercise on Dartmoor, when she fell into a fast-flowing stream, and was swept away by the strong current. She had been on the Moor with 10 other children from a secondary school, training for the Ten Tors expedition. D was a teacher at the school, and was team manager responsible for the training of the children for the Ten Tors expedition. D argued that C's death was the result of a tragic accident

[98] [2010] EWCA Civ 1476. [99] *ibid*, [29]–[30]. [100] *ibid*, [50].
[101] [2011] EWCA Civ 1182, [13]. [102] [2011] EWHC 2263 (Ch) [46].
[103] [2012] EWHC 1777 (QB) [134]–[135] (Owen J), and on appeal: aff'd [2013] EWCA Civ 410.

when she fell into the stream, whilst being assisted by a well-intentioned scout master unconnected with the school. **Held (trial):** no breach by D. The group was 'cold and wet', but did not appear to be 'completely exhausted', and were capable of continuing: 'some risk is inherent in many socially desirable activities. The Ten Tors event, and the training that those who participate must undergo, is a classic example ... the question in any individual case is whether the social benefit of any activity is such that the degree of risk that it entails is acceptable'. **Held (on appeal):** however, in a reframed case on appeal, another teacher, Miss Timms, was held in breach for failing to be at a tor checkpoint when due, because she had overshot and got lost without adequate explanation. Ultimately, however, causation failed. In *McErlean v Rt Rev Monsignor MacAuley*,[104] C slipped on an icy pavement, whilst accompanying school children to choir practice for a forthcoming nativity play. No breach was found. The court noted that, 'practising for a nativity play or taking part in choir practice is a desirable activity', and s 1 'added nothing to the common law'. In *Hopps v Mott Macdonald Ltd*,[105] Graham Hopps, C, an engineer, was travelling in Basrah in a vehicle which crossed an improvised explosive device, and was badly injured. He claimed that the MOD should have provided armed forces with better armoured vehicles which would have provided greater protection to the occupants. No breach was proven. The court held that s 1 could apply just as much to employment activities in the theatre of war, as it could to D who provides public amenities or socially-valuable activities such as the playing of sports. Taking the precautionary step advocated by C (retaining employees at the airport until better vehicles were available) would 'prevent the desirable activity of reconstruction of a shattered infrastructure after a war in a territory occupied by HM forces, particularly when failure to expedite that work would carry with it risks to the safety of coalition forces and civilian contractors in Iraq as a whole'.

Hence, employment activities can well fall within the phrase of 'desirable activities'.

THE *BOLAM/BOLITHO* FRAMEWORK FOR BREACH ANALYSIS

§7.11 The *Bolam/Bolitho* framework establishes a two-step test by which to determine breach, *viz*, to consider: (1) whether D's act or omission was supported by a body of peer professional opinion, i.e., whether D acted in accordance with a practice accepted as proper for an ordinarily competent D by a respectable body of professional opinion ('the *Bolam* test of breach'), and (2) whether that peer professional opinion is defensible/rational/logical ('the *Bolitho* gloss'). Where both limbs of the test are met, D is not in breach.

This two-part test represents the current framework that applies to professional breach (per Beatson J in *French v Thames Valley Strategic HA*[106]).

The *Bolam* test

The test, derived from the direction to the jury given by McNair J in *Bolam v Friern Hosp Management Committee*, a case of alleged medical negligence, states:

> [a doctor] is not guilty of negligence if he has acted in accordance with a practice accepted as proper by a responsible body of medical men skilled in that particular art ... Putting it the other way

[104] [2014] NIQB 1, [12]. [105] [2009] EWHC 1881 (QB) [93]. [106] [2005] EWHC 459 (QB) [9]–[10].

> round, a man is not negligent, if he is acting in accordance with such a practice, merely because there is a body of opinion who would take a contrary view.[107]

Also called the test of 'peer professional opinion', the *Bolam* test of breach requires that expert evidence be adduced by D to prove that the act or omission of D met the reasonable standard of care, and did not fall below it. The evidence is to be given by one or more of D's 'peers', who operates in the same broad field of activity.

In *Bolam*, Mr Bolam, C, a travelling salesman, suffered from mental illness, and attended the Friern Hospital to undergo electro-convulsive therapy. When administered, the electric current passing through the brain caused convulsions. D, the treating psychiatrist, did not warn C of the risk of bodily fracture during the convulsions. During the treatment, C lay in a supine position with a pillow placed under his back, his lower jaw supported by a mouth gag, a male nurse standing at each side of the bed in case he should fall from it, but otherwise no restraints or relaxant drugs were used. During the second treatment, C's hip joints were dislocated, and his pelvis on each side was badly fractured by the head of the femur being driven through the pelvic bone. C claimed that the ECT should have been administered with relaxant drugs (which would have precluded the risk of fracture altogether) and manual restraints, and that he should have been warned of the risk of fracture (1:10,000 probability). C's expert evidence supported the use of relaxant drugs and restraints to reduce or eliminate the risk of fracture. **Held:** no breach. D's expert evidence, which prevailed, was that relaxant drugs carried considerable risks because of the difficulty in getting the dosage right and not inducing heart stoppage; and manual restraints were generally ineffective to eliminate fractures. In *Davies v Univ Hosp of North Staffordshire NHS Trust*,[108] Tracy Davies, C, had a brain tumour, and claimed that, had a scan been carried out in Jan 2001 by her treating doctor, D, the tumour would have been detected. The various diagnoses, of C's recurrent headaches and vomiting, were frontal sinusitis or migraine, with neurological problem 'unlikely'. C suffered loss of vision and other damage. (The tumour was also misdiagnosed as being malignant, which was admitted as a breach.) **Held:** no breach. D's diagnosis of sinusitis or migraine was a reasonable diagnosis, and a reasonable course of action in the circumstances in Jan 2001, and accorded with a responsible body of professional opinion.

This *Bolam* test of breach is not be confused with the *Bolam* standard of care which was addressed in Chapter 6. The two passages of McNair J's instruction to the jury address two different legal matters.

Expanding the *Bolam* test

§7.12 Although both *Bolam* and *Bolitho* were medical negligence claims, the *Bolam* test of peer professional opinion is a test of professional negligence *generally*. More controversially, the *Bolam* test of breach has been applied in the context of the non-professional D too.

The *Bolam* test represents the '*locus classicus* of the test for the standard of care required of a doctor or *any other person professing some skill or competence*' (according to Lord Browne-Wilkinson in *Bolitho v City and Hackney HA*[109]). The Table below sets out authorities that support the application of the test of breach in broader professional contexts:[110]

[107] [1957] 1 WLR 582 (QB) 587. [108] [2014] EWHC 4004 (QB) [62]. [109] [1998] AC 232 (HL) 239.
[110] Note that, although *Bolam* was relevant in each, negligence was not necessarily proven pursuant to that test.

The wider application of *Bolam*

- architects: *Nye Saunders and Partners v Alan E Bristow*;[a]
- building project managers: *Royal Brompton Hosp NHS Trust v Frederick A Hammond*;[b]
- quantity surveyors, and contractual management specialists: *Ampleforth Abbey Trust v Turner & Townsend Project Management Ltd*;[c]
- valuers of shares: *Zubaida v Hargreaves*;[d] or property: *Blemain Finance Ltd v E Surv Ltd*;[e] or precious chattels/paintings/artifacts: *Thomson v Christie Manson & Woods Ltd*;[f]
- chartered surveyors and property consultants: *Capita Alternative Fund Services Ltd v Drivers Jonas (a firm)*;[g]
- structural and civil engineers: *Cooperative Group Ltd v John Allen Associates Ltd*;[h]
- educators of children with special needs (say, autistic children): *S v Chapman*;[i]
- geologists: *Mirant-Asia Pacific Ltd v Oapil*;[j]
- general providers of educational services of young pupils: *Phelps v Hillingdon LBC*;[k] educational services for pupils with learning difficulties: *Carty v Croydon LBC*;[l] or as providers of professional training: *Abramova v Oxford Institute of Legal Practice*;[m]
- teachers, specifically: *Liennard v Slough BC*;[n]
- social workers: *MS v Lincolnshire CC*;[o]
- lawyers: *D Morgan plc v Mace & Jones (a firm)*;[p]
- traffic engineers/highway authorities: *Lovell (Nee Geraghty) v Leeds CC*;[q]
- chartered accountants: *Goldstein v Levy Gee (a firm)*;[r]
- underwriting agents/insurers: *Henderson v Merrett Syndicates*.[s]

[a] (1987) 37 BLR 92 (CA).
[b] [2000] EWHC Technology 39, [26], [34].
[c] [2012] EWHC 2137 (TCC).
[d] [1995] 1 EGLR 127 (CA)
[e] [2012] EWHC 3654 (TCC).
[f] [2005] EWCA Civ 555.
[g] [2011] EWHC 2336 (Comm).
[h] [2010] EWHC 2300 (TCC).
[i] [2008] EWCA Civ 800.
[j] [2004] EWHC 1750 (TCC).
[k] [2000] UKHL 47, [2001] 2 AC 619.
[l] [2005] EWCA Civ 19, [2005] 1 WLR 2312.
[m] [2011] EWHC 613 (QB), [2011] ELR 385.
[n] [2002] EWHC 398 (QB).
[o] [2011] EWHC 1032 (QB).
[p] [2010] EWHC 3375 (TCC).
[q] [2009] EWHC 1145 (QB).
[r] [2003] EWHC 1574 (Ch), [2007] Lloyd's Rep PN 18.
[s] [1995] 2 AC 145 (HL).

In *Nye Saunders & Partners v Alan E Bristow*, Stephen Brown LJ stated that the *Bolam* test 'applied to any profession *or calling* which required special skill, knowledge or experience'.[111] Other judges have applied the *Bolam* test of breach to 'callings' too. Similar phraseology was used by Morritt LJ in *Adams v Rhymney Valley DC*[112] – who stated that

[111] (1987) 37 BLR 92 (CA) 103. [112] [2000] EWCA Civ 3035, [2000] Lloyd's Rep PN 777 (CA) [57].

the *Bolam* test 'does not depend on the actual possession of the relevant qualification', and that it applies wherever 'the act in question can only safely be done by a person with the necessary skill to do it'.

> In *Adams v Rhymney Valley DC*,[113] the Adams family (parents, and three children aged 7, 4 and 3) were tenants of a terrace house in New Tredegar. Shortly before they moved in, the owners of the accommodation, D, had replaced the windows in the terrace with hardwood-framed windows of standard design as part of a refurbishment of all its 9,000 dwellings. The windows were equipped with a key-operated lock. The keys for the windows were hung on a shoelace on the keyrack in the kitchen. The house had no smoke alarms. One morning, Mr Adams awoke to find the staircase on fire. He alerted his wife, who was sleeping upstairs with the children. He could not reach them because of the smoke and flame, and when he went outside for air, the door slammed shut on him and he could not get back in; Mrs Adams tried desperately to save the children, but could not reach the key downstairs, and, unable to unlock the bedroom windows, finally managed to smash a hole in one window. Mrs Adams fell out, suffering severe injuries. The three children all died in the fire. Had Mrs Adams been able to open the window, she and the children would probably have escaped. C claimed that D should have installed push button windows instead of key locks. **Held:** no breach. The decision to provide a lock with a removable key was supported by the evidence of window designers/installers. D was not in breach in not consulting with widespread opinion, and in not installing smoke alarms in the council accommodation.

There was a division of opinion in the Court of Appeal:

- the majority (Morritt LJ and Sir Christopher Staughton): providing safe windows was a 'calling' to which the *Bolam* test applied, because judgments had to be exercised about the conflict between the need to provide a means of escape or rescue in the case of fire, and the need to prevent children climbing or falling out of windows, especially in upper floors. In 1989/90, it was very common for houses to have lockable windows with removable keys on the first and upper floors, and that decision was one that a competent window designer/installer would have made at that time;
- the dissenter (Sedley LJ): the *Bolam* test had no relevance, because nobody in D's office professed to exercise any relevant design skill for windows. Instead, on an assessment of the quadrant of factors (probability; gravity; cost of precautions; third party considerations, such as security from burglary too), push button locks ought to have been provided, instead of locks with removable keys.

Hence, as *Adams* aptly demonstrates, the application of the *Bolam* and *Bolton v Stone* tests of breach **can** result in different outcomes – because where D is undertaking a task requiring specialist skills, and where the *Bolam* test of breach properly applies, the court must accept the opinion of a body of responsible practitioners called by D, unless that opinion contravenes the *Bolitho* test (below).

More recently, in *Bowen v National Trust*,[114] Mackay J went so far as to say that the application of the *Bolam* test of breach to areas beyond the 'learned professions' was 'now well-established'. The Scottish Outer House also observed, in *ICL Tech Ltd v Johnston Oils Ltd*,[115] that the concept of a 'profession' is 'a developing one, and also porous at its boundaries', but it was

[113] [2000] EWCA Civ 3035, [48] (Staughton LJ), [58], [60] (Morritt LJ), [16], [28] (Sedley LJ).
[114] [2011] EWHC 1992 (QB) [7]. [115] [2012] CSOH 62, [23].

no longer crucial to the application of the *Bolam* test, precisely because the test was no longer limited to the 'recognised professions'.

In *Bowen v National Trust*, a school group was visiting Felbrigg Hall in Suffolk, owned by D, for outdoor educational activities, and took shelter during some rain under a large beech tree, about 160–180 years old. Without warning, a large branch fractured from the trunk and fell on the group. One child was killed, three were seriously injured and the rest traumatised. The various relatives/injured claimed that D failed to carry out a competent risk assessment of the tree (albeit that it was conceded that no tree is absolutely safe). **Held:** no breach. Tree inspectors giving evidence on behalf of D considered that the risk assessment on an old tree which showed signs of stress and defects was that the affected branches should not be cut out, given the relatively low use of the path beneath; it would have been different, had the tree stood next to a carpark or highway. A responsible body of tree inspector opinion supported not cutting down the branch which caused the fatality and injuries. In *Wattleworth v Goodwood Road Racing Co Ltd*,[116] Simon Wattleworth, C, was driving his Austin Healey car on the Goodwood motor-racing circuit, and lost control of his car, collided with a tyre-fronted earth bank on the inside of the track, and was killed. His estate argued that the owners/operators of the circuit, D, negligently designed or selected the tyre structure fronting the bank at the relevant part of the bend. **Held**: no breach. A responsible body of experts in motor-racing safety supported the particular tyre wall at that bend (earth-filled lorry tyres laid house-brick fashion, fronting the earth bank). D had chosen a reasonable safety barrier, 'whether or not one puts it in precise *Bolam* terms'.

§7.13 Minority peer professional opinion, or such opinion which is drawn from a small body, can still constitute valid *Bolam* evidence so as to refute breach.

Variations in peer professional opinion are expected, indeed common. The House of Lords noted, in *Maynard v West Midlands Regional HA*, that, '[t]here is seldom any one answer, exclusive of all others, to problems of professional judgment'.[117] The fact that there may be a very small body of peer professional opinion to draw upon does not negate *Bolam* evidence on behalf of D. It is not a case of 'counting heads' and coming up short. A small number of tertiary specialists can constitute a 'responsible body of medical opinion', such that any judicial reference to a 'substantial body of medical opinion' (per *Hills v Potter*[118]) is not meant in a 'quantitative sense'.

In *De Freitas v O'Brien*,[119] Patricia De Freitas, C, 37, suffered severe back pain, and scans showed disc degeneration at the L4/5 level. She underwent surgery by D, an experienced spinal surgeon. The surgery was unsuccessful, C suffered a leakage of cerebro-spinal fluid, was transferred to intensive care, and was left with inflammation of a membrane covering the spinal cord. She was left with crippling pain, and virtually confined to bed thereafter. 'No-one reading her case notes could fail to have the deepest sympathy for her'. **Held:** no breach proven. D was a spinal specialist who only took referrals from orthopaedic and neuro-surgeons engaged in a wider field of surgical practice. There were only 11 specialist spinal surgeons in England at the time who could be regarded as constituting peer opinion, as to whether accepted medical practice would have countenanced surgery on C. Two of them supported surgery on C, whereas the other experts would not have recommended surgery.

[116] [2004] EWHC 140 (QB). [117] [1984] 1 WLR 634 (HL) 638 (Lord Scarman).
[118] [1984] 1 WLR 641 (QB) 653. [119] (1995) 25 BMLR 51 (CA).

That small number of specialists constituted a responsible body of medical opinion, justifying D's decision to operate.

Hence, the *Bolam* test may still be satisfied by the existence of a small number of peers in the field who considered D's conduct as meeting the reasonable standard of care – even if the majority of peers considered that D's practice was negligent. The fact that the *Bolam* evidence may be a minority view does **not** render it 'unreasonable' or 'irrational', pursuant to *Bolitho's* gloss. In *McCallister v Lewisham and North Southwark HA*[120] (where no breach was found in respect of the treatment given), Rougier J stated:

> Even though he may not have been actually acquainted with it, the current literature does not indicate that, in deciding to operate, [D] blundered or went outside a body of respectable medical opinion. This was a borderline case, and although ... [D] can immerse himself in a school of thought which would have condoned intervention here, I am bound to say that I think that school was very much in the minority.

§7.14 Where two bodies of conflicting (but respectable) peer professional opinion are put forward, one for C and the other for D – and where both opinions satisfy the *Bolitho* gloss – the better view is that the court cannot prefer C's body of opinion over D's, by means of a 'superiority analysis'. Breach will be refuted on the basis of the *Bolam* evidence adduced on D's behalf.

i. The traditional House of Lords' position. The court's role, when applying the *Bolam* test, is not to venture into a consideration of two contrary bodies of opinion, to select which, of C and D's expert opinion, it prefers. That would require the court to undertake a 'superiority analysis', in what would amount to a 'battle of the experts'. Regardless of the fact that such a battle is frequently played out in the courtroom, the task for the court has been stated in fairly restrictive terms, by the House of Lords:

> It is not enough to show that there is a body of competent professional opinion [for C] which considers that there was a wrong decision, if there also exists a body of professional opinion, equally competent, which supports the decision [by D] as reasonable in the circumstances ... A court may prefer one body of opinion to another: but that is no basis for conclusion of negligence [against D] ... a judge's "preference" for one body of distinguished professional opinion to another also professionally distinguished, is not sufficient to establish negligence in a practitioner [D] (*Maynard v West Midlands Regional HA*[121]).
>
> [the court must] remember that it is no part of its task of evaluation to give effect to any preference it may have for one responsible body of professional opinion over another, provided it is satisfied by the expert evidence that both qualify as responsible bodies of medical opinion (*Sidaway v Governors of Bethlem Royal Hosp*[122]).
>
> it would be wrong to allow such assessment to deteriorate into seeking to persuade the judge to prefer one of two views both of which are capable of being logically supported. It is only where a judge can be satisfied that the body of expert opinion cannot be logically supported at all that such opinion will not provide the benchmark by reference to which [D's] conduct falls to be assessed (*Bolitho v City and Hackney HA*[123]).

[120] (QB, 15 Dec 1993) [no pp]. [121] [1984] 1 WLR 634 (HL) 638, 648 (Lord Scarman).
[122] [1985] 1 All ER 643 (HL) 659 (Lord Diplock). [123] [1997] 4 All ER 771 (HL) 779 (Lord Browne-Wilkinson).

That inability to choose C's evidence over D's has been described by lower English courts as 'uncontroversial' (per *Kingsberry v Greater Manchester Strategic HA*[124]), and the 'correct approach' (per *M v Blackpool Victoria Hosp NHS Trust*[125]), and has been oft-applied where the court expressly admitted that two schools of reasonable thought existed and that it was not permitted to undertake any superiority analysis (per *Tuke v Mid Essex Hosp Services NHS Trust*[126]). As the Court of Appeal noted in *Marriott v West Midlands Regional HA*, 'it is not open to simply prefer the expert evidence of one body of competent professional opinion over that of another, where there was a conflict between the experts called by the parties'.[127]

In *Bellarby v Worthing and Southlands Hosp NHS Trust*,[128] patient C, 49, suffered from Crohn's disease for almost 25 years. Seriously ill, he was admitted as a hospital in-patient for almost three months, and also suffered deteriorating vision which was eventually diagnosed as candida. C alleged that this condition was mistreated, in that his treating doctors, D, used intravenous Amphotericin instead of Fluconazole. **Held:** no breach proven. Despite the greater use of Fluconazole in later years, the use of Amphotericin in 1999 was not negligent at the time, especially when candida might have seeded elsewhere in C's body. There were two possible approaches to treatment (said the court); each was logical on the evidence; and both were supported by a respectable body of opinion. The question 'was not whether one treatment was to be preferred to another, but whether [D's] treatment was unreasonable as described in *Bolam*, *Maynard* and *Bolitho*.' It was not.

That view, however, has recently been eroded by some significant case law to the contrary, where that is precisely what an adjudicating court *has* done – preferred one body of medical opinion to the other.

ii. A superiority analysis, nevertheless? The question is whether the test of breach is actually a three-step framework: (1) the *Bolam* test; (2) the *Bolitho* gloss; and (3) a superiority analysis. That would be contentious – but it has some support.

In the 2007 decision of *Smith v Southampton University Hosp NHS Trust*,[129] the trial judge held that both D doctors were not negligent, but her findings were later criticised by the Court of Appeal on this basis:

> She appears to rely exclusively on the *Bolam* test. Thus, she merely says that [Ds' expert] is highly reputable and that it had not been suggested that he did not represent the view of a responsible body of gynoncological surgeons. With great respect to the deputy judge, I do not think this is good enough. Where there is a clear conflict of medical opinion, the court's duty is not merely to say which view it prefers, but to explain why it prefers one to the other. This, in my judgment, is all the more so when the expert whose view is preferred accepts a substantial element of what the less favoured expert describes as basic good practice – in this case, keeping your scissors shut unless you can see what you are doing. In such circumstances, it is not sufficient, in my view, simply to say that [the expert] is representative of a responsible body of medical opinion and that, as a consequence, [D] was not negligent.

This is not an isolated instance. For example, in *Dowdie v Camberwell HA*,[130] the court accepted that the two distinguished expert witnesses for D had testified that D's conduct was 'within the

124 [2005] EWHC 2253 (QB) [11]. 125 [2003] EWHC 1744 (QB) [24]. 126 (QB, 1 May 2003) [32].
127 [1999] 1 Lloyd's Rep Med 23 (CA). 128 [2005] EWHC 2089 (QB) [98]–[99], [112].
129 [2007] EWCA Civ 387, [44]. 130 (QB, 1 Jul 1997) [no pp].

range of acceptable practice', but that 'does not oblige me to accept their evidence and, on this issue, I accept the evidence of [C's] experts'. In *Townsend v Worcester and District HA*[131] too, the court referred to 'choosing between the experts'.

Importantly, however, the rejected opinion adduced for D, in all of these cases, did **not** fail the *Bolitho* threshold, in that it was not considered illogical and unsupportable or indefensible. It was simply not the peer professional opinion which the courts preferred. There is, of course, a world of difference between an opinion that is rejected because it lacks a logical basis (as required by *Bolitho*), and one that is rejected because, whilst logical, another opinion is more plausible. Were a 'preferability' analysis to be incorporated as a *third stage* of the analysis of breach, it would significantly depart from the House of Lords' statements reproduced above. Indeed, it seems that Lord Scarman would (per *Maynard*) describe it as an 'error of law'.[132]

A preferability analysis, of course, does introduce a 'battle of the experts'. The onus upon C's experts inevitably alters – instead of seeking to argue that D's expert opinion was illogical and indefensible due to one of the *Bolitho* reasons (outlined below), C's experts would seek to argue that, whilst a reasonable and logical point of view was adopted by D, their own view was preferable. In that assessment, the wisdom of hindsight would have considerably more room for operation. C's body of peer professional opinion, which proposed a procedure that would have precluded or minimised the adverse outcome for C, would arguably be preferable. In addition, although the medical paternalism signified by the *Bolam* test was rightly tempered by the *Bolitho* gloss, it would surely be incorrect to permit a court (where the judge is a lay person with no formal medical training) to reject a reasonable body of expert opinion adduced on D's part in favour of an expert opinion that it considered preferable. That was never the judicial role envisaged by the House of Lords in *Sidaway*, *Maynard* or *Bolitho*, and to require that third step – a superiority analysis – strains both legal precedent, and the propriety of the court's role in professional negligence suits.

Anticipating the other view?

§7.15 It is not legally necessary that D should have considered and reflected upon the alternative avenues available to him (including the peer professional opinion adduced in C's favour), and made a deliberate choice between those opinions. It is sufficient if D's conduct is supported by a respectable body of peer professional opinion.

The *Bolam* test of breach does *not* require D to 'second-guess' what an alternative peer professional opinion may think, or investigate the alternatives that others with specialist skills might favour, and then conduct a cost-benefit analysis of the various options before coming to his decision, in order to preclude a finding of negligence. It is sufficient that D acts according to *one* body of peer professional opinion – and what matters is the end result, and not the processes by which it came to be given.

This point proved contentious in *Adams v Rhymney Valley DC*,[133] where the Court of Appeal held, by majority, that there was no difference between D, who decided to follow a particular practice because, on the basis of his experience, it was a reasonable and accepted professional practice; and D, who sat down in a chair and mused upon **all** the alternative practices open to him and then consciously selected the one to follow. Both Ds would escape

[131] (1994) 23 BMLR 31 (QB) [no pp]. [132] [1984] 1 WLR 634 (HL) 639.
[133] [2000] EWCA Civ 3035, [30], [43] (Sir Christopher Staughton), [59] (Morritt LJ), [19] (Sedley LJ, dissenting).

a finding of breach if their conduct accorded with accepted professional practice. (By contrast, the dissenter, Sedley LJ, considered it to be a 'requirement of the *Bolam* test' that D consider and evaluate the alternatives.) The majority considered Sedley LJ's view to be untenable, as an unacceptable re-writing of the *Bolam* principle, and that it 'would drastically alter the law of negligence'. The very point of *Bolam* was to give D a defence to a claim in negligence if he acted in accordance with a practice that was accepted as proper by a reasonable body of persons who practised the same 'art'. D did not have to anticipate that other body of opinion, and then actively consider and then reject that opinion. What mattered to liability was the act or omission by D, and whether it fell below the standard of reasonable care, and not the thought processes which preceded it. That principle can be applied to D's considerable advantage.

In *Camerata Property Inc v Credit Suisse Securities (Europe) Ltd*,[134] C, a company owned by a wealthy shipping businessman, invested in a 5-year bond issued by Lehman Bros, on the advice of Credit Suisse, D, for US$12m. On 8 Oct 2008, Lehman Bros was declared bankrupt, and C lost all or most of its investment. C claimed that D's advice was negligent, and that it would have otherwise sold the bond before the investment was lost. D's officer, who was C's relationship manager and adviser, had not properly read the information provided to him by C; and C would naturally and properly assume that his adviser would be aware of such information, and would have it in mind when advising C. **Held:** no breach. Ultimately, D's investment advice was sound; and was not to be condemned as negligent because of failings in the process that led to that advice. In *Smith v West Yorkshire HA (t/a Leeds HA)*,[135] a baby boy, C, suffered from quadriplegic cerebral palsy, allegedly because of the negligent management of his mother's labour by the medical staff at D's hospital. C claimed that D's medical staff mis-interpreted the trace readings on the cardiotocograph ('CTG'), recording the foetal heartbeat and the rate of maternal contractions. C argued that one responsible body of professional opinion took the view that the trace was of a baby who was unwell. Another body of professional opinion took the view that the trace was of a baby who was well (and D himself considered that the CTG was within acceptable limits). **Held:** no breach proven. If there were different bodies holding respectable but significantly different opinions on CTG trace interpretation, D's conduct was not compromised by the fact that he failed to take into account that the other respectable opinion could reasonably take a different view.

Reliance on professional guidelines

§7.16 D's compliance with the protocols and guidelines produced by professional bodies does not, of itself, preclude breach. However, it will constitute very strong evidence of D's adherence with a reasonable body of professional opinion, so as to satisfy the *Bolam* test of breach.

As the High Court was anxious to point out in *Zarb v Odetoyinbo*,[136] professional protocols and guidelines still have to satisfy the *Bolitho* scrutiny – and hence, it must follow that a failure to comply with them cannot, of itself, be regarded as irrational. However (said the court), D's compliance is a 'major obstacle' to any finding of breach of duty (as it was there, where the Guidelines of the Royal College of General Practitioners were complied with by D), and it was 'difficult to envisage' when a set of guidelines would not be *Bolam*-compliant.

[134] [2011] 2 BCLC 54 (CA) [199]. [135] QB, 27 May 2004, [27]–[28]. [136] [2006] EWHC 2880 (QB) [110].

Obversely, D's failure to comply with professional guidelines will render it difficult to satisfy the *Bolam* test, and expert evidence notwithstanding, D will find it difficult to justify that non-compliance.

In *Thomson v James*,[137] patient C, a young child, was not given a measles vaccination by D, his GP, because it was contra-indicated in the case of convulsions, which C may have experienced. **Held:** breach proven. D ought to have been aware of the Dept of Health and Social Services (DHSS) advice that, even if a child had a history of convulsions, the vaccination could be administered with special precautions, *viz*, the simultaneous injection of immunoglobulin. Failure to comply with DHSS guidelines on measles vaccination was crucial to that finding.

Where D's expert refers to a 'seminal' article in the area that supported D's conduct, that has also tended to carry great weight when determining *Bolam*-compliance (as it did, for example, regarding an article discussing the treatment of angina, and the utility of heart by-pass surgery, in *Shaw v McGill*[138]).

The *Bolitho* 'gloss'

§7.17 According to the *Bolitho* test, the court is required to disregard peer professional '*Bolam*' opinion, where that professional opinion is not responsible or capable of withstanding logical analysis. However, the *Bolitho* test cannot be used to permit the court to choose, or to prefer, one peer professional opinion over another, where *both* have a logical basis.

The test, and reasons for its introduction

Unsurprisingly, the *Bolam* test of medical breach – whereby D was exculpated if he acted in accordance with a practice accepted as proper by a responsible body of practitioners – was judicially criticised on several counts (and across a range of jurisdictions):

i. it was 'over protective and deferential' toward D (per *Foo Fio Na v Dr Soo Fook Mun*[139]);
ii. it had the potential to be satisfied 'by the production of a dubious expert whose professional views existed at the fringe of medical consciousness' (per *Khoo v Gunapathy d/o Muniandy*[140]);
iii. there was a perception that the medical profession was 'above the law', that the *Bolam* test deprived courts of the opportunity of 'precipitating changes, where required, in professional standards' (per *Hajgato v London HA*[141]), and that the courts were being 'dictated to' rather than exercising their judgment (per *Burne v A*[142]);
iv. the reality was that 'professions may adopt unreasonable practices. Practices may develop in professions ... not because they serve the interest of the clients, but because they protect the interests or convenience of members of the profession' (per *F v R*[143]);

[137] (1996) 31 BMLR 1 (QB). [138] (QB, 31 July 1998).
[139] [2007] 1 MLJ 593, [2006] MLJU 518, (Federal Court of Appeal, 29 Dec 2006) [26].
[140] [2002] 2 SLR 414 (CA) [63]. [141] (1982), 36 OR (2d) 669 (Ont SCJ) [56] (Callagan J).
[142] [2006] EWCA Civ 24, [10].
[143] [1983] 33 SASR 189 (Full Ct) 191 (King CJ) (although this was a disclosure case). Also: *Scott v Lothian University Hosp NHS Trust* [2006] ScotCS (OH) [33], [36].

v. there was a sense that the *Bolam* test did not adequately protect the community against medical practices that could not withstand critical scrutiny, and that more judicial safeguards for the public were necessary (per law reform opinion[144]);
vi. it was contended that a judicial scrutiny of medical expert opinion was no different from the type of careful analysis that a judge must make in respect of other professional evidence, be it 'a judgment by an accountant, lawyer, underwriter or other professional' – if the court was the final arbiter in respect of these professionals, then so too should it be with the medical profession (per *Wisniewski v Central Manchester HA*[145]).

It follows that, pursuant to the now-'commonplace'[146] *Bolitho* test, the court is the final arbiter of breach. In *Bolitho v City and Hackney HA,*[147] Lord Browne-Wilkinson stated the test thus:

> in cases of diagnosis and treatment there are cases where, despite a body of professional opinion sanctioning D's conduct, D can properly be held liable for negligence (I am not here considering questions of disclosure of risk) ... that is because, in some cases, it cannot be demonstrated to the judge's satisfaction that the body of opinion relied upon is reasonable or responsible. In the vast majority of cases, the fact that distinguished experts in the field are of a particular opinion will demonstrate the reasonableness of that opinion. In particular, where there are questions of assessment of the relative risks and benefits of adopting a particular medical practice, a reasonable view necessarily presupposes that the relative risks and benefits have been weighed by the experts informing their opinions. But if, in a rare case, it can be demonstrated that the professional opinion is not capable of withstanding logical analysis, the judge is entitled to hold that the body of opinion is not reasonable or responsible.

It will be very difficult to apply *Bolitho* where a distinguished expert in the field considered D's allegedly-negligent conduct to be reasonable (noted, e.g., in *Cowley v Cheshire and Merseyside Strategic HA,*[148] where *Bolitho's* caveat was rejected by the court). Indeed, more recently, a court was not prepared to invoke the *Bolitho* gloss, holding that it would be a 'very bold and inappropriate step for a court to find, in effect, that the authors of two leading world textbooks on orthopaedic surgery had described a surgical technique which could not be logically supported' (per *Ecclestone v Medway NHS Foundation Trust*[149]).

To hold that the medical opinion proffered by experienced specialists should be departed from has been termed a 'rare' occurrence (*In re B (a child)*[150]), 'very seldom' occurring (*M v Blackpool Victoria Hosp NHS Trust*[151]), and only to apply in exceptional circumstances, where 'the evidence shows that a lacuna in professional practice exists' (*French v Thames Valley Strategic HA*[152]). It has been said that peer professional opinion under the *Bolam* test 'should not lightly be set aside' (*AB v Leeds Teaching Hosp NHS Trust*[153]). It would have to be so

144 See, e.g., *Ipp Report*, [3.10] and [3.24], citing the major enquiry in NZ in: *Committee of Enquiry into Allegations Concerning the Treatment of Cervical Cancer at National Women's Hosp and into Other Related Matters* (1988).

145 [1998] EWCA Civ 596, [1998] PIQR P324 (CA) P335, citing the trial judge.

146 *Kingsberry v Greater Manchester Strategic HA* [2005] EWHC 2253, 87 BMLR 73 (QB) [11].

147 [1998] AC 232 (HL) 243 (Lord Browne-Wilkinson).

148 [2007] EWHC 48 (QB) [55]. Also: *Ndri v Moorfields Eye Hosp NHS Trust* [2006] EWHC 3652 (QB) [35].

149 [2013] EWHC 790 (QB) [47].

150 [2000] 1 WLR 790 (Fam Ct) 796 (Otter LJ). Also: *Calver v Westwood Veterinary Group* [2001] PIQR 168 (CA) [31] (Simon Brown LJ); *E v Castro* [2003] EWHC 2066 (QB) [99].

151 [2003] EWHC 1744 (QB) [42].

152 [2005] EWHC 459 (QB) [112].

153 [2004] EWHC 644 (QB) [226].

irrational that it '[could] not be logically supported at all' (*French*[154]). A degree of '*Wednesbury* unreasonableness' was required in one case (*Kushnir v Camden & Islington HA*[155]), although in *Joyce v Merton Sutton and Wandsworth HA*,[156] that term was disapproved of, given that it is an administrative law concept that was 'directed to very different problems and [its] use, even by analogy, in negligence cases can ... only serve to confuse'.

Further, the fact that the expert evidence adduced on behalf of D is a minority view of accepted medical practice does not, of itself, render that view illogical, irrational or irresponsible. Nevertheless, that may be more likely, if that minority opinion was based on a dubious expert whose professional views existed at the fringe of medical consciousness, or if D's expert adhered to out-of-date ideas (per *McGovern v Sharkey*[157]). However, the expert's competence and 'respectability' matter, for *Bolitho's* gloss. Recently, Green J provided an important vignette, when he remarked that lengthy NHS experience 'is a matter of significance' when considering D's expert to be logical and defensible; that an expert retired for 10 years 'and whose retirement is spent expressing expert opinions, may turn out to be far removed from the fray and much more likely to form an opinion divorced from current practical reality'; and that 'many judges and litigators have come across so called experts who can "talk the talk" but who veer towards the eccentric or unacceptable end of the spectrum. Regrettably there are, in many fields of law, individuals who profess expertise but who, on true analysis, must be categorised as "fringe"' (per *C v North Cumbria Univ Hosp NHS Trust*[158]).

Nevertheless, there is a body of English case law which shows that courts **are** prepared, on unusual occasion, to characterise peer professional opinion as lacking 'logical analysis', or as being 'irresponsible' or 'irrational', per *Bolitho*. These labels are, however, only helpful when 'fleshed out' with examples. Indeed, given the number of occasions upon which *Bolitho's* gloss has been applied, it is doubtful whether the test application quite warrants the moniker of a 'rarity'.

The *Bolitho* factors

The following Table identifies the factors which have indicated to the court that the requisite logical analysis of the body of peer professional opinion was absent:[159]

The *Bolitho* factors

	Factor	Case example/s
I	The peer professional opinion has overlooked that a 'clear precaution' to avoid the adverse outcome for C was available, so that the outcome could have been easily and inexpensively	In the pre-*Bolitho* case of *Hucks v Cole*[a] (1968), a patient suffered from septicaemia, causing various sores and yellow spots on her fingers and toes. D, the treating GP, put C on a 5-day course of tetracycline antibiotics, but ceased them when the sores showed signs of improvement, although he knew that the septic spots contained streptococcal infection

[a] [1993] 4 Med LR 393 (CA) (decided in 1968).

[154] [2005] EWHC 459 (QB) [9]–[10].

[155] QB, 16 Jun 1995, citing: *Bolitho* [1993] 4 Med LR 381 (CA) 392 (Dillon LJ).

[156] (1995) 27 BMLR 124 (CA) 156. [157] [2014] NIQB 117, [43]. [158] [2014] EWHC 61 (QB) [25(vi)].

[159] See further, Mulheron, 'Trumping *Bolam*: A Critical Legal Analysis of *Bolitho's* "Gloss"' (2010) 69 *CLJ* 609, from which this section of the chapter is substantially derived.

Factor	Case example/s
avoided – even if a reasonable body of medical opinion would have agreed with D's conduct. The *Bolam* test 'is not a licence for professionals to take obvious risks which can be guarded against'.[b] However, it is unlikely that *Bolitho* will be activated, to render *Bolam* evidence 'illogical', if D's medical conduct under scrutiny involved high complexity and uncertainty, such that there was no 'clear precaution'.	and organisms that could lead to puerperal fever, and that penicillin could kill streptococcal infection. The next day, C contracted puerperal fever. A number of distinguished doctors gave evidence, for D, that they would not have treated C with penicillin either. **Held:** breach proven. Penicillin was a clear precaution. In *Lowe v Havering Hosp NHS Trust*,[c] D left an 8-week gap between consultations with C, a patient, who had dangerously high and uncontrolled blood pressure, and who then suffered a major stroke. D had 'suspicions' that C was not diligently taking his medication, which emphasised the need to see C more frequently; and especially when C was a relatively young man who had a wife and dependent family, and for whom a disabling stroke would be devastating (a social, rather than a medical, consideration, but one which a reasonable D ought to have taken into account). **Held:** breach proven. More frequent appointments were easily arranged. In *French v Thames Valley Strategic HA*,[d] C was born prematurely (29 weeks), and suffered from brain damage and cerebral palsy. Her mother suffered from pre-eclampsia, and claimed her obstetrician and gynaecologist, D, delivered C prematurely by caesarean section, and that but for the premature delivery, C's injuries would probably have been avoided. **Held:** no breach proven. This area was vested with technical difficulty; and in the case of pre-eclampsia, literature advised that the best timing of delivery was 'a matter of opinion and judgment, with few facts or absolute guidelines', and where 'the pathological findings are so controversial and contradictory'.
II The peer professional opinion supports a practice that *guarantees* an adverse outcome for C – unless limited resources, and D's co-existing duties towards other parties, render the practice *Bolam*-compliant.	In *Garcia v St Mary's NHS Trust*,[e] patient C underwent heart bypass surgery, completed by 7.00 pm. At 11.53 pm, C coughed, lost consciousness, and suffered an acute post-operative bleed into the chest area, a recognised complication to this surgery. A 'crash call' was placed at 11.54 pm; the anaesthetic team arrived at 11.56 pm; at 11.58 pm, the cardiothoracic registrar on-call was notified at home; he arrived in the recovery room at 00.25 am; and by 00.40 am, the bleeding was under control. C was left brain-damaged. The neurological experts agreed that the length and severity of a period of hypotension/hypoperfusion of 30 minutes meant that there would be severe neurological damage. C claimed that, unless there was

[b] *Adams v Rhymney Valley DC* [2000] EWCA Civ 3035, [2000] Lloyd's Rep PN 777, [40].
[c] (2001) 62 BMLR 69 (QB).
[d] [2005] EWHC 459 (QB) [112].
[e] [2006] EWHC 2314 (QB) [88], [91]–[93].

Factor	Case example/s
	an on-call registrar staying at the hospital overnight to deal with such emergencies, the inevitable delay condemned C to severe brain damage. **Held:** no breach proven. The practice of having no specialist registrar on site was defensible, given the co-existing duties which registrars had to other patients and to co-employees.
III The peer professional opinion failed to weigh, or to properly direct its attention to, the comparative risks and benefits of D's practice. It is the process, rather than the ultimate decision, that activates the *Bolitho* test under this scenario. However, even if an alternative course had a very low risk to C, that does not necessarily activate the *Bolitho* gloss. The law will not insist upon a course of conduct that completely eliminates the risks of an adverse outcome, if that system is not workable.	In *Wiszniewski v Central Manchester HA*,[f] patient C was showing an abnormal foetal heartbeat prior to birth. Ultimately, C suffered irreversible brain damage in the 13 minutes immediately prior to his birth because, as he moved down the birth canal, the umbilical cord wrapped round his neck and had a knot in it, so that he was effectively being strangled. The attending obstetrician, D, adduced evidence that a respectable school of medical practitioners would not have moved immediately to intervene in a birth, at the sign of possible trouble with the foetal heartbeat. **Held:** breach proven. The alternative course of intervening to perform an artificial rupture of the membranes which, whilst itself had a small risk, was preferable to exposing C to the risk of brain damage by not intervening. In *Garcia*,[g] facts previously, no breach proven. The risk of post-operative bleeding into the chest area following heart by-pass surgery was 1 in 1,000. Having a specialist registrar on site for such an event might have reduced/eliminated the risk of C's brain damage. However, the hospital system had to be designed to accommodate the 'reasonably foreseeable' event, and not the 'rare occurrence'. The hospital's practice was *Bolam*-compliant.
IV The peer professional opinion endorses D's practice, but that practice contravenes widespread public opinion. One of the justifications for scrutinising *Bolam* evidence is to safeguard community expectations of acceptable practice.	In *AB v Leeds Teaching Hosp NHS Trust*[h] (the Nationwide Organ Retention Group Litigation), various doctors, D, failed to inform the relatives (mainly parents) of children who had died either at, or shortly after, birth, that a post-mortem examination of their children involved the removal of organs (brains, hearts, lungs) for later scientific examination. The parents had no opportunity for objection and/or refusal. The joint expert report stated that the practice in 1992, when this happened, was not to be explicit with parents about the details of post-mortems, an almost universal practice up to 1999/2000. **Held:** breach proven. Even if the practice was universally accepted, it was 'irresponsible conservatism' on the part of the medical profession, exhibited by the national scandal that gave rise to the group litigation in the first place.

[f] [1998] EWCA Civ 596.
[g] [2006] EWHC 2314 (QB) [96].
[h] [2004] EWHC 644 (QB).

	Factor	Case example/s
V	The peer professional opinion cannot be correct, when taken in the context of the whole factual evidence, or in the context of advances in scientific knowledge.	In *Tagg v Countess of Chester Hosp Foundation Trust*,[i] patient C suffered a bowel injury during a gynaecological operation. **Held:** breach proven. D's expert surgeon gave evidence supporting the surgical practice adopted by D. However, that expert opinion was 'neutralised by the unreliability of the factual evidence about what happened and about what was found at the operation'. In *Hucks v Cole*,[j] facts previously, one reason for disregarding the *Bolam* evidence adduced for D was that the peer professional opinion ignored advances in medical knowledge, i.e., the potential use of penicillin. In *Lillywhite v UCL Hosp NHS Trust*,[k] although the *Bolitho* test was not expressly applied to discount *Bolam* evidence on behalf of sonologist D, that is effectively what occurred. C, baby Alice, was born with a severe malformation of her brain, caused in the early stages of foetal development by the failure of her fore-brain to divide into two. As a result, she was severely brain-damaged, quadriplegic, and unable to use her limbs or to talk. **Held (trial):** no breach in failing to identify that three parts of the brain – a cavum septum (CSP), anterior horns from the lateral ventricles, and a falx – were absent. Peer opinion adduced for D was that D must have identified echoes mimicking the brain structures. **Held (CA, 2:1):** the peer professional opinion was 'neither possible nor plausible ... when looked at in the context of the evidence as a whole; and, in the case of the lateral ventricles, the only suggested explanation indicated negligent unawareness of the-then state of the art'.
VI	The peer professional opinion was not internally consistent – in that the expert endorsed D's practice, but then said that peer professional opinion would not have done that, but quite the opposite.	In the *Organ Retention Litig*,[l] facts previously, D's peer professional opinion agreed that parents were entitled to have their wishes in respect of their deceased child's body respected and complied with. Gage J could not perceive how those wishes could be respected, without the parents being told that organs from their children might be kept and not buried with the bodies. In *Taaffe v East of England Ambulance Service NHS Trust*,[m] patient C, 50, suffered chest pains, and her son called an ambulance. C had a history of hypertension, a family history of cardiac disease, and no pre-existing history of significant indigestion, which was the nature of the pain she described.

[i] [2007] EWHC 509 (QB) [64].
[j] On this point, see, e.g.: *Khoo v Gunapathy d/o Muniandy* [2002] 2 SLR 414 (CA) [65]–[66].
[k] [2005] EWCA Civ 1466, [106].
[l] [2004] EWHC 644 (QB) [235].
[m] [2012] EWHC 1335 (QB) [69].

Factor	Case example/s
	D, the paramedics, noted that C's pain had eased by the time they arrived, and two ECGs appeared normal. No detailed history was taken, and D did not advise C to attend hospital for investigations, because she was visiting her GP the next day. Five days later, C suffered a heart attack and died. C's estate claimed that D should have taken her to hospital or advised her to attend hospital. Expert evidence supported D's decision not to take her to hospital. **Held:** breach proven. D's expert evidence was internally inconsistent – having said that it was essential for a paramedic 'to look at the full picture', that did not occur here: that evidence was 'not consistent with the need to look at all relevant information in making the decision, nor logical'.
VII The peer professional opinion adhered to the wrong legal test (i.e., referring to the wrong standard of care expected of D); or contended what *that expert* would have done, rather than the view of a respected body of medical experts.	In *Hutchinson v Leeds HA*,[n] surgeon D had allowed faecal impaction to cause the disintegration of patient C's posterior-rectal wall, thereby requiring C, a young woman who was being treated by D for acute myeloblastic leukaemia, to undergo surgery and to have a colostomy. **Held:** breach proven. D's expert adhered to the standard that D had not committed 'an error so gross and/or so crass that no reasonably competent doctor would ever have committed', but that was not the *Bolam* standard of care. Hence, D's expert had 'set a yardstick by which to assess the acts or omissions of [D] and his team, which is unjustified, and which must affect the quality of this part of his evidence, and I do not accept it'.

[n] (QB, 6 Nov 2000) [78].

These factors constitute the grounds, to date, upon which English courts have been prepared to reject peer professional opinion as being indefensible and 'not capable of withstanding logical analysis'.

The effect of the SARAH Act 2015

As discussed in Chapter 6, the implementation of the Social Action, Responsibility and Heroism Act 2015[160] would appear to have no impact upon the standard of care relevant for Ds who engage in heroic or socially-beneficial activities. The common law already views such Ds sympathetically. However, whether s 3 of that Act is quite so benign in its impact upon proof of breach is rather less clear.

[160] In force 13 Apr 2015.

s 3 The court must have regard to whether the person, in carrying out the activity in the course of which the alleged negligence or breach of statutory duty occurred, demonstrated a predominantly responsible approach towards protecting the safety or other interests of others.

As the author has discussed elsewhere,[161] the abovementioned provision suffers from three distinct uncertainties. First, the use of the word, 'predominantly', is odd, because *Bolam* is clearly not a 'numbers game', such a position has been clearly rejected at common law. Secondly, whether the 'responsible approach' is to be assessed by a *Bolam* assessment, as qualified by a *Bolitho* (judicially-undertaken) scrutiny, or whether it is solely to be a judicial assessment which re-introduces the banned-at-common-law superiority analysis, is unclear. Thirdly, the provision appears to apply to any type of D, whether a professionally-qualified party (the traditional, but not exclusive, province of the *Bolam* test) or not. At the time of writing, the SARAH Act has not been judicially considered.

Where the *Bolam/Bolitho* framework does *not* apply

There are some circumstances in which it will be inappropriate for the court to rely upon peer professional opinion at all. In such cases, it is not a question of merely determining whether there was a respectable body of expert opinion to support D's (non-negligent) version of events, but rather, the court will weigh the evidence on both sides, and may properly prefer that of C's expert witness to that of D's. Certainly, expert evidence may not always be a pre-requisite in professional negligence cases, a point reiterated in *Royal Brompton Hosp NHS Trust v Hammond.*[162]

Indeed, in some cases, the battle-lines are drawn thus: D will argue that the alleged breach is a matter of expert judgment that falls within *Bolam*, given that peer professional opinion can then be properly adduced to uphold the practice (subject to the *Bolitho* caveat) – whereas C will argue that the alleged breach does not fall within *Bolam* at all because it involved no expert judgment whatsoever, and hence, it is for the court to form its own view, on all the evidence, and to prefer one expert's opinion to that of the other, as a valid course.

There are **three** scenarios in which the *Bolam* test has no room for application:

No body of peer professional opinion

§7.18 The *Bolam* test does not apply, if there is no evidence of an existing '*body of professional practice*' in respect of D's conduct. In that event, the court will hear all the evidence (expert and factual) and form its own view as to breach.

The allegedly-negligent incident may be so unusual or extraordinary that there will be no *Bolam* evidence to adduce, upon which the court could safely rely. In such cases, the court may hear expert evidence adduced by C and D, and decide for itself whether D's conduct fell below the standard of reasonable care. Hence, peer professional opinion may be helpful, but will not be determinative.

[161] Mulheron, 'Legislating Dangerously: Bad Samaritans, Good Society and the Heroism Act 2015' (2016) *Modern Law Review* [forthcoming].

[162] [2002] EWHC 2037 (TCC), 88 Con LR 1, [19].

In *Michael Hyde & Assoc Ltd v JD Williams & Co Ltd*,[163] a heating system was installed in C's premises during the conversion and refurbishment of old cotton mills. D was the architect. Six months after completion, textiles being stored at the premises by C showed 'phenolic yellowing', whereby anti-oxidants in plastic packaging can migrate to textiles and be absorbed by the textiles. C alleged that D ought to have been aware of the risk of discolouration and warned C of it. D contended that it was not aware of the process, and that those within the textile industry, such as C, ought to have known about its dangers and C could not blame others for its own shortcomings. **Held:** breach proven. The *Bolam* test of breach did not apply in this case; the court could assess the question of breach for itself. In *AB v Tameside and Glossop HA*,[164] a series of patients, C, allegedly suffered psychiatric illness for the way in which they were informed by the Glossop Health Authority, D, that they might be at risk of infection from contact with a former healthcare worker who had tested HIV-positive at D's clinics. There had been only one broadly similar incident in the whole of England before this litigation, at a time when the public's understanding of HIV/AIDS was far different. **Held:** no breach proven, in selecting the method of communicating the information to C. In *Ampleforth Abbey Trust v Turner and Townsend Project Management Ltd*,[165] new boarding accommodation was built for Ampleforth College, C, a school in North Yorkshire, for which D was project manager. The works were completed much later than expected. The builder claimed extensions of time and additional payments; whereas C sought liquidated damages of £750,000 for the delay. The whole project was carried out by the builder under letters of intent that C issued from time to time; the contract itself was not signed until long after completion, and hence, C never had any entitlement to liquidated damages. C sued D for professional negligence, alleging that D should have had the builder sign the building contract, so that C would have had a right to pursue liquidated damages for delay and would have achieved a better outcome in its dispute with the builder. **Held:** breach proven. However, the court stated that it obtained from the expert evidence very 'limited' assistance, because it was 'extremely rare for construction projects of any significance to be completed under letters of intent', an exceptional case, and there was no 'body of practice' to support it.

In *Hyde*, the *Bolam* test was discounted for two reasons – because the issue involved no *specialist* skill (discussed below); and because the incident was unusual, and the experts' evidence as to whether they would have further investigated the risk of discoloration 'amounted to no more than an expression of personal opinion as to what the witness would or would not have done, thereby falling short of being evidence of a responsible *body* of architects, or a recognised *practice* within the profession ... [there is] little to suggest that there were two recognised but contrary views of an accepted *practice* governing the decision in question'.[166] In *AB*, Brooke LJ noted that D's suggestion that the *Bolam* test governed the case was wrong, 'because there simply was no adequate well of professional experience on which the court could usefully draw in the present case'. Rather, the court 'has to perform the familiar role of considering the factual evidence carefully, listening to the expert evidence, and forming a view as to whether, in all the circumstances, [D] fell below the standards reasonably to be expected of them'.[167] Similarly, *Ampleforth Abbey* was 'not, properly speaking, a *Bolam* case at all' – the experts were merely saying what they would have done in a similar situation if project-managing the contract (e.g., they emphasised the importance of the protection provided by a contract, rather than mere letters of intent; and the nature of the risks and disadvantages if

[163] [2000] EWCA Civ 211, [2001] PNLR 8.
[164] (1996) 35 BMLR 79 (CA).
[165] [2012] EWHC 2137 (TCC) [101]–[102].
[166] [2000] EWCA Civ 211, [10] (original emphasis).
[167] (1996) 35 BMLR 79 (CA) 93.

the contractor were to walk off site with no contract in place), in other words, they gave their 'personal opinions or reactions'.

In *Royal Brompton* too,[168] HHJ Lloyd QC rejected *Bolam*-type evidence as being determinative, where 'the purposes or the upshot of the expert's opinion is no more than a statement of belief as to what he would have done in the circumstances, presented as evidence of practice'. Such evidence falls short of being evidence of a responsible *body* of experts, or a recognised *practice* within the profession (per Stephen Brown LJ in *Nye Saunders*[169]). In short, it is of 'little assistance' (per *199 Knightsbridge Development Ltd v WSP UK Ltd*[170]). In such cases, the court is entitled to make up its own mind; but it can certainly use the expert evidence adduced on either side to 'understand what would go through the mind of a professional person in those cases, where what would be common sense to the rest of the world would not, or might not, be sensible in that profession or occupation' (per *Royal Brompton*[171]).

In *Royal Brompton*, new buildings were constructed for C's Royal Brompton and National Heart and Lung Hospitals in Chelsea, for which D was project manager. C claimed that D and the architect failed to ensure that a contract drawing correctly showed the extent of the land available for site offices and other temporary purposes. **Held:** breach proven. D should have checked the drawing to make sure that C's instructions had been properly interpreted by the architect, and referred the drawing on to C instead of merely filing it. The parties accepted, for this part of the claim, that much of what the experts said about what a project manager should do with a drawing received from an architect, 'was not truly evidence of practice, but of personal reaction'. The court prefaced its decision on this part of the claim, 'if expert evidence was needed', doubting that it was.

Questions of fact

§7.19 Questions of fact are solely for the court to decide, and are not determined by *Bolam* peer professional opinion.

The court adjudicates questions of fact, to which the *Bolam* test does not apply; whereas, regarding whether or not D met acceptable standards of medical practice, *Bolam* certainly applies. Sometimes, a case will involve **both** questions.

In *Penney, Palmer and Cannon v East Kent HA*,[172] cytology screeners, D, reported four cervical smears taken from patients C as negative. Hence, there was no timely follow-up or diagnostic or therapeutic intervention, and each C went on to develop invasive adenocarcinoma of the cervix. **Held:** breach proven. The question of whether or not cancerous cells were visible on the slides was a question of fact for the court to decide. On the balance of probabilities, cancerous cells were on the slides. By contrast, whether D should have observed cancerous cells on the slides was a question of breach, to be assessed on the *Bolam* test. The conclusion that, in respect of these four slides, the cytoscreeners did not meet the required standard of care, was valid on the face of the expert evidence. Given that, on each slide, there were a small number of inflamed groups of endocervical cells showing changes in nuclear and cytoplasmic morphology, the smears ought to have been classified, at least, as 'borderline'.

168 [2002] EWHC 2037 (TCC), 88 Con LR 1, [20]. 169 (1987) 37 BLR 92 (CA). 170 [2014] EWHC 43 (TCC) [105]. 171 [2002] EWHC 2037 (TCC) [20], [75], and [104]. 172 (2000) 55 BMLR 63 (CA).

Of course, where the *Bolam* test does not apply, then the court may select one expert's explanation over that of another – because, whilst the court is not supposed to prefer one body of medical opinion to the other, where both represent respected medical practice, experts' explanations *of fact* fall outside the *Bolam* test.

In *Fallows v Randle*,[173] this approach was applied, where contrary explanations occurred, between C's and D's experts, as to why a 'Fallope' ring was not in place when a second operation was carried out, when it ought to have been.

Not matters of 'expert judgment'

§7.20 Given that the *Bolam* test applies to matters requiring 'expert judgment', i.e., matters where special skill or expertise is required and for which the court needs evidence on what constitutes the relevant 'body of practice', matters falling outside 'expert judgment' are not governed by that test. Rather, these matters fall to be determined by the court's forming its own view as to breach.

The *Bolam* test applies 'where the court *cannot answer the question* without expert evidence, as to the body of professional practice prevailing at the time, where the negligence lies in not following established practice' (per *Royal Brompton v Hammond*[174]). HH Judge Lloyd QC outlined the two reasons why *Bolam* evidence is needed: (1) 'the court would not otherwise know of it, as a matter of common sense (or judicial notice), or as a matter of expertise which the court should possess', and (2) 'as a matter of policy, a professional person should not be held liable without the court being satisfied that any competent professional would have done otherwise'. In other words, *Bolam* evidence is required to give the court information as to the relevant 'body of practice' which the court is unable to determine for itself.

Hence, once the expert strays into territory where he simply gives his own personal reaction as to what he would have done in the scenario; or provides an opinion that does not require specialist skill at all, then the court does not need that evidence to determine breach – it makes that assessment for itself (per *Michael Hyde v JD Williams*[175]), albeit that peer professional opinion may still sometimes be helpful on the point.

In *Worboys v Acme Investments Ltd*,[176] Sachs LJ gave the example of where a court could find a breach of duty against the professional D, without resort to *Bolam* evidence – where, say, 'an architect omitted to provide a front door to the premises'. Expert judgment requires the exercise of some special skill or expertise – but providing a visible and accessible means of access to premises does not require architectural skill and expertise, so the court can decide for itself whether the failure to provide such a door is a breach, without recourse to expert *Bolam* evidence. In *Wembridge v Winter*,[177] there was a large explosion of fireworks stored in a steel shipping container on a farm near Lewes in East Sussex. Two people were killed in the explosion.

[173] (QB, 7 May 1996), aff'd: [1997] 8 Med LR 160 (CA).

[174] [2002] EWHC 2037 (TCC), 88 Con LR 1, [17], [20].

[175] [2001] PNLR 233 (CA) [25], citing: *Nye Saunders and Partners v Alan E Bristow* (1987) 37 BLR 92 (CA) 103 and *Gold v Haringey HA* [1988] 1 QB 481 (CA) 490.

[176] (1969) 4 BLR 133, 139, and cited in: *Royal Brompton* [2002] EWHC 2037 (TCC) [18].

[177] [2013] EWHC 2331 (QB) [223].

Their estates and various firefighters and police officers sued for injuries sustained. Mr Winter, D1, gave inadequate or misleading information to firefighters at the scene about the contents of the container. East Sussex Fire and Rescue Service, D2, were sued for failing to evacuate the fireground. **Held:** breach proven. The *Bolam* test of breach did not apply to this scenario. There were no different schools of thought about highly technical matters in dealing with fireworks explosions, and whether/when to evacuate the fireground; rather, the 'problem is the speed and complexity of events, rather than making allowance for different intellectual or technical approaches'.

There are numerous facets of professional practice, however, where it is a very finely-balanced judgment as to whether or not the matter truly falls to be determined by *Bolam* evidence. For example, the case law is not always entirely consistent about whether the assessment of risks and benefits is a matter which properly falls within the *Bolam* test of breach. In *Bolitho*,[178] Lord Browne-Wilkinson observed that '[t]he assessment of medical risks and benefits is a matter of clinical judgment which a judge would not normally be able to make without expert evidence'. On the other hand, in *Michael Hyde v JD Williams & Co*[179] (the phenolic yellowing case), the court was of the view that whether D should have further investigated the risk of discoloration did not require any special architectural skills, but was simply an exercise in discounting the risk, and the factors relevant to that risk could be assessed by the court itself. The trial judge held that the factors governing that risk assessment 'are not peculiar to architectural or engineering practice. It was a matter of weighing risk against benefits: the risk was a known risk of some form of discoloration on materials; the potential effect of *any* form of discoloration on garments which were going to be kept in the distribution centre was obviously a matter of great concern ... this had to be weighed against the benefits of lower cost and a more flexible heating system'. Further investigations should have been carried out.

Similarly, whilst only matters of 'clinical judgment' in medical practice fall within the province of the *Bolam* test, the phrase has been widely interpreted, to permit *Bolam* evidence to determine the question (subject to *Bolitho's* caveat). That the following instances were taken to amount to 'clinical judgment' may appear somewhat surprising, but nevertheless, they fell within the *Bolam* test of breach:

- the nature of communications between nursing and physician staff, when a patient is discharged, because any decision about discharge from hospital involves an exercise of professional judgment by the medical professional to either authorise the discharge or to refer the patient to a colleague because of continuing worrying symptoms:

In *Rehman v University College London*,[180] patient C was discharged following abdominal surgery, but where her bowel had (unknown to staff) been perforated during the operation, and where C later suffered severe peritonitis, her condition became life-threatening, and she required further urgent surgery. C claimed that the hospital discharged her too early, that she was in obvious pain at the point of discharge by the nursing staff who authorised her departure, and that had she not been discharged, the perforated bowel would have been diagnosed and repaired earlier. C argued

[178] [1998] AC 232 (HL) 243. [179] [2000] EWCA Civ 211.

[180] [2004] EWHC 1361 (QB) [72]–[74], citing, e.g.: *Chapman v Rix* [1994] 5 Med LR 239 (HL) 245 (decided 21 Dec 1960) (Keith LJ, dissenting); and M Jones, *Medical Negligence* (3rd edn, Sweet & Maxwell, 2003).

that this case concerned, essentially, a breakdown of communication – the nursing staff ought to have informed the medical staff that C was in pain and did not wish to go home, that this was not a case of clinical judgment, and that a hospital was no different from any other work place where news was not communicated between employees. **Held:** breach proven. *Bolam* applied, so that expert evidence was admissible on how a responsible nurse would act when particular symptoms manifested, and on whether it would be entirely within the nurse's discretion to make up his own mind at the point of discharge.

- managing and organising hospital staff to meet on-call responsibilities – as the court noted in *Garcia v St Mary's NHS Trust*, '[o]bviously, this issue does not relate to medical or surgical diagnosis or techniques. What it relates to is staffing levels. But it has been argued before me on the footing that the *Bolam/Bolitho* principles apply to that question as well',[181] and the court accepted that:

In *Garcia v St Mary's*, facts previously, the claim concerned whether it was reasonable for the hospital not to make provision for an on-call cardiothoracic registrar to stay overnight in the hospital. Without that measure, patient C claimed (and the court agreed) that there was an inevitable half-hour delay built into the system between the 'crash call and the commencement of a re-sternotomy', which was a system which condemned C to suffer brain damage. **Held:** no breach proven. *Bolam* applied, and the professional practice governing staffing levels survived *Bolitho* scrutiny (as discussed previously).

- acquiring information from a patient about his symptoms – as the court remarked in *Burne v A*, '[t]his skill, while an important aspect of clinical practice, sits at the threshold rather than at the centre of it'.[182]

In *Burne*, doctor D sought to gain information from a mother over the telephone about what symptoms her child, C, was showing. C was vomiting at school and experiencing headaches. C had been born prematurely, and with a hydrocephalic condition that required him to be fitted at the age of nine weeks with a ventriculo-peritoneal shunt. This device continuously drained excess fluid from the brain cavity, and any blockage of it was potentially critical. This had occurred at least once previously. Following a conversation between mother and D, a diagnosis of upper respiratory infection was made by telephone. The following day, C's condition worsened, he was admitted to hospital, and it was found that the shunt had become blocked, leading to a heart attack and brain damage. **Held:** regarding the information-gathering technique used here, *Bolam* evidence was relevant. D's questioning fell short of the reasonable standard of care, given that 'this was no ordinary patient'. The medical evidence on both sides was that making enquiry about C's condition by a series of 'open' questions, to help with diagnosis, was acceptable professional practice. The trial judge disagreed, holding that, in relation to C whose particular vulnerability was known to D, 2–3 direct, leading, 'closed', questions about C's vomiting and drowsiness would have led to a correct diagnosis of a blocked shunt. (Ultimately, a retrial was ordered, because the medical experts at trial had not been asked to address the *Bolitho* point specifically, i.e., whether their view could be so lacking in logic that it should be rejected by the court.)

[181] [2006] EWHC 2314 (QB) [88].

[182] [2006] EWCA Civ 24, [13] (Sedley LJ).

OTHER POTENTIAL TESTS OF BREACH

Contravening specific duties of care

§7.21 The content of the duty of care which D owes C may, in some cases, also define whether D has breached that duty of care.

Where D is under a specific, and more narrowly-focused, duty than the general duty to exercise reasonable care to avoid or to minimise the risk of harm to C, and D contravenes the duty, that will constitute a breach, e.g.:

- a doctor is under a specific duty to warn a patient of material or significant risks associated with an operative procedure or treatment (as examined in Chapter 3). Hence, failure-to-warn of a specific risk of that kind will constitute breach;
- a driver is under a specific duty to exercise reasonable care towards other road-users. Breach may be constituted by, e.g., failing to provide any, or any proper lookout; losing control of the vehicle; failing to apply the brakes in time, or at all; failing to stop, steer, or otherwise control his vehicle so as to avoid a collision.

Contravening relevant standards or rules

§7.22 In determining whether D took all reasonable steps to reduce or eliminate the risk of harm to C, a court may have regard to the governing rules or standards which apply to D's conduct. However, adherence to, or departure from, those rules/standards is *not* conclusive on the question of breach.

Compliance or otherwise with building standards arises particularly in the context of occupiers who are sued for faulty premises. D's failure to comply with industry or professional construction standards (such as the relevant British Building Standard) does not **necessarily** entail a breach, so as to lead to liability under the Occupiers' Liability Act 1957. According to Staughton LJ in *Green v Building Scene Ltd*,[183] 'it is one thing to lay down ... standards, with [the] objective [of avoiding accidents], and another to define what is reasonably safe in all the circumstances of a particular case.' Conversely, the Court of Appeal reiterated in dicta, in *Perry v Butlins*,[184] that compliance with professional standards does not necessarily preclude liability on the part of occupier D (no building regulations directly bore upon the issue there). Nevertheless, compliance with relevant building standards is often referred to as a relevant pointer to the conclusion that occupier D was not in breach of his common duty of care (as occurred, e.g., in *McGivney v Golderslea Ltd*[185]). Further principles, relevant to the standard of care, and proof of breach, on an occupier's part, are discussed in Chapter 12.

The same principle applies, say, where an amateur referee does not comply with the 'Laws of the Game' for rugby union, as issued by the Council of the International Rugby Football Board. Departure from those rules does not **automatically** impute breach by that referee either. It will depend upon the circumstances (see e.g. the discussion of *Vowles v Evans* in Chapter 6).

[183] [1994] PIQR P259 (CA) P269. [184] [1998] Ed CR 39 (CA).

[185] [1997] EWCA Civ 2656, (2001) 17 Const LJ 454.

Contravening the 'making it worse' rule

Scope of application, and derivation

§7.23 The 'making it worse' test of breach provides that breach is proven where D makes C's condition worse than it would have been without D's intervention.

The test has very narrow application – and has been the subject of much criticism in any event. Its application appears to be limited to two fields of endeavour:

- where the 'good Samaritan' D goes to the aid of someone who is injured or imperilled, and in 'wading in' and assisting, makes C's condition worse than it would have been without D's intervention; and
- where D is an emergency services provider (and, in this context, the test is reconsidered under 'Public authority liability', in Chapter 13).

Feasibly, this test may be more difficult for C to prove, because D's conduct may fall below the reasonable standard of care, and yet **not** make the situation for C worse, in that the outcome (e.g., death) was always destined for C in any event. In that event, D will be excused. A rule of breach that is harder to satisfy for C is yet a further bulwark against successful claims being brought against either category of D. This reflects a judicial concern 'not to discourage benevolence and altruism' (as the Court of Appeal put it in *McLoughlin v O'Brian*[186]) or Samaritanesque help.

The making-it-worse test of breach has some scant support at Court of Appeal level in *Kent v Griffiths* where, by its inexcusable delay, the ambulance **did** make the situation for C worse than it would have been, had they not undertaken to intervene.

> In *Kent v Griffiths*,[187] Mrs Kent, C, was pregnant, and became seriously ill at home with a severe asthma attack. Her GP attended C at home, and urgently called an ambulance to transfer her to hospital. A 999 call was placed by the GP and accepted by the ambulance service, with two follow-up calls eliciting assurances that an emergency ambulance was 'on its way'. The ambulance was delayed, and C suffered both a miscarriage and brain damage as a result of the delay in reaching hospital. **Held:** breach proven. An assumption of responsibility/reliance 'crystallised' when the first 999 call was accepted: '[t]he acceptance of the call established the duty of care'. Had the GP who had called the ambulance been told that it would take some 40 minutes to arrive at the patient's house, the patient's husband could have driven her to hospital himself, thereby saving crucial minutes.

Lord Woolf MR cited, with approval, the well-known Canadian case of *Horsley v MacLaren (The Ogopogo)*,[188] where the making-it-worse rule was advocated too – but in that case, the actions of the rescuer, in seeking to save Mr Matthews, C, when he fell overboard from D's cruiser, 'cannot be said to have worsened Matthews' condition'. Some further dicta support for the application of the rule in the good Samaritan context was evident in *Capital and Counties plc v Hampshire CC*, where Stuart-Smith LJ observed that, if a doctor 'volunteers his assistance, his only duty as a matter of law is not to make the victim's condition worse'.[189]

[186] [1981] QB 599 (CA) 611 (Stephenson LJ), appeal allowed: [1983] 1 AC 410 (HL), but this point was not criticised.

[187] [2001] QB 36 (CA) [49]. [188] [1972] SCR 441 (SCC) 452, [1971] 2 Lloyd's Rep 410, 412.

[189] [1997] QB 1004 (CA) 1035 (the other members of the CA agreed). For further discussion, and criticisms, of the making-it-worse test, see: Mulheron, *Medical Negilgence: Non-Patient and Third Party Claims* (Ashgate Publishing, 2010), pp 207–10.

Criticisms of the test

There are several difficulties with the 'making it worse' test:[190]

i. as a test of breach, it may be inconsistent with the outcome of the *Bolam* test of breach (i.e., peer professional opinion may suggest that whatever D did fell below the standard of care, even if it did not actually make C's condition worse that if he had done nothing). Breach tests which produce different results may lead to a lack of coherency in the law;
ii. as stated, the test seems to have been endorsed specifically where the law is reluctant to find good Samaritans and emergency service providers negligent, and a more difficult test of breach accords with that sympathetic attitude. However, it is highly questionable whether it is needed in those scenarios in any event. It will be recalled, from Chapter 6, that the standard of care applicable to both the good Samaritan and the emergency services provider is likely to be suppressed by two factors – emergency 'battle' conditions, and a *Bolam*-standard that does not attribute to D any skills which he did not profess to have;
iii. the test seems more aligned with causation than it is to breach. If good Samaritan D intervenes to assist C, but C's outcome would have been dreadful (e.g., fatal) anyway, and D's lack of reasonable care did not make C's condition worse than was pre-ordained before D intervened, then D's conduct did not cause C's injury (i.e., death) (per the 'but-for' test explored in Chapter 8). That does not mean that there was no breach – but rather, that there was no causal link established. The same problem was evident, obversely, in *Kent v Griffiths*. The intervention by the ambulance D, 40 minutes late, meant that C's husband did not drive her to hospital; if he had done so, then on the balance of probabilities, C's physical damage and the loss of her baby would have been avoided. However, that is a causal, and not a breach, enquiry;
iv. the principle outlined at the commencement of this section states that D must make the situation worse than if he had done nothing (for that is the interpretation which this author places upon the Court of Appeal statements identified earlier). However, there is another possible interpretation of the 'making it worse' rule which has been suggested academically, i.e., that D made C's condition worse 'than if timely and competent treatment had been provided by [D]'.[191]

Surely, in the good Samaritan or emergency service provider scenarios, the better course is to apply the usual *Bolam* test of breach – as indeed applied in *Cattley v St John Ambulance Brigade*[192] (discussed in Chapter 6), where there was a strong body of evidence from those skilled in first-aiding and other highly-qualified medical specialists, that D's officers treated C's injuries in accordance with the ordinary skills to be expected of a St John Ambulance first-aider trained in accordance with the First Aid Manual.

THE DOCTRINE OF *RES IPSA LOQUITUR*

Setting the context

Meaning, effect and rationale

§7.24 C may seek to rely on the doctrine of *res ipsa loquitur*, wherever difficulty is encountered in proving breach, but C alleges that, nevertheless, it must have been negligence that caused

[190] Some of these points are also made in, e.g.: A Grubb, 'Medical Negligence: Duty of Care and *Bolam*' (1998) 6 *Medical L Rev* 120; and see too: I Kennedy and A Grubb, *Principles of Medical Law* (Oxford University Press, 1998) 301; M Jones, *Medical Negligence* (3rd edn, Sweet & Maxwell, 2003) 112; K Williams, 'Litigation against English NHS Ambulance Services and the Rules in *Kent v Griffiths*' (2007) 15 *Medical L Rev* 153, fn 34.

[191] Williams, 'Medical Samaritans: Is there a Duty to Treat?' (2001) 21 *OJLS* 393, 394.

[192] QB, 25 Nov 1988.

his injury or damage – for what other rational and feasible explanation could there be? The accident would not ordinarily occur without negligence.

Literally, the phrase, *res ipsa loquitur*, means that 'the thing speaks for itself'.[193] Whatever else may be said about the doctrine, the notion that it is as simple and transparent as this phrase suggests should be immediately dismissed. As a doctrine, it is not of ancient origin – its source has been traced[194] to an 1863 decision.

In *Byrne v Boadle*,[195] a flour barrel fell from D's shop window on to C, who was a passerby below. **Held**: '[t]his is one of those cases in which, I think, a presumption of negligence by defendant is raised, and it was for him, who had all the means of evidence and knowledge within his reach, to meet it'.

Two years later, Erle CJ gave what has come to be regarded as the classic exposition of the principle:

In *Scott v London and St Katherine's Docks*,[196] Mr Scott, C, a customs-house officer, entered D's dock, and while passing under a crane, was injured when some bags of sugar fell onto him from the crane platform. There was no warning of the danger, and no explanation as to how the sugar bags came to fall. **Held:** the doctrine applied.

> where the thing is shewn to be under the management of [D] or his servants, and the accident is such as in the ordinary course of things does not happen if those who have the management use proper care, it affords reasonable evidence, in the absence of explanation by [D], that the accident arose from want of care.

For much of its existence, though, the doctrine has been bedeviled by judicial inconsistency and, at times, barely-concealed antipathy – per such remarks as, 'the one thing that can certainly be said ... is that "it has not been allowed to speak for itself"' (per *Anchor Products Ltd v Hedges*[197]); that if the phrase 'had not been in Latin, nobody would have called it a principle' (per *Fred Ballard v North British Rwy Co*[198]); and that it simply amounts to an 'exotic ... phrase to describe what is, in essence, no more than a common sense approach' (per *Lloyde v West Midlands Gas Board*[199]). Its effect was well-articulated in *MacDonald v York County Hosp*:

> In certain situations, [C's] burden of proving negligence on the part of [D] is difficult, if not impossible, because [C] does not know how his injury or loss occurred and, consequently, cannot plead any act or omission amounting to negligence on the part of [D]. Only in situations where the exact cause of the accident is unknown can the maxim of *res ipsa loquitur* have any application ... *Res ipsa loquitur* is a circumstantial rule of evidence based on the concept that, when an accident occurs under circumstances where it is so improbable that it could have happened without the negligence of [D], the mere happening of the accident gives rise to an inference that [D] was negligent.[200]

[193] *Oxford Dictionary of Law* (6th edn, Oxford) 463.
[194] *Ratcliffe v Plymouth and Torbay HA* [1998] Lloyd's Rep Med 162 (CA) 178 (Brooke LJ).
[195] (1863) 2 H&C 722, 159 ER 299 (Ch) (Pollock CB).
[196] (1865) 3 H&C 596 (Exch) 598, 159 ER 665, 667.
[197] (1966) 115 CLR 493 (HCA) 496, and cited in: *Schellenberg v Tunnel Holdings Pty Ltd* [2000] HCA 18, [121].
[198] 1923 SC (HL) 43, 56 (Lord Shaw). [199] [1971] 1 WLR 749 (CA) 755 (Megaw LJ).
[200] [1972] 3 OR 469 (HC) 486–87 (Addy J).

In other words, the doctrine's rationale is that, in some cases, 'it would be palpably unfair to require [C] to prove something which is beyond his reach, and which is peculiarly within the range of [D's] capacity of proof' (per *Hanrahan v Merck Sharp & Dohme (Ireland) Ltd*[201]). There is an 'evidential gap' here for C – and the doctrine implies that it would be unfair for the consequences of that 'gap' to rest on C.

There may also be circumstances in which, say, a video recording speaks for itself ('*res ipsa videtur*', as the court termed it in *McKeown v British Horseracing Authy*,[202] but that did not apply in that case). The application of *res ipsa loquitur*, in the particular context of defective products, is considered in 'Defective products' (an online chapter).

Terminology

As a matter of terminology, *res ipsa loquitur* has been called everything, from a 'maxim' to a 'rule of evidence'.[203] Indeed, the topic has descended into jingoistic judicial debate. Some judges have suggested that it indicates 'when a *prima facie* case of negligence is proven' by C (per *Ratcliffe v Plymouth and Torbay HA*[204]) but that it does not raise any presumption (per *Wilsher v Essex AHA*[205]). Others have stated that it **does** raise a 'presumption of negligence', albeit that 'it would be dangerous to allow presumptions to be substituted for ... negligence' (per *Byrne v Boadle*[206]). Some others term it as 'a rule of evidence', but not a rule of law (per *Lillywhite v UCL Hosp NHS Trust*[207]), but some other jurisdictions believe that English judges *have* indeed elevated it to a rule of law (per *Schellenberg v Tunnel Holdings Pty Ltd*[208]). To top it all off, some English judges have refused to call it a 'doctrine' at all (per *Lloyde v West Midlands Gas Board*[209]).

However, in this section, *res ipsa loquitur* is referred to as a 'doctrine', for the sake of convenience.

Raising (and rebutting) the doctrine

To raise the application of the doctrine, C will need to prove the criteria outlined in the following Table (drawn, in most part, from Erle CJ's judgment in *Scott v London and St Katherine's Docks Co*). The doctrine's application can, however, be rebutted by D – or, more colloquially, '[t]he *res* [or thing], which previously spoke for itself, may be silenced, or its voice may, on the whole of the evidence, become too weak or muted' (per *Lloyde v West Midlands Gas Board*).

201 [1988] ILRM 629 (SC) 634–35, cited in: *Lindsay v Mid-Western Health Board* [1993] 2 IR 147 (SC) 168.

202 [2010] EWHC 508 (Admin) [165].

203 In the case law, all of the following appear: a 'maxim', a 'rule of law', a 'guide', a 'principle', an 'approach', a 'manner of reasoning', a 'presumption', an 'exotic label', a 'forensic tool', a 'diagnostic theory', a 'brocard', an 'aid' and 'a doctrine'.

204 [1998] Lloyd's LR (Med) 162 (CA) 177 (Hobhouse LJ).

205 [1987] QB 730 (CA). Also: *Lloyde v West Midlands Gas Board* [1971] 1 WLR 749 (CA) 755 (Megaw LJ).

206 (1863) 2 H&C 722 (Exch) 727, 159 ER 299, 301.

207 [2005] EWCA Civ 1466, [87] (Buxton LJ). Also: *Lindsay v Mid-Western Health Board* [1993] 2 IR 147 (SC).

208 [2000] HCA 18, [69] (Gaudron J) ('it is, in [Australia], no more than a Latin phrase describing a permissible process of reasoning. The same is true in Canada. However, it may enjoy some higher status as a principle of law or evidence in the UK').

209 [1971] 1 WLR 749 (CA) 755 (Megaw LJ), cited with approval: *Ratcliffe v Plymouth and Torbay HA* [1998] Lloyd's LR (Med) 162 (CA) 177.

D may do this, via any of the avenues noted by Brooke LJ in *Ratcliffe v Plymouth and Torbay HA*[210]), also outlined in the Table.

C's raising an inference of negligence, via the doctrine:	D's means of displacing an inference of negligence:
• Incontrovertible facts about the act and outcome must 'speak for themselves'; • D had exclusive or sole control over the thing which caused C's damage or injury; • D has no plausible innocent explanation of what caused the accident to occur; **and** • The accident was of a type that does not normally occur in the absence of negligence.	• Too many facts are contested; • D lacked sole or exclusive control over the thing that caused C's damage or injury; • D can offer a plausible 'innocent' explanation of what happened to C, which does not connote any negligence on D's part; or • No rational explanation is possible, but D took all reasonable care and skill and was not negligent.

If any of these four criteria fail for C, then without an inference of negligence to assist him, C must seek to prove that a breach caused the damage of which he complains in the ordinary way – which may be very difficult, if C has no direct evidence by which to substantiate his case.

Dealing with each criterion in turn:

Incontrovertible facts

§7.25 The first criterion of the doctrine is that the incontrovertible facts about the act and outcome must 'speak for themselves'. If there is contested evidence on the very facts said to give rise to the injury, then the doctrine cannot apply.

To invoke the doctrine, C must be able to point to the 'existence of an unchallenged and unchallengeable fact' or facts (per *Doherty v Reynolds*[211]).

> In *Cassidy v Ministry of Health*,[212] Mr Cassidy, C, entered hospital to undergo an operation to repair two stiff fingers, and emerged with four stiff fingers and a 'useless' left hand, which he alleged was due to negligent surgery. **Held:** the doctrine of *res ipsa loquitur* applied.

On the other hand, in circumstances of contested evidence as to what actually happened to C, two factors tend to disprove this criterion for C:

i. **Disputed expert evidence.** Wherever the cause of C's injury is contested by expert opinion, than *res ipsa loquitur* is inappropriate – in *Ratcliffe*,[213] Hobhouse LJ said that '[w]here expert and factual evidence has been called on both sides at a trial, [the doctrine's] usefulness will normally have long since been exhausted'.

> In *Croft v Heart of England NHS Foundation Trust*,[214] Arthur Croft, C, suffered an injury during his birth at Solihull Hospital, Birmingham, due to an obstetric brachial plexus injury. C suffered injury

[210] See points (4), (5) and (6) in: [1998] Lloyd's Rep Med 168 (Brooke LJ).
[211] [2004] IESC 42, [no pp] (Keane CJ). [212] [1951] 2 KB 343 (CA). [213] (1998) 42 BMLR 64 (CA) 85.
[214] [2012] EWHC 1470 (QB). See too: *Doherty v Reynolds* [2004] IESC 42, where the same injury (in an adult) could not give rise to the doctrine's application either.

to the nerves in his neck, and a permanent weakening and loss of function in his right arm, allegedly due to the negligence of the midwifery team. The court noted that, in a previous case in the Chester CC on the same injury in 2009, over 80 pieces of learned literature on the cause of obstetric brachial plexus injuries, plus expert evidence from biomechanical engineers, orthopaedic surgeons, and obstetric experts, were reviewed over a 10-day trial. **Held:** C could not rely on the doctrine, given the disarray of expert evidence on the issue: '[no] conclusion can be drawn as to whether the majority of [obstetric brachial plexus injuries] are probably caused by traction, probably caused by propulsion, or probably caused by a combination of both'. C had to prove his case in the usual way (but failed).

ii. The procedure was complex and technical. The more inherently-dangerous or uncertain the procedure, the more difficult is C's task of raising the doctrine – because matters can go tragically amiss, without any negligence at all. Birth is one such procedure, having been described by Denning LJ in *Whitehouse v Jordan* as the 'most dangerous process in the life of anyone'.[215] Complex surgery for gender reassignment is another (per *Bergman v Haertsch*[216]). Indeed, the modern English judicial view is that it is 'doubtful' whether the doctrine has much room to apply in most medical negligence cases (*Thomas v Curley*[217]).

Obversely, the doctrine is more likely to apply where the task was reasonably orthodox, routine and mechanical, but produced an entirely unexpected damage (said Buxton LJ in *Lillywhite v UCL Hosp NHS Trust*[218] – where the doctrine did **not** apply). It can also apply, where a procedure has an excellent safety record (despite its complex and technical nature), because there are so many design and manufacturing protections in place. The maintenance of aircraft is one such category. One time, the 'perils of airflight' would not have permitted the doctrine to apply, but the Privy Council confirmed that those days were well behind:

In *George v Eagle Air Services Ltd (Saint Lucia)*,[219] Hughes Williams, C, a mechanic working for D, an airline in St Lucia, serviced and repaired D's aircraft. He was flying with a pilot on a flight from St Lucia to Union Island, when the plane crashed as it was about to land at Union Island, and both were killed. C's estate claimed that the pilot must have been negligent. **Held:** the doctrine of *res ipsa loquitur* applied: '[t]his was [D's] aircraft, their flight and their pilot. Aircraft, even small aircraft, do not usually crash, and certainly should not do so. And, if they do, then, especially where the crash is on land as here, ... it is not unreasonable to place on them the burden of producing an explanation which is at least consistent with absence of fault on their part'. However, D did not suggest any explanation for the crash, and hence, failed to displace the inference of pilot negligence.

Sole or exclusive control

§7.26 The second criterion of the doctrine is that the thing which inflicted the damage upon C must have been under the sole management and control of D (or of someone for whom D was responsible).

[215] [1980] 1 All ER 650 (CA) 652. [216] (NSW SC, 22 Jun 2000) [49] (Abadee J).
[217] [2013] EWCA Civ 117, [10], [17], citing: *Ratcliffe v Plymouth and Torbay HA* [1998] Lloyds Rep Med 162 (CA) 177.
[218] [2005] EWCA Civ 1466, [85]. [219] [2009] UKPC 21, [2009] WLR 2133, [13].

According to *Scott v London & St Katherine Docks Co*,[220] the 'thing' under D's control may be, say: the premises where D's activities were conducted and where C suffered injury; the particular activity which D was conducting; or the equipment used by D (i.e., the dock and the crane; or the plane, in *George v Eagle Air*).

In *Ward v Tesco Stores Ltd*,[221] Ms Ward was shopping at a Tesco's store, when she slipped on some yoghurt which had been spilt on the floor (how it got there was unknown). C sued for the personal injury suffered. C could not prove how long the yoghurt had been there. **Held (2:1):** the doctrine succeeded. The floor was the *res* or 'thing' here, over which D had sole control.

However, if C cannot prove that degree of control on D's part (C squarely bearing the burden of proof), then no inference of negligence is possible. C may confront several problems on this point:

i. Several Ds. If several Ds were involved, then C may be unable to identify which one was responsible for the particular damage (a problem that can often arise where several doctors participated in the operative procedure on C).

In *Donne Place Investments Ltd v McDonnell*,[222] a dispute arose between developer C, and architect and project manager D, regarding two sites in Chelsea. Their agreement was terminated before the developments were finished. C claimed that D had caused undue delay in performing its obligations under the building contracts, e.g., it took 9 months to obtain awards for three party walls, before construction works could commence. C relied on *res ipsa loquitur* to argue that the delay was negligent. **Held:** *res ipsa loquitur* could not apply. The task of securing the party wall awards was not in D's sole control; rather, a surveyor had been appointed who was responsible for much of that project work. D was not responsible for the appointment of all subcontractors, and hence, the relevant activities were not within D's sole control.

ii. Lack of control over the object/instrument. Another potential complication is whether D had the requisite control, when an object or instrument was in the sole custody or possession of C, the injured party.

Conceivably, this problem could arise in the employment context, when a machine is being operated by employee C, whilst on the employer's, D's, premises. This commonly precludes the doctrine in that context. On the other hand, medical negligence scenarios are quite different. As Hobhouse LJ said in *Ratcliffe*: 'it is commonplace that [patient C] will not have fully known what occurred, particularly if the relevant procedure was an operation carried out under anaesthetic. The procedures were under the control of [doctor D]'.[223]

No innocent explanation

§7.27 The third criterion of the doctrine is that D must have no plausible innocent explanation of why C suffered the injury. D's burden, to rebut an inference of negligence, is *not* to prove an 'innocent' explanation on the balance of probabilities – only that the explanation is 'plausible'.

In seeking to rebut the doctrine, D's plausible innocent explanation may owe a great deal to the uncertainties of the scientific process by which the accident happened, or the inscrutability of

[220] (1865) 3 H&C 596, 601, [1861–73] All ER Rep 246, 248. [221] [1976] 1 WLR 810 (CA).
[222] [2011] EWHC 930 (TCC). [223] [1998] Lloyd's Rep Med 168 (CA) 65.

the human body, etc. To be 'plausible', D's explanation must be something more than 'theoretically or remotely possible' (per *Smith v Sheridan*[224]), but less than the standard of proof on the balance of probabilities (per *Lillywhite v UCL Hosp NHS Trust*[225]).

This principle has been evident in various contexts – e.g., in product liability, engineering and medical accidents – where a plausible explanation was possible, thus rebutting the doctrine's application:

> In *Carroll v Fearon, Bent and Dunlop Ltd*,[226] a tyre burst on C's car, causing the car to crash. Given that the tyre exploded several years after it left the factory, and had been regularly used since, the tyre's failure 'might have resulted from any one of a number of possible causes, including ... misuse or abuse, or inadequate repair of earlier damage'. In *United Marine Aggregates Ltd v GM Welding & Engineering Ltd*,[227] a serious fire broke out in a large aggregate processing plant owned by UMA, C, situated at Murphy's Wharf on the Thames, near Greenwich. C claimed that the fire was caused by hot work being carried out by contractors, D, who were doing repair work at the wharf, by setting fire to the rubber lining in a steel hopper or chute (the actual cause of the fire was never determined). The same method of working had been used without incident for almost 20 years; so arguably this fire must have had something to do with how the work was being carried out by D. C had changed the lining material in 2006, and it was possible that it was more combustible than the previous materials. That went 'some way to undermining any reliance' on *res ipsa loquitur*. In *Ratcliffe v Plymouth and Torbay HA*,[228] C underwent a successful operation on his right ankle, and received a spinal anaesthetic to relieve post-operative pain. Thereafter, he was left with a serious neurological defect, from his waist downwards. An MRI scan showed a lesion in the thoracic spine. C claimed that this must have been caused by the spinal anaesthetic being administered at the wrong place, and claimed *res ipsa loquitur*. The anaesthetist responsible for the spinal injection, D, stated that he had administered it at the lumbar spine. There was a plausible explanation for the paralysis, i.e., some asymptomatic weakness in C's central nervous system which the stress of the surgery could have 'brought to life'. Hence, *res ipsa loquitur* could not apply.

Hence, providing some sort of plausible innocent explanation is a common 'safety avenue' for D, by which to rebut the doctrine. Uncertainty is a valuable commodity, when it comes to rebutting an inference of negligence. As was memorably put in one Canadian case:

> The human body is not a container filled with material whose performance can be predictably chartered and analysed ... Because of this, medical science has not yet reached the stage where the law ought to presume that a patient must come out of an operation as well as or better than he went into it.[229]

On the other hand, remote and implausible possibilities as to why C suffered the injury will not be good enough to rebut the doctrine. Wherever D's explanation is considered to be 'entirely theoretical and based on speculation' (to quote *Lindsay v Mid-Western Health Board*[230]), then the doctrine cannot be rebutted, and an inference of negligence may arise.

224 [2005] EWHC 614 (QB) [113] (implausible explanation; negligence proven).

225 [2005] EWCA Civ 1466, [60], citing: *Ratcliffe* [1998] Lloyd's Rep Med 162 (CA) point 5 (Brooke LJ).

226 [1998] PIQR 416 (CA), cited in: *Divya v Toyo Tire and Rubber Co Ltd* [2011] EWHC 1993 (QB) [69].

227 [2012] EWHC 779 (TCC) [273]. 228 [1998] Lloyd's L Rep 162 (CA).

229 *Girard v Royal Columbian Hosp* (1976), 66 DLR (3d) 676 (BCSC) (Andrews J), and cited in, e.g.: *Lindsay v Mid-Western Health Board* [1993] 2 IR 147 (SC) 166–67.

230 [1993] 2 IR 147 (HC) [6] (Morris J).

In *Lindsay*, patient C, 8, was admitted for an emergency appendectomy under general anaesthetic. After the operation, it appeared initially that C was beginning to regain consciousness in the normal manner, but then she experienced a series of seizures, and sank into a coma. C suffered from irreversible brain damage, and never regained consciousness. By trial, C had been in a deep coma for 18 years. C claimed that her condition was due to a 'hypoxic insult' which she had suffered during the course of the operation, as a result of a reduction in, or withdrawal of, her oxygen supply. Anaesthetist D put forward the explanation that C had suffered from a viral infection. This was rejected; it was not a plausible explanation. The more likely explanation for C's damage (said the court) was the withdrawal of or reduction in oxygen supply.

The accident does not normally occur without negligence

§7.28 The fourth criterion is that the accident must be of a type that does not normally occur in the absence of negligence. Hence, D can rebut the doctrine by proving, not that there was an innocent explanation, but that D was not negligent.

D may rebut any inference of negligence under *res ipsa loquitur* by explaining that, irrespective of the adverse outcome (which cannot be explained by medical science), D exercised all reasonable care and skill during the activity or procedure. The doctrine will then have no room to operate. This acts as an *alternative* avenue to the innocent explanation avenue of rebuttal. This was confirmed by Stuart-Smith LJ in *Delaney v Southmead HA*: 'it is always open to [D] to rebut a case of *res ipsa loquitur*, either by giving an explanation of what happened which is inconsistent with negligence, or by showing that [D] had exercised all reasonable care'.[231]

Where things fall from a height onto C, innocent explanations may be hard to come by; and it will also be difficult for D to show that things fall without negligence (whether that negligence be framed as to how the thing was secured in place, where it was placed, or what security measures were placed around it to stop it falling). Where the flour bag dropped from the shop window in *Byrne v Boadle*,[232] and the sugar bags fell in *Scott v St Katherine Docks Co*,[233] the doctrine was established in each case. Slipping hazards in food halls and in supermarkets ('yoghurt pots and pieces of fruit like grapes and cherries appear to be frequent culprits', per *Bovaird v Westfield Shoppingtowns*[234]), or slipping on water near a drinks dispensing station on a cruise ship (as occurred in, e.g., *Dawkins v Carnival plc (t/as P&O Cruises)*,[235] also give rise to the doctrine – which will be impossible to rebut if D did not have a reasonable system of inspection and frequent cleaning in place which would have detected a spillage sometime before C's accident.

In *Ward v Tesco Stores Ltd*,[236] facts previously, **held:** the doctrine of *res ipsa loquitur* applied. Slipping on yoghurt on a floor was not something that would occur in the ordinary course of things, if floors are kept clean and spillages dealt with as soon as they occur. The incident required some explanation from Tesco, D, to show that the accident did not arise from any want of care on its part. D could not do that. The evidence was that the spillage had been on the floor long enough for it to have been cleaned up by a member of staff. It did not matter that C could not prove that the yoghurt had only been there for a few seconds. Whenever there was slippery liquid on the floor of

[231] (1995) 26 BMLR 111 (CA) 118. [232] (1863) 159 ER 299 (Exch). [233] (1865) 3 H&C 596, 159 ER 665.
[234] [2007] NIQB 123, [13]. [235] [2011] EWCA Civ 1237
[236] [1976] 1 WLR 810 (CA) (Lawton and Megaw LJJ; Ormrod LJ dissented).

the supermarket, D should know that it was not an uncommon occurrence, and that if it was not promptly attended to, it would cause a serious risk to customers, which was consistent with fault on D's part. In *Saldanha v Fulton Navigation Inc*,[237] Kennedy Saldanha, C, was First Engineer on board D's ship, the *Omega King*. It was lying at anchor off the coast of Wales, when the weather conditions deteriorated and became severe. The vessel began to drag anchor, the master decided to weigh anchor, the anchor would not come up because the locking pin on the chain stopper was jammed, so C was instructed to inspect and fix the pin, to save a potentially dangerous situation for ship and crew. While C was doing that, a large wave broke over the bow, and he fell against a nearby bollard and was injured. C sued D, his employer, in negligence. **Held:** the doctrine of *res ipsa loquitur* applied, because 'there is a very strong inference that ships do not get into this type of situation without negligence having occurred. Either the problems should be sufficiently foreseen so as to be avoided at an early stage [or] it is usually possible to alleviate the effects of wind, waves and current by appropriate engine and rudder manoeuvres short of actually weighing anchor and steaming away'. D could not provide a rational explanation of how the dangerous situation arose without negligence on its part.

On the other hand, D may well succeed in rebutting the doctrine in this way:

In *Lindsay v Mid-Western Health Board*,[238] facts previously, **held:** *res ipsa loquitur* could not apply. Although there was no innocent explanation possible (see above), no negligence could be proven: '[it] was for [anaethesist D] to establish that, from beginning to end of this anaesthetic procedure, there was no negligence on its part. This it did decisively ... and so the case returned to [C's] bailiwick to prove negligence'. Ultimately, C could not prove that D lacked reasonable care, and failed in her claim.

Of course, this element of the doctrine raises a significant issue regarding burden of proof – is it for D to prove he was not negligent on the balance of probabilities where the doctrine is raised, or is it for C to still prove that D was negligent in the usual way? It has been a vexed question, as discussed below.

The burden of proof

§7.29 The applicable burden of proof, where the doctrine of *res ipsa loquitur* is raised by C, is not entirely clear in English law, but the preferential view is that D bears an evidentiary burden, where the doctrine is raised.

It is trite law that C must prove his case of negligence on the balance of probabilities. However, the uncertainty surrounding the burden of proof, where *res ipsa loquitur* is pleaded, is attributable to some judicial language which has been either vague or somewhat inconsistent. Three possibilities have been raised in the case law.

Option #1: D cannot rebut the inference, because an irrebuttable presumption arises

The first possibility is that C raises the inference (by establishing the four criteria discussed above), and thereafter, the '*res*' (the thing) speaks for itself. The *res* raises an irrebuttable presumption of negligence to be drawn – and there is no point in D bearing any burden, because

[237] [2011] EWHC 1118 (Admlty), [2011] 2 Lloyd's Rep 206. [238] [1993] 2 IR 177 (SC), quote at 185.

negligence is made out, and nothing that D could provide by way of evidence could rebut the presumption.

This possibility was noted by the Court of Appeal in *Ratcliffe v Plymouth and Torbay HA*,[239] as being *res ipsa loquitur* in its 'purest form', whereby the thing 'does truly speak for itself'. A couple of examples were given: a surgeon cuts off a patient's right foot, instead of the left: or a swab is left in the operation site.

However, Brooke LJ remarked, in *Ratcliffe*,[240] that this scenario is likely to be very unusual, for two reasons: (i) D is likely to bring some factual evidence to bear on the question of what precisely happened: '[i]t is likely to be a very rare medical negligence case in which [D] takes the risk of calling no factual evidence, when such evidence is available to them, of the circumstances surrounding a procedure which led to an unexpected outcome for a patient'; and (ii) once C adduces expert evidence as well, the thing is not 'speaking for itself' any longer, and even if D were not to call any evidence at all, 'the judge would be deciding the case on inferences he was entitled to draw from the whole of the evidence (including the expert evidence), and not on the application of the maxim in its purest form'. Indeed, any suggestion of an irrebuttable presumption of negligence has been strongly disfavoured in English case law since.

Option #2: D bears an evidentiary burden

This second possibility is the mid-spectrum position, whereby D bears an evidentiary burden only. C can use the doctrine to raise a *rebuttable* inference or presumption of negligence on D's part, where the four criteria are satisfied. D must then rebut the presumption (if he can) by either establishing a plausible innocent explanation for what happened to C; or that whatever happened to C cannot be explained, but that no negligence occurred. If D can achieve this, then no inference of negligence can be drawn. The persuasive burden of establishing negligence still (and always) remains with C, and C must prove his claim in negligence in the usual way, 'without that initial advantage' (per *Hussain v King Edward VII Hosp*[241]).

This view was specifically approved by the Supreme Court recently in *David T Morrison & Co Ltd (t/a Gael Home Interiors) v ICL Plastics Ltd (Scotland)*, where Lord Reed noted that the doctrine 'belongs to the law of evidence, and refers to circumstances from the establishment of which an inference of negligence can be drawn, so as to shift the evidential burden of proof to [D]'.[242] Additionally, that D only bears an evidentiary burden has derived much Court of Appeal support too (e.g., in *Lloyde v West Midlands Gas Board*,[243] and *Bhamra v Dubb (t/as Lucky Caterers)*,[244] where the court approved shifting the evidential burden to D as being a concept 'simply ... of common sense', and in *Bull v Devon AHA*[245] too, where the court noted that, 'delays in summoning and securing the attendance of the registrar or consultant were so substantial as to place upon the authority the evidential burden of justifying them', which onus was not discharged).

It follows, under this option, that *res ipsa loquitur* does not shift the persuasive (or legal) burden of proof – that always rests on C. Once D has discharged the evidentiary burden which the doctrine raises, it remains for C to prove negligence in the ordinary way.

[239] (1998) 42 BMLR 64 (CA) 82–83. [240] *ibid*, 65–66.

[241] [2012] EWHC 3441 (QB) [35]; and see too: *Hay v Grampian Health Board* (1994) 25 BMLR 98 (CSOH) [202].

[242] [2014] UKSC 48, [4]. [243] [1971] 1 WLR 749 (CA) 755 (Megaw LJ).

[244] [2010] EWCA Civ 13, [31]–[34]. [245] (1989) 22 BMLR 79 (CA) 101 (Slade LJ).

Option #3: D bears the persuasive burden

A third possibility is that the persuasive burden shifts to D under the doctrine, so that, once raised, D must disprove negligence on the balance of probabilities. It is not for C to prove that he was negligent; it is for D to prove that he was not. This would effectively transfer the persuasive onus to D to disprove negligence.

This approach was advocated in *Cassidy v Ministry of Health*,[246] where the Court of Appeal held that the legal burden lay on hospital authority D to prove that there had not been any negligence on its part in the post-operative treatment of C's hand, left useless after the operation (which burden D could not discharge).

However, subsequent English authority strongly suggests that, on this point, *Cassidy* is no longer good law. In *Ratcliffe*,[247] Hobhouse LJ said that '[t]he burden of proving the negligence of [D] remains throughout upon [C]'. This was reiterated recently in *Hussain v King Edward VII Hosp*,[248] where Eady J remarked that, '[o]ne should never lose sight of the simple fact that the burden of proof remains on [C] throughout ... That is why [D] is only required to show a plausible alternative explanation in order to rebut a prima facie case.'

Conclusion on burden

It appears that the more-countenanced view is that D only bears an evidentiary burden, where the doctrine is raised against him. This is entirely defensible, given the point mentioned in the Ontario case of *Phillips v Ford Motor Co*,[249] that shifting the persuasive burden to D 'would come dangerously close to a fictional use of the maxim as a foundation for the doctrine of strict liability', whereby adverse outcome equals liability.

Of course, there is much sympathy for C, in these sorts of cases. The doctrine is said to apply precisely because, in the procedure in question (say, a surgical operation), C 'rarely knows anything; what has happened is known only to the [D]' (per *Lindsay v Mid-Western Health Board*[250]). However, the weight of English authority shows that it is only intermittently effective.

Two concluding notes

Although the doctrine of *res ipsa loquitur* is often considered relevant to proof of breach, it is probably more pertinent to proof of causation. As described in *Lloyde v West Midlands Gas Board*, the doctrine 'enable[s] [C] to succeed because, *although the precise cause of the accident* cannot be established, the proper inference on balance of probability is that the cause, whatever it may have been, involved a failure by [D] to take due care for [C's] safety'.[251] In *Corby Group Litigation v Corby DC* too, the court noted that, '[t]here is also reliance upon the doctrine of *res ipsa loquitur*, so far as causation is concerned'.[252] Hence, arguably it is proof of causation – rather than proof of breach – which is truly at the heart of the doctrine.

Finally, it is perhaps fair to say that, whilst the English judiciary's reception to *res ipsa loquitur* has been mixed, litigants' reliance on it has been equally uncertain. They have sometimes

[246] [1951] 2 KB 343 (CA). [247] [1998] PIQR P170 (CA) P186. [248] [2012] EWHC 3441 (QB) [12].
[249] [1971] 2 OR 637 (HC) 653. [250] [1993] 2 IR 147 (SC) 183.
[251] [1971] 1 WLR 749 (CA) 755, cited, e.g., in: *Kyriakou v Chase Farms Hosp NHS Trust* [2006] EWHC 2131 (QB) [52].
[252] [2009] EWHC 1944 (TCC) [702].

taken the unusual step of asking for judicial guidance on the doctrine, because of apparent inconsistencies amongst previous judgments (as occurred in *Ratcliffe v Plymouth and Torbay HA*[253]). Even within cases, confusion can reign supreme. In *Bull v Devon AHA*,[254] while negligence was ultimately proven, only one member of the Court of Appeal (Slade LJ) used *res ipsa loquitur* as the basis for that conclusion. In *Fallows v Randle*,[255] the court noted the utility of the doctrine, but decided in C's favour without relying on the doctrine at all. Courts have also sometimes remarked that the doctrine's application was 'misconceived' by the parties (per *Graham v Watt-Smyrk*[256]), whilst an eye-popping turnaround about the doctrine can be evident on D's part.

In *Brown v Merton, Sutton and Wandsworth AHA*,[257] patient C underwent an epidural anaesthesia, developed severe pain when receiving second doses, and developed quadraplegia. The anaesthetist D initially denied any application of *res ipsa loquitur*, but then conceded liability on that basis.

The doctrine does indeed have a chequered application in English jurisprudence.

The comparative corner: **Some Commonwealth vignettes of the doctrine**

British Columbia: In *Rabachuk v Cooke*,[258] patient C had a hernia operation. A plastic sheath was found at the surgical site, and was removed two weeks after the initial operation. **Held:** *res ipsa loquitur* was invoked to infer negligence on surgeon D's part, in failing to detect the loss of the sheath from the operative instrument. The court referred to the following 'incontrovertible facts': that '1.The foreign body was left in the patient and not discovered until after the operation was complete. 2. The sheath was of sufficient size (1cm x 2cm) to be seen and a visible component of the instrument used. 3. There had been difficulty in the operation of the instrument'.

New Brunswick: In *Cosgrove v Daudreau and Hotel-Dieu d' Edmundston*,[259] a surgical sponge was left in C's abdominal cavity, and it was discovered and removed 18 months later. Surgeon D adduced no evidence at trial as to how the sponge came to be left at the surgical site. **Held:** *res ipsa loquitur* applied: 'in the ordinary course of things', a sponge or lap pad is not left behind in the abdominal cavity after surgery, and it was probably left there as a result of D's negligence in not performing an adequate sponge count.

New Zealand: In *MacDonald v Pottinger*,[260] a pair of forceps was left in C's body after a complicated medical operation. Surgeon D, who performed the procedure, had been assisted by several others. **Held:** *res ipsa loquitur* did not apply. The procedure was never under the sole control and management of D.

Alberta: In *Clare v Ostolosky*,[261] C suffered a failed tubal ligation. **Held:** *res ipsa loquitur* did not apply. There was a reasonable explanation as to why a later tubal pregnancy was

[253] (1998) 42 BMLR 64 (CA) 73 ('[counsel] told us that there is a good deal of inconsistency as between different judges trying medical negligence cases about the way they should handle the operation of the maxim in these cases (if indeed, contrary to the views ascribed to some judges, it applies at all in this type of litigation). ... he invited us to give some guidance about the appropriate way to approach the maxim in medical negligence litigation').

[254] (1989) 22 BMLR 79 (CA). [255] [1997] 8 Med LR 160 (CA). [256] (QBD, 24 Nov 1986).

[257] [1982] 1 All ER 650 (CA). [258] [2001] BCSC 1349, [8] (Grist J). [259] (1981), NBR (2d) (QB) [28]–[33].

[260] [1953] NZLR 196. [261] (2001), 300 AR 341.

possible, and why C's right fallopian tube still remained open; a 'spontaneous reanastomosis does occur without any effect upon the tube or its appearance'.

Malaysia: In *Udhaya Kumar v Penguasa Hosp*,[262] baby C suffered severe brain injury from contracting encephalitis. **Held:** *res ipsa loquitur* did not apply. D's diagnosis and treatment of C's high fever was plausible.

WHAT DOES *NOT* PROVE BREACH

D's view, pre-accident

§7.30 The fact that D evidenced some intention, prior to the event or accident, to take a precautionary step that would, on the balance of probabilities, have prevented the injury or harm to C, is not, of itself, proof of breach.

Suppose that D was well aware of (i.e., had foreseen) the risk of injury to C, and had some precautionary steps within its contemplation. However, D did not implement these precautionary steps for whatever reason (e.g., lack of time or money or motivation). Then the injury to C occurs.

The fact that D did not implement those steps is no automatic proof of breach. The reasons for not implementing may have been reasonable. Alternatively, D may have, mistakenly, considered the precautionary step to be necessary to meet the standard of reasonable care, whereas such a step was more onerous than the law expected of a reasonable D. Under either scenario, the failure by D to take that step is not conclusive proof of breach, because a reasonable D may have acted no differently to prevent the risk of injury or damage.

In *Tomlinson v Congleton BC*[263] (the diving in the lake case), Council D was aware that its notices forbidding swimming and diving in the lake were commonly ignored, and that several accidents had resulted from swimming. In a meeting prior to C's accident, D resolved to plant vegetation (e.g., prickly bushes) around the shore, to prevent people from entering the water. However, it had not carried this out, due to financial shortages. **Held:** no breach proven.

On the other hand, if D had specifically foreseen that a precautionary step were possible, and with hindsight should indeed have been taken to reach the reasonable standard, then breach will be proven.

In *Reffell v Surrey CC*,[264] a school girl, C, put her hand through a glass plate door at D's school, when it was swinging. Replacement of the panel with toughened glass or with grilles or wooden slats would have prevented the injury. That precaution had been proposed by D's officers before the accident. **Held:** breach proven.

An expert organisation's opinion

§7.31 The fact that an expert organisation advocates that a precautionary step ought to have been taken by D to prevent the risk of injury or harm to C, is not, of itself, proof of breach.

[262] [2004] 2 MLJ 661 (HC Muar). [263] [2003] UKHL 47, [2004] 1 AC 46, [51], [55].
[264] [1964] 1 WLR 358 (QB) 365.

It is always for the court to determine whether a reasonable D should have taken a precautionary step to avoid the risk of injury or harm to C. An expert organisation's opinion as to what D should have done may simply have pitched the required standard of care too high. D must achieve reasonableness, not perfection.

In *Darby v National Trust*,[265] Mr Darby, C, died by drowning in a pond at Hardwick Hall. A Water and Leisure Safety Consultant to the Royal Society for the Prevention of Accidents gave evidence that, as a minimum, 'No Swimming' notices should be installed around all deep water, given that 450 people die of drowning each year in the UK. **Held**: no breach proven. (This case is discussed further in Chapter 12, regarding occupiers' liability; D was not required to erect a sign for such an obvious danger.)

A change of system, post-accident

§7.32 The fact that D took precautionary steps *after* C suffered the injury or harm which, had they been implemented before the event, would probably have prevented that injury or harm, is not, of itself, proof of breach.

A responsible D may put in place a system, post-accident, that will prevent it from happening again – but that does not enable the court to draw any inference of negligence; after all, D may be 'ultra-cautious' after an accident, without realising that what he believes to be necessary to avoid future liability was not, actually, legally mandated (per *Yates v National Trust*[266]).

In *Staples v West Dorset DC*,[267] the Court of Appeal noted that, once Council D knew that a visitor had slipped off the edge into the sea, 'they posted warning notices. [But] the fact that they took that action after the accident does not enable me to draw the inference that, in order to discharge the common duty of care to the visitor, they should have done so before the accident occurred'. Besides, hindsight is not the prism through which the court must look, when assessing breach. As Lord Pearce was quoted in *Ratcliff v McConnell*,[268] the crucial issue is 'how the matter appeared, *before the accident*, to a reasonable person in [D's] position'.

In *Ratcliffe*, a student, C, climbed over a pool fence at night, and suffered tetraplegia from diving into the shallow end of the pool. Post-accident, the pool-owner, D, implemented a number of further preventative steps (e.g., marking out the depth of water on the side of the pool, further warning signs in the changing room). In *Orchard v Lee*,[269] an accident happened in the school courtyard and walkway area, when school friends playing a game of tag collided with C, a lunchtime assistant supervisor at the school. Running around the courtyard and walkways was quite common among the young boys before the accident and broke no rules. However, after the accident, the rules were changed and notified to pupils, and the layout of the area was changed to discourage running. **Held, in both cases:** no breach proven.

Nevertheless, the fact that precautionary steps were taken after the accident does have the effect (as pointed out in *Stimpson v Wolverhampton MBC*[270]) of 'clearly show[ing] that there were additional steps which [D] might have taken' – and that some of them may have been cheap to implement, prior to the mishap.

[265] [2001] EWCA Civ 189, [2001] PIQR P17, [10]. [266] [2014] EWHC 222 (QB) [72].
[267] [1995] PIQR P439 (CA) 445.
[268] [1999] 1 WLR 670 (CA) [42] (emphasis added), citing: *McGlone v British Rwys Bd* 1966 SC (HL) 1, 17.
[269] [2009] EWCA Civ 295, [2009] PIQR P16. [270] CA, 22 May 1990.

In *Cunningham v Reading FC*,[271] concrete terraces were repaired within days of a serious hooliganism incident, at a cost of slightly less than £3,000. In *Stimpson*, a large sign was erected after a golfer visiting the premises was hit in the mouth by a golf ball struck by C – the sign prohibited the playing of golf in the park and gave notice of an on-the-spot fine for anyone found to be contravening the notice. **Held, in both cases:** breach proven.

Inherent risks

§7.33 The failure by D to remove an inherent risk cannot amount to a breach, for the nature of an inherent risk is that it cannot be removed through the exercise of reasonable skill and care. However, inherent risks can give rise to breach in one of two ways, *viz*, failure-to-warn, and failure to detect/report.

Inherent risks were defined in *Chester v Afshar*[272] – and the fact that such a risk manifests in a procedure/at a venue/during an event does not prove breach, because no precautionary step could have removed it.

For example, as Hale LJ pointed out in *Sussex Ambulance NHS Trust v King*,[273] employees whose occupations in the public service are inherently dangerous (i.e., fire fighters, police officers, and ambulance technicians) cannot expect their employers to remove those risks, because reasonable care will not remove them – they must be accepted as part of the job. What those employees can expect is that the employer will take reasonable steps to remove the risks which it would be negligent to disregard (by the provision of a safe system of work, safe equipment, etc, as discussed in 'Employers' liability', an online chapter). On that basis, inherent risks share some similarities with inevitable accidents.

Two ways that breach can arise are as follows:

i. C was not warned about material inherent risks, so as to make an informed decision as to whether or not to proceed with the procedure (as discussed in Chapter 3); and
ii. it was D's responsibility to detect, identify, report upon, or guard against any inherent risks that were apparent in a procedure/business, but failed to do so. For example, in the auditing context, the inherent risk that financial accounts may be misstated, due to the nature of the client's type of business, its environment, and the nature of the accounts, may lead to an overly-positive report by the auditor. As stated in *Barings plc v Coopers & Lybrand (a firm)*,[274] '[a]n important part of the process of planning an audit is to identify the inherent risks affecting the client, and to devise procedures which will afford the auditor a reasonable expectation of detecting material misstatements arising from those risks'. Similarly, there is an inherent risk of abuse, as noted by Lord Millett in *Lister v Hesley Hall Ltd*:[275] 'in boarding schools, prisons, nursing homes, old people's homes, geriatric wards, and other residential homes for the young or vulnerable, there is an inherent risk that indecent assaults on the residents will be committed by those placed in authority over them, particularly if they are in close proximity to them and occupying a position of trust'. Those who own/operate such facilities may be in breach for failing to prevent such abuse (although that claim failed in *Lister*).

[271] [1992] PIQR P141 (QB) 153. [272] [2004] UKHL 41, [2005] 1 AC 134, [72].
[273] [2002] EWCA Civ 953, [2002] ICR 1413, [21]. [274] [2003] EWHC 1319 (Ch) [503].
[275] [2001] UKHL 22, [2002] 1 AC 215, [83].

Relevance of 'gross negligence'

§7.34 There is no general requirement in English law that breach can *only* be proven by 'gross negligence'. However, in very limited circumstances, that test of breach is appropriate; and the parties may also agree, via contractual terms, that D's liability will be limited, in that D cannot be liable except for gross negligence.

The suggestion that D should **only** be liable for breach if guilty of 'gross negligence' has been made in a few contexts in which D was sympathetically-placed – but largely without success.

Meaning. The precise meaning of 'gross negligence' is unclear, as case law pertinent to awards of exemplary damages (canvassed in Chapter 11) illustrates. The phrase can carry any one of **three** possible meanings: (1) a grave departure by D from the standard of reasonable care; (2) conduct that amounts to either wilful or reckless disregard for C's welfare (i.e., D possesses a certain intent); or (3) conduct that causes an onerous level of damage to C. In what sense the term is used in the following contexts has often been left quite unclear.

General rule. The contexts in which the need to prove 'gross negligence' have been argued/mooted are multifarious. In the case of the 'good Samaritan' who attempts a rescue or who tries to assist a victim, the ambulance officers argued, in *Cattley v St John Ambulance Brigade*,[276] that the conduct complained of should be 'manifestly short of the standard to be expected', amounting to gross negligence, before they should be held in breach, but that submission was rejected outright by the court. Judge Prosser QC remarked that such a test was not known to English negligence law, and 'would be confusing and ... unnecessary'. (Interestingly, the view that good Samaritans should only be liable for 'gross negligence' has indeed received legislative enactment in jurisdictions other than England, where 'good Samaritan statutes' have been introduced.[277])

Recently, in *ICL Tech Ltd v Johnston Oils Ltd*,[278] the Scottish Outer House confirmed that C did **not** have to prove that the supplier of a hazardous substance or a dangerous product (LPG gas, in that case), D, should only be liable if it had demonstrated gross negligence – a position which reflects English law too. In the context of barristers who provide specialist advice, HH Judge Brown QC noted, in *West Wallasey Car Hire Ltd v Berkson & Berkson*,[279] that previous references (e.g., in *Saif Ali v Sydney Mitchell & Co*[280]) to the need to prove a 'blatant error' on D's part should **not** be read to mean that 'gross negligence' was required.

Hence, the test of gross negligence is extremely rare in English negligence law, insofar as a test of breach is concerned. Indeed, in *West Wallasey*, Judge Brown stated that 'gross negligence' has not been the test of breach in the tort of negligence, 'since at least 1910 upon the case law'.[281] However, there are a couple of exceptions to this general rule.

Exceptions. In the case of amateur referees, the Court of Appeal rejected the submission, in *Smoldon v Whitworth*,[282] that a referee should only be liable for breach if he had shown a deliberate or reckless disregard for the safety of player C. That was framed as a test of gross negligence, and was comprehensively rejected. However, as the discussion of participants and

[276] QB, 25 Nov 1988 [no pp available].

[277] See: Mulheron, *Medical Negligence: Non-Patient and Third Party Claims* (Ashgate Publishing, 2010), ch 6.

[278] [2012] CSOH 62, [13].

[279] [2009] EWHC B39 (Merc), [2010] PNLR 14, [30].

[280] [1980] AC 198 (HL) 220–21 (Lord Diplock).

[281] [2009] EWHC B39 (Merc), [2010] PNLR 14, [32], citing: *Ridehalgh v Horsefield* [1944] Ch 205 (CA) 237.

[282] [1997] PIQR 133 (CA) 138–39.

spectators in Chapter 6 demonstrates, the standard of care required of participants is so lowly-set that proof of gross negligence **will** be required in that context.

Furthermore, proof of gross negligence may be required, if the contract between C and D states that D will **only** be liable for that substandard performance. The following clause – as used in *Camerata Property Inc v Credit Suisse Securities (Europe) Ltd*[283] – provides an example:

> we shall not be liable for any losses, liabilities, costs, claims, damages, expenses, demands ... incurred or suffered by you ... other than Costs arising directly as a consequence of the gross negligence, fraud or wilful default of us or any of our directors, officers, or employees.

Some English judges have clearly been uncomfortable with the use of 'gross negligence' – witness, e.g., the comments in *Tradigrain SA v Internek Testing Services*,[284] that the term, 'although often found in commercial documents, has never been accepted by English civil law as a concept distinct from civil negligence'. However, having cited that case, the Court in *Camerata* preferred the view that, where used in contract to limit D's liability for negligence, the term must mean something different from 'mere' negligence, and that it was capable of meaning that D acted with 'serious disregard of or indifference to an obvious risk'. (Interestingly, the *Camerata* term survived the test of 'reasonableness' in the Unfair Contract Terms Act 1977.)

[283] [2011] EWHC 479 (Comm) [161], citing: *Red Sea Tankers Ltd v Papachristidis (The Ardent)* [1997] 2 Lloyd's Rep 547 (HL) 586 (Lord Mance).

[284] [2007] EWCA Civ 154, [23] (Moore-Bick LJ).

8

Causation of damage

INTRODUCTION

§8.1 In his negligence suit against D, C can only recover damages from D where D caused, or materially contributed to, C's harm; or where, exceptionally, some weaker causal link is established between D's breach and C's harm.

In most cases, C will have to prove a causal link between D's breach and his own damage on the balance of probabilities. In rare cases, something less than proof on the balance of probabilities will be sufficient to fix D with liability in negligence for causing C physical, property or economic damage.

A few introductory points will predicate the difficult issues which arise under this element.

Principles, with a splash of 'common sense'

Causation is, arguably, the most doctrinally complex of the elements of negligence. In most cases, the application of causation principles is straightforward. In other cases, however, some judicial statements verge on the despairing, when discussing the area's difficulties. Recently, in *Zurich Ins plc v UK Branch v Intl Energy Group Ltd*, Lord Mance admitted that 'the courts are still working out the implications' of previous appellate rulings on causation,[1] whilst in *Sienkiewicz v Greif (UK) Ltd*, Lady Hale 'pit[ied] the practitioners, as well as the academics, who have to make sense of our judgments in difficult cases' in this nook of the law.[2]

Indeed, at one end of the spectrum, some senior appellate judges have described causation as a question of mere pragmatism and 'common sense'. In *BAI Run-Off Ltd v Durham (the Trigger Litigation)*,[3] Lord Mance noted that causation '[n]ormally ... reflect[s] a common sense understanding of what is ordinarily understood when we speak of a cause'; in *Stapley v Gypsum Mines*,[4] Lord Reid said that causation 'must be determined by applying common sense to

[1] [2015] UKSC 33, [1] (Lord Mance).
[2] [2011] UKSC 10, [2011] 2 AC 229, [167]. To those categories, students should be added!
[3] [2012] UKSC 14, [2012] 1 WLR 867, [55].
[4] [1953] AC 663 (HL) 681.

the facts of each particular case'; while in *McGhee v National Coal Board*,[5] Lord Wilberforce decried that causation 'is not based on logic or philosophy, [but] on the practical way in which the ordinary man's mind works in the everyday affairs of life'.

At the other end of the spectrum, however, some judges have vigorously disagreed with that notion. In *Six Continents Retail Ltd v Carford Catering Ltd*,[6] Laws LJ said that 'an appeal to common sense is sometimes apt to be little more than an alibi for want of principle', and likened causation to 'metaphysics'. In similar vein, Lord Hope remarked, in *Chester v Afshar*,[7] that 'commonsense on its own, and without more guidance, was no more reliable as a guide to the right answer than an appeal to the views of the traveller on the London Underground'. Lord Nicholls, dissenting, in *Gregg v Scott*,[8] remarked that, if the majority's view were to prevail, it would be to liken the law to the 'proverbial ass'; and Laws LJ (again) compared causation to 'philosophical thickets' (in *Rahman v Arearose Ltd*[9]). Lord Matthews put it succinctly in *Percy v Govan Initiative Ltd*: 'no doubt this is one of the most difficult areas of the law'.[10]

In the midst of the brouhaha is C, who may find great difficulty in linking D's breach (whether admitted or proven) to the damage which C alleges. This has been especially evident in two oft-litigated contexts: medical incidents (which 'often raise particularly difficult questions of causation'[11]) and workplace illnesses. Sometimes, the evidence cannot say whether D's breach had any, or any significant, part to play in C's damage – and the scientific knowledge is not robust or advanced enough to satisfy the traditional causation principles. Alternatively, the facts themselves may not be sufficiently ascertainable, so as to point towards, or away from, a causal link.

The principles in this chapter seek to set out how causation may be established by C (upon whom the burden of proof always rests). However, given the judicial comments above, and more so than in any other chapter in this book, the principles espoused herein seek to represent legal propositions which are defensible by reference to majority judicial viewpoints – whilst acknowledging that, with the courts still feeling their way, some of the principles will be open to debate, particularly under the exceptional theorems of causation.

A note on terminology

The notion of 'factual causation' is used in some contexts, to describe whether D's negligent conduct played a legally sufficient role in bringing about C's harm. That topic is considered in this chapter. It is to be distinguished from the ancillary subject of remoteness of damage (sometimes called 'legal causation'), which deals with whether D *ought* to be held liable to pay damages for that harm (discussed in Chapter 9). It follows that establishing a causal link between D's breach and C's damage does not necessarily mean that liability will follow.

Lord Nicholls explained the diverse, but unified, concepts, in *Kuwait Airways Corp v Iraqi Airways Co*[12] as follows: 'the extent of [D's] liability for [C's] loss calls for a twofold inquiry: whether the wrongful conduct causally contributed to the loss; and, if it did, what is the extent of the loss for which [D] ought to be held liable. The first of these inquiries, widely undertaken as a simple "but for" test, is predominantly a factual inquiry'.

[5] [1973] 1 WLR 1 (HL) 5. [6] [2003] EWCA Civ 1790, [18]–[19]. [7] [2004] UKHL 41, [2005] 1 AC 134, [83]
[8] [2005] UKHL 2, [43]. [9] [2001] QB 351 (CA) [32]. [10] [2011] ScotCS 177 (OH) [16].
[11] *Bank of Credit and Commerce Intl SA (in liq) v Ali (No 2)* [2002] EWCA Civ 82, [70] (Robert Walker LJ).
[12] [2002] 2 AC 883 (HL) [69].

The second enquiry (remoteness) is just as important as the first – as the Supreme Court noted in *R v Hughes*,[13] if factual causation was conclusive or sufficient for liability, it would expand the boundaries of liability far too widely: 'if a woman asked her neighbour to go to the station in his car to collect her husband, [she] would be held to have caused her husband's death if he perished in a fatal road accident on the way home'. In *Chester v Afshar*,[14] Lord Bingham (dissenting, but not on this point) also emphasised that a literal application of factual causation, 'applied simply and mechanically, gives too expansive an answer: "But for your negligent misdelivery of my luggage, I should not have had to defer my passage to New York and embark on *SS Titanic*"'. Holding the wife and the baggage handlers liable in negligence respectively, in these examples, would be a legal nonsense.

Further, where D1, D2 and D3 act as 'joint tortfeasors', as 'several concurrent tortfeasors', or as 'independent tortfeasors', each D did cause *some* injury to C. The question then is how to apportion responsibility among them. That difficult issue – which arises when liability has already been established, and where quantification of the damages per D is at issue – is considered in 'Multiple defendants' (an online chapter).

The role of policy

It should be acknowledged, at the outset, that policy considerations and value judgments infuse the analysis of causation, to an equivalent extent as they find a role in remoteness enquiries. For example, the topic of intervening acts involves considerations of 'reasonableness' – which *always* invokes value judgments, as Ward LJ pointed out in *Corr v IBC Vehicles Ltd.*[15]

This can lead to an impression, at least, of imprecision in legal reasoning – although some call it an exercise in pragmatism. As Laws LJ remarked in *Rahman v Arearose Ltd*,[16] '[t]he common law on the whole achieved just results, but the approach has been heavily pragmatic'. The impression of controversy is also enhanced by the number of bare majority judgments with which the area is afflicted (e.g., 3:2 majorities in both *Gregg v Scott* and *Chester v Afshar*). Clearly, reasonable judicial opinion will differ on the causation enquiry.

This chapter will consider the following 12 topics in turn:

A nutshell of the causation analysis

Pre-requisite	C suffered compensable damage
The first step	The classic 'but-for' test (that rules out legally irrelevant causes)
Exception #1	The doctrine of material contribution to risk
Exception #2	The doctrine of material contribution to damage
Exception #3	The *Bolitho* causation theorem
Exception #4	The *Chester v Afshar* causation theorem
Severance	Intervening acts in the causal chain

[13] [2013] UKSC 56, [23]. [14] [2004] UKHL 41, [8].

[15] [2006] EWCA Civ 331, [37] (not adversely commented upon on appeal).

[16] [2000] EWCA Civ 190, [2001] QB 351, [31].

A weaker causal link	Causation and 'pure omissions'
Reframing the 'damage'	Loss of a chance claims
Supervening event #1	D damaged an already-damaged C
Supervening event #2	Innocent reasons would have led to the same damage
Evidentiary	The burden of proof

PRE-REQUISITE: PROOF OF COMPENSABLE DAMAGE

§8.2 The tort of negligence is not actionable *per se*. C must have suffered some legally-recognised compensable damage, to found a cause of action.

This is 'trite law', requiring 'no reinforcement by an anxious parade of supporting authority' (per *Clough v First Choice Holidays and Flights Ltd*[17]). In *Gregg v Scott*,[18] Baroness Hale reiterated that, 'damage is the gist of negligence. So it can never be enough to show that [D] has been negligent. The question is still whether his negligence has caused [C's] actionable damage'.

However, proving damage has been problematical in two particular instances in English law.

The *de minimis* threshold of damage

The general principle

§8.3 Per the principle of '*deminimis non curatlex*' – 'the law does not take account of trifles' – it is only damage (physical, psychiatric, property or economic) which meets a minimal threshold of harm which the law will compensate. Both pleural plaques, and 'loss of a chance' personal injury claims, are not compensable injuries in English law.

If C's symptoms, which allegedly flow from D's breach, are'trifling', then they will lack 'the significance required to turn the non-actionable into the actionable' (per Maurice Kay LJ in *Hussain v CC of West Mercia Constabulary*[19]). In *Cartledge v E Jopling & Sons Ltd*[20] too, the court emphasised that it will always be a question of fact and of degree, but that C's injury had to be 'beyond what can be regarded as negligible', or 'real damage, as distinct from purely minimal damage'.

In the following cases, the physical symptoms suffered by C were **not** sufficient injury to constitute actionable damage, and hence were not worthy of compensation:

> In *Hussain v CC of West Mercia*, Mr Hussain claimed that the police's actions placed him 'under stress', leading to physical symptoms of anxiety, *viz*, discomfort and numbness in his arm and leg (the action was actually brought under misfeasance in public office – which tort is not actionable *per se* either). In *Reilly v Merseyside HA*,[21] Mr Reilly was trapped in a lift, a 'most unpleasant experience', during which he suffered anxiety and fear, and had some physical consequences (vomiting and sweating).

[17] [2006] EWCA Civ 15, [30]. [18] [2005] UKHL 2, [217]. [19] [2008] EWCA Civ 1205, [19].
[20] [1963] AC 758 (HL) 771–72. [21] (1994) 23 BMLR 26 (CA) 29, 30.

Furthermore, where C has only suffered some anxiety-based disorder, then that type of damage does not, on its own, surmount the *de minimis* principle. C must prove some actionable *physical* injury, to graft onto that claim the anxiety disorder which falls short of a recognised psychiatric injury. It will be recalled, from Chapter 5, that the only freestanding mental injury claim which is permitted in English law is where a recognised psychiatric injury was suffered by C. This was at the root of the extraordinary *Pleural Plaques* litigation, otherwise known as *Johnston v NEI Intl Combustion Ltd (sub nom Grieves v FT Everard & Sons*[22]).

Pleural plaques are physiological changes to the lung lining, which are usually asymptomatic. The Scottish Inner House described them in *AXA General Ins Ltd v Scottish Ministers*:[23]

> Pleural plaques are physical changes in the pleurae: two layers of tissue comprising the visceral pleura, the inner layer which covers the lungs, and the parietal pleura, the outer layer which lines the ribs and chest wall ... Upon radiological examination, pleural plaques present as areas of fibrous tissue ... They are normally bilateral and almost exclusively found on the parietal pleura. Over time, they may increase in size and number and become calcified. They can measure more than 10cm across and up to 1cm in thickness, and may fuse into larger sheets as they become more extensive. They are caused by exposure to asbestos and are therefore associated with the construction, shipbuilding and steel industries. Their precise aetiology is unknown, but may involve prolonged inflammation due to cells reacting to, and attempting to engulf, inhaled asbestos fibres. They have a latency period of 20 years or more. In the vast majority of cases, pleural plaques are asymptomatic, causing no discomfort, impairment of the pulmonary function, or external marks. Nor do they actuate, or contribute to, more serious and potentially fatal conditions such as lung cancer, mesothelioma or asbestosis. Nevertheless, their existence evidences significant previous exposure to asbestos, which of itself represents a greatly increased risk of contracting such diseases.

Interestingly, in 1963, the House of Lords endorsed the view that those who sustained physiological changes from inhaled substances **did** suffer actionable damage.

> In *Cartledge v E Jopling & Sons Ltd*,[24] various employees, C, suffered death or serious injury from lung damage caused by inhaling fragmented silica. (This was a limitation problem, concerning the question of when the cause of action accrued.) Given that the silica fragments would be visible on an X-ray (if taken); would reduce C's lung capacity in a way which would be evident in cases of unusual exertion; made C more susceptible to contracting tuberculosis or bronchitis; and would reduce C's life expectancy because of their presence; all of that was sufficient, in combination, to constitute compensable 'damage'.

Subsequently, some first-instance decisions in the mid-1980s held that pleural plaques constituted actionable injury too (and modest sums, ranging between £1,500 and £31,250, were awarded to the affected Cs in *Church v MOD*,[25] in *Sykes v MOD*[26] and in *Patterson v MOD*[27]). None of these decisions was appealed, and, hence, a practice evolved, among English insurers, of settling pleural plaques claims, brought by employees wrongfully exposed to asbestos, for modest payments. Then, a challenge was brought by some insurers on this key question, as to whether these employees had actually suffered any legally-compensable damage. The House of Lords saw the outcome very differently in 2006.

[22] [2006] EWCA Civ 27, aff'd: [2007] UKHL 39, [2008] 1 AC 281, with Lord Hope's quote in Table at [42].
[23] [2011] CSIH 31, [9]. [24] [1963] AC 758 (HL). [25] (1984) 134 NLJ 623.
[26] (1984) 134 NLJ 783. [27] CA, 29 Jul 1986.

In *Johnston v NEI Intl Combustion Ltd*, 10 employees, C, were negligently exposed by their employers, D, to asbestos dust in their workplaces. Each C had developed pleural plaques, and alleged that it meant that they were at risk of developing long-term asbestos-related diseases (because the plaques signified exposure to asbestos); plus they had suffered some physiological change to their lungs; plus they had suffered anxiety (although only one C, Mr Grieves, had suffered a genuine psychiatric illness, *viz*, depression, and hence, his case was legally different, per Chapter 5). **Held (CA, 2:1; and HL, 5:0):** all Cs failed. The nine test Cs who had only suffered pleural plaques, and anxiety-based disorders, had suffered no actionable damage.

Of course, had the employees suffered a negligently-caused physical injury in this case, then that may have led to other damages consequences for them. For example, had that injury created the chance that C would suffer some other physical damage (i.e., some disease or illness) in the future, then C's general damages would be increased to reflect the chance of that physical injury manifesting (per *Gregg v Scott*[28]). Additionally, any fear or anxiety about developing a future disease would also be compensated under the 'pain and suffering' or 'loss of amenity' heads of damage, as a 'tag' to the physical injury claim. However, the main point of the *Pleural Plaques* litigation was that 9 out of the 10 test Cs could not prove that they had suffered any physical injury at all (even though pleural plaques certainly amounted to a physiological change in the human body) – and hence, there was nothing to which their anxiety-based disorders could attach. They could not recover.

Given the dissenting judgment of Lady Justice Smith in the Court of Appeal, and the prior case of *Cartledge*, it is useful to set out the contrasting viewpoints from the *Pleural Plaques* litigation:

The contrasting reasoning in the *Pleural Plaques* litigation

Why the plaques did not constitute damage (CA majority, all of HL):	Why the plaques did constitute damage (Smith LJ):
• none of the individual components of the alleged 'damage' constituted damage – the fibre penetration which resulted in the formation of the pleural plaque + the risk that pleural plaques could give rise to disease + C's anxiety generated about this risk – as Lord Hope said, '0 + 0 + 0 = 0'; Looking at the individual components: • a mere physiological change in the body is not sufficient to constitute damage. English law requires a *de minimis* threshold of damage, and something which is symptomless, having no adverse effect on any bodily function, and no effect on appearance, does not meet that threshold;	• the pleural plaques were an *injury*, because they were 'an abnormal tissue change', and were also a *disease*, because 'they were capable of progression'; • symptoms could result from large amounts of plaques (coughing, breathlessness), and it was not the symptoms which were the injury, but the plaques themselves. Symptoms merely showed how serious the injury was;

[28] [2005] UKHL 2, [67] (Lord Hoffmann).

Why the plaques did not constitute damage (CA majority, all of HL):	Why the plaques did constitute damage (Smith LJ):
• the pleural plaques did not increase susceptibility to asbestos-related or other diseases or shorten life expectancy (cf. *Cartledge*, where silica dust damage *did* increase susceptibility to TB and bronchitis, and *did* reduce life expectancy); • no claim could be made for the chance of contracting a future disease, unless that risk was based upon some existing physical injury – and none existed here. Policy reasons also dictated against pleural plaques being damage: • it would encourage stressful litigation by employees against employers; • the litigation may be driven by claims managers; • the costs of the litigation would far exceed the damages recovered; • some Cs may accept final awards and therefore preclude themselves from ever claiming for asbestos-related diseases that they might develop in the future.	• it was no different from a skin lesion on the outside skin – both hidden plaques and lesions were a 'tissue change' and, therefore, constituted an injury to the body.

As Lord Hoffmann remarked in *Johnston*, '[b]ecause people do not often go to the trouble of bringing actions to recover damages for trivial injuries, the question of how trivial is trivial has seldom arisen directly'.[29] However, be that as it may, the case was an object lesson in illustrating that, without compensable damage, there is no actionable negligence.

Other perspectives

The appellate decisions which declared pleural plaques not to be physical injury represented a sea-change in English common law – which attracted some vehement media commentary at the time:

Media comments on the *Pleural Plaques* litigation

'***Asbestos Condition not Compensable: UK Court***', *Reuters* (26 Jan 2006):
'The Association of British Insurers and their members are delighted with an outcome which could prevent 100,000 court cases, thereby saving the industry £1–1.4 billion'.

'***A Wrong-Headed Ruling on Asbestos***', *The Independent* (27 Jan 2006):
'The claimants and their representatives are seriously concerned at the implications of the Appeal Court's decision. The General Secretary of *Amicus*, the trade union which brought the case, condemned the judgment as "dreadful": "[it] harms many of our members who have been exposed in their working lives to asbestos. We believe that people with pleural plaques should be compensated, and we will fight on'.

[29] [2007] UKHL 39, [2008] 1 AC 281, [8].

Subsequently, the Scottish Parliament enacted legislation specifically to overrule the House of Lords' decision. The Damages (Asbestos-related Conditions) (Scotland) Act 2009 was passed, to provide (per s 1) that asbestos-related pleural plaques, and certain other asbestos-related conditions (pleural thickening and asbestosis), constituted personal injury which was **not** negligible, and which was actionable under Scots law. Unsurprisingly, insurance companies who were potentially 'on the hook' to pay out pleural plaque claims under Scottish employers' liability insurance policies, brought a petition for judicial review, seeking a declaration that the 2009 Act was unlawful. That application, in *AXA General Ins Ltd v Scottish Ministers*, failed. The Scottish Inner House noted that: '[i]n deciding that, notwithstanding *Johnston*, in Scotland pleural plaques should be, and have always been, a condition for which compensation should be paid and that, in effect, the insurers of negligent employers would be liable to meet claims for that compensation, the Scottish Parliament was, as a matter of political judgment, entitled to take into account that such insurers had, for a significant period, accepted such liability'.[30]

The 'loss of a chance' claim

Essentially, suppose that C cannot prove that D's breach caused his physical injury, on the balance of probabilities. There was a 25% probability that the breach caused C's harm; but there was a 75% probability that some innocent (non-tortious) reason caused C's injury. The finding that D's breach had a 25% chance of causing C's injury will not satisfy the traditional test of causation (considered in the next section), and C will lose his case.

However, by framing the damage in a different way – not as the physical injury, but as the loss of a chance – C may seek to prove that, because of D's negligence, C lost a 25% chance of a better outcome. Had the 25% chance that breach caused the injury not been 'in play', then C's prospects of avoiding the adverse outcome would have improved.

This type of claim (as discussed later in the chapter[31]) has met with a distinct lack of success in English law in *personal injury* litigation, but has garnered more traction in *economic loss* claims. This is a rare instance in which courts have proven to be more, rather than less, sympathetic towards Cs who have only suffered from economic loss. In any event, it is convenient to analyse traditional causation principles first, for they provide a proper context in which 'loss of chance' claims can be considered as a means of circumventing the traditional means of proving causation.

THE FIRST STEP: THE CLASSIC 'BUT-FOR' TEST

§8.4 The conventional test of causation – the 'but-for' test – states: 'would C's harm have happened, but for (or absent) D's breach? If probably not, then D's breach caused C's harm. However, if C's harm would probably have happened anyway, then D's breach did not cause that harm.'

The 'but-for' test of causation is sometimes referred to as a '*causa sine qua non*' (literally, 'a cause without which not'). The expression, 'but for', means in this context, 'were it not for'. The purpose of the test is to exclude causes of C's injury which the law regards as being legally insignificant, or 'irrelevant' (per *Corr v IBC Vehicles Ltd*[32]).

[30] [2011] CSIH 31, [93]. [31] See pp 469–77.
[32] [2006] EWCA Civ 331, [18] (Ward LJ), and not doubted on further appeal.

In general, the key to the test's application is hypothetically to fix D's breach, and then to ask whether the damage would have happened to C in any event – if the answer to that is, 'yes, C's damage would probably have happened anyway', then D's breach did not cause C's damage. In *Allied Maples Group Ltd v Simmons and Simmons*,[33] Stuart-Smith LJ remarked that to ask whether a ***positive act*** by D caused C's harm is 'a question ... of historical fact' (i.e., take the act away hypothetically, and would the damage still have occurred?), whereas in the case of ***omissions***, it depends upon a hypothetical enquiry as to what would have happened if D's omission had been corrected. Lord Browne-Wilkinson described it, in *Bolitho v City and Hackney HA*,[34] as 'the factual inquiry [which] is, by definition, in the realms of hypothesis'. In most cases, no absolute answer is possible – except in unusual cases (discussed below) where certainty, and not probability, rules the day.

The leading English authority for the 'but-for' test is an unusual case of medical negligence.

> In *Barnett v Chelsea and Kensington Hosp Management Committee*,[35] William Barnett, C, was employed as a night watchman at the Chelsea College of Sciences and Technology. On the night of 31 Dec 1965, C's colleague was attacked by an intruder at the college with an iron crowbar around 4 am, and taken to St Stephen's Hospital, Chelsea, D, for checking. C and his injured colleague then returned to Chelsea College. Around 5 am, C had a cup of tea with his colleague and the senior watchman on duty. All three men started vomiting immediately afterwards, and for the second time that day, C visited the casualty department of St Stephen's – this time as a patient – shortly after 8 am. The three men asked the duty nurse to fetch a doctor. Delays occurred, partly because the nurse suspected that the men had been excessively drinking. The nurse telephoned a doctor, D, on an upper floor. D's response was: 'Well, I'm vomiting myself, and I have not been drinking. Tell them to go home, and go to bed, and call in their own doctors – except [the injured colleague] who should stay because he is due for an X-ray later this morning'. C left the hospital, went back to the College, lay down on the floor to rest, and died later at 1.30 pm. The medical evidence was that all three men had been poisoned by arsenic, deliberately introduced into the tea. The coronial verdict was 'murder by person or persons unknown'. Mrs Barnett sued D, on behalf of herself and two of her children, as dependants of C. **Held:** negligence failed.

Would Mr Barnett's damage (i.e., death) have occurred, but for D's breach (their failing to admit and to treat him)? Unfortunately yes – death was inevitable from enzyme disturbance induced by arsenical poisoning. Had the breach been fixed, and Mr Barnett examined in the hospital emergency room, he would have been admitted to a ward, a blood and urine specimen taken, and an antidote to arsenic poisoning administered. However, because that antidote had to be given within 75 minutes (maximum) of the ingestion to reverse the disturbance of the enzyme processes, causation had to fail, because the death would have occurred in any event. Mr Barnett had presented to hospital too late.

The importance, and limits, of probability

The usual 'probability' scenario

§8.5 Any cause which is assessed as being, on the balance of probabilities, the source of C's harm, is legally assessed as being the sole, or certain, cause of C's harm. In that regard, at law, 51% = 100%.

[33] [1995] 1 WLR 1602 (CA) 1609–10. [34] [1998] AC 232 (HL) 239. [35] [1969] 1 QB 428.

Causation is a balance-of-probabilities assessment, but having been assessed, D is either fully liable or not liable at all – '[i]n determining what did happen in the past, a court decides on the balance of probabilities. Anything that is more probable than not, it treats as certain', according to Lord Diplock in *Mallett v McMonagle*.[36] While the expression, '51% = 100%', is a mathematical nonsense, it is legally rational and defensible. If there is an underlying uncertainty as to what precisely caused C's harm, the law disregards this in the search for pragmatic, and rough-at-times, justice.

In that regard, the 'but-for' test is truly a misnomer, because (as Sir Igor Judge pointed out in *Clough v First Choice Holidays and Flights Ltd*[37]), the words 'can mislead. They may convey the impression that C's claim for damages for personal injuries must fail unless he can prove that D's negligence was the only, or the single, or even chronologically the last cause, of his injuries ... [but] such an impression would be incorrect'. In the majority of negligence cases, there is D's breach, and also an innocent (non-tortious) reason for C's damage, both contributing to the maelstrom of C's factual story. C's task is to prove that, on the balance of probabilities (i.e., >50%), his harm would not have occurred, had D's breach not happened. As remarked in *Various Claimants v Flintshire CC*,[38] usually 'one is not dealing with certainties' as to the cause/s of C's problems.

It is not necessary for a trial judge to attribute percentages to the breach and to the innocent cause – in fact, it is probably easier **not** to descend into percentage discussion, according to Lord Ackner in *Hotson v East Berkshire AHA*:[39] '[u]nless there is some special situation, e.g. joint defendants, where the apportionment of liability between them is required, there is no point or purpose in expressing in percentage terms the certainty, or near certainty, which [C] has achieved in establishing his cause of action'.

There are thousands of cases which could usefully illustrate the 'but-for' test, where both negligent and innocent reasons for the damage were 'in play'. An illustrative example from each of the two most problematical contexts of causation – medical and employment scenarios – will suffice:

In *McWilliams v Sir William Arrol & Co Ltd*,[40] William McWilliams, C, was employed by Sir William Arrol, D, as an experienced steel erector. In the Kingston shipbuilding yard, Port Glasgow, he was working about 70 feet above the ground, on the steel lattice work of a tower crane being constructed, when he fell to his death. A safety belt, which would have prevented the death, had been available until 2–3 days before the accident, but was then transferred to another site. C's widow sued D, alleging that the failure to provide C with a safety belt was in breach of s 26(2) of the Factories Act 1937.

- *the innocent cause*: there was a **strong probability** that C himself would have elected **not** to wear a safety belt on the occasion of the accident, even if provided. His colleagues gave evidence that C did not normally wear a safety belt, even when working at greater heights than 70 feet. Sometimes, when conditions were dangerous (windy), some steel-workers did, but conditions were not windy that day;
- *the negligent cause*: there was a **very slight possibility** that C would have worn a safety belt, if it had been provided.

[36] [1970] AC 166 (HL) 176. [37] [2006] EWCA Civ 15, [44].
[38] (QB, 26 Jul 2000) [25] (Scott Baker J). [39] [1987] AC 750 (HL) 793.
[40] [1962] 1 WLR 295 (CA) 300 (Viscount Kilmuir LC), 307 (Hodson LJ).

Held: causation failed. (Separately, it was not proven that D should have exhorted or instructed C to use a safety belt. By virtue of the statutory wording, employees could 'elect to use' safety belts.)

In *Hotson v East Berkshire AHA*,[41] Stephen Hotson, C, 13, fell out of a tree at school, and fractured his left femoral epiphysis (hip joint). When he presented at D's hospital, it was not correctly diagnosed and treated, and he was sent home with instructions to take pain-killers. C returned five days later, in great pain, and a correct diagnosis was made. By that time, the hip joint had turned necrotic, due to ruptured blood vessels and a lack of blood supply to the joint. C was left with permanent disability. There were two potential causes of C's harm:

- *the innocent cause*: the original crush and fracture from the fall left insufficient blood vessels intact to keep the epiphysis alive, no matter what the treatment or how promptly it occurred – essentially, the blood vessels running along the back of the femoral neck contained about one-half of the total blood supply to the epiphysis, and if they were ruptured by the fall, that would doom the hip to necrosis, regardless of delay (assessed at 75% probability);
- *the negligent cause*: there were enough intact blood vessels surviving after the fall to keep the epiphysis alive, but these were subsequently (over the 5-day negligently-caused delay) occluded by pressure caused by bruising or bleeding into the joint, leading to necrosis (assessed at 25% probability).

Held: causation failed.

Hence, even if a breach by D occurs, and it has some causative effect on C's sustaining harm, causation will only be proven if the breach *probably* caused that harm. In legal terms, the breach then *definitely* caused that harm. In *Hotson*,[42] that simply could not be proven. The finding that too many blood vessels had been ruptured by the fall 'amounted to a finding of fact that the fall was the *sole* cause of the avascular necrosis' (Lord Bridge); that even 'before admission to hospital and therefore before the duty was imposed upon the doctor properly to diagnose and treat, the epiphysis was doomed' (Lord Ackner); and that 'when Stephen Hotson arrived at the authority's hospital for the first time, he had no chance of avoiding [necrosis]' (Lord Mackay).

The exclusive 'certainty' club

§8.6 Where C's harm would have occurred with absolute certainty because of some innocent (non-tortious) causes, regardless of D's breach of duty, then the breach did not cause the harm. Conversely, proving causation to the standard of certainty is **not** required in negligence law.

The leading case of *Barnett* (arsenic poisoning) was an example of a causal link being precluded with absolute certainty. Even had D's breach been hypothetically fixed in that case, the death of Mr Barnett would certainly have occurred, regardless. Conversely, if C can prove with 100% certainty that D's breach caused his harm, and that no innocent agent was in play, then causation will inevitably be proven. However, these scenarios are very unusual – and proving causation to a level of absolute certainty is **not** required on C's part.

[41] [1987] AC 750 (HL).

[42] *ibid*, with quotes at: 782 (Lord Bridge), 792 (Lord Ackner), 789–90 (Lord Mackay).

In *Bull v Devon AHA*,[43] baby Stuart Bull, C, claimed that a county hospital which was built over two sites failed to have an adequate system in place for summoning the obstetrician, D, which led to a 68-minute delay between delivery of first twin Darryl and C (the latter suffered profound mental disability with spastic quadriplegia). There were two possible causes canvassed for this tragedy:

- *the innocent cause*: where uni-ovular twins share the same placenta during pregnancy, one twin may draw more than its fair share of nutrient at the expense of the other (foeto-foetal transfusion), which may deprive the second twin of oxygen. It was common ground between *all* the medical experts that C had suffered some measure of foeto-foetal transfusion to Darryl;
- *the negligent cause*: hypoxia occurred during the negligent birthing process, depriving C of sufficient oxygen in those 68 minutes.

Held: negligence proven. The innocent cause of foeto-foetal transfusion was entirely discounted by the trial judge as causing C's disabilities, partly because C had grown as fast as Darryl after birth. Hypoxia was the sole cause, held the trial judge.

However, the Court of Appeal noted that the trial judge sought to place the blame for C's harm at D's door to a standard higher than was necessary, noting of hypoxia that, '[i]t would have sufficed for him to make the less unqualified finding that this cause was established on the balance of probabilities ... however, he was entitled to make such a finding'.

Therefore, *Bull* properly belongs, with *Barnett*, in a fairly rare cadre of cases in which the 'but-for' test operated in the realm of certainty.

No fractional damages

§8.7 Where D's breach has a <50% probability of causing C's harm, C cannot recover a fraction of the total damages, on the basis that there was a possible chance that his injury was caused by that breach. In other words, 49% = 0%. However, it is important to distinguish discounting at liability stage (which is not permitted) from discounting at damages assessment stage (which is allowed).

In quantification terms, if C can show a >50% chance that, but for D's breach of duty, he would not have suffered the injury, C recovers **full** damages, and there is no question of fractional damages (say, 75%) being awarded to take account of the fact that there was a 25% chance that negligence did not cause the injury. As Lord Ackner stated in *Hotson*,[44] C's loss is 'not discounted by reducing his claim by the extent to which he has failed to prove his case with 100% certainty'.

Conversely, where there was a <50% chance that D's breach caused C's harm, C cannot recover fractional damages. Stephen Hotson was not entitled to recover 25% of what a fully-compensated-for necrotic hip injury would have been worth. To reiterate, at liability stage, 49% = 0%; and 51% = 100%.

Despite the House of Lords' rulings on the subject, the point has proven somewhat contentious, where judicial attempts have been made to discount damages at liability stage:

[43] (1989) 22 BMLR 79 (CA). [44] [1987] AC 750 (HL) 792.

> In *Bagley v North Herts HA*,[45] the trial court held that it should assess C's claim on the basis that D was negligent, 'and then make the necessary discount' for the 5% risk that her baby would have been stillborn anyway, even absent medical negligence. In *Hotson*, Lord Ackner held this approach to be 'clearly wrong'.[46] C had proven her case with 'near certainty', and she ought to have recovered 100% of the damages assessed. To discount 'would be to propound a wholly new doctrine, which has no support in principle or authority, and would give rise to many complications in the search for mathematical or statistical exactitude'. In *Tahir v Haringey HA*,[47] the trial judge had reduced C's harm (spastic gait and bowel/bladder problems, worth £30,000) to the proportion (13%) of the delay for which D was negligently responsible (2–3 hours, of a total 20-hour period in which a spinal operation on C was not performed – only D's delay of 2–3 hours was negligent). Hence, at trial, C was awarded £4,000 for his injuries (13% of £30,000). The Court of Appeal unanimously overruled this decision: 'this arithmetic or apportionment or proportionate method ... is not a valid method of assessing damages ... in adopting this approach, the learned Deputy Judge fell into error. [C] had failed to prove that any of his loss of amenity was caused by the negligent delay'.

On the other hand, where C actually proves D's liability in negligence and suffers damage, then the assessment of damages may properly involve an evaluation of chances in the future which could affect C's damages. In the *Creutzfeldt-Jakob Disease Litig*,[48] where the Department of Health had committed a breach in not informing treating doctors that they should tell those being treated with human growth hormone about the risk of contracting Creutzfeldt-Jakob disease, liability was proven (via rather unorthodox means, as explained shortly) – but then, the assessment of the damages **could** reflect discounts for possibilities. Take the head of damage, future loss of earnings, which was part of the damages assessment for these claimants. Adjustments for chances 'arise only at the quantification stage; e.g., what were the chances of a [CJD recipient] being promoted [at work], but for the onset of CJD? If he had a 25% chance, that chance will be reflected in the assessment of loss of earnings.' Obversely, if there was a chance of C's ceasing employment for non-CJD-related reasons, a discount would be similarly appropriate. However, those questions arise at quantification – at the liability stage, it is all or nothing.

Legal points about the balance-of-probabilities assessment

Epidemiological and statistical evidence

§8.8 Epidemiological and statistical evidence can be used, in some cases, to prove the causal link between breach and damage. However, neither can be used to reverse the burden of proof, so as to place the burden on D to disprove causation.

Epidemiological evidence. Such evidence seeks to establish causation by comparing a class of persons suffering from condition X, who were exposed to the suspected disease-causing agent, with the general population's contraction of condition X. According to Akenhead J in *Re Corby Group Litig*,[49] 'epidemiology is that branch of medical science which addresses epidemics. In practice, it is a statistical-based discipline which seeks to investigate, collate information, and

[45] (1986) 136 NLJ 1014 (QB) 1015 (Simon Brown J). [46] [1987] AC 750 (HL) 793.
[47] [1998] Lloyd's Rep Med 104 (CA) (trial judgment on 12 Nov 1993).
[48] (1998) 54 BMLR 104 (QB), quote at 107–8. [49] [2009] EWHC 1944 (TCC) [706].

analyse whether medical conditions or diseases have occurred in any given country, or part of a country, to an extent which is over and above what might otherwise be expected'. There are two aspects to its use (according to French J in *Reay v British Nuclear Fuels Ltd*[50]), *viz*, association and cause: '[t]he purpose of epidemiological studies ... is to make an assessment of the probability (a) that there is an association between the [exposure and the disease] and (b) that the association, if any, is causal'. Those two limbs to epidemiology were later confirmed by the Supreme Court in *Sienkiewicz v Greif (UK) Ltd*.[51]

The scenario can arise where, say, it is alleged that a doctor's failure to implement infection controls, or a local authority's dumping of toxic waste near residential areas, caused damage (i.e., disease or infirmities) to a class of persons.

In *Corby Group Litig*,[52] 18 Cs brought a group litigation order, alleging that birth defects (i.e., shortened or missing legs, arms and fingers) occurred in children born 1986–99, near a British Steel site east of Corby, which had been reclaimed by the Corby BC, D. The defects allegedly occurred because the mothers ingested or inhaled cadmium, nickel and other heavy metals whilst pregnant. This came about because, during the reclamation works, D allegedly followed a 'dig and dump' policy of burying slurry, and the method of transporting metals led to airborne contamination. The purpose at trial was to decide the generic issue as to whether any breach of duty by D 'had the ability to cause upper and/or lower limb defects of the type complained of'. **Held:** generic causation proven. Epidemiological evidence showed that there was an unexplained cluster of birth defects to the children of mothers living in Corby during 1986–99; plus evidence pointed to continuing breaches of the duty of care owed to C, which led to the extensive dispersal of contaminated materials from 1985–97.

Notwithstanding the support for epidemiological evidence in *Corby*, two caveats apply:

- in *Reay*,[53] French J noted that an assessment of causation will always depend upon the court's acceptance (or non-acceptance) of the credibility of the epidemiological evidence itself: '[t]he fact that epidemiologists or another scientist would, or would not, find an association and/or a cause to be established to his satisfaction is most helpful to a judge, but only within the limits imposed by their respective disciplines'; and
- it is not legally permissible to argue along the lines that, 'a group of us have this disease, and D's breach was the common factor, and it is all too much of a coincidence to attribute our disease to anything else, so it is up to D to prove that his breach was **not** the cause of our disease'. Such an argument would unacceptably reverse the burden of proof on causation. As discussed later,[54] that burden always rests on C in English law.

Statistical evidence. Convoluted statistical theories can also assist to prove causation in difficult cases, where otherwise it would be impossible to prove whether or not D's breach caused C's harm:

In *Creutzfeldt-Jakob Disease Litig, Group A and C Plaintiffs*,[55] several young children, Cs, who showed signs of stunted growth, were injected with human growth hormone (HGH) in a clinical trial. This type of HGH was capable of infecting injectees with Creutzfeldt-Jakob disease, a brain-wasting and untreatable condition that consigned its sufferers 'to unimaginable suffering and certain death'.

[50] (1994) 5 Med LR 1 (QB) 12. [51] [2011] UKSC 10, [80] (Lord Phillips). [52] [2009] EWHC 1944 (TCC) [689], [885].
[53] (1994) 5 Med LR 1 (QB) 12. [54] See pp 483–86. [55] (1998) 54 BMLR 100 (QB).

Cs were told of the CJD contamination of HGH, and their risk of developing CJD, some years after the trial. Some Cs contracted CJD, whilst others sustained psychiatric injury from the worry that they would do so. For any HGH injections administered after 1 July 1977, and which contained a sufficient titre of the CJD agent to be lethal, they were 'negligent injections', for by that date, the risk of CJD contamination causing brain-wasting was known. For any injections which contained a sufficient titre of the CJD agent to be lethal and which were given prior to that date, those were 'innocent injections'. Some Cs received HGH treatment both before and after 1 July 1977, and contracted CJD. However, it was impossible to say whether C received the 'tainted' injection before or after 1 July 1977. CJD could be caused by a single injection containing a sufficient titre of the CJD agent, and it had no cumulative effect. **Held:** for those Cs who received more doses after 1 July 1977 than prior to that date, causation succeeded.

Notwithstanding the complicated mathematical evidence in the case, ultimately a fairly 'rough and ready' statistical analysis was applied. Morland J treated the lethal dose received by C as a so-called 'an Ace of Spades'. If C received 27 doses after the cut-off date and 25 before that date, then it was slightly more likely that the Ace was in the pile of 27. More than one 'Ace' per C was unlikely, given the rarity of CJD contamination.

The drawing of inferences

§8.9 Where the causal chain of events by which C's damage occurred is not capable of precise proof, the court may rely on an inference to establish a causal connection between D's breach and C's harm.

Where direct proof of what happened to bring about C's harm is impossible, then recourse may be sought to the doctrine of *res ipsa loquitur* (discussed in Chapter 7). Alternatively, the court may be prepared to draw an inference that the causal link was proven – which necessarily requires that the court 'be prepared to take a reasonably robust approach to causation' (per *Roadrunner v Dean*[56]). Inferences are especially useful where the court is not inclined expressly to rely on *res ipsa loquitur*, although some of the reasoning is similar under both.

In *Drake v Harbour*,[57] Toulson LJ explained that two pre-requisites apply for an inference of causation:

i. C's damage must be of a type that would ordinarily follow from the proven breach against D: 'where [C] proves both that [D] was negligent, and that loss ensued which was of a kind likely to have resulted from such negligence, this will ordinarily be enough to enable a court to infer that it was probably so caused, even if [C] is unable to prove positively the precise mechanism';
ii. any other causal explanation was improbable: '[t]he court must consider any alternative theories of causation advanced by [D] before reaching its conclusion about where the probability lies. If it concludes that the only alternative suggestions put forward by [D] are, on balance, improbable ... it is legitimate to infer that the loss was caused by the proven negligence'. However, Toulson LJ noted that there is no reversal of the burden of proof under this requirement; 'rather, it is a matter of applying common sense'.

[56] [2003] EWCA Civ 1816, [29]. [57] [2008] EWCA Civ 25, quotes at [28].

In *Drake v Harbour*, D negligently undertook electrical rewiring of C's house whilst C was absent, when installing festoon lights in the loft. Old cabling was used for the festoon lights, and D failed to inspect it properly. The lights were plugged into a light socket, and the house was then destroyed by a fire which was seated in the loft, whilst D's workers were absent overnight. **Held:** how the fire started was not conclusively determined. But it was 'more likely than not', via an inference, that the insulation of the festoon lights' cabling was damaged, causing arcing and overheating.

However, the 'Sherlock Holmes' inferential approach to causation, i.e., that if every other causal link between the breach and the damage has been ruled out as being unlikely, then whatever causal argument left, however implausible, must be the relevant cause of the damage, is not an acceptable route by which to prove causation in English law (per *Rhesa Shipping Co v Edmunds, The Popi M*[58]). As recently confirmed in *Graves v Brouwer*,[59] the upshot of that scenario is that C has not proven its case on causation on the balance of probabilities. The court is not required to choose between two implausible causes, and ignore the option that C simply failed to prove the cause of the damage. This topic is considered further in 'Defective products', an online chapter.

Exceptions to 'but-for' causation

The 'but-for' test is not the exclusive test of causation. The limits of that test have been widely acknowledged. In *Kuwait Airways Corp v Iraqi Airways Co (Nos 4 and 5)*,[60] Lord Hoffmann remarked that 'it would be an irrational system of tort liability which did not insist upon there being some causal connection between the tortious act and the damage. But causal connections can be of widely differing kinds'. In essence, the 'but-for' test cannot (per Sir Igor Judge in *Clough v First Choice Holidays*[61]) be treated 'as a single, invariable test applicable to causation issues'.

In *Fairchild v Glenhaven Funeral Services Ltd*, Lord Nicholls noted that any exception to the 'but-for' test is just that – an *exceptional* scenario:

> In the normal way, in order to recover damages for negligence, [C] must prove that but for [D's] wrongful conduct, he would not have sustained the harm or loss in question. He must establish at least this degree of causal connection between his damage and [D's] conduct before [D] will be held responsible for the damage. Exceptionally this is not so ... [and] a lesser degree of causal connection [is sufficient]'.[62]

There are **four** exceptions to the 'but-for' test, the most important of which is the *McGhee/ Fairchild* exception. Its application has arisen particularly in the contexts of employment and medical negligence.

EXCEPTION #1: THE 'MATERIAL CONTRIBUTION TO RISK' EXCEPTION

Suppose that C cannot prove that D's breach caused his harm on the balance of probabilities. There is at least one innocent cause, and the breach itself, swirling around in the factual matrix – but it is beyond the ken of scientific or medical knowledge to say which of these probably caused C's harm. The respective causes may have operated solely, or in combination to an

[58] [1985] 1 WLR 948 (HL). [59] [2015] EWCA Civ 595, [30].

[60] [2002] UKHL 19, [2002] 2 AC 883, [127], citing: *Bonnington Castings Ltd v Wardlaw* [1956] AC 613 (HL) and *McGhee v National Coal Board* [1973] 1 WLR 1 (HL).

[61] [2006] EWCA Civ 15, [43]. [62] [2002] UKHL 22, [2003] 1 AC 32, [37].

unknown degree, or not at all, to bring about C's damage. It is impossible to say – exposing a so-called 'evidential gap'.

An express reference to that 'gap' has arisen in several of the most difficult causation-in-negligence cases in English law, *viz*, *Gregg v Scott*,[63]*Fairchild v Glenhaven Funeral Services Ltd*,[64] *McGhee v National Coal Board*[65] and *Wilsher v Essex AHA*.[66] Into that gap has stepped 'the doctrine of material contribution' in a couple of the aforementioned cases, i.e., a series of legal principles have been developed as a pragmatic solution to the causal conundrum.

Essentially, C can prove causation under this theorem, only where he can align his case with *McGhee/Fairchild* (or with the so-called 'enclave' which developed from that line of authority that includes *Sienkiewicz v Greif (UK) Ltd*[67] and *Barker v Corus UK Ltd*[68]). Causation will fail, however, if C's scenario aligns with the *Wilsher* scenario; while the 'doubling the risk' doctrine has a very limited application. It is also necessary to correctly distinguish *McGhee/Fairchild* scenarios from *Bonnington*-type 'material contribution to damage' scenarios, as the legal ramifications are different for each. These difficult issues are discussed in this and the following sections.

The *McGhee/Fairchild* scenario

§8.10 According to the *McGhee/Fairchild* principle, C can prove a sufficient causal link where D's breach materially contributed to the risk of C's suffering damage. The doctrine applies where the following conditions are satisfied:

i. only one 'candidate' (agent) could have caused C's harm; and C was exposed to that agent, both tortiously (because of D's act or omission), and innocently, for a reason other than D's breach. That innocent exposure could be brought about because of some naturally-occurring environmental exposure to the agent; by C's own conduct by which he exposed himself to the agent; or by some lawful exposure to that agent which was brought about either by D or by some other party;
ii. D failed to take precautions against the risk of the agent causing C harm (i.e., proof of breach);
iii. D's breach preceded C's suffering the precise harm which that agent causes;
iv. C cannot (because of the current limits of scientific knowledge) prove, on the balance of probabilities, that his harm was the result of the particular exposure to the agent which that D's breach brought about; and
v. the highest that C can prove is that D's breach materially increased the risk of harm to him (somewhere between the balance of probabilities and *de minimis*).

In the *McGhee/Fairchild* scenario, the 'but-for' test will fail, because there are tortious and innocent contributors to C's harm, and none of them surmounts the 50% threshold of probability required for the 'but-for' test to apply. Nevertheless, under the exceptional theorem of causation known as 'the material contribution to the risk exception', C can still establish a sufficient causal link.

The abovementioned principle is derived from the leading cases of *McGhee v National Coal Board* and *Fairchild v Glenhaven Funeral Services Ltd*,[69] which, in turn, have been interpreted

[63] [2002] EWCA Civ 1471, [53] [64] [2002] UKHL 22, [150].
[65] [1973] 1 WLR 1 (HL) 7. [66] (1984) 135 NLJ 383 (QB).
[67] [2011] UKSC 10, [2011] 2 AC 229, [167]. [68] [2006] UKHL 20, [2006] 2 AC 572.
[69] See especially, *Fairchild* [2003] AC 32 (HL) [2] (Lord Bingham), [61] (Lord Hoffmann), [170] (Lord Rodger).

and clarified by subsequent cases, *viz*, *Sienkiewicz* and *Barker v Corus*. There are five conditions for the exception to apply, all of which must be satisfied.

Dealing with each pre-requisite in turn:

Pre-requisite (i): Only one 'candidate' (agent) could have caused C's harm; that agent had both 'guilty' and 'innocent' incidents; C was exposed to both

The single agent is absolutely crucial to the *McGhee/Fairchild* principle. Indeed, as the '*Fairchild* enclave' of authority (as it was termed recently by the Supreme Court in *Zurich Ins plc UK Branch v Intl Energy Group Ltd*[70]) has developed, it has become increasingly apparent that, if this exceptional theorem is to be contained within reasonable limits, this pre-requisite must apply.

This was emphasised in *Fairchild*[71] itself, where Lord Bingham stated that, '[i]t is one thing to treat an increase of risk as equivalent to the making of a material contribution where a single noxious agent is involved, but quite another where any one of a number of noxious agents may, with equal probability, have caused the damage'. Lord Hutton agreed that *McGhee's* principle could only apply, 'where there is only one causative agent'. Lord Hoffmann dissented on this point in *Fairchild*, but later considered his view to have been wrong, in *Barker v Corus UK Ltd*.[72]

If there are multiple agents in play, then the *Fairchild/McGhee* exception cannot apply (instead, it will be a *Wilsher* scenario, where causation will not be proven, as discussed below). If *Fairchild* were to extend to multi-agent cases as well, then identifying the contribution of each particular agent to C's harm would be 'well nigh impossible and highly artificial' (per Lord Scott in *Barker v Corus*[73]).

In *Fairchild v Glenhaven Funeral Services Ltd*,[74] three test cases were brought by employees (Arthur Fairchild *et al.*, C), who were wrongfully exposed to significant quantities of asbestos dust in their workplaces by their employers, D. Each employee suffered from mesothelioma. For each C as against each D, there were essentially two possible causes of his mesothelioma:

- C's exposure to asbestos which one particular employer, D, did not take adequate precautions to prevent ('*the guilty asbestos*'); or
- C's exposure to asbestos which those other employers who had employed C during his career did not take adequate precautions to prevent ('*the innocent asbestos*').

It was impossible to prove scientifically which employer's asbestos fibre/s had caused C's mesothelioma on the balance of probabilities. It was also not clear whether it was one fibre, or an accumulation of fibres, that caused mesothelioma – all that science could say was that the greater the exposure to asbestos, the greater the risk of contracting the disease; but that, once contracted, further exposure did not worsen the disease. **Held:** causation succeeded against each D. The breach by each D increased the likelihood of mesothelioma being suffered by C.

In *McGhee v National Coal Board*,[75] James McGhee, C, worked in a brick kiln in hot and dusty conditions whereby brick dust adhered to his sweaty skin. His employer, National Coal Board, D, committed no breach of duty in respect of these working conditions. However, D failed to provide adequate washing facilities, thus requiring C to cycle home after work with his body still caked in brick dust.

[70] [2015] UKSC 33, [1] (Lord Mance), [102] (Lord Hodge).
[71] *ibid*, with quotes at: [22] and [115], and see too, [149] (Lord Rodger), and [72] (Lord Hoffmann).
[72] [2006] UKHL 20, [2006] 2 AC 572, [23]. [73] *ibid*, [64]. [74] [2003] 1 AC 32 (HL). [75] [1973] 1 WLR 1 (HL).

C contracted industrial dermatitis (a condition caused by abrasive brick dust removing the upper skin layer, exposing the tender skin beneath). Brick dust adhering to the skin was a recognised cause of industrial dermatitis; and providing showers to remove it after work was a usual precaution to minimise the risk of the disease. There were two possible causes of C's dermatitis:

- the brick dust which abraded the skin, and which ought to have been washed off before his ride home if shower facilities had been provided ('*the guilty brickdust*'); or
- the brick dust which abraded C's skin during his work in the brick kiln during working hours, and against which D had no duty to provide preventative measures ('*the innocent brickdust*').

It was impossible for C to prove that, had D provided washing facilities, then on the balance of probabilities, the dermatitis would not have occurred. The 'but-for' test failed. Even if the brickdust had been washed off before C's ride home, C's dermatitis may still have been suffered in any event. **Held:** nevertheless, causation succeeded.

This exceptional theorem has some key points, under its first pre-requisite.

One D or multiple Ds. The 'innocent exposure' to the harmful agent needs to be clarified. Of course, *McGhee* and *Fairchild* were entirely different cases. In *McGhee*, there was only one D, but that employer D had exposed C to brickdust, both innocently and tortiously. In *Fairchild*, there were numerous employer Ds, all of whom were in breach by exposing C wrongfully to asbestos dust in each of those employment stints – but insofar *as each particular D* was concerned, C had been exposed to that D's 'tortious asbestos dust', but C had been exposed to asbestos dust by someone else altogether (so that was 'innocent' asbestos dust, as far as that particular D was concerned, as it certainly was not his). Hence, in *McGhee*, there truly was innocent exposure; whereas in *Fairchild*, all of the asbestos dust was tortious when looked at as a whole, but when taking each employer D individually, any other asbestos dust caused by another employer was the innocent dust, as far as that employer D was concerned. For that reason, *Fairchild* shares a close commonality with *McGhee*, and both fit within the five-pronged principle articulated at the commencement of this section.

Additionally, the 'innocent exposure' which C suffered could be caused by something else altogether. The *McGhee/Fairchild* one-agent exception also applies, to enable C to prove a sufficient causal link, where C was exposed to the harmful single agent via (1) his own contributory negligence, or (2) some natural occurrence which is completely out of either C's or D's control (e.g., some environmental exposure to the agent). Post-*Fairchild*, the House of Lords held that the exception applies to those 'one-agent' scenarios too. Dealing with each in turn:

Contributory negligence. The fact that some exposure to the harmful agent was brought about by C's failure to take reasonable care to protect himself against that agent will mean that C's damages will be reduced to the extent of that contributory negligence. However, C's ability to prove causation via the weaker causal link supplied by the *Fairchild/McGhee* exception against some party D who also exposed him to that same harmful agent, is unaffected by any contributory negligence. Once again, the harmful agent in the relevant case was asbestos dust:

In *Barker v Corus (UK) plc*,[76] Mr Barker died of mesothelioma. He had been wrongfully exposed to asbestos dust on three occasions during his working life – for six months when working for Corus, D1; for six weeks when working for another employer, D2 (now insolvent); and for three short periods over

[76] [2006] UKHL 20, [2006] 2 AC 572, [48]. Two other appeals, of Mr Patterson and Mr Murray, were conjoined in this appeal, but they did not involve any contributory negligence.

7 years, when working as a self-employed plasterer (when he failed to take reasonable precautions against asbestos for his own safety). Mrs Barker, C, sued D1 and D2 under the FAA. **Held (HL):** C's damages were reduced by 20%, to reflect Mr Barker's contributory negligence. However, Mr Barker's own negligence did not prevent the application of the *Fairchild* theorem. (Additionally, under the *Fairchild* theorem, each employer should only be liable for that proportion of the damages which represented his contribution to the risk that the employee would contract mesothelioma, as discussed in 'Multiple defendants', an online chapter.)

A natural event. Even where C is exposed to the harmful agent innocently, because that agent occurs naturally in the environment, the *McGhee/Fairchild* exception still applies, for C's benefit.

In *Sienkiewicz v Greif (UK) Ltd*,[77] Enid Costello, C, 74, died of mesothelioma. She was an office worker at a factory at Ellesmere Port from 1966–84. Her employer, Greif (UK) Ltd, D, manufactured steel drums, and during that work, asbestos dust was released around the factory, wrongfully exposing employees to that dust. C's duties took her all over the factory, including areas contaminated with asbestos. Whilst C had not been exposed to asbestos during any other employment, she was exposed to a low level of asbestos in the general atmosphere, given that she lived in close proximity to Ellesmere Port (in common with all other residents of that area). It could not be proven when C contracted mesothelioma (i.e., whether it was a fibre to which she was exposed during her employment, or during her exposure to the atmospheric asbestos dust). **Held:** causation proven, as a *Fairchild* scenario.

The application of the *Fairchild* exception, in any circumstances where D materially increased the risk that C would suffer damage, but where some other source of that risk was also present – whatever source that might be – has been affirmed at the highest appellate level. In *Barker v Corus*,[78] Lord Hoffmann (who gave the leading speech) commented that, for the purposes of the *Fairchild* exception, 'it should be irrelevant whether the other exposure was tortious or non-tortious, by natural causes or human agency or by C himself'. Similarly, in *Zurich Ins v Intl Energy Group*, Lord Mance noted that *Fairchild's* 'special rule' applied, wherever C had been exposed to 'asbestos dust originating from different sources over the same or different periods'.[79]

The 'single agent'. What is meant by a 'single agent' – sufficient to invoke the application of this exceptional theorem of causation – has provoked some real uncertainty. In *Sienkiewicz*, for example, Lord Brown doubted whether the distinction was easily recognisable in some cases (and even doubted whether it should continue to base an exception to 'but-for' causation which was any wider than asbestos causing mesothelioma).[80] Obviously, judges have been concerned to ensure that the *McGhee/Fairchild* exception is not applied too widely, so as to circumvent the 'but-for' test.

It seems that it does not matter that there were different mechanisms, or ways, in which the single agent acted to bring about C's harm. However, C's condition must have 'the same distinctive aetiology and prognosis', no matter which innocent or tortious exposure he suffered (as Lord Walker put it in *Barker*[81]). In the same case, Lord Scott said that he would regard different

[77] [2011] UKSC 10, [2011] 2 AC 229. In a conjoined appeal, Dianne Willmore alleged tortious exposure to asbestos whilst a pupil at school, together with environmental exposure. Both Cs succeeded on causation.

[78] [2006] UKHL 20, [17]. [79] [2015] UKSC 33, [3]. [80] [2011] UKSC 10, [187].

[81] [2006] UKHL 20, [114] (Lord Walker).

types of asbestos as constituting a single agent, whilst Lord Hoffmann gave an example of what would **not** involve the 'single agent' necessary for the *McGhee/Fairchild* exception to apply, i.e., where C 'suffers lung cancer which may have been caused by exposure to asbestos or some other carcinogenic matter, but may also have been caused by smoking, and it cannot be proved which is more likely to have been the causative agent'.[82] Undoubtedly, this particular aspect of pre-requisite (i) will continue to develop jurisprudentially.

Pre-requisite (ii): D failed to take precautions against the risk of the agent causing C harm

Proving that D was culpable for exposing C to the harmful agent is necessary, in order to establish causation under the *McGhee/Fairchild* principle. As the Court of Appeal pointed out in *Rolls Royce Industrial Power (India) Ltd v Cox*,[83] '[a]lthough *Fairchild* assists [C] in relation to causation, it does not relieve them of the requirement to prove a breach of the duty of care on the part of [D]'. The wrong can be a negligent breach of duty, or a breach of statutory duty – the point is that there must be a wrong (per *Zurich Ins plc v Intl Energy Group*[84]).

In some cases (e.g., in *Fairchild* itself), breach (in failing to provide safety precautions to prevent the inhalation of asbestos) was admitted. In cases where breach cannot be proven though, there is no room whatsoever for the exception to apply.

In *King v King*,[85] C, 22, had a vaccination course for typhoid and cholera at D's surgery before a trip to Morocco. About six hours after the second vaccination, C suffered a stroke. C alleged that D should not have given him the injection because he had a boil and a temperature, which materially increased the risk of an adverse reaction. (C could not prove that the vaccination caused his stroke on the balance of probabilities.) **Held:** the claim failed, as there was no breach. In *McGhee*, 'the problem ... arose because there had been a breach of duty by [D], and the question to be decided was whether that breach was causative' of C's dermatitis, whereas in this case, 'that prerequisite to such an enquiry is missing'.

Pre-requisite (iii): D's breach preceded C's suffering the precise harm which that agent causes

Brick dust was the **only** explanation for Mr McGhee's dermatitis and (as explained subsequently by the House of Lords in *Wilsher*[86]), the failure 'to take a precaution against brick dust causing dermatitis was followed by dermatitis caused by brick dust ... I can see the common sense, if not the logic, of holding that, in the absence of any other evidence, the failure to take the precaution caused or contributed to the dermatitis'. Similarly, mesothelioma is caused by the inhalation of asbestos particles (per *Fairchild*).

In some medical cases, the application of the *McGhee/Fairchild* exception has been tested on the basis that one agent may have operated tortiously, or innocently, or a mixture of both, to bring about a patient's harm – but the patient cannot prove which applies on the balance of probabilities. If the agent has **never** been known to cause that damage, however, then the exception simply cannot apply.

[82] *ibid*, [64] (Lord Scott), [24] (Lord Hoffmann). [83] [2007] EWCA Civ 1189, [3].
[84] [2015] UKSC 33, [3]. [85] CA, 9 Apr 1987 (Croom-Johnson LJ).
[86] [1988] AC 1074 (HL) 1091–92 (Lord Bridge), approving: [1987] QB 730 (CA) 779 (Browne-Wilkinson V-C, dissenting).

In *Kay v Ayrshire and Arran Health Board*,[87] toddler Andrew Kay, C, was admitted to hospital with pneumococcal meningitis. During treatment, he was negligently given an overdose of penicillin, which was immediately counteracted by remedial treatment. After recovering from the meningitis, C was found to be deaf. There were two possible causes of C's deafness (neither of which could be proven on the balance of probabilities):

- C already was at risk of neurological damage from the meningitis ('*the innocent cause*');
- C was overdosed with penicillin, which increased the risk of suffering some neurological injury ('*the guilty cause*').

Held: there was no evidence that an overdose of penicillin had ever caused, or even contributed to, deafness. Hence, C's deafness had to be regarded as resulting solely from the meningitis: '[t]he principle in *McGhee* would only fall for consideration if it was first proved that it was an accepted medical fact that penicillin in some cases caused or aggravated deafness ... because the necessary factual background cannot be established on the evidence in this case, this difficult question does not arise'.

Just as problematically in *Kay*, there were 'two competing causes of deafness, namely meningitis and penicillin', but these agents (alleged to bring about neurological damage) were quite different. One was a drug, and one was a bacterium. It could not be a *McGhee*-type case in any event, because it failed pre-requisite (i).

Pre-requisite (iv): C cannot (because of the current limits of science) prove, on the balance of probabilities, that his harm was the result of the exposure to the agent which D's breach brought about

As explained earlier, C has an 'evidential gap', in that there is no objective basis upon which science or medicine can determine whether or not C would have developed the harm anyway, even if D's breach had never occurred. The whole point of the exception is to assist C with this dilemma.

Undoubtedly the exception is policy-driven. As Toulson LJ explained in *Intl Energy Group Ltd v Zurich Ins plc*,[88] in the case of employment scenarios, *Fairchild* demonstrates 'the protective approach which the courts have taken towards the health of employees, and the difficulty of knowing the particular moment of exposure which has caused the onset of the disease' – in such cases, a 'broader test' of causation is appropriate.

In any case in which it can be proved that D's breach either did, or did not, cause C's harm on the balance of probabilities, reliance on *McGhee/Fairchild* is inappropriate. Hence, the *CJD* case[89] was 'a different problem of causation' from that arising in *McGhee*, as was *Hotson v East Berkshire AHA*.[90]

Presently, the contracting of mesothelioma from asbestos exposure falls within this 'evidential gap'. Where someone is exposed to asbestos fibres, those fibres may not trigger the malignant mutation necessary to form a mesothelioma tumour, it appears to depend on different fibres interacting to bring about a series of genetic alterations, ending with a malignant cell in the pleura.[91] Further, the point at which a tumour does form, i.e., 'present and assured of growth ... [so] has passed the stage where that mutation may die off' (as described in the *Trigger Litigation*[92]), is not presently capable of being ascertained scientifically, so that it is not

[87] 1987 SC 145, 168–69 (Lord Griffiths).
[88] [2013] EWCA Civ 39, [24].
[89] (1998) 54 BMLR 100 (QB), quote at 106.
[90] [1987] AC 750 (HL).
[91] *Zurich Ins v Intl Energy Group Ltd* [2015] UKSC 33, [1] (Lord Mance).
[92] [2011] 1 All ER 605 (CA) [51] (Rix LJ).

possible to tell which particular fibre/s caused the mutation. However, that gap in scientific knowledge may be rectified in time to come, in which case the usual 'but-for' test will apply in that scenario (and 'the problem which gave rise to the *Fairchild* exception will have ceased to exist', per *Sienkiewicz v Greif (UK) Ltd*[93]). That day, however, lies in the future.

Pre-requisite (v): The highest that C can prove is that D's breach materially increased C's risk of harm

Whether D materially increased (i.e., added to) the risk of harm to C is a question of degree. It lies somewhere between the balance of probabilities and *de minimis*.

Courts have been reluctant to be too specific as to what amounts to something more than a *de minimis* contribution. Lord Reid stated, in *Bonnington Castings Ltd v Wardlaw*, that 'any contribution which does not fall within that [*de minimis* scope] must be material. I do not see how there can be something too large to come within the *de minimis* principle, yet too small to be material'.[94] Some sort of quantitative assessment as to whether a contribution to risk was greater than *de minimis* is not a path that the Supreme Court has been willing to go down – rather, in *Sienkiewicz*, Lord Phillips said that it 'must be a question for the judge on the facts of the particular case.'[95] Although, in *Zurich Ins v Intl Energy Group*, Lord Mance referred to a requirement, under the *Fairchild* principle, that D had exposed C to '*significant* quantities of asbestos dust', that is not to impute that the contribution had to be 'significant' in probability terms.[96] Something greater than *de minimis* is all that is required.

In the case of occupational disease cases (such as mesothelioma), the courts have also declined to set a minimum period of employment which C must satisfy, in order to succeed on the *Fairchild* principle – although some patients have found the *de minimis* threshold too difficult to surmount.

In *Sienkiewicz*, facts previously, **held:** causation proven. Greif, D, wrongfully exposed Mrs Costello, C, to asbestos dust, which increased the environmental exposure to which C was already subject by 18%. That incremental exposure in the workplace materially increased her risk of contracting mesothelioma, over and above the *de minimis* threshold. In *Rolls Royce Industrial Power (India) Ltd v Cox*,[97] C was employed by D as a welder, during which he stripped down large boilers and was exposed to asbestos for 'at least a few months'. C had been exposed to asbestos at other stages of his working career too. C suffered mesothelioma. **Held:** causation proven. Three months was sufficient to fall within the *Fairchild* exception (indeed, D conceded that one week of exposure would be greater than *de minimis*). In *King v King*,[98] facts previously, **held:** causation failed. Any hope of relying on *McGhee* was precluded because there was 'no evidence that the inoculation of an unhealthy patient increased the risk of a neurological reaction'.[99] Hence, administering the vaccination did not contribute to C's risk of stroke in any way that was greater than *de minimis*. In *Brown v Lewisham and North Southwark HA*,[100] Mr Brown, C, was sent from London to Blackpool by train and taxi, following heart by-pass surgery, when he was physically unfit to travel. Ultimately, C suffered from

[93] [2011] UKSC 10, [142] (Lord Rodger), and also, [208] (Lord Dyson).
[94] [1956] AC 613 (HL) 621. Also: *Nicholson v Atlas Steel Foundry and Engineering Co Ltd* [1957] WLR 613 (HL) 622.
[95] [2011] UKSC 10, [108]. [96] [2015] UKSC 33, [3] (emphasis added). [97] [2007] EWCA Civ 1189, [21]–[22].
[98] CA, 9 Apr 1987 (Balcombe LJ).
[99] See also, for similar result: *Murray v Kensington and Chelsea and Westminster AHA* (CA, 11 May 1981), citing the *de minimis* threshold in *Bonnington Castings Ltd v Wardlaw* [1956] AC 613 (HL).
[100] (1999) 48 BMLR 96 (CA) 106. Also: *McDonald v Tees HA* (CA, 21 Oct 1996) (Brooke LJ; with Aldous LJ and Lord Woolf MR agreeing, and upholding the trial judge's view that causation failed).

serious blood-clotting, which occluded the common iliac vein, compromising blood supply to his left leg, and led to his left leg being amputated after it turned gangrenous. There were three possible causes of the blood-clotting (none of which could be proven on the balance of probabilities):

- C's journey to Blackpool had contributed to enlarge or extend deep vein thrombosis which was already in his left leg when he left the hospital by train and taxi, and the presence of which should have ruled out his travelling (*guilty blood-clotting circumstances*);
- a blood clot may have formed in C's leg, sometime before his transfer, but where doctors at London were not negligent in failing to diagnose that before agreeing that C could return to Blackpool (*innocent blood-clotting circumstances*);
- blood clotting may have been caused by administering heparin after the transfer, because heparin given after by-pass surgery could cause the onset of heparin-induced thrombocytopena thrombosis (*innocent blood-clotting circumstances*).

Held: causation failed. There was one agent for the damage, *viz*, blood clotting, and occlusions which led to the amputation were the precise damage which blood-clotting could cause. However, when C arrived at Blackpool hospital, there were no objective symptoms that the journey had, in fact, caused an extension or aggravation of the deep vein thrombosis which C was found to be suffering. Any impact from the journey was very insignificant, and did not overcome a *de minimis* contribution to C's injury.

The *Wilsher* scenario

§8.11 According to the *Wilsher* principle, where C was exposed to multiple causal agents which could give rise to the risk of harm to C, but which of those agents caused C's harm cannot be proven on the balance of probabilities, then the *McGhee/Fairchild* 'material contribution to risk' test cannot apply, and causation must fail.

The *Wilsher* scenario differs from *McGhee/Fairchild* because there is no 'one agent' in play which may have had an innocent or a guilty contribution to C's harm. Rather, there are several different agents in play, any of which may have caused C's harm, and none of which surmounts the balance-of-probabilities threshold. Causation must fail, in the *Wilsher* scenario.

In *Wilsher v Essex AHA*,[101] Martin Wilsher, C, was a very premature baby, who was cared for in a special care baby unit by a team of doctors and nurses. C required oxygen, and during the first 36 hours of his life, a mistake occurred. Instead of inserting the catheter in C's umbilical artery to read his arterial blood oxygen levels, a junior doctor inserted the catheter into his umbilical vein, which read venous blood. Due to the lower-than-expected readings of blood oxygen levels, more oxygen was mistakenly administered. C was 'supersaturated' with oxygen for up to 8–12 hours. After inserting the catheter, the junior doctor asked a senior registrar to check what he had done. The registrar inspected the X-ray with the junior doctor, but failed to detect that the catheter was misplaced, and subsequently, when replacing the catheter, did exactly the same thing himself. It was not the insertion of the catheter into a vein instead of an artery which was negligent (it was a difficult task), but rather, the failure to detect, from the X-ray, that the catheter was wrongly placed. C ultimately developed the incurable eye condition, retrolental fibroplasia (RLF), which resulted in blindness. There were five possible causes of C's RLF (none of which could be proven on the balance of probabilities):

[101] [1988] AC 1074 (HL).

- super-saturation of oxygen within the first 30 hours of C's life, via the doctors' mistake – excess oxygen could have a toxic effect on the immature blood vessels in C's retina, leading to RLF (*the guilty cause*);
- hypercarbia (hypercapnia) – the presence in C's blood of an abnormally high concentration of carbon dioxide (*an innocent cause*);
- intra-ventricular haemorrhage – ruptured blood vessels within the ventricle of C's heart (*an innocent cause*);
- apnoea – a temporary cessation of breathing, from a reduction in nasal airflow, a common occurrence in newborn babies (*an innocent cause*);
- patent ductus arteriosus – the ductus is a blood vessel connecting the pulmonary artery directly to the aorta, and where it fails to close, that produces a murmur, affecting pulmonary circulation (*an innocent cause*).

C suffered from *all five* conditions in the first two months of his life. **Held:** causation failed. Due to factual disputes, a re-trial was ordered (and the case settled before that re-trial). Similarly, in *Kay v Ayrshire and Arran Health Board,*[102] facts previously, there were two possible causes of C's deafness: meningitis and penicillin. **Held:** causation failed. Even if penicillin was proven to have been a possible cause of deafness (which it was not), C would have failed, because it was a multi-agent *Wilsher* case.

In *Barker v Corus,*[103] the House of Lords reiterated that *Wilsher* did not fall within the *McGhee/Fairchild* scenario. There, C's dermatitis could only have been caused by brick dust. In *Wilsher*, by contrast, 'a failure to take preventative measures against one out of five possible causes is no evidence as to which of those five caused the injury'.[104]

Of course, the *McGhee/Fairchild* exception would be capable of far wider application – and would assist far more Cs over the causal threshold – if multi-agent causes that did not satisfy the balance-of-probabilities test were nevertheless sufficient to establish a causal link, merely because each agent materially contributed to the risk of injury to C. However, English negligence law is not that liberal. It is not enough that D contributed to the overall risk that C suffered damage (per *Clough v First Choice Holidays and Flights Ltd*[105]). Were that to be the law, then it would constitute (in the words of Nourse LJ in *Fitzgerald v Lane*[106]) 'a benevolent principle [which] smiles on these factual uncertainties and melts them all away', and would entail (per Lord Rodger in *Fairchild*[107]) 'an obvious injustice to the defendants'.

Finally, it is useful to contrast *Wilsher* with the earlier (1981) case of *Murray v Kensington and Chelsea and Westminster AHA.*[108]

In *Murray*, C was a very premature baby who sustained RLF and blindness during his hospital treatment, due to the over-administration of oxygen during the first dire days of his existence. The baby's treatment could be divided into two periods: the first 36 hours, and the next 3–4 weeks. During both periods, the oxygen levels administered to the baby were elevated, but the trial judge held that it was only the first period that was negligent (which was doubted on appeal). In any event, the medical evidence was that '[w]e cannot say what was the cause of the blindness – whether it was

102 [1987] 2 All ER 417, 1987 SC 145 (HL).

103 [2006] UKHL 20, [18]–[24] (Lord Hoffmann), [64] (Lord Scott), [114] (Lord Walker).

104 [1988] AC 1074 (HL) 1091.

105 [2006] EWCA Civ 15, [38] (Sir Igor Judge).

106 [1987] QB 781 (CA) 800 (Nourse LJ) (*Fitzgerald* was delivered before *Wilsher* (HL), but pre-empted the outcome).

107 [2002] UKHL 22, [149] (Lord Rodger).

108 CA, 11 May 1981.

caused by a mistake in the first 36 hours, or whether it occurred during the next 3–4 weeks (when there was no negligence). We simply cannot say'. Hence, there were two possible causes of C's RLF:

- super-saturation of oxygen in hours 1–36 of C's life ('*the guilty oxygen*');
- super-saturation of oxygen in weeks 1–4 ('*the innocent oxygen*').

Held: the excess ambient oxygen for the first 36 hours of C's life played only a minimal, if any, part in the onset of RLF and the consequential blindness, i.e., it did not meet the *de minimis* threshold, and made no material contribution to the risk of blindness.

Although, at first glance, the facts in *Murray* and *Wilsher* bear passing resemblance to each other, they are, in fact, entirely different cases. Were the *de minimis* threshold to have been crossed, then *Murray* would have been a *McGhee/Fairchild*, rather than a *Wilsher*, scenario, and C would have been entitled to recover in full for his blindness. As it was, he had been abandoned by his parents at birth, and this action was brought by his foster parents – unsuccessfully, as it turned out.

Limiting the scope of the *McGhee/Fairchild* exceptional theorem

The impact of *Sienkiewicz*

§8.12 English law remains currently unsettled as to the extent to which the *Fairchild* exception can be applied beyond the scope of its precise facts (i.e., where D is one of a number of employers who committed a breach by tortiously exposing C to asbestos, and where C later suffers mesothelioma), to where C suffers harm from other occupational illnesses/injuries, from medical negligence, or from pharmaceutical products, where C was exposed to one harmful agent, both tortiously and innocently.

As has been evident from preceding discussion, the *McGhee/Fairchild* exception has been considered in medical negligence cases (e.g., *Brown*, *King v King*) – wherein, as in *McGhee* itself, there was one D, and it was claimed that D had exposed C to the risk of harm via one agent, both tortiously and innocently.

However, where D has exposed C to a harmful agent, but so too have other parties exposed C to that same agent by committing breaches of duty similar to those of D, then some judicial statements in *Sienkiewicz v Greif (UK) Ltd*,[109] seem to suggest that the application of the *Fairchild* exception **only** occurs where C suffers mesothelioma as a result of the wrongful exposure to asbestos, and that it should not be extended more widely than that. For example, Lord Brown considered that 'mesothelioma cases are in a category all their own', and that other types of Cs should expect to have to adhere to the traditional causation principles, whilst Lord Rodger referred to the *Fairchild* exception as a 'special rule' applying to mesothelioma.

Since *Sienkiewicz*, some judges have also considered the *Fairchild* exception to be a narrow one. In *Zurich Ins plc UK Branch v Intl Energy Group*,[110] Lord Mance (writing for the majority) referred to *Fairchild*, *Barker v Corus*, and *Sienkiewicz* as 'operating within what might be called the *Fairchild* enclave, to govern liability between victims and those who, in breach of duty, had exposed them to asbestos dust'. In *Re J (children)*,[111] Lady Hale remarked that the

[109] [2011] UKSC 10, [174], [186] (Lord Brown), [113] (Lord Rodger).

[110] [2015] UKSC 33, [1] (Lords Hodge, Clarke and Carnwath agreeing).

[111] [2013] UKSC 9, [2013] 2 WLR 649, [41].

Fairchild exceptional theorem 'applies only where [C] has contracted mesothelioma, has been exposed to asbestos from more than one source, and it cannot be shown which source was responsible for the disease ... in *Sienkiewicz*, the Supreme Court made it clear that this is a special rule, created only because of the special difficulty of proving causation in mesothelioma cases'. Furthermore, in *Jones v Sec of State for Energy and Climate Change*,[112] Swift J considered the effect of *Sienkiewicz*, and stated that, '[i]t does not appear that there is any appetite in the appellate courts for extending the *Fairchild* exception to cases involving diseases other than mesothelioma'.

However, in *Zurich*, Lord Hodge (also writing for the majority in a separate judgment) remarked that the *Fairchild* exception 'is not confined to mesothelioma', and that 'the boundaries of the *Fairchild* enclave ... are not coterminous with liability for mesothelioma, and that the precise boundaries of the *Fairchild* principle, like those of *McGhee*, may have to be worked out in other cases'.[113] Furthermore, there was nothing in *Fairchild* itself that indicated that it should be solely restricted to its own facts. *McGhee* did not involve mesothelioma, but dermatitis – and the House of Lords expressly based *Fairchild* on *McGhee's* reasoning. Indeed, Lord Bingham contemplated that the *Fairchild* principle would become 'the subject of incremental and analogical development', whilst Lord Hoffmann noted that, whilst the actual rule in *Fairchild* should be limited to cases where an employee was wrongfully exposed to asbestos, '[t]hat does not mean that the principle is not capable of development and application in new situations'.[114] Furthermore, the abovementioned suggestions, in and since *Sienkiewicz*, that the scope of the *McGhee/Fairchild* exception should be restricted to asbestos/mesothelioma, in the case of multiple Ds against none of whom can 'but-for' causation be established, were dicta only, as those cases were not directly concerned with, say, medical or pharmaceutical contexts.

Certainly, at *quantification-of-damages* stage, the apportionment of damages among various defendants, stipulated in s 3 of the Compensation Act 2006, only applies to mesothelioma cases (discussed shortly). However, on the current state of authority, whether the *Fairchild* principle (in establishing a causal link *at liability stage*) is restricted only to cases of mesothelioma where multiple Ds are involved, remains unsatisfactorily unsettled.

The employer versus the insurer: what was the insured event?

§8.13 Notwithstanding a line of authority which states that the *Fairchild* exception renders employer D liable for contributing to *the risk of the employee contracting mesothelioma* by wrongfully exposing that employee to asbestos, more recent authority has endorsed the view that the employer contributed to *the disease suffered by the employee*, thus enabling the employer to 'lay off' its liability for damages to a third party insurer.

It is perhaps of limited comfort, when examining this difficult legal area, to realise that Roman jurists apparently had the same difficulty in the first century BC, when deciding who was responsible in law for the death of a slave, where a number of people struck the slave, but it was impossible to say who struck the fatal blow.[115] Centuries later, and in the interval between *McGhee* (1973) and *Fairchild* (2003), there was much judicial debate, at the highest appellate

[112] [2012] EWHC 2936 (QB) [543].

[113] [2015] UKSC 33, quotes at [98] and [109], respectively, and also [127] (Lord Sumption).

[114] [2003] AC 32 (HL), with quotes at [34] and [74] respectively.

[115] Noted by Lord Rodger in *Fairchild*, *ibid*, [158]–[160] – the remedy accruing to the owner of that slave.

level in England, as to precisely what damage D was liable for. That debate continues to this day – and assumed particular importance in 2012, in a dispute between insured employers and their insurers.

McGhee was interpreted by the House of Lords in *Wilsher v Essex AHA* (1987) to mean that the 'guilty' brick dust contributed to Mr McGhee's actual *injury*, the dermatitis. In *Wilsher*,[116] Lord Bridge stated that '*McGhee* laid down no new principle of law whatever'. Rather, the inference could be drawn, in *McGhee*, that 'the consecutive periods when the brick dust remained on the body probably *contributed cumulatively to the causation of the dermatitis*'. However, that was definitely **not** what *McGhee* stood for. The medical evidence was that C's dermatitis may well have occurred, even if only the brick dust from the brick kiln had been on C's skin and had been immediately showered off after work ended for the day. D's failure to provide the showers (i.e., the breach) merely increased the risk of C's contracting dermatitis, it did not contribute to C's actual injury (at least, the evidence could not establish that).

Three decades later, in *Fairchild*, the House of Lords admitted that a new principle of causation – a 'material contribution to *the risk* of injury' – is precisely what *McGhee* **did** create, and that Lord Bridge's interpretation of *McGhee* was incorrect.[117] The result of this exceptional theorem was that D may be liable to pay damages to C for an injury for which D was entirely fault-free, in the sense that it was possible that Mr McGhee's dermatitis was caused solely by particles of 'innocent brickdust'. D was liable in negligence merely for materially increasing the risk of harm to C – and that was an entirely new method of proving the causal link, despite Lord Bridge's assertion to the contrary. Lord Hoffmann summarised the principle of what D was liable for, in the *McGhee/Fairchild* scenario, in this way: 'a breach of duty which materially increased the risk should be treated *as if* it had materially contributed to the disease ... the House [in *McGhee*] treated a material increase in risk as sufficient in the circumstances to satisfy the causal requirements for liability. That this was the effect of the decision seems to me inescapable'.[118] Lord Nicholls described it as a 'less stringent causal connection'.[119] In *Barker v Corus*,[120] Lord Hoffmann (who gave the leading speech) again reiterated the view that '[t]he purpose of the *Fairchild* exception is to provide a cause of action against D who has *materially increased the risk that C will suffer damage* and may have caused that damage, but cannot be proved to have done so because it is impossible to show, on a balance of probability, that some other exposure to the same risk may not have caused it instead'.

These two contrasting schools of thought – that D contributed to the risk of C's injury, versus that D contributed to C's actual injury – came to the fore in *Durham v BAI (Run-Off) Ltd (the Trigger Litigation)*.[121] This litigation essentially concerned a dispute between those employers rendered liable under the *Fairchild* exception for their employees' mesothelioma, and the employers' third party insurers. It was crucial to the case – because of the contractual wording of the insurance policies – that each insured employer's conduct contributed to employee C's actual disease, and that it did not merely contribute to the risk of C's suffering the disease. That is because the insurance policies were triggered, only where each employer's conduct

[116] [1988] AC 1074 (HL) 1087, quote at 1090 (Lord Bridge, with whom the rest of the court agreed).

[117] [2003] 1 AC 32 (HL) [22], [34] (Lord Bingham), [44]–[45] (Lord Nicholls), [70] (Lord Hoffmann), [150] (Lord Rodger).

[118] *ibid*, [65] (original emphasis). Only Lord Hutton preferred the view that materially increasing the risk of the onset of mesothelioma 'involved a substantial contribution to the disease suffered by [Mr Fairchild]': [109], [116].

[119] *ibid*, [44]. [120] [2006] UKHL 20, [17] (emphasis added). [121] [2012] UKSC 14, [2012] 1 WLR 867.

contributed to C's suffering '*personal injury by accident or disease*', or '*bodily injury or disease*' arising from that employment. Merely contributing to *the risk of C's suffering disease* was not an insured event for which the insurer had agreed to provide cover to the employers under the various policies.[122]

Ultimately, the Supreme Court divided on the issue. The majority (for whom Lord Mance delivered the leading judgment[123]) held that the insurance policies were triggered, because each employer's conduct had, on a 'weak or broad causal link', caused C's mesothelioma where it was proved that the employer had in fact exposed C to asbestos dust. As Lord Mance subsequently explained his view, the *Fairchild* exception meant that 'the ordinary requirements of causation (proof on a balance of probability) were modified as between the [employee C] and the responsible [employer D], so as to make the latter liable for the mesothelioma because of the risk of sustaining mesothelioma to which the victim had been exposed during the relevant period' – and that the same sort of 'weak' or 'broad' meaning of causation should be carried through to the insurance policies which covered the insured employer (per *Zurich Ins plc UK Branch v Intl Energy Group Ltd*[124]). This viewpoint may have rendered the insurers liable under the policies, but it also tended to veer the law back to the views of Lord Wilberforce in *McGhee* and Lord Bridge in *Wilsher*, that the dust contributed to C's actual injury – which view was so roundly rejected by the majority in *Fairchild* itself. Lord Hoffmann considered it 'inescapable' in *Fairchild* that it was the 'creating of a material risk of contracting mesothelioma' for which D was liable to C, and nothing more than that (as nothing more than that could be proven, scientifically – D's particular dust may not have caused, or contributed to, C's disease at all). In any event, the majority's decision in the *Trigger Litigation* meant that the necessary causal requirement was met, in the case of mesothelioma, where the employer negligently exposed C to asbestos during the insurance period, so that the insurer had to indemnify the employer against that insured liability.

Lord Phillips vehemently dissented in the *Trigger Litigation*,[125] holding that an employer's liability under the *McGhee/Fairchild* exceptional theorem did **not** mean that D had, in any sense, caused C's mesothelioma, but only meant that D had created the risk of causing the disease. On that basis, the insurance policies were not available to cover the employers' liability, because the trigger point – D's causation of a disease – had not been met. In other words, merely contributing to the risk of their employees contracting mesothelioma was not an insured event. Lord Phillips' reasoning of what, precisely, D was liable for under the exceptional theorem adheres closely to the views of the majority in *Fairchild*. Clearly, Lord Phillips regarded the majority's view in the *Trigger Litigation* as entirely policy-driven, to enable the employers to lay off their liability to their third party insurers, and not in accordance with strict precedent.

As the *Trigger Litigation* aptly demonstrates, these are not merely semantic matters of terminology. Millions of pounds of insurance exposure turns upon their outcome. This author considers that the views of Lord Phillips in the *Trigger Litigation* and of Lord Hoffmann in *Fairchild* are far preferable to the strained interpretation that Lord Bridge adopted in *Wilsher*, and which the majority preferred in the *Trigger Litigation*. Even given the developing scientific knowledge of how mesothelioma is caused, the fact presently remains that any D rendered liable under the *McGhee/Fairchild* exception may be paying damages for C's harm to which his particular asbestos dust contributed nothing. All that can be established is that D's wrongful conduct exposed his employee C to *a risk* of contracting mesothelioma. For now, that is as

[122] The various wordings were slightly different, set out in *ibid*, [7]–[9], but the nub of the issue remained the same.
[123] See, especially, *ibid*, [59], [71]–[74]. [124] [2015] UKSC 33, [21]. [125] [2012] UKSC 14, [131]–[134].

much as the scientific evidence will permit. While the *Trigger Litigation* may ultimately have been a policy decision to ensure that employers subjected to a weaker causal theorem were able to recoup their liability from their insurers, the majority decision obscures the doctrinal basis which underpins this exceptional theorem of causation.

Defective products

§8.14 Whether the *Fairchild* exception applies to render a producer liable for contributing to the risk of a consumer suffering harm from a defective product remains somewhat unsettled in English law. On a differential scenario, however, the 'market share' theorem of liability has not been imported into English law to date.

The actions available to C where he is injured by a defective product – *viz*, in negligence, and under the Consumer Protection Act 1987 – are discussed in 'Defective products', an online chapter, where causation is covered in some detail. As noted previously, given that, in *Sienkiewicz*, some members of the House of Lords seemed to suggest that the 'material contribution to risk' exceptional theorem should be restricted to mesothelioma claims when multiple Ds are in play, the *Fairchild* principle may not be transposed to defective product claims more generally – although (so far as the author's searches can ascertain) a determinative case is yet to arise on that point.

The issue is potentially significant, however, where: C consumes a drug over a time period; that drug is manufactured by multiple producers D; C consumes the drug from each manufacturer; one or more capsules of the drug were contaminated; C suffers damage from that consumption; but it is impossible to ascertain which manufacturer made the defective capsule which C consumed. This is a 'material contribution to risk' scenario, to which the *Fairchild* theorem could potentially apply.

Twisting that scenario somewhat: suppose that a drug is defective in that each and every capsule of it does not meet the public's legitimate expectations as to safety; the drug is manufactured by numerous producers who supply the entire market with the drug under a generic name; it is not possible to ascertain which particular manufacturer produced the drug capsules which were consumed at any given time by C; but each capsule was harmful to C. As Lord Hoffmann pointed out in *Fairchild*,[126] that is not a 'material contribution to risk' scenario of the type which arose in *Fairchild*. At any given employer's premises, there could have been many innocent asbestos fibres which did not trigger mesothelioma for Mr Fairchild; his exposure to those asbestos fibres at the hands of many employers merely increased the risk of his injury, i.e., contracting mesothelioma. However, there are no innocent capsules of this defective drug; so consuming those capsules at the hands of many manufacturers does not increase the risk of C's consuming a tainted capsule.

In the abovementioned scenario, the Californian Supreme Court developed a 'market share' theorem of liability in *Sindell v Abbott Laboratories*,[127] which concerned the anti-miscarriage drug diethylstilbestrol, or DES. The theory applies in the case of a interchangeable substance such as a generic drug, where the specific manufacturer of the substance used by each consumer is unknown, but the product manufactured by different manufacturers is the same. According to the theory, each manufacturer is liable only to the extent of its own market-share. However, no case to date has imported the 'market share' doctrine into English law.

[126] [2002] UKHL 22, [2003] AC 32, [74]. [127] 607 P 2d 924 (SC Cal, 1980).

Apportionment of damages

The common law reversed

The principles governing apportionment as between Ds under the *Fairchild* principle are considered in detail in 'Multiple defendants' (an online chapter). The section below provides a brief summary for present purposes.

In *Fairchild*, the House of Lords did not need to answer the question as to whether the liability of C's various employers, D1, D2, D3, etc, whose tortious conduct each materially increased the risk of mesothelioma to C during his various employments with them, was joint and several; or whether each of D1, D2, D3, etc, was severally liable only for the proportionate contribution which his asbestos had made to C's risk of developing the disease.

In 2006 in *Barker v Corus UK Ltd*,[128] a majority of the House of Lords favoured the proportionate (or 'aliquot') liability solution, i.e., that the liability of each of D1, D2, D3, etc, should be attributed according to each D's relative degree of contribution to the risk, measured by reference to factors such as the duration and intensity of C's asbestos exposure during his employment with each D. Under this solution, no one D would be liable for the whole of C's damage; each would have its exposure to damages capped by the proportion which it bore for the overall damage C suffered. Indeed, this common law solution still receives support to this day. In *Zurich Ins plc v Intl Energy Group*,[129] Lord Mance (for the majority) considered that it was both 'coherent and understandable' as to why joint and several liability was not adopted in *Barker*, as a *quid pro quo* for the weaker causal theorem which D had to endure, courtesy of *Fairchild's* theorem. Indeed, in *Zurich*, it was held (unanimously) that *Barker v Corus* remains part of the common law of England and Wales.[130]

However, the effect of *Barker v Corus* was subsequently (indeed, almost immediately) reversed by s 3 of the Compensation Act 2006, but **only** in respect of mesothelioma cases. Hence, where the *Fairchild* exception applies, D1, D2, D3, etc's liability is joint and several. That has the (beneficial-to-C) effect of enabling C to recover full compensation from **any** of D1, D2, D3, etc, who is found liable under the *Fairchild* exception and who is solvent, as each of them is severally liable.

Further, for the *Sienkiewicz*-type scenario too, where there is environmental exposure to asbestos swirling in the factual matrix, and where C ultimately suffers mesothelioma, the Supreme Court confirmed in that case that s 3 of the Compensation Act applies – just as it does in the *Barker v Corus* scenario – as to render employer D fully liable for any damages, on a joint and several basis.

No insured employer

Where employee C, who has suffered from mesothelioma from wrongful workplace asbestos, is unable to trace any solvent employer with an attached viable insurer, that would leave C without any practical hope of obtaining damages, even where the *McGhee/Fairchild* exception theoretically applied.

Parliament saw fit to remedy this gap in redress, by enacting the Mesothelioma Act 2014.[131] Under that Act, an insurance fund was created (via the contribution of insurers), by which any

[128] [2006] UKHL 20, [2006] 2 AC 572. [129] [2015] UKSC 33, [27].

[130] *ibid*, [28], [31], The point was important, because the law of Guernsey governed the contracts of insurance in the case; Guernsey had not enacted the equivalent of s 3 of the Compensation Act 2006; and the common law of Guernsey was identical to English common law on this point.

[131] Received Royal Assent on 30 Jan 2014.

eligible employee will recover damages according to a schedule, based in part upon C's age. It is estimated that approximately 300 eligible employees will claim per year (which will reduce year upon year), and that the average compensation package will be about £123,000 (plus £7,000 towards legal expenses[132]).

An insurer for only 'part of the period'

Where an employer has exposed an employee to asbestos, and insurer D has covered the insured employer for only **some** of the period for which that employer had negligently exposed C, the question arises as to whether insurer D is liable for the employee's full loss or for only a proportionate part of it. That was the issue in *Zurich Ins plc v Intl Energy Group Ltd.*[133]

Where the 2006 Act does **not** apply, then under *Barker v Corus*, the employer is only liable proportionately for the extent of exposure for which that employer was responsible. It follows consistently, therefore, that the insurer's obligation to indemnify that insured employer should be limited to proportionate liability too.

> In *Zurich Insurance*, IEG, formerly Guernsey Gas, the employer, employed Mr Carre, C, for 27 years, from 1961–88, exposing him to asbestos wrongfully throughout that period. Mr Carre died of mesothelioma. During those years of exposure, IEG had insurance cover for only 6 years with Zurich Insurance (1982–88). **Held:** Zurich Insurance should only cover employer IEG for 6/27ths of the period of C's exposure to asbestos (22% of that period), and hence, was only liable to insure IEG for 22% of the damages to which C was entitled (22% of £278,500), consistent with the proportionate liability established by the common law in *Barker v Corus*. Guernsey law, which governed this dispute, had not enacted any equivalent to s 3 of the Compensation Act 2006.

However, in jurisdictions where the 2006 Act **does** apply (as in England), then the employer is jointly and severally liable for the entirety of C's damage (overturning the proportionate liability favoured in *Barker v Corus*). Further, under the *Trigger Litigation*, the outcome for insurers was that employee C's mesothelioma was caused 'in, a broad sense, in each and every period of any overall period of exposure', rendering the insurer fully liable under the employer's insurance policy. Consistent with this view of transporting a 'weak' or 'broad' concept of causation into the insurance context between employer and insurer, a majority of the Supreme Court in *Zurich Insurance* held that an insurer which provided insurance for a limited period of C's total exposure will be exposed to the **whole** of the C's damages claim, if employer D wrongfully exposed employee C to asbestos during that period of insurance. This rather onerous view, however, is subject to an important caveat.

The *quid pro quo* was that the insurer should be able to seek contribution from any successive co-insurers, or from the employer itself, in respect of any periods of exposure to which the employer exposed C, and for which the insurer had not covered that insured employer, under the Civil Liability (Contribution) Act 1978. In that regard, the

[132] See Dept of Work and Pensions, *News Article* (dated 6 Mar 2014), available at: <https://www.gov.uk/government/news/asbestos-victims-to-get-123000-in-compensation>.

[133] [2015] UKSC 33, [51]–[52], [54] (Lord Mance, for the majority), and [104] (Lord Hodge, also for the majority). Lords Sumption, Reed and Neuberger dissented.

Supreme Court sought to relieve the heavy burden which would otherwise be placed upon an insurer (via a combination of the 2006 Act and the *Trigger Litigation*), by creating a new equitable right of recoupment for insurers in *Fairchild*-type cases. Hence, an insurer who insured an employer for only part of the exposure period to asbestos giving rise to employee C's mesothelioma should indemnify the employer in full – but with a right to recover contributions on a pro rata basis from successive insurers of the employer and from the employer itself. Lord Mance (for the majority) acknowledged that this was a policy-driven response to the weaker causal theorem created by *Fairchild*, in yet another conundrum thrown up by asbestos litigation: 'by introducing into tort and liability insurance law an entirely novel form of causation in *Trigger*, the courts have made it incumbent on themselves to reach a solution representing a fair balance of the interests of victims, insureds and insurers.'[134] Lord Hodge (also for the majority) approved of this solution too, being one that 'the London insurance market is prepared to live with' – and it also permitted an employee to recover his damages from one employer/one insurer, 'in a straightforward way' (rather than having to pursue several parties to obtain the totality of his damages), thereby leaving any dispute over contribution to be dealt with between employers and their insurers.[135]

The preceding discussion under this section, 'Exception #1', starkly demonstrates the evolving, complex and divisive landscape to which the *McGhee/Fairchild* exception has given rise. Piecemeal judicial responses to each new problem associated with asbestos exposure has fragmented the law to the point where consistency and certainty of reasoning seem to be something of a mirage. However, any further legislative clarification or codification in the area appears very unlikely.

The 'doubling the risk' theorem

§8.15 According to the 'doubling the risk' causal theorem, where:

i. D's breach exposed C to a harmful agent;
ii. C was also exposed to that same agent, or to some other agent, for innocent reasons (i.e., for reasons other than D's breach) (the innocent agent);
iii. D's breach preceded C's suffering the precise harm which the harmful agent causes; and
iv. the risk of injury created by D's breach was more than double the risk of injury which C faced from the innocent agent, then D's breach caused C's harm. The test has only been applied intermittently. However, where C suffers from mesothelioma because D wrongfully exposed C to asbestos in the workplace, the 'doubling the risk' test does not apply.

The 'doubling the risk' theorem is another means of proving a 'material contribution to risk', where C cannot prove that D's breach caused C's harm, on the balance of probabilities. Under the theorem, C must seek to prove that the risk of injury from innocent exposure to a harmful agent was Y%, and that the risk of that same injury from D's breach was 2.1 x Y% – in that event, then D's breach materially contributed to the risk of C's injury. The theorem has been applied from time to time in a variety of contexts, as the following sample of cases shows:

[134] *ibid*, [51]. [135] *ibid*, [105]–[106].

Emergence of the 'doubling the risk' theorem

Year of case	C's harm	The facts
2002	DVT	In *XYZ v Schering Healthcare Ltd (the Oral Contraceptive litigation)*,[a] the case concerned the risk of developing deep vein thrombosis from two different types of oral contraceptive. The parties, and Mackay J, agreed that C could succeed only if the epidemiology showed that the risk of harm arising from contraceptive A (for which no warning had been given) was at least twice that arising from contraceptive B (for which appropriate warning had been given).
2007	Bladder cancer	In *Novartis Grimsby Ltd v Cookson*,[b] C suffered bladder cancer. He had been tortiously exposed to carcinogens during his employment at a dye works, and non-tortiously exposed to cigarette smoke as a regular smoker. Both were potent causes of bladder cancer. If the risk of bladder cancer from carcinogenic exposure was more than double the risk of bladder cancer from smoking, C could succeed. This was proven, and hence, C succeeded.
2007	Mesothelioma	In *Jones v Metal Box Ltd*,[c] C was held to be entitled to succeed, if he could show that the risk of mesothelioma arising from asbestos exposure at work had more than doubled the risk arising from environmental asbestos exposure. The judge found that the risk had been more than doubled, and C succeeded.
2008	Lung cancer	In *Shortell v BICAL Construction Ltd*,[d] C died of lung cancer. He had been exposed to asbestos by his employer, D, and had no other asbestos exposure, but had been a fairly heavy smoker. Both asbestos and cigarette smoking are common causes of lung cancer. D conceded that if C could prove that the risk of contracting lung cancer from asbestos exposure at work had more than doubled C's risk of contracting lung cancer from smoking, C would succeed. This was proven.

[a] [2002] EWHC 1420 (QB).
[b] [2007] EWCA Civ 1261.
[c] Cardiff CC, 11 Jan 2007 (HHJ Hickinbottom).
[d] QB, 16 May 2008 (Liverpool District Registry).

The 'doubling the risk' theorem has the **disadvantage** to C that it is potentially more onerous than the *McGhee/Fairchild* test, because an exposure which materially increased the risk under the *Fairchild* exception (in a sense that it made a greater than *de minimis* contribution to C's harm) may not, in fact, have doubled the risk of disease caused by the innocent exposure. Also, the theorem can only be applied where there is a sufficiently-good quality of epidemiological evidence to support the assessment of relative risks. However, the **benefit** to C of the 'doubling the risk' test is that it can equally apply to multi-agent scenarios (where cause A is one agent, and cause B is a different agent) as to single agent cases, thereby avoiding the *Wilsher* problem of multi-agent causes.

Whether the 'doubling the risk' theorem could be correctly applied was very much at issue in *Sienkiewicz v Greif (UK) Ltd.* C argued that the theorem did not follow the *Fairchild* line of authority, whereas D relied upon the theorem and submitted that it was not met. At first instance[136] (affirmed by the Court of Appeal), Judge Main accepted the application of the 'doubling the risk' theorem to C's mesothelioma case. However, C failed, because the risk of mesothelioma from D's exposing her to asbestos in the factory did not double the risk of contracting mesothelioma from environmental exposure which she already faced because she lived in Port Ellesmere:

In *Sienkiewicz v Greif (UK) Ltd*, facts previously, the figures were:

- the environmental exposure created a risk of mesothelioma of 24 cases per million;
- the occupational exposure created a risk of an extra 4.39 cases per million;
- thus, the occupational exposure was modest, and increased the already-existing risk of mesothelioma due to the environmental exposure by only 18%;
- hence, C had not shown that the (negligent) occupational risk had more than doubled the risk from (innocent) environmental exposure.

However, ultimately, the Supreme Court rejected the 'doubling the risk' theorem as a means of establishing a causal link in cases where C contracted mesothelioma after being wrongfully exposed to asbestos in the workplace.[137] According to Lord Phillips, special features about mesothelioma, the gaps in knowledge about the disease, the potential unreliability of the epidemiological data and the importance of C's own characteristics and behaviour, all combined to make it inappropriate to decide causation on epidemiological data. Essentially, a test of 'doubling the risk' was a 'tenuous basis' for deciding that 'the statistically probable cause of a disease is also the probable biological cause'. In such cases, C could rely on the ordinary 'material contribution to risk' test in *McGhee/Fairchild.* The Supreme Court did not rule out the 'doubling the risk' test as being potentially applicable in other contexts though (e.g., for medically-caused injuries) – although Lady Hale considered that there were considerable problems in adopting the test in **any** context. Notwithstanding, anything said about using the 'doubling the risk' test, in **any** context other than mesothelioma, was only dicta in *Sienkiewicz.*

As a result of *Sienkiewicz*, the current position is that the 'doubling the risk' test survives as a causal theorem which is exceptional to the 'but-for' test, but that it is inappropriate for mesothelioma cases. As Swift J noted in *Jones v Sec of State for Energy and Climate Change*,[138] '[i]t is plain that the majority in *Sienkiewicz* considered that the test can be used in appropriate circumstances, although there was obvious concern about over-reliance on epidemiological evidence alone'.

In *Jones v Sec of State for Energy and Climate Change*, three lead Cs suffered from lung cancer, having been exposed to carcinogens, from dust and fumes, at the Phurnacite Plant. Each C was also a regular smoker, and exposed to carcinogens from that source, plus the scientific evidence was that each C would have been subject to environmental exposure to carcinogens too (albeit usually at a low level). 'All these factors are likely to have played some part in the carcinogenic processes going on in [Cs'] bodies, processes which are, by their nature, wholly random.' **Held:** causation failed. The 'doubling of risk' theorem was appropriate to consider here, but no C could satisfy it.

136 Liverpool CC, HHJ Main, 15 Dec 2008.

137 [2011] UKSC 10, [83] (Lord Phillips), [160]–[161] (Lord Rodger), [169]–[170] (Lady Hale), [189]–[191] (Lord Mance).

138 [2012] EWHC 2936 (QB) [8.62].

The 'hunting cases'

§8.16 Where there is an evenly-split probability that each D caused C's harm, but it cannot be proven which D was culpable, the 'but-for' test cannot be met (as no cause will be >50%). However, an exception to the 'but-for' test is permitted in order to establish a causal link.

The 'but-for' test does not handle a *Cook v Lewis*-type scenario, one of the so-called 'hunting cases' emanating from Canada, where there was precisely a 50% probability that each one of two hunters caused C's harm – but which hunter caused C's harm could not be proven.

> In *Cook v Lewis*,[139] Mr Cook, D1, and Mr Akenhead, D2, hunting for blue grouse during the hunting season, fired almost simultaneously at a covey of grouse in a clump of trees, where Mr Lewis, C, was crouched. C received several shots in the face, and lost his eye. C sued D1 and D2, but could not prove from which gun the offending shot which damaged his eye was fired. If C had asked, 'would my lost eye have happened, but for D1's breach?', the answer would be, 'yes, it may have happened anyway, due to the negligence of my co-hunter, D2'. **Held:** both D1 and D2 could be liable (a new trial was ordered).

In *Fairchild v Glenhaven Funeral Services Ltd*,[140] Lord Nicholls expressly approved of *Cook v Lewis* as a valid exception to the 'but-for' test, because the scenario involved an 'evidential difficulty ... [which] justifies a relaxation in the standard of causation required. Insistence on the normal standard of causation would work an injustice'. If D1 and D2 did not share culpability in this type of case, then the 'unattractive consequence' would be that C would go uncompensated, even though one of the two hunters negligently injured him. Indeed, in *Dickie v Flexcon Glenrothes Ltd*, the court remarked that it would be 'repugnant to any legal system that both hunters should escape liability',[141] while in *Fairchild*, Lord Nicholls called the outcome in *Cook v Lewis* a 'value judgment'.[142] Indeed, the analogy with *Fairchild* is close. One (or more) of the shots from the hunters' guns caused C to lose his eye, just as one (or more) of the asbestos fibres at the employers' premises caused C's mesothelioma. The asbestos fibre is akin to the bullet – it is impossible to say which employer/gun it came from, but each D created the risk that his fibre/bullet was the 'guilty' agent of C's injury. Hence, the hunting cases and the scenario in *Fairchild* both represent acknowledged exceptions to 'but-for' causation.

EXCEPTION #2: THE 'MATERIAL CONTRIBUTION TO DAMAGE' EXCEPTION

The *Bonnington* principle

§8.17 According to the *Bonnington* principle, C can prove causation if D's breach materially contributed to C's actual harm, in circumstances where D's breach exposed C to a harmful agent, and where C was also exposed to that agent innocently – but where the tortious exposure had a cumulative effect upon the severity of the injury which C suffered. Under this principle, D is liable where his breach exposed C to an agent which increased *the severity of C's injury* (whereas the *McGhee/Fairchild* principle applies where D's breach exposed C to an agent which only increased *the risk of injury* to C).

[139] [1952] 1DLR 1 (SCC, Locke J dissenting). See too: *Summers v Tice*, 199 P 2d 1 (1948).
[140] [2002] UKHL 22, [39]–[40]. [141] [2009] ScotSC 143 (Kirkcaldy, Sheriff Peter J Braid) [136].
[142] [2002] UKHL 22, [40].

The *Bonnington* principle provides a further exception to the classic 'but-for' test, because C cannot prove that D's wrongful act in exposing C to a harmful agent caused C's injury on the balance of probabilities – and, yet, D can be rendered liable in negligence. *Bonnington* applies where (unlike under the *McGhee/Fairchild* principle) the harmful agent did undoubtedly contribute to C's *damage* (and not just to the *risk* of that damage). Yet, C may have suffered an equal degree of damage from the innocent exposure to the harmful agent, without D's wrongful exposure – medical evidence cannot say. Therein lies the causal conundrum which *Bonnington* addresses.

Bonnington itself arose out of occupational exposure to harmful agents in the workplace. However, it has notably been applied in medical cases too.

In *Bonnington Castings Ltd v Wardlaw*,[143] Mr Wardlaw, C, developed pneumoconiosis as a result of inhaling silica dust whilst working at his employer's, D's, factory. C worked in the 'dressing shop', where minute particles of sand swirled around constantly in the atmosphere when C was operating the pneumatic hammers. This was 'innocent silica dust', because there was no means of collecting and neutralising it. However, a considerable amount of silica dust also emanated from the swing grinders, which was 'negligent dust', because D allowed the dust extraction plant for those grinders to become clogged and ineffective, which was a breach of statutory duty. The exposure to the 'negligent silica dust' had materially aggravated (to an unknown degree) C's pneumoconiosis, but C might have developed that disease in any event, from his exposure to the 'innocent silica dust' from the pneumatic hammers. It was impossible to say. **Held:** causation proven. D's breach made a material contribution to C's disease. In *Bailey v MOD*,[144] C was operated on for a gallstone problem, which was competently performed, but there was a negligent lack of aftercare by D, which weakened her condition. C then developed acute pancreatitis, a naturally-occurring illness, which was not a consequence of D's negligence, but which weakened her still further. A few days after her operation, and without knowing how great a contribution each (negligent aftercare and pancreatitis) had made to C's overall weakness, save that each was material, C was too weak to protect her airway when she vomited, leading her to choke on her vomit. This resulted in cardiac arrest which, in turn, led to hypoxic brain damage. **Held:** causation proven. D's breach, the post-operative care, made a material contribution to the injury, per the *Bonnington* principle.

The fact that a *Bonnington* scenario is an exception to the 'but-for' test was explicitly acknowledged by the Court of Appeal in *Bailey v MOD*. In any case of 'cumulative causes', the 'but-for' test has to be modified. Waller LJ explained the point this way: '[i]f the evidence demonstrates, on a balance of probabilities, that the injury would have occurred as a result of the non-tortious cause in any event, [C] will have failed to establish that the tortious cause contributed ... [but] in a case where medical science cannot establish the probability, but can establish that the contribution of the negligent cause was more than negligible, the 'but for' test is modified, and [C] will succeed'.

A comparison with the *McGhee/Fairchild* principle

In several respects, for the *Bonnington* principle to apply, the same conditions must be met as were required for the *McGhee/Fairchild* exception – but with one key difference. Referring to those pre-requisites, whether overlapping or different:

[143] [1956] AC 613 (HL). [144] [2008] EWCA Civ 883, [2009] 1 WLR 1052, [46].

i. Same agent. As an overlapping condition, the *Bonnington* principle applies where C has been exposed to one agent, both tortiously and innocently.

In *Bonnington* itself, the sole agent was silica dust to which C was exposed (negligently from the swing grinders, and innocently from the pneumatic hammers), whereas in *Bailey*, it was C's generally weakened state (negligently from D's lack of medical care, and innocently from pancreatitis) which contributed to C's injury.

ii. Proof of breach. As an overlapping condition, a wrongful exposure to the harmful agent must be proven against, or conceded by, D.

iii. A *de minimis* contribution. As an overlapping condition, a material contribution to C's injury from D's breach is any contribution greater than *de minimis*, but smaller than balance of probabilities (51%).

However, the big difference between the principles is that, in *Bonnington*, it was medically possible to prove that the inhalation of the 'negligent silica dust' actually contributed to C's injury. D's breach in wrongfully exposing C to silica dust did not increase *the risk of harm*; it increased *the actual harm* to C. Neither the innocent nor the guilty agent got over the balance of probabilities threshold, and it was impossible to say how great a contribution each actually made to C's injury. By removing the negligent exposure to the harmful agent which D brought about, C **may** have suffered the harm anyway.

By contrast, in *McGhee*, it was not possible to say whether or not the lack of a shower had in fact contributed to C's dermatitis; it had only increased the risk of contracting that dermatitis; and in *Fairchild*, it was not possible to say at which employer's premises the employee had inhaled the relevant asbestos fibre which led to the fatal mesothelioma condition, but all of the employers had exposed that employee to the risk of contracting mesothelioma. Hence, in *McGhee/Fairchild* scenarios, D's breach exposed C to the **risk** of injury only, and the duration of D's exposing C to the harmful agent did not increase the severity of C's injury in any way (because one single exposure was sufficient). All that the duration of exposure dictated was that the risk of C's suffering the injury increased correspondingly. That is the major difference between the principles.

In *AB v MOD (the Atomic Veterans case)*,[145] 10 former servicemen, Cs, alleged that they had suffered various types of cancer from exposure by D to ionising radiation during thermonuclear tests in the Pacific Ocean region in the 1950s. The case turned on limitation periods, but causation was also relevant. There were many potential causes of Cs' cancers, other than ionising radiation. 'But-for' causation could not be proven, because even if Cs' exposure to the ionising radiation had not occurred, their cancers may have developed in any event. However, Cs argued that expert evidence showed that their exposure to radiation had materially increased their risk of developing cancers. **Held:** causation failed per the *McGhee/Fairchild* exception, because it could not be said that there was *one agent* in play that was responsible for Cs' cancers. Ionising radiation was one possible agent; but two Cs had smoked 20 cigarettes a day for >20 years, introducing the multi-agent *Wilsher* problem. There were 'multiple potential causes [of Cs' cancers], some of which had not even been identified'. The *Bonnington* principle could not apply either. The exposure to ionising radiation did not increase the actual harm to C, but only increased the risk of harm. Cs could not prove that their exposure to radiation had made a material contribution to their cancers. The case fell outside the *Bonnington* principle for that reason.

[145] [2012] UKSC 9, [2013] 1 AC 78.

Damages under the *Bonnington* principle

§8.18 Under the *Bonnington* principle, D is liable to compensate C for the proportion of C's divisible injury which is attributable to D's breach.

Typically, the *Bonnington* principle can only apply if the injury is divisible, i.e., where the injury which C suffers is termed, by law, a 'divisible injury', because it is 'dose-related' or 'time-related'. For divisible injuries, each dose of exposure contributes to the extent of injury that C suffers. The tortious component of the exposure (caused by D's breach) makes a material contribution to the disease (for further discussion of 'divisible' versus 'indivisible' injuries, see 'Multiple defendants', an online chapter).

In *Bonnington* itself, pneumoconiosis was a divisible disease, in that the severity of the disease was entirely dependent upon the quantity of dust inhaled. In *Bailey* too, C's weakened condition was treated as a divisible injury. In both, causation succeeded. By contrast, in the *Atomic Veterans* case, Cs' cancers were an indivisible injury, and the *Bonnington* principle did not apply, hence causation failed. As Swift J put it in *Jones v Sec of State for Energy and Climate Change*, '[c]ancer is an indivisible condition; one either gets it or one does not. The condition is not worse because one has been exposed to a greater or smaller amount of the causative agent'.[146]

In *Bonnington* itself, no apportionment as between tortious and non-tortious exposure to the silica dust was assessed, and C was awarded damages against his employer D on a 100% basis. D had not argued otherwise. However, that particular aspect of *Bonnington* no longer applies.

In *Jones v Sec of State for Energy and Climate Change*,[147] Toulson LJ noted that, since *Bonnington* was decided, 'there have been a number of decisions involving divisible conditions (such as industrial deafness, vibration white finger, and types of lung disease) in which liability had been apportioned as between different defendants and/or as between tortious and non-tortious exposures to the causative agent'. Apportionment of damages, as between D's breach and the non-negligent causes that contributed to C's injury, is judicially mandated now. D will be liable in respect of the precise share of the disease for which he was responsible – albeit that, in *Sienkiewicz*, Lord Phillips remarked that the apportionment 'may necessarily be a rough and ready exercise'.[148]

Conclusion

Principally, C will seek to prove that, had D's breach been hypothetically fixed, C's damage probably would not have happened (per the classic 'but-for' test, per *Barnett v Chelsea and Kensington Hosp*[149]). If C cannot do so, these are his exceptional options:

- D's breach materially contributed to the risk of C's suffering harm, injury or disease, where that risk was created both tortiously, and innocently, via C's exposure to a sole harmful agent;
- C's risk of contracting injury or disease from D's breach, in exposing C to a harmful agent, at least doubled the risk of C's contracting that injury or disease from an innocent exposure to that same or another agent – although that causal principle is inappropriate where C suffers mesothelioma from asbestos exposure; or

[146] [2012] EWHC 2936 (QB) [554]. [147] [2012] EWHC 2936 (QB) [531].
[148] [2011] UKSC 10, [2011] 2 AC 229, [17]. [149] [1969] 1 QB 428.

- D's breach, in exposing C to a harmful agent, materially contributed to C's actual injury or disease – but where C's harm may have happened anyway, due to an innocent exposure to that same agent.

In each scenario, there has been a 'material contribution' by D to either C's risk of harm, or to C's actual harm. Causation is, exceptionally, proven – even though C cannot prove, on the balance of probabilities, that D caused his harm.

EXCEPTION #3: THE *BOLITHO* CAUSATION THEOREM

The causal theorem adopted by the House of Lords in *Bolitho v City and Hackney HA*[150] permits a causal link, where an omission by D does not meet the 'but-for' test.

The leading case and theorem explained

§8.19 Where D (1) commits a breach by omission; and (2) alleges that, even had he hypothetically fixed that breach by some positive act, C's damage would still have occurred (thus defeating the 'but-for' test), C may establish a causal link between D's original omission to act and C's ultimate damage (per the *Bolitho* causal theorem) by proving that *either:*

i. on the balance of probabilities, D would have done a further act, X, in order to prevent C's harm (although there was no legal duty on D to do X); *or*
ii. D would not have done the further act X to prevent C's harm, and it would have been negligent of D not to have done X (because the continuing proper discharge of D's duty towards C required that he do X).

The *Bolitho* causation theorem arose out of a medical negligence (failure-to-attend) case, but it has been applied or considered beyond that context – e.g., in cases of alleged legal negligence (*D Morgan plc v Mace & Jones (a firm)*[151]), and allegedly negligent pensions annuity advice (*Beary v Pall Mall Investments (a firm)*[152]).

It potentially arises where D's negligence is an omission. When the court asks, 'would C's harm have occurred, but for that omission?', the answer may well be: yes, C's harm would have occurred anyway, because hypothetically fixing that breach (by D's acting positively to fix it) would not have prevented C's damage. That is because D would not have done a further positive act, X, to prevent C's harm. If that version of hypothetical events is accepted by the court, then 'but-for' causation should fail (as C's harm would have happened anyway). However, an exception to the 'but-for' test has been judicially-crafted, per the principle above, so as to create a causal link between D's breach (the omission) and C's damage, and to render D liable, in these limited circumstances.

Limb #1: Under the first limb of the *Bolitho* causal theorem, the court does not make any finding of fact as to what D actually did after his omission – rather, the court must assess what D *would* have done in a hypothetical situation, had he fixed that omission. The credibility of D's evidence will be crucial under this limb. D undoubtedly will say that he would not hypothetically have done anything further, having fixed the original breach – and if the court believes that, then the first limb of *Bolitho* must fail (unless some TP might have intervened to prevent

150 [1998] AC 232 (HL). 151 [2010] EWHC 3375 (TCC). 152 [2005] EWCA Civ 415, [31].

C's harm, which is sufficient to prove the causal link, as discussed below). To reiterate, D was under no legal duty to do that further act X, but it is a matter of credibility as to whether, having fixed the breach, he would have done so (as C will allege).

Given that the first limb of *Bolitho*'s test is in the realm of the hypothetical, as to what D would have done, had the omission been hypothetically fixed, then if D fails to give evidence in the trial, the court may draw inferences damaging to D, as to what D would have done. The Court of Appeal noted, in *Wisniewski v Central Manchester HA*,[153] that if D chooses not to turn up to the trial to attest what he would have done (D, in that case, had moved to Australia and refused to return to England for the trial, or to have his evidence taken in Australia by an appropriate official), 'it may be easier for [C] to set up an affirmative case on that issue, which is liable to be strengthened if, for no good reason, [D] is unwilling to submit himself to questioning before the judge as to what he would probably have done'. The *Bolitho* causal theorem succeeded in *Wisniewski*.

There is, however, an **alternative** method of proving the causal link, even if limb #1 fails.

Limb #2: Under *Bolitho's* second limb, C must prove that D would not have done that further positive act X, and it would have been negligent for D not to have done that act X. In other words, D cannot escape liability by saying that C's damage would have occurred in any event, because he would have committed some other breach (breach #2) after the original omission (breach #1).

The second limb depends upon *Bolam* evidence, i.e., what a body of peer professional opinion would have regarded as reasonable conduct, upon redressing the breach-by-omission. In *Bolitho*, Lord Browne-Wilkinson noted that a *Bolam* assessment did **not** have any relevance to the first limb of the *Bolitho* test, but that it 'is central to the second [limb]'.[154] In no other aspect of causation is *Bolam* relevant, except under this second limb of *Bolitho's* causal theorem.

In *D Morgan plc v Mace & Jones (a firm)*,[155] Coulson J described the two *Bolitho* limbs as the 'would' and the 'should' limbs, respectively, and that they were entirely alternative routes for C to pursue. The 'should' limb was to counter any possibility that D could escape liability by saying that he would have failed to do something that a reasonably careful doctor would have done.

In *Bolitho v City and Hackney HA*,[156] Patrick Bolitho, C, 2, suffering from croup, was treated in hospital under the care of a paediatrician, D. D saw C in the morning looking a little better, and C ate a large lunch. However, after lunch, C's health (and especially his breathing) deteriorated. Two urgent calls were put through to the senior registrar and to D, but no doctor responded. C suffered cardiac arrest and brain damage, being without oxygen for 10 minutes until he was resuscitated. D gave evidence that, had she attended C when the crash call was put through, she would not have intubated C to clear his airways, because she had been satisfied at C's earlier presentation, so she would not have believed that C had blocked airways. So (submitted D), the outcome would have been the same for C, because if the breach (failing to attend after the crash call) was fixed, C's harm would have happened anyway, as she would not have done further act X (i.e., intubated). Applying the causal theorem, **held:** causation failed:

- **limb #1:** C argued that, having fixed the alleged omission and turned up to Patrick's bedside, D would have intubated Patrick – but D's evidence was that she would not have, and that was believed by the court. Hence, the first avenue by which to prove the causal theorem failed;

[153] [1998] PIQR P324 (CA) P343 (in some reported versions of this case, its name is *Wiszniewski*).
[154] [1998] AC 232 (HL) 240. [155] [2010] EWHC 3375 (TCC) [392]. [156] [1998] AC 232 (HL).

- **limb #2:** C argued that, if D had not intubated Patrick, that further omission would amount to negligence – but a reasonable body of medical opinion considered that it was reasonable not to intubate C, given his earlier presentation that morning. Hence, the second avenue by which to prove causation also failed.

Although the theorem was developed in *Bolitho* itself, it did not obtain for C, in that case, any positive outcome in establishing causation. Ironically, though, later claimants – especially in the medical context – have had better success in using the theorem to establish causation in cases of breach-by-omission.[157] For example:

In *Wisniewski v Central Manchester HA*,[158] Philip Wisniewski, C, suffered irreversible brain damage in the 13 minutes immediately prior to his birth because, as he moved down the birth canal, the umbilical cord was wrapped round his neck and had a knot in it (a very rare occurrence), so that he was effectively being strangled during delivery. The alleged omission on the part of the gynaecologist, D, was that he did not perform an artificial rupture of the birth membranes. Had that occurred, then C alleged that the presence of a substance, meconium, would have been revealed, which would have led to birth by caesarian section, rather than via birth canal delivery. Ultimately, that would have avoided the hazards of a natural birth. Applying the *Bolitho* exception, **held:** causation proven:

- **limb #1:** if D had fixed the omission hypothetically (i.e., ruptured the membranes), the court was satisfied that D would have done further act X, *viz*, performed a caesarian section (D did not attend trial – and an adverse inference was drawn against him, that he would have proceeded to perform a caesarian). Hence, causation was proven under this avenue;
- **limb #2:** if D had not done X (performed a caesarian), the court was satisfied that it would have been negligent for him not to have done so, as a decision to delay rupturing the membrane, and to continue observation, was not consistent with a responsible body of medical opinion. Hence, this limb of the theorem succeeded for C too.

In *Wright v Cambridge Medical Group*,[159] Lord Neuberger MR justified *Bolitho's* causal theorem on two policy grounds. Limb #2 was essential, as it would be an 'affront to justice if D could escape liability by contending that, if he had not been negligent as alleged, the same damage would have occurred because he would have subsequently committed a different act of negligence'. Furthermore, wherever D commits a breach of duty by omission, D has deprived C of the opportunity of being treated appropriately. If C had been given that opportunity, he should have a claim for damage for the first breach – no matter what happens afterwards.

Extending the *Bolitho* causal theorem to 'out-of-house' scenarios

§8.20 As an extension of the original *Bolitho* causal theorem, C may establish a causal link by proving that, once D had hypothetically corrected his breach-by-omission, then *either:*

i. on the balance of probabilities, a third party (TP) would have done a further act, X, in order to prevent C's harm (although there was no legal duty on TP to do X); *or*
ii. neither D nor TP would have done further act X to prevent C's harm, and it would have been negligent of D and of TP not to have done X.

[157] See also, for mixed results, e.g.: *Holt v Edge* [2006] EWHC 1932 (QB) [57], [61], [75], aff'd: [2007] EWCA Civ 602; *Jones v South Tyneside HA* [2001] EWCA Civ 1701, [22]–[27]; *Zarb v Odetoyinbo* [2006] EWHC 2880, [17].
[158] [1998] Lloyd's Rep Med 223 (CA).
[159] [2011] EWCA Civ 669, [2013] QB 312, [57].

Notably, in *Bolitho*, all the factors making up the causal theorem – the original breach-by-omission, and then the hypothetical enquiry as to what D would, or should, have done if that breach had been fixed – were 'in-house'. However, in *Gouldsmith v Mid Staffordshire General Hospitals NHS Trust*,[160] the *Bolitho* analysis was applied when the original omission was by D, a GP, for a failure-to-refer, and thereafter the court had to assess what *another* party – a surgeon in a specialist tertiary hospital – would have done, had the referral occurred. It was held, by majority, that the *Bolitho* causal theorem could nevertheless apply.

In *Gouldsmith v Mid Staffordshire*, Irene Gouldsmith, C, entered hospital with blood circulation and ulceration problems. She was treated with anti-coagulation drugs. C claimed that her treating physician, D, failed to refer her to a specialist tertiary hospital, when problems with her left hand were encountered; and that had she been referred, some more radical treatment than anti-coagulation would have been considered urgent and necessary while the limb was still viable; that a vascular specialist surgeon would have operated on a lesion on her left subclavian artery; and that her left hand thumb and fingers would have been saved (ultimately, they were all amputated). **Held (trial):** causation failed. **Held (CA, 2:1):** causation proven, and the case was remitted back to trial for an assessment of damages. Applying the *Bolitho* exception:

- limb #1: if D had hypothetically fixed the omission (i.e., referred C on to a specialist tertiary hospital), another surgeon would have done a further act X (i.e., performed surgery) – a medical expert from the tertiary hospital gave evidence that, had C been referred, a digit-saving operation would have been conducted. Hence, this first avenue of proving causation succeeded for C;
- limb #2: did not arise, given that limb 1 was answered in C's favour.

Of the majority, Wilson LJ held that there was 'no relevant difference' between the *Gouldsmith* and *Bolitho* situations, and Pill LJ was also content to adopt *Bolitho* as the correct approach.[161]

However, potential problems in extending the *Bolitho* theorem in this way were noted by the dissenter, Sir Maurice Kay:

> factual circumstances involving hypothetical reference elsewhere put different obstacles in the way of [C], when compared with the entirely 'in-house' circumstances of *Bolitho* ... It seems to me that it was such difficulty that led Lord Hoffmann in *Gregg v Scott* to opine that, where it is the hypothetical response of a *non-party*, rather than the act of [C], [D], or someone for whom [D] is responsible, that is in issue, the question should be approached on the basis of loss of a chance rather than proof on a balance of probability. However, that is a road down which neither counsel in the present appeal, and neither of the other members of the court, wish to travel on this occasion.[162]

A similar third-party '*Gouldsmith*-type' could have arisen in the *Creutzfeldt-Jakob Disease Litigation*, which was decided around the same time as the *Bolitho* case – but the *Bolitho* theorem was not referred to:

In *CJD Groups A and C v Sec of State for Health*,[163] the patients, C, received human growth hormone (HGH) treatment, and their treating doctors (endocrinological paediatric clinicians) were not informed of the remote risks of Creutzfeldt-Jakob Disease (CJD) arising out of the injections of HGH.

[160] [2007] EWCA Civ 397. [161] Respectively, *ibid*, [53]–[60] and [26], [37].
[162] *ibid*, [49]–[50]. [163] (1998) 54 BMLR 104 (QB) 110.

It was the Dept of Health which committed the breach, by failing to send out letters to the treating doctors, informing them of the risk. **Held:** causation proven. As part of the causal chain, C had to prove, on the balance of probabilities, that their treatment would have been stopped by their treating doctors, had the doctors been properly informed by the Dept. The court held that, because '[t]he endocrinological paediatric clinicians being so small in number and a close-knit group, ... peer pressure would have been such that no clinician would have stood out alone and continued treatment'.

Hence, it was a *Gouldsmith*-type scenario, although *Bolitho* was not referred to. Further causal difficulties, to which a robust 'statistical approach' was adopted (discussed previously in the chapter[164]), were also resolved in C's favour.

EXCEPTION #4: THE *CHESTER v AFSHAR* CAUSAL THEOREM IN 'FAILURE-TO-WARN' CASES

The causation principle in *Chester v Afshar*[165] arises exclusively in failure-to-warn medico-legal jurisprudence – where patient C concedes that, had a warning of material risks been given prior to a medical procedure or treatment as required by law (discussed in Chapter 3), C would have proceeded with the procedure or treatment in any event. Exceptionally, however, the failure-to-warn can be causally responsible for C's harm when the risk manifests, under a principle which the majority called, in *Chester v Afshar*, a 'narrow modification' to the 'but-for' test. Subsequently, the case has been widely considered to be an example of where English courts departed from conventional causation 'for policy reasons', to permit C to recover damages.

However, for the most part, causation in failure-to-warn cases follows the general 'but-for' test, which will be considered first in this section.

The general rule

§8.21 As a general rule, the 'but-for' test applies to the failure-to-warn scenario – would C's damage (caused by the manifestation of a material inherent risk) have occurred, but for D's failure-to-warn of that risk? If the harm which befell C would not have happened, because C would have declined the treatment, causation is proven. If the harm would have happened anyway, because even armed with information about material risk, C would have proceeded with the treatment, causation fails. The better view is that determining what C would have done is assessed, in English law, according to a 'hybrid objective/subjective' test (i.e., by reference to what a reasonable person in that patient's position, and with his particular hopes and concerns, would have chosen to do, had the warning about material risks been properly given by D).

Different approaches

A central debate in failure-to-warn scenarios is whether the causal link should be assessed *subjectively* (by seeking evidence from *that particular patient* as to what he would have chosen to do); *objectively* (by reference to what a reasonable patient would have done); or by a *hybrid* objective/subjective analysis (according to the principle above).

There have been judicial indications in English law that the test certainly has a subjective component. In *Chatterton v Gerson*, it was said that patient C 'must prove ... that, had the duty not been broken, she would not have chosen to have the operation'.[166] In *Smith v Barking*,

164 See pp 416–18. 165 [2005] 1 AC 134 (HL). 166 [1981] QB 432, 442.

Havering & Brentwood HA too, the court said that, '[b]oth counsel invited me to accept that, in the end, the matter must be one for decision on a subjective basis. As a matter of principle, this must plainly be right, because the question must be: if this plaintiff had been given the advice that she would have been given, would she have decided to undergo the operation or not?'.[167]

However, a purely subjective test has two considerable difficulties:[168]

- having suffered harm from the medical treatment, the patient invariably will say that, in hindsight, he would not have had the treatment. Such a response is understandable, but not necessarily credible: '[t]hat is not to impugn [C's] honesty as a witness. It is simply that ... in the light of the terrible results of his operation, hindsight is almost bound to rule' (per *Smith v Salford HA*[169]); and 'one would need almost to be a saint to answer such questions objectively – i.e., without allowing one's reaction to be influenced by the knowledge of what had, in fact, happened and appreciation of the vital significance of the question' (per *Smith v Barking, Havering and Brentwood HA*[170]). Indeed, even commencing proceedings against doctor D surely indicates C's subjective belief that he would not have proceeded with the treatment if due warning had been given (a point made by the Supreme Court of Canada in *Reibl v Hughes*[171]).
- moreover, C's credibility – in seeking to convince the court that he would not have had the operation – is all-important under a purely subjective test. Any adverse findings which the trial judge makes about C's credibility may influence the finding on causation, and be difficult to reconsider on appeal (a point explicitly made in the Australian case of *Percival v Rosenberg*[172]).

A purely objective test in failure-to-warn litigation is not without problems either. As the Ipp Committee pointed out,[173] when reviewing Australian negligence law, an objective test could ignore what that particular patient would have done; it may not sit well with a patient for whom certain risks are subjectively-significant and who is not necessarily acting rationally; and the test answers, 'what should have happened' rather than 'what would have happened', had the warning been given.

According to English case law, however, it is plain that a hybrid test is favoured. Most recently, in *Montgomery v Lanarkshire Health Board*,[174] the Supreme Court referred to the prospect of the patient's evidence being affected by hindsight, but referred to other evidence by which to assess whether that patient would have proceeded with a vaginal birth (and concluded that she would not have done so, but would have opted for a caesarean section). In other words, a patient's answers have been judicially tempered and tested against a consideration of various objective factors as to what a reasonable person in that patient's position would have done.

Relevant factors under the hybrid test

The following factors have figured as relevant, in failure-to-warn causation.[175] However, none of them is conclusive, and more than one may have to be balanced in the scales, before coming to a conclusion on the crucial question: would the patient have proceeded anyway?

[167] QB, 29 Jul 1989.

[168] Both noted, e.g., in: *Review of the Law of Negligence: Final Report* (Sep 2002) ('*Ipp Report*') [7.40].

[169] (1994) 23 BMLR 137 (QB) 149. [170] [1994] Med LR 285 (QB) 289 (Hutchinson J). [171] [1980] 2 SCR 880, 898.

[172] (WAFC, 25 May 1999) 3, 19. [173] *Ipp Report*, [7.38]. [174] [2015] UKSC 11, [104].

[175] See, for these factors in an Australian context, R Mulheron, 'Observations upon Causation in Recent "Failure to Warn" Cases' (2000) *National Law Rev* 2. Further factors mentioned therein, but which have no illustrative counterpart in English law to date, include: whether patient C nominated the form of treatment, not the doctor D; whether C feared medical disease and strongly desired an investigative procedure; whether C had an immutable image of the procedure's outcome; and whether C was unwilling to undergo any other alternative procedures to address the medical problem.

i. **Was the procedure advisable or necessary for medical or therapeutic reasons?** If patient C was in such chronic pain or suffering that an operation or some treatment was needed from a therapeutic point of view, then that indicates that, no matter whether or not D gave the risks information, C would have persisted with it.

In *Chatterton v Gerson*,[176] surgeon D performed an operation on patient C to block the sensory nerve between a painful post-operative scar in the right groin and her brain, in order to relieve pain. C alleged that D failed to warn her that permanent numbness to her right leg could result. C gave evidence that she would have chosen not to have the procedure, and that she was learning to put up with her condition. **Held:** no breach proven; and causation failed too: '[t]he whole picture ... is of a lady desperate for pain relief'. In *Hills v Potter*,[177] patient C underwent an operation at the Radcliffe Infirmary, Oxford, to alleviate spasmodic torticollis, a deformity of the neck. From the operation, C was paralysed from the neck down. **Held:** no breach proven; and causation failed too: 'having regard to the evidence as to the gravity of her condition, I think it is more likely than not that she would have agreed to go ahead with the operation, notwithstanding'.

ii. **Did the patient have prior positive experiences of medical treatment which pointed in favour of the treatment?** If patient C had tried the operation or treatment previously, with no adverse consequences, then that can be one factor suggesting that the patient would have proceeded with the treatment. Similarly, if C's previous experiences with alternative treatments/procedures were unhappy ones, that may indicate that C would have been prepared to have the new treatment in any event, even if the risks had been duly warned about.

In *Chatterton v Gerson*, facts previously, patient, C, had undergone the blocking operation on a previous occasion, and whilst not successful, it did not produce the level of numbness in the right leg that C suffered the second time around. **Held:** causation failed. In *Sem v Mid Yorkshire Hosp NHS Trust*,[178] Miss Fishwick, C, underwent a hysterectomy and other gynaelogical procedures. They were not successful, and left C an invalid, largely confined to her room and her bed. C alleged that, had she been warned of the risks, she would have undertaken less interventionist methods, such as pelvic floor exercises, physiotherapy, change of diet and a bladder drill programme. **Held:** causation failed. Non-surgical procedures had been tried previously for C, to alleviate her symptoms, but none proved satisfactory. It was likely that, even if offered warning of the surgical treatment actually undertaken, C would still have elected it. Also, C had been prepared, in the past, to undertake repeated investigations and surgical procedures, even when given very full warnings about the risks involved, e.g., when given the choice between a laparoscopy and a laparotomy, C decided to undergo the more invasive procedure. All of this indicated that C would have proceeded in any event.

However, even C's prior bad experiences with a procedure may not clinch causation in C's favour, where warnings were not given. The court may still consider that C would have proceeded, regardless.

In *Jones v North West Strategic HA*,[179] Jack Jones, C, suffered from cerebral palsy and brain impairment, because of oxygen starvation for about 15 minutes during his natural birth. His shoulder was lodged behind his mother's pelvic bone, in a condition of shoulder dystocia (an obstetric emergency). Babies can tolerate asphyxia for about 7–8 minutes without permanent damage, but after 9–10 minutes, some brain damage is likely. C alleged that his mother should have been

[176] [1981] QB 432, 445. [177] [1984] 1 WLR 641 (QB) 653.
[178] [2005] EWHC 3469 (QB). [179] [2010] EWHC 178 (QB).

advised, as part of her antenatal care, of the risk of shoulder dystocia, and told of the possibility of having a caesarean section as an alternative to natural birth. If C's mother had been warned of that risk, she would have opted for a caesarean, and Jack would have been born without damage. During the birth of Jack's elder sister, Rebecca, there was some slight shoulder dystocia, and C's mother said that she found that to be very dramatic, scary and traumatic. She claimed that she did not want that repeated, and would have opted for a caesarean. D's evidence was that a natural birth was far preferable for Mrs Jones and C. **Held:** causation failed. The evidence given by Mrs Jones was important, but other objective factors (below) suggested that she would have proceeded with natural birth in any event.

iii. Was the patient strongly motivated either to undergo, or forego, the treatment because of employment or family reasons? If patient C desperately needed the surgery to be profitably employed in his chosen field of work, then that may be a factor precluding a causal link, because C would have proceeded with the surgery, even if the risks information had been given.

In *McAllister v Lewisham and North Southwark HA*,[180] Ms McAllister, C, had brain surgery to rectify a neurological defect in her left leg. C was warned of the risk that the surgery could make her leg worse, but not of the risk of haemiplegia which, in fact, manifested. **Held:** causation proven. Rougier J was satisfied that C would not have had the operation, had the risk of haemiplegia been disclosed, because she would have wished to first seek security in her job, and could not afford any lengthy period of sick leave. In *Smith v Salford HA*,[181] Mr Smith, C, had been off work as a window cleaner for several months, with a back complaint. C claimed that he was not warned of the risks of damage to the spinal cord during surgery to fix a congenital spinal fusion. **Held:** causation failed. The court was satisfied that C would have proceeded with the operation, even if the warning had been given, given his need to return to work. (However, C succeeded in negligence on the separate ground of failure to treat with adequate care by the use of an inappropriate instrument.)

Furthermore, if the well-being and/or health of C's spouse or family was uppermost in C's mind in wishing to proceed with the operation, then that is a factor that will likely disprove causation.

In *Winston v O'Leary*[182] (an Irish case), John Winston, C, underwent a vasectomy operation after the birth of his 7th child. His wife had recently given birth to their youngest child. The couple managed a family-run news agency which was stressful and time-consuming, and a full-time undertaking. The birth of the couple's 2nd-last child had been difficult, and hence, the Winstons considered their family was complete. Unfortunately, the vasectomy left C with very considerable long-term pain and disability. He alleged that his surgeon, C, did not warn of him the risk of long-term pain. **Held:** causation failed. C's evidence was that the procedure was simple, he was 'anxious' to undergo it, and his wife's continued ill-health was an issue uppermost in his mind. Furthermore, there was nothing to indicate that C was unusually cautious, or the kind of patient who would have backed away at the mention of a remote risk.

iv. Was the patient strongly motivated by personal reasons? Patient C's psychiatric condition or religious convictions may point in favour of proceeding with, or alternatively declining, the treatment. Psychiatric evidence can prove crucial in this regard.

[180] [1994] 5 Med LR 343 (QB). [181] (1994) 23 BMLR 137 (QB). [182] [2006] IEHC 440 (MacMenamin J).

In *Sem v Mid Yorkshire Hosp NHS Trust*,[183] facts previously, **held:** causation failed. A joint psychiatric report indicated that C 'would have been highly dissatisfied with any treatment intervention other than surgery, on the basis that individuals with the tendencies towards illness behaviour exhibited by [C] tend to seek out more dramatic interventions rather than more conservative ones. Given that her symptoms were at least partly psychogenic in origin, conservative intervention was most unlikely to mollify them in any way. Thus, if the surgery had not taken place in July, it would have occurred a few month[s] later, after a more prolonged period of continuing complaint [by C]'. In *Jones v North West Strategic HA*,[184] facts previously, **held:** causation failed. Mrs Jones had an antipathy to blood transfusions, as she was brought up as a Jehovah's Witness. She also had a medically-acknowledged phobia of blood transfusions. It was not accepted that C's mother would have still been willing to have a caesarean, with its added risk of bleeding, and the possible need for a transfusion.

v. Did comparative treatments or procedures objectively carry far less risk? If the procedure which C underwent carried a risk about which C was properly warned – but another procedure carried a much-lower-to-nil risk, and C was not informed about that at all, then that objective risk is relevant when determining whether C would have undergone the higher-risk treatment anyway.

In *Montgomery v Lanarkshire Health Board*,[185] Mrs Montgomery, C, was concerned about the prospect of a natural birth, given her small size, and because she had been advised that it was a large baby (this was common for diabetic mothers, such as C). C was not advised of the risk of shoulder dystocia with a large baby, and that an elective caesarean would reduce the risk of injury to her and to the baby to almost nil. **Held:** had C been duly advised of the risk of shoulder dystocia and of the alternative, C would probably have elected to have her baby by caesarean section, in which case the baby would have been born unharmed. In *Birch v UCL Hosp NHS Foundation Trust*,[186] Mrs Birch, C, underwent an angiogram to exclude the possibility of an artery aneurysm. This required that a catheter be inserted from the groin to the brain. C was properly warned that undergoing the procedure of cerebral angiogram carried with it a 1% risk of a stroke. This risk materialised. However, C was not told that an MRI scan was an alternative diagnostic procedure which, although not as good a diagnostic procedure as the cerebral angiogram, carried no risk of stroke at all. **Held:** failure-to-warn of the comparative risks amounted to a breach. Further, causation was proven, because if C had been properly informed, she would not have consented to the angiogram. C's evidence was that she would have chosen the MRI scan, and objective factors supported this – she had had poorly-controlled diabetes for many years, and had previous ischaemic lesions in the immediate past which had resolved spontaneously without the need for risk-carrying tests. All this would have persuaded C to adopt the low-risk alternative which could not lead to a stroke.

vi. The patient trusted his medical advisers, and was strongly influenced by their recommendations. If patient C was accustomed to trusting the advice of his medical advisers, then the inference may be drawn that he was likely to proceed with the recommended operation (about which proper risk warnings were not given), thus precluding a causal link – as occurred in both of the following cases:

[183] [2005] EWHC 3469 (QB), quote at [55]. [184] [2010] EWHC 178 (QB).
[185] [2015] UKSC 11, [104]. [186] [2008] EWHC 2237, [81].

In *Chatterton v Gerson*,[187] facts previously, a respected neurosurgeon who was also treating patient C recommended that she give the procedure another try, which advice she trusted. In *Jones v North West Strategic HA*,[188] facts previously, C's doctor recommended that a natural birth was the safest course for her and for her baby Jack. During evidence, C said that she 'put her trust in the doctor'. That put C 'in the mainstream of patients in 1992, rather than in the category of the unusual patient who would take a course contrary to the doctor's advice (at least where it did not conflict with her attitude to transfusions).'

This factor tends to be cited by judges, where other factors also point against a causal link, so as to emphasise that C would have had the operation anyway. For example, in *Sem v Mid Yorkshire Hosp NHS Trust*,[189] the court made the broad generalisation that C 'acting as a reasonable patient ... would have been likely to follow the surgeon's advice. Patients do normally follow the advice of a consultant, and I cannot see in this case any factors which lead me to suppose that [C] would have done otherwise'.

The factor is very 'light-weight', however, because even if the patient shows some tendency to follow the 'doctor knows best' philosophy, other factors may nevertheless show that C would have decided against the treatment/operation, thus proving causation.

In *Birch v UCL Hosp NHS Foundation Trust*,[190] facts previously, **held:** causation proven. Cranston J was not satisfied that Mrs Birch, C, would have agreed to a catheter angiogram, had that been explained to her as being a necessary tool by which to eliminate an aneurysm – even though she took the view of 'doctor knows best' – given her history of poor health, and previous positive experience with low-risk tests.

The *Chester v Afshar* exception

The principle and reasoning

§8.22 Under the *Chester v Afshar* theorem, causation is established where patient C proves that, whilst he would or might have needed to proceed with the operation/treatment (for therapeutic or other reasons), he would have deferred that operation/treatment until a later occasion, had D provided proper warning of material risks. However, since it was delivered, *Chester* has been narrowly construed and infrequently applied.

The controversial decision of *Chester v Afshar*[191] provides an avenue in which a patient, C, may concede that, had the risks information been given, he still would or might have needed an operation or treatment – which supposedly should preclude a causal link – but C would have chosen to have the operation at a later time, at another venue, and with another doctor.

In *Chester v Afshar*, Dr Afshar, D, failed to warn Miss Chester, C, of a 1–2% risk of serious neurological damage resulting from a lumbar surgical procedure. C had suffered episodes of lower back pain for six years, and towards the end of that period, she could 'hardly walk' for the pain. The operation was undertaken, and C developed cauda equina syndrome. The operation was performed carefully and competently, but it was common ground at the trial that the risk ought to have been

[187] [1981] QB 432, 445. [188] [2010] EWHC 178 (QB), quote at [66].
[189] [2005] EWHC 3469 (QB) [54]. [190] [2008] EWHC 2237 (QB). [191] [2004] UKHL 41, [2005] 1 AC 134.

disclosed.[192] The appeal turned on the issue of causation. The surgery was elective. C argued that, had she been informed of the small risk of cauda equina syndrome, she would have sought advice on alternative treatments, surgeons and risks, and the operation would not have occurred when it did. C accepted that it was likely that she would have required the procedure at some future stage because of the pain that she had long endured, and that, at any later time, the same small risk of cauda equina syndrome would have been present. **Held:** causation proven.

If C would have undergone the operation in any event, even if the warning of cauda equina syndrome had been given, then the 'but-for' test of causation should have failed. However, according to the House of Lords' majority, justice required a 'narrow and modest' modification of the traditional 'but-for' test.[193] Notably, the two most senior Law Lords strongly dissented, and rejected that any exception to the 'but-for' test should have been created in this scenario. Contrasting the judicial points of view:[194]

The disparate points of view in *Chester v Afshar*

The majority (Lords Steyn, Walker and Hope) – to find causation would ...	The dissenters (Lords Bingham and Hoffmann) – no causal link should have been found, because ...
• vindicate the right of patient C to make an informed choice as to whether, and if so when and by whom, to be operated on – it can be a more complex decision than simply whether or not to undergo the operation. To find against C would be to 'strip [the duty to warn] of all practical force and devoid of all content. It will have lost its ability to protect the patient' (Lord Hope); • reiterate the importance which the medical profession itself places upon risks disclosure (Lord Hope); • reward the honest patient who cannot say that he would have declined the operation, if he had been warned (Lord Hope);	• the fact that patient C would have needed the operation at some point in the future meant that the 'but-for' test of causation was not met; • the fact that C would have had the operation at a different date/time from when she did have it is irrelevant, because changing the timing of the operation was 'irrelevant to the injury she suffered ... [t]hat injury would have been as liable to occur, whenever the surgery was performed and whoever performed it' (Lord Bingham), and 'the risk could have been precisely the same, if she had had it at another time or by another surgeon' (Lord Hoffmann); • to allow C to succeed would be as logical as telling C that the odds on No 7 coming up on the roulette wheel are 1 in 37 on Monday, so C goes away and comes back on Tuesday. 'The question is whether one would have taken the opportunity to avoid or reduce the risk, not whether one would have changed the scenario in some irrelevant detail ... the risk [to C] would have been precisely the same, whether it was done then or later, or by that competent surgeon or by another' (Lord Hoffmann);

[192] Noted in: *Chester v Afshar* [2002] EWCA Civ 724, [15].

[193] [2004] UKHL 41, [24] (Lord Steyn).

[194] The quotes in the Table are locatable at: [87] (Lord Hope), [8]–[9] (Lord Bingham), [31] (Lord Hoffmann), [94] (Lord Walker).

The majority (Lords Steyn, Walker and Hope) – to find causation would ...	The dissenters (Lords Bingham and Hoffmann) – no causal link should have been found, because ...
• be fair, because the injury suffered by C was not some coincidental injury (such as an interruption in anaesthesia) which occurred in the operation, but was the precise injury that D should have warned C against (Lord Walker); • reflect the reasonable expectations of the public in contemporary society, in reinforcing patient autonomy and control in their own decision-making (all majority Lords).	• if a failure-to-warn of a breach + the occurrence of the very injury which should have been warned about are enough to prove negligence, then other claims where C probably would have consented to the operation even if properly advised (because C was in pain, or it was required for therapeutic reasons) should succeed too (Lord Bingham); • the law did not have to reinforce the duty to warn, which 'few doctors in the current legal and social climate would consciously or deliberately violate', by requiring the payment of 'potentially very large damages' by D (or his insurer) (Lord Bingham); • there was no justification for creating a special causation rule for doctors – doctors should not be made insurers, especially where the operation was carefully and competently performed (Lord Hoffmann).

The limitations of *Chester v Afshar*

The causal theorem in *Chester v Afshar* has not been much applied in English law, so far as can be ascertained – which is an odd outcome, given the amount of ink which has been devoted to it.

Indeed, in *Chester* itself,[195] Lord Hope remarked that the modification was required 'in the unusual circumstances of this case', suggesting that the approach was not intended to have a general or wide application. Later cases have noted *Chester's* 'policy' nature – that it, e.g., was 'a policy decision with no application to cases like this' (per *Clough v First Choice Holidays and Flights Ltd*[196]); was an unusual decision where, 'for policy reasons, the courts have departed from conventional causation principles' (per *Reynard v Exquisite Cuisine Ltd*[197]); and 'depended peculiarly on the facts of that case' (per *Stephen v Peter*[198]). In *Wright v Cambridge Medical Group*,[199] Elias J remarked that this causal exception was due to the fact that there was a duty to warn, a breach of it and an infringement of C's personal autonomy – it was certainly not because surgeon D had increased the risk of an adverse outcome in the operation: '[t]he basis of liability was that the obligation to warn was an important protection of patient autonomy which should not be undermined, even if it is clear that the patient would have taken the risk of having the operation in any event ... It was quite arbitrary when that risk would materialise; the risk was the same whenever the operation occurred. The majority only imposed liability in order to give an effective remedy for breach of the right to warn'.

To emphasise *Chester v Afshar's* limitations/non-applications, as evident from case law since:

[195] *ibid*, [85]. [196] [2006] EWCA Civ 15, [42]. [197] [2005] CSOH 146, [51].
[198] [2005] CSOH 38, [26]. [199] [2011] EWCA Civ 669, [107].

i. Where C is clear: he would have opted for a different course of conduct. C's position may be that he would have proceeded with treatment #2, had the material risks associated with treatment #1 been provided. If this scenario applies, then the causal theorem in *Chester v Afshar* does not apply. The narrow facts of *Chester v Afshar* were that C was not informed of the material risks for treatment #1, and then proceeded with treatment #1 in an uninformed way. If C argues that, had he been warned about treatment #1, he would have undergone another form of medical treatment altogether, which did not carry the same risk at all, then that is a straightforward application of the 'but-for' test. The ratio of *Chester v Afshar* does not apply in that type of case. Two remarkably similar, and tragic, cases, from Scotland and England, illustrate the point:

In *Khalid v Barnet & Chase Farm Hosp NHS Trust*,[200] Fahima Khalid, C, was born with severe brain damage as a result of oxygen starvation (hypoxia) during labour. Had C been born by caesarean section 20 minutes earlier, she would not have sustained any damage. The labour involved a 'trial of scar' or 'trial of labour', because C's mother had a scar in her uterus from the caesarean birth of her first child. This scar carried a known, but small (about 2%), risk of rupture during the subsequent labour. C's mother had 'plainly set her heart on a normal delivery for her second child'. According to the evidence, in 30% of trial of scar pregnancies, natural delivery is abandoned in favour of a caesarean, as such pregnancies are high risk. C alleged that her parents should have been told of the risk of rupture if proceeding with a natural birth, and of the caesarean alternative. **Held:** causation succeeded. *Chester v Afshar* was raised in argument, but discounted as being 'irrelevant'. A natural labour undoubtedly led directly to the delay in C's delivery, whereas terminating the labour would have led to an earlier caesarean. Causation was proven on 'but-for' principles, and '[t]he problem that arose in *Chester* does not arise'. In *Montgomery v Lanarkshire Health Board*,[201] facts previously, the Scottish Inner House noted that *Chester v Afshar* did not apply: 'the situation in which the majority in *Chester v Afshar* considered that liability should exist was one where (1) a warning of risk would have resulted in the patient seeking further advice elsewhere, and (2) with resultant uncertainty as to whether the patient would have undergone at a future date *an identical procedure in which the same risk might or might not have materialised*'.

ii. Where no credible evidence is given by C. As noted in *REM v Mid Yorkshire Hosp NHS Trust*,[202] the *Chester v Afshar* causation exception will only arise where C gives credible evidence, accepted by the court, that if the warning had been given, C would not have had surgery then, but would or might have had surgery at some later time. It is only then that C 'could possibly rely on the loosening of the conventional approach to the problem of causation which underpinned the decision in *Chester v Afshar*.' In that case, the court was satisfied that if C had been warned of the risk, C 'would have elected for precisely the surgery which was, in fact, performed some weeks later' – thus rendering *Chester* inapplicable on the facts.

More recently, in *Meiklejohn v St George's Healthcare NHS Trust*,[203] Robinson J reiterated that, even if it is argued, along *Chester* lines, that C would have postponed the treatment or operation to another occasion when the risk probably would not have developed, if 'there is simply no evidence in support of such a proposition', then the argument cannot possibly succeed. On appeal,[204] the Court of Appeal confirmed that *Chester's* theorem, 'based on narrow facts far from analogous to those we are considering', did not apply, because C trusted his medical adviser and would have accepted her advice.

[200] [2007] EWHC 644 (QB) [3], [68].

[201] [2013] CSIH 3, [51] (emphasis added). The Supreme Court similarly disapplied *Chester's* theorem: [2015] UKSC 11, [105].

[202] [2005] EWHC B3 (QB) [37]. [203] [2013] EWHC 469 (QB) [163]. [204] [2014] EWCA Civ 120, [34]–[36].

iii. Limited to medical negligence. In *Beary v Pall Mall Investments (a firm)*,[205] the Court of Appeal indicated that *Chester v Afshar* should not extend beyond the realms of medical failure-to-warn, to claims for negligent financial advice.

Several reasons were given for this: (1) the *Chester* majority clearly provided that this narrow modification of 'but-for' causation was exceptional; (2) it was justified by the particular policy considerations that applied to a breach of the doctor's duty to advise a patient of the disadvantages and dangers of proposed treatment – but the policy considerations applicable to the duty to give proper financial advice 'are quite different'; and (3) to extend *Chester* to all cases of negligent financial advice was 'breathtakingly ambitious, contrary to authority and ... wrong.' The view had been expressed earlier, in *White v Paul Davidson & Taylor*,[206] that the principle in *Chester v Afshar* did not apply to legal negligence either – the 'special importance' of fully disclosing material risks to patients was the policy reason underpinning *Chester* (said Lady Justice Arden), but that was not translatable to the context of professional negligence generally.

Hence, in combination, these factors demonstrate why *Chester v Afshar's* causal theorem has had a very limited application, since it was handed down. It was stated to be an 'exceptional case', and case law in the decade since confirms that.

Notably, in *Chester v Afhsar*, there were several references to the similar Australian decision of *Chappel v Hart* – which coincidentally achieved a positive result for C, and also by a bare majority.

The comparative corner: An Australian vignette

In *Chappel v Hart*,[207] Mrs Hart, C, was a principal education officer, and a singing teacher. Due to ongoing throat infections, she was advised that the best treatment would be the removal of the pharyngeal pouch in the oesophagus. There was a risk of a loss of function of C's vocal cords, but it was so remote that it was 'not even mentioned in some clinical textbooks'. The surgery was elective, although the evidence was that C would have had to have surgery sooner or later. During the procedure, C's oesophagus was perforated, an infection called mediastinitis followed, which damaged C's laryngeal nerve, and led to paralysis of her right vocal cord. C's surgeon, Dr Chappel, D, an ENT specialist, advised C of the risk of perforation, but not of the risk of loss of her voice. C had to retire from her employment, following paralysis of her vocal cord. The risk of voice loss was material for C's employment, and should have been disclosed. **Held (3:2):** causation proven, even though C probably would have required the operation in the future in any event. To find causation was 'conducive to better health care' (Kirby J).

INTERVENING ACTS IN THE CAUSAL CHAIN

Even where the 'but-for' test is satisfied, the requisite causal link may still fail. The law imposes a number of 'exclusionary devices', which circumscribe D's liability where his acts or omissions are considered too 'remote' in law. The doctrine of intervening acts (or *novus actus interveniens*[208]) is one such legal device.

[205] [2005] EWCA Civ 415, [38]. [206] [2003] EWCA Civ 1511, [40]–[42].

[207] [1998] HCA 55, 195 CLR 232 (Gaudron, Gummow and Kirby JJ; with McHugh and Hayne JJ dissenting).

[208] Latin for 'a new intervening act': E Martin and J Law, *Oxford Dictionary of Law* (6th edn, Oxford University Press, 2006) 361.

These occur where D1 is the party who commits a breach; but the most direct agent of C's harm is something other than D1's conduct – something that constitutes a separate and independent cause of C's injury, intervening between D1's breach and C's damage. The intervening act is connected factually with D1's breach, however, in that the breach created the opportunity for that 'something else' to occur (i.e., the intervening act would not have occurred, had the breach not occurred) – if there is no factual connection between D1's breach and the intervening act, then that act is truly a supervening event (another legal conundrum which is dealt with in a later section of this chapter[209]).

Whilst most judges seem to consider that intervening acts are best dealt with as an issue of causation, others have favoured the view that the topic fits better within remoteness of damage. In *Chubb Fire Ltd v Vicar of Spalding*,[210] the Court of Appeal considered that it was a distinction without importance – and that it is a doctrine used to determine whether a wrongdoing D 'will be responsible for certain consequences of that negligence and the damages that are claimed to flow from those consequences'.

The characteristics of an intervening act

§8.23 Where D1 has committed a breach of duty against C, an intervening act can be due to any of the following: (1) unreasonable or deliberate behaviour of D2, which occurs after D1's breach; (2) criminal or negligent conduct committed by either an identified or an unknown third party (TP); (3) conduct on TP's part which was neither negligent nor criminal; (4) careless conduct by C himself, which exacerbates or brings about his own injury; or (5) some naturally-occurring event. An intervening act will only be upheld where it would be fair and just to relieve D1 of all liability for C's damage, because D1's breach lost its causative potency in light of the 'new cause'. Whilst it will assist proof of an intervening act if the act was (1) unreasonable, (2) reckless, (3) deliberate, or (4) unforeseeable, none of these is a pre-requisite for proving an intervening act.

The principle underlying the law's willingness to recognise intervening acts is one of fairness, as Lord Bingham made plain in *Corr v IBC Vehicles Ltd*: '[i]t is not fair to hold [D] liable, however gross his breach of duty may be, for damage caused to [C] not by [D's] breach of duty but by some independent, supervening cause (which may or may not be tortious) for which [D] is not responsible'.[211] Hence, a value judgment inevitably enters an assessment of what constitutes a break in the causal chain. Essentially, it comes down to the question: what **should** D be liable for, damages-wise? Whether the intervening act has the effect of relieving D1 from liability for his earlier negligent conduct 'depends on whether it is just that this should be so ... considerations of policy loom large in the analysis ... although they are generally concealed beneath the legal concepts used to justify the result' (per *Wright v Cambridge Medical Group*[212]). This infusion of policy can make the operation of the doctrine of intervening acts difficult to predict with any confidence.

As the aforementioned principle shows, an intervening act can be any one of several possibilities – C's own conduct, D2's later act, the act of an entirely unknown TP, or a natural event. However, defining the essential characteristics of that *novus actus interveniens* may well be a fruitless exercise. Judges have rarely agreed on them: indeed, in *Horton v Evans*,[213] Keith J remarked that, '[t]he guiding principle is that there is no guiding principle'.

[209] See pp 477–83. [210] [2010] EWCA Civ 981, [63] (Aikens LJ).
[211] [2008] UKHL 13, [2008] 1 AC 884, [15]. [212] [2011] EWCA Civ 669, [2013] QB 312, [110].
[213] [2006] EWHC 2808 (QB) [53].

The characteristics noted in the abovementioned principle are derived from the judgment of Evans-Lombe J in *Barings plc v Coopers & Lybrand (a firm)*.[214] In fact, intervening acts have been judicially described in various terms: an act that was 'so unforeseeable as not to be something likely to flow from the original negligence [of D1]' (per *Knightley v Johns*[215]); 'a new cause which ... can be described as either unreasonable or extraneous or extrinsic' (per *The Oropesa*[216]); an act that was 'reckless ... shutting his eyes to the obvious risks that existed [for C]' (per *Wright v Lodge*[216a]); and 'an independent, supervening event' (per *Humber Oil Terminal Trustee Ltd v Sivand, Owners*[217]). Clearly, it will be a fact-sensitive enquiry, in which a range of conduct may constitute a 'new cause'.

There are two oft-repeated *common* elements emerging from the abovementioned judgments, however, as to what will constitute an intervening act. First, D1's breach must be so 'obliterated' or 'eclipsed' by the intervening act that it deprives D's breach of its causative potency. Secondly, it would not be fair or just to hold D1 responsible for C's damage.

The effect of an intervening act

§8.24 Where an intervening act occurs, D1's breach is not considered to have been legally responsible for C's damage, and D1 will avoid liability altogether, for any damage on, and from, the occurrence of that intervening act. It is a mixed question of fact and of law, as to whether an intervening act breaks the 'chain of causation' between D's breach and C's damage.

An intervening act is considered by law to be a new cause of C's injury. It severs the causal link between D's breach (negligent though it was) and C's harm. It is true that C's injury would not have occurred, but for D's negligence – but the intervening act severs the **legal** effect of D's breach. D's breach is no longer the legally operative cause of C's harm.

Hence, an intervening act represents an all-or-nothing outcome for C. Where an intervening act is found, then D1 'walks way' without incurring any liability in negligence at all. This is especially important, when the intervening party may be unidentified, or lacking any assets with which to satisfy a judgment. D1 may well have represented the only feasible option for C to recover compensation for his injury. For this reason – and similarly to the court's reluctance to find in favour of D1 on the 'all-or-nothing' defence of *volenti* (see Chapter 10) – intervening acts are a fairly rare creature in English negligence law.

The lack of judicial enthusiasm for the device of the *novus actus interveniens* is also due to two pieces of legislation.

First, where C's own conduct is alleged to have constituted an intervening act, the alternative is to hold that C carelessly contributed to his own injury and was contributorily negligent (pursuant to the Law Reform (Contributory Negligence) Act 1945). That statute entails apportionment, and not an all-or-nothing outcome (as per Chapter 10). It means that D1 is liable for some damages, notwithstanding C's careless conduct (e.g., in *Dalling v JR Heale & Co Ltd*,[218] there was no intervening act, but contributory negligence of 33% was assessed against C, for the damages relating to the incident to which C contributed).

Secondly, where D2's conduct is alleged to have broken the causal chain, the court may instead find that D1 and D2 both contributed to C's harm – which will invoke an apportionment between the defendants, pursuant to the Civil Liability (Contribution) Act 1978. Again, that outcome will prevent D1 from 'walking away' from any liability 'scot-free'.

[214] [2003] EWHC 1319 (Ch) [838]. [215] [1982] 1 WLR 349 (CA) 366. [216] [1943] 1 All ER 211 (CA) 215. [216a] [1993] PIQR P31 (CA) P37. [217] [1998] EWCA Civ 100 (Evans LJ). [218] [2011] EWCA Civ 365.

Where an intervening act occurred, then in some cases, D1 will not be liable for any damages whatsoever, as C suffered no harm prior to that point. However, in other cases, D1 will be liable for the immediate effects of D1's breach, but not for the damage caused by the intervening act. In other words, the intervening act stops the extent of the D1's liability for damages.

This principle of intervening acts involves a mixed question of fact and of law. This was confirmed in *Roberts v Bettany*, where Buxton LJ remarked that, although the doctrine of *novus actus interveniens* is 'sometimes talked of as, and presented as, simply a question of causation, which at first sight might appear to be an issue of fact, it is well recognised that the matter is more complex than that. The issue is one of law, whereby the court has to be satisfied that the acts of the third party were sufficient as a matter of law to exculpate [D1] from liability for the particular result, proximate or distant though it might have been, of his negligent act'.[219] Whether something constituted an intervening act will always involve *some* degree of value judgment, thus rendering it a policy question too, and divorcing it from a purely factual assessment (per Lord Nicholls in *Kuwait Airway Corp v Iraqi Airway Co (Nos 4 and 5)*[220]).

Particular contexts

Of the multitude of cases which have turned on the question of whether or not an intervening act was committed, it is useful to give some contrasting examples in different contexts. Diagrammatically, the various leading cases in this section are illustrated below:

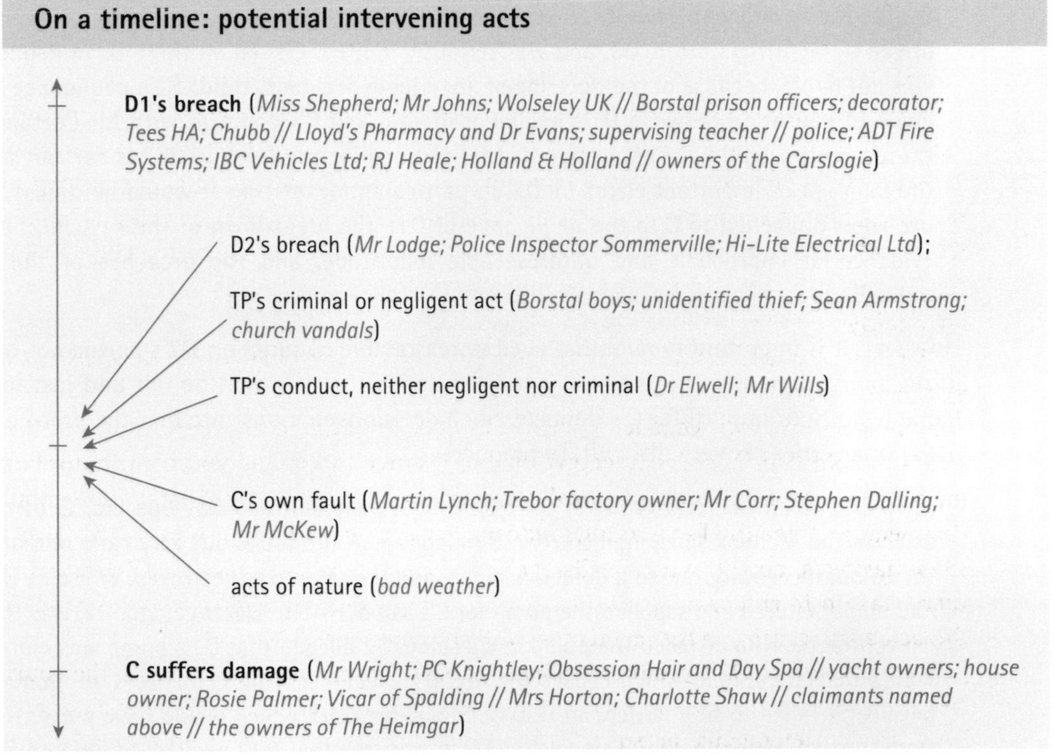

Dealing with each in turn:

[219] [2001] EWCA Civ 109, [12]. [220] [2002] UKHL 19, [2002] 2 AC 883, [70].

D2's acts or omissions

Reckless behaviour on D2's part, amounting to a disregard for the consequences of his conduct, may be sufficient to break the causal chain between D1's breach and C's harm. Alternatively, D2's conduct may have been unforeseeable, rather than reckless. That can also constitute an intervening act for which it would not be fair to hold D1 liable to C:

In *Wright v Lodge*,[221] Miss Shepherd, D1, was driving along a busy roadway when her Mini car petered out and came to a stop on the eastbound carriageway. Conditions were very foggy, with visibility down to 60 yards. D1 was negligent in not getting her passenger to help push the car off the carriageway onto the verge, which would have been an easy task. Mr Lodge, D2, was driving his articulated lorry at about 60 mph (in a 50 mph speed zone), and had to swerve and brake to avoid D1's Mini. His lorry overturned, and crossed over into the westbound carriageway, colliding with Mr Wright's, C's, vehicle. **Held:** D2's conduct amounted to a *novus actus interveniens* between D1's negligence and C's harm. D2 was driving recklessly, at a speed which was obviously unsafe for his vehicle and contrary to the law, and in thick fog. Although D2 would not have had to swerve and brake if D1's car had not been negligently left where it was, the accident was wholly attributable to D2's reckless driving. 'It was unwarranted and unreasonable', and D1's conduct was excluded as being causative of the accident. In *Knightley v Johns*,[222] due to his negligent driving, Mr Johns, D1, overturned his car at the end of a one-way tunnel in Birmingham. Police Inspector Sommerville, D2, was called to the scene, but forgot to close the tunnel in the chaos. He then instructed PC Knightley, C, and a colleague, to ride the wrong way down the tunnel to close it. In doing so, C was hit by an oncoming car driven by Geoffrey Cotton, D3, and was seriously injured. C sued all three Ds in negligence. D3 was not liable, because of the doctrine of 'inevitable accident'. **Held:** D2's negligence broke the chain of causation between D1's negligent driving and C's collision with Mr Cotton. None of these events would have happened, had D1 not negligently overturned his car, but thereafter, the long list of important errors by D2, in particular, meant that it would be unjust to attribute what happened to C to the negligence of D1: 'the breakdown of the system ... provid[ed] evidence of improbable and unforeseeable ineptitude, and the breaches of the standing orders'.

However, it is important to note that even unreasonable conduct on D2's part is not conclusive of an intervening act. The court may still determine that it would be fair and just to hold D1 liable (wholly or in part) for C's damage. Such decisions demonstrate that the proof of a *novus actus interveniens* is very difficult, in practice.

In *Hi-Lite Electrical Led v Wolseley UK Ltd*,[223] Obsession Hair and Day Spa Ltd, C, owned a hair salon in the Mailbox shopping centre in Birmingham. A fire broke out very early one morning, in the colour dispensary, due to a defective pump, and the salon was destroyed. Wolseley UK Ltd, D1, had manufactured and supplied the pump for C's salon. Hi-Lite Electrical Ltd, D2, was the electrical contractor who installed the pump in C's salon. D2 alleged that D1's pump was manufactured with an electrical fault which caused the fire. D1 alleged that D2 committed an intervening act, because it failed to fit a device, an RCD (a circuit-breaker), which would have prevented the fire from starting. **Held:** no intervening act by D2. It was true that D2's negligent failure to fit the RCD

[221] [1993] RTR 123 (CA) 129–30 (Parker LJ). [222] [1982] RTR 182 (CA) 189–90 (Stephenson LJ).
[223] [2011] EWHC 2153 (TCC) [182]–[208], [239] (Ramsey J).

failed to prevent the fire, and this was 'essentially unreasonable conduct'. However, the cause of the fire was the defective pump, and D2's failure to fit the RCD did not deprive D1's defective pump 'of its causative potency'.

Where D1 breached its duty of care to C in failing to take reasonable steps to prevent harm from occurring to C, D1 cannot argue that D2 failed to detect the same problem which D1's own breaches of duty failed to detect, and that D2's failure to fix the problem constituted a break in the causal chain. To find that D1 could escape liability in such a scenario would be unfair, and as a matter of 'simple and common sense', cannot be sustained (per *Carillion JM Ltd v Phi Group Ltd*[224]).

In *Carillion JM Ltd v Phi Group Ltd*, the Chiltern Railways train servicing depot near Wembley Football Stadium was designed and built in 2004–6, whilst the new stadium was being constructed. Carillion, C, was the contractor engaged to build the depot. Robert West Constructing, D1, was the engineering firm which undertook the soil excavations, and Phi Group, D2, was engaged to perform 'soil nailing work'. To create space for the depot, substantial excavations had to be made into the clay ground, leaving 70°–80° slopes each side. Those slopes became unstable in 2005, due to instability in the shear face and upper layers of the London Clay. Remedial work was done. However, later on, the deep-lying layers also became unstable. Apparently, London Clay is well-known for giving rise to different types of instability. C sued D1 for failing to redesign the works following the slip in 2005, which would have revealed the extent of the deep-lying instability that occurred later. D1 argued that C's reliance on D2, when the 2005 slippage happened, broke the chain of causation between D1's failure to redesign the works and the ultimate damage caused by the later slippages of the clay slopes. **Held:** D2 did not break the chain of causation. If D1 had acted carefully and competently *at the various stages of the project*, then the deep-seated instability would have been picked up and addressed. The causal chain was not broken, simply because D2, C or anyone else, might or should have realised the existence of the deep-lying instability.

The criminal or negligent acts of TP

A TP's criminal or negligent acts may conceivably break the chain of causation, where TP enters the scenario unheralded, neither known nor reasonably foreseeable by D1, and then creates havoc. In this scenario, English law supports the proposition that TP's acts may constitute a *novus actus interveniens*, severing the chain between D1's breach and C's damage.

In *Chubb Fire Ltd v Vicar of Spalding*,[225] three teenage boys (TP) entered the medieval parish church of St Mary and St Nicholas, at Spalding, whilst it was briefly unlocked and unattended. They took two dry powder fire extinguishers from the kitchenette next to the vestry, and discharged them around the church, including onto the organ. The cleaning-up operation was complex, laborious and expensive (costing about £250,000). The Vicar of Spalding, C, sued Chubb Fire Ltd, D1, who had supplied the dry powder extinguisher to the church in 1999, alleging that D1, when supplying the extinguisher, owed a duty to warn the church that any discharge of the extinguisher was likely to cause a mess. Had that warning been given, C said that he would not have had a dry powder extinguisher in the church. D1 argued that the vandals' acts were a *novus actus interveniens*.

[224] [2011] EWHC 1379 (TCC) [146].

[225] [2010] EWCA Civ 981. See too: *Lamb v Camden LBC* [1985] QB 625 (CA) (damage by squatters an intervening act).

Held: there was an intervening act by the vandals TP, and D1 was not liable for the damage caused by their independent acts. It would not be fair to hold D1 liable for that damage, some seven years after the extinguishers were provided. Also, TP's acts were deliberate and criminal, by persons for whom D1 had no responsibility and over which D1 had no control. Although vandals entering an unlocked church was foreseeable, the precise combination of events that led to such damage to the church was not reasonably foreseeable in 1999.

On the other hand, where D1's alleged wrongdoing is a failure to supervise or control the actions of that TP, who then ends up either injuring or killing C (these cases were discussed in Chapter 3), arguably the direct cause of C's injury was TP's wrongful or criminal act. Yet, that TP's conduct will **not** constitute an intervening act, according to English case law. The intervention is certainly foreseeable, given the violent or dangerous characteristics of TP – but even foreseeable events can constitute intervening acts. The more significant problem is that to hold that TP's act broke the chain of causation would permit D1 to evade liability, when the very duty cast upon D1 was to supervise or control TP. In *Dorset Yacht Co Ltd v Home Office*,[226] Lord Reid noted that, if what was relied on as a *novus actus interveniens* is the very thing which is likely to happen if D1 commits a breach of the duty which he owed, then D1 cannot rely on the intervening act.

In *Dorset Yacht Co Ltd v Home Office*, Borstal officers, D1, owed a duty to take reasonable care to prevent seven Borstal boys under their control, TP, from escaping from custody on Brownsea Island and causing damage to C's yacht moored nearby in Poole Harbour. **Held:** TP's criminal behaviour did not sever the chain of causation between the Borstal officers' lack of supervision of TP and the property damage which ultimately occurred to C's yacht. In *Stansbie v Troman*,[227] a decorator, D1, was working alone in C's house, and went out to buy wallpaper. He left the front door unlocked, despite being warned not to. Whilst he was away, an unidentified thief, TP, entered the house and stole items. **Held:** TP's deliberate act was not an intervening act, and D1 was liable for the lost items. D1's duty, in decorating the house, was to take reasonable care to guard the house against thieves.

Of course, if a mentally-ill person, TP, injured C for some other reason – e.g., attacking someone in a pub whilst drunk – then that may be an intervening act, given that the mental illness is **not** the provocation for TP's behaviour, it is some new and quite independent cause. That case has yet to arise in English law.

In any event, *Chubb* was distinguished from *Dorset Yacht*, because in *Dorset Yacht*, D1 was under a duty to take reasonable steps to supervise the Borstal boys, whereas in *Chubb*, D1 had no duty to protect the church from the violence of vandals; it had no control over the vandals, nor any responsibility for them.

TP's conduct which is neither negligent nor criminal

In some cases, TP gets involved in the 'story', and is neither negligent nor criminal, and yet, it is that TP's acts that are the most direct cause of C's suffering harm. For such an act by TP to be an intervening act, it must be unreasonable or unforeseeable. Further, if TP's intervention (or the effects of that intervention) were foreseeable to D1, then to uphold it as an intervening act is very unlikely.

[226] [1970] AC 1004 (HL) 1030. [227] [1948] 2 KB 48.

In *Horton v Evans*,[228] Cathy Horton, C, a high-earning lawyer, businesswoman, athlete and priest, was mis-prescribed some medication (dexamethasone) for a minor ailment (4 mg per day, instead of 0.5 mg per day), and her health deteriorated very markedly. C sued the GP who prescribed the wrong dose, and settled on confidential terms. C also sued pharmacist, Lloyds Pharmacy, D1, who dispensed the script, on the basis that they were negligent in not questioning the prescription and in proceeding to dispense the medication as prescribed. The medication was also mis-prescribed by another GP, Dr Elwell, TP, a few weeks later, whilst C was holidaying with her mother in New York State. C asked TP for a repeat prescription, of 4 mg a day, based upon C's showing TP the bottle of the previous prescription. TP based his prescription on viewing that label, which act D1 argued had the effect of breaking the chain of causation between any breach by D1 and C's deterioration in health. **Held:** TP's act was not an intervening act. TP was not negligent in prescribing C with the prescription which he did. Furthermore, it could not be said that D1's failure to question the GP's prescription was so eclipsed by TP's intervention that D1's conduct could properly be relegated to no more than a mere occurrence in the history of events. D1 should reasonably have foreseen the reliance which might be placed by a physician on the label on the bottle, and bore a 'real responsibility' for why TP thought that C had been prescribed 4 mg a day. In *Wilkin-Shaw v Fuller*,[229] Charlotte Shaw, C, 14, fell into a fast-flowing stream while on a training exercise on Dartmoor, was swept away by the strong current, and drowned. She had been on the Moor with 10 other children from the Kingsley School, North Devon, training for a Ten Tors expedition. C's mother sued the supervising teacher and school, D1, in negligence, on behalf of C's estate. The trip was undertaken in bad weather. Trevor Wills, TP, a scoutmaster, encountered the group at Watern Tor, when they were cold, distressed and wet, and advised them to cross at Walla Brook, where the accident occurred. (TP died prior to trial, and his police witness statement was relied upon.) **Held:** D1 were not negligent (although, on appeal, another D was found in breach, but 'but-for' causation failed). In any event, TP's conduct **would** have been an intervening act in advising the group that it was possible to cross the Walla Brook, and in guiding them to the crossing point where he oversaw the crossing. The effect of TP's intervention was to countermand D1's instructions: 'the intervention of a third party, anxious to help and apparently authoritative, would have broken the chain of causation. It could not have been foreseen that [the children] would have disobeyed instructions' given by the project leader and other responsible adults about the risks of water crossings (note that, on appeal, it was doubted whether TP's advice was indeed negligent).

C's own conduct

C's own conduct may break the causal chain if it amounts to 'unreasonable conduct' – but even then, it may not be sufficient to allow D1 to escape liability, for D1's breach may still remain the effective cause of C's damage (per Gross LJ in *Borealis AB v Geogas Trading SA*[230]). In *Mueller Europe Ltd v Central Roofing (South Wales) Ltd*, Stuart-Smith J noted, too, that even where C's conduct was reckless, it does not necessarily follow that C committed a *novus actus interveniens*.[231] (Both of these statements were made in the context of breach of contract, but the test for an intervening act is the same for both negligence and breach of contract.)

Hence, it comes as no surprise that it can be very difficult to establish that C's own conduct amounted to a break in the causal chain. It may well trigger a finding of contributory

[228] [2006] EWHC 2808 (QB).

[229] [2013] EWCA Civ 410, [53], affirming: [2012] EWHC 1777 (QB) [136]–[137].

[230] [2011] 1 Lloyds LR 482, [45].

[231] [2013] EWHC 237 (TCC) [122].

negligence against C (and hence reduce D1's liability for damages), but it will not sever the chain and exculpate D1 altogether. There are several reasons for the judicial unwillingness to hold C accountable as having committed an intervening act:

- if D1's duty of care towards C was to guard C against the very misfortune which befell C by virtue of C's own conduct, then it will be virtually impossible for C's conduct to break the chain of causation:

  In *Reeves v Commr of Police*,[232] Martin Lynch was put in a police cell whilst on remand for credit card fraud. He was on a suicide observation watch by the police, D1. Between observations, he hanged himself in his cell. **Held:** his act of suicide did not sever the chain of causation between D1's breach and the death of C. The very duty which D1 owed to C was to exercise reasonable care to prevent his taking his own life.

- if C's conduct was a panic or reflex reaction, in light of an emergency which D1's negligence created, then it will not amount to an intervening act – that would 'be wrong as a matter of principle'. As Lord Hoffmann stated in *SAAMCO's* case,[233] where D's breach lands C in a predicament, then C's 'reasonable attempt to cope with the consequences of D's breach of duty does not negative the causal connection between that breach of duty and the ultimate loss':

  In *Trebor Bassett Holdings Ltd v ADT Fire and Security plc*,[234] a large confectionery factory in Pontefract, owned by Trebor Bassett Holdings, C, was destroyed by fire in 2005, causing damage estimated at over £100m. The fire originally started in the popcorn production area where popcorn caught fire. Employees thought that the fire had been put out satisfactorily, but that was wrong, and a catastrophic fire followed. ADT Fire and Security, D1, provided a CO_2 fire suppression system for the popcorn machinery. D1 argued that C's own negligence broke the chain of causation between any defects in that suppression system and the destruction of the factory, because hardly any of C's employees were aware that the suppression system could be manually activated, and even fewer knew how to trigger it. **Held:** C's lack of staff training was negligent, but was not an intervening act. C's employees were striving to deal with the emergency which had been created by the lack of effectiveness of D1's CO_2 suppression system. Also, by the time that the fire was visible, when staff could manually activate the system, that would have come too late to have any causal effect. In *The Oropesa*,[235] *The Oropesa* steam ship was hit by D1's steam ship, the *Manchester Regiment*. The Master of *The Oropesa* decided to embark in a lifeboat, in rough and stormy weather, to get to the other ship and confer with her Master on what should be done to save the crews. Before the lifeboat could reach *Manchester Regiment*, it capsized and sank, drowning nine occupants, including the sixth engineer, C. **Held:** C's getting into the lifeboat with the Master was not an intervening act between D1's negligence in causing the collision, and C's ultimate drowning. C and his Master had not 'done something which was outside the exigencies of the emergency'. They were placed in this awful predicament by D1's negligence.

- if D1's original tort affected C physically or psychiatrically (or both), and put C in a position of vulnerability, whereby C was prone to act to the detriment of his own physical well-being, then it is very unlikely that C's conduct will be legally treated as breaking the chain of causation.

232 [2000] 1 AC 360 (HL). 233 [1997] AC 191 (HL) 218.

234 [2011] EWHC 1936 (TCC), quote and points from section M4.

235 [1943] P 32 (CA), quote at 39 (Lord Wright).

In *Corr v IBC Vehicles Ltd*,[236] Mr Corr, C, suffered a very serious and disfiguring head injury at a car factory in Coventry, for which his employers, D1, were liable. As a result of that head injury, C became depressed. Six years later, he committed suicide by jumping off a multi-storey carpark. C's estate brought an action against D1 for the consequences of the suicide. **Held:** C's suicide was not an intervening act. Although the suicide had been a deliberate conscious act, it had been the result of a depressive illness which was caused by D1's tort. In *Dalling v RJ Heale & Co Ltd*,[237] Stephen Dalling, C, was injured at work in 2005 when he fell about 5 metres whilst working as a ceiling fitter. His employer, RJ Heale, D1, admitted breach for the fall. However, three years later, C had a second accident, when he fell over backwards in a pub, having had too much to drink, and suffered a further head injury. **Held:** C's pub accident was not a *novus actus interveniens*. The first head injury played some part in the second accident, and the second accident could not sever the chain of causation between D1's original breach and C's ultimate damage. The original head injury had impaired C's judgment and ability to control his drinking. Both C and D1 had made substantial contributions to the happening of the second accident (33% CN was attributed to C). In *Wieland v Cyril Lord Carpets Ltd*,[238] Mrs Wieland, C, was injured in a bus accident, due to driver D1's negligence. She had to wear a neck collar and a brace afterwards, which affected her ability to use her bi-focals. C fell down some steps at her office, whilst in the company of her son. **Held:** the fall was not an intervening act, and hence, D1 was liable for the additional damage caused by that fall.

Notwithstanding the causal difficulties associated with C's conduct, C's own carelessness and unreasonable behaviour **can** constitute a *novus actus interveniens* at law (even if it was reasonably foreseeable to D). As Lord Reid stated in *McKew v Holland & Hannen & Cubitts (Scotland) Ltd*,[239] C's unreasonable conduct may have been entirely foreseeable, 'but that does not mean that [D] must pay for damage caused by the *novus actus*.'

In *McKew v Holland*, Mr McKew, C, was injured at work, caused by the breach of his employer, D. His back and hips were badly strained, he could not bend, and on several occasions his left leg suddenly 'went away from' him. A couple of weeks later, C was offered a tenancy of a flat in Glasgow, and went to inspect it. The flat was reached by a steep staircase with no handrail. When coming down the steps, C was carrying his young child, and his left leg 'vanished under him'. He threw his daughter back, and then, 'instead of toppling down head first, I threw myself and I landed on my feet'. C jumped about 12 feet from the top of the stair to the next landing, badly breaking his ankle. C claimed that the effect of the original breach was to weaken his leg and make him more prone to fall. D argued that C undertook a very hazardous exercise for which he, alone, was solely responsible. (If D was liable for the damage caused by the second accident, damages were agreed at £4,915, while if D was not, they were agreed at £200.) **Held:** the second accident was an intervening act. The second injury was caused by C's disability, which in turn was caused by D's breach, but C 'did something which a moment's reflection would have shown him was an unreasonable thing to do ... he chose to descend in such a way that, when his leg gave way, he could not stop himself'.

Acts of nature

An intervening act may be some 'exceptional natural event' (per dicta in *Kuwait Airways Corp v Iraqi Airways Co*[240]). In *Humber Oil Terminal Trustee Ltd v Sivand, Owners*,[241] the hypothetical

[236] [2008] AC 884. [237] [2011] EWCA Civ 365. [238] [1969] 3 All ER 1006 (QB) 1009–1111.
[239] 1970 SC (HL) 20, 25. [240] [2002] UKHL 19, [2002] 2 AC 883, [127]. [241] [1998] EWCA Civ 100.

example was given of an earthquake which disrupts repair work to C's vessel which D1 had negligently performed; and the actual example of *Carslogie Steamship Co Ltd v Royal Norwegian Govt*[242] was cited, where an intervening act occurred due to bad weather.

In *Carslogie*, C's ship, *The Heimgar*, collided with D's ship, *The Carslogie*, due to D's negligence. Temporary repairs were carried out to *The Heimgar* at Port Glasgow to make her seaworthy, but she had to make her way to New York where permanent repairs were to be carried out. She met heavy weather, and suffered damage which rendered her unseaworthy. That damage required 30 days of repairs; whereas the collision's effects required 10 days of repair. The repairs were done concurrently. **Held:** C was not able to recover the costs of the 10 days of repairs. The bad weather intervened to overtake the original tortious conduct of D; 'I cannot see that [C] sustained any damages in the nature of [tortious recovery against D] by reason of the fact that for I0 days out of the 30, she was also undergoing repairs in respect of the collision'.

Subsequent medical treatment

§8.25 Where C is injured by D1's breach and requires medical treatment as a result, and that treatment is negligently peformed by healthcare practitioner D2, that negligent medical treatment will not constitute an intervening act – unless the medical negligence is so gross and egregious as to be unforeseeable.

In *Wright v Cambridge Medical Group*, Elias LJ was of the view that intervening acts only apply where the new act is unforeseeable (which is not a view uniformly held among all judges, as discussed previously). In any event, it is (said Elias LJ) entirely foreseeable that hospital doctors and other medical professionals 'will be negligent from time to time', and that only medical negligence that was 'gross or egregious' could break the chain of causation, albeit that such a degree of negligence will be very difficult to prove.[243]

Even medical negligence with very serious outcomes for C will not break the chain of causation, where such negligence is foreseeable; and not grossly negligent. Hence, where C is injured at work or in a road accident, and there is subsequent negligence by a doctor brought in to treat the original injury, but who in fact made it worse, that medical treatment is very unlikely to constitute a *novus actus interveniens*.

In *Webb v Barclays Bank plc and Portsmouth Hospitals*,[244] Elizabeth Webb, C, contracted polio when 2 years old, and her left knee was left with a disability. While employed at Barclays Bank, D1, C stumbled over a protruding flagstone in their forecourt, C hyper-extended that knee, and was left with a grossly unstable knee. A long-term calliper was recommended, but C initially refused because of childhood experiences with callipers, but after terrible pain developed, she tried a calliper, without success. Her surgeon, Dr Jeffrey, D2, suggested an above-knee amputation of the left leg, which C accepted. After it was performed, it became apparent that an amputation had not been necessary to treat the condition. C sued D1 in negligence for failing to properly maintain the forecourt, and also sued D2 for negligent medical advice. **Held:** D2's medical negligence did **not** constitute a *novus actus interveniens*. D1's original wrongdoing remained a causative force of the amputation, as it had increased C's vulnerability and reduced her mobility. The medical intervention

[242] [1952] AC 292 (HL). [243] [2011] EWCA Civ 669, [2013] QB 312, [111].
[244] [2001] EWCA Civ 1141.

was plainly foreseeable, and given D2's conduct was negligent, but not grossly negligent, it would not be just and equitable to relieve D1 of all liability for the amputation. 'In short, the negligence in advising amputation did not eclipse the original wrongdoing. The Bank remained responsible for their share of the amputation damages. The negligence of Dr Jeffrey was not an intervening act breaking the chain of causation'. D1's responsibility was assessed at 25% and the doctor's (D2's) at 75%. In *Wright v Cambridge Medical Group*, Clarice Wright, C, 11 months, contracted chickenpox. She developed a high temperature and tachycardia, and was admitted to hospital on 9 April. Within a couple of days, C developed a very serious infection which went undiagnosed at the point of her discharge on 12 April. The bacteria seeded into part of C's hip-bone, infecting the bone on 13 or 14 April. C was taken by her mother to see her GP, D1, on 15 April, but the GP failed to arrange for C to be seen (this was a conceded breach). C was admitted to hospital again on 17 April, and eventually seen by a specialist paediatrician on 20 April, but a proper diagnosis of septic arthritis was not made until 21 April. C was left with a permanently unstable hip, and a discrepancy in leg length. Had D1 referred her to hospital on 15 April, as he should have done, and had C then been prescribed the right type of antibiotic in hospital, she would have fully recovered. No claim against the hospital was brought by C (which was 'highly unfortunate', said the court). **Held (2:1):** the negligent treatment which C received in hospital was not an intervening act. D1's delay retained its causative potency, because the less time that C was in hospital before the critical point of no return was reached re the infection, the more chance there was of not being able to give appropriate treatment. The GP's negligent delay did indirectly increase the risk of C's injury and was to that extent causally related to the injury.

Turning to a different scenario, that of 'wrongful conception' claims (discussed in Chapter 2), the leading case of *MacFarlane v Tayside Health Board*[245] confirmed that the parents' failure to either place an unplanned child for adoption, or to abort the child once the unplanned pregnancy was confirmed, will not constitute an intervening act, limiting the doctor D's liability for damages arising from the negligently-performed sterilisation operation. As Lord Slynn remarked, '[t]here was no legal or moral duty to arrange an abortion or an adoption of an unplanned child'.

CAUSATION AND 'PURE OMISSIONS'

Where it is alleged that D did not control or supervise TP with adequate care, or did not warn C of TP's propensities for violence – and then TP harms C – TP's acts are **not** an intervening act. As discussed in the previous section, it would not be legally logical for D to escape liability on the basis of an intervening act, when the very wrong alleged against D is that he should have taken steps to prevent TP from harming C.

However, a separate legal issue is how the causal link is proven in the case of 'pure omissions'.

§8.26 Where D's breach amounts to a 'pure omission' – including an omission to supervise or monitor a third party (TP), thereby providing TP with an opportunity to negligently or intentionally harm C's person or property – D's omission can cause C's harm, on the basis that D *created the opportunity* for that harm to occur. It is an indirect means of establishing causation, albeit that the 'but-for' test will be met in such cases.

[245] [2000] 2 AC 59 (HL), quote at 68 (Lord Slynn).

Pure omissions or non-feasances can undoubtedly constitute a 'cause' of harm in English law, based upon the more elliptical method of proving that D *created the opportunity for harm to occur.* Some classic 'omissions' cases (discussed earlier in Chapter 3) demonstrate this.

In *Haynes v Harwood*,[246] a carter, D, left a horse-drawn van unattended in a crowded street, and the horses bolted when a boy threw a stone at them. C, a police officer, suffered injury in stopping the horses before they injured a woman and children who were in the path of the bolting animals. The most directly responsible causes of the damage were:

- the actions of the mischievous boy; and
- the inherent nature of the animals, susceptible to sudden noise and movement.

The carter merely created a source of danger by leaving his horses unattended in a busy street, but that was sufficient for causation.

In *Goldman v Hargrave*,[247] an occupier of a West Australian station property, D, failed to douse a burning tree which had been struck by lightning. He felled the tree, preparatory to its being removed by a contractor. Unfortunately, the fire spread to adjoining land when gusty hot winds blew up. The direct and immediate causes of the disaster were:

- the naturally windy conditions and tinder-dry land; and
- the actions of the contractor in not removing the tree sooner.

The occupier was liable to the adjoining landowners in negligence.

Hence, pure omissions on D's part have not precluded causation in English law, quite the reverse.

Similarly, where D fails to prevent damage to C, brought about by the deliberate or criminal acts of TP who was under the control or supervision of D, causation can be established against D on the same basis. D committed no positive act against C, of course – TP did that – but D may still be liable in negligence, on the basis of this weaker causal link of creating an opportunity for harm to occur.

In *Dorset Yacht Co Ltd v Home Office*,[248] facts previously, **held:** causation proven: 'the injurious interference with the boats was caused by the acts and omissions of [D's] officers in bringing the Borstal boys to Brownsea Island and keeping them there under detention for compulsory training and yet taking no care for the safety of [Cs'] boat and the other boat or boats in the immediate vicinity of the place where the boys were being kept'. In *Carmarthenshire CC v Lewis*,[249] a kindergarten, D, was liable for failing to keep its premises secure, allowing toddler David to escape onto the main road into the path of Mr Lewis's lorry. Mr Lewis, C, was killed in trying to avoid David. **Held:** causation proven. The kindergarten created an opportunity for harm to occur to C.

It should be reiterated that, in these scenarios, the 'but-for' test is actually met. If D's breach had been hypothetically fixed (i.e., if the Borstal boys had been properly supervised, and if David had not been allowed to go wandering off), then the damage to C would not have occurred.

[246] [1935] 1 KB 146 (CA) (also known as *Hynes v Harwood*). [247] [1967] 1 AC 645 (PC).
[248] [1970] AC 1004 (HL) 1053 (Lord Pearson). [249] [1955] AC 549 (HL) 571.

Hence, these scenarios are not exceptions to the 'but-for' test. They are truly applications of it, but in a particular circumstance.

Similarly, were a duty of care to be owed by a 'Bad Samaritan' to C, whom that bystander did not rescue or assist (which is not presently the case, as discussed in Chapter 2), the causal link would be capable of being proven on the basis that D's failure to rescue/assist created the opportunity for C's harm to occur. The dilemma can be demonstrated by means of Lord Keith's example of the blind man (from *Yuen Kun-Yeu v A-G of Hong Kong*[250]), who is observed to walk over the edge of a cliff, and the bystander, D, shouts no warning at all. There are two innocent potential causes of the blind man's death or injury – his own disability, and the natural topography of the land – together with the breach, i.e., D's failure to shout the warning. D did not create the terrain or the disability, but his failure to shout created the opportunity for the harm to happen to the blind man. Hence, despite Lord Rodger's assertion in *Mitchell v Glasgow CC*, that, in the case of a person watching a child drown in a pool or a blind man walking out into traffic, that observer 'plays no part in the events',[251] a successful causal link would nevertheless be likely in 'Bad Samaritan' cases.

'LOSS OF A CHANCE' CLAIMS

What 'loss of a chance' means

§8.27 'Loss of a chance' claims arise when C frames his damage (resulting from D's breach) as the loss of a chance either to avoid a worse outcome or to gain a better outcome – and not as personal injury, property damage, psychiatric injury, or economic loss.

'Loss of chance claims' arise where C is having difficulty in proving a causal link between D's breach and the traditional forms of damage (physical, property, psychiatric or economic). This is to be distinguished from scenarios where C has already proven D's liability in negligence (including causation) – then lost chances, or the prospect that the outcome for C may get much worse, can be recovered as heads of damage. That is a **quantification** issue. In *Grieves v FT Everard & Sons Ltd*,[252] Lord Scott confirmed that, if D's breach caused C some physical injury, so that a tortious cause of action has accrued to C, then C 'can recover damages not simply for his injury in its present state, but also for the risk that the injury may worsen in the future, and for his present and ongoing anxiety that that may happen'. However, those matters that may occur in the future, which could diminish C's damages, 'have nothing to do with C's inability to prove causation to a balance of probabilities or the doctrine of loss of a chance; by the time this stage of the argument is reached, [C] will already have succeeded on the issue of causation' (per *Aercap Partners 1 Ltd v Avia Asset Management AB*[253]).

However, it is quite another matter, where C cannot prove that D's breach caused any actionable physical injury on the balance of probabilities – and so, in order to found a claim for damage which the tort of negligence requires, lost chances have been framed *as damage themselves*. This is a far more controversial proposition than merely claiming lost chances as heads of damage consequent upon already-proven injury. As Baroness Hale put it in *Gregg v Scott*, using loss of a chance is a 'radical way of defining [C's] damage'.[254]

[250] [1988] AC 175 (PC) 192. [251] [2009] UKHL 11, [2009] 1 AC 874, [55].
[252] [2007] UKHL 39, [2008] 1 AC 281, [67] (emphasis added).
[253] [2010] EWHC 2431 (Comm) [76] (Gross LJ). [254] [2005] UKHL 2, [2005] 2 AC 176, [209].

In some contexts (notably, in economic loss cases), the law **may** compensate that 'lost chance' as a type of damage. However, English law has set its face against awarding C compensation for a reduced chance of a more favourable outcome in personal injury claims (at the widest), and in medical negligence claims (at the narrowest). The basis for the distinctions can be finely-drawn and policy-driven, and the reasons for rejecting loss of a chance claims (especially in medical negligence) can be multifarious (and differ across judgments in the one case) – all of which adds considerably to the complexity of this area of causation.

Each context is considered in turn.

In the medical negligence context

§8.28 Where a breach by a healthcare practitioner, D, has not caused patient C's physical injury on the balance of probabilities, C may yet have lost a chance of a better outcome which can be measured in percentage terms. However, to date, English law does not uphold a compensable claim, where C has lost a chance of better outcome of <50%. However, the prospect of a successful 'loss of a chance' claim has not been entirely ruled out, judicially.

Leading cases, and outcomes

In the two leading House of Lords' decisions on this point – principally, in *Gregg v Scott*, and much earlier in *Hotson v East Berkshire HA* – neither C had any success. The reasons were wide-ranging. The area has been complicated somewhat by the fact that, in *Gregg v Scott*, the dissenters, Lords Hope and Nicholls, vehemently disagreed with the proposition that a loss of a chance claim should not be recognised for physical injury claims – and Lord Phillips, of the majority, did not entirely rule out the prospect of a future successful claim. Nor was it entirely ruled out in *Hotson* either.

> In *Gregg v Scott*,[255] Malcolm Gregg, C, consulted Dr Scott, his GP, D, about a lump under his arm. D diagnosed it as a benign lump of fatty tissue, without further investigation. Nine months later, non-Hodgkin's lymphoma was diagnosed. During that period of delay in achieving the correct diagnosis, C's chance of cure (i.e., survival disease-free for 10 years) dropped from 42% to 25%. C could not prove, on the balance of probabilities, that the delay caused the non-Hodgkin's lymphoma. C sued D for the loss of a chance of a cure over the 9-month period of delay. **Held:** the lost chance of better survival prospects was not a compensable harm. In *Hotson v East Berkshire HA*,[256] the trial judge held that, when Stephen Hotson, C, 13, first presented at the hospital following a fall from a tree, he had a 25% chance of avoiding necrosis of his hip joint. However, 5 days later, after the hospital, D's, negligently-delayed diagnosis and treatment of his hip, the hip joint was doomed to necrosis, and whatever 25% chance existed, of saving the hip joint, when he first turned up to hospital, was lost. **Held:** the lost 25% chance was not a compensable harm.

Later, in *Barker v Corus UK Ltd*,[257] the House of Lords confirmed that *Fairchild's* exceptional theorem of causation did not permit the *Gregg v Scott*-type lost chance to be compensated for.

[255] [2005] 2 AC 176 (HL). [256] [1987] AC 750 (HL).
[257] [2006] UKHL 20, [2006] 2 AC 572, [5] (Lord Hoffmann), also, [57] (Lord Scott).

The contrasting viewpoints in *Gregg v Scott* are noted in the following Table:[258]

The contrasting viewpoints in *Gregg v Scott*

The majority (Lords Hoffmann and Phillips and Baroness Hale) held that the claim for a lost chance was not compensable because ...	The dissenters held that the claim was compensable because ...
• this was analogous to *Wilsher's* case, because it was a multi-agent case, in which no one cause achieved the balance of probabilities threshold. The problem in both *Wilsher* and *Gregg* was that, whilst the doctors', Ds', breaches undoubtedly increased the risk of harm to their patients, Martin Wilsher and Malcolm Gregg, a mere increase in risk is not enough in multi-agent cases to render Ds liable. In *Gregg*, there were three possible causes of C's lost chance of survival in the 9 months: the missed diagnosis (the breach); C's lifestyle; and C's genetic make-up. To hold that the breach merely increased the chance of a bad outcome for Mr Gregg (an early death) was not sufficient. Otherwise, D would have been liable in *Wilsher* for increasing the chances of the baby sustaining RLF. Hence, *Gregg* was a *Wilsher*-type case – the articulation of the damages was different (the former articulated it as a lost chance, and the latter articulated it as blindness), but both were multi-agent cases. Hence, the *McGhee/Fairchild* 'single agent' exception could not apply to either of them (Lord Hoffmann); • neither *Hotson* (who lost a 25% chance of a good outcome) nor *Gregg* (whose chance of a good outcome reduced from 42% to 25%) was a true 'loss of a chance' case at all – what chance had each C lost? On the balance of probabilities, they were both always doomed to an adverse outcome at the point of breach, because Stephen Hotson had a 75% chance that his hip joint would turn necrotic from the minute he fell from the tree, and Malcolm Gregg had a 58% chance of not surviving the cancer at the point of the missed diagnosis (Baroness Hale, Lord Phillips);	• before the negligence, Mr Gregg had a less-than-evens chance (45%) of avoiding the deterioration in his condition which ultimately occurred, and the delay did not extinguish this chance, but reduced it by roughly half – what has to be valued is what the patient has lost, and this patient lost *some* chance of survival (from 45% down to 25%). That 'lost chance' was calculable, whether the prospects of survival were better or less than 50% at the time that the negligent diagnosis occurred (Lord Hope);

[258] The points are at: [2005] 2 AC 176 (HL) [90], [114], [172], [189]–[190] (majority); [43], [121] (dissenters).

The majority (Lords Hoffmann and Phillips and Baroness Hale) held that the claim for a lost chance was not compensable because ...	The dissenters held that the claim was compensable because ...
• if causation was upheld in *Gregg*, then it would have to be on a 'piecemeal' basis to remedy a perceived injustice, and 'the coherence of our common law would be destroyed' (Lord Phillips), plus it would lead to much uncertainty in many medical negligence cases (Lord Hoffman); • as a policy reason, if C succeeded in *Gregg*, then 'possible rather than probable causation' would be the basis for liability, and that 'would be so radical a change in our law as to amount to a legislative act. It would have enormous consequences for insurance companies and the NHS ... any such change should be left to Parliament' (Lord Hoffmann); • Mr Gregg's 'lost chance' was not borne out in reality, because he was very much alive at trial, and with good prospects of survival. A loss of a chance claim would be difficult to prove where C had >50% prospects of a good outcome at trial. *Gregg* was a much weaker case than *Hotson*, because Stephen Hotson was doomed to endure a necrotic hip joint at the point of breach (according to the trial judge), and he had lost whatever chance he had of avoiding that outcome – whereas, at the point of breach, Mr Gregg's chances of survival lay in the future, and happily, the chance of an adverse outcome had not materialised (Baroness Hale).	• 'it cannot be right to adopt a procedure having the effect that, in law, a patient's prospects of recovery are treated as non-existent whenever they exist, but fall short of 50%. If the law were to proceed in this way, it would deserve to be likened to the proverbial ass' (Lord Nicholls).

The principle of *Gregg v Scott* has been followed since, in a variety of medical negligence cases involving missed diagnoses, where the breach did not cause C's eventual damage on the balance of probabilities. To mention a couple:[259]

In *Beech v Timney*,[260] Joseph Beech, C, 35, suffered from recurring headaches and consulted his GP, Dr Timney, D, in Mar 2003. His blood pressure was recorded to be 110/80, but C claimed that it was recorded inaccurately, and was actually 180/100. D attributed C's headaches to ergonomic factors, and recommended postural exercises, and C also had his wisdom teeth removed. C consulted D again in May 2003, complaining of facial pain and 'bad heads'. In Nov 2003, C had a catastrophic stroke, which caused severe and permanent disability. C claimed that, had D measured and correctly recorded his high blood pressure, C would have embarked on a pharmaceutical treatment regime

[259] *JD v Mather* [2012] EWHC 3063 (QB) (missed cancerous growth); *Oliver v Williams* [2013] EWHC 600 (QB) (missed ovarian cancer).

[260] [2013] EWHC 2226 (Admin) [82].

which would probably have prevented the stroke. However, the medical evidence was that C would probably have suffered the stroke, even if D had started that treatment in Mar 2003, because such a programme had to be in place for 3–5 years before a 50% reduction in stroke risk occurred. By Nov 2003, the treatment would have had 'negligible' effect. **Held:** causation failed. Whatever chance of a better outcome that C may have lost, because the treatment was not started in Mar 2003, could not be claimed: 'the case falls squarely within the parameters of [*Gregg v Scott*]'. In *Carter v MOJ*,[261] Cheryl Carter, C, 34, was an inmate of D's prison, Cookham Wood, and claimed that, on three separate occasions, she consulted a medical officer as to the significance of a lump in her right breast, but it remained untreated. Eventually, after C's release, a large 10cm x 8cm tumour was diagnosed, for which C required chemotherapy and a mastectomy. C argued that, had she been referred for specialist treatment when she first alerted the medical officer with her concerns about the lump, the breast cancer prognosis would have been 'materially better than the one resulting from the eventual referral in November 2005 at the behest of her then GP'. **Held:** breach proven, but 'taking into account potential difficulties in distinguishing her case from that of [*Gregg v Scott*], the quantum of her claim may, at best, be moderate.'

Could a 'loss of chance' claim succeed in the future?

Despite their outcomes which rejected loss of a chance claims where C has suffered personal injury, neither *Hotson*nor *Gregg v Scott* entirely ruled out 'loss of chance' claims, according to senior English judiciary. Although Lord Bridge, in *Hotson*, perceived formidable difficulties in the concept of 'the lost chance of a better medical result which might have been achieved by prompt diagnosis and correct treatment', Lord Mackay remarked that it would be unwise to lay down a rule that a patient could never succeed by proving loss of a chance in a medical negligence case.[262]

The Court of Appeal has since indicated the same. In *Wright v Cambridge Medical Group*,[263] Lord Neuberger MR said that *Gregg v Scott* 'does not conclusively shut out, as a matter of strict logic', loss of a chance claims, and that, in this 'difficult area', 'the question would be appropriate for reconsideration by the Supreme Court'. However, no recovery for loss of a chance was countenanced in *Wright*, because, 'at this level, we should probably not expand the loss of a chance doctrine into the realm of clinical negligence'. Elias LJ agreed that *Gregg v Scott* 'effectively precludes this court from applying those principles to personal injury – and particularly clinical negligence – cases'.

For example, proving that C lost a 'chance of a better outcome' would appear to be crucial to the prospects of distinguishing *Gregg v Scott*. In *Hotson*, on the balance of probabilities (in fact, with a 75% probability), too many blood vessels were ruptured by the fall from the tree, and the hip joint was doomed to turn necrotic. Even prior to the occurrence of D's breach, a certain outcome was 'ordained', regardless of the delayed diagnosis and treatment. According to Lord Bridge in *Hotson*, '[t]he debate on the loss of a chance cannot arise where there has been a positive finding that ... the damage complained of had already been sustained or had become inevitable'.[264] That was sufficient to rule out any 'loss of chance' claim in that case. Similarly,

[261] [2010] EWHC 60 (QB), [30].

[262] [1987] AC 750 (HL), with quotes at 782 and 786, respectively. See too: *Bank of Credit and Commerce Intl SA (in liq) v Ali (No 2)* [2002] EWCA Civ 82, [71] (Robert Walker LJ).

[263] [2011] EWCA Civ 669, [2013] QB 312, with quotes at [84] and [93], respectively.

[264] [1987] AC 750 (HL) 782, 792. Lord Ackner agreed, at 793.

Mr Gregg's chances of survival were already less than the balance of probabilities (around 42%) when he first presented with the lump under his arm. Hence, whilst the delay reduced his chances of survival by about 20%, at the point of breach, Mr Gregg probably would not have survived anyway. Ostensibly, neither had lost a 'chance of a better outcome'.

Clearly, there has been a great deal of disquiet about that proposition, at senior judicial levels. It will be recalled that the dissenters in *Gregg* considered that a dropped chance of survival from 42% to 25% was something of value that C had lost. Other appellate judges have agreed, with Laws LJ commenting, in *Coudert Bros v Normans Bay Ltd (t/a Illingworth, Morris Ltd)*, that surely it should not be necessary for Mr Gregg to prove that he had >50% of a cure, in order to recover any damages for loss of a chance, because if it was, then 'I am driven to an unhappy sense that the common law has lost its way'.[265] In other contexts of professional negligence (e.g., solicitors who did not issue writs in time, such as in *Kitchen v RAF Assn*,[266] or in breach of contract cases, such as *Chaplin v Hicks*[267]), general damages have been awarded for loss of a chance, even though the chance lost was < 50%.[268]

In any event, if C **did** lose something which was assessed as a >50% prospect of a better outcome for C at the time of D's breach, then it would clearly be a distinguishable scenario from *Gregg v Scott*. This has been suggested, in dicta, by the Court of Appeal since.

> In *Yearworth v North Bristol NHS Trust*,[269] C and another five men were diagnosed with cancer, and were treated with a course of chemotherapy. The treating hospital, D, advised C that the treatment might damage their fertility. C agreed to produce samples of semen prior to the start of the treatment, so that it could be stored at D's fertility unit. The sperm was to be stored in liquid nitrogen (at minus 196°C) at D's facility, free of charge. Unfortunately, the amount of liquid nitrogen in the tanks in which it was stored fell below the requisite level, and the automatic topping-up of the levels did not work. The sperm perished irretrievably. **Held:** no damage occurred, as loss of the sperm did not constitute 'personal injury': 'it would be a fiction to hold that damage to a substance generated by a person's body, inflicted after its removal for storage purposes, constituted a bodily or "personal injury" to him ... We must deal in realities'. Also, no loss of a chance was compensable either.

The *Yearworth* court held that *Gregg v Scott* 'compelled a conclusion that, unless [C] were to demonstrate a greater than even chance that the lost sperm could have been used in order to achieve conception, then ... they could not claim in respect of such physical damage to their overall ability to become fathers'. This indicates the sort of distinguishable case that may succeed in the future.

An alternative claim

Although proving that C lost a compensable chance of a better outcome may not be legally possible, nevertheless, Baroness Hale pointed out, in *Gregg v Scott*,[270] that someone in Mr Gregg's position would have been entitled to a smaller type of damages claim 'on conventional [but-for causation] principles', had the claim been framed differently at trial – *viz*, damages for the following, as caused by the delayed diagnosis:

265 [2004] EWCA Civ 215, [68]. In the same case, Waller LJ also expressed 'disquiet' about the trial judge's conclusions and the CA's dismissal of the appeal in *Gregg*.

266 [1958] 1 WLR 563 (HL) 576–77. Also: *Cook v Swinfen* [1967] 1 WLR 457 (HL) 460.

267 [1911] 2 KB 786.

268 Noted, e.g., in: *Dyne, Hughes & Archer (a firm) v Cross* (CA, 11 Apr 1990).

269 [2009] EWCA Civ 37, [2010] 1 QB 1, [23]–[24].

270 [2005] UKHL 2, [2005] 2 AC 176, [205]–[207].

- any extra pain and suffering and loss of amenity resulting from the delay of diagnosis of 9 months. If the misdiagnosis had not happened and the cancer been detected straightaway, C would likely have enjoyed a longer period before more radical chemotherapy, and C would be entitled to damages for that ('to reflect the acceleration in his suffering'); and if the pain and suffering was greater because of 'the anguish of knowing that his disease could have been detected earlier', then that too would be compensable;
- any financial losses that C suffered during that delay of 9 months would also be recoverable;
- finally, any loss of expectation of life caused by the delay would be compensable – had C been treated when he should have been treated, 'his median life expectancy then would have been x years, whereas given the delay in treatment, his median life expectancy from then is x minus y ... There might therefore be a modest claim in respect of the "lost years".'

This alternative type of claim was taken up subsequently:

> In *JD v Mather*,[271] JD, C, consulted his GP, D, on 8 Mar 2006, being concerned about a growth in his right groin. C complained that the growth was growing, itching and bled when he had scratched it. D diagnosed it as a seborrhoeic wart, and nothing to worry about. The groin lesion turned out to be cancerous. It was diagnosed correctly in Oct 2006. The evidence was that, as at Mar 2006, C's chances of a cure (i.e., survival for >10 years), with an ulcerated primary tumour with at least one regional nodal micrometastasis, was <50%. **Held:** C's principal claim was unsustainable, per *Gregg v Scott*. However, the failure to diagnose the tumour reduced C's life expectancy by three years, which was compensable (damages to be agreed, or tried).

In the economic context

In comparison with the less-than-sympathetic view which English law adopts towards loss of chance claims in medical negligence, the loss of an economic chance has been permitted in two situations, *viz*, where (1) the loss is of a chance to secure a legal right (where rights are treated as equivalent to the loss of a property right), and (2) the loss is of a chance to follow up an economic opportunity. Recently, in *McCrindle Group Ltd v MaClay Murray & Spens*, the Scottish Outer House reiterated that 'it is important ... to distinguish those cases which involved the loss of a right, and those which did not.'[272]

Loss of legal rights

§8.29 Where D's breach causes C to lose a legal right, then even if the prospects of successfully pursuing that legal right fall short of the balance of probabilities, C may prove that the lost chance is compensable. It is sufficient that C had reasonable prospects of converting that legal right into an economic benefit.

The types of legal rights that the law has compensated for under loss of a chance, include the following:

> In *Chaplin v Hicks*,[273] C lost a contractual entitlement to compete for a prize. In *Kitchin v RAF Assn*,[274] C lost the chance of pursuing his legal claim (a right to sue) because his solicitors, D, failed to file the claim within the limitation period, such that D's negligence deprived C of a right of action.

[271] [2012] EWHC 3063 (QB) [43]–[48]. [272] [2013] ScotCS 72 (OH) [123] (Lord Hodge).
[273] [1911] 2 KB 786. [274] [1958] 1 WLR 563 (CA).

In these 'loss of right'-type cases, the court has to quantify that lost right, which (according to the Court of Appeal in *Parabola Investments Ltd v Browallia Cal Ltd*[275]) is a case of assessing the prospects, in percentage terms, of C's obtaining a positive outcome from the exercise of that right. C does not have to prove that he would have obtained an economic benefit, via that right, on the balance of probabilities: '[r]ather, it estimates the loss by making the best attempt it can to evaluate the chances great or small (unless those chances amount to no more than remote speculation), taking all significant factors into account'. More recently, the Court of Appeal suggested, in *Lillington v MOD*,[276] that C's lost right to seek a promotion due to negligently-caused injury could also fall within the *Gregg v Scott*-type loss of a chance cases (albeit that the suggestion was not taken up by counsel in that case).

Loss of economic opportunity

§8.30 Where D's breach causes C to lose the chance to pursue economic opportunities, then C has not lost a legal right, but rather, an opportunity to pursue an economic benefit. C must prove the so-called '*Allied Maples* conditions' in order to prove that causal link.

This type of claim is 'more in the realm of cases concerned with negligent failure to advise, where the client is deprived of information which he might have used to his economic benefit, rather than the loss of an item of property such as a right' (as explained in *McCrindle*[277]). In order to recover damages for the lost chance, C must prove three steps ('the *Allied Maples* conditions'):

i. on the balance of probabilities, C would have taken action to obtain the financial opportunity (either on his own account, or by approaching a third party);
ii. if acquiring the financial benefit depends on the hypothetical action of a third party (TP), then C must also prove that there was a real or substantial chance that the third party would have conferred the benefit on C; and
iii. C must prove, on the balance of probabilities, that he would have accepted that benefit.

This is an application of the principle in *Mallett v McMonagle*,[278] in that the court applies a balance of probabilities approach to proof of past facts and events.

> In *Allied Maples Group Ltd v Simmons & Simmons*,[279] Allied Maples, C, lost the chance to negotiate a warranty or other protection in a share purchase agreement, as a result of their solicitor's, D's, negligent failure to advise. **Held:** causation failed. C had to prove on balance of probabilities that he would have negotiated with the seller to obtain the benefit of the warranty, and C also had to prove that there was a real and substantial chance that the seller would have conferred the warranty. These could not be proven.

The *Allied Maples* scenario is distinguishable from the 'loss of right' case, because, in *Allied Maples*, D's negligent failure to advise did not cause C to lose a legal right. It merely deprived C of information which he might have used positively in negotiating further benefit. As the court in *McCrindle* put it, the *Allied Maples* court 'was not valuing a lost right, but was dealing

[275] [2010] EWCA Civ 486, [25] (Toulson LJ).
[276] [2015] EWCA Civ 775, [4] (Vos LJ) (lost chance to pass an exam and become a corporal).
[277] [2013] ScotCS 72 (OH) [125]. [278] [1970] AC 166 (HL). [279] [1995] 1 WLR 1602 (HL).

with the prior question of causation'.[280] The *Allied Maples* approach is difficult to apply, however, because the court must assess what TP would have done, and whether C would have accepted the benefit. Judging what one party hypothetically may have done is difficult enough – but judging what C would have done, where his interests were not necessarily aligned with TP's, can be even more so. It is an exercise in reconstruction and hypothesis, which is highly dependent upon the evidence given by the parties, well after D's breach occurred, as to what they would have done, had the breach not happened.

In *Dayman v Lawrence Graham*,[281] Mrs Fielding, C, sold her house and bought another. She was subsequently declared bankrupt, due to her indebtedness to Royal Bank of Scotland. C's solicitors, D, handled the sale and purchase, but did not recommend to C to negotiate her release from debts to RBS in return for payment of the sale proceeds. **Held:** causation proven. Applying the *Allied Maples* approach: (1) C proved, on the balance of probabilities, that she would have approached RBS; (2) there was a real or substantial chance that RBS would have responded to such an approach by proposing a deal to C; and (3) on the balance of probabilities, C would have accepted that deal.

In any event, the support for 'loss of a chance' claims in the economic context cannot be translated to the personal injury context, where English law has set its face against the loss of a better physical outcome as a compensable damage. It is one of the rare instances in which C's claim for economic loss is treated more favourably than where C suffers from some physical detriment allegedly arising from D's breach.

SUPERVENING EVENT #1: D2'S SUPERVENING TORT DAMAGED AN ALREADY-DAMAGED CLAIMANT

§8.31 Intervening acts have some factual linkage to D1's original breach, in that the breach created the opportunity for the intervening act to occur (i.e., the intervening act would not have occurred, had the original breach not occurred). By contrast, supervening acts are unrelated to the original tort, and are coincidental in occurrence.

This section concerns the unusual, but problematical, scenario of where D1 and D2, via separate and consecutive acts, injure C, such that D1 caused C a particular injury – but that same injury would have happened anyway at a later date (but prior to trial), courtesy of D2's unrelated act. These scenarios are treated as supervening events. According to the Court of Appeal in *Rahman v Arearose Ltd*, they arise where 'the effects of the first tort, which caused injuries to [C], were obliterated by the second [tort]', i.e., different and unrelated torts committed at entirely different times against the same C.[282] Supervening events may also occur where D caused C's harm – but naturally-occurring events in C's life would have led to the same injury.

The scenario causes legal difficulties. A number of English judges have acknowledged the conundrum: '[t]he law's approach to causation is pragmatic, where there are several concurrent or successive factors operating to cause injury' (per *Reynard v Exquisite Cuisine Ltd*[283]); the task of allocating liability involves 'swings and roundabouts', and some 'inevitable imprecision' (per Moore-Bick LJ in *Smithurst v Sealant Construction Services Ltd*[284]); and cases which

[280] [2013] ScotCS 72 (OH) [131] (Lord Hodge).
[281] [2008] EWHC 2036 (Ch) (Judge Hodge QC).
[282] [2000] EWCA Civ 190, [2001] QB 351, [31].
[283] [2005] CSOH 146, [51].
[284] [2011] EWCA Civ 1277, [43].

involve supervening events 'all raise, in one form or another, the question: on what disabling supervening events is [D1] entitled to rely to reduce or extinguish the consequences of his tort? Put another way: from what further misfortunes of [C] should [D1] be held entitled to benefit?' (per *Gray v Thames Trains Ltd*[285]).

Notably, there is **no** question of these successive tortfeasors being ***concurrent*** tortfeasors (see 'Multiple defendants', an online chapter), as the supervening acts arose from respective torts committed by separate Ds which were quite unrelated, and which did not concurrently cause a single indivisible injury. Hence, the Civil Liability (Contribution) Act 1978, whereby responsibility for damages can be apportioned between D1 and D2, does **not** apply. It will be the court's responsibility to arrive at a just conclusion, on the evidence, as to the respective damage caused by each D, 'even if it can only do it on a broad-brush basis which then has to be translated into percentages' (as Laws LJ noted in *Rahman*[286]). Wherever the original and supervening torts are concurrent torts, the discussion in this section is irrelevant. In the case of concurrent torts, the 1978 Act must be applied to apportion liability between the concurrent tortfeasors, unless the second tort constitutes an intervening act.

In *Webb v Barclays Bank plc*,[287] facts previously, **held:** Mrs Webb's employer, and the negligent doctor, were concurrent tortfeasors, and hence, apportionment under the 1978 Act applied. Once the Bank's liability for the period up to the amputation was assessed (£53,000), then the liability for the effects of the amputation were apportioned between bank and doctor, in the proportions of 25% and 75%, to reflect that the doctor's negligence 'was much more responsible for the amputation and all that went with it'.

Successive tortfeasors

§8.32 According to the *Baker v Willoughby* principle, where D1 causes C a tortious injury, but that same injury would have occurred later, via a separate, successive and unrelated act committed by D2, D1's liability for damages does not cease at the point at which D2's tort occurs. The 'causation principle' provides that D2 should only be liable for the damage which he inflicted upon C, and no more, i.e., D2 has damaged an already-damaged C.

Baker v Willoughby's principle arises where there are two successive tortfeasors, and two separate acts, which meant that the damages arising from C's injury, caused by D1's act, would have occurred via D2's tort in any event. Under the principle, D1 cannot 'benefit' from D2's tort, and use D2's tort to reduce the extent of damages for which D1 is liable. Specifically, D1's liability for damages does not cease, or cut off, at the point at which D2's tort occurs; D1's liability extends beyond D2's tort. D2 can only be liable for the additional damage which his tort causes, bearing in mind that he has damaged an already-damaged C. Hence, D2 appears to get off relatively lightly from the effects of his negligence against C.

In *Baker v Willoughby*,[288] Mr Baker, C, was injured by the negligent driving of Mr Willoughby, D1, in a car accident in 1964. C's left leg and ankle were left permanently stiff. In 1967, and just before his trial against D1, C was working in a scrap metal yard alone, and was shot in the left leg by two robbers, D2, in an armed robbery. His left leg had to be amputated. D2 (committing the tort of assault)

[285] [2009] UKHL 33, [2009] AC 1339, [97] (Lord Brown). [286] [2001] QB 351 (CA) [23].
[287] [2001] EWCA Civ 1141, [51], citing trial judge Rougier J. [288] [1970] AC 467.

were never located, and hence, were never sued. The events were entirely unrelated, there was no question of C's being unable to evade the robbers because of his 'gammy leg', which ruled out an intervening act. The question arose as to what damages D1 was liable for. **Held:** D2's tort could not reduce the amount of the damages which D1 had to pay for the particular disabilities caused by D1's breach. Hence, D1 had to pay damages for C's stiff leg (even though it had actually been amputated as a result of the second tort), to the extent that the heads of damage for the stiff leg were still applicable to C, i.e., damages for loss of mobility, damages for loss of amenity and enjoyment of life, and damages for loss of earnings.

There were two key points in *Baker v Willoughby*, re D2's liability for damages:[289]

i. if the robbers, D2, had been capable of being sued, then D2 would have damaged an already-damaged man, and would only have been liable for the very limited damages of the costs of the artificial limb used by C, and damages for pain in the stump of the leg (for those were 'extra damages' incurred by the second tort, the assault of shooting). Additionally, had the robbers D2 been sued, then they would have been liable to Mr Baker, C, for any *additional* loss of earnings brought about by the amputated leg, which were over and above the lost earning capacity which he already suffered by virtue of the stiff leg. D2 has to 'take his victim as he finds him'. By virtue of the causation principle, where D2 has injured an already-injured C (where that injury was inflicted by D1), then D2 is only liable for the 'extra' damage which his negligence caused. If no extra damage was caused (because the injury caused by D1 merged into the injury inflicted by D2), then C is not entitled to recover anything from D2. In *Baker*, however, there was additional damage;
ii. if D1 was only liable for the damages for which he was responsible (i.e., loss of mobility, loss of amenity and enjoyment of life) up to the second tort (the shooting) but not beyond, then that would create an injustice. D2 would still only be liable for the additional damages caused by the shooting. That would then leave a 'gap in the damages' after the shooting, in that C would be left without any damages for the continuing loss of amenity and loss of mobility which the car accident caused him. That is why D1's liability for damages must continue beyond the second tort.

It is a controversial principle which has drawn considerable judicial criticism since. Courts have shown no inclination to extend the principle beyond its strict facts (i.e., successive torts against C by D1, and then D2). Where the subsequent event was a naturally-occurring infirmity (per *Jobling v Associated Dairies Ltd*[290]), or C's own action (per *Gray v Thames Trains Ltd*[291]), the principle does not apply (discussed below).

The principle in *Baker v Willoughby* was, in truth, earlier espoused in the Court of Appeal in 1962 – and has been applied since, with similar controversial results:

In *Performance Cars Ltd v Abraham*,[292] C's car was involved in a collision with D1's car, which damaged the rear wing of C's car. It was not repaired, by the time that C's car was involved in a second accident with D2's car, due to D2's negligent driving. The front wing of C's car was damaged, and to fix the damage, the whole of the lower part of the car would have to be repainted (costing £75).

[289] [1970] AC 467 (HL) 493 (Lord Reid).

[290] [1982] AC 794 (HL) 809 (Lord Edmund-Davies), 815 (Lord Russell).

[291] [2009] UKHL 33, [2009] 1 AC 1339, [76], [96] (Sir Anthony Clarke MR).

[292] [1962] 1 QB 33, quote at 40 (Lord Evershed MR).

The same respray would have been required to make good the damage from the first and the second accidents. C sued D1 and recovered judgment for the cost of the respray (£75), but D1 did not satisfy the judgment. C then sued D2 to recover the cost of the respray. **Held:** C could not recover any sum for the respray from D2. D2 had damaged an already-damaged car, and was only liable for the 'extra' damage which his tort caused. There was no *extra* damage, and hence, C could recover nothing from D2: 'the necessity for respraying was not the result of [D2's] wrongdoing, because that necessity already existed'. Given that D2 had injured an already-injured car, 'the damage claimed did not flow from [D2's] wrongdoing. It may no doubt be unfortunate for [C] that the collisions took place in the order in which they did'. In *Rahman v Arearose Ltd*,[293] Mr Rahman, C, branch manager of the Burger King chain at King's Cross, London, was assaulted one night by two gang members. C suffered a fractured orbital wall of his right eye. That assault was due to the negligent system of work established by his employer, D1. The eye injury was medically treated by D2, and a bone graft attempted, but due to D2's negligence, C was blinded, because his optic nerve was severed during the operation. C suffered serious PTSD and depression, with severe impact upon his earning capacity. **Held:** D1, the employer, was liable for the psychiatric injuries (and economic consequences) sustained by C throughout the ordeal of both torts, and for a period of three years beyond the second tort. D2 was liable for the remainder of the future economic loss.

On a timeline: supervening events

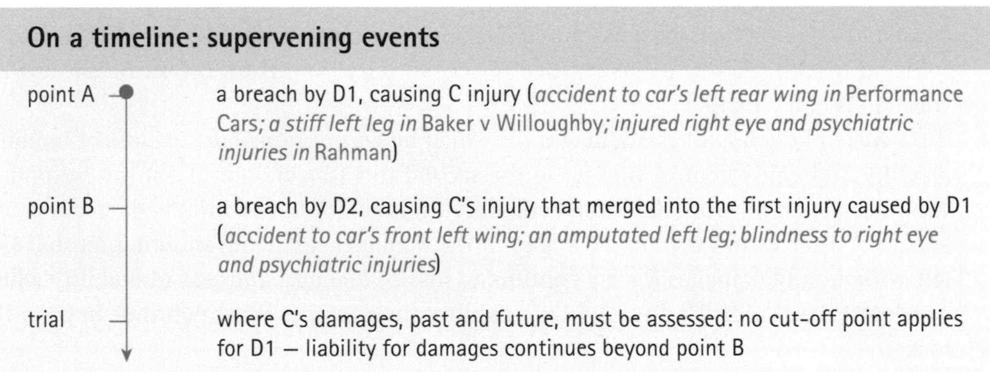

Judicial reaction to the *Baker v Willoughby* principle

It is fair to say that judicial reaction to the correctness of the *Baker v Willoughby* principle – by imposing on D1 liability for damages, for that period after the actions of D2 which 'obliterated' the effects of D1's tort – remains divided.

In favour of the outcome, the Court of Appeal remarked, in *Halsey v Milton Keynes General NHS Trust*,[294] that the decision produced a just and fair result for D1 and D2, albeit that it could cause inconvenience to C if D1 could not be found, or was insolvent. The court reasoned that, as 'a matter of logic and common sense, [*Performance Cars*] is clearly correct', because C was entitled to recover damages from D1 for the losses inflicted by him, and from D2 for any *additional* losses inflicted by him. If D1 was unlocatable or insolvent, then C would not be fully compensated for all the losses that he had suffered from the two accidents, but 'that is not a reason for making each defendant liable for the total loss'. But by corollary, D2 cannot

[293] [2001] QB 351. [294] [2004] EWCA Civ 576, [2004] 1 WLR 3002, [66]–[70].

be responsible for the consequences of the injury caused by D1, because D2 did not cause C's damage, it had already occurred.

On the other hand, the outcome in *Baker v Willoughby* has been doused in, not cold, but frozen water, by some subsequent judicial statements. For example:

- in *Jobling*,[295] Lord Edmund-Davies could discern 'no convincing juristic or logical principles supportive of the decision in *Baker v Willoughby*, and none were there propounded', and that the result was 'unrealistic'; whilst Lord Keith noted that *Baker* was 'mistaken in approaching the problems common to the case of a supervening tortious act and to that of supervening illness wholly from the point of view of causation', that the result in *Baker* was 'not acceptable'; and Lord Bridge doubted that the ratio of *Baker* 'could be sustained', but may be best regarded as 'a decision on its own facts';
- in *Heil v Rankin*,[296] Otton LJ agreed with Lord Keith in *Jobling* that the principle in *Baker*, of 'ignoring the occurrence of a second tort when awarding damages against [D1], could not be justified on any identifiable juristic basis, but rather was a just and practical solution to avoid the barrier to full compensation that would arise if the normal rules were applied to their full extent';
- in *Gray v Thames Trains*,[297] Lord Rodger labelled *Baker v Willoughby* as 'uncomfortable company';
- in *L(R) v Minister for Health and Children*,[298] the Irish High Court noted that the problem of supervening events occurring before the date of assessment of damages was a 'vexed question', for which neither *Jobling* nor *Baker* had provided a 'clear or persuasive solution'. In fact, the Irish Court was quite damning of the House of Lords' consideration of supervening events, noting that 'the outcome of their extensive consideration of the subject was defeat, in the sense that they were unable, individually or collectively, to convincedly adopt a set of principles to apply, both in circumstance of the supervening event being tortious and non-tortious'.

However, despite these numerous reservations, *Baker v Willoughby* retains its standing as authoritative law in England.

SUPERVENING EVENT #2: NON-TORTIOUS REASONS WOULD HAVE LED TO THE SAME DAMAGE

§8.33 According to the *Jobling* principle, where D has caused some injury to C – and then, after the initial tort but prior to trial, C suffers from an infirmity or illness which would have caused the same injury in any event – D cannot be liable for damages beyond the point at which the naturally-occurring physical infirmity arose.

Where D's breach causes C injury – but a subsequent non-tortious event would, on the balance of probabilities, have caused C the same type of injury in any event – D must not be liable for more damages than is fair and just.

According to the principle derived from *Jobling v Associated Dairies*,[299] D is not liable to C for the effects of the breach, after the point at which C would have suffered the same damage

[295] [1982] AC 794 (HL) 808–9 (Lord Edmund-Davies), 815 (Lord Keith), 821 (Lord Bridge).
[296] [2001] PIQR Q3, [17]. [297] [2009] UKHL 33, [2009] 1 AC 1339, [76].
[298] [2001] IEHC 64, [2001] 1 IR 744, [16]. [299] [1982] AC 794 (HL).

through supervening illness – even though C would have (hypothetically) continued to suffer that very disability from D's breach, if the supervening infirmity had not arisen. There is a limit, or cut-off, to D's responsibility for the damage to C:

> In *Jobling v Associated Dairies Ltd*, Mr Jobling, C, suffered a back injury which was caused by the breach of statutory duty by his employer, Associated Dairies Ltd, D. This impairment reduced his earning capacity, because he could only be given light duties. Three years later (and before trial), C was found to be suffering from a spinal disease, myelopathy, an unrelated illness, which would have precluded his continuing to work in any event. The question arose as to what damages D should be liable for. **Held:** D could only be liable to C for damages up to the point at which the naturally-occurring infirmity arose, but not beyond that. D's liability ceased at that point.

If Mr Jobling's condition had arisen post-trial, such that he had already obtained damages for D's breach, but then it turned out that he was unable to work because of his naturally-occurring infirmity, his damages payout would never be reassessed, to take account of the fact that C would have been disabled from work, even had D's negligence not occurred. In that respect, Mr Jobling is perceived to be at a disadvantage – even though courts typically reduce damages assessments for any C, to take account of the 'vicissitudes of life' (i.e., future contingencies affecting earning capacity, as discussed in Chapter 11).

As Lord Diplock noted in *Mallett v McMonagle*,[300] whatever discounting of the damages must occur in this scenario is solely a question of assessment of damages, and not strictly of causation *per se*. Lord Keith agreed with this view in *Jobling*: 'when an event ... has actually happened prior to the trial date, that event will fall to be taken into account in the assessment of damages'.[301]

The *Jobling* principle is also applied where C would have suffered the same damage via *his own conduct*, and not via illness or infirmity. The important point is that, where it is not a case of two successive tortfeasors D1 and D2, the *Jobling* principle continues to apply.

> In *Gray v Thames Trains Ltd*,[302] Mr Gray, C, was a passenger on a train which was involved in the Ladbroke Grove rail crash near Paddington. The crash was caused by the negligence of Thames Trains, D. In the accident, C suffered only minor injuries, but later suffered from PTSD. While being treated for that, C became enraged at a drunken pedestrian, Mr Boultwood, who had stepped in front of his car. He went to the house of his girlfriend's parents, took a knife, located the pedestrian, and stabbed him to death. C gave himself up to the police, pleaded guilty to manslaughter, and thereafter was detained indefinitely in a mental prison facility. C sued D for damages relating to his conviction, detention, feelings of remorse, and guilt, and damage to his reputation. It was accepted that he would not have committed the killing, but for the PTSD. **Held**: C could not claim damages for any lost earnings for the period after his arrest and detention for manslaughter, as that would have meant that his earning capacity ceased in any event. D was not liable to compensate C for his losses after the arrest, following *Jobling*.

Notably, *Gray* was a different case from *Jobling*, though. In *Jobling*, C was 'overtaken before trial by a wholly unconnected and disabling illness', i.e., that of myelopathy, but that event had nothing to do with D's conduct. By contrast, in *Gray*, C was 'overtaken before trial' by arrest and detention which prevented him from working because of the manslaughter, but C would

[300] [1970] AC 166 (HL) 178. [301] [1982] AC 794 (HL) 813.
[302] [2009] UKHL 33, [2009] AC 1339, quote at [49].

not have committed that manslaughter, if he had not been suffering from the PTSD which was a direct consequence of D's negligently-caused train crash. Nevertheless, despite this difference, the *Jobling* principle applied. Various judges in *Gray* justified the application of *Jobling* as follows:[303]

- C was 'wholly blameless' for the back condition that stopped D's liability for damages in *Jobling*, so it would be a 'strange conclusion' if, in *Gray*, C could 'ignore a vicissitude for which he has been held responsible (if only to a diminished extent)';
- the outcome was consistent, because Mr Gray had been lawfully detained, first in prison and then in a psychiatric prison hospital, for the public's protection. Hence, it would inconsistent with the policy underlying these orders by a criminal court, for a civil court to award Mr Gray damages for loss of earnings relating to the period when he was subject to those orders.

Summarising the two leading cases in diagrammatic form:

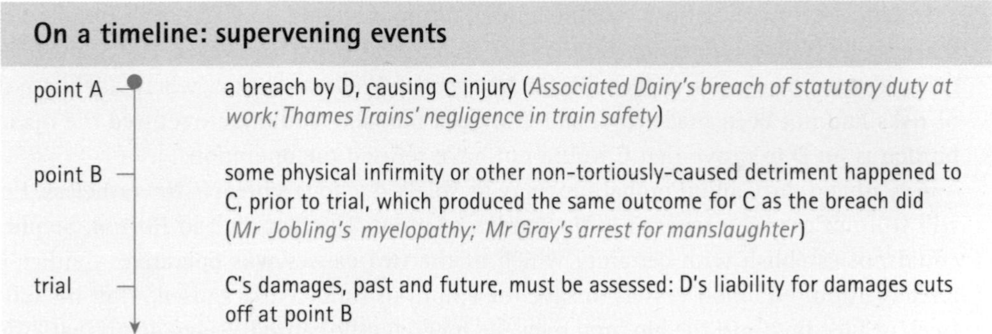

Hence, the *Jobling* principle cannot be applied – to limit the damages payable by D1 – where there are successive tortfeasors (D1, and then D2) who have both committed breaches against C and which have caused the same injury to C. That scenario is governed by the *Baker v Willoughby* principle. As Lord Rodger put it in *Gray v Thames Trains*,[304] it would not be right to put *Gray, Jobling*, and like cases, in the 'uncomfortable company' of *Baker v Willoughby*.

THE BURDEN OF PROOF

§8.34 The burden of proving that D's breach caused C's damage always rests with C. English law has refused to reverse the burden of proof, where C has confronted an 'evidential' gap in proving a causal link between D's breach and C's damage, whether due to factual uncertainty or the obfuscatory effects of D's breach.

The general position

The burden of proving causation must be discharged by C on the balance of probabilities. It is a basic tenet of English law. Judicially: '[C] must prove not only negligence or breach of duty, but also that such fault caused or materially contributed to his injury' (per *Bonnington Castings*

[303] [2009] UKHL 33, with quotes at [202] (Lord Brown), [75] (Lord Rodger), respectively.
[304] *ibid*, [76].

Ltd v Wardlaw[305]); and '[i]t is established on high authority (*Bolitho, Wilsher*) that the burden of proof on causation lies, and remains, on [C]' (per *Shawe-Lincoln v Neelakandan*[306]).

It has been judicially acknowledged that this burden can be extremely onerous – even impossible – in some cases in which evidential gaps confront C. For one thing, the origin of some conditions can be medically and factually impossible to ascertain. In *Bull v Devon AHA*,[307] in an action against doctors for negligent delivery of C as a baby, the Court of Appeal noted that, 'in very many cases of cerebral palsy ... or brain damage, the cause is never discovered' (albeit that causation was proven in *Bull* itself: '[t]he onus was on [C] Stuart ... the hypoxia which occurred at birth was of such a degree that it did cause [C's] disability, and [the trial judge] found that [C] had excluded the possibility that there was another cause').

If a judge is faced with two theories for C's damage – 'one of which he regard[s] as extremely improbable, and the other of which he regard[s] as virtually impossible' – it is not a matter of choosing one over the other. The correct approach is to hold that C has failed to discharge the burden of proof (per *Skelton v Lewisham and North Southwark HA*[308]).

In failure-to-warn actions too, the burden of proof resting on C has occasionally drawn controversy. In *Smith v Barking, Havering & Brentwood HA*,[309] however, Hutchinson J categorically rejected an earlier suggestion (in *Heywood v Wellers*[310]) that, where adequate disclosure of risks had not been made to C, and C alleged that she would have refused the operation, the burden is on D to prove that C would not have refused the operation.

Any uncertainty about probability may be solely due to D's breach. Nevertheless, English law will still not permit a reversal of the burden of proof. The fact that, in *Hotson*, Stephen Hotson could not establish with certainty which of the two causes was operative – either too many already-ruptured blood vessels to save the epiphysis (innocently caused, after his fall from the tree), or bleeding into the hip joint over the (negligently-caused) 5-day delay that killed off the rest of the intact blood vessels – rested entirely with the hospital doctors, D. After five days of bleeding and haematoma, it was impossible to say how many intact blood vessels existed when C was first seen at the hospital. As Lord Hoffmann remarked in *Gregg v Scott*, 'the need to prove causation was more unfair on Hotson, since the reason why he could not prove whether he had enough blood vessels after the fall was that the hospital had negligently failed to examine him'.[311] Hence, however unfair it may seem, if C cannot prove causation on the balance of probabilities because of D's own omissions and breach, that will not reverse the burden of proof – *Hotson* bears testament to that.

Twists and turns

There have been some twists in English law, which appellate courts have been at pains to correct.

For example, in *Keefe v Isle of Man Steam Packet Co Ltd*[312] (an employment case), the Court of Appeal was sympathetic towards C, where her lack of ability to prove causation was attributable to D:

> In *Keefe*, Mr Keefe's widow brought a deafness claim on her husband's, C's, behalf, against his former employer, D. The Dept of Employment's Code of Practice required D to measure noise in its

305 [1956] AC 613 (HL) 620 (Lord Reid). 306 [2012] EWHC 1150 (QB) [80] (Lloyd Jones J).
307 (1989) 22 BMLR 79 (CA) 110. 308 [1998] Lloyd's Rep Med 324 (QB).
309 QB, 29 Jul 1989. 310 [1976] 1 QB 446, 459. 311 [2005] UKHL 2, [2005] 2 AC 176, [88].
312 [2010] EWCA Civ 683.

premises and, if exceeding a certain level, to reduce the noise or to provide ear protectors. However, D never measured the noise levels (a breach of duty), and there was engineering evidence of excessive noise levels in the ships in which C had served. **Held (trial):** C failed; C could not prove exposure to excessive levels for periods in excess of 8 hours with any regularity. **Held (CA):** negligence proven; C's loss of hearing was caused by excessive noise on D's vessels.

The Court of Appeal in *Keefe* made several observations which, had they applied in *Hotson*, may have assisted Stephen Hotson to prove his claim. For one thing, Longmore LJ noted C's difficulty in proving D's breach of duty in not taking noise measurements, and that 'it hardly lies in [D's] mouth to assert that the noise levels were not, in fact, excessive. In such circumstances the court should judge [C's] evidence benevolently and [D's] evidence critically ... [D] who has, in breach of duty, made it difficult or impossible for [C] to adduce relevant evidence must run the risk of adverse factual findings. To my mind this is just such a case'.[313] The case is starkly similar to Stephen Hotson's difficulties.

Nevertheless, *Keefe* does **not** authorise a reversal of the burden of proof. In *Shawe-Lincoln v Neelakandan*[314] (a medical case), C argued that *Keefe* warranted a 'benevolent' treatment of C's case there too, given that the effect of D's negligence (no hourly neurological observations) had been to deprive C of evidence about the deterioration of his neurological condition. However, Lloyd-Jones J concluded that there could be no reversal of the burden (on the authority of *Bolitho*, *Bonnington*, etc): '[r]ather, *Keefe* is concerned with the weight which is to be attached to evidence and the circumstances in which the court may draw inferences'. In *Shawe-Lincoln*, it was not appropriate to draw an inference in favour of C either.

A rare House of Lords' indication that the burden of proof should shift to D occurred in the judgment of Lord Wilberforce who, in *McGhee v National Coal Board*, remarked: 'it is a sound principle that where [D] has, by breach of a duty of care, created a risk, and injury occurs within the area of that risk, the loss should be borne by [D], unless he shows that it had some other cause'.[315]

However, the House of Lords has since strongly reiterated that there can be **no** shift of the burden of proof in causation. Lord Wilberforce's opinion in *McGhee* was categorically overruled by *Wilsher*,[316] with Lord Bridge calling it a 'minority opinion'. In *Fairchild*,[317] Lord Bingham confirmed that Lord Bridge's dismissal of Lord Wilberforce's sentiments was entirely correct, while Lord Hutton remarked that, whatever the differing position in other jurisdictions may be, English precedent did not support the reversal of the burden of proof, as a matter of law. Further, in *Fairchild*, Lord Nicholls stated that any exceptions to the 'but-for' test are just that, true exceptions, and that the *Fairchild* exception itself 'is emphatically not intended to lead to such a relaxation whenever [C] has difficulty, perhaps understandable difficulty, in discharging the burden of proof resting on him'.[318] In *Bonnington Castings Ltd v Wardlaw*,[319] the House of Lords had already overruled an earlier decision which **did** shift the burden to D, *viz*, *Vyner v Waldenberg Bros Ltd*,[320] where it was held that the burden was on an employer to show that the breach of safety regulation was not the cause of an accident to the employee.

[313] *ibid*, [18]–[19]. [314] [2012] EWHC 1150 (QB) [80]–[81]. [315] [1973] 1 WLR 1 (HL) 6.
[316] [1988] AC 1074 (HL) 1087, and confirmed in: *Graham v Re-Chem Intl Ltd* (QB, Forbes J, 16 Jun 1995).
[317] [2002] UKHL 22, [22] (Lord Bingham), [10] (Lord Hutton); and also: [131], [144] (Lord Rodger).
[318] *ibid*, [43]. Also: *Barker v Corus UK Ltd* [2006] UKHL 20, [104] (Lord Walker).
[319] [1956] AC 613 (HL) 620. [320] [1946] KB 50 (CA).

The comparative corner: Reversing the burden of proof

Given the difficulties caused by the burden always resting on C, a couple of examples from other jurisdictions – of how the burden could feasibly be shifted – may be of interest.

i 'once [C] demonstrates that a breach of duty has occurred which is closely followed by damage, a *prima facie* causal connection will have been established. It is then for [D] to show, by evidence and argument, that [C] should not recover damages' (per the **Australian** decision of *Chappel v Hart*,[321] where the burden was ultimately not shifted, but where Kirby J described this formulation as 'compelling');

ii C must prove that D, by his breach, created a risk that the injury which actually occurred would occur. Once the court is 'convinced' that D had a 'substantial connection to the injury', then D has the burden of disproving causation, because an 'inference' of causation has arisen (per the **Canadian** decision of *Snell v Farrell*,[322] where Sopinka J described that formulation as explaining the outcome of *McGhee v National Coal Board*).

Were these formulations to be the English law, then that would have a marked impact in the two areas in which causation has had the most difficulty to date, *viz*, in medical and in employment negligence – e.g., having proved that oxygen was over-administered in *Wilsher v Essex AHA*, the doctors would have had to establish that one of the other four possible reasons was responsible for baby Martin's RLF, and not the excess oxygen; and having proved that the employer in *Fairchild* owed a duty to protect the employee from the risk associated with a single noxious agent like asbestos, and that the employer breached that duty by exposing the employee to that very risk, the employer would have to prove that it was not *his* period of employment that caused that employee to contract the disease of mesothelioma.

From the law reform perspective, however, the Australian Ipp Committee strongly opposed the notion that the burden of proof of causation should shift to D, under any circumstances. The Committee gave three reasons:[323]

- the evidentiary gap confronting C exists just the same for D, who may also find it impossible to discharge the burden of proof too;
- the reversal (if it were permitted) could feasibly apply, regardless of whether there was an evidentiary gap at all, but simply to cast on D the task of proving that C's damage was due to something other than his breach; and
- there was a consequent risk that courts would find in favour of C too readily by defining too widely the scenarios in which the 'but-for' test of causation should be departed from.

[321] (1998) 72 ALJR 1344 (HCA).
[322] [1990] 2 SCR 311 (SCC) 326–27.
[323] *Ipp Report*, [7.33]–[7.36].

9

Remoteness of damage

INTRODUCTION

Remoteness is the fourth limb of the negligence action, and represents the final opportunity for the court to circumscribe D's liability. This element asks whether the damage complained of, although factually caused by D's act or omission, was legally too remote. This principally (but not solely) involves an enquiry as to whether the kind or type of damage was reasonably foreseeable by D at the relevant time. As a general rule, D cannot be liable in law for damage that was not reasonably foreseeable.

The remoteness enquiry serves two limiting purposes, as a 'control mechanism' in ring-fencing D's liability: (1) it is the final element which C must prove, in order to make the cause of action complete; and (2) it provides the basis upon which the quantum of C's damages will ultimately be assessed, and ensures that D is not necessarily liable for **all** of the damage which his breach has caused – for C cannot recover from D any part of his damage which is adjudged to be too remote.

What the remoteness enquiry addresses

Remoteness is directed towards the *kind or type of damage* suffered by C. Is the damage, which is causally linked to D's breach, of the type for which the law regards D as properly being liable? Or is the damage too remote – too distant or unrelated – from the breach, to be fairly laid at D's door?

As a matter of terminology, the remoteness limb is sometimes referred to in modern jurisprudence as 'causation-in-law' or 'legal causation'. This distinguishes it from the factual enquiry as to whether D's breach caused the damage in fact, which is the function of the 'but-for' and other causation tests (per Chapter 8). In most remoteness problems, the damage would not have occurred, but for D's breach – but the purpose of remoteness is to ring-fence the 'but-for' consequences of a negligent act or omission. However, the label, 'legal causation', is something of a misnomer. As the Court of Appeal noted in *Robb v FT Everard & Sons Ltd*,[1] whilst remoteness is essentially an issue of law, the test of reasonable foreseeability (which applies at the remoteness stage) certainly requires findings of fact. Moreover, in *Jolley v Sutton LBC*,[2] Lord

[1] [1999] EWCA Civ 1022. [2] [2000] 3 All ER 409 (HL) 416.

Steyn instructed that remoteness is a fact-specific enquiry, requiring an 'intense focus on the circumstances of each case'.

Indeed, remoteness is a notoriously unpredictable area within the negligence action – driven, as it is, by 'common sense' (per *Barings plc v Coopers & Lybrand (a firm)*[3]), 'an immediately intuitive response' (per *Kuwait Airways Corp v Iraqi Airways Co*[4]), and by 'current ideas of justice and morality' (per *Overseas Tankship (UK) Ltd v Morts Dock & Engineering Co Ltd (The Wagon Mound)*[5]). When judges speak in such terms, then ascertaining the line between damages which D should lawfully bear, and those which should not fairly be transferred to D in the law's eyes, can be problematic ('riddled with indeterminacy', as one judge aptly put it[6]).

A few decades ago, Lord Denning optimistically remarked, in *SCM Ltd v WJ Whittall*,[7] that whereas 'lawyers are continually asking the question' whether or not damage is too remote, 'judges are never defeated by it. We may not be able to draw the line with precision, but we can always say on which side of it any particular case falls'. However, the number of successful appellate decisions discussed in this chapter would appear to indicate that not all judges share such a robust view! For example, in *Jolley v Sutton LBC*,[8] in a typically difficult remoteness scenario, the Court of Appeal unanimously disagreed with the trial judge, and the House of Lords unanimously overruled the Court of Appeal and reinstated the trial judge's view that Justin Jolley's damage was not too remote – hardly a model of predictability!

Finally, in addition to the arbitrary and fact-specific enquiry which remoteness inevitably entails, it is also invested with a decent 'dollop' of pragmatism. This is especially evident in economic loss cases, where D's exposure can be quite exacting. In the case of negligent audits/accountancy oversights, one court commented that 'an auditor is watchdog, not a bloodhound' (per *Re Kingston Cotton Mill Co (No 2)*[9]), while another acknowledged that the advisee company and directors 'have generally left the scene, headed in most cases for government-supervised liquidation or the bankruptcy court. The auditor has now assumed centre stage as the remaining solvent [D], and is faced with a claim for all sums of money ever loaned to or invested in the client' (per *Bily v Arthur Young & Co*[10]). Hence, judicial pragmatism under this element provides a valuable, if somewhat unpredictable, ring-fence around the quantum of damage for which D is liable.

Framework for analysis

A convenient framework for the remoteness enquiry is encapsulated in the Table below:

Nutshell analysis: Remoteness of damage

Checklist of issues to consider:

1 Whether the kind or type of C's damage was reasonably foreseeable (subject to the *Page v Smith* exception)
2 Whether C had any pre-existing vulnerability to that type of damage (and its legal effect)

[3] [2003] EWHC 1319 (Ch) [819]. [4] [2002] UKHL 19, [2002] 2 WLR 1353, [71].
[5] [1961] AC 388 (PC) 422. [6] *Perre v Apand Pty Ltd* [1999] HCA 36, 198 CLR 180, [82] (McHugh J).
[7] [1971] 1 QB 337 (CA) 346. [8] [2000] 3 All ER 409 (HL). [9] [1896] 2 Ch 279 (CA) 288 (Lopes LJ).
[10] P 2d 745, 763 (Cal Sup Ct 1992), both cited in *Barings plc v Coopers & Lybrand* [2003] EWHC 1319 (Ch) [822].

3 Whether the type of damage (even reasonably foreseeable damage) should be irrecoverable because:
   - the type of damage fell outside the scope of D's duty to avoid causing C damage;
   - there were too many causal links between D's breach and C's damage; or
   - reasons of public policy precluded recovery of C's damage.

Miscellaneous issues:

- The ongoing relevance of *Polemis*
- The difference between contract and tort

The issues in this framework will be considered in turn.

THE KIND OR TYPE OF DAMAGE

From *Re Polemis* to *Wagon Mound*

§9.1 The kind or type of damage suffered by C, as a result of D's act or omission, must have been reasonably foreseeable (per *Wagon Mound No 1*, which overruled the 'direct consequences' test, i.e., that D should be liable for any injuries which were 'directly caused' to C by D's negligent act, whether or not that injury was reasonably foreseeable).

According to the Privy Council in *Overseas Tankship (UK) Ltd v Morts Dock & Engineering Co (Wagon Mound No 1)* in 1961,[11] 'it is the foresight of the reasonable man which alone can determine responsibility'. Two years later, Lord Pearce reiterated, in *Hughes v Lord Advocate*,[12] that D are 'liable for all the foreseeable consequences of their neglect. When an accident is of a different type and kind from anything that [D] could have foreseen, he is not liable for it'. Reasonably foreseeable damage can be unlikely, but not so unlikely as to be 'brushed aside as far-fetched' (per *Wagon Mound*). This principle of remoteness in English law had its genesis in Sydney Harbour, of all places:

> In *Wagon Mound (No 1)*,[13] Morts Dock, C, owned the timber Sheerlegs Wharf at Morts Bay, Balmain, in Sydney Harbour, and conducted ship-building, ship-repairing and general engineering at the wharf. The wharf itself, plus the vessel, *The Corrimal*, which C was refitting at the wharf, were severely damaged by fire on 1 Nov 1951, which happened in a most unusual way. C's employees were working on *The Corrimal* with welding equipment, whilst a vessel, the *Wagon Mound*, was moored at Caltex Wharf on the north shore of Sydney Harbour. Overseas Tankship, D, chartered the *Wagon Mound*, and whilst filling it with bunkering oil, D's chief engineer negligently allowed a large quantity of oil to spill into Sydney Harbour, which D did not attempt to clean up. Meanwhile, C instructed its workmen not to undertake any welding work until it asked Caltex Oil whether C's workmen could safely continue their work on *The Corrimal*. C were told 'yes', that the oil was inflammable. C's management also believed that bunkering oil in the open, and floating on water, was inflammable. Unfortunately, two days later, the oil near Sheerlegs Wharf was ignited, and a fierce fire burnt the wharf and *The Corrimal*. The fire ignited because a cotton rag was floating on some debris in the oil;

[11] [1961] AC 388 (PC, on appeal from NSWSC) 424. [12] [1963] AC 837 (HL) 857.

[13] [1961] AC 388 (PC) 422–23, 425–26.

the cotton was set on fire by molten metal falling from Sheerlegs Wharf during welding; the cotton rag caught fire; those flames set the floating oil alight; and the flames then spread over the surface of the water in Sydney Harbour, reaching Sheerlegs Wharf itself. **Held:** fire damage to C's wharf was too remote to be compensable at law. That fire damage was the direct consequence of the oil's escape, but D could not reasonably be expected to have known that the oil would catch fire. Property damage from pollution was foreseeable; but damage by fire was unforeseeable.

The Privy Council overruled the then-current test of remoteness – *viz*, the *Polemis* 'direct consequences' test, which had been in force since 1921 – which was unfortunate for Morts Dock, C, given that the direct link between D's breach and their damage was, in fact, upheld:

In *Re Polemis and Furness, Withy & Co Ltd (Re Polemis)*,[14] Mr Polemis, C, owned the Greek steamship, *Thrasyvoulos*, which was chartered to Furness, Withy & Co, D, in 1917, for trading purposes, for the duration of the war. The vessel was loaded with cargo at Lisbon (*viz*, cases of benzine and/ or petrol and iron), and whilst being unloaded at Casablanca, it was discovered that some of the benzine/petrol had leaked *en voyage* in rough weather, and a lot of petrol vapour had accumulated in the hold, due to that leakage. Cases of benzine had to be transferred to another part of the ship, and D's stevedores placed heavy planks across the hatchway, to use as a platform for transferring the cases. However, with the ship's heaving, and due to D's stevedores' negligence, several cases hit a plank, causing it to fall into the hold. A rush of flames immediately occurred in the hold, and the ship was destroyed by fire. The fire arose from a spark igniting petrol vapour in the hold, which was caused by the falling board creating a spark. **Held:** the loss of the ship was not too remote. D (via their employed stevedores) were liable for all the direct consequences of the negligence, even though those consequences (i.e., the spark, the falling board) and the type of damage (damage by fire) could not reasonably have been foreseen.

The *Polemis* 'direct consequences' test is generally viewed to have been a **wider** test of remoteness, embracing more damage within its net, than the test of reasonable foreseeability. Certainly, the *Wagon Mound* approach is a more favourable test for D than was the *Polemis* test (as Morts Dock discovered, to its cost). As noted in *Essa v Laing*,[15] the test of reasonable foreseeability acts as a real control mechanism upon the ambit of claims for which D ought to be liable.

The meaning of 'reasonable foreseeability'

Test of foreseeability at other stages

§9.2 The test of reasonable foreseeability, for the purposes of remoteness, differs from that test at duty of care and breach stages, because it is focused on the kind or type of damage which resulted *from the accident or event which occurred.*

Some courts have suggested that there is **no** difference in the foreseeability analyses across the tort of negligence – whether considered at duty of care, breach, or remoteness stages. In *Jolley v Sutton LBC*,[16] Lord Hoffmann suggested that the test of foreseeability in *Wagon Mound* was relevant to the establishment of a duty of care, or remoteness, 'according to taste'. In *Corr v IBC Vehicles*,[17] Ward LJ noted that, 'there are considerable overlaps between the elements

[14] [1921] 3 KB 560 (CA). [15] [2004] EWCA Civ 2, [2004] IRLR 313, [37]–[38].
[16] [2000] 1 WLR 1082 (HL) 1091. [17] [2006] EWCA Civ 331, [2007] QB 46, [9].

of the scope of the duty of care, any break in the causal chain and remoteness of damage. Questions of foreseeability are the common thread, but into which compartment one places it, and even whether it matters where one places it, are not matters which are always abundantly clear'. In *Foster (nee Billington) v Maguire*[18] too, the Court of Appeal said that the question of whether C's damage was of the kind or type that was reasonably foreseeable was a question which overlapped between duty of care and remoteness, and which could be 'telescoped into one issue of fact'.

However, not all judges have treated the test of foreseeability as a seamless continuum. In *Corr v IBC Vehicles Ltd*,[19] Lord Bingham indicated that the query at remoteness stage is extremely focused – 'foreseeability is to be judged ... with reference to the *very accident which occurred*' – to be contrasted with the test at duty stage, which Lord Hoffmann described in *Jolley v Sutton LBC* as extremely general: 'whether injury *of some kind* was foreseeable'.[20]

In light of these comments, it is suggested that there is a distinct difference in the test of foreseeability at duty and remoteness stages. At remoteness stage, while it is not necessary that all the causal steps leading from breach to damage are foreseeable, the court will pay close attention to *precisely what damage* C sustained *as a result of the accident which occurred.* By contrast, at duty stage, the task is more general (as discussed in Chapter 2) – i.e., was it reasonably foreseeable that *some* damage could likely result from D's act or omission?

Furthermore, the remoteness enquiry depends upon what could reasonably have been foreseen at the time of D's breach, and not later (per *C Czarnikow Ltd v Koufos (The Heron II)*[21]).

General principles

§9.3 The kind or type of damage may be construed quite widely, so as to encompass the reasonable foreseeability of 'some personal injury' arising from D's breach. The specific kind or type of personal injury (e.g., damage by disease, damage by burns) is not required in that context. However, although the legal position remains unsettled, the better view is that reasonable foreseeability of a more specific kind of damage may still be required for property damage.

This principle has undergone some significant change over the past 50 years or so, at least in the context of personal injury. Under older cases, the kind or type of injury which had to be reasonably foreseeable was defined quite narrowly, e.g.:

- injury by burns:

  In *Hughes v Lord Advocate*,[22] Post Office employees, D, were working on telephone cables below a street in Edinburgh. They removed the manhole cover, put a canvas shelter tent over it, and put four red warning paraffin lamps around the hole, per normal procedure. Soon after 5 pm, when it was dark, D left the site for their 15-minute tea break, removing a ladder from the manhole and pulling a tarpaulin cover over the entrance to the shelter. Russell Hughes, 8, C, and his 10-year-old uncle, decided to enter the shelter, taking one of the paraffin lamps with them to explore the manhole. The lamp was either knocked or dropped into the manhole, and a violent explosion occurred, sending flames 30 ft into the air. C fell into the manhole from the force of the explosion, and was badly burnt. The accident occurred because, when the lamp fell down the hole and broke, some paraffin escaped, and enough vaporised to create an explosive mixture which was detonated by the naked

[18] [2001] EWCA Civ 273, [21]. [19] [2008] UKHL 13, [2008] 1 AC 884, [11] (emphasis added).
[20] [2000] 1 WLR 1082 (HL) 1091 (emphasis added). [21] [1969] 2 AC 350 (HL). [22] [1963] AC 837 (HL).

light of the lamp. **Held:** C's burn injuries were not too remote. Damage from burns was foreseeable, whether those burns were caused by explosion of vapour or the (more likely) ignition of liquid paraffin. The cause of the accident was a known source of danger, the lamp, but the risk of burns had happened unpredictably. The explosion of vaporised paraffin was an unforeseeable way for this accident to happen. But the end result – injury by burns – was not unforeseeable. If the lamp had simply fallen over and broken, C likely still would have been burned, possibly seriously.

- injury by disease:

  In *Tremain v Pike*,[23] William Tremain, C, was employed as a herdsman by farmer, Mr Pike, D. C contracted Weil's disease (leptospirosis) through contact with rats' urine. C alleged that he was infected by using or washing in contaminated water, or handling bales of hay, which contained the urine, because of an infestation of rats around the farm buildings. **Held:** C's damage (injury by disease) was too remote. Reasonably foreseeable damage caused by rat-associated disease was disease associated either with rat bites or food contamination, but contamination through exposure to rats' urine was very rare, and there was no evidence that the farming community knew, or ought reasonably to have foreseen, that a disease could be contracted by merely handling matter contaminated by rats. The possibility of contracting Weil's disease was a remote one which could not reasonably be foreseen, and the damage was irrecoverable.

- injury/damage by explosion:

  In *Vacwell Engineering Co Ltd v BDH Chemicals Ltd*,[24] Vacwell Engineering, C, had a laboratory in Surrey, and purchased a chemical, boron tribromide, from BDH Chemicals, D, in glass ampoules. A Russian physicist, Mr Strouzhinski, was working in the lab, removing the labels from these glass ampoules by immersing the ampoules in sinks of water, when an explosion occurred, killing Mr Strouzhinski, and seriously damaging the lab. The probable cause of the explosion was that Mr Strouzhinski had put or dropped these ampoules into the sink, the ampoules broke releasing the chemical, it reacted violently with water in the sink shattering other ampoules in the sink, and it all caused a violent explosion. **Held:** C's damage was not too remote. D committed a breach in failing to warn C of the risk of explosion of the chemical if it came into contact with water. It was foreseeable that, in the ordinary course of industrial use, D's chemical could come into contact with water and cause a violent reaction and an explosion, and that some damage to persons and property could result.

- damage by fire:

  In *Overseas Tankship (UK) Ltd v Miller Steamship Co Pty (Wagon Mound (No 2))*,[25] the case arose out of the same facts as in *Wagon Mound I*, but this time, the owners of the two ships damaged by fire, *The Corrimal* and the *Audrey D*, sued the charterers of the *Wagon Mound*, D, for negligently discharging the bunkering oil into Sydney Harbour. It will be recalled that, in *Wagon Mound (No 1)*, it was held that D did not know, nor could it have reasonably foreseen, that bunkering oil was capable of being set alight when spread on water. That was how the evidence was led, because the wharf owners, Morts Dock, C, would have been compromised, had it been proven that damage by fire was reasonably foreseeable, because their own actions in resuming welding would have given rise to a potential finding of contributory negligence, which was, at that time, a complete defence in New South Wales. Hence, Morts Dock had sought to rely on the *Polemis* 'direct consequences' test

[23] [1969] 1 WLR 1556 (Exeter Assizes) 1560.
[24] [1971] 1 QB 88 (Rees J).
[25] [1967] AC 26 (PC, on appeal from NSWSC).

of remoteness, and failed with that argument. In *Wagon Mound (No 2)*, C led different evidence to show that damage to their ships by fire **was** reasonably foreseeable. **Held:** Cs' damage was not too remote. The discharge of so much bunkering oil must have taken a good while, and a vigilant ship's engineer would have noticed that discharge, and ought to have known that it was possible to ignite this kind of oil on water (and that this had actually happened previously). Hence, damage by fire, whilst unlikely, was reasonably foreseeable.

These are the principal older cases.

However, in the context of personal injury, more recent case law has held that the kind or type of injury should be defined much more broadly to amount to 'some physical injury' to C (per *Jolley v Sutton LBC*[26]). This is a far more sympathetic-to-C principle than was evident in *Tremain v Pike* – for the wider the type of damage, the more likely that C's damage will fall within the requisite description.

In *Jolley v Sutton LBC*, the council, D, owned a block of council flats in Surrey, where an abandoned and derelict boat was left by some unknown person on a grassed area where children played. Flat residents complained to D about the boat, and D put a warning sign on it, but the boat was not removed for two years (until after the accident). Justin Jolley, C, 14, and his friend, rather poignantly planned to repair the boat and take it to Cornwall to sail it. C had the strength and ability to jack up the boat onto a car jack and some wooden blocks, to repair and paint underneath it. One day, while C was under the boat, it rocked (for some unexplained reason), and before he could get out from underneath, it fell onto him, broke his back, and rendered him a paraplegic. **Held:** C's type of damage was not too remote – 'some physical injury', as a result of meddling with the boat, was reasonably foreseeable. It would have been much more likely for C to have been injured by climbing onto the boat, and falling through its rotten deck, than the boat falling on top of him. However, it was reasonably foreseeable that young boys could try to mimic adult behaviour by repairing a boat, and that in doing so, a propped-up boat could collapse, causing C injury.

This case essentially reduced to **two** competing arguments: whether the trial judge was correct to define the type of damage along the lines that, 'children would meddle with the boat at the risk of some physical injury' – or whether the Court of Appeal was correct in defining the type of damage more narrowly, that 'children would be drawn to the boat, climbing upon it, and being injured by the rotten planking giving way beneath them'. The former (wider) view prevailed, as being the type of damage which should be reasonably foreseeable – and clearly, C's injury (caused by the boat falling on top of him, having jacked it up) fell within that description of the requisite type of damage. Curiously, the narrower views of the relevant type or kind of injury which were adopted in *Tremain v Pike* and *Vacwell Engineering* were not even referred to in *Jolley*. In any event, the wider view has been recently applied, again to C's benefit:

In *Hicks v Young*,[27] Kristopher Hicks, C, 23, caught Michael Young's, D's, taxi late at night in Bath to go home. After arriving at the intended address and letting C's companion out, D then drove off with C still in the taxi. The reason for this is that D believed that C and his companion were going to 'do a runner' without paying for the fare, and D intended to return with C to the taxi rank to sort out the matter. On that journey, C jumped out of the taxi when it was travelling at 20 mph, hit

[26] [2000] 1 WLR 1082 (HL) 1091.

[27] [2015] EWHC 1144 (QB), quote at [33]. See too, for further application: *ST v Maidstone and Tunbridge Wells NHS Trust* [2015] EWHC 51 (QB) (dicta only; causation ultimately failed).

his head hard, and suffered serious brain injury. **Held:** D was negligent (subject to C's contributory negligence). It may not have been foreseeable that C would jump out at that speed, but that was irrelevant. It was foreseeable that C would try to leave the taxi when it was moving, and that he may have suffered a bruised knee, broken wrist, etc. Catastrophic injury was less foreseeable, but it was the kind of damage which occurred, 'namely personal injury, which is required and not of the precise mechanism by which it occurred'.

However, an equivalent widening of the kind or type of damage, to equate to 'some property damage', has not been evident. Those types of Cs cannot take advantage of the benevolently-wide view of what amounts to a 'type of damage'. The aforementioned cases of *Wagon Mound (No 1)*, *Wagon Mound (No 2)* and *Vacwell* demonstrate a fairly narrow interpretation of the kind of property damage suffered (and *Vacwell's* description of the type of damage was approved in *Free Grammar School of John Lyon v Westminster CC*[28]).

§9.4 C's damage is not too remote, merely because the extent of C's damage is greater than was foreseen, or which could have been reasonably foreseeable, by D. D cannot limit his liability by contending that the *extent* of C's injuries could not have been reasonably foreseeable.

In *Hughes v Lord Advocate*, Lord Reid stated that D 'is liable, although the damage be a good deal greater in extent than was foreseeable'. In *Jolley v Sutton LBC*, Justin Jolley's paraplegia was a type of damage which was reasonably foreseeable, notwithstanding the severity of those injuries. In *Vacwell Engineering Co Ltd v BDH Chemicals Ltd*, it was also irrelevant that the magnitude of the explosion and the extent of the damage (i.e., the death of the Russian scientist, and the severe damage to the lab) was not foreseeable.

While this principle is often evident in the case of the 'egg-shell skull claimant' (who has a particular vulnerability to the damage which befell him), the rule has **general** application, applying equally to persons of normal fortitude (as with Russell Hughes, Justin Jolley and the Russian scientist working in Vacwell's lab).

Albeit that the abovementioned cases involved personal injury sustained by C, the principle is just as applicable to both greater-than-foreseen property damage (per *Vacwell Engineering*) and economic losses too:

In *Barings plc (in liq) v Coopers & Lybrand*,[29] the Barings group collapsed in February 1995, caused by the unauthorised trading on the Singapore International Monetary Exchange (SIMEX) by Nicholas Leeson (NL), the general manager of Barings Futures (Singapore) Ltd, C, who incurred losses for the group of about £791m. Those losses had been funded by other members of the Barings group, in ignorance of the trading activities for which the funds were being used. C sued Deloitte & Touche (Singapore), D, who were its auditors in 1992–93, claiming negligence because the auditors did not detect the unauthorised trading of NL. **Held:** D's audits were negligent, in failing to pick up NL's efforts to conceal significant losses in C's accounts. The damage flowing from losses, made by unauthorised trading in the course of a securities trading business of the type being operated by C, was foreseeable and not too remote. That the scale of those losses turned out to have been much greater than a reasonable auditor could have foreseen did not legally matter.

[28] [2012] UKUT 117 (Upper Tribunal, Lands Chamber) [78]–[79].

[29] [2003] EWHC 1319, [2003] PNLR 34 (Ch).

Hence, if C suffers a particularly severe case of injury, then C must prove that his damage was not unforeseeable damage of a different kind from that which was foreseeable, but simply more extensive damage of the same kind.

§9.5 C's damage is not too remote, merely because the precise manner or sequence of events giving rise to that damage was not foreseen, nor reasonably foreseeable, by D (i.e., it is the type of damage which must be reasonably foreseeable). Nevertheless, whilst that precise chain of events need not be foreseeable, there must be a *causal* link between D's breach and C's damage. As a further principle in C's favour, the precise chain of events between D's wrongdoing, and the ultimate damage that befell C, does not have to be reasonably foreseeable.

The abovementioned authorities of *Hughes v Lord Advocate* and *Jolley v Sutton LBC* provide ample authority for that in the context of C's physical injury. Provided that no 'new and unexpected factor' occurred that could be regarded as a *novus actus interveniens*, the fact that D could not have reasonably foreseen *the precise mechanics of just how the accident occurred* is no escape for D. The important point is whether C was 'injured as a result of the type or kind of accident or occurrence that could reasonably have been foreseen' (per Lord Reid in *Hughes v Lord Advocate*[30]); whether 'the accident is of a class that might well be anticipated as one of the reasonable and probable results of the wrongful act' (per Greer LJ in *Haynes v Harwood*[31]); and whether C can prove 'foreseeability, not as to the particulars, but the genus' (per Lord Hoffmann *in Jolley v Sutton*[32]). To the extent that decisions such as *Doughty v Turner Manufacturing*[33] held that an unforeseeable sequence of events rendered C's damage too remote, those have not been followed (and given the precedential hierarchy, courts since have expressly followed the reasoning in *Hughes* rather than in *Doughty*, as in, e.g., *Hadlow v Peterborough CC*[34]).

Remoteness arguments arise, in practice, when the 'precise form' by which C suffers his injuries was unlikely, but C argues that the class of accident was entirely foreseeable, and thereby produced a kind or type of damage which was foreseeable. The sequence of events in *Jolley* and *Hughes* were most unlikely, even fanciful – involving, as they did, the unpredictable activities of children – but in both, the damage was compensable. Other cases of physical injury have demonstrated the same principle – in both a medical and an employment context. For example:

In *Wisniewski v Central Manchester HA*,[35] Philip Wisniewski, C, suffered severe and irreversible brain damage during the 13 minutes immediately prior to his birth, because as he moved down the birth canal, the umbilical cord was wrapped round his neck and had a knot in it, effectively strangling him. His mother had been admitted to D's hospital three hours earlier. Had her care not been negligently mismanaged, a doctor would have carried out an artificial rupture of the membranes, which would have led to C's being born by caesarean, thus obviating the hazards of a natural birth. The strangling of C by the umbilical cord was very rare (1–2 a year, in a busy teaching hospital), and D argued that the damage was too remote to be compensable (a far more likely harm was the risk of damage by oxygen starvation whilst C was in the womb). **Held:** C's damage was not too remote. The foreseeable kind or type of damage was hypoxia (oxygen deprivation to the brain), and it made no

30 [1963] AC 837 (HL) 852. 31 [1935] 1 KB 146 (CA) 156. 32 [2000] 1 WLR 1082 (HL) 1091.
33 [1964] 1 QB 518 (CA). 34 [2011] EWCA Civ 1329, [15]–[22].
35 [1998] EWCA Civ 596, [1998] Lloyd's Rep Med 223. See similarly, in the medical context: *Loraine v Wirral Univ Teaching Hosp NHS Foundation Trust* [2008] EWHC (QB), and approved in: *ST v Maidstone and Tunbridge Wells NHS Trust* [2015] EWHC 51 (QB) [193].

difference that the precise mechanism by which the hypoxia arose was not foreseeable. In *Hadlow v Peterborough CC*,[36] Jean Hadlow, C, 63, was employed as a teacher at a secure unit for young women operated by Council D. She was due to teach a class of three women. The unit's policy was that no member of staff would be alone with a group of more than two young women. C's teaching assistant (TA) would normally have been present. The foreseeable source of danger here was a risk of attack on C. On this day, however, C was about to be left alone (her TA was due to arrive late), and C hurried to the door of the classroom to attract the attention of a carer to stay behind. In doing so, C tripped on a chair in her rush and badly injured herself. **Held:** C's damage was not too remote. The accident did not happen in the most likely way (i.e., an attack), but the risk of physical injury was foreseeable. It was unnecessary to show foreseeability of the precise chain of events leading up to the accident.

The precise sequence of events leading to C's consequential psychiatric injury does not need to be foreseeable either:

In *Corr v IBC Vehicles Ltd*,[37] Mr Corr, C, was a maintenance engineer employed by IBC Vehicles Ltd, D, at its Coventry factory. In 1996, C was badly injured whilst trying to remedy a fault on the automated presses which produced panels for Vauxhall vehicles. The automated arm threw a panel in C's direction without warning. C would have been decapitated, had he not ducked. His right ear was severed. Thereafter, C suffered disfigurement, bad headaches, PTSD and severe depression. He was treated by electro-convulsive therapy, was frequently hospitalised, and assessed as a high suicide risk. Six years after the accident, C committed suicide by jumping from the top of a multi-storey carpark. D admitted breach, but argued that C's suicide was too remote to be compensable, and because C was not technically insane at the time of his death, and could invoke personal autonomy, such that D was not 'his keeper'. **Held:** C's suicide was not too remote. Lord Bingham noted that suicide as a result of a severe depression was 'not uncommon', and that '[i]t was well known that between 1 in 6 and 1 in 10 sufferers from severe depression kill themselves'. Although some behaviour of severely depressed people could be 'so unusual and unpredictable as to be outside the bounds of what is reasonably foreseeable, suicide cannot be so regarded'. Also, given the extent and severity of C's physical injuries, some psychological harm, as a concomitant of physical harm suffered by C, was reasonably foreseeable. (By contrast, Lord Scott held that the risk of C's suicide was between 2–4%, which was 'possibly foreseeable', but not 'reasonably foreseeable'. However, Lord Scott too found for C, on the basis that depression was definitely foreseeable, such that the extent of the damage (suicide) did not need to be so.)

The treatment of *pure* psychiatric injury, and the remoteness rules applicable thereto, are considered shortly, under the next principle.

The principle that the sequence of events giving rise to C's consequential economic loss does not have to be foreseeable is also well established. In a complex business world, D may have no idea of the complicated financial arrangements into which C, the victim of his negligence, has entered, and the chain of events leading to C's losses may be very unlikely – and yet, C's economic losses will not be too remote on that score.

[36] [2011] EWCA Civ 1329.

[37] [2008] UKHL 13, [2008] 1 AC 884, with quotes at [5], [13] (Lord Bingham), [28] (Lord Scott), respectively. The other members of the House concurred with Lord Bingham on this point.

In *Conarken Group Ltd v Network Rail Infrastructure Ltd (Rev 1)*,[38] Network Rail, C, was responsible for the rail track system, and awarded train-operating companies franchises to operate on different parts of the system. C entered into 'track access agreements' to pay those train companies damages, should the rail network be unusable. In fact, Conarken's, D's, driver negligently caused damage to the parapet walls of a railway bridge, causing rubble to be strewn on railway tracks in Yorkshire. The line was closed for five days while repairs were carried out. **Held:** the contractual payments required from C to the train companies was not too remote. A revenue-earning asset was affected, and the complicated business arrangements entered into by C did not render that particular loss uncompensable. It was part and parcel of foreseeable economic loss arising from an accident such as this.

However, it is one thing to hold that D may be liable, even though the precise chain of events leading to C's accident was not a reasonably foreseeable chain of events. Nevertheless, C must still prove the requisite causal link between D's breach and his damage. If D's breach played no causal part at all in the accident which befell C, then it does not matter whether or not the chain of events is foreseeable – causation, and the negligence action as a whole, will fail. As the Court of Appeal stated in *Green v Sunset & Vine Productions Ltd*,[39] the principle in *Jolley* has 'no relevance at all to a case in which D's negligent act has not in fact played any causative role in the loss and damage suffered by C'.

In *Green v Sunset & Vine Productions*, Willie Green, C, an experienced driver of historic racing cars, was driving a Maserati in a Goodwood Revival race meeting, when he lost control of the car, was flung out, and the car ran over his legs, causing severe injury. C alleged that the car had hit a kerb cam set up by D, and that this impact caused the car to veer off the track. **Held:** C's damage was not caused by the kerb cam. The presence and installation of the camera did not materially cause the accident; the accident would probably have happened, even had it had not been there. Without causation, then the fact that it was reasonably foreseeable that a car passing over the kerb cam might lead to injury to a driver, even if the precise chain of events leading to C's accident was not a reasonably foreseeable chain of events, was irrelevant.

Exception to the requirement of reasonable foreseeability

There is **one** exception in English law – where an unforeseeable type of damage (i.e., psychiatric injury) **can** properly be recovered at law.

§9.6 Where D's breach puts C in a 'zone of physical danger' but where C suffers from psychiatric injury, then foreseeability of the risk of physical injury is sufficient, whether or not that psychiatric injury was reasonably foreseeable. If that psychiatric injury was indeed unforeseeable (as being remote and fanciful), then some physical injury will be reasonably foreseeable, precisely because C was put in that zone of physical danger ('the *Page v Smith* principle'). Otherwise, where C suffers pure psychiatric injury for reasons unconnected with being put in any 'zone of physical danger', C must prove that his psychiatric injury was reasonably foreseeable, in accordance with the usual *Wagon Mound* principle.

[38] [2011] EWCA Civ 644, [2011] BLR 462, [148]–[155]. [39] [2010] EWCA Civ 1441, [44].

Set down in the controversial decision of *Page v Smith*,[40] this is the **only** circumstance in English law where a type of damage that was unforeseeable is, nevertheless, compensable (as discussed in Chapter 5).

> In *Page v Smith*, Mr Page, C, was involved in a minor car accident with a car being driven by Mr Smith, D, when D turned in front of C carelessly. C suffered no physical injury, but three hours after the accident he began to feel exhausted. That exhaustion manifested as ME, or chronic fatigue syndrome, which C had suffered in mild form previously, and which he now suffered in a chronic and intense form. **Held (trial):** C won. **Held (CA):** C lost. Psychiatric reaction of this sort was not foreseeable in a person of ordinary fortitude as a result of what happened to C in that car accident. **Held (HL, by majority):** C could recover; his psychiatric condition was not too remote: 'it was enough to ask whether [D] should have reasonably foreseen that [C] might suffer physical injury as a result of [D's] negligence, so as to bring him within the range of [D's] duty of care. It was unnecessary to ask, as a separate question, whether [D] should reasonably have foreseen injury by shock; and it is irrelevant that [C] did not, in fact, suffer any external physical injury'.

Strictly speaking, however, this is **not** an exception at all, because Lord Lloyd (delivering the majority judgment) attributed this generous-to-C legal principle to the lack of distinction between the two types of personal injury (physical and psychiatric), insofar as medical science is concerned:

> The test ought to be whether [D] can reasonably foresee that his conduct will expose [C] to risk of personal injury ... There is no justification for regarding physical and psychiatric injury as different 'kinds' of injury. Once it is established that [D] is under a duty of care to avoid causing personal injury to [C], it matters not whether the injury in fact sustained is physical, psychiatric or both ... In an age when medical knowledge is expanding fast, and psychiatric knowledge with it, it would not be sensible to commit the law to a distinction between physical and psychiatric injury, which may already seem somewhat artificial, and may soon be altogether outmoded. Nothing will be gained by treating them as different 'kinds' of personal injury, so as to require the application of different tests in law.[41]

The *Page v Smith* principle applies, whether the psychiatric injury was 'pure' in nature, or consequential upon physical injury. It renders unforeseeable consequential psychiatric injury recoverable at law:

> In *Simmons v British Steel plc*,[42] Mr Simmons, C, was employed as a burner by British Steel, D, at Clydebridge Steel Works. He tripped and fell off the burning table and hit his head on a metal stanchion. Headgear protected him from a very serious head injury, but he suffered a bump, eye disturbances and discharge from his ear. C had complained to D about what he saw as an unsafe system of work, but nothing had been done. The physical injuries were not particularly onerous (£3,573), but C also suffered: (1) exacerbation of a pre-existing skin complaint, psoriasis, and (2) depression, brought on by extreme anger because the accident had occurred despite his attempts to avert it, and without apology from D. Also, D's medical officer refused to allow C to return to work, and D's HR officers failed to visit or take any interest in C, which angered C and caused him to become preoccupied with the accident. **Held:** both further consequences were not too remote at

[40] [1996] AC 155 (HL) 190 (Lord Lloyd, with whom Lords Ackner and Browne-Wilkinson concurred; Lords Keith and Jauncey dissented).

[41] [1996] AC 155 (HL) 188. [42] [2004] SC (HL) 94, [2004] PIQR P33.

law. Personal injury was a reasonably foreseeable result of D's breach, even if the exacerbation of the skin complaint and the depressive illness were not reasonably foreseeable. C was put in the zone of physical danger by D's breach, and hence, there was no reason to distinguish between physical and psychiatric forms of personal injury.

Of course, if the psychiatric injury itself **was** reasonably foreseeable, then compensation for it does **not** fall within this exceptional rule – because *Wagon Mound (No 1)* states that any kind of damage that is foreseeable is recoverable, and not too remote (as illustrated by *Corr v IBC Vehicles*, where Mr Corr's depression and suicide *were* held to be foreseeable). It is only for *unforeseeable* psychiatric damage that the exceptional rule in *Page v Smith* has room to apply.

Even then, *Page v Smith* applies in only very limited circumstances. In *Pratley v Surrey CC*,[43] the Court of Appeal pointed out that *Page v Smith's* view that there is 'no stark divide between physical and mental injury' arose specifically in circumstances where C was in the zone of danger, at risk of physical injury, but suffered psychiatric injury instead. As discussed in more detail in Chapter 5, for other types of pure psychiatric injury claims, *viz*, for secondary victims, for stress-at-work claims (of which Ms Pratley's case was an example), for elevated primary victims, and for the residuary type of claimant, C must prove that his *psychiatric* injury was foreseeable (i.e., in compliance with the usual *Wagon Mound* principle).

Some judges have commented, from time to time, that *Page v Smith* may require reconsideration. For example, in the *Pleural Plaques* litigation,[44] both Lord Scott and Lord Rodger indicated that the principle may be revisited in the future. To date, however, the House of Lords/ Supreme Court has not seen fit (nor perhaps had the opportunity) to revise the principle – and until it does, unforeseeable psychiatric injury will be compensable if suffered by C who was at the risk of foreseeable physical injury created by D's negligence.

Nevertheless, even if C's damage was reasonably foreseeable, it may **not** be recoverable. Three reasons, pertinent to remoteness, may preclude C's recovery of compensation for such damage – the damage fell outside the scope of D's duty to prevent; too many causal chains; and public policy. Before dealing with those, however, it is necessary to consider the position, at law, of the fragile, vulnerable, 'egg-shell skull' C.

THE POSITION OF 'EGG-SHELL' CLAIMANTS WITH PRE-EXISTING VULNERABILITIES

§9.7 Provided that it was reasonably foreseeable that a person of normal physical fortitude would suffer *some* damage of the type that was suffered by C ('the normal fortitude' rule), then an 'egg-shell skull' C, who suffers from some unforeseeable manifestation of injury because of his abnormal physical susceptibility, is able to recover compensation for the *full* extent of his damage, even where the manifestation of that abnormal susceptibility was not reasonably foreseeable. D must 'take his victim as he finds him' (the 'egg-shell skull' rule). The same applies to those who suffer from abnormal psychiatric susceptibility (with the exception of the *Page v Smith*-type victim of psychiatric injury noted in §9.6 above, who is not subject to the normal fortitude rule).

[43] [2003] EWCA Civ 1067, [2004] PIQR P17, [42]–[43].

[44] *Johnston v NEI Intl Combustion Ltd* [2007] UKHL 39, [77] (Lord Scott), [95]–[97] (Lord Rodger).

The 'normal fortitude' rule

The 'egg-shell skull' C is treated rather beneficently by English law. In the absence of any special knowledge about C's vulnerability, it must be reasonably foreseeable that the kind of damage suffered by C would be suffered by a person of normal fortitude or robustness as a result of D's breach (the so-called 'the normal fortitude rule'). That is, it must be reasonably foreseeable, to a person in D's position, that a person of 'customary phlegm' or 'with a normal standard of susceptibility'[45] would suffer *some* damage of the type that was suffered. As Lord Bingham stated in *Corr v IBC Vehicles Ltd*, under the remoteness enquiry, 'foreseeability is to be judged ... with reference, not to the actual victim, but to a hypothetical [victim]'.[46]

If, however, it is unforeseeable that an ordinarily-robust C would suffer any damage of the type that was suffered, then the damage suffered by C will be too remote at law. In other words, where C is so vulnerable that he – alone, exceptionally and extraordinarily – suffers some damage from D's breach, where a person of normal fortitude would not suffer any such damage, that damage is not reasonably foreseeable.

The normal fortitude rule applies, whether C has suffered from physical or psychiatric damage:

Physical injury: In *Bourhill (or Hay) v Young*, Lord Wright provided a hypothetical example of an egg-shell skull C of the physical variety: '[o]ne who suffers from a terrible tendency to bleed on slight contact, which is denoted by the term, "a bleeder", cannot complain if he mixes with the crowd and suffers severely, perhaps fatally, from being merely brushed against'.[47]

Psychiatric injury: the rule of normal fortitude applies to all Cs, with the exception of the so-called *Page v Smith*-type 'primary victim', who constitutes an exception to the normal fortitude rule, given that Mr Page suffered a recurrence of CFS (as discussed in Chapter 5). This was reiterated in *White v CC of South Yorkshire Police* ('[t]he law expects reasonable fortitude and robustness of its citizens, and will not impose liability for the exceptional frailty of certain individuals'[48]).

The 'egg-shell skull' rule

This is sometimes referred to by the maxim that the wrongdoer must take his victim *talem qualem* (as he finds him). It seems to originate from the judgment of Kennedy J in *Dulieu v White & Sons*:

> If a man is negligently run over [by D], or otherwise negligently injured in his body, it is no answer to the sufferer's claim for damages that he would have suffered less injury, or no injury at all, if he had not had an unusually thin skull or an unusually weak heart.[49]

Any person run over by D would have suffered from *some* physical injury from that accident, thus satisfying the rule of normal fortitude. Then, if C happens to be an 'egg-shell skull' C, the full extent of C's injury is compensable.

Hence, it is important to keep the 'rule of normal fortitude' distinct from the 'egg-shell skull' rule. They are different rules, and operate for different purposes. As the House of Lords explained in *White*, the 'rule of normal fortitude' is a rule of liability, because it is an essential component under the remoteness limb.[50] On the other hand, the 'egg-shell skull' rule is a rule of

[45] *Bourhill (or Hay) v Young* [1943] AC 92 (HL) 110 (Lord Wright), 117 (Lord Porter).
[46] [2008] UKHL 13, [2008] 1 AC 884, [11].
[47] [1943] AC 92 (HL) 109, [1942] SC 78, 92.
[48] [1999] 2 AC 455 (HL) 463.
[49] [1901] 2 KB 669, 679.
[50] [1999] 2 AC 455 (HL) 474.

quantum whereby, as a result of a breach of duty, the damage inflicted by D proves to be more serious than expected because of C's abnormal physical susceptibility, and that can properly be taken into account in assessing the quantum of C's damages. Where an exceptionally frail C *can* satisfy the rule of normal fortitude, this principle of remoteness applies in C's favour, by permitting C (or his estate, if he dies) to recover compensation for the full extent of C's damage, however extraordinary or abnormal that damage may be. As Laws LJ explained in *Rahman v Arearose Ltd*,[51] the egg-shell skull principle:

> is a principle designed to protect vulnerable claimants ... It is a modification of the usual rule that a negligent D is liable for damage which he should reasonably foresee. Its justification is that it promotes the basic rule in this area, which ... is that every tortfeasor should compensate the injured C in respect of that loss and damage for which he should justly be held responsible.

As a practical caveat, however, the quantum of the egg-shell skull C's damage may be reduced or discounted, to take into account that C would have been susceptible in the future to the type of damage that befell him. This discount would reflect the 'ordinary vicissitudes of life' which C was likely to endure, given his 'egg-shell' state (e.g., in *Page v Smith*,[52] Mr Page's damages for his psychiatric condition were discounted by 40%, under this caveat).

§9.8 The 'egg-shell skull' rule applies, whether C has suffered from physical or psychiatric damage. Despite some judicial uncertainty, the better view is that the egg-shell skull rule also applies where C suffers economic damage.

The physically-injured C. Least controversially, the 'egg-shell' rule applies to the physically-injured C:

> In *Smith v Leech Brain & Co Ltd*,[53] a small amount of molten metal was splattered in a factory, due to unsafe work practices employed by the factory owners, Leech Brain, D. Some molten metal splashed onto Mr Smith's, C's, face and lip. Due to a predisposition to cancer, the burn injury to C's lip developed into a cancerous state, and three years after the accident, C died of cancer. **Held:** C's death was not too remote. It was not necessary for a reasonable employer in D's position to have foreseen that a burn would cause cancer, and that C would die. It was only necessary that D could reasonably foresee the type of injury C suffered, *viz*, injury by burn (which was proven). The amount of C's damage depended upon his constitution and characteristics, but D was liable for the full consequences.
> In *Robinson v Post Office*,[54] Keith Robinson, C, slipped on some oil on a ladder whilst engaged as a technician at the Post Office, D, and grazed his shin. He was given an anti-tetanus serum injection eight hours later, and nine days later, developed encephalitis which resulted in brain damage and paralysis. This was a rare reaction, but more likely where the patient had had a previous dose of the serum (as in C's case). **Held:** D was liable for the full extent of D's injuries, including the brain damage and paralysis. Provided that some physical injury caused by slipping was foreseeable (as was the medical treatment which followed it), D had to take this victim as it found him, even where the amount of injury C suffered depended entirely upon C's allergy to the second serum injection.

Similarly, if C, a haemophiliac, suffers some accidentally-inflicted wound caused by D's negligence, then D will be liable to C, because a non-haemaphiliac would have suffered *some*

[51] [2001] QB 351 (CA) [30]. [52] *Page v Smith* [1993] PIQR Q55 (QB) 76–77 (Otton J).
[53] [1962] 2 QB 405, 415. [54] [1974] 1 WLR 1176 (CA).

damage from that wound. The fact that C may **die**, as a result of blood loss, invokes the 'egg-shell skull' rule.

The psychiatrically-injured C. Where C has an 'egg-shell skull' personality or mental state, and suffers psychiatric injury as a result of D's breach, then in *Page v Smith*, Lord Lloyd stated that, '[t]he negligent [D] ... takes his victim as he finds him. The same should apply in the case of psychiatric injury. There is no difference in principle ... between an eggshell skull and an eggshell personality.'[55] Hence, even though the normal fortitude rule does not apply to *Page v Smith*-type victims (see above), the egg-shell rule certainly does.

In *Page v Smith*,[56] the negligent car-driver Mr Smith, D, could not have reasonably foreseen that Mr Page, C, would suffer extreme chronic fatigue syndrome after the car accident, but C was an egg-shell skull personality, due to his previous condition of myalgic encephalomyelitis. **Held:** C's damage was not too remote. Lord Browne-Wilkinson stated that D 'did owe a duty of care to prevent foreseeable damage, including psychiatric damage. Once such a duty of care is established, D must take C as he finds him'. In *Simmons v British Steel plc*[57] Mr Simmons, C, suffered a knock to the head after a fall due to D's negligence, and suffered from exacerbation of a pre-existing skin complaint, psoriasis, and also depression. **Held:** both consequences were not too remote. D had to take its victim as it found him, including the possibility of exacerbation of pre-existing conditions and anger leading to depression. 'It does not matter whether a psychologically more robust individual would have recovered from the accident without displaying either condition'.

The economically-injured C. C may be an egg-shell skull victim, economically speaking, in various ways. C may be highly-paid, say, a famous actor – and if he is injured via some act of negligence by D, then D must take that victim as he finds him, when it comes to an assessment of the heads of damage pertaining to past and future economic loss (albeit that this example may also be considered pertinent under principle §9.4 above, to do with the unforeseeable extent of C's economic losses). Alternatively, as a result of D's negligence, impecunious C may have to incur expenditure to mitigate his losses, and that expenditure is more expensive than it would have been, had C been financially better-off. C cannot take advantage of a cheaper option X; instead, he must pursue the more expensive option Y. Alternatively, C may be liable, contractually, to pay financial penalties to third parties, if D damages C's property. In that context, C is an economically-vulnerable egg-shell victim, who had incurred additional expenses. Are those further expenses recoverable from D, or are they too remote?

The current legal position is that the law aligns the economically-vulnerable C with his other egg-shell counterparts. According to *Lagden v O'Connor*,[58] where C's expenditure was increased, due to his impecuniosity, D had to take his victim as he found him, so that if it was reasonably foreseeable that C would have to borrow money or incur some other kind of expenditure to mitigate his damages, then that expenditure was compensable and not too remote.

In *Lagden v O'Connor*, Mr Lagden, C, was involved in a car accident with Mrs O'Connor, D, in Oxford. C was unemployed at the time. While his car was being repaired, C required another car, and had to hire one at a cost of £659. Due to C's straitened financial circumstances, C could not afford to pay for the hire of a replacement car from his own pocket, and so signed an agreement with a

[55] [1996] AC 155 (HL) 189. See too: *MacDonald (or Cross) v Highlands and Islands Enterprise*, 2001 SCLR 547, 2001 SLT 1060 (SCOH) (stress at work; collapse and breakdown; suicide followed; not too remote).

[56] *ibid*, 182. [57] [2004] UKHL 20, 2004 SC (HL) 94, [56] (Lord Rodger).

[58] [2003] UKHL 64, [2004] 1 AC 1067.

credit-hire company, whereby it provided a hire car by way of the provision of a 26-week credit facility. The fees charged by the credit-hire company were reflected in a higher rate for the car hire than the equivalent 'spot hire rate' charged by traditional car hire firms. D disputed the claim for £659 car hire as being too remote. **Held (3:2):** C's damages were not too remote. An impecunious C who could not afford to hire a replacement car at commercial rates, or to obtain a loan, had no option but to obtain a credit hire package, and was entitled to recover the whole costs from D. It was reasonably foreseeable that there would be some car owners who would be unable to obtain a replacement car other than by use of a credit hire company.

Previously, the law was not nearly as kind to the impecunious egg-shell C. According to *The Liesbosch Dredger v SS Edison (Owners)*,[59] the financial circumstances of the injured C, and whatever additional expenses he was put to because of his 'financial embarrassment', were too remote. Lord Wright (with whom the other members of the House of Lords agreed) explained this principle as one of policy – that C's additional expenses, if arising from his own impecuniosity, arose from some cause 'extraneous to and distinct in character from the tort'.[60] If the impecuniosity was not traceable to D's tort, then the expenses incurred by reason of that impecuniosity were too remote ('[i]n the varied web of affairs, the law must abstract some consequences as relevant, not perhaps on grounds of pure logic, but simply for practical reasons'[61]).

In *The Liesbosch*, the dredge *Liesbosch* was used in the Greek port harbour of Patras. The dredge sank due to the fouling of its moorings by D's vessel, *The Edison. The Liesbosch* owners, C, had all their resources invested in the dredging contract, and their deposit under that contract would be forfeited if the dredging work was delayed. C could not afford to buy another dredge, so hired one, *The Adria*, from Italy. It involved high hiring costs, and was more expensive to run than if C had been able to purchase a dredge. C claimed from D all the costs and expenses caused by their hiring *The Adria.* **Held:** C was only able to recover the market price of a comparable dredger at the time of the loss, and the costs of transporting it to Patras and insuring it – but not the additional costs incurred by hiring *The Adria.* Those hiring costs were incurred because C were impeded in the performance of the dredging contract by its own impecuniosity, and were too remote.

Three reasons were given by the House of Lords in *Lagden*,[62] for the change of view from its decision in *The Liesbosch*:

i. First, 'the law has moved on' since *The Liebosch* decision, so that the overriding and correct test of remoteness today is whether C's economic loss was reasonably foreseeable. The principle that D must take his victim as he finds him applies equally to the economic state of his victim, in the same way as it applies to his physical and mental vulnerability. Hence, D had to take C as he found him, if C would have to borrow money or incur some kind of expenditure to mitigate his damages;[63]
ii. In the 70 years since *The Liesbosch* was decided, the general classification of C's impecuniosity as 'extraneous' or 'extrinsic' was not defensible. It could still be that some loss attributable to C's impecuniosity could be too remote in some cases, but it was no longer correct at law to say that the consequences that flowed from impecuniosity were simply too remote;[64]
iii. The rule in *The Liesbosch* has been distinguished so often that its authority has been greatly reduced (e.g., in *Alcoa Minerals of Jamaica Inc v Broderick*,[65] the Privy Council noted that

[59] [1933] AC 449 (HL). [60] *ibid*, 461. [61] *ibid*, 460. [62] [2003] UKHL 64, [2004] 1 AC 1067.
[63] *ibid*, [61] (Lord Hope). [64] *ibid*, [102] (Lord Walker). [65] [2002] 1 AC 371 (PC) [36] (Lord Slynn).

'courts have, from time to time, distinguished it or sought to set limits to its scope'), so that the time had come to refute the rule altogether.

Accordingly, the Court of Appeal recently, in *Haxton v Philips Electronics UK Ltd*,[66] expressly followed the view of *Lagden*, holding that the claimed head of economic damage which was consequential upon the death of C's husband (i.e., the diminution in the value of a litigation claim) was not too remote. In the context of property damage to Network Rail's, C's, track which produced some consequential economic loss for C (i.e., an obligation to pay sums to the rail companies under track access agreements, for every hour that the railtracks were unusable), the Court of Appeal also permitted that consequential economic loss in *Conarken Group Ltd v Network Rail*,[67] relying on *Lagden*.

THE 'SCOPE OF DUTY' ENQUIRY

A further control mechanism

§9.9 Notwithstanding that C's damage was reasonably foreseeable, it must fall within the scope of the duty which D owed C, to protect C by the exercise of reasonable care. Otherwise, C's damage will be regarded as being too remote to be compensable.

This particular principle provides a further 'escape route' for D, even where C's damage was reasonably foreseeable in *Wagon Mound* terms. It arises where a duty to avoid that damage did not fall within the *scope of D's duty* to prevent harm befalling C. This scope-of-duty enquiry is another control mechanism, in addition to the ring-fence already provided by the test of reasonable foreseeability. It requires that even foreseeable damage has to be fairly regarded as being within the scope of D's duty towards C.

As remarked by Evans-Lombe J in *Barings plc (in liq) v Coopers & Lybrand*,[68] the use of the 'scope of duty' argument by a negligent D, as a means of imposing a 'control mechanism' to ring-fence the bounds of foreseeable damage, is a rather 'modern development'. Its lineage appears to have commenced in the 1990 decision of the House of Lords in *Caparo Industries plc v Dickman*,[69] in which Lord Bridge stated that '[i]t is never sufficient to ask simply whether A owes B a duty of care. It is always necessary to determine the scope of the duty by reference to the kind of damage from which A must take care to save B harmless'. Since then, in *D Pride & Partners v Institute for Animal Health*,[70] Tugendhat J referred to the remoteness enquiry as one directed to 'the scope of the duty of care'; and in *Corr v IBC Vehicles Ltd*,[71] Lord Bingham explicitly considered, under the remoteness enquiry, that Mr Corr's, C's, damage (suicide) did not fall outside the scope of the duty of care owed to him by his employer.

In contrast, some judges appear to regard the scope-of-duty argument as fitting into either duty or remoteness elements. It will be recalled, from Chapter 2, that the establishment of any novel duty of care category requires that three elements are satisfied, per the 'necessary ingredients' of a duty of care laid down by Lord Bridge in *Caparo v Dickman*[72] – the first of which is that there is reasonable foreseeability of some kind of harm or damage arising from

[66] [2014] EWCA Civ 4, [2014] WLR 2721, [22]–[23]. [67] [2011] EWCA Civ 644, [2011] BLR 462, [150].
[68] [2003] EWHC 1319 (Ch) [807]. [69] [1990] 2 AC 605 (HL) 627. [70] [2009] EWHC 685 (QB) [102].
[71] [2008] UKHL 13, [2008] 1 AC 884, 893. [72] [1990] 2 AC 605 (HL) 609.

D's breach, and the third of which is that it must be 'fair, just and reasonable' for a duty of care to be imposed. In *Jolley v Sutton LBC*,[73] Lord Hoffmann considered that whether one discussed the foreseeability of C's injury as 'outside the scope of the duty' or 'too remote' was 'according to taste'; and in *Union Camp Chemicals Ltd v CRL TCL Ltd*,[74] Judge Thornton QC regarded the concepts as synonymous: 'in ascertaining whether the damage complained of falls within the scope of that duty ... the court may disallow recovery by use of the twin threshold tests for liability in negligence: the relevant damage is too remote, and it is neither fair and reasonable to allow recovery'.

Hence, it is clear that there is a great deal of overlap between the concept of a duty of care, and the 'scope of the duty' enquiry at remoteness stage. To exclude C's reasonably foreseeable damage on the basis that it is not within the scope of D's duty to prevent is driven by policy considerations which seek to protect D from paying for certain types of harm, notwithstanding that the harm was causally linked to D's breach – and whether these policy reasons are dealt with under duty of care, or remoteness, and whether they are attributed the label of 'not fair, just and reasonable', or 'beyond the scope of duty', seems to depend upon judicial preference rather than upon any clear analytical approach.

An excellent illustration of the conundrum is contained in the hypothetical mountaineering example provided by Lord Hoffmann in *South Australia Asset Management Corp v York Montague Ltd*[75] (the *SAAMCO case*). There was no doubt that D, the doctor, owed a duty to C, the mountaineer, as his patient. However, the question was whether the damage suffered by the mountaineer was within the scope of the doctor's duty to prevent – an issue which pertained to remoteness of damage.

> To paraphrase the *mountaineering example in SAAMCO*, suppose a mountaineer, C, is due to undertake a difficult climbing expedition, and is concerned about the fitness of his knee. He goes to a doctor, D, who negligently makes a superficial examination, and pronounces the knee fit. C goes on the expedition, which he would not have undertaken if D had told him the true state of his knee. C suffers a head injury when caught in an avalanche, which is an entirely foreseeable consequence of mountaineering, but has nothing to do with his knee. **Hypothetically, held**: C's injury was entirely and reasonably foreseeable (per *Wagon Mound*). However, the damage resulting from the head injuries are too remote. To hold D liable for the head injuries 'offends common sense because it makes the doctor responsible for consequences which, though in general terms foreseeable, do not appear to have a sufficient causal connection with the subject matter of the duty. The doctor was asked for information on only one of the considerations which might affect the safety of the mountaineer on the expedition. There seems no reason of policy which requires that the negligence of the doctor should require the transfer to him of all the foreseeable risks of the expedition'. In other words, injury to mountaineer C, if the knee gave way, was foreseeable and not too remote, because the scope of the doctor's duty was to advise on the fitness of the knee. On the other hand, head injuries caused by an avalanche were foreseeable, but too remote, because the duty was not so wide as to prevent all injuries occurring to C.

A number of real-life cases illustrate D's attempt to argue that C's damage fell outside the scope of D's duty of care to C, rendering the damage too remote. Selecting some contrasting cases by way of example, where the injuries were not too remote:

[73] [2000] 1 WLR 1082 (HL) 1091. [74] [2001] All ER (D) 95 (TCC) [98]. [75] [1997] AC 191 (HL) 213.

In *Corr v IBC Vehicles Ltd*[76] facts previously, Mr Corr, C, committed suicide several years after his ear was severed in a workplace accident. IBC Vehicles, D, argued that suicide was too remote, and that while an employer owes a duty of care to an employee to provide a safe system of work, C's suicide fell outside the scope of the duty of care owed by D as his employer, because there was no duty on the employer to protect employee C *from self-harm*. C was not technically insane at the time of his death, and could invoke personal autonomy and self-determination, such that the employer was not 'his keeper'. **Held:** the suicide was not too remote. D owed C a duty, as its employee, to take reasonable care to avoid causing him physical injury. C's conduct in taking his own life stemmed from that breach, and did not fall outside the scope of the duty which his employer owed him. In *Jolley v Sutton LBC*[77] facts previously, it was conceded by Council D that it ought to have removed the boat, as it represented a danger and an allurement for children who may have been tempted to play on it. There was a risk that children would have suffered minor injuries if the rotten planking gave way beneath them. However, it was argued that any injury caused by the propped-up boat collapsing fell outside the scope of D's duty to prevent. **Held:** the injuries were not too remote. D would have incurred no extra expense to eliminate that risk of the boat collapsing – if it had removed the boat (as it conceded that it ought to have done, and which it did after the accident happened), then the more unlikely sequence of injury would not have happened. Hence, the injuries suffered (paraplegia) were within the scope of D's duty to prevent.

– and where C's injuries lay outside the scope of D's duty to C:

In *R v Croydon HA*,[78] Mrs R, C, a nurse trained to work with the mentally disabled, applied for a job at the Croydon HA, D, as a community nurse. To be considered for this work, C had to undergo a medical examination, including a chest X-ray. Dr Manners, D, a radiologist, negligently failed to report a significant abnormality on C's X-ray which would have required C to be referred to a cardiologist, who would have diagnosed primary pulmonary hypertension (PPH). PPH, an untreatable condition, diminished limited life expectancy, and was exacerbated if the sufferer became pregnant. D accepted that C would not have become pregnant had she been diagnosed with PPH. C became pregnant four months after commencing her employment, became ill, and was diagnosed with PPH. After the birth of her child, C was unable to return to employment which involved dealing with difficult and potentially violent mental patients. C developed reactive depression and was retired on the grounds of ill health. C claimed the pregnancy and the costs of raising her child as damages resulting from the negligent reading of the chest X-ray. **Held:** the pregnancy and all the losses flowing from it were too remote. The pregnancy itself, and the costs of raising the child, etc, were foreseeable consequences of the failure to diagnose PPH. D's duty as a radiologist was to observe and report on abnormalities which could have affected her fitness for work as an employee of the health authority. However, it was not within the scope of the radiologist's duty to advise C on abnormalities which might render some activities wholly unconnected with employment problematical. Briefly put, C's 'domestic circumstances were not D's affair'. In *Pritchard v JH Cobden Ltd (No 1)*,[79] Mr Pritchard, C, was involved in a car accident with Mr Parrott, D, an employee of JH Cobden, who was driving an articulated lorry. C suffered brain damage resulting in left-sided hemiplegia, blindness in right eye, defective intelligence, concentration and memory and a severe personality change. This led to a breakdown of his marriage and eventual divorce. He sought (and recovered at trial) damages in respect of the additional cost of maintaining two households as a result of his divorce. **Held:**

[76] [2008] UKHL 13, [2008] 1 AC 884.
[77] [2000] 1 WLR 1082 (HL).
[78] [1998] 2 Lloyd's Rep Med 44 (CA).
[79] [1987] 2 WLR 627 (CA).

the damages for maintaining his wife were too remote, such that C was not entitled to damages to compensate him for the break-up of his marriage.

Hence, where domestic consequences for C are wrought by virtue of D's breach, those consequences may very well be outside the scope of D's duty.

The *SAAMCO* principle

The basic principle

§9.10 The *SAAMCO* principle applies in the particular scenario of negligent valuations, i.e., the provision of information on which C relies. The valuer, D, owes a duty to a lender, C, to protect C against losses which C might suffer, if the valued security is worth less than the sum at which D valued the security. However, the scope of D's duty is not to protect C against losses incurred because of a fall in the property market – even where (1) that property downturn was foreseeable, and (2) C would not have lent the money at all, had the valuation been carefully undertaken.

The *SAAMCO* principle, named after the case (a series of three appeals) in which it was espoused – *South Australia Asset Management Corp v York Montague Ltd*[80] – is a particular application of the scope-of-duty test. Again, foreseeably-occurring damage is excluded under this principle, because the duty owed by D can be regarded as limited to one kind of damage, and not to another. Essentially, C's losses, attributable to the fall in the property market, lie outside the scope of D's duty.

In *the SAAMCO case*, various banks, C, loaned money to developers of the London Docklands project, on the basis of valuations provided by various valuers, D. The valued properties were used as security for the mortgages, but were negligently over-valued. They proved to be inadequate security, when the borrowers defaulted on their loans and the security was called in (i.e., realised) by C. As a result, C suffered loss. While that loss was caused, in part, by the negligent over-valuations of the security (without which C would never have lent the money at all), the loss was also caused, in part, by a substantial fall in the value of property generally over the loan period. The question arose as to what amount of loss D were properly responsible for. **Held (CA[81]):** D were liable for *all the loss suffered* by C, including that referable to the fall in property prices. C would not have entered into the loans, but for the representations they had received from valuer D, and it was fair and reasonable that all the foreseeable losses flowing from that negligent advice should be recoverable from D. **Held (HL):** C was entitled to recover damages, measured by the difference between the true value of the security, and those shown on the negligent valuations, at the date that the loans were made. Whatever losses occurred in the property market after that date were too remote from the negligent valuations, and were not recoverable.

The reasoning of the House of Lords was that the valuer D's duty is **not** so wide as to protect lender C against **all** losses that it suffered because it entered into transactions on the strength of that valuation (even if C proves that it would not have lent the money at all). The scope of D's duty is not to protect C against all the consequences of entering transactions, thinking that the property was worth what valuer D said. Hence, the fall in the property market which adversely affected C's ability to use the security to meet a defaulting borrower's obligations was not to be

[80] [1997] AC 191 (HL). [81] [1995] QB 375 (CA).

laid at valuer D's door. It was also legally irrelevant that a drop in the property market which affected the property values was foreseeable.

Diagrammatically, the difference between the Court of Appeal and the House of Lords can be illustrated below, with reference to the transaction in *SAAMCO v York Montague* itself:

SAAMCO: The Court of Appeal and the House of Lords contrasted

-£15m–the negligent valuation of the property by the valuer D

-£11m–the amount the lender C loaned to the developer by way of mortgage over that property, on 3 Aug 1990

-£5m–what the property was actually worth, at the date of D's valuation

- £2.5m – following the fall in the property market, this is what the property sold for on 5 Aug 1994, when the borrower defaulted on the loan, and lender C redeemed the security

What the **Court of Appeal** held to be the compensable damage (the lender would not have lent at all if the valuation had been accurate; all foreseeable losses were recoverable):

	£11m (the amount loaned)
Less:	£2.5m
	£8.5m

What the **House of Lords** held to be the correct compensable damage (given that the lender did not have security over a property of the value which it thought it had):

	£15m
Less:	£5m
	£10m

Hence, on a time-line, the much later event, i.e., the date at which the security was redeemed in 1994, could be ignored. Lender C could not recover for this fall in the property market, that was too remote, and hence, the £8.5m was not the appropriate measure. Rather, the consequence of D's valuation being wrong was that lender C had £10m less security than it thought it had. If lender C had held that amount of security when it extended the loan, C would have suffered no loss, when it came time for the property to be redeemed. The HL reasoning ignored any fluctuations in the market, and what lender C actually redeemed the property for.

Limitations

The *SAAMCO* principle has its limits, however. To mention a couple:

i. It seems that there is an important distinction to be drawn, between (a) where D provides information to C on which C relies, but where D does not advise C to follow a course of action (whereupon D will not be liable for all of the consequences arising from C's reliance on the information, per *SAAMCO*); and (b) where D actually advises C to pursue a certain course of action (and C does, and where D will be liable for the reasonably foreseeable consequences of C's acting in reliance on that advice).

For example, in Lord Hoffmann's mountaineering example, doctor D did not advise or recommend his patient to go mountaineering; all he did was to say that the patient's knee was robust, and it was up to the patient as to whether to proceed with the expedition. On the other hand, investment advice is often more directive, in that C is advised to undertake the investment. In

Rubenstein v HSBC Bank plc,[82] Rix LJ noted that an investment adviser, D, 'with his statutory duties of various kinds', owes C a wider duty of care, to avoid **all** foreseeable losses, if D recommends a particular investment, and then some flaw in the investment turns out materially to contribute to a loss of that investment. In this case, the investment adviser, D, 'so to speak, put him in it'. In that scenario, the scope of D's duty will not reduce the foreseeable and compensable damages.

In *Aneco Reinsurance Underwriting Ltd (in liq) v Johnson & Higgins Ltd*,[83] Aneco, C, sought reinsurance for part of the liabilities which it undertook for Lloyds syndicates. C engaged Johnson & Higgins, D, reinsurance brokers, to obtain that reinsurance. The reinsurance was obtained, but ultimately, most of the policies were avoided by the relevant underwriters, because of non-disclosure of material facts concerning the true nature of the underlying insurance which C was undertaking. C sued D for failing to exercise reasonable care and skill in obtaining the reinsurance on its behalf. D claimed that the correct measure of damages was the value of the reinsurance cover which C lost when the cover was avoided (worth about £10m). C claimed that, had D made full disclosure of the material facts to the underwriters, then reinsurance cover of the kind which C required would not have been available in the London market on commercial terms, C would not have entered into the Lloyds syndicate at all, and hence, the full losses it suffered, of around £30m, would not have been suffered. **Held (2:1):** C's full damage of £30m was not too remote. The scope of D's duty was to obtain satisfactory reinsurance, or if unprocurable, to tell C that no such reinsurance was available or that none was available on acceptable terms. D knew that C would not accept the risk otherwise, and would not have entered the Lloyds syndicate. D was advising C here, as to what course to take. Hence, whatever loss C suffered from entering that transaction was recoverable.

Nevertheless, drawing the appropriate distinction between an 'information' case (which invokes *SAAMCO*) and an 'advice' case (which exposes D to a potentially wider scope of duty) is not easy to do in some cases (as exemplified by the discussion of Richards LJ in *Andrews v Waddingham*,[84] which was held to be an 'information' case; and in *Baillie v Bromhead & Co (a firm)*,[85] where the court frankly admitted that neither counsel was able to 'characterise what quality it was which placed a case in one category or the other').

ii. It is always necessary to establish a causal link between D's breach and C's economic loss, on the 'but-for' test – even where the economic loss suffered by C was reasonably foreseeable. If the 'but-for' cause of C's loss was C's own financial difficulties (unrelated to D's investment advice), together with the effects of a property crash, then that will bring about the failure of C's claim, regardless of whether or not the damage was within the scope of D's duty to avoid (per *Bateson v Savills Private Finance Ltd*[86]).

Failure-to-warn scenarios

§9.11 Where healthcare professional D fails to warn patient C of a material or significant risk which ought to have been warned about; C opts to have the surgical treatment or procedure; and *another* risk (which was not material or significant, and which did not need to be warned about) manifests, it is presently uncertain as to whether the injury arising from that different risk was too remote to be compensable.

[82] [2012] EWCA Civ 1184, [103]. [83] [2001] UKHL 51, [2002] PNLR 8, [16]–[17].
[84] [2006] EWCA Civ 93, [46]–[47]. [85] [2014] EWHC 2149 (Ch) [22]. [86] [2013] EWHC 719 (QB) [33].

The 'scope of duty' test suggests that the healthcare practitioner's, D's, liability should be limited to those particular risks of which mention ought to have been made, and which have actually manifested or eventuated. This scenario arguably fits within the previously-mentioned 'information' scenario of *SAAMCO's* mountaineering example provided by Lord Hoffmann – i.e., the warning as to risks is not a recommendation to the patient, C, to follow a course of action (i.e., it is not an advice scenario), but rather, information upon which C can base a decision as to whether or not to proceed with the medical treatment or procedure. That invokes a narrower 'scope of duty' enquiry, according to *SAAMCO*.

Undoubtedly, the fact that C suffered the remote risk satisfies the 'but-for' test of causation, in that C would not have undertaken the treatment or procedure, had warning of the material risk been given as it legally should have been. If patient C undergoes an operation which he would not have undergone, but for the negligent failure-to-warn, then any detriment resulting from the operation should be regarded as caused by the negligent failure-to-warn, in a strict 'but-for' analysis.

However, as the discussion in this chapter demonstrates, remoteness is quite a separate enquiry. On the grounds of fairness and policy, it is highly arguable that the **only** detriment for which damages should be awarded in C's favour are those against the risk of which D should have warned.[87]

Thus far, this conundrum has not been directly answered in English law, so far as the author's searches can ascertain. It is significant, however, that in the leading failure-to-warn case of *Chester v Afshar*,[88] the particular risk which manifested for patient C – paralysis caused by nerve damage – was said to be the precise risk against which warning ought to have been given. The majority noted that it was **not** a coincidental risk which damaged C: '[i]f a patient in the position of Miss Chester had been injured by some wholly unforeseeable accident of anaesthesia ... or because the operating theatre was struck by lightning ... the injury could have been described as coincidental ... [However] the misfortune which befell C was the very misfortune which was the focus of the surgeon's duty to warn'. This suggests that any coincidental damage could have been regarded as being too remote to be compensable.

The comparative corner: An Australian vignette

In *Hribar v Wells*,[89] King CJ gave this example (with a hypothetical scenario in brackets):

'There may be operations (*say, a dental operation*) which result in detriments which are quite unrelated to the risk against which it was the surgeon's duty to warn ... It may be, in some cases, that the detriment against which the surgeon should have warned (*say, the risk of permanent numbness of tongue and lips, following the administering of a particular anaesthetic*) does not materialise at all, but other detriments against the risk of which warning was ... not required (*say, the risk of unclean instruments being used during the procedure*) do ensue.'

King CJ did not have to answer the conundrum, but it was suggested that the other detriment might be too remote.

[87] See: Mulheron, 'Observations upon Causation in Recent "Failure to warn" Cases' (2000) *National L Rev* 2, [36]–[39].

[88] [2005] 1 AC 134, [94] (Lord Walker).

[89] (1995) 64 SASR 129 (FC) 130, and also 146–47 (Duggan J).

TOO MANY CAUSAL LINKS

§9.12 Where there are numerous links between D's breach and C's damage, then even reasonably foreseeable damage may be too remote to be recoverable.

Although this principle may seem to be more appropriately dealt with under the causal element, the language of some cases suggest that it is a remoteness issue.

In *Hyde v Tameside AHA*,[90] Lord Denning MR cited the well-known sequence of Benjamin Franklin: 'For want of a nail, the shoe was lost; for want of a shoe, the horse was lost; and for want of a horse, the rider was lost: and for want of a rider, the battle was lost'. In other words, if D negligently failed to nail soldier C's horseshoe directly, then the harm arising to C (and others) from the lost battle would be too remote from D's breach to be recoverable. Those long causal chains have been pointed to in some cases, in order to render the damage too remote. Two cases are worth contrasting:

In *Hyde v Tameside AHA*, Eric Hyde, C, was admitted to hospital for the treatment of a suspected disc lesion. By the 12th night of his admission, C convinced himself (wrongly) that he was dying of cancer, and was going to die in the next hour or so, and he tried to kill himself. In the middle of the night, he got out of his bed on the third floor, smashed the window, jumped out, landed on a parapet and flung himself from there on to the roadway outside. The attempted suicide failed, and C suffered quadriplegia. He sued the hospital, D, in negligence. **Held (at trial):** C recovered £200,000. **Held (CA):** C's damage was too remote. 'If the nurses had reported [C's] depression to the doctors, then the doctors might have called in a consultant psychiatrist. If a consultant psychiatrist had been called in, he might have ordered some treatment which might have had some effect on the depression. If it did have some effect on [C's] depression, it might have prevented him from attempting to commit suicide. All these consequences might have followed. But I think it wrong that the law should chase consequence upon consequence – possibility upon possibility – right down on a hypothetical line – so as to award damages to a man who attempted to commit suicide ... the damages are far too remote' (Lord Denning). In the alternative, no reasonable D would have reasonably foreseen that this C would try to commit suicide (per Watkins LJ).

In *McFarlane v Tayside Health Board*,[91] a sterilisation (vasectomy) operation was performed for Mr McFarlane, which was unsuccessful. However, this was not detected, and the parents were advised that they could dispense with other forms of contraception. A healthy child, Catherine, was subsequently conceived, and Mr and Mrs McFarlane, C, sought to recover, inter alia, the costs of maintenance of Catherine's upbringing. **Held**: that head of damages were rebutted, with a suggestion that the damage was almost too causally remote: 'there are several successive stages from the allegedly negligent advice [that Mr McFarlane was sterile] before one reaches the incurring of the maintenance costs; the intercourse without protection, the conception of the child, the carrying of the child to her birth, and the acceptance of the baby as a further member of the family with all the obligations towards her which parenthood involves. The cost of the maintenance of the child seems to me to be a loss near the limits of the causal chain' (per Lord Clyde). Nevertheless, causation was proven, and the costs of Catherine's upbringing were not rejected on this ground, but for policy reasons (per Chapter 2).

[90] QB, 13 Apr 1981. [91] [2000] 2 AC 59 (HL) 104.

It follows that, if there are 'several successive stages' between breach and damage, then not only may one of those interim events constitute a *novus actus interveniens*, but the damage itself may be too remote to be compensable in law.

POLICY: A 'FINAL ARBITER'

§9.13 Even if C's damage was reasonably foreseeable, reasons of public policy may render C's damage too remote.

It is perhaps unsurprising that the unruly horse, otherwise known as policy, infuses this last element of negligence as it has elsewhere in the tort – allowing the court to determine for what damages D *ought* to be liable. The Singapore Court of Appeal expressed the position perfectly in *Sunny Metal and Engineering Pte Ltd v Ng Khim Ming Eric*,[92] when it said that the remoteness enquiry:

> unlike that of causation, presents a much larger area of choice in which legal policy and accepted value judgment must be the final arbiter of what balance to strike between the claim to full reparation for the loss suffered by an innocent victim of another's culpable conduct and the excessive burden that would be imposed on human activity if a wrongdoer were to be held to answer for *all* consequences of his default.

Hence, reasonable foreseeability of damage is not determinative, if public policy precludes recovery of damage which was causally connected to D's breach. This factor has largely, perhaps, been subsumed under the 'scope of duty' enquiry – albeit that some cases have discussed the preclusion of recovery in policy terms.

> In *Pritchard v JH Cobden Ltd (No 1)*,[93] facts previously, **held:** the damages for maintaining C's wife were too remote, as it would be against public policy, and open to abuse, to bring into personal injury litigation considerations relevant to matrimonial proceedings.

On the other hand, suicide is a form of personal injury that is 'not beyond the pale' nor too remote on policy grounds. The law does not 'draw up its skirts and refuse all assistance to [a suiciding C]' (per Bingham LJ in *Saunders v Edwards*[94]), notwithstanding that the act might prompt religious condemnation, and was previously-criminalised. Provided that the suicide arises out of depression, and that the depression is causally linked to the breach, the law will not consider it to be uncompensable (per *Corr v IBC Vehicles*).

[92] [2007] SGCA 36, (2007) 113 Con LR 112, [56]. [93] [1987] 2 WLR 627 (CA).
[94] [1987] 1 WLR 1116 (CA) 1134.

10

Defences

INTRODUCTION

§10.1 There are six defences to the tort of negligence. The burden of proof rests with D, when seeking to prove any of these defences.

The defences available in negligence comprise the following: (1) contributory negligence, i.e., that C carelessly contributed to his own injury; (2) *volenti*, i.e., that C fully and freely assumed the risk of injury created by D's breach; (3) illegality, i.e., that C was engaged in an illegal purpose when harmed by D; (4) exclusion clauses, i.e., that D can take advantage of a limitation of liability clause in his agreement/contract with C; (5) therapeutic privilege, i.e., that D withheld information about material risks from C, because disclosure might harm C's health and well-being; and (6) necessity, i.e., that D's negligence was committed because it was necessary to save life, limb or property.

The burden of proof rests with D (e.g., for necessity, see *Southport Corp v Esso Petroleum Co Ltd*[1]). It is not for C to prove that no defence applies; D bears the persuasive burden to convince the court that it does.

All but one – contributory negligence – is a complete defence. Contributory negligence is a partial defence, and (probably) cannot serve as a complete defence.

This chapter does not traverse other 'defences', such as the doctrines of 'inevitable accident' and *res ipsa loquitur*, which are relevant to the proof of breach (as discussed in Chapter 7). These doctrines arguably do not shift the burden of proof from C, but are ways in which breach may be (dis)proven. Nor does the chapter re-examine the doctrine of 'common employment', which did provide an effective defence for an employer until its abolition, when the Law Reform (Personal Injuries) Act 1948 was passed (see 'Employers' liability', an online chapter).

CONTRIBUTORY NEGLIGENCE

Preliminary matters

§10.2 Contributory negligence means that, notwithstanding D's breach of duty, C was at fault for contributing towards his own damage. The defence is a statutory, not a common law, defence, prescribed by the Law Reform (Contributory Negligence) Act 1945.

[1] [1954] 2 QB 182 (CA).

The defence of contributory negligence has operated in its present statutory form in England from the mid-20th century. The Law Reform (Contributory Negligence) Act 1945 ('the 1945 Act') provides:

> s 1(1) Where any person suffers damage as the result partly of his own fault and partly of the fault of any other person or persons, a claim in respect of that damage shall not be defeated by reason of the fault of the person suffering the damage, but the damages recoverable in respect thereof shall be reduced to such extent as the court thinks just and equitable having regard to the claimant's share in the responsibility for the damage.

Two practical matters are worth mentioning at the outset. First, any assessment of contributory negligence by the trial judge is a decision which will not be interfered with on appeal unless the trial judge 'has gone fundamentally wrong' (per *Dixon v Clement Jones Solicitors (a firm)*[2]) or where 'some error in the judge's approach is clearly discernible' (per *Smith v Nottinghamshire Police*[3]). The types of 'identifiable error' necessary, for appellate intervention, include: where the trial court omitted to mention a material fact about C's behaviour (as in *Stapley v Gypsum Mines Ltd*[4]); or recklessness was attributed to C where none existed (as in *Jackson v Murray*[5]); or the appellate court disagreed as to which party should bear the greater share of responsibility (another reason for overturning the apportionment in *Jackson*). Otherwise, if the appellate court disagrees with the (albeit wide) range of appropriate apportionment in which reasonable opinion may fix contributory negligence, then that can also justify appellate overrule (as in *Stapley*, where contributory negligence was varied from 50% up to 80%) – but if the trial judge's assessment of contributory negligence is within that range, albeit that it was 'about as favourable to [C] as it could be, having regard to his behaviour', that will be non-appealable (per *Silverlink Trains Ltd v Collins-Williamson*[6]).

Secondly, C cannot obtain insurance for his own wrongdoing. Hence, as one leading Torts commentator has remarked, 'the only significant group of people who are called upon to pay for the consequences of their negligence are accident victims themselves'.[7]

The defence of contributory negligence entails four elements (per *Badger v MOD*):[8]

The framework for contributory negligence

1. C was partly at fault in bringing about his own injury or harm
2. There must be a causal link between C's contributory negligence and his injury
3. The apportionment of contributory negligence must take into account the relative blameworthiness of C's and D's conduct, *and* the extent of their fault in causing C's damage
4. C's damages must be reduced by an amount which is just and equitable

Alternative allegations

Wherever contributory negligence arises as a potential allegation, the acts or omissions which raise that defence may give rise to other legal arguments too – although their legal bases and

[2] [2004] EWCA Civ 1005, [51]. [3] [2012] EWCA Civ 161, [36]. [4] [1953] AC 663 (HL) 682–83.
[5] [2015] UKSC 5, [36]–[37]. [6] [2009] EWCA Civ 850, [61].
[7] P Cane, *Atiyah's Accidents, Compensation and the Law* (7th edn, Cambridge University Press, 2006) 56.
[8] [2005] EWHC 2941 (QB) [6] (Stanley Burnton J).

ramifications are quite distinct (per *Gregory v Shepherds (a firm)*[9]). For example, C's acts or omissions may amount to:

- an intervening act, brought about by C's own carelessness, as both of the following held:

  In the Scottish case of *Sabri-Tabrizi v Lothian Health Board*,[10] Ms Sabri-Tabrizi, C, alleged that, due to surgeon D's negligence in performing a surgical sterilisation, she remained fertile. C became pregnant, had this pregnancy terminated, fell pregnant again, and gave birth to a stillborn child. She claimed damages for both pregnancies, but failed. Re the second pregnancy, C's decision to have unprotected intercourse after the first pregnancy was a *novus actus interveniens*. In *McKew v Holland & Hannen & Cubitts (Scotland) Ltd*, Mr McKew, C, was injured at work, caused by his employer's, D's, breach. His back and hips were badly strained, and on several occasions his left leg suddenly 'went away from' him. Despite that, after inspecting a flat in Glasgow, C decided to descend a steep staircase with no handrail, carrying his young child. His left leg 'vanished under him', and he jumped about 12 feet to the landing below. C's conduct was unreasonable, and a *novus actus interveniens*. C 'must have realised ... that he could only safely descend the stair if he either went extremely slowly and carefully, so that he could sit down if his leg gave way, or waited for the assistance of his wife and brother in-law. But he chose to descend in such a way that, when his leg gave way, he could not stop himself'.

- an ability on C's part to prove any breach on D's part, given C's acts or omissions:

  In *Venner v North East Essex AHA*,[11] C was advised to cease taking the contraceptive pill before a sterilisation operation, and to take other contraceptive precautions. C ignored that advice, and was pregnant when the operation took place. In answer to a question as to whether there was any chance that she could be pregnant, C answered 'no', and no further questioning or investigations were done before the operation. C sued D in negligence, for failing to ascertain that she might be pregnant. **Held:** no negligence by D. There was no breach by D, in not 'prying further into the intimate details' of C's life: '[w]here a mature and sensible woman is asked a question to which only she knows the answer, then she bears a real responsibility to give an accurate and truthful answer ... if a woman conducts herself in that way contrary to advice, and then gives an answer which is less than frank, it can scarcely be said that the operating gynaecologist is responsible for the continuing pregnancy'.

However, these are all-or-nothing outcomes. In modern times, courts prefer to apportion fault (if, indeed, there is fault on both sides) under the 1945 Act.

A partial, or a total, defence?

§10.3 The predominant view in English law is that contributory negligence *cannot* operate as a complete defence.

Can C be the sole author of his own misfortune, even though D was negligent towards him? In other words, can contributory negligence of 100% be awarded against C? Prior to the enactment of the 1945 Act, contributory negligence operated as a complete defence at common law.[12] However, under the 1945 Act, dicta are divided.

The 'no' case. The weight of Court of Appeal authority is that a 100% deduction for contributory negligence is not correct in law (per *Pitts v Hunt*,[13] and *Anderson v Newham College*

[9] (Ch, 8 Feb 1999) [4.3]. [10] [1998] SC 373 (OH) 377. [11] QB, 19 Feb 1987.
[12] *Commr of Police v Reeves* [2000] AC 360 (HL) 364 (Lord Hoffmann). [13] [1991] 1 QB 24 (CA) 48.

of Higher Education[14]). As these cases pointed out, a 100% attribution of negligence to C is seemingly at odds with a finding that D was, in some way, at fault too. After all, the reduction of damages permitted under the 1945 Act is not triggered, unless C's damage is 'partly the fault of any other person' (per s 1(1)). Further, the fact that the statute refers to C's damages 'being reduced' and that the court must assess C's 'share in the responsibility for the damage' means that C should recover some damages and that D must also share in that responsibility. As Sedley LJ stated in *Anderson*, '[i]f there is liability, contributory negligence can reduce its monetary quantification, but it cannot legally or logically nullify it'.[15] Moreover, 100% contributory negligence sits very uneasily with the inherent trust and confidence, or imbalance of power and bargaining position, which the relationship between C and D may entail (note, e.g., the police–prisoner relationship in *Reeves v Commr of Police*,[16] where the trial judge had held 100% contributory negligence against C who hanged himself in custody, but where 50% was eventually held on appeal, given the responsibility of the police in preventing suicides in custody).

In *Pitts v Hunt*, Andrew Pitts, C, 18, sued Mark Hunt, 16, D, for damages for personal injuries received when he was travelling as a pillion passenger on a motor cycle driven by D. The two friends regularly used the bike to go trail bike-riding together. On this occasion, they attended a disco, drank a great deal and then set off home. Their motorcycle collided with another car, and D was killed, while C was severely injured. During the journey, they had behaved in a reckless, irresponsible and idiotic way, shouting, blowing the horn and driving at pedestrians on the verge of the road. D's estate claimed that, by C's getting on the motorcycle as a pillion passenger, knowing D to be drunk, unlicensed and uninsured, C had voluntarily assumed the risk. **Held (trial):** 100% CN. **Held (CA):** at the most, 50% CN, dicta (separately, illegality applied, defeating the claim).

The 'yes' case. The proposition that contributory negligence can be a complete defence does have some support in dicta at House of Lords' level, with Lord Reid stating, in *Imperial Chemical Industries Ltd v Shatwell*, that 'it does not matter in the result whether one says 100% contributory negligence or *volenti*'.[16a] There have been occasional dicta in lower courts too, supporting the notion that contributory negligence can be a complete defence (per *Mitchell v W S Westin Ltd*,[17] *Jayes v IMI (Kynoch) Ltd*,[18] and *Pratt v Intermet Refractories Ltd*[19]) – although these were all disapproved in *Anderson*. In favour of the 'yes' case is that, conceivably, D's negligence may have brought about the *accident* in which C was involved; but C's own negligence was 100% responsible for C's *damage* (as s 1(1)'s language actually requires). Further, if the degree of fault is so great on C's part, then fine assessments of negligence on D's part (say, < 5%) are virtually meaningless according to *Jayes*, and equate to a finding of 100% contributory negligence.

The comparative corner: A complete defence

Australian law reform opinion favoured permitting 100% CN against C (i.e., that it become an absolute, rather than just a partial, defence – a change to Australian substantive

[14] [2002] EWCA Civ 505, [10]–[18]. [15] [2002] EWCA Civ 505, [18].

[16] [2000] AC 360 (HL). See also: *Barings plc v Coopers & Lybrand* [2003] EWHC 1319 (Ch) [837] (100% CN was 'a contradiction in terms', per Evans-Lombe J).

[16a] [1965] AC 656 (HL) 672. [17] [1965] 1 WLR 297 (CA) 305 (Sellers LJ), 308–9 (Pearson LJ).

[18] [1985] ICR 155 (Goff LJ) 158–59. [19] (CA, May LJ, 21 Jan 2000).

law[20]). The Ipp Committee justified its view thus: 'denying C any damages need not be viewed as inconsistent with a finding that D was negligent ... there may be cases in which C's relative responsibility for the injuries suffered is so great that it seems fair to deny C any damages at all ... apportionment of damages is concerned with the issue of appropriate remedy, not with liability. It does not follow from a decision that C should be denied any damages at all, that D was not at fault. Such a decision only means that, as between the two parties at fault, C should bear full legal responsibility for the harm suffered'.[21] Not all Australian commentators agreed: 'it is difficult to justify a conclusion that [D's] conduct was negligent and caused [C] injury, yet at the same time finding that [C] is not "worthy" of any compensation whatsoever').[22]

The 'last opportunity' rule

§10.4 The 'last opportunity' rule was overruled by the 1945 Act.

The 'last opportunity' rule[23] was ascribed to *Davies v Mann*,[24] where C's donkey was hit by D's cart, but the donkey had been let loose by C's carelessness; D's negligence was the last opportunity to avoid the damage to the donkey, and C recovered in full. Hence, the rule provided that if, in the chain of events, the last opportunity to prevent C's harm rested with D, then the sole cause of C's harm was D's own fault – even where C had committed some prior wrongdoing himself. In effect, D's act or omission was the whole cause of C's loss, and C would be able to recover damages, notwithstanding that contributory negligence.

The rule was implemented in response to the common law position that, otherwise, any contributory negligence on C's part afforded D a complete defence. In those pre-1945 Act days, an all-or-nothing outcome had the potential to wreak real injustice as between the parties. Indeed, one of the purposes of the 1945 Act was to 'do away with the injustices' of the 'last opportunity' rule, and enable the apportionment of damages as between C and D, both of whom were at 'fault' (per *Sahib Foods Ltd v Paskin Kyriakides Sands (a firm)*[25]).

Transferred contributory negligence

§10.5 If D is vicariously liable for an employee's wrongdoing, or if C is claiming under certain statutes, then D can take advantage of any contributory negligence finding which was made against a wrongdoing party.

Vicarious liability against D for an employee's negligence will be reduced by the percentage of contributory negligence found against the wrongdoer C.

In *Silverlink Trains Ltd v Collins-Williamson*,[26] Silverlink, D, was vicariously liable for its train guard who, having seen passenger Mr Collins-Williamson, C, being 'idiotic' and 'playing the fool' while the train was stationary, gave a signal for the driver to start. **Held:** 50% CN awarded, which could thereby reduce D's damages liability.

[20] Cf: *Wynbergen v Hoyts Corp Pty Ltd* (1998) 72 ALJR 65 (HCA) (CN could not be a 100% defence).

[21] *Ipp Report*, [8.22], [8.24]. [22] M Shircore, 'Drinking, Driving and Causing Injury' [2007] *QUTLJJ* 22.

[23] Also called the 'last clear chance rule'. [24] (1842) 10 M&W 546.

[25] [2003] EWHC 142 (TCC) [72]. [26] [2009] EWCA Civ 850.

Additionally, under some statutes, contributory negligence on the part of another party also will reduce C's damages. For example, the damages recoverable by a Dependant will be reduced by the amount of the contributory negligence of the Deceased (pursuant to s 5 of the Fatal Accidents Act 1976 (as discussed in Chapter 11); and a child's damages against a healthcare practitioner under the Congenital Disabilities (Civil Liability) Act 1976 will be reduced by the extent of his parent's contributory negligence in causing that child be to be born disabled (per s 1(7)).

The elements

When seeking to prove the defence of contributory negligence, the framework for the defence necessarily involves that D prove some fault on C's part, a causal link, and it may even involve some aspects of remoteness, according to judicially-developed principles. In that respect, it somewhat resembles the analysis which C himself must follow, if suing D in negligence. However, when it comes to contributory negligence, it is a nonsense to talk of C's owing any duty of care to D (per Lord Denning MR in *Froom v Butcher*[27]). Rather, the correct question to ask is whether C took reasonable care of himself and/or of his affairs in the circumstances.

Dealing with the four elements of the defence in turn:

Element #1: Fault

§10.6 C must have been partly at fault in bringing about his own injury or loss. D must prove that C should reasonably have foreseen that, if C did not conduct his affairs in accordance with the standard of reasonable care, C might contribute toward his own injuries. C's conduct must be judged against that reasonable standard, although the law takes into account *that particular* C's characteristics and background, or any emergency circumstances in which D's breach placed C, when assessing C's conduct.

Reasonable foreseeability. As with any analysis of breach (per Chapter 7), it is necessary to apply the test of reasonable foreseeability (per *Jones v Livox Quarries*[28]), i.e., whether a reasonable person in C's position ought reasonably to have foreseen that C's acts or omissions might contribute to his own injury or harm. It is an objective test which applies. As Stanley Burnton J stated in *Badger v MOD*, in an employee–employer context, 'it is not necessary to show that [C] *personally* foresaw harm ... [and] the foreseeability need not be of the *precise way* that the damage or injury is caused'.[29] This is important – it may be perfectly obvious to a passenger who gets into a car with a drunk driver of the risks of doing so, but the risks of C's conduct may be less foreseeable to C where there is a knowledge imbalance in the parties' relationship.

Meaning of 'fault'. The trigger for the defence is worth recalling: 'Where any person suffers damage as the result partly of *his own fault* and partly of the fault of any other person ...' (per s 1(1) of the 1945 Act). Under the wide definition of 'fault' in s 4 of that Act, that fault may be negligence, but it may equally be some other tort such as breach of statutory duty, battery or assault. Given that the definition encompasses an 'act or omission which gives rise to liability

[27] [1976] QB 286 (CA) 291 (original emphasis). See too: *Badger v MOD* [2005] EWHC 2941 (QB) [7]; *Sahib Foods Ltd v Paskin Kyriakides Sands (a firm)* [2003] EWCA Civ 1832, [62].

[28] [1952] 2 QB 608 (CA) 615–16 (Denning LJ).

[29] [2005] EWHC 2941 (QB) [11]–[12] (emphasis added).

in tort', C's fault has encompassed both a lack of reasonable care on C's part, as well as C's intentional act.

In *Murphy v Culhane*,[30] Timothy Murphy, C, 29, a self-employed builder, went with some other men to beat up John Culhane, D, at his house. There was a fracas, and during the struggle, D struck C on the head with a plank, and killed him. D was convicted of manslaughter. C's widow brought an action against D for damages under the FAA 1976. **Held:** even if C's widow were entitled to damages under the FAA (which she was not), they would fall to be reduced under the LR(CN)Act 1945, because the death of C was the result partly of his own fault (i.e., going to D's house with the intention of beating him up), and partly of the fault of D. In *Reeves v Commr of Police*,[31] Mr Lynch, C, tried to hang himself in the Kentish Town police station, whilst on remand for credit card fraud, and died shortly thereafter. The police, D, knew that C was a suicide risk, because of earlier self-harming incidents when he had been in police custody. The police surgeon advised that C should be kept under regular observation. C tied his shirt through the flap in the cell door, which had been left down. At the time of his suicide, C was found to be of sound mind. **Held:** 50% CN found. Since C's intentional act was whilst of sound mind, CN could succeed. Responsibility was apportioned equally between C and D.

Notably, C's religious beliefs which contribute to C's harm are not 'fault', and cannot trigger the defence. In the absence of any directly-relevant English authority, a British Columbia case illustrates the point.

In *Hobbs v Robertson*,[32] Mrs Hobbs, C, a Jehovah's Witness, 35, died because of massive blood loss during a hysterectomy. Prior to surgery, C signed a document, 'Refusal to Permit Blood Transfusion', the legal effect of which was to deny her doctors, D, the opportunity to transfuse C with blood or blood products that would have saved her life. Contributory negligence was not pleaded by D, 'undoubtedly because it cannot be said that adherence to a sincerely held religious belief amounts to fault for purposes of apportioning liability'. **Held:** C's claim failed because the Refusal was a term of the doctor–patient contract, and it constituted an express agreement by C to assume the risk of harm (even death) if the surgeon could not transfuse. C was not at fault in this scenario.

Proving breach. The test of contributory negligence is whether a reasonable person in C's position would have acted in the same manner as C did. The relevant enquiry 'is not whether [C's] conduct fell below the standard reasonably to be expected *of him*, but whether it fell below the standard reasonably to be expected of a person in his position: did his conduct fall below the standard to be expected of a person of ordinary prudence?' (per *Badger v MOD*[33]). Hence, in the usual course, C's conduct must be judged against the standard of a reasonable person. However, that is subject to two caveats:

i. Occasionally, the characteristics of *the particular* C have been taken into account to decide whether C attained the standard of reasonable self-care. These broadly reflect the matters which could affect the standard of care applicable to D too (discussed in Chapter 6). For example, the more sophisticated and knowledgeable C is – the fact that C 'should have known better' – the more likely contributory negligence is to be held. By contrast, if C is: naive and unknowledgeable; a child; or mentally-incapacitated, then it is less likely that the defence will be triggered – or, at least, any contributory negligence will be much reduced.

[30] [1977] QB 94 (CA). [31] [2000] AC 360 (HL). [32] [2004] BCSC 1088, [78], [91]–[92] (Pitfield J).
[33] [2005] EWHC 2941 (QB) [7], citing: *Froom v Butcher* [1976] QB 286 (CA) 291.

In *Gibson v Grampian Health Board*,[34] Mr Gibson, C, underwent a bowel examination under general anaesthetic at D's hospital, and for that purpose, an intravenous cannula was inserted in the back of his hand. Unfortunately, when C left hospital later that day, so too did the cannula in his hand. It was removed by his GP later that evening, after a period of severe pain. **Held:** no negligence was proven; but had it been, contributory negligence of 20% would have been held because had C 'been simply a rather naive patient with no previous experience of hospital, I should have been inclined to exclude contributory negligence altogether. [C], however, has unfortunately had a long experience of hospital treatment of one kind or another, and I find it hard to believe that he was in fact as naive as he sought to appear'. In *Jackson v Murray*,[35] Miss Jackson, C, 13, was let off on a winter's evening by the school bus, just opposite her parents' farm, and she ran from behind the bus directly into the path of Mr Murray's, D's, car, and was severely injured in the collision. D was driving negligently, in that he did not reduce his speed from 50 mph, even when seeing the stationary school bus ahead. **Held:** 50% CN, given C's youth. A 13-year-old 'will not necessarily have the same level of judgment and self-control as an adult ... she had to take account of D's car approaching at speed, in very poor light conditions, with its headlights on ... the assessment of speed in those circumstances is far from easy, even for an adult, and even more so for a 13-year-old'. In *Dalling v RJ Heale & Co Ltd*[35a], Stephen Dalling, C, was injured at work in 2005, and recovered damages for that injury, against his employer, D. In 2008, C then suffered a second accident, where he fell backwards in a pub and suffered a further head injury, having had too much to drink. C alleged that the additional injuries in 2008 were causally related to his first head injury, because that head injury had impaired his judgment and his ability to control his drinking. **Held:** D liable for negligence, because the first head injury had a causative effect in relation to the second accident. However, 33% CN awarded against C.

Where D's breach has caused C to suffer from mental instability, and then C contributes to his own injury or death (via suicide or other acts of self-harm), English law countenances that some finding of contributory negligence will nevertheless be possible against C as a matter of law:

In *Reeves v Commr of Police*, facts previously, Mr Lynch, C, was of sound mind, but mentally-disturbed, when he hanged himself whilst on remand. 50% CN was awarded against C. In *Corr v IBC Vehicles Ltd*,[36] Mr Corr, C, worked on the assembly line of a Vauxhall vehicle factory in Coventry. Whilst he was fixing an automated machine, the machine suddenly picked up a steel plate and threw it. If C had not ducked, he would have been decapitated. As it was, he lost his right ear and suffered serious facial injuries, plus severe depression. Six years later, C committed suicide by jumping from a multi-storey carpark. **Held:** no CN found against C, given that evidence on the point was not given at trial. However, the majority (Lords Scott, Mance and Neuberger) held that 20% CN would have been appropriate, given that C was not insane, retained personal autonomy, was not an automaton, and made the decision to end his life. (Lords Bingham and Walker, dissenting, held that C's mental instability was the doing of his employer, and that CN against C was not appropriate.)

ii. Where D's breach places C in a situation of peril or danger, then the standard of care expected of C will likely be reduced, such that contributory negligence is less likely to be found. This is particularly evident where rescuer C suffers some injury during the rescue, sues D whose negligence put him in that boat, and D argues that the rescuer was contributorily negligent during the rescue.

[34] (1985) OH Cases (15 Mar 1985) (Lord Murray). [35] [2015] UKSC 5, [41].
[35a] [2011] EWCA Civ 365, [26]–[27]. [36] [2008] AC 884 (HL) [18].

In *Baker v TE Hopkins & Son Ltd*,[37] Dr Baker, C, went down into a well filled with carbon monoxide gases, on D's premises, to try to save two workers who had entered the well, and died in the rescue attempt. C had asked to be lowered down with a rope tied to him, despite warnings against it, but all three men died. C's estate sued D; and CN was alleged against C. **Held:** no CN found: 'the court should not be quick to accept criticism of the rescuer's conduct from the wrongdoer who created the danger'.

Hence, predicting the outcome of contributory negligence pleas may be very difficult without knowing the characteristics of *that particular* C. It is not always a case of how the law should have expected a reasonable C to have conducted himself.

Element #2: Causation

§10.7 C's lack of reasonable care for his own safety and well-being must, in part, have caused or contributed to his *injury or harm*. However, it is not necessary to prove that C's lack of reasonable care caused or contributed to *the accident*.

It is not enough that C failed to act prudently in looking out for his own health or well-being. A causal link must be proven between that lack of prudence and C's injury or harm – notwithstanding that establishing that 'causal link' is **not** referred to in s 1(1) of the 1945 Act. The burden of proving that causal link (as with all elements of the defence) rests with D (per *King v Medical Services Intl Ltd*[38]).

In order to rely on the defence, D does **not** need to prove either of the following:

- that C partly caused *the accident* to occur. This distinction was reiterated recently by the Supreme Court in *Jackson v Murray*.[39] For example, by failing to wear a seatbelt, passenger C will have partly caused his own *injuries*, but he will not have caused the accident itself, if driver D ran a red light and collided with another vehicle – nevertheless, the defence can be proven against C (per *Froom v Butcher*,[40] where contributory negligence of 20% was held against C, for failing to wear a seatbelt).
- that C caused his own injuries, *on the balance of probabilities*. All that D needs to show is that some act or omission on C's part *contributed to* identifiable injury or harm to C. On that basis, as judicially acknowledged in *Badger v MOD*,[41] establishing a causal link between C's own wrongdoing and his damage may be 'impossible, and a broader and less defined approach is necessary'. What it may come down to is for D to prove that C's unreasonable behaviour caused, in part, his own injury, rather than (as Denning LJ memorably put it in *Jones v Livox Quarries Ltd*[42]) merely being part of C's 'history'. A hypothetical scenario was provided by the British Columbia Supreme Court in *Bevilacqua v Altenkirk*[43] – suppose that C takes the wrong bus due a careless lack of attention, and is then a victim of the bus driver's negligent driving. Had the passenger not made his own mistake, his injury would not have happened, causally-speaking; but there was only a 'fortuitous connection', an accidental link, between C's fault and his injury, and hence, C could not be contributorily negligent. This invokes a remoteness-type enquiry (as discussed in Chapter 9).

[37] [1959] 1 WLR 966 (CA). [38] [2012] EWHC 970 (QB [282]. [39] [2015] UKSC 5, [20]. [40] [1976] QB 286 (CA).
[41] [2005] EWHC 2941 (QB) [14] (the employee's smoking was accepted to be a substantial cause of his death).
[42] [1952] 2 QB 608 (CA) 616. [43] [2004] BCSC 945 (Groberman J) [39].

In *Beasley v Alexander*,[44] a car accident occurred, where Paul Alexander, D, turned across the path of Marcel Beasley's, C's, motorcycle. C suffered severe brain damage in the accident. **Held:** D was negligent; and no CN applied. C was travelling too fast; but even if he had been travelling at a 'top safe speed', there would nonetheless have been an accident in which he would have sustained serious injury. C's injury would have happened anyway, regardless of his negligence; and hence, C's negligence did not cause his damage.

Causation dilemmas can arise whenever it is alleged that C **failed** to do something, and that omission contributed to his own downfall – the court must then operate in the realms of the hypothetical, and that 'less defined approach' cited in *Badger* may be necessary. A couple of examples, in the medical context, illustrate the conundrum:

i. Where it is alleged that patient C failed to give sufficient information about his symptoms to doctor D, then D has to prove the requisite causal link as follows – that, on the balance of probabilities: D's diagnosis would have been different if he had received the information; that C would have taken whatever steps that the treatment had required; and D's treatment (had he given it) would have forestalled or prevented C's injury or harm. If, however, D's diagnosis would probably *not* have been different, had the information been disclosed by C, then it cannot be said that C contributed to his downfall, because the information held back would have made no difference. Then, the defence of contributory negligence will fail.

In the **Ontario** case of *Taylor v Morrison*,[45] Mr Taylor, C, was a reticent patient, and did not disclose his symptoms at two appointments with his GP, D. He was not diagnosed with severe coronary heart disease; heartburn was initially diagnosed. **Held:** D was liable in negligence; and no CN found. C 'would have taken *some steps* to manage his risk factors if he had been diagnosed with coronary heart disease and advised of the life threatening consequences of a failure to do so'. That part of the causal link was made out. However, D also had to establish that, had C disclosed his symptoms at two appointments, he would have diagnosed and investigated a cardiac cause for his presentations, and C's life would then have been extended. However, D could not prove that he would have diagnosed a cardiac cause – 'Nor am I satisfied that, had [C] made disclosure, [D's] diagnosis would have been different'. Hence, no CN found.

ii. Where it is alleged that C failed to attend an appointment with D, and thereby lost the opportunity to receive further information or assistance that would have probably prevented C's injury, the court must be satisfied, on the balance of probabilities that, if C had attended as he ought to have done, then that would have produced a better outcome for C. That establishes the causal link between C's omission, and C's injury. Only then can contributory negligence be made out. If, however, C's turning up would not have produced a better outcome for C, then there is no causal link, and no contributory negligence will arise. Particularly difficult causal problems arise, if C's turning up to the appointment would have produced a better outcome, but only coincidentally and incidentally.

In the **Ontario** case of *Rupert v Toth*,[46] patient C died of inverting papilloma, which was not diagnosed and treated properly by D before turning malignant and invading C's cranial cavity. C had missed a follow-up appointment, and D argued that, had C turned up, D was intending to tell C

[44] [2012] EWHC 2197 (QB). [45] (Ont SCJ, 19 Jul 2006) [133], [153].
[46] (2006), 38 CCLT (3d) 261 (SCJ) [140]–[141].

certain information at the follow-up appointment, and C would have undergone further surgery to have an inverting papilloma removed, thereby increasing his life expectancy. **Held**: D negligent; but CN of 50% held. In the **British Columbia** case of *Bevilacqua v Altenkirk*,[47] patient C underwent a vasectomy operation, but it failed, and a third child was born to C and his wife. Surgeon D admitted negligence, for misreading the post-operative laboratory report and telling C (incorrectly) that his sperm count was zero and that it was safe to cease other forms of contraception. However, C failed to return to his urologist for a post-operative examination three months later. Had he done so, the urologist would have re-read the laboratory report and discovered D's mistake in time to prevent subsequent conception of the third child (albeit that the post-operative examination was to physically check for any early signs of the vas recanalising, and not for the purposes of checking a post-operative sperm count). Hence, C's failure to turn up was a cause of his damage (the birth of the third child) – but was it an *effective cause* of C's damage? **Held:** no CN. There was no causal link between C's non-attendance and the birth of the third child, because the return to the urologist did not deal with the risk that the laboratory report had been misread; it was to deal with 'a separate risk – that of the *vas* being in the early stages of recanalisation. In failing to go for an examination by Dr Chartrand, Mr Bevilacqua assumed the risk that early-stage recanalisation might go undetected. He did not assume a risk that the operation failed from the outset to render him sterile. While Dr Chartrand would undoubtedly have corrected Dr Altenkirk's error had Mr Bevilacqua attended for a re-examination, that would have occurred only incidentally – it was not the purpose for which a re-examination was required'.

It is suggested that these cases would be decided in the same way in English law.

Element #3: Comparative responsibility

§10.8 Under the 1945 Act, the apportionment of contributory negligence must take into account the relative blameworthiness of C's and D's conduct, and the extent to which that fault caused the damage (i.e., the causative potency of their acts).

The assessment of contributory negligence against C must entail a comparative assessment of culpability or fault of C and D (i.e. of their degrees of departure from the reasonable standard of care), **and** of the relative importance of the acts of C and D in causing C's damage (i.e., the causative potency of their acts), when assessing the apportionment of damages which C and D must each bear (per *Stapley v Gypsum Mines Ltd*[48]).

This is not an easy, nor precise, evaluative step, however. As the Supreme Court pointed out in *Jackson v Murray*, the court is not comparing 'like with like' – it is comparing D's breach of a duty which the law required of him, with C's lack of reasonable care for his own interests.[49] Moreover, translating the facts of one accident to those of another is not a good general guide to apportionment (per *Groves v Studley*[50]).

It follows that, if D should bear 'the lion's share of responsibility', C's contributory negligence is likely to be assessed at well below 50%. In the employment context, this comparison is particularly important, in that while the injured employee may have failed to take due care in what he was doing, that lack of care may be modest and 'far outweighed by the breaches of

[47] [2004] BCSC 945, [39]–[47], with quote at [44].

[48] [1953] AC 663 (HL) 682. Also: *Badger v MOD* [2005] EWHC 2941 (QB) [16]; *O'Connell v Jackson* [1972] 1 QB 270 (CA) 277–78.

[49] [2015] UKSC 5, [27].

[50] [2014] EWHC 1522 (QB) [44].

duty [by the employer] which had placed him in the position in which he found himself' (per *Milroy v BT plc*,[51] where 30% contributory negligence was found). However, if C was significantly more at fault than was D, contributory negligence is likely to be 50% or greater.

In *Stoddart v Perucca*,[52] Sally Stoddart, C, 14, was riding her horse, Trigger, along a bridleway near Sunderland, when she emerged into a road, colliding with D's campervan and trailer. D was driving at approximately 35 mph, and the speed limit was 60 mph. The horse reared and fell on C, causing serious injury. C was an experienced rider, riding since she was seven, and Trigger was a dependable horse. **Held:** 50% CN. C was 'significantly more at fault in terms of simple blameworthiness than [D]', especially given that D was well within the speed limit and keeping a good lookout. C 'was an experienced rider who knew this road well and was doing something foolish when she rode out without looking'. However, that was balanced against the greater 'causative potency' that D's driving a car (a 'potentially dangerous weapon'), posed to C. In *Badger v MOD*,[53] Mr Badger, C, died of lung cancer as a result of being exposed wrongfully to asbestos whilst working as a boiler maker for the MOD, D. C also smoked, which was causative of his cancer. **Held:** 20% CN. Significantly greater blame was to be attributed to employer D, than to C, as D was guilty of statutory breaches at a time when the dangers of asbestos were well-known. Further, not all of C's smoking was blameworthy. In *Stapley v Gypsum Mines Ltd*,[54] Mr Stapley, C, and his colleague, Mr Dale, were told by their employer, D, to bring down a dangerous roof (an underground stope), and not to work beneath it, in the meantime. Their efforts to bring down the roof failed, so C then proceeded to work beneath the roof in breaking up gypsum. The roof collapsed and killed him. **Held:** 80% CN, as C's conduct in entering the stope contributed more immediately to the accident created by the dangerous roof.

It will be rare for a pedestrian to bear a greater share of responsibility than the driver, given the causative potency of a car being driven by D ('a car is potentially a dangerous weapon, and accordingly, the attribution of causative potency to the driver must be greater than that to the pedestrian'[55]).

In *Jackson v Murray*,[56] facts previously, **held:** 50% CN held (reduced from 90% at trial and 70% on appeal). D's conduct 'played at least an equal role to that of [C] in causing the damage, and was at least as blameworthy'. The dangerous nature of a car being driven at speed and D's failure to modify his driving, plus that C was only 13 at the time, was to be balanced against C's knowledge of the road, the risks of traffic, and the need to exercise care when crossing the road. In *Ayres v Odedra*,[57] C stood in front of D's car at a traffic light in a traffic-calming area of Leicester, drunk and having dropped his trousers, and D moved forward in his car and ran over C, severely injuring him. **Held:** 20% CN. C deliberately placed himself in the road in front of D's car, remained there when he should have known that the traffic lights were likely to change and D would want to move forward, and where his drunken state and dropped trousers hampered his ability to move freely and out of the way of D's car.

Element #4: Reduction

§10.9 The damages recoverable by C will be reduced to the extent that the court thinks just and equitable, having regard to C's share in the responsibility for C's damage (where that 'damage' may constitute C's death, personal injury, property damage, or economic damage).

[51] [2015] EWHC 532 (QB) [37]. [52] [2011] EWCA Civ 290, [18].
[53] [2005] EWHC 2941 (QB) [55]. [54] [1953] AC 663 (HL) 682 (Lord Reid).
[55] The Supreme Court quoted the Extra Division, Inner House, Court of Session with approval on this point, *ibid*, [15], although the ultimate percentage was varied.
[56] [2015] UKSC 5, [39]–[44]. [57] [2013] EWHC 40 (QB) [153].

There is no *de minimis* principle applying to contributory negligence in English law – 'the words of s 1(1) ... do not seem to leave much room for an application of the *de minimis* principle ... [but] I very much doubt if they permit ... no reduction at all because the court thinks it just and equitable that there should be no reduction' (per *Boothman v British Northrop Ltd*[58]). Therefore, it is not possible for C to argue that his own contribution to his injury was so negligible that it can be disregarded – once C is found to have been at fault within the language of s 1(1), *some* reduction in his damages is obligatory.

In some scenarios, the range of percentage of contributory negligence is reasonably fixed by case law. For example, where passenger C fails to wear a seatbelt and suffers injury in a car accident, the Court of Appeal noted, in *Froom v Butcher*,[59] that the range of contributory negligence will appropriately fall between 15–25%. That extent of any reduction of a passenger's damages by reason of contributory negligence must be proportionate, given that domestic rules governing contributory negligence must be compatible with the principles underpinning the EU Directives governing motor insurance (per *Candolin v Pohjola*[60]). The range identified in *Froom* has been confirmed by the English Court of Appeal as being appropriate for domestic law in *J (a child) v Wilkins*.[61]

The 'damage' suffered by C, recovery for which is reduced under the 1945 Act, is defined to include 'loss of life and personal injury' (per s 4). However, contributory negligence may also be found in the context of both property damage (per *Wessanen Foods Ltd v Jofson Ltd*,[62] in dicta) and economic loss (per *Playboy Club London Ltd v Banca Nazionale Del Lavoro Spa*,[63] where 15% was held).

The doctor–patient context: a policy and a comparative vignette

§10.10 Notwithstanding that the doctor–patient relationship exhibits two characteristics, *viz*: (1) trust, confidence and reliance by the patient on the doctor's knowledge, skill and care, and (2) vulnerability on the patient's part, given his illness/injury and the information imbalance, a patient can nevertheless be found to have contributed to his own damage.

Any professional relationship, and the defence of contributory negligence, are not necessarily comfortable bed-fellows. It is **not** the same scenario as in the other more common applications of contributory negligence – say, a passenger not wearing a seatbelt who sues the negligent driver, an employee who fails to exercise due care for his own safety in circumstances where his employer has provided an unsafe system of work, or where a lawful entrant is drunk and falls over some hazard left on the land by the negligent occupier – where the litigants are in a relatively equal position with respect to the ability to control their own welfare.

In the context of medical negligence, English courts have been quite resistant to the notion of contributory negligence, but not necessarily averse to it altogether.

In *Pidgeon v Doncaster HA*,[64] C sued for a 'false negative' cervical smear test, and which showed a pre-cancerous condition that should have warranted further investigation and treatment. Invasive

[58] (1972) 13 KIR 112 (CA, Stephenson LJ), and reiterated by: *Badger v MOD* [2005] EWHC 2941 (QB) [15].
[59] [1976] QB 286 (CA). [60] [2005] ECHR I-5745 (ECJ, Case C-537/03). [61] [2001] PIQR 179 (CA) [21].
[62] [2006] EWHC 1325 (TCC) [209]. [63] [2014] EWHC 2613 (QB) [63]–[64].
[64] [2002] Lloyd's Rep Med 130 (CC Sheffield, 23 Nov 2001).

cervical cancer, in fact, developed. **Held:** C's damages were reduced by two-thirds (from £55,000 to £18,500), because of C's refusal to follow medical advice and to undergo further smear tests in the intervening period between the false negative and the correct diagnosis. In *Hardaker v Newcastle HA*,[65] a diver decided to re-immerse himself in water, and then delayed making the emergency call, once he recognised the symptoms of decompression illness. His claim against D, which operated the decompression chamber, for systemic negligence, failed. Contributory negligence was raised, but was not necessary to deal with. In *Gouldsmith v Mid-Staffordshire General Hosp NHS Trust*,[66] a patient with ulceration and circulatory problems in her left hand had 'not fully co-operate[d] with treatment' prescribed for her – but there was no allegation of contributory negligence there. In a somewhat similar Irish case, *Byrne v Ryan*,[67] a patient suffered a failed sterilisation and then failed to attend hospital for her six-week check-up as advised. She had acted 'imprudently' and 'negligently', but 'no case of contributory negligence was pleaded against C, nor was it urged on me that her failure to take the advice offered to her on her discharge from the hospital amounted to such', so the court did not consider the issue further.

The area is ripe with judicial differences of opinion, however. A comparative analysis of Australian and Canadian jurisprudence reveals a surprising disparity in the application of contributory negligence to cases of medical negligence. There have been four scenarios, in particular, in which patients have failed to take reasonable measures of 'self-care'.

A comparative corner: **Commonwealth examples**

Failing to provide full information. As the Ontario court put it in *Lurtz v Duchesne*,[a] the law cannot expect a doctor to 'act as a clairvoyant', whilst the Alberta court pointed out, in *Rose v Dujon*,[b] that '[b]oth parties in the doctor-patient relationship have obligations – the doctor to the patient, and the patient to himself – and inherent in the discharge of such obligations is the need to communicate fully with each other. To be effective, communication must be bilateral. Doctors are not mind readers'. In the Queensland case of *Locher v Turner*,[c] C was diagnosed with and treated for colon cancer. That diagnosis by her GP was negligently-delayed (attributing the symptoms to irritable bowel syndrome to begin with). **Held:** 20% CN. The evidence suggested that C had been suffering from bowel troubles which were much more frequent and indeed serious than she had disclosed to D.

Failing to attend follow-up/recommended appointments. Where C was told (in certain and unambiguous terms) to return for a follow-up visit or to book another appointment, and failed to do so, then numerous Commonwealth authorities support a finding of CN. Some courts have been sympathetic to the patient who does not keep an appointment, make a follow-up phone call, etc, although the reasons for denying any CN have been carefully articulated (e.g., there was some plausible explanation for C's non-attendance; or that it was more the responsibility of D to ensure that C followed up). In the New South Wales case of *Kalokerinos v Burnett*,[d] C consulted her GP, who advised her to come again if she continued to suffer from having vaginal bleeding; but he failed to arrange an alternative referral to a specialist that was more convenient to C. C's

[a] (Ont SCJ, 16 Apr 2003) [157].
[b] (1990), 108 AR 352 (Alta QB) [148].
[c] [1995] QCA 106.
[d] [1996] NSWCA 324, [40]–[41] (per Clarke JA) (overturning trial judge's finding of no CN).

[65] (QB, 15 Jun 2001). [66] [2007] EWCA Civ 397, [8]. [67] [2007] IEHC 207.

condition worsened, and she suffered daily vaginal bleeding, but for more than four months did not return to the GP or seek any further medical attention. She was eventually diagnosed with cervical cancer. **Held:** 20% CN. In the Western Australian case of *Le Brun v Joseph*,[e] C was making good progress with physiotherapy, but failed to keep two appointments. **Held:** no CN. The reasons for non-attendance were plausible.

Failing to seek medical treatment. Wherever C ignores a condition which, as a matter of common sense, ought to have been checked out; or where C knows of a particular propensity to a medical condition in the family but ignores 'warning signs', CN is possible. Some Commonwealth courts may also be unimpressed with patients who discharge themselves post-operation without permission. In the Alberta case of *Strichen v Stewart*,[f] C knew of a history of cancer in her close family and had been recommended to attend for yearly check-ups. She failed to turn up for mammograms, and was then diagnosed with breast cancer. **Held:** no liability against D. Otherwise, 35% CN would have applied. In the Malaysian case of *Tan Ah Kau v Govt of Malaysia*,[g] C discharged himself from hospital, while in post-operative recuperation. **Held:** 20% CN. He 'felt that the facilities at home were better since his wife and children could take care of him', but that was careless behaviour. In the **British Columbia** case of *Zhang v Kan*,[h] C failed to insist to her GP that she have an amniocentesis test, when C knew that, due to her age, she was at high risk of having a child with Down's Syndrome. A child with that condition was born. **Held:** 50% CN. C was 'a sophisticated and experienced businesswoman' who had researched the topic of amniocentesis, and did not submit to the test, against her gynacologist's advice.

Failing to follow instructions. Patients frequently disregard their doctor's instructions, which has sometimes cost the patient damages. In the Alberta case of *Dumais v Hamilton*,[i] C disregarded D's, her surgeon's, instructions not to smoke in the week following a 'tummy tuck' operation. C did smoke immediately after the operation, which caused necrosis of the tissue, leaving areas of disfigurement. **Held:** 50% CN.

[e] [2006] WADC 200.
[f] [2004] ABQB 612, [90].
[g] [1995] MLJU 183 (HC).
[h] [2003] BCSC 5, [61]–[63].
[i] [1998] ABCA 218, [15]–[17].

On the other hand, some Commonwealth judges have considered contributory negligence by a patient to sit most uneasily with the concept of medical negligence, where vulnerable, sick, worried and unknowledgeable patients put themselves in the hands of competent medical practitioners for advice and treatment. As the Irish High Court said, in *Ryan v Bon Secours Hospital*,[68] '[i]n the doctor/patient relationship there is a total reliance placed by the patient upon the doctor', and that the doctor–patient relationship was distinguishable from the employer–employee scenario, because a patient 'cannot be presumed to have any prior knowledge regarding the nature of his ailment, what possible diagnoses might be open, what tests might be appropriate, the significance of any such tests, or any possible or appropriate treatment', whereas 'a finding of contributory negligence can be made against an employee who has acted

[68] [2004] IEHC 77 (also reported under the name, '*Philp v Ryan*', at the same neutral citation).

in a way which perhaps lacked ordinary common-sense, or was contrary to some training which he had received'. The Fiji High Court called the possibility of contributory negligence against a patient, in *Moli v Bingwor*, as a 'startling proposition'.[69]

Notably, English law suggests that the doctor–patient relationship does *not* represent a fiduciary relationship. In *Sidaway v Governors of Bethlem Royal Hospital*,[70] Lord Scarman said (in his minority opinion, but no other member disagreed with this observation) that the relationship simply could not be compared to that of a solicitor-client or trustee-beneficiary (confirming Dunn LJ's view in the court below,[71] that the fiduciary relationship 'has been confined to cases involving the disposition of property, and has never been applied to the nature of the duty which lies upon a doctor in the performance of his professional treatment of his patient'). Subsequently, in *R v Mid Glamorgan Family Health Services Authy; ex p Martin*,[72] Popplewell J reiterated that, in *Sidaway*, the 'notion of fiduciary relationship was expressly disavowed'. This is in contrast to some other Commonwealth jurisdictions (including Australia and Canada), where the doctor–patient relationship has been expressly held to be fiduciary in nature.[73] It is ironic, then, that contributory negligence seems to be more frequently countenanced where the doctor–patient relationship is seen as a fiduciary relationship involving trust and confidence, than in a jurisdiction where it is not so acknowledged.

A greater acknowledgment of a patient's personal responsibility and self-determination is the most obvious reason to support an extended interplay between contributory and medical negligence – supported by Lord Steyn's statement, in *Chester v Afshar*, that '[i]n modern law, medical paternalism no longer rules'.[74] English judges have been equally willing to acknowledge that times have moved on from when 'doctor knew best',[75] and in extra-curial comment, Lord Woolf observed that '[t]he contemporary approach is a more critical approach'.[76] Whilst those observations have been made within the context of what a patient can expect of a doctor, surely the sentiment has equal ramifications for what a doctor may *expect of a patient*. In other words, if the pendulum is swinging toward a less indulgent attitude toward patients, then they may come to be treated exactly as would road users, employees and invitees – whereby a reasonable standard of care is expected of them all. A greater use of contributory negligence would take into account the *reality* that an effective doctor–patient relationship simply cannot exist in a vacuum of misinformation or non-cooperation – it is a relationship of 'shared responsibility'.[77] Moreover, it is hardly likely that contributory negligence would subvert the principles of trust and reliance upon which the doctor–patient relationship is based. Undoubtedly the trial judge, when assessing the percentage reduction warranted, will give due weight to

[69] [2003] FJHC 279 (no CN).
[70] [1985] AC 871 (HL) 884.
[71] [1984] QB 491 (CA) 515.
[72] (1993) 16 BMLR 81 (QB).
[73] e.g., in Canada: *McInerney v MacDonald* (1992), 93 DLR (4th) 415 (SCC) [17], [19] ('The relationship between physician and patient is one in which trust and confidence must be placed in the physician. The physician-patient relationship is a fiduciary relationship': La Forest J). In Aust: *Breen v Williams* [1996] HCA 57, [15], [19] ('the doctor acquires an ascendancy over the patient'; '[w]hilst duties of a fiduciary nature may be imposed upon a doctor, they are confined and do not cover *the entire* doctor-patient relationship'); *Johnson v Biggs* [2000] NSWCA 338 (Giles JA) ('the doctor has a fiduciary relationship with the patient, in which the patient places trust in the doctor to listen to the patient's concerns').
[74] [2004] UKHL 41, [16].
[75] e.g.: *AB v Leeds Teaching Hosp NHS Trust* [2004] EWHC 644 (QB) [115 (re organ harvesting); *B v An NHS Hosp Trust* [2002] EWHC 429 (Fam) [94] (re disabled patients); *R v Bournewood Mental Health Trust, ex p L* [1998] UKHL 24, [1999] AC 458 (HL) 473–74 (re mental health legislation for incapacitated patients).
[76] Lord Woolf, 'Are the Courts Excessively Deferential to the Medical Profession?' (2001) 9 *Med L Rev* 1.
[77] A term used, e.g., in: *Tai v Hatzistavrou* [1999] NSWCA 306, [56].

the high standards of conduct which are required of a doctor, plus the comparative assessment of fault will make it almost inconceivable that the patient will be *more* at fault for his injury than the doctor. It can be used as a measured defence. For these reasons, the author considers that contributory negligence ought to take a more prominent role in English medico-legal jurisprudence than it has to date.

VOLUNTARY ASSUMPTION OF RISK (*VOLENTI*)

What *volenti* means

Definition

§10.11 *Volenti* means that there was a voluntary undertaking by C to absolve D from the legal consequences of a breach of duty by D, where C had full knowledge of both the nature and extent of the risks of injury created by that breach. Where it applies, *volenti* is a complete defence.

The defence of *volenti* is derived from the maxim, '*volenti non fit injuria*' – 'to he who is willing, no harm is done'.

It was described by Lord Reid in *Imperial Chemical Industries Ltd v Shatwell* in these terms: C 'who freely and voluntarily incurs a risk of which he has full knowledge cannot complain of injury if that risk materialises and causes him damage'.[78] In *Smith v Baker*, Lord Herschell stated that the maxim was 'founded on good sense and justice. One who has invited or assented to an act being done towards him cannot, when he suffers from it, complain of it as a wrong'.[79] As Buxton LJ noted, in *Reeves v Commr of Police*, the defence means that, both in fact and in law, 'the whole blame for [C's] death [or injury or loss] must rest on [C's] shoulders'.[80]

The defence is difficult (although not impossible) for D to establish. Proof that C has accepted the risk of D's negligence, and has absolved D from the consequences, is to set a very high threshold.

Alternative pleas

Alongside the many judicial reservations surrounding the defence, *volenti's* practical import has been substantially lessened because of the existence of *apportionment* under the Law Reform (Contributory Negligence) Act 1945, which relieves a court from having to decide cases on an 'all or nothing' basis. That makes contributory negligence a much more attractive defence – which has long been judicially-recognised. For example, in *Nettleship v Weston* (where *volenti* failed), Lord Denning MR noted that, whereas once *volenti* was 'used almost as an alternative defence to contributory negligence', its use had become 'severely limited' ever since contributory negligence became a partial defence.[81] In *ICI Ltd v Shatwell*, Lord Pearce cited that '[a]pportionment of loss through contributory negligence ... can so often provide a fair result'.[82]

Furthermore, C's foolhardy actions may also have constituted a *novus actus interveniens*, severing the chain of causation between D's negligent act or omission, and C's injury (this plea was made, unsuccessfully, in *Reeves*, *Corr v IBC Vehicles Ltd*, and *North v TNT Express (UK) Ltd*).

The defence of illegality may also be pleaded in conjunction – that C's behaviour was illegal or unlawful in some way (per *ex turpi causa oritur non actio*). For example, this alternative plea

[78] [1965] AC 656 (HL) 671. [79] [1891] AC 325 (HL) 360. [80] [1997] EWCA Civ 2868, [1999] QB 169 (CA) 175.
[81] [1971] 2 QB 691 (CA) 701. [82] [1965] AC 656 (HL) 684.

occurred, unsuccessfully for D, in *Lane v Holloway*[83] (the defence of illegality is considered later in this chapter, online).

The elements

The defence of *volenti* entails a four-part analysis:

The framework for *volenti*

1. C knew of, and appreciated, the specific risk of injury posed by D's activities
2. C voluntarily consented to that risk of injury, expressly or impliedly
3. The defence does not destroy the content of the duty which D owed to C
4. The defence is not barred at law

Dealing with each in turn:

Element #1: Knowledge of risks

§10.12 C must have known of, and appreciated, the *specific* risk of injury which he suffered (a mere knowledge of the *general* risks associated with D's activities is insufficient). The predominant view is that C's appreciation of risk should be judged objectively, and not subjectively. C must consent to the *specific* risk of the injury which occurred.

Knowledge and appreciation. Knowledge of the risks, on its own, is not sufficient to prove the defence. Without a full appreciation of the risk, the defence can have no application. Age can inhibit that full appreciation – although even children (albeit older children) can be taken to have appreciated the risks of what they were doing – while a close involvement in a trade or profession may enhance such an appreciation of the risks posed by 'things' in a workplace.

Given that C must have knowledge of the *specific* risk which he is running, that renders the defence of *volenti* much narrower in its operation, as it will be a harder task for D to show that C knew of the specific risk which he had supposedly undertaken.

Volenti applied in the following cases:

In *Titchener v British Rwys Board*,[84] D was driving a train when Ms Titchener, C, 15, ran across the unfenced train track. She knew that it was a line which trains used, and that it would be dangerous to cross it, but said that 'it was just a chance I took', to visit the brickworks on the other side of the track, with her boyfriend, for a 'kiss and a cuddle'. She was struck by the train. C voluntarily accepted the risk of being hit by the train. In *ICI Ltd v Shatwell*,[85] brothers George and James Shatwell, C, were qualified shotfirers working at ICI's, D's, quarry. They bored 50 shotholes and inserted electric detonators, and needed to test the circuit for continuity, which should have been done by connecting long wires so that the men could go to a shelter some 80 yards away and test from there. C did not have sufficient wire with them, and decided to test with only short wires. A detonator nearby exploded, causing C serious injury. They sued D for breach of statutory duty, but *volenti* applied.

[83] [1968] 1 QB 379 (CA). [84] [1983] 1 WLR 1427 (HL). [85] [1965] AC 656 (HL).

C knew that they were dealing with a dangerous quantity of explosive when they entered on the foolhardy course.

However, given the age/specific risks point noted above, *volenti* failed in the following:

In *McGlone v British Rwys Board*,[86] C, 12, was mucking around with some young friends, and climbed a transformer tower. He touched live wires with his arm, and was severely burnt. However, *volenti* failed because a boy that young did not have a proper appreciation of the risk from live wires.

Sporting cases. It will be recalled that the standard of care is suppressed, in sporting and recreational pursuits (per Chapter 6), so that proving breach in that context may be difficult, thus affording D a complete 'defence'. Even where breach is proven, C may have nevertheless consented to run the risks of participating in a sport where D has complied with the laws and rules set by the governing body. However, C will not consent to run risks which are posed because those laws are not complied with. That is a *specific* risk to which C will not have consented. To contrast some cases:

In *Slack v Glenie*,[87] Andrew Glenie, C, was riding a motorcycle and sidecar combination around a race track at D's Matchams Leisure Park in Hampshire, with Peter Lain as his passenger, when the motor cycle went out of control and hit the fence on the inner side of the race track. PL was killed, and C was rendered paraplegic. Racing with specially constructed motor cycle and sidecar combinations was a recognised but inherently very dangerous sport, and at international level, the sport was governed by the Federation Internationale Motocycliste (FIM). D's track did not comply with the FIM safety standards, in that there was no clear in-field run-off. **Held:** *volenti* failed, because although C freely and voluntarily rode on the track and knew that the inner fence was there and of the risks of hitting it, C did not know that the hazard would be unacceptable on any track where FIM Track Standards applied. Hence, C did not have a full appreciation of the nature and extent of the risk presented by the fence. In *Watson v British Boxing Board*,[88] Michael Watson, C, was a professional boxer engaged in a professional fight with Chris Eubank for the WBO super-middleweight fight at the Tottenham Spurs Football Club. The fight, organised by the British Boxing Board, D, was stopped in the final round, when C was clearly in trouble. He returned to his corner, and fell unconscious. There was chaos in and around the ring. After seven minutes, C was seen by a doctor; and was taken by the ambulance on standby to hospital, 30 minutes later, and then to a specialist neurosurgery hospital. C had sustained a brain haemorrage, and was left with very serious brain damage. **Held:** negligence proven; but *volenti* failed. C had consented to the risk of physical injury in the fight, but he had not consented to the risk that there would be inadequate medical treatment and attention, should he be seriously injured in the fight. In *Simms v Leigh Rugby Football Club Ltd*,[89] Mr Simms was playing a game of rugby, when he collided with a concrete wall around the football ground, and broke his leg. The by-laws governing the conduct of the game were complied with, by a matter of some three inches. **Held:** *volenti* applied: 'footballers who go to the Leigh ground, go to that ground willingly accepting the risks that arise from playing the game under the rules of the League, on a ground approved by the League'.

Subjective or objective? The question arises as to whether C's appreciation of the risk must be judged on a subjective basis (i.e., what that particular C appreciated about those risks), or on an objective basis (what a reasonable person in C's position should have appreciated). If

[86] 1966 SLT 2 (HL). [87] [2000] EWCA Civ 145.
[88] [2001] QB 1134 (CA). [89] [1969] 2 All ER 923 (Assizes Liverpool) 928.

subjective, then C would presumably have a greater chance of defeating this element (and the defence would apply more narrowly, as a result), if he could show that, whatever others may have appreciated about the danger, *he* did not appreciate it.

The preponderance of English law has supported an objective test (although, as noted previously, the age of C will always be relevant when asking whether C appreciated the relevant risks). In *Bennett v Tugwell*, Ackner J supported an objective test – it does not matter what C 'feels or inwardly consents to, but what his conduct or words evidence that he was consenting to'.[90] Other cases endorse this notion too:

In *Wooldridge v Sumner*,[91] C was run over by a race horse at a racetrack, having been told by the master of the course to step back from the track, but having ignored the instruction. C had no real knowledge or awareness of the nature and behaviour of horses ('a person ignorant of equine behaviour'). However, that would not have precluded the defence from applying, because the defence turned upon what a *reasonable* person in C's position should have appreciated in respect of the risks posed by horses at a racetrack (dicta only, as there was no negligence by D). In *ICI v Shatwell*[92] too, the court suggested that reasonable shot firers in C's position should have appreciated the risks of handling explosives in defiance of regulations.

An oddity arises where C is intoxicated, and where that affects his judgment as to the risks that he was running. Where an objective test applies, then D could take advantage of the defence against that intoxicated C, because a reasonable person in the same circumstances would have been perfectly cognisant of the risks. Under a subjective test, the drunk C will likely not have appreciated the risk, and hence, *volenti* could not apply. Hence, the drunk C would be better off under a subjective test; whereas D would prefer an objective test, as the drunkenness could be ignored when considering a reasonable person in C's position. This point was made by Stocker LJ in *Morris v Murray*, where the objective test – of what C *ought* to have appreciated – was upheld.

In *Morris v Murray*,[93] Mr Morris, C, 25, was drinking at a pub with Mr Murray, D, all afternoon. D had a pilot's licence for a light aircraft, and suggested that C should go on a flight with him. C agreed. C drove them to the airfield; tried to start the engine by turning the propeller; bought the fuel for the plane and helped to fill it up; and asked D whether they had to 'radio in' before taking off. Hence, C was a willing and involved participant in the whole endeavour. Flying conditions were poor, with strong winds, poor visibility, low cloud and occasional drizzle, and the flying club had cancelled all club flying on the day. D was not aware of this, and took off for the joyride, which was described as 'short and chaotic'. D took off down wind when he should have taken off on a different runway and into the wind. The plane went up almost vertically about 300 ft, stalled and plunged to the ground, killing D instantly and severely injuring C. The autopsy on D showed that he had a blood alcohol content equivalent to 17 whiskies. **Held (trial):** *volenti* failed; C was awarded £130,000 for his injuries. **Held (CA):** *volenti* applied. C fully knew of the risks of flying with D, having drunk with him all afternoon. He was not entirely sober, but sober enough to appreciate the risk, being 'merry', but not 'blind drunk', when he took the flight with D. C's actions did not suggest that his faculties 'were so muddled that he was incapable of appreciating obvious risks ... flying with a drunken pilot is great folly'. Also, C had consented to the *specific* risk of suffering serious injury or death if D fell below the standard of a reasonable pilot controlling the plane.

[90] [1971] 2 WLR 847 (QB) 851. [91] [1963] 2 QB 43 (CA). [92] [1965] AC 656 (HL) 682. [93] [1991] 2 QB 6 (CA).

Stocker LJ would not go so far as to say that the appreciation of risk should *always* be judged objectively – although he suggested that it certainly should, if C was intoxicated.[94]

Element #2: Voluntary consent

§10.13 C must voluntarily agree, expressly or impliedly, to waive any claim for loss or injury that he might suffer from D's breach of duty.

As remarked in *Nettleship v Weston*,[95] the fact that C knows of the risk of injury is **never** enough for *volenti* to apply: 'nothing will suffice, short of *an agreement* to waive any claim for negligence'. This does not mean that a contract must have existed between C and D, however. It requires consent.

Express or implied. C's express agreement to 'run the risk' is rarely given. More frequently, C's consent will be given impliedly, as occurred, e.g., in *Titchener*, *ICI v Shatwell*, and *Morris v Murray*. In the last-mentioned, C knowingly and willingly embarked on a flight with a drunken pilot, where the flight served no useful purpose, there was no need or compulsion to take it, it was 'just entertainment'. The court noted it to be 'much nearer to the dangerous experimenting with the detonators in *Shatwell*'.

Voluntariness. The consent of C must not be obtained by way of compulsion or undue influence.

In *Morris v Murray*, the lengthy drinking session was participated in by both C and D, and there was no bullying or coercion towards C to get into the plane with D. Quite the reverse; C drove them to the airfield himself.

Employment cases, such as *ICI v Shatwell*, are difficult, however, where dangerous activities are being carried out in the course of that employment. Although the two employed shotfirers who tested the explosives circuit were subject to the defence and could not recover compensation, the court acknowledged that any consent of C may be 'shaped' by his need to maintain employment, rather than from any implied agreement to run the risks (indeed, the need for a free assumption of risk 'makes it as a rule unsuitable in master and servant cases owing to the possible existence of indefinable social and economic pressure'[96]). **Any form of compulsion or pressure on employee C, however indefinable or implied, will vitiate the defence**, as the following cases showed:

In *Read v J Lyons & Co Ltd*,[97] Miss Read, C, an employee of the Ministry of Supply, was required to inspect the filling of shell cases with explosives, at a munitions factory during the war. She had to be present in the shell-filling shop for that purpose. One day, an explosion in the shell-filling shop killed a man and injured C seriously. Negligence was proven; and *volenti* did not apply. C was only on the premises because she was required to work there as an employee: 'had she been a free agent she would not have remained there'. In *Williams v Port of Liverpool Stevedoring Co Ltd*,[98] C, a stevedore, was injured during the unloading of a vessel, where a dangerous system of unloading was undertaken by the whole gang at their instigation (not at C's). *Volenti* did not apply, as it was difficult for one man to stand out against his gang. It would have been different if C had instigated the dangerous system himself.

[94] *ibid*, 17. The decision was unanimous, but the other members of the Court did not comment on this point.
[95] [1971] 2 QB 691 (CA) 701. [96] [1965] AC 656 (HL) 687–88.
[97] [1947] AC 156 (HL) 157. [98] [1956] 1 WLR 551 (Assizes Liverpool).

In *Morris v Murray*,[99] the Court of Appeal remarked that the defence had been 'in retreat' in the employment context. Subsequently, in *Davies v Global Strategies Group (HK) Ltd*,[100] it was acknowledged that there had been 'very few examples' where employer D could take advantage of the defence against employee C.

It has been said that *volenti* can be a defence in sporting injury cases, where 'injuries (even career ending ones) are part and parcel of the rough and tumble of competitive sport' (per *Collet v Smith*[101]), or 'where participants accept known risks of a lawfully conducted sport' (per *Lee North v TNT Express (UK) Ltd*[102]). However, in spite of these assurances, successful cases in the sporting context are difficult to find in English law (the previously-mentioned rugby case of *Simms v Leigh Rugby Football Club Ltd*[103] is a rare example).

Consent to D's breach of duty. The point of the defence is that C must consent to (or accept) D's acting below the standard of reasonable care, and the risks which flow from that. In *Wooldridge v Sumner*,[104] Diplock LJ remarked that '[t]he consent that is relevant is not consent to the risk of injury, but consent to the lack of reasonable care that may produce that risk'.

Volenti has no room to operate, where C accepts the risk of injury in ordinary, non-negligent, circumstances. As the court put it in *Browning v Odyssey Trust Co Ltd*,[105] it is not to the point that spectators accepted the risk of injury by being close to the action at a dangerous sporting event conducted by D – D must show that C accepted the risk of injury created *by D's breach of duty*.

In *Corbett v Cumbria Kart Racing Club*,[106] Peter Corbett, C, was riding a motorcycle with a sidecar passenger at Moped Mayhem, an amateur event for moped enthusiasts, when the vehicle came off the track, careered across the grass, through a tyre barrier, before finally colliding with an ambulance parked in the service road immediately behind the barriers. C suffered severe brain injuries, and sued the owner/operator of the track, D. C signed a competitor signing-on sheet, saying that he would satisfy himself before taking part that the venue and track were acceptable to him with regard to its features and layout and were satisfied with it. **Held:** *volenti* was not pleaded, and was doomed to fail. Signing that form was not a consent to waive the risks of injury created by D's breach in positioning the ambulance where it was, and by putting up inadequate barriers.

Factors against voluntary consent. Various factors will negative a finding that C voluntarily consented to take the risk of injury caused by D's breach – some are transparently logical, while others are perversely challenging. They include:

- where C takes precautionary steps before engaging in D's activity, he clearly demonstrates that he was concerned about his own safety and well-being, and cannot be taken to have agreed, expressly or impliedly, to waive any claim for damages owing to D's failure to measure up to the standard of reasonable care.

In *Nettleship v Weston*,[107] passenger C, teaching driver D to drive, was shown a comprehensive insurance policy which covered passengers; and then C was injured by D's negligence. **Held:** *volenti* failed. C's enquiry made *Nettleship*, said the court in *Murray v Morris*, an 'unhopeful ground for a *volens* plea'.[108]

[99] [1991] 2 QB 6 (CA) 17. [100] [2009] EWHC 2342 (QB) [86].
[101] [2011] EWHC 90208 (Costs) [27] (dicta only, as the case settled). [102] [2001] EWCA Civ 853, [11].
[103] [1969] 2 All ER 923 (Assizes Liverpool) 928. [104] [1963] 2 QB 43 (CA) 69.
[105] [2014] NIQB 39, [17]. [106] [2013] EWHC 1362 (QB) [89].
[107] [1971] 2 QB 691 (CA). [108] [1991] 2 QB 6, 14.

- where rescuer C is plunged into an emergency to assist X because of D's conduct, the defence will not apply, as C cannot be taken to have consented to the risk of injury during that emergency.

  In *Baker v TE Hopkins & Son Ltd*,[109] facts previously, **held:** *volenti* failed. C may well have had knowledge of the risk that he was running, being medically-trained, but he did not freely and voluntarily take that risk, being placed in the position of rescuer in an emergency.

- where C commits suicide, that does not mean that C voluntarily consented to that injury (death). Indeed, if C was not of sound mind (i.e., if he suffered from a recognised psychiatric illness) and harmed or killed himself, the defence is not available to D, as C is not truly a volunteer.

  In *Corr v IBC Vehicles Ltd*,[110] facts previously, Mr Corr's, C's, suicide was not an act to which C consented voluntarily, and with his eyes open. Rather, it was 'an act performed because of the psychological condition which the employer's breach of duty had induced'. In *Kirkham v Anderton*,[111] Mr Kirkham, C, killed himself while on remand at the Risley Remand Centre. C's estate sued the police for failing to pass on information about C's suicidal tendencies to the prison authorities, and for not completing the appropriate form which would have identified to the prison that C was a suicide risk. Again, *volenti* did not apply, because C was not of sound mind. C had 'shout[ed] at the magistrates in court, when they remanded him in custody to Risley, that if he was sent there, he would never come back' and that he 'wanted to do away with himself'. The court concluded that it was 'quite unrealistic to suggest that Kirkham was truly *volens*. His state of mind was such that, through disease, he was incapable of coming to a balanced decision, even if his suicide was deliberate'.

  In *Kirkham*, it was suggested though, obiter, that if C is of sound mind and commits suicide, where there is a breach of duty by D towards C, then the defence could potentially apply.

- where C helped to create the very event which caused the mishap and which placed D in a difficult position, then while C's behaviour may have been irresponsible, foolish, offensive, stupid or dangerous, that behaviour does not, of itself, impute that C voluntarily consented to the risk of injury.

  In *North v TNT Express (UK) Ltd*,[112] Lee North, C, was drinking in a wine bar, and left after closing time (1.00 am) with some friends. He stepped into the path of a large articulated lorry, and asked the lorry driver, D, for a lift home. When the lorry driver refused, C climbed up on to the front bumper of D's lorry, clung on for about 100 m to the windscreen wiper, whilst the lorry drove off slowly, and then the wiper came out, and C fell off. C was struck by the lorry, suffering internal injuries. C sued D in negligence. **Held:** *volenti* did not apply. That C 'was behaving in an offensive and thoroughly irresponsible fashion, displaying a complete lack of regard for his own safety', did not mean that he voluntarily consented to the risk of suffering injury.

- C cannot be taken to have consented to an injury which was 'out of all proportion to the occasion'; incidental injuries may be consented to, but not 'savage' injuries (the following case concerned battery, or trespass to the person, but the same point would feasibly apply where the suit was brought in negligence too).

[109] [1959] 1 WLR 966 (CA). [110] [2008] AC 884 (HL) [18].
[111] [1990] 2 QB 283 (CA). [112] [2001] EWCA Civ 853, [16].

In *Lane v Holloway*,[113] Mr Lane, C, 64, was a retired gardener, living in a quiet court. Backing onto that court was Mr Holloway's, D's, café (D was 23). One night, C and D got into a fight, with C calling D's wife a 'monkey-faced tart'. D punched C in the eye, which required 19 stitches and hospitalisation for a month. D pleaded that, by entering into a fist fight, C consented to the risk of injury. **Held:** *volenti* could not apply. D's punch caused C very severe injury. Given the differences in their ages, and that C was infirm and 'full of beer', the prospect of proving *volenti* was 'inconceivable'.

Element #3: No destruction of D's duty

§10.14 *Volenti* cannot succeed if C's conduct is the very act which D had a duty to prevent. To hold the defence effective in that case would empty that duty of all content.

This has been called the 'very thing' principle. If D is under a duty of care to prevent C from acting as he did, then to hold that D could take advantage of *volenti* – by C's doing that very act – would be to use the defence to empty the duty of any content. That cannot be permitted, and the defence will fail in that scenario. Where the defence has succeeded, D was negligent, but it was **never** D's duty to stop C from doing what s/he did.

In *Titchener v British Rwys Board*, it was not the British Railways Board's duty to stop Ms Titchener from running across the train line. In *Morris v Murray*, it was not Mr Murray's duty to stop Mr Morris from getting into the plane with him and embarking on the drunken flight. The defence succeeded in both cases, as the defence did not destroy the content of the duty which D owed to C.

However, where the police, D, are under a duty to prevent C's suicide whilst in custody, then C's suicide in custody could not give rise to *volenti*, because it is the police's very duty to prevent that harm to C. There is no distinction, for this purpose, between C who is of sound mind and C who is mentally disturbed. In either case, once D is under a duty to prevent the suicide, the defence cannot apply if C commits suicide.

In *Reeves v Commr of Police*,[114] facts previously, **held:** *volenti* failed. D owed a duty of care to Mr Lynch to exercise reasonable care to prevent his suicide whilst in their custody, when D knew he (Mr Lynch) was a suicide risk – and the defence could not apply, when C did the very thing that D was supposed to exercise reasonable care to avoid. To uphold the defence would be to destroy that duty altogether. In *Kirkham v Anderton*,[115] facts previously, **held:** *volenti* failed. C was not of sound mind, so could not voluntarily consent to the risk of injury. C's suicide was the very act which the police had a duty to prevent (by communicating that fact to the prison authorities, who had no inkling of his suicidal tendencies).

Subsequently, in *Stone & Rolls Ltd (in liq) v Moore Stephens*,[116] Langley J described *Reeves* as an unusual case, and called it the 'very thing' test. Where this unusual situation arises, the defence cannot apply. In fact, the 'very thing' test can arise, to preclude *volenti*, in economic loss negligence cases too.

In *Spreadex Ltd v Sekhon*,[117] Dr Sekhon, C, was an experienced spread better, and Spreadex Ltd, D, was a spread betting company. C carried out a large number of spread betting transactions with D,

[113] [1968] 1 QB 379 (CA). [114] [2000] AC 360 (HL). [115] [1990] 2 QB 283.
[116] [2007] EWHC 1826 (Comm) [59]–[63], [65], aff'd: [2009] UKHL 39, [2009] 1 AC 139 1.
[117] [2008] EWHC 1136 (Ch) [164].

but then D closed out all of C's positions at a time when C owed D about £695,000. C claimed that D ought to have closed his open positions, against his will, earlier, and had D done so, C would then not have owed D any money, or at least, owed D much less money. C relied upon a rule, COB 7.10.5, that D 'must close out a private customer's open position if that customer fails to meet a margin call made for that position for five business days following the date on which the obligation to meet the call accrues'. **Held:** D could not rely on *volenti*, because of that rule. One purpose of the duty imposed on D by COB 7.10.5 was to protect C against himself. It was incompatible with that duty that C could agree to give up the benefit of that duty and keep spread betting.

Element #4: Bars to *volenti*

§10.15 *Volenti* may be barred in two respects – either by statute; or because the defence would be repugnant to public policy at common law.

Statute. *Volenti* cannot be pleaded against a passenger (i.e., someone who 'is carried in or upon the vehicle') who is injured by D, the negligent driver (i.e., the 'user') of the motor vehicle, by virtue of s 149(3) of the Road Traffic Act 1988. The predecessor of s 149 (s 148 of the Road Traffic Act 1972) was considered in *Pitts v Hunt*,[118] and held by the Court of Appeal to preclude a plea of *volenti*.

In *Pitts v Hunt*, facts previously, **held:** *volenti* did not apply. The effect of s 148(3) (the predecessor section) meant that it was no longer open to the driver of a motor vehicle to say that his passenger had willingly accepted a risk of negligence on his part.

That principle was affirmed, more recently, by the Court of Appeal in *Joyce v O'Brien*.[119]

Apart from the scenario of getting into a vehicle with a drunk driver, the provision may also apply (to protect the injured C) where, say, C was not wearing a seatbelt, was riding illegally in the back tray of a utility, or decided to leave the vehicle whilst it was moving (given that the provision covers C who is 'entering' or 'alighting' the vehicle too). However, the preclusion of *volenti* where passengers are injured in motor vehicle accidents does not apply to passengers in aircraft accidents, and hence, the court did not have regard to the provision in *Morris v Murray*.

Common law. It may be 'repugnant', at common law, for the defence to succeed. For example, where C is a rescuer who acted out of compassion and instinct to try to save the life of another, then *Baker v TE Hopkins & Son Ltd* demonstrates[120] that *volenti* cannot apply. Willmer LJ held that, 'once it is determined that the act of the rescuer was the natural and probable consequence of [D's] wrongdoing, there is no longer any room for the application of *volenti*. It would certainly be a strange result if the law were held to penalise the courage of the rescuer by depriving him of any remedy'.

Miscellaneous issues

Theoretical bases

The 'theoretical bases' for the defence of *volenti* have been described as being one of **four** possibilities:

[118] [1991] 1 QB 24 (CA). [119] [2013] EWCA Civ 546, [10]. [120] [1959] 1 WLR 966 (CA) 983 (Willmer LJ).

i. C waived any claim for injury caused by D's negligent acts or omissions (per *Nettleship v Weston*[121]);
ii. there was no duty of care owed to C by D, because C's very foolish behaviour exempted D from owing any duty of care to C which he would otherwise have owed (per *Wooldridge v Sumner*[122]);
iii. C's consent reduced the reasonable standard of care expected of D, to such an extent that no breach on D's part could be proven (per the English Law Commission[123]); or
iv. that C's consent negatived any causal link between D's breach and C's damage, because C voluntarily caused his own injury, excluding any causal effect of what D did (per *Moore Stephens v Stone Rolls Ltd*[124]).

It was noted, in *Reeves v Commr of Police*,[125] that there was probably not a lot to choose between some of these – although the first appears to fit better with more recent successful applications of the defence (as in *Morris v Murray*[126]). However, the lack of clear theoretical delineation of the defence adds to the impreciseness and uncertainty which hallmarks its modern judicial treatment.

Reasons for *volenti's* problems

The criticisms of the defence of *volenti* have been manifold, and from many quarters:

- when D, who enjoys a stronger bargaining position than C, tries to rely on *volenti*, it is unfair – for how can that vulnerable C be taken to have absolved a more powerful or knowledgeable D from the legal consequences of an unreasonable risk of harm created by that D? (per *Bowater v Rowley Regis Corp*[127]);
- the elements of the defence are 'ill-defined'. The House of Lords acknowledged, in *Moore Stephens v Stone Rolls Ltd (in liq)*, that the principle was 'far from precise'.[128] *Volenti* was described in *Wooldridge v Sumner* as being a doctrine, 'expressed or obscured by the maxim *volenti non fit injuria* [which] ... applicable originally to a Roman citizen who consented to being sold as a slave'.[129] One gains the impression that Roman times is precisely where the doctrine ought to have remained!
- in *ICI Ltd v Shatwell*, Lord Reid described *volenti* as having 'a chequered history', in that it has gone through stages of being oft-used, and then hardly used at all.[130] Indeed, in that case, having said that *volenti* was a 'dead or dying defence', it was then applied against the negligent employee Cs;
- *volenti* has sometimes been rendered a virtual 'dead letter', by reason of a strand of authority which suggests that the defence is not available wherever it was alleged that C accepted the risks created by D's *negligent acts or omissions*. For example, in *Titchener v British Rwys Board*,[131] C was taken to have accepted the risk of D's train being operated properly, i.e., in the 'ordinary and accustomed way', but she would not have accepted the risks of injury, had D's train which injured C been driven negligently (which were, of course, not the facts of that case), because those risks 'would not have been within the risks that [C] had accepted'. On this interpretation, *volenti* has no practical application, because it is only where D is negligent that

[121] [1971] 2 QB 691 (CA) 701. [122] [1963] 2 QB 43 (CA) 67.
[123] *Liability for Psychiatric Illness* (Rep 249, 1998), fn 70. [124] [2009] UKHL 39, [2009] 1 AC 1391, [178].
[125] [1999] QB 169 (CA) 175, aff'd: [2000] 1 AC 360 (HL). [126] [1991] 2 QB 6 (CA) 15.
[127] [1944] KB 476 (CA) 480–81 (Goddard LJ). [128] [2009] UKHL 39, [178]. [129] [1963] 2 QB 43 (CA) 69.
[130] [1965] AC 656 (HL) 671–72. [131] [1984] SC(HL) 34, 52, 57.

the defence is sought to be relied upon by D. However, on the alternative view, C is taken to have accepted the risks of injury, *should D act negligently*. For example, in *Nettleship v Weston*, the defence applied (said the court) where C agrees, 'expressly or impliedly, to waive any claim for any injury that may befall him due to the lack of reasonable care by [D] or, more accurately, due to the failure of [D] to measure up to the standard of care that the law requires of him.'[132] This view has been upheld in cases such as *Morris v Murray*, so as to give the defence *some* room in which to operate successfully.

Interaction with statute

Where C dies as a result of D's negligence, and C's estate brings a claim under the Fatal Accidents Act 1976, the defence of *volenti* can be successfully pleaded against C's estate.[133]

The defence also applies under the Occupiers Liability Act 1957 (per s 2(5)), and under the Occupiers Liability Act 1984 (per s 1(6)), for risks voluntarily accepted by lawful entrants and trespassers, respectively. It was confirmed, in *Geary v JD Wetherspoon plc*,[134] that the defence 'is precisely the same as the position at common law'. This topic is discussed further in Chapter 12.

There is also a *volenti*-type provision in the Animals Act 1971 (per s 5(2)), although some courts have been keen to emphasise that the provision should be given its 'ordinary English meaning' (per *Cummings v Granger*[135]), or 'a broad construction untrammelled by any technicalities which may have attached to the common law defence of *volenti*' (per *Flack v Hudson*[136]). Liability for animals is considered in the identically-named online chapter.

THERAPEUTIC PRIVILEGE

Where it applies

§10.16 Therapeutic privilege is a defence specifically available to a healthcare practitioner, D, which excuses D from complying with the legal obligation to disclose to a patient, C, the risks associated with medical treatment, where it is reasonably considered that such disclosure would seriously harm C's health or welfare.

The defence of therapeutic privilege[137] has been approved at the highest level in England (in dicta). Most recently, in *Montgomery v Lanarkshire Health Board*,[138] the Supreme Court remarked that a doctor is 'entitled to withhold from the patient information as to a risk if he reasonably considers that its disclosure would be seriously detrimental to the patient's health'. Three decades earlier, in *Sidaway v Governors of Bethlem Royal Hospital*,[139] Lord Templeman noted that the duty to disclose was 'subject always to the doctor's own obligation to say and do nothing which the doctor is satisfied will be harmful to the patient', while Lord Scarman also accepted that a doctor can 'withhold from his patient information as to risk, if it can be shown that a reasonable medical assessment of the patient would have indicated to the doctor that disclosure would have posed a serious threat of psychological detriment to the patient'.

132 [1971] 2 QB 691 (CA) 701. 133 EWLC, *Claims for Wrongful Death* (Rep 263, 1999) [2.3].
134 [2011] EWHC 1506 (QB) [35]. 135 [1977] QB 397 (CA) 407. 136 [2000] EWCA Civ 360, [2001] QB 698, [36].
137 Also termed the 'therapeutic exception' and 'doctor's privilege'.
138 [2015] UKSC 11, [88] (Lords Kerr and Reed, with whom the other members of the Court agreed).
139 [1985] AC 871 (HL) 889 (Lord Scarman), 904 (Lord Templeman).

Subsequently, in *Chester v Afshar*,[140] Lord Steyn accepted that 'there may be wholly exceptional cases where, objectively in the best interests of the patient, the surgeon may be excused from giving a warning'.

Court of Appeal authority has supported the defence too, although not by that name. In *Wyatt v Curtis*, it was said that a doctor, 'would be bound to place in the balance the potential emotional distress that might be caused to the patient by reopening a question over which it was likely that she would have agonised in making her difficult decision',[141] while in *Thake v Maurice*, withholding information about risks was said to be justified if it 'might have caused worry or concern to the [patient]'.[142] The following cases are perhaps the closest application of the defence in English law to date (although again, not by name):

> In *Pearce v United Bristol Healthcare NHS Trust*,[143] obstetrician D did not warn Mrs Pearce, C, an expectant mother, of the increased risk of stillbirth as a result of a delay in delivery, if they were to 'let nature take its course' without any Caesarian or medical intervention. The baby died *in utero* and was delivered stillborn. **Held:** no negligence; the risk did not have to be disclosed because, inter alia, 'when one bears in mind Mrs Pearce's distressed condition, one cannot criticise Mr Niven's decision not to inform Mrs Pearce of that very, very small additional risk [of stillbirth]'. In *AB v Leeds Teaching Hosp NHS Trust*,[144] the organs of children who had died of natural causes were harvested and retained, post-mortem, without the parents' consent. Some parents suffered recognised psychiatric injuries as a result. **Held:** the information about harvesting the organs was considered to be necessary, albeit likely to be distressing to parents. Gage J accepted, obiter, that, 'there may be some circumstances in which a clinician might have been justified in giving no details to parents of a post-mortem examination'. However, disclosure in this case ought to have occurred.

As acknowledged in *Sidaway*,[145] therapeutic privilege was originally derived from US medico-legal jurisprudence (per *Canterbury v Spence*[146]), which described it as a physician's 'privilege to keep the information from the patient'.

Despite the high-level endorsement of the defence, both its definition and its application present real legal difficulties. For a start, there are considerable divisions as to the *type* of patient, and the kind of potential *harm*, that should trigger the defence. Moreover, it is unclear whether reasonable non-disclosure is an objective assessment based upon what reasonable medical opinion dictates, or by what the court considers appropriate. These difficulties are discussed in the next section.

The elements

The elements of the defence are two-fold:

> **The framework for therapeutic privilege**
>
> 1 Patient C would suffer relevant harm if doctor D disclosed a material risk associated with medical treatment
>
> 2 D's decision not to disclose was reasonable and in C's 'best interests'

[140] [2004] UKHL 41, [2005] 1 AC 134, [16]. [141] [2003] EWCA Civ 1779, [21]. [142] [1986] QB 644 (CA) 680.
[143] (1998) 48 BMLR 118 (CA). [144] [2004] EWHC 644 (QB) [238].
[145] [1985] 871 (HL) 889 (Lord Scarman). [146] 464 F 2d 772, 789 (1972).

Dealing with each in turn:

Element #1: The requisite harm

§10.17 Therapeutic privilege is triggered where there is likely to be some 'harm' to patient C, if the risks are disclosed by healthcare practitioner D. However, the type of harm which triggers the defence is not settled in English law.

In *Montgomery*, the Supreme Court referred to risks disclosure being 'seriously detrimental to the patient's health', but without any further articulation about the type of harm required. In fact, there are three potential types of detriment to C, should risks be disclosed, which are quite disparate. All three have some degree of support on the present state of English case law.

i. The prospect of mental harm. The risk of serious *psychological* harm or emotional stress to C, if the risks are disclosed by D, is clearly a trigger for therapeutic privilege in English law – as made plain by the definition of the defence by Lord Scarman in *Sidaway*. Additionally, *Pearce* was a case in which information about the risk of stillbirth was validly not disclosed because it was likely to cause a distressed expectant mother further distress. This is the most common type of harm which is likely to prompt the defence.
ii. The prospect of physical harm. The prospect of *physical* harm to C (say, a heart attack in a patient who suffers an unstable cardiac arrhythmia,[147] or the risk of 'hysterical blindness'[148]), if the risk was disclosed, is rarer and more controversial. English judges have only rarely explicitly referred to the risk of physical harm to C as being a trigger for the defence. In *Pearce*,[149] Lord Woolf CJ stated, in dicta, that D was entitled to take account of the effect that disclosure might have on 'the state of the patient at the particular time, both from the physical point of view and an emotional point of view'. However, whether extending the defence beyond the scope of psychological harm to physical harm constitutes an 'unwarranted extension' of the privilege, is a matter of some debate in jurisdictions elsewhere.[150]
iii. Foregoing treatment. Controversially, if disclosure of the risk would cause C to forego the treatment which D believes to be in the 'best interests' of C, that is a potential 'harm' that could trigger the defence, in the view of some judges. For example, in *McCallister v Lewisham and North Southwark HA*, Rougier J stated (obiter) that therapeutic privilege applied 'where a doctor may be genuinely and reasonably so convinced that *a particular operation is in the patient's best interests* that he is justified in being somewhat economical with the truth where recital of the dangers is concerned'.[151] Similarly, in *Poynter v Hillingdon HA*, Sir Maurice Drake noted, in dicta, that if there was any possibility that giving information about risks would have deterred the patient, or in that case, 'the parents [of the patient] from consenting to the operation, which those experts strongly believed to be in the best interests of Matthew, I think it is arguable that they were entitled to withhold that information'.[152] However, in *Montgomery*, Lords Kerr and Reed appeared to dismiss this definition of harm, noting that therapeutic privilege is not intended to 'subvert' the duty to disclose, by preventing the patient from choosing a path which D considers to be contrary to his 'best interests'.[153]

[147] See, e.g., the American Psychiatric Assn, *Principles of Informed Consent in Psychiatry: Resource Document* (No 960001, Jun 1996) (at <www.psych.or/archives/960001.pdf>).

[148] e.g., *Battersby v Tottman* (1985) 37 SASR 524 (Full Ct) 527.

[149] [1999] PIQR 53 (CA) 59.

[150] Further: Mulheron, 'The Defence of Therapeutic Privilege in Australia' (2003) 11 *J of Law and Medicine* 201.

[151] QB, 15 Dec 1993 (no therapeutic privilege; a failure-to-warn of risks associated with brain surgery proven).

[152] (1997) 37 BMLR 192 (QB) 206.

[153] [2015] UKSC 11, [91].

Undoubtedly, proving that C may have foregone the treatment if the risks had been disclosed is an easier avenue for D to plead the defence than proving that serious psychological or physical harm would follow from that disclosure. However, there are two principal difficulties with the notion that foregoing treatment constitutes 'harm' to the patient.

First, it means that D is permitted to make up C's mind for him that a certain treatment is the best option – thereby introducing a strong element of medical paternalism. To similar effect, the American case generally attributed as being the origin of therapeutic privilege, *Canterbury v Spence*, described the very notion of foregoing therapy as harm to be 'paternalistic' and incorrect.[154]

Secondly, if a patient is concerned about whether or not to undergo treatment, then arguably, the patient's anxiety about the risk does not constitute a 'harm' that triggers therapeutic privilege, but means that the risk is, legally-speaking, significant or material and *should* therefore be disclosed, because that particular patient attaches significance to it. If the law supports the notion that D may withhold risk information if it would cause the patient to decline treatment, then that is directly in conflict with when a duty to warn is triggered in the first place.

Element #2: D's decision was validly held

§10.18 D's decision to withhold from C information about material risk must have been reasonably and objectively formed. Whether that is to be determined by *Bolam* evidence or by the court's assessment is not entirely settled in English law.

In *Montgomery*, doctor D must '*reasonably* consider' that the disclosure of risks information would harm the patient,[155] whilst in *Chester v Afshar*, Lord Steyn endorsed the defence only where it is '*objectively* in the best interests of the patient'.[156] How, though, is that objectivity to be measured? If, according to a body of reasonable medical opinion, C was the type of patient likely to suffer harm if the risks were disclosed, then the defence could be upheld under a *Bolam*-type assessment.[157] On the other hand, if peer opinion was only one factor in deciding whether the defence applies, then it is a court-based assessment. As it happens, both schools of thought have been judicially supported in England.

Plainly, in *Sidaway*, Lord Scarman preferred the second view, noting that '[o]n ... the defence, medical evidence will, of course, be of great importance'[158] (but not, by implication, determinative). On the other hand, it was suggested by Rougier J in *McCallister v Lewisham and North Southwark HA*[159] that therapeutic privilege 'comes within the umbrella of a question of clinical judgment', i.e., under a *Bolam* assessment. In permitting the defence in *Pearce v United Bristol Healthcare NHS Trust*,[160] and in citing it in *Montgomery*, those respective courts did not specifically address the issue.

This division in view, as to whether or not therapeutic privilege is decided by a *Bolam* assessment, is yet another hallmark of its difficulty. As discussed in Chapter 3, English law has rejected a strict *Bolam* assessment of whether a warning of a particular risk ought to have been given, in favour of the 'reasonable patient' test. Arguably, to re-introduce a *Bolam* assessment

[154] 464 F 2d 772, 789 (1972). [155] [2015] UKSC 11, [88] (emphasis added), [85].

[156] [2004] UKHL 41, [2005] 1 AC 134, [16].

[157] A *Bolam* assessment is (per Lord Scarman's formulation in *Sidway* [1985] AC 871 (HL) 881) that, 'a doctor is not negligent if he acts in accordance with a practice accepted at the time as proper by a responsible body of medical opinion even though other doctors adopt a different practice'.

[158] [1985] AC 871 (HL) 889. [159] QB, 15 Dec 1993. [160] (1998) 48 BMLR 118 (CA).

for the defence would be a retrograde step, and inconsistent with the way in which the primary duty to warn is assessed.

Caveats

Once patient C asks a direct question about whether a risk may occur as a result of a procedure, then healthcare practitioner D must provide an honest and complete answer – and the defence will have no room to operate. The law does not support evasiveness on D's part. Both *Sidaway*[161] and *Pearce*[162] support that proposition (in the latter, Lord Woolf CJ agreed that 'if a patient asks a doctor about the risk, then the doctor is required to give an honest answer').

Further, in some cases where the defence could have applied, D may be exculpated for other reasons. For example, as in *Poynter v Hillingdon HA*,[163] there may be no duty to disclose the risk in the first place; or there may well have been a failure-to-warn of an objectively-significant risk, but there was no causal link, because C probably would have proceeded with the treatment in any event.

The practice corner

The GMC's guidance, *Consent: Patient and Doctors Making Decisions Together*,[a] states:

'You should not withhold information necessary for making decisions for any other reason, including when a relative, partner, friend or carer asks you to, unless you believe that giving it would cause the patient serious harm. In this context, "serious harm" means more than that the patient might become upset, or decide to refuse treatment'.

'Whilst this guidance is laudable for its efforts to promote patient autonomy,[b] some dicta in English case law is at variance with this passage – *McCallister* and *Poynter* indicated that a prospect of forgoing treatment **could** justify non-disclosure, while *Pearce* supported non-disclosure where it was likely to cause a patient emotional distress'.

[a] GMC (1 Jun 2008) [16].
[b] Also emphasised, *ibid*, [1], [3], [4], [9].

NECESSITY

The scope

§10.19 D is not liable, where his tortious act or omission was necessary to preserve the health and safety of the person or property of another, or of D's own person or property. However, whether the defence of necessity can apply to defend D's negligence is unsettled in English law.

The defence of necessity certainly may apply where D has committed an *intentional* tort against C. It has applied to defend D's otherwise tortious actions where those were undertaken to prevent injury or damage to persons or property, in scenarios of: false imprisonment (per *Austin v Commr of Police*[164] and *R v Bournewood Community and Mental Health NHS Trust,*

[161] [1985] AC 871 (HL) 898 (Lord Bridge). [162] [2000] PIQR 53 (CA) 54.
[163] (1997) 37 BMLR 192 (QB). [164] [2007] EWCA Civ 989, [2008] QB 660, [49].

ex p L[165]); battery (per *In re F (Mental Patient: Sterilisation*[166]); trespass to land (per *Cope v Sharpe (No 2),*[167] *Rigby v CC of Northamptonshire,*[168] and *Esso Petroleum Co Ltd v Southport Corp*[169]); private nuisance (*Esso Petroleum*); the rule in *Rylands v Fletcher* (*Rigby*); and trespass to chattels (per *Cresswell v Sirl*[170]). The defence has notable application where medical treatment is administered without consent (as discussed in Chapter 14).

The defence of state necessity is a particular application of this defence. Whilst said, in *Bici v MOD*, to be 'closely and imprecisely related to (and in some cases perhaps identical with) a separate concept of necessity', it has a very narrow application. It is available to 'the government and indeed individuals, who take action in the course of actual or imminent armed conflict and cause damage to property or injury (including possibly death) to fellow soldiers or civilians' (per *Bici*[171]), and is 'limited to situations in which the interests of the individual member of the armed services must, of necessity, be subordinated to the attainment of the military objective' (per *Smith v MOD*[172]). It is closely linked with the so-called 'combat immunity' (discussed in Chapter 2), and will not be considered further in this chapter.

More interestingly for the purposes of a non-intentional tort such as negligence, various courts have opined that the defence of necessity **does** apply to torts *in general*. For example, in *R v Bournewood Community, ex p L*, Lord Goff considered that the defence, 'has its role to play in all branches of our law of obligations – in contract ... in tort (see *In re F (Mental Patient: Sterilisation*[173]), and in restitution, ... and in our criminal law. It is therefore a concept of great importance. It is perhaps surprising, however, that the significant role it has to play in the law of torts has come to be recognised at so late a stage in the development of our law'.[174] Subsequently, in *Rigby v CC of Northamptonshire*, Taylor J said that '[t]here is a surprising dearth of authority as to the nature and limits of necessity as a defence in tort',[175] while in *Austin v Commr of Police*, Tugendhat J noted that 'necessity is recognised in text books as a general defence in tort'.[176]

However, in two leading cases in which the defence was raised in the context of negligence – in *Southport Corp v Esso Petroleum Co Ltd*[177], and in *Rigby v CC of Northamptonshire*[178] – D was sued for another tort as well as in negligence. The defence of necessity proved effective for D in both, to rebuff the intentional torts alleged against him; and nothing in the cases ruled out the defence's application to negligence.

The elements

The defence has two elements – both of which could feasibly be met, where D is sued in negligence:

The defence of necessity

1 D was confronted with an emergency when he acted negligently against C
2 The emergency in which D acted negligently was not caused by D's *prior* fault

[165] [1999] 1 AC 458 (HL). [166] [1990] 2 AC 1 (HL). [167] [1912] 1 KB 496. [168] [1985] 1 WLR 1242 (QB).
[169] [1956] AC 218. [170] [1948] 1 KB 241. [171] [2004] EWHC 786 (QB) [90]. [172] [2011] EWHC 1676 (QB) [97].
[173] [1990] 2 AC 1 (HL). [174] [1999] 1 AC 458 (HL) 488–90. [175] [1985] 2 All ER 985 (QB) 993.
[176] [2005] EWHC 480 (QB) [49], citing: *Halsbury's Laws* (4th ed), 'Torts', [372].
[177] [1954] 2 QB 182 (CA). [178] [1985] 1 WLR 1242 (QB).

Element #1: An emergency

§10.20 An emergency arises, wherever D's acts or omissions were necessary to prevent injury or harm to C, to a third party, to the general community, or to D himself.

The emergency in which D is involved must generally entail that D acted to prevent death or serious injury. This has been expressed as a subjective test, i.e., that D must believe at the time that he acted that it was necessary to do so in order to prevent death or serious injury (per *ZH v Commr of Police*[179]). The first limb was met in both of the following:

> In *Rigby v CC of Northamptonshire*, Mr Rigby's, C's, gunsmith shop was burnt out when D, the police, fired a canister of CS gas into the building, trying to flush out a dangerous armed psychopath who had broken into the shop. The canister set C's shop ablaze. No fire-fighting equipment was available at the time, because a fire engine which had been standing by was called away. C claimed that D should have used another CS gas device (the Ferret) which involved no fire risk; and that D was negligent in firing the gas canister when no fire-fighting equipment was promptly available. C sued for several causes of action: trespass to land; the escape of a dangerous thing pursuant to *Rylands v Fletcher*; private nuisance; and *negligence*. **Held:** trespass failed, because the defence of necessity was available to D. The fact that there was a dangerous psychopath in C's gunshop, and his arrest was urgently required, created an emergency. However, D was negligent to fire the canister, when fire-fighting equipment was absent, and damages were awarded to C for that negligence (see second limb below). In *Esso Petroleum Co Ltd v Southport Corp*, D's oil tanker was stranded in the Ribble River estuary, and ran onto the revetment wall. Her master jettisoned 400 tons of oil cargo, to prevent the tanker from breaking up. The tide carried the oil slick to the foreshore and it entered (and closed) the Marine Lake (owned by C), extending for about 7.5 miles. It cost C a great deal to fix the damage. C sued the ship-owner, D, in trespass to land, nuisance, and negligence. **Held:** trespass to land and nuisance failed (the defence of necessity was available to D). The oil had to be discharged, as the lives of the crew were at stake, had the oil not been jettisoned. (Negligence was pleaded against the master, not the ship-owner, D.)

Absent any threat of death or serious injury, however, the defence is likely to fail.

> In *North v TNT Express (UK) Ltd*,[180] facts previously, Lee North, C, climbed onto D's lorry and fell off, suffering injuries. **Held:** the defence of necessity was not available to D. D did not fear an imminent attack by C or his friends. 'What he was faced with was an irritating inebriate impeding his progress in circumstances which had the potential to become violent, but had not done so, and might never do so'.

Element #2: No prior fault

§10.21 D must not have been at fault in causing the very emergency in which he then commits the tortious act or omission for which he is sued by C.

In *Esso Petroleum*, it was said that 'no one can avail himself of [the defence of] necessity, produced by his own default'.[181] In *Rigby*, Taylor J confirmed that the defence does not apply, 'if the need to act is brought about by negligence on the part of [D]. Once that issue is raised, [D]

[179] [2012] EWHC 604 (QB) [42]. [180] [2001] EWCA Civ 853, [9].

[181] [1954] 2 QB 182 (Denning LJ) 198, eventually aff'd: [1956] AC 218 (HL) 235.

must show, on the whole of the evidence, that the necessity arose without negligence on [D's] part'.[182] In other words, D must have acted reasonably.

In *Esso Petroleum*, C's claim was brought against the ship owners, and the only negligence alleged was against the master for faulty navigation of the vessel. Hence, on a pleadings point, it was not the ship owner's negligence that caused the emergency. Hence, the defence of necessity could apply, as the ship owner was not at fault. In *Rigby*, it was not negligent of the police, D, to not have a Ferret device; and D had not been negligent in bringing about the emergency. The only alternative was to fire the CS gas cannister into the shop (a trespass for which the defence of necessity was available) – but D was negligent in firing the CS cannister with no fire-fighting equipment present, and for the damage resulting from that negligence, necessity could not apply.

The law reform corner: Rescue

As the **Irish Law Reform Comm** has noted,[183] the defence of necessity may apply for D's benefit, where D 'dives in' to rescue C, but acts negligently in the rescue and harms C, and where the need for C's rescue was not brought about by D's own negligence (but did not cite any authority where the defence had applied in that scenario).

182 [1985] 1 WLR 1242 (QB) 1254.

183 *Civil Liability of Good Samaritans and Volunteers* (CP 47, 2007) [4.55].

11

Remedies

INTRODUCTION

This chapter considers the principal categories of damages which typically arise for discussion (if not for application) in the tort of negligence: compensatory damages (including those awarded in the event of a tortiously-caused death); aggravated damages; exemplary damages; nominal damages; and restitutionary damages. The chapter does **not** purport to give an exhaustive treatment of the subject of damages in negligence, nor does it cover the *manner* in which damages may be paid (e.g., via lump sums, structured settlements and periodic payments).[1] Instead, it focuses on key heads of damage, terminology and some of the controversial issues associated with these categories.

Injunctive relief may also be sought for the tort of negligence. This remedy, however, is more frequently associated with property-based torts (such as Private Nuisance), and readers are referred to relevant discussion of different forms of that remedy in Chapter 16.

The remedy of an apology remains under-utilised in English law to date. In 2006, the NHS Redress Act[2] was enacted, under which the Secretary of State can, by regulation, establish a scheme for the purpose of enabling redress to be provided to patients without recourse to civil proceedings. Certain types of 'qualifying liabilities in tort' can be covered by a scheme, *viz*: those arising from a breach of a duty in relation to the diagnosis, care or treatment of a patient, or from any act or omission by a healthcare professional. 'Redress' under the Act includes an apology.[3] However, no scheme has yet been established. Otherwise, in litigation generally, the Irish High Court explained the problem well in *O'Connor v Lenihan*[4] – where C failed in their attempt to sue D for harvesting the organs of their two deceased children without permission, because C had suffered no recognisable damage: 'no award of damages would be even half as useful in easing their feelings of anger and distress as a forthright and sincere and appropriately tendered apology ... But the problem is that our legal system is not conducive to such

[1] For comprehensive treatments, see, e.g.: H McGregor, *McGregor on Damages* (19th edn, Sweet & Maxwell, 2012); the EWLC's work programme on damages: *Structured Settlements and Interim and Provisional Damages* (CP 125, 1992; Rep 224, 1994); *Damages for Personal Injury: Non-Pecuniary Loss* (CP 140, 1996; Rep 257, 1998); *Damages for Personal Injury: Medical, Nursing and Other Expenses; Collateral Benefits* (CP 144, 1996; CP 147, 1997; Rep 262, 1999); *Claims for Wrongful Death* (CP 148, 1997; Rep 263, 1999); *Damages Under the Human Rights Act* (Rep 266, 2000); and Dept for Constitutional Affairs, *The Law on Damages* (CP 9, 2007).

[2] NHS Redress Act 2006, s 1(1), 1(4). [3] Section 3(2). [4] [2005] IEHC 176 (Peart J).

steps being taken by [D] ... once fault might be seen to be acknowledged by such an apology'. Of course, where D admits liability in negligence, an apology may be issued to C (as occurred, e.g., in *Ellison v Univ Hosp of Morecambe Bay NHS Foundation Trust*[5]).

The comparative corner: Statutory apology

In Australia, it has been acknowledged that an apology is important in encouraging potential Cs to avoid the courtroom. Every Australian state and territory has enacted provisions for apologies arising out of negligently-caused personal injury. Using Western Australia's statute as illustration,[6] an 'apology' means 'an expression of sorrow, regret or sympathy by [D] that does not contain an acknowledgment of fault by [D]', and its effect 'does not constitute an express or implied admission of fault or liability by [D] in connection with that incident'.

It is also possible that criminal sanctions may follow a negligent act or omission. For example, occasionally D's negligence that results in the death of C may be sufficiently severe and gross as to attract criminal penalty for gross negligence manslaughter (per *R v Adomako*[7] and *R v Misra*[8]); a prosecution of a negligent employer may ensue under s 3 of the Health and Safety at Work Act 1974; and the Corporate Manslaughter and Corporate Homicide Act 2007 may apply where an organisation owed a relevant duty of care to C, and committed a 'gross breach' of that duty (note that the common law offence of manslaughter by gross negligence against corporations was abolished by this Act[9]).

Turning now to the principal remedy of compensatory damages:

COMPENSATORY DAMAGES

§11.1 Insofar as is practicable, the assessment of damages in negligence should proceed on the basis of full compensation. However, C is under a duty to take reasonable steps to mitigate the loss caused by D's negligence.

As with all tort claims, the sum paid to the negligently-damaged C should put him 'in the same position as he would have been in, if he had not sustained the wrong for which he is now getting his compensation' (per Lord Blackburn in *Livingstone v Rawyards Coal Co*[10]). This means that C is 'entitled to be compensated as nearly as possible in full for all pecuniary losses ... Subject to the obvious qualification that perfection in the assessment of future compensation is unattainable, the 100% principle is well established and based on high authority' (per Lord Steyn in *Wells v Wells*[11]).

The duty to take reasonable steps to mitigate was explained recently in *Totham v King's College Hosp NHS Foundation Trust*[12] to mean that 'there will often be a range of potentially reasonable options for C to choose from when mitigating her loss. Provided her choice is within

[5] [2015] EWHC 366 (QB). [6] Civil Liability Act 2002, ss 5AF–5AH.
[7] [1995] 1 AC 171 (HL) 176–77 (Lord Mackay). [8] [2004] EWCA Crim 2375, [25]. [9] Section 17.
[10] (1880) 5 App Cas 25, 39. [11] [1999] AC 345 (HL) 382–83, citing *Livingstone, ibid.*
[12] [2015] EWHC 97 (QB) [13].

that range, D cannot reduce his liability by arguing that [C] should have chosen a cheaper option from that range'. Whilst D may well benefit from the steps taken by C to mitigate his loss (i.e., that the damages are reduced), the obverse is also true: C can recover the costs of taking reasonable steps to mitigate. In such cases, however, the standard of reasonableness is not high, given that C has been 'put in a position of embarrassment' as an innocent party (per *PL Private Finance Ltd v Arch Financial Products LLP*[13]).

Pecuniary versus non-pecuniary damages

§11.2 Non-pecuniary damages are awarded for 'intangible' heads of damage which are not capable of precise quantification, whereas pecuniary damages are awarded for the loss of a calculable sum of money, and are usually divided into past (pre-trial) and future (post-trial) pecuniary damages. Special damages are awarded for expenditure actually incurred by C as a result of D's negligence, whereas general damages are 'damages at large', to be estimated by the court.

Non-pecuniary damages cover losses which are 'not easily translated into monetary terms',[14] and which are awarded for the loss of something other than a sum of money. General damages may overlap with, but are not the same as, non-pecuniary damages. As the *Oxford Dictionary of Law* states, general damages are 'given for a loss that is incapable of precise estimation'.[15] Damages for pain, suffering and loss of amenity fall into both categories; but the loss of future earnings and future costs of care are general damages, but are also pecuniary damages.

Dealing with some principal heads of non-pecuniary damages:

Pain and suffering, and loss of amenity (PSLA). Whilst pain and suffering covers 'worry, upset, anxiety, and frustration, arising from an injury and any subsequent medical treatment, as well as actual physical pain and suffering',[16] loss of amenity damages means an award for the reduction of C's enjoyment of life, due to physical or mental impairment which C's injury causes him. It includes things such as: the inability to engage in recreational past-times and sports; loss of sexual enjoyment; C's worry about impending death, or about the future of a disabled spouse/child without C's being there to care for him and support him – all of that sounds in loss of amenity damages.

According to *Lim Poh Choo v Camden and Islington AHA*,[17] a key distinction between the heads is that pain and suffering is subjective and reflective of C's personal awareness (i.e., if C is permanently unconscious and incapable of feeling any pain, nothing is awardable for this head); whereas damages for loss of amenity are awardable for 'the deprivation of the ordinary experiences and amenities of life', and that is a 'substantial loss, whether C is aware of it or not'.

The assessment of damages for pain, suffering and loss of amenity (PSLA) has been said to be 'one of the commonest tasks of a judge sitting in a civil court, [and yet] also one of the most difficult ... Since no monetary award can compensate in any real sense, these damages cannot be assessed by a process of calculation'.[18] They are 'necessarily artificial, and involve a value judgment' (per *Ellison v Univ Hosp of Morecambe Bay NHS Trust*[19]) and are 'inevitably

[13] [2014] EWHC 4268 (Comm) [331]. [14] *Butterworths Concise Australian Legal Dictionary* (1997) 277.

[15] E Martin and J Law (eds) (6th edn, Oxford University Press, 2006) 238. [16] *ibid*, 292.

[17] [1980] AC 174 (HL) 189 (Lord Scarman), approving: *Wise v Kaye* [1962] 1 QB 638 (CA).

[18] Foreword to the First Edition by Lord Donaldson in: *Guidelines for the Assessment of General Damages in Personal Injury Cases* (Judicial College, Oxford University Press, 1992).

[19] [2015] EWHC 366 (QB) [10].

impressionistic' (per *Totham v King's College Hosp Trust*[20]). However, the *Guidelines for the Assessment of General Damages in Personal Injury Cases* (now in its 12th edition[21]), seeks to provide guidance, so that courts may achieve consistency and confidence in making PSLA awards. It has been acknowledged that they 'represent current best practice based on up-to-date judicial decisions and medical knowledge' (per *Beesley v New Century Group Ltd*[22]). The *Guidelines* also now reflect that a 10% uplift in general damages for PSLA is necessary for most personal injury cases tried after 1 April 2013, following the non-recoverability of ATE premiums and solicitors' success fees from that date (per *Simmons v Castle*[23]). The Table below gives some examples of approximate PSLA awards (including the 10% uplift):

Guidelines for PSLA in English law: a sample

Scenario	Circumstances	Amount (£)
Tetraplegia/ Quadriplegia	Full awareness of disability, with an expectation of life of >25 years, retaining powers of speech, sight and hearing, but needing help with bodily functions; with physical pain, respiratory issues and depression	262,350–326,700
Very severe brain damage	Some insight and ability to follow basic commands, recovery of eye opening, and sleep and waking patterns, postural reflex movements, but with little speech; double incontinence; needing full-time nursing care	227,975–326,700
Total blindness and deafness	Ranking with the most devastating injuries	326,700
Total loss of taste and smell	Rarely does this injury occur alone; it is normally associated with brain injury or infection, so this amount is added to those injury markers	31,625
Impotence	Total impotence and loss of sexual function and sterility for a young man; with award depending upon, e.g., age and psychological reaction	119,900
Female infertility	Complete infertility, from anxiety or disease, with severe depression; and depending upon whether the affected woman already has children	92,950–136,950
Loss of both arms	Amputation above the elbows	194,700–242,550
Loss of both legs	Amputation above the knees, with award depending upon, e.g., severity of phantom pains; psychological effects; and the success of prosthetics	194,700–227,975
Very severe facial scarring for female	Facial scarring in relatively young women, typically teens to early 30s, with very disfiguring cosmetic effect and severe psychological reaction	39,160–78,650

20 [2015] EWHC 97 (QB) [17].

21 Judicial College (Oxford University Press, Sep 2013). The 13th edn of the *Guidelines* is expected in Sep 2015.

22 [2008] EWHC 3033 (QB) [17].

23 [2012] EWCA Civ 1039, [2013] 1 WLR 1239.

Loss of expectation of life. Where C's natural life expectancy is shortened as a result of D's negligence, then damages for that expected shortened lifespan were abolished by s 1(1)(a) of the Administration of Justice Act 1982 (except to the limited extent provided by s l(l)(b), where C's awareness of that shortened life expectancy can be taken into account when assessing his damages for PSLA).

No damages for C's fear of impending death can be awarded either. In *Hicks v CC of South Yorkshire Police*,[24] Lord Bridge stated that 'fear, by itself, of whatever degree, is a normal human emotion for which no damages can be awarded'. Lord Bridge analogised C's fear of death to the living person's free-standing claim for distress or anxiety who suffered no physical injury (per Chapter 5) – neither has any claim to damages.

Loss of consortium. Also called 'loss of society', this was a head of damage that awarded a spouse a sum to compensate for the deprivation of the love, companionship and support of C, the injured partner, as well as for loss of services in the home, society and sexual relations. That head has been abolished in English law by statute.[25] The 'nearest modern equivalent' (said the English Law Commission[26]) is a claim for bereavement where a spouse dies as a result of D's negligence (per s 1A of the Fatal Accidents Act 1976, discussed below).

Loss of congenial employment. This head of damage is intended to reflect that D's negligence deprived C of a 'much loved job and vocation' (per *Malvicini v Ealing Primary Care Trust*[27]). Where there is no realistic prospect of C's returning to that job (and where the evidence suggests that employers would be dissuaded from taking the risk of offering C a job in any event), then the loss of work which C found stimulating and satisfying sounds in damages. The sums are usually modest, in the range of £5,000–£7,000 (per *Davison v Leitch*[28]). In *Malvicini*, the sum awarded was £5,000, for the inability to return to a nursing career, and in *Davison*, £6,500, for the inability to return to a career in finance.

Pecuniary damages are those which are awarded to cover the loss of a sum of money. They include special damages, which cover things to which an actual figure can be reliably attached and which can be quantified with certainty (e.g., 'out-of-pocket' medical expenses, past costs of care for which receipts can be furnished, past lost earnings as calculated by payslips and tax records, the costs of travel to/from hospitals or medical centres). Dealing with some principal heads of pecuniary damage:

Past and future costs of care (including gratuitous care). An injured C is entitled to recover damages, equivalent to the value of the care provided to C. If this is provided by commercial carers, then the damages will be calculated according to their bill for those services.

If the care is provided gratuitously by voluntary carers, then that amount is recoverable by C, *to be held on trust* for the voluntary carer, to enable that voluntary carer to receive recompense for his services to the Deceased (per *Hunt v Severs*[29]). The voluntary carer himself (stated Lord Bridge[30]) 'has no cause of action of his own against [D]. The justice of allowing the injured claimant to recover the value of the services so that he may recompense the voluntary care has been generally recognised ... the law now ensures that an injured C may recover the reasonable

[24] [1991] UKHL 9, [1992] 2 All ER 65, 68.

[25] Administration of Justice Act 1982, s 52, and Law Reform (Miscellaneous Provisions) Act 1970, ss 4, 5.

[26] *Damages under the Human Rights Act* (2000) [4.64].

[27] [2014] EWHC 378 (QB) [102].

[28] [2013] EWHC 3092 (QB) [61].

[29] [1994] 2 AC 350 (HL) 361, endorsing: *Cunningham v Harrison* [1973] QB 942 (CA) 952 (Lord Denning).

[30] *ibid*, 358, 363.

value of gratuitous services rendered to him by way of voluntary care by a member of his family'. The point of *Hunt v Severs* is that the loss is that of the carer for whom C holds the damages on trust, and is not the loss of C himself. Hence, if D and the carer are one and the same party (as they were in *Hunt v Severs*), then D will not be required to pay the cost of that gratuitous care to C (for otherwise, D, the wrongdoer, would be paying damages to himself as carer). As the English Law Commission noted, the ratio of *Hunt v Severs* is that it 'denies damages for gratuitous services to a tortfeasor-carer'.[31] In such cases, it will be practically prudent for the care to be provided by someone other than the wrongdoer-carer – which has been judicially acknowledged as likely to lead to C's care being provided by professional carers rather than by a wrongdoer relative himself (per *Lowe v Guise*[32]). When assessing the costs of gratuitous care provided by family members, commercial care rates should generally be discounted by 25–30% to reflect that the voluntary carer will not need to make tax and NI contributions (per *Evans v Pontypridd Roofing Ltd*[33]).

If in-patient care to C is provided by the staff of a hospice, then those costs are also recoverable by C (or by his Estate, if he dies), for they are directly analogous to claims that are now accepted as being recoverable under the principle in *Hunt v Severs*. For example, in *Drake v Starkey*,[34] approximately £10,000 was permitted for this head of damage – there was 'no reasonable basis for distinguishing St Joseph's, a charitable Foundation, from a private individual or from one of Mr Wilson's family members or friends. St Joseph's staff provided very similar services to those provided by his family member, and which they would have carried on providing, but for the fact that they were no longer able to cope with the deterioration in Mr Wilson's health'.

Where relatives or friends of the injured party provide nursing and other care to the injured victim, C, and given up paid employment to do so, then the loss equates to any remunerative employment which they have given up in order to care for C, albeit that the compensation is capped at the commercial cost of that care (the 'ceiling principle') (per *Totham v King's College Hosp*[35]).

Past loss of earnings. These are usually calculable fairly precisely, on the basis of past payslips, and the days of absence incurred by reason of C's injury or illness, and can be computed on the basis of the multiplicand (the lost *net* earnings per year) and the relevant multiplier (the years between the tortious act and trial). As such, past lost earnings are treated as special damages.

Future loss of earnings. This is often a highly-contentious head of pecuniary damage. Where C was either employed, or self-employed, and had to stop work because of injury or illness caused by D's negligence, then C may claim a sum for the prospective loss of earnings. The sum may be discounted to reflect the fact that C may not have worked the whole period between when he became injured/ill and when he retired (say, because as a self-employed, the work may not have been available to him, or he may have chosen not to take it).

Courts typically use the multiplicand (the annual lost earnings) and multiplier (the number of years of expected future loss) method of calculation, subject to complaints by D that C had a 'residual earning capacity' which could validly reduce either component of the equation (as evident, e.g., in *Malvicini v Ealing Primary Care Trust*[36]). Loss of earnings, via this technique, is illustrated, for readers' benefit, under the calculations required for an FAA claim (discussed below).

[31] *Damages for Personal Injury: Medical, Nursing and Other Expenses; Collateral Benefits* (1999) [1.12].

[32] [2002] EWCA Civ 197, [16].

[33] [2001] EWCA Civ 1657, [36]–[37].

[34] [2010] EWHC 2004 (QB) [40]–[43], with quote at [41(6)].

[35] [2015] EWHC 97 (QB) [22].

[36] [2014] EWHC 378 (QB) [102].

One of the most contentious issues arising under this head of damage arises where C's life expectancy is shortened, such that C is likely to die prior to retirement age, and/or will be unable to take advantage of any pension entitlements. The period in which C will (likely) not be alive to receive such earnings and pension entitlements are called 'the lost years'. The question arises as to whether C can only make a claim for loss of earnings during the period for which he was expected to live, or whether he can also claim in respect of those 'lost years'. Of course, it is not expected that C himself will be able to take advantage of such damages, but rather, compensation for the 'lost years' would form an available fund to support C's actual or likely dependants during those years.

For an adult C whose life expectancy is shortened, the House of Lords held, in *Pickett v British Rail Engineering Ltd*,[37] that C is permitted to recover the value of his lost earnings during the 'lost years', net of any living expenses and other expenses which C would have incurred during those years (had he lived). One of the reasons that prompted this view in *Pickett* was that, should C obtain judgment against D or settle his claim against D, that barred any cause of action which his dependants might otherwise have under the Fatal Accidents Act 1976 – and it was unfair that C could not recover for those lost years of earnings (net of living expenses) which he could then pass on to his Estate; and that his dependants could not recover the financial losses which accrued to them, as dependants, either. Otherwise, said Lord Salmon, 'Parliament would surely have made it plain that no judgment in favour of the deceased or settlement of his claim could bar a claim by his dependants under the FAA'.[38]

However, the aforementioned case of *Totham* (outlined in detail overpage) suggests that this issue about the recovery of earnings for the 'lost years' remains one of real contention and uncertainty where C is a child (in that case, C was seriously-injured during the course of her birth, was 7 at the time of trial, had a life expectancy of 47 years, and claimed damages for her loss of earnings and pension between the ages of 47 and 93). On the one hand, according to the Court of Appeal in *Croke v Wiseman*,[39] child C (who was also injured at a very young age, 21 months) could not recover lost earnings for those 'lost years', because in the case of a seriously-injured child, future dependants was far too speculative a proposition by which to create a fund for persons 'who will in fact never exist'. On the other hand, in *Iqbal v Whipps Cross Univ Hosp NHS Trust*,[40] the Court of Appeal considered itself bound by *Croke*, but opined that *Croke* was inconsistent with *Pickett* and with the principle of full compensation, and should be reconsidered at the highest appellate level (the case settled before it reached the House of Lords). In *Totham* itself, Mrs Justice Laing was obviously deeply uncomfortable with the view in *Croke*. Her preferred view was that D's negligence had deprived C, a child, of both earnings and pension entitlement (net of living expenses) during the 'lost years', and that '[s]he should, in principle, be compensated for that loss. There is no rational basis for allowing such claims by adults, but refusing to allow them when made by children'. Given *Croke*, however, no recovery for the 'lost years' was permissible.

Future treatments and therapies, transport costs, medical aids, etc. The multiplier–multiplicand method of computation is typically adopted for these heads of damage too. D will typically argue that such heads are not properly quantified, or too speculative, whilst C must convince the court that the claims are reasonable, and that the assessment of the chances of those future events should be reflected in the amount of damages awarded.

[37] [1980] AC 136 (HL), overruling: *Oliver v Ashman* [1962] 2 QB 210 (CA). [38] *ibid*, 145.
[39] [1982] 1 WLR 71 (CA). [40] [2007] EWCA Civ 1190.

Illustrative example of damages recovery for a living C

In *Totham v King's College Hosp NHS Foundation Trust*, Eva Totham, C, suffered severe brain injuries during her delivery at King's College Hospital in 2007. D accepted liability, but quantum was in dispute. The total damages awarded to C at trial (when C was aged 7) were: £10,135,511. Some of the heads of damage were as follows (to the nearest thousand):

General damages: £275k Past gratuitous care: £60k Past holidays and leisure (adjustments required): £41k Past paid care: £48k Past orthotics: £9k Past treatment and therapies: £50k Past accommodation: £150k Past travel & transport: £7k	Future treatment and therapies: £245k Future orthotics: £6k Future travel & transport: £226k Future aids & equipment: £455 Future education: £45k Future accommodation: £1.5m Future IT: £500k Future holidays: £475k	Annual care and case management in periodical payments: from ages 7 to 12: £96k; from ages 12 to 19: £157k: from age 19: £250k Lost years: £0 Future child care: £0 (C's having children was too unlikely on the medical evidence)

The conventional sum

§11.3 Where a child is born alive as a result of wrongful conception (i.e., the occurrence of a pregnancy) or wrongful birth (i.e., the continuation of a pregnancy), a conventional award compensates the parents for their loss of autonomy.

Wrongful conception and wrongful birth actions were considered in Chapter 3. A 'conventional sum' (£15,000) was first awarded in favour of the parental Cs in *Rees v Darlington Memorial Hosp NHS Trust*,[41] hence its nomenclature of the '*Rees* award'.

What the award is for. Actually, such an award (for £5,000) was suggested by Lord Millett three years earlier in *McFarlane v Tayside Health Board*[42] itself, for the parents' deprivation of autonomy to limit the size of their family – but no other member of the House took up the suggestion, and so it was not awarded.

However, in *Rees*, the award was made, by majority. Lord Millett explained again, in *Rees*, that the award in cases such as *McFarlane* should be 'modest', and should be 'by way of general damage, not for the birth of the child, but for the denial of an important aspect of their personal autonomy, *viz*, the right to limit the size of their family. This is an important aspect of human dignity, which is increasingly being regarded as an important human right which should be protected by law ... the parents have lost the opportunity to live their lives in the way that they wished and planned to do ... whether characterized as a right or freedom, [it] is a proper subject for compensation'.[43] Lord Bingham also remarked that the award should not be 'nominal' or 'derisory', but should 'afford some measure of recognition of the wrong done'.[44]

Caveat. The *Rees* award cannot be awarded where a child dies during pregnancy and is stillborn. According to *Less v Hussain*[45] (where that scenario tragically occurred), '[w]hen the

[41] [2003] UKHL 52, [2004] 1 AC 309. [42] [2000] 2 AC 59 (HL). [43] [2003] UKHL 52, [123].
[44] *ibid*, [8]. [45] [2012] EWHC 3513 (QB) [180].

law allows deviation from the compensatory principle, every incremental development needs careful consideration. The existence of a legal wrong remains the starting point'. Given that the award is for the loss of autonomy by parents who are suffering from the 'mixed blessings' of parenthood which they did not expect, then if their child dies *in utero*, the basis of a *Rees* award is absent.

The dissenting viewpoint. Nevertheless, for the sake of interest, the dissenters in *Rees* (Lords Steyn and Hope) put forward several cogent reasons as to why the conventional award was a 'misstep', no matter how sympathetic the position of the parental Cs:[46]

i. although only Lord Millett suggested the conventional award in *McFarlane*, 'it would be wrong to assume that the majority did not consider it' there. Hence, the conventional award ran counter to the majority view in *McFarlane*. Further, in subsequent wrongful conception cases (such as *Parkinson v St James and Seacroft Univ Hospital NHS Trust*[47]), the suggestion of a conventional sum was not raised at all, when it could have been – plainly because, after *McFarlane*, 'it was thought that this avenue was no longer open';
ii. the conventional award could not be regarded merely as a 'gloss' in *McFarlane* (as it was described by Lord Bingham in *Rees*). Rather, it represented 'a radical and most important development which should only be embarked on after rigorous examination of competing arguments';
iii. neither English nor overseas authority supported such an award for the deprivation of personal autonomy, which 'underlines the heterodox nature of the solution adopted';
iv. a conventional award went beyond the 'permissible creativity for judges'. Not only did it seek to constitute a 'backdoor evasion of the legal policy' in *McFarlane*, but it should only be rendered lawful by Parliament;
v. quantifying the conventional award is difficult. It cannot be derisory; yet any award will fall well short of what would be needed to meet the aim of compensating parents for the wrong done to them.

Heads of damage available to the Estate

Where C dies as a result of D's tortious conduct, C's estate may bring a 'survival action' on behalf of the Deceased against D, in order to recover damages which were sustained by the Deceased between the date of the tort and the date of his death, pursuant to the Law Reform (Miscellaneous Provisions) Act 1934 ('the 1934 Act'). This action was discussed in Chapter 1. The section below considers some key points about the assessment of those damages.

Recoverable damages

§11.4 Since 1983, the damages recoverable in a survival action are limited to certain types – loss of earnings, special damages, physical injury, PSLA, funeral expenses, and care and assistance for the Deceased.

As originally enacted, the 1934 Act permitted the Estate to recover a wide array of damages on behalf of the Deceased. However, since s 1 of the Administration of Justice Act 1982 took effect on 1 January 1983, the heads of damage are much curtailed. Practically speaking, none of those heads (apart from funeral expenses) will be awarded at all, if the Deceased died at the point of, or shortly after, D's tort against that Deceased.

[46] [2003] UKHL 52, with quotes at: [41]–[46], [75]. [47] [2001] EWCA Civ 560.

The principles governing the recovery of loss of earnings, special damages, and the costs of care and assistance provided to the Deceased prior to his death, follow the same pattern as for a living C (discussed above).

The Estate is able to recover for any ***physical injury*** and ***PSLA*** sustained by the Deceased as a result of D's tort, prior to the Deceased's death. A sizable award to the Estate is likely, where the Deceased suffered a lengthy period (e.g., of several months) of illness and pain, and prolonged medical treatment, prior to his death – such as generally applies in mesothelioma cases arising from wrongful asbestos exposure. A separate award can be made for the Deceased's reduced ability to care for a spouse during the period leading up to his death, according to *Lowe v Guise*.[48] However, as with all heads of damage under the 1934 Act, if the medical evidence does not establish that any physical injury or PSLA was sustained by the Deceased prior to his death – e.g., if unconsciousness or death occurred instantaneously, or very promptly after D's negligence – then the Estate will be unable to recover anything under this head (per *Hicks v CC of South Yorkshire*[49]). Where the Deceased is conscious, or part-conscious, for some time before his death, then *some* damages under this head have been awarded.

Short time-frames of pain and suffering under the 1934 Act

- death within **5 minutes** – no damages awarded in *Hicks v CC of South Yorkshire* – Sarah Hicks, 19, and her sister Victoria, 15, died in the Hillsborough stadium disaster on 15 April 1989. Their parents claimed that, at the moment of death, Sarah and Victoria each had an accrued cause of action for their injuries, but failed. Theirs was a 'swift and sudden death' from traumatic asphyxia. The medical evidence was that the victim would lose consciousness within a matter of seconds from crushing of the chest, cutting off the ability to breathe, leading to death within 5 minutes. Sarah had suffered some 'superficial bruising', probably sustained post-loss of consciousness. The girls' fear of impending death (as a free-standing anxiety claim) did not create a cause of action which survived for their estates' benefit either.
- death within **an hour** – £1,100 awarded in *Hayes v South East Coast Ambulance Service NHS Trust*[a] – Paul Hayes suffered an asthma attack at home, and an ambulance was urgently summoned. He was treated, but suffered a cardiac arrest, and died within an hour (and was not conscious for much of that time). The court noted that Mr Hayes' 'period of suffering was very short'.
- death within **6 days** (when much of that was spent in a coma) – £5,000 was awarded in *Amin v Imran Khan & Partners*[b] – Zahid Mubarek died in prison, six days after he was violently attacked by his cellmate at Feltham Young Offenders Institution and clubbed to death with a wooden table leg. C lay in a coma until the life support machine was turned off; screams were heard when the attack happened, and C was 'barely conscious' when discovered. His period of consciousness during and after the attack, before the coma, was unknown, but undoubtedly entailed 'a period of intense and horrifying conscious pain'.

[a] [2015] EWHC 18 (QB) [150].
[b] [2011] EWHC 2958 (QB) [80], [83].

The question has arisen as to whether this fairly unsympathetic attitude of the English courts towards damages recovery under the 1934 Act contravenes the ECHR. Undoubtedly, rather stingy (if any) damages are available to the Estate where the Deceased survives for very little time after D's tortious act. The European Court of Human Rights suggested, in *Keenan v*

[48] [2002] EWCA Civ 197, [38].
[49] [1991] UKHL 9, [1992] 2 All ER 65, 65–66.

UK[50] (in which C's son committed suicide whilst in prison), that the damages available to the Estate of the Deceased is an 'ineffective remedy' – 'not in the sense that more money would make it an effective remedy, but in the sense that it is too little to be worth pursuing ... [the finding in] *Hicks* ...makes it extremely unlikely that any damages at all would be awarded for a brief period of suffering before a violent death; and if any damages were awarded, they would be at most a few hundred pounds'. Nevertheless, in spite of this disquiet, *Hicks* remains good law, and was approved in *Johnston v NEI Intl Combustion Ltd.*[51]

An award of the Deceased's reasonable ***funeral expenses*** to the Estate is also possible, under s 1(2)(c) of the 1934 Act (e.g., in *Rabone v Pennine Care NHS Trust*, £2,499;[52] and in *Devoy v William Doxford & Sons Ltd*, £3,044[53]). If a claim is brought under both the 1934 Act, and also by a Dependant under the Fatal Accidents Act 1976 ('the FAA'), then funeral expenses can alternatively be claimed under the latter. However, claiming them under the 1934 Act may be preferable, because their amount will not be reduced by the extent of the Dependant's contributory negligence in bringing about the death of the Deceased (whereas such a reduction will occur under the FAA).[54] Where the Deceased dies instantaneously, then the reality is that funeral expenses will be all that the Estate will recover.

Illustrative example under the 1934 Act

In *Beesley v New Century Group Ltd*,[a] Mrs Beesley, the widow of her husband, John Lambie, recovered the following award of damages under the 1934 Act. Her husband died in November 2006, as a result of contracting malignant mesothelioma, caused by wrongful exposure to asbestos while he was employed by D.

General damages for PSLA: From June 2005, Mr Lambie was breathless, tired, aching and sweating, could not work or even drive, and slept most of the time. He suffered severe pain and impairment of function and quality of life throughout 17 months, with much more extreme pain and suffering towards the end of his life. An award at the upper end of the scale was justified: £72,000.

Special damages: bedding, extra heating, telephoning, special food, lotions and ointments, clothing: £3,000; plus the cost of paying tradesmen to perform home and garden work which Mr Lambie would otherwise have performed: £750; plus the cost of a cancelled holiday: £3,682.

Care and assistance: Throughout Mr Lambie's illness, Mrs Beesley provided care and assistance, attending to his needs, including those at night, increasing ultimately to full-time care, in very difficult circumstances. Claim calculated as care and assistance on an average of 8 hours per day, over the 17-month period, at a rate of £8.43 ph (discounted by 25% for non-commercial care): £25,000.

Pre-death loss of earnings: Mr Lambie was a self-employed builder and decorator, who stopped working in June 2005. The full year before his illness was an indicator of Mr Lambie's income, and discounted somewhat to take account that work may not be available or he may have decided not to work on as many days: £13,500.

Funeral expenses: £1,790.

TOTAL (approx): £120,000.

[a] [2008] EWHC 3033 (QB), [14]–[23], [31]–[34], [87].

[50] [2001] ECHR 242, [8] (Sir Stephen Sedley, sitting in the ECHR).

[51] [2007] UKHL 39, [2008] 1 AC 281, [89] (Lord Rodger). [52] [2012] UKSC 2, [49]. [53] [2009] EWHC 1598 (QB) [49].

[54] EWLC, *Claims for Wrongful Death* (1999) [2.13], fn 103, citing: *Mulholland v McCrea* [1961] NI 135, concerning the Law Reform (Miscellaneous Provisions) Act (Northern Ireland) 1937.

Non-recoverable damages

§11.5 Certain heads of damages are not recoverable by the Estate under a survival action: damages for loss of expectation of life; fear of impending death; bereavement; earnings for the 'lost years'; or exemplary damages.

Just as with a living injured C, the Deceased's Estate cannot recover for the Deceased's loss of expectation of life or fear of impending death (discussed previously).

Moreover, no damages for the pain of bereavement are payable to members of the Deceased's Estate under the 1934 Act – that claim can **only** be made under the FAA, as a lump sum award prescribed by the legislature and to prescribed parties (discussed below). As remarked upon in *Thompson v Arnold*,[55] bereavement damages under the 1934 Act were abolished by s 1 of the Administration of Justice Act 1982, marking a key distinction between the 1934 Act and the FAA. In *Hicks*, the House of Lords noted that both loss of expectation of life, and pain of bereavement, were 'conventional awards [which] had long been felt to be anomalous'.[56]

Additionally, the Deceased's Estate cannot claim damages for lost earnings for the Deceased's 'lost years'. C himself can claim that head of damage whilst living (discussed above), but that claim does not survive for the benefit of C's estate (per s 4 of the Administration of Justice Act 1982[57]).

Exemplary damages are not recoverable under the 1934 Act either, per s 1(2)(a)(i) of that Act,[58] even if C would have been able to claim these, had he lived (see, e.g., *Amin v Imran Khan & Partners*,[59] where such damages were erroneously claimed). This reflects the general aversion to this type of damages at common law (discussed below). In *Hicks*, the House of Lords reiterated that the parents' claims under the 1934 Act, regarding the deaths of their two daughters at Hillsborough, were 'not brought for the sake of the money that may be awarded, but rather to mark the anger of these parents and other bereaved relatives at what occurred. But whatever justification there may be for that anger has no relevance to damages in a civil action for negligence, which are compensatory, not punitive'.[60]

Heads of damage available to Dependants under the FAA

The cause of action instituted by Dependants of a tortiously-killed Deceased under the Fatal Accidents Act 1976 was considered in Chapter 1. It will be recalled that the category of Dependants is statutorily-prescribed under that Act.

§11.6 The purpose of an FAA award is to provide the Dependants of the Deceased with a capital sum to cover the material comforts (i.e., financial support, and the value of services) which the Deceased would have provided to those Dependants, had he not died. Any amounts awarded under the FAA must be awarded to the Dependant/s *individually*, and not as a group.

Although it is commonly considered that FAA damages are only awarded for financial or pecuniary loss accruing to the Dependant, some non-pecuniary heads of damage are certainly recoverable.

The purpose of an FAA award is to provide the Dependant/s of the Deceased with a capital sum, 'which with prudent management, will be sufficient to supply them with material benefits

[55] [2007] EWHC 1875 (QB) [20]. [56] [1991] UKHL 9, [1992] 2 All ER 65, 66.

[57] This provision overruled the opposite position at common law: *Gammell v Wilson* [1982] AC 27 (HL).

[58] Inserted by s 4 of the Administration of Justice Act 1982.

[59] [2011] EWHC 2958 (QB) [40]. [60] [1992] 2 All ER 65 (HL) 68.

of the same standards and duration as would have been provided for them out of the earnings of the Deceased, had he not been killed by the tortious act of [D]' (per Lord Diplock in *Mallett v McMonagle*[61]). The amount awarded to the Dependant/s is not expected 'to be preserved intact', but should be used up gradually, and exhausted, over the relevant period (per *Taylor v O'Connor*[62]). An FAA damages award forms, in theory, a gradually dwindling fund which, as the years go by, is both reduced by current expenditure, and added to by the interest on the remaining capital.

Each Dependant must be regarded separately, so that, per s 3(2), 'any amount recovered, otherwise than as damages for bereavement, shall be divided among the dependants in such shares as may be directed'.

The principles governing the award of pecuniary damages to the Dependant/s have largely been judicially-driven, courtesy of House of Lords' decisions in *Mallett v McMonagle*,[63] *Graham v Dodds*[64] and *Taylor v O'Connor*.[65] Although it is not possible to do justice to the range of those principles herein, the Table below describes the components which go to make up an FAA award:

The equation:

amount of annual loss to Dependant (the '***multiplicand***') – this covers (1) the loss of financial income which the Dependant would have received from the Deceased, and (2) the loss of the value of services (in monetary terms) which the Deceased would have provided to the Dependant, had he lived

multiplied by:

the number of years during which the Deceased would have provided financial support to the Dependant, had the Deceased lived (the '***multiplier***') – calculating the multiplier is a difficult and imprecise exercise, and solely at the judge's discretion. The factors to be taken into account, in calculating the multiplier, will consist of (1) the age of the Deceased when he died; (2) how much 'working life' the Deceased likely had left, had he not died; and (3) the expectation of life of the Dependant/s. Hence, the size of the multiplier 'is normally based upon the prospective length of the joint lives of the Deceased and the Dependant' (per *Spittle v Bunney*[a]).

Subtotal (lump sum)

Less:

Discounting of the lump sum – to take into account various factors, *viz* (1) the inherent imponderables (or 'vicissitudes') of life for the Deceased (i.e., he may have been struck down by a disease which prevented him from working as long as intended); (2) if in a hazardous occupation, the Deceased may have suffered a premature death or incapacitating injury; (3) a discount should be applied to reflect that the Dependants will receive an accelerated benefit in the form of a lump sum.

Add:

Interest component for pre-trial years – damages under the FAA are divided into two parts: pecuniary loss pre-trial (on which interest is payable); and pecuniary loss post-trial (on which no interest is payable).

TOTAL (£££)

[a] [1988] EWCA Civ 16, [1988] 1 WLR 847, 855.

[61] [1970] AC 166 (HL) 175. [62] [1971] AC 115 (HL) 143. [63] [1970] AC 166 (HL) 176–77, 184–85. [64] [1983] 1 WLR 808 (HL, Northern Ireland) 816–17. [65] [1971] AC 115 (HL) 143.

The multiplier should be calculated from the date of death, because 'everything that might have happened to the deceased after that date remains uncertain' (per *Cookson v Knowles*[66]). In practice, the court typically determines the pre-trial multiplier (i.e., x years between the Deceased's death and trial), plus the post-trial multiplier (i.e., y years that the Deceased would supposedly have provided the Dependant/s with financial support) to be applied to the multiplicand to assess the post-trial losses.

In *Spittle v Bunney*, Kate Hall, the Dependant, aged 3 years 2 months, was walking with her mother on a footpath in Barnsley when D's van mounted the pavement, injured Kate, and killed her mother, aged 28. **Held**: the maximum period to be covered by the FAA award would be until Kate reached 22 years, 18.5 years from the Deceased's death. Kate would probably have proceeded to tertiary education of some sort, 'be it Sixth Form College, Polytechnic or University', meaning dependence until she was 22. By trial, 7.5 years had already elapsed; and the multiplier from trial to end of dependency was 11 years.

Before turning to the pecuniary and non-pecuniary heads of damage recoverable under the FAA, it should be reiterated that an award of reasonable funeral expenses may be recovered under the FAA, pursuant to s 3(5) (to recall, these are also recoverable under the 1934 Act, per s 1(2)(c)).

Pecuniary damages (for lost financial support provided by the Deceased)

This section covers some issues concerning the assessment of the Dependant's pecuniary damages:

i. **The loss of financial support per year.** The most common financial support lost by the Dependant is the loss of earnings/money being brought into the household by the Deceased, for the benefit of that Dependant, had the Deceased not died as a result of D's tort.

   It is judicial practice (see, e.g., *Dodds v Dodds*[67]) to divide a family's expenditure into four columns, to assess what amount of the Deceased's earnings would have been spent on the Dependant/s:

1	2	3	4
expenses benefiting the Deceased exclusively	expenses benefiting the Deceased's spouse exclusively	expenses benefiting the Deceased's individual Dependants (say, children) exclusively (pocket money, presents, sports fees)	expenses relating to the whole family, from which the Dependant/s derive some benefit, along with the Deceased (rent, mortgage, repairs, rates)

ii. **Prospects of promotion.** A court may take into account, especially for a young Deceased, the prospect that he would have been promoted in the future, thus increasing his earnings.

66 [1979] AC 556 (HL) 576. 67 [1978] QB 543, 551, 553.

In *D v Donald*,[68] Mr Donald, a soldier, was killed in a motorcycle accident due to D's negligent driving. Mrs Donald sued under the FAA on behalf of herself and her daughter (the Dependants). D argued that, because of his disciplinary problems in the army (bounced cheques, driving offences), Mr Donald would not have been promoted, and indeed might well have been discharged from military service for disciplinary reasons. **Held**: the Army thought well of the soldierly qualities of Mr Donald, and believed he was capable of promotion. Although he had suffered demotion because of disciplinary problems, this was only a temporary set-back, with the object of spurring improvement. The Army did its best to mould a good soldier, rather than waste its investment by a discharge. Mr Donald had a good chance of promotion to Lance Corporal, which could be taken account of in the FAA damages assessment.

iii. Business losses. The FAA does not give a right of recovery for the loss of business profits suffered by the surviving business partner, when his business partner, the Deceased, is tortiously killed. The FAA only provides a right of recovery for a loss of a dependency which is founded in the familial relationships outlined under the FAA.

In *Burgess v Florence Hosp for Gentlewomen*,[69] Mr and Mrs Burgess were professional dancing partners. Mrs Burgess died as a result of medical negligence. Their earning capacity as a couple was greater than their individual abilities to earn an income as professional dancers. **Held**: Mr Burgess could not recover for the loss of his income as a dancer after Mrs Burgess's death. The fact that Mr Burgess happened to be husband of the Deceased did not enable him to claim a dependency on the death of the other partner where the amount claimed arose out of their business relationship.

However, if the relationship is *primarily* that of family membership, where the Deceased provided financial support or services for other members of the family, it does not matter that their financial arrangements took the form of a business partnership. That financial support now lost to the familial parties will be recoverable under the FAA. In *Welsh Ambulance Services NHS Trust v Williams*,[70] the Court of Appeal reiterated that the 'products of a business relationship with the deceased are not recoverable', but that '[t]he court will look at the substance of the relationship and the real nature of the support provided'.

In *Cape Distribution v O'Loughlin*,[71] Mr O'Loughlin, the Deceased, had owned a number of properties, which he managed and developed prior to his negligently-caused death. Mrs O'Loughlin inherited the properties and tried to manage them as her husband had done, but this was unsuccessful, so she sold some of the properties and lived on the income. She brought an FAA action. **Held**: Mrs O'Loughlin was a Dependant, because had he lived, the Deceased would have gone on managing and enhancing the property portfolio as before. Her loss of dependency was the cost of replacing the Deceased's skills as manager, according to the value of someone with that level of flair and business acumen which would result in the successful development of the property portfolio. Mrs O'Loughlin 'lost the services of Mr O'Loughlin as the manager of the family assets, and that loss is capable of being valued in money terms'.

iv. The loss to the Dependant of benefits-in-kind. What the Dependant expected to receive from the Deceased may not have been earnings, but benefits-in-kind. The value of that lost benefit – e.g., the use of a company car of which the Deceased had the use – is also recoverable under an FAA action (per *Dodds v Dodds*[72]).

[68] [2001] PIQR Q5 (QB) [32], [49]. [69] [1955] 1 QB 349. [70] [2008] EWCA Civ 81, [52].
[71] [2001] EWCA Civ 178, [16]–[17]. [72] [1978] QB 543, 546.

Non-pecuniary damages (for lost services provided by the Deceased)

Alternatively, the Dependant may claim under the FAA for various heads of damage, because the Deceased provided *services*, quantifiable in monetary terms, which the Dependant must now pay for.

i. **Care services which the Deceased provided to the Dependant.** Wherever the Dependant required care and assistance for a medical or disabled condition which the Deceased provided to that Dependant, then the Dependant is entitled to recover damages for the value of that care and assistance – on the basis that the Dependant will now have to pay others for that care, following the Deceased's death.

   Unsurprisingly, the calculation of this head of damage may be complex. For example, the value of care and assistance may be calculated at the rate of payment for a home help, or 'notional nanny' (per *Spittle v Bunney*,[73] facts previously). However, if the Dependant continued to have the care and assistance given by friends and relatives in place of the Deceased, then a discount of 25% may be appropriate, given that these other carers would not pay tax or NI contributions (see, e.g., *Devoy v William Doxford & Sons Ltd*[74]). However, if the Dependant would have been receiving 24-hour care from outside carers or in a residential home, even if the Deceased had continued living, then the Dependant cannot recover those costs of care by way of FAA damages.

ii. **Domestic services which the Deceased provided to the Dependant.** If the Dependant reasonably expected to receive benefits from the Deceased, such as domestic house-keeping, gardening, child-minding, etc, had the Deceased lived, then the Dependant may claim damages under the FAA to compensate for the loss of that benefit. These are recoverable, even if the services had been provided, and were likely to be continued to be provided, gratuitously by the Deceased to the Dependant.

   > In *Devoy v William Doxford & Sons Ltd*,[75] the Deceased died of mesothelioma due to D's negligence. Had he lived, the Deceased would have continued to carry out gardening and DIY around the house, from which his widow, the claimant/Dependant, would have benefited. However, 'as [the Deceased] got older, particularly as he would have been still undertaking the care of [his widow, who suffered from Parkinson's disease], he may well have reduced the amount of DIY and gardening that he did himself'.

iii. **The Deceased's 'private attention' to the Dependant.** The Dependant can be awarded FAA damages to recognise that the Dependant lost the personal attention which the Deceased gave in providing the services of which the Dependant is now deprived by the Deceased's death.

   Of course, since the enactment of s 3 of the Administration of Justice Act 1982, the Dependant is not entitled to any award for the loss of society (or consortium) of the Deceased. However, the Dependant may still claim that he has lost, not just domestic services, but the extra value derived from having such help provided by a spouse or close family member (per *Regan v Williamson*[76]). For example, in *Regan* itself, the Dependant child's loss of dependency, for the loss of the services of his mother, was increased to reflect the benefit of the personal attention to a child's upbringing which a mother provided, and which could not be replaced by a housekeeper, nanny or child minder. This head of damage is not only applicable to claims by children who have lost their mothers, but *more generally*. As the court noted in *Beesley v New*

[73] [1988] EWCA Civ 16, [1988] 1 WLR 847, 852–53. [74] [2009] EWHC 1598 (QB) [63].
[75] [2009] EWHC 1598 (QB) [76]. [76] [1976] 1 WLR 305 (QB) 308–9.

Century Group Ltd,[77] such awards for the loss of 'intangible benefits is now well established', and that '[i]n principle, there is no reason for differentiating between the position of children and spouses in connection with the availability of such awards'.

iv. **Special damages incurred by the Dependant.** If the Dependant has incurred expenses, because the Deceased is no longer available to provide the Dependant with services-in-kind (e.g., the cost of an alarm service for the Dependant; the cost of a door intercom; or the cost of transport which the Deceased would otherwise have provided to the Dependant), then those are recoverable as FAA damages.

Remarriage/divorce prospects

i. **Prospects of the Dependant's re-marriage.** At common law, a Deceased widow's prospects of remarriage had to be taken into account in order to assess her FAA damages, where her husband was tortiously-killed.

However, that common law position, much-criticised,[78] has now been statutorily abolished. Section 4 of the Law Reform (Miscellaneous Provisions) Act 1971 provided that, in assessing the claim of a widow, neither her prospects of remarriage nor her actual remarriage would be taken into account – and this provision is now enacted as s 3(3) of the FAA. The provision is not all-embracing, though. In fact, it is quite narrowly-drafted. For example, a widower's prospects of remarriage, and an unmarried Dependant's prospects of marriage, are both unaffected by s 3(3), so must be taken into account when assessing FAA damages. Back in 1974, these anomalies prompted one judge to say that '[t]his may be thought to call for consideration by the legislature' (per *Hay v Hughes*[79]), an amendment which has not occurred to date.

ii. **The Deceased's divorce prospects.** Where a marriage breakdown between the Dependant and the Deceased was likely at the time of the Deceased's death, given the Deceased's 'scant regard for the marriage vows', then that will lead to reduced damages for the Dependant spouse under the FAA (per *D v Donald*[80]). This may seem harsh, because a widow, entirely innocent and blameless, is to be 'penalised' because her husband (the Deceased) strayed and showed little commitment to the marriage – but the court 'cannot ignore that evidence'.

In *D v Donald*, facts previously, at the time of his fatal accident, soldier Mr Donald, the Deceased, was having an affair with a young woman without his wife's knowledge and whilst his wife was pregnant. **Held**: the fact that the Deceased had cheated on his wife, showing scant regard for his marriage vows, meant that there must have been a substantial chance that the marriage would have failed. The court weighed 'heavily in the balance the fact that Mrs D loved her husband, and for herself had a responsible and committed attitude to the marriage and to her child ... she would not easily have given up'. Nevertheless, the multiplier of dependancy had to be discounted; although the Deceased was only 25 when he died, the multiplier was assessed at only 11.

What of *benefits* accruing to the Dependant from the Deceased's death?

Generally speaking, any benefits accruing to the Dependant as a result of the Deceased's death must be disregarded, i.e., not to be treated as reducing the FAA award. This can appear to lead to something of a windfall for the Dependant.

[77] [2008] EWHC 3033 (QB) [83]–[85]. [78] Noted in: EWLC, *Claims for Wrongful Death* (1999) [2.32].
[79] [1975] QB 790 (CA) 796. [80] [2001] PIQR Q5 (QB) [58]–[60].

How to treat benefits which accrue to the Dependant, arising from the Deceased's death, has long been a problem in FAA damages assessment. For example, under the FAA 1846, any damages recoverable by a Dependant under the Law Reform (Miscellaneous Provisions) Act 1934 (the 1934 Act) had to be offset against any damages awarded under the FAA 1846 – the Dependant could not 'doubly recover', he could only recover his 'net loss'. Indeed, if the Dependant brought an FAA 1846 action, and it was not clear, at that time, whether or not any survival action under the 1934 Act would be brought by the Estate, then when assessing the FAA damages, the court had to make the best estimate it could of the likely benefits to be obtained under the 1934 Act, and then deduct that sum from the FAA award. Confirmed in *Davies v Powell Duffryn Colleries Ltd*[81] (arising out of a mine explosion in D's colliery in 1938), this became known as the 'common law rule of deduction'. It illustrated the restrictive, more pro-D, view adopted by earlier courts towards the FAA.

However, over time, certain benefits accruing to the Dependant (e.g., insurance, pensions) were not offset against FAA awards, so that the Dependant did not have his FAA sums reduced accordingly. Damages recovered under the 1934 Act are not to be offset against damages obtained under the FAA, as made plain by s 1(5) of the 1934 Act, which states that rights conferred by the 1934 Act are in addition to those conferred by the FAA. Moreover, from 1983, benefits flowing to the Dependant from the Deceased's death could be disregarded, per s 3(1) of the Administration of Justice Act 1982, which inserted s 4 of the FAA: 'benefits which have accrued or may accrue to any person from [the Deceased's] estate or otherwise as a result of his death shall be disregarded'. This provision 'entirely swept away the common law rule of deduction' and also 'swept all benefits into oblivion' (per *Welsh Ambulance Services v Williams*[82]). It represents a far more beneficent view towards Dependants.

At least on its wording, the apparent intent of s 4 was to ensure that benefits accruing to the Dependant from the Deceased's death, such as death benefit payouts, life insurance payments, bequests under the Deceased's will, returns of bonds or unused premiums, etc, should not be deducted from an FAA award to the Dependant. They should not be taken into account at all. On the other hand, any benefits which the Dependants would have enjoyed or received anyway, regardless of whether the Deceased had died or had lived, would be treated as reducing the FAA award, because they did not accrue from the Deceased's death. However, things have not been nearly that simple. The interpretation and application of s 4 has proven problematical. To mention a couple:

- the meaning of 'benefit' has been contentious. It has transpired that a 'benefit' does not have to be of a solely monetary or pecuniary nature. For example, where D's tort kills a child's parent (with whom that child had been living); where no care or support had been, or was likely to be, provided to that child by the surviving parent, at the time that the other parent died, but where the surviving parent then takes over the care and responsibility for the upbringing of that child – then that care given to the Dependant child is a 'benefit which has accrued as a result of the Deceased's death', and hence, it must be disregarded under s 4, in the assessment of FAA damages. It follows that the Dependant child can claim for the costs of those services rendered by the surviving parent. The important point is that, if the new care arrangements for the Dependant child would **never** have happened, had the Deceased parent not died, then that new care regimen is a 'benefit' accruing from the Deceased's death, and that benefit has to be disregarded under s 4. Hence, the cost of it can be claimed under the FAA. However, if

[81] [1942] AC 601 (HL) 601–2. [82] [2008] EWCA Civ 81, [33].

the benefit would have happened anyway, regardless of whether the Deceased had lived or died, then the cost of it cannot be recovered as FAA damages, as it did not accrue from the Deceased's death.

In *Stanley v Saddique*,[83] the Deceased mother was killed in a car accident caused by D's negligence. Her son, the Dependant, aged 6, went to live with his re-married father and his new stepmother. **Held**: the Dependant recovered £10,000 for the loss of services of his mother (calculated by the cost of a nanny/housekeeper). The fact that the Dependant was receiving better care from his stepmother than could have been expected from his own mother (a finding at trial) was a benefit which accrued to him from his mother's death, and fell within s 4. That benefit of moving to a better home environment, 'as a result of his absorption into the family unit, consisting of his father and stepmother and siblings, should be wholly disregarded' for the purposes of assessing the Dependant child's damages. It was only after the mother's death that the Dependant child's father settled down, married and created a new home to which the Dependant moved. Hence, the benefit accrued as a result of Deceased's death. In *Hayden v Hayden*,[84] the Dependant was 4 when her mother, Mrs Hayden, was killed in a car accident, due to Mr Hayden's, D's, negligent driving. The family had lived together when Mrs Hayden died, and Mr Hayden then raised the Dependant, giving up work to do so. The Dependant's FAA claim against her father included the cost of her father's care (referable to the costs of a nanny). **Held**: the cost of Mr Hayden's care services could not be recovered by the Dependant. She 'remained in the family home with her father and, for a time, with her older brothers and sisters until they left home. She continued to be looked after by him'. There was no 'benefit' accruing to the Dependant that had to be disregarded under s 4, because all the father was doing was 'discharg[ing] his parental duties, many of which he had been carrying out in any event, and would be expected to continue to do ... the continuing services of the father are not a benefit which has accrued as a result of [this mother's] death'.

- any financial income or payments to the Dependant (even *ex gratia* payments) have to be disregarded when assessing FAA damages to the Dependant, if those payments would never have become available to that Dependant, had it not been for the Deceased's death. Those payments fall within s 4, and the Dependant's FAA damages must be assessed without regard to them. Effectively, the Dependant may appear to receive 'additional damages' or 'double compensation',[85] by virtue of the FAA action. However, if the payments would have been made to the Dependant anyway, then they cannot be disregarded; the FAA award must take them into account.

In *Arnup v MW White Ltd*,[86] the Deceased, Kevin Arnup, was killed at work because of his employer's, D's, negligence. After he died, his widow, Mrs Arnup, the Dependant, received two payments: £129,000 from a Benefit Scheme, and £100,000 from a Benefit Trust. Mrs Arnup sued D under the FAA. **Held**: both amounts had to be disregarded under s 4, when judging her FAA damages. Both amounts would not have been paid, had Mr Arnup not died. Hence, both were benefits coming to the Dependant as a result of that death, and both were to be left out of account.

The complexities involved in an FAA assessment of damages can be illustrated by two examples:

[83] [1990] EWCA Civ 16, [1992] QB 1 (CA) 14 (Purchas LJ), 20 (Ralph Gibson LJ).

[84] [1992] 1 WLR 986 (CA) 999–1000.

[85] EWLC, *Claims for Wrongful Death* (1999) [2.52]–[2.53].

[86] [2008] EWCA Civ 447, [25]–[26], [28].

Where husband in a long-standing marriage died, leaving a widow:

In *Beesley v New Century Group Ltd*,[a] facts previously, Mrs Beesley brought an FAA action against D, for the death of her husband from mesothelioma. Mr Lambie died in November 2006, aged 62. The medical evidence was that but for the mesothelioma, Mr Lambie's life expectancy would have been another 22 years.

Had he not been ill, Mr Lambie would have worked substantially until he was 65, although he would have taken more Fridays off; and then, from 65–70, he would have carried on working, but with even more Fridays off, as well as having longer holidays with Mrs Beesley, when their foster children had moved out. Mrs Beesley gave evidence that Mr Lambie wanted to take more Fridays off; and that his willingness and ability to run a business in London, away from his home in Lincolnshire, indicated that he wouldn't have kept up the same workload. After he was 70, he would have essentially retired.

It was appropriate to discount Mr Lambie's earnings from the date of his death to age 65 by 10%, and from 65–70 by 20%, for the vicissitudes of life which Mr Lambie may have suffered during that time.

Mrs Beesley's loss of income dependency was partly offset by £3,000 pa paid to her by Mr Lambie for a small amount of casual clerical work provided by her to him. Mrs Beesley was paid in excess of the market rate, because they were married. A deduction of £1,500 was made to reflect Mrs Beesley's services to the business (which was not a loss of dependency).

Mr Lambie was a builder and decorator, skilled at DIY and in maintaining his substantial 5-bedroom home and 3 acre garden. After his death, Mrs Beesley had to pay for those services: estimated at £2,000 pa. With a multiplier of 3.5 years to trial, that loss was approx £7,000. Post-trial, Mr Lambie might not have carried out these tasks for the whole of his remaining life, but it was reasonable to assume he could continue providing these services until age 75, and at a steadily reducing level thereafter. Hence, with a multiplier of 10, that equalled £20,000 for domestic services which would have been provided by the Deceased.

Bereavement damages of £10,000 were awarded under the FAA (discussed below), given that Mrs Beesley was the Deceased's spouse.

Finally, Mrs Beesley was entitled to a non-pecuniary award under *Regan v Williamson*,[b] because there were 'considerable advantages in having jobs around the house and garden done by a husband at his own time and convenience, rather than having to go out to find and choose commercial providers, and to have to work around the hours that suit them for the work in question' (assessed at £2,000).

[a] [2008] EWHC 3033 (QB) [12], [17], [85].
[b] [1976] 1 WLR 305, and cited, *ibid*, [79].

Where an older family member died, leaving behind younger family members:

In *Drake v Starkey*,[a] James Wilson died in 2007, aged 75, of mesothelioma, contracted as a result of his exposure to asbestos whilst working for D in the early 1950s as a boiler erector at Dartford power station. An FAA action was brought against D, on behalf of Mr Wilson's two daughters, six grandchildren and four great-grandchildren. All were entitled to recover under the FAA (as all were Dependants).

[a] [2010] EWHC 2004 (QB).

Re daughter, Catherine Drake: Catherine, having four children and being a single mother, was struggling financially. Her shopping trips with her father were undertaken as part of their love and companionship and her wish to spend time with him, and the trips were a convenient way for him to do his shopping and, simultaneously, to make financial provision for her and her family. Mr Wilson paid for her shopping on most occasions that they shopped together (averaging about £20 pw). Mr Wilson also liked to speak to Catherine on the phone and invariably provided her with £35 pm towards her mobile phone bill. Mr Wilson was clearly determined to assist Catherine and her children regularly (assessed as £1,460 to Catherine pa).

Re daughter, Tina Starkey: Mr Wilson gave Tina £20 pw in cash, so that his regular payments to each daughter were approximately the same. He also gave Tina additional cash for her son's school dinners, which he laughingly described as being in return for her doing his washing. Mr Wilson also occasionally bought Tina and her family presents for their home, e.g., a new TV, items that she could not afford (assessed at £1,040 to Tina pa; and £331 pa for her son's school dinners, i.e., £1.70 x 195 school days).

Re the grandchildren and great-grandchildren: Mr Wilson gave each of his 10 grandchildren and great-grandchildren £20 each Christmas and on each of their birthdays. He was meticulous in never missing these present-giving occasions (assessed at £40 per Dependant).

The Dependants' claims were 'scaled down' to 80%, to 'take account of the casual nature of the payments that were made'. All up, the payments by Mr Wilson totalled £2,617.50 pa, and represented about 24% of his net income.

The agreed multipliers were 2.7 years from death to trial, and 2.88 for future loss.

Total sum payable to the Dependants: £14,604.

Bereavement damages

§11.7 Bereavement damages were not recoverable at common law, but *are* recoverable under the FAA by certain statutorily-prescribed claimants.

The common law position. The common law has never awarded damages for the pain of a relative's bereavement following the Deceased's tortiously-inflicted death at D's hands. For example, as noted in *F v Wirral MBC*, '[t]he negligent killing of a child gave no cause of action for the loss by a parent of the delight in the company of a child, nor for the grief and loss suffered'.[87] The House of Lords reiterated this in *JD v East Berkshire Community Health NHS Trust*: 'when someone negligently kills another, at common law his relatives have no right to recover damages for the distress and loss which this causes them'.[88] The simple reason for this unsympathetic rule was articulated in *Baker v Bolton*[89] – the death of a human being could not be complained of as an injury in a civil court.

Under the FAA. When the FAA was first enacted in 1846, it reproduced that common law rule, only permitting Dependant/s to recover the loss of pecuniary benefit caused by the Deceased's death, and not for any grief or the loss of the Deceased's society – which was then re-enacted in s 3 of the FAA 1976.

[87] [1991] Fam 69 (CA) 104 (Ralph Gibson LJ). [88] [2005] 2 AC 373, [102] (Lord Rodger).

[89] (1808) 1 Camp 493, 170 ER 1033 (Lord Ellenborough).

However (and based upon a recommendation by the English Law Commission[90]), that position was changed, whereby s 3(1) of the Administration of Justice Act 1982 introduced a claim for 'bereavement damages' for the first time. These damages are now recoverable under FAA, s 1A. The Law Commission considered[91] that such an award was justified because, *inter alia*, it would mitigate the effects of statutorily abolishing the common law claim for loss of expectation of life; and it performed a symbolic function of providing some recognition by society of the importance which a loss of human life represents.

Entitled claimants. Only certain persons, itemised in s 1A(2) of the FAA, can claim bereavement damages, *viz*: the spouse (or civil partner) of a deceased spouse (or partner); the parents of a deceased unmarried minor child; or the mother of an illegitimate unmarried minor child. Note that minor or adult children cannot recover such damages if their parents are killed by D's tort.

In *Hicks v CC of South Yorkshire*,[92] a bereavement claim was recoverable in respect of Victoria, 15, but not in respect of Sarah, 18 (who was not a minor). In *Rabone v Pennine Care NHS Foundation*,[93] Mr and Mrs Rabone could not recover any bereavement award in relation to the negligently-caused suicide of their daughter Melanie, who was >18 at the time. In *Beesley v New Century Group Ltd*,[94] the widow of Mr Lambie was able to recover a bereavement award, as spouse of the Deceased.

In *White v CC of South Yorkshire*, the House of Lords noted that the restricted class of claimant for bereavement damages, i.e., that 'Parliament ... decided that the only persons who can claim bereavement damages are parents and spouses', was a legislative policy decision – and that '[t]he spectre of a wide class of claimants in respect of bereavement led to an arbitrary, but not necessarily irrational, rule'.[95]

It will be recalled from Chapter 1 that the first element of an FAA action is that D can only be liable under an FAA action if D would have been liable to the Deceased, had the Deceased lived. The same position applies to a claim for bereavement damages under the FAA. In *JD v East Berkshire*, the House of Lords explained that 'a surgeon operating on a child will readily foresee that, if he is careless and the child dies, her parents will suffer extreme distress which may well make them ill. Nevertheless, her parents will have no common law right to damages for that distress or illness. They may have a claim for bereavement damages under s 1A of the FAA – but only because the surgeon *owed a duty of care to their daughter*, as his patient.'[96] Of course, if the parents have suffered something more than mere distress, *viz*, a recognised psychiatric injury, then they may recover separately, according to the rules governing that area of negligence (per Chapter 5).

The ceiling of recovery. The amount for bereavement damages is fixed at £11,800 under s 1A of the FAA. The sum started at £3,500, increased to £7,500, and then to £10,000, until then to its current level.

In *F v Wirral MBC*, the Court of Appeal noted that, given the legislature's decision to fix the sum for bereavement damages, 'the law does not require or permit the court to value the nature and extent of the loss and grief suffered by a particular parent in respect of the child'.[97] Some judges have expressed a level of disquiet, though, about the limited amount. In *White*, the House of Lords noted that '[m]any people feel that the statutory ceiling [then £7,500] is an

[90] EWLC, *Personal Injury Litigation: Assessment of Damages* (1973) [172]–[180].
[91] EWLC, *Claims for Wrongful Death* (1999) [2.66]–[2.67]. [92] [1992] 2 All ER 65 (HL) 67 (Lord Bridge).
[93] [2012] UKSC 2, [58] (Lord Dyson). [94] [2008] EWHC 3033 (QB) [79]–[87] (Hamblen J).
[95] [1998] UKHL 45, [1999] 2 AC 455, 492 (Lord Steyn). [96] [2005] UKHL 23, [2005] 2 AC 373, [102] (Lord Rodger).
[97] [1991] Fam 69 (CA) 104 (Ralph Gibson LJ).

inadequate payment to someone like Mr Hicks, who lost his two daughters in such horrifying circumstances'.[98]

In fact, the ceiling is just that – the award could be less. If the Deceased was guilty of any contributory negligence in bringing about his own death, or if the Dependant was liable for any negligence in causing the Deceased's death, the bereavement award will be reduced by that amount.

Is reform needed?

The fact that the Estate cannot recover more than funeral expenses, where there is no dependency claim or bereavement award which any of the Deceased's relatives can claim under the FAA, gave rise to the argument, in *Cameron v Network Rail Infrastructure Ltd*,[99] that a new tort should be created, 'damages for wrongful death', to fill a lacuna in the common law, and in order for the court to meet its obligations under Art 2 of the ECHR. That lacuna arguably existed because of the restricted class of persons entitled to sue for damages where a loved one was tortiously killed.

> *Cameron v Network Rail* arose out of the Potters' Bar train disaster in May 2002, in which a number of people were killed. The Deceased, Mrs Agnes Quinlivan, died instantaneously, when debris from the railway bridge fell onto her whilst she was walking below the bridge. Her daughters sued D claiming damages for breach of the Deceased's right to life under Art 2.

As the court noted, '[w]hat lies at the heart of this application is that under English law ... there is a restricted class of person able to bring proceedings on behalf of a Deceased person or his/her estate, which does not include the daughters of a Deceased person who were not financially dependent upon that person. The only right which was available to this family was the recovery of funeral expenses, which is quite insufficient to provide "just satisfaction" ... to the family within the meaning of human rights jurisprudence'.[100] However, ultimately, no tort for 'wrongful death' was created – because the court did not need to consider it. D was not acting as a public authority in regard to the maintenance of the points and track at Potters Bar at the material time, so any Art 2 claim was 'bound to fail'.

Further, the restricted class of claimants who can claim a bereavement award prompted recent judicial comment, in *Hayes v South East Coast Ambulance Service NHS Foundation Trust*.[101] The FAA makes no provision for bereavement damages to surviving minor children, yet that restricted category of eligible claimants does not (said the court) render the FAA incompatible with the HRA 1999.

The law reform corner: Bereavement damages

Draft legislation to widen the categories of C for bereavement damages was recommended by the English Law Commission in *Claims for Wrongful Death*,[102] to include a child, a brother, a sister, or a fiancé, of the Deceased, or a person who had lived with the Deceased as husband or wife for at least two years prior to the tort. However, that recommendation remains unenacted.

[98] [1999] 2 AC 455 (HL) 510. [99] [2006] EWHC 1133 (QB). [100] *ibid*, [2], [49].
[101] [2015] EWHC 18 (QB) [152]. [102] (Rep 263, 1999) [6.31].

AGGRAVATED DAMAGES

§11.8 Aggravated damages are compensatory in character, to compensate for indignation, hurt feelings, humiliation, mental anguish and the like.

Aggravated damages are appropriate 'where there are aggravating features about the case which would result in C's not receiving sufficient compensation for the injury suffered if the award were restricted to a basic [compensatory] award' (per Lord Woolf MR in *Thompson v Commr of Police*[103]). They are 'awarded for feelings of distress or outrage as a result of the particularly egregious way or circumstances in which the tort was committed, or in which its aftermath was subsequently handled by D' (per Lord Neuberger in *Ashley v CC of Sussex Police*[104]).

However, Lord Devlin commented in *Rookes v Barnard* that 'aggravated damages ... can do most, if not all, the work that could be done by exemplary damages'.[105] A precondition of aggravated damages, according to Lord Devlin, was that D's conduct 'must have been offensive, or accompanied by malevolence, spite, insolence or arrogance'. However, as the English Law Commission noted, this would presumably have been the kind of oppressive conduct which would give rise to exemplary damages.[106] Further, take the statement of Finlay CJ in *Conway v Irish National Teachers Organisation*,[107] that aggravated damages must 'be, in part, a recognition of the added hurt or insult to [C] who is being wronged, and in part also a recognition of the cavalier or outrageous conduct of [D]'. The latter aspect, concentrating as it does upon *D's* conduct, is more properly the province of exemplary, not aggravated, damages.

Nestling as they do between compensatory and exemplary damages, aggravated damages tend to blur across both boundaries. Their very rationale is difficult to pinpoint.

Non-availability for negligence

§11.9 Although the law is not entirely settled, the predominant judicial view is that aggravated damages are not available for negligence claims.

In the leading case of *Kralj v McGrath*,[108] D's negligent treatment of C was, according to the court, 'horrific', 'completely unacceptable' and 'outrageous' – but it was **not** considered to be appropriate to an award of aggravated damages: 'it would be wholly inappropriate to introduce into claims ... for negligence, the concept of aggravated damages', because the aim of compensatory damage was to restore C to the position he would have been in, had the tort not been committed, and 'not to treat those damages as being a matter which reflects the degree of negligence or breach of duty of [D]'.

In *Kralj v McGrath*, Mrs Kralj, C, sued her obstetrician, D, for negligence, where C was subjected to a delivery without anaesthetic that caused excruciating pain, and during which D put his arm inside C in an effort to turn the second twin, who was lying in a transverse position, by manual manipulation of its head. These efforts were unsuccessful and the baby was later delivered by caesarean section, was born disabled, and died of her injuries eight weeks later. **Held:** negligence proven, but no aggravated damages.

[103] [1998] QB 498 (CA) 516. [104] [2008] UKHL 25, [2008] 1 AC 962, [102].
[105] [1964] AC 1129 (HL) 1230. [106] *Damages Under the Human Rights Act* (2000) [4.69].
[107] [1991] 2 IR 305 (SC) 317 (Finlay CJ). [108] [1986] 1 All ER 54 (QB) 61.

That non-availability of aggravated damages for negligence was confirmed by the Court of Appeal in *AB v South West Water Services Ltd*,[109] and has been followed in other first-instance decisions, e.g., in *Appleton v Garrett*[110] (which was a trespass to the person case); and *Hall v Gwent Healthcare NHS Trust*.[111] Even where D is a governmental official, or where negligence was pleaded in company with intentional torts, the non-availability of aggravated damages in negligence has been reiterated:

> In *Alleyne v Commr of Police*,[112] Michael Alleyne, C, was 'a man of good character'. One morning, 14 police homicide and other officers forced entry to C's flat. Shortly before, a teenager had been stabbed to death by three men with knives, and C's son was suspected of being one of them. While being handcuffed and pinned to the ground, C sustained injury to his right eye and a fracture to his right ankle. **Held:** C's injuries were negligently inflicted, in breach of a duty of care owed to him by officers entering the flat. However, neither aggravated nor exemplary damages were 'appropriate or recoverable'.

The reason for their non-availability is that, where the court is being asked to compensate C for his mental anguish, anger, indignation, hurt, distress and the like, then such matters will have *already* been adequately compensated for within the component of general damages for PSLA. In *Kralj v McGrath*,[113] Woolf J awarded some compensation for the mental distress suffered by Mrs Kralj as a result of the negligently-caused horrific birth and the unnecessary suffering to which she was put, but as an aspect of *compensatory* damages. Those damages could be increased if the impact of what happened to C made it more difficult for C to recover her health and well-being. Similarly, in the public nuisance case of *AB v South West Water*, the 'real anxiety or distress' caused by drinking contaminated water was compensable by way of PSLA, because '[t]he ordinary measure of compensatory damages will cover all they have suffered as a result of that breach, physically, psychologically and mentally. Full account will be taken of the distress and anxiety which such an event necessarily causes'.[114]

Hence, there is the distinct problem of double-compensation, where aggravated damages are awarded. For example, in the Australian decision in *Tan v Benkovic*,[115] an award of $40,000 in aggravated damages was revoked on appeal, because 'hurt and distress' had already been compensated in general damages, and there was an 'unexplained overlap' (said the court).

However, some doubt about the non-availability of aggravated damages for negligence arises from the curious case of *Ashley v CC of Sussex Police*[116] (which, like *Alleyne*, concerned a police raid, but one in which C was shot dead by member of the Sussex Police Special Operations Unit, during a drugs raid). Although the claim by C's estate was instituted in both assault and battery, and in negligence, the police, D, conceded liability in negligence, **and** that aggravated damages would be available for that tort – which concessions prompted the House of Lords to draw an inference that 'the Chief Constable is determined to avoid, if he can, a trial of liability on the assault and battery claim'. However, Lord Neuberger remarked that it was not clear why aggravated damages 'should not logically be recoverable in some categories of negligence claims. In the present case, it must have been reasonably foreseeable ... that a negligently mishandled armed police raid could result in just the sort of mental distress or shock that aggravated damages are intended to reflect ... it would be reminiscent of the bad old days of forms of action if

[109] [1993] QB 507 (CA) 523, 527–528. [110] [1996] PIQR P1 (QB) P5–P6.
[111] [2004] EWHC 2748 (QB) [23]. [112] [2012] EWHC 3955 (QB) [177].
[113] [1986] 1 All ER 54 (QB) 61–62. [114] [1993] QB 507 (CA) 532.
[115] [2000] NSWCA 295, [35]. [116] [2008] UKHL 25, [23] (Lord Bingham).

the court held that [C's] claim could result in aggravated damages if framed in battery, but not if framed in negligence'.[117] This observation was not cited in *Alleyne*; aggravated damages were simply ruled out as being inappropriate for the negligent infliction of injuries.

The law reform corner: Aggravated damages

The uncertainty of how to treat consequential damages for mental distress has troubled the English Law Commission. In 1997, it recommended the enactment of legislation to establish that aggravated damages may be awarded to C to compensate for his mental distress, even for negligence actions: per *Aggravated, Exemplary and Restitutionary Damages*.[118] In 2000, it also hedged its bets, stating that it '*appears* that aggravated damages *may* not be recovered in an action for negligence': per *Damages under the Human Rights Act*.[119]

No 'back door' recovery

§11.10 Where stand-alone mental anguish or distress occurs to C (i.e., mental distress that is not parasitic upon any physical injury), such damages cannot be recovered via aggravated damages.

As discussed in Chapter 5, English law decrees that a recognisable psychiatric injury must be proven to have been sustained by C, as a minimum threshold for recovery of negligently-inflicted pure mental harm. Aggravated damages cannot be used to recover that which the law of Tort otherwise bans.

No English case demonstrates this point, but some Australian authority illustrates the proposition well:

> In *Hunter Area Health Service v Marchlewski*,[120] baby Maria was severely injured during birth, due to the admitted negligence of D's hospital staff. Maria lived only four weeks. Her parents, C, sued D in negligence, and claimed aggravated damages because of the high-handed and arrogant manner in which D decided that Maria was 'not a candidate for resuscitation' if her condition deteriorated. **Held (trial):** C was awarded aggravated damages, because the non-resuscitation decision 'without the parents' concurrence, aggravated the damage that they would otherwise have suffered. The strong belief of C in the future life of Maria, however unsoundly based that may have been, meant that the pain and anguish C suffered was exacerbated by D's action during the four weeks of Maria's life'. **Held (NSWCA):** the aggravated damages were overturned.

In what is equally true of English law, the New South Wales Court of Appeal held that it was legally wrong for C to recover damages for pure, stand-alone mental distress (which is not consequent upon some other injury) by the 'back door' of an aggravated damages claim. Such a claim would seek to circumvent the obstacles which have been deliberately placed by the law in the path of 'secondary victim' psychiatric illness claims, so that, '[i]n a field where policy and precedent preclude or limit compensation for mental distress or injured feelings, policy and precedent ought not to be trumped by an appeal for aggravated damages'.[121]

[117] *ibid*, [102]. [118] (Rep 247, 1997) [2.42]. [119] (Rep 266, 2000), ch 4, fn 129 (emphasis added).
[120] [2000] NSWCA 294, [88]. [121] *ibid*, [117].

EXEMPLARY DAMAGES

While the *principal* purpose of the law of negligence may be to compensate those harmed by D's unintentional, careless and accidental wrongdoing, *punishment* of that negligent D has occupied an increasingly prominent position in English legal debate. The long arm of punishment is an especially interesting topic, insofar as negligent professional Ds (and their employers and insurers) are concerned.

The position in English law

§11.11 Although an award of exemplary damages for negligence is not legally ruled out in English law, it has not occurred to date – principally because of the effects of *Rookes v Barnard*, which restricts the availability of exemplary damages to three categories only. However, the 'cause of action' test – whereby situations in which exemplary damages should be awarded ought to be limited to causes of action where the law would have awarded exemplary damages before *Rookes v Barnard* – has been rejected. In any context, exemplary damages can be awarded, 'if, and only if' the amount of compensatory damages is inadequate to punish D.

By virtue of *Rookes v Barnard*[122] in 1964, exemplary damages are disallowed – and English law is 'still toiling in [its] chains'[123] in this respect – except in three circumstances:

i. where they are necessary to punish oppressive, arbitrary, or unconstitutional acts by government servants (e.g., where immigration officers unlawfully detain a foreign national,[124] or where police officers display oppressive and insulting behaviour towards a prisoner[125]);
ii. where D's purpose is to make a profit from his tort – a category which typically applies where the 'activities of [D] were commercially motivated for profit' (per *Breslin v Mckevitt*[126]), or where D, 'with a cynical disregard for [C's] rights, has calculated that the money to be made out of his wrongdoing would probably exceed the damages at risk' (per *Rookes v Barnard*[127]). This is the category under which exemplary damages for the publication of defamatory material are customarily awarded (as discussed in Chapter 15).The aim of this category is truly to reverse an unjust enrichment accruing to D – i.e., to 'redistribute to [C] the gains or benefits which [D] made or hoped to make', so as to achieve 'redistributive justice, rather than the imposition of a penalty' (per *Breslin*); or to 'not punish [D], but to prevent his unjust enrichment'.[128] Further, the making of confiscation orders against D in criminal proceedings does not preclude the award of exemplary damages – especially where criminal proceedings provide no compensation to C (per *Borders (UK) Ltd v Commr of Police*[129]);
iii. where exemplary damages are specifically provided for by statute – e.g., against publishers of news-related material under the Crime and Courts Act 2013, s 34 (but only if claimed: s 34(5)).

At the time of *Rookes v Barnard*, exemplary damages had never been awarded in negligence. In *Cassell & Co Ltd v Broome*, Lord Diplock took the view that *Rookes* 'was not intended to extend the power to award exemplary or aggravated damages to particular torts for which they had not previously been awarded: such as negligence or deceit'.[130] Such a statement seemed

[122] [1964] AC 1129 (HL) 1226–27. [123] *A v Bottrill* [2002] UKPC 44, [2003] 1 AC 449, [42].
[124] *VS v Home Office* [2014] EWHC 2483 (QB) (point not determined).
[125] *Thompson v Commr of Police* [1998] QB 498 (CA). [126] [2011] NICA 33, [140].
[127] [1972] AC 1027 (HL) 1227 (Lord Devlin). [128] [2009] EWHC 225 (QB) [68].
[129] [2005] EWCA Civ 197. [130] [1972] AC 1027 (HL) 1130–31.

to set the cursor at 1964 – and as exemplary damages for negligence were not available as at that date, then they could not be available for negligence at all. However, that 'cause of action' test is no longer good law. While the House of Lords showed no inclination later in *Kuddus v CC of Leicestershire*[131] to permit the recovery of exemplary damages for negligence, *Kuddus* explicitly overruled the 'cause of action' test – and overruled *AB v South West Water*,[132] where the Court of Appeal had endorsed the 'cause of action' test.

In *Kuddus*, Mr Kuddus, C, returned to his flat, where a friend had been staying, to find much of his property gone. C reported the theft to the police, D. Later, a police constable forged C's signature on a document withdrawing the complaint. C sued D for misfeasance in public office. At the time of *Rookes v Barnard*, exemplary damages had not been awarded for that tort. **Held:** the 'cause of action' test should be abandoned. In principle, exemplary damages could be awarded for misfeasance in public office.

Lord Slynn (with whom the majority of the House agreed, on this point[133]) considered that the 'cause of action' test artificially restricted the proper development of the common law, and preferred that exemplary damages should be available for most torts. He noted that the three categories in *Rookes v Barnard* might fall to be reconsidered in time, and that it was the 'features of the behaviour' of D ('an outrageous disregard of [C's] rights', said Lord Nicholls), rather than the cause of action, which was crucial to determining whether to award exemplary damages. Hence, the general consensus in *Kuddus* was that English courts can only award exemplary damages in Lord Devlin's *three categories of case* – **but** that it was not necessary to restrict exemplary damages to pre-1964 causes of action for which they had then been recognised. Lord Scott, on the other hand, decried the need, in *Kuddus*, for exemplary damages at all in a civil system – a minority view with which some lower courts since have expressed sympathy (per *Parabola Investments Ltd v Browallia Cal Ltd*[134]).

It follows, from *Kuddus*, and from categories i and ii of *Rookes v Barnard*, that legally-speaking, exemplary damages are not entirely ruled out in an appropriate case of negligence. However, they have not figured in negligence in English law to date.

According to *Rookes v Barnard*, 'if, and only if, the amount [of compensatory damages] is inadequate to punish [D] for his outrageous conduct, to mark the disapproval of such conduct and to deter [D] from repeating it' can exemplary damages be awarded (thereby acknowledging that compensatory awards may have, themselves, some capacity to punish).[135] This 'if and only if' formula was cited with approval in *Cassell* as 'a most valuable and important contribution to the law of exemplary damages'.[136]

The law reform corner: Exemplary damages

In 1997, the English Law Commission recommended[137] that the rule in *Rookes v Barnard* be abandoned, and that exemplary damages should be available in any scenario where D had

[131] [2002] AC 122 (HL). [132] [1993] QB 507 (CA).

[133] [2002] 2 AC 122 (HL) [26] (Lord Slynn), [45] (Lord Mackay), [68] (Lord Nicholls), [89] (Lord Hutton), but contrast [107]–[121] (Lord Scott).

[134] [2009] EWHC 901 (Comm) [208]. [135] [1964] AC 1129 (HL) 1228 (Lord Devlin).

[136] [1972] AC 1027 (HL) 1089 (Lord Reid).

[137] *Aggravated, Exemplary and Restitutionary Damages* (1997), Recommendation #18.

deliberately and outrageously disregarded C's rights. Had this reform been enacted, it would have encompassed some of the negligence scenarios that have occurred elsewhere which have attracted the punitive remedy. However, the Draft Bill proposed by the Law Commission to achieve this outcome has never seen the light of day.

§11.12 For claims against public authorities concurrently in tort and for infringements of the ECHR, exemplary damages are not to be awarded for the latter.

The same facts may give rise both to a claim in tort (e.g., for negligence, trespass to the person, whether assault or battery or false imprisonment), or under s 7 of the HRA 1998 for infringement of a Convention right. However, exemplary damages are not awarded for ECHR infringements (per *Ala Anufrijeva v Southwark LBC*).[138]

Practical problems

Albeit that such damages have never been awarded against a negligent D in English law, there are two problems of practicality where exemplary damages are concerned: what triggers their award, and how the awards are quantified. Dealing with each in turn:

The requisite trigger

§11.13 Where exemplary damages for negligence have been awarded in other jurisdictions, the level of D's culpability, necessary to trigger an award, has varied between: gross negligence, reckless conduct and wilful conduct.

The trigger for exemplary damages has been the subject of much judicial debate elsewhere. When New Zealand abolished the right to court-ordered compensatory damages for accidental personal injury and introduced its no-fault statutory compensation scheme, it retained the right of C to pursue exemplary damages at common law.[139] This led to various victims of accidents trying to increase their quantum of compensation via the avenue of exemplary damages, and inevitably, one of these attempts ended up in the Privy Council.

In *A v Bottrill*,[140] the negligent wrongdoing of D, a gynaecologist, consisted of the 'wholesale misreading of cervical smears [of patients] in the Gisborne area' of New Zealand. In A's case, had the slides been correctly interpreted, she would have avoided radiation treatment and a hysterectomy. When subsequent investigations showed that D's false reporting rate for cervical smear slides was at least 50%, the matter became a national concern in New Zealand. The Privy Council granted a re-trial in this case.

The influence of the accident compensation scheme upon exemplary damages was directly at issue. The New Zealand Court of Appeal adopted the view that a narrowly-defined trigger for exemplary damages was warranted, as the statutory bar upon common law actions for

138 [2003] EWCA Civ 1406, [55(e)].

139 Accident Insurance Act 1998 (NZ), s 396(1), and see too: *Donselaar v Donselaar* [1982] 1 NZLR 97 (CA).

140 [2002] UKPC 44, [2003] 1 AC 449, [5], [9].

damages should not prompt the courts to extend the role of exemplary damages to reflect any perceived inadequacies or shortfalls in that statutory compensation.[141] On appeal, however, the Privy Council dismissed this 'floodgates' concern as ill-founded, and favoured the view[142] that a wider trigger for exemplary damages was the state of the law at the time that the accident compensation scheme came into force, and presumably Parliament was content with that when it permitted exemplary damages to be pursued under the scheme. Ultimately, regarding what conduct should trigger an award of exemplary damages, the Privy Council divided 3:2.[143] The case also featured the rare spectacle of Tipping J having articulated a particular trigger for exemplary damages in an earlier case,[144] then changing his mind in the *Bottrill* appeal court and propounding a narrower test,[145] only to see his original test endorsed by the Privy Council!

Three 'grades' of wrongdoing have been sufficient triggers, as the following Table shows:

The comparative corner: The spectrum of negligent wrongdoing

- *'gross negligence'*: only a flagrant departure from the reasonable standard of care – showing an appalling level of skill, and a standard of conduct distantly removed from the prudent behaviour of the reasonable D – can equate to gross negligence. According to the majority of the Privy Council in *Bottrill*, gross negligence **can** justify an award of exemplary damages.[146] Although the 'test of outrageousness would usually involve intentional wrongdoing coupled with an element of flagrancy, cynicism, oppression or the like', neither this, nor conscious recklessness by [D], was necessary as a matter of law. Gross negligence requires, inescapably, a judgment about 'degrees of negligence', as acknowledged in *Bottrill* – but this was justified because, whatever trigger is adopted, '[t]he reality is that there will be an element of forensic uncertainty in borderline cases'. In the Irish case of *Cooper v O'Connell*,[147] a dentist's work was described as 'seriously negligent', but exemplary damages were ruled out, as gross incompetence was not a sufficient trigger (and there was no evidence of wilful or reckless misconduct by D).
- *reckless conduct*: this occurs where D was aware of the risks inherent in his conduct and proceeded anyway, recklessly indifferent to the consequences for C's safety and welfare. The minority in *Bottrill*[148] preferred this trigger for exemplary damages, because (1) it justified punishment of D, closely approaching intentional harm; and (2) gross negligence involved too much uncertainty about degrees of negligence. (This trigger has since been adopted as correct by the Supreme Court of New Zealand.[149])
- *wilful wrongdoing*: this trigger requires wilful conduct (notwithstanding that the action is framed in negligence, and not as a trespass to the person). It means deliberate, wilful wrongdoing by D, calculated to harm. This trigger was adopted by the minority in *Bottrill*, as an alternative to recklessness. Obviously, this will be the toughest trigger to prove. In the Victorian case of *Backwell v AAA*,[150] D, the doctor responsible for a donor

[141] *Bottrill v A* [2001] 3 NZLR 622 (CA) [79]–[80], [118]–[119]. [142] [2002] UKPC 44, [54]–[63].
[143] *ibid* (Lords Nicholls, Hope and Rodger; Lords Hutton and Millett dissented).
[144] *McLaren Transport Ltd v Somerville* [1996] 3 NZLR 424 (HC) 434.
[145] *Bottrill v A* [2001] 3 NZLR 622 (CA) 664–65 (Tipping J).
[146] See *A v Bottrill* [2003] 1 AC 449 (PC, from NZCA) [27], [33], [35]. [147] (SC, Keane J, 5 Jun 1997).
[148] *Bottrill* [2003] 1 AC 449 (PC) [26], [75], [82]. [149] *Couch v A-G* [2010] NZSC 27.
[150] [1997] 1 VR 182 (CA) 211.

insemination program, mistakenly inseminated a patient, C, with semen from a donor of incompatible blood type. D then recommended termination, falsely telling C that if she carried forth and miscarried, her identity might be revealed through publicity, that she might have difficulties getting treated again at any clinic in Australia, and that the clinic itself might be forced to close if the mistake came to light. It warranted exemplary damages. Ormiston JA noted that '[a]lthough it was a claim in negligence, the deliberate acts of a party are relevant to determining whether that party has acted in contumelious disregard of the other party's interests'.

Clearly, the appropriate trigger for exemplary damages in negligence is an area in which judicial opinion differs markedly, and vests the law with an unwelcome uncertainty.

Quantifying awards

§11.14 Quantifying awards for exemplary damages is highly imprecise, because the court is charged with the task of fixing the size of a penalty or fine.

In those jurisdictions in which exemplary damages have been awarded for negligence, courts have despaired of their quantification as a mere 'matter of impression' (per *Backwell v AAA*[151]) or a 'forensic lottery' (per *Phillip v Whitecourt General Hosp*[152]). In *Broome v Cassell & Co Ltd*, Lord Reid noted that there was no limit upon the monetary penalty which exemplary damages represented, 'except that it must not be unreasonable'.[153] The amount must be linked to the amount awarded to C as compensatory damages, because under the 'if and only if' formula in *Rookes v Barnard*, compensatory damages must be taken into account in determining how much punishment exemplary damages should impose.

Canadian jurisprudence has benefited from the detailed direction to the jury by the Supreme Court of Canada in *Whiten v Pilot Insurance Co*,[154] that quantifying exemplary damages awards should take account of: the harm caused (was it directed specifically at C?); the degree of D's misconduct (was it an isolated event, or oft-repeated?); the relative vulnerability of C (were the parties in a relationship of trust and confidence, or complete strangers?); any advantage or profit gained by D; and any other fines or penalties imposed on D.

Awards have tended to be modest in other jurisdictions where exemplary damages have been awarded for negligence. None of the exemplary damages awards in the following cases exceeded the compensatory damages awarded.

The comparative corner: Vignettes of exemplary damages amounts

In the Australian case of *B v Marinovich*,[155] a male psychiatrist, D, had sexual relations with a female patient during a consultation, knowing of her then-vulnerable psychiatric state and that she had been sexually abused as a child. Thereafter, D pressured C to keep the matter secret from her spouse; and charged her for the consultation ($30,000 awarded). In

151 [1997] 1 VR 182 (CA) 215–16 (Ormiston JA).
152 [2004] ABQB 2, [278] (Watson J).
153 [1972] AC 1027 (HL) 1086–87.
154 [2002] SCC 18, [94], directions 3–4. Also: *McIntyre v Grigg* (2006), 43 CCLT (3d) 209 (Ont CA) [82]–[87].
155 [1999] NTSC 127.

Backwell v AAA,[156] facts previously ($60,000 awarded). In the **Canadian** case of *Coughlin v Kuntz*,[157] a surgeon, D, performed a non-urgent surgical procedure (an operation on the cervical spine) which the College of Physicians and Surgeons (BC) had requested not to be performed until further investigations about it could be carried out ($25,000 awarded). In the **Irish** case of *Philp v Ryan*,[158] a patient's prostate cancer went undiagnosed. The treating doctor, D, falsified a clinical note to give the impression that he had advised C to have a further test carried out, and D's legal advisers, when told of alteration by D about a week prior to trial starting, failed to inform C's legal advisers (€50,000 awarded).

Policy objections

Exemplary damages in negligence have been considered in rather disparaging terms by some judges. For example, in *Kuddus v CC of Leicestershire*, Lord Scott labelled them 'an anomaly'.[159]

The uncomfortable interplay between aggravated damages (compensatory in nature) and exemplary damages (punitive in nature) has already been mentioned. Additionally, there are several policy objections to an award of exemplary damages for negligent wrongdoing (and for such damages more generally). These were explored in law reform studies in England and Wales,[160] in Ireland,[161] and in Ontario.[162] Summarising these:

Windfall to C. In *Broome v Cassell & Co Ltd*,[163] Lord Reid called an award of exemplary damages, 'a pure and undeserved windfall at the expense of [D]'. C has already been fully compensated for his harm or injury – and he then benefits from the fact of D's punishment. Furthermore, if D is a public service provider, and is not insured for the exemplary damages award, then C's windfall may be at the expense of the public good that D's activities provide. Also, at a time when insurance funds are coping with large payouts to seriously injured Cs affected by negligence *simpliciter*, it was distasteful to grant a C parasitic and windfall damages. On the other hand, as Lord Diplock memorably stated in *Broome v Cassell*, C 'can only profit from the windfall if the wind was blowing his way'.[164] The Privy Council also remarked, in *W v W*, that exemplary damages constitute a fine on D, but it was better than seeing the monies disappear into consolidated revenue.[165]

No purpose. Negligence law is concerned with the compensation of injured victims, whereas the sole purpose of exemplary damages is to discharge the traditional criminal role of punishment and deterrence. In any event, aggravated damages can adequately compensate C for any outrage or humiliation suffered by C (per *Daniels v Thompson*[166]). On the other hand, exemplary damages may be perceived to vindicate the strength of the law (per *Rookes v Barnard*[167]); to fufil the 'social purpose' of 'teach[ing] [D] that tort does not pay' (per *Broome v Cassell*[168]); to assuage C's desire for revenge and self-help which, if pursued, might endanger the peace of good society (per *Lamb v Cotogno*[169]); and give C a sense of empowerment and control (e.g., in

156 [1997] 1 VR 182 (CA), with special leave refused: *AAA v Backwell* (HCA, M25/1996, 5 Aug 1996).
157 (1989), 42 BCLR (2d) 108 (CA).
158 [2004] IESC 105.
159 [2001] UKHL 29, [2002] 2 AC 122, [119].
160 *Aggravated, Exemplary and Restitutionary Damages* (CP 132, 1993), and subsequent *Report* (Rep 247, 1997).
161 *Aggravated, Exemplary and Restitutionary Damages* (CP 12, 1998), and subsequent *Report* (Rep 60, 2000).
162 *Report on Exemplary Damages* (1991).
163 [1972] AC 1027 (HL) 1086.
164 *ibid*, 1126.
165 [1999] UKPC 2, [1999] 2 NZLR 1, [6].
166 [1998] 3 NZLR 22 (CA) 29.
167 [1964] AC 1129 (HL) 1226 (Lord Devlin).
168 [1972] AC 1027 (HL) 1130 (Lord Diplock).
169 (1987) 164 CLR 1 (HCA) 9.

Backwell v AAA: 'I am looking for that it never happens to anybody else. I would hate anybody to go through what I have been through').[170]

Uncomfortable interplay with the criminal law. The lower standard of proof in civil proceedings may be ill-suited to punishment. In *Broome v Cassell*, Lord Reid stated that, '[i]t is no excuse to say that we need not waste sympathy on people who behave outrageously. Are we wasting sympathy on vicious criminals when we insist on proper legal safeguards for them?',[171] while Lord Diplock held that punishment, deterrence, vindication and condemnation were not the legitimate functions of Tort law and should occur only within Criminal law.[172] Furthermore, if D has already been convicted and/or fined, then what basis is there left to support exemplary damages for the same conduct? In *AB v South West Water*,[173] an award of exemplary damages was struck out because, *inter alia*, of D's conviction and fine; while in *Devenish Nutrition Ltd v Sanofi-Aventis SA (France)*,[174] Lewison J concluded that a previous fine was 'not conclusive in itself', but a 'powerful factor' against exemplary damages.

The financial means of D. If D's financial circumstances are relevant, when determining what sum would be necessary to deter and to punish that D, then this could constitute a severe intrusion into D's affairs, could increase the costs of disclosure, could lead to disproportionate litigation against asset-rich Ds, and could give C a competitive advantage over D if they were competitors of C's.[175]

Effect of an award. The deterrent effect of exemplary damages may be lessened if the award of compensatory damages was already very large. Also, cynicism of the law may result from large exemplary damages awards in defamation for injury to reputation, but where dreadful injury to C's person does not warrant an award.[176]

Logistics of the litigation compromised. Settlements may be more difficult to negotiate where C holds out hopes for exemplary damages; or it may be difficult for D to settle when the exposure to exemplary damages awards is unpredictable.[177]

The corporate D. It is pointless to punish a corporate D with exemplary damages, as that punishment will inevitably fall upon innocent shareholders (or employees, if redundancies become necessary).[178]

The insured D. There is no punitive effect on D, where he is insured for exemplary damages. Further, if insurers had to bear such burdens under compulsory statutory insurance schemes, then the awards would raise premiums for all insureds, to spread the burden among many who were not wrongdoers.[179]

Multiple Ds. In the case of jointly liable Ds, then per *Broome v Cassell & Co Ltd*,[180] there should only be one award of exemplary damages, limited to whatever is necessary to punish the *least* culpable D. Hence, the most responsible D 'obtains a benefit' by having joint, but less culpable, co-Ds.[181] Several liability, in respect of exemplary damages, is another possible solution to the conundrum.[182]

Multiple Cs. If C receives an award of exemplary damages, then so too may other Cs have suffered, especially where D's conduct reflected systemic, rather than isolated, failure. A financial

[170] (1996) Aust Torts Rep ¶81–387. [171] [1972] AC 1027 (HL) 1087.
[172] *ibid*, 1127–28. [173] [1993] QB 507 (CA) 527 (Stuart Smith LJ).
[174] [2007] EWHC 2394 (Ch) [64].
[175] See, e.g. OLRC (1991) 51–53 (two dissenting Commissioners); EWLC (Rep 247, 1997) 86, 141.
[176] Irish LRC (CP, 1998) 110, 113. [177] OLRC (1991) 1. [178] Irish LRC (CP, 1998) 39.
[179] EWLC (CP, 1993) 146, and (Rep 247, 1997) 91. [180] [1972] AC 1027 (HL) 1063–64, 1090, 1105, and 1122.
[181] EWLC (CP, 1993) 87, and (Rep 247, 1997) 80. [182] OLRC (1991) 59, and endorsed by EWLC, *ibid*, 157–61.

windfall may accrue to one C, to the exclusion of others who have not sued or who may sue at a later time (e.g., in *A v Bottrill*, the Privy Council, in granting a re-trial, did not address the question of how exemplary damages should be handled, when potentially hundreds of affected patients existed).

Vicarious liability. There is no punitive or deterrent effect on D, if the burden of the award is automatically shifted to the employer under the doctrine of vicarious liability (and whether the doctrine should be disapplied if related to D's own financial means is a difficult policy question[183]).

Although the English Law Commission considered that the arguments for retaining or abolishing exemplary damages in tort were 'finely balanced',[184] the numerous policy objections, together with the blurred distinction between aggravated and exemplary damages, and the difficulty in identifying what triggers exemplary damages, suggests to this author that such damages should be abolished in English negligence law.

NOMINAL DAMAGES

§11.15 Nominal damages cannot be awarded in negligence, given that the tort requires actual proof of damage.

Nominal damages are awarded in the 'traditional sum' of £2 (per *TCP Europe Ltd v Perry*[185]) or £1 (per *AB v MOJ*[186]). They are capable of being awarded for torts which are actionable *per se* (i.e., without proof of damage), such as for trespass to the person, because they signify or vindicate that a cause of action has been made out, but no actual damage has occurred to C (per *The Mediana*[187]). As noted in the *Oxford Dictionary of Law*, nominal damages are 'a token sum of damages awarded when a legal right has been infringed, but no substantial loss has been caused'.[188] Nominal damages are also awardable for breach of contract (for which proof of damage is not required either). Of course, if actual loss *has* been sustained by C, then that loss will be duly compensated by an award of substantial damages, in place of nominal damages.

However, nominal damages are entirely inappropriate for negligence, given that, '[p]roof of damage is an essential step in establishing a claim in tortious negligence' (per *Heaton v AXA Equity and Law Life Ass Soc plc*[189]). Hence, if C cannot prove that any injury or harm flowed from D's breach of duty, then no cause of action is possible, and there can be no question of nominal damages being awarded, even where proof of breach has been made out.

In *Capita Alternative Fund Services (Guernsey) Ltd v Drivers Jonas (a firm)*,[190] Capita, C, purchased a factory-outlet-centre at the Chatham Historic Dockyard in Medway, Kent. C sued Drivers Jonas, D, a firm of valuers, for negligently valuing the property. C alleged that it paid too much. **Held (trial):** D was negligent in advising and valuing the property, and there was proof of substantial damages. **Held (CA, 2:1):** the trial judge was entitled to find substantial damages. However, if there had not been any loss established, then in contract, C would be entitled to nominal damages only; but in negligence, the claim would fail altogether.

183 EWLC (Rep 247, 1997) 79, 89–90. 184 *ibid*, 101. 185 [2012] EWHC 1940 (QB) [124].
186 [2014] EWHC 1847 (QB) [55]. 187 [1900] AC 113 (HL) 116.
188 E Martin and J Law (eds) (6th edn, Oxford University Press, 2006) 356.
189 [2002] UKHL 15, [2002] 2 AC 329, [8(1)] (Lord Bingham). 190 [2012] EWCA Civ 1417.

RESTITUTIONARY DAMAGES

§11.16 Although restitutionary damages have been awarded for some torts, there has been no such award for the tort of negligence to date.

Meaning and policy goals

An award of restitutionary damages means that the damages are 'assessed according to the gains made by the wrongdoer [D], rather than the loss to the claimant [C]'.[191] Where awarded, C may receive an award much larger than the actual loss suffered.

The Irish Law Reform Commission remarked that English courts 'have tended towards a restitutionary approach to damages in several [tort] cases, and in a few instances have awarded damages on the basis of the gain to [D]. They have at times gone to great lengths, however, to characterise such awards as compensatory', which has strained the rationale.[192] That Commission further noted that, in seeking to deprive D of his 'ill-gotten gains', restitutionary damages 'do not place as onerous a burden on [D] as do exemplary damages'.[193] This may make this form of award more palatable for the compensatory policy goals which the law of negligence seeks to achieve.

Distinction between proprietary and non-proprietary torts

Restitutionary damages have been awarded for various proprietary torts, i.e., torts that serve to protect C's interest in or over real or personal property, *viz*, for: trespass to land (per *Whitwham v Westminster Brymbo Coal & Coke Co*[194] – 'if [D] has, without leave of [C], been using [C's] land for his own purposes, [D] ought to pay for such user'); for detinue (per *Strand Electric and Engineering Co Ltd v Brisford Entertainments*[195] – 'the claim for a hiring charge is ... not based on the loss to [C], but on the fact that [D] has used the goods for his own purposes'); and for interference with an easement of light (per *Carr-Saunders v Dick McNeil Associates Ltd*[196] – awarding damages to 'take account of ... the profit which [D] would look to in the development of their site'). Occasionally, it has been judicially suggested that restitutionary damages should be more widely available for proprietary torts. In *Stoke-on-Trent CC v WJ Wass Ltd (No 1)*,[197] Nourse LJ remarked that, '[i]t is possible that the English law of tort, more especially of the so-called "proprietary torts", will in due course make a more deliberate move towards recovery, based not on loss suffered by [C], but on the unjust enrichment of [D] ... But I do not think that that process can begin in this case [or] ... at this level of decision'.

To date, however, there has been no award of restitutionary damages for negligence, so far as the author's searches can ascertain. Indeed, for non-proprietary torts generally, English courts have been reluctant to make any such award. In *Halifax Building Socy v Thomas*,[198] no restitutionary award was made for fraudulent representation (deceit) – with Peter Gibson LJ remarking that 'there is no decided authority that comes anywhere near to covering the present circumstances', and that 'it cannot be suggested that there is a universally applicable principle

[191] EWLC (Rep 247, 1997) [3.3]. [192] (CP 12, 1998) [8.17]–[8.18]. [193] (Rep 60, 2000) [6.01].
[194] [1896] 2 Ch 538 (CA) 542. [195] [1952] 1 All ER 796 (CA) 801 (Denning LJ).
[196] [1986] 2 All ER 888 (QB) 896 (Millett J). [197] [1998] 1 WLR 1406 (CA) 1415.
[198] [1996] Ch 217 (CA) 227.

that, in every case, there will be restitution of benefit from a wrong'. Citing *Halifax*, the English Law Commission noted that, '[i]t is unclear whether or not restitutionary damages are available for non-proprietary torts ... it may well be that an account of profits or other restitutionary measures of damages will also become more widely available in tort'.[199] Since then, in 2011, Lord Kerr acknowledged the concept of restitutionary damages in Tort in *Lumba v Sec of State for the Home Dept*,[200] but made no specific reference to their availability in negligence.

[199] *Damages Under the Human Rights Act* (2000) [4.76].

[200] [2011] UKSC 12, [2012] 1 AC 245, [254].

Part II

Specific negligence regimes

12

Occupiers' liability

THE CAUSE OF ACTION DEFINED

This chapter concerns the liability of occupiers of premises, D, towards either lawful visitors or trespassers, C, who are injured (or killed) whilst on those premises.

§12.1 The law of occupiers' liability is governed, in English law, by two statutes:

- the Occupiers' Liability Act 1957 ('the OLA 1957'), which governs the liability of an occupier of premises to his lawful visitors. An occupier owes any lawful visitor a 'common duty of care', the terms of which are 'a duty to take such care as in all the circumstances of the case is reasonable to see that the visitor will be reasonably safe in using the premises for the purposes for which he is invited or permitted by the occupier to be there' (per s 2(2)); or
- the Occupiers' Liability Act 1984 ('the OLA 1984'), which governs the liability of an occupier to trespassers (or unlawful visitors). An occupier does not owe a 'common duty of care' to a trespasser; rather, the occupier's duty of care is far more limited.

The law of occupiers' liability is a true mix of statutorily-stated principles and common law negligence. Both Acts impact, to some degree, as to whether the occupier owed a duty of care or breached that duty, and the defences available to him; whilst causation and remoteness are *entirely* governed by the common law.

Where the Acts apply, it has been judicially clarified that their provisions were truly intended to *replace* the common law, rather than merely to consolidate it (per *Maloney v Torfaen CBC*[1]). As Carnwath LJ explained in *Maguire v Sefton MBC*,[2] the law of occupiers' liability 'had become over-complicated by subtle distinctions derived from the case law over several decades', and that the reform proposals 'were not pure codification in the strict sense. They were ... codification-plus; that is, sorting out the law by a combination of re-statement, and amendment, as necessary'.

Where the statutes are not applicable

It is convenient, at the outset, to briefly dispose of those situations where the Acts do **not** apply at all:

[1] [2005] EWCA Civ 1762, [11] (Laws LJ). [2] [2006] EWCA Civ 316, [32].

- for persons who are exercising public right of way, the ordinary principles of negligence (or protective provisions under the Highways Act 1980) apply, e.g., where C tripped over: a pothole in a footpath and broke her leg (in *McGeown v Northern Ireland Housing Executive*[3]); or a defective manhole in a public pathway while delivering milk (in *Holden v White*[4]); or a pothole on a dilapidated bridge (in *Greenhalgh v British Rwys Board*[5]). None of these were 'visitors' under the OLA 1957, and the OLA 1984 does not apply either;
- entrants who access D's premises under the 'right to roam' rights contained in the Countryside and Rights of Way Act 2000, or via an access agreement under the National Parks and Access to the Countryside Act 1949, are excluded from the OLA 1957 (s 1(4)), and are governed by a modified version of the OLA 1984 (per s 1(6A)), the terms of which lie outside the scope of this book;
- C must be *an entrant* onto the occupier's land, for either Act to apply. If some activity occurred on the occupier's premises which caused injury to C who was *passing by*, occupiers' liability cannot apply.

> In *Gabriel v Kirklees MBC*,[6] Tashan Gabriel, 6, C, was struck in the left eye by a stone or mud thrown by other children from the occupier's building demolition site. Once it was clear that C was not on the demolition site at the time he was injured, the OLA claims fell away, and C's action was brought in negligence (successfully).

- the entrant onto D's premises must be of the wrongdoing human variety! If, say, bees trespass onto D's land seeking the nectar of flowering oil seed rape, and D sprays the crop to kill weavils, and that spray is deadly to the bees, it is not possible to allege that D owed any duty of care to the bees or to their owner, as 'trespassers'. In *Tutton v AD Walter Ltd*,[7] the court held that the bees could not be classified as trespassers, because 'trespassers, in the eyes of the law, are wrongdoers. It is unreal to look at bees in this light. Bees are useful insects; their use to the neighbourhood in which they forage is universal'.

Employees who are visitors to an occupier's site

Where an employee is injured on **his own employer's premises** during the course of his employment, his employer *does* technically owe that employee a duty of care under the OLA 1957 (i.e., there is nothing in the Act to preclude the employee from being a visitor). However, given that the employer also owes a common law duty to provide a safe system of work and a safe workplace (see 'Employers' liability', an online chapter), there is no material advantage which the OLA 1957 provides to an injured employee, over and above the ordinary principles of negligence. Insofar as duty of care is concerned, the Court of Appeal noted, in *Priestley v Nottingham HA*,[8] that the 'the common duty of care imposed by the OLA 1957 adds nothing to [the employer's] common law duty'. A perusal of OLA cases confirms that few employee-versus-employer actions involving state of the premises are brought under the OLA 1957 (albeit

[3] [1995] 1 AC 233 (HL), decided under the Occupiers' Liability Act (Northern Ireland) 1957, but the position was said to be the same under the OLA 1957 (England and Wales).

[4] [1982] QB 679 (CA). [5] [1969] 2 QB 286 (CA). [6] [2004] EWCA Civ 345, [4].

[7] [1986] QB 61, 75 (Denis Henry QC, sitting as a Deputy High Court Judge).

[8] CA, 22 Jan 1986. See, on the same point: *Anness v Goodyear Tyre & Rubber Co (GB)* (QB, 9 Nov 1983); *David v Honeywell Normalair-Garrett Ltd* [2005] EWHC 351 (QB) [92].

that some instances do exist, e.g., where an employee lorry driver slipped on spilt fuel on his employer's petrol station: *Holt v Holroyd Meek Ltd*[9]).

Where an employee, C, is injured, during the course of his employment, **whilst working at other premises** occupied by D2, then authorities show that it *may* be easier for the employee to pursue his employer, D1, rather than the occupier, D2. The employee will be owed a duty of care by both employer and occupier, but on different bases (the former as a common law duty in negligence and the latter because of the common duty of care owed under s 2(2), OLA 1957). An employee may feasibly recover against both defendants. As Lord Keith noted in *Ferguson v Welsh*,[10] if the employee is operating under an unsafe system of work, and thereby suffers injury on the occupier's premises, that occupier would not ordinarily be liable under the OLA 1957, for failing to tell that employee how to do his work – unless there were 'special circumstances' (which did apply in the following case):

> In *Lough v Intruder Detection and Surveillance Fire and Security Ltd*,[11] Mr Fulton, the owner of a country home, D2, was having a new security system installed. Balustrades and banisters on the stairs and landings had been taken away for renovation. The security installers, including John Lough, C, were nevertheless permitted to work inside the house. Inexplicably, C fell off a stairs landing when coming down the stairs. **Held:** occupier D2 was liable under the OLA 1957 for failing adequately to warn C that the stairs and landing were unprotected and for permitting them to work there in the first place. C's claim in negligence against his employer, D1, also succeeded.

However, the court will often place more weight on the duty owed by the employer than that of the occupier. Also, regarding breach, more precautionary steps may be expected of a reasonable employer than of a reasonable occupier (per *Jones v BBC*[12]). In the following cases, the employer, D1, was liable in negligence – but not the occupier, D2, whose premises he was working at:

> In *Hannington v Mitie Cleaning (South East) Ltd*,[13] Stanley Hannington, C, was employed as a contract cleaner by Mitie Cleaning, D1, and worked regularly at factory premises of De La Rue Cash Systems, the occupier, D2. C was required to empty refuse into a large skip in the yard, which had a heavy lid that was left standing open. On a windy day, while C was emptying refuse, the lid blew closed, injuring him. The employer, D1, was negligent, because this accident was readily foreseeable, and D1 should have put in place a safe system of work for this. D2, however, was not liable under the OLA 1957, because occupier D2 could reasonably expect employer D1 to do safety assessments and inspections on the premises, which it had not done. In *Makepeace v Evans Bros (Reading) (a firm)*,[14] David Makepeace, C, who was an employee of Evans Bros, painters and decorators, D1, was touching up paint work at a major residential development on the Thames, and was working from a tower scaffold. The site developer, Alfred McAlpine Construction Ltd was the occupier, D2, and had provided the scaffold which D1 erected inappropriately. It collapsed, seriously injuring C. D2 was held not to be liable to C under the OLA 1957. The employer, D1, was of good repute, and erecting scaffolding was an ordinary part of doing this type of work. Occupier D2 was not liable under the OLA 1957 in failing to instruct D1's employee how to use the scaffold, that was D1's task.

Where an employee, C, is injured on an occupier's premises during the course of his employment, the occupier's liability may assume legal importance for two reasons. First, if the employer is

[9] [2002] EWCA Civ 1004, [7]. [10] [1987] 1 WLR 1553 (HL) 1564. [11] [2008] EWCA Civ 1009.
[12] [2000] All ER (D) 283 (Jun) [153] [13] [2002] EWCA Civ 1847, [38].
[14] [2000] EWCA Civ 171, [2000] BLR 287, [2001] ICR 241 (CA) 246.

liable to C, that employer may seek contribution from the occupier under the Civil Liability (Contribution) Act 1978, which requires a legal analysis as to whether the occupier was liable to C as a visitor under the OLA 1957 (as in, e.g., *Lough v Intruder Detection and Surveillance Fire and Security Ltd*). Secondly, if the employer is uninsured, in liquidation, or is otherwise unable to meet any judgment against it, then attention will swiftly turn to whether C can recover compensation from the occupier of the premises where the mishap occurred.

The framework

There are various preconditions for any entrant to establish under either statute. Thereafter, given the separation which English law maintains between lawful visitors and trespassers, the next task is to ascertain which of the two Acts applies to the fact scenario – which is not an entirely straightforward task, in some cases. Finally, the provisions of the appropriate statute, and relevant principles of negligence law, must be correctly applied, in order to determine whether or not D is liable for the injury which befell C on the premises.

Nutshell analysis: **Occupiers' liability**

Pre-conditions for the Acts to apply:

i D must be an 'occupier'
ii The incident occurred at relevant 'premises' to which the Acts apply
iii The danger was a 'static/occupancy danger', not an 'activity danger'

Which of the two Acts applies to C's circumstances?
The elements to establish liability:

1 Duty of care
- for visitors: per s 2(1), OLA 1957
- for trespassers: per s 1(3), OLA 1984

2 Breach of the duty
- for visitors: establish the standard of care (including any elevated standard of care for unaccompanied children, per s 2(3)(a)); then prove breach of that standard; and then check whether D is absolved from breach by virtue of any of the statutory 'escape hatches', *viz*, specialist visitors, per s 2(3)(b); warnings, per s 2(4)(a); and/or independent contractors, per s 2(b)(b);
- for trespassers: similarly, establish the standard of care; then prove breach; and then check whether D is absolved by virtue of the solitary statutory 'escape hatch', *viz*, warnings, per s 1(5)

3(a) Causation – per the common law
3(b) Remoteness – per the common law

Defences – various (depending upon the statutory action), including:

- Contributory negligence
- Acts of strangers
- *Volenti*
- Exclusion of liability

Remedies

Dealing with each in turn:

PRE-REQUISITES FOR THE LEGISLATION TO APPLY

Precondition #1: An 'occupier'

An occupier under the OLA 1957 is one who would be treated as an occupier *at common law* (per s 1(2)). Under the OLA 1984, the meaning of an occupier is related back (via s 1(2)) to its meaning under the OLA 1957. Otherwise, neither Act defines an occupier, and hence, recourse must be had to the common law.

The test of control

§12.2 D is an occupier where he has control over the premises where the mishap occurred. D can be an occupier without being the owner, or the person in physical possession, of those premises. More than one person may exercise the requisite control over the premises, as 'joint occupiers'.

In the leading authority of *Wheat v E Lacon & Co Ltd*,[15] Denning LJ stated that an 'occupier' was 'simply a convenient word to denote a person who had a sufficient degree of control over premises to put him under a duty of care towards those who came lawfully on to the premises'. It is not to be given a meaning derived from what it means, say, under the Licensing Act 1964 (per *Bushell v Newcastle Licensing Justices*[16]), or from the law of property – for occupiers' liability, the 'governing criterion is simply control' (per *Seymour v Flynn*[17]).

It is a wide definition, covering occupiers who may be ostensibly 'in the background', but who nevertheless exert the necessary control. Hence occupiers include the following:

- where D, an owner of a building, leases flats to tenants, he will still be regarded as retaining control of the communal staircases, roof gutters and communal balconies of those premises:

  In *Jordan v Achara*,[18] Albert Jordan, C, a meter-reader employed by the London Electricity Board, visited a house owned by Mr Achara, D, to read the meter. The house was divided into six flats, and the meter was in the basement, down a flight of stairs. C could not find a light for the stairs leading to the basement, and used his handtorch. His foot caught on worn carpet on the stairs, he fell, and injured his back. **Held**: D was liable under the OLA 1957; the accident occurred in a communal non-leased area over which D had control.

- where D, a building owner, licenses a person to occupy the premises, with the owner retaining the right to do repairs in all areas of the licensed premises, he retains control of all those premises, even though that party is virtually an 'absentee occupier'. Notably, the licensee may *also* have sufficient control over the premises to be an occupier:

  In *Wheat v E Lacon & Co Ltd*,[19] the Lacon brewers, D, owned a pub, 'The Golfer's Arms'. Mr Richardson was the publican of the pub (which was on the ground floor), and lived with his wife on the first floor, marked 'Private'. D could enter the premises to view the state of repair. During the summer, D allowed Mrs R to take in paying guests, who included Mr and Mrs Wheat, C, who lived on another area of the first floor. There was no direct access between the pub on the ground floor, and C's

[15] [1966] AC 552 (HL) 577 (the events occurred in 1958, and hence, preceded the enactment of the OLA 1957).
[16] [2004] EWCA Civ 767, [25].
[17] CA, 4 Feb 1992, Steyn LJ.
[18] [1988] 20 HLR 607 (CA) 611.
[19] [1966] AC 552 (HL).

accommodation on the first floor, but a back staircase went down from the first floor. One night, W went down to buy some drinks from the bar. He was found at the foot of the staircase with a fractured skull, from which he died. An electric light in the vestibule above the stairs had no bulb in it at the time of the accident. **Held**: D was an occupier of the upper floors, vestibule and back staircase, because D kept for themselves a right to do repairs, giving D a residuary degree of control. R, with his licence to occupy, and Mrs R, who took paying guests, were also occupiers of the upper floor areas. However, D did not have the degree of occupational control as to be responsible for day-to-day matters such as changing a lightbulb, and hence, were not liable. In *Maddocks v Clifton*,[20] the visitor, Mrs Maddocks, C, suffered serious injury at the stables of Burtons Farm, when she fell down a ladder. The farm, land and buildings (including the stable block) were owned by Mrs Clifton, D2. Her mother, D1, ran a stabling business as a licensee, and C paid a fee to D1 to stable her horse there. **Held**: D1 and D2 were joint occupiers of the stables. D2 had some degree of control over the stables as owner of the stables; she lived close by; and knew that people such as C frequently accessed the stables. As licensee conducting a business in the stables, D1 also had the requisite control over the premises.

- where an owner employs an independent contractor to do continuous work on the premises, both the owner and the independent contractor may be sufficiently in control, at the time of the accident, to be occupiers. However, a contractor doing work on an intermittent or temporary basis will not be so treated:

In *Collier v Anglian Water Authy*,[21] the East Lindsey DC owned the seaside promenade, and the Anglian Water Authy was responsible for maintaining its structural condition. Both were joint occupiers, towards a young girl who tripped over an obstacle on the promenade. On the other hand, in *Prentice v Hereward Housing Assn*,[22] where grass outside properties was not cut according to a reasonable maintenance schedule by the Housing Assn, that contractor was not an occupier, and could not be liable for injuries suffered by a resident of a nearby house.

It is evident from *Wheat v Lacon* and the abovementioned cases that there may feasibly be *joint* occupiers in any given case, where both assume sufficient control. As Denning LJ described, occupier D 'may share the control with others. Two or more may be "occupiers". And whenever this happens, each is under a duty to use care towards persons coming lawfully on to the premises, dependent on his degree of control'.[23] The standard of care expected of joint occupiers is discussed below.[24]

However, the extent of control is always a question of fact and of degree – and, in that regard, the line between 'scant' and 'non-existent' control may be very fine indeed. Two cases can be contrasted:

In *Bailey v Armes*,[25] Matthew Bailey, 7, C, together with his young friends, frequently passed through the living room of the flat belonging to the Armes, D, and climbed through a window onto a supermarket asphalt roof. The supermarket was operated by the Cullens. C fell from the roof, and suffered serious head injuries, which caused seizures, paralysis and psychiatric consequences. D had no

[20] [2001] EWCA Civ 1837. [21] CA, 1 Jan 1983.

[22] QB, 29 Apr 1999, subsequently overturned on appeal, re the truthfulness of witness statements, but not on this point: [2001] EWCA Civ 437.

[23] [1966] AC 552 (HL) 568. [24] See pp 609–15. [25] CA, 11 Feb 1999.

permission from the Cullens to allow the children onto the roof, and the Cullens did not know it was happening. The roof was clearly not part of D's flat, but it was argued that, since D controlled access to the roof through the window of their flat, they had acquired *de facto* control over the roof itself, and therefore occupied the roof. **Held:** D did not have sufficient control over the supermarket roof, or over who gained access to the flat roof, to render them occupiers of the roof.

In *Harris v Birkenhead Corp*,[26] the Birkenhead Corp, D, was developing housing. One house was owned by Mrs Gledhill, rented to Mrs Redmond (described as a 'good and careful tenant'), and managed by a firm of real estate agents who collected the rent, etc. When ready to resume the house, D served the tenant with a notice of entry, and the tenant left 5–6 months later, telling the estate agents of her departure. D did not know that the house was vacant at that point. However, D did know, from previous experience, that houses left vacant in this area were promptly attacked by vandals, broken into and trashed. A few months after the tenant left, Julie Harris, 4, C, entered into the vacant house to play, fell out of a smashed window on the top floor, and suffered serious head injuries. **Held:** D, having the immediate right of control of the property, became its occupier as soon as the tenant had left it vacant. Knowing the property was empty, D did nothing about providing any protection against trespassers such as C. Neither the tenant nor Mrs Gledhill was an occupier after the tenant left, for D had asserted its right to control this property after the notice to enter was given, even if that 'control' was fairly 'symbolic'.

The landlords of premises

§12.3 A landlord is technically an occupier over leased premises, if he has retained sufficient control over them. However, under modern law, that landlord is more appropriately liable to a visitor under s 4 of the Defective Premises Act 1974.

It might seem, on the face of it, that a landlord should be liable under s 2 of the OLA 1957, to see that a visitor (whether a tenant or someone else) is reasonably safe in using the leased premises, at least in respect of those areas of the leased premises over which the landlord retains sufficient control to be an occupier under the *Wheat v Lacon* test.

However, it was recently held, in *Drysdale v Hedges*,[27] that whilst s 2 of the OLA 1957 is of 'general application', a landlord's duty of care to keep premises reasonably safe is defined more particularly by s 4 of the Defective Premises Act 1972, and it is that particular duty which should prevail over the general occupier's duty. In the court's view, 'I cannot think that Parliament intended both sections to define a landlord's duty'. Hence, any visitors injured when entering a landlord's premises must proceed under s 4, which provides:

> s 4(1) Where premises are let under a tenancy which puts on the landlord an obligation to the tenant for the maintenance or repair of the premises, the landlord owes to all persons who might reasonably be expected to be affected by defects in the state of the premises a duty to take such care as is reasonable, in all the circumstances, to see that they are reasonably safe from personal injury or from damage to their property caused by a relevant defect.
>
> (2) [This] duty is owed if the landlord knows (whether as the result of being notified by the tenant or otherwise) or if he ought ... to have known of the relevant defect.

[26] [1976] 1 WLR 279 (CA).

[27] [2012] EWHC 4131 (QB) [74] (John Leighton Williams QC, sitting as a Deputy High Court Judge).

That 'visitor' can include a tenant, because the wording of s 4(1) did not suggest any intention to exclude the tenant from the category of 'persons ... affected by defects in the state of the premises'.

> In *Sykes v Harry*,[28] the tenant, C, suffered carbon monoxide poisoning and brain damage from a defective gas fire in the leased premises, eight years after taking up the tenancy from landlord, D. **Held**: D was in breach of his duty under s 4 of the 1972 Act. D had failed to service the gas fire regularly or at all himself, or to check or enquire of C as to the whether he had it serviced during the 8-year period. D knew about the importance of regular servicing, and that the fire had never been serviced, that he did not expect the fire to be serviced by the tenants, and all of that meant that he was 'put on enquiry that there was a real risk that these defects had occurred'.

However, in order for a visitor to proceed under s 4 of the 1972 Act, there must be some 'relevant defect', in that the premises must be 'not in good repair', as the court put it in *Drysdale v Hedges*.[29] In that regard, something is not a defect, simply because it is potentially dangerous or hazardous – under s 4(3), a defect must have been an act or omission by the landlord which would constitute a failure to carry out his obligation of maintenance or repair. Furthermore, the duty to repair under s 4(1) cannot be equated with a duty to 'make safe' and to remove all potential hazards from the premises. It follows that a glass panel in a front door which is not made of strengthened glass (as in *Alker v Collingwood*[30]), or a set of external steps which are painted and hence become more slippery when wet (as in *Drysdale*), are not 'relevant defects' for which the landlord could be liable under s 4. They may be hazardous in certain circumstances (i.e., if a visitor slips and crashes through the glass, or a tenant slips on the painted steps in the rain), but they are not 'out of repair'. For these types of scenarios which are not caught by s 4 of the 1972 Act, the landlord is under a common law duty of care (in negligence), when carrying out repairs and maintenance at the premises, to take reasonable care not to create an unnecessary risk of injury to a visitor (including a tenant) (per *Drysdale*[31]). Further discussions of a landlord's duties are beyond the scope of this book.[32]

Precondition #2: 'Premises' to which the legislation applies

A wide variety

§12.4 The premises to which the OLAs apply can cover a range of premises, from land to buildings, and from structures to movable vessels.

According to the OLA 1957, s 1(3)(a), premises are defined as 'any fixed or movable structure, including any vessel, vehicle or aircraft'. The OLA 1984 provides the same (via a combination of s 1(2) and s 1(9)).

A sample of case law shows a wide array of 'things' which have been alleged to give rise to occupiers' liability (not all succeeded, but all of them constituted premises to which the Acts could apply):

[28] [2001] EWCA Civ 167, [2001] QB 1014, [11]. [29] [2012] EWHC 4131 (QB) [82].

[30] [2007] 1 WLR 2230 (CA). [31] [2012] EWHC 4131 (QB) [102].

[32] See further, e.g.: M Pawlowski, 'Injury Sustained as a Result of Slippery Steps' (2012) 16 Landlord and Tenant Rev 236; Irish LRC, *The Law Relating to the Liability of Builders, Vendors and Lessors for the Quality and Fitness of Premises* (WP 1, June 1977).

- *land*: a dairy farm (*Simpson v Al Dairy Farms Ltd*[33]); a block of land with a sheer 5-metre drop from open grassland down to a carpark (*Harvey v Plymouth CC*[34]); a mountainside with an unfenced bluff (*Simkiss v Rhondda BC*[35]); a beach (*Proctor v Young*[36]); the grassy verge beside a road (*Taylorson v Bourne Leisure Ltd*[37]); and a council park (*Allen v Stoke-on-Trent CC*[38]).
- *buildings or fixed structures*: the roof of a building (*Young v Kent CC*[39]); an artificial pool (*Evans v Kosmar Villa Holidays plc*[40]); a sea wall or a quay against which a boat could moor pursuant to a mooring licence (*George v Coastal Marine 2004 Ltd (t/as Mashfords)*[41]); dilapidated football terraces (*Cunningham v Reading Football Club*[42]); a hotel room (*Lewis v Six Continents plc*[43]); a factory (*Rae v Mars (UK) Ltd*[44]); a concrete wall (*Kolasa v Ealing Hosp NHS Trust*[45]); a motor-racing circuit (*Wattleworth v Goodwood Road Racing Co Ltd*[46]); an airport runway (*Monarch Airlines Ltd v London Luton Airport Ltd*[47]); the floor of a takeaway shop (*Laverton v Kiapasha (t/as Takeaway Supreme*[48]); a ladder in horse stables (*Maddocks v Clifton*[49]); a cleaning storeroom (*Andrews v Initial Cleaning Services Ltd*[50]); and a rubbish tip (*McNamara v North Tyneside MBC*[51]).
- *movable structures*: a machine used to drill out a tube tunnel (*Bunker v Charles Brand & Son Ltd*[52]); scaffolding (*Gillingham v Ash Scaffolding Co Ltd*[53]); a movable windmill mast (*Jones v BBC*[54]); a fridge in a hotel (*Shtern v Cummings (Jamaica)*[55]); and an exercise machine in a leisure centre (*Maguire v Sefton MBC*[56]).
- *vessels of all descriptions*: a barge (*Hillen v ICI (Alkali) Ltd*[57]); a ship (*Symonds v Norfolk Lines Ltd*[58]); and a trailer super-structure of the type attached to a lorry (*Bubb v Vanguard Engineering*[59]).

Defective premises

§12.5 Liability under the Occupiers' Liability Acts arises only if the premises are dangerous *and defective*. Premises which are inherently dangerous do not attract the operation of the Acts, if those premises are not *also* defective. Premises are *not* defective, if they are in good repair, and/or operate as intended, and/or have features which are entirely expected and patent (i.e., obvious).

Premises may be inherently dangerous, but that does not, of itself, render them defective. If there was 'nothing wrong' with the state of the premises at which an accident occurred – i.e., the premises were in proper condition, operating as they were meant to, and/or had features which were expected and obvious – then the OLAs will **not** apply. This principle applies, whether the premises are man-made or naturally-occurring. In many of these cases, it was not the premises which were unsafe; what was unsafe was the activity in which C was engaged in, on or around those premises.

[33] [2001] NPC 14. [34] [2009] EWHC 2936 (QB). [35] CA, 1 Jan 1983. [36] [2009] NIQB 56.
[37] [2009] EWHC 3786 (QB). [38] CA, 14 Feb 1989. [39] QB, 14 Mar 2005. [40] CA, 23 Oct 2007.
[41] [2009] EWHC 816 (Admlty). [42] QB, 19 Mar 1991. [43] CA, 12 Dec 2005. [44] [1990] 1 EGLR 161 (QB).
[45] [2015] EWHC 289 (QB). [46] [2004] EWHC 140 (QB). [47] [1997] CLC 698 (QB, Comm).
[48] [2002] EWCA Civ 1656. [49] [2001] EWCA Civ 1837. [50] [2000] ICR 166 (CA). [51] CA, 21 Feb 1997.
[52] [1969] 2 QB 480. [53] CA, 22 May 1990. [54] [2007] All ER (D) 283 (Jun). [55] [2014] UKPC 18.
[56] CA, 23 Feb 2006. [57] [1936] AC 65 (HL). [58] QB, 15 Jun 1990. [59] QB, 17 Jun 1983.

Man-made premises. In the following sample of cases,[60] there was something inherently *dangerous* about the premises, but nothing *defective*, and hence, occupier D could **not** be liable under either OLA:

> In *Ogwo v Taylor*,[61] Mr Taylor, D, occupier of a small terraced house, used a blow lamp to burn off paint from the fascia boards beneath the house eaves, and set fire to the premises. The fire brigade were called. Fireman Mr Ogwo, C, squeezed through a narrow hatch into the roof space with his hose, but suffered serious burns. There was nothing defective about the premises. If D had failed to warn a fireman of the presence of some dangerous chemical or explosive material or other 'unexpected danger or trap', it would be different, but here, the attic, although a dangerous place in which to fight a fire, contained no special hazard. In *Burke v Southern Education and Library Board*,[62] Miss Burke, 15, C, climbed a back school gate in a palisade iron fence, but became impaled on the splayed top of the gate, and seriously injured her left arm. The pales at the front of the school were rounded at the top for aesthetic reasons, but the fences at the back were regarded as more vulnerable to intruders. The gate was not out of repair, it was maintained in good condition. The splayed tops were dangerous due to their pointed tips, but only if someone climbed up onto them, and they contained no hidden dangers. In *Geary v JD Wetherspoon plc*,[63] Ruth Geary, C, attended a work drinks party at a Wetherspoon pub in Newcastle, which had a grand open staircase in the centre, with sweeping banisters on both sides. When leaving, C climbed onto a banister to slide down it, fell backwards onto the marble floor four metres below, and broke her back, suffering tetraplegia. Whilst dangerous, there was nothing defective about the staircase, and the risk of falling off the slippery and slanting surface was obvious. The banister was slightly lower than usual, but the 'waiver' of a recommendation as to height was 'the kind of thing which happens on building projects in the UK every single day'.

Just because a structure (say, a building's flat roof) is high enough so that someone could fall from it and suffer serious injury does not render the premises defective either. The height may make the roof inherently dangerous, but there must be *something further* to make it defective, and render the occupier liable. Similarly, a climbable tree is not defective simply because it can be climbed, and an occupier is under no duty to fence it off (per *Simkiss v Rhondda BC*[64]). On this important point, two cases can be contrasted:

> In *Young v Kent CC*,[65] Master Young, 12, C, attended a youth club at a school which was owned by the Council, D. C was playing football with other children, when the football was kicked or thrown onto the roof of the school building. That block had a flat roof and a number of skylights set into it. C climbed onto the flat roof to retrieve it, jumped on one of the skylights whilst up there as a 'prank', fell through to the floor below, and severely injured himself. The skylight through which he fell was brittle. **Held**: D was liable under OLA 1984. 'The roof was an inherently dangerous place for a child, particularly having regard to the brittle nature of the skylight'.

[60] See too: *McDonagh v Kent AHA* CA, 7 Oct 1985 (O'Connor LJ) (steep staircase; awkward, but not out of repair; no liability).

[61] [1988] AC 431 (CA) 438 (Stephen Brown LJ), 439 (Neill LJ), appeal dismissed.

[62] [2004] NIQB 13, [27].

[63] [2011] EWHC 1506 (QB). Similarly: *Kolasa v Ealing Hosp NHS Trust* [2015] EWHC 289 (QB) [46] (wall above a 10-metre drop to the road below not dangerous or defective; '[w]hat was unsafe was the activity of sitting on the wall').

[64] CA, 22 Feb 1983. [65] [2005] EWHC 1342 (QB) [29], [34] (but 50% CN held).

In *Keown v Coventry Healthcare NHS Trust*,[66] Martyn Keown, 11, C, climbed an external fire escape which ran up the outside of a hospital building in Coventry, while showing off to his sister and her friend. He slipped on a rung, fell about 30 feet to the ground, fractured his arm, and sustained serious brain damage. **Held:** the OLA 1984 did not apply. The fire escape was not dangerous merely because it was high and able to be climbed. If the fire escape had been fragile, in a state of disrepair, or had some structural deficiency, then it would have been arguable that C suffered his injury by reason of dangers due to the state of the premises – but those were not the facts of the case. C's injury was not arising from 'the state of the premises', but from how he chose to use those premises.

In *Keown*, the Court of Appeal (per Longmore LJ) said that any suggestion that the OLA applied in *Young* because a flat roof was inherently dangerous was wrong, but if the judge 'was only saying that a roof with brittle skylights is dangerous premises, [then] that would be less controversial'.[67] In *Siddorn v Patel*,[68] another falling-through-a-skylight case, the skylight was not in a state of disrepair, the premises were not dangerous and defective, and hence, no duty could be imposed upon an occupier under the OLA 1984.

Naturally-occurring features of land. Even if natural features are inherently dangerous, or enable entrants to use them to engage in risky activities, that does not attract liability under the OLAs, absent any defective or latently dangerous features of that land. It follows that there is no obligation upon an occupier, D, to fence off or guard those natural features to stop visitors or trespassers from using them, and doing themselves an injury.

Steep cliffs which allow for rock-climbing or hang-gliding; water-holes which allow for swimming; mountainsides which allow for skiing or mountaineering – all of these features of the land are naturally-occurring, and contain no dangers which cannot be reasonably expected. In *Donoghue v Folkestone Properties Ltd*, Lord Phillips concluded that, regardless of which OLA is applicable, '[i]t does not seem to me that a person carrying on such an activity can ascribe to the "state of the premises" an injury sustained as a result of a mishap in the course of carrying on the activity – provided, of course, that the mishap is not caused by an unusual or latent feature of the landscape'.[69] The following two cases illustrate:

In *Tomlinson v Congleton BC*,[70] John Tomlinson, 18, C, went swimming in a lake in a disused quarry in a country park owned by two local authorities, D. Swimming in the lake was prohibited, and there were prominent warning notices stating, 'Dangerous water: no swimming'. D was aware that the notices were frequently ignored by park visitors, and that several accidents had resulted from swimming in the lake. On a hot day, C entered the lake, stood in shallow water up to his knees, dived from that standing position, and struck his head on the sandy bottom, breaking his neck. D had intended planting vegetation around the shore to prevent people from going into the water, although that had not occurred at the time of the accident, due to a shortage of financial resources. **Held (HL[71]):** arguably, the OLA 1984 did not apply. There was nothing about this lake that made it any more dangerous than any other stretch of open water. C 'suffered his injury because he chose to indulge

[66] [2006] EWCA Civ 39, [12]–[13], [29]. [67] *ibid*, [13]. See too, in separate judgment, [30] (Lewison J).

[68] [2000] EWHC 1248 (QB) [27]. [69] [2003] QB 1008, [2003] EWCA Civ 231, [35].

[70] [2003] UKHL 47, [2004] 1 AC 46, [26]–[29] (Lord Hoffmann), quote at [26], citing Lord Phillips, *ibid*, [53] (but Lord Hoffmann considered the case, assuming that the OLA 1984 did apply). Cf. Lord Hutton's view that the dark and murky water was a 'state of the premises' attracting the OLA 1984's application (at [53], [64]).

[71] The claim failed at first instance, succeeded by a majority in the CA [2002] EWCA Civ 309 (Ward and Sedley LJJ, Longmore LJ dissenting), but failed unanimously on further appeal to HL.

in an activity which had inherent dangers, not because the premises were in a dangerous state'. In *Weir-Rodgers v SF Trust Ltd*,[72] Geraldine Weir-Rodgers, C, was sitting with friends close to a cliff edge, admiring the sunset over the sea. She stood up, slipped on some loose rocky material close to the cliff edge, lost her footing, and fell down the sheer cliff-face into the sea. C suffered severe injuries. **Held:** D was not liable under the equivalent Irish statute. Someone sitting adjacent to a cliff 'must be prepared for oddities in the cliff's structure or in the structure of the ground adjacent to the cliff, and he assumes the inherent risks associated therewith'.

§12.6 Obversely, 'defective' premises – to which the OLAs apply – are those which are out-of-repair, do not operate as intended, or have some feature (whether man-made or naturally-occurring) which is unusual, unexpected, or latent.

In *Donoghue v Folkestone Properties Ltd*,[73] Lord Phillips MR said that the 'obvious situation' in which a duty on an occupier, D, in respect of his premises is likely to arise, is where D knows that an entrant may come across a danger on those premises which is unexpected and latent (i.e., a feature which is not readily discoverable by reasonable inspection). A few samples of leading cases will illustrate:

Man-made premises. If the man-made premises (or a man-made object on the premises) provides latent, unexpected or peculiar dangers, so as to expose the visitor or trespasser to the risk of injury without knowing it, then the OLA 1957 or the OLA 1984 respectively applies, as to potentially render the occupier, D, liable. The OLAs applied in the following cases on that basis:[74]

In *Donoghue v Folkestone Properties Ltd*,[75] Mr Donoghue, 25, C, and an experienced navy diver, attended a Christmas party with friends. He dived from a slipway into Folkestone Harbour shortly after midnight, and struck his head on a grid, or pile, under the water adjacent to the harbour wall. He broke his neck and suffered tetraplegia. The pile was a latent feature which was covered with water when the tide was in, and was not visible in the dark in any event. In *Garner v Walsall Hospitals NHS Trust*,[76] Mr Garner, C, attended an A&E Dept for a cut to his arm, when he slipped on a manhole cover near the hospital carpark, injuring his back. The cover was slightly concaved (probably because of heavy vehicles rolling over it prior to the accident – it was replaced by a stronger cast iron cover after the accident), and some slimy substance had accumulated in that shallow depression in the manhole cover, causing C to slip. The dark slime was not visible or noticeable. In *Harvey v Plymouth CC*,[77] Mr Harvey, C, fell about 5 metres from an open grassy recreational area onto a carpark, by falling through a fence that had been constructed along the edge of the land, but was not securely fixed in the land, which the grass obscured from view.

The latent danger posed by the premises might be very transient and brief – but that will be sufficient to attract the operation of the OLAs.

In *Simpson v A1 Dairies Farms Ltd*,[78] some unknown person set a hay barn on D's farm on fire in the middle of the night. Mr Simpson, C, was a firefighter in the team that responded to the emergency. A drain in the farmyard, which was usually clearly visible, was covered by standing water from the firefighting operations. C stepped into it and twisted his back. **Held**: D was liable under OLA 1957.

[72] [2005] 1 IR 47 (SC) [17]. [73] [2003] EWCA Civ 231, [2003] QB 1008, [33].

[74] See too: *Rae v Mars (UK) Ltd* [1990] 1 EGLR 161 (C fell into pit in a poorly-lit storeroom; 'hazardous and unexpected').

[75] *ibid*, [58]. [76] [2004] EWCA Civ 702. [77] [2009] EWHC 2936 (QB). [78] [2001] NPC 14, [11].

The drain, being obscured from view, was a latent danger, and D ought to have warned the firemen about it.

Naturally-occurring features. Latent and unexpected dangers arising on or in natural premises may also trigger liability under the OLAs.

In *Rhind v Astbury Water Park Ltd*,[79] Jamie Rhind, 20, C, was playing football in a park next to a lake, which was a flooded disused gravel pit. Notices near the lake said: 'Private Property. Strictly NO Swimming Allowed'. The ball went into the water, and to retrieve it, C took a running dive into the shallow water and hit his head on a fibreglass container, which was lying on the bed of the lake, half-covered in silt. C suffered tetraplegia. **Held:** the OLA 1984 applied. This was distinguishable from *Tomlinson*, where C had taken a similar dive in shallow water and hit his head on the lake bottom (coincidentally, situated about five miles from Mr Rhind's accident). Here, the latent danger posed by the container on the lake bed meant the injury was due to 'the state of the premises'.

Premises dangerous to children

§12.7 Premises which would not present any dangers to an adult of full capacity *may* be dangerous and defective for a young child who is less able to appreciate, or to guard against, obvious risks (thereby invoking the application of the OLAs).

Where a young child lacks the capacity to recognise that premises are dangerous, then the OLAs will apply if the premises were *dangerous*, but not necessarily *defective* in the sense described in the previous section. Even if the risks posed by the premises would be obvious to an adult, an occupier can still be liable, because the young child lacked a genuine and informed choice to avoid that risk (per *Tomlinson v Congleton BC*[80]). In fact, in *Tomlinson*, Lord Hoffmann suggested that there could be other scenarios in which C lacked any genuine or informed choice, and may run obvious risks for that reason, *viz*, employees whose work requires them to take the risk; or 'the despair of prisoners which may lead them to inflict injury on themselves'.[81] However, it is the naivety of children with which the case law has principally been engaged.

The point at which premises become dangerous for a child is, according to the Court of Appeal in *Keown v Coventry Healthcare NHS Trust*,[82] 'a question of fact and degree'. Longmore LJ gave the example of a toddler suffering injury who crawls into an empty and derelict house through a very small gap, whilst Lewison J referred to a child's small head being trapped between stair banisters or his small foot being trapped in a lattice walkway. Those banisters or latticework may be in perfectly good repair, and pose no risk to an adult – but it is enough if the premises are dangerous to that child. Two cases may be usefully contrasted:

In *Perry v Butlins Holiday World (t/as Butlins Ltd)*,[83] a young child of 3 fell on top of a very low wall, 36 cm high, cutting his ear badly. **Held**: the premises were dangerous, and D was liable under the OLA 1957. A taller person would not have been injured if he had fallen near the wall, but 'the wall was very low. Apart from very old people, the section of the population most vulnerable to falls is the very young and therefore the very short. The lower the wall, the more likely that a short person will fall on to it or on to its top edge, rather than against its side'.

[79] [2004] EWCA Civ 756, [7]. [80] [2003] UKHL 47, [2004] 1 AC 46, [46] (Lord Hoffmann).
[81] *ibid.* [82] [2006] EWCA Civ 39, [12] (Lewison J), and [31] (Longmore LJ). [83] CA, 28 Nov 1997.

In *Keown*,[84] facts previously, **held:** D was not liable under the OLAs. Martyn Keown, C, was 11 when he climbed and fell off the fire escape. At that age, he appreciated, not only that there was a risk of falling, but also, that what he was doing was dangerous and that he should not have been climbing the exterior of the fire escape.

Precondition #3: The type of danger posed by the premises

§12.8 At common law, a distinction was drawn between the liability of an occupier for the dangerous design, physical features, or state of repair of the premises ('static dangers'), and for dangerous activities which the occupier permitted on the premises ('activity dangers').

At common law, pre-OLA 1957, the law of occupiers' liability – and the graduated duties of care which were owed to different classes of entrant – was restricted to dangers due to 'the state of the premises'. Where the danger arose from activities on the premises, on the other hand, any duty arising was governed by the general rules of negligence, in which those different graduated duties had no role to play.[85]

In *Glasgow City Corp v Muir*,[86] six young children were at D's country mansion tea-room and were buying sweets at the counter. They were scalded when two men, with the manageress's permission, carried a heavy urn of boiling tea through the shop, and accidentally dropped it. **Held**: this concerned an activity danger, and not a danger to do with the state of the premises (the latter would have meant an enquiry as to D's duty to these children as invitees). D was not liable in negligence, because the manageress was not required to clear the children out during the urn's transit through the shop, or take any other precautionary steps, to guard them against scalding.

The debate about 'occupancy' versus 'activity' dangers under the OLAs

§12.9 Although the matter is not free from doubt, the better view is that the OLAs govern the liability of an occupier in relation to static (i.e., occupancy) dangers, but do not govern the occupier's liability in relation to 'activity dangers'. Rather, the latter must be addressed under the ordinary principles of negligence.

Section 1(1) of the OLA 1957 provides that the purpose of the Act is to replace the common law rules of occupiers' liability, so as 'to regulate' the duty which an occupier owes to his visitors 'in respect of dangers *due to* the state of the premises or to *things done or omitted to be done on them*'. Section 1(1)(a) of the OLA 1984 uses the same wording: the Act 'shall have effect, in place of the rules of the common law, to determine whether any duty is owed by [an occupier] ... by reason of any danger *due to* the state of the premises or to *things done or omitted to be done on them*'.

However, whether these provisions encompass **both** static and activity dangers is somewhat uncertain. Judicial opinion was divided in *Tomlinson v Congleton BC*[87] – and other decisions have reflected this:

[84] [2006] EWCA Civ 39, [12], [29].

[85] See: *Fairchild v Glenhaven Funeral Services Ltd* [2001] EWCA Civ 1881, [113]–[121]; and *Jones v BBC* [2007] All ER (D) 283 (Jun) [148]. Earlier: *London v Graving Dock Co Ltd v Horton* [1951] AC 737 (HL) 745, 752, 776–77; and *Abbott v Dunster* [1954] 1 WLR 58 (CA) 62.

[86] [1943] AC 448 (HL) 463–64.

[87] [2003] UKHL 47, [2004] 1 AC 46.

View #1: activity dangers are covered. On the face of the italicised wording above, the OLAs appear to apply to both static **and** activity dangers.

This view is also judicially supported. According to Lord Hobhouse in *Tomlinson*,[88] the Acts cover both dangers, so that if shooting, or speed boats in swimmers' areas, are permitted on occupier D's premises and injure entrants there, then one or other of the Acts potentially applies. Further, in *Stimpson v Wolverhampton MBC*,[89] where a visitor to the Council's public park was hit in the mouth by a golf ball while walking through the park where golf was prohibited, the Council owed a duty of care under the OLA 1957 because the hitting of golf balls (i.e., an activity) was a possible danger to park visitors. In *Revill v Newbery*,[90] Evans LJ expressly reserved his opinion as to whether the OLAs could apply where an occupier was carrying out activities on his land, while the view that the OLAs cover occupancy and activity dangers has been followed in first-instance decisions since *Tomlinson* (e.g., *Poppleton v Trustees of Portsmouth Youth Activities Committee*[91]).

View #2: only static dangers are covered. If Parliament's intention, when enacting the OLA, was to reproduce the common law position – and s 1(2) suggests this, in that the OLA 1957 'will not alter the rules of the common law as to the persons on whom a duty is imposed' – then only static dangers were governed by the common law of occupiers' liability. Furthermore, s 2(2) refers to 'care ... to see that the visitor will be reasonably safe in using the premises', again indicating that only static dangers are covered. This is explicable, given that, as the Privy Council affirmed recently in 2014, the OLA 1957 had a very specific purpose, *viz*, to 'replace different levels of duty towards different classes of visitor by a uniform "common duty of care" to all lawful visitors' (per *Shtern v Cummings (Jamaica)*[92]). It only had to achieve this for static dangers, because the graduated duties only applied for those types of dangers.

There is a deal of judicial support for this view. In *Tomlinson*, a majority of the Lords considered that the only risk to Mr Tomlinson arose out of what he chose to do when diving into the lake, and not out of the state of the lake,[93] and hence, there was no static danger which could give rise to a duty on the occupier's part under the OLAs. In *Revill v Newbery*,[94] Neill LJ also held that the ordinary principles of negligence, and not the OLA 1984, applied wherever an occupier was doing dangerous activities on his land. Since *Tomlinson*, differently-constituted Courts of Appeal have preferred this second view too – e.g., in *Keown v Coventry NHS Trust*,[95] '[i]f an adult or a child chose to create danger by climbing [drain pipes or trees], any such danger was due to such person's activity, not the state of the premises', and hence, the OLAs could not apply; in *Bottomley v Todmorden Cricket Club*,[96] Brooke LJ held that, 'the OLA 1957 was concerned only to replace the old common law rules relating to the occupancy duties of an occupier'; and in *Fairchild v Glenhaven Funeral Services Ltd*, the Court said that Act's wording is 'a fairly strong indication that Parliament intended the Act to be concerned with what used

[88] *ibid*, [69]. His Lordship disagreed with other members of the House on this particular point, but agreed with the result.

[89] CA, 22 May 1990. [90] [1996] QB 567 (CA) 579.

[91] [2007] EWHC 1567 (QB) [38]. The trial judge's findings of breach were overruled on appeal, but the CA did not address comment to this aspect of the trial judge's decision.

[92] [2014] UKPC 18, [17].

[93] [2003] UKHL 47, [2004] 1 AC 46, [27] (Lord Hoffmann, with whom Lords Nicholls and Scott agreed).

[94] [1996] QB 567 (CA) 575–76.

[95] [2006] EWCA Civ 39, [2006] 1 WLR 953, [28] (Lewison J), and [7], [9] (Longmore LJ).

[96] [2003] EWCA Civ 1575, [31].

to be described as "occupancy liability".'[97] First-instance decisions have followed that view too (e.g., *Siddorn v Patel*[98]).

Any significance?

Does it make any legal or practical difference to occupier D, whether activity dangers are treated under the OLAs or under the ordinary duty of care imposed by the law of negligence?

Where injured visitors are concerned, the answer seems to be 'no'. In *Makepeace v Evans Bros (Reading)*,[99] Mantell LJ observed that it was 'of no practical importance, save possibly as a pleading point', while the Court of Appeal stated, in *McCook v Lobo*,[100] that it is 'inappropriate and unnecessary to treat potential liability at common law ... as distinguishable from the common duty of care owed by an occupier of premises under the OLA 1957, unless a distinct simultaneous duty also arises: for example, from the relationship of employer and employee'. For activity dangers on D's premises, a duty of care will inevitably be owed at common law, due to the 'closeness in time and space' between the occupier and the entrant who suffered the injury. Moreover, the standard of care expected of an occupier is the same, whether under the OLA 1957's common duty of care or under negligence's reasonable standard (discussed later in the chapter[101]).

Insofar as trespassers are concerned, it would seem to make little difference either. If the trespasser was injured by reason of the occupier's activity, then even if the OLA 1984 did not apply, it will nevertheless 'guide' the application of the ordinary principles of negligence to that scenario. This was confirmed by the Court of Appeal in *Revill v Newbery*.[102] Where the occupier slept in his shed in order to protect his property at night from vandals and thieves, and shot a burglar attempting to enter the shed only intending to frighten him and not to shoot him, negligence succeeded against the occupier (subject to contributory negligence). In so finding, Neill LJ (with whom the other members agreed) confirmed that the provisions governing the imposition of a duty of care and the standard of care in the 1984 Act were 'very helpful in defining the scope of the duty owed at common law to an intruder who comes on premises in the middle of the night', and that 'the question of liability at common law is to be determined on the same lines as if one were considering a breach of duty under s 1 [of the OLA 1984]'.

Admittedly, the dividing line between activity and static dangers can be very finely-drawn:

In *Fairchild v Glenhaven Funeral Services Ltd*,[103] John Hussey, C, died from mesothelioma, having spent about two years being exposed to asbestos dust and fibre while working at the Barking and Battersea Power Stations in the early 1950s. He worked as a welder for Babcock, specialist suppliers of boilers and associated pipework, at the power stations, during which time the boilers and pipework were lagged with asbestos material (by other unidentifiable contractors employed at these enormous sites). Several hundred tonnes of lagging material would be used in a typical power station at that time, and there was a great deal of asbestos dust or fibre in the atmosphere when the lagging work was carried out. C's allegations of wrongdoing related to the dust raised in the course of those lagging activities. **Held**: this concerned an activity, and not a static, danger; it was 'not concerned with Mr Hussey suffering injury from something in the static condition of those two power stations which posed an unusual danger'.

[97] [2001] EWCA Civ 1881, [2002] 1 WLR 1052, [129]. [98] [2007] EWHC 1248 (QB) [21].
[99] [2001] ICR 241(CA) [7]. [100] [2002] EWCA Civ 1760, [12]. [101] See pp 609–13.
[102] [1996] QB 567 (CA) 575–76. [103] [2001] EWCA Civ 1881, [2002] 1 WLR 1052 (CA) [120], [149].

Ultimately, the practical effect of the difference is how to frame the appropriate cause of action. Where C cannot base his case on a danger due to 'the state of the premises', no claim under the OLAs can possibly be made. C must then point to *some activity on the occupier's part which was conducted negligently* – or, indeed, to *some other cause of action altogether*, such as breach of statutory duty (as in, e.g., *Swift v Yorkshire Electricity Group plc*,[104] where a successful action was brought by a visitor under reg 9 of the Electricity Supply Regulations 1937, which required that outdoor electricity substations be fenced or otherwise protected, 'so as to prevent access to the electric lines and apparatus therein by any unauthorised person'). This will typically depend upon whether the occupier, D, assumed responsibility for the entrant's safety in all the circumstances (on an objective basis), and whether there was a corresponding reliance by the entrant on D (per *Risk v College*[105]), although sometimes the tri-partite *Caparo* test will be employed in the alternative, by which to seek to establish that the occupier owed C a duty of care (per *Yates v National Trust*[106]). The success in bringing a claim against an occupier in ordinary negligence, for an activity danger, has been very mixed:

In *Geary v JD Wetherspoons plc*, facts previously, this was an obvious danger to which the OLA 1984 did not apply. Further, nothing about the events in the pub that night showed that D assumed any responsibility to C, who slid down the banisters. If D had organised banister-sliding competitions, there may well have been an assumption of responsibility, but those were not these facts. **However,** in *Fowles v Bedfordshire CC*,[107] Mr Fowles, C, attended a gym centre owned by the Council, D, and on his first visit, received some instruction as to the use of gym mats for forward somersaults. However, he was not made sufficiently aware of the dangers of uncontrolled rolls, and was not told to use the mats only with supervision. On another occasion, C used the mats with a friend without supervision, and suffered serious injury. Here, D had assumed responsibility to C, giving rise to a duty of care at common law, because D assumed the task of teaching and advising C about the mats, failed to do that adequately; and gave C unrestricted access to the crash mats without warning him of the need for supervision.

WHICH ACT APPLIES?

An entrant, C, would **always** prefer to be within the bounds of the OLA 1957, rather than the OLA 1984. An occupier, D, automatically owes a duty of care ('the common duty of care') to *all* his visitors (as defined in s 2(1), OLA 1957), and the question at issue is whether D has discharged, or breached, that duty. On the other hand, the first question under the OLA 1984 is whether the occupier owes a duty of care to the trespasser *at all*. If any of the three prerequisites for a duty of care under that Act is not satisfied (and case law confirms that they are quite hard to satisfy), then no duty is owed.[108]

Moreover, under the OLA 1957, the common duty of care requires the occupier to do whatever is reasonable to see that his visitor would be reasonably safe in using the premises. On the other hand, re trespassers, the query is whether the danger was one against which, in all the circumstances, the occupier might reasonably have been expected to offer the trespasser **some** protection. Breach is harder to establish. As Lord Phillips MR stated in *Donoghue v Folkestone*

[104] CA, 7 Nov 1997. [105] [2013] EWHC 3869 (QB) [104]–[109] (liability was not proven).
[106] [2014] EWHC 222 (QB) [52] (liability was not proven). [107] [1995] PIQR P380 (CA).
[108] See, under the Northern Ireland statute: *Burke v Sthn Education and Library Bd* [2004] NIQB 13, [27] (Higgins J).

Properties Ltd, the duty of care imposed under OLA 1984 'is significantly less exacting' than the common duty of care imposed under OLA 1957.[109]

Wherever C enters D's premises under a statutory power of entry – say, a fire officer (*Simpson v Al Dairies Farms Ltd*[110]), a police officer, or an electricity meter-reader (*Jordan v Achara*[111]) – he is treated as a lawful visitor (per s 2(6), OLA 1957), whether or not D agrees to that visitor being on his land.

Visitors versus trespassers

A 'visitor' is described, in s 1(2) of the OLA 1957, as 'the same ... as the persons who would at common law be treated as ... invitees or licensees'. For the purposes of the OLA 1984, persons within its bounds (i.e., trespassers) are 'persons other than his visitors' (per s1(1)). At common law, a trespasser was defined as 'one who goes on [D's] land without invitation of any sort, and whose presence is either unknown to [D] or, if known, is practically objected to' (per *Robert Addie & Sons (Colleries) Ltd v Dumbreck*[112]).

The reference in s 1(2) to the common law harks back to the meaning of a 'visitor' which applied, prior to the OLA 1957, when there was a variety of types of lawful 'visitors' (per *Robert Addie*[113]). Different duties were owed to each class – stricter or looser – depending upon the type of entrant:

Type of entrant (in descending order of importance) – and the relevant duty owed by the occupier	Example
the contractual entrant – a duty to make the premises reasonably fit and safe for the purpose required by the contract	where a member of a club enters the club premises, given that the Constitution is the contract between the body corporate and each member (per *Gesner v Wallingford Labour Party Supporters' Assn Club*[a])
an invitee, who has some economic interest in being on the premises, shared with the occupier – a duty to exercise reasonable care to prevent damage arising from unusual dangers which he knows or ought to know exist	someone who enters a cinema to see a movie or who enters a shop to buy some clothes
an express licensee, who has no mutual economic interest in being on the premises, but who is expressly permitted by the occupier to be there – a duty to warn of concealed dangers of which the occupier knows, and to act with reasonable care to prevent the premises from misleading or entrapping the licensee	someone who is invited to the occupier's home as a party guest, someone visiting church, or a pupil attending school

[a] CA, 26 May 1994 (Hobhouse and Hoffmann LJJ) (no pp available).

[109] [2003] EWCA Civ 231, [2003] QB 1008, [31]. [110] [2001] EWCA Civ 13.
[111] CA, 14 Mar 1988. [112] [1929] AC 358 (HL) (Viscount Dunedin).
[113] *ibid*. For the examples and duties given in the Table, see, e.g.: Irish LRC, *Occupiers' Liability* (Rep 46, 1994) [2.1].

Type of entrant (in descending order of importance) – and the relevant duty owed by the occupier	Example
an implied licensee, who has no express invitation to be on the premises – as for express licensees	someone enticed onto the premises by an allurement, or who is habitually on the premises without any express consent to be there and which the occupier knows about but does not prevent
a trespasser – a duty not to either wilfully/intentionally or recklessly harm the trespasser, and to treat him with 'ordinary humanity'	anyone who should not be on the premises – e.g., young children, burglars, people taking a shortcut

On the recommendation of the English Law Reform Committee (*Third Report: Occupiers' Liability to Invitees, Licensees and Trespassers*) in 1954,[114] these categories were amalgamated within the designated class of 'visitor', to whom an occupier owes a *single* common duty of care under the OLA 1957. The Law Committee (with the notable exception of Kenneth Diplock QC, later Lord Diplock) rejected the complex and technical distinctions ('the old Byzantine distinctions', as Brooks LJ termed them[115]) which depended upon the type of entrant. Some judges were delighted by the reform. In *Roles v Nathan*, Lord Denning remarked that the OLA 1957 'has been very beneficial. It has rid us of those two unpleasant characters, the invitee and the licensee, who haunted the courts for years, and it has replaced them by the attractive figure of a visitor, who has so far given no trouble at all'.[116]

However, the categorisation between visitor and trespasser has become somewhat complicated, in that some entrants who appear to be lawful visitors can take on the mantle of a trespasser by their behaviour, whilst some who appear to be unlawful visitors can claw their way into the more comfortable confines of the OLA 1957 by proving that they were implied licensees. Each scenario is considered in turn:

Downgrading a 'visitor' to trespasser status

§12.10 If the visitor *enters/uses* the occupier's premises in the manner intended, but then exceeds the bounds of permission by not using the premises as permitted when the accident occurred, the visitor will be treated as a trespasser.

According to s 2(2) of the OLA 1957, the common duty of care is imposed upon the occupier to ensure that a visitor 'will be reasonably safe in using the premises for the purpose for which he is invited or permitted by the occupier to be there'. Hence, once the entrant transgresses the bounds of permission, the OLA 1984, and not the OLA 1957, applies. The metaphor given by Scrutton LJ in *The Carlgarth* illustrates well: '[w]hen you invite a person into your house to use

[114] (1954) (Cmd 9305). [115] *Donoghue v Folkestone Properties Ltd* [2003] QB 1008, [2003] EWCA Civ 231, [60].
[116] [1963] 1 WLR 1117 (CA) 1122.

the staircase, you do not invite him to slide down the banisters, you invite him to use the staircase in the ordinary way in which it is used'.[117] (The tragic facts of *Geary v JD Wetherspoons plc*, mentioned previously, exemplified that metaphor in 'real life'.)

A few examples show how a visitor can 'slide down the banisters' from the OLA 1957 to OLA 1984:

Visitors who become trespassers

Scenario	Case example
Where a tenant of leased premises enters a part of the building which is not within those leased premises and which the landlord had not given authority to the tenant to access	In *Siddorn v Patel,*[a] Miss Siddorn, C, went up to the flat garage roof after dark, with friends, in order to dance. She accessed the roof through a bedroom window which was in the leased premises, but the roof was not. C inadvertently stepped on a skylight on the roof, plunged through it, and sustained serious head and orthopaedic injuries.
Where a visitor lawfully enters premises, but then does something which (albeit not expressly unauthorised) goes beyond the bounds of his permission to be there	In *Keown v Coventry Healthcare NHS Trust,*[b] facts previously, Martyn Keown's access to the hospital grounds was permitted, as a thoroughfare between streets, but no permission was given to climb the fire escape. (Note: it was also suggested that C may *always* have been a trespasser, because children were not permitted to play in the grounds at all.) In *Kolasa v Ealing Hosp NHS Trust,*[c] Slawomir Kolasa, C, was taken to a hospital A&E department for treatment, after being attacked. In between being seen by medical staff, C went outside and sat on a concrete wall edging a roadway used by ambulances. C fell off the wall into the road 10 metres below, and suffered serious spinal injuries. C was a legal visitor to the hospital when he was brought to A&E, but his act of climbing on the wall was not an act covered by his general permission to be on the hospital site as a patient.
Where a visitor has permission to enter and use a building or grounds, except for a part of the building or grounds to which access or use has been expressly forbidden (orally or in writing), and he	In *Hillen v ICI (Alkali) Ltd,*[d] stevedores were unloading a barge, and walked onto an inadequately-supported hatch cover to unload some of the cargo. The barge owner had clearly told them not to do that. In *Tomlinson v Congleton BC*[e] and *Rhind v Astbury Water Park Ltd,*[f] two young men ignored the respective occupiers' clear

[a] [2007] EWHC 1248 (QB).
[b] [2006] EWCA Civ 39, [3] (Longmore LJ).
[c] [2015] EWHC 289 (QB) [42].
[d] [1936] AC 65 (HL) 69–70 (Lord Atkin).
[e] [2003] UKHL, [2004] 1 AC 46.
[f] [2004] EWCA Civ 756, [4] (Latham LJ, quoting trial judge at [55]).

[117] [1927] P 93, 110 (Scrutton LJ).

Scenario	Case example
nevertheless accesses/uses the excluded part. However, if any written signs were either ambiguous, misleading a reasonable person in the visitor's position to believe that access was not forbidden; or not prominently visible, then he would remain a lawful visitor	and unambiguous warning notices (e.g., 'Dangerous Water. No Swimming', in *Tomlinson*, and 'Strictly No Swimming Allowed' in *Rhind*), and entered the water to swim/dive (in *Rhind*, those who paddled or lay in the shallows would be visitors, but at the point of diving, would become trespassers). In *Darby v The National Trust*,[g] Kevin Darby, C, drowned in a pond at Hardwick Hall one warm August night, while playing a game of 'hide-e-boo' in the centre of the pond with his young children. The water was described as murky and cold. There were no warning notices around the pond, but there was a small notice at the carpark entrance which gave information on opening hours, charges, etc, and also said, 'Bathing and boating not allowed', in legible but inconspicuous lettering. C was treated as a visitor to the grounds.
Where a person has permission to visit premises for a set period of time, and exceeds that time	In *Stone v Taffe*,[h] Mr Taffe, a publican, D, invited some friends to a pub for a party. At 10.30 pm, the licence for serving alcohol expired. The party continued until after 1.00 am. Mr Stone, C, a guest at the pub, fell down stairs which were in total darkness, and died. The only reason that C remained a visitor was that D, as occupier's employee, did not clearly delimit the time to the guests, and there was no calling of time or any other indication that the party had ended. Had that occurred, then after that time, C would have been a trespasser on the premises.

[g] [2001] EWCA Civ 189, [2001] PIQR P17 (CA) [10].
[h] [1974] 1 WLR 1575 (CA) 1583 (Megaw LJ).

Of course, merely because there has been an accident involving the visitor's use of the occupier's premises does not mean that the visitor exceeded those bounds. The injured visitor may have been using the premises exactly as they were intended to be used.

In *Poppleton v Trustees of the Portsmouth Youth Activities Committee*,[118] Gary Poppleton, 25, C, visited a leisure centre at Portsmouth, operated by D, to engage in 'bouldering', which is simulated rock-climbing without ropes. C, a relatively inexperienced climber, mimicked a move by a friend, and attempted a risky leap from a wall, somersaulting in the air and falling onto the matting below (a 'dyno move'). C landed on his head, and suffered tetraplegia. **Held:** the OLA 1984 did not apply, because C was not a trespasser. There was nothing wrong with the premises, the simulated climbing wall was used just as it was intended.

[118] [2008] EWCA Civ 646, [2009] PIQR P1, [7] (May LJ).

Upgrading a 'trespasser' to visitor status

Given that trespassers were owed such a minimal duty of care at common law, given that occupiers would rarely act with intentional or reckless malevolence towards them, and given that the 'ordinary humanity' standard was so nebulous, the trespasser charted very unsympathetic legal waters. Hence, trespassers frequently sought to be treated as implied licensees, because then an occupier owed a somewhat higher duty, rendering a breach easier to prove (see Table at pp 602–3). Traditionally, at common law, there were two principal ways in which a trespasser could achieve this. The first applied exclusively to child entrants via the doctrine of allurement, while the second – proof that the trespasser was an implied licensee – was of more general application. It remains debatable whether, post-OLA, either of these has a role to play in the modern law of occupiers' liability.

The doctrine of allurement

§12.11 An occupier who permitted an allurement to exist on his premises gave an implied licence to child trespassers to enter those premises, thus rendering the child a lawful visitor (i.e. a licensee) at common law. Whether the doctrine applies under the OLA 1957 remains somewhat unsettled.

An allurement has been judicially described as something that 'combine[s] the properties of temptation and retribution as to be properly called a trap'.[119] Under the doctrine, alluring things can be inanimate or living. They have included, e.g., a dangerous piece of machinery such as a turntable (*Cooke v Midland Great Western Rwy of Ireland*,[120] where the trespassing boy, 4, fell from the turntable while playing and died); or an open cellar where painting was going on, protected at ground level by a flimsy bar against which a child leant over, and fell through it into the cellar (*Jewson v Gatti*[121]); and a shrub with poisonous berries growing in the Botanic Gardens in Glasgow (*Glasgow City Corp v Taylor*,[122] where a young boy, 7, died from eating them).

Does the doctrine still apply, post-OLA, to assist a child trespasser? There are contrasting viewpoints:

View #1: the doctrine has no place in modern occupiers' liability law. Given that the trespasser benefits from a more generous duty under the OLA 1984 than applied at common law, there is less need for the doctrine to apply. Moreover, in *Keown v Coventry Healthcare NHS Trust*,[123] Lewison J (in the Court of Appeal) disparaged the doctrine, calling it 'a throw-back to [an] old idea'. The fact that the fire escape was attractive to children, because of the challenge and the dare of climbing it, did not alter C's status as a trespasser.

View #2: the doctrine continues to have relevance in modern occupiers' liability law. The doctrine continues to receive judicial endorsement in post-OLA cases. For example, in *Swain v Puri*, McCowan LJ noted that, '[i]t is ... important that there was, in this case, no allurements to children present on the [occupier's] land'.[124] In *Burke v Southern Education and Library Board*,[125] a case decided under the equivalent Northern Ireland statute, the

119 *Latham v R Johnson & Nephew Ltd* [1913] 1 KB 398 (CA) 416 (Hamilton LJ).

120 [1909] AC 229 (HL) 241–42 (Lord Collins).

121 (1886) 2 TLR 381.

122 [1922] 1 AC 44 (HL) 50 (Lord Buckmaster), albeit that this was not a case of trespass, as the shrub was growing in the open gardens.

123 [2006] EWCA Civ 39, [32].

124 [1996] PIQR 442 (CA) 450 (another falling-through-a-skylight case).

125 [2004] NIQB 13, [27].

High Court held that a palisade iron fence was not an allurement, thus signifying that the doctrine may still have some status. Moreover, the wording of s 2(1) is odd. The definition of 'visitor' refers to the common law definition of a visitor – which included an implied licensee who achieved that status via the doctrine of allurement. It would have been easy enough for the Legislature to exclude the doctrine, if it had so wished. Furthermore, although a child trespasser is better protected now under the OLA 1984 than he was at common law, it is by no means automatic that he will be owed a duty under that Act (and, even if he is, the standard of care expected of the occupier will not be as high as it is under the OLA 1957). Hence, the doctrine of allurement still provides some legal attractiveness (no pun intended!).

The former view appears, to this author, to be the better one, albeit that it is one of the unsatisfactory features of the OLA 1957 that this issue continues to pose uncertainties in the law of occupiers' liability.

An implied licence to enter

§12.12 An implied licence arose at common law where the occupier granted no express permission to an entrant to use/enter his premises, but impliedly permitted the trespasser's presence. The doctrine has since been applied under the OLA 1957.

The rule of an implied licence was developed because not all trespassers were perceived to be alike: young children were not 'in the same bag as burglars or poachers', as the Court of Appeal put it in *Videan v British Transport Commn.*[126] This (said the Court) prompted 'the shifts to which generations of judges have been put, to escape the rule. They have, time and again, turned a trespasser into a licensee so as to give him a remedy for negligence when otherwise he would have none'.

According to *Phipps v Rochester Corp*,[127] an occupier who resigns himself to the occasional presence of trespassers on his premises, or who does not fence his land or keep his gate closed against trespassers, does not convert that trespasser into a licensee. On the other hand, an implied permission can be carved out where the occupier knew that trespassers used or entered the occupier's premises frequently, and did not take steps to stop that. The dividing line between implied permission (which elevates the trespasser to visitor status) and mere toleration (whereby the trespasser remains just that) may be quite blurred, but it is a matter of degree – as Lord Dunedin said, in *Robert Addie v Dumbreck*, the toleration must be so blatant as to amount to a permission and an implied licence.[128]

> In *Cooke v Midland Great Western Rwy of Ireland*,[129] the railway company, D, kept a dangerous turntable on their land close to a public road. D knew that children were in the habit of playing on the turntable, and that they could obtain easy access through a well-worn gap in a fence. D were bound by statute to maintain that fence. Master Cooke, 4, C, was seriously injured on the turntable whilst playing on it. **Held:** C was an implied licensee, not a trespasser. He played on the turntable frequently, with the tacit permission of the railway company. (The doctrine of allurement also applied, as mentioned above.)

[126] [1963] 2 QB 650 (CA) 663.

[127] [1955] 1 QB 450 (QB) 455–56 (Devlin J, citing: *Salmond on Torts* (11th edn) 571) (trespasser held to be a licensee).

[128] [1929] AC 358 (HL) 372.

[129] [1909] AC 229 (HL) 235, 240, 241. Also: *Lowery v Walker* [1911] AC 10 (HL) (trespasser also a licensee).

That an implied licence can *still* be used as a legal device by which trespassers can gain 'access' to the OLA 1957 received obiter approval by differently-constituted Courts of Appeal in *Maloney v Torfaen CBC*[130] and in *Harvey v Plymouth CC*[131] (the attempt failed in both cases). It was accepted in both cases that, post-OLA 1957, an occupier could confer an implied licence by conduct, but it would be a question of fact, in light of the circumstances at the time of the accident.

In *Maloney v Torfaen CBC*, Mr Maloney, C, took a shortcut from a pub to his flat late at night, across a sloping grass bank owned and occupied by the Council, D. C slipped and fell from the unfenced bank onto a concrete pedestrian subway next to the bank, and suffered significant brain damage. C claimed that he was crossing the grassy bank as an implied licensee, given that there was a well-worn path on the bank, indicating regular use. **Held** (at trial, aff'd on appeal): there was no implied licence to use the embankment as a footpath. Photographic evidence did not support well-worn usage; no evidence was called from other residents of nearby housing estates that they commonly used the embankment as a shortcut; and neither of the two previous accidents at this spot had involved using the grass bank to gain access to the flats. Hence, there were no grounds for implying that D consented to a tenant of the flats in C's position walking on the bank, late at night, as a means of getting home.

Having determined whether the preconditions for the OLAs to apply are met, and if so, which Act applies to the scenario, it is necessary to assess whether the cause of action is made out. Dealing with each Act in turn:

VISITORS UNDER THE OCCUPIERS' LIABILITY ACT 1957

This section will deal principally with the statutory incursions which are made upon the ordinary negligence action by the OLA 1957.

A duty of care toward a visitor

To reiterate, an occupier owes any lawful visitor a 'common duty of care', by virtue of s 2(2) of the OLA 1957, 'to take such care as in all the circumstances of the case is reasonable to see that the visitor will be reasonably safe in using the premises for the purposes for which he is invited or permitted by the occupier to be there'.

An implied contractual term

§12.13 The common duty of care is automatically implied in any contract between an occupier and a contractual visitor (per s 5, OLA 1957).

In *Maguire v Sefton MBC*, the Court of Appeal noted that 'authority on the workings of s 5 barely exists'.[132] However (it said), the implication of that common duty of care has the following legal consequences:

- the purpose of s 5, according to *Sole v WJ Hallt Ltd*,[133] was to reduce the higher duty which an occupier owed to a contractual visitor at common law, and to equate contractual entrants with

[130] [2005] EWCA Civ 1762, [25]. [131] [2009] EWHC 2936 (QB) [17]–[28]. [132] [2006] EWCA Civ 316, [16].
[133] [1973] QB 574, 578 (Swanwick LJ), and cited in *Maguire v Sefton MBC* [2006] EWCA Civ 316, [19].

other lawful visitors. Under pre-OLA 1957 case law, an occupier was under a *stricter* duty to ensure that its premises were 'reasonably fit for purpose' (e.g., in *Francis v Cockrell*,[134] the visitor bought a ticket for a seat on a structure at a public exhibition, and it contained an implied term that the structure should be reasonably fit for purpose).

- it is **not** open to a court, in light of s 5, to imply a term into the contract which imposes upon the occupier a *stricter* standard of care than the common duty of care requires.

  In *Maguire v Sefton MBC*,[135] Paul Maguire, C, suffered an accident on an exercise machine which he was using at a leisure centre operated by the Council, D. C successfully sued the machine's manufacturer (Precor) in negligence, but the question was whether he could succeed against D under the OLA 1957. C paid £20 per month for his subscription to D's leisure facility. The trial judge implied a term into the contract between C and D that 'any machine that C was to use on the premises was safe to be used'. **Held**: this implied term was too strict (i.e., absolute) to comply with the common duty of care, and was struck out. All that s 2 required was that D would see that the exercise machine would be reasonably safe.

- in most cases in which an entrant visits an occupier's premises pursuant to a contractual right of entry, nothing will turn on the term implied by s 5, because the common duty of care arises on the occupier's part under the OLA in any event (a point noted in *Wattleworth v Goodwood Road Racing Co Ltd*,[136] where the user of the circuit, who was killed when his car hit a tyre-bank on a bend, entered the racing circuit pursuant to a contract of hire, and hence, the common duty of care was an implied term of that contract).

A duty to take positive steps

Section 2(2) of the OLA 1957 states that the occupier, D, must take reasonable steps to '**see** that the visitor is safe' (emphasis added). It follows (per *Proctor v Young, Coleraine BC*[137]) that the common duty of care is more than a duty to avoid negligent acts – it compels D to exercise reasonable care to fix omissions. Hence, D must take reasonable steps to protect his visitors from dangers which he did not himself create.

The requisite standard of care

§12.14 The common duty of care under s 2(2) requires D to meet the standard of reasonable care. It is *not* a strict or absolute standard of care.

The common duty of care is **not** a duty to ensure that there are no defects or hazards on the premises; nor is it a guarantee that the visitor will be safe when entering or using the premises – those articulations are too strict and absolute (per *West Sussex CC v Pierce*[138]). The requisite standard is one of reasonableness. It was not the intention of the OLA 1957 to cast a more onerous obligation on the occupier than did the common law at its highest (per *Cole v Davies-Gilbert*[139]). This principle has been evident, in the retail and workplace scenarios, as the following duo of cases shows, respectively, in which **neither** of the relevant occupiers was liable under the OLA 1957:[140]

[134] (1869–70) LR 5 QB 501, 509–10. [135] [2006] EWCA Civ 316, [19]–[24]. [136] [2004] EWHC 140, [96].
[137] [2009] NIQB 56, [48]. [138] [2013] EWCA Civ 1230, [18].
[139] [2007] EWCA Civ 396, [34]. See too: *Proctor v Young* [2009] NIQB 56, [47].
[140] See too: *Burns v Thamesdown BC* (CA, 14 Nov 1991, Lloyd LJ) (clock dislodged from wall; no liability).

In *Laverton v Kiapasha (t/as Takeaway Supreme)*,[141] a customer, C, slipped on a wet floor in shop-keeper D's takeaway food shop. However, the law does not insist that the floor be kept dry, regardless of the weather and of customers walking in water: '[t]o suggest otherwise [as was held at trial] is a counsel of perfection imposing a near strict liability which the law does not at present do'.[142] Precautionary steps could have been taken (mopping up constantly, closing the shop in wet weather), but these were aimed at meeting strict liability, not the standard expected of the shop-keeper by the OLA 1957. In *Fryer v Pearson*,[143] Mr Fryer, a gas fitter, C, visited the home of the Pearsons, D, to fit a new gas fire. C laid out a dust-sheet in front of the hearth of the fire, but knelt on the carpet to the side of the fire to inspect the fire that he was taking out. A needle entered his knee, and permanently remained there despite surgery. The presence of a needle on carpet in a home did not mean that the Pearsons were in breach of their common duty of care to C. How the needle came to be there was unclear, but given the evidence that Mrs Pearson vacuumed every day, and did not sew in that room because of its poor light, there was no liability on D's part.

However, certain matters will impact upon that standard of care, where lawful visitors are injured on an occupier's premises.

§12.15 The precautionary steps expected of a reasonable occupier, in order to meet the relevant standard of care:

- may be more onerous, where the visitor is a child (per s 2(3)(a), OLA 1957), but subject to important qualifications;
- may be less onerous, if the occupier is a joint occupier whose extent of control of the premises is less than another occupier's.

Some matters, however, do not affect the standard of care (e.g., where the visitor was a member of the emergency services, or where the occupier is a charitable organisation).

Child entrants

According to s 2(3)(a) of the OLA 1957, an occupier must be prepared for child visitors to be less careful than adults. This puts an onus on the occupier to take more precautionary steps than he would take to reasonably safeguard an adult. The provision has been teased out by some (at times, difficult-to-reconcile) judicial treatment and qualifications.

- where the occupier, D, can reasonably expect that the child **would** be accompanied to the premises and/or supervised by a parent or guardian – and the danger to the child is one that would be obvious to that parent or guardian – then it is not necessary for D to take precautionary steps to reasonably protect the child, as if he were unaccompanied or unsupervised. In other words, where the presence of a parent or guardian was reasonably expected, then the standard of care is not elevated by reason of s 2(3)(a), and a breach will be more difficult to prove against that occupier, D, because a *reasonable* occupier would not be required to take whatever precautionary steps would have been necessary to protect an unaccompanied child (per Devlin J in *Phipps v Rochester Corp*[144]). As noted in *Smyth v Smyth*,[145] the age of the child will dictate whether some parental supervision was required in the circumstances (the child was 12 there,

[141] [2002] EWCA Civ 1656. [142] [2002] EWCA Civ 1656, [23].
[143] (CA, 15 Mar 2000) [7]. [144] [1955] 1 QB 450, 472, a pre-OLA case.
[145] [2003] NIQB 19 (QB) (no breach either, as C was well aware of the risks posed by playing in the yard).

and parental supervision was not expected). In *Simkiss v Rhondda BC*,[146] Dunn LJ considered whether the child should reasonably have been accompanied to the premises as 'the first question for consideration'.

Courts have certainly been prepared to hold that some degree of parental supervision was reasonably expected by the occupier, thereby making it easier for the occupier to meet the standard which the common duty of care required. Neither of the following relevant occupiers was liable:

> In *Simkiss v Rhondda BC*, a child of 7, C, was playing with her friend of 10, and slid down a slope on a blanket. Unable to stop, C fell over the unfenced bluff on a mountainside (owned by the local authority, D) onto the road below. Children often played unaccompanied on the mountain. Given that there were a large number of flats across the road (where C came from), and a housing estate nearby, many children lived in the vicinity, with no nearby playground. C argued that D ought to have anticipated that children would play there by themselves since it was, in effect, a recognised playground for the children from the flats. However, D was not liable under the OLA 1957. The danger of an unfenced bluff on a mountainside was obvious to an adult, and D 'were entitled to assume that adult parents would act reasonably and not permit their children to play there unless the parents were satisfied that the children would not do stupid things on the [premises]'. In *Phipps v Rochester Corp*, the developer, D, was entitled to assume that parents would not leave their children, including C, 5, and his 7-year-old sister, unaccompanied to go to a site where building operations, involving trenches and machinery, were ongoing. D was not liable for C's broken leg, which he sustained when falling into a trench being dug for sewerage pipes.

On the other hand, where supervision or guardianship could **not** be expected (or could **not** be expected around-the-clock), then more will be expected of the occupier D, as the following occupiers found to their cost – notably, in contrast to the abovementioned cases, the following were in 'organised settings', and probably for that reason, the burden on occupier D was heightened:

> In *Ward v Hertfordshire CC*,[147] Master Ward, 8, C, was a pupil in D's primary school, and was unsupervised in the playground until 8.55 am, when the bell sounded for school. During this time, C raced between the flint walls, and fell and struck his head against one. There had been previous similar accidents involving other pupils, and the school staff knew that children were prone to race between the flint walls. The walls could have been rendered to make them safer, for £400–£1,000. No supervision of the children in the playground at that time of the morning was expected. Hence, the precautionary step should have been taken by a reasonable occupier. In *Perry v Butlins*,[148] the premises were a holiday camp conducted by Butlins, D, and 'children are what Butlins is for'. At a venue for children's entertainment shows provided by D, C, a child of 3, fell against a low wall and cut his ear. It would reasonably be expected by D that young children would be there, possibly not as closely supervised as if they were in a public place; that they would eagerly respond to requests for audience participation; and would generally be running around when, to an adult, 'walking would seem to have sufficed'. Hence, D should reasonably have constructed the wall without its being so low and with a hard, sharp edge.

[146] (1983) 81 LGR 460 (CA). [147] [1970] 1 WLR 356 (CA) 359 (Lord Denning MR). [148] (CA, 28 Nov 1997).

- if some accompaniment for young children was expected, and the hazards presented by the premises would not be obvious to a parent or guardian (let alone to the child), then a reasonable occupier, D, must take reasonable precautionary steps to draw the hazards to the parent or guardian's attention. However, if a young child is injured or killed on D's premises, it is not necessary for D to then prove that the child's guardian or parent was negligent. As the Court of Appeal put it in *Marsden v Bourne Leisure Ltd*,[149] these cases can sometimes descend into an unfortunate 'blame game', with the parent alleging that the occupier 'ought to have foreseen that there will be unaccompanied small children on its site and taken precautions', and with the occupier 'blaming the parent for losing control over the child'.

  In *Marsden v Bourne Leisure Ltd (t/as British Holidays)*, Matthew Marsden, 2½, C, drowned in a pond in Greenacres Holiday Park, owned by D, where he was holidaying with his parents and younger brother. He disappeared whilst his mother was talking on the phone, and by the time he was found, he had drowned. Three days before C's death, his parents had been given a welcome pack with a plan showing the layout of roads, lakes, ponds, the river and the beach. **Held:** D not liable under the OLA 1957. Giving further warnings to C's parents about the dangers posed by waterways and to keep an eye on their children, would have made no difference – they were described as already 'responsible, attentive and caring', and were already well aware of the dangers of the site for small unaccompanied children. Moreover, C's parents were not negligent (and D did not need to prove that they were). 'Short of keeping hold of the two children at all times when outside the caravan, there is nothing more the Marsdens could do. Small children can disappear in a moment'.

- a more mature child will be treated as possessing the same appreciation of danger as an adult, thereby reducing the burden on occupier D to take extra precautionary steps to avoid the risk of injury to that child.

  In *Burke v Southern Education and Library Board*,[150] facts previously, re the 14-year-old girl, C, who was impaled on the pointed school gate, a reasonable school occupier, D, was not required to erect warning signs not to climb the gate, because while 'school authorities must be prepared for children to be less careful than adults, [C] was well aware that the gate was there for a purpose and was not to be climbed'. In *Simkiss v Rhonddha BC*,[151] where the elder child playing on the mountain was 10, the court said that regard should be given to the 'natural ability of children of these ages ... not to do anything stupid'.

- whilst the presence of alluring objects **may** help to 'elevate' a child trespasser to visitor status (per the doctrine of allurement, above), the law is more certain where that child is *already* a lawful visitor. An occupier, D, will be reasonably expected to take further precautionary steps where a child's presence was encouraged, even implicitly, because there was a 'trap or allurement' on D's premises. The most reasonable step might be to remove the allurement altogether, failing which D will not have met the standard of care. Both of the following occupiers could have done more, and were in breach:

  In *Jolley v Sutton LBC*,[152] the Council, D, owned and occupied the common parts of a block of council flats in Surrey, including a grassed area where children, including Justin Jolley, 14, C, commonly

[149] [2009] EWCA Civ 671, [14], [16], citing: *Phipps v Rochester Corp* [1955] 1 QB 450 (CA) 469 (Devlin LJ).
[150] [2004] NIQB 13, [33], referring to the NI equivalent legislation, which is the same on all material terms.
[151] (CA, 22 Feb 1983).
[152] [2000] 1 WLR 1082 (HL), citing the trial judge: [1998] 1 Lloyd's Rep 433 (QB) 439–40.

played. A derelict boat was brought on a trailer and left on the grassed area, abandoned, unfenced, and uncovered. Eventually a sticker was placed on the side of the trailer, 'Danger: do not touch this vehicle unless you are the owner'. C and a friend tried to repair the boat with a plan to take it sailing at Cornwall. The boys pulled the boat off the trailer, and in order to repair the holes in the hull, jacked it up and set it on wooden blocks. One day, while working underneath the jacked-up boat, the boat crashed down onto C, breaking his back, causing paraplegia. D was liable under the OLA 1957, because D should have removed the boat well before the accident, not only because it was an eyesore (which tenants frequently complained about), but also because 'it was a trap or allurement to children'. In *Glasgow City Corp v Taylor*,[153] a pre-OLA 1957 case, Master Taylor, 7, died from eating poisonous berries from the *atropa belladonna* shrub growing in the Botanic Gardens in Glasgow. D was liable, as the shrub could have been isolated and fenced off; warning signs could have been erected; and it was not reasonable for parents to accompany a child at all times in a public park such as this.

The scenario of joint occupiers

As discussed previously,[154] who may be considered to be an occupier depends upon what degree of control is exercised by that party – and, on that basis, joint occupiers are legally feasible. However, the extent of a joint occupier's control will dictate what is required on the part of that occupier to attain the standard of care (per *Wheat v E Lacon & Co Ltd*[155]).

It may well turn out that both occupiers failed to attain the standard of care expected, but one was less culpable than the other, rendering him less liable to C, under the Civil Liability (Contribution) Act 1978.

In *Andrews v Initial Cleaning Services Ltd*,[156] a cleaning contractor, D1, kept a cleaning storeroom on the client's (D2's) premises. Ms Andrews, C, a cleaner, rested her bag on a sink in the storeroom, and the sink came loose from the wall and fell on her, causing her to fall back and hit her head. **Held**: both D1 and D2 were occupiers; but D1 were 75% liable and D2 only 25%. D1 had employees on the premises daily, with a supervisor, they knew of the sink's defect and failed to notify D2 about it, and were far the more culpable occupier than D2.

On the other hand, it may be that the extent of the occupier's control was so limited that he did whatever was necessary to attain the requisite standard of care. Occupiers who are virtually 'in absentia' have less expected of them by the law than a joint occupier who is involved in the day-to-day operation of the premises, and on that basis, neither of the following occupiers was liable:

In *Wheat v Lacon*, facts previously, the landlord, D, the brewers, was not liable under the OLA 1957. The standard of care expected of D was to ensure that the pub's structure was reasonably safe, and that the system of lighting was efficient, but D was not expected to see that the lights were switched on, that the bulb was in the socket, or the rugs were laid safely on the floor. Those daily matters were for the Richardsons, the licensees. In *Shtern v Cummings (Jamaica)*,[157] Adele Shtern, C, was visiting D's hotel in Jamaica, when she received an electric shock when opening a fridge door in the hotel. D owned the hotel and land, but staff of another company were responsible for the

[153] [1922] 1 AC 44 (HL) 50 (Lord Buckmaster), albeit that this was not a case of trespass, as the shrub was growing in the open gardens.

[154] See pp 589–92.

[155] [1966] AC 552 (HL) 578, 581.

[156] [2000] ICR 166 (CA).

[157] [2014] UKPC 18, [20]–[22].

day-to-day operation of the hotel business. The mere fact that D owned the fridge, contents, and hotel, did not render D an occupier liable under the OLA (Jamaica's legislation was modeled on the UK's OLA 1957). D was not operationally responsible for the running of the hotel.

By contrast, where the premises has a structural defect, rather than a transient hazard, then the failure to meet a reasonable standard of care may be easier to point to, on the part of the 'absentee' occupier:

In *Maddocks v Clifton*,[158] facts previously, the daughter who owned the stables where visitor Mrs Maddocks kept her horses was liable under the OLA 1957. The standard of care expected of her would not extend to the 'mere transient features of the stables, such as movable items', as those would be under the control of her mother, the other joint occupier, in running her livery business. However, for matters concerning the condition of the structure (e.g., the defective ladder), that was in the daughter's control.

Matters that do not affect (either elevate or reduce) the standard

Some matters have been mentioned by courts as being of no relevance to the question of whether more, or less, ought to have been expected of the occupier, D, being sued.

Although emergency service providers, such as ambulance personnel and firemen, are well-accustomed to visiting hazardous and unfamiliar premises by virtue of their employment, and must be taken to be cognisant of the risks that may arise during the course of their dangerous occupation, there is nothing lesser expected of an occupier, D, toward that type of visitor. D must still see that the fireman, etc, is reasonably safe for the purposes for which he is summoned to the premises. That was confirmed by the Court of Appeal in *Simpson v A1 Dairies Farms Ltd*[159] (where, as previously discussed, D had a duty to warn a firemen of a transient danger, *viz*, the presence of a drain temporarily covered by standing water).

A charitable occupier, D, is not subject to a lower standard of care, compared with profit-making occupiers, either. As the House of Lords memorably stated in dicta, in *Marc Rich & Co AG v Bishop Rock Marine Co Ltd (The Nicholas H)*,[160] hospitals are 'subject to the same common duty of care under the OLA 1957 and 1984 as betting shops or brothels'.

Proving breach

Whether an occupier is in breach of the common duty of care is a question of fact and, for that reason, it has been said that 'authority will be of little assistance' when deciding whether or not the occupier was in breach (per Smith LJ in *Lough v Intruder Detention and Surveillance Fire & Security Ltd*[161]).

Proving a breach of duty is precisely the same for an occupiers' liability suit as it is for an ordinary negligence action. Hence, readers are referred to Chapter 7 for detailed discussion. A summary of those issues, together with supporting authorities under the OLA 1957, are contained in the first section below. There are also a number of statutory 'escape hatches' available under the OLA 1957, which may serve to absolve the occupier, D, from any finding of breach. Although these escape hatches are, properly-speaking, defences for D against the

[158] [2001] EWCA Civ 1837, [8]. [159] [2001] NPC 14 (CA) [11].
[160] [1995] UKHL 4, [1996] 1 AC 211, 228. [161] [2008] EWCA Civ 1009, [10].

visitor's claim, they are so specific to defeating breach that they are conveniently discussed in the section below.

A brief revision of the ordinary principles of negligence

§12.16 The ordinary principles of proving breach apply to a visitor's claim against an occupier, D. Hence: D must have either foreseen the danger posed by the premises, or the danger must have been reasonably foreseeable. The court must then identify the potential precautionary steps which could have been taken by D, and then assess (by virtue of the usual quadrant of factors) whether those steps *should* have been taken by a reasonable occupier in D's position. The court may have regard to the practice of other occupiers and/or the requirements of relevant building standards. The law does *not* require D to take precautionary steps (including warnings) about obvious risks posed by the premises.

Reasonable foreseeability. The occupier, D, must have either foreseen (appreciated) that the state of the premises did, or would, pose a danger to a visitor's safety, or it must have been a reasonably foreseeable danger (i.e., a reasonable occupier would have appreciated that the state of the premises was, or would become, a danger). Foreseeability of the event giving rise to the visitor's injury is 'critical' to the visitor's claim against the occupier, 'whether put at common law or under the common duty of care' (per Laws LJ in *Wombwell v Grimsby Fish Dock Enterprises*[162]). If what occurred on the premises was so remote and unlikely as to be unforeseeable (i.e., a 'mere possibility' at best), then no reasonable occupier would have taken precautionary steps to guard against the risk of that danger manifesting (even if some could be identified that would have precluded the event from occurring). Where the accident had *never* happened on the premises previously, then that is 'not conclusive, but it is helpful' to proving that the danger was unforeseeable (per Swinton Thomas LJ in *McGivney v Golderslea Ltd*[163]) – or, as Waller LJ put it in *Simkiss v Rhondda BC*,[164] no previous incident tends to offset 'to a great extent' any obverse argument that the risk of injury was foreseeable. It is certainly not required by law that an occupier should foresee (where a similar accident has never happened before) that C may act foolishly under the influence of alcohol (per *Tacagni v Penwith DC*[165]). By corollary, if the risk had eventuated prior to the visitor's accident, then D was at least alerted to the risk, and to the possibility that precautionary steps could be taken to avert the risk of injury. The fact that these precautionary steps were not taken does not, of itself, indicate breach – whether those steps **should** have been taken by a reasonable occupier is an *entirely different* question, depending upon the 'quadrant of factors' (below[166]). In the following cases, a similar accident had never happened previously, it was unforeseeable, and the occupiers were **not** liable under the OLA 1957:

In *Lewis v Six Continents plc*,[167] Christian Lewis, 22, C, was staying at a hotel owned by hoteliers, D, for a work training course. At 1 am, C fell out of his second floor room through the sash window, and suffered severe head injuries when hitting the pavement 35 ft below. The accident was unforeseeable, so D was not liable under the OLA 1957. Nothing distinguished this hotel from the ordinary run of hotels, or distinguished this guest from other typical hotel guests. No such accident had ever

[162] [2008] EWCA Civ 831, [12]. [163] [1997] EWCA Civ 2656. [164] (1983) 81 LGR 460 (CA) (no pp available).
[165] [2013] EWCA Civ 702, [20]. [166] See below, and for more detail, **Chapter 7**.
[167] [2005] EWCA Civ 1805, [22], [29].

occurred at this hotel; and it was not reasonably foreseeable that an adult would lean so far out the window to get fresh air, to see something going on outside, or even to be sick, that D should have limited the distance to which the window could be opened. Blocked sashes would not have allowed C to fall out, but as the event was not reasonably foreseeable, a reasonable hotelier would not have taken that precautionary step. In *McGivney v Golderslea Ltd*,[168] Mr McGivney, 18, C, was visiting a friend in a block of flats at Finchley Road, and when coming down the stairs, tripped on the bottom step, reached forward, and his hand went through a glass pane on the front door. No other accident like this had ever occurred in the block. In one sense, the accident was possible; but 'as a matter of common sense', it was unforeseeable. In *West Sussex CC v Pierce*,[169] Lewis Pierce, 9, C, cut his thumb on the underside of a water fountain at school, whilst he was 'up to mischief' in the playground during school playtime. There was a possibility that such an accident could occur (but about 8,000 of these water fountains had been installed around the country, and no report of any accident had ever been made). A mere possibility does not equate to reasonable foreseeability. The sharp edge could have been bevelled or padded, but it did not require that, for such a remote risk of injury.

However, reasonable foreseeability will always depend upon the circumstances – and in the following cases, the occupier, D, should have foreseen the accident which happened to the visitor, and was liable:

In *Maddocks v Clifton*,[170] facts previously (the stables ladder case), a previous complaint had been made about the potential dangers posed by the ladder, and felt had been applied to each rung after that. The complaint meant that D should have been aware of the physical danger posed by the ladder. In *Bunker v Charles Brand & Son Ltd*,[171] Mr Bunker, C, was working in a tube tunnel which was being drilled out by a machine operated by Charles Brand, D (D was not C's employer, hence the claim was brought under the OLA 1957). The normal way to reach the front of the machine was by walking on the rollers, using a girder as a handhold, but C's foot slipped off onto the rollers which moved, and he fell. Such an accident had never happened in the past, but that did not absolve D from taking further precautions. D should have put down planks beside the rollers, or lashed planks on top of the rollers, to provide a sure-footed method of getting to the front of the machine.

Precautionary steps. When assessing breach, a court will consider what precautionary steps the occupier *could* have taken, in order to avoid or prevent the injury to the visitor. Apart from the erection of warning signs, the types of precautionary steps commonly alleged in occupiers' liability cases include: removing the structure which was the source of the danger altogether; concealing or covering the danger; making it more difficult (or impossible) for the entrant to gain access to the premises by putting up physical barriers; refusing the visitor permission to enter the premises at all; organising security patrols of the premises; or providing better education about the dangers of the premises to a class of persons of whom the entrant was one.

Whether any of those steps should have been taken by the occupier, D, will depend upon an assessment of the quadrant of factors, derived from *Bolton v Stone*,[172] *viz*, the probability of the injury occurring; the gravity of the injury should it happen; the cost of those precautionary steps; and any impact of those steps on the social utility of D's activities, or on those similarly

168 [1997] EWCA Civ 2656. See too: *Nessa v Walsall MBC* (CA, 18 Dec 2000).
169 [2013] EWCA Civ 1230, [18]. 170 [2001] EWCA Civ 1837, [12].
171 [1969] 2 QB 480, 489. 172 [1951] AC 850 (HL).

situated to D (per *Tomlinson v Congleton BC*[173]). As with all negligence scenarios, it is a balancing exercise. The Court of Appeal spoke for all occupiers when it said, in *Allen v Stoke-on-Trent CC*,[174] that '[t]here is clearly a balance to be struck between placing burdens on city councils which they find it impracticable to fulfil, and allowing councils to ignore their responsibilities [as occupiers]'.

Of course, many occupiers undertake activities of real social utility, which brings the fourth factor (and s 1 of the Compensation Act 2006, discussed in Chapter 7) into play. For example, in *Tomlinson* (the lake diving case),[175] the Council D was not liable for breach. The social value derived from using the beaches of the lake for purposes of sunbathing, paddling, playing with children ('the harmless recreation of responsible parents and children with buckets and spades on the beaches', said Lord Hoffmann) would have to be prohibited if the beaches were planted up with prickly bushes and shrubs to prevent access to the lake. This was relevant, *whether the entrant was a trespasser or a lawful visitor.* Lord Hoffmann reiterated that 'there is an important question of freedom at stake', in that it was unjust for the 'harmless' activities of responsible third parties to be prohibited by some so-called duty on the occupier's part to safeguard 'irresponsible visitors against dangers which are perfectly obvious'. Similarly, in *Simkiss v Rhondda BC*[176] (the sliding-over-the-bluff case), the Court of Appeal noted, that, '[i]f the exercise of reasonable care required the Borough Council to fence off this bluff, it seems to me it would also require them to fence every natural hazard in the Rhondda Valley which was adjacent to housing estates. The Borough Council are in no special position compared with other occupiers. There are many parts of the country with open spaces adjacent to houses where children play unattended, and this is to be encouraged'. Indeed, *Tomlinson* (and other cases like it since[177]) reflect the modern reality that this type of tension will commonly be resolved *against* the injured visitor. Lord Hobhouse expressed the point in this way:

> Does the law require that all trees be cut down because some youths may climb them and fall? ... [or] require the coastline and other beauty spots to be lined with warning notices? ... [or] require that attractive waterside picnic spots be destroyed because of a few foolhardy individuals who choose to ignore warning notices and indulge in activities dangerous only to themselves? The answer to all these questions is, of course, no ... the arguments for [C] ... attack the liberty of the individual to engage in dangerous, but otherwise harmless, pastimes at his own risk and the liberty of citizens as a whole fully to enjoy the variety and quality of the landscape of this country.[178]

Notably, in Lord Scott's words, 'of course there is some risk of accidents arising out of the *joie-de-vivre* of the young. But that is no reason for imposing a grey and dull safety regime on everyone'.[179]

To take just a few cases of visitors injured on the occupiers' premises by way of illustration – some have failed to prove breach[180] (in addition to *Tomlinson* and *Simkiss* above) –

[173] [2003] UKHL, [2004] 1 AC 46, [34]. Also: *Stimpson and Wolverhampton LBC* (CA, 22 May 1990, Sir Roualeyn Cumming-Bruce).

[174] (CA, 14 Feb 1989, Woolf LJ). [175] *ibid*, [2003] UKHL, [2004] 1 AC 46, [46]. [176] (CA, 22 Feb 1983).

[177] *Evans v Kosmar Villa Holidays* [2007] EWCA Civ 1003, [2008] 1 WLR 297, [41]; *Hampstead Heath Winter Swimming Club v London Corp* [2005] EWHC 713 (Admin) [41]; *Proctor v Young* [2009] NIQB 56, [44].

[178] [2003] UKHL, [81]. [179] *ibid*, [94].

[180] See also, e.g.: *Ferrari v The National Trust* [2004] NIQB 56; *Gallagher v Haven Leisure Ltd* (QB, 10 Dec 2003); *Horton v Jackson* (CA, 28 Feb 1996); *Gallagher v Haven Leisure Ltd* (QB, 10 Dec 2003).

In *Burke v Southern Education and Library Board*,[181] (re C who was impaled on the school fence), the risk of injury from the splayed tops of the fence was held to be 'remote or slight', because it was most unlikely that anyone would climb the gate, and the danger from the tops, if the gate was climbed, was 'obvious'; there was a high risk of stabbing; but the suggestion that the splayed tops be covered or replaced, or that the fence be removed altogether, would have a serious cost, because the fence protected the school from vandals. In *Wombwell v Grimsby Fish Dock Enterprises*,[182] Mr Wombwell, C, had just bought a boat, and went to the docks to put equipment on it. At the same dock was another boat, whose fire cylinders (filled with liquid Halon gas) were lying on the quayside near a fence. C somehow extracted the safety pin on a cylinder, and it exploded, causing C serious injuries. The probability of the injury occurring was 'so remote as to be, in practice, unforeseeable'; and guarding against the risk of a visitor removing the safety pin of the cylinder would have required either an absolute prohibition against the storage of cylinders on the quayside, or some locked cage for their storage. These steps would seriously restrict the safety of the boats moored there, and would involve expense and inconvenience.

– whilst, in others, the quadrant was balanced in favour of a finding of breach on the occupier's part:[183]

In *Cunningham v Reading FC*,[184] Mr Cunningham, C, was an on-duty police officer at a football match between Reading and Bristol City at Reading Football Stadium (of which Reading FC was occupier, D). Bristol City fans violently attacked Reading fans and invaded the pitch, throwing lumps of concrete torn up from the dilapidated terraces. One of these struck C, injuring him. The probability of this incident was very high, given that the same had occurred four months previously, so D 'had been put on full notice of the potential danger from this state of affairs and had done nothing whatsoever to remedy it'. Serious injury could result from this hooliganism behaviour. If the club had repaired concrete on the terraces, eliminated major cracking and portions of crumbling concrete, that would have made throwing missiles more difficult for spectators (and repair works cost less than £3,000 – which were done within four days of the incident). In *Stimpson v Wolverhampton MBC*,[185] Ms Stimpson, C, was walking through D's public park when a golf ball hit her in the mouth. The probability of an accident was high, as park attendants said that people regularly played golf in the park, despite being told not to, and there had been some complaints from the public who had previously been struck by golf balls. There was a risk of serious injury, although other visitors hit by balls had not been seriously injured. D could have instructed staff to admonish offenders more strongly, erect notices prohibiting golf; and rigorously enforce on-the-spot fines.

The fact that an occupier, D, showed some intention, prior to C's accident, to take a precautionary step that would have prevented C's injury; and/or that an expert organisation/individual advocates that a precautionary step ought to have been taken by a reasonable occupier, are not proof of breach. Both may have contemplated a precautionary step which was far more onerous than the law expected of a reasonable occupier. On that basis, the occupier was not liable in the following cases:

[181] [2004] NIQB 13, quote at [31]. [182] [2008] EWCA Civ 831 (Sir John Chadwick).

[183] See also, e.g.: *Kincaid v Hartlepool BC* (CA, 5 Dec 2000); *Scout Assn v Barnes* [2010] EWCA Civ 1476; *Reffell v Surrey CC* [1964] 1 WLR 358 (QB) 365.

[184] [1992] PIQR P141 (QB) 153.

[185] (CA, 22 May 1990). It will be recalled that this 'activity danger' case was dealt with under the OLA 1957.

In *Tomlinson v Congleton BC*[186] (the diving in the lake case), the Council, D, was aware that its notices forbidding swimming and diving in the lake were commonly ignored and that several accidents had resulted from swimming in the lake. In a Council meeting prior to T's accident, D resolved that it would plant vegetation around the shore, to prevent people from going into the water. It had not carried out this plan, because of a shortage of financial resources. In *Darby v The National Trust*[187] (the Hardwick Hall drowning case), a Water and Leisure Safety Consultant to the Royal Society for the Prevention of Accidents gave evidence that 'No Swimming' notices should have been installed around all deep water, given that 450 people die of drowning each year in the UK. However, the court disagreed, holding that such a sign was not legally required for such an obvious danger.

Post-accident steps. That the occupier, D, took precautionary steps after C's accident which, on the balance of probabilities, may have prevented or avoided C's injury, is not, of itself, proof of breach. A number of steps (from marking out the depth of water on the side of the pool, to erecting warning signs in the changing room) were taken in *Ratcliff v McConnell*[188] (after a student who climbed over the fence at night suffered tetraplegia from diving into that pool), but it was reiterated that hindsight is not relevant. The important issue is 'how the matter appeared before the accident to a reasonable person in the [occupier's] position'. In *Staples v West Dorset DC*[189] too, once the Council knew that a visitor had slipped off a sea wall into the sea, then 'as responsible occupiers, they had to do what they could to prevent a recurrence, so they posted warning notices. [But] the fact that they took that action after the accident does not enable me to draw the inference that, in order to discharge the common duty of care, they should have done so before the accident occurred'.

Nevertheless, the fact that precautionary steps were taken after the accident does have the effect (as the Court of Appeal pointed out in *Stimpson v Wolverhampton MBC*[190]) of showing that there were additional steps which the occupier might have taken (there, a large sign was erected after the golf ball hit C in the mouth, prohibiting the playing of golf in the park, and imposing an on-the-spot fine). It also may indicate just how cheap the precautionary step would have been, had it been implemented prior to the mishap (e.g., in *Cunningham v Reading FC*,[191] the concrete terraces were repaired within days of a serious hooliganism incident, at a cost of less than £3,000). In both cases, breach on the part of the occupier was held.

The practice of other occupiers. In determining whether the occupier, D, took all reasonable steps to protect the visitor, a court is entitled to take into account the practice of other occupiers, as *Bolam*-type evidence of what peer opinion would regard as reasonable.

In *Proctor v Young*,[192] Miss Proctor, C, an experienced horsewoman, was exercising a race horse on a beach and suffered a fall when the horse stumbled in a hole on the beach. C suffered tetraplegia. Other beach occupiers (usually Councils) had the custom to only ban horse riding on the beach between 10.30 am and 6.00 pm to avoid injury to other beach users (this accident occurred at 9.30 am). **Held:** no breach under the OLA 1957: 'there is good reason why this practice has been followed for many years without mishap ... Any additional signage, zoning or banning would be wholly disproportionate in the circumstances. A ban that did exist between 10.30 am and 6.00 pm

186 [2003] UKHL 47, [2004] 1 AC 46, [51], [55].
187 [2001] EWCA Civ 189, [2001] PIQR P17 (CA) [10].
188 [1999] 1 WLR 670 (CA) [42], quoting Lord Pearce in *McGlone v British Rwys Bd* 1966 SC (HL) 1, 17. *Ratcliff* was decided under the OLA 1984, given that C was a trespasser.
189 [1995] PIQR P439 (CA) 445.
190 (CA, 22 May 1990).
191 [1992] PIQR P141 (QB) 153.
192 [2009] NIQB 56, quote at [45].

was ... more than sufficient to ensure the reduction in risk to horses/beach users during those hours'. Further, occupiers were not bound to introduce zoning in order to protect horse riders; 'a considerable social utility and amenity of beaches' could be compromised if Councils zoned off areas from normal public use.

However, *Bolam* evidence is *not* conclusive on the question of breach. It may be mere good fortune that an accident had not occurred earlier under that practice; or knowledge and standards may have moved on since the practice was adopted by D. The *Bolitho*-type gloss – requiring the court to examine a practice against logic and commonsense – applies equally to occupiers' liability cases as to any other context of negligence.

In *Cunningham v Reading CC*,[193] facts previously, **held:** breach proven under the OLA 1957. In 1984 when the incident occurred, the Reading ground was well up to the average condition of other third and fourth division grounds, but it was 'no excuse' for D to show that their unsafe ground was equalled by a unsafe grounds elsewhere.

Merely because other occupiers ('the norm') tend to construct their premises in a different way than does the occupier, D, does not necessarily indicate that D was in breach:

In *Baines v York CC*,[194] Mrs Baines, C, visited D's pool, caught her foot between the back of the steps leading into the pool and the pool wall, and badly twisted her ankle. Since this pool was built in 1970, recessed steps actually built into the wall of the pool had become of more general use. **Held**: no breach under the OLA 1957. It was reasonable for D to maintain steps of this type, as they had advantages, and were in wide usage at one stage. No similar accident had ever happened either in D's pool or in pools of which D was aware; and to rebuild the pool so that integral steps were built would have been costly.

Building standards. The requirements of relevant building standards or other industry standards may also be relied upon as evidence of reasonable practice by the occupier D (although, again, it will not be conclusive, as the standard itself might be proven to be illogical or irrational). The following cases can be contrasted:

In *Slack v Glenie*,[195] Mr Slack, C, was riding a motor cycle and sidecar combination round a racetrack at a leisure park owned by D, with Peter Lain as his passenger. He lost control, and hit the fence on the inner side of the race track. Mr Lain was killed, and C rendered a paraplegic. The inner fence was a non-obvious hazard, because its design did not comply with acceptable standards of race track design (under international track standards). D breached the OLA 1957 (subject to a finding of contributory negligence). **However,** in *Wattleworth v Goodwood Road Racing Co Ltd*,[196] Simon Wattleworth, C, was racing at the Goodwood motor-racing circuit, came out of a bend, lost control and collided with a tyre-fronted earth bank on the inside of the track, and was killed. His widow alleged that Goodwood Road Racing Company Ltd, D, the owners and operators of the circuit, were liable under the OLA 1957, and that her husband's death was caused by negligent design or selection of the tyre barrier. However, D properly instructed motor safety governing associations, liaised closely with them, followed their detailed recommendations 'to the letter', and

193 [1992] PIQR P141 (CA) 153. See too, *Reffell v Surrey CC* [1964] 1 All ER 743 (QB) 747 ('I cannot help thinking that the defendants have been lucky that there has been no previous accident at this door').

194 (CA, 14 May 1992, Balcombe LJ). 195 (CA, 19 Apr 2000).

196 [2004] EWHC 140 (QB), [2004] PIQR P25, [106].

had no reason to think that the tyre barriers recommended as appropriate in 1998 by those bodies were inappropriate.

Where the occupier's premises were built in accordance with building standards in force at the time of construction, that will assist to prove that no breach occurred – D's conduct must be compared with the standards at the date of construction of the hotel, and not at the date of C's accident. An occupier does **not** owe a continuing duty to engage in a constant process of updating existing buildings, by rebuilding or refurbishment, so as to reflect changes in building standards (unless those standards compel certain action to be taken, such as the removal of asbestos); that would be too onerous a duty on an occupier (per *McGivney v Golderslea Ltd*[197]).

In *McGivney*, facts previously, even though C broke a glass pane in the door of the residential block, that glass complied with relevant building standards at the date that it was built. Had the block been built at the time of the accident, the regulations in force would have required stronger and thicker glass to be used. C argued that the glass in the door should have been replaced and brought up to current standards in order to comply with the common duty of care in the OLA 1957. This was rejected: 'it is quite impossible to say that these [occupiers] were in breach of that duty in failing to remove a pane of glass which complied with the regulations when it was installed and to replace it with more up to date safety glass'.

On the other hand, failing to build the premises in accordance with building standards applicable at the time will likely constitute a breach of duty (per *Japp v Virgin Holidays*[198]).

Obvious risks. Visitors are compelled, by law, to accept responsibility for the *obvious risks* that they choose to run, when undertaking inherently-risky activities on D's premises. Whatever injuries are suffered are not injuries for which occupier, D, is liable. There is no duty upon D to warn (or to better warn) or to fence off against an obvious risk. The reason was baldly stated by Lord Hobhouse in *Tomlinson* – 'no purpose was in fact served by the [occupier's] warning: It told the visitor nothing he did not already know'.[199] In *Tomlinson*, Lord Hoffmann reaffirmed that, '[i]f people want to climb mountains, go hang gliding, or swim or dive in ponds or lakes, that is their affair ... the balance between risk on the one hand and individual autonomy on the other ... is a judgment which the courts must make and which in England reflects the individualist values of the common law'.[200] Hence, to the extent that cases[201] prior to *Tomlinson* permitted recovery by visitors who dived into seas or waterways and suffered broken necks by hitting their heads on shallow beds, those cases may now be considered to be of doubtful authority.

However, as the Court of Appeal reiterated in *Evans v Kosmar Villa Holidays plc*,[202] that 'core reasoning' in *Tomlinson* **only** truly applies when C chooses to run an 'obvious risk'. Whether or not a risk of danger was 'obvious' depends, in part, upon whether the thing was natural or man-made – risks arising from man-made structures tend to be legally viewed as being less obvious. Also, it depends upon an objective, rather that a subjective, assessment (although the

[197] [1997] EWCA Civ 2656. [198] [2013] EWCA Civ 1371, [20].

[199] [2003] UKHL 47, [2004] 1 AC 46, [71], [74]. Applied since, in another diving-into-shallow-water case, in *Vaughan v MOD* [2015] EWHC 1404 (QB).

[200] [2003] UKHL 47, [2004] 1 AC 46, [45]–[47].

[201] e.g., *O'Shea v Kingston-upon-Thames* [1995] PIQR P208; *Harrison v Thanet DC* (QB, 22 Sep 1997).

[202] [2007] EWCA Civ 1003, [39].

visitor's capacity to appreciate the dangers are relevant as to whether a risk should have been obvious). An adult injured visitor of full capacity cannot argue that, however 'obvious' the risk may have been to others, it was not obvious *to him*, because he mistakenly assessed the risk (per *Evans v Kosmar Villa Holidays plc*[203]).

All of the following scenarios involved 'obvious risks', and in **none** was the occupier liable:

'Obvious risks' associated with visitors' activities

- swimming in murky, cold, deep water, with the risks of getting cramp or exhaustion; 'the pond had no relevant characteristics making it more dangerous than any other pond', and its hazards were obvious, and 'entirely typical of such ponds': *Darby v National Trust*[a]
- diving into shallow water in an inflatable pool (where C helped to fill the pool himself, so could not have been unaware of its depth): *Risk v College*[b]
- diving into a swimming pool without checking the depth, or at night when the depth was not visible ('[t]here is no uniformity in shape, size or configuration of swimming pools'): *Ratcliff v McConnell*[c]
- diving from a cliff into clean and clear water where a protruding underwater shelf was clearly visible: *Bartrum v Hepworth Minerals and Chemicals Ltd*[d]
- climbing over a sharp pointed fence, where the clear purpose was to keep trespassers out: *Burke v Southern Education and Library Bd*[e]
- riding a horse on a beach with potholes and channels in soft sand, whether naturally-made crevices and holes or made by beach-goers: *Proctor v Young*[f]
- slipping on an algae-covered seaward rock at the Cobb at Lyme Regis which had a pronounced 1:5 slope: *Staples v West Dorset DC*[g]
- going for a hillside walk where there was no clearly-defined path, down a steep gradient where footing was insecure and unstable, towards a cliff edge, which the walker fell over: *Cotton v Derbyshire Dales DC*[h]
- slipping on a wet floor in a busy takeaway shop which, in wet weather, had water and dirt walked in by customers, creating a slippery floor: *Kiapasha (t/a Takeaway Supreme) v Laverton*[i]
- jumping off a 'bouncy castle' in such an exuberant and spectacular manner as to land on a hard surface in an uncontrolled fashion: *Humber v Fisher (t/as Children's Party Bouncers)*[j]

[a] [2001] EWCA Civ 189, [15]. Also: *Tomlinson v Congleton BC* [2002] EWCA Civ 309, [47] (Longmore LJ).
[b] [2013] EWHC 3869 (QB) [89] (the risk was 'even more obvious' than in *Tomlinson*).
[c] [1999] 1 WLR 670 (CA) 680–81 (Stuart-Smith LJ).
[d] (QB, 29 Oct 1999).
[e] [2004] NIQB 13, [33].
[f] [2009] NIQB 56.
[g] (1995) P1QR 439.
[h] (1994) The Times, 20 Jun.
[i] [2002] EWCA Civ 1656.
[j] (CA, 3 Feb 2000) (no reasonable prospects of appeal).

On the other hand, the dangers posed by mechanical or other man-made apparatus tend to be viewed, at law, as less obvious dangers, thus potentially attracting liability for the occupier, D, under the OLA 1957. In each of the following cases, D well knew of the danger, but the visitor, C, did not (and D was liable):

[203] [2007] EWCA Civ 1003, [2008] 1 WLR 297, [42].

'Non-obvious risks'

- stairs and landings were unprotected by stabilising balustrades, which had been removed for renovations, but the house owner did not warn security system installers of that: *Lough v Intruder Detention, etc Security Ltd*[a]
- a ladder which provided access to the loft but was not properly secured to the wall, as it ended below the level of the loft floor with a gap between ladder and loft floor: *Maddocks v Clifton*[b]
- windows in a house, constructed in the 1950s, did not have a lintel above the window frame, making the collapse of the brickwork above the window far more likely than if a lintel had been in place, and which a joiner could not have known, merely by looking at the window: *Eden v West & Co*[c]
- poisonous berries on a bush, which looked just like edible 'grapes or cherries' to a young child: *Glasgow City Corp v Taylor*[d]
- a piece of gym equipment which involved barbells and fixed railings, and which amputated C's finger, when her hand was placed on the machine during exercises: *Ireland v David Lloyd Leisure Ltd*[e]

[a] [2008] EWCA Civ 1009, [14].
[b] (CA, 19 Nov 2001) [4], [18].
[c] [2002] EWCA Civ 991, [2003] PIQR 2.
[d] [1922] 1 AC 44 (HL) 50 (Lord Buckmaster), a pre-OLA case.
[e] [2013] EWCA Civ 665, [26].

Where the visitor ran an obvious risk, then the failure by the occupier, D, to warn/fence/provide protection against that obvious risk will not render D liable, merely because: (1) the visitor inadvertently, rather than deliberately, ran the risk (e.g., dived into a pool, not realising that it was the shallow rather than the deep end) – for, as the Court of Appeal said in *Evans v Kosmar Villa Holidays plc*, 'a brief state of inadvertence ... could be said of almost all accidents';[204] (2) the visitor was acting 'in the exuberance of youth, and in the spirit of the moment' (per *Evans*[205]); (3) many people, other than C, were taking the same obvious risks on that particular occasion (per *Tomlinson v Congleton BC*[206]); or (4) D knew (or had reasonable grounds to believe) that any notices that it *had* erected were frequently ignored, that visitors commonly ran the risk, or that several accidents had already occurred at the premises ('[t]he fact that such people take no notice of warnings cannot create a duty to take other steps to protect them'[207]).

On the other hand, if the visitor is too young or incapacitated to properly appreciate a risk of injury that would be obvious to an adult, then the occupier, D, will be liable if warnings/fencing/precautionary steps were not taken against that obvious risk (per the pre-OLA case of *British Rwys Board v Herrington*[208]), but borne out in particularly tragic circumstances recently:

> In *Pollock v Cahill*,[209] Mr Mark Pollock, C, 39, had been blinded as an adult, but nevertheless undertook many impressive athletic rowing and yachting endeavours. He was visiting a summer regatta, and stayed at the house of Mr and Mrs Cahill, D. At some point during the night, C fell through the second-floor window, which was open, and suffered paraplegia in the fall. **Held:** a breach of duty was proven against the occupiers. The risk of an open window would have been obvious to a sighted person, but not to this particular visitor. C had stayed in the house before, and D knew of C's

[204] [2007] EWCA Civ 1003, [28]. [205] *ibid.* [206] [2003] UKHL 47, [2004] 1 AC 46.
[207] *Tomlinson*, *ibid*, [46] (Lord Hoffmann). [208] [1972] AC 877 (HL). [209] [2015] EWHC 2260 (QB), quote at [53].

disability. Further, the fact that C was 'a resourceful blind person was irrelevant to the risk created by an open window'.

Statutory 'escape hatches' for the occupier, D

There are **three** defences available to an occupier, D, to absolve a finding of breach under the OLA 1957. Although the statute does not state where the burden of proof lies, it has been judicially said that the burden is on D to establish the defences (per *George v Coastal Marine 2004 Ltd (t/as Mashfords)*.[210] More than one defence may apply in any given scenario.

Re skilled visitors to the premises

§12.17 Where a visitor, C, has specialist skills pursuant to his calling, and enters the premises of the occupier, D, to exercise those skills, D can expect C to appreciate and guard against any special risks ordinarily incidental to that calling, to the extent that D allows C to do so (per s 2(3)(b), OLA 1957).

Known as the 'skilled visitor' defence, it has **three** components:

i. **C must have suffered the injury in the exercise of his calling.** A 'calling' does not require that C be a professional person (it could be a trade or any specialist activity), or that C was visiting as an employee. None of the following occupiers was liable, because each visitor was skilled in their own way:

   In *Proctor v Young*,[211] facts previously, the visitor was an experienced horsewoman, and the Council, D, was entitled to expect that type of visitor to appreciate the risks inherent in riding horses over a beach of soft sand, with man-made and natural holes and crevices in the sand. In *Wombwell v Grimsby Fish Dock Enterprises*,[212] facts previously, the dockside operator, D, was entitled to expect that only responsible seafarers would be quayside, and would realise the hazards of removing the pin from a fire cylinder belonging to another boat, while holding the cylinder in a dangerous horizontal position. In *Roles v Nathan*,[213] the owner/occupier of the Manchester Assembly Rooms, who was having problems with the old coke-heating boiler, was entitled to expect two chimney sweeps (the Roles brothers, C) whom they had engaged to clean the long (70 ft) flues, to know that carbon monoxide fumes from the boiler were dangerous (C ignored the warnings, the boiler was relit, and next morning, the chimney sweeps were found dead in the boiler room, overcome by fumes). In *Bamforth v Jones*,[214] an ambulance man, C, fell over a pile of books sitting on the floor of the landing, as he was walking backwards carrying the sick occupier, D, in a carrying chair. Speedy transfer/evacuation and continuous observation of D was essential, given that D had fallen unconscious during an epileptic fit. A special risk ordinarily incidental to the calling of an ambulance man was the risk of injury from a sudden strain arising from slipping while walking backwards carrying a heavy patient, and D was entitled to expect C to guard against it, notwithstanding the urgency, by asking for better lighting or the removal of obstructions.

ii. **The risk must have been ordinarily incidental to C's calling.** Whatever risk C encountered during his visit to D's premises and which caused him injury cannot be an entirely different and unrelated type of risk, which has nothing to do with C's trade or profession. In each of the

[210] [2009] EWHC 816 (Admlty), [2009] 2 Lloyd's Rep 356, [34]. [211] [2009] NIQB 56, [43].
[212] [2008] EWCA Civ 831, [16] (Sir John Chadwick) [19] (Waller LJ), affirming the trial judge's decision on this point.
[213] [1963] 1 WLR 1117 (CA) 1125. [214] (CA, 20 Mar 1991).

abovementioned cases, the risks were ordinarily incidental; but in the following cases, they were **not**, and hence, D could not be absolved from breach:

In *Gillingham v Ash Scaffolding Co Ltd*,[215] an experienced scaffolder, C, was not warned that an entire handrail in one of the 'lifts' of the scaffolding was missing, and stumbled or fell through that gap. The occupier (who was not C's employer, and hence his OLA claim as a visitor) argued that it was entitled to expect that C would appreciate and guard against the risk of missing parts of handrails. However, this mishap arose because someone from D's firm partially dismantled the scaffolding without giving any warning to those working on it. The fact that parts of a handrail were missing had nothing to do with C's special skills or with the technical aspects of scaffolding work. In *Roles v Nathan*, facts previously, Lord Denning gave the hypothetical example: had the chimney sweeps been descending to the cellar of the Manchester Assembly Rooms and the stairs had given way because they were defective, then that would not be a special risk incidental to their callings as chimney sweeps.

iii. **D, as occupier, must have allowed C to appreciate the risk and to guard against it.** Lack of lighting or invisible warnings for C may mean that D cannot be absolved of breach towards that skilled visitor. Two cases may be contrasted:

In *Hughes v Midnight Theatre Co*,[216] a production and stage manager, C, was setting up the scenery and the lighting at a theatre (owned by D), requiring him to work on different stages and in different scenarios. C stepped back on the stage to check the position of a piece of scenery, and fell down some steps behind him. **Held**: the defence under s 2(3)(b) succeeded for D. 'The stepped arrangement undoubtedly constituted a risk', but it was 'the sort of irregular arrangement that one, particularly somebody of [C's] calling, would expect to find in a theatre'. Furthermore, the auditorium was sufficiently lit when the accident happened, D had provided sufficient lighting facilities for the auditorium.

In *Woollins v British Celanese Ltd*,[217] a post office engineer, C, was trying to unhook a length of cable, and put his foot on some hardboard roofing, went through, fell and broke his leg. The owner of the building where he was working, D, had put a warning that the roofing was unsafe, but it had been put behind a door and not in a natural place for a person to see it. **Held**: the defence under s 2(3)(b) failed for D. A special risk incidental to C's work might be live wires (if engaged in electrical work), but accessing parts of the workplace was not a special risk ordinarily incident to the calling of an engineer: '[i]t was an ordinary risk incident to the premises themselves'.

Re warnings conveyed to the visitor

§12.18 Where the occupier, D, warns visitor, C, of a danger posed by the state of the premises, which warning was sufficient to enable C to be reasonably safe, then D is not in breach of the common duty of care (per s 2(4)(a), OLA 1957).

As mentioned above,[218] the common law already provides that obvious dangers do not need to be warned about, or fenced off, or otherwise guarded against, by the occupier, D (see, e.g., *Darby v National Trust*[219]). Hence, this defence is *only* relevant, to absolve D, where the danger is latent or hidden from the visitor. It has two components:

[215] (CA, 22 May 1990). [216] (CA, 1 Apr 1998, Auld LJ). [217] [1966] KIR 438 (CA) 440. [218] See pp 616–22.
[219] [2001] EWCA Civ 189. See too, the cases referred to in the Table at p 622 above.

i. There must be a warning. This can be written, or oral (often the subject of a finding of credibility, where the visitor and the occupier differ on what was said), or by some other means (e.g., by hand gestures). The defence succeeded for the following occupiers:

In *George v Coastal Marine 2004 Ltd (t/as Mashfords)*,[220] Mr George, C, was attempting to moor his boat near the seawall. A wharfinger, D, gesticulated by hand gestures to C where his boat should stop, so that it would not berth unsafely, given that the beach sloped up closer to the seawall. D also orally warned C to back up the boat by 12 ft, otherwise, the boat would 'ground hollow'. C did not want to move the vessel any further back, as he was concerned about the stern overhanging the end of the quay wall. The vessel did 'ground hollow', and was damaged. Sufficient warnings were given to C to position his boat differently. In *Roles v Nathan*,[221] the occupier's employees told the chimney sweeps, C, not to come back that evening, and not to attempt to seal up the sweep-hole while the fire under the boiler was still alight, but to come back next morning, and make sure that the fire was out before attempting to seal the sweep-hole. C ignored those warnings.

Another legal consequence of D's posting a warning – quite apart from making out this defence – is that the risk of injury will then be reasonably foreseeable, for why, otherwise, would D have posted it? For example, in *Woollins v British Celanese Ltd*[222] (where the warning was posted in a place which the visitor could not see, and hence, a breach was made out), the court questioned whether, were it not for the warning sign, the injury to the post office engineer, who went through a roof, would have been foreseeable at all.

ii. The warning must be sufficient to enable reasonable safety. The presence of a warning alone is not enough to exculpate D. The warning cannot be hidden, or in a hard-to-find place where a reasonable visitor would not look (as in *Woollins*, although the case actually turned on s 2(3)(b)'s skilled visitor defence, and not on this defence), or in a place remote from the site of danger itself (as in *Darby v National Trust*, where the notice was at the carpark and not at the lake, although as it was an obvious danger, no warning was ultimately required). Also, the warning may need to provide the visitor with more detailed information than to simply advise that the premises were dangerous.

In *London Graving Dock Co Ltd v Horton*,[223] the example was given of two rotten footbridges. It would not be enough for D to put up a notice, 'This bridge is dangerous', if there was a safe bridge 100 yards away. D would need to put a notice, 'Do not use this footbridge. It is dangerous. There is a safe one further upstream', because only then would the warning be enough to enable the visitor to be reasonably safe.

The occupier's independent contractor

§12.19 Where the occupier, D, engages an independent contractor to do construction, maintenance or repair to the premises, and visitor C is harmed by a danger arising from that work, then provided that D acted reasonably in entrusting the work to an independent contractor, and had reasonably satisfied himself that the contractor was competent and that the work was properly done, D is not in breach of the common duty of care (per s 2(4)(b), OLA 1957).

[220] [2009] EWHC 816 (Admlty) [52]. [221] [1963] 1 WLR 1117 (CA) 1123–24.
[222] [1966] KIR 438 (CA). [223] [1951] AC 737 (HL).

The general rule at common law is that an employer can only be vicariously liable for the acts or omissions of his employee, and not for those of his independent contractor. There are certain exceptions in which an employer **will** be liable for the wrongs of his independent contractor (e.g., where he selected the contractor negligently, or where the work performed by the independent contractor was unlawful or extra-hazardous), as discussed in Chapter 18.[224] However, where an employer of the independent contractor is *also an occupier* of premises which posed a danger to visitor C because of the state of those premises, the common law is replaced by s 2(4)(b), which adopts the *general* rule, i.e., non-liability of the employer towards C for the acts of his independent contractor, *except in closely-defined circumstances.*

Of course, any visitor who is injured because of the acts or omissions of the occupier's independent contractor may well seek to sue *that contractor* in negligence – but an action against the occupier may be desirable or necessary for numerous reasons, *viz*, if the contractor was uninsured (per *Mackin v SV Drumgath Parish*[225]), or has gone into liquidation and has no assets with which to satisfy a judgment, or cannot be located. In those scenarios, whether the injured visitor can successfully pursue the *occupier* becomes vitally important.

There are **four** components to the defence in s 2(4)(b):

i. **C's injury caused by a danger created by an independent contractor.** The defence only applies to absolve the occupier, D, where the person responsible for the danger was truly an independent contractor engaged by D. If the party who created the danger was not engaged by D in that capacity, then the defence will not be engaged either. The defence will not excuse D from breach, if the party creating the danger was either D's employee (in which case D will be vicariously liable) or a virtual stranger coincidentally on the scene.

    In *Jones v BBC*,[226] Stuart Jones, C, was working as a sound recordist for the BBC during a TV recording of the lowering of a modern windmill mast. Whilst C was passing under the inclined mast, the windmill rotor fell onto C's back, rendering him a paraplegic. The accident happened at a farm in Pembrokeshire, owned by Mr and Mrs Orbach, D. Two farmworkers from the farm community, including Mr Brown, helped to lower the mast. **Held**: it could not be said that D left the responsibility for lowering the mast to Mr Brown. Further, Mr Brown was not an independent contractor. Hence, s 2(4)(b) could not apply, to excuse D. Mr Brown had relatively little experience in lowering the windmill, having done it twice before (and on one of those, an accident happened).

ii. **C's injury was due to faulty execution of work of construction, maintenance or repair by the contractor.** Even though this component refers to '*faulty execution*' of work, the section also applies to any faulty *omissions* on the contractor's part – the occupier, D, is absolved from liability for both types of wrongs.[227] The contractor's work must relate to the state of the premises, because the defence will only apply where the OLA 1957 applies, and it will be recalled[228] that a precondition of the application of the Act is that C was injured by an occupancy/static danger. The defence succeeded for the occupier in the following cases:

    In *Smith v Storey (t/as Rushworth and Storey)*,[229] a shopkeeper, D, had a new shopfront installed, including glass-panelled doors installed by a glazier firm. When leaving the store, Mr Smith, 60, C, accidentally broke the glass plate and suffered bad cuts. Any shopkeeper (or householder) knows

[224] See pp 1012–15. [225] [2008] NIQB 118, [25]. [226] [2007] All ER (D) 283, [151].

[227] e.g., *AMF Intl v Magnet Bowling Ltd* [1968] 1 WLR 1028 (QB) 1042–43.

[228] See pp 589–91. [229] (CA, 26 Jun 1980, Sir David Cairns).

that there is some risk of glass being broken, but is entitled to assume that a glazier is far more competent than himself to choose a reasonably safe glass for his purpose. It was not reasonable to expect D to ask whether there was a better glazing choice. In *Prentice v Hereward Housing Assn Ltd*,[230] the occupier had a good defence, where the grass was not cut by the contractor in accordance with a reasonable maintenance schedule (i.e., an omission).

iii. **D, the occupier, acted reasonably in entrusting the work to an independent contractor.** Evidence which will support this element includes where D: had previously employed the contractor for the same type of task and was completely satisfied with the contractor's performance (*Dyson v LE Sims & Partners Ltd*[231]); had put the work out to tender and chose the successful tenderer on an objective professional basis (*Ferguson v Welsh*[232]); or engaged the 'best possible expert' (i.e., the manufacturer of the premises) to do the work (per *Maguire v Sefton MBC*[233]). In each of these, the occupier could rely on the defence:

In *Dyson v LE Sims & Partners Ltd*,[234] publishers Penguin Book Ltd, D, owned a warehouse which had a leaky roof. They engaged Sims (who had previously done a smaller job for them competently) to repair it. Mr Dyson, C, a surveyor and engineer from design firm Arups, came to inspect the roof. While up on the roof, he inadvertently stepped off a wooden platform and onto brittle vinyl roofing material, plunged through it to the warehouse floor, and was killed. D acted reasonably in entrusting the roofing work to Sims, including providing proper safety precautions. In *Ferguson v Welsh*, Sedgefield DC, D, engaged an independent contractor (Mr Spence) to carry out demolition works on their site, while prohibiting any subcontracting without D's consent. Mr Spence engaged subcontractors (the Welsh brothers) without D's knowledge or consent. Mr Ferguson, C, an employee of the Welsh brothers, was severely injured when part of the building collapsed. D had put out the demolition to competitive tender, and also had no way of knowing that Mr Spence was likely to contravene the prohibition on subcontracting, or 'bring in cowboy operators who would proceed to demolish the building in a thoroughly unsafe way'. In *Maguire v Sefton MBC*, Mr Maguire, C, was using an exercise machine at D's leisure centre, and arranged for the machine to be maintained by its manufacturer and supplier (Precor). The machine failed shortly afterwards, injuring C. D was entitled to believe that it had engaged 'the best of all experts in relation to the Precor machines'. D knew nothing to suggest that the machines were sensitive or likely to go wrong, nor could it have conducted inspection or maintenance of the machines itself.

iv. **D took reasonable steps (if any were possible) to satisfy himself that the independent contractor was competent, and that the work had been properly done.** This element is one of degree, making it a difficult element to apply. In *Ferguson v Welsh*,[235] Lord Keith clarified that D's duty to take these reasonable steps arises *during* the work, and not merely *after* the work is done; but that it is not necessarily expected that D should supervise the contractor's activities on a daily or regular basis.

The more technically-proficient the work, the less checking that was reasonable for the occupier to do (per *Haseldine v Daw and Son Ltd*,[236] a pre-OLA case in which the occupier was not expected to check the repair of a lift which a contractor had serviced). But if the work was fairly prosaic, then checks are more to be expected, and the occupier may well

[230] [2001] EWCA Civ 437, [2001] 2 All ER (QB) 900, and earlier: QB, 29 Apr 1999.
[231] (CA, 27 Nov 1984). [232] [1987] 1 WLR 1553 (HL) 1560–61. [233] [2006] EWCA Civ, [30].
[234] (CA, 27 Nov 1984). [235] [1987] 1 WLR 1553 (HL) 1553, 1560. [236] [1941] 2 KB 343 (CA).

lose the protection of this defence if the contractor's work turns out to be faulty (per *Martin v Martin Baker Engineering Co Ltd*[237]). Further, if D had very serious misgivings about how the contractor's work was progressing, the protection of the defence is likely to be lost (per *Clark v Hosier & Dickson Ltd (in liq)*[238]). Neither of the following occupiers could rely on the s 2(4)(b) defence:

> In *Martin v Martin Baker Engineering*, a new building was being built for Martin Baker, D, by Giltspur Engineering. Both were occupiers of the premises. Mr Martin, C, a visitor, walked over an area near the entrance covered with large pieces of loose cardboard which concealed a scaffolding board underneath, causing a hidden trap. C caught his right foot, tripped, and suffered serious injury. Martin Baker did not satisfy themselves that Giltspur were looking after safety properly, and it required no technical expertise to see the cardboard lying outside the door and do something about it. In *Clark v Hosier & Dickson*, a theatre touring company, D, engaged Hosier to renovate their premises. Whilst excavating for foundations, Hosier unearthed and then reburied a mains electricity cable unsafely, and without showing its correct location. Mr Clark, C, a gates installer working on site, hit that cable when drilling. D's employee had realised that Hosier's workers had no adequate supervision on site, he had misgivings as to their competence, and he should have contacted the architect or the Electricity Board when the matter of the mains cable arose. The theatre company was in breach of its common duty of care.

It is apparent, from *Ferguson v Welsh* (above), that English law is averse to holding an occupier liable to *an employee of the independent contractor*, on the basis that the occupier had not taken reasonable care to see that the independent contractor's work methods were competent and safe. Sedgefield DB, as occupier, was not liable to the Welsh brothers' employee, as they had selected the contractor carefully, and did not have to supervise the contractor's methods. In the 2014 case of *Yates v National Trust*,[239] the court rationalised that outcome (in dicta, as *Yates* concerned an activity danger) on a policy basis – it is one thing to render an occupier liable if he wrongfully entrusted the work to a contractor, and that contractor's work harmed a visitor; but if an occupier was liable to the contractor's *employee or subcontractor* where the contractor performed the work negligently, then there was 'very much more scope for an employee to be injured than for an ordinary visitor', and it would place an intolerable burden on an occupier to see that the contractor's *employee* was reasonably safe. Separately, in the case of extra-hazardous activities, a person who engages an independent contractor may be liable for the acts or omissions committed by that contractor (towards anyone – the contractor's employee or anyone else), as discussed in Chapter 18. But where occupiers have taken reasonable care to select competent and safe contractors, *Ferguson* and *Yates* demonstrate the difficulty for any employee of the contractor to successfully sue the occupier. The s 2(4)(b) defence is likely to avail the occupier of protection from liability.

Where the contractor lacks insurance. If visitor C's injury is due to a danger brought about by the contractor's work, and the contractor is uninsured (but the occupier, D, did not know and had not checked that), can D still be shown to have satisfied himself that the independent

[237] (QB, 21 Dec 1983, Hirst J). See too, pre-OLA: *Woodward v Mayor of Hastings* [1945] KB 174 (occupier liable for icy steps at school; 'no esoteric quality' about cleaning snow-covered steps).

[238] [2003] EWCA Civ 1467, [21]–[23].

[239] [2014] EWHC 222 (QB) [52]. The ordinary principles of negligence applied, and occupier D was not liable to the contractor's employee, who was injured on D's premises whilst an employee of the independent contractor (arborist).

contractor was competent, or does D's failure to check the insurance position preclude his reliance on s 2(4)(b) and expose D to an action for liability to the visitor?

§12.20 The failure of the occupier to ascertain from its independent contractor that it carried public liability insurance is not, of itself, sufficient to constitute a breach of the duty to select an independent contractor with reasonable care. However, an exceptional duty to enquire about the independent contractor's insurance will be imposed on the occupier when two factors are present: (1) the independent contractor was carrying out a hazardous activity with a clear risk of injury to the public; and (2) the occupier itself would not have performed, nor been permitted to perform, the hazardous activity without the requisite insurance. This exceptional duty to enquire will be discharged if the occupier asks the independent contractor whether it carries a public liability insurance policy, and that query is answered affirmatively (albeit wrongly).

According to differently-constituted Courts of Appeal in *Naylor (t/as Mainstreet) v Payling*[240] and *Glaister v Appleby-in-Westmorland TC*,[241] occupier D does **not** owe a stand-alone duty to visitor C to ensure that the contractor has appropriate insurance to cover injuries suffered by the public (of whom C is one) through the negligence of that contractor. Of course, one way in which D may satisfy himself about the contractor's competence is by checking whether he had insurance cover, but that is not mandatory. D could feasibly meet that requirement via, say, checking whether the contractor was licensed or checking with previous clients who had engaged this contractor.

In *Naylor v Payling*, Mr Payling, C, was ejected from the Main Street nightclub in Rotherham by a door steward who acted negligently in doing so. C suffered severe head injuries. Mr Naylor, D, owned and ran the nightclub. The security contractor who provided the door stewards had provided security services at the nightclub as D's independent contractor for 18 months. It turned out that they did not hold any public liability insurance policy for the injuries to C. D admitted that he had never enquired of the security contractor as to whether they carried public liability insurance. **Held**: D, as occupier, selected the security contractor with reasonable care. The security contractor had provided employees who were licensed by the local authority as accredited individuals to carry out security; D had satisfied himself that the security officers were properly accredited; D had no reason to consider their work unsatisfactory before this incident occurred; no untoward incident had happened before C's injury in D's club; and D had obtained good references about them from the previous owner. There was no duty on D to check their insurance position.

Naylor clarified the position, from the earlier and confusing decision in *Gwilliam v West Hertfordshire Hospitals NHS Trust*.[242] Both members of the majority in *Gwilliam* (Lord Woolf CJ and Waller LJ) seemed to suggest that a free-standing duty on the occupier to check the contractor's insurance cover did exist, but Waller LJ later clarified, in *Naylor*,[243] that this is **not** what he intended.

In *Honeybourne v Burgess*, the Scottish Outer House concluded, from its perusal of the relevant English authorities, that 'properly analysed, they do not support the proposition that an occupier has ... a "free-standing" duty ... to take any steps to satisfy himself that an independent

[240] [2004] EWCA Civ 560, [2004] PIQR P36, 615. [241] [2010] PIQR 123 (CA).
[242] [2002] EWCA Civ 1041, [2003] QB 443. [243] [2004] EWCA Civ 560, [55]–[59].

contractor has insurance cover'.[244] Hence, occupier D can meet the s 2(4)(b) defence, even where the contractor is not insured.

However, Neuberger LJ made the point, in *Naylor*,[245] that the more hazardous the task for which the contractor was engaged, then the greater the care which the law will expect of an occupier when selecting that contractor – and a failure to ascertain whether the contractor was insured **may** show that the occupier did not discharge suitable checks to avail himself of s 2(4)(b), especially if the contractor was uninsurable due to its history. Those were not the facts in *Naylor*, because the activities of a bouncer did not 'fall within the type of hazardous activity which was under consideration in *Bottomley*'.

In *Bottomley v Todmorden Cricket Club*,[246] Mr Bottomley, C, suffered very serious facial and other injuries at the Todmorden Cricket Club's, D's, annual fundraising fete. Chaos Encounter, a two-man stunt team, had been engaged by D, as independent contractors, to conduct a pyrotechnic (bonfire and fireworks) display. The men from Chaos invited C to help them carry out their show. His task was to prime the mortars by lowering gunpowder in a plastic bag into the mortar. However, the contents of the mortar tube ignited and exploded in C's face, causing him severe burns and a broken arm. Chaos Enterprises, the independent contractor, carried no public liability insurance. **Held**: D was directly liable to C, for failing to select Chaos Encounter with reasonable care. Chaos asked C to assist when he had had no training or experience in the use of pyrotechnics. Chaos presented D with no safety plan for the event, nor did D ask for one, when D knew beforehand that Chaos intended to perform a potentially dangerous stunt involving pyrotechnics. D professed not to know that C was to be involved, which only went to show 'the extent of the club's ignorance as to what was going on'. If D had taken reasonable care to inquire into Chaos's credentials, it would have found that they were largely unaware of the basic safety requirements needed, and 'an amateurish organisation in a field which required the highest degree of professionalism to avoid danger'. Further, in deciding whether a pyrotechnic stunt performer was competent, an enquiry about insurance was necessary, and proper checks would have revealed that Chaos had no public liability insurance. If a failure to have insurance in such a dangerous field was because Chaos was unable to procure it, that might suggest either a history of claims or insufficient funds to pay the premiums – indicating that 'short-cuts' on safety might also have been taken. Insurance cover was very relevant to Chaos's experience, reliability and general suitability to carry out the pyrotechnic display.

However, even where hazardous activities are being arranged or conducted by the independent contractor, *Gwilliam* suggests that merely asking, and receiving an affirmative answer, that insurance was in place, is sufficient.

In *Gwilliam*, Mrs Gwilliam, 63, C, was injured when using a 'splat-wall', which entailed bouncing from a trampoline and adhering by Velcro to a wall. The splat-wall was hired from Club Entertainments by D's hospital, as part of its fair activities. It was arranged that the hospital, D, would take advantage of Club Entertainment's public liability insurance policy, D not having insurance itself for this equipment. Unfortunately, the splat-wall was set up by Club Entertainment's employees negligently, and C was injured; and even worse, Club Entertainment's public liability insurance cover expired some 4 days before C's accident. **Held:** D was not liable, for it had selected Club Entertainments as its independent contractor with reasonable care. Although the hospital selected Club Entertainments from the phone book, the hospital had no reason to doubt the competency of

[244] 2006 SLT 585, 2006 SCLR 227 (OH) [24]. [245] [2004] EWCA Civ 560, [38], with quote at [58] (Waller LJ).
[246] [2003] EWCA Civ 1575.

their staff. Further, D was under a duty to enquire into the insurance position of Club Entertainments, because operating the splat-wall was a hazardous activity and the hospital accepted that it would have had to carry public liability insurance if this had been its own equipment. However, the hospital's fund-raising manager *did* enquire of Club Entertainments as to their insurance position, and told the contractor that, 'you have to make sure that insurance is put in hand, that is basic', to which the contractor had said that it had the necessary insurance. According to the majority, that was sufficient for the hospital to meet the requirements of s 2(4)(b). The hospital's rep did not ask to see the policy, but (held Woolf MR) he was not required to ask to see it. To impose that sort of burden on an employer would be 'an unreasonable requirement', and in any event, checking the terms of the policy would not preclude the possibility that Club Entertainment's own conduct could somehow void the policy. Hence, there was no breach of duty by the employer, and C failed in her claim.

Hence, in *Honeybourne v Burgess*,[247] Smith J noted that establishing a duty on the part of the occupier to have ascertained about insurance could be a distinctly 'pyrrhic victory' for C, where the enquiry was made, the answer was wrong, D had no duty to do anything further, and C has no deep pocket against which to sue. Hence, *Gwilliam* showed that 'discharge of the duty did not, as a matter of fact, produce a situation whereby the injurious event was covered by any insurance at all ... It is, of course, not difficult to envisage the sort of difficulties that could arise if occupiers were required to check certificates'.

Causation/remoteness

§12.21 Whether the occupier's, D's, breach caused visitor C's damage (including the 'but-for' test), and whether that damage was too remote at law to be foreseeable, are governed by the usual principles of negligence.

The usual principles governing causation and remoteness, discussed in Chapters 8 and 9 respectively, apply with equal force to actions brought under the OLAs.

For example, even if occupier D had taken precautionary steps to protect visitor C, if C's injury probably would have happened anyway, causation will fail. This will occur if, say, C was so determined to gain access to the premises that no further fencing would have stopped him (*Scott v Associated British Ports*,[248] where two young boys were playing truant and 'surfing' on moving train wagons); or C had shown himself to be 'quite indifferent to any notices' in the past (i.e., it was 'fanciful' that any additional notices would have mattered) (*Ratcliff v Harpur Adams Agricultural College*[249]). Plainly, whatever C says on the subject of what he would have/not have done, is not conclusive. C's statement will be tested against the objective evidence.

One potential remoteness problem is where occupier D should have taken precautionary steps to prevent a risk of certain injury to visitor C, and had that step been taken, C would not have entered the premises. However, the step was not taken (which was a breach by the occupier), C **did** enter the premises – and then suffered a different type of injury altogether. Is the injury which actually manifested too remote to be recoverable at law? A causal link is certainly established, because C would not have suffered his injury, but for the occupier's breach. However, it will be recalled (from Chapter 9) that this scenario is reminiscent of the

[247] 2006 SLT 585, 2006 SCLR 227 (OH) [20]. [248] (CA, 22 Nov 2000) [16].

[249] (QB, 7 Nov 1997, Judge Brunning QC) [48], although ultimately no duty of care was owed by D on appeal: [1999] 1 WLR 670 (CA).

'mountaineer-caught-in-the-avalanche' example provided by Lord Hoffmann in *South Australia Asset Management Corp (SAAMCO) v York Montague Ltd.*[250] In that case, the House took the view that the law should **not** penalise D's wrongful conduct by shifting onto him the **whole** risk of consequences which followed from D's breach (and hence, the injury that manifested to C would be too remote). Of course, to shift the whole consequences to the occupier would help to deter wrongful conduct, but that is not the English legal position. In the context of occupiers' liability, there is a leading illustrative authority:

In *Darby v The National Trust*,[251] facts previously, the pond at Hardwick Hall was not systematically patrolled, although wardens would periodically discourage people from swimming, telling them of the danger of Weils disease (a disease transmitted from rats' urine). The court held that the risk of contracting Weils disease required a notice, and the cost of the sign would have been minimal. However, there was no breach on the part of the National Trust in not warning against the dangers of drowning in the pond – because that danger was obvious. Hence, the drowning was too remote (or, as the court put it, outside the scope of D's duties as an occupier). Weils disease 'was not the kind of risk or damage which Mr Darby suffered, and any duty to warn against Weils disease cannot ... support a claim for damages resulting from a quite different cause'. The risk of catching Weils disease and the risk of drowning 'are of an intrinsically different kind, and so are any dependent duties'.

TRESPASSERS UNDER THE OCCUPIERS' LIABILITY ACT 1984

At common law, things frequently looked bleak for injured trespassers. According to *Robert Addie v Dumbreck*,[252] an occupier was under a duty not to deliberately, intentionally, or recklessly harm a trespasser. Viscount Dunedin gave this example: 'if the person is a trespasser, then [the occupier] ... may not shoot him; and he may not set a spring gun, for that is just to arrange to shoot him without personally firing the shot.'

In *Robert Addie*, the occupier colliery owner was not liable when C, a little boy of 4, wandered into a field being used as a dump for the deposit of ashes from the pithead of a colliery, and was accidentally killed when he sat on an unprotected iron wheel. There was no intentional or reckless conduct on D's part – he was using the land in the course of his business, and was under no obligation to protect trespassers.

The status of the *Robert Addie* principle was, however, muddied by *British Rwys Board v Herrington*,[253] in which Lord Pearson stated that the occupier's duty to a trespasser was slightly higher – 'a duty to treat the trespasser with ordinary humanity' (whatever that might mean). It was sufficient, at any rate, to ensure compensation to the child trespasser in that case.

In *Herrington*, the railway authority was liable in negligence towards C, 6, who wandered from a meadow which was a popular play-spot with children onto an electrified railway line and was electrocuted. He gained access because the fence was dilapidated. The station master knew that children had been seen on the line, and that the fence was out of repair.

[250] [1997] AC 191 (HL) 212. [251] [2001] EWCA Civ 189, [2001] PIQR P27, [6], [22], [25].
[252] [1929] AC 358 (HL) 365 (Lord Hailsham LC), with Viscount Dunedin's examples at 376.
[253] [1972] AC 877 (HL) 882–83, 922 (Lord Pearson).

Of *Herrington*, the Court of Appeal said in *Ratcliff v McConnell*[254] that there was a real 'difficulty of seeing its precise ratio', while in *Donoghue v Folkestone Properties Ltd*,[255] Brooks LJ described it as a case in which '[t]he five law lords spoke with different voices when they tried to identify the occasions on which an occupier's duty to a trespasser might arise. They also spoke with different voices when they sought to identify the content of that duty'.

Unsurprisingly, a reference to the Law Commission occurred just two months after *Herrington* was handed down, and led to the *Report on Liability for Damage or Injury to Trespassers and Related Questions of Occupiers' Liability*,[256] and eight years later, the OLA 1984.

Whilst the law may not be quite as unsympathetic now towards trespassers who are injured by the state of an occupier's premises as it was in the day of *Robert Addie*, the pre-requisites for establishing a cause of action under the OLA 1984 for occupiers' liability is littered with considerable legal challenges. There are some trespassers for whom judges have expressed great sympathy – 'a moment of misplaced youthful exuberance'[257] with life-long consequences in the form of tetraplegia, or an accident which had 'the most appalling consequences, a promising life is now destined to be spent in a wheelchair'[258] – but where the trespasser has left the court with an 'empty pocket'. This is primarily due to the tough legal stance which both the Legislature, and the courts, have generally adopted towards trespassers under the OLA 1984.

A duty of care toward a trespasser

The duty to a trespasser has been reformulated[259] on a statutory basis.

§12.22 An occupier, D, will owe a trespasser, C, a duty of care if three conditions are met (per s 1(3), OLA 1984):

(a) D was aware of the danger or had reasonable grounds to believe that it existed;
(b) D knew, or had reasonable grounds to believe, that C was in the vicinity of the danger, or that he might come into that vicinity; and
(c) the risk is one against which, in all the circumstances of the case, D might reasonably be expected to have offered C some protection.

All three criteria must be met. Although the section does not say so, the Court of Appeal stated in *Donoghue v Folkestone Property*[260] that each criterion is time-specific: it must be evaluated in light of C's characteristics, and the circumstances prevailing, when C suffered the injury.

The danger on the premises

§12.23 Under s 1(3)(a), the particular danger to trespasser C must be specified; and it is of that danger that occupier D must have had the requisite knowledge.

The relevant 'danger' which the premises posed to trespasser C must be strictly identified, e.g., a fire escape which was unguarded and unfenced (*Keown v Coventry Healthcare NHS Trust*[261]);

[254] [1999] 1 WLR 670 (CA) [33]. [255] [2003] EWCA Civ 231, [67]. [256] EWLC (Rep 75, 1976).
[257] *Rhind v Astbury Water Park Ltd* [2004] EWCA Civ 756, [18].
[258] *Ratcliff v McConnell* [1999] 1 WLR 670 (CA) [49].
[259] Per EWLC, *Damage or Injury to Trespassers and Related Questions of Occupiers' Liability* (Rep 75, 1976).
[260] [2003] EWCA Civ 231, [2003] QB 1008, [18]. [261] [2006] EWCA Civ 39.

a steep unfenced grassy slope which dropped to a concrete pedestrian subway (*Maloney v Torfaen CBC*[262]); a pool of unfenced shallow water (*Ratcliff v McConnell*[263]); a fibre-glass container half-submerged in the bed of a lake (*Rhind v Astbury Water Park*[264]); or a readily-climbable roof which had a brittle skylight (*Young v Kent CC*[265]). It follows that the more narrowly-defined the danger, the more likely that occupier D will say that he was not aware, nor had reasonable grounds for believing, that the danger existed on his premises. How the danger is defined can make a material difference to the outcome of s 1(3)(a).

In *Scott v Associated British Ports*,[266] two young boys, 16 and 13, engaged in the practice of 'surfing', i.e., climbing onto moving train wagons via an access ladder and jumping off as the wagons started to accelerate. Both boys were playing truant from school, and glue-sniffing, meaning that their judgment was probably impaired. They fell, and suffered limb amputations. **Held (at trial):** the danger of the premises was of young boys 'surfing'. The railway authority, D, was not aware of their premises being used for that, and hence could not be liable. **Held (CA):** the danger should be defined more widely as the risk of injury or death caused by moving trains. On that basis, D knew that trespassers, including children, were regularly on or near the railway tracks. Hence, s 1(3)(a) was satisfied (but, as causation failed, that was dicta). Similarly, in *Young v Kent CC*,[267] facts previously (the skylight case), **held:** the fact that children were known to congregate and meet near the passageway of the school, which had a readily climbable means of access to the flat roof, was enough to meet the criterion in s 1(3)(a), notwithstanding that there was no evidence to suggest that D knew that children actually stood or jumped on the skylights, which is actually what caused the injury to C.

As s 1(3)(a) provides, actual knowledge by occupier D of the risk of danger to trespasser C is sufficient. That will be a matter of the evidence *in toto*. For example, in *Young v Kent CC*,[268] the requisite knowledge on the Council, D's, part, was derived from witnesses at the youth club ('children frequently went up onto this roof, and the club staff knew of it, because Mr Richards was regularly calling them to come down'), plus the school itself admitted that it had been experiencing problems with trespass and vandalism and in particular access to the roof prior to the incident.

The other type of knowledge permitted by s 1(3)(a) – that D had 'reasonable grounds to believe that the danger exists' – means 'shut-eye' knowledge, i.e., that D knew of certain 'primary facts' that provided reasonable grounds for believing that the risk of injury existed (per *Swain v Puri*[269]). It does not require proof of any malice or bad faith on D's part.[270] D is also **not** required to meticulously inspect his premises for possible dangers, so as to give rise to a form of constructive knowledge (i.e., that D ought to have taken steps to acquire knowledge of the dangers). Neither of the following occupiers had the requisite 'shut eye' knowledge (and they certainly had no actual knowledge) of the dangers which their premises posed, and hence, the trespassers failed under s 1(3)(a):

In *Rhind v Astbury Water Park Ltd*,[271] facts previously, the Water Park operators had not been aware of the fibreglass container on the bed of the lake, nor were there reasonable grounds to believe that

[262] [2005] EWCA Civ 1762, [2006] PIQR P21 (CA), where Laws LJ regarded this as arguable, at [29].
[263] [1999] 1 WLR 670 (CA). [264] [2004] EWCA Civ 756. [265] [2005] EWHC 1342 (QB) [25], [29].
[266] CA, 22 Nov 2000, [6], [16]. [267] [2005] EWHC 1342 (QB) [31], [33]. [268] *ibid*, [22], [33].
[269] [1996] PIQR P442 (CA) P446 (Pill LJ), P448 (Evans LJ).
[270] *Milne v Express Newspapers (No 1)* [2004] EWCA Civ 664, [43]. [271] [2004] EWCA Civ 756.

it existed. Following the accident, it took a diver using a snorkel and mask and feeling carefully over the bed of the lake to find it at all. It would have been different if there had been some object or spike in the lake of which D was aware, but those were not these facts. In *Swain v Puri*, Carl Swain, 9, C, together with his young brother, gained access to an abandoned warehouse owned by D, by climbing over a 7 ft-high corrugated fence, at a section where some barbed wire was missing. The boys climbed onto the roof, and C then fell through a skylight about 25 ft to the floor. Reasonable inspection would have revealed the gap in the perimeter wire, but D did not know of that gap, and furthermore, was not required to inspect its fencing, looking for dangers. There were no facts upon which to base 'shut-eye' knowledge, and D was not liable.

In the vicinity

§12.24 Under s 1(3)(b), occupier D must have the requisite knowledge that trespasser C was, or might come, in the vicinity of D's premises. The enquiry is time-specific, depending upon the time of day or the time of year of the accident.

The same standard of knowledge is required of occupier D under this limb as was required under s 1(3)(a), i.e., either actual or 'shut-eye' (i.e., some reasonable grounds to believe) knowledge. Also, it is enough if occupier D had reasonable grounds to believe that, not the trespasser himself, but a class of persons of whom the trespasser was one, was in the vicinity, or might come within the vicinity, of danger.

For example, the requisite knowledge will be proven if: D had seen footholds in the perimeter wall but had never personally seen trespassers (*Swain v Puri*[272]); D had seen trespassers on his premises prior to the accident and asked them to leave (*Young v Kent CC*[273]); D had been notified of trespassers' access to the premises by some responsible third party, say, a Health and Safety Executive (*Young v Kent CC*); or D was aware that his premises formed a natural and frequently-used route for trespassers from one place to another (argued, but not proven, in *White v St Albans CDC*[274]).

On the other hand, 'reasonable grounds for believing' that a trespasser might be in the vicinity is **not** proven by factors such as: the mere fact that D's premises could be entered relatively easily by a trespasser (*Higgs v Foster (t/as Avalon Coaches)*[275]); or that D had installed security lights, chain-link fencing, or other precautionary steps, to deter access to the premise (*White v St Albans' CDC*). Significantly, just because D has taken precautions against trespassers does **not** prove that he had reasonable grounds for believing that a trespasser was likely to come into the vicinity of a danger.

In *Higgs v Foster (t/as Avalon Coaches)*, Mr Higgs, C, a police officer, was investigating a suspected stolen trailer which had been parked in the service yard of a supermarket. To observe it better, C entered the premises where Avalon Coaches, C, kept its buses. With no torch to help him, he fell into an uncovered inspection pit, and suffered serious injuries, forcing him out of the police force. D's usual practice was to park a coach over that pit, but this night, there was about 10 feet uncovered at the back of the coach. **Held**: C was a trespasser under the OLA 1984; but there were no reasonable grounds for D's believing that trespassers would be in the vicinity. In *Maloney v Torfaen CBC*,[276] there was no photographic evidence to show that the steep grassy slope was being used

[272] [1996] PIQR P 442 (CA) P446 (Pill LJ). [273] [2005] EWHC 1342 (QB) [23].
[274] CA, 2 Mar 1990. [275] [2004] EWCA Civ 843, [10].
[276] [2005] EWCA Civ 1762, [20], [29] (Laws LJ), affirming the trial judge's conclusion on that pre-requisite.

as a pedestrian short-cut, no complaints from nearby residents, and no requests to the Council to create a proper footpath – so there was neither actual nor 'shut-eye' knowledge that trespassers were in the vicinity.

The pre-requisite is time-specific, as noted previously. Hence, the occupier may not know, or have reasonable grounds to believe, that a trespasser was in the vicinity of danger, if the accident occurred at night (as in *Maloney*, where C was crossing a steep grassy slope in the pitch dark), or in freezing weather (as in *Donoghue v Folkestone Properties*,[277] where the accident happened on a cold, dark, mid-winter night, quite different from 'children swimming or diving in the harbour at high tide on a sunny August bank holiday weekend'). At some times of the day or the year, trespassers could be considered to be such a rare occurrence that a reasonable occupier could safely discount the possibility.

Some protection

§12.25 Under s 1(3)(c), it must have been reasonable for occupier D to offer trespasser C some protection. D does not have to provide any protection to a trespasser against obvious risks. This element is likely to fail, where C was of sufficient age and capacity to fully appreciate the danger for himself.

For obvious dangers, occupier D does **not** need to provide C with any protection. The principles canvassed previously,[278] about what constitutes an obvious risk and how the law treats a *visitor* who runs an obvious risk and is then injured, apply equally to the case of a *trespasser*. In *Tomlinson v Congleton BC*,[279] Lord Hoffmann stated that, with respect to obvious dangers, 'plainly there can have been no duty under the 1984 Act. The risk was not one against which [a trespasser] was entitled under s 1(3)(c) to protection'. The following cases involved obvious dangers, for which D was **not** liable under the OLA 1984:

> In *Tomlinson*, facts previously, diving into water of unknown depth was an obvious danger, against which it was not reasonable for the occupier to provide the trespasser with protection other than warning signs. In *Keown*, although C was only 11, he fully appreciated the dangers of climbing the fire escape, the risk of falling was obvious. In *Kolasa v Ealing Hosp NHS Trust*, the wall from which the hospital patient fell had obvious risks, and was of an adequate height, and nothing further by way of deterrent (raising its height, or putting some rail or other deterrent on top of it) was warranted. In *Bartrum v Hepworth Minerals and Chemicals Ltd*,[280] Mr Bartrum, C, visiting a recreational site, dived from a cliff on a quarry face into a pool, striking his head on a protruding shelf under the surface of the water which was clearly visible. He did not dive far enough out from the cliff face. The danger here 'was so obvious to any adult that it was not reasonably to be expected of [D] that they would offer any protection'.

For adult trespassers of full capacity, it will be difficult to satisfy s 1(3)(c) so as to establish a duty of care. As demonstrated in *Donoghue v Folkestone Properties Ltd*,[281] adults can be expected to look out for dangers on premises upon which they are trespassing, in which case, why should a reasonable occupier guard against those dangers? For child trespassers who are too young to heed a written or oral warning, more (e.g., physical barriers) may be expected of

[277] [2003] EWCA Civ 231, [2003] QB 1008, [77] (Brooke LJ). [278] See pp 615–23.
[279] [2003] UKHL 47, [2004] 1 AC 46, [50]. [280] QB, 29 Oct 1999, Turner J. [281] [2003] EWCA Civ 231, [41].

an occupier in providing them with some protection (per *Herrington v British Rwys Board*[282]). Even so, English courts have not been particularly sympathetic to child trespassers. For example, the 9-year-old boy who got through the barbed wire fence and fell through the roof in *Swain v Puri*;[283] the 14-year-old girl who was impaled on the fence in *Burke v Southern Education Library Board*[284] and a 15-year-old girl who trespassed onto railway lines in *McGinley or Titchener v British Rwys Board*[285] were all old enough to appreciate the dangers which they were running, and not trespassers for whom the occupiers might reasonably be expected to offer some protection.

Setting the standard of care, and proving breach

§12.26 The standard of care expected of an occupier, D, towards a trespasser, C, is to 'take such care as is reasonable, in all the circumstances of the case, to see that he does not suffer injury on the premises by reason of the danger concerned' (per s 1(4), OLA 1984). The assessment of breach requires the court to consider the precautionary factors which a reasonable occupier could have taken to provide some protection to C; and to consider those, in light of s 1(4).

The occupier, D, is not under a duty to ensure that a trespasser cannot enter the premises; or to light premises at night to ensure that trespassers can see their way about; or to otherwise ensure that the premises are 'fit for trespassers to trespass in' (per *Herrington v British Rwys Board*,[286] and approved under the OLA 1984 in *Swain v Puri*[287]). As noted previously, D does not need to check his premises for hidden dangers either.

Although the usual quadrant of factors applies, all that the occupier is required to do is to provide *some* protection. The case law to date indicates that, where the presence of trespassers was known to occur, and there were low-cost precautionary measures available to deter them and which were not taken, then breach may be proven (e.g., in *Young v Kent CC*,[288] there was a clear precautionary measure to prevent access to the roof, *viz*, to fence off the passageway to stop access to the roof, which the school should have done).

On the other hand, where the precautionary steps would entail cost, to either D personally or to third party interests, then breach is very unlikely. As the Court of Appeal remarked in *Mann v Northern Electric Distribution Ltd*,[289] 'no amount of security measures will keep out a sufficiently determined trespasser' (the trespasser, 15, was *very* determined there, climbing a high wall to get into an electricity substation, where he was electrocuted, suffering severe burns and leg amputation). Further, *Keown* confirms that the resources available to D impact on the precautionary steps which could reasonably be expected of D under s 1(4):

> In *Burke v Southern Education and Library Bd*[290] (the impaling on a fence case), the suggested precautionary steps (covering the sharp points on the gate, removing this type of gate) would expose the school to increased vandalism and arson, which had been serious problems in the past. In *Keown v Coventry Healthcare NHS Trust*[291] (the fire escape case), there were precautionary steps available (fencing off the fire escape, arranging for a patrol of the grounds by security guards, fencing off the entire grounds from the public), but they were not considered necessary. The resources of

[282] [1972] AC 877 (HL) 940. [283] [1996] PIQR P442 (CA). [284] [2004] NIQB 13, [29].
[285] [1983] 1 WLR 1427 (HL) 1433–34. [286] [1972] AC 877 (HL) 909 (Lord Morris).
[287] [1996] PIQR P442 (CA) 450 (McCowan LJ). [288] [2005] EWHC 1342 (QB) [33].
[289] [2010] EWCA Civ 141, [18]. [290] [2004] NIQB 13. [291] [2006] EWCA Civ 39, [2006] 1 WLR 953, [17], [24].

a NHS were 'much more sensibly utilised in the treatment and care of patients, together with the proper remuneration of nurses and doctors, rather than catering for the contingency (one hopes infrequent) that children will climb where they know they should not go'. Also, if the whole premises were fenced off (which is exactly what happened after the accident), that would render the hospital ground 'a bit like a fortress', which would destroy the amenity to the general public of passing through the grounds to neighbouring streets and of children harmlessly playing in the grounds. Further, it would set a wrongful precedent, in that 'occupiers of buildings up and down the country will have to "child-proof" their buildings in case children try to climb them'.

Given the actual or 'shut-eye' knowledge which occupier D must have about the danger and the presence of trespassers in the vicinity in order to owe any duty of care under s 1(3), it would be surprising if an occupier could owe a duty of care, and yet, be found not to be liable for breach because the incident of trespassing had never occurred previously. Yet, that rather odd legal result **has** manifested.

In *Platt v Liverpool CC*,[292] the Council, D, was undertaking a rehousing programme, and the empty houses gave rise to regular problems with vandals, scavengers, drug addicts and playing children. D covered the houses' doors and windows with metal sheets, and arranged for employees to check them daily and report if the shuttering was damaged. D also erected a strong 8-ft high metal fence. One day, David Platt, 14, C, got inside an empty house with some friends. The house collapsed, and C was killed. There was a gap of about 8 inches where some metal sheeting had been slightly lifted at one side of the fence, just big enough for a child to go under. **Held**: D did not breach the OLA 1984. There was no evidence that children had ever either climbed the fence or entered through the gap. 'The position might have been different if it was known that children had habitually been wriggling through the 8-inch gap but there was no evidence ... of that kind whatsoever'.

Statutory 'escape hatch' for the occupier, D

Contrary to the position under the OLA 1957, there are not three statutory escape hatches for an occupier D under the OLA 1984, but only **one**.

§12.27 If an occupier, D, has warned trespassers about the dangers posed by the state of the premises, that will absolve D from breach (per s 1(5), OLA 1984).

The law relating to this provision is the same as under s 2(4)(a) of the OLA 1957, *viz*, there is no duty upon an occupier to warn, or otherwise protect a trespasser (by means of physical obstacles), against an *obvious risk*.

In *Ratcliff v McConnell*,[293] Luke Ratcliff, C, a student at an agricultural college, climbed over a 7-ft gate at night, dived into an open-air swimming pool owned by the college, without checking the depth, and suffered tetraplegia when hitting his head on the bottom of the pool. **Held:** no breach under the OLA 1984. More warning signs and other obstacles were not necessary to deter trespassers, given the obviousness of the risk to any adult.

DEFENCES

§12.28 An occupier, D, may rely upon the defences of contributory negligence, and the acts of a stranger. In addition, *volenti* is statutorily-provided; and the common duty of care under the OLA

[292] CA, 1 May 1997. [293] [1999] 1 WLR 670 (CA) [36]–[37].

1957 can be modified or excluded by express agreement between D and the visitor. Whether D can validly exclude liability for loss or damage suffered by a trespasser is unclear on the present state of the law.

Contributory negligence

Despite the defence not being explicitly referred to under either Act, a lack of care for his own safety and well-being on the part of either a trespasser or a lawful visitor will attract the defence of contributory negligence for the occupier. Higher expectations of behaviour may be expected of a visitor who is a highly-experienced professional.

In *Rae v Mars (UK) Ltd*,[294] facts previously, a surveyor fully familiar with visiting hazardous premises to carry out surveys was liable for 33% CN for failing to turn on his torch when walking into a dark room, where he fell into a pit. In *Slack v Glenie*,[295] facts previously, C, the racing rider, was 50% contributorily negligent, because he knew that he would be riding on a fast track with no brakes, in circumstances where the stability and control of his machine depended largely on the skill of a passenger with whom he had never ridden before, whose experience related to a different type of track, and with whom he had no established means of communication. Also, C could have done more to lessen the impact, by pulling on the lanyard and disconnecting the power.

Although age may suppress the standard of care expected of C, child trespassers may suffer fairly significant findings of contributory negligence under the OLA 1984.

In *Young v Kent CC*,[296] facts previously, C, 12, was found liable for 50% CN, for stepping or jumping on the brittle skylight. In *Keown v Coventry Healthcare NHS Trust*,[297] facts previously, C, 11, had his damages reduced at trial by 67% for undertaking what the trial judge described as a 'foolhardy and rash enterprise' in climbing the fire escape; but, on appeal, C lost altogether, for no static danger was involved, the OLA 1984 hence did not apply, and no other cause of action was available to C.

If C would have rejected any training about the hazards present on the occupier's, D's, premises, that will justify some finding of contributory negligence (25%, in the case of *Ireland v David Lloyd Leisure Ltd*,[298] the amputated-finger-in-the-gym case).

The remaining principles associated with this defence, discussed in Chapter 10, will not be repeated herein.

Acts of strangers

An occupier does not owe a duty of care to avoid injury to visitors when it is the negligence of a stranger which caused the injury (per *H&N Emanuel Ltd v GLC*[299]).

Volenti

The *volenti* defence is available against a lawful visitor (per s 2(5), OLA 1957) and against a trespasser (per s 1(6), OLA 1984). These provisions preserve (and reproduced, according to *Geary v JD Wetherspoon plc*[300]) the common law defence. Hence, it has two constituent

[294] [1990] 3 EG 80 (QB). [295] CA, 19 Apr 2000, [11]. [296] [2005] EWHC 1342 (QB). [297] [2006] EWCA Civ 39. [298] [2013] EWCA Civ 665, [34]. [299] [1971] 2 All ER 835 (HL) 838. [300] [2011] EWHC 1506 (QB) [36].

elements: that C (1) knew of the risks of danger; and (2) freely and voluntarily consented to bear the consequences of that risk (per *Ratcliff v McConnell*[301]). Its effect is that entrant C exempts the occupier, D, from any obligation towards his safety. However, if the risk was obvious, and the entrant ran the risk anyway, then the OLAs will technically not apply at all (see discussion previously). In any event, the defence succeeded in the following cases:

> In *Ratcliff v McConnell*, C, the student who dived into the pool in the dark, had been told by the school's staff that the pool was closed and contained dangerous chemicals; he knew that its levels were kept low during winter; he deliberately climbed over a wall 7 ft high; he knew that there was no standard depth profile in pools, and did not know the depths where he was diving; he knew that alcohol might affect his judgment (having had 4 pints); and ignored the notice at the gate, although saw the word, 'WARNING'. In *Geary*, C was not drunk when leaving the pub, and she knew the risks of sliding down the banisters. In both cases, C was aware of the risk and willingly accepted it. In *Kolasa v Ealing Hosp NHS Trust*, re the man who fell off the hospital wall, he was somewhat drunk, but he nevertheless 'willingly accepted the risk of climbing over the wall', and s 1(6) was expressly held to exempt the hospital, D, from liability (among other reasons).

Of course, the defence cannot apply, if C did not know that the occupier's premises did not comply with the relevant building standards, because then it cannot be proven that C had full knowledge or appreciation of the risk of danger, and hence, the first element of the defence will fail (per *Slack v Glenie*[302]).

Exclusion by agreement or otherwise

Under s 2(1) of the OLA 1957, the occupier's common duty of care extends to 'all his visitors, except in so far as he is free to and does extend, restrict, modify or exclude his duty to any visitors by agreement or otherwise'. In accordance with usual contractual principles, any 'agreement' between visitor C and occupier D must suitably incorporate the exclusion clause; the clause will be construed against D who is seeking to rely on it (e.g., if the clause excludes D's liability for accidents to 'spectators and ticket-holders', but C is a competitor, the exclusion will not apply); and absent any contractual document, D must draw the clause specifically to C's attention and obtain his express or implied assent (per *White v Blackmore*[303]). The erection of warning signs does not, of itself, enable D to rely on s 2(1) – that is clearly the effect of the statutory escape hatch in s 2(4)(a).

Section 2(1) must now be read in the light of the Unfair Contract Terms Act 1977, which applies to **business** occupiers, i.e., where D occupies the premises 'used for business purposes of the occupier' (s 1(3), UCTA 1977). Any attempt to exclude D's liability for death or personal injury is strictly prohibited; and for property and other damage, the exclusion must be reasonable in all the circumstances, for D to rely upon it (s 2, UCTA). Where the visitor accesses premises for recreational or educational purposes, then if D is providing those services at his premises for a business purpose, the terms of UCTA apply to restrict what D can exclude; otherwise, UCTA does not apply, and D can validly exclude liability for liability towards those visitors.

[301] [1999] 1 WLR 670, [47]. For other applications of the *volenti* defence against an entrant, see, e.g.: *Titchener v British Rwys Board* [1983] 3 All ER 770 (HL); *Proctor v Young* [2009] NIQB 56, [35].

[302] CA, 19 Apr 2000, [10], citing the trial judge.

[303] [1972] 2 QB 651 (CA) 656–57.

In *Monarch Airlines Ltd v London Luton Airport Ltd*,[304] Monarch Airlines, C, owned a 737 plane (with an insured value of US$30m), which was damaged when it was taking off from Luton Airport, owned by D. Approximately 130 square metres of paving blocks on the runway became displaced and struck the aircraft, causing about £500k worth of damage. It was agreed that C was a visitor to the airport, and that the runway was premises. However, cl 10 of D's standard conditions excluded liability for damage to aircraft arising from any act, omission, neglect or default on the part of the airport company or its employees (unless done intentionally or recklessly). **Held:** the clause excluded liability for D's negligence (even though negligence was not referred to). The clause also met the standard of reasonableness in UCTA 1997.

However, whether a business occupier can validly exclude liability towards *trespassers* (whether for personal injury, property damage, or other) is unclear, given that the OLA 1984 and UCTA 1977 do not refer to the issue at all, and nor does any judicial authority to date, so far as the author's searches can ascertain.

REMEDIES

§12.29 An award of damages is the principal remedy under the OLAs. However, unlike visitors, trespassers cannot recover for property damage.

For lawful visitors, damages for both personal injury and property damage are recoverable (the latter is provided for under s 1(3)(b), OLA 1957).

However, for trespassers, the only damages recoverable are for death or personal injury (including 'impairment ... of mental condition') (per s 1(9), OLA 1984). Although there is no binding authority on point, it is likely that this would cover a recognisable psychiatric injury (as applies in negligence), and not pure mental distress of some lower order. Recovery for property damage is explicitly barred by s 1(8), OLA 1984.

Hence, the question arises as to whether the common law duty to a trespasser as expressed in *Herrington* (i.e., a duty of 'ordinary humanity') has survived the enactment of the OLA 1984 – given that no such bar on property damage was applied at common law. However, in *Tomlinson* (CA),[305] Ward LJ expressed the view that, when determining a duty of care to a trespasser arising from the state of the premises (which Ward LJ held to be the case here, but which was ultimately overturned on appeal, the House of Lords holding that Mr Tomlinson was harmed from an *activity danger*, not a static, danger), it was 'essential to use the 1984 Act as a template for judgment in each and every case', and that 'the question [of duty] depends solely upon whether the three criteria of section 1(3) are satisfied'. This point was not dealt with on appeal. Further, in *Donoghue v Folkestone Properties Ltd*, where a duty of care under s 1(3) was not established (albeit that the case concerned C's personal injury), none of the Court of Appeal judges sought recourse to the *Herrington* common law duty. These authorities suggest that the common law does **not** operate alongside the 1984 Act.

[304] [1997] CLC 698 (QB, Comm). [305] [2002] EWCA Civ 309, [19]–[21].

13

Public authority liability

This chapter considers the liability of public authorities in negligence. It applies many of the principles discussed in Chapters 2 and 3, when assessing the duty of care (if any) owed by a public authority, where that authority's acts or omissions cause C loss or damage. Inevitably, as a result of the analysis adopted by the courts in this area of negligence, proof of breach is closely intertwined with the duty of care analysis.

INTRODUCTION

§13.1 In the context of suits in negligence, 'public authorities' are those entities which are established by statutory instrument (including delegated legislation), and/or which have responsibility for exercising a statutory duty or a statutory power which has, as its aim, the provision of some public service. Statutory *duties* are imposed where a statutory scheme requires a public authority to take action in a particular province of activity, whereas statutory *powers* arise where a statute empowers the public authority to take action at its discretion.

A public authority may comprise the following: health authorities; the police; local planning, education, etc, authorities; government departments; entities established for road, general transport, or other aspects of public safety; emergency services (e.g., fire brigade, ambulance, coastal rescue); and executives, commissions and agencies which are set up under relevant statutes and which engage in public services (e.g., the collection of tax revenue, or workplace health and safety).

Notably, some of the cases cited in this chapter arose because C sued a private entity (D1), and that party then sought to **join** the public authority as a third party (D2), seeking contribution or indemnity from that public authority for C's damage (as, e.g., in *Furnell v Flaherty (t/as Godstone Farm)*[1]). Of course, where D1 proves that the public authority, D2, was liable to C in respect of the same damage, then D1 may claim a contribution under s 1(1) of the Civil Liability (Contribution) Act 1978 from public authority D2. Hence, the cases do not always arise from direct suits by C against the public authority.

[1] [2013] EWHC 377 (QB).

Direct versus vicarious liability

As Dyson LJ pointed out in *Carty v Croydon LBC*,[2] most relevant cases concern whether the public authority was vicariously liable for the negligence of its employees (per the principles discussed in Chapter 18). However, direct liability on the part of the public authority may be pursued concurrently – as, e.g., in *X v Bedfordshire CC*,[3] *Phelps v Hillingdon LBC*,[4] *Neil Martin Ltd v HMRC*,[5] *Carty v Croydon LBC* and in *Furnell v Flaherty (t/as Godstone Farm)*[6] – although not always successfully.

Allegations of direct liability against a public authority may suffer from two problems. First (per Dyson LJ in *Carty*), they are likely to be based on decisions by a public authority which are heavily policy-laden, and hence, which may be non-justiciable (discussed shortly). Secondly, the pragmatic sentiments of Lord Slynn in *Phelps v Hillingdon LBC* are worth noting: '[s]ince the public authority can only act through its employees or agents, and if they are negligent vicarious liability will arise, it may rarely be necessary to invoke a claim for direct liability'[7] – albeit that, in claims against local education authorities in that case, Lord Slynn stated that it would not be right to strike out the vicarious liability claims, and since the direct claims were so closely linked with them, the latter would not be struck out either.

This chapter concentrates upon allegations of direct liability against a public authority, for negligence on that entity's part in its dealings with C – although it is noteworthy that allegations about wrongdoing on the employee's part, and by the public authority itself, can become conflated in the judicial discussion.

Ancillary causes of action

In *McCreaner v MOJ*,[8] for example, where a former prisoner claimed that he spent four months longer in jail than he should have, claims were brought against the operators of the jail, D, for false imprisonment, negligence, misfeasance and breach of the Human Rights Act 1998 (but only negligence succeeded). Actions in negligence against a public authority may also commonly be accompanied by claims for occupiers' liability, private nuisance, or breach of statutory duty.

The inter-relationship of negligence with breach of statutory duty is not without difficulty (as discussed in 'Breach of statutory duty', an online chapter). Breach of statutory duty is a different tort from negligence (for one thing, it does not require proof of any duty of care), but where proven, it gives a freestanding right to claim damages, quite independent of any tort of negligence being proven against the public authority. For example, it will be impossible to establish C's right to a breach of statutory duty against the public authority, in cases in which the statute imposes a statutory duty, or creates a statutory power, which is for the benefit of the public as a whole (per *Gorringe v Calderdale MBC*[9]); or even where the duties cast on a public authority were intended to benefit a limited subclass, Parliament may not intend that there should be a remedy by way of damages (per *Welsh Water v Barratt Homes Ltd (Rev 1)*[10]). That the statute confers a private right of action is an absolute pre-requisite to the availability of the tort of breach of statutory duty.

[2] [2005] EWCA Civ 19, [36]. [3] [1995] AC 633 (HL). [4] [2001] 2 AC 619 (HL). [5] [2007] EWCA Civ 1041. [6] [2013] EWHC 377 (QB). [7] [2001] 2 AC 619 (HL) 658. [8] [2014] EWHC 569 (QB). [9] [2004] UKHL 15, [2004] 1 WLR 1057. [10] [2013] EWCA Civ 233, [35].

If, as a matter of construction of the statute, Parliament did not intend that the tort of breach of statutory duty would be available in the event that the public authority either does not perform the duty at all, or performs it without reasonable care, an action in negligence may still be available against the public authority – on the basis that the public authority assumed responsibility for the well-being of a specific person. A Health Authority provides a good example. Under s 1(1) of the National Health Service Act 1977, '[i]t is the Secretary of State's duty to continue the promotion ... of a comprehensive health service'. That statutory duty is not enforceable by a private individual in an action for breach of statutory duty – and yet a health authority or hospital trust which provides medical treatment under that public law duty can still owe a duty of care, directly and systemically, to a patient. It does so, solely because it has assumed responsibility for a specific patient's welfare, just as a doctor in private practice may do.

The framework

The framework of analysis for public authority liability in negligence is set out in the following Table:

Public authority liability in a nutshell

Preliminary matters:

i The *East Suffolk* principle
ii The policy versus operational distinction
iii The 'pure omissions' principle

Modes of establishing a duty of care – proving 'something more', where:

1 Public authority created or increased the danger to C, by a positive act (i.e., 'made it worse')
2 Public authority assumed responsibility to C specifically, over and above acting in the general public interest
3 Public authority and C were in a proximate relationship, and policy favoured a duty of care (per *Caparo*), or
4 Public authority owed a duty to C, entirely unconnected with the statutory duties or functions being exercised

The impact of the ECHR

Dealing with each element in turn:

PRE-REQUISITE LEGAL ISSUES

The *East Suffolk* principle

The general principle

As Sir Anthony Clarke MR noted in *X v Hounslow LBC*, '[t]here has, in recent years, been much discussion as to the relationship between the tort of negligence and statutory powers and duties'.[11] In some respects, part of that discussion is now only of historical significance, given the judicial views and turnarounds over time.

§13.2 Public authority, D, does not owe a duty of care to C, merely by undertaking a statutory duty or statutory power without reasonable care, or by its failing to perform a statutory duty or a statutory power at all. In other words, a duty of care towards C cannot arise *automatically* out of a statutory duty or power that the public authority exercised, or failed to exercise, properly for C's benefit.

The abovementioned '*East Suffolk*' principle has a long pedigree, having been emphatically stated by the House of Lords in the 1941 case of *East Suffolk Rivers Catchment Board v Kent*.[12] In Lord Romer's words, '[w]here a statutory authority is entrusted with a mere power, it cannot be made liable for any damage sustained by a member of the public [C], by reason of a failure to exercise that power'. *East Suffolk* itself was a case where a statutory power was allegedly exercised without reasonable care:

> In *East Suffolk Rivers Catchment Board v Kent*, an exceptionally high spring tide caused around 30 breaches in a sea wall on the Suffolk coast, and 50 acres of marsh pastures on C's land were flooded. The breaches were not the result of negligence. East Suffolk Rivers Catchment Board, D, constituted under the Land Drainage Act 1930, s 34(k)(a), had the statutory power to repair, inter alia, any existing drainage work, including the walls or banks which guarded C's farm. In exercising those statutory powers, D undertook repairs to the wall. However, the work was performed so inefficiently that the flooding continued for several months (164 days); if reasonable skill had been exercised, the wall would have been repaired in about two weeks. C's pasture land was severely damaged whilst covered by salt water for all that period. **Held:** D was not liable in negligence, merely because it persisted in a method of repairing the breach that was fundamentally flawed, and which no reasonable entity would have undertaken in that way.

However, over time, the same principle has been applied, even where the public authority failed to exercise the statutory power *at all* (i.e., cases of 'pure omission') –

> In *Stovin v Wise*,[13] Mr Stovin, C, was riding his motorcycle along a road in Wymondham, when Mrs Wise's car emerged from a junction into his path, causing a collision in which C was severely injured. The trial judge held that Norfolk CC, D (joined as a third party), was partly liable for the accident, as the local highway authority. D knew that the junction was dangerous, in that road users' views were restricted by a bank on adjoining land, which meant that they approached the junction 'blind'. Previous accidents had occurred there, and nearly a year before the accident, D's officers had accepted that a serious visibility problem existed, and had recommended that part of the bank be removed if the landowner agreed. The cost to contour the bank was estimated at around £1,000, but C's accident occurred before D got around to doing any remedial work on the bank. **Held (3:2):** D was not liable in negligence; no duty of care was owed by D to C to improve the visibility at the intersection.

[11] [2009] EWCA Civ 286, [40]. [12] [1941] AC 74 (HL) 102.

[13] [1996] AC 923 (HL). Lords Goff, Jauncey and Hoffmann (who gave the principal judgment) were in the majority; with Lords Slynn and Nicholls dissenting.

– and even where the public authority failed to exercise a statutory *duty*:

> In *Gorringe v Calderdale MBC*, Mrs Gorringe, C, was driving uphill to a crest in the road around 50 mph, and was just short of the crest when she braked, having seen the top of a bus coming in the opposite direction. The front wheels of her car locked, and it skidded across the road into the side of the bus. C was seriously injured, including significant brain damage. At the bottom of the downslope, a driver had no view of the road beyond the crest and or of a vehicle approaching from the opposite direction until they were both close to the crest. That crest was also hazardous, in that the change of gradient from uphill to downhill was 25 metres maximum, so that any car going 50 mph (within the speed limit) was at risk of becoming momentarily airborne, plus the road narrowed at the crest. The only traffic warning sign in place stated, 'Uneven Road'. C sued the Council, D, as highway authority, for failing to put adequate signs and road markings, to warn of the road's contours and to reduce speed. C alleged that s 39 of the Road Traffic Act 1988, which imposed general duties upon highway authorities in respect of road safety, could form the basis of a common law duty of care. **Held:** D did not owe C a duty of care to place markings or signage on/near the road, warning motorists to slow down and to exercise care.

In fact, up until *Anns v Merton LBC*[14] in 1978, there was no English authority which supported the notion that a statutory power could potentially give rise to a common law duty of care on a public authority's part. However, in *Anns*, where the Merton LBC failed to carry out building inspections to ensure compliance with building by-laws as it had the statutory power to do under the Public Health Act 1936, it was held to be liable in negligence to the adversely-affected building owners as a result.

However, the dogma that a 'statutory may' could not give automatic rise to a 'common law ought' (as Lord Hoffmann put it in *Stovin v Wise*[15]) was reaffirmed by Lord Browne-Wilkinson in *X v Bedfordshire CC* in 1995. It was unanimously held (in one of the conjoined appeals, *E v Dorset CC*) that it was **not** legally correct 'to superimpose on the statutory machinery for the investigation and treatment of [C's] special educational needs a duty of care to exercise the statutory discretions carefully' (although *East Suffolk* was not referred to, oddly enough). In *X*, Lord Browne-Wilkinson said, 'in order to found a cause of action flowing from the careless exercise of statutory powers or duties, [C] has to show that the circumstances are such as to raise a duty of care at common law. The mere assertion of the careless exercise of a statutory power or duty is *not sufficient*'.[16] The point was reiterated (albeit by a bare majority) in *Stovin v Wise* in 1996. Unlike in *East Suffolk*, *Stovin* was a case of pure omission, where nothing was done to exercise the statutory power at all. However, the same ethos applied – to fix the authority with a duty of care required something more than its not exercising a statutory power, not fulfilling a statutory duty, or doing so with even a flagrant lack of care.

Subsequently, in 2004 in *Gorringe v Calderdale MBC* (another highway authority 'pure omission' case), the House of Lords reaffirmed the *East Suffolk* principle – albeit that Lord Steyn called the topic of negligence and statutory duties and powers, 'a subject of great complexity, and very much an evolving area of the law. No single decision is capable of providing a comprehensive analysis'.[17] Subsequent appellate cases have applied the *East Suffolk* principle, in cases of **both** positive acts and omissions to act by a public authority, as the following cases, respectively, show:

[14] [1978] AC 728 (HL). [15] [1996] AC 923 (HL) 948.
[16] [1995] 2 AC 633 (HL) 734–35 (emphasis added). [17] [2004] UKHL 15, [2004] 1 WLR 1057, [2].

In *Jain v Trent Strategic HA*,[18] D applied its statutory powers incorrectly and negligently, to remove patients from J's care home, causing J severe economic losses. That positive act by Trent Stratetic HA, D, could not, of itself, found a duty of care towards the care home owner, C. In *Neil Martin Ltd v HMRC*,[19] the HMRC omitted to issue a certificate, as requested by C, as they were under a statutory duty to do under the Income and Corporation Taxes Act 1988. That could not give rise to an automatic common law duty to process the application with reasonable efficiency in C's favour – 'the duty which s 561(2) ICTA does impose – a duty to issue a tax certificate to an applicant in respect of whom the relevant conditions are satisfied – does not, of itself, give rise to a common law duty owed to the applicant to process the application with reasonable expedition. Powerful support for that conclusion is found in the passages in *Stovin v Wise* and *Gorringe.*'

Reasons for the *East Suffolk* principle

There are several reasons for the *East Suffolk* principle, regardless of whether the court is dealing with a statutory duty or a statutory power.

Statutory duties:

- where Parliament has not given C any right to claim statutory compensation, should a public authority not fulfil a statutory duty set out in the Act (or fulfil it carelessly), then the same legislative policy would ordinarily exclude any duty of care (and liability in negligence) arising (*Stovin v Wise*, Lord Hoffmann);
- if the policy of the statute is that no tort of breach of statutory duty is available, by which a public authority is liable to pay damages because the statute conferred a private right of action, then 'the same policy would ... exclude the use of the statutory duty in order to create a common law duty of care that would be broken by a failure to perform the statutory duty ... I do not accept that a common law duty of care can grow parasitically out of a statutory duty not intended to be owed to individuals' (*Gorringe*, Lord Scott[a]);

Statutory powers:

- where a public authority is given a statutory power, then Parliament has chosen to bestow on that authority a discretion, rather than to impose a duty – and 'the fact that Parliament has conferred a discretion must be some indication that the policy of the Act conferring the power was not to create a right to compensation' via a duty of care being imposed (*Stovin v Wise*, Lord Hoffmann[b]).

[a] [2004] 1 WLR 1057 (HL) [71].
[b] [1996] AC 923 (HL) 953.

As Turner J noted in *Furnell v Flaherty (t/as Godstone Farm)*, 'it should now be taken as settled law that no liability will arise in negligence out of a mere failure, without more, by a public body to confer a benefit by its *omission* to fulfil a public statutory duty or to exercise a statutory power, however irrational such failure may turn out to be have been'.[20] As *Jain* and *East Suffolk* demonstrate, the same applies where a public authority has committed a *positive* negligent act in acting under a statutory power or duty.

[18] [2009] UKHL 4, [2009] 1 AC 853. [19] [2007] EWCA Civ 1041, [2008] Bus LR 663.
[20] [2013] EWHC 377 (QB) [51] (emphasis added).

The discounted *Wednesbury* test

§13.3 Any former suggestion that a public authority, when exercising its discretion under a statutory power, owes a duty of care to C (and breaches that duty), *only* where that public authority has conducted itself so unreasonably and irrationally that no public authority would have exercised its discretion in a similar way (i.e., the *Wednesbury* test), has now been judicially discounted.

The area of public authority liability in negligence has been 'muddied' by the judicial suggestion that it was possible to base a duty of care upon a statutory power – in that any failure to exercise its discretion under that statutory power, or some positive act of exercising its discretion under that power, would expose a public authority to negligence, but **only if** that authority's conduct was so unreasonable or irrational that no reasonable public authority could have behaved in that way.

Conduct that is 'unreasonable' in this way invokes the concept of *Wednesbury* reasonableness (per *Associated Provincial Picture Houses Ltd v Wednesbury Corp*[21]) – a public law concept. This proposition received support at the highest appellate level – i.e., by Lord Browne-Wilkinson in *X v Bedfordshire CC*, and by Lord Slynn in *Barrett v Enfield LBC*.[22] For example, in *X*, the House of Lords accepted that, in deciding, in the exercise of their statutory powers, not to take Cs into care, it was arguable that those decisions could be 'so unreasonable that no reasonable local authority could have reached them' (albeit that the claim was ultimately struck out for policy reasons under the *Caparo* test, discussed shortly).

However, mixing private law and public law concepts in that way has caused considerable difficulty. In fact, the law has 'twisted and turned' on the point, such that Lord Hoffmann was forced to admit (in *Gorringe v Calderdale MBC*) that 'it may have been ill-advised to speculate' upon the circumstances in which a public law statutory duty could base a common law action in negligence.[23] The timeline in the Table below outlines these twists and turns of judicial opinion.[24] Nevertheless, the law on this point is (as Turner J indicated in the passage from *Furnell* above) now settled, in light of the House of Lords' unanimous decision in *Gorringe*. It is not necessary to prove that the public authority was '*Wednesbury* unreasonable' in order to prove breach; and the fact that the public authority may have been '*Wednesbury* unreasonable' in exercising its statutory power does not invoke a duty of care being owed on its part.

In *Furnell v Flaherty (t/as Godstone Farm)*,[25] Godstone Farm in Surrey, owned and operated by D1, offered a range of recreational agricultural and farming activities, intended to be suitable for families with young children. Farm visitors were encouraged to touch and stroke a variety of animals and pets, which necessarily involved a risk of *E coli*, resulting from contact with the animals' excrement. Good standards of cleanliness, washing facilities, etc, were provided. However, Godstone Farm became the source of a very serious outbreak of *E coli* in 2009, and although there were no deaths among the visitors, twins Aaron and Todd Furnell, C, fell very seriously ill, and almost died. D1 denied liability in negligence, and sought to join the Health Protection Agency, D2, and Tandridge DC, D3, as third parties. D1 alleged that D2 and D3 were aware of the *E coli* outbreak traceable to the farm before she was, but that they took no adequate steps to act upon that knowledge, and prevent the

[21] [1948] 1 KB 223 (HL).

[22] [2001] 2 AC 550 (HL) 566, citing: Lord Browne-Wilkinson in *X v Bedfordshire CC* [1995] AC 633 (HL) 749.

[23] [2004] UKHL 15, [2004] 1 WLR 1057, [26], [31].

[24] The citations of cases referred to therein appear elsewhere in the chapter.

[25] [2013] EWHC 377 (QB). The timeline in the Table is drawn from the discussion in this case.

exposure of visitors to the infection; and that, after being informed of the *E coli* outbreak, D2 and D3 did not promptly arrange to involve an Outbreak Control Team per the Outbreak Control Plan for Surrey and Sussex, nor did they promptly visit the farm themselves, but merely liaised with D1, the owner, by phone. It was not suggested that the farm should be closed to the public, but only that extra signage about handwashing should be put up around the farm. **Held:** no duty of care was owed to C by D2 or D3. In light of *Gorringe*, even if D2 and D3's omissions to act to limit the outbreak of *E coli* could be considered as 'irrational' or 'unreasonable', that could not give rise to a duty of care owed to C. (Ultimately, no duty of care was owed on any other basis either.)

A timeline of the two-stage test (now recanted): the twists and turns of judicial opinion

1995 – in *X (Minors) v Bedfordshire CC*, Lord Browne-Wilkinson said that it was neither 'helpful nor necessary to introduce public law concepts' when determining whether a statutory power could base a duty of care. Nevertheless, a public authority's exercise of a statutory discretion could be negligently exercised (and hence, a duty of care owed by that authority to C, the intended beneficiary of that statutory discretion) if the statutory power was exercised so unreasonably that the public authority's conduct 'falls altogether outside the ambit of the statutory discretion', or where the public authority 'decided an issue so carelessly that no reasonable public authority could have reached that decision'.

1996 – in *Stovin v Wise*, Lord Hoffmann suggested a 2-part test for imposing a duty of care on a public authority:

(1) it failed to exercise a statutory power, which was irrational or 'unreasonable', in the sense used in *Bedfordshire*); and
(2) there were exceptional grounds as to why the policy of the statute required compensation to be paid to persons who suffered loss because the statutory power was not exercised by the public authority.

The first limb clearly invoked public law concepts, *viz*, that the public authority's failure to exercise a statutory power amounted to the *Wednesbury* test of unreasonableness;

2001 – in *Barrett v Enfield LBC*, Lord Hutton doubted this approach. To apply, as a 'preliminary test, the public law concept of *Wednesbury* unreasonableness', was not the preferred course. He preferred another 2-part enquiry: whether the decision of the public authority was justiciable (via an operational versus policy distinction); and whether the *Caparo* framework meant that a duty of care should be imposed;

2001 – in *Larner v Solihull MBC*, Lord Woolf (writing for the Court of Appeal) stated that, in exceptional cases, a common law duty of care could be owed by a public authority (e.g., a highway authority), if that authority 'acted wholly unreasonably' in failing to exercise a statutory power (thus reinstating the *Stovin* view);

2003 – additionally, in *Health and Safety Executive v Thames Trains Ltd*, arising out of the Ladbroke train disaster, the Court of Appeal anticipated that the *Stovin v Wise* 2-stage test could be applied, to ask whether the HSE had irrationally failed to act under a statutory duty, and thereby, could owe a duty of care to C (a strike-out application of the negligence claim was refused);

2004 – however, in *Gorringe*, Lord Hoffmann recanted on his earlier remarks in *Stovin v Wise* – 'it may have been ill-advised to speculate on such matters', and that, 'I find it difficult to imagine a case in which a common law duty can be founded simply on the failure (however irrational) to provide some benefit which a public authority has power (or a public law duty) to provide'. *Larner* was expressly disapproved in *Gorringe*; Lord Hoffmann noted that there should never have been a duty of care upheld in *Larner*;

2007 – in *Neil Martin Ltd v HMRC*, and applying *Gorringe*, a common law duty on HMRC's part to C could not arise on the basis that the acts or omission of an unidentified employee in the Furness tax office were irrational in the *Wednesbury* sense (but a duty of care was separately owed on another basis, later);

2010 – in *Connor v Surrey CC*, Laws LJ held that *Wednesbury* is 'not a touchstone of liability for negligence', in cases where a public authority acts unreasonably. However, a duty could arise on *Caparo* principles;

2013 – in *Furnell v Flaherty (t/as Godstone Farm)*, Turner J remarked that, in *Gorringe*, 'Lord Hoffmann took the opportunity to catch and kill the hare which had been set running by his own reference, in *Stovin*, to a possible '2-stage test', and that, following *Gorringe*, the approach taken in *Thames Trains* 'would no longer be permissible', and that *Larner's* reasoning 'cannot survive *Gorringe*' either.

The policy versus operational distinction

§13.4 Where a public authority has exercised its discretion under a statutory duty or power which is purely policy in nature, courts cannot assess such decisions in a negligence action, because Parliament intended for those decisions to be made by that authority alone. Hence, any purely policy decision of a public authority is 'non-justiciable', and is not capable of founding a duty of care owed to C.

When exercising statutory powers or duties, a public authority frequently has to exercise discretion in its decision-making, in seeking to fulfil those powers and duties for public purposes. In that regard, there is a distinction to be drawn between policy matters and operational decisions.

In *Anns v Merton LBC*,[26] Lord Wilberforce held that *policy* decisions are not 'justiciable', because Parliament intended for those decisions to be made by a public authority, and it was not for the courts to interfere with those decisions via civil litigation.

In *Barrett v Enfield LBC*,[27] some examples of non-justiciable decisions were given: a public authority has to allocate limited financial resources between different recipients, all of whom are in need; or has to make a decision which involves the weighing of competing public interests; or needs to balance desirable social aims (e.g., rehabilitation) against the risk to the public which is inherent in pursuing those social goals.

However, *operational* decisions are capable of basing an action in negligence against a public authority. These are decisions where the authority must practically execute those policy decisions, and where C is alleging that the practical manner in which the act was performed was negligent.

[26] [1978] AC 728 (HL) 754. [27] [2001] 2 AC 550 (HL) 587.

In *Dorset Yacht Co Ltd v Home Office*,[28] the policy of implementing rehabilitation and social re-integration via Borstal training was a policy matter; but how the Borstal boys were supervised at night whilst on Brownsea Island was operational. In *Connor v Surrey CC*,[29] Laws LJ gave the example of an education authority deciding whether or not to close a school as a policy decision; but laying on a bus to take pupils on a school trip and then the bus having an accident due to the driver's carelessness, as operational matters which are justiciable.

However, not every operational matter gives rise to a duty of care. As the Privy Council pointed out in *Rowling v Takaro Properties Ltd*,[30] policy decisions by a public authority are exempt from any action in negligence (because 'a question whether it has been made negligently is unsuitable for judicial resolution') – but the fact that a decision is operational does not automatically mean that a duty of care will attach. That question must be decided by the relevant duty of care tests that apply to a public authority.

Undoubtedly, the distinction between policy and operational issues is problematical. Lord Wilberforce acknowledged, in *Anns*, that the distinction could be difficult to draw, and was 'probably a distinction of degree; many "operational" powers or duties have in them some element of "discretion". What could be said was that, 'the more "operational" a power or duty may be, the easier it is to superimpose upon it a common law duty of care'.[31] It was nevertheless acknowledged by the House of Lords, in *Phelps v Hillingdon LBC*, that 'there is some validity in the distinction'.[32] Certainly, the principle that purely policy decisions are non-justiciable has been reiterated since, although some senior judges have stated that purely policy decisions will rarely arise in practice. In *Carty v Croydon LBC*, Dyson LJ remarked that '[t]hese cases are comparatively rare';[33] in *Barrett v Enfield LBC*, Lord Slynn noted that many cases will comprise a mix of policy and operational decisions;[34] and in *Connor v Surrey CC*, the Court of Appeal opined that mixed policy/operational cases are 'likely to be a large class of instances', where the court's decision as to whether or not a duty is owed 'will be sensitive to the particular facts'.[35]

The 'pure omissions' principle

§13.5 The reluctance of English law to impose a duty of care in respect of pure omissions applies as equally to a public authority, D, as to a private entity or individual.

In cases such as *Stovin v Wise* and *Gorringe*, the relevant public authority, D, failed to remove a hazard that it knew about, rather than creating one itself. Hence, each D committed a pure omission. The many policy reasons which prevent a duty of care from being owed by a private entity or individual in the case of pure omissions (discussed in Chapter 3) apply equally to a public authority.

In *Stovin v Wise*, it was argued that, whilst it may be unreasonable to expect a private landowner to spend money for the benefit of others (including C), a public authority is

[28] [1970] AC 1004 (HL). [29] [2010] EWCA Civ 286, [2011] QB 429, [78]–[79].
[30] [1988] AC 473 (PC, on appeal from NZ) 501. [31] [1978] AC 728 (HL) 754. [32] [2001] 2 AC 619 (HL) 658.
[33] [2005] EWCA Civ 19, [2005] 1 WLR 2312, [21]. [34] [2001] 2 AC 550 (HL) 561.
[35] [2010] EWCA Civ 286, [2011] QB 429, [103].

expected to spend its resources on making roads reasonably convenient and safe, and hence, the pure omissions principle did not apply. However, that argument was rejected. It was true (said Lord Hoffmann) that some arguments justifying the pure omissions principle could **not** apply to a public authority (e.g., it could hardly argue the 'why pick on me?' argument, given that it often singly had the financial and physical resources, and legal powers, to eliminate the source of harm to C). However, the policy reasons negating a duty of care in the case of pure omissions applied equally to a public authority, to preclude a duty of care.

In *Stovin v Wise*, the Norfolk CC, D, did not bring about the dangerous configuration and poor visibility at the road junction, and hence, there was no positive act of negligence. However, D had carelessly failed to remove the danger. It was more than a mere bystander, because it had a statutory power to remove this source of danger, although it was not under a statutory duty to do so. The fact that D had done nothing at all brought it within the realm of 'pure omissions'; and the fact that Parliament had entrusted it with general responsibility for highways, and given D the statutory power to improve and repair them, did not create any duty of care on D's part.

Of course, there are recognised exceptions to the general principle that D should not be liable for pure omissions, as discussed in Chapter 3 (e.g., in *Goldman v Hargrave*,[36] there was a positive duty on the part of an adjoining landowner to prevent fire or harmful matter from crossing the boundary to C's premises). However, those are exceptional cases. There is no such exceptional duty to be imposed, merely because D is a public authority whose sphere of activity is to provide services for the public's benefit. The House of Lords was not inclined to create a further exception to the general rule of pure omissions, in relation to road safety, in either *Stovin v Wise* or in *Gorringe* – nor indeed, was the Supreme Court prepared to create a new exception to the general rule about omissions in the recent police-999-call case of *Michael v CC of South Wales Police*,[37] in spite of an express invitation by the C's estate to do so (as discussed in Chapters 2 and 3).

ESTABLISHING A DUTY OF CARE

Where C's grievance is that the public authority was not exercising its statutory duties and powers properly, then as the House of Lords reiterated (per the *East Suffolk* principle), that scenario is not sufficient to give rise to a duty of care on that authority's part. Something more is required to fix a duty of care.

Defining that 'something more', however, has been prone to difficulties. There are, according to an analysis of the case law (and confirmed by the Supreme Court in *Michael*, although none was successful there), a few different ways in which a duty of care may be imposed upon a public authority in favour of C, in the course of its exercising statutory powers and duties, as shown in the diagram overpage.

[36] [1967] 1 AC 645 (PC). [37] [2015] UKSC 2, [2015] 2 WLR 343, [102], [130].

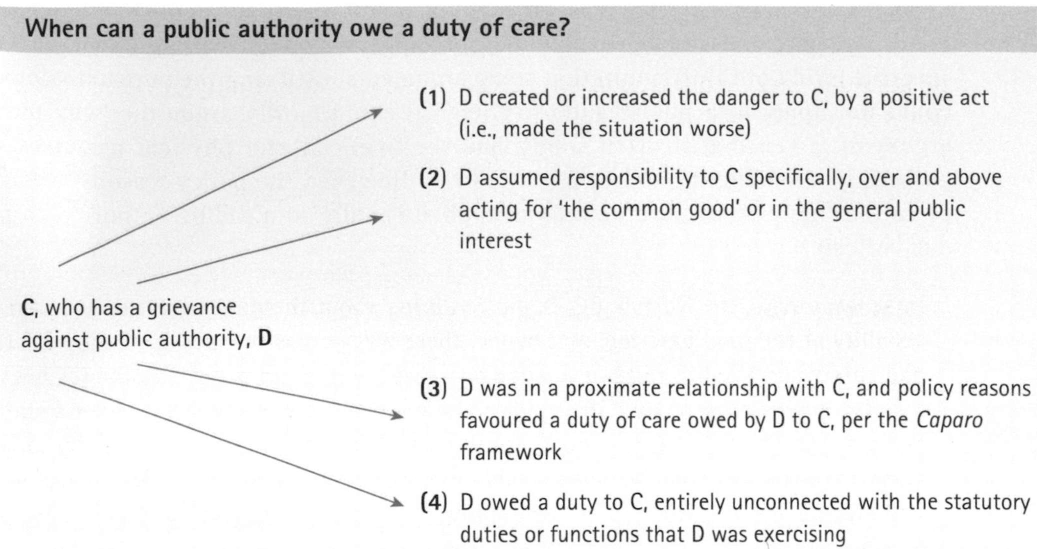

Dealing with each in turn:

The 'making it worse' principle

§13.6 A public authority may owe a duty of care to C where, by some act, the authority has put C in a worse position than if the authority had done nothing at all, i.e., if the authority introduced a new hazard or source of danger for C which was not previously there.

This principle requires that the public authority created a new danger for C, or positively increased the danger to C by what the public authority did. Where that public authority has put C in a worse position than if it had nothing at all, a duty of care may be owed to C.

This necessarily requires the following equation: what would have happened to C if the public authority had done nothing ('Harm X'); and what happened to C when the public authority did something in the exercise of its statutory power or duty ('Harm Y'). If Harm Y > Harm X, then that public authority is liable in negligence to C.

The principle has received strong appellate support in English law – although successful applications of it are relatively rare. In *East Suffolk*,[38] Lord Romer said that where a public authority has a statutory power and, 'in the exercise of their discretion, they embark upon an execution of the power, the only duty they owe to any member of the public [C] is not thereby to add to the damages that he would have suffered, had they done nothing'. In *X v Hounslow LBC*, Sir Anthony Clarke MR also noted that a duty of care may be owed by a public authority 'where [D] has created or increased the danger to [C]'[39] (although that was not such a case). One notable successful case of this principle occurred in the context of emergency services:

> In *Capital & Counties plc v Hampshire CC*, facts previously in Chapter 2,[40] the fire fighters actually made the damage worse than if they had not turned up at all, by ordering the sprinkler system to be turned off, allowing the fire to seat and spread.

[38] [1941] AC 74 (HL) 102. [39] [2009] EWCA Civ 286, [60]. [40] See pp 85–88.

Otherwise, several cases have demonstrated that it is difficult to prove a duty of care owed by a public authority on this 'making it worse' principle. In none of the following did the public authority make matters worse for C, and in no case was a duty of care imposed under this principle (or, indeed, on any other basis):

In *Gorringe*,[41] Mrs Gorringe's case for D's failing to install better road signage and road markings could not be attributable to a new source of danger negligently introduced by the highway authority, Calderdale MBC. Hence, no duty of care could be owed on that basis. In *Furnell v Flaherty*, no duty of care was owed, because D2 and D3 had not made the situation worse. That may have happened, had their employees visited the farm and, acting negligently, spread the *E coli* infection. However, nothing that they did made the situation worse than it would have been, if they had done nothing whatsoever about the *E coli* outbreak on the farm. In *East Suffolk Rivers Catchment Board v Kent*, the Catchment Board persisted in a method of repairing breaches of the sea wall that was fundamentally flawed and quite ineffectual – but having embarked upon the repairs, it could not be said that the damage to C's marsh pastures was greater than if D had done nothing.

Assuming responsibility for C, rather than for 'the common good'

§13.7 A public authority may owe a duty of care to C where, in undertaking its statutory powers or duties, that authority had assumed responsibility for the safety or welfare of C *as an individual*, rather than merely acting for the common good or in the public interest.

In short, an assumption of responsibility by a public authority generates a private law obligation to exercise reasonable care towards C specifically, an obligation which will found a claim in negligence. This point was made by both Lords Hoffmann and Brown in *Gorringe v Calderdale MBC*.[42]

Although the *East Suffolk* principle does not permit a duty of care to be based solely upon a public authority's statutory power or duty, a duty may certainly be imposed if the authority has entered into a legal relationship with C, to whom the authority assumed specific responsibility. Speaking extra-curially, Lord Hoffmann remarked that the existence of statutory powers or duties that govern the public authority's functions were 'simply irrelevant to whether a common law duty is owed', and that a common law duty is created, 'if at all, by what the public body has actually done: whether it assumed responsibilities or done acts which, if they had been done by a private body, would have given rise to a duty of care'.[43] It is a very fact-dependent enquiry.

The court will search, in such cases, for whether the public authority was acting primarily for the injured C, or for the common public good (per *Furnell v Flaherty*[44]). In the former, a duty of care is likely to be owed, but in the latter, it will be precluded. As with all 'duty of care' enquiries, policy considerations infuse the analysis. Dealing with a sample of scenarios in which this test of duty has been applied:

Emergency services. All three emergency services can be summoned on a 999 call, but their treatment, at law, is quite disparate.

[41] [2004] UKHL 15, [2004] 1 WLR 1057, [70] (Lord Scott). [42] [2004] UKHL 15, [38], [100], respectively.

[43] 'Reforming the Law of Public Authority Negligence' (Bar Council Law Reform Lecture, 17 Nov 2009), and cited in: *Furnell v Flaherty (t/as Godstone Farm)* [2013] EWHC 377 (QB) [52].

[44] [2013] EWHC 377 (QB) [62].

Re the **fire brigade**, it owes a duty of care to the owners of burning buildings, and not to any one owner in particular. As established in *Capital & Counties plc v Hampshire CC*,[45] the fire brigade has 'a general public law duty to make provision for efficient fire-fighting services'. Re the **police** too, its primary obligation is to protect the public at large (dicta in *Kent v Griffiths*) – '[i]n protecting a particular victim of crime, the police are performing their more general role of maintaining public order and reducing crime ... there is therefore a concern to protect the public generally'.[46] This was discussed in Chapter 2. As a general rule, both act for the 'common good', and assume responsibility to no person in particular.

However, where C calls 999 to access the **ambulance service** and where that service accepts that emergency call, the ambulance service assumes personal responsibility for the well-being of, and owes a duty of care to, that particular patient, C – 'in the case of fire, the fire service will normally be concerned not only to protect a particular property where the fire breaks out, but also to prevent fire spreading ... there is therefore a concern to protect the public generally'. But the ambulance 'was different' (per ratio in *Kent v Griffiths*) again as discussed in Chapter 2.

For the common good, versus for C in particular

- the ambulance was a part of the health service, it transported patients to and from hospitals, and was part of the system of 'providing services of the category provided by hospitals' – and Health authorities assume responsibility for particular patients within their care;
- the ambulance service was not providing services equivalent to those provided by the police or the fire service. Criminal activity, and the spread of fire, put other members of the public at risk, and those services must act in the public's interests in combating them. However, in the case of Mrs Griffiths' emergency call, 'the only member of the public who could be adversely affected was Mrs Griffiths. It was for [C] alone for whom the ambulance had been called'. Hence, the ambulance assumed responsibility for C in particular, rather than for the common good;
- a situation could theoretically arise where the ambulance service was being called upon to rescue or assist large numbers of the public, in which case a conflict could arise between the C and the public at large – but that was not the case for Mrs Griffiths. There was no explanation as to why the ambulance failed to turn up promptly in answer to the several 999 calls which were placed by her husband and her attending GP.

Health authorities. An NHS Trust or health authority which has the responsibility of conducting a hospital owes a direct duty of care to patients in that hospital. As acknowledged in *X v Bedfordshire CC*,[47] the negligent acts or omissions of a nurse, a GP, or other healthcare professional employees are capable of constituting a breach of the duty of care (if any) owed directly by the health authority, if those acts signify systemic negligence on the health authority's part. As clarified in *Gold v Essex CC*,[48] it is not that they are operating under statute that renders health authorities liable, but because there is an assumption of responsibility for the well-being of those patients, individually. The allegation of systemic negligence against a health authority has been considered in Chapter 7, and the direct liability of such an authority, where it fails to control the acts or omissions of a dangerous patient (per *Selwood v Durham CC*[49]), has also been considered in Chapter 3.

[45] [1997] QB 1004 (CA), as described *ibid*, [70]. [46] [2001] QB 36 (CA) [45]. [47] [1995] AC 633 (HL) 740.
[48] [1942] 2 KB 293 (CA) 304–5. [49] [2012] EWCA Civ 979, [42], [52].

However, some health protection entities may be more likely to owe duties for the common good, rather than to any one C in particular.

In *Furnell v Flaherty (t/as Godstone Farm)*,[50] facts previously, **held:** no duty of care was owed by either the Health Protection Agency, D2, or the Tandridge DC, D3. Their mere knowledge of an outbreak or potential outbreak of *E coli* from the farm fell far short of giving rise to an assumption of responsibility on their part, towards the twins who suffered infection as visitors to the farm.

For the common good

- those likely to be affected by any omissions on the part of D2 or D3 were not limited to an identified person (e.g., the patient in *Kent v Griffiths*), or to a limited class of persons (e.g., employees or quasi-employees of the type of Ms Selwood in her case against Durham CC). Rather, the potential victims of the *E coli* outbreak could encompass the actual visitors to the farm, and also an indeterminate class of people to whom the infection could be spread by contact with faecal matter carried away by visitors – hence, the prospect of indeterminate liability;
- there were no proximate dealings between D2 and D3, and the visitors to the farm – they had no direct communications or contact in the days prior to the *E coli* outbreak. The police had far greater contact with C in *Smith v CC of Sussex Police*,[a] and yet, no duty of care was owed there;
- public authorities have to strike a balance between competing legitimate interests. Otherwise, defensive practices would prevail; a public authority would be prone to err on the side of caution, and hence, deciding what, if any, enforcement action to take, and when, should be uncluttered by considerations of exposure to civil suit. 'Bad decisions can, where appropriate, be met with internal disciplinary consequences and/or public law challenges'.

[a] [2009] 1 AC 225 (HL).

Taxation matters. The HMRC acts in the public interest in assessing and collecting taxes and other revenue, so that such monies may be spent for the 'common good'. Where mistakes occur in HMRC's performance of its statutory powers and duties, no automatic duty of care arises (per the *East Suffolk* principle). However, in particular cases, a legal assumption of responsibility may have arisen on HMRC's part, towards a particular taxpayer.

In *Neil Martin Ltd v HMRC*,[51] re certain tax deduction schemes for subcontractors involved in the construction industry, declarations have to be made and signed in support of (i) an application for a registration card and (ii) an application for a tax certificate. Mr Martin, C, a subcontractor, completed and signed the declaration in support of an application for a tax certificate, but not for a registration card. However, when the forms arrived at the HMRC Furness office, an unidentified HMRC staff member mistakenly processed them as applications for a registration card, without the authority of C. That led to delay. **Held:** HMRC owed a common law duty of care to C, by completing a declaration in support of an application for a registration card without C's authority.

[50] [2013] EWHC 377 (QB), with points in box at [87]–[89].

[51] [2007] EWCA Civ 1041.

For C, in particular

- what happened here went beyond an administrative mistake made in the ordinary course of processing the application. In completing a declaration in support of an application for a registration card, the HMRC employee took it upon himself to apply on behalf of C – an application which C had chosen not to make;
- the HMRC employee was not processing an application which had been made: he was assuming an authority to make an application which had not been made. In those circumstances, HMRC assumed a responsibility to C.

Road safety. A highway authority does **not** assume responsibility towards any individual road user, in respect of its failure to improve the roads or highways by installing further road markings, or removing hazards, or erecting further signage (per both *Stovin v Wise*[52] and *Gorringe v Calderdale MBC*[53]).

For the common good

- highway authorities promote road safety in the public interest, and not just for C, or for a class of C such as (1) careless drivers partly to blame for their own accidents, or (2) drivers (such as Mrs Gorringe) who did not know the area, or (3) injured drivers;
- where careless drivers harm C on the road, then drivers (or more accurately, their insurers, or compulsory third party insurance) must take responsibility for the damage caused to C, and not the relevant highway authority;
- the burden on a highway authority, if a duty were owed to individual road-users, would be too burdensome, as C's injury, caused by a careless road-user, 'may have a wider impact upon his family, his economic relationships, and the burden on the public services'.

Land protection. In *East Suffolk*, the fact that council D went onto C's land and sought to deal with the breaches in the seawall from that land did not mean that D had assumed a legal responsibility towards C, the affected landowner.

For the common good

- there were about 30 breaches of the seawall, including those that skirted C's land, so the workmanship required on D's part was quite widespread, and certainly not solely focused on C's land;
- D was working 'for the common good', in seeking to protect the landholdings of all owners who might be at risk from the high spring tide.

Accommodation for the homeless. Where a housing authority administers a scheme of social welfare to provide housing for those in need (e.g., the homeless), then that scheme is intended to confer benefits upon the public, at the public expense. It **cannot** be said to be a statutory

[52] [1996] AC 923 (HL). [53] [2004] 1 WLR 1057 (HL), with quote in box at [35].

power or duty (however the scheme may be framed) merely for the private benefit of those homeless persons.

In *O'Rourke v Camden LBC*,[54] Mr O'Rourke, C, a homeless person, sued Camden LBC, D, the local authority in the area in which he was 'sleeping rough', on the basis that D had failed in its statutory duty, under the Housing Act 1985, to provide him with council accommodation at the public expense. **Held:** D did not owe C any duty of care (nor was any action for breach of statutory duty available to C).

For the common good

- the local authority, D, did not assume responsibility towards a homeless person, C, as an individual. Even though it was foreseeable to D that some may have to 'sleep rough' if D did not provide everyone who needed it with council accommodation, that was not sufficient, of itself, to impose a duty of care;
- any scheme for providing social housing has a general public interest, because 'proper housing means that people will be less likely to suffer illness, turn to crime, or require the attention of other social services. The expenditure interacts with expenditure on other public services such as education, the National Health Service, and even the police. It is not simply a private matter between [C] and the housing authority [D]';
- just because Parliament has authorised D to spend money on housing the homeless 'does not necessarily mean that it intended cash payments to be made by way of damages to persons who, in breach of the housing authority's statutory duty, have unfortunately not received the [housing] benefits which they should have done'.

No bright-line distinction between the various duty of care tests governing public authority liability can be maintained. However, the *Caparo* test has frequently been applied, as an alternative to the assumption of responsibility test.

The *Caparo* framework

§13.8 A public authority may owe a duty of care to C where, in undertaking its statutory powers or duties, that authority was in a closely-proximate relationship with C, and where public policy supports the imposition of a duty on that authority.

As an alternative to the assumption of responsibility test of duty of care, the traditional *Caparo* framework has been employed frequently in modern negligence jurisprudence involving a public authority D (as the analysis of suits against the police, in Chapter 2, demonstrated). Some further contexts in which that analysis has occurred are discussed below.

The overriding impression from the case law is that *Caparo's* third limb, that of policy, is indeed an 'unruly horse', where claims against a public authority are concerned – and that it is a horse that has bolted off course at key times, causing even more confusion in the rest of the stable of public authority cases.

[54] [1998] AC 188 (HL), with points in box at 193.

Reasonable foreseeability

§13.9 The fact that it was foreseen, or reasonably foreseeable, that C could suffer injury or loss if a benefit or service was not provided by a public authority pursuant to a statutory duty or power, or was provided carelessly, is not sufficient, of itself, to give rise to a duty of care on that authority's part.

Proof that the harm suffered to C, by virtue of a public authority's acts or omissions, was reasonably foreseeable, is always a pre-requisite for the establishment of a duty of care – but it is **never** sufficient on its own. That incontrovertibly follows from the modern *Caparo* framework. The proposition applies equally in the context of the liability of a public authority in negligence as it does to any other type of D.

As is common under the *Caparo* test, the first limb is generally easily satisfied. For example, in *Dorset Yacht Co Ltd v Home Office*,[55] it was reasonably foreseeable that unsupervised Borstal boys would cause damage if they tried to escape from Brownsea Island; in *Gorringe v Calderdale MBC*,[56] it was foreseeable that a driver unfamiliar with the area, such as Mrs Gorringe, would take the top of the crest at too much speed; in *X v Bedfordshire CC*,[57] the local authority accepted that it could foresee damage to neglected and abused children living in the area for which it had responsibility for social services, if it carried out its statutory duties negligently; and in *E v Dorset CC*,[58] it was 'plainly foreseeable that if [statutory] powers were exercised carelessly, a child with special educational needs might be harmed, in the sense that he would not obtain the advantage that the statutory provisions were designed to provide for him'. But as Lord Hoffmann reiterated in *Gorringe*, it is **never** enough that a highway authority might reasonably have foreseen that, in the absence of warnings or road markings, some road users might be injured.

The other two limbs have posed far greater difficulties for litigants who sue public authorities.

Proximity and public policy

§13.10 The statutory relationship that governs a public authority and C does not, of itself, create any requisite proximity sufficient to prove a duty of care. There must be other aspects of their relationship which give rise to that duty. Indeed, the policy and proximity factors tend to be 'merged' in the judicial analysis of claims against public authorities.

In *East Berkshire*, Lord Bingham remarked that, '[t]he focus of debate is on whether it is fair, just and reasonable to impose a duty of care on health care and child protection professionals involved in cases such as these. But it is acknowledged ... – and in my view rightly – that this question cannot be divorced from consideration of proximity'.[59]

That observation has been fully apparent in a number of different contexts in which public authorities have been sued by aggrieved parties. To provide a sample:

Prison authorities. Prison authorities act by virtue of statutory powers and duties, and a *Caparo*-type analysis applies where claims are brought against that prison authority – whether C was a third party injured by the acts of prisoners (as in *Dorset Yacht*) or a prisoner himself

[55] [1970] AC 1004 (HL). [56] [2004] UKHL 15, [2004] 1 WLR 1057. [57] [1995] AC 633 (HL).
[58] Part of the litigation in *X v Bedfordshire CC* [1995] 2 AC 633 (HL) 762.
[59] [2005] UKHL 23, [20] (Lord Bingham).

(as in *R (Amin) v Sec of State for the Home Dept*[60]). The custodial relationship is typically one in which the prison authority has 'actually done acts or entered into relationships ... which give rise to a common law duty of care' (per Lord Hoffmann in *Gorringe*).

Social welfare services for neglected and abused children.[61] Suits on behalf of children who claim that they were neglected and abused, and that the public authority was negligent in not doing more to protect them from such abuse when exercising its statutory functions and duties, have typically been analysed using the *Caparo* test. The law has evolved considerably in this field – indeed, it has effected quite a turnaround, which is best analysed in **four** stages.

i. **The *Bedfordshire* cases.** The starting point is the complex decision of *X (Minors) v Bedfordshire CC; M (A Minor) v Newham LBC; E (A Minor) v Dorset CC*,[62] a series of cases that went to the House of Lords, on what was termed 'a question of great importance and difficulty' common to each case: 'may a child maintain an action for damages (whether for breach of statutory duty or common law negligence) against a local authority for steps taken or not taken in relation to the child by that authority as the responsible social services authority?. In *Bedfordhire* and *Newham*, in particular, it was alleged that each public authority negligently failed to carry out statutory powers to take children into care, which had the purpose of protecting children from child abuse.

In *X v Bedfordshire CC*, five children of the same family, C, had been victims of appalling maltreatment and neglect, which had been brought to the notice of Bedfordshire CC, D, by several parties – GPs, teachers, neighbours, relatives, the NSPCC, a health visitor and a social worker. However, for several years, D's officers failed to act. The children were locked outside the house for long periods in the bitter cold, the 5-year-old was left 'in charge' of the 3- and 2-year-olds, some children had cigarette burns on their skins, their beds were sodden with urine and their home was in a filthy state, the walls smeared with faeces, and some of the children were seen stealing food from time to time. D, the public authority responsible for social services where the children lived, refused to put the children on the Child Protection Register, despite strong recommendations from health workers. **Held** (5:0[63]): no duty of care was owed by D to the children, and the claims were struck out. In *M v Newham LBC*, KM, a young girl, C, was put on the child protection register, after a social worker was concerned that C was being sexually abused. C was interviewed by a social worker and psychiatrist, D1, and afterwards, C's mother, TP, was told that C had been sexually abused, and that XY (the mother's current partner) was the abuser. When TP privately asked C, after the interview, whether XY had abused her, C shook her head and said 'no'. TP relayed this to D1, but she was not believed (her information was perceived as an attempt to protect her partner, and to persuade C to retract the allegation). C was removed from her mother's custody, made a ward of the court, and placed with foster parents. When viewing the taped interview about a year later, TP realised that C had not identified XY as the abuser, but rather, a cousin who had previously lived at the house

[60] [2004] 1 AC 653 (HL), albeit that it concerned investigations into a racially-motivated murder of a prisoner by another, but was not a negligence claim. However, in *Selwood v Durham CC*, Dame Janet Smith noted that, '[t]he Home Office was held to have assumed responsibility towards the youth who was killed. The killer had a history of violence. That case could be analysed as an assumption of responsibility or a duty on the Home Office of supervision and control': [2012] EWCA Civ 979, [49].

[61] See, further, Mulheron, *Medical Negligence: Non-Patient and Third Party Claims* (Ashgate Publishing, 2010), ch 10, from which some of the material in this chapter (especially the tables, case descriptions and some textual analysis) is derived.

[62] [1995] 2 AC 633 (HL) 651 (quote by Sir Thomas Bingham MR, CA), and see too, Lord Browne-Wilkinson at 730.

[63] Lords Jauncey, Lane, Ackner, Browne-Wilkinson (who delivered the main judgment), and Nolan.

and had the same first name as TP's partner. C was reunited with her mother TP after almost a year, and both alleged that this separation had caused them psychiatric harm. They sued the employed psychiatrist D1 in negligence; and the local authority, D2, and the health authority, D3, for vicarious liability (no direct duty of care on the part of D1 and D2 was alleged). **Held** (4:1[64]): no duty of care was owed to either mother or to her child; their claims were struck out.

A duty of care was precluded from being owed to C under *Caparo's* third limb on policy grounds. This reasoning applied as equally to a local authority as to employed doctors, social workers and psychiatrists who treat abused children.[65] Hence, there is a great deal of overlap in public authority cases, between the entity itself and its employed servants through whom the public authority is acting, when acquitting its statutory powers and duties (and all are encompassed within the meaning of D, in the following Table).

Proximity and public policy analysis against a duty of care to the child

- the statutory system established for the protection of children at risk from abuse or neglect was inter-disciplinary. It involved the police, educational bodies, healthcare professionals, local authorities, health authorities, etc, and required recommendations and decisions of a joint nature. To hold that, out of all these parties, only the local authority or their employed professionals were subject to a duty of care, would be manifestly unfair. But equally, to extend the duty to all would lead to huge problems of contribution among all these parties;
- dealing with children at risk is very complex and delicate. D has to consider the physical health of the child, the desirability of not disrupting the family unit, the harm potentially caused by wrongfully leaving the child *in situ* versus the harm potentially caused by removing the child wrongfully, the dangers of acting too soon or not soon enough – working all the while with parents who are, themselves, often in need of help. Introducing a legal duty of care into this fragile mix was fraught;
- imposing a duty of care on D would lead to 'defensive practices' – D would likely adopt a more cautious and time-consuming approach (i.e., not acting until 'concrete facts' were known about abuse or neglect, possibly too late to prevent injury to the child). Child abuse investigations would be prejudiced because of the increased workload per case; and defending litigation would divert money and human resources away from deserving cases;
- where D recommended that the child be removed from the home, and the parents naturally wished to keep the child with them, conflicts, deep feelings and hostility were likely. All of this could result in fertile litigation, unless the law deemed such litigation to be impossible;
- it was not as if the wronged child had no other remedy. Complaints procedures, and references to local authorities' Ombudsmen schemes, were possible – and even if compensation might not be possible under these avenues, that would not justify imposing a tortious duty of care;
- the law must proceed incrementally, and by analogy with decided cases. The purpose of the statutory social welfare scheme was to protect the weak (children). Under similar scenarios – e.g., the victims of crime versus police, investors versus regulators of financial markets – the law did not cast a duty of care on the 'protector'. Hence, no close legal analogies could be found;
- re very young children, given the suspension of their limitation periods until majority, the prospect of 'sleeper actions' for long-ago grievances would place the legal system under an intolerable and uncertain burden.

[64] Lord Nolan dissented in this case. [65] [1995] 2 AC 633 (HL) 754.

The traditional duty of care on D's part, in the scenarios of *Bedfordshire* and *Newham*, was not to cause physical harm to the neglected or abused child during a physical examination of the child. However, the duty could not be extended any more widely than that, to cover a duty to avoid psychiatric or economic injury caused to the children, for the various reasons noted in the Table.

However, although the House's decision was unanimous, the policy factors were certainly not all tending one way. Sir Thomas Bingham MR strongly dissented in *Bedfordshire/Newham* (CA), and would have found a wider duty of care than simply not to damage a child examinee during an interview/examination. Ultimately and ironically, the policy reasoning in the Master of the Rolls's judgment came to represent the current law – and in the most extraordinary precedential circumstances.

ii. Post-*Bedfordshire*. Four years after *Bedfordshire*, in *Barrett v Enfield LBC*,[66] a differently-constituted House of Lords decided to limit *Bedfordshire* to its facts, to distinguish it, and to permit a neglected and abused child to sue a local authority in negligence – albeit in a slightly different scenario.

In *Barrett v Enfield LBC*, Keith Barrett, C, 10 months old, was admitted to hospital suffering from injuries inflicted by his mother. Thereafter, he was placed under the care of Enfield LBC, D, until he was 17. During this time, C endured almost 10 different foster home care arrangements, had sporadic contact with his mother which did not go well, was separated from his half-sister, and suffered various physical and psychiatric disorders. C alleged that the social workers employed by D, and the local authority itself, were under a duty to act in *loco parentis*, and to provide him with the standard of care which could be expected of a reasonable parent, including a duty to provide a home and education, to take reasonable steps to protect him from physical, emotional, psychiatric or psychological injury, and to promote his development. **Held:** D owed C a duty of care. C's claims against both social worker and local authority were not struck out, as there were potential actions against both.

The factual situation in *Barrett* – while involving local authorities and employees working in the child protection field, just as *Bedfordshire* did – was significantly different from *Bedfordshire*, because the latter held that no duty could be imposed by authorities (and their employees) who were *investigating* whether or not to take a child into care, with all the difficult policy decisions which that involved. In *Barrett*, on the other hand, the child was *already* taken into care, and claimed that D then assumed parental responsibilities over him. The House of Lords agreed. It was plausible that acts or omissions on the part of the local authority *during the period of care orders* could found a claim in negligence. That difference in fact situation, from *Bedfordshire*, changed the proximity/policy analysis considerably in *Barrett*.

Policy analysis in favour of a duty of care

- just because the law should not permit a child to sue his parents about the manner of his upbringing did not mean that a child should be precluded from suing a public authority which is under a statutory duty to take him into care and to make arrangements for his future. The comparison

[66] [1999] UKHL 25, [2001] 2 AC 550, 568–69 (Lord Slynn); and recently affirmed in: *OPO v MLA* [2014] EWCA Civ 1277, [57].

between parent and public authority was not apt, because the authority has to make a type of decision which a parent in a normal family relationship does not have to make, *viz*, whether the child should be placed for adoption, or with foster parents, or in a residential home;

- there was no inter-disciplinary system set up by statute for protecting the child in *Barrett*, in that other disciplines were not closely involved in the same way as for the children in *Bedfordshire*;
- deciding whether to remove a child from his parents because of the fear of sexual abuse was a very delicate one for a public authority, but C was already removed from his mother, and the duties of the public authority were 'not so delicate, although questions did arise as to whether [C] should remain with particular foster parents';
- if liability were to be imposed, a public authority *may* adopt a more cautious and defensive approach to its duties, but defensive practices were not to be given 'great weight';
- although the relationship between a social worker and a child's parents is frequently one of conflict, particularly in a case of child abuse, that consideration is of less weight when the child is already placed in care;
- there was a statutory procedure for complaints and for investigating grievances, but if C has suffered psychiatric injury, then civil litigation should not be excluded merely because other avenues of complaint might exist;
- in *Barrett*, C was not a member of a wide class of persons which the public authority was obliged to seek to protect, but was an individual person who had been placed in the care of D by statute.

In *Barrett*, C did **not** attempt to rely upon a common law duty of care, generated by the fact that the local authority was exercising statutory powers. Undoubtedly, the *East Suffolk* principle was well and truly recognised by this time. However, the fact that Enfield LBC could take C into care at all was **only** because of its statutory powers or duties; it could not have done so without them. Nevertheless, once it chose to assume that parental responsibility, then a duty of care could attach, by virtue of its proximity to C, and because policy reasons favoured a duty of care being owed.

Yet a further shift in judicial mood – against the public authority – was evident in the 2000 case of *S v Gloucestershire CC*.[67] The Court of Appeal remarked that the 'child abuse cases' which might be brought against local or health authorities (or their employees) were **not** bound to fail, and that there was no question of any 'blanket immunity' operating in such cases, in a public authority's favour.

iii. The ***East Berkshire*** 'revolution'. The most significant development was the *East Berkshire* (Court of Appeal) decision, a series of three conjoint appeals, in which various mistaken allegations of child abuse and mistreatment had been made: *JD v East Berkshire Community Health NHS Trust; RK and MAK v Dewsbury Healthcare NHS Trust; RK and AK v Oldham NHS Trust.*[68]

In *Oldham* and *Dewsbury*, both the child and the parental claimant/s brought actions in negligence for alleged psychiatric harm that each suffered because of the separation that they endured because of the mistaken diagnoses of child abuse. The question for the Court of Appeal was whether doctors, and vicariously or directly, health authorities, could be liable to the

[67] [2001] 2 WLR 909 (CA), [2011] Fam 313, 338.
[68] [2003] EWCA Civ 1151, [2004] QB 558 (Lord Phillips MR, with Hale and Latham LJJ concurring).

children in negligence. However, only *Dewsbury* is of direct relevance. In *Oldham*, the child MK sued the health authority D, but she was held (at first instance) **not** to have suffered a recognisable psychiatric injury because of her very young age (less than 12 months), and that decision was never appealed,[69] so the case is not relevant for the child's claim. In *East Berkshire*, the child did not sue at all – the claim in negligence was brought *only* by the mother, JD. Hence, only *Dewsbury* is of direct relevance to a child's claim against a public authority.

In *RK and MAK v Dewsbury Healthcare NHS Trust*,[70] RK, C, suffered from Schamberg's disease (a progressive pigmented purpuric dermatitis or capillaritis), which showed by purple patches on the skin. Her father MAK took C to her GP with bruising on the legs, but the marks disappeared after treatment, and no diagnosis of Schamberg's disease was made. Subsequently, when C was 9, her swimming teacher expressed concern about marks on the insides of her legs, and a paediatrician, D1, diagnosed that the marks were suggestive of abuse. C's mother was told that C had been sexually abused, and, as a result, her father and elder brother were told that they should not sleep at home when C was released from hospital. In the hospital, in front of other ward patients and visitors, MAK was told that he was not allowed to see his daughter, C. Finally, a correct diagnosis was made of C's condition, and it was accepted by the Dewsbury Healthcare NHS Trust, D2, that no abuse had occurred. C sued paediatrician D1 and health authority D2, claiming psychiatric injury. **Held:** D arguably owed C a duty of care; a strike-out application could not succeed.

In allowing this claim in negligence by the child RK to proceed, the Court of Appeal took the most unusual step of **not** following the House of Lords' precedent in *Bedfordshire*. The Court of Appeal unanimously concluded that the law had moved on since the days of *Bedfordshire*, especially since the implementation of the Human Rights Act 1998: 'it will no longer be legitimate to rule that, as a matter of law, no common law duty of care is owed to a child in relation to the investigation of suspected child abuse and the initiation and pursuit of care proceedings. It is possible that there will be factual situations where it is not fair, just or reasonable to impose a duty of care, but each case will fall to be determined on its individual facts'.[71] Ultimately, the Dewsbury NHS Trust did not dispute the Court of Appeal's decision to allow RK's action in negligence to proceed against it.

When the trio of cases went on appeal to the House of Lords in *East Berkshire*, that appeal **only** concerned whether any duty of care could be owed by doctors, local authorities, and health authorities, to a *wrongfully-accused parent*. The child's claim was not in direct contention in that appeal. Quite what the House of Lords would do in *JD v East Berkshire* about the Court of Appeal's departure from *Bedfordshire* (HL), re *the child's claim*, provoked some uncertainty. However, the House of Lords unanimously accepted the lower court's view that the policy reasons that underpinned *Bedfordshire* (HL) were, by and large, eroded, albeit that Lord Bingham called the Court of Appeal's non-adherence to *Bedfordshire* a 'bold' step.[72] Ironically, the dissenting view of Sir Thomas Bingham MR in *Bedfordshire/Newham* (CA)[73] ultimately

[69] Noted in: [2004] QB 558 (CA) [121] and in the HL decision: [2005] UKHL 23, [2005] 2 AC 373, [19].

[70] In *RK and MAK v Dewsbury Healthcare NHS Trust*, RK was the child, and MAK was her father. Both brought actions in negligence, but MAK's claim is considered shortly.

[71] [2003] EWCA Civ 1151, [2004] QB 558, [83]–[84].

[72] [2005] UKHL 23, [2005] 2 AC 373, [21]. The remainder of the HL did not specifically comment upon the CA's failure to follow the precedent of *Newham/Bedfordshire* (HL).

[73] [1995] 2 AC 633 (CA) 662–64.

came to define the current law – a duty of care was owed by a public authority to the neglected or abused child, wider than a duty not to injure the child during a medical examination.

Policy reasons in favour of a duty of care to the child

- only very serious acts/omissions would justify a breach of any duty owed by a public authority, D, to a child, C – few claims would succeed, so there was no prospect of opening the 'floodgates';
- no greater defensive measures would be taken by D if it knew that a duty to the child was owed, other than a knowledge that it should be sound in the performance of its statutory duty;
- just because a policeman, financial regulator, or teacher may not be liable to third parties is hardly relevant; each new case – including those involving public authorities – must be judged on its particular facts;
- the fact that actions could be brought for lengthy periods (because of the suspension of limitation periods whilst C was still a minor) was not cogent. It was Parliament's view that children should be able to prosecute for civil wrongs done to them, up to 21 years of age. If that was to be disallowed on 'policy grounds', by precluding any duty of care being owed by D, then courts would be substituting their own policy for Parliament's;
- the first claim on policy is that wrongs should be remedied – and no strong policy grounds went against that, in the context of negligently-conducted investigations of alleged child abuse or neglect;
- no other redress for compensation was possible for the neglected or abused child against D, except for an action brought in negligence (no HRA claim was possible in domestic courts, given that the conduct pre-dated the implementation of the HRA on 2 October 2000).

Hence, over a relatively short period, the reasoning in *Bedfordshire* came to be overturned, such that, now, it is 'well established that a local authority which carries out investigations into suspected child abuse owes a duty of care to a child who is potentially at risk ... [including] a duty to take reasonable steps to avoid or prevent her from suffering personal injury' (per *NXS v Camden LBC*[74]). The law in this area has moved on, as Lord Nicholls said in *East Berkshire*, 'remarkably swiftly'.[75]

Still, a Court of Appeal departure from House of Lords' authority, set a short number of years previously, is always going to be exceptional. The fact that it happened in *East Berkshire* may be attributed to a confluence of circumstances, *viz*, English law's need to take account of the ECHR and that *Bedfordshire* was heard in 1995, before the HRA came into force, so that none of the opinions referenced the ECHR; because the 'facts were of extreme character' (per Lord Bingham in *Kay v Lambeth LBC*[76]); and because the children in *Bedfordshire* ultimately recovered large amounts of reparation for violation of Art 3 when they took their claim to the European Court of Human Rights.

Indeed, the Court of Appeal's refusal to follow the *Bedfordshire* (HL) authority handed down just a few years previously owed a great deal to its view that the law had moved on since the days of *Bedfordshire*, especially since the implementation of the HRA in 2000:

[74] [2009] 3 FCR 157 (QBD) [6]. [75] [2005] UKHL 23, [2005] 2 AC 373, [82].
[76] [2006] UKHL 10, [2006] 2 AC 465, [45] (Lord Bingham).

> In so far as the position of a child is concerned, we have reached the firm conclusion that the decision in *X (Minors) v Bedfordshire CC* cannot survive the Human Rights Act. Where child abuse is suspected, the interests of the child are paramount. Given the obligation of the local authority to respect a child's Convention rights, the recognition of a duty of care to the child on the part of those involved should not have a significantly adverse effect on the manner in which they perform their duties. In the context of suspected child abuse, breach of a duty of care in negligence will frequently also amount to a violation of Article 3 or Article 8. The difference, of course, is that those asserting that wrongful acts or omissions occurred before October 2000 will have no claim under the Human Rights Act. This cannot, however, constitute a valid reason of policy for preserving a limitation of the common law duty of care which is not otherwise justified. On the contrary, the absence of an alternative remedy for children who were victims of abuse before October 2000 militates in favour of the recognition of a common law duty of care once the public policy reasons against this have lost their force. It follows that it will no longer be legitimate to rule that, as a matter of law, no common law duty of care is owed to a child in relation to the investigation of suspected child abuse and the initiation and pursuit of care proceedings.[77]

iv. Post-*East Berkshire*. Nevertheless, the decision in *East Berkshire* did not mean that local authorities, health authorities, etc, are always to be exposed to successful suits from neglected or abused children. A court will still have to ask whether there is anything *about the circumstances in the particular case* which would render a duty imposed on the public authority, in favour of C, to be fair, just and reasonable.

In *X v Hounslow LBC*,[78] over the course of a weekend, four local youths moved into the flat of X and Y, who were child-like in their mental capacities, with very low IQs. X was autistic too. The youths subjected X and Y to frequent and degrading sexual and physical assaults during the weekend. X and Y sued Hounslow LBC, D, in whose housing they resided, alleging that D owed them a duty of care to protect them, as vulnerable adults, from the criminal acts of others, and that D should have relocated X and Y to other accommodation, when their social workers realised that X and Y might be subject to attacks and were frightened of youths who were using their flat for illicit activities. **Held:** D did not owe a duty to protect these two tenants from the criminal acts of others.

Proximity and public policy analysis against a duty of care to a child

- the fact that there was a legal (tenancy) relationship between C and D, pursuant to which C lived in the flat, did not create a sufficient proximity between them (and D was not in breach of any of its obligations under the tenancy);
- D did not assume any responsibility to C, so as to impose upon it a duty to take reasonable care of these vulnerable adults, by removing them from the flat to temporary emergency accommodation. Both the Social Services Dept and the Housing Dept were seeking to carry out their statutory functions, and no more;
- no-one within D, the Council, had created the danger faced by C, or had assumed specific responsibility for C's safety (not even X and Y's assigned social worker);

[77] [2003] EWCA Civ 1151, [2004] QB 558, [83]–[84].

[78] [2009] EWCA Civ 286, [2009] 3 FCR 266.

- under the *Caparo* test, it was not fair, just and reasonable to impose a duty of care. There was an important difference between where children assert that a duty of care is owed to them, and a case (like this) where C were vulnerable adults living in the community. D had specific obligations in respect of children under the Children Act 1989 which were different from those which applied re adults, and where D has parental responsibility.

Wrongfully-accused parents. The benevolent turnaround of the law, in the child C's favour, has not been matched for the parental C who has been wrongfully-accused of sexually or physically abusing their children or those within their *loco parentis* care. That was the upshot of the House of Lords' decision in *JD v East Berkshire Community Health NHS Trust; RK and MAK v Dewsbury Healthcare NHS Trust; RK and AK v Oldham NHS Trust.*[79]

i. **Pre-*East Berkshire*.** In one of the conjoined appeals in the 1995 *Bedfordshire* litigation (the *Newham* case), a wrongfully-accused mother's claim in negligence against a psychiatrist and social worker was struck out by the House of Lords as disclosing no cause of action (although the parental claim was merely a secondary issue in that case, the main question being the neglected children's claims, discussed above).

In 2001, in *L and P v Reading BC*,[80] the Court of Appeal had refused to strike out a negligence claim brought by a wrongfully-accused *father* against a social worker and a police officer, on the grounds that (1) there was an 'arguable case' that there was a relationship of proximity between the social worker and police officer and *both* the child *and the father*, based upon a legal assumption of responsibility and a 'special relationship' between them; and (2) then-recent authorities (e.g., *Osman v UK*[81]) suggested that extreme care had to be taken in striking out claims in what was an evolving area of the law.

However, also in 2001, the Privy Council held that a wrongfully-accused father could **not** be owed a duty of care by a social welfare department and by its employed healthcare professionals.

> In *B v A-G (NZ)*,[82] a social worker had made a complaint to the effect that B, the father of two daughters aged 7 and 5, had sexually abused his younger daughter. The social worker believed this incorrectly. The relevant Act imposed on the Director General of Social Welfare a duty of inquiry, where he knew or had reason to suspect that any child or young person was suffering or likely to suffer from ill-treatment. B and his daughters claimed damages in respect of the allegedly negligent way in which the complaint had been investigated by the clinical psychologist and the social worker involved. **Held:** the Privy Council refused to strike out the claim in negligence brought by the daughters; but the father's claim was struck out as disclosing no cause of action.

ii. ***East Berkshire* (HL).** In the three conjoint appeals in *East Berkshire*, each parental C was falsely and negligently accused of abusing or harming his or her child, and as Lord Nicholls said, '[t]he primary question before the House is whether doctors and, vicariously or directly, health trusts are liable in damages to a parent in such a case. Hand-in-hand with this is a parallel question concerning the liability of a local authority in respect of its investigation of suspected

[79] [2005] UKHL 23, [2005] 2 AC 373. [80] [2001] EWCA Civ 346, [2001] 1 WLR 1575 (CA).
[81] [1999] 1 FLR 193 (ECtHR). Also: *Barrett v Enfield LBC* [1999] UKHL 25, [2001] 2 AC 550.
[82] [2003] UKPC 61 (Lord Nicholls, who delivered the judgment, was in the majority in *East Berkshire*).

child abuse.' *Dewsbury's* facts (re Schamberg's disease) have already been considered above. The other two conjoined cases also concerned false accusations of abuse against the parent, RK and JD respectively.

In *RK and AK v Oldham NHS Trust*, RK was the father of baby MK. When MK was two months old and was being lifted from a lounge settee, she screamed with pain, and was taken to hospital. Hospital notes incorrectly recorded that MK had been 'yanked up' from the couch. A paediatrician, D, diagnosed MK as having an 'inflicted injury', a fractured femur, and did not investigate further the possibility of a diagnosis of *osteogenesis imperfecta* ('brittle bones'). The welfare authority obtained an interim care order, MK was discharged from hospital into the care of an aunt – and thereafter sustained further similar fractures while in her aunt's care. After further tests, a diagnosis of brittle bone disease was made, and after eight months of separation, MK was returned to the care of her parents. Both parents (RK and wife AK), C, suffered psychiatric injury, and sued D directly in negligence, and his employer health authority vicariously. **Held (4:1):** no duty of care was owed to the parents, C. In *JD v East Berkshire Community Health NHS Trust*, JD was a registered children's nurse, and mother of son M. M had suffered from severe (medically-investigated) allergic reactions all his life. When M was 5, he was diagnosed by a paediatrician, D, as suffering from Munchausen's Syndrome by Proxy (a condition in which a person inflicts harm upon another, such as a child, to garner medical attention). It was concluded that M's condition had been fabricated by his mother JD JD herself was unaware of this opinion. M was put on the 'At Risk' register. Later, when M was an in-patient at Great Ormond Street hospital, JD happened to see a handwritten note that she was fabricating M's condition and harming him. When M was eventually confirmed to have severe allergic problems, M was removed from the 'At Risk' register. JD alleged that she suffered psychiatric injury as a result of the misdiagnosis of M's condition, and that she had not returned to nursing since the negligent misdiagnosis was made, thereby suffering economic loss. (Mother and child were not separated in this case.) **Held (4:1):** no duty of care was owed to JD (C in this case).

Both were majority decisions: Lord Bingham dissented strongly in both cases.

Hence, the highest legal protection that will be afforded to parents suspected of abusing or mistreating their children is that D must act in good faith, and must not act recklessly, without caring whether the allegation of abuse is well founded or not (per *East Berkshire*[83]).

The various policy reasons against a duty of care being owed to a wrongfully-accused parent in *East Berkshire* apply,[84] whether D was a local authority or health authority being sued directly in negligence, or the employed professionals charged with carrying out the specific tasks of social welfare.

Proximity and public policy analysis against a duty of care to the parent/s

- the relationship between D and the parent will frequently be one of irreconcilable conflict, 'poles apart'. D's duty to act in the best interests of the child (i.e., to remove him and to report the suspicion of abuse) might mean acting adversely to the personal interests of the parent (to keep the child within the home, for any suspicion not to be reported, and to give the parent the presumption of innocence). At the time of the investigation, D does not know whether there has been abuse by the parent, which means that, at that point, the interests of child and parents are diametrically

[83] [2005] UKHL 23, [2005] 2 AC 373, [74], [90] (Lord Nicholls), [138] (Lord Brown).

[84] [2005] UKHL 23, [2005] 2 AC 373, with quotes in box at: [126] and [86], respectively.

opposed: '[i]t will always be in the parents' interests that the child should not be removed. Thus, the child's interests are in potential conflict with the interests of the parents';

- there is a serious risk that vexatious claims, or even seriously-grounded claims with the aim of restoring the parent's reputation, could be brought years after D's decisions concerning the child were made;
- if D owed a duty to the parents, then D, as those responsible for the protection of a child against criminal conduct, would owe suspected perpetrators a duty of care to prevent foreseeable harm to them, which would be extraordinary;
- D already had sufficient burdens here – having to consider the short-term and long-term welfare of the child; making decisions on limited information; deciding what to tell family members. It would be wrong to add to the burdens by having potential claims by aggrieved parents in the back of their minds;
- child abuse and mistreatment is a serious social problem ('appallingly prevalent in our society'), and D played a vital part in combating the risk and in protecting the vulnerable from such harm. It was best attacked by relieving D of the fear of legal proceedings brought by parents arising out of their investigations. Uncompensated innocent parents pay the price, but that is a necessary price;
- the potential for indeterminate liability arises, with potential suits from a range of possible abuser (e.g., other relatives, school-teachers, babysitters, neighbours, total strangers);
- where D negligently allows a child to die, and the parent suffers a recognisable psychiatric injury, then unless that parent can prove that he is a 'secondary victim' (per Chapter 5), he cannot recover – and there the child is lost forever. There is even less reason to permit a parent to recover for psychiatric injury when *temporarily* separated from his child after wrongful accusations of abuse;
- it is no answer to say, 'impose a duty on D towards the parent, but excuse D if he has met the reasonable standard of care'. Imposing any duty to the parent would be an 'insidious' influence on the healthcare practitioner's conduct (not consciously though, as D are 'surely made of sterner stuff' than that); and it would expose D to the risk of costly and vexing litigation in trying to prove no breach;
- shared information between parent and D, and involving parents in the decision-making process, is an ideal and should be done as fully as is compatible with the child's best interests. But it is quite a step from this to saying that D personally owes a suspected parent a duty sounding in damages.

As mentioned, Lord Bingham dissented in *East Berkshire* (HL), and would have allowed the parents' claims to proceed to trial. Notably, his Lordship also dissented in *Bedfordshire* (CA), prior to his elevation to the House of Lords, re the *child's* claim, and that dissenting viewpoint eventually prevailed in *East Berkshire* (CA). However, it is difficult to envisage the parental C enjoying Lord Bingham's dissent becoming law, given the bulwark that continues to be presented to such claims.

iii. **Post-*East Berkshire*.** Undoubtedly courts which have considered parental claims since *East Berkshire* have felt enormous sympathy for parental victims who are confronted with wrongful accusations. For example, in *AD v Bury MBC*,[85] Wall LJ stated that he 'shared the sympathy ... for any parent wrongly accused of injuring their child'; while in *Hinds v Liverpool CC*,[86] the court noted that, 'I can understand Mr Hinds' predicament at having lost contact permanently

[85] [2006] EWCA Civ 1, [32]. [86] [2009] 1 FCR 475 (QB) [67].

with RH and RQ, and contact with RM, and can only sympathise'. In *R v Reading BC*,[87] the court observed that the father's dilemma must be 'the most terrible experience that a father can face, being falsely accused of sexually assaulting his 3-year-old daughter'.

Nevertheless, when policy precludes litigation against a public authority which is acting in the interests of the wider community, then there is 'always a price to be paid by individuals' for that policy (according to the police case of *Van Colle v CC of Hertfordshire*[88]) – and in the present scenario, those individuals who 'pay the price' are wrongfully-accused parents, whose damage goes uncompensated. In *Trent Strategic HA v Jain*, the House of Lords reiterated the *East Berkshire* principle emphatically: 'the authority of the *Newham/Bedfordshire* case, for the proposition that no duty of care was owed *to the mother*, remains unshaken. The social worker's, and the council's, statutory duty had been owed to the child. That duty provided no basis for the imposition on the authority of a duty of care owed to the mother.'[89]

iv. **Extensions of the *East Berkshire* (HL) principle.** Since *East Berkshire*, the principle has undergone a number of extensions and clarifications – many of which have been brought about in decisions in which frustrated and devastated parental Cs have tried to distinguish *East Berkshire* (often with 'ingenuity and skill'[90]), but with a singular lack of success.

East Berkshire concerned D's conduct of investigations of child mistreatment, where D's decision about the separation of child from parent was an *evaluative* one. However, no duty of care will be owed to the parental C where D's wrong was more 'operational' in character either.

In *L (a minor) and B v Reading BC*,[91] the court held that C, a father, had not sexually abused his daughter L in any way, and was very critical of statements made by a social worker and police officer, Ds, about their interview with L, and of their professional conduct as a whole. L went to live with her father, and C claimed damages for loss of employment and for depression suffered as a result of the wrongful accusations. In seeking to distinguish *East Berkshire*, C accused the social worker and police officer of negligent operational activities/decisions, arguing that L had been removed from the family home on the basis of an error-prone interview; and that L's responses and demeanour had not been not recorded. **Held:** D owed C no duty of care. 'The interviewing of a child, and the relaying of the contents of that interview, are just as much part of the investigation as the evaluation of that and other material to decide whether intervention is necessary ... a duty of care cannot exist for some purposes in the course of an investigation into child abuse and cease to exist for other purposes because of a shift in the factual matrix. It either exists for all purposes in the investigation, or for none'.

Furthermore, the *East Berkshire* rule covers the whole gamut of potential Ds in such cases – social service departments, social workers, doctors and healthcare professionals generally, plus local authorities and health authorities, whenever any one of them is sued directly for negligence. In *Lawrence v Pembrokeshire CC*, Auld LJ said that, '[i]t is immaterial that social workers, not doctors, place children on the Child Protection Register or take them into care, since child protection work requires social service departments to work closely with the police, doctors, community health workers, the education service and others'.[92]

[87] [2009] EWHC 998 (QB) [1]. [88] [2008] UKHL 50, [2009] 1 AC 225, [139] (Lord Brown).
[89] [2009] UKHL 4, (2009) 106 BMLR 88, [25] (Lord Scott) (emphasis added).
[90] As the court remarked in *AD v Bury MBC* [2006] EWCA Civ 1, [16].
[91] [2006] EWHC 2449 (QB) [28] (Keith J). [92] [2007] EWCA Civ 446, [2007] 2 FCR 329, [22].

Hence, although the health authorities and local authorities were sued *vicariously* in *East Berkshire*, a parental C will not succeed in claiming a duty of care was owed to him where that authority was sued directly for systemic negligence. As the Court of Appeal stated, in *L and B v Reading BC*, 'the approach of the [*East Berkshire*] majority seems to us to apply both to cases of vicarious liability and to cases of what may be called a direct liability [of an NHS Trust or local authority involved in abuse investigations]'.[93]

Additionally, the *East Berkshire* rule covers the *whole* investigative process, both during the initial period of the investigation into alleged child abuse, after an interim care order has been made, after a final care order is made, and right up until proceedings have been discharged (per *AD v Bury MBC*[94]). It also covers the scenario (distinguishable from *East Berkshire* itself) where the claim is directed to the period *after* children were removed from their parents and taken into care, and where a decision was made that there was insufficient evidence to keep them there, but the children were *still* retained in care, contrary to D's statutory powers (per *Williams v Hackney LBC*[95]).

In short, numerous attempts in parental suits to distinguish *East Berkshire* have failed, rendering this line of authority one of the strongest bulwarks in modern duty of care jurisprudence.

Foster/adoptive parents. Despite the legal obstacles facing parental Cs who have been wrongfully accused of sexually or physically abusing children in their care, not all parental Cs have met with such disfavour under the *Caparo* test. Several courts have permitted claims brought by natural, foster or adoptive parents under different scenarios, on the basis that a duty of care was arguable. To give a sample:[96]

> In *W v Essex CC*,[97] a foster child abused the parents' own four children, giving rise to psychiatric injury on the part of those parents, C. It was arguable that the local authority, D, owed a duty of care to C in placing that child whom they knew to have a history of having abused other children.
>
> In *A v Essex CC*,[98] the local authority, D, owed adoptive parents, C, a duty of care in relation to information provided to C about the placed child, who turned out to be aggressive and with a history of aggression towards family members. C suffered physical and psychiatric injury; and the adoptive child threw an iron at their natural child. D knew that the adoptive child had a history of aggression, and that the adoptive father was mentally fragile. D could owe a duty of care to both the adoptive parents and to C's natural children who were at risk from the adoptive child.

In *East Berkshire* itself, Lord Bingham (dissenting) noted that it was not as if parents had *never* had the ability to bring a suit against those public authorities who were engaged in child protection, and that was one reason for upholding a duty of care in favour of a wrongfully-accused parental C. However, the majority's viewpoint prevailed, which rendered the wrongfully-accused parent more aligned with the law's (unsympathetic) attitude towards the wrongfully-accused suspect than with its view of the aggrieved foster parent.

[93] [2007] EWCA Civ 1313, [2008] 1 FLR 797, [33], overturning the decision, [2006] EWHC 3206 (QB), in which Keith J refused to strike out the father's claim, because it was arguable that the Council owed the father a 'direct' duty of care. The father had already failed to establish that he was owed a duty of care by the social worker on the basis of an operational-versus-policy distinction: [2006] EWHC 2449 (QB). Instead of seeking permission to appeal from that, the father sought leave to amend his claim to allege breach of a direct duty of care. Keith J permitted the amendments, considering that if a duty were owed, it would not conflict with the duty owed to the child, and hence, would not fall within the reasoning applied in *East Berkshire* (HL). The CA overturned that decision.

[94] [2006] EWCA Civ 1, [2006] 1 WLR 917, [22].

[95] [2015] EWHC 2629 (QB) [101]–[102].

[96] See too: *Merthyr Tydfil County BC v C* [2010] EWHC 62 (QB) (an arguable duty of care owed).

[97] [2001] 2 AC 592 (HL).

[98] [2003] EWCA Civ 1848, [2004] 1 WLR 1881.

Educational services. As part of the long-standing system of public education (now encompassed in the Education Act 1981), local education authorities have responsibility for the performance of statutory duties, e.g., in relation to children with special educational needs, such as dyslexia. Failure to diagnose and/or treat such conditions has exposed these public authorities to increasing litigation.

i. The *Bedfordshire* cases. It will be recalled that *X v Bedfordshire CC*[99] concerned five appeals. Three of them, *E v Dorset CC*, *Christmas v Hampshire CC* and *Keating v Bromley LBC*, related to negligence claims against education authorities (directly and vicariously) for breach of their statutory duties towards children with special educational needs.

> In *E v Dorset CC*,[100] it was common ground that E had learning difficulties amounting to dyslexia. His parents sought an assessment of how these difficulties could be addressed, and the local education authority, D, concluded that E could be appropriately placed in an ordinary county school. His parents disagreed with the assessment and placement. E sued D, alleging that D negligently failed to make proper assessment of or provision for his special educational needs. Also, D provided a psychology services which advised E's parents in their assessments of E's learning difficulties, and the parents claimed that they relied upon it. **Held:** D did not owe any duty of care to assess or to provide for E's special education needs. However, D did owe a duty of care to E and to his parents, in providing the psychology service, given that once D decided to offer a psychological advice service, then that statutory body was 'in the same position as any private individual or organisation holding itself out as offering such a service. By opening its doors to others to take advantage of the service offered, it comes under a duty of care to those using the service to exercise care in its conduct. The position is directly analogous with a hospital conducted, formerly by a local authority now by a health authority in exercise of statutory powers ... the authority running the hospital is under a duty to those whom it admits, to exercise reasonable care in the way it runs it'. In *Christmas v Hampshire CC*, C had severe behavioural problems and learning difficulties, especially in learning to read. His parents asked the headmaster of his primary school and members of the teaching staff for advice and investigation into C's condition. The headmaster told C's parents that C did not have any special learning difficulty. The headmaster then referred C to an advisory service run by D, for an assessment of C's learning difficulties, and reported back that C had 'no serious handicaps, but that it was mainly a question of a good deal of regular practice'. At a secondary school to which C moved eventually, he was diagnosed with 'a severe specific learning difficulty'. C claimed that both headmaster and advisory service were negligent (and D was vicariously liable for that negligence) in failing to ascertain that C had a specific learning difficulty, failing to assess the nature of his learning difficulty, failing to diagnose dyslexia, and failing to refer him to an educational psychologist. **Held:** a duty of care was owed to C.

It was reiterated in *Dorset* that, even if D failed to exercise its statutory powers carefully, that could not, of itself, sustain an action in negligence. Although *East Suffolk* (1941) was not adverted to, this case demonstrates an application of that principle. In *Christmas*, and unlike in *Dorset*, there was no attempt to fashion a common law duty out of a statutory power – 'the negligence complained of has nothing to do with the Act of 1981: ... nor is there any allegation of any failure to operate the statutory regime. The claim is a pure common law claim based on a duty of care owed by a headmaster and educational advisor to a pupil'.[101] In that regard, the

[99] [1995] 2 AC 633 (HL). [100] [1995] 2 AC 633 (HL), with quotes in case description at 762–63.
[101] *ibid*, 765–66.

headmaster of private or public schools, or a teaching advisor, is under a duty to his pupils to exercise skill and care in advising on their educational needs. To hold otherwise 'would fly in the face, not only of society's expectations of what a school will provide, but also of the fine traditions of the teaching profession itself'.

ii. The *Phelps* effect. In 2000, five years after *Bedfordshire*, the House of Lords, in *Phelps v Hillingdon LBC*,[102] re-examined the position of poorly-educated children – again in a series of four conjoined appeals. Three of the children were dyslexic, and the other suffered from Duchenne Muscular Dystrophy. In *Phelps* (the only one which went to full trial), C was examined by an educational psychologist who was employed by the local education authority, D. Again, as with *Dorset/Hampshire*, D was operating within a statutory framework, in that it was under a duty to make an assessment of the special educational needs of any child, and had to seek educational, medical and psychological advice in that regard.[103]

> In *Phelps v Hillingdon BC*, Pamela Phelps, C, aged 11, had learning difficulties, but the educational psychologist, M, reported that she could find no specific weaknesses with C. M was employed by the Hillingdon Educational Psychology Service, an entity set up by the local authority, D, to help C's poor progress in reading and writing. C received 6 hours per week in special needs teaching in English and Maths, which was not specifically designed for a dyslexic pupil. In her last three years at school, C missed many teaching periods because of ill-health and truancy (allegedly of a psychological origin because of her educational failure). Towards the end of her school education, C was discovered to be dyslexic, and her reading age was assessed as someone of 7.9 years. C claimed that she left school with fewer skills than she would have learned, had she been correctly assessed, diagnosed and treated earlier. C sued the psychologist (and D, vicariously), and D directly, alleging that, via the negligent diagnosis, C had suffered economic loss, given the employment opportunities that were denied to her. **Held**: C was owed a duty of care by the psychologist M; the action could not be struck out.

The House of Lords (per Lord Slynn) observed that a requisite proximity existed, as between psychologist and child, in respect of the child's educational needs, which was based upon an assumption of responsibility that was *imposed*, rather than *assumed*, by the psychologist towards that child:

> where an educational psychologist is specifically called in to advise in relation to the assessment and future provision for a specific child, and it is clear that the parents acting for the child and the teachers will follow that advice, *prima facie* a duty of care [in favour of the child] arises ... It is not so much that responsibility is assumed as that it is recognised or imposed by the law.[104]

Furthermore, no policy reasons dictated against a wide duty of care being imposed on the educational psychologist. In particular, the appeals review procedure did not give 'sufficient redress' for the wrong alleged here; the imposition of a wider duty of care was unlikely to lead to defensive practices; and to impose a duty on the psychologist would still only require the attaining of reasonable, not unreasonably high, standards of practice from educational defendants.[105]

[102] [2001] 2 AC 619 (HL).

[103] [2001] 2 AC 619 (HL) 666 (Lord Nicholls), citing: Education (Special Educational Needs) Regulations 1994 (SI 1994/1047), reg 6.

[104] [2001] 2 AC 619 (HL) 654, reversing: [1999] 1 WLR 500 (CA).

[105] [2001] 2 AC 619 (HL) 653–55. See also, Lord Clyde's discussion of policy factors at 672.

Importantly, though, the public authority **itself** could, in law, owe a duty of care to a child who complained of poor education, according to *Phelps*, obiter. There were two reasons for that:

- where a public authority is exercising its statutory powers, if it appointed a psychologist who was transparently neither qualified nor competent to carry out its statutory duties or powers, in regard to children with special educational needs, then a duty of care on the public authority's part was certainly possible; and
- any 'operational negligence' on the part of a public authority could give rise to a duty of care on that public authority's part – provided that the tri-partite *Caparo* test was met.

However, this was dicta, because Pamela Phelps, C, succeeded against public authority D on the basis of vicarious liability; and according to Lord Slynn, 'I do not consider that the case of direct liability on the part of Hillingdon BC is made out, nor indeed was necessary'.[106]

iii. The *Carty* case. In *Phelps*, the relevant Ds were medically-qualified healthcare professionals. Four years later, in *Carty v Croydon LBC*,[107] it was the first time that the Court of Appeal had been asked to decide whether an education officer could owe a duty of care to children with special educational needs. He could.

> In *Carty v Croydon LBC*, Leon Carty, C, claimed that, over a substantial period of his schooling, the officers employed by the local education authority, D, failed to provide him with suitable education. C sued D vicariously for the negligence of its education officer, and for a direct or corporate duty of care. C claimed that the education officer failed to assess and issue a statement of special educational needs, including speech therapy, allowing C to remain at one school, and then failed to re-assess C after the breakdown of his placements in other schools. **Held:** the education officer owed a duty of care to C, because that officer (a) acted as a person with special skills and relevant experience in operating in the statutory framework established to cater for special educational needs; (b) actually undertook specific educational responsibilities towards C; and (c) entered into a particular relationship with C, re his special education needs.

However, a duty was not owed, merely because of any failure to exercise the statutory powers under the Education Act 1981 carefully – a reiteration of the *East Suffolk* principle.

Immigration matters. The fact that the Home Secretary acts pursuant to the Immigration Act 1971 in exercising his statutory powers (e.g., to give indefinite leave to remain in the UK) does not give rise to a duty of care in favour of any individual, C (e.g., who claims that his leave to remain was withheld or delayed).

> In *Home Office v Mohammed*,[108] six Iraqi Kurds, C, who reached the UK between 1999–2001, were eventually found to be entitled to be granted indefinite leave to remain. The first of these was granted in 2007; and the last in 2009, partly because the applications had been put on hold pursuant to a prior policy which was subsequently held to be unlawful, and partly because the Home Office, D, failed to implement the appropriate ministerial policy. C sued D in damages for negligence. **Held:** no duty of care was owed to C.

[106] [2001] 2 AC 619 (HL) 657. [107] [2005] EWCA Civ 19, [2005] 1 WLR 2312, [86].
[108] [2011] EWCA Civ 351, [2011] 1 WLR 2862, and with quote in box at [26].

Proximity and public policy analysis against a duty of care re immigration matters

- when undertaking activities to do with immigration assessment, enforcement, detention, asylum, residency, etc, immigration officers of the Home Office were acting as public servants, with their primary duty to the State;
- to owe duties to individuals who may be affected adversely by immigration officers' activities could entail an actual or potential conflict of interest, between, say, the safety of the general public, and C's interests;
- in *Rowley v Sec of State for Work and Pensions,*[a] C alleged negligence by the Child Support Agency, D, re the maintenance on which C and her children depended. Analogously, D owed its duties to the State, and not to C;
- there were other forms of redress available to C – C could invite the parliamentary Ombudsman to adjudicate and recommend payment of compensation. If the Home Office failed to comply with such a recommendation, then 'like all decisions of public authorities, [it] must meet legal standards of good faith, rationality and more'.

[a] [2007] EWCA Civ 598.

De-registration of business proprietors, causing economic loss. In *Jain v Trent Strategic HA,*[109] the damage complained of by C was pure economic damage (whereas several cases considered previously in this chapter have concerned personal injury, psychiatric injury, or consequential economic injury). No duty of care was owed, primarily for policy reasons.

In *Jain v Trent Strategic HA*, Mr and Mrs Jain, C, ran a nursing home, Ash Lea Court, to cater for the mentally-ill and infirm. Most of the residents were elderly. The business was closed down by executive action taken against them by the predecessor of the Trent Strategic HA, D, who issued a notice that their nursing home should close. To achieve the closure, D applied, *ex parte* and without notice, to a magistrate for the cancellation of registration of C's nursing home, under the Registered Homes Act 1984, with immediate effect. Ultimately, it turned out that the application was made without any just cause. C sued to recover for the severe economic losses caused by D's conduct. **Held:** no duty of care was owed to C by D.

Proximity and public policy analysis against a duty of care towards business proprietors

- the purpose of the statutory powers exercised by D to cancel registration was to protect the interests of the residents in nursing homes. Whenever a cancellation order was issued, the interests of the proprietors of that nursing home, C, could be affected – and to consider the possibility of economic injury to C could give rise to a potential conflict of interest between residents and owners C, as it would always be in the interests of C that the nursing home should remain open for use (just as it would always be in the interests of an accused parent to keep an abused child in the home, a point made in *JD v East Berkshire*, where no duty was owed either);
- where economic loss is sustained by C, because of D's exercise of statutory powers, there is even less reason than in cases of personal injury to hold that a duty is owed. This case was analogous

[109] [2009] UKHL 4, [2009] 1 AC 853 (HL), with point in box at [26] and [37].

to *Harris v Evans* (the bungee-jumping case considered in Chapter 4), where the Health and Safety Executive issued a certificate requiring the owner of the bungee jumping crane facility to either modify its operations or close down. The primary focus of that statutory purpose was to protect the physical safety of members of the public using those facilities – which must prevail over any duty of care to the proprietor of the facilities who had suffered economic damage on account of the public authority's 'misconceived' conduct;

- the procedures governing the cancellation of nursing home registrations showed 'a lamentable lack in the statutory procedures ... of reasonable safeguards for [owners such as Mr and Mrs Jain] against whom these applications, *ex parte* and without notice, can be made'; but the remedy for that was not to impose on D an 'inappropriate duty of care owed to the proprietors of the nursing homes in question. It lies in the formulation and application of procedural safeguards comparable to those attendant upon *ex parte* applications in the High Court';
- the fact that there was no other form of redress available to C for the ruination of their nursing home business was not sufficient to establish a duty of care (although it was always one factor to be balanced in the scales, when assessing policy under the third limb of *Caparo*).

Where an aggrieved C claims that the de-registration process at D's hands caused him economic losses, then the availability to C of other remedies and recourse will be relevant, and tends to count *against*, the imposition of a duty of care on D (per the removal of a dentist from an NHS list, in *Jowhari v NHS England*[110]).

The incremental test

§13.11 The incremental test by which to ascertain whether a duty of care should be owed has been explicitly relied upon in some public authority cases.

It will recalled from Chapter 2 that the incremental test was proposed by Lord Bridge, in *Caparo Industries plc v Dickman*, as a cross-check upon the analysis derived from proximity and policy and/or from the assumption of responsibility/reliance tests.[111]

Interestingly, the deep division within the House of Lords in *East Berkshire*,[112] as to whether or not a wrongfully-accused parent should be owed a duty of care, was reflected in their application of the incremental test. For Lord Bingham (dissenting), recognition that a duty of care should be owed to a wrongfully-accused parent was a 'small, analogical and incremental development' in the law, given that it was now accepted that a duty may be owed to a child. On the other hand, for Lords Nicholls and Rodger of the majority, whatever the law said about the child's claim gave 'no guidance on how "wrongly suspected parent" cases should be decided', and that it by no means followed that local authorities, health authorities, and employed professionals, owed any similar duty of care to the parents. Plainly, then, what is an incremental step and a close hugging-of-the-coastline to one judge is a 'long jump' to others!

In *Home Office v Mohammed*,[113] the Court of Appeal rejected any duty of care on the Home Office's part towards six Iraqi Kurds who were not issued with indefinite leaves to remain

110 [2014] EWHC 4197 (QB) [44], [47]. 111 [1990] 2 AC 605 (HL) 618 (Lord Bridge).
112 [2005] UKHL 23, [2005] 2 AC 373, with the respective views at: [36], and on the other hand, [83], and [106].
113 [2011] EWCA Civ 351, [2011] 1 WLR 2862, [27].

for a number of years, on the basis that the incremental test did not call for such a duty. Sedley LJ remarked that, '[a] number of leading cases touch on the continuing possibility of incremental change at the margins of common law liability, not in order to commend it, but in order not to exclude it. Incremental change has both attractions and problems, not the least of which is that it can go in more than one direction'. In any event, the policy reasons did not call for an duty being imposed, where none had been imposed previously in any similar case.

Conclusion

It is obvious from the abovementioned discussion that *Caparo* is a frequently-applied test in the context of public authority negligence liablity. In *Connor v Surrey CC*,[114] Laws LJ paid particular heed to the application of the *Caparo* test, and summed it up in this way: '*Caparo*, though it is no rule-book, represents the modern backdrop against which to judge any putative negligence claim ... And though there seems to be something of a shift from the sharp-edged rule of immunity for policy decisions found in *X v Bedfordshire CC* towards the looser spectrum from strategic to specific decision-making found in *Barrett* and later authorities, the corpus is a principled whole'.

However, it is equally obvious from this section that many Cs claimed for negligently-inflicted *pure psychiatric injury* (arising from enforced separations from family members, etc) – and notably, the corpus of principles governing that particular area of negligence (discussed in Chapter 5), tends to be conflated with the *Caparo* test in a fairly haphazard way, where public authorities are sued. In fact, some cases involving psychiatric injury suffered by parental Cs (e.g., *JD v East Berkshire*) followed a straight *Caparo* analysis, whereas other suits brought by parents against a public authority for that type of injury (e.g., *W v Essex CC*) entailed judicial discussion of whether C was a primary victim or a secondary victim (with discussion of the inevitable subprinciples which that analysis requires). Ultimately, the results of the respective analyses may not differ, but the lack of consistency in how such cases are approached adds to the uncertainty in this field of negligence law.

An incidental duty of care

§13.12 A public authority may owe a duty of care to C when it performs activities carelessly during the course of undertaking its statutory duties or powers, but where those activities are quite separate from the nature of the statutory functions ordinarily undertaken by that authority.

This scenario will be quite rare. In *Home Office v Mohammed*,[115] Sedley LJ gave examples of a gas meter reader who lights a cigarette in C's premises and causes severe property damage, or an environmental health officer who is inspecting C's premises and who breaks the restaurant's china carelessly. Although the public authority (through its employees) is acting in the normal discharge of its statutory function, the way in which these accidents happen is quite unconnected with the particular functions which the public authority was meant to perform. Yet a duty will be owed to C.

[114] [2010] EWCA Civ 286, [2011] QB 429, [102].

[115] [2011] EWCA Civ 351, [2011] 1 WLR 2862, [12]. The restaurant china example was recently affirmed in: *Jowhari v NHS England* [2014] EWHC 4197 (QB) [44].

IMPACT OF THE ECHR

Regarding negligence suits against public authorities, the ECHR has prompted **four** interesting developments of note. Dealing with each in turn:

Paths worn to the European Court of Human Rights

§13.13 For any alleged negligent conduct on the part of a public authority occurring after 2 October 2000, ss 7 and 8 of the Human Rights Act 1998 enabled C to bring proceedings in the English domestic courts against that public authority for a contravention of a Convention article, for which English courts may award damages for that contravention.

For events occurring **prior** to 2 October 2000, the **only** avenue for an aggrieved C was to take his action to the European Court of Human Rights in Strasbourg, and seek compensation via that avenue. C could not plead a violation of their Convention rights in the domestic courts, because prior to 2 October, those rights were not incorporated into domestic law by the 1998 Act. Before seeking a remedy for breach of their Convention rights in Strasbourg, C must have exhausted their domestic remedies via litigation in the English courts – hence, the importance of the duty of care analysis handed down by the House of Lords.

Having met a hard rock-face in English negligence law, in which they were owed no duty of care by the relevant public authorities, the separate Cs in *Bedfordshire/Newham* (facts previously) did precisely that.

In *Z v UK*,[116] four of the abused and neglected child Cs in *Bedfordshire* (one child ceased his action due to the express wishes of his adoptive parents) alleged contraventions by the public authority, D, of Art 3 (the right to freedom from torture or inhuman or degrading treatment or punishment) and Art 13 (the right to an effective remedy). **Held:** Art 3 was violated because the neglect and abuse suffered by the four children reached the threshold of inhuman and degrading treatment required; the treatment was brought to D's attention in 1987; D was under a statutory duty to protect the children and had a range of powers available to them, including the removal of the children from their home; the children endured abuse and neglect, without D's intervening, for 4.5 years; the child psychiatrist who examined them called it the most horrific experiences that she had treated in her career; and the Criminal Injuries Compensation Board also found that the children had been subject to appalling neglect over an extended period and suffered physical and psychological injury directly attributable to a crime of violence. D failed to protect these applicant children from serious, long-term neglect and abuse. Art 13 was also contravened, because no action in the domestic courts was available, given that the abuse occurred prior to October 2000. Cs were awarded, in combination, £320,000 (including £32,000 to each, by way of non-pecuniary damage), the level of horrific abuse reflected in the award. However, there was no violation of Art 6 (discussed below).

In *TP and KM v UK*,[117] both mother (TP) and daughter (KM), from the *Newham* case, alleged violations of Art 8 (the right to a private and family life) and Art 13. **Held:** Art 8 was violated, because of the failure to immediately disclose to the mother the video interview with M. Had that video been *promptly* shown to the mother, she would have realised who was identified by M, and it

[116] (2001) 34 EHRR 97, [2001] 2 FLR 612 (ECtHR).

[117] (2001) 34 EHRR 42, [2001] 2 FLR 549 (ECtHR) [30], [80]–[83], [115]–[117].

would have avoided the lengthy period of separation which followed, and which caused psychiatric disorders to both mother and child. Art 13 was violated because Cs had no avenues of compensation from the Ombudsman or from any other complaints regime available to them. Each C recovered £10,000.

In *RK and AK v UK*,[118] the same parties as in the *Oldham* 'brittle bone' litigation (which formed part of the *East Berkshire* trilogy of cases), AK and RK (mother and father, respectively, of baby MK), brought a claim in the European Court of Human Rights for violations of Arts 8 and 13. **Held:** Art 8 was not contravened, because mere errors in judgment by health and other professionals in potential abuse situations did not render their conduct incompatible with the requirements of Art 8: '[t]he authorities, medical and social, have duties to protect children, and cannot be held liable every time their genuine and reasonably held concerns are proved retrospectively to have been misguided'. There had been sufficient reasons for the authorities to have taken protective measures, which were proportionate to the aim of protecting baby MK, plus as soon as a further fracture occurred to MK whilst in her aunt's care, further tests were quickly pursued, and within weeks, MK was returned home. However, breach of Art 13 occurred, given the lack of remedy available to the parents as a result of *East Berkshire*.

For events which occurred after October 2000, however, a plea of contravention of the ECHR can (and often is) brought in domestic law against a public authority.

The Art 6 problem

§13.14 Where policy reasons mean that it would not be 'fair, just and reasonable' to impose a duty of care on the public authority under the *Caparo* test, that will preclude a duty of care, but will not entail a violation of Art 6.

Negligence suits against public authorities gave rise to an instance of legal misunderstanding on the part of the European Court of Human Rights, which had important effects on these types of suits in domestic law for some time.

It will be recalled that the *Bedfordshire/Newham* abuse cases, and the victim-of-crime case of *Osman v Ferguson*, were all struck out by the House of Lords as disclosing no cause of action. This was because, as a matter of public policy, it was not fair, just and reasonable to impose a common law duty of care on the relevant public authorities, to the abused children, to their parents, or to victims of crime where the police failed to investigate and suppress crime, respectively. The disappointed claimants in these cases took their cases to the European Court of Human Rights – and in *Osman v UK*, that Court held that precluding a duty of care from arising, for policy reasons, conveyed an immunity which infringed Art 6. That view, however, was ultimately overturned. A time-line of the significant milestones (in the Table below) conveys the twists and turns of judicial opinion.[119]

Hence, it is now incontrovertible that, where it would not be 'fair, just and reasonable' to impose a duty of care on the public authority under the *Caparo* framework, then that will preclude a duty of care, but it will not entail a violation of Art 6. Of course, aggrieved claimants will have harsh outcomes in some cases. As the House of Lords said in *Seal v CC of South Wales*

[118] (2009) 48 EHRR 29 (ECtHR) [36]–[37], [45].

[119] See: *Osman* [1999] 1 FLR 193 (ECtHR) [149]–[151; *Barrett* [1999] UKHL 25, [2001] 2 AC 550, 559; and *Z v UK* (2001) 34 EHRR 97, [2001] 2 FLR 612 (ECtHR) [100]–[101].

Police,[120] the rule in *East Berkshire* that precludes a duty of care from being owed towards a wrongfully-accused parent does not constitute a denial of that parent's access to the courts in violation of Art 6, but is merely 'the price to be paid for the established principle (and the assurance it provides) of protecting various classes of prospective defendants against claims in negligence.'

A time-line of important events re ECHR and public authorities

1993–Osman v Ferguson – Mr Osman's claim, and his father's estate's claim, in negligence against the police was struck out by the House of Lords as disclosing no cause of action, on the basis of the core *Hill* principle (i.e., the public policy reasons derived from *Hill v CC of West Yorkshire*), per Chapter 2

1995–the *Bedfordshire* and *Newham* claims were struck out by the House of Lords as disclosing no cause of action

1998–Ahmet Osman took his case to the ECtHR, in *Osman v UK*, arguing that the core *Hill* principle had the effect of precluding a duty of care being owed by the police in domestic law, which infringed his Art 6 rights. The court agreed, stating that the core *Hill* principle is based on the view that:

> '... the interests of the community as a whole are best served by a police service whose efficiency and effectiveness in the battle against crime are not jeopardised by the constant risk of exposure to tortious liability for policy and operational decisions ... while the Government have contended that the exclusionary rule of liability is not of an absolute nature and that its application may yield to other public-policy considerations, it would appear ... that [*Osman*] proceeded on the basis that the rule provided a watertight defence to the police and that it was impossible to prise open an immunity which the police enjoy from civil suit in respect of their acts and omissions in the investigation and suppression of crime ... an application of the rule, without further enquiry into the existence of competing public-interest considerations, only serves to confer a blanket immunity on the police for their acts and omissions during the investigation and suppression of crime, and amounts to an unjustifiable restriction on an applicant's right to have a determination on the merits of his or her claim against the police in deserving cases'.

1999–in *Barrett v Enfield LBC*, Lord Browne-Wilkinson explained why the ECtHR had misunderstood (in *Osman v UK*) the effect of the role of policy in precluding a duty of care:

> '[i]n English law, the decision as to whether it is fair, just and reasonable to impose a liability in negligence on a particular class of would-be defendants depends on weighing in the balance the total detriment to the public interest in all cases from holding such class liable in negligence as against the total loss to all would-be plaintiffs if they are not to have a cause of action in respect of the loss they have individually suffered', and that any decision to preclude a duty on policy grounds is not a 'blanket immunity' of the type that would invoke a contravention of Art 6, as the *Osman* court had held.

2001–in *Z v UK* (the *Bedfordshire* application to Strasbourg), the four abused children also alleged a violation of Art 6, per the finding in *Osman v UK*. However, the ECtHR 'ate its words' from *Osman*:

[120] [2007] UKHL 31, (2007) 97 BMLR 172, [75].

'The Court considers that its reasoning in *Osman* was based on an understanding of the law of negligence which has to be reviewed in the light of the clarifications subsequently made by the domestic courts ... The Court is satisfied that the law of negligence as developed in the domestic courts since *Caparo* and *Barrett* includes the fair, just and reasonable criterion as an intrinsic element of the duty of care, and that the ruling of law concerning that element in this case does not disclose the operation of an immunity. In [this] case, ... the inability of the applicants to sue the local authority flowed, not from an immunity, but from the principles governing the substantive right of action in domestic law. There was no restriction on access to court ... The applicants may not therefore claim that they were deprived of any right to a determination on the merits of their negligence claims. Their claims were properly and fairly examined in light of the applicable domestic legal principles concerning the tort of negligence.'

2001–in *TP and KM v UK* (the *Newham* application to Strasbourg), the ECtHR rejected any claim for violation of Art 6, on the same basis as in *Z v UK*.

The strike-out problem

The abovementioned twists and turns had important ramifications for the use of the strike-out procedure too. Under CPR 3.4(2), a statement of claim can be struck out if it discloses no cause of action on its face (even assuming that all facts pleaded by C are proven to be true). Hence, where a court holds that a duty of care cannot be owed, whether on the basis of a lack of proximity or for policy reasons (or both), the strike-out procedure is highly-useful for D. It is an oft-used litigious tactic for public authorities, to seek to defeat negligence suits brought against them before the expenses of a full trial are incurred.

However, in *X v Bedfordshire CC*,[121] Lord Browne-Wilkinson noted that it was undesirable to strike out claims which were arising in developing areas of the law, without full exploration of the facts at trial. Post-*Osman v UK*, English courts manifested even more reluctance to strike-out claims on the basis that no duty of care was owed. In *JD v East Berkshire*,[122] the Court of Appeal noted that *Osman* had 'led to an understandable reluctance on the part of the English courts' to strike out – as evident, e.g., in the aforementioned public authority cases of *Barrett v Enfield LBC*, *W v Essex CC*, *Phelps v Hillingdon LBC* and *L (A Child) v Reading BC*.

However, some senior English judges sought to downplay that line of argument. For example, in *Kent v Griffiths*,[123] Lord Woolf MR remarked that, 'it would be wrong for *Osman* to be taken as a signal that ... the courts should be reluctant to dismiss cases which have no real prospect of success. Courts are now encouraged, where an issue or issues can be identified which will resolve or help resolve litigation, to take that issue or those issues at an early stage of the proceedings so as to achieve expedition and save expense. There is no question of any contravention of Art 6 of the ECHR in so doing'. Additionally, in *Smith v CC of Sussex Police; Van Colle v CC of Hertfordshire Police*,[124] Lord Brown observed that, '[e]ither a duty of care arises on these facts or it does not. No useful purpose would be served by allowing the action to go to trial for facts to be found and then for further consideration to be given to the applicable law'.

[121] [1994] 2 WLR 554 (CA) 557–58, 575 (Bingham LJ). [122] [2003] EWCA Civ 1151, [15].
[123] [2001] QB 36 (CA) [38]. [124] [2008] UKHL 50, [2009] 1 AC 225, [140].

These points of view were ultimately accepted by the Strasbourg court in *Z v UK*,[125] which concurred that the striking-out procedure was 'an important feature of English civil procedure, performing the function of securing speedy and effective justice ... By means of this procedure, it can be determined at an early stage, with minimum cost to the parties, whether the facts as pleaded reveal a claim existing in law'. No violation of Art 6 was involved in the use of the striking-out procedure in either *Z v UK* or in *TP and KM v UK*.

In modern case law, the strike-out procedure is still utilised where public authorities dispute that any duty of care exists at all. For example, in 2013 in *Furnell v Flaherty (t/as Godstone Farm)*, Turner J held that any attempt to drag in the Health Protection Authority and the Tandridge CC to the litigation should be struck out, on the basis that he was 'unpersuaded that any further evidence could salvage the case on the existence of a duty of care', and that 'novelty is no substitute for merit'.[126]

Amending the common law to fit with the ECHR?

§13.15 Where a public authority contravenes an ECHR right and causes C injury or damage, it is *not* necessary for the English common law to provide a common law remedy in negligence for every instance. In some cases, C may be left solely to his remedy under the ECHR.

Where C's suit in negligence against a public authority fails because no duty of care was owed to C – but where the public authority has nevertheless violated one of the Articles of the ECHR – then, as Lord Rodger remarked in *JD v East Berkshire*,[127] the English court hearing the case has two options:

i. to award C compensation for violation of the ECHR rights – assuming that the conduct of the public authority post-dated the implementation of the HRA (on 2 October 2000); or
ii. to modify domestic common law, so as to provide C with a basis for recovery under that common law.

In the case of a neglected or abused child, English courts were prepared to follow the second of these avenues (given the turnaround from *Bedfordshire* (HL) to *East Berkshire* (CA)). However, that trend appears to be 'the exception to the rule'.

In other (and later-decided) contexts in which a public authority has been sued, the House of Lords has sternly resisted the temptation to amend the common law, so as to 'fill the gap'.

The parental suit in *East Berkshire*[128] itself was one such example. Given that the events in the *East Berkshire* cases arose pre-October 2000, the parental Cs could not seek damages in the **domestic** courts for any possible breach of a Convention right. As to the second avenue, whether the common law should change, in the parents' favour, was a subject of mixed views. Lord Rodger seemed to leave the question open – 'I should wish to reserve my opinion as to whether, in such a case, it would be appropriate to modify the common law of negligence rather than to found any action on the provisions ... of the Human Rights Act 1998';[129] while Lord Bingham (dissenting) strongly believed that it **should** be modified:

> the question does arise whether the law of tort should evolve, analogically and incrementally, so as to fashion appropriate remedies to contemporary problems, or whether it should remain essentially

[125] (2001) 34 EHRR 97 (ECtHR) 119–20. [126] [2013] EWHC 377 (QB) [94]. [127] [2005] UKHL 23, [117]–[118].
[128] [2005] UKHL 23, [2005] 2 AC 373. [129] *ibid*, [118].

static, making only such changes as are forced upon it, leaving difficult, and, in human terms, very important problems to be swept up by the Convention. I prefer evolution.[130]

Subsequently, the question as to whether the *East Berkshire* principle needed modifying, for the English common law to comply with Art 8 (the right to a private and family life), arose for direct judicial consideration in *Lawrence v Pembrokeshire CC*. The Court of Appeal unanimously held that the *East Berkshire* principle **did** survive the implementation of Art 8 into domestic law, and that the common law did **not** require modification.

In *Lawrence v Pembrokeshire CC*,[131] Mrs Lawrence, C, and her family, had come to the notice of the Council's, D's, child protection team in 1999. Eventually, after sporadic investigations, D placed C's children on the Child Protection Register in April 2002, because it was thought that they were at risk of physical and/or emotional harm from C or their father. They were removed from the register in June 2003. C complained to the Ombudsman about maladministration and a failure to follow due procedure by D, and in December 2004, the Ombudsman upheld these complaints. C was paid £5,000 by D in compensation. C then sued D for damages for psychiatric injury, alleging negligence *and* a violation of her Art 8 right, because of the conduct of D's social workers towards her and her children, in placing the children's names on the Child Protection Register. **Held:** the claims, both in negligence and under Art 8, were struck out.

The reasoning as to why the English common law did **not** require amending, to render the *East Berkshire* principle compatible with Art 8, may be summarised as follows:[132]

- *East Berkshire's* mantra was that to recognise a duty of care towards the wrongfully-accused parent would conflict with the more pressing duty to the child to protect him from the risk of parental abuse when suspected – and nothing about the implementation of Art 8 into domestic law, or the ability of the parents to bring a claim under s 7 of the HRA for violation of Art 8, had changed that conflict;
- the whole point of the *East Berkshire* principle was to forestall possible harm to a child, by robust and timely intervention, when the public authority suspected parental abuse of children. Strasbourg jurisprudence had already accepted that interference with family life, to preserve the interests of safety and welfare of children when parents were suspected abusers, could be legitimate, proportionate and necessary in a democratic society under Art 8(2). Hence, the common law rule was compatible with Art 8 and did not need amending;
- where a parent sued under Art 8 for interference with family life, the public authority had to justify its conduct. If this were to be literally translated into a common law duty of care, it would require the public authority to prove that it was not in breach of duty, a reversal in the burden of proof which would amount to a 'plain distortion' of common law negligence. It was not necessary, or correct, for domestic law to be developed in this way;
- the advent of Art 8 into domestic law did not undermine the primary need to protect children from the risk of abuse from their parents. The *East Berkshire* rule was consistent with the protection of family life, and with Art 8.

[130] *ibid*, [50]. [131] [2007] EWCA Civ 446, [2007] 2 FCR 329.

[132] [2007] EWCA Civ 446, [34]–[55] (Auld LJ), with Richards and Scott-Baker LJJ concurring, the latter delivering a short judgment.

There is no doubt that parental Cs who are wrongfully accused of molesting or neglecting their children are on the wrong end of a common law principle which is fairly unsympathetic to the damage which they may suffer as a result of the wrongful accusation. The view that the English common law should not be too hasty to adapt, to provide a common law remedy for a Convention violation, is not restricted to wrongfully-accused parents, however.

It was also evident in the privacy-based suit in *Wainwright v Home Office*,[133] arising out of an unlawfully-performed strip search of prison visitors, albeit that the tort of misuse of private information has cautiously and incrementally developed since *Wainwright* (see 'Privacy', an online chapter). Similarly, in *Jain v Trent Strategic HA*,[134] the House of Lords considered whether the English common law should modify the duty of care principles, so as to provide an action in negligence on the part of the proprietor of a business affected by D's conduct, where it was highly arguable that Art 1 (the right to peaceful enjoyment of his possessions), and Art 6 (the right to a fair and public hearing), would have been violated (had the acts of this public authority taken place before the Act came into force). However, it was held that the English common law, which governed not only *Jain*, but other cases involving business proprietors who are the victims of public authority mistakes (e.g., *Harris v Evans*[135]) should **not** be amended. This left C without a remedy at common law, but unfortunately, that was the price to be paid for coherent legal principle. Most recently, the Supreme Court has held, in *Michael v South Wales Police*,[136] that, whatever C's rights under Art 2 (the right to life) may be, English common law would **not** recognise a duty of care owed by the police to a pre-identified victim who was killed by a third party, where the police could reasonably have taken steps to prevent that death. Lord Toulson reiterated that the possibility of an ECHR claim was no good reason for creating a parallel common law claim or for creating wider duties of care.

UNENACTED LAW REFORM

Perhaps unsurprisingly, given the complexity of principles outlined in this chapter, the English Law Commission proposed to reform the law associated with litigation against the public authority. In its Consultation Paper, *Administrative Redress: Public Bodies and the Citizen*,[137] the Commission proposed that, insofar as negligence suits against a public authority were concerned, certain 'truly public' activities by public authorities should be remedied via a specialised statutory scheme of redress, whilst any cases which did not satisfy the 'truly public' test would be 'determined under the normal rules of tort law'.

However, this proposal was, as Sedley LJ put it bluntly in *Home Office v Mohammed*,[138] 'sent to the sea-bed by central government'. The final report of the Commission summarised the situation bleakly:[139]

The law reform corner: Administrative redress: public bodies and the citizen

The English Law Commission proposed very significant changes:

> 'The analysis of court-based remedies was divided between those available in judicial review and those available in private law. In private law, the primary focus was on negligence ...

[133] [2004] 2 AC 406 (HL) [34]. [134] [2009] UKHL 4, [2009] 1 AC 853. [135] [1998] 1 WLR 1285 (CA).
[136] [2015] UKSC 2, [126]–[127]. [137] (CP 187, 2008). [138] [2011] EWCA Civ 351, [2011] 1 WLR 2862, [22].
[139] (Rep 322, 2010) [1.16]–[1.22].

In private law, we suggested that the current system was untenable. The uncertain and unprincipled nature of negligence in relation to public bodies, coupled with the unpredictable expansion of liability over recent years, has led to a situation that serves neither claimants nor public bodies. Furthermore, recent developments in the tort of misfeasance in public office have rendered its continuance of limited value and inappropriate as a cause of action. Breach of statutory duty is not a suitable cause of action in relation to most forms of administrative wrongdoing.

In light of this, we argued in favour of the reform of court-based administrative redress in both public and private law ... We provisionally proposed the reform of court-based redress in both public and private law. This would have led to the creation of a specific regime for public bodies [comprising] ... a requirement to show "serious fault" on the part of the public body, rather than merely ... – in tort – negligence ...

In private law, we provisionally proposed placing certain activities – those which can be regarded as "truly public"– within a specialised statutory scheme ... Cases which did not satisfy the "truly public" test would have been determined under the normal rules of tort law'.

However, it ultimately concluded that:

'This project was notable in that the key stakeholder – Government – was firmly opposed to our proposed reforms. This opposition was expressed both in the formal response and in discussions at both ministerial and official level. Government's formal response was a single document agreed across Government. This is extremely unusual, if not unique, in recent times ... In light of this, we feel that it is impractical to attempt to pursue the reform of state liability any further at this time'.

In *Home Office v Mohammed*,[140] Sedley LJ called this law reform episode 'a debacle'. In particular, he remarked that it was a 'troubling comment on the functioning of the separation of powers that the state's independent law reform advisory body has had to abandon a project affecting the liability of government ... principally because the control exercised by government over Parliament would frustrate any reform, however wise or necessary, which would make government's life more difficult'. Nonetheless, the reform has faltered for lack of a political will. Hence, the complex fabric of legal principle outlined herein will continue to bedevil actions which are brought by aggrieved citizens against public authorities.

[140] [2011] EWCA Civ 351, [2011] 1 WLR 2862, [23].

Part III

Other selected torts

14

Trespass to the person

INTRODUCTION

This chapter considers **three** different torts: battery (unlawful physical touching); assault (an apprehension or threat of unlawful touching); and false imprisonment (unlawful confinement or constraint). While their common aim is to protect the integrity of C's person, the ingredients of each tort are quite disparate.

As a preliminary matter of terminology: trespass to the person is a *form* of action, but assault, battery and false imprisonment are *causes* of action.

Trespasses versus actions on the case

§14.1 Assault, battery and false imprisonment are torts of trespass, and not actions on the case. That differentiation continues to have significant effects upon current legal doctrine, i.e., these torts are actionable *per se*, and the recovery of damages is not subject to the principles of remoteness which apply to actions on the case.

As explained by Buxton LJ in *Wainwright v Home Office*,[1] the distinction between torts of trespass and torts of 'action of the case' arose in much earlier (medieval) times. A trespass encompassed a *direct* and wrongful interference by D with the person, land or goods of C, such that an action in trespass was pleaded when the damage was caused directly, rather than indirectly. On the other hand, an action on the case consisted of a claim arising from an act or statement which *indirectly* caused C damage. By having to prove the chain of causation (which required an examination 'on the case'), that distinguished actions on the case from trespasses.

Unfortunately, the categorisation of trespasses to the person is an ongoing source of confusion. The Irish Law Reform Commission has stated[2] that assault, battery, false imprisonment, and the tort of *Wilkinson v Downton* are indeed 'the modern elements of the generic writ of trespass to the person'. However, some judges disagree. For example, the tort in *Wilkinson v Downton*

[1] [2001] EWCA Civ 2081, [2002] QB 1334, [66]–[72], and also see Lord Hoffmann on appeal: [2003] UKHL 53, [2004] 2 AC 406, [8]. See too: the explanations of 'trespass', 'trespass on the case', and 'action on the case', in: *Oxford Dictionary of Law* (6th edn, 2006); J Penner, *The Law Student's Dictionary* (Oxford University Press, 2008) 7, 296–7; and *Butterworths Concise Australian Legal Dictionary* (Butterworths, Sydney, 1997) 10, 396.

[2] *Non-Fatal Offences Against the Person* (Rep 45, 1994) ch 1, fn 25, and [2.2].

(considered in the identically-named online chapter) is **not** a trespass to the person, it is a form of 'an action on the case' – Lord Hoffmann stated, in *Wainwright v Home Office*, that the tort 'ha[s] nothing to do with trespass to the person'.[3] Furthermore, in the *Wainwright* Court of Appeal below, Buxton LJ remarked that false imprisonment has been 'unhappily' categorised as a tort of trespass to the person too.[4]

Another source of confusion is that it is probably a misnomer to call trespasses to the person torts of **intentional** conduct – each **can** be proven by intentional conduct, but the type of intent necessary on D's part significantly differs among them (and negligence may be sufficient for battery, as discussed below).

Nevertheless, the distinction still continues to hold good, in general terms: trespasses to the person consist of the direct infliction of force upon C, whereas actions on the case consist of harm inflicted indirectly – and, if intentional, that is the tort of *Wilkinson v Downton*; and if unintentional, that invokes the tort of negligence. The distinction between trespass to the person and an action on the case also has some important consequences for C:

i. Trespasses to the person are actionable *per se*, i.e., without proof of damage. The very act constitutes the tort, and it is not necessary to prove that C suffered actual damage. It is the very application of force or restraint applied to C, or the act of total confinement, that constitutes the tort. Even if that causes no loss or injury to C, the tort is proven, and nominal damages will be granted to C, to record that the tort was committed (an 'elementary' proposition, per Lord Dyson MR in *Lumba v Sec of State for the Home Dept*[5]). In that respect, the torts of trespass to the person vindicate the personal integrity of C, and the right not to suffer any infringement of that integrity (per *Ashley v CC of Sussex Police*[6]).

   In *Ashley*, James Ashley, C, was shot dead by PC Christopher Sherwood of the Sussex Police Special Operations Unit, during an armed raid at C's home, which had formed part of police investigations into drug trafficking, and a stabbing of a man by an alleged associate of C. At the time of the shooting, C was unarmed. The Chief Constable, D, admitted negligence re the pre-raid planning and briefing, and that as a result of that negligence, C was killed. D accepted liability in damages for all consequential damage caused by the shooting. However, D denied C's assault and battery claims, and any aggravated and exemplary damages claims flowing from that. **Held (HL, 3:2):** assault and battery could proceed to trial. The torts were 'rights-centred' rather than 'loss-centred', and it was for C 'to demonstrate that the right in question should not have been infringed at all'.

   On the other hand, there can be no cause of action in negligence (or under the tort of *Wilkinson v Downton*) unless C has suffered some actionable injury or damage that was causally related to D's wrongdoing.

ii. It is not necessary for C, in trespass actions, to prove that the harm suffered by him was reasonably foreseeable. The damage to C may be remote and unforeseeable (in negligence terms), but will still be compensable in a trespass action. If damage to C is caused by the trespass, then it is only necessary to prove that the interference *caused* that damage, and D will then be liable to compensate for that injury, even if highly-unusual to the point of being unforeseeable.

[3] [2003] UKHL 53, [2004] 2 AC 406, [47].
[4] [2001] EWCA Civ 2081, [2002] QB 1334, [67] (Buxton LJ).
[5] [2011] UKSC 12, [2012] 1 AC 245, [64].
[6] [2008] UKHL 25, [2008] 1 AC 962, [60], and with quote in case description at [22] (Lord Scott).

This is a notable difference, of course, from the principles of an action on the case (such as negligence, or the tort of *Wilkinson v Downton*), where liability under those torts is limited to the type of damage that D foresaw, or should have reasonably foreseen, as liable to result from his acts, by virtue of the element of remoteness.

In *Breslin v McKevitt*,[7] an action was brought against the Real Irish Republican Army, and five individuals representing that organisation, for the planting of the Omagh bomb in the Omagh town centre on 15 August 1998. It killed 29 people and injured hundreds, and damaged a substantial part of the commercial centre of Omagh. Several parties, C, survived the bombings, but suffered physical and psychiatric injuries. They sued for assault and battery. **Held:** D was liable in battery. Any question of whether any of C's injuries were too remote was irrelevant, where trespass was concerned.

As a result of these distinctions, at least two considerable advantages flow from the trespass action. As Buxton LJ put it in *Wainwright v Home Office*, '[t]here are therefore powerful reasons why [C] will be well advised to seek to categorise his claim as sounding in trespass. Once he has passed through that door, he not only is able to recover for unforeseeable damage, but also is relieved of the issues of duty of care and of fairness, justice and reasonableness that are applied to limit recovery in negligence'.[8]

Ancillary actions

Assault, battery and false imprisonment are often pleaded together, arising out of the one fact scenario. Ancillary causes of action which may accompany these torts can feasibly include: the tort of *Wilkinson v Downton*; negligence; intimidation; malicious prosecution; fraudulent misrepresentation; an action under the Protection from Harassment Act 1997; malicious procurement of a search warrant;[9] and misfeasance in public office (relevant, e.g., where prison officers' conduct has resulted in the confinement of prisoners[10]).

In some respects, the torts of trespass to the person take a mid-spectrum role. In *Salmon v Police Service of Northern Ireland*,[11] it was said that they occupy the legal territory – an 'in-between position' – between negligence (which requires mere carelessness) and misfeasance (which requires proof of malice).

Scenarios which give rise to the causes of action considered in this chapter may also involve infringements of the ECHR, where D is a public authority. Specifically, claims for infringement under the ECHR – for intentional deprivation of life in violation of Art 2, or for breach of C's rights to be free from 'inhuman or degrading treatment or punishment' under Art 3, 'the right to liberty and security of person' under Art 5, and 'the right to respect for family and private life' pursuant to Art 8 – may feature.

§14.2 Assault and battery are both torts and crimes. Where D is acquitted of the crimes, a civil suit for those torts may still be maintained, and their prosecution would not constitute double

[7] [2009] NIQB 50, [272], appeal dismissed: [2011] NICA 33.

[8] [2001] EWCA Civ 2081, [2002] QB 1334, [71], and not disapproved on appeal.

[9] A relatively newly-created tort, discussed in: *Fitzpatrick v Commr of Police* [2012] EWHC 12 (QB) [142], citing: *Keegan v CC of Merseyside* [2003] 1 WLR 2187 (CA) and *Gibbs v Rea* [1998] AC 786 (PC).

[10] See, e.g.: *R v Deputy Governor of Parkhurst Prison, ex p Hague* [1992] 1 AC 58 (HL) 164; and also: *Prison Officers' Assn v Iqbal (Rev 1)* [2009] EWCA Civ 1312, [2010] 1 QB 732, [41]–[42].

[11] [2013] NIQB 10, [23].

jeopardy. The appropriate standard of proof in an action in tort remains the *civil* standard of proof.

As the House of Lords reiterated in *Ashley v CC of Sussex Police*, the prosecution of C's civil actions, based on assault and battery, is not a 'collateral attack' on D's acquittal. Rather, '[i]t raises issues different from those on which the criminal charges against [D] turned, issues which were not relevant to and could not be raised in the criminal trial. Nor will the prosecution of the civil action place [D] in double jeopardy. There are no penal consequences for adverse findings in the civil courts'.[12]

In civil proceedings for assault and/or battery, even if the D's conduct is of the utmost gravity (leading to C's murder, rape, grievous bodily harm, etc), the relevant standard of proof is the civil standard, i.e., proof on the balance of probabilities. Just because very serious allegations of wrongdoing are in issue does not mean that the standard of proof becomes higher (per *Re H and R (Child Sexual Abuse: Standard of Proof)*,[13] and applied subsequently in *Shah v Gale*[14]).

The Court of Appeal of Northern Ireland summarised, in *Breslin v McKevitt*,[15] why the civil standard of proof should appropriately be applied to trespasses to the person brought in tort. First, the claim is usually for compensatory damages and, hence, remains a civil action, notwithstanding that the conduct giving rise to the trespass is also criminal. Secondly, a trespass action 'remain[s], in effect, litigation between two private sets of individuals', such that the action is not being prosecuted by the State. In combination, it is **not** appropriate to apply the criminal standard of proof of 'beyond reasonable doubt' to cases of trespasses to the person brought in tort.

Turning now to the torts themselves:

ASSAULT AND BATTERY

§14.3 The distinction between assault and battery is that assault is the threat of the application of force, whereas battery is the infliction of force.

Both assault and battery entail **direct** interferences, by virtue of their both being trespasses. However, in *Collins v Wilcock*,[16] Goff LJ explained their difference succinctly: '[a]n assault is an act which causes [C] to *apprehend* the infliction of immediate, unlawful, force on his person; a battery is the *actual* infliction of unlawful force on another person'. In that sense, the torts are parasitic upon each other, and protect the integrity of C's person. However, an assault may occur without any battery occurring (e.g., D showing his fists to C without hitting him); and a battery may occur without any assault (e.g., where D hits C from behind and takes C entirely by surprise).

The framework

The elements of the two torts differ, in accordance with the definition in *Collins v Wilcock* (previously):

[12] [2008] UKHL 25, [2008] 1 AC 962, [24] (Lord Scott). [13] [1996] 1 FLR 80 (HL) 96 (Lord Nicholls).
[14] [2005] EWHC 1087 (QB). [15] [2011] NICA 33, [21]–[25].
[16] (1984) 1 WLR 1172 (CA) 1177–78 (emphasis added).

Nutshell analysis: Assault and battery

Elements of the torts:

	Battery:	Assault:
1	Direct application of force (i.e., contact) by D against C	An overt, deliberate and hostile act by D, indicating an intention to inflict force on C
2	D possessed the requisite intent	D had capacity to carry the intention into immediate effect
3		C apprehended the immediate infliction of force
	Defences:	
•	Consent	
•	Provocation	
•	Prevention of crime, disorder or ill-discipline	
•	Self-defence	
•	Contributory fault	
•	Necessity (and the analogous statutory 'best interests' defence)	

Elements of battery

Element #1: Direct application

§14.4 The infliction of force (i.e., contact) upon C must be direct rather than indirect, to constitute a battery. That application of force must be deliberate, physical and hostile (in the sense that it lacked C's consent). Inflicting fear, discomfort, or psychiatric injury on C is not sufficient to constitute the necessary application of force, for the purposes of battery.

The law draws a dividing line between direct force (properly the province of battery) and indirect force (which is only actionable under a tort that derives from an action on the case, such as negligence or the tort of *Wilkinson v Downton*). That line is finely-drawn at times – and the application of force can be very short-lived, and yet **still** constitute a battery – as the following Table shows:

Direct force

The following constitute direct applications of force, so as to constitute a *prima facie* battery:

- touching C with D's hand (per *Wainwright v Home Office*),[a] where C, the brother of a prisoner whom he was visiting, was touched inappropriately by a prison officer, D, during an unlawfully-conducted strip search, without C's consent; and per *Collins v Wilcock*,[b] where a police constable, D, in restraining a woman suspected of prostitution from walking away from him, took hold of her arm – D committed a battery in these cases;

[a] [2003] UKHL 53, [2004] 2 AC 406.
[b] (1984) 1 WLR 1172 (CA).

- hitting C with a rifle or other instrument (per *Lavery v MOD*[c]);
- injuring C by using a bomb, missile, or explosion, even where intended to detonate after an interval of time (per *Breslin v McKevitt*, the Omagh Bombing case[d]);
- hitting C's horse, upsetting that horse and causing C to fall off (per Buxton LJ in *Wainwright v Home Office*[e]);
- shooting C (per *Bici v MOD*[f]);
- deliberately setting a trained police dog upon a member of the public in order to detain or apprehend that person (per *Roberts v CC of Kent*[g]).

However, the following may **not** constitute **direct** application of force:

- digging a hole in the ground into which C falls and injures or traps himself (dictum in *R v Clarence*;[h] an example given in *Oxford Dictionary of Law*;[i] and affirmed in *Wong v Parkside NHS Trust*,[j] where Hale LJ called such an act the intentional infliction of physical harm by indirect means);
- putting sulphuric acid in a hand-drying machine to hide it, intending to remove it later, but the next user, C, hit the on-switch, and the acid flew out onto C's face – in *DPP v K*,[k] criminal battery succeeded in reliance on the dictum in *Clarence*, but given the dicta of Hale LJ in *Wong*, this scenario may also be arguably too indirect. In *Wainwright* (CA),[l] *DPP v K* was called 'controversial', and the Irish LRC stated that it could be 'questioned';[m]
- putting rocks on a train line to derail a train, injuring the occupants; or stringing a wire between trees on each side of a road to bring down a motorcyclist – two examples of indirect applications of force given by the Irish LRC.

[c] [1984] NI 99 (QBD) 106.
[d] [2011] NICA 33, [16]–[17], approving the trial judge: [2009] NIQB 50, [12].
[e] [2002] QB 1334, [67]. This scenario occurred in: *Dodwell v Burford* (1670) 1 Mod Rep 24, 86 ER 703.
[f] [2004] EWHC 786 (QB) [67].
[g] [2008] EWCA Civ 1588, [21].
[h] (1888) 22 QBD 23, 45 (Stephen J), and cited in: *Breslin v McKevitt* [2011] NICA 33, [16].
[i] (6th edn, 2006) 546.
[j] [2001] EWCA Civ 1721, [2003] 3 All ER 932, [9].
[k] (1990) 91 Cr App R 23 (Div Ct), [1990] 1 WLR 1067.
[l] [2002] QB 1334, [67].
[m] *Non-Fatal Offences Against the Person* (Rep 45, 1994) [1.50].

For a battery to occur, D's act must be deliberate and without consent. The term, 'applying force', is to overstate the position. It does not require violence. As Lord Goff remarked in *F v West Berkshire HA* (when referring to the scenario of medical or surgical treatment), 'any touching of another's body is, in the absence of lawful excuse, capable of amounting to a battery and a trespass'.[17] That is, any unwanted contact is, prima facie, sufficient.

In earlier times, it was said that the application of force must be 'hostile' – that is what 'turn[ed] a touch into a battery' (per *Cole v Turner*[18]). That 'hostility' could encompass a range of things – malice, ill-will, anger (although these are not strictly required for hostility: *Wilson v Pringle*[19]), threatening conduct, or touching C with unfriendly words. Indeed, many batteries will be hostile in that sense. However, in modern parlance, hostility means something quite different – that D touched C without consent (whether express or implied). In *F v West Berkshire*,[20]

[17] [1990] 2 AC 1 (HL) 73. [18] (1704) 6 Mod 149, 87 ER 907 (Holt CJ).
[19] [1987] QB 237 (CA) 253. [20] [1990] 2 AC 1 (HL) 73.

Lord Goff referred to various potential batteries which entail no hostility: a doctor's careful touch; a 'prank that gets out of hand', or 'an over-friendly slap on the back'.

In *Collins v Wilcock*,[21] facts previously, the police constable, D, touched C deliberately, but without an intention to do more than restrain her temporarily. But lack of consent was proven; D was acting contrary to C's legal right not to be physically restrained, unless a power of arrest was being lawfully exercised (which was not being attempted here). In *Wainwright v Home Office*, facts previously, the prison officers were not acting with any hostility or ill-will towards Alan Wainwright, when conducting a search for drugs, and touching him in his armpits and on his penis, but nevertheless, battery was conceded.

Merely creating fear, angst, distress or discomfort to C does not constitute a battery. To cite an example given in *C v D*,[22] if D deliberately touches C's genitals without C's consent, that is a battery; if D videotapes C whilst C is naked but without any intention of touching C, that cannot be battery (or an assault). The latter must be brought under the tort of *Wilkinson v Downton* (discussed in an online chapter of that name). Furthermore, making silent calls to women, causing them fear that the caller D would turn up on their doorstep, thereby causing them psychiatric injury, does not constitute the 'application of force' necessary for the tort to apply – battery requires some kind of physical contact between D and his victim/s (*R v Ireland*[23]).

If *DPP v K*[24] is a correct illustration of the tort of battery, then it also illustrates that an act can start off lacking all intent to inflict force either wilfully or recklessly (in that case, the acid was put in the dryer in a moment of panic), but recklessness can follow (D left the acid in the machine and departed the toilets, when it could have been removed). In other words, the requisite intent can develop mid-course, rather than right at the inception of D's conduct.

§14.5 However, as an exception to the tort of battery, bodily contact which arises from the exigencies of everyday life are not legally actionable.

This point was reiterated in *Collins v Wilcock*.[25] There are many instances in which people are exposed to physical contact in ordinary life – e.g., the inevitable jostling on the train or tube; shaking hands; tapping someone on the shoulder to gain their attention; hearty congratulatory slaps on the back – and none is actionable as a battery. It all depends (said Goff LJ in *F v West Berkshire*) on whether the touching 'transcends the norms of acceptable behaviour', and whether the physical contact between C and D has 'gone beyond generally accepted standards of conduct'.

Element #2: The requisite intent

§14.6 Three types of intent on D's part can suffice for a battery: (1) a wilful intent to apply force to C; (2) a reckless indifference as to C's suffering the application of force; or (3) most controversially, the negligent application of force.

Wilful intent is the most common instance of battery. In *Collins v Wilcock*, for example, the police constable deliberately touched C's arm – and intentional actions of that sort frequently satisfy this element of battery.

[21] (1984) 1 WLR 1172 (CA). [22] [2006] EWHC 166 (QB) [87].
[23] [1998] AC 147 (HL). [24] [1990] 1 WLR 1067 (Div Ct).
[25] [1984] 1 WLR 1172 (CA) 1177 (Goff LJ), and approved in: *F v West Berkshire HA* [1990] 2 AC 1 (HL) (Lord Goff).

Somewhat less usually, **recklessness** may suffice. That was described, in *Bici v MOD*, as a sort of 'subjective recklessness', in that D 'appreciated the potential harm to [C], and was indifferent to it'.[26] Indeed, one of the reasons for including recklessness in the tort of assault is that, 'in many cases, the dividing line between intention and recklessness is barely distinguishable' (per *R v Venna*[27]).

In *Breslin v McKevitt*,[28] facts previously, **held:** battery proven. The IRA phoned three warnings to police and a Samaritan worker, alerting them to a planted bomb (and with the code, 'Martha Pope', indicating that the warning might refer to an actual, rather than hoax, bomb). This may have indicated that the bomb was intended to be discovered before it exploded. However, by planting a large car bomb in the centre of a busy town on a Saturday afternoon, injury and death were likely, and those who planted the bomb were recklessly indifferent in doing so.

More controversially still, **negligence** may suffice to make out a battery too. Of course, where D has acted unintentionally and negligently in causing some harm to befall C, then the natural cause of action is to pursue a claim in negligence. Indeed, some judges believe that to be the **only** cause of action that can be brought. In *Wilson v Pringle*,[29] Croom-Johnson LJ categorically stated that, 'the distinction ... has to be drawn between an unintended accident (when the action must be brought in negligence) and a deliberate accident (when it may be brought in trespass to the person).' However, there is still a line of authority in English law – which has never been expressly overruled – which countenances that negligence on D's part, in inflicting the force on C, is sufficient for a battery (provided always that the application of force is direct). In the *Omagh Bombing* case,[30] the Northern Ireland High Court helpfully traced that line of authority. Summarising this in the following Table:

The case lineage

1617 – in *Weaver v Ward*,[a] C and D were exercising with live ammunition, when D shot C, but D claimed that he had not shot C intentionally. C sued D in trespass. **Held:** C's claim could proceed; D could be liable in trespass if he acted negligently, even though he had no intention to shoot C;

1891 – in *Stanley v Powell*,[b] D fired at a pheasant, but a pellet from the gun glanced off a tree branch and accidentally wounded C. **Held:** C could not recover in trespass, as there was no wilful intent or negligence on D's part in shooting as he did – but proof of negligence would have sufficed for trespass;

1951 – in *National Coal Board v JE Evans & Co (Cardiff)*, *Stanley v Powell*[c] was approved;

1958 – in *Fowler v Lanning*,[d] Diplock J opined that battery could be proven if D acted either intentionally or negligently; and without either, there could be no battery;

[a] (1617) Hobart 135, 80 ER 284.
[b] [1891] 1 QB 86.
[c] [1951] 2 KB 861 (CA) 876.
[d] [1959] 1 QB 426, 439.

[26] [2004] EWHC 786 (QB) [67]. [27] [1976] QB 421 (HL) 429.
[28] [2011] NICA 33. [29] [1986] EWCA Civ 6, [1987] QB 237, 247.
[30] [2009] NIQB 50, [7]–[12], with this lineage noted on appeal: [2011] NICA 33, [14], with the caveat: '[t]his dichotomy of opinion is one on which there is no final or conclusive decision in this jurisdiction'.

1964 – in *Letang v Cooper*,[e] Mrs Letang, C, was sunbathing in the carpark of a Cornish country hotel, when Mr Cooper, D, drove his Jaguar over C's legs, because he did not see her there. C sued in both negligence and battery, more than three years after the event. Her action in negligence was statute-barred; and she was not permitted to bring the action in battery because it was caught by the 3-year limitation period too. However, the Court of Appeal divided as to what cause(s) of action were open to C. Lord Denning MR (with whom Danckwerts LJ agreed) suggested that unintentional and negligently-caused injury could **not** give rise to battery, but only to negligence ('instead of dividing actions for personal injuries into trespass (direct damage) or case (consequential damage), we divide the causes of action now according as whether D did the injury intentionally or unintentionally. If one man intentionally applies force directly to another, C has a cause of action in assault and battery; ... if he does not inflict injury intentionally, but only unintentionally, C has no cause of action today in trespass. His only cause of action is in negligence'); whereas Diplock LJ followed his earlier view in *Fowler v Lanning*, holding that negligent acts which 'inflict direct personal injuries' on C, 'could be described indifferently, either as a cause of action in negligence or as a cause of action in trespass';

2004 – in *Bici v MOD*,[f] two Kosovar Albanians, passengers in a car travelling in Kosovo, were shot at by British soldiers, D, who were part of a UN peacekeeping operation in Kosovo in 1999. Mohamet Bici, C1, was shot in the face but not killed. D's shots were aimed at a third party on the roof of the car, Fahri Bici, who *was* killed. There was no intent on D's part to shoot C1. C1 brought his claim against D in both battery and negligence. Battery succeeded for C1, as a negligent trespass. D did not intend to shoot C1; and D was not reckless (it was not proven that D must have appreciated that it was likely that there were passengers in the car but gave no thought for their safety). However, D were guilty of negligence, in using unreasonable force in the circumstances, and in shooting C1 as the wrong, unintended, person;

2009 – in *Breslin v McKevitt* (the *Omagh Bombing* case[g]), the High Court of Northern Ireland concluded that *Fowler v Lanning* (never overruled) means that a trespass (e.g., battery) 'may be committed negligently' in English law.

[e] [1965] 1 QB 232 (CA) 239 (Denning LJ), 243–44 (Diplock LJ).
[f] [2004] EWHC 786 (QB).
[g] [2009] NIQB 50, [11], [16(c)].

As noted in *Letang* above, the distinction between trespass and negligence could be important, re the relevant limitation periods which apply to the tort (although the law has since changed, so as to render the distinction not so important, as discussed in 'The beginning and end of liability', an online chapter). Also, as *Bici* demonstrates, the defence of self-defence applies slightly differently between the torts (in negligence, self-defence applies if D's conduct is reasonable, so that breach will fail; whereas in battery, self-defence applies if D reasonably perceived that he would be imminently attacked, and used reasonable and proportionate force to protect himself). Further, in trespass, C does not have to prove any damage, it is the vindication of C's bodily integrity which is at the forefront of the torts, whereas the principal purpose of negligence is to achieve compensatory redress for the damage suffered. Additionally, if damage does result from D's act, it is not necessary to prove, in trespass, that it was foreseeable (as discussed in the Introduction), whereas that is a key element of the negligence action. Finally, pleading a duty of care on D's part may be completely artificial, as in the *Omagh Bombing* case itself – it was untenable to argue that the IRA owed a duty of care to members of the public, in conducting its bombing campaign and political activism; the case could only sensibly be pleaded as a case of intentional battery to the person.[31] Hence, any merging of trespass and negligence creates some difficult issues.

Unsurprisingly, there is clearly some unease, in English judicial circles, in encompassing negligent conduct within the realm of trespass to the person. In *Prison Officers' Assn v Iqbal*,[32] Smith LJ asserted that, '[i]t is well-established that all forms of trespass require an intentional act. An act of negligence will not suffice' (citing *Letang v Cooper*). In addition, in *Wainwright v Home Office*,[33] and in a passage approved on appeal by Lord Hoffmann,[34] Buxton LJ made the point that, given all the legal advantages that trespass offers (no foreseeability test, no policy requirements for any duty of care, actionable *per se*), 'there are strong policy reasons that the tort of trespass to the person should be limited to its proper sphere', and that Lord Denning MR's view in *Letang v Cooper* was preferable. In *Wilson v Pringle*,[35] the Court of Appeal held that *Weaver v Ward* could only be brought in negligence these days, and not in trespass. Notwithstanding these misgivings, however, the concept of a 'negligent battery' has, it seems, not yet been demolished as a line of authority.

§14.7 The requisite intent on D's part, to prove a battery, is to deliberately *apply force* to C, rather than an intent to cause harm or injury to C.

C may suffer no physical damage from the battery, but still, the tort can be proven – provided that D intended to *apply force* to C. As Buxton LJ explained in *Wainwright v Home Office*[36] (and approved on appeal[37]), 'any intended "hostile" touching founds an action for battery, even if there is no intention thereby to cause injury or actual physical harm'. That point had already been made in *Wilson v Pringle* – '[a]n *intention to injure* is not essential to an action for trespass to the person. It is the mere trespass by itself which is the offence'.[38]

In *Wilson v Pringle*, Peter Wilson, C, and Ian Pringle, D, both 13, were two schoolboys finishing a maths class. As they left the classroom and were walking along the school corridor, D pulled at C's school bag via the shoulder strap, and C fell to the ground, injuring his hip. C sued D in both negligence and battery. **Held:** the case should go to trial for battery (and for negligence, in the alternative). It did not matter if D did not intend to cause C any injury via this act of horseplay, provided that he intended to apply force to C.

§14.8 The doctrine of 'transferred malice' is a particular application of a negligently-inflicted, and actionable, battery.

The 'doctrine of transferred malice' applies where D intended to apply force to X; but the 'wrong person', C, was the recipient of that force. It is negligent of D to have inflicted it on the wrong person – yet, nevertheless, D can be liable to C for battery, in those circumstances.

[31] [2011] NICA 33, [14]. [32] [2009] EWCA Civ 1312, [2010] 1 QB 732, [71].
[33] [2001] EWCA Civ 2081, [2002] QB 1334, [71]. [34] [2003] UKHL 53, [2004] 2 AC 406, [47].
[35] [1986] EWCA Civ 6, [1987] QB 237. [36] [2001] EWCA Civ 2081, [2002] QB 1334, [69].
[37] [2003] UKHL 53, [2004] 2 AC 406, [47] (Lord Hoffmann expressed general agreement with Buxton LJ's sentiments).
[38] [1986] EWCA Civ 6, [1987] QB 237, 249 (emphasis added).

The principle was cited and approved by Elias J in *Bici v MOD* (where, as noted in the Table above, the soldiers intended to shoot the person riding on the roof of the car, but the passenger, C1, was shot as well). In fact, targetting one person, and inflicting force on another, has long constituted a battery in both English and Northern Irish case law, as Elias J explained in *Bici*:

> In *James v Campbell*,[39] D was involved in a fight at a parish dinner, and struck C by mistake, giving him two black eyes. **Held:** battery proven. In *Ball v Axten*,[40] D aimed to hit a farmer's dog, and mistakenly hit the farmer's wife, C, instead, as she was trying to shield the dog. **Held:** battery proven (although Elias J doubted whether the doctrine of transferred malice could properly apply as between animal and human, and that negligence would be the preferable cause of action there). In *Livingstone v MOD*,[41] a soldier, D, fired a round at rioters who were attacking the soldiers, and mistakenly hit C with one of the bullets. **Held:** battery possible, because D intentionally applied force to the rioter who was struck. 'Similarly, if a soldier fires a rifle bullet at a rioter intending to strike him, and the bullet strikes that rioter and passes through his body and wounds another rioter directly behind the first rioter, one whom the soldier had not seen, both rioters have been "intentionally" struck by the soldier and, assuming that the force used was not justified, the soldier has committed a battery against both'.

Elias J described these decisions as 'sound law',[42] and hence, endorsed the proposition that a negligently-inflicted battery ('negligent' only in the sense that an unintended person was the recipient of the force) is nevertheless actionable.

That particular, and narrowly-applied, type of negligently-inflicted battery, as illustrated in *Bici*, may well represent the limits of negligence within the tort of battery.

Elements of assault

The elements of the tort of assault, definitively set out in *Collins v Wilcock*,[43] were usefully restated in *Mbasogo v Logo Ltd*[44] – it 'requires an overt act indicating an immediate intention to commit a battery, coupled with the capacity to carry that intention into effect, causing another to apprehend the infliction of immediate and unlawful force'. The tort is actionable *per se*. Hence, the tort embodies three elements:

Element #1: An overt act, and intention

§14.9 For the tort of assault, D must commit an overt act, with an intention to inflict force immediately or imminently upon C. That intention may be wilful or reckless. An intention to inflict future force is not sufficient.

An 'overt' act means a word or deed which is openly done by D. Something said or done can be sufficient to cause an apprehension of immediate personal violence.

> In *Hepburn v CC of Thames Valley Police*,[45] the example was given: D does not assault C by merely passively standing in front of C, getting in their way and refusing to move; but it is an assault to

[39] (1832) 5 Car & P 372, 172 ER 1015. [40] (1866) 4 F&F 1019, 176 ER 890.

[41] [1984] NILR 356, 361 (Hutton J). [42] [2004] EWHC 786 (QB) [68]–[71].

[43] [1984] 1 WLR 1172 (QB) 1177 (Goff LJ).

[44] [2006] EWCA Civ 1370, [2007] QB 846, [74]–[75]; and earlier, at trial: [2005] EWHC 2034 (QB) [35], citing: *R v Ireland* [1998] AC 147 (HL) 161–63 (Lord Steyn).

[45] [2002] EWCA Civ 841 (Sedley LJ), and cited in: *Magill v Royal Group of Hospitals* [2010] NIQB 10, [61].

take active measures to block or obstruct C from moving in a particular direction with some threat of physical interference if he does so. In *R v Ireland*,[46] Lord Steyn gave the example: a man accosting a woman in a dark alley, saying, 'come with me or I will stab you', can constitute an assault by words.

D must intend to inflict immediate force on C. An intention to inflict force or violence *in the future* is not sufficient – C must apprehend *immediate* force or violence.

In *Mbasogo v Logo Ltd*,[47] a coup was allegedly organised against the President of the African State of Equatorial Guinea (a country rich in oil and gas), by a group of Special Forces soldiers who had served in South Africa, and mercenaries. An advance group of 20 Special Force soldiers was to gain intelligence and prepare and participate in the attack. The coup failed, but the President feared that he and his family would be abducted, incapacitated, seriously injured, or killed, in the attempts to overthrow his government. **Held:** assault failed. No overt act was proven – the presence of an advance group in the country; plus numerous mercenaries in Zimbabwe preparing to load arms *en route* for Equatorial Guinea, were not overt acts causing the apprehension of immediate violence. In *Tuberville v Savage*,[48] D clapped his hand upon his sword and said to C, 'If it were not assize-time, I would not take such language'. **Held:** there was no threat of immediate force, and hence, no assault. Any intention to inflict injury later, when the judges were not in town, was not sufficient.

The relevant intent can be either wilful or reckless, i.e., 'any act by which [D], intentionally or recklessly, causes [C] to apprehend immediate and unlawful personal violence' (per Lord Hope in *R v Ireland*[49]). The meaning of recklessness, in this context, was described in *Bici v MOD* in these terms: 'it would have to be shown that [D] must subjectively have appreciated that, by his conduct, [C] would be put in fear of the immediate application of a battery, and [D] must have been indifferent as to this possibility'.[50]

Hence, and to reiterate from the Introduction, the fact that it was reasonably foreseeable that C would be put in fear of imminent violence from D's acts is not sufficient. The requisite *intent* must be present, in order for assault to be made out (per *Bici v MOD*[51]). That has been a very long-standing proposition: in 1669, according to *Tuberville v Savage*, 'the intention as well as the act makes an assault. Therefore, if one strikes another upon the hand, or arm, or breast in discourse, it is no assault, there being no intention to assault'.[52]

§14.10 The doctrine of 'transferred malice' does not apply to the tort of assault.

Notably, whilst the doctrine of 'transferred malice' can apply in the tort of battery, *Bici* rules out the doctrine for the tort of assault. It is C, who is targeted with the threat, who has standing to sue for the tort, and no-one else. This element of the tort requires that D intend to put C – and not some other person – in fear of imminent violence.

In *Bici v MOD*,[53] facts previously, there was also a claim by C1's cousin who was travelling with C1 in the same vehicle. Skender Bici, C2, (unlike C1) was not shot, but suffered psychiatric injury from the

[46] [1998] AC 147 (HL) 162. [47] [2005] EWHC 2034 (QB) [38], aff'd on appeal: [2006] EWCA Civ 1370, [2007] QB 846.
[48] (1669) 1 Mod 3, 86 ER 654.
[49] [1997] 4 All ER 225 (HL) 239, citing: *R v Savage* [1992] 1 AC 699 (HL) 740 (Lord Ackner).
[50] [2004] EWHC 786 (QB) [78]. [51] *ibid*, [77].
[52] I Mod Rep 3. In the second sentence of this quote, references to 'assault' would mean 'battery' in the modern English law of trespass.
[53] [2004] EWHC 786 (QB) [74]–[81].

soldiers', D's, attack. C2 argued that he was put in personal fear for his own safety when the shots were fired by D at his vehicle, and he claimed in assault. **Held:** assault failed. D were not specifically targeting C2 at all; and there was no basis to hold that D intended to put C2, personally, in fear of imminent violence. Also, D did not satisfy the test of reckless conduct, in firing upon the car upon which C2 was travelling.

Element #2: The requisite capacity

§14.11 The general rule is that D must have the capacity to carry out his intention to inflict force with immediate or imminent effect. Exceptionally, however, liability is still proven if D does not have the capacity, but C apprehends that he does.

General rule. According to *Mbasogo*,[54] C must prove the long-standing requirement that D had the means and capacity to carry out a threat of force into immediate effect. That had long been the law – in 1849, in *Cobbett v Gray*,[55] Pollock CB remarked that if D raised his fist towards C within striking distance, that may be an assault; but if D says, whilst standing some distance away, 'I'm going to hit you', that is not an assault. Hence, D's merely uttering threatening words or acts towards C will not amount to any assault, if there is no capacity to carry them into effect.

In *Mbasogo v Logo Ltd*,[56] facts previously, **held:** assault failed. There was no fear of an immediate application of force. There was no evidence that any of the 'advance group' were armed, or had done anything before they were apprehended, or that there was any prospect of a surprise attack by mercenaries that would overrun the small Equatorial Guinea army presence. In *Thomas v NUM*,[57] picketing miners, D, shouted threats to so-called 'scab miners', C, who broke the picket lines (being ferried into the mines via coaches) to work the mines during long-running strikes. **Held:** assault failed. D had no capacity to put into effect their threats of violence, whilst they were held back from the vehicles in which C were travelling.

Exception. There is some appellate authority which suggests that D does not need to have capacity to carry out his intention with immediate effect, provided that C has an apprehension that D will act imminently. In other words, C may not know that D did not have the capacity to commit violence against him, but fearing that prospect (i.e., violence) is sufficient.

In *R v Ireland*,[58] D made repeated phone calls to three women, C, in which D remained silent. The calls lasted sometimes a minute, sometimes for several minutes. **Held:** those nuisance calls constituted assault. The possibility of immediate personal violence being feared by C in such cases is sufficient. That case also held (at CA level) that if D points an unloaded or toy gun at C, but C does not know that it is unloaded or is an imitation gun, then that constitutes an assault too.

It is not entirely settled as to how strong this exceptional line of authority is, given that, in *Mbasogo*,[59] the Court of Appeal explained *Ireland* away on the basis that it said nothing about D's capacity to carry the intent into effect.

[54] [2006] EWCA Civ 1370, [2007] QB 846, [75], citing: *Stephens v Myers* (1834) C & P 349; *Cobbett v Grey* [1849] 4 Ex 729, 744; *Reid v Coker* [1853] 13 CB 850, 860.

[55] (1849) 4 Ex 729 (CA) 744. [56] [2006] EWCA Civ 1370, [2007] QB 846.

[57] [1986] 1 WLR 20 (CA) 62, cited *ibid.*

[58] [1998] AC 147 (HL) 149; and below: [1996] EWCA Crim 441 (Swinton Thomas LJ).

[59] [2007] QB 846, [2006] EWCA Civ 1370, [76]–[77].

Element #3: The requisite apprehension

§14.12 C must have apprehended the application of immediate force (i.e., contact) from D.

As will be seen in the next section, C can be wholly unaware that the tort of false imprisonment is being committed against him. However, the tort of assault requires awareness on C's part of the threat of imminent interference or violence. This point was particularly evident in the *Omagh Bombing* case[60] (which, although a decision of the Court of Appeal of Northern Ireland, is, it is submitted, a proposition equally as applicable to English law).

> In *Breslin v Mckevitt*, assault was not pleaded, only battery for the deaths and injuries caused by the Omagh bombing. However, some people knew of the warning before the explosion. The Court of Appeal acknowledged that it 'can be persuasively argued that the planting of the bomb, and the giving of a short and unclear warning, causing reasonable apprehension of imminent violence, coupled with the capacity of carrying out the threatened explosion, constituted an assault in law'.

However, the apprehension of contact does not have to provoke any type of mental injury in C, in order for the tort to be made out. The tort is actionable *per se*, as dealt with under 'Remedies', below.

The defences applicable for both assault and battery are discussed after the analysis of the remaining tort of trespass to the person: false imprisonment.

FALSE IMPRISONMENT

False imprisonment claims frequently arise where C alleges that the powers of arrest or of detention have been infringed by the police, or by prison or immigration detention authorities. However, as the cases herein demonstrate, C may complain that his personal liberty has been violated by D in many other scenarios too.

Definition

§14.13 False imprisonment is the unlawful deprivation of C's liberty, by D's imposing a constraint upon C's freedom of movement from a particular place.

This definition is derived from *Collins v Willcock*.[61] False imprisonment was categorised there as a trespass to the person, although (as noted in the Introduction[62]), some judicial sentiment[63] says that it fits uneasily as a trespass, and would be better being treated as an action on the case. In any event, it will be recalled that trespasses to the person (including false imprisonment) 'enjoy' three notable advantages over an action on the case (such as negligence, or the tort of *Wilkinson v Downton*). First, false imprisonment is actionable *per se* (confirmed in *Lumba v Secretary of State for the Home Dept*[64]). Secondly, there is no requirement that any damages flowing from the false imprisonment must be reasonably foreseeable – even unforeseeable damage arising from a trespass is compensable. Thirdly, claims for pure mental harm falling short of a recognised psychiatric injury are compensable in false imprisonment.

[60] [2011] NICA 33, [15]. [61] [1984] 1 WLR 1172 (HL) 1177 (Lord Goff). [62] See pp 689–90.
[63] e.g., Buxton LJ's view in *Wainwright v Home Office*, which passage was endorsed by the HL in the same case.
[64] [2011] UKSC 12, [2012] 1 AC 245, [63] (Lord Dyson MR), [181] (Lord Walker), [197] (Lady Hale), [252] (Lord Kerr).

Re its elements, Lord Bridge suggested, in *R v Deputy Governor of Parkhurst Prison, ex p Hague*,[65] that the tort has only two: 'the fact of imprisonment, and the absence of lawful authority to justify it'. However, more latterly, the Supreme Court confirmed, in *Lumba*,[66] that the tort has, in fact, **three** elements, in that the imprisonment must be intentional too. Also, as to Lord Bridge's second 'ingredient', it is for D to prove that the constraint was lawful, and hence, those justifications are properly dealt with under 'Defences'.

> Nutshell analysis: **False imprisonment**
>
> **Elements of the tort:**
>
> 1 C's freedom of movement was constrained
> 2 D possessed the requisite intent
> 3 D's act caused C's constraint (subject to qualification)
>
> Defences (as for assault and battery, above)
> Remedies

As the court put it recently in *VS v Home Office*,[67] 'the Court's role is to guard liberty with jealous care' – and the elements of the tort continue to reflect that strict position.

Element #1: A constraint

The nature and scope of the constraint

§14.14 The constraint upon C's freedom of movement may be imposed by physical or non-physical boundaries.

Although it was said, in very early expositions of the law, that 'every imprisonment includes a battery', the modern position is that it is **not** necessary, in order to constitute false imprisonment, that C should be physically touched (per *Bird v Jones*,[68] and affirmed more recently in *Alleyne v Commr of Police*[69]).

The boundaries which constrain C's freedom of movement may be physical, e.g., a flat or a room (*AT v Dulghieru*[70]), a police car or police station (*Commr of Police v ZH*[71], and *Rowlands v CC of Merseyside Police*[72]), a house and car (*Lawson v Dawes*[73]), or a prison or detention cell (*Lumba*), to cite a few.

In *AT v Dulghieru*, four young women, C, nationals of Moldova, were victims of an unlawful conspiracy to traffic women into the UK for the purposes of sexual exploitation and prostitution. The women were held in a flat at Earls Court in London against their will, taken to and held in various brothels in London, sexually abused and physically threatened by a married couple who were key figures in the conspiracy, D1 and D2, and by various customers. **Held:** the false imprisonment of C was created by the appalling treatment at Ds' hands, in confining them to the flat, then in brothels, for 1–2 months. Each was terrified of escaping, even had the opportunity arisen.

[65] [1992] 1 AC 58 (HL) 162. [66] [2012] 1 AC 245, [29] (Lord Dyson MR). [67] [2014] EWHC 2483 (QB) [30].
[68] (1845) 115 ER 668, 7 QB 742 (Patteson J). [69] [2012] EWHC 3955 (QB) [171]. [70] [2009] EWHC 225 (QB).
[71] [2013] EWCA Civ 69. [72] [2006] EWCA Civ 1773, [2007] 1 WLR 1065. [73] [2006] EWHC 2865 (QB).

An area the size of Oxford Circus was capable of constituting an area of constraint in *Austin v Commr of Police*.[74] However, as the Irish Law Reform Commission has noted, '[t]here is little authority on the question of how large the area of confinement may be. It has been suggested that it would be tortious to confine a person in a large country estate or the Isle of Man'.[75]

In *Austin*, Ms Austin, C1, took part in a demonstration involving at least 3,000 people at Oxford Circus on May Day 2001. During the demonstration, police imposed a cordon around the crowd. From about 2.20 pm, no-one was allowed to leave, except with police permission, and some were prevented from leaving for over seven hours. Some people, such as Mr Saxby, C2, were not taking part as demonstrators, but were in the region for work purposes and got caught up in the melee. The day was wet and chilly; there were no toilet facilities; and the conditions in which C1 and C2, and others, were held, became very difficult. **Held:** the confinement within the police cordon constituted a constraint sufficient to make out the tort (although, ultimately, a defence succeeded).

However, non-physical enclosures will do just as well for the tort. Nothing need be said; and no barriers may be in place – and yet a confinement still be proven. Via implied suggestions or threats, the constraints must coerce the will of C, such that C believes that he cannot freely leave or move about. In the early 1919 case of *Meering v Grahame-White Aviation Co Ltd*,[76] the Court of Appeal confirmed that false imprisonment could feasibly occur anywhere in which C's liberty is restrained, 'in the open field, or in the cage in the streets ... so long as he hath not his liberty freely to go at all times to all places whither he will'. Similarly, in *Bird v Jones*,[77] Coleridge J remarked that, 'though little may be said, much is meant and perfectly understood. [C] ... feels that he has no option, no more power of going in any but the one direction prescribed to him than if [D] had actually hold of him: no return or deviation from the course prescribed is open to him. And it is that entire restraint upon the will which ... constitutes the imprisonment'.

In *Commr of Police v ZH*, ZH, C, 16, who suffered severe autism and epilepsy, was taken by his day school carers to the local swimming pool. He went to the poolside, became fixated by the water, and would not move (a common reaction of autistic sufferers to water). C also had an aversion to being touched. After 30 minutes, the pool manager called the police, D, who found C still standing poolside. The officers approached C, introduced themselves, and touched him 'gently' to see whether he would respond. C moved closer to the pool edge, and both officers took hold of his jacket, but C jumped into the pool. He was removed by lifeguards and police, and then restrained poolside by 5–7 officers, put in handcuffs and leg restraints, detained in a police van, and kept there until released to his carers, all of which took about 40 minutes. C suffered PTSD afterwards, and an exacerbation of his epilepsy. **Held:** false imprisonment proven, from when C was restrained poolside until released from the police van (battery and assault also proven, by D touching C before he jumped, whilst C was being lifted out of the pool, and whilst being restrained by the poolside after he was lifted out).
In *Lawson v Dawes (Decd)*,[78] Ms Lawson, C, was seeking a business liaison with Mr Dawes, D, by which she would front a modelling agency. They agreed to meet for an interview, and over a period of 4 days, C was raped, forced to take crack cocaine, and threatened if she left the premises. C was

[74] [2009] UKHL 5, [2009] 1 AC 564, affirming: [2007] EWCA Civ 989, [2008] QB 660 (the HL appeal only concerned whether C's Art 5's rights had been infringed. Hence, references in this chapter will be to the CA decision, where the common law action was determined).

[75] *Non-Fatal Offences Against the Person* (Rep 45, 1994) [2.10], citing: Street, *Law of Torts* (8th edn, 1988) 28.

[76] [1918–19] All ER Rep 1490 (CA) 1503, citing: *Termes de la Ley*.

[77] (1845) 115 ER 668, 7 QB 742, 748.

[78] [2006] EWHC 2865 (QB), with C's quote at [40].

also driven about in a car by D, when she feared that he was high on drugs and alcohol. C did not seek to escape at various points during the ordeal: 'I just wanted to get out of the situation, but I could see no way out. I was really scared. I remained cool on the outside while inside every cell in my body was on red alert'. **Held:** false imprisonment proven.

The comparative corner: A Commonwealth vignette

Elsewhere, false imprisonment has arisen in a variety of scenarios – from a department store to the family home:

Australia: in *Myer Stores Ltd v Soo*,[79] Mr Soo, C, was approached by a store detective, Mr Evans, in the hi-fi section of Myers department store, and asked to go to the security office, where he was questioned for an hour. C asked to be interviewed in the hi-fi dept, but that was refused. He was accompanied ('frog-marched') to the security office, led by Mr Evans, followed by the police a few paces behind; a bystander would readily appreciate that C was being escorted; and was not allowed to proceed at his own pace and by his own route to the security office. C was (wrongly) accused of having shoplifted a Waterford crystal vase and other items. **Held:** false imprisonment proven, from when C was spoken to in the hi-fi section until he left the security room: 'the police intentionally restrained the freedom of movement of [C] by actively escorting him, and passively by making known to him their clear intention to ask him some questions about shoplifting ... it was made clear to [C] that he had no option but to follow Evans, and by being followed by the police, it was made clear to him that he had no choice in fact – his freedom of movement had been totally restrained'. D's words and conduct constituted imprisonment.

Canada: In *ADY v MYY*,[80] a child, C, brought an action against his parents for false imprisonment. Over an 8-year period, C was regularly hit with a belt and wooden paddle, confined for days or weeks to a locked bedroom where the furniture was eventually removed; forced to eat left-over food; berated for stupidity and character defects; and bore marks of physical abuse. C had been diagnosed with Attention Deficit Disorder and hyperactivity. **Held:** false imprisonment proven. 'A child is entitled to expect the family home to be something of a haven; not Utopia but generally safe, fair, and supportive. Within the home, a child may legitimately expect discipline and guidance given with affection and respect.' Here, however, C was subject to frequent verbal and physical abuse, physically confined and isolated, and made to feel worthless.

§14.15 Any restraint of C's movement must be total or whole. A partial restraint, i.e., restraining C's movement in one direction only, will not suffice.

If C cannot prove that his movements were wholly restrained, either by physical or by non-physical boundaries, then there will be no 'imprisonment'. As affirmed recently in *Patel v Sec of State for the Home Dept*, '[t]he tort is only committed whilst [C] is wholly deprived of her liberty'.[81] The constraint must be total. C is not imprisoned if free to move in a particular direction, but not in another: '[a] prison may have its boundary large or narrow, visible and

[79] [1991] 2 VR 597 (Vic CA). [80] (1994), 90 BCLR (2d) 145 (SC). [81] [2014] EWHC 501 (Admin) [240].

tangible ... it may itself be movable or fixed, but a boundary it must have' (per Coleridge J in *Bird v Jones*[82]).

In *Bird v Jones*, part of Hammersmith Bridge, used as a public footway, was sectioned off by temporary fencing for seating paying members to watch a regatta on the River Thames. Mr Bird, C, wanted to pass along the bridge, and tried to climb over the fence. Mr Jones, D, the clerk of the Bridge Co, pulled C back, but C succeeded in climbing over the fence. D then stationed two policemen to prevent C from proceeding along the footway in the direction he wished to go. C was told that he could go back the way he had come, and walk along the other side of the bridge, but he refused, and stayed there in the enclosure for 30 minutes. **Held (2:1):** false imprisonment failed. Only a partial obstruction occurred in this case, and that could not constitute an imprisonment. In *Alleyne v Commr of Police*,[83] Michael Alleyne, C, was in his flat when about 14 police officers forced entry, as part of a police operation to track down the murderer of a teenager, Ben Kinsella, who had been stabbed to death. C's son had been identified as one of the killers, and the police obtained a search warrant for his flat (where C was living too). During the commotion, C was forced to the floor, his right eye was injured, and his ankle was broken. C sued for battery, false imprisonment and negligence. The false imprisonment was alleged to cover the entire period from when he was handcuffed in the flat, to when he was taken to the police station for questioning and examined by a medical officer and able to leave the station – over four hours later. **Held:** only negligence proven. Assault/battery failed (defences being available). False imprisonment also failed; C was not detained by implied threat or otherwise. He had willingly answered questions, and was taken to the police station for an examination by the medical officer, rather than for the predominant purpose of detaining him for questioning.

Indeed, whether C was subject to a total or partial restraint (i.e., which side of the line between wrongful or lawful D's actions amounted to) can be a very finely-balanced assessment. At times, a decision may emphasise (in D's favour) that C was not under any physical locks or restraints – although it is clearly evident, from the aforementioned authorities, that physical restraints are unnecessary to make out the tort. The following case illustrates the fine margins that can apply on this question:

In *Bournewood Mental Health NHS Trust, ex p L*,[84] Mr L, C, 48, was autistic, profoundly mentally retarded and unable to speak (hence, had always been incapable of consenting to medical treatment). C was often agitated, with no sense of danger, and often hit and harmed himself. He had lived at the Bournewood Hospital for over 30 years, until discharged to live in the community with paid carers on a trial basis. One day, at his regular day care centre, C became very agitated and violent towards himself. A social worker recommended that C be taken to hospital by ambulance, given in-patient treatment, and seen by a psychiatrist. C was assessed by a psychiatrist as being in need of in-patient treatment. C made no attempt to leave, and was transferred to the behavioural unit at the hospital. He was not detained formally under the Mental Health Act 1983, as it was deemed unnecessary, given that C appeared to be fully compliant, did not resist admission, and showed no signs of wanting to leave. C's carers objected to the treatment which C had received by healthcare professionals, D, in the ambulance and at hospital. **Held (3:2):** there was no false

[82] (1845) 115 ER 668, 7 QB 742, 744 (Denman CJ dissenting).

[83] [2012] EWHC 3955 (QB).

[84] [1999] 1 AC 458 (HL). Lords Goff, Lloyd and Hope were in the majority; Lords Nolan and Steyn dissented. For observations in case description, see: 485–86 (Lord Goff), 495 (Lord Steyn).

imprisonment of C. According to the majority: C was not kept in a locked ward after he was admitted to hospital, as he had shown no wish to leave. Although the treating doctors contemplated that he might have to be compulsorily detained under the Mental Health Act 1983, that 'did not give rise to his detention in fact at any earlier date'. According to the dissenters: C was imprisoned, because he was detained when D intentionally assumed control over him to a degree as to amount to complete deprivation of his liberty. In his 'best interests', any possible resistance by him was overcome by sedation and by close supervision of him in hospital, and if he had wanted to leave, he would have been physically prevented from doing so. The suggestion that he was free to go was 'a fairy tale'.

However, if C's avenue of escape means that he must put himself at real risk of personal injury (say, escaping through a window of a locked room, or wading through water to get away from a building), or having to take a route that was so round-about that C's affairs would be delayed and inconvenienced, then that suggests that the constraint on C is indeed total (that proposition was noted by Denman CJ in *Bird v Jones* – and whilst he dissented on the facts, it has not been doubted in later cases).

§14.16 C may be falsely imprisoned, without being aware of the fact of that constraint.

C may successfully sue for false imprisonment, even if he was, say: asleep, unconscious or drugged during the constraint; held in a room without knowing that the door was locked from the outside; or otherwise unaware of the confinement (per *Meering v Grahame-White Aviation Co Ltd*[85]). A constraint will also occur if C lacked the capacity to refuse consent to the confinement, or was mentally retarded to the point where he did not appreciate the fact that he was being confined (dicta in *R v Bournewood Mental Health NHS Trust, ex parte L*[86]).

The reason for such a strict, pro-C, legal view was explained in *Murray v MOD*: '[t]he law attaches supreme importance to the liberty of the individual, and if he suffers a wrongful interference with that liberty, it should remain actionable'.[87] That principle was re-affirmed by the Supreme Court in *Lumba v Secretary of State for the Home Dept*.[88] However, any damages awarded to C in these circumstances would likely be nominal only (noted, obiter, in *POA v Iqbal*[89]), and as discussed under 'Remedies', below.

§14.17 Generally, D must have committed a positive act to bring about C's imprisonment. Where D breaches his contract by failing to act, which brings about C's confinement, that will not amount to the requisite positive act. Exceptionally, D can be liable for 'false imprisonment by omission', where C has a legal right to be released from the confinement, D is under a statutory or other duty to prevent C's continuing confinement, and fails to do so.

According to both older (*Herd v Weardale Steel, Coal and Coke Co*[90]) and more recent (*Prison Officers' Assn v Iqbal*[91]) authority, D is not liable for bringing about C's constraint, if all D did was to abstain from providing C with the means of escaping that constraint. In other words, D

[85] (1919) 122 LT 44, 53–54, [1918–19] All ER 1490 (CA) 1507 (per Atkin LJ).
[86] [1999] 1 AC 458 (HL) 485–86 (Lord Goff), 495 (Lord Steyn).
[87] [1988] 1 WLR 692 (HL) 703 (Lord Griffiths). [88] [2011] UKSC 12, [2012] 1 AC 245, [344].
[89] [2009] EWCA Civ 1312, [2010] 1 QB 732, [46] (Lord Dyson MR), [83] (Smith LJ).
[90] [1913] 3 KB 771, aff'd: [1915] AC 67 (HL) 77–78 (Lord Moulton). [91] [2009] EWCA Civ 1312, [2010] 1 QB 732.

must commit some **positive** act to impose the constraint on C. This invokes the difficult, and often unsatisfactory, line that is to be drawn between a positive act and a 'pure' omission (one which, it will be recalled from Chapter 3, has arisen in negligence too).

General rule. Under the general rule, confinement-by-omission is simply not sufficient to prove false imprisonment, as the following cases illustrate:

In *Herd v Weardale Steel*, Mr Herd, C, was a miner working in a deep shaft in a coalpit. He asked his employer, Weardale Steel, D, to be taken to the surface via the power-operated cage, after he (wrongfully) refused to work, but that request was not met until two hours later. There was no breach of contract here (the implied term in the contract was that C would be brought to the surface by the end of his shift). **Held:** false imprisonment failed. The fact that the only means of C's getting out were in the hands of his employer D did not render this an imprisonment, because C was contractually obliged to work in the coalpit during the time that he claimed that he was 'imprisoned'. D was not bound to operate the cage which was under its control at C's request, and C was not entitled, by any contractual relation with D, to demand that. In *Prison Officers Assn v Iqbal (Rev 1)*,[92] Mohammed Iqbal, C, was serving 15 years' imprisonment in HMP Wealstun. His normal weekday routine permitted him to leave his cell around 8.00–11.45 am, and again at 5.45–7.45 pm. However, following a pay dispute, the POA called a national strike, and hardly any prison officers turned up to the prison on that day. As a result, C was kept in his cell for the day. C sued for false imprisonment, for the six hours that he was confined to his cell when he would normally have been let out. **Held (2:1):** false imprisonment failed. The prison officers could not be liable for false imprisonment which occurred as a result of their failure (omission) to turn up to work at the prison. Their failure to let C out of his cell for the 6 hours was a 'pure omission'. Smith LJ also suggested that, if a co-prisoner, D, heard C, a fellow prisoner, complaining that he was still locked in his cell, and C called to D to get the key (which was available) and let him out, and D failed to do so, then D would not be liable to C for false imprisonment – D would not be under any duty to let C out of his cell; it would be a mere omission.

Where D breaches his contract (whether with C or with some other party), which indirectly brings about C's confinement, that does not necessarily amount to a positive act of confinement either.

In *Prison Officers Assn v Iqbal*, the prison officers, D, were under a contractual duty with their employer not to withdraw their labour via strike action; and D's failure to turn up to work constituted a breach of their employment contracts. However, that breach of contract with the employer did not mean that the exceptional scenario – that the prison officers should have taken positive steps to let C out of his cell and to positively comply with the prison Governor's instructions to let prisoners out for 6 hours a day – applied. The general rule applied; and there was no positive act of imprisonment. In *Herd v Weardale Steel*,[93] D did **not** breach his contract on the facts. However, Buckley LJ gave this example: even if C had been kept in the shaft at the end of his shift, due to mechanical problems with the lift, that would be a breach of contract by employer D, but it would **not** constitute false imprisonment: although D 'has not enabled C to get out, as under the contract he ought to have done, he has done no act compelling him to remain there'.

[92] [2009] EWCA Civ 1312, [2010] QB 732 (Lord Dyson MR, Smith LJ; Sullivan LJ dissenting) [66] (Smith LJ). The Governor could not be liable if he was acting with authority and in good faith: per *R v Deputy Governor of Parkhurst Prison, ex p Hague* [1992] 1 AC 58 (HL), and hence was not sued (at [28]).

[93] [1913] 3 KB 771, aff'd: [1915] AC 67 (HL) 77–78 (Lord Moulton).

Exception. Where a prison detention authority commits a so-called 'public law error' in detaining a prisoner beyond that which was lawful, then the tort of false imprisonment is established. According to Cranston J in *McCreaner v MOJ*, a 'public law error' encompasses where D did not act in accordance with a proper understanding of the law, or where D wrongfully exercised its discretion (i.e., acted for an improper purpose, or took account of irrelevant factors, or exercised a discretion in a *Wednesbury* unreasonable manner).[94] Two prison cases can be conveniently contrasted on this point:

> In *R v Governor of Brockhill Prison, ex p Evans (No 2)*,[95] the Governor, D, did not release a prisoner, C, on her prescribed release date, due to a miscalculation of the release date. D was mistakenly acting in accordance with the law as it had been previously thought to be, regarding how to credit days on remand for those serving concurrent sentences, and the mistake was genuinely made, and in good faith. C was detained 59 days beyond what was subsequently held to be her automatic release date. **Held:** false imprisonment proven. At the release date, prisoner C was not lawfully in the custody of the prison Governor. At that point, D had a duty to release C, and C had a right to be released. That 'pure omission' to release was actionable under the tort of false imprisonment. In *McCreaner v MOJ*, Kenneth McCreaner, C, a former prisoner, claimed that he was not released under home detention curfew (HDC) as soon as he should have been (that scheme permitted prisoners to be released early on curfew, monitored by the prisoner wearing an electronic device or tag). Following a decision of the Supreme Court in *Noone* (2010), there was a new purposive construction of a relevant Order which brought about a change at the point at which some prisoners could be eligibly released on HDC. C argued that he was not released for HDC when he should have been, due to the fault of the MOJ, and that he spent almost 4 months longer in prison than he should have. **Held:** no false imprisonment proven. A failure by the MOJ to recalculate C's eligibility date for HDC, in light of the *Noone* decision, was not a 'public law error'. C continued to be held by the MOJ in prison until his lawful release dates could be calculated, and any delay in that calculation led to his unlawful detention. However, that delay of itself did not constitute public law error; something more – acting for an improper purpose, or irrationality in a public law sense – was required, which was not evident here.

Given the unsympathetic tenor of the general rule, it is plain that exceptions by which omissions can constitute false imprisonment will be very rare.

Element #2: The requisite intent

§14.18 D must intend both to commit the act (or, more rarely, the omission) bringing about the constraint *and* to deprive C of his liberty – both are necessary. The requisite intent may be proven by either a wilful intent, or a reckless indifference as to whether a constraint would be likely to follow from the act. Malice on D's part is not required; and negligence on D's part in constraining C's freedom of movement is not sufficient to prove false imprisonment.

As with the torts of assault and battery, the tort of false imprisonment requires proof of intent – but it requires an intentional act **and** an intention to confine. In *Prison Officers Assn v Iqbal*,[96] Smith LJ gave this example:

[94] [2014] EWHC 569 (QB) [26]. [95] [2001] 2 AC 19 (HL). [96] [2009] EWCA Civ 1312, [2010] 1 QB 732, [72].

A security guard in a building locks the door to C's room, believing that everyone, including C, had gone home for the night, not realising that C is, in fact, still inside the building. The security guard could not be liable for the tort of false imprisonment, because he certainly committed a deliberate act, but he did not intend to deprive C of his liberty. Both elements of intent are required.

In common with other torts of trespass to the person, the fact that the interference (imprisonment) may be reasonably foreseeable is not sufficient to prove this element. An intent, amounting to wilful constraint or recklessness, are necessary to make out the tort of false imprisonment. Recklessness is proven if D 'realises that the likely consequence of his act or omission will be that [C] is imprisoned, and carries on with that act (or omission), regardless of that likely consequence' (per *Iqbal*[97]).

In *Iqbal*, the prison officers, D, had the requisite intent to commit the false imprisonment of C, by leaving him in his cell all day as a result of D's unlawful strike. D did not actually wish for the prisoners to be confined to their cells all day – but they knew that that was likely to happen, and went ahead with their unlawful strike action regardless, which was reckless. The first element failed, but this element of intent was proven.

In *Iqbal*, Smith LJ held that negligence would **not** suffice to make out the tort of false imprisonment (it will be recalled[98] that this proposition is less than clear for the tort of battery). This principle is important in protecting D against the practical day-to-day matters that may interfere with strict time-keeping, say, in a prison setting. Lord Dyson MR referred to these concerns as 'practical implications' – but they also highlight that negligence on D's part will not prove the tort. Otherwise, **any** delay by a prison officer in letting a prisoner out of his cell at the precise time mandated by the Governor's direction could result in a claim for false imprisonment, say, where the prison officer was delayed in opening the prisoner's cell through poor time-keeping on his part in arranging his daily routine.

§14.19 It is not strictly necessary that D's intent to confine C, and the act of confinement, coincide (although that coincidence will usually be present).

It is implicit, from the example given by Smith LJ in *Prison Officers Assn v Iqbal*,[99] that D's act of depriving C of his liberty, and the intent to deprive C of his liberty, may not necessarily coincide, and yet, the tort of false imprisonment could be made out.

Although such cases will be rare, it is conceivable that D's confinement of C was not, originally when it occurred, a false imprisonment at all, but that it became so. For example, suppose that D, a security guard, locks up industrial premises, failing to appreciate that either C is still in the building or that C has no key with which to exit the building. Once D becomes aware of C's existence and inability to escape the confines of the building, the requisite intent is formed, albeit that the confinement itself occurred prior in time.

Element #3: Causation

To reiterate, false imprisonment is actionable *per se*, i.e., without proof of actual damage. It is the very application of force or restraint applied to C that constitutes the tort. Where it causes

[97] [2009] EWCA Civ 1312, [2010] 1 QB 732, with points in text respectively at [73]–[74], [71] (Smith LJ), and [39].
[98] See pp 695–98. [99] [2009] EWCA Civ 1312, [2010] 1 QB 732, [72].

no actual loss or injury to C, nominal damages will be granted, to signify that a tort was committed.

General principle

§14.20 D's act must directly cause the constraint suffered by C. Merely providing the occasion for the confinement is not sufficient to prove the causal link.

Whilst D's act of confinement does not need to have caused C *damage*, it must have caused C's *constraint.*

That causal link should be contrasted with the position in negligence, where D, via his negligent conduct, may well be liable for providing the occasion for bringing about the harm suffered by C. It will be recalled, from Chapter 3, that such a scenario is particularly evident where a third party injures C, due to the negligent acts or omissions of D that facilitate the opportunity for that harm to be done. That liberal view of causation is **not** replicated in the tort of false imprisonment. Indeed, in *Iqbal*, Smith LJ remarked that '[t]he kind of causal link which will often suffice in the tort of negligence will not necessarily suffice for false imprisonment'.[100] On that basis, causation can be difficult to establish, as in the following cases:

> In *POA v Iqbal*, there was no sufficient causal link between the prison officers', D's, strike and the confinement of C in his cell all day on the day of the strike. D's strike certainly brought about the all-day confinement in cells, but the fact that D withdrew their labour did not directly lead to C being confined in his cell. The direct cause of that confinement was the Governor's direction not to let the prisoners out of their cells that day. Even though that direction may have been the inevitable and foreseeable result of the strike, nevertheless, on a strict causal analysis, D's strike was only the indirect act that provided the occasion for the Governor's decision. In *Davidson v CC for North Wales*,[101] Mrs Yates, D, a store detective, mistakenly thought that she had seen Mr Davidson, C, shoplifting, and she informed the police. C was arrested. The mistake was eventually determined, and C was released after two hours of detention. **Held:** false imprisonment failed. All D did was lay information before the police, for them to take such action as they thought fit. D merely created the opportunity for the imprisonment.

These cases also demonstrate that, while D's act or omission may have inevitably and foreseeably brought about C's confinement, that is not sufficient to establish liability – being a direct cause of the confinement is something quite different. In *Iqbal*,[102] Lord Dyson MR pointed out that it must have appeared equally as likely to both the store detective in *Davidson*, and the prison officers in *Iqbal*, that C's confinement of the shopper and the prisoner, respectively, would result. However, both provided the occasion for someone else (the police constable and the Governor, respectively) to constrain C. That is not sufficient to make out the requisite causal link.

Qualification to causation

§14.21 If C has been unlawfully constrained, but could have been lawfully constrained during that same period, it is not open to D to say, 'the detention would have happened anyway'. D is liable for the tort of false imprisonment.

[100] [2009] EWCA Civ 1312,[2010] 1 QB 732, [78].

[101] [1994] 2 All ER 597 (CA) 601–4.

[102] [2009] EWCA Civ 1312, [2010] 1 QB 732, [27].

This point is truly relevant to the question of whether D had lawful authority to detain/constrain C's movements and freedom under 'Defences', but it is convenient to deal with it under 'Causation'.

Where D could have lawfully constrained C, but because of some error (e.g., D acted outside its jurisdiction, or exercised a power in an unlawful manner), C is unlawfully constrained during that period, then the imprisonment is unlawful and unjustified. While it may be open to D in a negligence suit to say, 'I am not causally responsible for C's damage, because on the balance of probabilities, C would have suffered the same damage anyway, regardless of my breach', the same tack **cannot** be adopted by D in a false imprisonment suit. If C had been lawfully detained, then the confinement would have happened anyway, that is true; but the **wrongful** confinement would not have occurred – and the essence of the tort is the unlawful constraint upon C's liberty of movement.

In *Lumba v Sec of State for the Home Dept*,[103] Walumba Lumba, a citizen of the Democratic Republic of Congo, and Mr Kadian Mighty, a citizen of Jamaica, C, were each detained in prison, pending deportation, as foreign national prisoners. Non-British citizens could be deported if the Secretary of State 'deems his deportation to be conducive to the public good'. However, the Government's detention policies which applied for the period Apr 2006–Sep 2008, were held to be unlawful for a number or reasons (e.g., they were unpublished: 'notice is required so that the individual knows the criteria that are being applied and is able to challenge an adverse decision'). C sued for false imprisonment. The Government argued that, even had the reasons for the unlawful policies been corrected (e.g., the policies published), C would have been detained lawfully, and hence, their detention would still have occurred. It was accepted that each C 'had a very bad criminal record, and would undoubtedly have been kept in custody under the Secretary of State's published policies'. Hence, had the Government applied the published lawful policy rather than the unpublished unlawful policy, they would have inevitably reached the same decision: detain C, pending deportation. **Held (6:3):** false imprisonment proven, where the Government was operating detentions of convicted foreign prisoners under an unpublished policy. In *Roberts v CC of Cheshire*,[104] Mr Roberts, C, had been arrested and detained in a police cell. D, a custody officer, failed to conduct a timely review of a prisoner's detention at 5.25 am, as statutorily required. Had he done so, D would have authorised C's continued detention. The review was actually conducted at 7.45 am, and C's continued detention was authorised. D argued that C could only prove false imprisonment if he could show that, if the review had been carried out at the appropriate time, he would have been released. **Held:** false imprisonment proven, for the period 5.25–7.45 am. The fact that the detention would have carried on during that period if the review had been lawfully carried out at 5.25 am was 'nothing to the point'.

As Lady Hale pointed out in *Lumba*,[105] this is a very unusual scenario – in most cases, D does **not** have a choice in confining C either lawfully or unlawfully, because the confinement could usually not have been rendered justifiable. But, in cases like *Roberts* and *Lumba*, D does have a choice, which is where this qualification applies. In that sense, the causal argument, 'the damage would have been suffered by C anyway, because C could have been lawfully detained, but

[103] Lords Rodger, Brown and Phillips dissented, holding that there was no false imprisonment of C.

[104] [1999] 1 WLR 662 (CA) 667. The case is also known as *Roberts v Jones*.

[105] [2011] UKSC 12, [2012] 1 AC 245, [210] (Lady Hale was in the majority, with Lords Brown and Rodger dissenting).

as it happened, he was unlawfully detained', is **not** part of the tort of false imprisonment. There are several reasons for this view in C's favour (per *Lumba*[106]):

i. lawful authority to detain C either exists or it does not. It is not open to D to argue that the law should 'render lawful what is, in fact, an unlawful authority to detain, by reference to how [D] could and *would have* acted if it had acted lawfully, as opposed to how it *did in fact* act' (per Lord Dyson);
ii. false imprisonment, being actionable *per se*, and not requiring awareness on C's part of the imprisonment, means that the emphasis must be put on the fact of the unlawful constraint itself;
iii. if D could have exercised the power of confining C lawfully, but exercised it unlawfully, then that 'is a powerful reason for concluding that the detainee [C] has suffered no loss, and is entitled to no more than nominal damages. But that is not a reason for holding that the tort has not been committed' (per Lord Dyson). Indeed, in *Lumba*, C received nominal damages, as it was 'inevitable' that they would have been detained.

DEFENCES

There are numerous defences to trespass to the person. Indeed, this is one of the areas of Tort law in which the defences are so extensive and detailed as to almost match the elements themselves. Some defences are relatively long-standing and uncontroversial (e.g., self-defence), whilst others are more controversial (e.g., acting in C's 'best interests' under the Mental Capacity Act 2005, and contributory fault under the Law Reform (Contributory Negligence) Act 1945).

Although Lord Bridge stated, in *R v Deputy Governor of Parkhurst Prison, ex p Hague*,[107] that the second 'ingredient' of the tort of false imprisonment was 'the absence of lawful authority to justify it', the modern view is that lawful justification for that constraint is a defence for which D, not C, bears the burden of proof. The House of Lords confirmed this in *Lumba*, '[a]ll that [C] has to prove in order to establish false imprisonment is that he was directly and intentionally imprisoned by [D], whereupon the burden shifts to [D] to show that there was lawful justification for doing so'.[108]

Dealing with the *principal* defences to trespasses to the person below:

Consent

§14.22 Where C consents, either expressly or impliedly, to the application of force or to a restraint/confinement to the degree and extent applied by D, there is no trespass. However, C's consent will be vitiated (and the trespass remains actionable) if the extent of force is unreasonable, or if providing that consent would be contrary to the public interest.

Consent to what would otherwise be a trespass may be express, or (more usually) implied, and it is a complete defence where it applies. Separate points of contention have arisen under the different torts.

106 The various points are at *ibid*, [239] (original emphasis), [62], [66], [71], [95], and cited recently in: *R (on the application of Das) v Sec of State for the Home Dept* [2014] EWCA Civ 45, [15].
107 [1992] 1 AC 58 (HL) 162.
108 [2012] 1 AC 245, [65]. Also: *Austin v Commr of Police* [2007] EWCA Civ 989, [2008] QB 660, [70].

Battery – general

Where battery is concerned, it will be recalled that, according to *Wilson v Pringle*, 'there are many examples in everyday life where an intended contact or touch is not actionable as a trespass' (e.g., the hand-shake), such contact being impliedly consented to, as 'generally acceptable in the ordinary conduct of everyday life' (per Lord Goff in *F v West Berkshire HA*[109]).

Additionally, in contact sports, the participants are 'taken impliedly to consent to those contacts which can reasonably be expected to occur in the course of the game, and to assume the risk of injury from such contacts' – and the same defence extends to horseplay or children's games which inevitably involve some physical contact (per *Blake v Galloway*[110]). The essential question is whether the application of force went beyond the consent granted by C.

> In *Blake v Galloway*, Master Blake, C, 15, and his friends, including Master Galloway, D, also 15, were taking a lunch break from their jazz quintet practice, when they engaged in spirited and vigorous horseplay, which entailed throwing twigs and pieces of bark chipping at each other. D picked up a small piece of bark and threw it back at C, striking C in the right eye, causing loss of sight in that eye. **Held:** battery succeeded, but the defence of consent applied. It could not be said that C impliedly consented to the risk of a blow on the lower part of his body only. Rather, C impliedly had consented to a blow to any part of his body or face, provided that the bark or stones were not thrown deliberately at the face or eyes by D (and they were not). Hence, the consent provided by C was in accordance with the tacit understandings or conventions of the horseplay.

In this context, consent may be somewhat aligned with the defence of *volenti non fit injuria* (voluntary assumption of risk). In *Murphy v Culhane*,[111] Lord Denning MR gave the example of a burglar, C, who bursts into D's house, D feels threatened, and picks up a nearby gun and shoots C: 'I doubt very much whether the burglar's widow will have an action for damages. The householder might well have a defence either on the ground of *ex turpi causa non oritur actio* [illegality] or *volenti*'.

Some instances of battery will likely remain actionable, however, even if C consents to them, because it is **not** in the public interest that consent should be given in the circumstances. Essentially, C's consent will be vitiated by public policy. In *F v West Berkshire*, Lord Griffiths acknowledged that, while 'the individual is the master of his own fate' generally, C's consent will be contrary to the public interest where, say, C participates in an unlawful bare knuckle prize fight (per *R v Coney*[112]), or where C engages in sexually perverse conduct that inflicts serious injury on C (per *R v Donovan*[113]).

Battery – medical treatment

§14.23 Where patient C has the capacity to give consent to medical treatment by D, and provides that consent, D's treatment is rendered lawful and D cannot be liable in battery. On the other hand, where no consent is provided by C who is of sound mind, then no matter how important or minor the intervention or well-intentioned the medical treatment might be, D commits a battery.

It is in the field of medical and surgical treatment that the interaction between battery and consent has been at its most problematical, with new and vexed issues brought before the courts on

[109] [1990] 2 AC 1 (HL) 13. [110] [2004] EWCA Civ 814, [2004] WLR 2844, [21]. [111] [1977] QB 94 (CA) 96.
[112] (1882) 8 QBD 534. [113] [1934] 2 KB 498.

numerous occasions. The discussion in this section samples only some of the leading medical battery cases for analysis.

The Diagram below sets out, in diagrammatic fashion, the various lines of analysis which may arise, where the interaction of medical treatment, trespass to the person, and lack of capacity, are concerned.

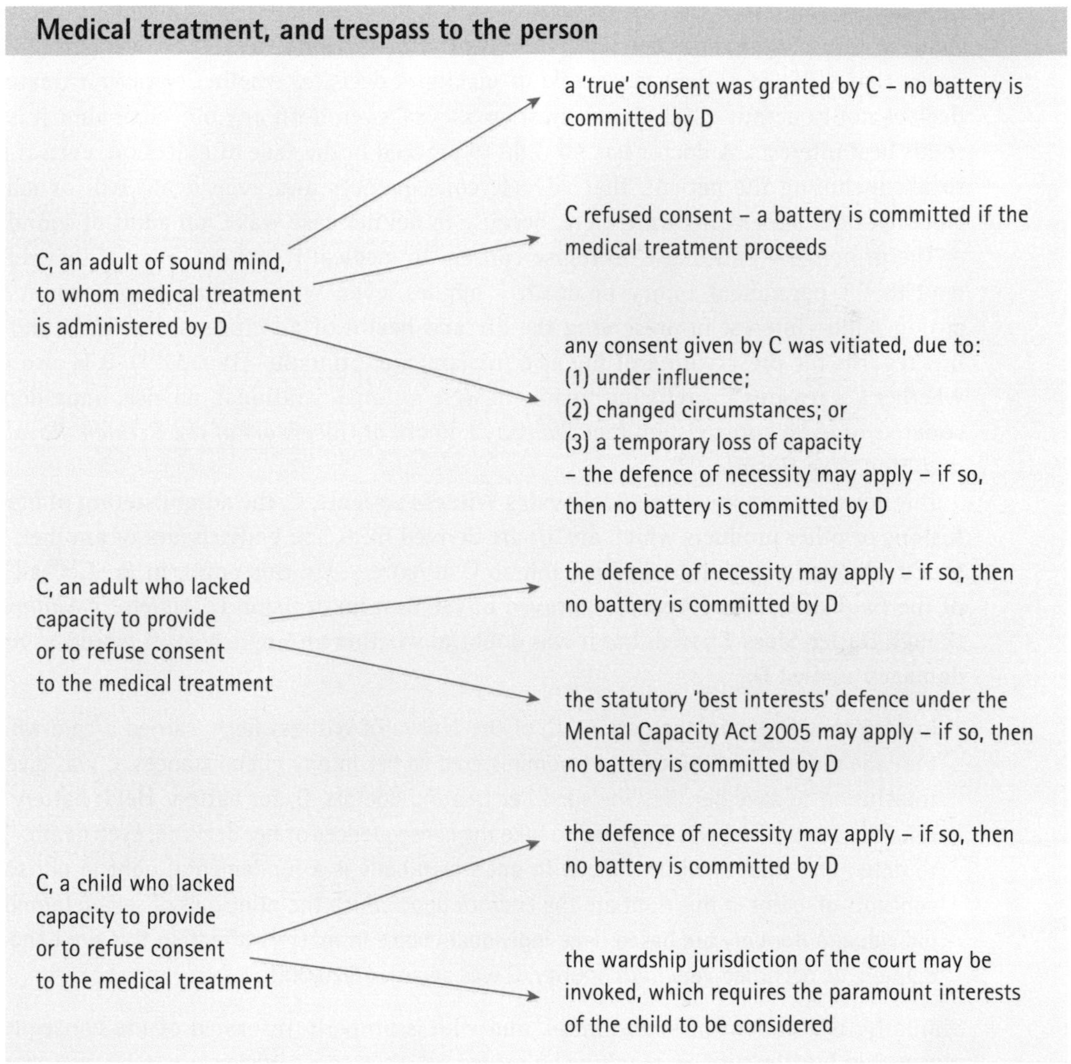

This section deals with the adult who had full capacity and was of sound mind.

A 'true' consent, or a 'true' refusal of consent. An adult of sound mind, C, has the right to decide whether he will or will not receive medical or surgical treatment (*Re T (Consent to Medical Treatment)*[114]). A true consent is one which is unimpaired by any external compulsion, and for which C has capacity, being competent and sound of mind.

[114] [1992] EWCA Civ 18, [1992] 3 WLR 782, [54].

In *F v West Berkshire HA*,[115] Lord Brandon confirmed that a healthcare practitioner, D, will be liable for battery, if C receives treatment involving the application of force ('however small') without C's consent, whilst Lord Goff stated that, 'the performance of a medical operation upon [C] without his consent is unlawful, as constituting both the crime of battery and the tort of trespass to the person'. This proposition is a vital one for healthcare practitioners, who ignore a patient's wish to refuse treatment at their peril, for they are likely to end up on the wrong end of a battery suit, albeit that the damages awarded may ultimately be nominal (it will be recalled that the tort is actionable *per se*). Subsequently, in *Airedale NHS Trust v Bland*,[116] Lord Goff noted that, '[i]f the patient is capable of making a decision whether to permit treatment, and decides not to permit it, his choice must be obeyed, even if on any objective view it is contrary to his best interests. A doctor has no right to proceed in the face of objection, even if it is plain to all, including the patient, that adverse consequences and even death will or may ensue'. Notably, both statements were dicta, because in neither case was C an adult of sound mind.

The principle – entitling C to refuse consent to medical treatment, even if that refusal may lead to C's permanent injury or death – applies, even when taking into account the 'very strong public interest in preserving the life and health of all citizens' (*Re T*[117]), and that 'the law regards the preservation of life as a fundamental principle' (*W v M*[118]). It is also irrelevant whether C's reasons for refusing treatment were rational, irrational, unwise, imprudent, unreasonable, or even non-existent (per *Sidaway v Board of Governors of the Bethlem Royal Hospital and Maudsley Hospital*[119]).

It follows that, in the case of Jehovah's Witness patients, C, the administering of blood transfusions or other products which are, or are derived from, the body tissues of another, may lead to a healthcare practitioner being liable to C in battery. On this point, in *Re T*,[120] all members of the English Court of Appeal approved of the Ontario decision in *Malette v Shulman*,[121] although Butler-Sloss J noted that it was doubtful whether an English court would have awarded damages against D.

In *Malette v Shulman*, the patient, C, of the Jehovah's Witness faith, carried a card which stated that she did not wish blood to be administered to her in any circumstances. C was given a blood transfusion to save her life. She sued her treating doctors, D, for battery. **Held:** battery proven. C refused consent, and was prepared to take the consequences of her decision, even death: '[t]he right to determine what shall be done with one's own body is a fundamental right in our society. The concepts inherent in this right are the bedrock upon which the principles of self-determination and individual autonomy are based. Free individual choice in matters affecting this right should, in my opinion, be accorded very high priority'. C was awarded $20,000.

Similarly, if a patient of sound mind, and who is properly informed of the consequences, requests that his life-support machine be turned off, then those wishes are to be respected, and for D to go against them and force treatment of C which C has not consented to will constitute a battery. Where C does indeed die, then in *Airedale NHS Trust v Bland*,[122] Lord Goff emphasised, in dicta, that there is no question of D having committed the crime of aiding, abetting or procuring C's suicide;[123] rather, D's conduct is treated, at law, as according a patient of sound mind

[115] [1990] 2 AC 1 (HL) 55. [116] [1993] AC 789 (HL) 891, and also Lord Keith (at 857).
[117] [1992] EWCA Civ 18, [1992] 3 WLR 782, [37]. [118] [2011] EWHC 2443 (Fam) [7].
[119] [1985] AC 871 (HL) 904–5 (Lord Templeman). [120] [1992] EWCA Civ 18, [1992] 3 WLR 782, [40].
[121] (1990), 67 DLR (4th) 321. [122] [1993] AC 789 (HL) 864. [123] Per the Suicide Act 1961, s 2(1).

his right to self-determination and personal autonomy. If a patient of sound mind is receiving artificial nutrition and hydration (ANH) and invasive procedures to evacuate waste products against his wishes, that would constitute a battery too (per dicta in *Bland*[124]).

In *B v An NHS Hospital Trust*,[125] Ms B, C, 43, suffered from a haemorrhage of the spinal column in her neck. She thereafter executed a Living Will stating that, should the time come when she was unable to give instructions, she wished for treatment to be withdrawn if she was suffering from a life-threatening condition, permanent mental impairment or permanent unconsciousness. However, C was told that the risk of re-haemorrhage was not particularly great, and after several weeks, C recovered sufficiently to leave hospital and return to work. However, a couple of years later, C suffered another bleed. She became tetraplegic, and also suffered such serious respiratory problems as to become dependent upon a ventilator. C claimed that the invasive treatment of the artificial ventilation was a battery. C retained full mental capacity to make her own decisions about her treatment in hospital, in spite of her disability. **Held:** a battery was committed, in artificially ventilating C against her wishes. C had the right to make a decision to decline future ventilation, and to die. However, only a 'small award of damages' should be awarded against D in the circumstances. In *St George's v S*, the patient was suffering a medical condition which was dangerous for both her and for her unborn child, but she declined the option of a Caesarian section. D obtained a court order to permit it to carry out the operation, to save both lives. **Held (on appeal):** a battery was committed, Notwithstanding the interest in saving the life of the unborn child, the operation interfered with C's right to personal autonomy, and contravened her express wishes.

§14.24 Where C's consent is vitiated (whether by undue influence or other external compulsion; by the circumstance of the treatment being entirely different from what C understood them to be; or by temporarily losing the capacity to decide), then a battery will be committed, unless the doctrine of necessity applies.

Where C, an adult of sound mind, gives consent or refuses consent, but that decision is vitiated, or rendered inoperative at law, then there is a further legal question that must usually be answered – whether the common law defence of necessity applies, such that D may nevertheless administer treatment lawfully and without a battery occurring. The defence of necessity is discussed later. The provisions of the Mental Capacity Act 2005 are also likely to be invoked.

Meanwhile, and necessity aside, at common law, C's consent to, or refusal of, medical treatment may be vitiated, or negatived, in one of **three** circumstances:

i. Undue influence or other external compulsion: C's refusal of medical treatment may be vitiated because it resulted, not from C's will, but from the will of others who are in a close relationship with C (e.g., C's spouse, parent, religious adviser). In that case, C's refusal will not have represented a 'true decision' (*Re T*[126]).

124 [1993] AC 789 (HL) 882.

125 [2002] EWHC 429 (Fam), [2002] 2 All ER 449 (alternative title: *Re B (Adult: Refusal of Medical Treatment)*). Butler-Sloss P remarked (at [95]) that, 'I would like to add how impressed I am with her as a person, with the great courage, strength of will and determination she has shown in the last year, with her sense of humour, and her understanding of the dilemma she has posed to the Hospital. She is clearly a splendid person, and it is tragic that someone of her ability has been struck down so cruelly. I hope she will forgive me for saying, diffidently, that if she did reconsider her decision, she would have a lot to offer the community at large'.

126 [1992] EWCA Civ 18, [1992] 3 WLR 782, [37] (Lord Donaldson MR).

ii. **A change of circumstances from what C had consented to:** As demonstrated in both *Malette* and in *B v An NHS Hospital Trust*, C may have indicated, in advance of the calamity, that he refused consent to medical treatment (by virtue of a Jehovah's Witness card, or a Living Will, respectively). If that indication remains legally viable at the time of the medical calamity, no matter what the change of circumstances, then any treatment by D which is contrary to those wishes will constitute a battery.

In *Airedale NHS Trust v Bland*,[127] Lord Keith affirmed the proposition that C may express a wish, in anticipation of the event, that if he, say, enters a condition such as a permanent vegetative state (PVS), then he is not to be given medical care (e.g., artificial treatment and hydration, or ANH), designed to keep him alive. Provided that C had capacity to make that decision, and understood the ramifications of it, then the English common law position is that to provide treatment to C, against his wishes, will constitute a battery against C. That view was implemented in *Re B (Refusal of Consent)*, discussed above, and also in *Re AK (Medical Treatment: Consent)*,[128] which concerned a patient affected by motor-neurone disease.

However, as Hughes J explained in *Re AK*, the court must consider prior instructions, wishes or expressions of intent with the greatest care, to ensure that they still represent C's wishes. Enquiries as to how long ago the instruction was given, what knowledge of alternatives C may have had, and whether any pressure was brought to bear on C in making that decision, will be necessary for the court's assessment. All of this may demonstrate that C refused consent to medical treatment in one situation, but not in another. His refusal to, say, accept a blood transfusion may have been a refusal of limited scope, e.g. 'I refuse to have a blood transfusion, so long as there is an effective alternative' or 'provided that my life is not in danger'. If, however, the medical calamity is outside the scope of the refusal granted, then C's refusal 'ceases to be effective. The doctors are then faced with a situation in which the patient has made no decision and – he by then being unable to decide for himself – they have both the right and the duty to treat him in accordance with what, in the exercise of their clinical judgment, they consider to be his best interests' (per *Re T*[129]). This scenario potentially invokes the defence of necessity – and the provisions of the Mental Capacity Act 2005 – discussed below.

iii. **A temporary loss of, or reduced, capacity:** C, as an adult patient of sound mind, may nevertheless temporarily lose capacity to give or refuse consent, by temporary factors such as unconsciousness, confusion, or the effects of fatigue, shock, pain or drugs. As Staughton LJ pointed out in *Re T*, C's understanding and reasoning powers may be seriously reduced by drugs or other circumstances, even without being actually unconscious, and even then, C's consent may be vitiated or negatived.[130] The defence of necessity will again arise for consideration.

Although the application of one factor is sufficient to render C's consent (or refusal of consent) inoperative at law, in rare cases, all three factors may operate in conjunction.

In *Re T*, Miss T, C, was 3 when her parents separated. Her mother was a devout Jehovah's Witness, but her father was not. C was brought up by her mother with a view to her becoming a Jehovah's Witness, although C was not a devout follower of that faith. When C was 34 weeks pregnant, she was involved in a car accident, and thereafter suffered serious pneumonia, plus an abscess on the lung. She was hospitalised, and received sedatives, antibiotics and other treatment. C had previously told the nursing staff that she did not wish to receive a blood transfusion, but enquired about alternatives,

[127] [1993] AC 789 (HL) 857. [128] [2001] 1 FLR 129 (Fam).
[129] [1992] EWCA Civ 18, [1992] 3 WLR 782, [33] (Lord Donaldson MR). [130] [1992] EWCA Civ 18, [59].

and also was reassured that a blood transfusion was unlikely. C became less aware of her surroundings, due to the effect of the drugs. C's baby was ultimately delivered by Caesarian section, and she would have benefited from a blood transfusion, but given her express wishes, was given paralysing drugs and ventilated. An application was made to court for directions by her partner and father. **Held:** C's refusal of consent to blood transfusions was vitiated. It was procured by the undue influence of her mother; her refusal was in the context that other alternatives, such as sugar solutions, could have been used which she had enquired about, and she never appreciated that her life could be in danger without blood; and her capacity to refuse consent at the time of the calamity was reduced because of the drugs with which she was being treated.

§14.25 Where a patient, C, undergoes a medical or surgical treatment or procedure at the hands of a healthcare practitioner D, then C must consent broadly to the general type of treatment or procedure, to refute an action for battery. However, where D failed to provide C with information about material risks associated with the treatment or procedure, the appropriate cause of action lies in negligence and *not* in battery.

Where patient C broadly consents to the treatment or procedure, but D fails to disclose the material or significant risks associated with medical or surgical treatment, it cannot be said that the consent of C is vitiated. The consent stands (and battery is hence impossible to sustain), and the relevant cause of action for C must lie in negligence (as discussed in Chapter 3).

The Irish Law Reform Commission succinctly stated the position (for English law too): '[w]here a patient consents in broad terms to the general nature and quality of a proposed procedure, such consent will not be ineffective, merely because it was obtained without disclosure of associated risks and possible alternative treatments'.[131] That principle is derived from *Sidaway v Board of Governors of the Bethlem Royal Hospital*,[132] from the judgments of both Lords Diplock and Scarman (although the latter dissented in the outcome, his views on the appropriate cause of action, i.e., that it would be 'deplorable' to base failure-to-warn cases on the tort of battery, have not been doubted since). The *Sidaway* reasoning was as follows:

i. it would fly in the face of English precedent,[133] which treated this aspect of a doctor's duty as a strand of negligence, and there was no justification for imposing a 'new and different rule' (or new cause of action). Where C is operated on without having had the material risks of the operation explained to him, he is not being operated on against his will, so as to make out an action in battery. Rather, D's provision of information about material risks is one part of the wider duty of care which D owes to his patient;
ii. to import the concept of 'battery + informed consent = no trespass to the person' from American legal doctrine (per *Canterbury v Spence*[134]) was unwarranted and undesirable – especially when 'a cynic might be forgiven for remarking' that treating the cause of action as negligence would have involved a shorter limitation period and thereby precluded C's claim in *Canterbury*, whereas the longer limitation period allowed for battery permitted it to proceed; and

[131] *Non-Fatal Offences Against the Person* (Rep 45, 1994) [1.122].

[132] [1985] AC 871 (HL) 883 (Lord Scarman), 894 (Lord Diplock),

[133] *Chatterton v Gerson* [1981] QB 432 (Bristow J); *Hills v Potter* [1984] 1 WLR 641 (QB) (Hirst J).

[134] 464 F 2d 772 (1972, Col CA).

iii. consent to a procedure or medical treatment 'is a state of mind personal to the victim of the battery', whereas the law of negligence permits D to treat patients objectively ('what would a reasonable patient wish to know about the operation ahead?'). The two are separate concepts, and are appropriately covered by different torts.

However, if the patient consented to some procedure of an entirely different nature, then the consent will be vitiated or negatived, and an action for battery will lie. In *Re T*,[135] Staughton LJ gave the example: '[a] patient who consents, even in the widest terms, to a dental operation under anaesthetic does not give a true consent to the amputation of a leg', while in *Chatterton v Gerson*,[136] Bristow J provided the example of a surgeon who carries out a circumcision instead of the tonsillectomy which the patient had consented to. The patient's consent will not be sufficiently broad to cover the entirely different procedure, and will be negatived.

False imprisonment

§14.26 There may be lawful confinement of C by reason of D's insistence upon C's performance of the contract between them. Hence, that contracted-for performance may constitute an implied consent to the restraint imposed by D.

Two early 20th-century cases highlight that C may have impliedly consented to his confinement by D, by virtue of his contractual relationship with D.

In *Herd v Weardale Steel, Coal and Coke Co*,[137] facts previously, where C was 'imprisoned' down a mine shaft until his employment shift had ended, **held:** no false imprisonment. C had no contractual entitlement to be returned to the surface before his shift ended. It will be recalled that, even if D had breached its contract with C, it was said, in dicta, that would not have constituted false imprisonment, because D's refusal of his request was a mere omission. In *Robinson v Balmain New Ferry Co Ltd*,[138] barrister Archibald Robinson, C, entered the turnstile onto the wharf of the Balmain New Ferry Co, D, intending to cross Sydney Harbour to Balmain. A sign near the turnstile stated: 'Notice. A fare of one penny must be paid on entering or leaving the wharf. No exception will be made to this rule, whether the passenger has travelled by the ferry or not'. C paid his penny, changed his mind about travelling because the next steamer was 20 minutes away from leaving, and sought to leave the wharf without paying the penny. C was restrained from leaving by D's employees, but eventually he succeeded in getting past them, squeezed himself through a narrow space between the entry turnstile and the bulkhead into the street. He sued D for false imprisonment. **Held:** no false imprisonment. C knew of the terms on which he entered the wharf, and D was entitled to prevent C from leaving the wharf without payment.

Both of these cases could be explained on different bases than the principle above, however. In *Herd*, the distinction between a positive act and an omission was brought to the fore in the court's reasoning, whereas in *Robinson*, C's restraint was only partial, as he could have left the wharf by means of the ferry which was due to arrive 20 minutes later. Nevertheless, the principle has never been overruled, and provides a useful defence for D, where D's behaviour does not constitute a breach of contract.

[135] [1992] EWCA Civ 18, [1992] 3 WLR 782, [58]. [136] [1981] QB 432, 443.
[137] [1913] 3 KB 771, aff'd: [1915] AC 67 (HL) 77–78 (Lord Moulton).
[138] [1910] AC 295 (PC) 299 (Lord Loreburn).

Necessity

General

§14.27 Necessity applies as a defence to trespasses to the person where D's act of trespass was required (1) in C's best interests, or (2) to avoid danger, or potential danger, to C or to others. Under either category, D's act of trespass must, additionally, have been reasonable in all the circumstances.

Necessity is a common law defence to a trespass to property (e.g., D's destroying C's property to stop the spread of fire) and to a trespass to land (e.g., D's entering upon C's property to stop fire spreading too) – and it can also lawfully serve as a defence to a trespass to the person. The defence will require clear facts before the threshold requirements of 'best interests to C himself, or danger to others' will be met.

The availability of the defence was endorsed, re *false imprisonment*, in *Austin v Commr of Police*[139] (in dicta, given that the 'breach of the peace' defence provided lawful justification for the imprisonment there) – and additionally, in the context of *assault, battery and false imprisonment*, in *R v Bournewood Community and Mental Health NHS Trust, ex p L*[140] (in which Lord Goff also reiterated the two threshold requirements noted in the principle above).

In *Bournewood Mental Health NHS Trust, ex p L*, facts previously, the House of Lords split on the issue of false imprisonment, with the majority holding that there was none. However, re the question of whether any detention of C would have been defendable on the basis of the doctrine of necessity: **Held (5:0):** the defence of necessity applied. The constraint of C was justified on the basis of necessity, because when C became agitated and violent, an emergency arose, and the constraints imposed upon C were in his best interests. That included the restraints imposed during C's journey by ambulance from the day centre to the A&E unit, a journey which was plainly justified by necessity. Additionally, all the steps taken in the hospital itself were taken in the best interests of C, and were justified on the basis of the common law doctrine of necessity.

Interestingly, in *Bournewood*, Lord Goff made the point that the defence of necessity 'has its role to play in all branches of our law of obligations ... It is perhaps surprising, however, that the significant role it has to play in the law of torts has come to be recognised at so late a stage in the development of our law'.

Nevertheless, the defence has come to have further, problematical, applications in the context of medical and surgical treatment, and to some extent, has been overtaken by the Mental Capacity Act 2005.

Medical treatment

§14.28 Where C, an adult, lacks the capacity to consent to medical treatment, such that it is impossible to ascertain C's wishes regarding actual or proposed medical treatment, then that treatment may be *administered*, and rendered lawful under the common law defence of necessity, to preclude a battery being committed by D. The treatment must be in C's 'best interests', for the defence to apply. Conversely, where C lacks the capacity to refuse medical treatment, then D can lawfully *withhold* life-saving medical treatment where that is in C's 'best interests', without being liable in tort or in crime.

[139] [2007] EWCA Civ 989, [2008] QB 660, [49].

[140] [1998] UKHL 24, [1999] 1 AC 458, 488, 490 (Lord Goff), with the later observation of Lord Goff's at 491.

Re adults who lack capacity to consent. Every adult is presumed to have the capacity to consent to, or to refuse, medical treatment, but that presumption can be rebutted – and capacity has absolutely nothing to do with the intelligence or education of the adult patient concerned (per *Re T*[141]). C's lack of capacity may be due to, e.g., an accident rendering C unconscious, and where an operation or other treatment is advisable before C recovers consciousness; or where (as in *Re F* itself[142]) C cannot, by reason of mental disability, understand the nature or purpose of an operation or other treatment; or where C is rendered speechless by a catastrophic stroke. In the case of an adult who is not of sound mind and lacks the capacity to either give or refuse consent to medical treatment which is necessary to preserve the life, health or well-being of C, the treatment may lawfully be given to C without consent, on the basis of the defence of necessity. The duty on healthcare practitioners D is to treat C in whatever way they consider, in the exercise of their clinical judgment, to be in his best interests (per *Re T*[143]). C's 'best interests' will be proven, if the treatment was required 'to save [C's] life, or to ensure improvement or prevent deterioration in [C's] physical or mental health' (per *Re F*[144]).

A Bolam-type analysis. The question of whether proposed medical treatment was in the 'best interests' of C, so as to invoke the defence of necessity, is to be determined by a *Bolam*-type[145] analysis, i.e., that the proposed treatment would be in accordance with a practice accepted at the time by a responsible body of medical opinion skilled in the particular form of treatment in question (per *Re F*[146]).

However, according to Lord Goff in *Re F* (and similarly to the '*Bolitho* gloss' applied under the tort of negligence, as discussed in Chapter 7), the medical opinion cannot properly be the final arbiter of the question. The ultimate decision as to whether the proposed treatment was in C's best interests is for the court to decide: 'expert opinions ... are listened to with great respect; but, in the end, the validity of the opinion has to be weighed and judged by the court'. Lord Goff noted that a 'best interests' assessment should entail, as 'good practice, [a duty] to consult relatives and others who are concerned with the care of the patient', and perhaps the views of an inter-disciplinary team too.[147] Furthermore, the 'best interests' analysis properly encompassed 'medical, emotional and all other welfare issues' (per *Re A (Male Sterilisation)*[148]).

In *F v West Berkshire HA (Re F)*, F, 36, the C, suffered from a serious mental disability, from a virus that she contracted at 9 months old, and was a voluntary in-patient at Borocourt Hospital (a mental hospital) since 14 years of age. C had the verbal capacity of a child of two, and the general mental capacity of a child of 4–5. She could not give consent for medical procedures. C was prone to aggression unless treated, but had a close relationship with her mother, who was her only relative and who visited her regularly. C formed a consensual sexual relationship with a male patient, P, in the same hospital. However, given her mental disability, C could not cope at all with pregnancy, labour or delivery, or care for a baby: it would be 'disastrous for her to conceive'. The hospital sought clarification that female sterilisation would be lawful. **Held:** the defence of necessity would apply, in respect of any battery action that may be brought. In *Simms v An NHS Trust*,[148a] a male patient, JS, 18, and a female patient, JA, 16, suffered in their teens from variant Creutzfeldt-Jakob disease (vCJD), and became bed-ridden but still remained partly conscious of their surroundings

141 [1992] EWCA Civ 18, [1992] 3 WLR 782, [33] (Lord Donaldson MR).

142 [1990] 2 AC 1 (HL). Also known as: *Re F (Mental Patient: Sterilisation)*.

143 [1992] EWCA Civ 18, [1992] 3 WLR 782, [37].

144 [1990] 2 AC 1 (HL) 66 (Lord Brandon).

145 *Bolam v Friern Hospital Management Committee* [1957] 1 WLR 582 (QB).

146 [1990] 2 AC 1 (HL) 66–68 (Lord Brandon).

147 *ibid*, 80.

148 [2000] 1 FLR 549 (Fam) 555.

148a [2002] EWHC 2734 (Fam).

and of loved ones. Both lacked capacity to make a decision about future treatment proposed for them. That treatment consisted of inserting a catheter into the front region of the brain, so as to enable Pentosan Polysulphate (PPS) to be infused in controlled dosages into the affected brain tissue. The treatment was untested on human beings, but had shown successful results in mice that suffered from other neurological diseases which involved the accumulation of abnormal proteins in the brain. Although JS and JA were from separate and unrelated families, each was at a broadly similar stage in the vCJD onset and progress, so the proposed treatment would be identical for both. **Held:** the defence of necessity applied. The treatment was *Bolam*-compliant. Although there was no direct experience of the treatment having occurred in the UK or of PPS being licensed in the UK to that point, evidence showed that a responsible body of medical opinion supported PPS treatment in the UK for these patients. Further, when balancing all the relevant considerations (their families' wishes, the welfare of JS and JA with and without the treatment, etc), it was in their best interests that the treatment should be carried out. In *Re T*, facts previously, **held:** the defence of necessity applied. It was in C's best interests that a blood transfusion be administered. There was no valid refusal of consent, so the doctors were justified in their treatment of Miss T (in providing her with blood and plasma), by the principle of necessity.

Emergencies not required. It is sometimes said (as in, e.g., *Re MB*[149]) that *Re F* stands for the proposition that medical or surgical treatment 'can be undertaken in an emergency even if, through a lack of capacity, no consent had been competently given, provided the treatment was a necessity, and did no more than was reasonably required in the best interests of the patient'.

However, it is important to emphasise that it is **not** necessary to prove that C was in a position of *emergency*, when D's battery occurred, in order for the common law defence of necessity to apply. In *Re F* itself, C was incapable of consenting to a sterilisation operation over many years, which could not properly be described as a 'permanent emergency'; and the two tragic patients in *Simms* were similarly-placed. Certainly, an emergency scenario may frequently give rise to the defence of necessity in medical treatment scenarios (per the example below), but it is **not** a pre-requisite to the defence applying.

Lord Goff's example in F's case: take a railway accident, in which injured passengers are trapped in the wreckage – those staff, bystanders and emergency staff who rush to aid the unconscious or who have to amputate a passenger's limb to free him from the wreckage do not commit batteries because of the defence of necessity. The ambulance staff who transport the passengers to hospital, and the hospital staff who confine the unconscious passenger in hospital, do not commit false imprisonment by reason of the defence either. Such conduct was reasonable in all the circumstances.

Withholding life-saving treatment. Where C's life can only be sustained via intrusive medical care to which C cannot consent because he lacks the capacity to give or to refuse consent, then the question arises: is the healthcare practitioner, D, under a legal duty to nevertheless maintain C's life, so as to lawfully invade the bodily integrity of C without his consent (i.e., commit a battery), where a *Bolam*-type analysis is that it is **not** in C's best interests to do so? According to the House of Lords in *Airedale NHS Trust v Bland*,[150] the answer to that question is 'no'.

There is no basis in English law whereby a court could give its consent, on behalf of an adult patient lacking capacity. On this point, English law departs from US law, as Lord Goff noted in *Bland*, who noted the approach of American courts to 'seek, in a case in which the patient is incapacitated from expressing any view on the question whether life-prolonging treatment

[149] [1997] EWCA Civ 3093, [17(3)]. [150] [1992] UKHL 5, [1993] AC 789.

should be withheld ..., to determine what decision the patient himself would have made had he been able to do so. This is called the "substituted judgment" test, and it generally involves a detailed inquiry into the patient's views and preferences ... However ... I do not consider that any such test forms part of English law in relation to incompetent adults, on whose behalf nobody has power to give consent to medical treatment'.[151]

Rather, in English law, the healthcare practitioner, D, has a duty to act in the 'best interests' of his patient – and in an appropriate case, that 'best interests' assessment may properly be **not** to prolong C's life by invasive medical treatment. Where C lacks capacity to consent, D's decision as to whether invasive medical treatment should be withheld in C's 'best interests' must be assessed according to *Bolam*, i.e., that withholding treatment is in accordance with a practice accepted at the time by a responsible body of medical opinion. In the words of Lord Browne-Wilkinson in *Bland*, 'if there comes a stage where the responsible doctor comes to [a *Bolam*-supported] conclusion ... that further continuance of an intrusive life support system is not in the best interests of the patient, he can no longer lawfully continue that life support system: to do so would constitute the crime of battery and the tort of trespass to the person. Therefore he cannot be in breach of any duty to maintain the patient's life. Therefore he is not guilty of murder by omission'.[152] Lord Goff explained the reasoning by reference to both law and to ethics: 'a doctor who is caring for such a patient cannot, in my opinion, be under an absolute obligation to prolong his life by any means available to him, regardless of the quality of the patient's life. Common humanity requires otherwise, as do medical ethics and good medical practice accepted in this country and overseas'.[153] It was clear, from *Bland*, that the views of C's immediate family, his treating team, and the independent specialists, all contribute to the 'best interests' analysis. More recently, the court in *W v M*[154] put it this way: 'due respect for the wishes and feelings of the patient, and for the wishes and feelings of other family members, has, of course, been a feature of the best interests assessment process since the decision in *Bland*'.

In *Bland*, Anthony Bland, C, then 17, but 21 at the time of trial, was injured at the Hillsborough football stadium disaster. He suffered very serious crush injuries, and due to prolonged deprivation of oxygen, his cerebral cortex was destroyed. C was in a persistent vegetative state (PVS) for over three years. As a result, C could not see, hear or feel anything, nor communicate in any way, nor exhibit any essential feature of individual personality. However, the brain stem which controlled the reflexive functions of C's body, *viz*, heartbeat, breathing and digestion, continued to operate. C received ANH through stomach and nose, and his excretionary functions were regulated by a catheter and by enemas, which could give rise to periodic infections. The medical opinion was that there was no prospect of C ever recovering from his condition, and that he would continue to live for many years under present medical treatment. C's parents, his treating medical team, D, and independent medical specialists, formed the view that no useful purpose was to be served by continuing that medical care, and that artificial ventilation, and ANH, and other invasive medical treatment, should be stopped. C's father stated, 'He certainly wouldn't want to be left like that'. A declaration was sought to withdraw C's life-saving treatment. **Held (5:0):** D would not commit a criminal offence by an omission, i.e., by ceasing C's life-saving treatment. In most cases, the 'best interests' of patient C will be to administer the medical treatment – but not in the case of Mr Bland, where the treatment had no therapeutic purpose, and where it was 'futile', because he had no prospects of recovery or of consciousness. Further, C would feel no pain and distress between the withdrawal of treatment and his death, as the consequences could be suppressed with sedatives.

[151] *ibid*, 871–72, [152] *ibid*, 883–84. [153] *ibid*, 867. [154] [2011] EWHC 2443 (Fam) [95].

However, where C is not in a PVS, but rather, is in a 'minimally conscious state' (MCS), then it will not be lawful to withdraw ANH from that patient.

In *W v M*,[155] C, 43, was preparing to leave for a skiing holiday with her partner. The night before leaving, she went to bed early with a headache. The following morning, her partner found C in a confused and drowsy state. C was taken to hospital, where she soon fell into a coma. C had suffered viral encephalitis which left her with extensive and irreparable brain damage. Thereafter, C was wholly dependent on others for her care, and fed via a gastrostomy tube. Her family and partner explored all options in the hope that she would recover consciousness, but without success. They decided (with the support of C's treating doctors) to apply for a court order authorising the withdrawal of ANH. **Held:** the application was refused. D could not lawfully discontinue and withhold all life-sustaining treatment, including ANH. This was a different type of case from *Bland.* C's life had 'positive elements', and her carers who cared for her full-time were of the firm view that ANH should not be withdrawn, and that C's quality of life could be improved to expose her to increased stimulation under a modified future care plan.

Some courts have authorised the withdrawal of ANH from a patient diagnosed, not in an MCS, but in a state somewhat short of a PVS (per *In Re D (Adult: Medical Treatment)*[156] and in *An NHS Trust v A and SA*[157] – where it was **not** in the best interests of the patient to be kept alive by ANH.

Procedural matters. Where C, an adult, lacked capacity and was of unsound mind, then historically the court exercised its jurisdiction, under the prerogative of the Crown as *parens patriae*, to protect the person and property of those unable to do so for themselves. That particular jurisdiction was abolished by s 1 of the Mental Health Act 1959, but the House of Lords clarified, in *Re F*,[158] that the court's inherent jurisdiction could still properly be employed for declaratory purposes,[159] for adults who lacked mental capacity. That judicial declaration could encompass rulings such as whether C had the requisite capacity to accept or refuse medical treatment, and (if capacity was lacking) whether the proposed treatment was in C's 'best interests', and hence lawful. This declaratory process closely resembled the *parens patriae* jurisdiction (noted in *W v M*[160]), and the Court of Appeal was at pains, in *Re MB*,[161] to set out a useful procedural guidance note as to steps that should be taken, where a healthcare practitioner or NHS Trust was requesting that the court give a declaration as to capacity, lawfulness, 'best interests', and/or necessity.

However, the Mental Capacity Act 2005[162] has since provided a comprehensive statutory regime for making decisions about adults who lack capacity. Some of that was new, and some of it drew upon procedures judicially-developed to that point. A new Court of Protection has been established, which seeks to determine questions of welfare for incapacitated adults (e.g., whether a bodily sample for DNA purposes could be taken from an adult to determine whether the applicant was that adult's daughter, as in *LG v DK*[163]). Discussion of that regime lies beyond the scope of this book.

§14.29 Where a child, C, has the capacity to give (or to refuse) consent, that consent is a 'true' consent, such that administering medical treatment to C in accordance with those wishes does not

155 [2011] EWHC 2443 (Fam). 156 [1998] 1 FCR 498 (Sir Stephen Brown). 157 [2005] EWCA Civ 1145.
158 *Re F (Mental Patient: Sterilisation)* [1990] 2 AC 1 (HL) 64 (Lord Brandon).
159 *Viz*, a declaration under RSC, Ord 15, r 16. 160 [2011] EWHC 2443 (Fam) [60].
161 [1997] EWCA Civ 3093, [62]. 162 Especially, ss 15–17. 163 [2011] EWHC 2453 (COP).

constitute a battery. However, where C lacks the capacity to consent to medical treatment, or C consents but his/her parents or guardian contend that the treatment is not in C's 'best interests', then the court can exercise its wardship jurisdiction, and, in doing so, is obliged to consider the 'best interests' of C, as the paramount consideration.

Where a child lacks capacity to consent to or to refuse medical treatment, or where it is uncertain as to whether the minor's consent is in his/her best interests, the court has a 'wardship jurisdiction', so that the High Court (Family Division) may give directions as to the medical treatment of a child. That assessment must be governed by what was in that child's 'best interests', which again invokes the common law defence of necessity (per *Re J (A Minor) (Wardship: Medical Treatment)*[164]). As the Court of Appeal explained, in the case of the conjoined twins Jodie and Mary (in *Re A (Children)*[165]) – where there was intense media questioning as to why the court should be involved at all where the case was more pertinent to criminal rather than tort law – the reason was powerfully put: 'Long, long ago, the sovereign's prerogative to protect infants passed to the Lord Chancellor, and through him to the judges, and it forms a part of the inherent jurisdiction of the High Court'.

Further, where a child is made a ward of the court, then the court requires all relevant expert, parental, and other evidence to be brought before the court, to enable it to decide whether or not the treatment or procedure was in the best interests of the minor. As remarked in *Re B (A Minor) (Wardship: Medical Treatment)*,[166] once a child is made a ward of the court, then, '[f]ortunately or unfortunately ... the decision no longer lies with the parents or with the doctors, but lies with the court. It is a decision which, of course, must be taken in the light of the evidence and views expressed by the parents and the doctors, but at the end of the day, it devolves on this court in this particular instance to decide'.

In *An NHS Trust v MB (A Child)*,[167] the patient was an 18-month-old child suffering from severe and degenerating spinal muscular atrophy. C was artificially ventilated and fed, but suffered pain and discomfort from associated medical procedures, and had a short life expectancy. However, he was not in a PVS, and was conscious of his surroundings. His treating doctors sought an application authorising the withdrawal of ANH. **Held:** the application was refused, but the court declared that withholding further procedures, such as CPR and the administration of intravenous antibiotics, which would involve the infliction of further pain, would be authorised.

Where the minor has capacity, is 16 years or over, and has consented to 'any surgical, medical or dental treatment', then D has statutory protection from any action brought in battery, as if that minor were of full age (per s 8(1) of the Family Law Reform Act 1969[168]).

Where the minor is under 16 years of age (and hence, the aforementioned provision does not apply), that minor may nevertheless be of 'sufficient understanding and intelligence' that his/her consent will be validly-given, and operative at law. That will preclude any action in battery from being brought against the healthcare practitioner, D, who provides that treatment (per *Gillick v West Norfolk and Wisbech AHA*[169]).

[164] [1991] Fam 33 (Fam). [165] [2000] EWCA Civ 254, [2001] 2 WLR 480.

[166] [1981] 1 WLR 1424 (CA) 1423–24. [167] [2006] EWHC 507 (Fam).

[168] Implementing the key recommendations in: *Report on the Age of Majority* (chaired by Latey J) (Cmnd 3342, 1967).

[169] [1986] AC 112 (HL).

In *Gillick*, Mrs Gillick, C, a mother of five daughters under the age of 16, challenged the legality of guidance issued in 1980 by the English Dept of Health and Social Security to health authorities, including West Norfolk AHA, D, which provided advice to doctors about the benefits of providing advice about contraception without parental consent to a mature child under 16. The guidance stated that it would be 'most unusual' to provide contraceptive advice to a child without parental consent, but that not to provide such advice, if requested by a child under 16, 'might cause some not to seek professional advice at all. They could then be exposed to the immediate risks of pregnancy and of sexually-transmitted diseases, as well as other long-term physical, psychological and emotional consequences which are equally a threat to stable family life', but that the advice given always remained for the clinical judgment of the doctor concerned. **Held (3:2):** the guidance was lawful. A strict age rule in relation to consent to medical treatment for those under 16 (as opposed to the clear rule for 16- and 17-year-olds in s 8 of the 1969 Act) would not take account of the growing maturity and capacity of the child. The significant factor in assessing the capacity of a person under 16 was not the age of the individual, but his or her ability to understand fully what was proposed.

In that regard, as the Irish Law Reform Commission noted, *Gillick* was based upon the proposition that the English common law 'recognised the independent decision-making capacity of persons under 16', or the so-called 'mature minor'.[170] It followed from *Gillick* that any action brought by that 'mature minor' for battery may be defeated by the defence of consent.

Statutory 'bests interests' defence

§14.30 Where D acts in C's 'best interests' within the meaning of the Mental Capacity Act 2005, then D is not liable in tort for his actions.

The Mental Capacity Act 2005 sanctions certain acts done by D, in connection with the care or treatment of C who lacks capacity (or where D reasonably believes that C lacks capacity) – including providing treatment or restraint (in narrowly-prescribed scenarios). According to s 1(4), the 'cardinal principle' was that 'an act done, or decision made, under this Act for or on behalf of a person who lacks capacity must be done, or made, in his best interests'. Section 4 prescribes the steps to be taken to determine what is in C's best interests. Furthermore, under s 4(7) of the Act, D is obliged to take into account the views of, amongst others, anyone caring for C, but only if it is *practicable and appropriate* to consult that carer.

This defence is closely analogous to, but doctrinally distinct from, the defence of necessity. Hence, when police officers, healthcare practitioners, or other authoritarian figures, D, restrain or touch C, with the intention of taking steps to take care of C who lacks capacity, then where D's acts would otherwise attract liability for trespass to the person, they will not do so, if D reasonably believed that (per Lord Dyson MR in *Commr of Police v ZH*,[171] in a convenient summary of the statutory position):

i. C lacked capacity, having taken reasonable steps to establish that;[172]
ii. those acts of restraint or touching were done in C's 'best interests';[173] and
iii. restraint or touching was necessary in order to prevent harm to C, and was a proportionate response.[174]

[170] *Children and the Law: Medical Treatment* (Rep 103, 2011) [2.16], [2.40].
[171] [2013] EWCA Civ 69, [39]–[40], [43]–[57]. [172] Per s 5(1)(a) and (b)(i).
[173] Per s 5(1)(b)(ii). [174] Per s 6(2) and (3).

As Lord Dyson MR noted, a 'striking feature' of the statutory defence of 'best interests' is that it is 'pervaded by the concepts of reasonableness, practicability and appropriateness. Strict liability has no place here ... D is under no liability to C in tort, for an act done in connection with the care or treatment of C, if he *reasonably* believes that it will be in C's best interests for the act to be done'.[175] This was important, for the 2005 Act 'does not impose impossible demands on those who do acts in connection with the care or treatment of others. It requires no more than what is reasonable, practicable and appropriate. What that entails depends on all the circumstances of the case'.[176]

In *Commr of Police v ZH*, facts previously, **held:** the statutory 'best interests' defence pleaded by the police, D, failed. There was no emergency scenario in which ZH was at imminent risk of jumping into the pool. He had been standing by the poolside, fixated by the water, for at least 40 minutes by the time D (two police officers) arrived. Had D consulted ZH's carer, which it would have been practicable and appropriate to do, the carer would have said that it was not uncommon for autistic people to become 'stuck' in the one place for a considerable time, and that ZH 'needed time'. Also, there were a number of lifeguards around the pool, keeping an eye on ZH's movements, so he was not in any danger from drowning if he did jump in. Then, once in the water, D should have stepped back and allowed the carers to deal with ZH (those carers would have advised that ZH would hate being touched and lifted out). D could not have reasonably believed that it was necessary to restrain ZH in order to prevent harm to him; and nor was the restraint proportionate. ZH could have been allowed to leave the pool from the shallow end or, when poolside, could have been released to his carers, rather than be put in handcuffs/leg restraints, etc.

The ECHR angle

Where C has capacity and refuses medical treatment. Where healthcare practitioner, D, 'respects the wishes' of C, a person of sound mind, to refuse medical treatment or surgery, then D's conduct is not a violation of the ECHR (and nor is the English legal principle authorising D's conduct incompatible with the ECHR).

In *W v M*,[177] Baker J confirmed that there could be no infringement of *Art 8* (right to respect for private and family life), where C decides to refuse medical treatment, because of the paramount importance of self-determination: '[p]ersonal autonomy is an important element of the Art 8(1) right. As the European Court has recently observed in *Jehovah's Witness of Moscow v Russia*, "The freedom to accept or refuse specific medical treatment, or to select an alternative form of treatment, is vital to the principles of self-determination and personal autonomy. A competent adult patient is free to decide, for instance, whether or not to undergo surgery or treatment, or, by the same token, to have a blood transfusion. However, for this freedom to be meaningful, patients must have the right to make choices that accord with their own views and values, regardless of how irrational, unwise or imprudent such choices may appear to others'."

Nor did Baker J consider that *Art 2* (protecting the right to life) or *Art 3* (prohibiting inhuman and degrading treatment) would be infringed in these circumstances.

Where C lacks capacity and treatment is withheld. Although *Bland* was decided before the HRA 1998 came into effect, the judicial opinion since then has affirmed that a declaration that the withholding or withdrawal of life-sustaining treatment from C, who lacks capacity but for whom that is in his 'best interests', is compatible with the ECHR.

[175] [2013] EWCA Civ 69, [40]. [176] *ibid*, [49].
[177] [2011] EWHC 2443 (Fam), [2012] 1 WLR 1653, [94], with the internal quote at: [2011] 53 EHRR 4 (ECtHR) [136].

In *An NHS Trust A v M*,[178] President Butler-Sloss held that ***Art 2*** (protecting the right to life) imposes a positive obligation to give life-sustaining treatment in circumstances where, according to responsible medical opinion, such treatment is in the best interests of C, but does not impose an absolute obligation to treat if such treatment would be futile. Further, **Art 3** (that 'no-one shall be subjected to torture or to inhuman or degrading treatment or punishment') was held not to apply to C, who is in a PVS. Rather, that Article 'requires the victim to be aware of the inhuman and degrading treatment which he or she is experiencing, or at least to be in a state of physical or mental suffering. An insensate patient suffering from PVS has no feelings and no comprehension of the treatment accorded to him or her. Article 3 does not ... apply'. In *Glass v UK*,[179] the European Court of Human Rights also held that, given that English law required a detailed 'best interests' assessment to be carried out, then there could be no breach of Art 2 if a 'do not resuscitate' note was added to C's medical records.

Even where C is not in a PVS, but rather, in a minimally-conscious state, *W v M*[180] confirmed that ***Art 3*** would still not be violated, if various medical treatment was withheld, on the basis that responsible medical opinion and other evidence supported the view that to do so was in C's best interests: 'in non-PVS cases, a patient may have some awareness and comprehension of the withholding and withdrawal of treatment. The impact of the withdrawal of treatment, the methods by which it is achieved, and the steps that can be taken to alleviate any suffering and distress are all part of the best interests assessment. Thus a decision by the Court, having carried out an assessment in accordance with established legal principles, that it is in the patient's best interests to withhold or withdraw treatment does not give rise to a breach of Art 3'. (In that case, it will be recalled that the withdrawal of medical treatment was held not to be in C's best interests.)

Finally, ***Art 8*** (protecting right to respect for C's private and family life) includes 'personal autonomy' as an important element (per *Jehovah's Witness of Moscow v Russia*[181]). However, given that the decision in *Bland* compels a court to take account of the wishes and feelings of the patient, and of other family members, as part of the 'best interests' assessment, an assessment that it would be in C's best interests to withhold or withdraw treatment does not give rise to a breach of Art 8 (per *W v M*[182]).

Prevention of crime, disorder or ill-discipline

§14.31 D may be lawfully justified in applying force or restraint to C when: exercising lawful powers of arrest or imprisonment; preventing a criminal offence; preventing an imminent breach of the peace and maintaining public order; or imposing parental authority. The application of the force or restraint must be both reasonable and proportionate in all scenarios, to constitute a valid defence.

Powers of arrest or detention

Where police officers, D, enter and search C's property, and/or effect an arrest, and C alleges that a trespass to the person was committed against him, D has a good defence, if it was necessary to use force on C, and that the force was reasonable. The following legislative provisions have proven to be relevant in various cases:

[178] [2001] Fam 348, [37], [49]. [179] [2004] Lloyd's Rep Med 76 (ECtHR). [180] [2011] EWHC 2443 (Fam) [92].
[181] (2011) 53 EHRR 4, [136]. [182] [2011] EWHC 2443 (Fam) [95].

Police and Criminal Evidence Act 1984, s 117:
Where any provision of this Act – (a) confers a power on a constable; ... the officer may use reasonable force, if necessary, in the exercise of the power [where, e.g., s 17(1) provides that 'a ... constable may enter and search any premises for the purpose ... (b) of arresting a person for an indictable offence'].

Criminal Law Act 1967, s 3(1):
A person may use such force as is reasonable in the circumstances in the prevention of crime, or in effecting or assisting in the lawful arrest of offenders or suspected offenders or of persons unlawfully at large.

Borders Act 2007, s 36(1)(a):
A person who has served a period of imprisonment may be detained under the authority of the Secretary of State while the Secretary of State considers whether [the Secretary must make a deportation order in respect of a foreign criminal].

According to *Farrell v Sec of State for Defence*,[183] s 3(1) can provide a defence to a civil action for assault or battery – the relevant question being whether D used reasonable force in the circumstances, in preventing crime, or in bringing about or assisting in C's lawful arrest. For both provisions, the burden is on the police, D, to prove that the force used was reasonable (per *Alleyne v Commr of Police*[184]).

In *Roberts v Kent CC*,[185] Mr Roberts, C, 57, had drunk a fair amount during a day's outing to London. When returning to Sittingbourne, Kent, C got into his car to drive to get a Chinese takeaway. PC Harris, D, observed C parked in his car, and asked C to give a breath specimen. C took off by foot, and D instructed Police Dog Oscar to chase him. A fight ensued between C and D, and Oscar bit C quite viciously, as he was trained to do when a police officer was being assaulted. That incident was a battery; but the legal question was whether the use of Oscar, in seeking to apprehend and detain C, was 'reasonable force'. **Held:** the use of Oscar was reasonable under s 3(1). Oscar reacted in the manner in which he had been trained. The force used to apprehend someone who was being sought for two suspected offences – driving under the influence, and refusing to give a breath specimen – was reasonable. In *Connor v CC of Merseyside Police*,[186] gang warfare was ongoing in Liverpool, and a public informant told police, D, that weapons used in previous shootings were stored at C's home. The police obtained a search warrant of C's premises because there were reasonable grounds for suspecting that there was a danger to the public. D raided C's property, and C and her children were 'put' in a police car for about 40 minutes during the raid. **Held:** no false imprisonment proven. The search powers were reasonably exercised. It was predictable that police officers, D, searching a house for firearms were likely to take precautions, including removing the occupants of the house who might obstruct the search or would put themselves and others in danger.

However, what of the situation where D's belief of what C was about to do was mistaken? It depends upon whether or not D's belief was **reasonable**:

i. **An unreasonable belief.** Where C does not obstruct or hinder the police, D, in the exercise of their powers – but D mistakenly and *unreasonably* believes that C was obstructing them – then

[183] [1980] 1 WLR 172 (CA) 178. [184] [2012] EWHC 3955 (QB) [104].
[185] [2008] EWCA Civ 1588. [186] [2006] EWCA Civ 1549, [68].

D **cannot** rely on the statutory defences. The use of force, in those circumstances, will amount to a battery, as it will not be justified (dicta in *Ashley v CC of Sussex Police*[187] – although that case was contested strictly on the grounds of self-defence, and not on the abovementioned provisions).

ii. A reasonable belief. However, if the police, D, believed that C was obstructing them, and that was mistaken but *reasonable*, then although the House of Lords in *Ashley*[188] left open the question as to whether the statutory defences could successfully apply to the torts of assault and battery, the question was addressed at first instance in *Alleyne*.[189] That court was satisfied that D mistakenly but reasonably believed that C was 'non-compliant' and obstructive, and the conduct of the police was lawful. The force used was reasonable, in light of what the key police officer reasonably believed: 'it would be wrong to set too exacting a standard of police officers required to make rapid entry in pursuit of a suspected violent murderer', especially in the 'brief seconds available to [D]'.

In *Alleyne v Commr of Police*, facts previously, C sued for battery, false imprisonment (for the period from when he was handcuffed in the flat, to when he was examined by a medical officer and able to leave the police station over four hours later), and negligence. **Held:** only negligence was proven. The torts of assault/battery, and false imprisonment, had good defences under the statutory provisions. C was a 'decent man facing an unexpected rapid forcible entry into his flat and who later gave his son's whereabouts to the police', and was 'not obstructing, and did not intend to obstruct, the police officers from entering the flat and searching it', that it was 'instinctive to pull away when seized by a police officer in these circumstances'. However, the police officer, D, who restrained C, mistakenly believed that C was 'non compliant' and was seeking to obstruct the police officers by pulling away, and the police officer was attacked by a violent dog during the affray too. D's belief as to C's behaviour was mistaken, but reasonable. The defence was proven.

Prison confinement

A prisoner is lawfully held in prison under a court-imposed sentence, pursuant to statutory authorisation (per ss 12(1) and 13(1) of the Prison Act 1952).

In a false imprisonment claim, the onus of establishing that a detention is justified lies on the police, the prison Governor, or other detaining authority (per *Williamson v A-G of Trinidad and Tobago*[190]). The abovementioned provisions lawfully authorise the restraint of prisoners within the bounds of the prison, by authority of the Governor. In light of these principles, the tort of false imprisonment failed in the following cases:

In *Prison Officers Assn v Iqbal (Rev 1)*, facts previously, Cs' detention in the cell all day, during the prison officers' strike, was at the direction of the prison Governor, who issued the order not to allow prisoners out of their cells during the course of the strike, because she had no choice in the matter; the strike had forced her hand. That excused the Governor from the tort of false imprisonment. However, this action was not against the Governor, but against the striking prison officers. In the circumstances of an unlawful strike which was in breach of their employment contracts, this statutory defence was **not** available to the prison officers themselves. In *R v Deputy Governor of Parkhurst Prison; ex p Hague*, there was a conjoined appeal: Mr Hague was perceived to be a trouble-maker,

[187] [2008] 1 AC 962 (HL). [188] *ibid*, [136].
[189] [2012] EWHC 3955 (QB) [171]. [190] [2014] UKPC 29, [23].

and was segregated from other prisoners at Wormwoods Scrubs for 28 days. Mr Weldon was strip-searched and detained in a strip cell for a day. Both argued the tort of false imprisonment, but failed: '[p]lacing Weldon in a strip cell, and segregating Hague, altered the conditions under which they were detained, but did not deprive them of any liberty which they had not already lost when initially confined'.

On the other hand, if the Governor has **not** authorised C's particular confinement within the prison, then that can lead to a claim for false imprisonment against the prison officers – but apparently **not** against the Governor. The latter will be excluded from liability because, 'if the [prison] officer deliberately acts outside the scope of his authority, he cannot render the Governor or the Home Office vicariously liable for his tortious conduct', because 'a prison officer who acts in bad faith, by deliberately subjecting a prisoner to a restraint which he knows he has no authority to impose, may render himself personally liable to an action for false imprisonment ... Lacking the authority of the Governor, he also lacks the protection of section 12(1)' (per dicta in *ex p Hague*[191]). Hence, if a prisoner locks C, a co-prisoner, in a shed in the prison grounds, that would **not** be authorised by the Governor, and could give rise to a claim for false imprisonment against the fellow prisoner, but not against the Governor. Similarly, in *Prison Officers' Assn v Iqbal (Rev 1)*,[192] it was confirmed that, if prison officers detain prisoners wrongfully, then those officers can be liable for false imprisonment, even where the Governor is excused by s 13(1) of the Prison Act 1952. The Governor may have the benefit of the statutory defence, but the prison officers will not. Nevertheless, if the prison officers themselves do not carry insurance, then a successful claim in tort against those parties is hardly likely to recover for C any measure of damages. Moreover, the suggestion, in *ex p Hague*, that a Governor cannot be vicariously liable for the tort of the employed prison officer must be read in light of the more recent authorities on that subject (discussed in Chapter 18).

However, the statutory defence in the Prison Act does not necessarily provide a blanket protection for a prison Governor, when not releasing a prisoner from imprisonment. The fact that a detaining authority (or one of its employees), D, reasonably believed that it had the necessary authority to keep C in detention does not afford D any defence, where there was a duty to release C. In that case, the detention will be unlawful, and D will be liable for the tort of false imprisonment (per *Patel v Sec of State for the Home Dept*[193]).

In *R v Governor of Brockhill Prison, ex p Evans (No 2)*,[194] facts previously, **held:** the tort of false imprisonment succeeded, for the 59 days of wrongful detention. Where there was a duty to release C, the Prisons Act did not protect the Governor from that tort.

Recently, false imprisonment cases have arisen, in relation to those who have been subject to deportation orders, whether under s 36(1) of the Borders Act 2007 or otherwise. In both *Assad v Sec of State for the Home Dept*[195] and *R (Francis) v Sec of State for the Home Dept*,[196] claims for false imprisonment on the part of foreign nationals who were convicted of criminal offences, sentenced to a prison term, and recommended for deportation, failed, on the basis that, under different statutes, the Secretary of State had the authority to detain those parties.

[191] [1992] 1 AC 146 (HL) 164 (Lord Bridge). [192] [2009] EWCA Civ 1312, [2010] 1 QB 732, [28]–[31].
[193] [2014] EWHC 501 (Admin) [240]. [194] [2001] 2 AC 19 (HL).
[195] [2015] EWHC 2281 (QB). [196] [2014] EWCA Civ 718, [2015] 1 WLR 567.

Parental authority over children

Children may be punished by the application of force, or confined, by their parents, who are exercising parental authority and/or discipline. Although no child has sued his parent in tort in English law,[197] so far as the author's searches can ascertain, the point has been examined in the context of a *criminal prosecution* for false imprisonment in *R v Rahman*.[198] Some observations therein are helpful to the defence of lawful justification in this context.

According to *Rahman*, any restriction on the child's freedom of movement would only amount to false imprisonment if it were an unlawful restraint – which could occur where any of the following applied:

- the parent has acted in contravention of a court order;
- the parent acted in contravention of the other parent's lawful rights and wishes; or
- the constraint of the child by the parent was 'for such a period, or in such circumstances, as to take it out of the realms of reasonable parental discipline'.

> In *Rahman*, Rummana Rahman, C, came to England from Bangladesh with her mother and father (the father being D), when she was 2-years-old. Her mother returned to Bangladesh shortly thereafter, and C was fostered out by D, with the consent and assistance of the local authority. When 14 and attending school, C did not wish particularly to see D or to go away with him. On C's way to school, D approached and grabbed hold of her, and pushed her into the back of a car. C was told that she was going to Bangladesh with D in order to visit her sick grandmother (whom she did not know). C struggled, and screamed for help out of the car window, and was noticed by two policemen who were coincidentally nearby. D was searched, and two airline tickets to Dacca were found on him, one a return ticket for himself and the other a single ticket for C. D initially pleaded guilty to false imprisonment, but then appealed that conviction. **Held:** false imprisonment proven, and was not erroneous at law.

The Court of Appeal concluded that '[i]t hardly needs stating that a parent will very seldom be guilty of that offence in relation to his or her own child. The sort of restriction imposed upon children is usually well within the realms of reasonable parental discipline and is therefore not unlawful'.

However, whether in crime or in tort, those bounds of parental appropriate behaviour can be exceeded by extreme behaviour, bringing about the child's unlawful confinement.

Imminent breach of the peace

Where C's restraint by the police, D, is necessary in order to avoid an imminent breach of the peace, the restraint will be justified at common law, even where D did not reasonably suspect that C, *in particular*, was committing, or about to commit, a breach of the peace. D may lawfully take preventive action against persons other than those committing a breach of the peace – even if that results in the confinement of C, an 'innocent party'. Four criteria are required to prove the common law breach of the peace defence (per *Austin v Commr of Police*[199]):

[197] Some relevant Canadian authority has been mentioned, *viz*: *ADY v MYY* (1994), 90 BCLR (2d) 145 (SC).

[198] (1985) 81 Cr App R 349 (CA).

[199] [2007] EWCA Civ 989, [2008] QB 660, [35] (Sir Anthony Clarke MR), the list in the text paraphrasing/combining the elements referred to therein. To reiterate, *Austin* was further appealed, only as to whether the police had acted incompatibly with Art 5 of the ECHR (they had not): [2009] 1 AC 564 (HL).

i. the police have taken all possible steps to ensure that an imminent breach of the peace was avoided, and that the rights of innocent third parties were protected (e.g., making sure that proper preparations have been made to deal with such a breach);
ii. the police reasonably believed that there was no other way of preventing an imminent breach of the peace, except by containing C (as one of a crowd or group);
iii. given that the defence of breach of the peace is an instance of the defence of necessity, the defence can only apply, so as to lawfully justify a confinement, in 'truly extreme and exceptional circumstances';
iv. the police action 'must be both reasonably necessary and proportionate'.

The following two cases provide a useful contrast, based upon the abovementioned principles:

In *Austin v Commr of Police*, facts previously (concerning the police cordon around a crowd of about 3,000 demonstrators in Oxford Circus), **held:** the restraint of C and others by the police, D, was lawfully justified to prevent an imminent breach of the peace. Even though a majority of the crowd were neither committing a breach of the peace nor threatening to do so, and even though the period of confinement was lengthy at 7 hours, it was necessary, because there was no means by which the risk of serious injury to persons and property could have been avoided, other than by cordon, and the release policy adopted, i.e., to leave it to the discretion of D to free individuals who obviously had nothing to do with the demonstration, but who were caught up in the cordon by being at Oxford Circus at the wrong time. No notice of the demonstration had been given to D beforehand, and so there was no opportunity for D to formulate a plan of crowd control. It was not practicable for D to release the crowd collectively earlier than they did, and there was no different release policy which could have been adopted. Even though D clearly recognised that not everyone in the crowd was a demonstrator, they could not say who was, or was not, likely to cause a breach of the peace. Hence, the restraint used, in cordoning off the whole crowd, was reasonable and proportionate.

In *R (Laporte) v CC of Gloucester Constabulary*,[200] Jane Laporte, C, a peace protester, was one of 120 passengers on three buses going to a demonstration at an RAF base at Fairford in Gloucestershire. The police, D, had intelligence that there were likely to be some violent protesters on the buses, including some members of a group called the Wombles. D were concerned that, if they permitted the bus to reach Fairford, there would be a serious risk of violence, so they stopped and searched the buses. The passengers, including C, were escorted back to London, and were not allowed off before they reached London. D had concluded, from the intelligence and what was found on the buses, that a breach of the peace would have occurred at RAF Fairford. However, D admitted that there was the potential risk that some peaceful protesters were caught up in the decision not to allow the buses to proceed, because it was not possible to be certain who was, or was not, intent on direct action. **Held:** the breach of the peace defence was not available. D acted unlawfully in not allowing the protesters to proceed to the demonstration and in sending them back on the bus to London. D's actions could not be lawfully justified, unless a breach of the peace was 'imminent', which it was not, at the time of D's actions.

In the alternative, the provisions of the Public Order Act 1986 may provide authorisation for the police's acts of crowd control, as it includes (in ss 12–14) a power to bring a procession to an end, to direct an assembly to disperse along a particular route, or to order an assembly to stay in a particular place so long as necessary to effect that dispersal. Interestingly, these

[200] [2006] UKHL 55, [2007] 2 AC 105.

provisions were not relied upon by the police D in *Austin* – but were nevertheless criticised in that case: 'the exceptional circumstances of this case suggest that ss 12–14 of the Act require further consideration and perhaps amendment for the future'.[201]

Self-defence

§14.32 Where D has committed a common law assault or battery, then for self-defence to apply, D must both (1) have an honest and reasonable belief that he was going to be imminently attacked by C, and (2) have used reasonable, necessary and proportionate force to protect himself.

Self-defence is one form of justification, for an otherwise unlawful interference with the bodily integrity of C. The defence also applies where D's force is applied to C when defending others.

However, the justification falls away, and the defence will fail, if D uses disproportionate force to protect himself or others. What is proportionate or reasonable force is a question of fact. However, as the High Court of Northern Ireland put it poetically in *McAleer v PSNI*,[202] whilst there needs to be some balance between the degree of aggression posed by C and the defensive behaviour of D who commits the assault, the law does not require that D 'should very nicely measure the weight of the blows'. Nevertheless, it must be the minimum force necessary for D to protect himself from C's imminent attack. In both of the following cases, the defence failed because of the disproportionate force used.

In *McAleer*, the police were attempting to arrest a man in Omagh town who was lying on the ground. A crowd of 15–20 people were gathered around the police (of whom there were four), shouting abuse and behaving in a hostile manner. Nicola McAleer, C, joined the group as an observer, and was then hit twice on the upper thigh with a baton by a constable, D. C sustained severe bruising. Self-defence did not apply. The court believed D's evidence that C was pushing against her, and abusing her, and that she did not obey the instruction of the police to step back. However, D did not sufficiently control her wielding of the baton so as to ensure that the minimum force was applied to an appropriate area of C's body, and hence, the response to C's actions was disproportionate and unlawful. In *Lane v Holloway*,[203] Mr Lane, C, 64, lived in a 'quiet court', which backed onto a café run by Mr Holloway, D, 23. C objected to the sounds of a juke-box from the café, and to customers relieving themselves at night in the courtyard, and tensions with D were high. One night, D's wife told C and his neighbour to keep quiet, C retaliated, 'Shut up, you monkey-faced tart'. D objected to this insult to his wife, and came down, whereupon C threw a punch at D's shoulder. D retaliated with a severe blow with his fist to C's face, which caused him a severe eye injury. Self-defence did not apply, especially given the disparity in their ages. Also, D, 'in anger, went much too far. He gave a blow out of proportion to the occasion'.

Further, at common law, where D was mistaken about the imminent attack that he (wrongly) believed was about to happen, then whether D honestly believed that he was under threat from C is **not** enough to make out the defence. D's belief must have been reasonable too. Evidence from witnesses of fact, who were there at the relevant time, will invariably be helpful to assess whether D's belief that he was under threat from C was reasonable. Two cases may usefully be contrasted on this point:

[201] [2007] EWCA Civ 989, [2008] QB 660, [74]. [202] [2014] NIQB 53, [7]. [203] [1968] 1 QB 379 (CA) 387.

In *Cross v Kirkby*,[204] Mr Harry Cross, C, was emphatically anti-hunting, and sought to disrupt those activities, including the hunt in which Mr William Kirkby, D, was involved. C armed himself with a baseball bat, and confronted D in an almost hysterical state. C screamed at D, 'you're ****ing dead', and then jabbed him twice in the chest and the throat with the baseball bat. D wrestled the bat off C, and struck him once on the side of the head. This blow cracked C's skull, causing serious injury. **Held:** self-defence succeeded. D used the same implement that had been used by C against him, and from this, he knew that being struck with a hard wooden implement was likely to cause him serious injury. Also, witnesses who saw C's attack and D's response said that they considered that D must have thought that he was facing serious injury. D did not aim a blow, but hit C instinctively, and had 'only done what was necessary in the circumstances' to protect himself.

In *Bici v MOD*, facts previously, **held:** self-defence failed. The soldiers, D, did not reasonably believe that Fahri Bici was about to shoot at them. The evidence did not support the soldiers' version, that Mr Bici was about to fire upon them. For one thing, the track made by the bullet through Mr Bici's body was inconsistent with his being shot whilst aiming his weapon at the soldiers. Also, where the gun came to rest after Mr Bici slumped down was not likely if the gun had been pointed at the soldiers.

As explained in *Bici v MOD*, self-defence operates differently in tort than it does in the criminal law. In the latter, D's belief only has to be honest (per *R v Palmer*[205]). The criminal proceedings, *R v Williams (Gladstone)*[206] clarified, too, that, '[e]ven if the jury come to the conclusion that the mistake was an unreasonable one, if [D] may genuinely have been labouring under it, he is entitled to rely on it'. This inconsistency between tort and criminal law – which renders the defence harder to prove in tort – has been justified on two bases (per Lord Bingham in *Ashley*[207]):

i. there is no reason in principle why the same test of self-defence should apply in both tort and criminal law, given that 'the ends of justice which the two rules respectively exist to serve are different'. Criminal law is principally punitive, and tort law is predominantly compensatory; and
ii. the defence, as it operated in tort, had not caused dissatisfaction or injustice.

Contributory fault

§14.33 Although the law remains unsettled, the better view is that the defence of contributory negligence does not provide a partial defence to D, where D has committed an intentional trespass to the person against C.

Under s 1(1) of the Law Reform (Contributory Negligence) Act 1945, any 'fault' on C's part can invoke the application of the defence, so as to reduce the damages payable by D to C, where the 'fault' committed by C which could trigger the operation of the defence includes any negligent act, breach of statutory duty, or indeed, 'act or omission which ... would, apart from this Act, give rise to the defence of contributory negligence'.

The views upon whether contributory negligence is possible, where D is sued for a trespass to the person, have become quite variant in English case law. A time line demonstrates how this uncertainty has emerged (where 'CN' means 'contributory negligence'):

[204] [2000] EWCA Civ 426, [34].
[205] (1971) 55 Cr App R 223 (PC), cited in *Bici*, *ibid*, [42].
[206] [1987] 3 All ER 411 (CA).
[207] [2008] UKHL 25, [2008] 1 AC 962, [3].

The case lineage

1977 – in *Murphy v Culhane,*[a] Timothy Murphy, C, was hit on the head by John Culhane, D, with a plank, and died as a result. D was guilty of manslaughter. C's estate sued D for damages under the Fatal Accidents Act 1976; and D admitted the battery, but argued that C's death was caused partly by his own fault, because he had initiated the criminal affray. C had, in fact, gone to D's place with some others, with a view to beating up D. **Held:** C's damages could be reduced for CN under the 1945 Act, because his death 'might be the result partly of his own fault, and partly the fault of [D]'. C was 'responsible', in part, for his own injury. However, Lord Denning MR held that it was open to D to raise both illegality and *volenti.*

2000 – in *Reeves v Commr of Police,*[b] a 'fault' on C's part (necessary to trigger the CN defence) means any act or omission which would have given rise to that defence at common law, i.e., C's fault must, *before the 1945 Act,* have permitted D to plead the defence of CN. However, prior to the 1945 Act, CN could **not** provide a defence to an intentional tort such as trespass to the person. Hence, under the 1945 Act, if C attacked D, and D 'hit back', then no defence of CN applied, and C was entitled to recover in full from D.

2004 – in *Bici v MOD,*[c] Elias J called the conundrum of whether CN was available for trespasses to the person a 'knotty question', and that authorities were divided. However, he did not rule it out altogether, especially holding that it would be a 'very rare case' if damages should be reduced in circumstances where D's conduct was an intentional and unjustified trespass to C's person, and C's conduct was merely negligent.

2008 – in *Parmer v Big Security Co Ltd,*[d] Mr Parmer, C, was being removed from a Walkabout pub in Croydon for disorderly conduct, when the doorman, Mr Colby, D, pushed him against a railing; C toppled over it and was badly injured, suffering serious brain damage. CN of 30% was attributed against C, on the basis that he was partly 'responsible' for the sequence of events which occurred, resulting in his injury.

2008 – in *Ashley v CC of Sussex Police,*[e] Lord Scott remarked, in dicta, that 'the rules relating to contributory fault can come into play and provide a just result', where D is accused of battery.

2011 – in *Co-operative Group Ltd v Pritchard,*[f] Miss Deborah Pritchard, C, an employee, had a dispute with the manager of the store, Mr Neville Wilkinson, D, where she worked, because D refused to grant her a day's holiday leave because she felt unwell. C, her sister, and a friend, went to the store to remonstrate with D, and a heated argument followed, during which D took hold of C's arms. C claimed that D had committed a battery, causing her to suffer a severe psychiatric injury. **Held (3:0):** D committed a battery, and the defence of CN was **not** available, to reduce the damages that would otherwise be payable to C.

[a] [1977] 1 QB 94.
[b] [2000] 1 AC 360 (HL).
[c] [2004] EWHC 786 (QB) [111].
[d] [2008] EWHC 1414 (QB).
[e] [2008] UKHL 25, [2008] 1 AC 962, [20].
[f] [2011] EWCA Civ 329.

It is apparent, from the timeline above, that whether or not the defence of contributory negligence applies to a trespass to the person committed by D depends solely upon how 'fault' has been interpreted, by which to trigger the defence's application. If its application depends upon whether contributory negligence was available to D who had committed a trespass to the person **prior to** the 1945 Act coming into effect (as *Reeves* held), then the defence cannot apply. However, if it depends upon a *different* (and wider) interpretation of 'fault' – i.e., whether C was 'responsible', in part, for his own injury (per *Murphy v Culhane*) – then the defence is available, if C's conduct contributed to the sequence of events culminating in D's battery of C.

The Court of Appeal's decision in *Pritchard* (in which the Court aligned with the *Reeves* view) highlighted the competing arguments on this point very well, and they are presented in the Table below:

The competing arguments

Yes, C *can* be contributorily negligent:	No, C should *not* be contributorily negligent:
• CN is appropriate, where C obviously puts himself in danger's path, or provokes the battery that ultimately results: e.g., if C voluntarily participates in a riot which is being attended by riot police, with all the obvious dangers and risks that the event entails, then C can be taken to have failed to take reasonable care for his own safety (per *Wasson v CC of Northern Ireland*[a]); or in *Murphy v Culhane*, where C's husband visited D's premises planning to attack D, and D retaliated; • giving the word, 'fault', its ordinary or colloquial meaning means that C, who provokes D to commit an act of battery or assault against him (either by words or actions) was 'at fault', and it was Parliament's intention that this **would** be a circumstance where C's damages could be reduced to reflect the justice and equity of the case. This position seemingly has merit, where C's conduct towards D is 'provocative, verging on the intimidatory'. However, this argument was rejected by Smith LJ in *Pritchard*, given *Reeves*' interpretation of 'fault': 'I do not think that the law permits me to so hold'; • Smith LJ noted that she reached the view that CN was not available 'with regret', because 'I think that apportionment ought to be available to [D] who has committed the tort of battery, where [C] has, by his misconduct, contributed to the happening of the incident, for example by provocative speech or behaviour'.	• at common law, CN was **not** a defence to an intentional tort. There were no definitive cases, prior to the 1945 Act, in which CN had provided a defence to a claim for damages for assault or battery (Aikens LJ in *Pritchard*); • re cases since the 1945 Act, *Murphy v Culhane* was not binding on the CA, and was not to be followed, given that the question asked there was whether C was 'responsible' for his own damage. However, the modern approach (since *Reeves*) was to ask whether C's conduct could have given rise to CN at common law (Smith LJ in *Pritchard*); • in many cases since the 1945 Act, whether CN was available as a defence was not fully argued; and the 'line of authority' stemming from *Murphy v Culhane* (i.e., all that mattered was that C was 'responsible' in some way) had been accepted without questioning its legal basis (Smith LJ in *Pritchard*); • CN was not a defence to the intentional tort of deceit either (per *Alliance & Leicester Building Socy v Edgestop Ltd*[b]). Hence, for consistency's sake and logic, nor should CN be available for the intentional torts of assault and battery (especially when these torts can be proven by recklessness too) (Aikens LJ in *Pritchard*); • the decision in *Parmer* (2008), which permitted a finding of CN, did not result from contested legal argument; the application of CN was conceded by C (Smith LJ in *Pritchard*).

[a] [1987] NI 420 (HC).
[b] [1993] 1 WLR 1462 (CA) (Mummery LJ).

In the 2014 case of *McAleer v PSNI*,[208] the High Court of Northern Ireland noted that it agreed with Lady Justice Smith's views, but that the law 'compelled' a finding, in that case, that contributory negligence was not available to D, where D (the police constable in that case) had committed a trespass to C's person. Given the 'reluctance' with which lower courts are declining to hold that contributory negligence could apply, the issue clearly cries out for some Supreme Court clarification.

If the defence were to apply, then as with the application of the defence in negligence (discussed in Chapter 10), it would be necessary to have regard **both** to causation and to blameworthiness, when apportioning the respective percentages as between C and D, under the 1945 Act.

> In *Bici v MOD*,[209] facts previously, D argued that if C chose to travel in a vehicle with someone who he knew to be firing a rifle in a potentially provocative and dangerous manner towards UN peace-keeping soldiers, then C was acting recklessly and contributed to his own injury. Furthermore, C knew that there was an embargo on the use of guns, and that his companion (who was actually killed) had been firing an AK-47 just prior to the shooting. **Held:** CN did not apply, and even if it did, the apportionment against C should be nil. 'Any imprudence on [C's] part was dwarfed by the acts of the soldiers', and 'even assuming that [C's] imprudence could fairly justify the epithet "negligent", this would not be one of the exceptional cases where contributory fault should be found'.

Provocation

§14.34 The law remains unsettled as to whether the defence of provocation is a separate defence from that of contributory negligence, and which could provide a defence for D, where D has committed an intentional trespass to the person against C.

There are **three** possible legal approaches, where C's behaviour provokes D's battery, assault or false imprisonment against C – and all three have derived some support in authorities. As a result, the status of provocation in English trespass law has remained very cloudy. Dealing with the three different approaches in turn:

i. Reject provocation outright. In *Lane v Holloway*[210] (where C called D's wife a 'monkey-faced tart'), and in which D punched C hard in the eye causing severe injury to C, C sued D for battery. D alleged that C's injuries were provoked by C's rude behaviour. Lord Denning MR held that any provocation by C could **not** constitute a defence (either full or partial) to the tort of battery (although it could remove any entitlement to aggravated or exemplary damages, by 'taking away any element of aggravation'). Salmon LJ also 'entirely rejected' any suggestion that D should be afforded a partial defence because C had 'behaved badly'.

However, subsequently, a decade later, in *Murphy v Culhane*,[211] Lord Denning MR distinguished *Lane v Holloway*, noting that it was a case in which C's conduct was 'trivial', and D's conduct was 'savage'. The defence of provocation could apply, however, where C's conduct was more serious than trivial, so that it would be fair to take that behaviour into account in mitigation of the damages.

[208] [2014] NIQB 53, [18]–[19]. [209] [2004] EWHC 786 (QB) [109], [111].
[210] [1968] 1 QB 379 (CA) 388 (Lord Denning MR), 390 (Salmon LJ). [211] [1977] 1 QB 94 (CA) 98.

ii. Embrace provocation within contributory negligence, and hence to permit both (or neither) as a defence, depending upon the view adopted about contributory negligence. The more important feature of the 1977 case of *Murphy v Culhane* was that C's provocative behaviour could constitute contributory 'fault', sufficient for the 1945 Act to apply for D's benefit. After all, in that case, C and his friends had attended D's premises, intending to 'beat up' D, which was described as provocative behaviour, and a reduction of damages under the 1945 Act was permitted.

However, as noted in the previous section, *Murphy* was not followed by the Court of Appeal in *Pritchard*, in that contributory negligence was **not** available where D had committed a trespass to C's person. Indeed, in *Pritchard*, Smith LJ expressly referred to C's 'provocative speech or behaviour', and entirely aligned it with contributory negligence, which did not afford D any defence (albeit that she formed that view 'with regret'). Importantly, provocation was not differentiated from contributory negligence, either by Smith LJ or the other Court of Appeal judges. The non-availability of contributory negligence meant the similar non-application of provocation.

iii. Differentiate these as separate defences, and allow that, whilst contributory negligence may be unavailable as a defence, provocation could be permitted. Some judicial support for this third approach – i.e., to differentiate provocation from contributory negligence, and to permit the former as a defence, even if the latter is disallowed – is apparent from the 2014 decision of the Northern Ireland High Court in *McAleer v PSNI*.[212] As the most recent (albeit non-precedential) word on the subject, these views are of great interest.

Given that contributory negligence 'has made its exit from the stage of trespass to the person cases' (said the High Court), the defence of provocation could warrant a separate, and 'higher profile' application, when defending trespass to the person actions, suggested that court (by reference to academic writings[213]). After all, by engaging in such provocative conduct, C has 'brought the trespass on himself. It is, as it were, a contribution charged to him on account of his own fault', that, 'legal integrity demands that, in a case where [C] provokes [D] into a measure of excessive force, he should not be permitted to recover full damages against [that D]', and that '[i]s it fair, reasonable or just that a plaintiff's provocation should be ignored? I think not. Where there is a synergistic interaction between the behaviour of [C] and [D], it may be appropriate to proceed on the basis that both were causative of the damage suffered by [C]'. However, the Northern Ireland High Court noted that the application of provocation to trespasses to the person was 'a vexed area of law', in which reasonable opinion could differ, as it had among English judges and also amongst Commonwealth jurisdictions.

It is arguable that *Pritchard* says nothing about the availability of provocation for a trespass to the person, because it was only concerned with the application of contributory negligence. Hence, the issue must be regarded as being presently unsettled in English law.

Moreover, the question arises as to what D would need to prove, to establish that he was provoked by C into committing a battery. In *McAleer*, the court noted[214] that 'provocation' was defined by the Oxford English Dictionary as 'something that provokes anger or retaliation', signifying that D must have lost control in some way. If D cannot prove that, then the defence is unlikely to apply.

[212] [2014] NIQB 53, [20]–[31].

[213] Citing: J Goudkamp, (2011) 127 *LQR* 519, and *McGregor on Damages* (3rd Supp to the 18th edn, [37-009A].

[214] [2014] NIQB 53, [31].

In *McAleer*, facts previously, the police constable did not swing her baton in C's direction with any anger, retaliation or loss of control. Rather, D 'took a measured decision of crowd control by use of a baton in light of the conditions that obtained at that moment'. She was not 'provoked' in the true or legal sense of the word.

REMEDIES

For cases involving pleas of false imprisonment, jury trials are possible – and hence, courts have sought to provide juries with guidance as to the amount which juries should award for damages. The Court of Appeal explained, in *Heil v Rankin*,[215] that judicial guidance has two objectives: to achieve consistency among cases, and to substantiate the public perception of fairness (and restraint).

Guidance was given, in respect of false imprisonment, in the 1997 case of *Thompson v Commr of Police*[216] (e.g., £500 for the first hour of false imprisonment, with a reduced rate on a sliding scale for each hour thereafter; and exemplary damages, if awarded, should be somewhere in the range of £5,000–£50,000). In 2006, in *Rowlands v CC of Merseyside Police*,[217] that hourly amount was increased to £600, 'to allow for inflation', and the minimum level of exemplary damages was also inflation-adjusted to £6,000.

In *Thompson*, Mr Hsu, C1, had a lodger who complained to the police that C1 was wrongfully preventing her from collecting her possessions from his home. Two police officers came to C1's house, and arrested C1 when he attempted to prevent entry to the house. C1 complained of physical assault (including being placed in a head lock and punched in the face and back) and racial abuse. He was put in a cell for about an hour. In his absence, his house was entered, and as well as the belongings of the lodger being removed, some of his own property was missing. The police falsely recorded that the reason for C1's arrest was that C1 had pushed a police officer in the chest. C1 sustained PTSD. Separately, Ms Thompson, C2, was lawfully arrested for a drink driving offence to which she pleaded guilty; instead of being bailed, C2 was put in a cell, pushed and shoved, and her hair pulled out, and she suffered bruising and pain. C2 was tried for assault occasioning bodily harm (for allegedly biting a police officer's finger during the struggle), and acquitted. Both C1 and C2 brought successful claims of false imprisonment, assault and malicious prosecution – **£10,000** awarded globally for these torts for Ms Thompson by way of basic damages; and for Mr Hsu, an amount of **£20,000** for compensatory damages.

Dealing with the types of damages that have been discussed where trespasses to the person have occurred:

Compensatory damages

§14.35 The principal remedy for the torts of trespass to the person is compensatory damages. Both general and special damages are potentially available.

It is surprising, perhaps, how low the damages awards may be, for trespasses to the person. Especially in the case of assault, for apprehended injury, the awards can be very modest, as

[215] [2000] EWCA Civ 84, [26]. [216] [1997] EWCA Civ 3083, [1998] QB 498 (CA).
[217] [2006] EWCA Civ 1773, [2007] 1 WLR 1065, [26].

admitted in *Shah v Gale*: '[i]t is obviously important to ensure that these damages do not run out of line with the size of damages awarded for personal injury and ... subject to aggravation, they will sound only at a modest level'.[218] The examples below, of cases previously considered in this chapter, demonstrate this adage:

Quantum of compensatory damages awards

In *AT v Dulghieru*, each C was awarded general damages for PSLA, of **£82,000–£125,000**. Aggravated and exemplary damages were also awarded (see below). Each C also claimed special damages, equal to the sum for the cost of Trauma-Focused Cognitive Behavioural Therapy sessions, resulting from the PTSD and depressive conditions that each had suffered, but no evidence was put before the court to justify that, so no award was made under that head.

In *Lawson v Dawes (Decd)*, C was awarded **£78,500** for PSLA, to reflect that the torts involved multiple rape, a 3–4 day terrifying ordeal, and C's symptoms had persisted to some extent for 6–7 years. Past loss of earnings from her hairdressing salon, to which business C never returned after the incident, were assessed at **£94,000** (less earnings during that time, including an interview with the *Mail on Sunday*); the lost opportunity to pursue 'session modelling work' was assessed at **£30,000**; future loss of earnings were assessed at **£12,000** over the next 18 years; and loss of the sale of C's business (she ended up 'simply handing the keys back to the landlord', when the business 'melted away') was assessed at **£25,000**. That was not double recovery, as C had both the asset of the hairdressing salon, and the means to go on making a modest income from it, before the incidents giving rise to this litigation.

In *Rowlands v CC of Merseyside Police*, Mrs Rowlands, C, complained to police about a rowdy and noisy party across the road, and when the police attended, C was arrested for an altercation with the police. She was handcuffed, taken to the station, and detained there for about 90 minutes. She was tried for assaulting a police officer in the course of his duty, and acquitted. C sued the police successfully for assault, battery, false imprisonment and malicious prosecution. Basic damages of **£6,350** were awarded globally for all the torts.

In *Shah v Gale*, Mr Naresh Shah, C, 45, an accountant, was at his home in Hounslow when his front door burst open and he was attacked. C suffered at least seven stab wounds to his chest and back, and died. X was convicted of C's murder. However, Kelly Anne Gale, D, was acquitted of all charges. C's family were unhappy with that outcome of the criminal proceedings. D admitted that, albeit in error, she had pointed out C's home as the home of a man against whom X had a grievance. C's family sued D in assault and battery, for her role that led to his murder. This action succeeded. The compensatory damages awarded to C's estate had to reflect X's entry into C's home in a terrifying manner with the intent to inflict injury on him, and the physical discomfort, distress and inconvenience suffered by C in the short time between when C's home was unlawfully entered and the knife attack occurred (which led to almost-instant death). That was assessed at **£750**, even allowing for the terrifying features during this period.

In *McAleer v PSNI*, C recovered **£3,000** in general damages for bruising, sleep disturbances and anxiety arising from the battery.

[218] [2005] EWHC 1087 (QB) [53].

§14.36 Given that trespasses to the person are actionable *per se*, if C has not suffered actual damage, an award of nominal damages is appropriate to record the fact that the tort was proven.

Despite trespasses to the person being actionable *per se*, English courts have been slow to conclude that C suffered no real damage as a result. Indeed, in *Iqbal*, Smith LJ remarked that, for the tort of false imprisonment, 'the circumstances in which nominal damages would be appropriate are rare almost to vanishing point ... there should *always* be an award of damages based on normal compensatory principles'.[219]

Where C suffers battery resulting in a fairly rapid death, such a case is not suitable for merely nominal damages either, but for compensatory damages suffered due to the battery (per *Ashley*,[220] where C died within one hour of being shot by D, and where compensatory damages were capable of being awarded).

In *Prison Officers Assn v Iqbal*, facts previously, **held (at trial):** false imprisonment proven, but C was only awarded **£5**, on the basis that he had exaggerated the hurt to his feelings caused by the confinement, and because the decision that he had been falsely imprisoned provided him with 'just satisfaction'. **Held (on appeal):** this quantum of damage would have been increased to **£120**, had the tort been made out (on appeal, the tort failed).

In *Iqbal*, the trial judge's decision as to quantum was reversed unanimously, and criticised[221] on **three** bases:

i. The sum of £5 should be increased because C suffered 'real damage in being confined to a small cell throughout the day, rather than having the relative freedom of A Wing, while carrying out cleaning work, for three hours, getting some exercise for half an hour, working out for an hour or so and telephoning his mother. That would have been a genuine and significant loss of freedom, albeit within the confines of the prison'.
ii. There was no room for the operation of 'just satisfaction', when assessing compensatory damages at common law. It was a concept used by the European Court of Human Rights, but not in English common law.
iii. The mere fact that C may have exaggerated his distress self-evidently did not mean that C's damages should, consequently, be nominal. Real damage means substantial damages.

The guidelines given in *Thompson* were in respect of a person enjoying freedom of movement, not a person who was incarcerated in prison already. Hence, a lower figure than the £500 for the first hour of wrongful confinement was appropriate. The quantum for the prisoner, Mr Iqbal, was assessed as: 6 hours x £20 per hour of false imprisonment (although, to reiterate, Mr Iqbal ultimately failed in his claim on appeal, and recovered nothing for false imprisonment).

Finally, even though damage is not required to be proven to make out a trespass to the person, the reality remains that, where some damage is alleged, the court will need to be satisfied that there is a causal link between D's assault, battery, or false imprisonment, and C's damage. If some other factor caused C's damage, then that damage will not be compensated for (albeit that nominal damages will be awarded for a tort which is actionable *per se*).

[219] [2009] EWCA Civ 1312, [2010] 1 QB 732, [83]. [220] [2008] 1 AC 962 (HL) [60] (Lord Rodger).
[221] [2009] EWCA Civ 1312, [2010] 1 QB 732, [44]–[49] (Lord Dyson MR).

In *Co-operative Group Ltd v Pritchard*,[222] facts previously, **Held:** a battery was committed by D. However, C was angry and irritated before the assault, and had a history of depression, anxiety and panic attacks. The assault accelerated, by between 1–2 years, a psychiatric state, including agoraphobia, that C would have suffered in any event, even if there had been no assault. Hence, damages could only be awarded to C for that 1–2 year period.

§14.37 In actions for trespass to the person, damages may be awarded for *pure* mental distress falling short of a psychiatric injury. This is in contrast to an action on the case where no physical damage is suffered by C, where compensable injury will only be proven by C's suffering a recognised psychiatric injury.

In most cases, a battery will cause some physical bodily injury to C, and, possibly, some consequential mental distress too – all of that is recoverable. Hence, in *Thompson v Commr of Police*,[223] concerning battery and false imprisonment, one C (Mr Hsu) suffered a recognised psychiatric injury (PTSD), but the other C, Miss Thompson, suffered only mental distress, and could nevertheless recover damages for that injury.

However, some physical touching of C may have occurred so as to amount to a battery (as in the case of sexual abuse), but without any compensable physical *injury* arising. Even so, C has a right to compensation for the indignity, distress and humiliation caused by that sexual abuse, without the need to prove any recognised psychiatric injury arising. In *AB v Nugent Care Society*,[224] the Court of Appeal was dealing with a case concerning allegations of historic sexual abuse at a children's home, and where the joint expert opinion was that C had not suffered from any psychiatric injury from the alleged acts of abuse. Nevertheless, '[u]nlike a cause of action in negligence, a cause of action in trespass to the person does not require proof of physical or psychiatric damage ... It follows that, in cases involving the sexual abuse of young people ... an absence of immediate physical or psychiatric damage does not mean that the right to a significant award of damages has not arisen'.

In the case of a threatened battery (i.e., an assault) or a false imprisonment, it is quite likely that C has only suffered emotional distress, with no physical injury at all – and he may not suffer any recognised psychiatric injury either. In such cases, C is able to recover for that 'pure' mental distress, without the need to prove a recognised psychiatric injury.

There is plenty of appellate support for that proposition in English law. The Court of Appeal noted, in *Laing Ltd v Essa*,[225] that the distinction between psychiatric injury on the one hand, and injury to feelings or emotions falling short of a recognised injury on the other, is not adhered to in the tort of false imprisonment: '[i]t is only in certain torts, such as defamation or false imprisonment, that damages for injury to feelings may form an element in damages', where no physical injury is sustained. Furthermore, in *POA v Iqbal*,[226] false imprisonment was not made out – but had it been, the Court of Appeal was prepared to compensate C for the mental distress caused by the 6-hour confinement.

The reason for this more generous approach was reiterated recently by the High Court of Northern Ireland (which adopts the English law's view in this regard). The tort of assault (and of false imprisonment too) 'affords protection from the insult which may arise from interference with a person. Thus, a further important head of damage can be the injury to feelings i.e. the indignity, the mental suffering, disgrace and humiliation that may be caused. Damages may

[222] [2011] EWCA Civ 329, [2012] QB 320, [21]. [223] [1997] EWCA Civ 3083, [1998] QB 498.
[224] [2009] EWCA Civ 827, [2010] WLR 516, [108]–[109]. [225] [2004] EWCA Civ 2, [2004] IRLR 313, [117].
[226] [2009] EWCA Civ 1312, [2010] 1 QB 732.

thus be recovered by a claimant for an assault which in fact has done him no injury at all' (per *McAleer v PSNI*[227]). In other words, where the protection of the dignitary interests of C is at the very essence of these torts, then the justifications for excluding anything less than a recognised psychiatric injury are not as paramount, nor as justifiable.

Aggravated damages

§14.38 Aggravated damages may be awarded to C for trespass to the person in exceptional circumstances, to compensate for injury to feelings, distress or indignity suffered as a result of D's outrageous or deliberately-violent conduct.

The principles governing an award of aggravated damages – a form of compensatory damages – have been discussed in Chapter 11, and will not be repeated in detail herein. As always, the two matters governing such damages are their trigger; and their quantum.

Triggers. The types of factors which may yield an award in C's favour for false imprisonment may include: a lengthy term of detention; where the breaches and unlawful acts giving rise to that detention showed callous and deliberate behaviour on D's part; where D lacked any remorse or even acknowledgement of that behaviour; where D attempted to cover up knowledge of that behaviour; and the potentially very severe consequences to C (or his/her family) (per *Patel v Sec of State for the Home Dept*[228]). In *AT v Dulghieru*,[229] a case of assault, battery and false imprisonment, the court granted aggravated damages for the injury to feelings, humiliation, loss of pride and dignity, and feelings of anger or resentment caused by D's actions, given that D's actions (in trafficking C for prostitution) 'was so appalling, so malevolent, and so utterly contemptuous of [Cs'] rights as to amount to exceptional conduct warranting an award of aggravated damages'. These cases demonstrate that very exceptional circumstances will be required to trigger aggravated damages for trespass to the person.

There has been some dispute about whether aggravated damages **should** be available for trespasses to the person. The Court of Appeal stated, in *Richardson v Howie*,[230] that damages for injured feelings, indignity, mental suffering, distress, humiliation, anger, etc, would normally be included as part of the general (compensatory) damages awarded to C, and that 'it is no longer appropriate to characterise the award of damages for injury to feelings as aggravated damages, except possibly in a wholly exceptional case'.

As it has turned out, however, that ruling has not precluded aggravated damages. In *AT v Dulghieru*, aggravated damages were awarded because C would not be adequately compensated for injuries to feelings if the award were restricted to general damages. Further, in the *Omagh Bombing* case,[231] the Court of Appeal of Northern Ireland agreed with the authors of *McGregor on Damages*, that '[i]f the scale or the horror of the assault increases the injury to [C's] feelings, the damage is aggravated, and hence the damages are aggravated'. Some appellate authority has suggested that whether injured feelings, distress, humiliation, etc, are part of general damages or aggravated damages does not much matter: 'the important factor is that they are primarily intended to be *compensatory*, not punitive' (per *Rowlands v CC of Merseyside Police*[232]).

[227] [2014] NIQB 53, [32]. [228] [2014] EWHC 501 (Admin) [332]. [229] [2009] EWHC 225 (QB) [62] (Treacy J).
[230] [2005] PIQR Q3 (CA) [23]. [231] [2011] NICA 33, [148].
[232] [2006] EWCA Civ 1773, [2007] 1 WLR 1065, [26] (Moore-Bick LJ) (emphasis added).

Quantum. Aggravated damages are unlikely to be as much as twice the general damages, except where the basic damages were 'modest' (per *Thompson*[233]). This principle poses a significant ceiling on the award.

Where C is claiming damages which may be claimed at common law under general and/or aggravated damages, and also under the HRA where infringements of the ECHR are proven, then there must be no double recovery (per *Patel v Sec of State for the Home Dept*[234]).

In *Patel*, C was also entitled to damages under Arts 5, 8 and 14 of £40,000 – i.e., £20,000 for interference with her family life in relation to her six family members in the UK and three family members in India; £10,000 for interference with her private life; £7,000 for interference with her Art 5 rights; and £3,000 for interference with her Art 14 right. Those sums awarded under the HRA were additional to, and not overlapping, the sums awarded for general and aggravated damages.

Quantum of aggravated damages awards: examples

In *Thompson v Commr of Police*, successful claims of false imprisonment, assault, and malicious prosecution – **£10,000** awarded globally for these torts for Ms Thompson by way of aggravated damages; and for Mr Hsu, the amount of **£20,000** for compensatory damages included a component for aggravated damages;

In *Patel v Sec of State for the Home Dept*, successful claims of false imprisonment were made out, for immigration and detention issues – **£30,000** was awarded (where £20,000 was awarded in general damages);

In *Breslin v Mckevitt*, successful claims of battery – **£30,000** per C;

In *AT v Dulghieru*, successful claims for assault, battery and false imprisonment – **£30,000–£35,000** per C;

In *Rowlands v CC of Merseyside Police*, re successful claims for assault, battery, false imprisonment, and malicious prosecution – **£6,000** awarded on appeal;

In *Shah v Gale*, damages were not awarded for Mr Shah's murder *per se*, but for the period of apprehended battery, the 'very short time when one or more men entered [C's] home and put him in fear of being attacked; this is the only element of this terrible incident that falls for [aggravated damages]', and it 'was over very quickly' – **£2,000**.

Exemplary damages

It will be recalled, from the discussion in Chapter 11, that the function and purpose of exemplary damages is to punish D, rather than to compensate C. The principles governing their triggers will not be repeated herein, but a few specific comments, particularly relevant to trespasses to the person, are worthy of mention.

§14.39 Exemplary damages may be awarded for assault, battery or false imprisonment, where the award fits within one of the *Rookes v Barnard* categories.

According to Lord Devlin in *Rookes v Barnard*,[235] exemplary damages can be awarded in three circumstances:

[233] [1997] EWCA Civ 3083, [1998] QB 498 (CA). [234] [2014] EWHC 501 (Admin) [331].
[235] [1964] AC 1129 (HL) 1226–27.

i. Where they are necessary to punish 'oppressive, arbitrary, or unconstitutional action by servants of the government', or so as to mark 'an arbitrary and outrageous use of executive power'. To contrast two trespass cases:

In *Rowlands v CC of Merseyside Police*,[236] exemplary damages were awarded under this category, given the 'catalogue of misconduct' on D's part. The arresting police officer physically restrained C without any legitimate reason for doing so; handcuffed her and placed her in a police car; deliberately caused her unnecessary pain by tugging on the handcuffs while she was in the car; procured her continued detention by giving false information to the custody sergeant to ensure that she was charged with an offence which he knew she had not committed; and he gave false evidence at her trial in an attempt to secure her conviction. The combined [basic damages + aggravated damages] totalled [6,350 + 6,000] = £12,350. However, that amount was not sufficient to punish the police for their conduct towards C, hence exemplary damages were warranted. In *ZH v Commr of Police*,[237] however, no exemplary damages were awarded: '[w]hilst the police action was in my judgment hasty and ill-informed, it was not arbitrary and oppressive. The police acted in a misguided, but well intentioned, manner'.

ii. Where D's purpose is to make a profit from his tort, such that D acts with a cynical disregard for C's rights, and has calculated that money to be made out of his wrongdoing will probably exceed the damages at risk. Two cases may be contrasted:

In *AT v Dulghieru*, exemplary damages were awarded under this category, because D deliberately acted with a view to making profit for themselves, which profits were likely to be in excess of what could subsequently be recovered from them by any legal process. Their trafficking activities generated huge benefits, shown by confiscation orders in the criminal proceedings, totalling around £786,000 (and these orders did not preclude an award of exemplary damages). In the *Omagh Bombing case*, C argued that exemplary damages were available under the 'profit-making' category, because the IRA typically carried out spectacular acts of atrocity in order to attract funding, recruits and support. However, this scenario did not fit within the traditional profit-making scenarios recognised under Lord Devlin's category, and no exemplary damages were awarded.

iii. Where exemplary damages are specifically provided for by statute (so far as the author's searches can ascertain, no statutes are relevant in the context of trespasses to the person).

In *Broome v Cassell & Co Ltd*, Lord Diplock reiterated that exemplary damages were potentially available for assault, battery and false imprisonment.[238] In *Kuddus v CC of Leicestershire*,[239] the point was also made that, in the realm of *false imprisonment*, exemplary damages had a vital role 'in buttressing civil liberties', and that, where *assault and battery* are committed by those in positions of executive power (e.g., by police or prison officers) who use their executive power in an arbitrary and outrageous way, exemplary damages had an important role 'in vindicating the strength of the law'. Although English law has rejected the 'cause of action' test proposed in *AB v South West Water Services Ltd*,[240] that point was never as significant for trespass to the person as it was in negligence – for, as at 1964, exemplary damages **had** been awarded for trespasses to the person, and hence, their availability was never in issue, post-*Rookes v Barnard*.

[236] [2006] EWCA Civ 1773, [2007] 1 WLR 1065 (CA). [237] [2012] EWHC 604 (QB) [157].
[238] [1972] AC 1027 (HL) 1131. [239] [2001] UKHL 29, [2002] 2 AC 122 (HL) [63] (Lord Nicholls).
[240] [1993] QB 507 (CA).

However, it is notable that the quantum of exemplary damages awards, for what constitutes *intentional* torts to C's person, have been relatively modest in leading English cases to date:

Quantum of exemplary damages awards: examples

In *Thompson v Commr of Police* – **£25,000** for Ms Thompson (reduced from £50,000 at trial); and **£15,000** for Mr Hsu (reduced from £200,000 at trial), because 'the whole incident was over in a matter of hours, and there is already an award of aggravated damages which has to be taken into account', plus the reduced sum was sufficient to register the court's 'strongest disapproval of what occurred'.

In *Patel* – **£15,000**;

In *AT v Dulghieru* – **£15,000** per C;

In *Rowlands v CC of Merseyside Police* – **£7,500**. C, in this case, was subjected to a lesser degree of violence than was inflicted on Ms Thompson and Mr Hsu, and hence, the award of exemplary damages should reflect that.

Apart from disputes about quantum of awards, the principal disputes concerning the availability of exemplary damages for trespasses to the person, which have emerged in the case law to date, are noted below:

i. **Where C sustained no actual damage.** It will be recalled that assault, battery and false imprisonment, are all actionable *per se*, i.e., without proof of actual damage. This means that it is possible that there will be no award of compensatory damages made to C. Can C still obtain an award of exemplary damages?

   On the one hand, the 'if and only if' principle would suggest 'yes', because no 'punishment' at all has been inflicted on D, if only nominal damages were awarded to C – so some award of exemplary damages would be warranted. Further, in *Lumba*, C was awarded nominal damages for the false imprisonment committed by the Government – and yet it was accepted by the Supreme Court that exemplary damages could be awarded to C (ultimately they were not, but the fact that C had received nominal damages was **not** one of those reasons).

   On the other hand, *Watkins v Secretary of State for the Home Dept*[241] – a case of misfeasance in public office – suggests that it is **not** possible for an award of exemplary damages where C (a prisoner in that case) had suffered no material damage. The House of Lords held that the law of tort should not be developed, so as to award exemplary damages solely for the purpose of punishment, in cases where C suffered no actual damage that would attract a compensatory award.

   Hence, although the position is somewhat unsettled, the better, and more authoritative, view is that exemplary damages are available, even where C receives only nominal damages for the trespass committed against him.

ii. **The categories of Lord Devlin should be expanded/superseded.** It may be impossible to prove that D was a public official or acting in the exercise of a public power, or that D was acting with a profit-making motive – and yet, the nature of D's trespasses to C's person was flagrant, deadly and brutal.

[241] [2006] 2 AC 395 (HL).

Nevertheless, courts have been unwilling to expand the availability of exemplary damages beyond Lord Devlin's three categories. Even the most horrific acts of trespass have not moved appellate judges to consider an expansion of those categories. The reasons usually postulated for this conservatism are: (1) the 'anomalous nature of the remedy', and (2) the fact that the availability of such damages have borne a 'longstanding restriction to very limited types of case by the highest judicial authority' (per *Breslin v Mckevitt (the Omagh Bombing case)*).

In the *Omagh Bombing case*,[242] facts previously, C argued that the batteries committed were part of a 'widespread and evermore brutal terrorist campaign' which 'led to death, serious injury and destruction', that the Omagh bombing 'was a continuation of other similar terrorist conduct', and that the bombing 'involved a deliberate disregard for the safety of ordinary people and a flagrant rejection of civilised and legal order and of the human rights of people who might be killed or injured by this conduct'. **Held:** exemplary damages were not awarded. None of the *Rookes v Barnard* categories was met, and there was no ground for extending their availability, even in this scenario where '[i]t is difficult not to have considerable sympathy for [C's] submission'.

Additionally, whether exemplary damages should be awarded against a *vicariously*-liable D is another legal 'hotspot', and is considered later in the chapter (online).

Vindicatory damages

§14.40 Vindicatory damages compensate C for the violation of his constitutional rights by D. The position is presently unsettled in English law, as to whether vindicatory damages are available for trespasses to the person, where the trespass concerns a violation of C's constitutional rights.

As Lord Bingham stated in *Ashley v CC of Sussex Police*, 'it is not the business of the court to monitor the motives of the parties in bringing ... what is, on the face of it, a well-recognised claim in tort'.[243] C's motive may well be to seek vindication for a strong sense of grievance or bitterness.

In *Ashley*,[244] the House of Lords upheld vindication as a purpose of tort law: '[a]lthough the principal aim of an award of compensatory damages is to compensate [C] for loss suffered, there is no reason why an award of compensatory damages should not also fulfil a vindicatory purpose'. Their purpose, though, is *compensatory* and not punitive – they are 'not to teach the executive not to misbehave. The purpose is to vindicate the right of [C], whether a citizen or a visitor, to carry on his ... life, ... free from unjustified executive interference, mistreatment or oppression' (per the Privy Council in *Merson v Cartwright (Bahamas)*[245]).

In *Merson v Cartwright*, Tamara Merson, C, succeeded in her suit against the Bahamian police for assault and battery, false imprisonment, malicious prosecution, and contravention of her constitutional rights. The Privy Council approved an award of **$100,000** by way of vindicatory damages, for the conduct of the Bahamian police and the A-G of the Bahamas. The award was 'high, but within the bracket of discretion available to the judge'.

The concept of vindicatory damages was apparently postulated by the Court of Appeal of Trinidad and Tobago in *AG of Trinidad and Tobago v Ramanoop*, 'as a head of loss in claims

[242] [2011] NICA 33, quote at [139]. [243] [2008] UKHL 25, [2008] 1 AC 962, [4].
[244] [2008] UKHL 25, [22] (Lord Scott). [245] [2005] UKPC 38, [18].

for breach of constitutionally protected rights and freedoms'.[246] Albeit that the United Kingdom does not have a written constitution, the question arises as to whether vindicatory damages are available where a trespass to the person is committed by the State against C, e.g., where the decision 'is taken at the highest level of Government to detain certain people, irrespective of the statutory purpose of the power to detain' (as Lady Hale put it, in *Lumba*[247]). If they are, then vindicatory damages would be particularly available in respect of the conduct of police, government officials, or prosecution authorities.

However, whether (and when) vindicatory damages are available for a trespass to the person is quite unsettled, on the present state of English law.

View #1. On the one hand, where D's trespass to C's person has caused a violation of a constitutional right, then some judicial opinion is that vindicatory damages should be available to C.

In *Ashley v CC of Sussex Police*,[248] Lord Scott stated, in dicta, that an award of vindicatory damages would be appropriate where a battery was committed by the police which caused C's death. In *Lumba (Congo) v Sec of State for the Home Dept*,[249] Lords Hope and Walker, and Lady Hale, supported an award of vindicatory damages: 'the conduct of the officials in this case amounted ... to a serious abuse of power and it was deplorable. It is not enough merely to declare that this was so. Something more is required, and I think that this is best done by making an award of damages that is not merely nominal'. Lords Hope and Walker assessed vindicatory damages at £1,000 per C, whilst Lady Hale preferred a lower award of £500, as a 'modest conventional sum'.

View #2. On the other hand, in *Lumba*,[250] other members of the majority rejected the concept of vindicatory damages for trespass to the person. Lords Dyson, Collins and Kerr considered that nominal damages would be sufficient for C. The introduction of vindicatory damages was termed, by Lord Dyson MR, as akin to 'letting ... an unruly horse loose on our law'. Three reasons were given:

- it was a 'big leap' to award vindicatory damages in any private claim against the executive;
- the limits of vindicatory damages was unclear: '[t]he implications of awarding vindicatory damages in the present case would be far-reaching. Undesirable uncertainty would result. If they were awarded here, then they could in principle be awarded in any case involving a battery or false imprisonment by an arm of the state. Indeed, why limit it to such torts? And why limit it to torts committed by the State?';
- the purpose of vindicatory damages was unclear, in that they were unnecessary and unjustified. Vindication was already available for C, via a combination of compensatory and exemplary damages.

Lord Collins was equally emphatic: '[n]or do I consider that the concept of vindicatory damages should be introduced into the law of tort. In truth, despite the suggestions to the contrary by the Privy Council in ... *Merson*, vindicatory damages are akin to punitive or exemplary damages'.

246 As noted in: *Lumba v Sec of State for the Home Dept* [2011] UKSC 12, [2012] 1 AC 245, [97] (Lord Dyson MR).

247 [2011] UKSC 12, [2012] 1 AC 245, [216]. Also: [97]–[99] (Lord Dyson).

248 [2008] AC 962 (HL) [23].

249 [2011] UKSC 12, quote at [176] (Lord Hope). All three were members of the 9-bench majority in this case.

250 [2011] UKSC 12, [2012] 1 AC 245, [101] (Lord Dyson MR), [237] (Lord Collins), [256] (Lord Kerr). Lord Phillips, a dissenting judge who considered that C's detention was not unlawful, agreed with Lord Collins' decision that vindicatory damages were not available (at [335]).

Furthermore, there was no proper analogy to be drawn between the conventional sum awarded in *Rees v Darlington Memorial Hospital NHS Trust*[251] (by which to register the violation of C's personal autonomy resulting from a failed sterilisation), and the award of vindicatory damages for a trespass to the person. Consequently (said Lord Collins), there was no basis 'in the present law' or 'in policy' for vindicatory damages. Lord Kerr considered that vindicatory damages should only be available in very limited circumstances, and only where other damages 'provides insufficiently emphatic recognition of the seriousness of [D's] default. That situation does not arise here. [D's] failures have been thoroughly examined and exposed'.

Hence, the position is presently unsettled as to whether vindicatory damages are available to C, in respect of a trespass to the person that also constitutes a serious infringement by an arm of the state.

[251] [2003] UKHL 52, [2004] 1 AC 309 (HL).

15

Defamation

INTRODUCTION

§15.1 Defamation enables C to obtain a remedy for injury to his reputation which is usually caused by D's written publications or oral statements. Defamation consists of two separate torts – libel and slander – a distinction which retains some limited significance in the modern English law of defamation.

Framework for the tort

Defamation can have a long-term effect – a 'propensity to percolate through underground channels and contaminate hidden springs' of C's reputation (per *Slipper v BBC*[1]). It is a technically difficult tort, in which the defences available to D assume equal, if not greater, prominence in the judgments as do the elements of the cause of action itself. The Defamation Act 2013, which took effect on 1 January 2014, overruled aspects of the common law, but preserved other aspects, adding to the complexity of the tort. Wherever the publication complained of began in 2013 and continues into 2014, the court is now likely to have to consider the position both at common law and under statute (per *Donovan v Gibbons*[2]).

The tort's framework is outlined below:

Nutshell analysis: Defamation

Pre-requisites:

i Identifying libel or slander
ii The matter is justiciable
iii A 'real and substantial tort' and 'serious harm'
iv Capacity of C to sue

Elements:

1 D made a defamatory imputation
2 The defamatory imputation identified C
3 The defamatory imputation was published

[1] [1991] 1 QB 283 (CA) 300. [2] [2014] EWHC 3406 (QB) [4].

Defences:

- Honest opinion (fair comment)
- Truth (justification)
- Peer-reviewed statements in scientific and academic journals
- Innocent dissemination
- Public interest (formerly *Reynolds*) privilege
- Common law qualified privilege
- Reportage
- Absolute privilege
- Consent and acquiescence
- Offer of amends

C bears the burden of proving the elements of the cause of action. It is common for D to plead a number of defences in a given fact situation, for which the burden lies upon D.

The tensions and complexities in defamation

Although the elements of the tort of defamation are easily stated, their application to fact scenarios can be difficult, as Lord Phillips pointed out in *Joseph v Spiller*:

> Over 40 years ago Diplock LJ in *Slim v Daily Telegraph Ltd*[3] referred to 'the artificial and archaic character of the tort of libel'. Some 20 years on Parker LJ in *Brent Walker Group plc v Time Out Ltd*,[4] commented on the absurdity of the 'tangled web of the law of defamation'. Little has occurred in the last 20 years to unravel the tangle.[5]

The tension in the tort is readily apparent. C wishes his reputation to be protected to the extent that the law will permit it. D wishes to invoke the freedom of expression which hallmarks a democratic society, to the extent that the law will permit it. Hence, the defences available in defamation are of particular import, as they mark out the restrictions upon 'free speech' which the law countenances.

Overarching these difficulties is the need for English courts to consider Strasbourg jurisprudence regarding the ECHR, to ensure that the common law of defamation properly takes account of Convention rights. On the one hand is Art 10: 'Everyone has the right to freedom of expression. This right shall include freedom to hold opinions and to receive and impart information and ideas without interference by public authority and regardless of frontiers'. For example, in *Thoma v Luxembourg*,[6] it was pointed out that the press 'plays an essential role in a democratic society', reporting information on matters of public interest, and acquitting its 'vital role' as 'public watchdog'. On the other hand is Art 8: 'Everyone has the right to respect for private life'. According to *Joseph v Spiller*,[7] reputation is firmly within the ambit of Art 8. In other words, reputation is but one aspect of privacy. In that case, Lord Phillips considered that the potential conflict between Arts 8 and 10 was 'obvious', and

[3] [1968] 2 QB 157 (CA) 171. [4] [1991] 2 QB 33 (CA) 46.
[5] [2010] UKSC 53, [2011] 1 AC 852, [2]. [6] (2003) 36 EHRR 21 (ECtHR) [45].
[7] [2010] UKSC 53, [75]. Also: *Pfeifer v Austria* (2007) 48 EHRR 175 (ECtHR) [35], [38].

'the fact that each right is qualified means that the law must strike an appropriate balance between the two'.

The scenarios which give rise to defamation in English law frequently involve politicians or sporting figures on the one hand, and the press on the other, both of whom may be well-resourced and willing to litigate issues (whether interlocutory or final) of real complexity. For example, in the recent case of *Yeo v Times Newspapers Ltd*,[8] the headline of D's newspaper article proclaimed, 'Top Tory in new Lobbygate row', where the article concerned a lunch meeting between journalists posing as consultants to a Far Eastern solar company and Mr Yeo MP, which was covertly filmed. Three different defences were pleaded by the newspaper, and two interlocutory applications were heard within six months of each other. When modern surveillance methods are added to the complexity which internet technology and twitter and blog communications represent, the emergence of a new 'breed of publisher' associated with 'internet libel', the differences or connections that may exist between online and print versions of articles, and the need to ensure that domestic law harmonises with the ECHR – the tort has assumed considerable legal difficulty.

The enactment of the Defamation Act 2013 ('the 2013 Act') which overlays, and at times reverses, the common law, has added a further layer of complexity. In March 2011, the Ministry of Justice published its *Draft Defamation Bill Consultation*,[9] which purported to deal with concerns about the 'chilling effect' which the current law on defamation was having upon freedom of expression.

The law reform corner: **Statutory reform**

The Draft Bill proposed to amend defamation, to rebalance the 'chilling effect' on freedom of expression, by:

- a new requirement of a threshold of causing 'substantial harm' before a statement could be defamatory;
- a new public interest defence, re 'publication on a matter of public interest', wider than the *Reynolds* defence;
- a new statutory 'truth' defence, where key elements of the common law justification defence would be clarified;
- a new statutory 'honest opinion' defence, where elements of the 'fair comment' defence would be clarified;
- new provisions updating and extending the defences of absolute and qualified privilege;
- the introduction of a 'single publication rule', to prevent an action being brought in relation to publication of the same material by the same publisher after the one-year limitation period had passed;
- provisions dealing with 'libel tourism'; and
- removal of presumption of a jury trial (i.e., a court must decide whether a jury trial is in the interests of justice).

[8] [2015] EWHC 209 (QB).

[9] CP3/2011 (Cm 8020), especially, 'Executive Summary', pp 5–6, and 'The Proposals', pp 8ff. The author was a member of an earlier Ministery of Justice/Civil Justice Council Working Group, established to consider the terms and effect of the draft Defamation Act 2010.

The 2013 Act embodies these proposals.

Ancillary actions

In an appropriate scenario, C may claim that the words of which he complains are not only defamatory, but also that they constitute a malicious falsehood. That latter action requires proof that: (1) D's statement was false; (2) D's statement referred to C's goods; (3) D published the statement; (4) D acted with malice; and (5) the statement either caused actual damage or was calculated to cause C financial loss (pecuniary damage). Having to prove malice may make malicious falsehood a more difficult tort to establish than defamation (per *Thornton v Telegraph Media Group Ltd*[10]). Of course, D may have acted with malice in publishing a defamatory imputation, but it is not a necessary element of defamation, and merely impacts upon some defences which may otherwise have applied. Malicious falsehood, like defamation, also involves Art 10's freedom of expression; but unlike defamation, does not involve Art 8, but rather, the right to protection of property (the First Protocol, article 1) (per *Ajinomoto Sweeteners Europe SAS v Asda Stores Ltd*[11]).

The law of privacy (see 'Privacy', an online chapter) may also overlap with the law of defamation, albeit that '[t]he relationship between defamation and the new cause of action of misuse of private information is not yet clear' (per Tugendaht J in *Terry (LNS) v Persons Unknown*[12]).

PRE-REQUISITES

Establishing libel or slander

Libel and slander are two different torts ('the two causes of action of a different genus', per *Barber v Pigden*[13]). Although appropriately treated, generically, as defamation – given that their elements, and the defences applicable thereto, are virtually identical – their distinction retains importance for two reasons. The requirement of proof of damage differs between them, and libel can constitute a crime whereas slander cannot (discussed further below).

The law reform corner: **Libel versus slander**

- the distinction between libel and slander has been statutorily abolished in some jurisdictions (e.g., Defamation Act 1992 (NZ), ss 2(1), 4; Defamation Act 2005, s 7 (NSW), and enacted in various other Australian States too);
- the Faulks Committee recommended that the distinction be abolished, because it was 'entirely attributable to historical accident, ... carrying a host of rules and exceptions, derived partly from precedent and partly from statute, which are illogical, difficult to learn, and ... [t]o an outsider, at least, appear contrary to normal precepts of justice';[14] whereas the Porter Committee wished to retain the distinction, to avoid 'trivial but costly litigation' and 'frivolous actions' if slander were treated as generously as libel.[15]

[10] [2010] EWHC 1414 (QB) [41]. [11] [2010] EWCA Civ 609, [2011] QB 497, [10], [28].

[12] [2010] EWHC 119 (QB) [96], quote at [78]. [13] [1937] 1 KB 664 (CA) 670.

[14] *Report of the Committee on Defamation* (Cmnd 5909, 1975) 20–21.

[15] *Report of the Committee on the Law of Defamation* (Cmnd 7536, 1948) [40], and cited *ibid*, 19, a claim which the Faulks Committee rejected as being most unlikely.

The distinction

§15.2 A libel is an act of defamation in permanent (usually written) form, whereas slander is an act of defamation in transient (usually spoken) form. Alternatively, libel is addressed to the eye, whereas slander is addressed to the ear.

One test for distinguishing between the two turns upon permanence versus transience. According to Lopes LJ in *Monson v Tussauds Ltd*, as well as publications in the form of printed matter or in handwriting, libels can comprise 'a statue, a caricature, an effigy, chalk marks on a wall, signs, or pictures'.[16] Slander, on the other hand, arises from the publication of a statement by gestures, spoken words or other sounds – something more transitory in nature. Given how frequently permanence can be achieved by modern technology, actions for slander have been remarked upon as being 'relatively rare (per *Smith v ADVFN plc*[17]) and 'relatively uncommon' (per *Maccaba v Lichtenstein*[18]). As an alternative test, it has been suggested that libel is addressed to the eye and slander to the ear (per *Youssoupoff v Metro-Goldwyn-Mayer Pictures Ltd*[19]).

Libel	Slander
• In *Youssoupoff v MGM Pictures Ltd*, the film, *Rasputin, The Mad Monk*, purported to depict the life of Rasputin, and it also portrayed that Princess Irina Alexandrovna of Russia had been raped or seduced by Rasputin (imputing unchastity by a married woman). The movie film was in a permanent form, because it consisted of a series of negatives linked together on a spool which could be projected on to a screen for an audience to see and hear time and again, and the spoken words accompanying the film were part of that defamatory matter ('part of the surroundings explaining that which is to be seen'). • In *Smith v ADVFN plc*,[a] a posting on a bulletin board (an online discussion forum), under a pseudonym, alleged that Smith was a scrounger, a bankrupt and a racist. This is libel, although Eady J analogised bulletin board discussions with 'casual conversations' which may be 'uninhibited, casual, ill thought out' and much like conversational 'repartee'. • In *Monson v Tussauds Ltd*,[b] Mr Monson, C, had been tried in Scotland for a shooting murder, with the verdict, 'not proven'. At an exhibition of wax figures at Madame Tussauds, in	• In *Clynes v O'Connor*,[c] a 'shouting match' occurred between neighbours, where one called the other a 'wife beater' and a 'drug dealer'. • In *Reachlocal UK Ltd v Bennett*, phone messages were left on C's customers' voicemails, accusing C of misrepresentations, deceit and 'scamming'. • In *Andre v Price*,[d] D made comments to a live studio audience on the Graham Norton show about her estranged husband, suggesting that he was a hypocrite and a liar.

[a] [2008] EWHC 1797 (QB).
[b] [1894] 1 QB 671 (CA).
[c] [2011] EWHC 1201 (QB).
[d] [2010] EWHC 2572 (QB).

[16] [1894] 1 QB 671 (CA) 692. [17] [2008] EWHC 1797 (QB) [16] (Eady J).
[18] [2004] EWHC 1580 (QB) [10]–[13] (Gray J). [19] (1934) 50 TLR 581 (CA) 587 (Slesser LJ).

Libel	Slander
London and in Birmingham, there were various wax effigies representing notorious murderers, and relics and models of the scenes of murders, in a room, 'Chamber of Horrors', which included an effigy of C with the gun, the clothes and a model of the scene. • In *Robinson v Chambers*,[e] D read aloud from a script, which was a libel. • In *Cooper v Turrell*,[f] D left a voicemail (a recorded message on C's solicitor's recording device), which was 'plainly a libel'.	• In *McManus v Beckham*,[g] D told customers in C's shop not to buy an autographed photograph of her husband, David Beckham, as 'they are all fakes', and that she did not want to see the customers 'being ripped off'.

[e] [1946] NI (No 2) 148, and cited in Irish Law Reform Comm, *Civil Law of Defamation* (CP 3, Mar 1991) 5.
[f] [2011] EWHC 3269 (QB) [78].
[g] [2002] EWCA Civ 939, [2002] 1 WLR 2982.

Unfortunately, the two tests will not always produce the same result. For example, voicemails are addressed to the ear, but are in permanent form – and were treated as potential slander by HHJ Richard Parkes QC in *Reachlocal UK Ltd v Bennett*,[20] but were said to be libel by Tugendhat J in *Cooper v Turrell*.[21] Other scenarios can pose difficulties too. If 'chalk on a wall' was considered by Lopes LJ to be a libel in *Monson*, then sky-writing a message, or writing in invisible ink which becomes briefly apparent when heat is applied, would constitute libels too (the former because 'the vapour takes some little time to disperse', said the aforementioned Faulks Committee); whereas sign language would constitute slander. Of course, the alternative test of 'libel to the eye, and slander to the ear', would mean that sign language was indeed libel.

Inevitably, the distinction between libel and slander has been blurred by various technological advances by which the spoken word or performance can achieve permanence. In light of this, some statutory provisions have designated some publications to be one category or the other, to avoid confusion.

Under the *Broadcasting Act 1990, s 166* (formerly Defamation Act 1952, s 1), 'the publication of words in the course of any programme included in a programme service' (where a programme service is defined by s 201 to cover TV, radio and digital broadcasts) shall be treated as publication in permanent form (i.e., as libel). Pursuant to the *Theatres Act 1968, s 4*, 'the publication of words' (defined to include pictures and gestures) in a play are to be treated as publications in permanent form (i.e., libel), but the Act does not apply to domestic performances of plays in private dwellings, play rehearsals, or performances to enable records and broadcasts to be made.

Its modern importance

While the distinction between libel and slander was 'not based upon principle but on historical grounds',[22] it retains importance in modern defamation law for two reasons.

[20] [2014] EWHC 3405 (QB) [21]. [21] [2011] EWHC 3269 (QB) [78].
[22] *Meldrum v ABC Co Ltd* [1932] VR 425 (SC) 430–31 citing: Holdsworth's History of English Law, Vol 8, 333–36.

§15.3 Libel is actionable *per se*, i.e., without proof of 'special damage'. On the other hand, the general rule is that, in the case of slander, C must prove that he suffered some 'special damage'. Slander is only actionable *per se* in stipulated exceptional circumstances.

C is presumed to have suffered some damage, where a libel has occurred – proof of damage is not an element of that cause of action. In reality, if no injury to C's reputation can be shown from the publication of a libel, then damages may be awarded for other reasons, e.g., to vindicate C, or to reiterate to others that C's reputation was unfairly sullied. However, theoretically at least (and subject to the requirement of a 'substantial tort' and the statutory 'serious harm' requirements, discussed below), nominal damages may be awarded for a libel (e.g., a parent company was recently awarded nominal damages of £100 for libel, where substantial damages were awarded separately to its subsidiary company, in *Reachlocal UK Ltd v Bennett*[23]).

For the purposes of slander, 'special damage' means that some specific *pecuniary loss* must have been suffered by C, as a result of the slanderous words (per *Sanders v Percy*[24]). Actual pecuniary loss is typically measured by a loss of income, i.e., the actual loss of money to C's 'hip-pocket'. Note that it is not proven by pointing to some injury or damage which could be measured by a monetary award – it certainly does not include damages for injury to business reputation, even though a monetary figure may be put on that (per *Lonrho plc v Fayed (No 5)*[25]). Rather, special damage is shown, e.g., where, say C lost customers,[26] or business or profit,[27] or valuable contracts,[28] as a result of the slander. If no special damage can be alleged, then no action can proceed (unless one of the exceptional categories applies).

Why does the law draw this distinction between libel and slander? In the early 1892 case of *Ratcliffe v Evans*,[29] Bowen LJ summed up the difference: where D publishes defamatory matter in permanent form, on paper or in print, then it inevitably is 'more permanent and more easily transmissible than oral slander', and hence, more likely to cause C damage – so the law more readily 'presumes, and in theory allows, proof of general damage'. Even earlier, in the 1829 case of *Clement v Chivis*,[30] the fact that libel should be actionable *per se* (whereas slander was not) was also justified because 'written slander' (as it was called then) 'is premeditated, and shows design', whereas slander often occurs in a heated 'off-the-cuff' exchange. For these reasons, English law has long been reluctant to presume damage for the more transitory slander.

Before turning to the two exceptions whereby slander is still actionable *per se*, it is worth noting that not one, but two, former exceptions, were overruled by s 14 of the Defamation Act 2013.

i. A slanderous imputation by D that C was suffering from some contagious or infectious disease was actionable *per se* – but that was a common law-created exception that seemed to have emanated from a different age. For example, in *Kerr v Kennedy*,[31] a slander falsely imputed that an author had leprosy. That was said to be 'so intrinsically outrageous that they ought to be actionable even if no pecuniary loss results', because that author (per Asquith LJ) 'may suffer no falling-off in his sales – his sales may rise – but he will be shunned and avoided'. As the *Explanatory Notes* to the Defamation Act 2013 note, the exception also applied in

23 [2014] EWHC 3405 (QB) [34]. 24 [2009] EWHC 1870 (QB) [9]. 25 [1993] 1 WLR 1489 (CA) 1501.
26 *Hopwood v Thorn* (1849) 137 ER 522 (CCP) (but no loss of custom here).
27 *English and Scottish Co-Op Prop Mortgage Socy Ltd v Odhams Press Ltd* [1940] 1 KB 440 (CA) 454–55.
28 *Lonrho plc v Fayed* [1993] 1 WLR 1489 (CA) 1508.
29 [1892] 2 QB 524 (CA) 530. 30 (1829) 109 ER 64 (KB) 174. 31 [1942] 1 KB 409 (KB) 411.

old cases where it was imputed that C had the plague, and venereal disease.[32] However, by virtue of s 14(2) of the Defamation Act 2013, C must now prove that he suffered 'special damage' as a result of such an imputation, in accordance with the general rule applying to slander;

ii. A slanderous and false imputation that a woman or girl was unchaste or had committed adultery was a statutorily-created category of slander which was actionable *per se*, per the Slander of Women Act 1891, s 1. This exception was judicially said to arise for two reasons: first, the imputation was cause for the woman to be shunned; and secondly, it was said to 'damage her prospects in the marriage market and thereby her finances', and hence, pecuniary damage could be presumed (per *Kerr v Kennedy*[33] – where an allegation by Lady John Kennedy, D, against Mrs Kerr, C, that C was a lesbian, was held to fall within the meaning of 'unchastity' in s 1, allowing Mrs Kerr to recover for slander). However, whether this category of slander, actionable *per se*, should have any place in modern society had been seriously doubted (both by the Irish Law Reform Commission in its 1991 study of defamation,[34] and by the English Ministry of Justice in its 2010 proposal for a Defamation Bill[35]). Ultimately, the Slander of Women Act 1891 was repealed by s 14(1) of the Defamation Act 2013. Now, any allegations of unchastity or adultery are subject to the general requirement of proving special damage.[36]

§15.4 Exceptionally, slander is actionable *per se* where D's slander imputes that:

i. C was guilty of an imprisonable criminal offence; or
ii. C was unfit, incompetent or dishonest, where C is carrying on a profession, trade, calling or business.

Dealing with each in turn:

i. C was guilty of a criminal offence punishable by imprisonment. This common law exception applies where the imputation is that C *actually committed* the offence. According to *Gray v Jones*,[37] this exception was created, so that proof of special damage was not required, because the slander would expose C to being shunned or avoided, and **not** because it would put him in danger of a criminal prosecution and loss of freedom. A slander which imputes that C was only suspected of an imprisonable offence is not sufficient to invoke this exception. Hence, when D said, in *Simmons v Mitchell* (1880), 'haven't you heard that [C] is suspected of having murdered his brother-in-law?', that slander was not actionable *per se*.[38] The exception is still litigated:

In *Noorani v Calver*,[39] C was the Deputy Chairman of the West Kirby and Thurstaston branch of the Wirral West Conservative Association. D was Chairman. Allegedly, D said to C, in the presence of C's teenage daughter: 'No wonder you have depression, married to a Islamist terrorist. He is a refugee. He is a troublemaker. We should get rid of these people and rebuild the country'. D denied the conversation; and in any event, C did not allege special damage. **Held:** this alleged slander was actionable *per se*. Section 1 of the Terrorism Act 2000 created terrorism as a specific crime. D may not have specifically alleged that C 'was a bomber or an assassin', but D's words related to 'the commission of serious and specific criminal offences'. In *Sanders v Percy*,[40] D was a court listing officer. C had sued

[32] (2013) [80]. [33] [1942] 1 KB 409 (KB) 411. [34] *Civil Law of Defamation* (CP 3, Mar 1991) 40.
[35] *Draft Defamation Bill Consultation* (CP 3, 2011).
[36] *Explanatory Notes to the Defamation Act 2013* (2013) [79]. [37] [1939] 1 All ER 798 (KB) 800.
[38] (1880–81) LR 6 App Cas 156 (PC, on appeal from the CA for the Windward Islands (Grenada)).
[39] [2009] EWHC 561 (QB) [2], quote at [16]. [40] [2009] EWHC 1870 (QB).

in several actions in the Barnet County Court. In one action, a District Judge asked D to check with C's solicitors about a matter. During that telephone conversation, D allegedly said to C's solicitor that, 'You should report your client to the benefits office, as I believe he is a benefit fraudster who is not going to disclose the fact that he is receiving a settlement'; that D had reported C 'for benefit fraud'; and that D had 'once called the police, as he was driving his car without a tax disc'. **Held:** this alleged slander about benefit fraud imputed an imprisonable offence, and was actionable *per se*. However, the allegation about driving without a tax disc was not actionable *per se*, because the offence was only punishable by a fine.

ii. **Unfitness, incompetence or dishonesty, when carrying on a profession, trade, calling or business.** This was originally a common law-created exceptional category, but was then embodied in the Defamation Act 1952, s 2, whereby proof of special damage is **not** required, 'in respect of words calculated to disparage the plaintiff in any office, profession, calling, trade or business held or carried on by him at the time of the publication'. In this provision, 'calculated' means 'likely', but not on the balance of probabilities; 'disparage' means 'discredit'; and the test is objective (per *MacCaba v Lichtenstein*[41]).

Section 2 changed the common law which had preceded it, in two respects. First, the common law had required that D's imputation had to refer to C *in his specific occupation.*

In *Jones v Jones*,[42] D alleged that C, a schoolmaster, had committed adultery with the wife of the school caretaker. The slander did not relate to C's calling – it did not impute any adverse imputation upon his ability to teach; but it seriously prejudiced C's job as the schoolmaster and might lead to his dismissal. **Held:** because the slander did not relate to C's calling as a schoolmaster, the slander was not actionable *per se*.

Section 2 removed that requirement. It provides that the slander is actionable *per se*, 'whether or not the words are spoken of the plaintiff in the way of his office, profession, calling, trade or business'. These words were presumably intended to remove the need for the slander to be specifically directed at C's calling.

In *Andre v Price*,[43] Katie Price, D, gave an interview on the Graham Norton show in front of a live studio audience, in which she alleged that her estranged husband, Peter Andre, C, had had an affair with her former manager (and his current manager), Claire Powell. Hence, the alleged defamatory meaning was that C had committed adultery with his manager whilst he was still married to D. **Held:** the slander related to a professional context, i.e., an affair with C's manager. Whilst the imputation did not relate to C in his occupation as a pop star and TV personality, it was nevertheless directed to C in a professional context. For that reason, it was prima facie actionable *per se*. However, the statement did not 'disparage' C to the level of serious discredit which s 2 required, and hence, was not actionable at all under s 2.

Secondly, the common law (per *Robinson v Ward*[44]) was that C could sue for slander as being actionable *per se* if the imputation related to C's holding of an 'office of profit', because imputations about C were likely to cause financial damage; whereas if C merely held an 'office of honour', i.e., an honorary office with no salary or recompense, then imputations were unlikely to cause damage, and were not actionable *per se*. In *MacCaba v Lichtenstein*,[45] it was held that

[41] [2004] EWHC 1580 (QB) [2]. [42] [1916] 2 AC 481 (HL). [43] [2010] EWHC 2572 (QB) [101]–[105].
[44] (1958) 108 LJ 491. [45] [2004] EWHC 1580 (QB) [21].

the distinction between the two offices did **not** survive s 2's enactment, and that **all** slanderous imputations relating to C's holding of office were actionable *per se*.

In *MacCaba v Lichtenstein*, C was CEO of an IT company. D alleged, in a conversation, that C had committed adultery with young married Jewish women. C claimed that this was likely to disparage him in his business, because he was accused of perversely using his position and power to seduce young married women, and because many of C's business dealings took place with fellow members of the orthodox Jewish community, whose members took a strict view about adultery and marital infidelity. C also was a director/trustee of an orthodox Jewish school in north London, and of a charitable foundation which had the advancement of the orthodox Jewish religion and further education as its object. No special damage was alleged by C, and s 2 was relied upon. **Held:** the slander was actionable *per se*. C held offices of 'honour' – and under s 2, the alleged slanders were capable of disparaging C within the orthodox Jewish community, given the clientele of his business. Many businessmen would be wholly unaffected, in relation to their business, by an accusation of adultery – but not C.

Slanders which disparage companies in their business are also actionable *per se* under s 2, without proof of special damage.

In *Reachlocal UK Ltd v Bennett*,[46] C carried on the business of providing online advertising and marketing services for their customers, including search engine advertising and boosting the profiles of their customers by raising their rankings on search engines (i.e., search engine optimisation). A competitor, D, made various phone calls to C's customers, accusing C of scamming those customers. As a result, C lost customers. **Held:** the slander was actionable *per se* (although there was a substantial special damage claim here).

§15.5 Libel may constitute a crime as well as a tort, if the public interest requires a prosecution, whereas slander is not a crime.

The public interest may require a prosecution if a libel had the tendency to cause a breach of the peace and if the public interest requires a prosecution (per *Gleaves v Deakin*[47]). On the other hand, slander is not in itself a crime in English law, although some spoken words may amount to, say, blasphemy (a crime at common law) or treason (punishable under the Treason Act 1351, as updated).

The matter is justiciable

§15.6 An alleged defamation may be non-justiciable for an English court, for reasons of either (1) jurisdiction or (2) subject matter.

An English court only has jurisdiction over a defamation claim if C alleges damage to his reputation in England and Wales. C is only entitled to recover damages which flow from the publication within the jurisdiction of the English court – which usually requires that the words were published[48] or broadcast[49] in this jurisdiction.

46 [2014] EWHC 3405 (QB) [22]. 47 [1980] AC 477 (HL).
48 *Maharaj v Eastern Media Group Ltd* [2010] EWHC 1294 (QB) [2].
49 *Berezovsky v Russian Television and Radio Broadcasting Co* [2010] EWHC 476 (QB).

Jurisdiction

Section 9 of the Defamation Act 2013 is directed towards curtailing 'libel tourism'. Under s 9(2), an English court will not have jurisdiction to determine a defamation action, unless it is satisfied that, 'of all the places in which the statement complained of has been published, England and Wales is clearly the most appropriate place in which to bring an action in respect of the statement'.

Prior to the Act taking effect, that had already been the common law position. If C's connection with the English jurisdiction was tenuous; and if publication abroad was far more substantial than any which occurred in England, then 'the weaker the presumption in favour of England and Wales being the natural forum for the claim' (per *King v Lewis*[50]). If C had taken either criminal or civil proceedings (or both) in another jurisdiction in respect of the defamatory allegations complained of, then that also indicated that the other jurisdiction was the natural forum (per In *Karpov v Browder*[51]).

Similarly, according to the *Explanatory Notes*, 'if a statement was published 100,000 times in Australia, and only 5,000 times in England, that would be a good basis on which to conclude that the most appropriate jurisdiction in which to bring an action in respect of the statement was Australia, rather than England. There will, however, be a range of factors which the court may wish to take into account including, e.g., the amount of damage to C's reputation in this jurisdiction compared to elsewhere, the extent to which the publication was targeted at a readership in this jurisdiction compared to elsewhere, and whether there is reason to think that C would not receive a fair hearing elsewhere'.[52]

Internet publication provides particular opportunities for 'libel tourism'. Recently, in *Sloutsker v Romanova*,[53] Warby J pointed out that C must prove that D committed a 'real and substantial tort' in the English jurisdiction (as discussed in the next pre-requisite) – and that an English court 'should not be shy of allowing foreigners who publish via the internet to be sued in this jurisdiction, given that such publishers will have chosen to disseminate their information via a global medium'.

> In *Sloutsker v Romanova*, D, a journalist, alleged that Mr Sloutsker, C, arranged for a contract 'hit' on X whilst X was being transferred to prison in Moscow, and tried to bribe the head of a Russian court to increase the length of X's prison sentence. These allegations were published in four publications: a blog post written by D on the website of the Moscow-based radio station; two articles on the website of a Russian online newspaper; and a radio programme of which a transcript was posted online. The publications were all in Russian, and two were in English. **Held:** the action could proceed in England. The fact that D may have defamed C to more people in Russia than in England and Wales did not answer the question whether D had committed a real and substantial tort here. The sting of the allegations made via the online publications 'could easily have reached as many as 60,000 readers in this jurisdiction, and the Programme appears likely to have been heard or read here by several thousand at least', plus these were allegations of the utmost seriousness.

As pointed out in *Mengi v Hermitage*,[54] 'libel tourism' does not necessarily arise because C believes that the English *substantive law* of defamation is superior to that of the jurisdiction where he resides. Rather, the English jurisdiction may be attractive (rather than Tanzania, in that case), because of compulsory disclosure, a trial on oral evidence, judges who are free of

[50] [2004] EWCA Civ 1329, [27] (Lord Woolf MR). [51] [2013] EWHC 3071 (QB) (Simon J).
[52] (2013) [66]. [53] [2015] EWHC 545 (QB) [43]. [54] [2012] EWHC 2045 (QB) [74].

corruption, and a specialist defamation Bar. And although 'English procedure gives rise to the worryingly high costs, ... those costs can be perceived by litigants as better than any available alternative'.

Subject matter

Insofar as subject matter is concerned, English courts will not rule upon religious doctrinal issues, nor intervene in a dispute concerning the regulation or governance of religious groups. This is for several reasons. Courts are secular, and are removed from religious issues, while respecting the rights of religious worshippers. Also, disputes between the religious followers are likely to involve doctrines or beliefs which do not readily lend themselves to the sort of resolution which is the normal function of a court, and hence, there is a natural and inevitable limitation upon the judicial function. Further, questions of faith or doctrinal opinion cannot be easily determined by expert or factual evidence.

> In *Maharaj v Eastern Media Group Ltd*,[55] Mr Maharaj, C, who lived in India, complained of an article published in the *Sikh Times* in 2007, headed, 'Cult divides Sikh congregation in High Wycombe'. It allegedly claimed that C was the leader of a cult and an impostor, that he had disturbed the peace in the Sikh community of High Wycombe, that he promoted blasphemy and the sexual exploitation and abuse of women, and that he acted detrimentally to the Sikh community. This was said to be damaging to C's reputation, particularly among various Sikh communities in England, where there were over 850,000 followers, among whom it was likely that many would know of C and of the article. **Held:** the action for defamation was non-justiciable. Issues of a religious or doctrinal nature permeated the case. A court could not determine whether someone was morally and religiously fit to carry out the spiritual and pastoral duties of his office. Whether C was fairly described as 'an impostor' could not be isolated and resolved without reference to Sikh doctrines and traditions.

As stated in *Shergill v Purewal*, such issues fall 'within the territory which the courts, by self-denying ordinance, will not enter'.[56]

Proof of a 'real and substantial tort'

The *Jameel* principle

§15.7 Under the '*Jameel* principle', C must demonstrate a 'real and substantial tort' to proceed with a defamation suit. Otherwise an abuse of process will occur.

Being sued for defamation is 'a serious interference with freedom of expression' for D (per *Wallis v Meredith*[57]). According to *Jameel v Dow Jones & Co Inc*, the *quid pro quo* is that the 'game has to be worth the candle'.[58] This threshold exercise applies to **all** defamation suits (per *Thornton v Telegraph Media*[59]).

Several factors prompted this change in law, whereby a defamation action could constitute an abuse of process (per *Jameel*[60]). Pursuant to the overriding objective contained in r 1.1 of the

[55] [2010] EWHC 1294 (QB) [28], [30]–[31]. This point was not appealed, although others were: [2011] EWCA Civ 139.

[56] [2011] EWCA Civ 815, [1].

[57] [2011] EWHC 75 (QB) [64].

[58] [2005] EWCA Civ 75, [2005] QB 946, [6], [40], [57], [69], aff'd: *Jameel v Wall Street Jnl* [2006] UKHL 44, [2007] 1 AC 359.

[59] [2010] EWHC 1414 (QB) [91].

[60] [2005] EWCA Civ 75, [55].

Civil Procedure Rules, the courts have to deal with cases justly, which requires that they deal with cases 'proportionately' – and that means that courts are required to be more proactive and interventionist. That potential abuse of process becomes especially important where defamation suits are concerned, given that s 6 of the HRA 1998 requires the court, as a public authority, to administer the law in a manner which is compatible with Convention rights. Balancing Art 10 (right of freedom of expression) and Art 8 (the protection of individual reputation) requires the court to bring to a stop, as an abuse of process, defamation proceedings that are not serving the legitimate purpose of protecting C's reputation. Hence, the court should only compensate C if his reputation has been unlawfully damaged to a *required threshold of seriousness*. Further reasons for a threshold principle were put forth in *Thornton v Telegraph Media Group Ltd.*[61] For one thing, the well-known early libel case of *Sim v Stretch*,[62] in which no defamatory imputation was found, supports the notion that a threshold of seriousness **must** be demonstrated, such that the notion of a 'real and substantial tort' in defamation is not a new one. Moreover, for libel, the law presumes that damage has been suffered by C, which is a logical corollary only if the defamatory imputation has adverse effects upon C which are more than trivial.

The *Jameel* principle has since provided a useful 'escape hatch', and a legitimate ground upon which the proceedings can be struck out, should they not serve the legitimate purpose of protecting C's reputation. That scenario has been borne out in various cases, to D's advantage, where the limited advantages accruing to C, if successful, could not outweigh the expense to the parties, and the waste of court resources, if such a 'trivial case' went ahead:

i. where C cannot prove that his reputation suffered more than *de minimis*, or nominal, damage, because publication occurred to a very limited number of publishees, and was swiftly removed before it could be read by any number of people. Examples of *Jameel's* application include:

> In *Jameel v Dow Jones & Co Inc*, D published an article in the online edition of the *Wall Street Journal*, which was available to about 6,000 subscribers in England. The article had an internet hyperlink, which when followed, contained a list of names. The hyperlink, when combined with the article, implied that Mr Jameel, C, a Saudi businessman, had been one of the first financial supporters of Osama Bin Laden and Al-Qaeda, and that he was suspected of continued support for such terrorism, including the September 11 attacks. D proved that only five subscribers in England had followed the hyperlink and accessed the alleged defamation. Of these, two were unidentified but were said not to know C or to recollect reading his name; and three were 'in C's camp', i.e., C's agents, already. In *Kaschke v Gray*,[63] about four people posted comments to D's blog, which blog falsely suggested that C had been accused of being a member of the Baader-Meinhof terrorist group. In *Reed Elsevier UK Ltd v Bewry*,[64] Mr Bewry, C, complained of a sentence in a case digest published by LexisNexis on its subscriber-only law reports service. The case report was accessed by only three people whilst it was up, and after C complained, the digest was redrafted, and with no publication of the offending sentence thereafter.

Since *Jameel*, an action in defamation is unlikely to proceed on the score of one publishee – especially where 'strenuous efforts have been made to identify another publishee but they have not borne fruit' (per *Wallis v Meredith*[65]). However, if the imputation, even published to one person, was particularly grave and serious, then that will counter against a *Jameel*-type strike-out (a topic discussed further, under 'Element #3: Publication').

[61] [2010] EWHC 1414 (QB) [90]–[94]. [62] [1936] 2 All ER 1237 (HL). [63] [2010] EWHC 1075 (QB).
[64] [2014] EWCA Civ 1411, [41]. [65] [2011] EWHC 75 (QB) [57].

ii. where the imputation was of such a trivial nature that to proceed with it was not 'worth the candle' (to adopt an expression of Eady J's in *Schellenberg v BBC*[66]):

> In *Ecclestone v Telegraph Media Group Ltd*,[67] the *Daily Telegraph* published a diary piece about Petra Ecclestone's, C's, new fashion line, in which C was quoted as saying, 'I am not a veggie and I don't have much time for people like the McCartneys and Annie Lennox'. C claimed that publication of this comment was defamatory of her. **Held:** the imputation was not serious enough to be capable of being defamatory. The ordinary reasonable reader would not think adversely of C, because there is no obligation on a young person in today's society to be respectful to people such as Sir Paul McCartney; nor were people likely to think the less of C merely because she expressed herself as not having much time for him because of his vegetarianism.

iii. where no substantive vindication or benefit would be achieved by a defamation suit against D – say, where C has, prior to the litigation, exercised a right of reply to vindicate her reputation already and which had been published by D (per *Kaschke v Gray, Hilton*[68]); or where the opinions of many/all readers would be unlikely to be influenced, one way or the other, by any verdict in a defamation action (per *Lonzim plc v Sprague*[69]); or where C's background and serious criminal convictions would mean that any adverse effect upon his reputation that was caused by a defamatory imputation would be minimal, and hence, the damages and vindication obtained would be minimal (e.g., where C was a long-term prisoner, per *Williams v MGN Ltd*[70]); or where the minuscule number of publications complained of have long since been taken down by D, D having made it plain that they would not be republished, and there is no threat of any wider publication (per *Reed Elsevier UK Ltd v Bewry*[71]);

iv. where C, who resides in an overseas jurisdiction, had no connection with England, and had no reputation to protect in the English jurisdiction which was capable of being harmed (i.e., his 'reputation' was created and harmed via the one allegedly defamatory publication in England) (per *Karpov v Browder*[72]); or where C has little if any trading reputation in the UK which could be damaged by the imputation (per *Liberty Fashions Wears Ltd v Primark Stores Ltd*[73]) – by contrast, if C had 'some reputation here to protect', then a 'real and substantial tort' will be possible, if the allegations were seriously defamatory, and if their dissemination was widespread and could notionally have reached several thousands of readers (per *Sloutsker v Romanova*[74]).

The *Jameel* Court of Appeal itself regarded that a case which did not meet the requisite threshold of seriousness would be 'rare'[75] – after all, its effect is to deprive C of a shot at justice, on what may be a claim that has some merit. However, that view has shifted since. In *Thornton v Telegraph Media Group Ltd*, it was said that the *Jameel* principle was being applied 'with some frequency, and in a number of different, but related, contexts in defamation actions',[76] an impression confirmed even more recently by Warby J in *Ames v The Spamhaus Project*.[77] At the nub of the matter is that defamation actions will not be permitted to proceed, 'where the legitimate objective of vindication [for C] is not required or, at least, cannot be achieved without a wholly disproportionate interference with the rights of D' (per *Kaschke v Osler*[78]).

[66] [2000] EMLR 296 (QB) [14], and cited in: *Jameel* [2005] QB 946 (CA) [57]. [67] [2009] EWHC 2779 (QB).
[68] [2010] EWHC 1907 (QB) [4], [49], [58]. [69] [2009] EWHC 2838 (QB) [31].
[70] [2009] EWHC 3150 (QB) [11], [23]. [71] [2014] EWCA Civ 1411, [41]. [72] [2013] EWHC 3071 (QB) [73], [139].
[73] [2015] EWHC 415 (QB) [54]. [74] [2015] EWHC 545 (QB) [67]. [75] [2005] QB 946 (CA) [40].
[76] [2010] EWHC 1414 (QB) [62]–[63]. [77] [2015] EWHC 127 (QB) [33]. [78] [2010] EWHC 1075 (QB) [22].

The statutory 'serious harm' requirement

Given both the existence and the utility of the *Jameel* principle, it was something of a surprise that Parliament felt it necessary to implement a statutory 'serious harm' test. However, this is what it did, via s 1(1) of the Defamation Act 2013, which provides that a statement is not defamatory, 'unless its publication has caused, or is likely to cause, serious harm to the reputation of C'. It requires serious harm to reputation, and not serious distress or injury to C's feelings (per *Cooke v MGN Ltd*[79]).

It was clarified, in *Ames v The Spamhaus Project*,[80] that s 1(1) does not abolish the *Jameel* principle, but is *additional* to it. That was evident from the use of a different word – 'serious' rather than 'substantial' – and by the note, in the *Explanatory Notes*, that s 1(1) 'raises the bar for bringing a claim'.[81] In *Lachaux v Independent Print Ltd*,[82] Warby J added that, 'Parliament is presumed to know the common law, and to legislate by reference to it', and that the *Jameel* principle is a common law rule for this purpose. In Warby J's opinion, it is the statutory test which should be looked at first. If 'serious harm' is proven, then it is necessary to ask whether the tort was 'real and substantial'. Although Warby J noted that the answers to the two tests may be different in an appropriate case, that scenario has yet to come before the court. For now, however, s 1(1) adds a further layer of (arguably unwarranted) complexity to this pre-requisite.

Where 'a body that trades for profit' is concerned (and only then), s 1(2) provides that 'serious harm' must mean that the defamatory imputation 'has caused, or is likely to cause, the body serious financial loss'. Hence, serious actual or likely financial loss (i.e., special damage) is mandatory under the Act. At common law, a trading corporation could recover general damages (for, say, damage to its good name or to its commercial reputation, because they were things of value), even where the corporation could not prove that it had suffered any special damage (i.e., where damage to its reputation had not caused it some provable financial loss) (per *Jameel v Wall Street Journal*[83]). That common law position is now reversed.

When it comes to proving s 1's 'serious harm' requirement, it appears that, in some cases, evidence will not be required – it will be inferred, say, where C is accused, in a widely-disseminated publication, of being a terrorist or a paedophile (per *Cooke v MGN Ltd*[84]). In less severe cases, evidence of opinion poll surveys, or a selection of comments from a blog, or some other indication of what 'right thinking people' thought when they read the defamatory matter, may be useful (per *Cooke*). However, in *Ames*,[85] the court noted that it is indeed often very difficult for C to obtain witness statements that they read the defamatory imputations about C and thought the worse of C because of what they read.

As with the *Jameel* principle, steps taken to reverse or eradicate the defamatory imputation in the minds of readers will mean that there is little or nothing to achieve from the litigation. For example, providing C with a right of reply, or publishing an apology, will assist to disprove any 'serious harm'.

In *Cooke v MGN Ltd*, an article was published by D in the *Sunday Mirror*, 'Millionaire Tory Cashes in on TV Benefits Street'. The Midland Heart Housing Assn, and its CEO, Ms Ruth Cooke, C, alleged that the article was defamatory of them, because readers would think of them as 'dodgy landlords' associated with a particular street in Birmingham, where a number of residents dependent on social security benefits resided in poor quality accommodation. C alleged that the article caused the

[79] [2014] EWHC 2831 (QB) [30]. [80] [2015] EWHC 127 (QB) [49]–[51]. [81] (2013) [11].
[82] [2015] EWHC 2242 (QB) [44]. [83] [2006] UKHL 44, [2007] 1 AC 359, [26].
[84] [2014] EWHC 2831 (QB) [43]. [85] [2015] EWHC 127 (QB) [55].

Association serious harm, because as a non-profit association, it was dependent upon grant and contract income which depended on competitive tender, and that success in the tender process required a strong reputation for delivering high-quality housing services. **Held:** no serious harm proven, nor could it be inferred. A prompt apology was published by D, and the article was less accessible via internet searches than the apology was.

Capacity of C to sue

Governmental and public authorities

§15.8 A local authority and a public authority are not permitted to sue in defamation, although an individual councillor or Government officer may sue in defamation when suing in a personal capacity.

This rule, derived from *Derbyshire CC v Times Newspapers Ltd*,[86] means that 'the government of the day will not be a claimant' in defamation (per *Cook v Telegraph Media Group Ltd*[87]).

Several reasons underpin this lack of capacity to sue, as explained by Lord Keith in *Derbyshire*.[88] First, where C is a local authority, then it is temporarily under the control of the prevailing political party. On that basis, it is 'difficult to say that the local authority as such has any reputation of its own' – its reputation in the public's eyes is more likely to attach to the controlling political party, such that whenever the political party changes, the local authority's reputation itself will change. Secondly, if public criticism of the local authority occurs, then 'it is open to the controlling body to defend itself by public utterances and in debate in the council chamber', rather than via a defamation action. Thirdly, governmental bodies cannot sue for defamation because (said Lord Keith), '[i]t is of the highest public importance that a democratically elected governmental body ... should be open to uninhibited public criticism. The threat of a civil action for defamation must inevitably have an inhibiting effect on freedom of speech'. Fourthly (and as noted by the Court of Appeal in *Derbyshire*,[89] and also in *R (on the application of Comninos) v Bedford BC*[90]), a local authority lacks capacity to sue in defamation because, under Art 10 of the ECHR (directed towards the preservation of free speech), there was no pressing social need that a public authority should have the right to sue in defamation for the protection of its reputation.

The *Derbyshire* rule has been applied to prevent suits in libel by a government-owned corporation (per *British Coal Corp v NUM (Yorkshire Area) and Capstick*[91]). The rule also applies to political parties (per *Goldsmith v Bhoyrul*,[92] where Buckley J remarked that a democratically electable political party should be open to public criticism, and that the party itself lacked standing to sue in defamation).

However, the *Derbyshire* rule has its limits:

- public authorities are permitted to be *defendants* in libel actions;
- public authorities are permitted to bring claims for malicious falsehood; and
- individuals 'who hold authority or power in the state' (e.g., individual councillors, Government officers) may still sue in libel, provided that they are suing in their personal capacity. As

[86] [1993] AC 534 (HL) 540. [87] [2011] EWHC 763 (QB) [109].
[88] [1993] AC 534 (HL) 550, 534, 551, respectively (Lord Keith).
[89] [1992] QB 770 (CA) 771, 817 (Balcombe LJ). [90] [2003] EWHC 121 (Admin).
[91] (Unreported, 28 Jun 1996), cited in: *Steel & Morris v UK* [2005] EMLR 15 (ECtHR) [40].
[92] [1998] QB 459, 462–63.

pointed out in *McLaughlin v Lambeth BC*,[93] courts must be careful to ensure that claims by individuals who are connected to governmental bodies or public authorities must not be framed as attempts by those bodies to circumvent the *Derbyshire* rule. However (said Tugendaht J), the *Derbyshire* rule did permit individuals to sue for defamation, where what is impugned is their conduct in undertaking the business of a governmental body.

In *McLaughlin v Lambeth LBC*, the head teacher, governor, director and Chairman of the governors, of the Durand Primary School, C, sued in libel, complaining about three emails sent by an auditor employed by D. The school was run by D, and then by central government as an Academy School. D's emails alleged that Cs were personally responsible for mistreating and failing to support newly qualified teachers, and for acting with impropriety to the school's detriment. D claimed that C's suit should be struck out, on the basis that C were trying to circumvent the *Derbyshire* rule, which would have prevented the governing body of the school, a governmental body, from suing for defamation. **Held:** the *Derbyshire* principle did not preclude this suit, where the individual reputation of any person controlling or carrying on the day-to-day management of the affairs of a governmental body was allegedly impaired by D's publication. This action had been brought for the dominant purpose of vindicating C's individual reputations. In *Thompson v James*,[94] Mr James, C, CEO of the Carmarthenshire CC, was accused by D of doing everything in his power to protect the 'officers' club slush fund'. Another blog post by D referred to C 'and his cronies', financing deals before budget cuts were put through. **Held:** the imputation was directed at C, and not at the Council, and C had capacity to sue. '[D] is saying that [C] was either instrumental in setting up the fund, or at the very least, that he knew it was being set up so that he could benefit from it'.

- a member of a political party has the capacity to sue in defamation, if the publication refers or identifies him (per *Coad v Cruze*,[95] discussed below, and per *Tilbrook v Parr*[96] – although there, the Chairman of the English Democrats political party, Mr Tilbrook, lacked the capacity to sue the author of 'Bloggers4UKIP' for comments made about the party, as he was not sufficiently *referred to* in D's blog).

Companies and associations

§15.9 Companies, partnerships and incorporated entities, have the capacity to sue in respect of defamatory imputations which can be seen as having a tendency to damage that entity in its business. However, any unincorporated trade or professional association which merely consists of its members lacks standing to sue, either individually or collectively.

As O'Connor LJ put it in *Electrical, Electronic, Telecommunication and Plumbing Union v Times Newspapers Ltd*, 'unless one can attach a personality to a body, it cannot sue for defamation'.[97] Hence, the following entities may sue in defamation:

- companies – e.g., in *Hays plc v Hartley*,[98] C was a substantial public company and specialist recruitment agency, which sued for imputations by D that, via its employees, it committed or condoned gross acts of racism; and in *South Hetton Coal Co Ltd v North Eastern News Assn*

[93] [2010] EWHC 2726 (QB) [40]–[41], [46]. [94] [2014] EWCA Civ 600, [25].
[95] [2009] EWHC 3782 (QB) [27]–[28]. [96] [2012] EWHC 1946 (QB).
[97] [1980] QB 585 (CA) 595. [98] [2010] EWHC 1068 (QB).

Ltd,[99] a corporate employer sued in defamation for allegations made by D that the housing provided for its employees was unsanitary and that its pitworker employees were neglected. A trading corporation 'is entitled to sue in respect of defamatory matters which can be seen as having a tendency to damage it in the way of its business' (per *Derbyshire CC v Times Newspapers Ltd*[100]). It will be recalled that a company which is slandered can bring an action without proof of special damage, under s 2 of the Defamation Act 1952, if it is disparaged in its business (per *Reachlocal UK Ltd v Bennett*[101]). A trading corporation does **not** need to prove that it had suffered 'special damage' from a libel either – otherwise, it would have to wait until it had lost earnings, customers or contracts, and 'incalculable harm' could be done to it in the meantime (per *Jameel v Wall Street Journal*[102]). This proposition was affirmed, in *Meadows Care Ltd v Lambert*[103] (although special damage was pleaded by the owners of the children's care homes there). A company or association has no feelings to hurt, but it can recover general damages for the damage which the defamation did to its good name (per *Jameel*);
- incorporated trade and professional associations (limited by guarantee) – in *British Chiropractic Assn v Singh*,[104] C was such an entity, and could validly sue for imputations made by a scientist about the effectiveness of chiropractic treatments;
- partnerships (noted in *EEPTU v Times Newspapers*[105]) and charitable organisations (noted in *Thornton v Telegraph Media Group Ltd*[106]).

However, the following entities may **not** sue in defamation:

- a trade union, which is an unincorporated body, and without a quasi-corporate personality – it cannot sue in its own name for damages in relation to its own reputation, and nor can it sue for damages on behalf of each individual member who claims that the publication was defamatory of their several reputations (per *EETPU v Times Newspapers Ltd*[107]);
- an unincorporated association – in *EETPU*,[108] O'Connor J gave the example: suppose that D says, of the Longbeach Anglers' Association, that at the competition last Saturday they cheated. That is a defamatory statement; but the Association cannot maintain an action in its own name, because it has no personality of its own which is capable of being defamed. The individuals of the association who participated in the competition that day may successfully sue for defamation if the statement referred to them individually and sufficiently clearly. This raises a separate problem in Defamation (i.e., reference, and group defamation), which is discussed under Element #2, below.

ELEMENT #1: A DEFAMATORY IMPUTATION

There are two aspects to this first element – determining the meaning of the words complained of, and then deciding whether that meaning was defamatory.

Ascertaining the meaning

§15.10 The natural and ordinary meaning of D's words can be derived from: (1) their direct literal meaning; (2) a false (popular) innuendo – a meaning of the words which would be understood

[99] [1894] 1 QB 133 (CA) 146–47. [100] [1993] AC 534 (HL) 547 (Lord Keith).
[101] [2014] EWHC 3405 (QB) [22]. [102] [2006] UKHL 44, [2007] AC 359, [98]–[104] (Lord Hope).
[103] [2014] EWHC 1226 (QB) [19]. [104] [2010] EWCA Civ 350, [2011] 1 WLR 133, [10].
[105] [1980] QB 585, 595 (O'Connor J). [106] [2010] EWHC 1414 (QB) [37]. [107] [1980] QB 585. [108] *ibid*, 595–96.

by anyone by 'reading between the lines' and without knowing anything more by way of facts; or (3) a true (legal) innuendo – where a statement does not appear to be defamatory on its face, but is rendered defamatory because certain readers know of extrinsic circumstances or extraneous facts relating to C which render the words defamatory. With the exception of scenario (3), the court is required to determine the single meaning which the publication conveyed to the reasonable reader.

The court's task is to determine the single meaning of the words used (the only exception to this is where the words are capable of bearing a true innuendo, where two meanings arise from the words). The words cannot be treated as giving rise to two meanings which are inconsistent with each other (e.g., that C is guilty, and is reasonably suspected of a crime, to quote an example of Warby J in *Yeo v Times Newspapers*[109]). If the court considers that the meaning of the words, as alleged by C, is only possible from 'some strained or utterly unreasonable interpretation', the court will discard it. It has been said that a judge should only exclude a pleaded meaning if satisfied that it would be 'perverse to uphold it' (per *Jameel v Wall Street Journal*[110]). Courts will err on the 'generous' side, when deciding what meanings the words can bear ('[a]n exercise in generosity, not in parsimony', per *Berezovsky v Forbes*[111]).

Of course, the single meaning rule may not reflect reality at all. Different readers may have understood the words as bearing different possible meanings – but all that matters is what a court thinks is the one and only meaning that reasonable readers should have collectively understood the words to bear.

In *Cooke v MGN Ltd*, facts previously, **held:** the meaning of D's article was not merely that Ms Cooke, C, had a large house, and that her large salary provided 'colour' to the article. Rather, the natural and ordinary meaning of the words complained of were that Midland Heart, one of the well-off landlords of rented properties on James Turner Street, let houses to people in receipt of housing benefit, and made money from the misery of those residents; and that its CEO was personally responsible for this conduct of Midland Heart, and has herself profited and become rich from it, being paid a good salary and living in a large house in Gloucestershire. Whilst that was capable of being defamatory, it did not satisfy the 'serious harm' test.

The literal meaning

According to *Jones v Skelton*,[112] the ordinary and natural meaning of words may be of two types – the literal meaning, and the false innuendo. The most common is the literal meaning of the statement.

In *Johnson v MGN Ltd*,[113] professional footballer Glen Johnson, C, sued for defamation, for an article in *The People*, which stated: 'Glen Johnson will complete a sensational move to Liverpool this week. *People Sport* understands the Portsmouth right-back was given a tour of the Merseysiders' Melwood training complex in the build-up to Christmas. Reds' boss Rafa Benitez is keen to land him as soon as possible, and Liverpool will pay cash-strapped Pompey £9 million. Johnson missed the Boxing Day 4–1 home thrashing by West Ham reportedly through injury, but his appearance on Merseyside will

109 [2014] EWHC 2853 (QB), [2015] 1 WLR 971, [85].
110 [2004] EMLR 6 (CA) [6], [9]–[16], [23].
111 [2001] EMLR 45 (CA) [16] (Sedley LJ).
112 [1963] 1 WLR 1362 (PC, on appeal from Australia) 1370–71 (Lord Morris).
113 [2009] EWHC 1481 (QB) [12].

fuel suspicions that a deal is already done'. **Held:** the words were capable of being defamatory in their literal meaning, because they could convey to the reader that C had lied about being injured, to prevent his playing in the Boxing Day match.

A false (popular) innuendo

The second type of 'ordinary and natural meaning of words' is an inferred or indirect meaning. A false innuendo is a meaning which would be understood by anyone reading the words in their natural and ordinary meaning, but without knowing anything more by way of facts (per *Grubb v Bristol United Press Ltd*[114]).

In *Bestobell Paints Ltd v Bigg*,[115] professional decorators, D, painted a house with C's brown paint, which was sold under the registered trade mark, 'Carsons'. After about six months, the paint started to turn green in places, giving an unsightly appearance to the house. D complained to C that the paint was unsatisfactory, and asked for compensation. C alleged that D had mixed two different paints together, and that the work had been badly executed. D then put up a large sign on the house saying, 'This house is painted with CARSONS paint'. The house was near the South Circular Road in London, and very visible to numerous passersby. **Held:** the sign contained a false innuendo, that C's paint was inferior and changed colour.

A true (legal) innuendo

A true innuendo arises where a statement does not appear to be defamatory on its face, but is rendered defamatory because *certain readers only* will know of extrinsic circumstances or extraneous facts relating to C. Also called a 'meaning innuendo',[116] and a 'legal innuendo',[117] it arises where the facts are not part of general knowledge, but are specifically known to some reasonable readers/listeners only.

In *Cassidy v Daily Mirror Newspapers*,[118] Kettering Cassidy (aka Michael Corrigan) told a journalist that he was engaged to Miss X, and allowed a photograph of them together to be taken. The photograph, and an announcement of their engagement, were published in D's newspaper, with the caption, 'Mr M Corrigan, the race horse owner, and Miss [X], whose engagement has been announced'. In fact, Mr Cassidy was already married to Mrs Cassidy, C. She was not referred to in the photograph, and sued in defamation. **Held:** the photo and caption were defamatory of C, because of the imputation that she 'was an immoral woman who had cohabited with Corrigan without being married to him'. The announcement by a newspaper of a couple's engagement was an innocent statement on its face, but there would be readers who knew that one of the persons in the photograph was already married. Because of that, the statement was defamatory of C, the person's spouse. In *Baturina v Times Newspapers Ltd*,[119] Mrs Baturina, C, was the wife of the former Mayor of Moscow. The *Sunday Times* newspaper printed an article, 'Bunker billionairess digs deep', stating that C, 'Russia's richest woman', was 'believed to be' the owner of a house *Witanhurst*, described as London's largest residence after Buckingham Palace. C was alleged to have purchased *Witanhurst* through a 'front company' based in the British Virgin Islands. In the same year, the Russian President had enacted a decree requiring Russian officials to publish

[114] [1963] 1 QB 309 (CA) 333 (Upjohn LJ). [115] [1975] FSR 421 (Ch) 429.

[116] *Baturina v Times Newspapers Ltd* [2011] EWCA Civ 308, [23].

[117] *Grappelli v Derek Block (Holdings) Ltd* [1981] 1 WLR 822 (CA) 824–25.

[118] [1929] 2 KB 331 (CA). [119] [2011] EWCA Civ 308.

information about their (and their spouses') assets and income. C contended that, for those that knew of the effect of the Decree, then by not including *Witanhurst* in her list of assets, the article imputed that C had used a front company to hide her interest as beneficial owner of the house, and that she had failed to comply with Russian law. **Held:** a true innuendo was possible here. In *Johnson v MGN Ltd*,[120] facts previously, **held:** a true innuendo was contained in D's article, because a group of readers with knowledge of the Premier League Rules would realise that, as a player under contract with Portsmouth, the imputation was that Glen Johnson, C, was in breach of the Rules when he made an approach to Liverpool and supposedly visited their training ground whilst under contract.

Whether the imputation is defamatory

§15.11 A publication is defamatory if it substantially and adversely affects the attitude of other people towards C. Imputations which lower C in the estimation of right-thinking members of society generally, or which cause C to be shunned, ridiculed or avoided, will be defamatory.

According to *Thornton v Telegraph Media Group Ltd*,[121] C does not have to prove that the defamatory imputation, in fact, adversely affected the attitude of other people towards him; a tendency or likelihood of that is sufficient. As Tugendhat J noted, there have been several definitions of what is meant by the term, 'defamatory' (and not all of them have been consistent or identical) – and the distinction between personal and business defamation is important, even if they are not mutually exclusive.[122]

There is no rule in English law that C 'could have no reputation worth protecting', because of 'bad character' – a bad reputation does not preclude a person from suing in defamation, provided that he can establish that a publication has affected the attitude of other people towards him, adversely, to the required threshold of seriousness (otherwise, the *Jameel* principle will be triggered).

Personal defamation

§15.12 Personal defamation occurs where there are imputations as to the character or attributes of an individual.

Defamatory imputations of a personal nature consist of those which: lower C in the estimation of right-thinking members of society generally, by reason of some unethical, immoral, illegal or socially harmful conduct on C's part (per *Sim v Stretch*[123]); or expose C to hatred, ridicule or contempt (per *Berkoff v Burchill*[124]); or cause C to be shunned, scorned and avoided because of C's misfortune or something involuntary (e.g., disease, insanity, etc) (per *Youssoupoff v MGM Pictures Ltd*[125]).

The Table below provides an array of imputations which have been held to be either defamatory, or capable of being defamatory in a personal sense:

[120] [2009] EWHC 1481 (QB) [18]–[19].

[121] [2010] EWHC 1414 (QB) [93]–[96], citing: *Berkoff v Burchill* [1997] EMLR 139 (CA) [30].

[122] *ibid*, [34]. [123] [1936] 2 All ER 1237 (HL) 1240 (Lord Atkin).

[124] [1997] EMLR 139 (CA) 140. [125] (1934) 50 TLR 581 (CA) 587 (Slesser LJ).

Personal defamatory imputations: a sample

How it would adversely affect the attitude of a reasonable person:

- that C had **committed adultery** (i.e., engaged in an affair with someone else, whilst married) (per *Andre v Price* – D alleged that her estranged pop star husband, C, had an affair with her former manager (and C's then-manager); or that C entered into a **romantic relationship with another party, knowing him to be in stable, long-term and committed relationship,** and so knowingly encouraged his betrayal of his family and likely to lead to the breakdown of his relationship with his family (per *Contostavlos v News Group Newspapers Ltd*[a])
- that C demonstrated **weakness in character or judgment whilst in political office**, in not living up to the principles that C proclaimed (per *Cook v Telegraph Media Group Ltd*[b] – in campaigning for the RAF, when C claimed a £5 offertory donation for an RAF charity made during a memorial service to commemorate the Battle of Britain – C apologised for the 'serious error' in submitting the claim at all)
- that C showed **hypocrisy**, which on the part of a politician would adversely affect the attitude of people towards him in political office (dicta in *Cook*, not proven there)
- that C had acted **dishonestly**, whether in political office (dicta in *Cook*, as not proven there) or in business where C was described as a 'shyster', meaning someone who **engages in sharp, disreputable and dishonest practices**, and **attempting to blackmail** via imposing extravagant and unscrupulous demands before any possible takeover (per *Levi v Bates*[c] – former director/owner of Leeds United Football Club, C, was alleged to be a 'shyster', and that '[t]his unpleasant and dishonourable man will not succeed in his attempt to obtain money in an unscrupulous way, he is simply deterring would-be investors [in LUFC]')
- that, as an actor, C was not merely physically unattractive, but **actually repulsive in appearance** (per *Berkoff v Burchill*[d] – in a review of the film Frankenstein, the reviewer described 'the Creature' as marginally better looking than the actor Mr Berkoff, C, who was described as 'hideously ugly', making C an object of ridicule and lowering him in the estimation of the viewing public and in the view of those who may not hire him for a job)
- that C had committed a serious imprisonable offence, and/or was a member or supporter of the Baader-Meinhof terrorist group and **sympathised with, or was part of, terrorists' causes and activities** (per *Kaschke v Osler*,[e] and *Kaschke v Gray, Hilton*[f] – C was once suspected by the West German authorities to be a member of that group, was arrested by the West German police in the mid-1970s, and spent 3 months in prison, for which she was paid compensation for wrongful imprisonment)
- that C was a **willing beneficiary of 'cronyism' and 'back-scratching'**, even though he had kept 'within the letter of the law' (per *Miller v Associated Newspapers Ltd*[g] – where C was given a contract to improve Sir Ian Blair's image (under a so-called vanity contract), where they were old friends, skiing partners, had done business together, and the contract was not put out to tender, and lacked transparency)

[a] [2014] EWHC 1339 (QB) [11].
[b] [2011] EWHC 1134 (QB) [8]–[9].
[c] [2009] EWHC 1495 (QB) [82].
[d] [1997] EMLR 139 (CA).
[e] [2010] EWHC 1075 (QB).
[f] [2010] EWHC 690 (QB).
[g] [2010] EWHC 700 (QB).

- that C **supported or sympathised with serious criminal conduct, such as a notorious child abuser or child killer** (per *Thornton v Telegraph Media Group Ltd*[h] – dicta examples only)
- that C, a police officer, was suspected of **corruption** (per *Gregg v O'Gara*[i] – C was alleged to have had planted or interfered with evidence, in order to frame an innocent man of a serious crime)
- that C had a contagious or infectious disease (per *Villers v Monsley*[j] – C was described as: 'You old stinking, old nasty, old itchy old toad' (similar to imputations, from an earlier age, that C had leprosy or the plague)
- that C was **anti-Semitic** (per *Levi v Bates*[k] – not proven there though – although C was described as 'the Enemy Within', which was used by Nazis to describe the Jews, it did not mean here that D's words were anti-semitic – it was only used to describe 'dissidents' in this case)
- that C, an employee, was being **disloyal to an employer**, and was also **a liar** about his employment status and/or his activities (per *Johnson v MGN Ltd*[l] – it was alleged that C feigned injury to avoid playing for Portsmouth in a match and to conceal that he was having unauthorised talks with another club Liverpool, and that he had a tour of their training complex prior to that match (no such tour ever occurred)
- that C was **untruthful**, and also exhibited **unreasonable obsessive behaviour** (per *Trumm v Norman*[m] – allegations that C was guilty of some disreputable conduct, had not been truthful; was an obsessive whose behaviour had led to the breakdown of his marriage and the loss of contact with his children; and that he was not generally to be believed – a medical condition may actually provoke sympathy with the ordinary reader, but the allegation of obsessive disorders may lower C's estimation)
- that C was **a perpetrator of domestic violence, a drug-dealer, and a paedophile** (per *Clynes v O'Connor*[n] – in a dispute about the installation of CCTV in a front garden, one neighbour hurled abuse at her neighbour, that he was a 'wife beater', a 'drug dealer', a 'paedophile' and a 'perv')
- that C was portrayed by caricature, as having **ridiculous, absurd or unsuitable costumes or attitudes** (per *Dunlop Rubber Co Ltd v Dunlop*[o] – C, the inventor of the pneumatic tyre, assigned the invention to D and presented D with a portrait bust of himself to be used as a trademark, and was then shown in D's advertisements as a caricature adapted from the portrait bust, showing a man dressed in an exaggeratedly foppish manner, wearing a tall white hat and waistcoat, carrying a cane and eye-glass)
- that C, a well-known beauty therapist, was described by *Tatler* magazine, the famous fashion magazine, as a 'boot', meaning **'an ugly harridan'** (per *Winyard v Tatler Publishing Co Ltd*[p] – to call a women old, ugly or haggard would simply injure her feelings, but for a beauty therapist, potential clients might not wish her to be in charge of their beauty treatments)
- that C was suspected of having **mafia or cosa nostra connections** (per *Atlantis World Group of Cos NV v Gruppo Editoriale L'Espresso SpA*[q] – such that C was controlled by the mafia or cosa nostra, or had sufficient links that C should not have been granted a gaming licence in a casino)

[h] [2010] EWHC 1414 (QB).
[i] [2008] EWHC 658 (QB) [46].
[j] (1769) 2 Wils KB 403, (1769) 95 ER 886, 887.
[k] [2009] EWHC 1495 (QB) [82].
[l] [2009] EWHC 1481 (QB).
[m] [2008] EWHC 116 (QB) [15].
[n] [2011] EWHC 1201 (QB) [2].
[o] [1921] 1 AC 367 (HL, Ireland) 370.
[p] (Unreported, 16 Jul 1991), and cited in: *Berkoff v Burchill* [1997] EMLR 139 (CA) [149].
[q] [2008] EWHC 1323 (QB) [19].

- that C was a '**racist**' or a '**Nazi**' (per *Mitchell v Evening Chronicle*[r])
- that C **consorted with and had sexual relations with a prostitute** (per *Dwek v Associated Newspapers Ltd*[s] – capable of being defamatory, 'even as the third millennium approaches')
- that C **had committed a criminal offence**, and was involved in **dishonest dealings** (per *Shendish Manor Ltd v Coleman*[t] – D said, C 'is a crook and is only in business for a fast buck', and that 'I have to count my fingers to make sure that they are all there after shaking hands with him')
- that C had engaged in marriage as a **hypocritical sham**, to conceal the fact that one or both parties to the marriage was **homosexual**, and/or that the **Church of Scientology**, of which they were members, had ordered the marriage to hold C up as an example to the young (per *Cruise v Express Newspapers plc*[u])

[r] [2003] EWHC 1281 (QB) [6].
[s] [2000] EMLR 284 (CA) 294.
[t] (CA, 15 Jun 2001) [6].
[u] [1998] EWCA Civ 1269, [1999] QB 931.

Where allegations of criminal wrongdoing, corruption or impropriety, are made by D, then there are three possible levels of meaning: that C *was guilty* of serious wrongdoing (a 'Chase Level 1' meaning); that there *were reasonable grounds to suspect* C of wrongdoing ('Chase Level 2'); or that there are *reasonable grounds to investigate* whether C has engaged in wrongdoing ('Chase Level 3') (per *Chase v News Group Newspapers Ltd*[126]). All three may be defamatory.

Business defamation

§15.13 Business or professional defamation occurs where the imputation relates to an attribute of an individual, corporation, trade union, charity, or similar body, and the imputation relates to the way the profession or business is conducted.

Defamatory imputations may also be, separately, of a business nature (per *Thornton v Telegraph Media Group Ltd*[127]). They may consist of imputations which: do not relate to any moral fault or defect of personal character on the part of a business or professional person, C, but which impute a lack of qualification, knowledge, skill, capacity, judgment or efficiency on C's part (per *Drummond-Jackson v British Medical Association*[128]); or impute that the fitness or competence of C's goods/services fall below the required standard, and which are likely to cause adverse consequences to C's customers, patients or clients (per *Thornton*[129]); or deter people from dealing with C's business or firm (whether, say, refraining from providing financial support or business or employment services to C) (per *South Hetton Coal Co Ltd v North-Eastern News Assn Ltd*[130]).

For illustrative purposes, some of the imputations contained in the above Table of 'personal imputations' cover business reputation too. The Table below provides some further examples:

[126] [2002] EWCA Civ 1772, [46].
[127] [2010] EWHC 1414 (QB) [34].
[128] [1970] 1 WLR 688 (CA) 699.
[129] [2010] EWHC 1414 (QB) [38].
[130] [1894] 1 QB 133 (CA) 141.

Business defamatory imputations: a sample

How it would adversely affect the attitude of a reasonable person:

- that C **committed adultery, in order to further her business career** (per *Leech v Independent Newspapers (Ireland) Ltd*[a] – C was alleged to have had an affair with a Minister of the Government)
- that, in a sporting context, C **threw matches**, or **took performance enhancing drugs** (per *Dee v Telegraph Media Group Ltd*[b] – dicta examples only)
- that C, an entertainment group, were **cavalier in their approach to contractual obligations**, and should not be booked by venues and promotors for parties and other occasions (per *Joseph v Spiller*[c] – C were alleged to be grossly unprofessional and untrustworthy, they considered that 'contracts held no water', and that they were unlikely to honour any bookings made for them)
- that company C is insolvent, which might **deter banks from lending to that company** (per *Derbyshire CC v Times Newspapers Ltd*[d] – dicta example)
- that employer C provided terrible conditions in which to work/live, which imputations could **impede C's ability to hire the best qualified workers**, or make others reluctant to deal with C (per *South Hetton Coal Co Ltd v North-East News Assn Ltd*[e] – C, a colliery company, owned a number of cottages for its employees, of which D wrote that they were in an unsanitary state, unfit for habitation by the pitmen)
- that C set up, or benefited from, **a slush fund**, where the ordinary meaning of a slush fund was that the money was 'dirty money', being used for improper purposes, or obtained corruptly (per *Thompson v James*[f])
- that C was **dishonest** in his business dealings and **deliberately lied** to the *Financial Times* by making unfounded allegations against D which he knew to be untrue (per *Haji-Ioannou v Dixon Regus Group plc*[g])
- that C **lacked professional judgment** in how he practised and **recommended an unproven method** of anaesthetising patients **which was dangerous** for patients (per *Drummond-Jackson v British Medical Assn*[h] – there was no analogy between a professional person's technique and a trader's goods – goods are impersonal and transient; professional technique is 'relatively permanent, and it belongs to him'; C developed a special technique for dental anaesthetic; four scientists from Birmingham University, D, scientifically investigated the technique and claimed in the British Medical Journal that the technique 'must be regarded as having serious detrimental physiological effects, which may well have been the cause of the reported deaths')

[a] [2014] IESC 79.
[b] [2010] EWHC 924 (QB) [49].
[c] [2010] UKSC 53, [2011] 1 AC 852, [118].
[d] [1993] AC 534 (HL) 547.
[e] [1894] 1 QB 133 (CA) 135–36.
[f] [2014] EWCA Civ 600, [21].
[g] [2009] EWHC 178 (QB).
[h] [1970] 1 WLR 688 (CA) 698, 701.

On the other hand, a number of comments that may seem derogatory have been held **not** to be defamatory in nature as the table overpage illustrates.

Unsuccessful defamatory imputations

The imputation	Why it would not adversely affect the attitude of people towards C
C stated (and reported by D) that she disagreed with the pro-vegetarian views held by Sir Paul Macartney and Annie Lennox (*Ecclestone v Telegraph Media*[a])	C had not disagreed in such violent, excessive, abusive or disrespectful language that ordinary reasonable members of society might think the less of C. There was no suggestion of hypocrisy here. The opinion expressed was an acceptable one in a democratic society, on a subject where strong opinions are validly held
in *Levi v Bates*, facts previously, D wrote that some of C's remarks and conduct 'are so serious that they have been reported to the police'	reference that C had been reported to the police would not, of itself, convey to readers that C's conduct was criminal
D wrote an article about C, a tennis player, calling C the 'world's worst tennis pro', and stating: 'until his win at the Reus tournament near Barcelona, [Dee] had lost 54 consecutive professional tennis matches during his three years on the professional tennis circuit, and had therefore proved himself to be the worst professional tennis player in the world' (*Dee v Telegraph Media*[b])	the words did not suggest that D's performance fell below the standard generally required for his profession as a tennis player, because in every race, match or other sporting event, someone has to come last – losing is an occupational hazard of competitive sport. An allegation of poor sporting skill may dent a sportsman's pride rather, but not their professional reputation in a defamatory sense. Anyway, the ordinary reader will not necessarily have an adverse opinion – a sportsman on a losing streak might be unlucky, inexperienced, playing out of his league, lacking proper management, out of form, injured, or simply not as good; and several defeats followed by a famous victory could be regarded as creditworthy
C, author/journalist, wrote a book, *Seven Days in the Art World*, based partly on interviews with those in art circles. D published a book review, stating that C 'practices "reflexive ethnography", which means that her interviewees have the right to read what she says about them and alter it. In journalism we call this "copy approval" and disapprove'. The review also noted that C had 'a seemingly limitless capacity to write pompous nonsense' (*Thornton v Telegraph Media*[c])	some professionals (e.g., a dentist or doctor, or the standards of cleanliness in *South Hetton*) must attain only one minimum professional standard, but others such as writers are able to choose from a number of acceptable standards (what is suitable for an 'entertainment piece' of writing may not be acceptable for a 'thesis-type piece of writing). Copy approval may not suit the highest journalistic standards, but this was a 'fly-on-the-wall narrative', and the words used did not impute that C was conducting herself, in her business, badly or wrongfully, because she was free to adopt different standards for different readerships to whom the writing was directed. Moreover, the fact that a poor book review may discourage commercial publishers from dealing with a writer professionally, or a reader from reading the book, was not a business defamation

[a] [2009] EWHC 2779 (QB).
[b] [2010] EWHC 924 (QB) [49].
[c] [2010] EWHC 1414 (QB). There was no personal libel here either: [99]–[102].

The imputation	Why it would not adversely affect the attitude of people towards C
C, employed by the BBC as a junior assistant to enter data into databases, received feedback about job performance which indicated that errors had been made and which was critical of C's performance (*Daniels v BBC*[d])	this criticism of C's work concerned trivial errors, failure to communicate with colleagues, and speaking to customers rather than to fellow members of the team, to point to areas in which improvement could be made. No ordinary and sensible reader would think less of C, either in his personal or business reputation, as a result of what was said, because it was commonplace that people starting employment in a new job need to learn what to do, and there might be room for improvement
C, a model, actress and former Miss India, and contestant on Big Brother, alleged that other contestants made statements on the show alleging that she was promiscuous, of below average intelligence, and socially inferior (e.g., because of how she ate her breakfast cereal) (*Uppal v Endemol UK Ltd*[e])	referring to C as a 'piece of shit' was merely 'vile abuse', and reflected adversely on the person who uttered the statement, and not on C. Whatever the fellow contestants may have said about proposed sexual activity with C, nothing suggested that C would be a willing participant in the suggested activity, which defeated any imputation of promiscuity. Offensive racial stereotyping of people of Indian origin reflected, again, on the person who made the statement, and not upon C herself
C, a former postgraduate student at Swansea University, missed two exams, and following various procedures, was required to withdraw from his academic course. C relied on medical opinion that he suffered from CFS and anxiety (*Ibrahim v Swansea University*[f])	no reasonable person would, nowadays, think any the worse of someone who had suffered from either 'mental health difficulties' or from 'chronic fatigue syndrome and anxiety'. That allegation would not be capable of lowering C in the eyes of right-thinking members of society

[d] [2010] EWHC 3057 (QB) [48].
[e] [2014] EWHC 1063 (QB).
[f] [2012] EWHC 290 (QB).

Focusing on the reasonable reader/listener

§15.14 When determining whether or not an imputation was defamatory, the court will apply the standard of a 'hypothetical reasonable reader', or the so-called 'right-thinking member of society'.

That reader will have a number of important characteristics (per *Jeynes v News Magazines Ltd*[131]):

> [he is] not naïve, but he is not unduly suspicious either. He can read between the lines. He can read in an implication more readily than a lawyer, and may indulge in a certain amount of loose thinking, but he ... is not avid for scandal, [and] should not select one bad meaning where other non-defamatory meanings are available. Over-elaborate analysis is best avoided.

131 [2008] EWCA Civ 130, [14], principles 1, 2, 3 and 6. Also; *Trumm v Norman* [2008] EWHC 116 (QB) [17].

However, the hypothetical reasonable reader is 'a crude yardstick', because readers of any publication will differ enormously as to how they read articles, and how they interpret the words that they do read (per *Charleston v News Group Newspapers Ltd*[132]).

§15.15 To assess the view of the hypothetical reader/listener, the general rule is that the court will have regard to whether the opinion of a person from society as a whole towards C was adversely affected by the publication. However, in exceptional scenarios, the court may have regard to whether the opinion of a limited group of readers towards C was adversely affected by the publication.

The test is not whether a section of the public would think less of C, but whether the opinion of a reasonable reader/listener drawn from society as a whole towards C would be adversely affected by D's publication (per *Thornton v Telegraph Media Group Ltd*[133]).

The Court of Appeal pointed out, in *Ajinomoto Sweeteners Europe SAS v Asda Stores Ltd*,[134] that it would perhaps be easier for C if the English law of defamation assessed 'adverse effect' by having regard to whether it had that effect on 'a substantial number of people'. C would arguably have had a better chance of success than having regard to a hypothetical person from the whole general public. However, the tougher test of the hypothetical reasonable reader from the general public makes it more difficult for C to establish his case in defamation – thereby advancing the right to freedom of expression over the right to reputation.

Two consequences follow from the general rule:

i. the fact that both C and D may consider that a certain practice alleged against C should be 'disapproved of' is by no means proof of defamation – the case has to be tried against the standards of members of society generally (per *Thornton*[135] – where C's practice of giving interviewees 'copy approval' was agreed not to be appropriate for all types of authorship);
ii. just because *a subsection* of the general public might think the imputation defamatory of C is **not**, in general, relevant – what matters is whether the imputation is defamatory in the eyes of the wider general public.

In *Williams v MGN Ltd*,[136] Mr Williams, C, serving a life term for murder, sued for defamation for an article in which he was alleged to be a police informant, or a 'grass', regarding the identity of the party who funded the murder of a jewellery store owner in Nottingham in 2003. **Held:** the article was not defamatory of C. Any allegation of being a 'grass' was incapable of bearing a defamatory meaning in the eyes of the general public, as a matter of public policy. It will probably raise C's reputation in the eyes of that public. In *Ecclestone v Telegraph Media Group Ltd*,[137] facts previously, **held:** no defamatory imputation, as it could not be said that the general public would think adversely of Petra Ecclestone, C, for disapproving of those, such as Annie Lennox and Paul Macartney, who promoted the vegetarian lifestyle and choices. Just because a sector of the public could think the less of C who 'dissed' vegetarians, did not mean that the public in general would think worse of C for saying it. All that was being published by D was that C was not a vegetarian,

[132] [1995] 2 AC 65 (HL) 73–74 (Lord Nicholls).
[133] [2010] EWHC 1414 (QB) [77], citing: *Sim v Stretch* [1936] 2 All ER 1237 (HL).
[134] [2010] EWCA Civ 609, [2011] QB 497, [27]–[28], [31], [34].
[135] [2010] EWHC 1414 (QB) [98].
[136] [2009] EWHC 3150 (QB) [17]–[18], citing, e.g.: *Byrne v Deane* [1937] 1 KB 818 (CA) 832–33.
[137] [2009] EWHC 2779 (QB) [17] (Sharp J).

and did not have much time for people who were; but no ordinary reasonable reader would think less of C as a result.

However, in limited scenarios, the opinion of a limited group will suffice:

i. re a *business imputation* that C's goods or services fall below a required standard, that standard will usually be one that is set by the professional body or a regulatory authority, and hence, it is the members of that body/profession which will be more useful than the opinion of 'right-thinking members of society generally' (but for other types of business defamation, 'there may be more of a role for the opinion or attitude of right-thinking members of society') (per *Thornton*[138]);
ii. re *a true (legal) innuendo*, the court may also have regard to whether a certain group of readers knew of the extraneous facts said to give rise to the innuendo – it is not necessary that the general public would have known of the extraneous facts necessary to give rise to a legal innuendo.

In *Baturina v Times Newspapers Ltd*,[139] facts previously, the court had to consider whether some of the 400,000 UK-based Russian residents would have known of a Russian decree requiring disclosure of assets, giving rise to a legal innuendo, where C, wife of the former Moscow Mayor, had not declared her ownership of a grand house. C was required to identify specific readers who appreciated the innuendo that she had concealed her ownership of the house; her ownership of the house was published in the *Sunday Times*, but even though it was 'a national newspaper with a very wide circulation', there was 'no evidence to show that its circulation is wide among Russian inhabitants of England and Wales', so C had to call witnesses who knew of the Russian decree.

Focusing on the publication

The 'bane and the antidote'

§15.16 In order to determine the natural and ordinary meaning of the words, and whether they are defamatory, it is necessary to take into account the context in which the words appear, how the relevant material was set out and presented, whether inverted commas were used around the imputation, and whether an 'antidote' was sufficient to neutralise the defamatory 'bane'.

Any 'bane and antidote' contained in a publication must be read together (per *Jeynes v News Magazines Ltd*[140]). For example, the text may prove an antidote to a headline or photograph; or some curative words in a conclusion may prove an antidote to an earlier and derogatory part of the article; but if the curative words are 'tucked away', then the ordinary sensible reader would likely discount the antidote. In any event, the bane and antidote must be taken together (per *Dee v Telegraph Media Group Ltd*[141]).

i. **Headlines/photos versus text.** Where a headline or photograph, read alone, is defamatory in character, the reasonable and fair-minded reader must be taken to have read beyond the headline, and read the article itself. It means that a claim for defamation cannot be based on a headline or photograph in isolation from the rest of the article. The proposition that one part

138 [2010] EWHC 1414 (QB) [34], [38]. 139 [2011] EWCA Civ 308, [47].
140 [2008] EWCA Civ 130, [14], principle (5).
141 [2010] EWHC 924 (QB) [20], [22], [114], citing: *Chalmers v Payne* (1835) 2 CM&R 156, 159 (Alderson B).

of an article can be severed from another part of the article, because the ordinary reader will read one part and not another, was expressly rejected in *Charleston v News Group Newspapers Ltd*[142] – newspapers cannot be liable for what the headline says, alone. This is so, even though it is judicially acknowledged that many readers will not, in fact, have read the whole article at all (per *Kaschke v Osler*[143]), and even where editors know that an eye-catching headline or photograph will first attract the reader's attention and that a 'significant number will not trouble to read any further' (per *Charleston*).

In *Charleston*, the actor and actress, C, played the parts of Harold and Madge Bishop, a respectable married couple, in the popular Australian TV soap, 'Neighbours', well-known to millions of English viewers. The *News of the World* published an article with photographs which showed Cs' faces superimposed on the near-naked bodies of models in pornographic poses, and with a large headline, 'Strewth! What's Harold up to with our Madge?'. It was plain from the article that the superimposition had occurred without Cs' knowledge or consent: 'The famous faces from the TV soap are the unwitting stars of a sordid computer game that is available to their child fans ... The game superimposes stars' heads on near-naked bodies of real porn models. The stars knew nothing about it', and the rest of the article was indignantly critical of the makers of the 'sordid computer game'. C claimed that readers would have thought that C had been willing participants in the production of the pornographic photographs. **Held:** no defamatory imputation. No reader would have thought that C was involved, if they read the text as well. It did not matter if some 'limited readers' would have read only the headline or the photograph, and not the rest of the article. A reasonable reader must be taken to have read beyond the headline and photograph. In *Hamaizia v Commr of Police*,[144] a police press release had the headline, 'Three jailed for murder of Marvin Henry', and the release itself referred to 'five individuals involved in Marvin Henry's murder'. Two Cs claimed that the press release imputed that they were murderers, involved in the murder, whereas they were only convicted of matters involved in the lead-up to that murder. **Held:** no defamatory imputation. Despite the headline, the text of the press release made it clear that neither C was jailed for murder, nor convicted of murder; but only involved in the lead-up (Cs' convictions were for false imprisonment and grievous bodily harm, not for murder).

ii. **Inverted commas around words in headline.** If inverted commas are placed around the allegedly defamatory words, that does not preclude defamation, but it is a relevant factor to take into account when assessing the meaning of the offending words and the degree of gravity to be attached to them. A reasonable reader would assume that it was an allegation that had originally been made by someone else, akin to 'reportage'.

In *Kaschke v Gray, Hilton*,[145] and *Kaschke v Osler*,[146] Mr Gray, D1, published on his blog the heading, '"Baader-Meinhof" losing candidate joins diss-Respect', and Mr Osler, D2, published on his blog the heading, 'Respect member's "Baader-Meinhof link"'. The articles referred to Ms Kaschke, C. D1's article imputed that C was once suspected by the West German authorities to be a member of Baader-Meinhof, and D2's article falsely suggested that C had been accused of being a member of the Baader-Meinhof terrorist group. **Held:** C's reputation was only minimally damaged by articles, given the use of inverted commas, akin to reportage.

142 [1995] 2 AC 65 (HL) 72–73 (Lord Bridge), 74 (Lord Nicholls).

143 [2010] EWHC 1075 (QB) [19], and *Charleston v News Group Newspapers Ltd* [1995] 2 AC 65 (HL) [73].

144 [2014] EWHC 3408 (QB) [26]–[30]. 145 [2010] EWHC 1907 (QB) [19]. 146 [2010] EWHC 1075 (QB).

iii. **Different articles, containing bane and antidote.** Where an article relating to C is spread over several pages of the one publication for space or editorial reasons, or where different articles about C were printed in the one publication (freestanding, without connectors between them), then the key question is whether the articles were sufficiently closely connected as to be regarded as a single publication. If so, then the bane and the antidote appearing in different places must be read together – because a reasonable reader should be taken to have turned over the pages and found and read the other pages or other articles (even if, in reality, many people would only have read one of the relevant pages or articles (per *Dee v Telegraph Media Group Ltd*[147]).

In *Dee v Telegraph Media*, facts previously, an article on the front page of the *Daily Telegraph* used the heading, 'World's worst tennis pro wins at last', and named Robert Dee, C. It also referred to 'Full Story: S20' (p 1 of the Sports Supplement), where it said that 'Dee equalled the world record for the longest run of consecutive defeats, after his first three years on the international professional circuit saw him lose 54 matches in a row, and all of them in straight sets'. **Held:** the two articles were not defamatory. They had to be read together, as there was a very clear cross reference between them; and S20 contained an explanation/antidote to the headline.

The same principle, of whether articles were sufficiently connected as to be regarded as a single publication, applies in the case of articles appearing in different publications.

In *Galloway v Telegraph Media Group Ltd*,[148] Mr Galloway, C, founder of political party, Respect, opposed military action in Iraq in 2003 and sanctions against the Saddam Hussein regime. Articles appeared in the *Daily Telegraph* on 22 and 23 April 2003, said to have been based upon documents found in badly damaged government offices in Baghdad. The gist of the article on 22 April, published on the front page under the heading, 'Galloway in Saddam's pay, say secret Iraqi documents', was that G had received money from Saddam Hussein's regime, and had been granted special deals in the UN oil-for-food programme. The articles on 23 April reported that the documents suggested that G had demanded more money from the regime, but had been rebuffed. **Held**: whether the articles were defamatory (which they were) had to be judged by taking account of both sets of articles.

Intent

§15.17 Whether D intended the statement to be defamatory is irrelevant.

The only assessment which the court must make is how the hypothetical reasonable reader would have viewed the statement. What author/publisher D may have intended is not determinative – or even relevant – to that question (per *Jeynes v News Magazines Ltd*[149]). As Russell LJ put it in *Cassidy v Daily Mirror Newspapers Ltd*, '[l]iability for libel does not depend on the intention of the defamer; but on the fact of defamation'.[150]

This can have some fairly harsh results. D can be liable for defamation by true innuendo, even if D did not know (and could not reasonably have been expected to know, when he made the statement) of the extraneous facts which 'made apparently innocent statements defamatory' and thereby created the innuendo. The point was reiterated in *Baturina v Times Newspapers*

147 [2010] EWHC 924 (QB) [27]–[30]. 148 [2006] EWCA Civ 17, [65]–[66].
149 [2008] EWCA Civ 130, [14], principle (4), cited in: *Cook v Telegraph Media* [2011] EWHC 1134 (QB) [4].
150 [1929] 2 KB 331 (CA) 340, 354.

Ltd,[151] in the case of innuendo instituted by the wife of the former Mayor of Moscow (although, in that instance, the considerable journalistic resources available to newspaper D meant that the facts surrounding the Russian decree were probably known to D).

ELEMENT #2: IDENTIFICATION

In the vast majority of cases, the defamatory imputation will clearly identify C as being the person about whom D is allegedly casting defamatory imputations. However, if the defamatory words do not expressly identify C – and a number of problematical scenarios can arise – then C will be obliged to establish that the publication did refer to him.

General principles

§15.18 The defamatory imputation must refer to C, or be understood as referring to C (the latter of which is to be judged according to the ordinary reader). Whether the imputation actually referred to C is not to be judged by what D intended, knew, or could reasonably have foreseen.

Whether a defamatory imputation referred to C must be assessed by reference to precisely the same type of reader as is used to determine whether an imputation was defamatory in the first place, i.e., by reference to the reasonable reader, who can read between the lines, but who is not overly suspicious or prone to over-elaborate analysis (per *Jeynes v News Magazines Ltd*[152]). It is not necessary for *all* readers to consider that the defamatory imputation referred to that C. It is enough if *some* readers would have understood that to be the case.

It does not matter whether or not D intended to refer to C – he is equally as culpable if he did not aim his defamatory imputation at C, but C is nevertheless identified in such a way that other persons will read it as intended to refer to C. Additionally, D may not have foreseen that the imputation could defame C, as he did not know, nor could he have known, the facts which caused readers with special knowledge to connect the statement with C (per *Morgan v Odhams Press Ltd*[153]). In *Hulton & Co Ltd v Jones*, it was said that, rather than 'who was meant', the correct question was, 'who was hit'.[154]

Problematical scenarios

C not named in the publication: reference innuendo

§15.19 A reference innuendo arises where the defamatory imputation does not refer to C expressly, but where knowledge of extrinsic facts on the part of *some readers* is required to link the statement to C.

If, armed with extrinsic facts, readers would reasonably be led to believe that C was the person referred to in the statement, then C is referred to by means of a reference innuendo (per *Baturina v Times Newspapers*[155]).

[151] [2011] EWCA Civ 308, [24]. [152] [2008] EWCA Civ 130, [14]. [153] [1971] 1 WLR 1239 (HL).
[154] An exchange between court and counsel, noted in: *Bradley v Independent Star* [2011] IESC 17, [44].
[155] [2011] EWCA Civ 308, [23].

The facts relied upon to establish reference to C have to be supported by evidence. However, where there is no realistic prospect of establishing that readers of the publication would understand that the words referred to C, because insufficient people knew of the extrinsic facts necessary to refer to C, then defamation will fail.

In *Morgan v Odhams Press Ltd*,[156] Mr Morgan, a journalist, C, investigating a story about a dog doping gang, used information given by a kennel girl, Margo Murray, who was a key witness in the prosecution of the gang. At one point, MM left her lodgings and spent six days with C at his flat. MM was seen with C in public, sometimes in distress and hysteria. Newspaper D published two articles in the newspaper, including a blurred photograph of MM with her name underneath, with a headline, 'Dog doping girl goes into hiding', and stating that the witness was 'kidnapped last week by members of the gang' and 'kept in a house in Finchley'. The article did not name or describe C. C claimed that, by innuendo, the article defamed him by associating him with dog-doping and kidnapping. **Held:** the article was defamatory. The 'ordinary reader' could reasonably think that their witnessing of MM with C was consistent with C being a kidnapper, having terrified MM so that she did not try to escape. Six witnesses gave different reasons for thinking that the article referred to C; and two of them rang C to let him know of the article. In *Powell v Boldaz*,[157] Mr and Mrs Powell, C, complained of the treatment provided to their son by the GP practice, D, and their complaints were the subject of an HTV programme. D put up a notice in their surgery reception area: 'Following the HTV programme of 5th November, 1992 the Practice wishes to inform its patients that allegations of conspiracy, missing letters etc are lies and complete distortion of the actual facts – some of the allegations belong in the realms of fantasy'. C was not referred to in the notice. **Held**: a reference innuendo to C, formed from those who had watched the programme, was possible on these facts. In *Mosley v Focus Magazin Verlag GmbH*,[158] in an interview in *Focus* magazine, retired EEC Competition Commissioner, D, said, 'the worst one was the proceedings over the marketing of Formula 1. It was very clear that certain people were spending a great deal of money to destroy me. Fortunately, they did not succeed'. Max Mosley, C, the long-standing President of the FIA, alleged that the phrase 'certain people' referred to him. The FIA had been under formal investigation by the EEC re the enforcement of EU competition laws, regarding the staging, televising and promotion of F1 races. **Held:** the article did not refer to C. It was unlikely that those readers of *Focus* interested in F1 would have known or remembered the close involvement of C in this dispute, so no extrinsic facts linked C to this article.

C named in one place and not in another

§15.20 C may be identified in a defamatory statement which does not refer to him, if readers have seen other statements in linked publications which did refer to C.

This scenario is important for several reasons. Assessment of damages will be increased if both publications are taken to have referred to C. Also, the statement which actually refers to C may not contain any defamatory imputations at all, thereby requiring the two statements to be linked, in order to defame C.

Where C complains that he was defamed in articles in consecutive newspaper publications, but is only identified in one of them, sufficient linkages between them may mean that C was identified in **both** articles.

[156] [1971] 1 WLR 1239 (HL). [157] [2003] EWHC 2160 (QB) (also called *Powell v Boladz* in case reports).
[158] [2001] EWCA Civ 1030, [21], [30].

In *Hayward v Thompson*,[159] Jack Hayward, C, was a wealthy philanthropist living in the Bahamas, who had, during 1970–75, donated over £200,000 to the Liberal Party. The *Sunday Telegraph* published article #1 with the heading, 'Two more in Scott affair', discussing an alleged plot to murder Norman Scott. It did not mention C by name, but said that the names of two more people 'connected with' the plot, one of whom was 'a wealthy benefactor of the Liberal Party', had been given to the police. A week later, article #2 appeared in the same paper, 'New Name In Scott Affair', which named C, that he was a 'Bahamas-based millionaire, who once gave the Liberal party £150,000', and said that the police wanted to interview him. C claimed that both articles defamed him, for imputing that C was guilty, or reasonably suspected, of condoning a murder plot, and that C was the 'wealthy benefactor' in article #1. **Held:** both articles identified C, because article #2 made clear who was the 'wealthy benefactor' in article #1. In *Cook v Telegraph Media Group Ltd*,[160] the assistant of Frank Cook MP, C, made a £5 offertory donation at a Battle of Britain church service in 2006. C reimbursed his assistant, and then claimed the £5 donation as an expense, which was rejected. In 2009, three separate articles were published in the *Sunday Telegraph*: a front-page cover story, 'MP claimed £5 for church collection' (article #1); on p 2, 'I'm sorry, church claim was unfair' (article #2); and later in the newspaper, under the heading, 'COMMENT AND ANALYSIS – Now it is the people's turn to be heard'. C was named in articles #1 and #2, but #3 only referred to, 'as we report today, one Labour MP thinks it is appropriate to claim back from taxpayers the £5 he put in a church collection for an RAF charity, the most obvious conclusion that Labour is made up of people who will destroy the ethic of selfless public service'. **Held:** C was identified in article #3. Although not named, C was identifiable to those readers who had already read articles #1 or #2, and they were linked by the words 'as we report today'.

Internet hyperlinks are another area of controversy. Where C is not specifically referred to on a defamatory website page, but that webpage contains hyperlinks which clearly identify that C was being referred to on the website, then (per *Islam Expo Ltd v The Spectator (1828) Ltd*[161]), the hyperlinks are all part of the context, and may be used to reference C on the website.

In *Islam Expo Ltd v The Spectator*, Islam Expo Ltd, C, organised the bi-annual IslamExpo and Islamic exhibition. The *Spectator* published on its website an article, stating 'Demos sponsored and participated in a debate at IslamExpo and a seminar on "Political Islam". That's right: a left of centre think tank worked with a clerical fascist party to organise a conference about its racist, genocidal, theocratic political programme'. Although C was not named, it alleged that it was described as a 'clerical fascist party'. There were four hyperlinks in the article. Clicking on these, it was clear that C was the organiser of the conference. **Held:** C was sufficiently identified for a defamation action to proceed.

However, where C is named in sentence #1 in a publication, but not in sentence #2, and both contain defamatory imputations, then the ordinary reader would assume that, if D was prepared to name C in sentence #1, he would have named C in the other defamatory imputation too – so that the ordinary reader would consider that C was **not** the person referred to in sentence #2.

In *Coad v Cruze*,[162] Councillor Diana Coad, C, a Conservative councillor in Slough BC, complained of an election leaflet written by the Slough Party, D, which contained the words, 'Slough Conservatives under Investigation again! Police are investigating a Conservative councillor for suspected Perjury

[159] [1982] QB 47 (CA) 59, 65, 72–73. [160] [2011] EWHC 1134 (QB) [24]–[25].
[161] [2010] EWHC 2011 (QB) [25]. See too: *Ali v Associated Newspapers Ltd* [2010] EWHC 100 (QB) [28].
[162] [2009] EWHC 3782 (QB) [27]–[28].

offences. The Electoral Commission are investigating Conservative Cllrs Dexter Smith and Diana Coad for suspected election expenses irregularities'. C sued in defamation, for the imputation that she was under investigation for perjury, given that some readers would have known that C was the only conservative candidate standing in the ward. **Held:** the sentence about perjury did not refer to C. The ordinary reader would reasonably assume that, if the author of the leaflet was prepared to name C in the context of election expense irregularities, he would have named her in the perjury context too. That C was not named reasonably meant that she was not the person referred to.

Fictional characters

§15.21 If D describes a fictional character which reasonable readers could think was intended to refer to C, then C is sufficiently referred to.

As stated previously, D does not have to intend to make a defamatory imputation, nor does the reference to C need to be foreseeable. It may be completely accidental, and yet, defamatory.

In *E Hulton & Co v Jones*,[163] Thomas Artemus Jones, C, a barrister practising on the North Wales Circuit, occasionally wrote articles for the *Sunday Chronicle*, D. D's Paris correspondent wrote an article, describing a motor festival at Dieppe. It included some fictional events, and referred to 'Artemus Jones', a churchwarden at Peckham, who had committed adultery, and who was the 'life and soul of a gay little band that haunts the Casino and turns night into day, besides betraying a most unholy delight in the society of female butterflies'. C sued D for defamation. **Held:** defamation proven, regardless of D's intention to create an 'imaginary character'.

Notably, the newspaper publisher published a statement in the following issue of their paper, 'It seems hardly necessary for us to state that the imaginary Mr Artemus Jones referred to in our article was not Mr Thomas Artemus Jones, barrister, but, as he has complained to us, we gladly publish this paragraph in order to remove any possible misunderstanding and to satisfy Mr Thomas Artemus Jones we had no intention whatsoever of referring to him'. In modern terms, this would be an offer to make amends (discussed below).

Mistaken description or photographs

§15.22 If D publishes a defamatory imputation which contains words/photographs that describe/depict C – but D actually intended to refer to someone else – then C may still have been sufficiently referred to.

It depends upon whether the ordinary reader could reasonably have understood the words/photo to refer to C. As the court put it in *Newstead v London Express Newspapers Ltd*, '[i]f there is a risk of coincidence, it ought in reason to be borne, not by the innocent party to whom the words are held to refer, but by the party who puts them into circulation'.[164]

As pointed out in *O'Shea v MGN Ltd*,[165] the difficulty in 'look-alike' cases is that it casts an 'impossible burden' on the publisher, D. For example, where a defamatory imputation arises from a photo uploaded to an internet site, the image of which looks similar to C's appearance, D is not expected to perform extensive researches to avoid that similarity of appearance. If the law did require D to do this, it would 'place an impossible burden on a publisher if he were

[163] [1910] AC 20 (HL) 24, affirming: [1909] 2 KB 444 (CA). [164] [1940] 1 KB 371 (CA).
[165] [2001] EWHC (QB) 425, [43]–[48], quote at [44].

required to check if every true picture of someone [he published] resembled someone else who, because of the context of the picture, was defamed'.

In *O'Shea v MGN Ltd*, a newspaper published a lawful advertisement for an adult internet service featuring, with her agreement, a photograph of a young woman. That party very closely resembled C, who complained of defamation. **Held:** no defamatory imputation here.

However, where D uses the wrong photograph – C's, instead of the correct party's – then reference is likely. Also, where the description could reasonably refer to C, and not to the correct party who was intended, then reference to C is also likely.

In *Mitchell v Evening Chronicle*,[166] Garry Mitchell was a prisoner at Frankland Prison, Durham. The *Newcastle Evening Chronicle*, D, published an article, 'The few who bred race hatred', which stated 'Chronicle names and shames those holding vile racist views. This gathering of shame exposes 16 of the North-East's most notorious race hate campaigners', and stated, as one of 16 men, 'Garry Mitchell of Emily Street, Gateshead, a long-standing active Nazi and Combat 18 activist, convicted of racial assault in 1993, when he was sentenced to 18 months. Last year he was jailed for 10 years for rape and burglary'. The words were published with a photograph of C, who also had the name, Garry Mitchell, but who was not the prisoner Garry Mitchell that D was referring to. **Held:** the article referred to C. For those readers who knew what C looked like, they could conclude that the words did refer to C, and that the newspaper had published a photograph of the wrong man; and for those readers who did not know what C looked like, they could reasonably understand the words to refer to C. In *Dwek v Macmillan Publishers Ltd*,[167] a photograph of dentist C, and a woman, was published in D's book. The photo caption erroneously stated that it was of Dodi Fayed, and that the woman was a prostitute. C sued for defamation. **Held:** the photograph and caption were capable of referring to C. It was possible that C's friends or acquaintances would have recognised him from the photograph and formed the view that he consorted with prostitutes.

Group defamation

§15.23 If a defamatory imputation refers to a group of persons (i.e., a group 'at large'), and does not refer to any individual person within that group, then no action in defamation can lie by a member of that group. However, where the group is limited, and D's statement may reasonably be taken to refer to C, as a member of that group individually, then C is sufficiently identified.

For a member of a group to be able to sue for defamation, where that member is not named specifically, then the member must prove that the defamatory statement was reasonably understood as referring to him (per *Knupffer v London Express Newspaper*[168]).

A corporate entity cannot be 'put up' as C, where it has no legitimate complaint of its own, but is purely a front for an impermissible group defamation action (dicta in *British Chiropractic Assn v Singh*[169]).

For those entities which do not have standing to sue in their own right – e.g., a trade union, or an unincorporated association – this principle has grave ramifications, as members of the union/association will not be able to sue in defamation either, if the imputation is aimed at the

[166] [2003] EWHC 1281 (QB). [167] [2000] EMLR 284 (CA) 293–94.
[168] [1944] AC 116 (HL) 121–22. [169] [2010] EWCA Civ 350, [2011] 1 WLR 133, [10]–[12].

union/association as a whole, without identifying any particular members of the union/association as to impair their reputations individually (per *EETPU v Times Newspapers Ltd*).[170] The same applies to a profession – if D says, 'all lawyers are rascals', that does not permit any lawyer in the jurisdiction to sue for defamation.[171] Members of the group will need to show that D's statement referred to them individually and with sufficient clarity. For example, to reiterate the example in *EETPU*,[172] of D's stating that the Anglers' Association cheated at a competition – if a limited number of individuals competed last Saturday, and were easily identifiable, then D's statement referred to them individually and sufficiently clearly. However, group defamation has been difficult to establish in English law to date, even where the number in the group was relatively small:

> In *Knupffer v London Express Newspapers*,[173] Mr Knupffer, C, a Russian living in London, was a member of the Young Russia Party. In 1938, C was appointed head of the British branch of the party. In 1941, D's newspaper article stated, 'The quislings on whom Hitler flatters himself he can build a pro-German movement within the Soviet Union are an emigré group called Mlado Russ or Young Russia. They are a minute body professing a pure Fascist ideology ... The vast majority of Russian emigrés repudiate these people, but Hitler is accustomed to find instruments among the despised dregs of every community'. The British branch of the party comprised 24 members, and worldwide, had over 2,000 members. C claimed that the article defamed him. **Held:** no defamation possible. That some witnesses said that their minds went to C when they read the article was because they happened to know C as the leading member of the Party in England; but nothing in the article referred to C as an individual. In *Braddock v Bevins*,[174] Mrs Braddock, C, was Labour MP in Liverpool. D, a political opponent, said in an election address: 'I am profoundly disturbed by the aims of the Soviet Government. I am convinced that our civilization is gravely threatened by the fanatical desire to shackle their barbaric will on mankind. I am horrified that the Socialist MP for the Division and her friends in Abercromby should persistently take sides with the Soviet Government and the British Communist party'. C and three of her supporters sued for defamation. **Held:** the three supporters could not sue, because they were not referred to. They were all prominent among C's supporters, but nothing distinguished them as being the 'friends' referred to. The words were not capable of referring to any one of them as an identifiable individual, although it was 'perhaps somewhat near the border line'.

ELEMENT #3: PUBLICATION

§15.24 There can be no defamatory publication which is published only to C himself.

The whole point of defamation is that serious harm has been caused, or is likely to be caused, to C's reputation, which arises from publication of the imputation *to a third party*. If it was only necessary to prove that the publication caused C distress or injury to feelings, then publication to C alone would do. However, for defamation, there can be no publication which is limited to C himself (per *Ibrahim v Swansea University*[175]). Thus, for example, any letter posted by D to C, which only C opens and reads, cannot be defamation.

[170] [1980] QB 585. [171] An example given by O'Connor J in *EEPTU*, *ibid*, 595–96.
[172] *ibid*, 595–96. [173] [1944] AC 116 (HL). [174] [1948] 1 KB 580 (CA) 587, quote at 589.
[175] [2012] EWHC 290 (QB) [14].

When publication occurs

The single publication rule

§15.25 Under the common law, each separate publication by D gave rise to a separate cause of action ('the multiple publication rule'). However, that position is reversed by s 8 of the Defamation Act 2013, whereby a cause of action in defamation accrues on the date of the first publication, where D subsequently publishes the same or a similar statement ('the single publication rule').

Under the 'multiple publication' rule in *Duke of Brunswick v Harmer*,[176] a separate cause of action accrued for each individual publication of a libel, and each action was subject to its own limitation period. Indeed, each publication was a separate tort (per *Berezovsky v Michaels*[177]). This entitled C to identify all of the publications of a defamatory statement, and to claim for them separately as inflicting damage upon his reputation (per *Jameel v Dow Jones & Co Inc*[178]).

The ramifications of the 'multiple publication' rule were uncomfortable for publisher D. For example:

- when material was published in hard copy, and then again on the internet, that constituted separate publications, each giving rise to a tort (per *Loutchansky v Times Newspapers*[179]);
- where a book was published, and then reprinted, or a new softback edition published, those constituted separate publications (per an example in *Loutchansky*[180]); and
- where the material was published in separate jurisdictions, via the internet, then separate publications occur in whatever jurisdictions those words were heard or read. Hence, publication of the material in England involves tortious conduct separate from any tort involved in its publication abroad (per *Berezovsky v Michaels*,[181] thus rejecting a 'global publication' rule, analogous to a 'single publication rule').

However, as a result of s 8 of the Defamation Act 2013, and the introduction of the 'single publication' rule, it means that a cause of action in defamation will be treated as having accrued on the date of the *first* publication, if a person publishes a statement and subsequently publishes that or a substantially similar statement. This, of course, is less generous to C than the common law was.

Pursuant to s 8(4), though, where the manner of the subsequent publication is 'materially different' from the original publication, then they will be construed as being multiple publications (each subject to its own limitation period). The *Explanatory Notes* give this example: suppose an article was originally published by D on the web in a fairly obscure fashion, where several hyperlinks needed to be gone through to access it, but then it was promoted to a position where it could be directly accessed from the home page of D's website, thereby increasing the customer traffic that it received – that would be a separate publication, under s 8(4).

Natural and probable consequence

§15.26 Publication of the defamatory imputation must have been the natural and probable consequence of D's activity. Otherwise, D is not liable as 'publisher'.

176 (1849) 14 QB 185. 177 [2000] 1 WLR 1004 (HL) 1012 (Lord Steyn).
178 [2005] EWCA Civ 75, [24]. Also see, on further appeal: [2007] 1 AC 359 (HL) [48].
179 [2002] QB 783 (CA) [16]. 180 *ibid*, [63]. 181 [2000] 1 WLR 1004 (HL) 1014 (Lord Steyn).

C must establish that publication of the defamatory imputation was a natural and probable consequence of what D did (per *Theaker v Richardson*[182]). Failing that, D will not be liable for the publication.

In *Bezant v Rausing*,[183] Mr Bezant, C, objected to a letter written by Dr Rausing, D, containing a false allegation that C had been detained in public by a police officer. That letter was opened and read by C's daughter, Miss Bezant, who then showed it to other family members, all of whom were distressed and shocked. The letter was marked, 'private and confidential'. **Held:** no publication by D. D did not know that Miss Bezant would open and read the letter. C had argued that D was aware of the practice, within the Bezant family, of opening each other's mail, but that did not establish the 'natural and probable consequence' of D's sending the letter.

Republication

§15.27 If a reasonable person in D's position should have appreciated that there was a significant risk of repetition of D's defamatory imputation, either wholly or partly, then D will be liable for the additional damage caused by that original publication. However, if republication of the imputation was not reasonably foreseeable, then that repetition will break the chain, such that D is not liable for any additional damage caused by the republication.

'Republication damage' (as it was termed in *Collins Stewart Ltd v Financial Times Ltd*[184]) means that whole or partial repetition of D's defamatory imputation by a third party (TP) will entitle C to further damage against D – provided that such republication of D's imputation (whether in the media, on the internet, or otherwise) was reasonably foreseeable. According to *McManus v Beckham*,[185] C must prove that D 'foresaw that the further publication would probably take place, or that a reasonable person in D's position should have so foreseen [that further publication], and that, in consequence, increased damage to C would ensue'. The fact that a subsequent publication by TP only repeats the imputation in part is irrelevant; either whole or part will do, to entitle C to republication damages against D (*Collins Stewart*[186]). However, if that republication was not reasonably foreseeable, then D will not be liable for that republication damage (per *Slipper v BBC*[187]).

In *McManus v Beckham*, facts previously, whilst Victoria Beckham, D, may have told three customers in C's shop that the autograph on a photograph of her husband, David Beckham, was a fake, the incident received considerable press coverage, as a result of which C's business suffered a dramatic downturn. **Held:** it was arguable that a reasonable person in D's position should have appreciated that there was a significant risk that what she said would be repeated, in whole or in part, in the press, which would increase the damage to C caused by the slander, and that it was not unjust that D should be liable for it. That question should be left for trial.

About the publishee

Publication to solicitor/police

§15.28 Despite a very limited number of publishees, the more 'official' that publishee, the more likely it is that the action in defamation will at least be 'worth the candle', and not struck out as an abuse of process. It is a case-by-case analysis.

[182] [1962] 1 WLR 151 (CA). [183] [2007] EWHC 1118 (QB). [184] [2005] EWHC 262 (QB) [21].
[185] [2002] 1 WLR 2982 (CA) [42]–[43] (Laws LJ). [186] [2005] EWHC 262 (QB) [21].
[187] [1991] 1 QB 283 (CA).

A very limited number of publishees (i.e., recipients) may constitute too minor a matter to constitute 'a real and substantial tort' (per the *Jameel* principle, discussed previously under 'Pre-requisites'). However, it was pointed out in *Mardas v New York Times Co* that whether C fell foul of the *Jameel* principle 'cannot depend upon a numbers game', and that each case must be determined on its own facts, especially in light of who the publishee may be.[188] For example, a *Jameel* point was not successful in any of the following, where the sole publishee was:

> an immigration officer/police officer (per *Hughes v Alan Dick & Co Ltd*,[189] where C complained that someone from his former employer's office rang an officer of the UK Border and Immigration Agency alleging that C had been embezzling from his employer in Nigeria whilst employed there, and that C's wife might be carrying £100,000 in her luggage. This information was passed onto a police officer); or a public relations firm (per *Stelios Haji-Ioannou v Dixon*,[190] where the imputation against C, as a well-known businessman, was of a most serious nature, i.e., dishonesty, and where there was also republication in the *Financial Times*).

Where C can only point to a publication of the defamatory imputation to C's solicitor, as part of the dispute between C and D, then that technically fulfils the 'publication requirement'. However, again, such publication is subject to the *Jameel* principle. In some circumstances, publication to a solicitor, as the *sole* recipient of the alleged defamatory imputation, will be sufficient to go forth.

> In *Wallis v Meredith*,[191] an employee, D, whose employment with C had been terminated, conveyed an allegation in a letter to C's solicitor that he suspected that 'two burly men with East European accents who threatened me' may have been sent by C, given their demand that D apologise to 'the man that you have offended', which, D alleged, may have referred to one of C's employees with whom he had had a heated conversation. **Held:** the action was struck out on *Jameel* grounds, given that C's solicitor was unlikely to have thought worse of C, especially in light of C's denials of the D's imputation, and where C's solicitors were probably 'busily engaged in stating that [D's] allegation is false'; and given that D was entitled to express his concerns about what he said had happened, in measured tones, and it was appropriate that he should do so to C's solicitors. In *Sanders v Percy*,[192] facts previously, D's allegations about C's benefit fraud were only published to C's solicitor in a phone conversation; and moreover, the solicitor was noted not to have appeared to have believed them or acted on them to C's detriment. **Held:** the suit could proceed, and was not an abuse on *Jameel* grounds. The allegations against C were serious, and intended to persuade the solicitor to act to C's detriment; and D was a court officer acting or purporting to act in relation to court business.

Absent special factors, however, the general position, in *Wallis*, is that mere publication to C's solicitor, and to no other publishee, is 'not worth the candle' – that such publication was as 'numerically minimal as it could get', and in circumstances where solicitors were 'routinely the recipients of defamatory imputations about their clients (since most allegations of unlawful conduct are likely to be defamatory)'.

Publishees of a slander

§15.29 Given that slander is defamation in spoken form, C is permitted some latitude, when identifying precisely what was said and to whom.

[188] [2009] EMLR 8 (QB) 15.
[189] [2008] EWHC 2695 (QB), permission to appeal refused: [2009] EWCA 272.
[190] [2009] EWHC 178 (QB).
[191] [2011] EWHC 75 (QB) [60]–[62].
[192] [2009] EWHC 1870 (QB) [15].

In the case of slander, C may have learnt of 'the general gist' of what was supposedly said by D, but that is all. In Practice Direction 53, it is provided that 'the Claim Form must, so far as possible, contain the words complained of, and identify the person to whom they were spoken and when'.[193] However, it was held, in *Freer v Zeb*,[194] that if C does not know the name of the publishees to whom the slander was made, the court may, exceptionally, allow the claim to proceed, pending disclosure or D's providing further information to identify those publishees.

Hence, the purpose of the Practice Direction is to enable D to know what the case against him is, so as to be able to meet it; while the judicial exception gives C the opportunity to gather evidence to 'make his case'. However, without credible evidence, in the first place, that any publication of the slander has occurred, there can be no good cause in defamation.

Publication and the internet

Websites

§15.30 Publication over the internet takes place only if the material is accessed and downloaded by a third party (although whether the publication was sufficient to constitute 'serious harm' and to surmount the *Jameel* principle must be decided upon all the facts and circumstances). Publication may arise from webpage content, from Facebook and LinkedIn content and profiles, and from twitter postings.

According to *Gregg v O'Gara*,[195] for those websites where the number of 'hits' can be ascertained, then publication to readers of that website is established. However, where publication is alleged to have occurred on a website open to general access, C bears the onus to prove publication in the ordinary way (per *Al Amoudi v Brisard*[196]) – although an 'irresistible inference' (as it was described in *Gregg v O'Gara*[197]) can be drawn that publication did happen, as in the following:

> In *Steinberg v Englefield*,[198] a client, D, of law firm C, wrote a letter to C, alleging that the firm 'artificially and unprofessionally inflated their solicitor and own clients costs'. This letter was posted by D on the internet, and was accessible to anyone (including potential clients) who fed C's name into any standard search engine; and it was also posted on D's own professional website, and could be read by anyone who accessed that website. In *Gregg v O'Gara*, Mr O'Gara, D, published a book, *The Real Yorkshire Ripper*. Certain statements on his own website at www.yorkshireripper.co.uk and on a google discussion board, alleged that the senior investigating officer of the case, C, had engaged in serious misconduct in the investigations into the 'Yorkshire Ripper' hoax letters (for which John Humble was wrongly convicted for perverting the course of justice in 2006), including that D alleged that C had been party to the tampering of DNA evidence to incriminate Humble; and that C had been party to mistreating Humble during the investigation. D's website was one of the first on the search list when the 'Yorkshire Ripper' was entered into a standard search engine, and the google discussion board was easily locatable. C was contacted by people in different professions across the media, the law and the police, all of whom had become aware of D's allegations in circulation.

193 Para 2.2(2).
194 [2008] EWHC 212 (QB) [31], citing: *Best v Charter Medical of England Ltd* [2001] EWCA Civ 1588, [11]–[13].
195 [2008] EWHC 658 (QB) [48]. 196 [2006] EWHC 1062 (QB) [37].
197 [2008] EWHC 658 (QB) [52]–[53]. 198 [2005] EWCA Civ 288, [21].

However, for some websites, it is not possible to determine the number of 'hits', which can pose difficulties for proof of publication. For example, in *Beach Developments Ltd v Foskett*,[199] Eady J remarked that proof of publication was a 'real issue in relation to the Windows Live publications', as it could be difficult to establish that anyone actually read the statement posted up on a Windows Live website, before the site was modified and the statement removed.

Any imputations contained on D's facebook page (or which are available via links on that page) are published to those who view or access that page. 'Tweets' visible on D's twitter account are also published – and retweeting and hashtagging adds to the extent of publication, once viewed or retweeted.

In *Applause Store Productions Ltd v Raphael*,[200] Grant Raphael, D, set up a Facebook account, and created a link to a group entitled 'Has Mathew Firsht lied to you?', which suggested that D had not been paid money owed by Mr Firsht, C. A false profile was created by D for C, citing personal details of C, including his sexual preferences, relationship status, political and religious beliefs and age, plus referring to C's company. Facebook kept no records which showed how many users viewed or accessed either the profile or the group, but it was visible to over 850,000 members of the London network of Facebook. In *Lord McAlpine v Bercow*,[201] Sally Bercow, D, wife of the Speaker of the Commons and a TV personality, tweeted on her Twitter account, 'Why is Lord McAlpine trending? *innocent face*'. D's account had 56,000 followers. A contemporaneous BBC Newsnight report stated that Mr Messham had been abused at Welsh children's home 20 years previously by a leading Conservative politician from that time, and that the decision of the BBC not to name the person identified was a public controversy. When the tweet occurred, Lord McAlpine, C, was not otherwise in the public eye, and there was much speculation as to the identity of an unnamed previously-prominent politician. The tweet meant, in its natural and ordinary meaning, that C was a paedophile who was guilty of sexually abusing boys living in care. Also, the reasonable reader would understand the *innocent face* as being insincere and ironical.

Indeed, internet publication via Facebook or Twitter creates the potential for one defamatory imputation to spread 'virally', which is said to comprise a 'percolation' effect – a harmful factor which enhances C's damages (per *Rai v Bholowasia*[202]).

In *Reachlocal UK Ltd v Bennett*,[203] facts previously, D published a series of tweets on its Twitter page (with almost 4,000 followers) that ReachLocal, C, engaged in dishonest and deceptive practices and was scamming its customers. D also sent those tweets to other Twitter accounts (with 7,300 followers), and one of these retweeted material on his own Twitter page (with 90,000 followers). D also attracted attention to its Twitter page by using the hashtag #SearchWars, which topic had a large readership in a wider context of competition between search engines. D also published the imputations about C on its Facebook page and LinkedIn pages. All contributed to an eventual award of £75,000 of general damages.

However, the treatment of tweets and re-tweets is clearly still developing in defamation litigation. For example, recently in *Paris v Lewis*,[204] Judge Llewellyn QC, sitting as a Deputy High Court judge, noted that there were two aspects to tweets and re-tweets. First, tweets were likely to be ephemeral and replaced by newer tweets very quickly, and hence, were unlikely to be

[199] [2011] EWHC 198 (QB) [25]. [200] [2008] EWHC 1781. [201] [2013] EWHC 1342 (QB).
[202] [2015] EWHC 382 (QB) [173]. [203] [2014] EWHC 3405 (QB) [61].
[204] QB, Swansea District Registry, 14 Jul 2015.

read after a short time. Secondly, the re-tweet could mean that an original defamatory message could appear in a later timeline, and be published to a different publishee who had not read the original tweet. Obviously, these two aspects pull in different directions, and it will be a question for the court, in each case, as to whether the tweets gave rise to a 'real and substantial tort' (in this case, they did not).

Internet search engine providers and web hosts

§15.31 As a general rule, internet search engine providers and web hosts of content posted to the internet are facilitators for that publication, but do not publish nor authorise publication of the material themselves. However, where it is drawn to D's attention that a defamatory imputation has been posted to a website of which D is host, and D does not take steps to remove it within a reasonable time, then D is taken to have become the publisher of that imputation (via the doctrine of consent and acquiescence). Even where a defamatory imputation is drawn to D's attention, it must be feasible for D to block the sites which contain that defamatory content or to remove it from the website; otherwise no liability will lie for any continuing publication of the imputation.

The law of defamation has had to cope with the development of the internet age, by considering the liability (if any) of those entities which host internet content (web hosts, such as Google, Facebook and YouTube), or which provide search engines by which to 'mine' internet content (search engine providers, such as Google), and which facilitate access to the internet (internet service providers, or ISPs, such as AOL, Tiscali, or BT). Most significantly for Element #3, the question arises as to whether any of these entities are publishers.

General rule. Subject to the exception below, a **web host** simply provides a platform for other users to upload material, and is to be treated as a facilitator – it is neither a publisher nor an entity which authorised publication of the defamatory material. Its role is a passive one, merely facilitating postings on the internet (per *Tamiz v Google Inc*[205]). Eady J (at first instance) pointed to Google's stated policy of non-intervention, which reflected that its role as a platform provider was a purely passive one.

Similarly, for entities which provide internet search engines (per *Metropolitan Intl Schools Ltd v Designtechnica Corp and Google*[206]), and for those ISPs which enable internet access (per *Bunt v Tilley*[207]), they are not to be regarded as publishers either, as a general rule. Various reasons for the 'facilitator-not-publisher' role have been stated.

In *Metropolitan Intl Schools*,[208] Eady J held that an **internet search engine** such as Google was a mere facilitator, even where Google had taken steps to ensure that certain URLs were blocked from coming up on a search list, and where those URLs were pre-identified to it as containing defamatory material – it was 'unrealistic to attribute responsibility for publication to Google'. Eady J distinguished a search engine provider from a website host. The latter could 'merely press a button to ensure that the offending words will never reappear on a Google search snippet'. On the other hand, the process of search engines is automated, and searches are framed by those making the enquiry without any human input from Google, so that the mental element required for publication was missing. Moreover, there was a problem of practicality: search engine users could type in any search term that could elicit the offending words

[205] [2012] EWHC 449 (QB).
[206] [2009] EWHC 1765, [2011] 1 WLR 1743 (QB).
[207] [2006] EWHC 407 (QB).
[208] [2009] EWHC 1765, [56]–[64].

in a search list, in circumstances where it was not feasible for Google to block everything that contained those particular words: 'if the words are thrown up in response to a future search, it would by no means follow that the [ISP] has authorised or acquiesced in that process'. Hence, even following notification of the offending material, liability on the part of an ISP will be difficult to establish.

In *Bunt v Tilley*,[209] the liability of ISPs for communicating defamatory material via the services which they provided to consumers was rejected. Eady J explained that to impose liability on publisher D at common law, 'it is essential to demonstrate a degree of awareness, or at least an assumption of general responsibility, such as has long been recognised in the context of editorial responsibility'. Whilst that did not require that D should have to know of every defamatory word contained in a publication (editors and publishers frequently do not, yet are liable as publishers of the printed imputation), it was, nevertheless, essential that D 'must [have] a knowing involvement in the process of publication of *the relevant words*. It is not enough that a person merely plays a passive instrumental role in the process'. In other words, the ISP was akin to the post office – an instrument in the process of dissemination of information.

Exception. Given that 'publication' requires a mental element (per *Bunt v Tilley*, above), the impact of that requirement upon these types of entities has not always been consistently or definitively treated.

In the case of websites or blogs which are hosted by D, and where the offending material is drawn to D's attention, D may become a publisher, if D does not remove the imputation from the site. The governing principle for D's liability is that D consented and acquiesed, and hence authorised, the publication of the defamatory imputation. In the case of *Byrne v Deane*[210] – from another era, when an offending verse was posted on a golf club's noticeboard – the club proprietors were liable for publication of the verse by allowing it to remain on the noticeboard.

Drawing upon that old common law rule, HHJ Parkes held, in *Davison v Habeeb*,[211] that it was arguable that Google was a publisher, rather than a mere facilitator, if it was notified that particular material was appearing on a blog noticeboard for which it was responsible, and it remained published on that website and not taken down. Similarly, in *Godfrey v Demon Internet Ltd*,[212] where D continued to store a defamatory posting on its news server, after having been asked to remove it by C, D was responsible for the publications which occurred when that posting was later accessed. Subsequently, in *Tamiz v Google Inc*,[213] Eady J (at first instance) considered that, in the case of Google as a web host for a blog site, the mere fact that it had been notified of a complaint about defamatory content on that blog did not immediately convert Google's status or role into that of a publisher. It would be a 'fact sensitive' enquiry, depending upon whether D knew of the words complained of, their potential or actual illegality, or the extent that it had over their publication. The *Tamiz* Court of Appeal[214] (per Richards LJ) put the matter more specifically – that a web host such as Google could not properly be regarded as a publisher until it had had a reasonable time within which to act to remove the defamatory imputations; thereafter, it could be taken to be the publisher of the imputation.

In *Tamiz v Google Inc*, Google, D, provided a service called Blogger (at Blogger.com), a platform that allowed an internet user to create a blog (web log). One of these bore the name 'London Muslim'. Mr Tamiz, C, complained that eight comments posted on the blog defamed him. He complained about

[209] [2006] EWHC 407 (QB) [21]–[23] (original emphasis).
[210] [1937] 1 KB 818 (CA) 830 (Greer LJ), 834–35 (Slesser LJ).
[211] [2011] EWHC 3031, [42]–[48].
[212] [2001] QB 201.
[213] [2012] EWHC 449 (QB) [38].
[214] [2013] EWCA Civ 68, [35].

them to D, and his letter was received by D in early July 2011. On 11 August 2011, D forwarded the letter to the blogger; and three days later, the blogger voluntarily removed the comments. C sued D, as publisher of the allegedly defamatory comments during the period before their removal. **Held (trial)**: three comments were arguably defamatory, but D was not publisher of them, either before or after it was notified of C's complaint. D's response was 'dilatory', but not outside the bounds of a reasonable response. **Held (CA)**: given the 5-week period between notification and removal, it was arguable that D was publisher of the comments during some period prior to their removal.

Hence, the authorities to date clearly establish that publication requires a mental element, such that D only becomes a publisher, say, where specific defamatory material on identified web pages is drawn to D's attention – and even then, that may not be sufficient to fix liability on an ISP which operates search engines and which, practically speaking, are impossible to police. Separately, defences may be available for entities which adopt a role in internet communication and technology (discussed below).

Where the author of a posting on an internet website is anonymous, then the publisher of the website (if there is such an entity) will be the **only** D capable of being sued. This was always the common law (per *Byrne v Deane*,[215] where the author of the verse was unknown, yet the club secretary was held to have published it) – but it has taken on a more impactful dimension, given the extent of frequently-anonymous contributions to blogs which the internet revolution has facilitated.

Turning now to the numerous defences in Defamation:

HONEST OPINION (FAIR COMMENT)

§15.32 The statutory defence of honest opinion, contained in s 3 of the Defamation Act 2013, defends D from liability for expressing an opinion (comment) which was made honestly and not maliciously, and which was based on fact. The common law defence of fair comment has been abolished.

The statutory defence of honest opinion, now contained in s 3 of the Defamation Act 2013, replaces the common law defence of 'fair comment' (or honest comment, as it came to be called), which is abolished (per s 3(8)). The parliamentary decision to replace the fair comment defence was not particularly surprising, given that, in 2010 in *Joseph v Spiller*, the Supreme Court called it 'one of the most difficult areas of the law of defamation',[216] and in *Thornton v Telegraph Media Group Ltd*, Sir Charles Gray noted that it had 'not had an altogether easy ride over the years'.[217] Several of its elements were confusing, the subject of inconsistent judicial treatment, and difficult to apply.

The *Explanatory Notes* to the Act specify that s 3 'broadly reflects the current law, while simplifying and clarifying certain elements, but does not include the current requirement for the opinion to be on a matter of public interest'.[218] In that respect, the statutory honest opinion defence differs from the common law defence, in that the latter's purpose was to facilitate D's right to comment on matters of public interest, and upheld the public interest of everyone being free to express their honestly-held views on matters of public interest, provided that they do not act maliciously when doing so. The *Notes* further provide that, whilst the common law defence is abolished, it has not entirely lost its relevance: 'where uncertainty arises in the interpretation

[215] [1937] 1 KB 818 (CA). [216] [2010] UKSC 53, [2011] 1 AC 852, [1].
[217] [2009] EWHC 2863 (QB) [16]. [218] (2013) [19].

of s 3, case law would constitute a helpful but not binding guide to interpreting how the new statutory defence should be applied'.

According to s 3, the defence has **four** elements:

Elements of the defence

1 The statement complained of was a statement of opinion: s 3(2)
2 The statement complained of indicated, whether in general or specific terms, the basis of the opinion: s 3(3)
3 An honest person could have held the opinion on the basis of **either** any fact which existed at the time the statement was published **or** anything asserted to be a fact in a privileged statement published before the statement complained of: s 3(4)
4 The defendant held the opinion expressed (i.e., an absence of malice): s 3(5)

Dealing with each element in turn:

A statement of opinion (not a statement of fact)

§15.33 The defence of honest opinion protects statements of opinion (comment), whereas the defence of truth protects statements of fact.

As the Court of Appeal put it in *British Chiropractic Assn v Singh*, where D has made a clear assertion of highly damaging fact, then D 'must prove its truth, or lose'.[219] Honest opinion covers that other creature, 'comment' or 'opinion'.

What is the difference between a fact and an opinion/comment? It has been judicially acknowledged that '[m]uch learning has grown up around the distinction between fact and comment' (per Lord Nicholls, sitting as part of the Court of Final Appeal of Hong Kong in *Tse Wai Chun v Cheng*,[220] and affirmed in *Joseph v Spiller*[221]). Under the fair comment defence, there was certainly some confusion arising from the case law as to how to determine the distinction (e.g., 'the boundary between comment and fact may sometimes be hard to establish', but that, '[i]n recognition of its importance to protecting freedom of expression, the law allows some width to what can be held to be comment', per *Rath v Guardian News and Media Ltd*[222]).

Without intending to be exhaustive, the following factors pointing to the distinction have been made:

- where the statement is capable of verification as being true or false, it is a fact (per, e.g., *Gregg v O'Gara*[223] – where imputations that C, a serving police officer, framed an innocent person for a serious crime, and tampered with evidence in order to secure a conviction, were 'unambiguously imputations of fact'; and per *Donovan v Gibbons*[224] – where D's YouTube video showed a bucking polo pony, with a caption, 'Pharmapoloponies.com Louisa Donovan sold this polo pony as being suitable for children. Downright dangerous and a scandal they get away with

[219] [2010] EWCA Civ 350, [2011] 1 WLR 133, [22]. [220] [2001] EMLR 31 (commencing at p 777) (HKCFA) [17].
[221] [2010] UKSC 53, [2011] 1 AC 852 (SC) [3], [4], [105] [222] [2008] EWHC 398 (QB) [53].
[223] [2008] EWHC 658 (QB) [70]. [224] [2014] EWHC 3406 (QB) [18].

this', and where the fact of the horse's dangerousness was immediately apparent from viewing the video, constituting an allegation of fact) – whereas a comment is 'something which is or can reasonably be inferred to be a deduction, inference, conclusion, criticism, remark, observation, etc' (per *Branson v Bower*[225]);

- where the statement is in a part of a newspaper which is headed, 'Comment and Analysis', so that it is clearly distinguished, by style and position, from the news reports, then it is more likely to be treated as a comment, not fact (per *Cook v Telegraph Media Group Ltd*[226]). Similarly, if the article is evidently an opinion piece rather than a news column (per *Rath*[227] – re D's statement in an article, 'How money is not the only barrier to Aids patients getting hold of drugs' and, 'Matthias Rath is the multimillionaire vitamin salesman who aggressively sells his message to Aids victims in South Africa that Rath vitamin pills are better than medication. He has contributed in large part to a madness that has let perhaps hundreds of thousands of people die unnecessarily', this was arguably comment, because there was room for different views as to whether vitamin pills were better for Aids sufferers than medication, the word 'madness' was clearly an opinion, to say that C had 'contributed in large part' was also opinion because historians often differed about the contribution a particular person had made to a particular consequence, and because the article appeared as an opinion piece under the title Bad Science). Similarly, a statement which is contained in a critic's review piece (which 'any reader would appreciate, and which the reader will expect, to contain a subjective commentary by the critic') is comment (per *Associated Newspapers Ltd v Burstein*[228] – re a critical review of the opera);
- where D's statement attributes a certain state of mind to C, or hypothesises what that state of mind could be, then that is a comment, because D could not know that the state of mind he was attributing to C was correct. For example, comment occurs where, e.g., D states what C's 'secret motives' may have been (per *Cook v Telegraph Media Group*[229] – re the statement, of 'those who put their snouts in the trough', that they were 'individuals who ... decided to claim what they thought they could get away with, rather than what they could justify to their constituents', that attributes a belief to the MP that, when he made the claim, he did not believe that he could justify it to his constituents, that must be a comment);
- where D is expressing an opinion upon C's work product (e.g., a book, play, theatrical or sporting performance, music concert, etc), that is a comment (per *Dee v Telegraph Media Group*[230] – a statement that C, a professional tennis player, 'had lost 54 consecutive professional tennis matches during his three years on the professional tennis circuit, and had therefore *proved himself to be the worst professional tennis player in the world*', contained both comments, in italics, and statement of fact, in roman type; and per *Thornton v Telegraph Media Group*[231] – where a book reviewer noted C's 'seemingly limitless capacity to write pompous nonsense', and where such words of disapproval were comment, although the defence ultimately failed for another reason);
- where D makes a statement amounting to an inference of fact, where it would be obvious to a reasonable reader that the inference was not objectively verifiable, because D would not know that the inference that he was drawing was correct (an example also noted in the *Explanatory Notes*[232]). However, in a confusing twist of the law under fair comment, where D made a

225 [2001] EWCA Civ 791, [11]–[12] (Latham LJ). 226 [2011] EWHC 1134 (QB) [30].
227 [2008] EWHC 398 (QB). 228 [2007] EWCA Civ 600, [23] (re critical review of an opera).
229 [2011] EWHC 1134 (QB) [6], [24]. 230 [2010] EWHC 924 (QB) [8], [34], [119].
231 [2009] EWHC 2863 (QB) [5]. 232 (2013) [21].

statement amounting to an inference of fact, even where that inference *was verifiable*, it could still be treated as a comment – even though it would seem very close to being too far along the spectrum towards 'fact' to be a comment at all, and indeed, in *Joseph v Spiller*, Lord Phillips was doubtful as to whether this could satisfactorily be treated as a comment.[233]

The basis of the opinion

§15.34 To invoke the statutory defence, D's opinion must explicitly or implicitly state, in general terms, the basis of that opinion. It must identify, generally, what has led D to make the statement about C, so that the reader can understand what the comment is about and why D expressed the views about C that he did.

This principle, reiterated in *Joseph v Spiller*,[234] means that if D's comment does not refer to any basis to explain his comment, then the defence of fair comment could not apply at all. Hence, if D states that a barrister is 'a disgrace to his profession', then in order for the defence of fair comment to apply, D needs to state whether this is because he does not deal honestly with the court, or does not read his papers thoroughly, or refuses to accept legally aided work, or is constantly late for court, or wears dirty gowns. If D states that C 'is untrustworthy', 'unprofessional', or 'incompetent', with no other comment, then the defence must fail.

Section 3(3) repeats that position for the statutory defence of honest opinion.

However, according to *Joseph v Spiller*,[235] it is **not** necessary that D's comment must identify the matters on which it is based with sufficient particularity *to enable the reader to judge for himself* whether the comment was well founded. Comments on things such as a concert, play, or football match, will not enable readers to form their own view of the validity of D's criticism – and yet, all of these can give rise to the defence of fair comment. Any level of detail to enable the reader to ascertain whether D was justified in making the comment is not necessary, in order to trigger the defence.

In *Joseph v Spiller*, Cs were members of the groups of musical performers, 'The Gillettes', and 'Saturday Night at the Movies'. The group used an entertainment booking agency, D, as promotors. Under the terms of their contract, any further bookings at a venue in the following 12 months had to be arranged through D, but C arranged a performance directly with a venue in breach of that condition. D posted a notice on their website announcing that they were no longer accepting bookings for C, because C 'have not been able to abide by the terms of their contract', that 'it may follow that the artists' obligations for your booking may also not be met', and that 'instead, we recommend any of the following *professional* artists and bands'. C sued D in defamation, alleging that the posting bore the meaning that C 'were grossly unprofessional and untrustworthy, and unlikely to honour any bookings made for them to perform as The Gillettes or as Saturday Night at the Movies'. The defendants pleaded justification and fair comment. **Held (CA):** the defence of fair comment could not succeed, because the posting had not indicated the facts on which the comment was being made with sufficient particularity to allow a reader to judge how far the comment was well founded (given that the C's alleged breach of contract was not particularised). **Held (HL):** the defence was available. D's posting sufficiently identified C's breach, the posting did not state which contract and which term was at issue, or how it was allegedly breached – but D had

[233] [2010] UKSC 53,[2011] 1 AC 852, [114]. [234] *ibid*, [101]–[105]. [235] *ibid*, [101]–[102], [126].

identified, in general terms, what had led D to make the comment, i.e., an unparticularised breach of contract.

Honest opinion, based on an existing fact, or a privileged statement

§15.35 D's opinion must be one which was capable of being honestly expressed, and which is to be assessed objectively. The opinion must be based on a fact which existed at the time the statement was published, or based upon a privileged statement.

This element also existed under the fair comment defence, and the requirement of an 'honest person' holding that opinion has been carried over, under s 3(4)(a) of the 2013 Act. At common law, the element did not ask whether D made the comment honestly believing it to be justified and well founded (a subjective test). Instead, D had to prove that a hypothetical person could honestly express the relevant opinion as stated by D (an objective test, per *Branson v Bower (No 2)*[236]).

That 'hypothetical person' did not have to be a reasonable person; the defence was (and presumably still is) available to the unreasonable, offensive, obstinate, and prejudiced person – provided that it was possible to express the comments and viewpoints honestly, in light of the facts. As the court put it in *Burstein v Associated Newspapers Ltd*, the defence of fair comment 'deals with matters upon which strong opinions could legitimately be held ... without any scintilla of dishonesty on the part of those who hold them'.[237] Lord Phillips called this element 'bizarre and elusive' in *Joseph v Spiller*,[238] but nevertheless upheld it as a separate element of the defence. Section 3(4) reflects that viewpoint.

Otherwise, the *Explanatory Notes* provide that the intention of the 2013 Act was to 'avoid the complexities which have arisen in case law, in particular over the extent to which the opinion must be based on facts which are sufficiently true, and as to the extent to which the statement must explicitly or implicitly indicate the facts on which the opinion is based. These are areas where the common law has become increasingly complicated and technical, and where case law has sometimes struggled to articulate with clarity how the law should apply in particular circumstances'.[239]

According to s 3(4)(a), one of the conditions for the 'honest opinion' defence is that the facts upon which the comment is based must have existed, and been known to D, at the time of publication. This is one respect where D's state of mind and knowledge are relevant to this defence. At common law, this requirement had been stipulated by Eady J in *Lowe v Associated Newspapers*,[240] and endorsed by the Supreme Court in *Joseph v Spiller*,[241] for the defence of fair comment – and it has been carried over to the statutory defence. Hence, any fact pleaded to support fair comment must have existed at the time of publication. It must have been known to D, at least in general terms, at the time that D expressed the opinion. It is not sufficient for the defence if there is a fact that would have supported that opinion but which D was unaware of, but would have been supportive, had D known about it. Furthermore, if the circumstances indicate that the so-called 'fact' had no bearing at all on D's comment, then it will be dismissed as being irrelevant to support that opinion.

236 [2002] QB 737, [38]. 237 [2007] EWCA Civ 600, [2007] EMLR 21, [27].
238 *Joseph v Spiller* [2010] UKSC 53,[2011] 1 AC 852, [6]. 239 (2013) [22].
240 [2007] QB 580, [74]. 241 [2010] UKSC 53, [2011] 1 AC 852, [70]–[71].

In *Joseph v Spiller*, facts previously, the facts relied on by D in support of fair comment were that the entertainment group C had by-passed promoter D when accepting a re-engagement at one restaurant in early 2007 (fact 1); when D objected, C emailed D in March 2007 to say that 'your contract ... holds no water in legal terms' (fact 2); and C had cancelled another booking made for them by D 'when something better had come up', earlier in December 2005 (fact 3). **Held:** fact 3 could not be used to base the defence of fair comment. The principal nub of D's imputation was C's breach of re-engagement clause. D had made no fuss about the 2005 cancellation (which C had explained on the basis of clashing commitments), and it was not the 'breach of contract' referred to in D's posting in 2007. Hence fact 3 was irrelevant to any defence of fair comment.

§15.36 Where D's statement comments upon facts, some of which are true and some of which are false, D may still succeed with the statutory defence of honest opinion, provided that the comment was 'honest' in relation to the facts which were accurately stated.

This proposition was coded in s 6 of the Defamation Act 1952, but this provision has now been abolished, by s 3(8) of the 2013 Act. However, according to the *Explanatory Notes*,[242] the defence of honest opinion is still not precluded, if the truth of every allegation of fact is not proved – but that s 6 is no longer required, because D will be able to prove the elements in s 3, 'without needing to prove the truth of every single allegation of fact relevant to the statement complained of'. Presumably, then, the following cases would be decided the same way under the 2013 Act:

In *Rath v Guardian News and Media Ltd*,[243] facts previously, **held:** the defence of fair comment was arguable. D's statement was that 'Matthias Rath is the multimillionaire vitamin salesman who aggressively sells his message to Aids victims in South Africa that Rath vitamin pills are better than medication'. Some of the facts alleged were true, but some were not. C manufactured vitamin and other micronutrient products which he sold on the internet and through natural health outlets, but he did not sell them in South Africa. Rather, he donated these to community organisations in the townships of South Africa free of charge, to help tackle the recognised serious problem of malnutrition and micronutrient deficiency in patients with AIDS. In *Levi v Bates*,[244] facts previously, **held:** the defence of fair comment failed. What Mr Bates, D, wrote about Mr Levi, C, in the match day programmes and the letter to the club were 'riddled with material inaccuracies'. The defence could not be salvaged by s 6 of Defamation Act 1952, because those facts proved by D to be true 'fall well short of amounting to a sufficient substratum for the comments made by Mr Bates ... Mr Bates materially mis-stated the circumstances under which Mr Levi declined to transfer the shares which were the subject of the call option and, secondly, it was not true to say (as Mr Bates did) that Mr Levi had deterred would-be investors in the Club'.

Under the defence of fair comment, the substratum of facts upon which D's opinion is based must not only be true, but also, must be *completely* stated.

In *Branson v Bower (No 2)*,[245] Eady J provided this example: suppose that C was charged with child abuse, and D's newspaper article called for him to be suspended from his teaching post until the matter is concluded. A defence of fair comment could be legitimately raised, because the underlying factual substratum of the comment (*viz*, there are reasonable grounds to suspect that C may be

[242] (2013) [28]. [243] [2008] EWHC 398 (QB). [244] [2009] EWHC 1495 (QB) [159]–[160].
[245] [2001] EWCA Civ 791, [2002] QB 737, [37]–[38].

guilty of child abuse) are true. However, suppose that D did not mention certain further facts – that the proceedings against C had been dropped by the Crown Prosecution Service, because C had been acquitted at trial because of mistaken identity, or C had an alibi, or DNA testing excluded C. Any omission to refer to those extraneous facts would mean that the accuracy of the substratum of facts would be undermined. D would be unable to rely upon the defence of fair comment.

Absence of malice

§15.37 The statutory defence of honest opinion fails if D made the statement, not honestly believing in the truth of his opinion (i.e., that he made it with malice).

Malice was also capable of defeating the defence of fair comment, and that again applies, under s 3(5) of the 2013 Act. According to the Supreme Court in *Joseph v Spiller*,[246] it is a subjective enquiry, as to what D believed when making the comment.

Malice, in the context of fair comment, did not mean that D was motivated by spite or ill-will towards C (whatever motivated D to make the comment was not relevant or material). It simply meant (and means) that D did not hold the opinion which he expressed. In *Tse Wai Chun v Cheng*,[247] Lord Nicholls noted that, in the context of the fair comment defence, 'malice covers the case of D who does not genuinely hold the view he expressed. In other words, when making the defamatory comment, D acted dishonestly. He put forward as his view something which, in truth, was not his view. It was a pretence'. That same interpretation of malice applies under s 3(5) (per *Yeo v Times Newspapers Ltd*[248]). (Malice means something different under the common law defence of qualified privilege.)

The burden of proving malice in the context of fair comment was on C (that position continues under the statutory defence, per the *Explanatory Notes*[249]) – and that it will, in practice, be difficult for C to prove that D did not believe what he said at the time at which he said it.[250]

TRUTH (OR JUSTIFICATION)

§15.38 The defence of truth, contained in s 2 of the Defamation Act 2013, provides a defence for D if the imputation was 'substantially true'. The common law defence of justification has been abolished.

Although s 2's defence of truth replaces the common law defence of justification, the *Explanatory Notes* to the Defamation Act 2013 provide that s 2 'is intended broadly to reflect the current law while simplifying and clarifying certain elements'.[251]

A defamatory imputation is presumed to be false (the 'presumption of falsity', per *Gregg v O'Gara*[252]), and hence, the burden of proving that the imputation was true, or substantially true, rests on D (per *Ma v St George's Healthcare NHS Trust*[253]). Where applicable, it is a complete defence. The presumption of falsity is not incompatible with Art 10 – for whilst it has the potential to have a 'chilling effect' on the press (by having to prove the truth of what

[246] [2010] UKSC 53,[2011] 1 AC 852, [68], [69] and [108]. [247] [2001] EMLR 77, [24].
[248] [2015] EWHC 209 (QB) [27]. [249] (2013) [25]. [250] [2010] UKSC 53, [68], [108].
[251] *Explanatory Notes* (2013) [13]. [252] [2008] EWHC 658 (QB) [8], citing: *Belt v Lawes* (1882) 51 LJQB 359, 361.
[253] [2015] EWHC 1866 (QB) [7].

it reported), that presumption aims to safeguard C's right to protection of his reputation (per Art 8), and hence, is a justified restriction on D's freedom of expression under Art 10(2). This was confirmed by the European Court of Human Rights in *Wall Street Journal Europe SPRL v UK*.[254]

The defence of justification applies to anything D publishes which is true, notwithstanding that: (1) the publication may cause great harm to reputation, and distress and anger to C; (2) there may be no public interest in publishing the imputation; or (3) D acted with spite or malice in publishing the true facts about C (per Tugendaht J in *Terry v Persons Unknown*[255]). His Lordship raised the question as to whether the defence should require a public interest element, to give due regard to C's right to reputation in Art 8, and to give effect to an 1843 reform suggested by the Select Committee of the House of Lords on the Law of Defamation, that for the defence of justification to apply, publication must be 'for the benefit of the community'. However, his Lordship acknowledged that any such change was for an appellate court to determine.[256]

Elements of the defence

1 The imputation was one of fact
2 The defamatory imputation must be substantially true

An imputation of fact

§15.39 D's statement must be one of fact (a statement of comment which is true attracts the different defence of fair comment).

For the distinction between fact and comment, readers are referred to the discussion under 'Fair comment'. A comment is just as capable of being defamatory as is an assertion of fact, but the available defences differ.

Where D made a statement about C that was derogatory or disparaging of his character to suggest that C had conducted himself in some discreditable way, without identifying any particulars of that conduct, then the law treats this as a statement of fact, not as a comment. Hence, it follows that justification is a defence to such a comment (per *Brent Walker Group plc v Time Out Ltd*[257]).

D is entitled to plead any fact, whether or not it was known to him when he made the statement, in order to show that the imputation was true, or substantially so.

Where D alleges that C engaged in criminal conduct, then that will be justified by evidence that C had a criminal conviction (per the Defamation Act 1996, s 12(1)).

Substantially true

The fact that the imputations contained in D's publications turned out to be ultimately baseless does not alter the fact that, if they were substantially true at the time of the publication, then the defence is available to D.

[254] (2009) 48 EHRR (ECtHR) SE19, citing: *McVicar v UK* (2002) 35 EHRR 22 (ECtHR) [87]. Also: *Jameel v Dow Jones & Co Inc* [2005] EWCA Civ 75, [41], [67], [293].
[255] [2010] EWHC 119 (QB) [74]–[82], and see too: *Fraser v Evans* [1969] 1 QB 349, 360–61.
[256] *ibid*, [80]–[81]. [257] [1991] 2 QB 33, 44.

In *Ma v St George's Healthcare NHS Trust*,[258] a dispute arose in a hospital A&E ward, where Tao Ma, C, took her child who had cut her forehead. C behaved somewhat erratically in the waiting room. Various allegations which were said to be defamatory of C were contained in certain medical documents prepared by D's medical staff (i.e., a Children's Specialist Services Referral Form, and a Paediatric Liaison Health Visitor Referral Form). The allegations were that C was confrontational towards staff, argued vehemently with the child's father and tried to remove her daughter from the hospital before she could be examined, contrary to her father's wishes. C alleged that these imputed that her behaviour had been so reprehensible that it raised child safeguarding concerns for her daughter. Ultimately, it was held that no further action was required re safeguarding, and the Wandsworth social services file was closed. **Held:** D proved the defence of justification. D's staff who referred the incidents to social workers, via the aforementioned documents, were genuine as to their concerns about C's apparently irrational and erratic behaviour at the hospital, and its possible effects for her daughter. The fact that the social services file was ultimately closed did not mean that D's concerns were not genuine at the time that they were made.

The sting

§15.40 D does not need to prove that every single word contained in the imputation was true – but D does have to prove that the 'sting' of the imputation was true (or that, as s 2 requires, the words were 'substantially true').

According to the common law principle in *Chase v News Group Newspapers Ltd*, D 'does not have to prove that every word he published was true. He has to establish the "essential" or "substantial" truth of the sting of the libel'.[259] That position is embodied now in s 2(1) of the 2013 Act – it is enough that the imputation was 'substantially true'. If there are some words used by D which were not true, but those do not materially affect C's reputation, then D can still rely on the defence. The standard of proof is that of the balance of probabilities.

In *Dee v Telegraph Media Group Ltd*,[260] facts previously, D published an article that Mr Dee, C, 'had lost 54 consecutive professional tennis matches during his three years on the professional tennis circuit, and had therefore proved himself to be the worst professional tennis player in the world'. In fact, during that period, D had also played matches in domestic tournaments in Spain and had won some matches (and money) there. **Held:** the defence of justification succeeded. C had lost 54 consecutive matches in tournaments on the international professional circuit, which were under the jurisdiction of the ITF and the ATP. These were world ranking tournaments and attracted world ranking points; and his performance was the world record equalling worst-ever run of consecutive losses on the international professional circuit. The domestic Spanish tournaments, whilst 'professional' in the sense that prize money was offered, were not part of that circuit. In *Simpson v MGN Ltd*,[261] Danny Simpson, C, a premiership footballer, was said, in an article in the *Daily Mirror*, to be having an affair with celebrity Tulisa Contostavlos. The various imputations were (1) infidelity, that C had been unfaithful 'to his loyal partner Miss Ward', with whom he was in a long-term and committed relationship, living with their daughter and with another child expected, and (2) C had broken up an established family unit. In fact, C did not live with Miss Ward and daughter at the time of the affair with Ms Contostavlos, and had not done so for seven months. **Held:** the defence

[258] [2015] EWHC 1866 (QB) [47]. [259] [2002] EWCA Civ 1772, [34].
[260] [2010] EWHC 924 (QB). [261] [2015] EWHC 77 (QB).

of justification must fail for imputation (2). C and Miss Ward were not living together as a family when the relationship began, and it could not be true that C's infidelity broke up an established family unit.

The same principle applies, where it is not a mixture of words about C (some of which were true and some of which were not), but where it was a mixture of imputations. If separate defamatory imputations have been made by D against C, and if D fails to prove the truth of every one of those imputations, D can still rely on the defence of truth – provided that the false imputations do not 'seriously harm' C's reputation, when regard is had to the true imputations which have been proven against C. This is provided for now, in s 2(3) of the Defamation Act 2013, which replaces the previous s 5 of the Defamation Act 1952 (and its older terminology, that the false defamatory imputations should not 'materially injure' C's reputation).

However, it can be very difficult, on a case-by-case basis, to determine whether or not D has met the 'sting' of the imputation. In *Rothschild v Associated Newspapers Ltd*, Sir David Eady gave two helpful examples of the difficulties – and differences – that can arise:[262]

Scenario #1: D states that C (1) is dishonest; (2) stole monies from his employer; and (3) committed adultery. All of these allegations impute dishonesty. Suppose that C has not committed adultery, but has stolen funds from his employer. The 'sting' of (1) and (2) will be true, and D will have a defence against those. However, (3) is not true, and even though it may fall within the general allegation of dishonesty, it is an allegation of a separate and distinct nature, and it cannot be defended on the basis of justification.

Scenario #2: D states that C (1) was an embezzler; and (2) had embezzled £10,000. In fact, C had embezzled funds, but only to the tune of £5,000. The 'sting' of the allegation is that C embezzled funds, and the example given, whilst untrue, is of the same character as the general charge which has been established to be true. Hence, the defence of justification would apply to defend, successfully, both imputations.

Rothschild itself was an example of the second scenario:

In *Rothschild v Associated Newspapers Ltd*, Mr Rothschild, C, a banker and businessman, and Lord Mandelson, had been close friends for many years. The article stated that, 'Revealed: the astonishing story of the night Lord Mandelson was flown to Moscow by private jet to join a billionaire friend desperate to strike a deal that cost British jobs'. The imputation was that C, the 'billionaire friend', flew Lord Mandelson (then-EU Trade Commr) in his private jet to Moscow when he had no official reason to go there, and where, unknown to EU officials, Lord Mandelson and C attended a business dinner in Moscow, held to close a lucrative deal (with the American aluminium producer Alcoa and with a Russian oligarch); C must have foreseen that this would bring Lord Mandelson's integrity into disrepute; and expose him to accusations of conflict in his duties as EU Trade Commr. In fact, Lord Mandelson did not attend that Moscow dinner, nor discuss EU tariffs on aluminium or assist with the £500m deal. However, C did travel with Lord Mandelson, the oligarch, and others, to Siberia, to visit an aluminium smelter and foil plant. **Held:** the defence of justification succeeded. The 'sting' of the imputation was that C was involved in a web of relationships (with Lord Mandelson, and the oligarch), and that C wished to impress and keep close to that oligarch, partly by facilitating close contact with Lord Mandelson, which was true. The imputation that C arranged a meeting of the parties at the Alcoa dinner was false, but that was merely an example of the general 'sting'. The defence covered the general **and** the Alcoa imputations.

[262] [2013] EWCA Civ 197, [61]–[62].

Where the defamatory imputation concerns criminal wrongdoing, D will need to justify the relevant *Chase* level meaning (see previously) – i.e., proof of C's guilt; proof of reasonable grounds for C's guilt; or proof of the fact of an inquiry about C's guilt.

The repetition rule

§15.41 Where D repeats a defamatory statement made by a third person about C ('I have been told that ...', 'It is rumoured that ...'), D is as liable to C as if he had made the statement himself. When seeking to prove the defence of truth, D must prove the truth of that imputation, and not merely that the third party said it.

This proposition (expressed by Lord Devlin in *Lewis v Daily Telegraph*[263]) means that repeating a defamatory statement is as 'bad', in the law's eyes, as making the statement directly (per *Flood v Times Newspapers Ltd*[264]). The natural and ordinary meaning of the words used is not, 'X is the case', but that 'TP said that X is the case'. However, D, as publisher, is in the same position as if he had indeed stated, 'X is the case' (per *Curistan v Times Newspapers Ltd*[265]).

The repetition rule is a long-standing common law principle, 'reflect[ing] a fundamental canon of legal policy in the law of defamation dating back nearly 170 years, that words must be interpreted, and the imputations they contain justified, by reference to the underlying allegations of fact, and not merely by reliance upon some second-hand report or assertion of them' (per *Shah v Standard Chartered Bank*[266]).

It is also part of the 'repetition rule' that, if D repeats defamatory imputations made by TP, then the defence of truth in s 2 will require D to prove the truth of that imputation – it is not enough for D to merely prove that TP indeed made the statement. In that regard, s 2 has not abrogated the 'repetition rule' in any respect (per *Lachaux v Independent Print Ltd*[267]). Furthermore, the repetition rule, and its burdensome effect on D, is compatible with the ECHR (per *Berezovsky v Forbes Inc*[268]).

PEER-REVIEWED STATEMENTS IN SCIENTIFIC OR ACADEMIC JOURNALS

§15.42 Pursuant to s 6 of the Defamation Act 2013, the publication of D's statement will be privileged if it relates to a scientific or academic matter, and was subject to independent review.

The defence of peer-reviewed statements in scientific or academic journals was newly-introduced by the 2013 Act. It was implemented in response to the decision in *British Chiropractic Assn v Singh*.[269]

Elements of the defence

1 The statement relates to a scientific or academic matter which was published in a scientific or academic journal
2 Before the statement was published in the journal, it was subject to independent review by an editor or referee

263 [1964] AC 234 (HL) 283. 264 [2010] EWCA Civ 804, [88]. 265 [2008] EWCA Civ 432, [2009] QB 231, 261.
266 [1998] EWCA Civ 612, [1999] QB 241, 263. 267 [2015] EWHC 620 (QB) [42].
268 [2001] EWCA Civ 1251, [8]–[9]. 269 [2010] EWCA Civ 350, [2011] 1 WLR 133.

There were concerns, at common law, about the use to which defamation suits were being put. The effect of such suits could be, not only to stifle freedom of expression, but also to stifle proper and valid scientific debate.

In *British Chiropractic Assn v Singh*, the BCA, C, had, as its objects, promoting and maintaining high standards of conduct and practice among UK chiropractors. Dr Singh, D, a scientist and science writer, wrote an article in *The Guardian* in 2008, which stated that the BCA 'claims that their members can help treat children with colic, sleeping and feeding problems, frequent ear infections, asthma and prolonged crying, even though there is not a jot of evidence. This organisation is the respectable face of the chiropractic profession, and yet it happily promotes bogus treatments'. C sued D for defamation, and D pleaded fair comment. **Held (trial):** fair comment was not available. D's statements were of fact, not opinion. D's article concerned whether those responsible for C's claims were well aware that there was simply no evidence to support them, which was an issue capable of verifiable fact. This result would mean that D would have to prove that the imputations were factually true, or lose. **Held (CA):** fair comment was available. D's statement that there was not a jot of evidence was a statement of opinion backed by reasons. Whether or not evidence goes to support a claim (e.g., that a patient's condition improved after chiropractic treatment; chiropractic treatment works) is for debate; and whatever C or D state about what the evidence proves is an opinion. That opinion may be mistaken, but it can give rise to the defence of fair comment. Also, the words appeared under a general heading, 'Comment and Debate'.

The reasons behind the litigation were dealt with by the Court of Appeal with real misgivings:

> this litigation has almost certainly had a chilling effect on public debate which might otherwise have assisted potential patients to make informed choices about the possible use of chiropractic services ... [and] the questions raised by Dr Singh, which have a direct resonance for patients, are unresolved. This would be a surprising consequence of laws designed to protect reputation. By proceeding against Dr Singh, and not *The Guardian* ... the unhappy impression has been created that this is an endeavour by the BCA to silence one of its critics. Again, if that is where the current law of defamation takes us, we must apply it.[270]

Hence, s 6 affords protection for the author of the peer-reviewed critic – and the peer reviewer's assessment of D's statement is also protected, under s 6(4), as are the members of the journal's editorial board, under s 6(8). The *Explanatory Notes* provide that a 'scientific journal' includes a medical and engineering journal.[271] However, the s 6 defence would appear not to apply to the *Singh* scenario, given that the article was (presumably) not subject to refereeing nor published in an academic journal.

INNOCENT DISSEMINATION

§15.43 Where D re-publishes (i.e., distributes) defamatory statements as a secondary publisher, D is prima facie liable for publication of those statements, except where D has engaged in their innocent dissemination. In that scenario, D may seek to rely upon the common law defence of innocent dissemination (i.e., where D did not know that it was circulating a defamatory imputation) or on s 1 of the Defamation Act 1996. Operators of a website have a specialist statutory defence, under s 5 of the Defamation Act 2013.

[270] [2010] EWCA Civ 350, [2011] 1 WLR 133, [11]–[12]. [271] (2013) [44].

At common law

According to Romer LJ in *Vizetelly v Mudie's Select Library Ltd*,[272] the common law defence of innocent dissemination applies to those who had a 'subordinate part in disseminating' the material which contained the defamatory imputation. It contains three elements:

Elements of the defence

1. D did not know of the defamatory imputation contained in the material
2. Neither the material nor the surrounding circumstances puts D on notice that the material contained any defamatory imputation
3. D was not negligent

The common law defence survived the enactment of the statutory defence created by s 1 of the Defamation Act 1996. It has been judicially said that the common law defence has been superseded, but not abolished – and that it would not avail D, once D had it drawn to his attention that the words that it was disseminating were arguably defamatory (per *MIS Ltd v Designtechnica Corp*[273]). A concession made in *Godfrey v Demon Internet*,[274] that the defence had been abolished, was disapproved subsequently in *MIS v Designtechnica*.

The survival of the common law defence could be important, if element #1 was differently expressed, i.e., if it was sufficient for D to prove that he was aware that the imputation was defamatory, but had no knowledge that the imputation was indefensible, and could not be defended by truth, fair comment, etc. That interpretation would not need D to prove that he was unaware of the defamatory imputation itself. However, that view of the element was not judicially endorsed in *MIS v Designtechnica*.[275] Hence, whether the common law defence assists D to any greater extent than the statutory defence in s 1 does, is questionable.

This defence has application, both in the modern IT world, where, say, webblog hosts facilitate the publication of comments posted to those blogs – and in an earlier age when libraries, supermarkets and newsagents distributed written material. It succeeded in each of the following:

> In *Tamiz v Google*,[276] facts previously, the Court of Appeal noted that Google could not know, or reasonably ought to have known, of the defamatory statements appearing on its hosted blog until receiving C's complaint. Until that time, it was able to take advantage of the defence of innocent dissemination. In *Bottomley v FW Woolworth and Co Ltd*,[277] Woolworth, D, sold off a consignment of remaindered American magazines which contained a libel against C. D did not check every magazine for defamatory content, there was nothing in the nature of the individual magazine which should have led D to suppose that the magazine contained a libel, and it had not been negligent in failing to carry out a periodical examination of specimen magazines.

However, the defence did not succeed in *Vizetelly* itself, because D had been careless in the conduct of its affairs:

272 [1900] 2 QB 170 (CA) 180. Earlier: *Emmens v Pottle* (1885) 16 QBD 354, 357–58.
273 [2009] EWHC 1765 (QB) [68], [70]. Also: *Davison v Habeeb* [2011] EWHC 3031 (QB) [29].
274 [2001] QB 201. 275 [2009] EWHC 1765 (QB) [70].
276 [2013] EWCA Civ 68, [2013] 1 WLR 2151, [26]. 277 (1932) 48 TLR 521.

In *Vizetelly*, D owned a library. A circulating library book contained a defamatory imputation against C without D's knowing that it contained that libel. D's director gave evidence that he and the co-director alone exercised supervision over the books, that there were too many books to check them for libels, and the library did not employ readers because it was cheaper for D to run the risk of being sued for libel.

Nevertheless, the modern position is that the common law defence of innocent dissemination remains 'alive', and secondary publishers may avail themselves of that defence (per *Tamiz v Google Inc*[278]).

Statutory defence for secondary publishers

Secondary publishers may seek to rely on the defence in s 1 of the Defamation Act 1996, which has three elements:

Elements of the defence

1. D was **not** the author of the statement; or an editor having editorial responsibility for the statement or for the decision to publish it; or a commercial publisher which issues the material in the course of its business: s 1(1)(a)
2. D took reasonable care in relation to the publication: s 1(1)(b)
3. D did not know, nor had reason to believe, that what he did caused or contributed to the publication of a defamatory statement (i.e., that D was not aware that the words complained of were defamatory, and had no reason to believe that they were defamatory either): s 1(1)(c)

A number of examples of 'secondary publishers' who may seek to avail themselves of s 1's defence are listed in s 1(3). They include: printers, distributors, sellers of print publications, exhibitors of film recordings, sellers of films, broadcasters of live programmes where D had no effective control over the person who utters a slander, or the operator or provider of access to a communications system by which the statement is communicated (which would include internet service providers). Although the host of a web blog is not itemised in s 1(3), the section states that the court can have regard to these examples when deciding, by analogy, whether a secondary publisher ought to have the protection of that section.

For example, the statutory defence in s 1 has prima facie applied to the following scenarios, provided that the three elements noted above are proven:

- those entities which host blogs and provide a platform for the blogs – e.g., in *Tamiz v Google Inc*,[279] the fact that Google did not know of the defamatory imputation on the web blog, prior to C's notification of it, meant that it would have had an 'unassailable defence during that period' under s 1;
- Amazon, as an online bookseller, where a 'review' of the book generates a thread of discussion, some of which is defamatory – e.g., in *McGrath v Dawkins (Rev 1)*,[280] it was held that even with some limited pre-publication control of reviews (automated processes which would

[278] [2013] EWCA Civ 68, [21]–[22]. [279] [2013] EWCA Civ 68, [26] (Richards LJ).
[280] [2012] EWHC B3 (QB) [41].

provoke human intervention if certain forbidden words were used), Amazon did not become an 'editor': 'this is an illustration of the notorious "Catch-22" under which an ISP seeking to attract the statutory defence by taking reasonable care may find that it has instead forfeited it by becoming an editor. In the present case, Amazon took no steps in relation to the content of any of the statements, and no part in any decision to publish it, except by way of the automatic process referred to above';

- internet service provider which provided a news service – in *Godfrey v Demon Internet Ltd*, Demon, an ISP, D, received and stored a defamatory article on its news server, which had been posted by an unknown person via another ISP. Mr Godfrey, C, informed D of the defamatory nature of the article and requested its removal from their news server, but it remained available until its automatic expiry – here, the defence was not available, for once D had knowledge that the posting was defamatory, D had not taken reasonable care in relation to the statement.

Notably, the 2013 Act limits the circumstances in which a secondary publisher can be sued. No action can be brought against that secondary publisher of a defamatory imputation, unless 'it is not reasonably practicable for an action to be brought against the author, editor or publisher' (per s 10).

As an alternative statutory defence, D may be able to rely on Reg 19 of the Electronic Commerce Regulations 2002,[281] which provides an information service provider with an 'escape hatch', where it did not know of the defamatory imputation, nor would it have been apparent to that service provider, and where it acted expeditiously to remove the information or to disable access to it when it became aware of the information. This is considered to be a 'more liberal' defence than s 1 of the 1996 Act, partly because D does not have to show, under Reg 19, that it took reasonable care in relation to the publication (per *McGrath v Dawkins*[282]).

Operators of websites

An operator of a website, D, has a defence, where it can show that it was not the party which posted a defamatory statement on the website (per s 5 of the 2013 Act).

However, as with innocent dissemination and s 1 of the 1996 Act, C's notification to D that the website contains a defamatory statement about C will lose D the defence. According to s 5(3), if C can show that he cannot identify who posted the defamatory statement; but C gave D a notice of complaint about the statement, and thereafter, D failed to 'respond' to that notice, then D has lost the defence.

The Defamation (Operators of Websites) Regulations 2013,[283] also in force on 1 January 2014, sets out (in its Schedule) the actions that can be taken by operator D, as 'responses', to enable D to rely on the defence. These steps include: operator D sending the notice of complaint to the poster of the statement requiring that the defamatory post be removed (cl 2); and where D cannot contact the poster, then D must remove the statement from the website itself (cl 2(3)); or if D can contact the poster but the poster fails to take down the statement, then D must do so itself (cl 5). The Schedule also provides that, where the poster receives D's notice but refuses to remove the statement from the website, then operator D must inform C, the complainant, of that (cl 8) – although it is not clear, from the Schedule, whether operator D remains liable, and loses the defence afforded by s 5, if the poster of the statement will not remove the offending item.

[281] (SI 2002/2013), which transposed Art 14 of the E-Commence Directive into English law.
[282] [2012] EWHC B3 (QB) [43]. [283] SI 3028/2013.

At the time of writing, there has been no judicial consideration of the s 5 defence, so far as the author's searches can ascertain.

'PUBLIC INTEREST' PRIVILEGE (FORMERLY, THE *REYNOLDS* DEFENCE)

§15.44 Pursuant to s 4 of the Defamation Act 2013, the statutory 'public interest' defence replaces the common law *Reynolds* defence which had, as its focus, the protection of 'responsible journalism'. The statutory defence protects D for the publication of a statement (either of fact or of opinion) which is in the public interest, and where D reasonably believed it to be so.

It is impossible to ignore the previous '*Reynolds* privilege',[284] when construing the s 4 statutory defence enacted in the 2013 Act, for the *Explanatory Notes* state that 'it is based on the existing common law defence established in *Reynolds v Times Newspapers*, and is intended to reflect the principles established in that case and in subsequent case law'.[285] *Reynolds* was termed, by the Supreme Court in *Joseph v Spiller*, as '[t]he most significant development of the common law of defamation in recent times'.[286] Another judge noted that '[q]ualified privilege for the media has been radically altered by *Reynolds*' (*Mitchell v Evening Chronicle*[287]).

Hence, it is hardly surprising that the statutory defence seeks to build upon that ground-breaking common law defence – albeit that it is abolished by the 2013 Act[288] – but in a somewhat modified fashion. It has three elements:

Elements of the defence

1 The statement must be, or form part of, a matter of public interest: s 4(1)(a)
2 D reasonably believed that publishing the statement was in the public interest: s 4(1)(b)
3 D's statement may be of either fact or opinion: s 4(5)

General matters re *Reynolds*

§15.45 The statutory defence in s 4 of the 2013 Act applies to any statement-maker who publishes a statement in the public interest (whether a journalist or another person).

The *Reynolds* defence was also called the defence of 'responsible journalism', to reflect that journalists were the principal beneficiary of the defence. Notably, the *Reynolds* defence could apply to non-journalistic authors too, provided that they could prove its elements (as accepted in *Gregg v O'Gara*,[289] re a book author, although the defence failed there). That wider category of D has been transposed into s 4 of the 2013 Act.

Where applicable, the privilege achieved 'a fair balance ... between freedom of expression on matters of public concern, and the reputations of individuals' (per *Bonnick v Morris*[290]). If *Reynolds* privilege succeeded, then it meant that the balance was struck in favour of freedom

[284] *Reynolds v Times Newspapers Ltd* [2001] 2 AC 127 (HL). [285] (2013) [29].
[286] [2010] UKSC 53, [2011] 1 AC 852, [65]. [287] [2003] EWHC 1281 (QB) [29]. [288] Per s 4(6).
[289] [2008] EWHC 658 (QB) [70]. [290] [2003] 1 AC 300 (PC, on appeal from Jamaica) 309, [23] (Lord Nicholls).

of speech, and that an interference with C's right to reputation was proportionate (per *Flood v Times Newspapers Ltd*[291]).

The courts considered that the press required greater protection for their freedom of expression, over and above the defence of fair comment (per *Baturina v Times Newspapers*[292]). The defence was based on the public interest: journalists should be relatively free to report matters which it was in the public interest to place in the public domain, and journalists should take reasonable care to verify the accuracy of stories which may damage reputations. However, the *Reynolds* defence did not convey any blanket defence for statements made on political matters – the defence turned upon a case-by-case determination.

The decision in *Reynolds* was handed down in between the time that the HRA was enacted and its coming into force. The *Reynolds* privilege was meant to strike an appropriate balance between Art 10's right to freedom of expression and Art 8's right of an individual to protect his reputation which is an aspect of private life. However, neither of those Convention rights was pre-eminent or had 'presumptive priority' in the balancing exercise (per *Galloway v Telegraph Group Ltd*[293]). The European Court of Human Rights confirmed that the *Reynolds* defence was 'an exceptional defence', intended to ensure wide dissemination of news via the media, without fear of litigation, even if that involved making defamatory statements of fact which could not be proven to be true (per *Wall St Journal Europe Sprl v UK*[294]).

Dealing with the three elements of the statutory defence:

A matter of public interest

§15.46 The statement must be a matter of public interest. Whilst undefined in the 2013 Act, 'public interest' was the first element of the *Reynolds* privilege, and has a common law meaning. However, there is no presumption of public interest, in the reporting of political or any other matters.

In *Jameel v Wall Street Journal Sprl*,[295] Lord Bingham made the point that what engages the interest of the public may not be material which engages the public interest! When pleading or relying on the *Reynolds* defence, matters of public interest have included the following:

- MP's expenses claims alleged to have been improperly made (as in *Cook v Telegraph Media Group*[296]);
- police investigations of alleged police corruption (as in *Flood v Times Newspapers*,[297] and *Charman v Orion Publishing Group*[298]) – because corruption undermines the necessary public trust in those responsible for upholding the law and protecting the public, and the public has an interest in knowing that the police will rigorously investigate an allegation against one of their own;
- allegations of actual or suspected criminal activity by C (as in *Flood*;[299] *Reynolds*;[300] and *Jameel*[301]);

[291] [2010] EWCA Civ 804, [2011] 1 WLR 153, [107]. [292] [2011] EWCA Civ 308, [28].
[293] [2006] EWCA Civ 17, [80], [83]. [294] (2009) 48 EHRR SE19 (287) (EctHR).
[295] [2006] UKHL 44, [2007] 1 AC 359, [31]–[33]. [296] [2011] EWHC 1134 (QB).
[297] [2010] EWCA Civ 804, [2011] 1 WLR 153. [298] [2007] EWCA Civ 972.
[299] [2010] EWCA Civ 804, [2011] 1 WLR 153. [300] [2001] 2 AC 127 (HL).
[301] [2006] UKHL 44, [4].

- alleged involvement in terrorist activities – e.g., statements that US authorities were satisfied that the Saudi Arabian Monetary Authority was monitoring approximately 150 bank accounts of some prominent businessmen, to 'prevent them being used wittingly or unwittingly' for funnelling funds to terrorist organisations, and hence were providing co-operation in the fight against terrorism (as in *Jameel*).

According to *Jameel* (handed down after the HRA), Arts 8 (right to reputation) and 10 (right to freedom of expression) have *equal* weight, such that there was no presumption that publication was in the public interest.[302] Right to reputation is just as important as freedom of expression.

Under s 4(2) of the 2013 Act, the court must have regard to 'all the circumstances of the case', when determining whether the two elements of the statutory defence are made out. Additionally, s 4(4) requires the court to 'make such allowance for editorial judgment as it considers appropriate'. These two provisions seem to draw in certain matters dealt with under the *Reynolds* privilege, noted below:

Timing. *Reynolds* privilege had to be judged at the date of each (or ongoing) publication. Hence, the privilege could attach to a print newspaper and website publication, to protect D from defamation, when they were first published; but the privilege may be lost, especially in relation to an ongoing website publication, if further information comes to light, so that there is no continuing public interest in the ongoing website publication. According to *Flood v Times Newspapers*,[303] once further information arises which affects the standing of a website publication, any responsible journalist would appreciate that the allegations 'required speedy withdrawal or modification'. If this is not done, *Reynolds* privilege will be lost.

In *Flood v Times Newspapers*, Mr Flood, C, a serving police officer in the Extradition Unit, sued in defamation after *The Times*, D, published an article in its paper and on its website in June 2006, alleging that C corruptly sold intelligence information about wealthy Russian businessmen whom the Russian legal regime wished to extradite back to Moscow. There was a police investigation, C was removed temporarily from his post, was then cleared of any wrongdoing by a report in December 2006, and was returned to his post. D learnt of the report clearing C in September 2007, but the original article remained on its website unamended. D relied on *Reynolds* privilege for both print and website versions of the article. **Held:** neither publication attracted *Reynolds* privilege at the time of publication; but even if they had, the website publication would cease to be privileged after D learnt of the conclusions of the police investigation in Sept 2007, and did not withdraw or modify the website.

The traditional 'legitimate interest' test. Under *Reynolds* privilege, the inclusion of the defamatory statement by D had to make a real contribution to the story about C. According to Baroness Hale in *Jameel v Wall Street Journal Europe Sprl*,[304] there had to be 'a real public interest in communicating and receiving' the information as interpreted and relayed by the journalists in the article. A considerable degree of deference had to be paid to editorial judgment when deciding whether the inclusion of the defamatory material was justified.

[302] [2006] UKHL 44, [109].

[303] [2010] EWCA Civ 804, [53], [78], citing: *Loutchansky v Times Newspapers (Nos 2–5)* [2002] QB 783 (CA).

[304] [2006] UKHL 44, [147].

In *Jameel*, the report informed the public that SAMA was monitoring certain individual and company accounts, and to that end, the report reasonably included *names* of those large and respectable Saudi businesses and persons who were, after reasonable and professional inquiries, believed to be account-holders who were being monitored for funnelling. Including names was an important part of the story.

Lord Nicholls' 10 factors. In *Reynolds*, Lord Nicholls set out a list of 10 non-exhaustive matters which could usefully be taken into account, when deciding whether D's attempts to gather, verify and publish the information were responsible and fair. This balancing exercise represented an important element of the *Reynolds* privilege. The 10 matters were said to be 'non-exhaustive' and 'illustrative', and that the weight to be given to them would vary from case to case.[305]

Lord Nicholls' *Reynolds* factors

1. The seriousness of the allegation. The more serious the charge, the more the public is misinformed and the individual harmed, if the allegation is not true.
2. The nature of the information, and the extent to which the subject matter is a matter of public concern.
3. The source of the information. Some informants have no direct knowledge of the events. Some have their own axes to grind, or are being paid for their stories.
4. The steps taken to verify the information.
5. The status of the information. The allegation may have already been the subject of an investigation which commands respect.
6. The urgency of the matter. News is often a perishable commodity.
7. Whether comment was sought from the plaintiff. He may have information others do not possess or have not disclosed. An approach to the plaintiff will not always be necessary.
8. Whether the article contained the gist of the plaintiff's side of the story.
9. The tone of the article. A newspaper can raise queries or call for an investigation. It need not adopt allegations as statements of fact.
10. The circumstances of the publication, including the timing.

Whilst s 4 of the 2013 Act does not reproduce these factors, their consideration is surely covered by s 4(2)'s reference to 'all the circumstances of the case'.

Prior to the passing of the 2013 Act, it was apparent that the 'winds were blowing' more in favour of permitting journalist Ds to rely upon the *Reynolds* defence. This point was evident in the Court of Appeal decision in *Charman v Orion Publishing Group*,[306] where Ward LJ noted that, e.g.:

- 'weight must be given to the professional judgment of the journalist' – even if the court, in hindsight, would have exercised different editorial judgment, it was important to 'make allowance' for editorial judgment;
- the *Reynolds* factors were 'not intended to present an onerous obstacle to the media in the discharge of their function' and that *Reynolds* was intended to be 'liberalising', insofar as freedom of expression was concerned – a very pro-media statement indeed;

[305] [2001] 2 AC 127 (HL) 205. [306] [2007] EWCA Civ 972, [66], [75], and proposition 5.

- in *Jameel*, Baroness Hale stated that '[w]e need more such serious journalism in this country, and our defamation law should encourage rather than discourage it', which lower courts should take as 'sombre words of warning';
- Strasbourg jurisprudence since *Jameel* had been very supportive of the right of free expression, e.g., re the case in which the murder of Olaf Palme, the Swedish Prime Minister, was discussed in *White v Sweden*,[307] and where 'the public interest in publishing the information in question outweighed the applicant's right to protection of his reputation'.

This view may serve as a precursor to how the statutory defence will be considered, given the *Explanatory Note* that 'the current case law would constitute a helpful (albeit not binding) guide to interpreting how the new statutory defence should be applied'.[308]

An objective reasonable belief

§15.47 The second element of the statutory defence is that D must have reasonably believed that publishing the statement was in the public interest. This reflects the position under the *Reynolds* privilege, that the journalist must have believed the statement to be true.

This element of the statutory defence, stipulated in s 4(1)(b), puts onto a compulsory statutory footing the opinion of Lord Hoffmann in *Jameel*: '[i]n most cases, the *Reynolds* defence will not get off the ground unless the journalist honestly and reasonably believed that the statement was true'.[309] Subsequently, in *Cook v Telegraph Media Group*, Tugendaht J stated that *Reynolds* 'is not a defence which is available for the publication of statements which a journalist does not believe to be true'.[310]

However, it is a defence if D can prove that there was a public interest in the fact that the statement was made, when it may be clear that D, as author/publisher, does not believe it is true (the defence of 'reportage', discussed elsewhere in the chapter).

Notably, in *Charman v Orion Publishing Group Ltd*,[311] the Court of Appeal emphasised a further factor not referred to in *Reynolds* – whether C himself had put the 'attack on their character' in the public domain. If so, then that would weigh in favour of a *Reynolds* defence applying.

In *Charman v Orion Publishing Group Ltd*, C was a former detective constable in the Met Police who was 'handler' of an informant. Mr McLagan was an investigative journalist and author of a book, *Bent Coppers*, published by D. In the book, it was alleged that there were cogent grounds to suspect that C abused his position as police officer to receive payment from the informant, in return for the informant's protection, should the informant be arrested. The informant was ultimately arrested and imprisoned, and he alleged corruption against C, which was investigated and summarily dismissed. The book reported on the informant's trial. **Held:** the *Reynolds* defence succeeded. C had made a press announcement and asked for a statement on his behalf to be made in Parliament by his MP, which contributed to the successful defence.

The defence succeeded in both of the following:

[307] [2007] EMLR 1 (ECtHR) [26]. [30]. [308] (2013) [35]. [309] [2006] UKHL 44, [62].
[310] [2011] EWHC 763 (QB) [70]. [311] [2007] EWCA Civ 972, [11], [13], [57], [84].

Reynolds-type analysis

Jameel v Wall Street Journal Europe Sprl:[312]	*Reynolds* factors which favoured 'D's freedom of expression': • it was in the public interest to know that the US was stating that they were satisfied the Saudi authorities were providing co-operation in the fight against terrorism, when some were inclined to question that; • the article was written by an experienced specialist reporter; • it was approved by senior staff who themselves sought to verify its contents; • an editor telephoned the office of the Jameel Group the evening before publication, had spoken to a representative of the Group who asked for publication to be postponed for 24 hours so that Mr Jameel, who was in Japan for business, could be contacted, but the editor declined; • the article was unsensational and neutral in tone, and factual in content; • C's response was sought and the paper's inability to obtain a comment recorded; • per Lord Bingham, 'this was the sort of neutral, investigative journalism which *Reynolds* privilege exists to protect', and per Baroness Hale: 'if the public interest defence does not succeed on the known facts of this case, it is hard to see it ever succeeding'; • the article indicated that the accounts being monitored might be used by terrorists without the knowledge or connivance of the account holders, which neutralised any potential defamatory sting; • the refusal to delay publication did not lose D the defence; if Mr Jameel were asked whether he knew of any reason why anyone would want to monitor his account, he would likely have answered, 'no' in any event.
Charman v Orion Publishing Group Ltd:[313]	*Reynolds* factors which favoured 'D's freedom of expression': • re the nature of the information: the police served a public protection function, and where there was corruption or suspicion of it, it should be exposed and discussed; • much of the story came from B, a 'flawed character', but D made 'great efforts' to tap police and other sources; • D did further research to verify whether C was corrupt, and held interviews with the investigating officers; • the matters were investigated at the Central Criminal Court, and hence, 'they must command respect', plus the information given to D by the investigating officers was 'certainly high enough to warrant writing a story' about the allegations against C; • urgency was not a factor in this case, and greater care was expected, given the book format; • D made approaches to obtain C's side of the story, which were rebuffed; so D was entitled to assume that C would remain unco-operative if the allegations to be published had been put to him; • the book contained the gist of C's side of the story; • the tone of the book was exactly what one would expect of an objective investigative journalist – essentially factual in context and unsensational in tone, whereby D expressed no personal judgment but left it to the reader to form his own impression of the two officers concerned – '[t]hat seems to me to be a hallmark of responsible journalism'.

[312] [2006] UKHL 44, quotes at [35], [151].

[313] [2007] EWCA Civ 972, [2008] EMLR 16 (commencing at p 505) (quotes at [83]).

Fact or opinion

§15.48 The statutory defence applies, whether D's statement was one of fact or of opinion.

It was unclear, at common law, whether the *Reynolds* defence could be a defence to a comment. That issue was expressly left open in *British Chiropractic Assn v Singh*.[314] However, s 4(5) laid that to rest – the statutory defence in s 4 applies to either.

QUALIFIED PRIVILEGE

Common law qualified privilege

§15.49 According to common law qualified privilege, D will have a defence to defamation where D had a legitimate interest in speaking freely and informing readers of the published imputations, and the recipient had a corresponding interest to receive the information, provided that the publication was not made with malice.

Despite the evolution of *Reynolds* (now 'public interest') privilege, there was always a separate defence of qualified privilege – which has also been termed as 'traditional common law privilege' (per *Trumm v Norman*[315]) or 'traditional duty-interest qualified privilege' (per *Rai v Bholowasia*[316]). According to *Adam v Ward*, qualified privilege requires that 'the person who makes a communication has an interest or a duty, legal, social or moral, to make it to the person to whom it is made, and the person to whom it is so made has a corresponding interest or duty to receive it. The reciprocity is essential'.[317]

Elements of the defence

1 D had a legitimate interest in informing readers of the statement
2 Readers had a corresponding and legitimate interest in being informed about the statement
3 D was not motivated by malice

If the defamatory allegations are untrue, but these elements are proven, then the defence will succeed, notwithstanding that it is sure to leave C aggrieved (in *Jameel v Wall Street Journal Europe Sprl*, Lord Bingham stated that '[q]ualified privilege as a live issue only arises where a statement is defamatory and untrue'[318]).

Dealing with each element in turn:

A legitimate interest to inform

Whether D had a 'legitimate interest' (or, as sometimes it is termed, a duty, whether legal, social or moral) in speaking freely will depend upon all the circumstances. That interest may arise because of 'some public or private duty, whether legal or moral, on the part of [D] which

[314] [2010] EWCA Civ 350, [2011] 1 WLR 133, [31]. [315] [2008] EWHC 116 (QB) [42].
[316] [2015] EWHC 382 (QB) [45]. [317] [1917] AC 309 (HL) 334 (Lord Atkinson).
[318] [2006] UKHL 44, [2007] 1 AC 359, [32].

justifies his communicating it, or of some interest of his own which he is entitled to protect by doing so' (per *Horrocks v Lowe*[319]). The defence will also turn on D's relationship with the readers of the statement, and the way in which D disseminated the statement. Qualified privilege applied in the following:

> In *Akinleye v East Sussex Hosp NHS Trust*,[320] a doctor, C, employed by East Sussex NHS Trust, sued in defamation for an email sent from that Trust's medical director, D, to another medical director, to whose Pennine NHS Trust C had shifted. It stated that C's work was not good; that C's knowledge of echo-cardiography (ECG) was limited; that C was suspected of the theft of the Echo Machine at the hospital where he had worked; and that C did not pay rent and owed rent when he left. The defence applied, because the email was sent in response to an authoritative request by the medical director of one NHS Trust to D, as C's former employer, for any information relating to concerns about C during his employment at D's hospital. D had a duty to respond to the Pennine Trust's legitimate enquiry, and the Pennine Trust had a legitimate interest in knowing the answer to that enquiry. In *Ma v St George's Healthcare NHS Trust*,[321] facts previously, the defence applied to communications which voiced genuine concerns about the safety and safeguarding of a young child patient ('there would plainly be a duty on the part of a nurse or clinician to communicate those concerns to the appropriate quarter'). In *Trumm v Norman*,[322] Mr Trumm, C, complained of defamatory statements published by a union officer, D, regarding ongoing litigation between them, contained in a *Loco Journal* issue; 18,000 copies were distributed mainly to present and retired union members. The defence applied, because D had a duty to let its members know what it was spending its money on, including re legal settlements. C had allegedly created so much publicity about his disputes with the union, among its railway membership, that the publication was D's way of 'setting the record straight',and union members had a legitimate interest in reading the article.

Any words which were published will *prima facie* be subject to the qualified privilege, unless they are not relevant to the subject matter which is privileged. In both the following cases, the defence was made out:

> In *Akinleye*,[323] C argued that the email from D to the other medical director was 'excessive and out of scope', because it should not have referred to the unpaid rent, theft of the echo machine, or his allegedly limited knowledge of ECG. Given that there was a serious investigation underway into a real risk of danger to cardiac patients, D was entitled/bound to let Pennine Trust know of any information which might be relevant to an assessment of C's integrity and professionalism, so that it could 'form a complete picture'. In *Wallis v Meredith*,[324] where D writes to C's solicitors, in the midst of a commercial dispute between C and D, such correspondence will be covered by qualified privilege, on the basis of a common and corresponding interest, provided that it relates to the dispute at hand.

A legitimate interest in receiving

The corresponding and legitimate interest held by readers in being informed about D's statements is often financial (as in different contexts in *Akinleye*, re employment, and *Trumm*, re union membership funds).

[319] [1975] AC 135 (HL) 149 (Lord Diplock). [320] [2008] EWHC 68 (QB). [321] [2015] EWHC 1866 (QB) [53].
[322] [2008] EWHC 116 (QB). [323] [2008] EWHC 68 (QB) [20]. [324] [2011] EWHC 75 (QB) [61].

Common law qualified privilege will only be available as a defence for D, in relation to those readers who had an interest in being informed about the published statements. If there was publication to a *wider* group of readers (who did not have that interest), then the defence will fail, and D will be liable in defamation for publication to that wider group. In this respect, common law qualified privilege is a narrower defence than the public interest (or old *Reynolds*) qualified privilege, for publication to members of the general public could certainly be protected by *Reynolds* qualified privilege (per *Trumm v Norman*[325]).

In *Trumm v Norman*, as well as publication in *Loco Journal*, 200 further copies were distributed to people who were not union members (e.g., to the union's legal and financial advisers, and members of other unions), and were also published on the union website (hence, accessible to the general public). Although there were 18,133 hits on the website during one month, there was no direct evidence that any person read the words complained of on the website. **Held:** qualified privilege still applied. The union website was of specialist interest (compared with a website like BBC News), so it could not be inferred that non-union members had read the defamatory statements there. However, for copies of the journal sent to non-union members, D could not rely on the defence, as those readers did not have any interest in the union's affairs, over and above that of any ordinary member of the public. In *Levi v Bates*,[326] a letter was written by Mr Bates, D, the then-Chairman of Leeds United Football Club, to the club members, about Mr Levi's, C's, character and activities, describing C as a 'shyster'. **Held:** the letter was protected by qualified privilege. The Chairman of a football club had a legitimate interest in keeping the 'particularly committed supporters of the club' informed of matters affecting the club, and those members had a corresponding and legitimate interest in being informed about the club's financial affairs. However, the publication of D's statements in the match day programmes was not protected by qualified privilege. Even if the most reasonable and responsible way of communicating information of legitimate interest to supporters was via the match programmes, the non-members of the club, the away supporters, and one-off attendees, did not have the requisite legitimate interest in the contents of the match day programme or of being informed of the misconduct alleged on C's part by D. Also, the matchday programme was not a reasonable or proportionate way for D to communicate with those supporters – when their addresses were known to the club.

Absence of malice

D must not have been motivated by malice. In this context, malice means where D (per *Horrocks v Lowe*[327]):

i. did not believe that what he published was true, at the time that it was published;
ii. published untrue defamatory matter recklessly, without considering or caring whether or not it was true;
iii. was motivated (as the dominant motive) to publish the statement to give vent to his personal spite or ill-will towards C (even if he did believe that what he published was true); or
iv. was motivated to obtain some private advantage unconnected with the reason as to why it was privileged in the first place.

If any of those malicious indicators is proven, D loses the benefit of the privilege.

[325] *Trumm v Norman* [2008] EWHC 116 (QB) [43].
[326] [2009] EWHC 1495 (QB) [98].
[327] [1975] AC 135 (CA) 150 (Diplock LJ).

In *Cambridge v Makin*,[328] Jan Cambridge, C, an interpreter, was an unpaid non-executive director of the Chartered Institute of Linguists. Another interpreter, D, a member of the association, sent an email to many members of the profession, claiming that C had abused her position as an office holder to act on a conflict of interest to her own financial benefit. **Held:** malice by D proven; no qualified privilege possible. D's conduct, in making the allegations, was to be characterised as reckless, or 'wilful blindness'.

However, as Sir David Eady pointed out in *Ma v St George's Healthcare NHS Trust*, involving an allegation of dishonesty as it does in most cases, proof of malice in defamation trials is 'very rare'.[329] Furthermore, the fact that D's mindset about C 'is prejudiced and irrational' does not constitute malice (per *Rai v Bholowasia*[330]).

In *Akinleye*, it could not be inferred that D lacked any belief in the truth of his words, nor a desire to vent personal spite or any other improper motive against C, a locum employee whom he had known for only a matter of weeks, or that he would wish to damage his standing at his new hospital. No malice could be proven or inferred. In *Levi v Bates*, there was no malice, just because D's letter purported to advise club members of recent events to do with C's financial dealings, but actually referred to events which had occurred a long time ago; and character statements about C being a 'shyster' or a 'blackmailer' did not constitute malice either. In *Ma*, professional medical staff who were confronted with an erratic parent who wished to remove her child from A&E before her head injury had been fully assessed could not ignore the matter, and with the interests of the child at heart, properly referred the matter to social workers who had 'safeguarding' responsibilities.

There is no malice if D knows that his statement will injure C, but is acting in accordance with a sense of duty or in *bona fide* protection of his own legitimate interests (per *Horrocks v Lowe*[331]).

Statutory qualified privilege

§15.50 D's publication of any reports or other statements referred to in Schedule 1 of the Defamation Act 1996 are subject to qualified privileged under s 15(1) of that Act, provided that the publication was not made with malice.

D's report or statement is protected by qualified privilege, if D repeats another's defamatory statement under s 15, where that report or statement is of a type stipulated in Sch 1 of the Defamation Act 1996. A publication is protected under s 15(1), even if the statement's publication was not in the public interest; and D is not under any duty to check the accuracy of the statement.

Where s 15 applies, then it revokes the repetition rule. Otherwise, if it did apply, then as Laws LJ said in *Curistan v Times Newspapers Ltd*,[332] 'the privilege would be nullified [because] the privilege allows the publisher to rely on the fact that he is reporting what another has said ... The very purpose of the privilege is to facilitate what [a stipulated other] has said. It can only be done if the repetition rule is set aside'. In *Curistan*, it was confirmed that revocation of the repetition rule was compatible with the Convention, even though it may appear to 'tip the balance' in favour of D's right to freedom of expression, and against C's right to reputation under art 8.

328 [2012] EWCA Civ 85, [63]. 329 [2015] EWHC 1866 (QB) [56]. 330 [2015] EWHC 382 (QB) [161].
331 [1975] AC 135 (HL) 149–151. 332 [2008] EWCA Civ 432, [2009] QB 231, 261–62, 257.

Elements of the defence

1 The statement was 'a fair and accurate report' of a type described in Sch 1 of the 1996 Act
2 D was not motivated by malice

A fair and accurate report

Some reports and statements of D's (those in Sch 1, Pt 1), are automatically entitled to privilege, if they contain defamatory statements. They include where D has made a 'fair and accurate report' of parliamentary, court, or public enquiry proceedings, and of defamatory imputations made in those proceedings.

Other publications (set out in Sch 1, Pt 2), are entitled to privilege, but that is lost if, per s15(2), D was requested 'to publish in a suitable manner a reasonable letter or statement by way of explanation or contradiction', and failed to do so. This type of publication includes 'fair and accurate report' of a press conference that discusses a matter of public interest, or of the proceedings of a scientific or academic conference (these were added by s 7 of the Defamation Act 2013). It also covers statements issued by the police, that X has been charged with a criminal offence. Where any of these reports is defamatory, then it is protected under s 15.

Statutory qualified privilege has been 'judicially stretched', in some important respects. For example, D will be protected, even where the statement (say, a police report), a copy or extract of which D published, does not identify C – but D's publication goes further than the report did, and actually identifies C. The statutory qualified privilege extends to the publication of C's identity, and it remains a 'fair and accurate' report (per *Flood v Times Newspapers Ltd*[333]).

In *Flood*, Mr Flood, C, a serving police officer in the Extradition Unit, sued in defamation after *The Times* published an article, alleging that C had corruptly sold intelligence information about wealthy Russian businessmen whom the Russian legal regime wished to extradite back to Moscow. The article included information in a police press statement, and in addition named C (who had not been identified in the police statement) and included the details of the allegations made against him. C was removed temporarily from his post, was then cleared of any wrongdoing, and then returned to his post. *The Times* learnt of the report clearing C, but the original article remained on its website unamended. **Held:** statutory qualified privilege effectively extended to identifying or naming the relevant police officer as C.

Similarly, where an MP makes defamatory statements about C in Parliament, and D reports those statements about C in an article, but also intermingles, amongst the 'privileged passages', a number of other comments about C which were not made in Parliament and which are 'non-privileged passages', then that inter-mingling can *still* produce a 'fair and accurate report' of the parliamentary proceedings, such that the defamatory statements (which constitute a copy or extract of what the MP said) can retain the protection of qualified privilege under s 15 (per *Curistan*[334]) – provided that the extraneous material was not so excessive in quantity that it deprived the report of its quality of fairness.

In *Curistan*, Mr Curistan, C, a well-known businessman and chartered accountant in Northern Ireland, sued for the publication of an article, under the headline, '"IRA" developer in row over

333 [2010] EWCA Civ 804, [2011] 1 WLR 153, [28], aff'd: [2010] UKSC 1, [2010] 2 WLR 325.
334 [2009] QB 231, 237.

accounts', appearing in D's *The Sunday Times* in its Belfast edition. The article reported that an MP, Mr Robinson, had alleged in the House of Commons that C had laundered money for the IRA, and it also added the journalist's own statement that, in response to those allegations in Parliament, C had vigorously denied the allegations, had referred to the state of his accounts, but D's inquiries had revealed that C's claims about his company accounts were false. **Held:** the whole article was protected by qualified privilege, insofar that it reported allegations made in Parliament. There was a distinct report of what Mr Robinson said; the allegations of money-laundering were made by the MP and accurately reported by D; and the extraneous material (about financial malpractice) was not so excessive that it destroyed the fairness of the report. Hence, D's report of what Mr Robinson said was privileged.

Suppose that an MP makes a defamatory statement in Parliament which is protected by qualified privilege under s 15 – and then D not only repeats those statements in his report, but also uses words which appear to indicate that D believes that the statements are true (i.e. that D adopts them). D can lose the protection of qualified privilege under s 15, under the doctrine of adoption.

In *Curistan*,[335] the *Sunday Times* had not adopted the MP's (Mr Robinson's) statements made in Parliament. The word 'IRA' in the headline was in inverted commas; the MP's statements were set out without any express comment; and D's article did not express any opinion on the truthfulness or gravity of the MP's statements.

Absence of malice

The statutory privilege conveyed by s 15 is qualified in the usual sense, that the defamatory imputation cannot have been made by D with malice. In this context, 'malice' means 'where D knows that the allegation is false, or is reckless to whether it is true or false. It is an allegation of dishonesty' (per *Ifedha v Kilburn Times North West London Newspapers*[336] – where malice could not be proven).

REPORTAGE

§15.51 Reportage constitutes a complete defence, based upon the concept of 'neutral reporting'. It is now contained in s 4(3) of the Defamation Act 2013.

The defence was described, in *Roberts v Gable*, as 'a special form of common law qualified privilege with distinctive features of its own'.[337] Section 4(3) of the Defamation Act 2013 repeats the common law defence, reinforcing the elements that existed at common law:

Elements of the defence

1 The article reflected 'neutral reporting'
2 The article covered a subject of legitimate public interest

Where the defence applies, a journalist can defend the publication of a defamatory imputation, without having verified, or attempting to verify, the truth of the statement being reported. In

[335] [2009] QB 231, 252. [336] [2010] EWHC 2819 (QB) [26]. [337] [2007] EWCA Civ 721, [2008] QB 502, [60].

that respect, the defence is different from the 'public interest' defence, which requires that the journalist take *some* steps to verify the truth of the statement. Where the reportage defence does not apply, then if a journalist has sought to merely 'report' defamatory allegations, the other defence to which recourse must be had is the defence of truth.

Neutral reporting

§15.52 Neutral reporting means reporting defamatory imputations without adoption, embellishment, or subscribing to any belief in their truth.

In s 4(3), this element is described as 'an accurate and impartial account of a dispute to which C was a party'. At common law, this element, as described in *Charman v Orion Publishing Group Ltd*, demonstrated just how limited the defence's application is: '[t]he protection is lost if the journalist adopts what has been said and makes it his own, or if he fails to report the story in a fair, disinterested, neutral way'.[338] D's statement must be judged as a whole, and it must report, not the truth of the statements, but the fact that they were made, as attributed to another. Any connotation that journalist D has engaged in 'investigative reporting', i.e., 'acting as the bloodhound sniffing out bits of the story from here and there, from published material and unpublished material, not as the watchdog barking to wake us up to the story already out there', will preclude the defence.[339]

In *Roberts v Gable*,[340] journalist D wrote an article about a feud between different factions of the British National Party. The article contained allegations made by some BNP members that Mr Roberts, C, had committed theft of money collected at their 'grand rally', and had threatened violence. C sued for libel. **Held:** the defence of reportage applied. The article only reported the conflicting positions, and the allegations and counter-allegations, rather than taking sides. D had not adopted the allegations made, and D did not need to seek their verification.

Legitimate public interest

§15.53 D must prove that he was reporting on a matter of legitimate public interest in the same way as is necessary under the 'public interest' defence.

It was said, in *Roberts v Gable*,[341] that the defence of reportage should be treated 'restrictively' and would be 'relatively rare'. It has infrequently been successful in English law to date, and tends to have applied in relation to disputes between political opponents (per *Al-Fagih v HH Saudi Research & Marketing (UK) Ltd*[342]).

In *Flood v Times Newspapers Ltd*,[343] facts previously, **held:** the defence failed. If the D's report stated that an unidentified informant gave information which, if true, could incriminate a police officer in corruption, that will 'very rarely be justifiable reportage'. The subject matter will be in the public interest, but it would be tipping the scales too far in D's favour to hold that D did not need to take

[338] [2007] EWCA Civ 972, [2008] EMLR 16 (commencing at p 505) [48]. [339] *ibid*, [49].
[340] [2007] EWCA Civ 721, [2008] QB 502. [341] [2007] EWCA Civ 721, [74], [88].
[342] [2001] EWCA Civ 1634, [6]. [343] [2010] EWCA Civ 804, [2011] 1 WLR 153, [63].

reasonable steps to check the accuracy. In *Charman v Orion Publishing Group Ltd*,[344] facts previously, **held:** the defence of reportage failed. The book drew upon confidential material (tapes, information, private conversations), not just the court proceedings in the public domain, and purported to tell the 'inside story' of corruption in the Met Police. It was hardly a neutral, disinterested report. D 'was not simply reporting published material, but mixing that material with other information his enquiries had revealed, so as to write as the product of his own considerable researches'.

ABSOLUTE PRIVILEGE

§15.54 All participants in legal proceedings – judges, counsel, witnesses (including expert witnesses) and parties – enjoy an immunity from any suit in defamation, for words written or spoken in the ordinary course of any proceeding before any court or tribunal recognised by law. Absolute privilege also applies to protect statements made in Parliament. However, the privilege is subject to a number of exceptions.

This principle, which has a long-standing pedigree (per *Crawford v Jenkins*[345]) protects these participants, even where they have spoken untruthfully or maliciously.

Parliament. The purpose of the privilege is to preserve the right of Members of Parliament to speak their minds in Parliament without any risk of incurring liability for defamation. However, statements made outside Parliament are not protected by absolute privilege, even if they simply repeat what was said in the parliamentary chamber. If an MP, having 'spoken his mind' and defamed someone, elects to repeat his statement outside Parliament, then 'the paramount need to protect freedom of speech in Parliament does not require the extension of absolute privilege to protect such statements' (per *Buchanan v Jennings*[346]).

Court. Immunity here is grounded in public policy, and has a two-fold purpose. Within the courtroom, it means that the parties can 'discharge their duties without fear or favour and without the dread of an impending action' (per *Jones v Kaney*[347]). Outside the courtroom, the absolute privilege applies to out-of-court statements which can fairly be said to be part of the process of investigating a crime or suspected crime with a view to prosecution (per *Taylor v Director of the Serious Fraud Office*[348]); and also applies to affidavits, proofs of evidence and witness statements (per *Iqbal v Dean Manson Solicitors (No 2)*[349]). However, the privilege is subject to a number of exceptions. For example, it is lost, where 'the words used had no connection with the case in hand' (per *Primrose v Waterston*[350]), or had 'no reference at all to the subject-matter of the proceedings' (per *Iqbal v Dean Manson Solicitors*[351]). The absolute privilege applies to any court or tribunal which is recognised by law (as opposed to domestic tribunals which derive their authority from agreement or consent) (per *White v Southampton Univ Hosp NHS Trust*,[352] which held that the immunity applied to D's initiating letter sent to the General Medical Council).

344 [2007] EWCA Civ 972, [11], [13], and quote at [57].

345 [2014] EWCA Civ 103, [28]. See, e.g.: *Dawkins v Lord Rokeby* (1872–73) LR 8 QB 255 (Exch) 263 (Kelly CB); and *R v Skinner* (1772) Lofft 55, 56, 98 ER 529, cited in: *Jones v Kaney* [2011] UKSC 13, [11], [133].

346 [2005] 1 AC 115 (PC) [13], [17].

347 *ibid*, [134], citing: *Primrose v Waterston* (1902) 4 F 783 (CSIH) 793–94.

348 [1999] 2 AC 177 (HL) 215 (Lord Hoffmann).

349 [2013] EWCA Civ 149, [29].

350 1902 4 F 783, and cited in *Jones v Kaney*, *ibid*, [135].

351 [2013] EWCA Civ 149, [32].

352 [2011] EWHC 825 (QB) [14].

Notably, whilst a barrister no longer enjoys an immunity from suit, in respect of a claim in negligence brought against him by his own client (per *Arthur J S Hall & Co v Simons*[353]), that barrister still enjoys an absolute privilege from a claim in defamation in relation to statements made in the course of the conduct of legal proceedings (clarified, post-*Simons*, in *Medcalf v Mardell*[354]). The same applies to expert witnesses, who are potentially liable in negligence in relation to the evidence which they gave in court, or for the views which they expressed in anticipation of court proceedings – but they continue to enjoy an absolute privilege from defamation claims (per *Jones v Kaney*[355]).

Where D makes a defamatory statement in court, reports of those proceedings are subject to the defence of absolute privilege too (per s 14(3) of the Defamation Act 1996[356]), and the same applies to the reporting of defamatory statements in Parliament (per *Makudi v Baron Triesman of Tottenham*[357]).

CONSENT AND ACQUIESCENCE

§15.55 It is a complete defence to an action for defamation that C consented to, or acquiesced in, the publication complained of.

If C consented to the publication of the words he is suing for, then he cannot therefore complain about their publication or continued publication. Acquiescence is proven, where C knew of the words used by D, and did not object to their publication or continued publication.

In *Tamiz v Guardian News & Media Ltd*,[358] Mr Tamiz, C, sued the Guardian online newspaper for an article which contained a hyperlink to an article published in the Evening Standard, the latter of which referred to derogatory comments allegedly made by C about women in two places online: first, in a Facebook group called 'Girls in THANET...you are all slags, hoes, brasses and bheads' (the Facebook Group); and secondly, on his publicly available Facebook profile page. C sued for defamation, on the basis that he had never been a member of that Facebook page, and that to allege that he was a member of it imputed that he was a misogynist and sexist. **Held:** C consented to certain forms of wording used by D; or knowing that certain content was there and by not objecting to it, C had acquiesced to its publication.

AN OFFER OF AMENDS

§15.56 The offer of amends is a defence governed by the statutory regime in ss 2–4 of the Defamation Act 1996.

According to the Neill Committee,[359] which recommended the offer-of-amends reform, the regime was intended to provide a fair and reasonable exit route for D, who was being confronted with unreasonable demands from a 'manipulative or powerful' C, where D was being held 'over

353 [2002] 1 AC 615 (HL). 354 [2003] 1 AC 120 (HL) [52]–[54] (Lord Hobhouse).

355 [2011] UKSC 13, [2011] 2 WLR 823, [179].

356 The scope of the courts caught by the defence have been widened by s 7(1) of the Defamation Act 2013.

357 [2013] EWHC 142 (QB) [67], aff'd: [2014] EWCA Civ 179.

358 [2013] EWHC 2339 (QB) [68].

359 (Neill LJ, Chair), Supreme Court Procedure Committee, *Practice and Procedure in Defamation* (Jul 1991).

a barrel' for what it had spoken/written. The regime would 'help to focus minds on achieving realistic compromise, and thus reduce the cost, for a much wider range of litigants'. It would also fit in with the modern 'cards on the table' approach to litigation, and with the underlying premise of the Defamation Pre-action Protocol (per *Abu v MGN Ltd*[360]).

The effect of an offer. An offer to make amends concerns an *alleged* defamatory statement – once an offer is made by D and accepted by C, defamation proceedings cannot be commenced or continued. Hence, there is no definitive judicial finding of a defamatory imputation, where an offer to make amends has been offered and accepted. The procedure puts D to an election, in that D cannot make an offer to amend after he has served a defence in the action.[361] An offer to make amends by D has three components: an offer to 'suitably correct' the statement complained of and to make a 'sufficient apology' to C; an offer to publish the correction and apology in a 'reasonable and practicable manner'; and an offer to pay C compensation (either agreed, or if not, determined by the court).[362]

The effect of an acceptance, or non-acceptance, of an offer. Once C accepts an offer of amends, D cannot withdraw its offer of amends and then plead justification. A binding and legally enforceable contract comes into existence, and D is bound (subject to the court's having a very restricted residual discretion to allow D to resile from an offer of amends under the Defamation Act 1996). If D has made its offer of amends freely, on the basis of legal advice, then D is very unlikely to be allowed to resile from the offer (per *Warren v Random House Group Ltd*[363]).

If C and D cannot agree on the amount of compensation to be paid, then the court must determine that on the same principles as damages in defamation proceedings (discussed below). If C and D cannot agree on the steps to be taken for correction, apology and publication, then D can take what he thinks are 'appropriate steps', which the court will then take into account when determining the amount of compensation.[364]

How is compensation assessed? According to the Court of Appeal in *Nail v News Group Newspapers Ltd*,[365] C may recover the types of heads of damage that would ordinarily be awarded under compensatory damages; and exemplary damages and special damages are not precluded. An offer to make amends will be, of itself, a mitigating factor, given that C has effectively 'won' at that point, and any stress, hurt, anxiety, will be reduced from that point onwards. Damages will also be mitigated if the offer is made early, and with an agreed apology. Nevertheless, awards of compensation under the offer to make amends procedure may still be large.

An offer of amends in action – *Bowman v MGN Ltd*[a]

Facts: An article was published on the website of the *Mirror* newspaper, D, under the heading, 'Hannah Waterman new man revealed as Les Miserables star Simon Bowman', and that actress Ms Waterman was 'stepping out with ANOTHER actor since her split with former EastEnders and Strictly Come Dancing star Ricky Groves'. Mr Bowman, C, complained to D that the article, was

[a] [2010] EWHC 895 (QB) [17].

[360] [2002] EWHC 2345 (QB), [2003] 1 WLR 2201, [8], [9]. [361] Defamation Act 1996, ss 3(2), 2(5).
[362] Defamation Act 1996, s 2(4). [363] [2007] EWCA Civ 834, [2009] QB 600, [1]–[2], [54].
[364] Defamation Act 1996, s 3(4), (5).
[365] [2005] 1 All ER 1040 (CA) [19], [45]. Also: *Turner v News Group Newspapers* [2006] 1 WLR 707 (CA) 723.

posted for about 27 hours before being taken down, was inaccurate and caused him humiliation and distress. An apology appeared online, stating: 'Simon Bowman – An Apology: On Wednesday 6 January we suggested that Simon Bowman was Hannah Waterman's new man following her split from her husband Ricky Groves. Simon is a family friend, he has been in a serious relationship with someone else for 20 years, and there is no romantic relationship between him and Hannah. We apologise to him for the distress and embarrassment caused by our suggestion to the contrary'.

Held: this could only be defamation by innuendo – to say that C was going out with Ms Waterman would not of itself be defamatory, but would be to those in C's circle of friends, fans, relatives and theatrical acquaintances who knew that C had been in a relationship with another for 20 years.

Quantum: starting point: £8,500 in damages.

Factors for mitigation: prompt removal of the article from the website; an early apology; an early offer of amends by D, at which point C's stress and anxiety should have been correspondingly reduced.

Factors against mitigation: the apology was of modest size and placement – of which Eady J said, '[t]hat, of course, is par for the course. Journalists hardly ever give an apology comparable prominence to that of the original offending words. The mitigating effect will thus be proportionately reduced'. Plus, after the offer was made, D did not adopt a conciliatory approach, but rather, a 'take it or leave it' approach.

Verdict: discount of 50% warranted; C recovered £4,250.

REMEDIES

Damages

Assessing the quantum of the award: some governing principles

According to the Court of Appeal in *John v MGN Ltd*,[366] the purposes of an award of compensatory general damages for defamation are three-fold: (1) to compensate C for any genuine damage (injury) to his reputation; (2) to serve as an outward and visible sign to vindicate C's good name; and (3) to compensate for the distress, hurt feelings, embarrassment and humiliation which the defamatory publication has caused C. A differently-constituted Court of Appeal noted more recently, in *Times Newspapers v Flood*, that defamation suits 'are not primarily about recovering money damages, but about vindication of C's reputation'.[367]

Ultimately, choosing the right bracket or figure for compensation is largely a matter of impression and personal judicial evaluation. Having said that, a court will consider the following factors (as set out in, e.g., *Abu v MGN Ltd*,[368] *Levi v Bates*[369] and *Bowman v MGN Ltd*[370]):

- the gravity of the defamatory imputations – a 'bit of celebrity gossip' is at the less serious end of the scale, whereas allegations of serious criminal wrongdoing or which relate to the integrity or truthfulness of C, are at the more serious end;

[366] [1997] QB 586 (CA) 607; *Levi v Bates* [2009] EWHC 1495 (QB) [163]–[164].

[367] [2014] EWCA Civ 1574, [37].

[368] [2003] 1 WLR 2201 (QB) [13]. See too *Levi v Bates* [2009] EWHC 1495 (QB) [164].

[369] [2009] EWHC 1495 (QB). [370] [2010] EWHC 895 (QB) [14].

- the type of defamatory imputation – e.g., the measure of damages will be lower in the case of defamation by innuendo in an article only published on a website, than in the case of defamation by a natural and ordinary meaning published in a national newspaper; but the far-reaching nature of its distribution, via the internet, may also be a relevant factor in the award;
- the time period over which the publication appeared – the more 'short-lived' the defamation, the lower the award, especially where the words were removed from a website, or corrected by subsequent publication by D, almost as soon as the complaint was received from C;
- D's own behaviour – damages may be higher where D sought unsuccessfully to justify his statements about C, and carried on with those attempts in a public trial lasting many days; or where D's conduct was calculated to exacerbate the distress and hurt feelings suffered by C (e.g., in *Levi v Bates*,[371] D included, in the defamatory publications, details of C's home address, email address and reference to his number being in the telephone book, 'which was, in effect, an invitation to Leeds fans to pester Mr Levi');
- frequency of publication – several occasions over, say, 10 months will warrant higher compensation than just one publication in that period (as evident in *Levi v Bates* itself);
- the readership – whether the readership to which the publication was directed were persons whose esteem C particularly valued.

A number of these factors were evident in the following:

> In *Farrall v Kordowski*,[372] Mr Kordowski, D, published a website, solicitorsfromhell.co.uk, with an anonymous posting which criticised Miss Farrall's, C's, professional competency. Damages of £10,000 were awarded. The factors which were relevant to that assessment included:
>
> - the tone of the allegations was abusive and malicious;
> - they caused C great upset, given that the posting mentioned her employer and she had had to discuss it with the practice partners, and that it represented an unwarranted slur upon the competency and probity of a young member of the legal profession;
> - D, as publisher, had not admitted that there was no truth in the allegations made against C, nor issued any apology, which meant that vindication was important in the assessment of damages;
> - the duration of publication was limited (about a month), and with the extent of publication unknown; however, publication of defamatory statements on a website published them to a potentially very wide readership, and the statement was easily locatable via various search engines;
> - D had not attempted to verify the allegations before publication, gave C no opportunity to comment before publication, and the website itself allowed the option of 'delete a listing', and to ensure no future listing, but subject to payment of 'administration and monitoring costs' of a one-off payment of £299;
> - when C complained to D of the posting, D essentially demanded that F prove the allegations to be untrue, by asking C's employers for information about C, including file reviews and appraisals;
> - even after the posting was deleted from the website, traces remained on various search engines which showed what the posting would have been about, even if the precise posting was no longer capable of being read.

371 [2009] EWHC 1495 (QB), quote at [164].
372 [2010] EWHC 2436 (QB) (injunction), and subsequently: (QB, 28 Jan 2011, Lloyd Jones J, award of damages).

In *Bento v CC of Bedfordshire Police*,[373] a police press release, which was emailed to various local media, included the allegation that evidence obtained by the police showed that C (against whom charges had been dropped) had probably murdered his girlfriend. Bean J awarded damages of £125,000. Relevant factors included:

- the press release was not a national or worldwide publication, it was a limited publication. However, a news release published in the Bedfordshire section of the BBC news website can be accessed by anyone who is interested enough to look for it;
- it concerned an unjustifiable allegation of serious criminal conduct;
- the defence of truth was heard in open court, which increased the distress to C, although that was a limited aggravated factor, 'in view of the courtesy and restraint with which it was done'.

Certain matters must be **excluded** from consideration, where damages computations are concerned. For example, it is important to only compensate C for injury or distress caused by D's publication, and to isolate those elements of damage, and not to 'heap upon D' responsibility for distress which may have been caused to C by other publications for which D was not responsible. Further, any distress caused to those who are close to C is not compensable; it is not the function of a defamation award to compensate C's friends or relatives as if they were claimants too. Also, damages are not recoverable in respect of any privileged publications (per *Trumm v Norman*[374]).

Other relevant matters

The 'egg-shell skull' C. If C was more distressed than the usual person may have been by the defamatory publication, because C was over-sensitive and lacked a sense of proportion, it is nevertheless appropriate in defamation, as in other areas of the law, for a tortfeasor to 'take his victim as he finds him' (per *Bowman v MGN Ltd*[375]). On the other hand, if C was 'so robust that he would feel the injury less than others', then the damages award should reflect that (per *Trumm v Norman*[376]).

Factors governing mitigation of damages. Several factors may mitigate, or reduce, C's damages, e.g.:

- if C is alleged by D to have already had (prior to the defamation action) a 'general bad reputation', then evidence to that effect may be introduced for the purpose of mitigating damages; but D cannot introduce evidence of specific acts of misconduct (per the rule in *Scott v Sampson*,[377] and reaffirmed in *Berezovsky v Russian Television and Radio Broadcasting Co*[378]):

In *Berezovsky*, Mr Berezovsky, C, a high-profile and long-standing opponent of Russian President Vladimir Putin, sued in defamation for a TV documentary, shown on an English free-to-air channel, alleging, inter alia, that C was a knowing party to a criminal conspiracy to avoid his extradition back to Russia, and to obtain political asylum in Britain. **Held:** the TV programme was defamatory of C. (The claim that C had been defamed because of an allegation that C had been a party to the murder, by polonium poisoning, of Alexander Litvinenko in London, was abandoned at trial.) Re damages, it would be 'unreal' to ignore the fact that, in the eyes of many Russian people, C had the reputation

[373] [2012] EWHC 1525 (QB). [374] [2008] EWHC 116 (QB) [46]–[47].
[375] [2010] EWHC 895 (QB) [15]. Also: *Cleese v Clark* [2004] EMLR 3 (commencing at p 37) (QB) [40].
[376] [2008] EWHC 116 (QB) [55]. [377] (1881–82) LR 8 QBD 491, 499. [378] [2010] EWHC 476 (QB) [169], [176].

as a 'criminal on the run' from Russian justice, and he had been sentenced to 13 years imprisonment in his absence. On the other hand, many saw C as a political dissident working for justice and validly opposing the Putin regime. Hence, C did not have a settled 'general bad reputation'. Damages were assessed at £150,000, given: the seriousness of the allegation; it was false, had gone uncorrected for three years, and had caused C distress, and was calculated to put at risk C's leave to remain in the UK; and the need to serve the purpose of vindication.

- there may be a relatively limited number of copies of the publication sold or given away;
- in *Burstein v Times Newspapers*,[379] it was mentioned that C's own conduct, in provoking D's defamatory imputation or in engaging in a slanging match with D for which D was seeking retaliation, may be taken account of, to reduce the damages to which C is entitled – that C will normally receive a lower award of damages than a C who has been defamed without provocation.

Comparison with personal injury awards. The quantum of awards for pain, suffering and loss of amenity, in personal injury claims is a legitimate consideration to take into account in assessing a suitable quantum for hurt, distress, etc, in defamation actions (per *John v MGN Ltd*[380]). The *Judicial College Guidelines* for psychiatric damage (as discussed in Chapter 11) may be referred to as helpful (per *Garcia v Associated Newspapers Ltd*[381]). However, there is also a 'vindicatory element' to damages in defamation cases, which is not present in general damages assessments in personal injury awards (per *Leech v Independent Newspapers (Ireland) Ltd*[382]).

Companies. In the case of a business defamation, if that action is commenced by an individual, the damages awarded may include an award for injury to feelings; but if the action is brought by a corporation, the award of damages cannot include injury to feelings (per *Thornton v Telegraph Media Group*[383]). Hence, the damages recoverable by a company for defamation will be on the low side ('unlikely to exceed a low five figure sum', per *Beach Developments Ltd v Foskett*[384]), and that '[v]indication is what is really at stake, not money', in many such cases.

Excessive jury awards. As noted in *Cook v Telegraph Media Group Ltd*,[385] excessive jury awards have been awarded in some notable English cases. However, it has been held that such awards have interfered with D's freedom of expression under Art 10 (per *Tolstoy Miloslavsky v UK*,[386] where the award of £1.5 million was set aside as being a disproportionately large award against D).

In order to remedy the 'extremes' of jury awards, Parliament enabled judges in the Court of Appeal to have the power to substitute a proper award for an excessive jury award, per s 8 of the Courts and Legal Services Act 1990, and CPR r 52.10(3). For example, in *Rantzen v MGN Ltd*,[387] a jury award of £250,000 was replaced, under s 8, by an award of £110,000.

However, given the presumption against jury trials which is now enacted (per s 11 of the 2013 Act, discussed below), this problem may be lessened, if not resolved entirely.

Aggravated and exemplary damages

Defamation is a tort that may attract aggravated damages, where the court wishes to take account of aggravating conduct on D's part – to compensate for additional hurt to C's feelings,

[379] [2001] 1 WLR 579 (CA) [25]. [380] [1997] QB 586 (CA). [381] [2014] EWHC 3137 (QB) [299].
[382] [2014] IESC 79. [383] [2010] EWHC 1414 (QB) [35]. [384] [2011] EWHC 198 (QB) [29].
[385] [2011] EWHC 763 (QB) [107]. [386] (1995) 20 EHRR 442 (ECtHR), [1996] EMLR 152, [51], [54].
[387] [1993] EWCA Civ 16.

or in the context of vindication, injury to his reputation, brought about by D's conduct over and above that caused by the publication itself (per *Cairns v Modi*[388]). An award of aggravated damages compensates C 'for any salt that D has rubbed in the wound, over and above the injury caused by the defamatory publication(s)' – which means that C must have known of D's aggravating conduct (per *Henry v NGN Ltd*[389]). A company has no feelings, and hence, cannot recover aggravated damages (per *Collins Stewart v Financial Times*[390]). Malice alone, without the exemplary damages factors, only warrants aggravated damages (per *McGrath v Dawkins*[391]).

In the case of exemplary damages, two situations in which exemplary damages may be claimed are relevant for defamation suits: where (1) oppressive, arbitrary or unconstitutional action is committed by D, as servants of the government; or (2) D deliberately commits defamation, with the intention of gaining some advantage which will outweigh the compensation otherwise payable (e.g., the sale of newspapers which contain that defamatory article) (per *Rookes v Barnard*[392]).

The principles underpinning both categories of damages have been considered in further detail in Chapter 11.

Declaration of falsity

Summary disposal of a defamation action (per s 8 of the Defamation Act 1996) is possible, where it appears to the court that D has no defence to C's defamation claim which has a realistic prospect of success, and that there is no other reason why C's claim should be tried. As part of the summary procedure, the court may make a 'declaration of falsity', i.e., a declaration that D's statement was false and defamatory of C.[393] It may also order that D publish a suitable correction and apology.[394]

In many cases of summary disposal, declarations of falsity will be appropriate – but they are not for every case (e.g., if the extent of publication in England, and any connection between C and the jurisdiction, was very limited, per *Mahfouz v Brisard*[395]). Furthermore, declarations of falsity under s 8 are **not** obtainable following a trial of the claims. As Lord Phillips said in *Jameel v Dow Jones & Co Ltd*, 'English law and procedure does not permit the court to make a declaration of falsity at the end of a libel action ... The presumption of falsity does not leave the judge in a position to make a declaration to all the world that the allegation was false'.[396]

Injunctive relief

A court may grant an injunction, restraining D from publishing, or from further publishing, a defamatory statement, where it is clear that D, unless restrained, intends to continue publishing the defamatory imputations.

In *Gregg v O'Gara*,[397] a clear intent by D to continue publication was evident: from D's correspondence to numerous media organisations, repeating his allegations that C framed John Humble as the Yorkshire Ripper hoaxer and that the 'real Yorkshire Ripper' was, and remained, unknown and free; and when C had succeeded in having one of D's websites containing the defamatory material taken

388 [2012] EWCA Civ 1382, [2013] 1 WLR 1015, [28], [35]. 389 [2011] EWHC 1058 (QB) [7].
390 [2006] EMLR 5 (QB) (Gray J). 391 [2012] EWHC B3 (QB) [82], aff'd: [2013] EWCA Civ 206.
392 [1964] AC 1129 (HL) 1226 (Lord Devlin). 393 Per s 9(1)(a). 394 Per s 9(1)(b).
395 [2006] EWHC 1191 (QB) [23]–[24]. 396 [2005] QB 946 (CA) [67]. 397 [2008] EWHC 658 (QB) [77].

down, the website and content soon reappeared on another website, with D writing to the original web host to complain that they were 'weak-willed'.

Where a newspaper or other media is intending to publish, and indicates that it intends to justify the defamatory imputation (or to rely on some other defence, such as 'honest opinion' or 'public interest'), then an interim injunction is very unlikely to be obtained by C, to restrain D's publication of the article, even though it is defamatory (per the rule in *Bonnard v Perryman*,[398] as affirmed in *Fraser v Evans*[399]). The *Bonnard* common law rule is intended, of course, to preserve D's freedom of speech (per *Merlin Entertainments plc v Cave*[400]).

Notably, in *Terry (LSN) v Persons Unknown*,[401] when the professional footballer and English captain, John Terry, applied for an ex parte interim injunction to restrain the publication of certain information about his private life, the causes of action relied upon were breach of confidence and misuse of private information (for which interim injunctions can be granted), and not defamation.

Order to a newspaper to publish report

According to the Independent Press Standards Organisation's *Editors' Code of Practice 2015*,[402] cl 1(ii) states that, where a 'significant inaccuracy, misleading statement or distortion' in a newspaper article published by newspaper D is recognised, it must be 'corrected, promptly and with due prominence, and – where appropriate – an apology published'. However, if newspaper D refuses to publish such a correction, then there is no sanction available. That the IPSO's predecessor, the Press Complaints Commission, 'lacked teeth' when it came to enforcement of the Code, was judicially acknowledged in *Lord Ashcroft v Foley*.[403]

398 [1891] 2 Ch 269 (CA) 284–85.

399 [1969] 1 QB 349 (CA) 360.

400 [2014] EWHC 3036 (QB) [39].

401 [2010] EWHC 119 (QB).

402 The IPSO is charged with enforcing the Editors' Code of Practice (revised Mar 2015). This organisation took over the role previously exercised by the Press Complaints Commission on 8 Sep 2014. The Code is available in full-text at: <https://www.ipso.co.uk/assets/82/Editors_Code_of_Practice_A4_March_2015.pdf>.

403 [2011] EWHC 292 (QB) [69].

16

Private nuisance

DEFINING THE CAUSE OF ACTION

§16.1 A private nuisance is an act or omission by D which unduly interferes with C's reasonable use and enjoyment of his land, or of some easement or other right which C uses or enjoys in connection with that land.

The abovementioned paraphrase of *Dobson v Thames Water Utilities Ltd*[1] is a convenient description of the tort of private nuisance. Others include:

> the essence of private nuisance is ... an interference with land or the enjoyment of land ... [and] ... an invasion of [C's] interest in the possession and enjoyment of land ... The function of the tort ... is to control the activities of the owner or occupier of property within the boundaries of his own land, which may harm the interests of the owner or occupier of other land (per Lord Lloyd, and Lord Hope, respectively, in *Hunter v Canary Wharf Ltd*[2]).
>
> The controlling principles [of private nuisance] which are (a) the reasonable use of property, and (b) reciprocal regard for the interests of neighbours, reinforce an altruistic process of give and take (*Hirose Electrical UK Ltd v Peak Ingredients Ltd*[3]).

Private nuisance is an old tort – much older than negligence. Claims for nuisance 'can be found in reports of cases going back to the reign of Henry IV' (albeit that, as one judge drily pointed out,[4] undoubtedly it was not responsible for the exhortation in *Henry IV*, 'the first thing we do, let's kill all the lawyers'[5]).

The framework

The pre-conditions, elements, and defences for the tort may be summarised as follows:

[1] [2011] EWHC 3253 (TCC) [685]; and also: *Network Rail Infrastructure Ltd v Conarken Group Ltd* [2010] EWHC 1852 (TCC) [68]–[69], citing: *Clerk and Lindsell on Torts* (19th edn)'s definition, [20-01] and [20-02].

[2] [1997] UKHL 14, [1997] AC 655 (HL) 723 (Lord Hope).

[3] [2011] EWCA Civ 987, [1], citing: *Cambridge Water Co v Eastern Counties Leather plc* [1994] 2 AC 264 (HL) 299.

[4] *Barr v Biffa Waste Services Ltd* [2011] EWHC 1003 (TCC, Coulson J) [329] and fn 16.

[5] Pt 2, Act IV, Sc II.

Nutshell analysis: Private nuisance

Preconditions for the tort to apply:

i Capacity of C to sue
ii Capacity of D to be sued
iii A threshold level of inconvenience

Elements of the tort:

1 An interference by D with C's use and enjoyment of land
2 D committed an unreasonable user
3(a) D's interference caused C the requisite damage
3(b) The damage is not too remote to be recoverable at law

Defences to the tort:

- Statutory authority
- A right of prescription
- The independent contractor defence
- The 'common enemy' defence
- Proprietary estoppels
- Act of God
- Contributory negligence/*volenti*

Miscellaneous matter:

Claims under Art 8 of the ECHR

Other actions possible in conjunction

An action for private nuisance may be brought by C in conjunction with other claims, e.g., public nuisance; negligence; an action under *Rylands v Fletcher*; trespass to land; a HRA action for violation of Art 8 of the ECHR; a claim against the landlord of D's premises (where D is a tenant) for a breach of the covenant for quiet enjoyment; and/or a claim under the Protection from Harassment Act 1997.

Indeed, some overlap between private nuisance and other causes of action may be quite likely. For example, in *Corby Group Litigation v Corby BC*, the Court of Appeal said that '[it] is true that the same conduct can amount to a private nuisance and a public nuisance. But the two torts are distinct and the rights protected by them are different';[6] while, in *Colour Quest Ltd v Total Downstream UK plc*, it was said that claims in nuisance and in *Rylands v Fletcher* can overlap, and that, especially, 'repeated escapes can give rise to liability on both bases'[7] (a topic which is considered shortly). Further, one category of private nuisance – arising from physical encroachments from D's land to C's property – closely resembles trespass to land, a fact which has been judicially recognised (per *Network Rail Infrastructure Ltd v Conarken Group Ltd*[8]).

[6] [2008] EWCA Civ 463, [2009] 2 WLR 609, [30] (Dyson LJ). [7] [2009] EWHC 540 (Comm) [409].
[8] [2010] EWHC 1852 (TCC) [69] (Akenhead J), aff'd: [2011] EWCA Civ 644, 136 Con LR 1.

The costs of litigation

Private nuisance is a tort which is resplendent with fairly technical issues, which of itself, creates expensive and time-consuming disputes.

A further problem with private nuisance, both historically and currently, is that courts have not always provided clear and adequate guidance as to where the boundaries of the requisite 'give and take' are properly to be drawn. Many of the cases considered in this chapter are notable for the fact that they concerned a very simple problem – the emission of smells, noise or some other interference from D's land, which irritated and annoyed C – and took an inordinate amount of time and money to resolve, often at appellate level. Of course, no doubt some of this can be attributed to the bitter litigious disputes that can arise between neighbours too.

Modern courts have been fond of pointing out that, what begins as a neighbourly dispute can easily escalate into costly and time-consuming litigation, and with a pyrrhic victory at the end of it all. Differently-constituted Courts of Appeal have despaired that 'by now the total costs of this litigation, which has achieved nothing of use for the parties, must be greater than the expense of a constructive solution to the smell permeation problem by insulation works to the party wall' (*Hirose Electrical*[9]); that 'it is hard to understand how the process of resolving this narrow issue of law became so long, hard-fought and expensive ... [the case] has grown out of all proportion to its subject-matter', especially where the damages were 'unlikely to add up to more than a few tens of thousands', but with legal costs running at about £3 million per side (*Barr v Biffa Waste Services Ltd*[10]); and that '[t]his appeal concerns a disagreement between neighbours about a few yards of pedestrian access which, as is far too often the case, has escalated into bitter and costly litigation' (*Lester v Woodgate*[11]), a case in which the princely sum of £10 was awarded to C at first instance, but C then lost on appeal altogether.

PRE-REQUISITES FOR THE TORT

Precondition #1: Capacity of C to sue

The standing rules applicable to private nuisance are far more restrictive than in, say, the tort of negligence, given the former's emphasis upon protecting C's enjoyment of property.

A proprietary or possessory interest

§16.2 C, whose use and enjoyment of the land is affected by D's interference, must have either a proprietary or a possessory interest (amounting to a right to exclusive possession) in the land. A 'substantial link' between C and the land itself is not sufficient to establish standing.

The abovementioned principle, set by the House of Lords majority in *Hunter v Canary Wharf Ltd*,[12] is termed 'the *Hunter* rule of standing', and follows from private nuisance being a property-based tort.

In *Hunter v Canary Wharf*, two group actions were brought by Patricia Hunter – one for damages in private nuisance for interference with reception of television broadcasts in group members' homes on the Isle of Dogs (with 690 claimants), and the other for damages for private nuisance in respect of deposits

[9] [2011] EWCA Civ 987, [16]. [10] [2012] EWCA Civ 312, [3], [5], [48].

[11] [2010] EWCA Civ 199, [1], [16]–[17], [43]–[50].

[12] [1997] AC 655 (HL) 688 (Lord Goff), 695, 698–99 (Lord Lloyd), 707 (Lord Hoffmann), 716 (Lord Hope). Lord Cooke dissented on this point, 719.

of dust on their properties caused by the construction of the Limehouse tunnel (with 513 claimants). All group members who did not have the requisite proprietary or possessory interest were excluded from the group action. (Ultimately, legal aid for the action was then withdrawn, and the group actions collapsed.)

The standing rules applicable to private nuisance apply, by analogy, to the rule in *Rylands v Fletcher* (according to Lord Hoffmann in *Transco plc v Stockport MBC*[13]), as discussed in Chapter 17, and hence, the causes of action are treated interchangeably when citing illustrative cases in the Table below.

Those with lawful standing to sue

A freehold owner of land	In *Arscott v Coal Authority,*[a] residential property-owners adjacent to a property (Grove Fields) which was raised to provide playing fields, and which then caused flooding when the Taff River overflowed, had the necessary proprietary interest in their properties to enable them to sue under *Rylands v Fletcher.*
A person with a proprietary interest in an easement over land	In *Transco plc v Stockport MBC,*[b] Lord Hoffmann was 'willing to assume' that Transco's easement, which entitled it to maintain a gas pipe in an embankment, was a sufficient proprietary interest to enable C to sue under *Rylands v Fletcher.*
A tenant	In *Hunter v Canary Wharf Ltd,*[c] some group members were tenants of premises on the Isle of Dogs – they could validly remain in the group actions for private nuisance.
A landlord whose reversionary interest is interfered with	In *Hunter,*[d] this category was cited with approval.
A licensee with exclusive possession	In *Tinseltime Ltd v Davies,*[e] Fountain of Youth Ltd, a licensee, had exclusive possession to part of a building, 'The Old Creamery' – assisted by a clause in the licence which made provision for the licensor to have the right to *resume* possession in some circumstances. FOY had standing to sue in private nuisance. In *Olympic Delivery Authy v Persons Unknown,*[f] protestors at an Olympic site planned for the basketball venue prevented the ODA from accessing the site, with barricades and other conduct. The ODA had an exclusive licence to possess or occupy the land under a Licence Agreement, and had sufficient standing to sue in private nuisance. In *Crown River Cruises Ltd v Kimbolton Fireworks Ltd,*[g] a barge permanently moored in the Thames was fire-damaged by a fireworks display. The barge owner had exclusive use and occupation of the mooring, which was sufficient standing for nuisance/*Rylands.*

[a] [2003] EWHC 1690 (QB).
[b] [2003] UKHL 61, [2004] 2 AC 1, [47].
[c] [1997] UKHL 14, [1997] AC 655 (HL) 695.
[d] [1997] AC 655 (HL) 706–7, citing: *Rust v Graving Dock Co* (1887) LR 36 Ch D 113 (CA) 130.
[e] [2011] EWHC 1199 (TCC) [19], [21].
[f] [2012] EWHC 1012 (Ch) [17], [29].
[g] [1996] 2 Lloyd's Rep 533 (QB).

[13] [2003] UKHL 61, [2004] 2 AC 1, [47].

A person with exclusive possession to land, which is valid against all but the true owner of the land (a 'de facto possessor'[h])	In *Foster v Warblington UDC*,[i] the Council, D, discharged sewage into artificial oyster beds located on a foreshore which belonged to the lord of the manor. Mr Foster, C, was an oyster merchant who had, for many years, exclusively operated the oyster beds. No-one interfered with his occupation of the beds or his removal and sale of oysters from them. C had standing to sue in private nuisance, notwithstanding that he could not prove any title to the land; he had exclusive possession of that part of the foreshore.
A 'tolerated trespasser', who, whilst remaining in the premises, has actual and exclusive possession	In *Pemberton v Southwark LBC*,[j] Ms Pemberton, C, fell into rent arrears on her flat, but Council D agreed not to evict her. Thereafter, C made regular payments of 'rent' to D, so became a 'tolerated trespasser'. C sued in private nuisance for a cockroach infestation in the building. C had standing to sue – while 'precarious', her possession as a tolerated trespasser was exclusive and not unlawful; and she could not be evicted until she breached the conditions on which she was being allowed to stay.

[h] The description given by Lord Hoffmann in *Hunter v Canary Wharf Ltd* [1997] AC 655 (HL) 703.

[i] [1906] 1 KB 648 (CA) 668, 679–80.

[j] [2000] 1 WLR 1672 (CA) 1683–84. The status of the 'tolerated trespasser' still applies (per *Willis v Derwentside DC* [2013] EWHC 738 (Ch) [50]), but the precise ratio of *Pemberton* is now overruled by *Austin v Mayor and Burgesses of Southwark LBC* [2010] UKSC 28, [29], because the Housing and Regeneration Act 2008, Sch 11, 'restores tenancy status to all existing tolerated trespassers'.

By contrast, those with a mere beneficial ownership or non-exclusive possession of land do not have sufficient standing to sue in private nuisance or in *Rylands v Fletcher* (per *Colour Quest v Total Downstream UK plc*[14]). This restrictive view excludes a number of persons who may be aggrieved by the nuisance-creating activities of D – including many who actually occupy the affected premises.

Those with no standing to sue

Lodgers, an *au pair* girl, a resident nurse caring for an invalid, a live-in servant, temporary visitors to a house, and residents of retirement, children's or care homes	In *Hunter v Canary Wharf Ltd*,[a] all of these hypothetical examples were given, of Cs who would lack standing to sue in private nuisance.

[a] [1997] AC 655, 693.

[14] [2009] EWHC 540 (Comm) fn 71.

Children or relatives living with their parents in the family home	In *Hunter*, these parties were excluded from the group actions. The ability of a child living with her parents to sue in private nuisance – permitted in *Khorasandjian v Bush*[b] – was overruled in *Hunter*.[c]
A worker who suffers interference at the workplace	In *Hunter*,[d] the hypothetical example was given of a worker who receives harassing phone calls from D whilst at work – that worker could not sue for that interference to their peaceable enjoyment (rather, 'the employer is responsible for their welfare').
Spouses who do not have their name on the proprietary title (but who live in the home as non-exclusive licensees)	In *Malone v Laskey*,[e] C, was the wife of a company manager who lived in a company house (the husband was licensee of the premises, and his employer leased the house). She was injured when a bracket supporting a cistern fell from a wall in the toilet, caused by the vibrations of an engine operating on D's adjoining premises. C had no standing to sue in nuisance – a decision explicitly approved in *Hunter* (the case 'remains good law'[f]). Indeed, in *Hunter*, spouses who lacked the requisite proprietary title or exclusive possession were excluded from the group actions.
Someone with a contractual right to access/ use the property, but nothing more	In *Tate & Lyle v GLC*,[g] Tate & Lyle, C, had access to a sugar jetty, but that access was affected because the Thames river bed silted up, when D built adjacent terminals. C had to incur dredging expenses to enable vessels to reach the jetty – but as C had no proprietary right or exclusive possession to the jetty, it had no claim in private nuisance available to it (it did, however, have a claim in public nuisance, where the rules of standing are entirely different). In *Weller & Co v Foot and Mouth Disease Research Institute*,[h] auctioneers, C, sued to recover their lost profits attributable to the closure of a market where they carried out sales/auctions, following an outbreak of foot and mouth disease from D's premises at which experimental work was carried out in connection with the disease. C lacked standing to sue under *Rylands*, because they did not possess the requisite proprietary or possessory interest in the market: 'persons who have no interest in the property to which a danger has escaped have no claim for damages against the person who permitted the escape'.
A 'mere trespasser' (e.g., a casual intruder), or a temporary occupier	In *Alegrete Shipping Co Inc v Intl Oil Pollution Compensation Fund*,[i] Tilbury, C, processed whelks which were fished from the coastline between Tenby and Saundersfoot, but lost profits of approx. £650,000, when crude oil was spilled from the *Sea Empress*. C sued the owners of the *Sea Empress*. Had the claim been made under *Rylands v Fletcher*, C would have failed, as it had no requisite proprietary interest in the whelks (or in the coastline threatened by the oil) to base a claim.

[b] [1993] QB 727 (CA).
[c] [1997] AC 655, 694, 698 (Lord Goff), 715 (Lord Lloyd).
[d] [1997] AC 655, 672, 692, with the quote by Lord Cooke at 718.
[e] [1907] 2 KB 141 (CA).
[f] [1997] AC 655, quote at 678, and also 693–94.
[g] [1983] 2 AC 509 (HL) 510–11.
[h] [1966] 1 QB 569, with quote at 588.
[i] [2002] EWHC 1095 (QB (Admiralty)) [25].

Why the law changed, post-*Hunter*. The House of Lords majority in *Hunter* adopted a far stricter approach to standing in private nuisance than had hitherto been the view of the Court of Appeal in *Khorasandjian v Bush* – where all that was required was 'a substantial link' between C and the land.[15]

> In *Khorasandjian v Bush*, Miss Khorasandjian, C, 18, had formed a friendship with Mr Bush, D, 28, but broke off the friendship. D took it badly. Thereafter, D pursued a campaign of harassment against C, including assaults, threats of violence, and pestering C with unwanted phone calls to the home which C shared with her mother (the house was owned by C's mother). D was imprisoned for the threats and abusive behaviour. C sued D in private nuisance, to restrain him from 'harassing, pestering or communicating with' her. **Held** (2:1): an injunction could be granted in relation to the phone calls made to C at her home, even though C was a mere licensee there.

That view was followed by the Court of Appeal in *Hunter*,[16] but both it, and *Bush*, were overruled by the House of Lords in *Hunter*, the latter preferring the strict view of *Malone v Laskey* (1907, noted in the Table above),[17] but which had been departed from in the interim. As noted by Lord Cooke (dissenting) in *Hunter*,[18] the relevant standing rules in private nuisance are essentially a question of policy, rather than of legal analysis – and as summarised in the Table below,[19] reasonable opinion can indeed differ on that.

Justifications for a restrictive view of standing

- private nuisance is concerned with interference with the enjoyment of land, and the standing rules must reflect that – a wider test of standing would 'transform it from a tort to land into a tort to the person' (*Hunter*, Lord Goff);
- where C's complaint is about abusive phone calls, the 'gravamen of the complaint' lies in harassment – and the appropriate causes of action are invasion of privacy, a claim under the Protection from Harassment Act 1997 (unavailable to Miss Khorasandjian at the time), or the tort of *Wilkinson v Downton* – hence, other torts apply;
- nuisance cannot be permitted to create actionable interferences 'via the back door' – in *K v Bush*, 'what the Court of Appeal appears to have been doing was to exploit the law of private nuisance in order to create by the back door a tort of harassment which was only partially effective in that it was artificially limited to harassment which takes place in [C's] home' – not 'a satisfactory manner in which to develop the law' (Lord Goff again);
- C can reach an agreement with D, the creator of the nuisance, to permit the nuisance to continue for a payment, or to cease for certain times of the day – and such arrangements would not be 'practicable', if there were unidentifiable and unlimited numbers of people with whom D needed to make such an agreement;
- the wider test of a 'substantial link' is difficult to define;

[15] [1993] QB 727 (CA) 738–40 (Dillon LJ), cf 746 (Peter Gibson LJ, dissenting).
[16] [1996] 2 WLR 348 (CA) 365. [17] [1907] 2 KB 141 (CA). [18] [1997] AC 655, 717.
[19] The restrictive view is drawn from the majority in *Hunter* [1997] AC 655 (HL) 691–94, 707; *Khorandjian v Bush* (CA, Peter Gibson LJ, dissenting); *Hunter* [1993] QB 727 (CA) 365 (Pill LJ); and *Hunter* at first instance (Judge Havery QC). The wider view is drawn from the majority in *K v Bush* [1993] QB 727 (CA) 734–35 (Dillon LJ); *Hunter* (CA); and *Hunter* [1997] AC 655 (HL) 713–14 (Lord Cooke, dissenting)

- 'no great disadvantage' is suffered by those in a home with no standing to sue – practically, they will urge the title-holder to sue, who will recover damages for loss of amenity *for the land as a whole*. If they wish to sue for their personal injuries, they would have to pursue those damages in negligence in any event (given the restrictions which apply on recoverable damages in nuisance, discussed later);
- it would be 'ridiculous if, in this present age, the law is that the making of deliberately harassing and pestering telephone calls to a person is only actionable in the civil courts if [C] happens to have the freehold or a leasehold proprietary interest in the premises in which he or she has received the calls' – the social conditions had changed since *Malone v Laskey* in 1907 (Dillon LJ, *K v Bush*);
- private nuisance is an interference with the enjoyment of land, 'actionable by an occupier' – and the word, 'occupier', is an expression which can cover a variety of persons 'living there [in the household], who have been exercising a continuing right to enjoyment of that amenity' (*Hunter*, Lord Cooke);
- to deny standing to spouses not on the title deed was problematical: (1) it showed a 'rather light treatment of a wife, at least in today's society where she is no longer considered subservient to her husband'; (2) modern statutes, at least, give spouses a special status in respect of the matrimonial home; (3) standing in nuisance should not be bedevilled by whether the spouse not on the title has a proprietary equitable interest in the matrimonial home, a 'notoriously difficult' issue; (4) the rights of children have been recognised in international treaties, which should shape the common law in affording children standing to sue in private nuisance; (5) Art 8 of the ECHR also supports treating mere residence as a basis of standing at common law (Lord Cooke);
- other jurisdictions (e.g., Queensland, US) have permitted nuisance calls to a home to be an actionable nuisance.

Impact of the ECHR

§16.3 It has been judicially queried as to whether the aforementioned *Hunter* rule of standing complies with Art 8 of the ECHR.

When *Hunter* was decided,[20] the ECHR was not part of English law.[21] Whether the majority's preference for a narrow view of *locus standi* in respect of the property-based torts of nuisance and *Rylands v Fletcher* complies with the Human Rights Act 1998 remains somewhat uncertain.

In *McKenna v British Aluminium Ltd*,[22] Neuberger J remarked that there is a 'powerful case' for saying that the legal landscape has changed, and that the *Hunter* rule of standing was **not** compliant with Art 8.[23] He expressed sympathy with the argument that 'effect has not been properly given to Art 8.1 if a person with no interest in the home, but who has lived in the home for some time and had his enjoyment of the home interfered with, is at the mercy of the person who owns the home, as the only person who can bring proceedings'.[24] In *Hunter v Canary Wharf*,[25] Lord Cooke (dissenting) also had regard to Art 8 of the ECHR in supporting a wider view of standing (per the Table above).

[20] i.e., on 24 April 1997. [21] The Convention was incorporated as part of national law on 2 October 2000.

[22] [2002] Env LR 30 (Ch) [29], [52]–[53].

[23] Under Art 8.1: 'Everyone has the right to respect for his private and family life, his home and his correspondence'.

[24] [2002] Env LR 30 (Ch) [53].

[25] [1997] AC 655 (HL) 714, citing Art 8 cases: *Arrondelle v UK* (1982, re aircraft noise), and *Lopez Ostra v Spain* (1994, re fumes and smells from a waste treatment plant).

Unfortunately, the House of Lords did not comment upon this observation, when it considered the torts of private nuisance and *Rylands v Fletcher* subsequently in *Transco plc v Stockport MBC*,[26] and *Cambridge Water*.[27] Hence, whether the *Hunter* rule of standing accords with the Convention remains an open question.

Nuisances occurring prior to C's interest being acquired

§16.4 C can sue for damage caused by D's nuisance which was incurred prior to C's acquiring his interest, provided that: (1) the nuisance continued after C's acquisition, and (2) no double-compensation is imposed on D.

C may have the necessary proprietory or possessory interest in the affected land – but the damage arising from D's interference occurred (or at least started) prior to C's acquiring that interest. Can C sue for that damage? The answer is 'yes', provided that the nuisance was continuing after C's interest was acquired, and that D has not already paid the previous owner for remedial works. Otherwise, if C were to sue successfully for that damage too, double recovery would ensue, which cannot be permitted (per *Delaware Mansions Ltd v Westminster CC*[28]).

In *Delaware Mansions v Westminster CC*, Delaware, C1, sued the Council, D, which owned a London plane tree growing in the footpath four metres from the front boundary of C1's property, Delaware Mansions, in Maida Vale. C1 was the management company of the flats; and Flecksun, C2, acquired the freehold of Delaware Mansions from the developers, the Church Commissioners, in 1990. **Held:** there was a continuing nuisance here, because the encroachment of the roots from the tree was causing continuing damage to C2's land by dehydrating the soil and inhibiting rehydration, and that nuisance arose prior to C2's acquisition, and carried on during C2's ownership until underpinning and piling remedial works occurred in July 1992. Reasonable remedial expenditure may be recovered by the owner who has had to incur it, which was C2 in this case. D knew of, or ought to have reasonably foreseen, the nuisance caused by the plane tree roots, well before the remedial works were undertaken, much of which would not have been necessary if the plane tree had been immediately removed.

Precondition #2: Capacity of D to be sued

As was said by Lord Millett in *Southwark LBC v Mills and Tanner*, '[o]nce the activities complained of have been found to constitute an actionable nuisance, more than one party may be held legally responsible'.[29] In fact, the bases upon which separate Ds in private nuisance may be liable are quite different in principle.

The principles covered in this section pertain **only** to private nuisance suits – the rules governing the appropriate D in a suit under *Rylands v Fletcher* are somewhat narrower, and are covered in Chapter 17.[30]

The creator of the nuisance

§16.5 The principal D in private nuisance is the party who owns or occupies the land from which the interference arises. It is unnecessary for D to have any proprietary or possessory interest in

[26] [2003] UKHL 61, [2004] 2 AC 1. [27] [1994] 2 AC 264 (HL).
[28] [2001] UKHL 55, [2002] 1 AC 321, [11], [28], [33]. C1 did not feature in the appeal to the House of Lords.
[29] [1999] UKHL 40, [2001] 1 AC 1 (HL) 21 (Lord Millett). [30] See pp 924–5.

the land from which the nuisance emanates. However, the law remains somewhat unsettled as to the extent to which D, who creates a nuisance but does not do so from land which D owns or occupies, is an appropriate D in private nuisance. On more recent authority, interferences emanating from a public thoroughfare can properly arise in private nuisance.

It is evident, from the principle above, that the scope of potential defendants in private nuisance is potentially very wide, albeit still somewhat contentious.

The usual party sued in nuisance is he who creates or controls the nuisance-generating activity on the land of which he is an owner or occupier. This principle was exemplified in *Coventry v Lawrence*[31] – all six Ds in that case were either occupiers or owners. Where D is merely an occupier of land, that is perfectly sufficient for liability in private nuisance, because it gives D control. In *LE Jones (Insurance Brokers) Ltd v Portsmouth CC*,[32] Dyson LJ explained that, 'by virtue of his occupation, an occupier usually has it in his power to take the measures that are necessary to prevent or eliminate the nuisance. He has sufficient control over the hazard which constitutes the nuisance for it to be reasonable to make him liable for the foreseeable consequences of his failure to exercise that control so as to remove the hazard'.

More contentious scenarios arise, however, where D's activities do not arise out of land at all, but at sea; or from activities conducted on a public thoroughfare or from communal areas not belonging to D; or from the use of a 'thing' under the land rather than from on the land itself. None of these falls within the classic instance of a nuisance arising from D's ownership or occupation of his land.

The narrower view. In *Southport Corp v Esso Petroleum Co Ltd*,[33] Denning LJ held that the release of 400 tons of oil by shipowner, D, at sea, could not constitute a private nuisance, because it could not comply with the proposition by the House of Lords, in *Sedleigh-Denfield v O'Callaghan*,[34] that for D to be liable in private nuisance, he must be in 'possession and control of the land from which the nuisance proceeds', and that D is liable for 'a nuisance existing on his property'. Causing an interference from a ship at sea clearly could not satisfy that requirement. That view of Denning LJ's was endorsed by Lord Radcliffe in the House of Lords.[35]

More recently, the Court of Appeal took the same view in *Hussain v Lancaster CC*.[36] One of the reasons as to why no private nuisance could be proven by C against the tenants of a council estate who had vilified C with a long-running campaign of racial harassment, was that the interferences suffered by C 'did not involve the tenants' use of the tenants' land'. Rather, the tenants' anti-social behaviour was conducted from communal areas around, and outside of, C's shop. Hirst LJ referred to the *Sedleigh-Denfield* views, which the tenants' behaviour could not align with, and hence, it 'fell outside the scope of the tort'.

The wider view. More recent authorities have clearly adopted a view that a nuisance does **not** have to exist on D's property nor arise out of the use of his land. For example, transient trespassers, such as protestors, have been subject to a claim in private nuisance. Further, D may merely own or control a 'thing' which causes the nuisance, but not the land on or over which that 'thing' is positioned; nevertheless, where D deals with it in such a way as to cause interference with C's enjoyment of his land, then that has recently been sufficient for D to be potentially liable in nuisance.

31 [2014] UKSC 13, [2014] 1 AC 822 (26 Feb 2014); and later: [2014] UKSC 14, [2015] AC 106 (23 Jul 2014).

32 [2002] EWCA Civ 1723, [2003] 1 WLR 427 (CA) [11].

33 [1954] 2 QB 182 (CA) 196.

34 [1940] AC 880 (HL) 903 (Lord Wright) 919 (Lord Porter).

35 [1956] AC 218 (HL) 242.

36 [2000] QB 1 (CA) 23.

In *Olympic Delivery Authy v Persons Unknown*,[37] facts previously, **held:** an actionable private nuisance. Protestors at the Olympic site planned for the basketball venue prevented the ODA from gaining access to the site, because of some interferences, including playing boules on the access road to the venue. That stopped delivery vehicles, and effectively brought work on the site to a standstill.
In *Welsh Water v Barratt Homes Ltd (Rev 1)*,[38] Barratt, C, was granted planning permission to build a school and 98 houses on land. After a number of homes had been constructed, C gave notice, pursuant to s 106 of the Water Industry Act 1991, to Welsh Water, D, the sewerage services provider, that it intended to connect the development by its drains to the public sewer, owned by D, at a connection point under the highway. D refused to allow C to connect at that point (and instructed that the connection be made 300 metres away). D then poured concrete into the manhole and C's drainage pipe that it intended to use to connect with the public sewer. C had to place a temporary storage tank on the land to receive sewage from the houses and the school, which then had to be removed by tanker at great expense. D argued that it was not making use of its land in creating the concrete 'plug'. **Held:** no actionable nuisance (for other reasons). However, re capacity to be sued, D was suable. It was dealing with its sewer in a way that interfered with C's enjoyment of its land.

The Court of Appeal's statement in *Welsh Water*, that 'nuisance does not require a use by D of **its** land',[39] conflicts with some of the appellate views in *Southport Corp* and *Hussain*, but would appear to have the ascendancy in modern law.

It would follow, from a broad interpretation of an appropriate D to sue, that interferences emanating from a public thoroughfare **can** give rise to private nuisance. These do not fall easily into the recognised categories of private nuisance, however, and are more likely to be a trespass to land, or negligence (per *Network Rail Infrastructure Ltd v Conarken Group Ltd*[40]), or a public nuisance (per 'Public nuisance', an online chapter). Additionally, where D permits a dangerous thing to escape from a public thoroughfare, then liability under the rule in *Rylands v Fletcher* is also possible (per Chapter 17). However, the mere fact that D has created a nuisance from a public thoroughfare or public right of way is not, of itself, sufficient to *deny* D the capacity to be sued (as the statements in *Welsh Water*, and as the outcome in *Olympic Delivery Authy*, demonstrate).

Adoption and/or continuance of the nuisance

§16.6 Alternatively, D may be sued in private nuisance, where the nuisance has been created by others (e.g., trespassers, other residents, licensees), but D, as owner/occupier of the land, has adopted and/or continued the state of affairs which comprised the nuisance. If D did not have either actual or constructive knowledge of the nuisance, he cannot be said to have continued or adopted it. In that sense, D's liability in nuisance is *not* strict.

To *continue* a nuisance, D must know (either actually or constructively) of the nuisance-creating behaviour, but fail to bring it to an end, when D had both the reasonable means and the time to do so. To *adopt* a nuisance, D must both continue the nuisance, **and** make use of the nuisance for his own benefit (per *Sedleigh-Denfield v O'Callaghan*[41]). This category of D is particularly useful where the creator of the nuisance has no assets with which to meet a judgment, but the adopter or continuer of the nuisance has a 'deeper pocket'.

[37] [2012] EWHC 1012 (Ch) [9], [18], [29]. [38] [2013] EWCA Civ 233. [39] *ibid*, [57] (original emphasis).
[40] [2010] EWHC 1852, [70]–[71] (TCC, Akenhead J); point not the subject of appeal: [2011] EWCA Civ 644.
[41] [1940] AC 880 (HL) 894 (Viscount Maughan), 897 (Lord Atkin).

D may have encouraged the nuisance-creating activity to continue via some positive act. Alternatively, D may have known of the nuisance and failed to abate it (i.e., remove or limit it). Either type of behaviour has been sufficient to render D liable for continuing the nuisance. Clearly, where C has made complaints to D about the nuisance-creating activities being conducted by others, D will be fixed with the requisite knowledge, as evident in the following cases.

In *Lippiatt v South Gloucestershire CC*,[42] the Council, D, tolerated the trespass and interferences caused by a camp of gypsies on some Council land, and also provided the gypsy camp with toilets, water, rubbish skips, and other facilities. D had continued the nuisance. In *Octavia Hill Housing Trust v Brumby*,[43] Terri Brumby, C, lived in the same block of flats in southeast London as did Mrs Walker. The Housing Trust, D, owned and occupied the common areas around the flats in which the nuisance activities occurred (i.e., a 'trench' outside C's flat). C alleged that, over a period of four years, various visitors to Mrs Walker's flat undertook anti-social behaviour, that she complained about their activities to D, but that D failed to take any reasonable steps to abate them. C alleged that she also proposed steps to abate the nuisance, such as to bar access to the trench by some physical barrier or gate. A strike-out application failed; there was a potential actionable continuance here.

Given that D can be equally liable at law for continuance as for adoption of another's nuisance, the distinction between the two is not of crucial importance for liability purposes. Nevertheless, D will be held to have adopted the nuisance where he does something positive to continue the nuisance and takes a benefit from the nuisance. In this context, 'benefit' has been widely construed – from proof of some profit accruing to D, to something which enhanced D's policies as a public body. In the following cases, there was both continuance and adoption by D.

In *Page Motors v Epsom and Ewell BC*,[44] the Council, D, landlord of certain waste ground next door to Page Motor's, C's, car sales and repair garage, deliberately allowed gypsies to reside at that ground for several years (unlawfully, as trespassers), because it was considered important, for policy reasons, to tolerate the gypsies' presence. During that time, the gypsies' behaviour included: smearing tar on the roads and on the lock gates outside C's garage; burning tyres which caused thick black smoke over C's premises; damaging vehicles belonging to C and their customers by firing airguns, catapults, and other missiles; and permitting dangerous dogs to bite C's customers. D provided water to the campsite by means of a standpipe, and rubbish skips were put in place. D did not move the gypsies on for almost five years, in order to 'contain' the problem to one site within D's Borough, and to buy time to enable a solution to be found. In *Sedleigh-Denfield v O'Callaghan*,[45] Mr O'Callaghan, D, owned a ditch that ran beside Mr Sedleigh-Denfield's, C's, house at Mill Hill. In 1934, the Middlesex CC installed a pipe in the ditch for rainfall run-off without D's permission. The pipe was then connected to a manhole and sewer, and a grating installed. The mouth of the pipe was not protected by a grid, and hence, became blocked with refuse and debris in heavy rainfall. Middlesex CC was treated as a trespasser in the case. After 1934, D continued to use the pipe installed by the Council for his own benefit, in order to assist the run-off of water from his land. After very heavy rain, the pipe became blocked, the water was unable to escape, and C's land was flooded. It was held that D adopts a nuisance if 'he makes any use of the erection, building, bank or artificial contrivance which constitutes the nuisance', which he did here.

[42] [2000] QB 51 (CA). [43] [2010] EWHC 1793 (QB)[16] (Mackay J). [44] [1982] JPL 572 (CA).
[45] [1940] AC 880 (HL) 894–95 (Viscount Maugham).

Landlords and tenants

§16.7 A landlord will not be liable for acts of nuisance committed by his tenant, unless he has authorised those acts. The landlord authorises a tenant's acts of nuisance in two scenarios, where: (1) the landlord either actively participates in that nuisance or otherwise authorises the nuisance by his conduct (although the case law is unclear as to the extent to which a landlord who does nothing to correct the tenant's nuisance can still be liable for authorising it); or (2) the tenant's nuisance was certain, or highly likely, to result from the purposes for which the landlord let the premises to the tenant. Moreover, this principle complies with Art 8 of the ECHR.

This principle (per *Smith v Scott*[46]) was affirmed by the Supreme Court in *Coventry v Lawrence.*[47]

Clearly, a tenant's acts of nuisance are distinguishable from those of a trespasser. The law is more willing to hold that a landlord should be liable for the nuisance of trespassers than for the nuisance of his tenants. These are different, and 'distinguished', categories of cases, as the Court of Appeal was keen to point out in *Mowan v Wandsworth LBC.*[48] Whatever liability may be found against the landlord regarding trespassers (as in *Page Motors*[49] and *Lippiatt,*[50] canvassed above), those cases do not impact upon 'the well-established principles' by which the landlord is liable for tenants' nuisances.

First limb: Although it was said by the Supreme Court, in *Coventry v Lawrence,*[51] that the principles governing the liability of a landlord in nuisance are 'tolerably clear', the application of those principles yields some fairly borderline, and difficult-to-reconcile, cases.

A landlord (often a Council) who merely knows of the conduct of a troublesome tenant cannot be said to have expressly authorised that tenant to commit that nuisance-making activity. Hence, complaints to the Council by C, without more, are not sufficient to trigger a continuance of the nuisance on the Council's part.

In *Hussain v Lancaster CC,*[52] Mr and Mrs Hussain, C, owned a shop on D's housing estate. C alleged that, for several years, they had been subjected to a campaign of violent racial harassment by over 100 tenants living at D's estate, involving arson, thrown missiles, and verbal and physical threats. C had informed D about the harassment, and D had failed to take any action against the perpetrators. **Held**: D was not liable for continuing the nuisance, as it had not expressly authorised the harassment.

However, an authorisation will occur if the landlord participated directly in the commission of the nuisance. Although active participation is cited in modern case law (e.g., *Southwark LBC v Mills*[53]), Lord Neuberger admitted, in *Coventry v Lawrence,*[54] that there was 'little authority' on the issue, but that it was mainly a question of fact, turning principally on what the landlord did subsequent to the grant of the lease. Significantly, a majority in *Coventry* held that, 'the fact that a landlord takes steps to mitigate a nuisance can scarcely give rise to the inference that he has authorised it' by participating in the nuisance in some way (according to the dissenters, these mitigating steps contributed to an active participation by the landlords in the nuisance created by the motor-racing activities).

In *Coventry v Lawrence*, Terence Waters, a farmer/landowner in the Mildenhall area, obtained planning permission in 1975 to construct a sports stadium on part of his land, which was then used

[46] [1973] Ch 314, 321–22. [47] [2014] UKSC 46, [11]–[12]. [48] (2001) 33 HLR 56 (CA) [35].
[49] (1981) 80 LGR 337 (CA). [50] [2000] QB 51 (CA) [59]–[60]. [51] [2014] UKSC 46, [11].
[52] [2000] 1 QB 1 (CA). [53] [2001] 1 AC 1 (HL) 22 (Lord Millett) (participation certainly did not occur there).
[54] [2014] UKSC 46, [19], [23] (Lords Neuberger, Clarke and Sumption; Lords Carnwath and Mance dissenting).

for speedway racing, stock car racing, banger racing, and greyhound racing for 10 years. The local councils supported these various activities at the stadium, and permanent planning permission was renewed in 1985. In 1984, stock car and banger car racing started at the stadium, and after 10 years of that, Mr Waters obtained a Certificate of Lawfulness for that use. In 2002, permanent planning permission was granted for the use of the land as a motocross track to the rear of the stadium, subject to conditions limiting the use of the track to x days per year, within set hours, and below a maximum noise level. In 2006, Ms Lawrence and Mr Shields, C, purchased a house, 'Fenland', situated about 840 m from the motocross track. In 2008, C sued the various operators/occupiers/owners of the premises, D, in private nuisance, for the noise emanating from the track. As at 2006, motor sports had been taking place at the venue for many years, and these noisy activities were an established and dominant feature of the locality. **Held:** an actionable private nuisance was committed here – but the landlord Mr Waters was not liable for authorising it. The fact that the landlord did nothing to persuade his tenant to reduce the noise did not show participation. The fact that the landlord also erected a hay-bale wall around Fenland to discourage complaints and to keep down the noise also did not show participation.

In the absence of any direct participation, case law suggests that it is more likely that a landlord's authorisation is to be inferred from the circumstances, if D could have done something 'easy and cheap' to preclude the nuisance from occurring, but prevaricated and did nothing.

In *Hilton v Smith*,[55] James Smith, D, a landlord who owned a block of shops, knew that tenants of those shops (and possibly trespassers) were parking their vehicles so as to block a private roadway over which all the tenants enjoyed a right of way. This meant that Mr Hilton, an antiques dealer, C, the tenant of the last shop in the row, could not obtain access to his shop at all, and could not access his parking space when delivering and unloading furniture. The problem could have been solved by D's putting a hinged post, which could be locked in position, at the entrance to the roadway. D knew about the blockages, but did nothing to instruct the tenants not to park there. **Held**: D continued the nuisance, by standing by and doing nothing to stop the unauthorised parking. In *Chartered Trust plc v Davies*,[56] Miss Davies, C, leased premises from D, to conduct a business selling puzzles and executive toys. D represented that the retail premises would only be let to 'high class retailers'. Eventually, due to the property crash, retailers moved out, premises were left empty, a coffee shop put its tables such as to block access to shops at the back of the block where C's premises were, and then a pawnbroker moved into one of the outlets, hanging the traditional three balls over the arcade, which C alleged made the premises look like 'Pawnbroker's Arcade', and 'killed new business and deterred old'. **Held:** D continued the nuisance, by consenting to the pawnbroker's sign, and the coffee tables, being placed where they were, in such prominent and damaging positions. Also, D could have stopped the pawnbroker's clientele blocking access to C's store. They 'prevaricated and did nothing', and 'in failing to act to stop the nuisance ... continued the nuisance'.

While the above cases seem straightforward, the difficulty is that, in *Coventry v Lawrence*, Lord Neuberger stated that, 'even if a [landlord] has the power to prevent the nuisance, inaction or failure to act cannot, on its own, amount to authorising the nuisance'.[57] *Hilton* was not cited in that regard, and *Davies* was cited, but with neither approval nor disapproval as to whether there was a valid claim against the landlords in that case. Hence, the extent to which a landlord does

55 [1979] 2 EGLR 44 (CA) 46 (Ormrod LJ), 47 (Scarman LJ).

56 [1997] EWCA Civ 2256.

57 [2014] UKSC 46, [22].

nothing to stop the tenant's nuisance, and still escape liability because he did not 'authorise' it, is somewhat difficult to glean, on the current state of the case law.

Second limb: The other avenue for rendering a landlord liable for the nuisance of his tenant is that the nuisance must be 'certain' or 'very highly probable' to result from the letting.

It is not enough that the nuisance was foreseeable to a reasonable landlord in D's position. In that respect, in *Mowan v Wandsworth LBC*,[58] the Court of Appeal noted that, under the law in Queensland, 'a landlord may be held liable for the nuisance caused by the tenant if, at the time of the letting, it was reasonably foreseeable that the tenant would commit the nuisance [per *Aussie Traveller Pty Ltd v Marklea Pty Ltd*[59]]. That is not the law of England'. In *Coventry v Lawrence*[60] too, Lord Carnwath considered any test of foreseeability to be 'less stringent', unsupported by authority in England, and 'insufficiently rigorous'.

> In *Mowan v Wandsworth LBC*, Mrs Mowan, C, lived in a flat directly beneath Miss Abrahart's flat. Miss Abrahart had a mental disorder, and had been sectioned under the Mental Health Act 1983, with the police frequently receiving complaints about her behaviour. The Council, D, as landlord, received advice from the police that Miss Abrahart should be placed in a care home, but D had taken the view that she should 'live in the community'. C frequently complained to D about Miss Abrahart, re her blocking toilets and causing sewage to overflow, leaving taps running causing flooding, threatening to kill C, and causing noise by banging, chanting and moaning. C sued D, for adopting and/or continuing Miss Abrahart's nuisance. **Held**: D was not liable, because it did not expressly authorise the nuisance, nor was it certain to result from the letting. In *Coventry v Lawrence*, facts previously, **held:** leasing the stadium and track for motor-racing activities did not mean that a nuisance was inevitable or a nearly certain consequence. The stadium and track had been conducted in the past without creating any nuisance, and racing could have been conducted at suitable noise levels which did not entail a nuisance.

This point has entailed an issue under Art 8 of the ECHR. Clearly, the Court of Appeal in *Mowan* was reluctant about its decision, but remarked that 'we cannot accept the invitation to bend the common law so that it affords a remedy against the council. The principles are too well established for that. If they are to be altered, that must happen elsewhere. Accordingly ... there is no case for holding the council liable in nuisance ... this [is] a deplorable result; but the law in this court has already been stretched as far as it will go'.[61] In *Mowan*,[62] C had argued that, if the Council had not authorised the nuisance caused by a troublesome tenant, then C's lack of remedy would be incompatible with C's human right to respect for private and family life, and that the common law **should** provide C with an effective remedy against the Council. However, in dicta (because the case pre-dated the HRA's coming into force), the court expressed the view that there was no infringement of C's Art 8 rights, by refusing C's claim in nuisance, given that C had at least two 'adequate remedies' re the troublesome tenant, *viz*, the Council's decision in deciding not to pursue proceedings for repossession of Ms Abrahart's flat could be subjected to judicial review, and a landlord could be liable to a tenant, C, for breach of the tenant's right of quiet enjoyment under the lease.

[58] (2001) 33 HLR 56 (CA) [34] (Peter Gibson LJ), with points in case description at [26]–[27].

[59] [1998] 1 Qd R 1.

[60] [2014] UKSC 46, [56]. Although Lord Carnwath dissented on the outcome of landlords' liability, this observation does not conflict with the views of the majority on this point.

[61] (2001) 33 HLR 56 (CA) [18] (Sir Christopher Staughton).

[62] (2001) 33 HLR 56 (CA) [26], [38].

According to the House of Lords in *Southwark LBC v Tanner (No 2)*,[63] the landlord–tenant relationship should not be affected by importing implied warranties which are not found in the contract or imposed by statute. However, a landlord who continues a nuisance is liable in tort, which is 'independent of contractual arrangements, and depends upon the use and enjoyment of land', and hence, the *Tanner* principle is not contravened (per *Octavia Hill Housing Trust v Brumby*[64]).

Vicarious liability

§16.8 An employer can be vicariously liable for a private nuisance committed by an employee. In limited scenarios, the employer may also be vicariously liable for a private nuisance committed by an independent contractor.

Liability for the private nuisance of an employee is uncontroversial in this context. However, liability for an independent contractor is more contentious. According to the Court of Appeal in *Alcock v Wraith*,[65] C, who lived in a row of terraced houses, brought a claim against his neighbour, D, for the damage caused by water ingress and damp penetration from D's to C's premises, brought on by the negligent work of D's independent contractor. For the purposes of private nuisance and *Rylands v Fletcher*, Neill LJ noted the exceptions in which employer D would still be vicariously liable: where the independent contractor (1) withdrew support from C's land; (2) allowed the escape of fire to damage C's premises; or (3) was engaged in extra-hazardous acts. That scenario has been applied since.

In *Johnson (t/as Johnson Butchers) v BJW Property Devp Ltd*,[66] C's butcher shop suffered severe damage when a fire escaped from BJW's, D's, neighbouring premises. The fire was caused when Mr Young, an antique dealer, negligently interfered with D's fire grate during reconstruction works. The antique dealer was not an employee of D, but an independent contractor. **Held:** D was vicariously liable for that antique dealer's negligence. Mr Young's work involved a special risk, given the proximity of the fire grate to the potentially inflammable party wall.

However, if the independent contractor had exclusive possession of the premises when the act of interference/escape occurred, then D may avoid vicarious liability (per *RHM Bakeries (Scotland) Ltd v Strathclyde CC*[67]).

Some relationships simply **cannot** give rise to vicarious liability for private nuisances committed, *viz*: local authority and tenants; and local authority and travellers.

In *Lippiatt v South Gloucestershire CC*, facts above, there was no question (said the CA) that the Council, D, would be vicariously liable for any torts which may have been committed by travellers who had set up camp on D's land which they had entered as trespassers and which they occupied until eviction. However, D was directly liable in private nuisance for the interference to neighbouring farmers' enjoyment of their land which the travellers' activities caused. In *Hussain v Lancaster CC* too, the Council, D, could not be vicariously liable for the acts of its tenants (nor was D directly liable for their racial harassment, etc).

Precondition #3: The threshold principle

§16.9 Given that a private nuisance requires some 'give and take', C is expected to 'put up with' some degree of interference, with nuisance to be found only if the interference is over and above

[63] [1999] UKHL 40, [2001] 1 AC 1, [12]–[18]. [64] [2010] EWHC 1793 (QB) [16].
[65] (1991) 59 BLR (CA) 23 (Neill LJ). [66] [2002] 3 All ER 574 (QB (TCC)) [67]–[69].
[67] [1985] UKHL 9, citing: *Gourock Ropework Co Ltd v Greenock Corp* 1966 SLT 125.

that threshold. However, English law does ***not*** impose a 'numerical threshold' of inconvenience (e.g., days of noise, levels of smell) in order to determine whether or not an actionable nuisance has occurred. Rather, it is a question of fact and degree.

By its very phraseology, the tort of private nuisance has long insisted that there be some minimal level of interference – witnessed by judicial terminology such as D's nuisance causing C 'to suffer *significant* inconvenience and annoyance' (per *Dobson v Thames Water Utilities Ltd*[68]), that D's interference '*materially* impairs the comforts and convenience of life' (per *Hirose Electrical UK Ltd v Peak Ingredients Ltd*[69]), that C suffered 'a *real* interference' (per *Pusey v Somerset CC*[70]), and that any infringement to a right to light depends upon 'whether there is a *substantial* loss of light so as to render the occupation of the house less fit for occupation, and uncomfortable according to the ordinary notions of mankind' (per *Regan v Paul Properties DPF No 1 Ltd*[71]). In *Halsey v Esso Petroleum Co Ltd*,[72] it was said that there is no 'absolute standard' of what constitutes a private nuisance, it being a question of fact and degree whether the interference was sufficiently serious as to amount to a nuisance. Hence – and regardless of whether the interference caused physical damage or intangible effects to C's premises – if it is too minor or trivial to be worthy of compensation, it will not be actionable.

However, whilst that law is uncontroversial, there has been some significant judicial disagreement about whether a numerical threshold should apply to the tort of private nuisance. For example, that approach manifested in the following noise-related nuisance cases.

> In *Kennaway v Thompson*,[73] Mary Kennaway, C, built a house on Mallam Water, and sued the Cotswold Motor Boat Racing Club, D, for the noise of power-boat racing on that man-made lake. The Court of Appeal was required to fashion a remedy to 'protect [C] from the noise which the judge found to be intolerable but which will not stop the Club from organising activities about which she cannot reasonably complain'. It ordered an injunction limiting the number and spacing of international events, national events, and club events, and that no boats could create a noise of more than 75 decibels on D's water premises. In *Watson v Croft Promo-Sport Ltd*,[74] Croft, D, used an airfield for private motor-racing, which had been permitted since 1963. In 1998, the local planning authority granted a new planning permission for the motor-racing circuit. The circuit operated for about 200 days pa. For approximately 140 of those days, there was a high level of noise. The Watsons, C, whose homes were about 300 m from the circuit, contended that the high level of noise should be confined to 20 days a year, and that 40 days would be acceptable if D made financial compensation for the difference between 20 and 40 days. Simon J rejected C's argument that 20 days represented the threshold of nuisance – that was too low. Rather, the correct threshold was 40 noisy days each year (affirmed on appeal). An injunction was awarded on appeal, to protect C from the use of the racetrack for more than 40 days.

Subsequently, however, in *Barr v Biffa Waste Services Ltd* – which was an odour, rather than a noise, nuisance case – the Court of Appeal disapproved of any numerical threshold principle when determining whether an actionable nuisance has occurred. Rather, the thresholds in the above cases were directed towards *the remedy of future injunctive relief*. Carnwath LJ stated

[68] [2011] EWHC 3253 (TCC) [1067] (first instance) (emphasis added).
[69] [2011] EWCA Civ 987, [3] (emphasis added). [70] [2012] EWCA Civ 988, [19] (emphasis added).
[71] [2006] EWCA Civ 1391, [37] (emphasis added), citing: *Colls v Home Stores Ltd* [1904] AC 179 (HL).
[72] [1961] 1 WLR 683 (QB) 689–91. [73] [1980] EWCA Civ 1, [1981] QB 88 (CA) 94.
[74] [2008] EWHC 759, [2008] 3 All ER 1171 (QB) [64]–[66], and aff'd: [2009] EWCA Civ 15, [53]–[55], [87].

that '[t]here is no general rule requiring or justifying the setting of a threshold in nuisance cases'.[75] At first instance,[76] Coulson J had considered that, if some level of odour was inherent in the permitted activity, then it would be necessary to set a precise threshold, to distinguish between the acceptable and the unacceptable, and to determine 'the moment when "give" becomes "take"'. However, on appeal,[77] Carnwath LJ explained *Watson* and *Kennaway* on the basis that they were not 'setting a threshold for evaluating past nuisance', but rather, that their thresholds were 'set primarily for the purpose of control in the future, rather than assessing whether there had been a nuisance in the past or judging reasonable user.' Furthermore, while noise nuisance was 'susceptible' to the control of a numerical threshold level to help local residents 'order their lives accordingly', smell-type nuisances (as in *Biffa*) were entirely different. They were not susceptible to any numerical threshold principle, because D could not limit the smelly activities to particular days in advance; the smells were transient and unpredictable in timing and intensity; and there was no proven technology for assessing and setting enforceable limits to smells, as there was for noise.

In *Barr v Biffa Waste Services*, which was a group claim involving 152 households, the minimum threshold of inconvenience which C would have to put up with (given that the locality had long been used for tipping and waste landfill) was set by the trial judge as one odour complaint day each week (i.e. 52 days each year). Only two householders could prove that that threshold was exceeded, and hence, all the others failed at trial. **Held** (on appeal): Cs did not need to specify a precise limit of acceptable smell, and there was no accepted methodology for doing so. To apply that threshold test was erroneous; and without that threshold applying, then 'at least for a substantial part of the 5-year period, particularly in the summer, there was a serious interference with the ordinary enjoyment of their homes, judged by the traditional tests'. Their cases were referred back to trial.

Since *Biffa Waste*, it has again been confirmed, in *Pusey v Somerset CC*,[78] that setting a numerical threshold is 'a useful tool' for the purposes of setting injunctive relief, to regulate 'a potentially intrusive activity which should be allowed to continue in the future, but subject to restrictions on its frequency and duration' – but that no numerical threshold should be set by which to assess whether a nuisance had occurred in the first place.

Turning now to the elements of the tort:

ELEMENT #1: AN INTERFERENCE WITH USE AND ENJOYMENT OF LAND

§16.10 Whether D's activities have interfered with C's use and enjoyment of his land, sufficient to constitute an actionable private nuisance, is to be determined according to an objective standard.

It is not whether *the particular C* finds D's activities to be discomforting and inconvenient, but whether an objective person in C's person would have found them to be so (per *Hirose Electrical UK Ltd v Peak Ingredients Ltd*[79]), according to 'the standards of the average person' (per *Barr v Biffa Waste Services Ltd*[80]). As Knight Bruce VC put it in the oft-quoted statement in *Walter v Selfe*, the question is not judged 'merely according to elegant or dainty modes and habits of living, but according to plain and sober and simple notions among the English people'.[81]

[75] [2012] EWCA Civ 312, [46(v)]. [76] [2011] EWHC 1003 (TCC) [385].
[77] [2012] EWCA Civ 312, with quotes in text, and in case description, at [115]–[116], [139], [121].
[78] [2012] EWCA Civ 988, [26]–[29]. [79] [2011] EWCA Civ 987, [1] (Mummery LJ).
[80] [2012] EWCA Civ 312, [36]. [81] (1851) 4 De G&Sm 315, 322; (1851) 64 ER 849 (QB) 852.

Practically speaking, the task of proving an interference with C's use and enjoyment may depend upon a variety of types of evidence. C may give his own evidence of the effect of D's activities upon his use and enjoyment (e.g., a diary log of incidents, as in *Pusey v Somerset CC*[82] – although it is more helpful if such documentary evidence is contemporaneous with the nuisance, rather than years later, per *Barr v Biffa Waste Services Ltd*[83]). Evidence of prior complaints may be useful, but it is not definitive (in *Halsey v Esso Petroleum Co Ltd*,[84] the lack of complaints by residents around Esso's depot before bringing the action did not preclude, or invalidate, a successful action in private nuisance, as a matter of law – although in *Barr v Biffa Waste Services*, the fact that there were 'substantial and credible complaints ... over five years' by some neighbouring residents certainly assisted to prove that private nuisance was potentially actionable by *those* residents[85]). C may also adduce statements from witnesses of fact (i.e., other residents in the neighbourhood or vicinity of D's premises), and/or opinions from expert witnesses (e.g., engineers, arboriculturists, industrial noise specialists, mathematicians engaged in statistical modelling, and the like). Evidence from relevant statutory authorities responsible for monitoring or regulating environmental or workplace health and safety matters may also be relevant. In *Hirose*, the point was made that, if D's activities are complained about by C, but the relevant statutory authorities (e.g., the local authority, the Health and Safety Executive, or the Environmental Health Department) do not see fit to intervene or to object to D's activities, that will not be conclusive that C was not suffering a private nuisance; but such evidence will be relevant in the court's assessment of the (low) levels of discomfort and inconvenience being experienced by C – otherwise the statutory authorities would presumably have acted on the complaint on environmental or safety grounds). A site visit by the trial judge may also be helpful/warranted.

Types of interferences

C must prove a 'private nuisance in fact', i.e., an actionable interference with his use and enjoyment of land.

Actionable, and non-actionable, interferences

§16.11 There are four types of interferences which can give rise to private nuisance: (1) physical interferences; (2) intangible interferences; (3) interferences which prevent a natural feature from reaching C's land which has been acquired by right of prescription; and (4) interferences which constitute a failure-to-abate an actual or threatened encroachment.

It has been said that 'the forms which nuisance may take are protean' (i.e., widely varied), and that 'nuisance is a term used to cover a wide variety of tortious acts or omissions' (per Lord Cooke in *Hunter v Canary Wharf Ltd*[86]). The following Table provides descriptions of each type – in the case examples, that type of interference was, at least, **capable** of constituting a nuisance, but not all cases succeeded, because of the failure of one or more preconditions or elements of the tort:

[82] [2012] EWCA Civ 099, [15]. [83] [2012] EWCA Civ 312, [127]. [84] [1961] 1 WLR 683 (QB) 695–96.
[85] [2012] EWCA Civ 312, [41], [55]–[56], [140]–[141], citing Coulson J (trial judge).
[86] [1997] AC 655, 680 (Pill LJ), 710 (Lord Cooke, dissenting on the question of standing).

Types of private nuisance

Sources of the interference	Case examples
Physical interferences – D's acts cause physical damage or injury to C's land, or to C's interests in land (e.g. easements), or to things growing on or affixed to C's land	
Structural damage caused by vibrations, or subsidence damage caused by excavations or removal of support	*Sturges v Bridgman*[a] (from D's neighbouring meatworks (confectioner)) *Jones v Ruth*[b] (from D's neighbouring building works on his house) *Malone v Laskey*[c] (from D's neighbouring factory)
D fixing posters to, or inscribing graffiti on, C's buildings	*City of London v Samede*[d] (from the protest camp set up in the grounds of St Paul's Cathedral, London, in October 2011)
Acid rain, fireworks, metal strips, or other dangerous items fall onto C's property and cause damage	*St Helen's Smelting Co v Tipping*[e] (fumes from copper smelting works mixed with rain to cause acid rain which injured C's land) *British Celanese v AH Hunt*[f] (metal foil strips fell onto electricity substation)
Leakage or spread of things that cause damage, such as chemicals or sewage	*Cambridge Water Co Ltd v Eastern Counties Leather plc*[g] (escape of solvents) *Marcic v Thames Water Utilities Ltd*[h] (escape of sewage) *Foster v Warblington UDC*[i] (discharge of sewage)
Intangible interferences – D's acts cause intangible interferences that, in turn, cause discomfort or inconvenience to C's use and enjoyment of his land	
Odours	*Barr v Biffa Waste Services Ltd*[j] (from D's waste treatment and landfill site) *Dobson v Thames Water Utilities Ltd*[k] (from D's sewage treatment plants) *Milka v Chetwynd Animal By-Products (1995) Ltd*[l] (from D's meat knackers/animal rendering plant) *City of London v Samede*[m] (noted above) *Hirose Electrical UK Ltd v Peak Ingredients Ltd*[n] (a smell of curry/garlic produced by food additives manufactured by D) *Wheeler v JJ Saunders Ltd*[o] (from D's pig farm)

[a] (1879) LR 11 Ch D 852 (CA).
[b] [2011] EWCA Civ 804.
[c] [1907] 2 KB 141 (CA).
[d] [2012] EWHC 34 (QB).
[e] (1865) 11 HLC (Clark's) 642, 11 ER 1483.
[f] [1969] 1 WLR 959 (QB).
[g] [1994] 2 AC 264 (HL).
[h] [2002] QB 929 (CA).
[i] [1906] 1 KB 648 (CA) 668, 679–80.
[j] [2012] EWCA Civ 312.
[k] [2011] EWHC 3253 (TCC).
[l] (Carmarthen CC 19100, 2000), as cited in *Dobson*, *ibid*, [1024].
[m] [2012] EWHC 34 (QB).
[n] [2011] EWCA Civ 987.
[o] [1996] Ch 19 (CA).

Sources of the interference	Case examples
Noise	*Coventry v Lawrence*[p] (from D's motocross circuit) *Watson v Croft Promo Sport Ltd*[q] (from D's motor-racing circuit) *White v Lynch*[r] (dance music from D's restaurant late at night)
Smoke, dust, fumes and grit in the air	*Anthony v Coal Authority*[s] (from D's coalworks; plus a pungent smell of sulphur dioxide) *Hunter v Canary Wharf Ltd*[t] (from D's construction of the Limehouse Road Link and Limehouse Tunnel, for the dust caused) *City of London v Samede*[u] (hypothetical example: the 'traditional use of the highway by vehicular traffic might amount to a private nuisance if there was emission of exhaust fumes which caused decay to the fabric of the cathedral')
Activities on neighbouring land which are highly-visible and which damage C's land or interest in land	*Thompson-Schwab v Costaki*[v] (prostitutes and clients entering and leaving D's neighbouring premises) *Lippiatt v South Gloucestershire CC*[w] (a camp of gypsies on D's land)
Emission of high-frequency airwaves, or creation of electromagnetic fields	*Network Rail Infrastructure Ltd v Morris (t/a Soundstar Studio)*[x] (electromagnetic signals emitted from D's railway signalling box) *Bridlington Relay Ltd v Yorkshire Elec Bd*[y] (emissions from D's electricity high-tension cables)
Unstable structures on D's land which threaten to (or do) collapse onto C's land	*Birmingham Devp Co Ltd v Tyler*, dicta[z] (a house or wall on D's property, presenting a danger of collapsing onto C's property)
Interferences which prevent natural things from reaching C's land – activities by D which prevent, say, light or running water, from reaching C's land	
Natural light	*Regan v Paul Properties DPF No 1 Ltd*[aa] (interruption of natural light to C's maisonette in a flat complex by D's new building)

[p] [2014] UKSC 13; and [2014] UKSC 46. This case had many name changes over its history: *Moto-land UK Ltd v Lawrence* [2012] EWCA Civ 264; and at first instance: *Lawrence v Fen Tigers Ltd* [2011] EWHC 360.
[q] [2009] EWCA Civ 15.
[r] [2011] EWHC 1664 (QB).
[s] [2005] EWHC 1654 (QB).
[t] [1997] UKHL 14, [1997] AC 655.
[u] [2012] EWHC 34 (QB) [133].
[v] [1956] 1 WLR 335 (CA).
[w] [2000] QB 51 (CA).
[x] [2004] EWCA Civ 172.
[y] [1965] Ch 436.
[z] [2008] EWCA Civ 859, [52].
[aa] [2006] EWCA Civ 1391, [63].

Sources of the interference	Case examples
Physical encroachment (including failure-to-abate) nuisances – D does not create a natural hazard, but allows or causes the natural hazard to interfere with C's use and enjoyment of his land	
Mosquitoes, or biting insects, flying from D's property	*Dobson v Thames Water Utilities Ltd*[bb] (mosquitoes were attracted to D's sewage or waste treatment plants, and then troubled nearby residents)
An unstable thing on D's land	*Leakey v National Trust*[cc] (an unstable naturally-occurring mound of earth on D's property called 'Burrow Mump', prone to subsidence, which threatened C's adjoining land, and eventually slipped onto C's land)
Flood or fire spreading from D's land to C's adjoining land	*Green v Somerleyton*[dd] (spread of floodwaters from playing field) *Goldman v Hargrave*[ee] (D, owner of a Western Australian farm, failed to put out a fire in a burning red gum tree which had been struck by lightning)
Tree roots	*Berent v Family Mosaic Housing and Islington LBC*[ff] (roots of big London plane trees encroaching on C's premises) *Delaware Mansions v Westminster CC*[gg] (same)

[bb] [2011] EWHC 3253 (TCC).
[cc] [1979] EWCA Civ 5, [1980] QB 485.
[dd] [2003] EWCA Civ 198.
[ee] [1967] 1 AC 645 (PC, on appeal from the High Court of Australia).
[ff] [2011] EWHC 1353 (TCC), aff'd: [2012] EWCA Civ 961.
[gg] [2001] UKHL 55, [2002] 1 AC 321.

§16.12 Certain interferences to C's use and enjoyment of land cannot be protected by the tort of private nuisance, *viz*, the right to a view, and the right to flow of air.

There is an important distinction under this principle. An interruption to the flow or extent of natural light to C's premises is protectable in nuisance, but the interruption to C's view is not.

In *Regan v Paul Properties DPF No 1 Ltd*[87] Mr Regan, C, owned a maisonette in a flat complex in Brighton, 12 metres opposite D's new 5-storey building. Construction of D's building disrupted the light entering the maisonette, especially in the living room, and the enjoyment and comfort of the living room were significantly reduced. It affected ordinary activities in the living room such as reading, and forced C's family to use artificial light, or to utilise the part of the room close to the bay window, in full view of the occupants of the flats in the new development. **Held:** a private nuisance. There was a substantial interference with C's enjoyment of natural light in the living room: '[w]hat matters is not so much the amount of light that is taken, as the amount of light that is left' after the interference.

However, even if the construction, or presence, of D's building interferes with C's view, that is not actionable in private nuisance. That is a long-standing rule of English law (per *A-G v Doughty*[88] and *Fishmongers' Co v East India Co*[89]). That is not to say that an aggrieved C is

[87] [2006] EWCA Civ 1391, with quote at [63]. [88] (1752) 2 Ves Sen 453 (Ch). [89] (1752) Dick 163 (Ch).

totally without remedy when his view is blocked. If D's land is subject to a restrictive covenant that endows C with a right to a view, that is actionable; but in private nuisance, C has no remedy. As Lord Lloyd said in *Hunter v Canary Wharf*, '[t]he house-owner who has a fine view of the South Downs may find that his neighbour has built so as to obscure his view. But there is no redress, unless, perchance, the neighbour's land was subject to a restrictive covenant in the house-owner's favour.'[90]

D's building may restrict the flow of air onto C's neighbouring land, again without any action in private nuisance arising (per *Chastey v Ackland*[91]).

Radio, television and other signals

§16.13 In appropriate cases, interference with TV reception, and electro-magnetic interference, are capable of constituting an actionable private nuisance.

There has been no English case yet in which interference with television reception has amounted to an actionable nuisance. However, in *Hunter v Canary Wharf Ltd*,[92] a majority of the House of Lords held that, in appropriate cases, interference with TV reception **may** constitute a private nuisance (despite earlier authority to the contrary). The observations in *Hunter* were dicta only – its ratio concerned standing to sue.

> In *Hunter v Canary Wharf*, Patricia Hunter and others in the group claim, Cs, claimed damages for interference with TV reception, caused by the construction of Canary Wharf Tower on land developed by the London Docklands Devp Corp, D. The large Tower was about 250 m high; was clad in stainless steel with metal windows; and stood in the path of the television signals emitting from the BBC transmitter at Crystal Palace. Cs lived on the Isle of Dogs (mainly in Poplar), in an electromagnetic shadow, so they received either no TV signal at all, or a very blurred picture. This carried on from 1989 (when the Tower was built) to April 1992 (when a new relay transmitter was built and brought into service, and the aerials of Cs' homes were adjusted or replaced at no cost to the owners). This claim was for the period of the interference; it was instituted in private nuisance and negligence, but the latter was abandoned. **Held**: standing was determined restrictively, so the claim collapsed. However, interference with TV reception was held (3:2) to be capable of amounting to an actionable nuisance.
> In *Bridlington Relay Ltd v Yorkshire Electricity Board*,[93] the Electricity Board, D, caused electrical interference with C's TV reception, because of electro-magnetic radiation from high tension electrical cables installed by D. **Held:** no actionable interference. D merely interfered with a recreational facility, 'as opposed to interference with the health or physical comfort or well-being of C' (had it been the latter, the emission of the radiation could have constituted a private nuisance).

The majority in *Hunter* considered that interference with TV reception would be actionable in private nuisance **only** where that TV reception was 'so important a part of an ordinary householder's enjoyment of his property that such interference should be regarded as a legal nuisance' (per Lord Goff[94]). That level of importance may potentially be shown by:

- the length of time that C watched the television per week ('[c]ertainly, the average weekly hours for television viewing in this country, ... 24 hours per week, show that many people devote

[90] [1997] UKHL 14, [1997] AC 655 (HL) 699. [91] [1895] 2 Ch 389 (CA).

[92] [1997] AC 655 (HL) (on this point, Lords Goff, Hoffmann, and Cooke, were in the majority, with Lords Lloyd and Hope dissenting). See, especially, 719 (Lord Cooke).

[93] [1965] Ch 436, with quote at 447.

[94] [1997] AC 655 (HL) 684. For reasoning in the text, see 684–85 (Lord Goff), 719 (Lord Cooke).

much of their leisure time to watching television' (Lord Goff); and '[t]elevision has become a significant and, to many, almost an indispensable amenity of domestic life' (Lord Cooke) – in which case the amenity ancillary to C's land which was provided by receipt of a television signal could constitute more than the mere recreational activity referred to in *Bridlington*;

- television viewing which 'transcend[ed] the function of mere entertainment' for C who is from the demographic of the elderly and sick, since 'it must provide a great distraction and relief from the circumscribed nature of their lives'; or where C uses television for educational or business purposes.

The majority opinions suggest that, in the absence of an above distinguishing factor, interference with TV reception will not be an actionable nuisance. This result was justified in *Hunter* on the bases[95] that the ultimate responsibility for inadequate television reception in certain areas rests more with where the broadcaster sites its transmitter, rather than with the characteristics of D's building (and D cannot control what the broadcaster does) (Lord Cooke); and secondly, the problem was 'likely to become less and less important', given the availability of cable and satellite television (Lord Goff).

The dissenting views in *Hunter* (by Lords Lloyd and Hope[96]) are worth briefly noting. First, the right to unaffected TV reception did not affect C's proprietary or possessory interest in the land, but was merely a right of personal enjoyment, which the law of nuisance did not protect; secondly, the right to a nice view, and reception of TV signals, are highly analogous, especially where both are interfered with by the presence of D's building, and neither is actionable; and thirdly, in a dispute between D's property interest to build on his land and C's personal enjoyment of his land, D's interests must prevail, and no action in nuisance was possible.

Subsequently, in *Network Rail Infrastructure Ltd v Morris*,[97] an electromagnetic interference caused by D to C's business enterprise would have been actionable, but for the fact that the interference itself was unforeseeable. This reiterates that disruptions with the use of intangible signals for business purposes are capable of constituting an actionable interference under the modern law of private nuisance.

Isolated interferences versus a state of affairs

§16.14 Although a private nuisance may be easier to establish where the interference constitutes a 'continuing state of affairs', an isolated, one-off interference can *still* constitute an actionable private nuisance.

Where C is subjected to an isolated interference, that may point to a temporary interference only – and the duration of the interference is relevant to the question of 'unreasonable user' (under Element #2).

However, while isolated occurrences do not often constitute a nuisance, they **may** do – '[m]ost nuisances do arise from a long continuing condition; and many isolated happenings do not constitute a nuisance. It is, however, clear from the authorities that an isolated happening by itself [i.e., a first escape] can create an actionable nuisance' (per *British Celanese Ltd v AH Hunt (Capacitors) Ltd*[98]).

[95] [1997] AC 655 (HL), respectively at 684, 699, and 721.
[96] [1997] AC 655 (HL), respectively at 684, 699, and 721.
[97] [2004] EWCA Civ 172.
[98] [1969] 1 WLR 959 (QB) 969.

In *British Celanese v AH Hunt (Capacitors)*, AH Hunt, D, stored on its factory premises long strips of metal foil, necessary for manufacturing electrical conductors. D negligently failed to keep them covered and safe, and the foil strips were carried by the wind of a storm onto an electricity substation owned by the electricity board, and this led to a power failure over a wide area. The power loss, in turn, caused a power failure at British Celanese's, C's, factory, bringing its machines to a halt and damaging them, and causing a loss of production whilst they were fixed. This accident occurred in 1964. **Held**: an actionable private nuisance. The harm was reasonably foreseeable. This was not the first escape of the metal foil strips – a similar problem had occurred in 1961, and D had been warned to secure the foil strips more safely. However, *even if it had been the first escape*, an action for private nuisance would still have been possible (said the court).

The modern law of private nuisance does **not** maintain a clear division between isolated and continuing interferences. Several reasons were provided in *Colour Quest Ltd v Total Downstream UK plc*:[99]

i. the borderline between an isolated interference and a continuing state of affairs is quite blurred ('simply a matter of degree'[100]);

   In *Midwood v Manchester Corp*,[101] Manchester Corp, D, was statutorily authorised to supply electricity and electric lighting in Manchester. The insulation around one of D's electricity conductors which was laid in bitumen failed, electricity leaked out, and that caused the bitumen to become volatile and to produce inflammable gas. That gas accumulated for about three hours in that vicinity, wafted into a house next to Midwood's, C's, store, and then exploded. **Held**: there was a state of affairs sufficient to give rise to an actionable nuisance.

ii. '*Rylands v Fletcher* liability is a species of nuisance',[102] and whatever their other differences may be, the transitory nature of D's interference does not distinguish one cause of action from the other;

iii. older, more dogmatic, authorities which decreed that a continuing state of affairs was necessary for a private nuisance have been increasingly treated with caution. For example, *AG v PYA Quarries* held that 'a private nuisance always involves some degree of repetition or continuance. An isolated act which is over and done with, once and for all, may give rise to an action for negligence or an action under the rule in *Rylands v Fletcher*, but not an action for nuisance'.[103] However, this was noted in *Colour Quest* as being merely dicta, and not an accurate legal statement any longer.[104] Furthermore, in *Cambridge Water Co v Eastern Counties Leather plc*[105] (where percolating water contaminated by D made its way to C's borehole), Lord Goff remarked that what happened there was 'not an isolated escape, but a continuing escape resulting from a state of affairs ... Classically, this would have been regarded as a case of nuisance'. However, that case concerned a claim in *Rylands v Fletcher*, and hence, anything said about private nuisance was dicta only. As a result, *Colour Quest* held that *Cambridge Water* did not preclude an isolated escape from constituting a private nuisance, and hence, the one-off explosion at the Buncefield Oil Depot *could* feasibly give rise to a claim in private nuisance[106] (ultimately, however, the claim failed in *Colour Quest*, for other reasons).

[99] [2009] EWHC 540 (Comm) [410]–[421]. [100] *ibid*, [410]. [101] [1905] 2 KB 597 (CA), cited *ibid*, [413].
[102] [2009] EWHC 540 (Comm) [411]. [103] [1957] 2 QB 169 (CA) 192 (Denning LJ).
[104] [2009] EWHC 540 (Comm) [416]. [105] [1994] 2 AC 264 (HL) 306 (Lord Goff).
[106] [2009] EWHC 540 (Comm) [419]–[421], also citing *Clerk and Lindsell on Torts* (19th edn) [20-16].

Emanation

The general rule, and exceptions

§16.15 Generally, interferences amounting to a private nuisance emanate from land which D owns/occupies. However, there are exceptional cases in which an emanation from D's land is ***not*** strictly required for an actionable nuisance, although these exceptions are likely to be narrowly applied and construed.

In *Arscott v Coal Authority*, Laws LJ stated that '[t]he unifying factor in all [nuisance] categories is that there is some sort of invasion of [C's] land, or his enjoyment of it'.[107] Indeed, generally speaking, interferences in private nuisance reflect an emanation-and-invasion pattern, whereby something will emanate from D's land and thereby disrupt C's use and enjoyment of his land – e.g., odours spread, tree roots encroach, noise travels, or fumes combine with atmospheric moisture to create acid rain.

However, that is not a hard-and-fast rule in private nuisance. In *Hunter v Canary Wharf Ltd*,[108] Lord Goff remarked that the interference 'will generally arise from something emanating from [D's] land', but that, '[o]ccasionally activities on [D's] land are in themselves so offensive to neighbours as to constitute an actionable nuisance ... Such cases must however be relatively rare'. In similar vein, Lord Lloyd said that 'nuisance does not depend in every case on an activity, although it usually does'. In other words, some nuisances can just 'be' or 'exist' on D's land – without invading C's premises at all – and that will be sufficient to constitute an intangible interference so as to give rise to a private nuisance. Case law demonstrates that, thus far, these exceptional scenarios are fairly limited:

- in *Thompson-Schwab v Costaki*[109] (cited by Lord Goff in *Hunter*), the sight of prostitutes and their clients entering and leaving neighbouring premises constituted a nuisance, because it was an offensive sight to neighbours C (although, clearly, neither prostitutes nor clients encroached onto C's property);
- in *Bank of New Zealand v Greenwood*,[110] the glare reflected from the verandah of D's neighbouring greenhouse constituted a nuisance for C, although Lord Lloyd noted, in *Hunter v Canary Wharf Ltd*, that this case 'may go to the limit of the law of nuisance'.[111] However, the case has analogy with noise cases – sound waves and light waves have been affected in such a way as to cause interference with C's use and enjoyment of his land, and hence, arguably fit the 'emanation-and-invasion' pattern;
- where the interference is because of some threatened collapse of D's building or structure onto C's land, and C can establish that 'living in the shadow of the threat' constitutes an interference with his quiet use and enjoyment of his land, there can be an actionable nuisance, with no emanation, too. In *Birmingham Development Co Ltd v Tyler*,[112] that proposition was accepted, in dicta, as being correct – although there was, ultimately, no nuisance there, because of a lack of any well-founded fear of collapse. In *Hunter*, Lord Lloyd said that threatened encroachments could be actionable nuisances, because of 'a mere state of affairs on [D's] land which he allows to continue';[113]

[107] [2004] EWCA Civ 892, [95]. [108] [1997] AC 655 (HL) 685–86 (Lord Goff), 700 (Lord Lloyd).
[109] [1956] 1 WLR 335 (CA). [110] [1984] 1 NZLR 525 (HC).
[111] [1997] UKHL14, [1997] AC 655 (HL) 700. [112] [2008] EWCA Civ 859, [2008] All ER (D) 325 (Jul) (CA) [52].
[113] [1997] AC 655 (HL) 700.

- where D plugs a manhole and a drain with concrete, which causes sewage to build up in drains on C's land, rather than passing through to D's public sewer, there has, strictly speaking, been no emanation of something onto C's land from D's land either. Nevertheless, an action in private nuisance could theoretically lie (per *Welsh Water v Barratt Homes Ltd (Rev 1)*[114]).

Hence, both the following scenarios are feasibly possible to make out an actionable nuisance:

Emanation versus mere existence

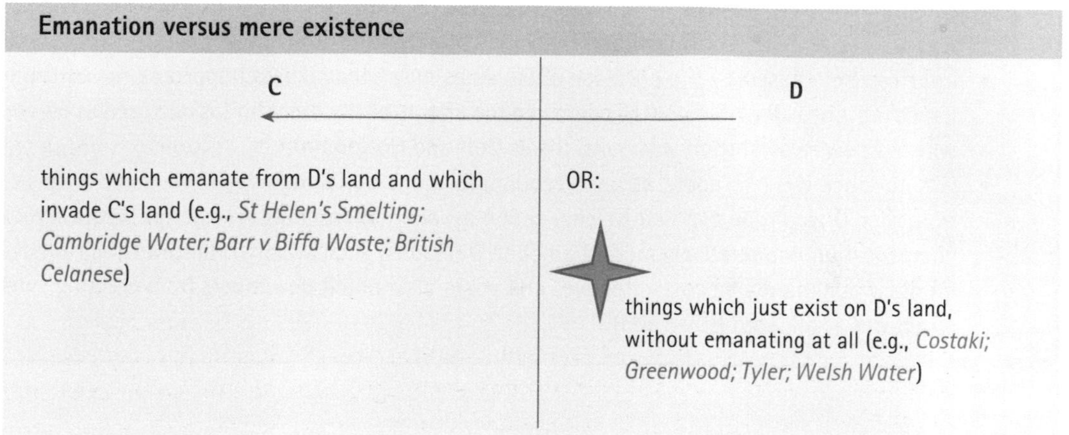

The mere presence of an 'inconvenient' building

In *Hunter* itself, the offending presence of the 250 metre-high Canary Wharf Tower on D's land, and its interference with C's television reception in the surrounding Isle of Dogs area, did **not** constitute an actionable nuisance (although it will be recalled that the majority held that interference with TV reception *could feasibly* be actionable). The building did not 'emanate'; it could not be treated as an exception to the general rule; and hence, it could not cause an actionable nuisance. According to Lord Goff,[115] the mere presence of the Tower was the deathknell of any claim for interference with TV reception (or, at least, a 'formidable obstacle' to its success). The numerous reasons which justified this view in *Hunter* are summarised in the Table below.[116]

Why a building on D's land, 'in the way', is not actionable in private nuisance

- *Hunter* concerned D's *constructing* a building; but if the mere presence of a building on D's land could give rise to an actionable nuisance, then C could complain about D's building, after C moved in and found that the building caused interference – given that it is no defence that C 'came to the nuisance' (Lord Goff);
- it is a long-standing general rule of English law that 'anyone may build whatever he likes upon his land' (Lord Hoffmann), as qualified by planning controls, restrictive covenants, or to some easement to which C is entitled. The London Docklands Development Corp, D, had not infringed any such restriction (Lord Goff);

[114] [2013] EWCA Civ 233, [58]–[60]. [115] [1997] AC 655 (HL) 685–66.
[116] See the reasoning variously at: 685–66, 701, 707, 710–11, 721, 727.

- if the presence of a building could be an interference, then a centuries-old line of authority – that flows of air, and views, are not actionable in private nuisance – would need overruling (Lords Goff and Hoffmann);
- even if potential problems caused by a building are not appreciated before it is built, or objections to its construction are not possible (as they were not with the Canary Wharf redevelopment, that being sanctioned as an 'Enterprise Zone' by the Government, so that planning permission for any construction was deemed), that was no reason to consider that the mere presence of the building was an interference (Lords Goff and Hoffmann);
- interferences caused by the presence of buildings may become 'less important', given the technological advances possible now to overcome the effects of the building (as occurred in *Hunter* itself, where a new relay station was built) (Lords Goff and Hoffmann);
- if a nuisance were to apply, as an exception, for large buildings which interfered with TV reception, then D would be exposed to legal action by 'an indeterminate number of [C's], each claiming compensation in a relatively modest amount. Defending such actions, whatever their merits or demerits, would hardly be cost-effective', and might also inhibit developers from erecting substantial structures at all (Lord Hoffmann).

Since *Hunter*, some judges have shown little inclination to uphold alleged nuisances which did not directly emanate-and-invade. In *D Pride & Partners v Institute for Animal Health*, C had no claim in private nuisance, because any interference 'has not been directly caused by anything emanating from [D's] land ... Nothing from [D's] land encroached on any land of [C's]'.[117] Additionally, in *Network Rail Infrastructure Ltd v Conarken Group Ltd*, the accidents did not give rise to actionable nuisance, partly because it was said that there was no encroachment onto C's land (although, indirectly, there clearly was some 'invasion').[118]

In *D Pride & Partners v Institute for Animal Health*, the owners and/or occupiers of livestock farms in Great Britain, C, alleged that the Dept of Environment, Food and Rural Affairs (DEFRA), D, caused, or failed to prevent the escape of, the foot and mouth disease from its animal research facility at Pirbright in 2007. The allegation was that the escape of the virus caused interference with the use or enjoyment by the farmers of their land, because of the restrictive measures imposed upon them by D, in that they could not move their stock or send their stock for slaughter. **Held**: no actionable nuisance. The premises from which the disease emanated was from Pirbright, owned by the Institute for Animal Health, not from DEFRA's (D's) land. In *Conarken*, Network Rail, C, sued Conarken and Farrell Transport Ltd, Ds, the employers of drivers who separately caused disruption to C's rail-lines. The driver of a tractor was taking a tractor along a road to a level crossing on the East Coast Main Line route, when his radio aerial made contact with overhead electrical cables. This caused an explosion, brought down powerlines onto the rail line, and caused suspension of services for 4–5 hours. In the other case, the driver of a loader carrying a piling rig collided with a lorry, both vehicles hit the parapet wall of a railway bridge, and debris fell onto C's railway line, with part of the lorry overhanging the line. A crane had to be manoeuvred onto the track to remove part of the debris. **Held**: neither incident was an actionable nuisance. These respective drivers created interferences when they were

117 [2009] EWHC 685 (QB)]133]–[134].
118 [2010] EWHC 1852 (TCC) [70], aff'd: [2011] EWCA Civ 644, 136 Con LR 1 (CA).

'simply exercising a common law or statutory right to pass and re-pass on the public highway. The undue interference with enjoyment category of nuisance is wholly inapt to describe what happened here'. Plus there 'was hardly an encroachment on to Network Rail's land'.

ELEMENT #2: AN UNREASONABLE USER

§16.16 Proof of an 'unreasonable user' requires the court to balance objectively the competing interests of D, the creator of the nuisance, and C, the person who is complaining of the interference. The essence of private nuisance is a 'give-and-take' balancing exercise, between D's right to make use of his property, and C's right to the peaceable use and enjoyment of his land.

General points

An 'unreasonable user' by D depends upon proof that D's use and occupation of his land caused such inconvenience and injury to C's use and enjoyment of **his** land that it should be actionable at law. D's conduct exceeded the threshold of 'give and take' which is the essence of the tort.

Notably, an 'unreasonable user' in the context of private nuisance is **not** to be equated with a lack of reasonable care in negligence. Liability in nuisance is strict, in that an 'unreasonable user' can be proven, even where D has exercised the **utmost** care to prevent the interference from occurring (as discussed later). In Lord Millett's view in *Southwark LBC v Mills*, the word 'reasonable', was liable to be misunderstood for that reason – rather, a 'reasonable user' requires proof that D's acts complained of must (1) be necessary for the common and ordinary use and occupation of land and houses; and (2) be 'conveniently done', so that it was 'done with proper consideration for the interests of neighbouring occupiers' such as C.[119] Certainly, the notion of an 'unreasonable user' has been judicially linked to the *reciprocity* which is at the heart of the tort. It has been described by Lord Goff in *Cambridge Water Co v Eastern Counties Leather plc* as the device by which liability under nuisance is 'kept under control ... the principle of give and take as between neighbouring occupiers of land';[120] by Bramwell B in *Bamford v Turnley* as 'give and take, live and let live';[121] and by Coulson J in *Barr v Biffa Waste Services Ltd* as, 'everyone must put up with a certain amount of discomfort and annoyance caused by the legitimate activities of his neighbours'.[122]

This second element of the tort is to be assessed by the court objectively (hence the terminology of '*reasonable* user). Typically, up to **five** 'balancing factors' have been referred to:

- the character of the neighbourhood;
- the duration, intensity and frequency of the interference;
- the public benefit or utility of D's activities;
- the presence of any malice on D's part; and
- the effect of planning permission for D's activities.

The outcome of that balancing exercise certainly does **not** depend upon how C or D would have assessed those factors themselves (per Lord Carnwath in *Coventry v Lawrence*[123]).

[119] [2001] 1 AC 1 (HL) 20–21, citing: *Bamford v Turnley* (1862) 3 B&S 62 (KB) 83–84, 122 ER 27 (KB) 32.
[120] [1994] 2 AC 264 (HL) 299. [121] (1862) 3 B&S 62 (KB) 83–84, 122 ER 27 (KB) 32.
[122] [2011] EWHC 1003 (TCC) [200], citing: *Clerk and Lindsell on Torts* (20th edn, Sweet & Maxwell, 2010) [20-10]. The outcome itself was overruled on appeal, but not this proposition.
[123] [2014] UKSC 13, [179], citing with approval: T Weir, *An Introduction to Tort Law* (2nd ed, 2006) 160.

Inevitably, the concept of an 'unreasonable user' does not lend itself to a neat analysis, or even to a readily predictable outcome. As Lord Cooke noted in *Hunter v Canary Wharf Ltd*: 'tidiness has not had a high priority in the history of the common law. What has made the law of nuisance a potent instrument of justice throughout the common law world has been largely its flexibility and versatility'.[124] Of course, what is 'flexible' to one is 'uncertain' to another. Witness, for example, Lord Wilberforce's statement in *Goldman v Hargrave*, 'the tort of nuisance, uncertain in its boundary'.[125]

The balancing exercise required under Element #2 is acutely important. After all, where D is using his land precisely in accordance with planning permission, in accordance with the zoning of the land, in compliance with the terms of any lease of the premises, in the absence of any negligence, and perhaps also conducting activities which are in the public interest, that D can still have committed an 'unreasonable user', and be liable for private nuisance, and be required to pay sizable damages.

Notably, as part of the 'give and take' principle, English law has adopted the view that a building (and, more specifically, its dividing walls) should be taken for what it is, 'warts and all'. Courts have been unsympathetic to C's argument that, had a third party constructed the premises more solidly, then the interference would not have occurred – and for that poor construction, either that third party or D should be liable in nuisance for the inconvenience being caused to C's use and enjoyment of his land. Certainly, it may have been possible to sound-proof the premises better; or porous walls could have been insulated to stop smells from wafting onto C's premises. But any failure to construct the premises better has not, thus far, constituted an actionable nuisance on the part of the third party or D.

In *Southwark LBC v Tanner and Mills*,[126] noise generated by ordinary day-to-day living in residential flats interfered with the enjoyment by other residents, due to the lack of adequate sound insulation between the flats. **Held**: no actionable nuisance on the part of the landlord (nor, implicitly, on the part of the residents). To be a nuisance, a resident's ordinary activities would have to be carried out in an unnecessarily burdensome way, such as by putting a TV or washing machine straight against a common wall. In *Hirose Electrical UK Ltd v Peak Ingredients Ltd*,[127] the smells generated by D's food additives manufacturing business were exacerbated by the fact that the block party wall between the adjoining warehouse units was porous and with considerable gaps. An insulated and sealed wall would have prevented, or reduced, the smells in C's premises. **Held**: no actionable nuisance on D's part.

Application to 'physical interference' nuisances

For interferences which cause physical damage to C's land, the law was more willing, in the past, to presume an unreasonable user, and to diminish (to the point of dismissing altogether) the significance of factors (such as the 'character of the neighbourhood') in the balancing exercise. Even if the area was noisy, smelly, and full of manufacturing industry, some physical interference with C's use and enjoyment can tip the balance in favour of an unreasonable user by D. It did so in the following cases:

124 [1997] AC 655 (HL) 711. 125 [1967] 1 AC 645 (PC, on appeal from Australia) 657.
126 [1999] UKHL 40, [2001] 1 AC 1 (HL) 15–16 (Lord Hoffmann).
127 [2011] EWCA Civ 987, [1], citing: *Cambridge Water Co v Eastern Counties Leather* [1994] 2 AC 264 (HL) 299.

In *St Helen's Smelting Co v Tipping*,[128] Mr Tipping, C, bought a 1,300 acre estate in Lancashire. He complained that his hedges, trees and shrubs were being damaged by pollution from St Helen's, D's, copper smelting works 1½ miles away. D argued that the area around Leeds was full of factories and chemical works, and that if C was entitled to complain, industry around Leeds would be brought to a halt. An actionable nuisance was proven. When D's activities caused a material injury to C's property, 'then there unquestionably arises a very different consideration'. C was entitled to damages, notwithstanding the locality's industrial nature. In *Crown River Cruises Ltd v Kimbolton Fireworks Ltd*,[129] facts previously, the firework display which damaged C's moored barge was of fairly short duration, for 15–30 minutes, but was sufficient to constitute an action in private nuisance.

St Helen's was approved, and described as a 'landmark case', in *Hunter v Canary Wharf Ltd*.[130] However, modern authorities tend to show that even serious physical damage to C's land does not necessarily favour an unreasonable user being found, and that a balancing exercise is relevant, regardless. There is certainly no general rule that D should be liable in nuisance wherever physical damage to C's property is caused by D's activities – that proposition was specifically rejected again recently in *Northumbrian Water Ltd v McAlpine Ltd*.[131]

In *Northumbrian Water*, McAlpine, D, a construction company, was redeveloping a site in Newcastle's city centre, which required large foundations to be sunk. During those excavations, a private sewer, not shown on any public plan (it was only on a 1908 plan in the Newcastle Discovery Museum), was breached, and concrete ran through that gap, into Northumbrian Water's, C's, public sewers, causing extensive damage. **Held:** no actionable nuisance. Redevelopment of an urban city centre site was a reasonable and normal use of the land. In this case, D was not engaged in any unusual methods of pile-driving, when constructing a new building for the city centre. There was no unreasonable user.
In *Ellison v MOD*,[132] the MOD operated the RAF Greenham Common Airbase, built during WWII. The Ellisons, C, lived at the foot of a valley near the airfield, and provided engineering services for agriculture. The other two Cs ran a sawmill and a motor cycle club. On 10 August 1986, a very intense storm occurred. At that time, 4 x 5,000 cubic metre bulk fuel storage tanks, plus pipelines and pump-houses, were being constructed, and the excavated spoil was tipped in piles at the edge of the base. After the storm, a vast amount of water flowed from the airbase into the valley, causing serious damage to Cs' property (cars, caravans, and whole sheds, moved; possessions were swept more than a mile away). C alleged that the MOD's positioning of the spoil interfered with the natural drainage of their land whereas, before the spoil was deposited, the natural rainwater flow passed safely along gullies and culverts on the airbase. **Held:** no actionable nuisance. Building the fuel storage tanks was a reasonable user of the airfield, because of the public interest in serving the 'national defence policy' by storing bulk aviation fuels, plus the relatively open and rural nature of the locality.

Undoubtedly, the balancing exercise under the element of 'unreasonable user' is more keenly-debated and contentious for 'intangible interference' nuisances than for cases where C has suffered some material damage to the fabric of his property – and it is to these factors that attention now turns.

Relevant factors for the balancing exercise

Dealing now, in more detail, with the five balancing factors of relevance under Element #2:

[128] (1865) 11 HL Cas (Clarks) 642 (HL) 650. [129] [1996] 2 Lloyd's Rep 533 (QB).
[130] [1997] AC 655 (HL) 705 (Lord Hoffmann). [131] [2014] EWCA Civ 685, [24]. [132] (1996) 81 BLR 101 (QB).

Character of the neighbourhood

§16.17 The character of the neighbourhood or locality in which the interference occurred is relevant to the balancing exercise required to assess whether D committed an 'unreasonable user'.

Essentially, the noisier and smellier the locality, the less likely that D's nuisance will be actionable, because C already must put up with a certain amount of ambient discomfort. The quieter the neighbourhood, the more likely that D's activities may be held to be an interference with C's use and enjoyment of his land. Hence, 'what may be a nuisance in a quiet rural area may not be in a busy town' (per *Hirose*[133]); or 'what would be a nuisance in Belgrave Square would not necessarily be so in Bermondsey' (per *Sturges v Bridgman*[134]).

Re 'intangible interference' nuisances. Character has certainly been applied to preclude private nuisances where the locality was already odorous/noisy. In the following cases, C failed in its claims:

In *Hirose Electrical v Peak Ingredients*,[135] Hirose, C, manufactured parts for mobile phones at commercial premises at an industrial estate at Milton Keynes. Peak Ingredient, D, manufactured food additives and coatings in the adjacent warehouse unit. C complained about the escape of odours (garlic, curry, peppery or spicy) from D's premises, and that D's food processing business made their premises smell 'like an Indian curry house'. The premises were in a light industrial estate; it was 'not the high class, genteel business park depicted by Hirose in its evidence'. The occupier of a unit on a light industrial estate must expect the possibility of disagreeable smells. In *Murdoch v Glacier Metal Co Ltd*,[136] the Murdochs, C, complained that Glacier's, D's, factory noise, kept them awake at night with the constant droning. C's sleep patterns were disturbed, and the noise exceeded levels which the WHO said could affect the restorative power of sleep. However, not only was the character of the neighbourhood essentially industrial, but there was also a noisy motorway nearby, so it was not a quiet locality at the best of times.

Nevertheless, even where a neighbourhood is already on the noisy or smelly side, C can **still** successfully complain of D's interference as being an actionable nuisance – although it will be necessary to show that D's activities seriously **increased** the interference over and above the disturbance caused by existing sources of noise or smell. The 'essence' of the nuisance, in such cases, 'lies ... in the introduction of a *new and more offensive form* of [nuisance]' (per *Barr v Biffa Waste Services Ltd*[137]). This principle has been applied, across a range of nuisances – noise, fumes and smells. In the following cases, actionable nuisances were proven:[138]

In *Halsey v Esso Petroleum Co Ltd*,[139] Mr Halsey, C, lived in a house near to Esso's, D's, oil distributing depot. Fuel oil had to be pumped from river tankers, to the depot, and then to road tankers. Some grades of oil had to be kept hot at all times, which required a boilerhouse to heat the fuel oil via steam. Two metal chimneys on the boilerhouse belched out noxious acid smuts containing sulphate and other noxious fumes. There had been occasional smells of oil for surrounding residences for many years, but those odours had been increasing in intensity and frequency, once D's depot started treating heavier grade oil, to the point of a 'particularly pungent smell, which

133 [2011] JPL 429 (Ch D) [103]. 134 (1879) 11 Ch D 852 (CA) 865 (Thesiger LJ).

135 [2011] EWCA Civ 987, quotes at [15] and [92]. 136 [1998] Env LR 732 (CA).

137 [2012] EWCA Civ 312, [74] (Carnwath LJ).

138 See too: *Polsue v Rushmer* [1906] 1 Ch 234 (CA) 249, 250, aff'd: [1907] AC 121 (HL) (printing presses situated around Gough Square, London, introduced a 'fresh noise' to the Square at night; a legal nuisance).

139 [1961] 1 WLR 683 (QB) 695–96.

goes far beyond any triviality, far beyond any background smell of oil'. In *Barr v Biffa Waste Services Ltd*,[140] 152 householders on the Vicarage Estate in Ware, Hertfordshire, sued Biffa for odours emanating from their waste treatment plant. Biffa obtained a permit for the tipping of pre-treated waste at the Westfill site in 2003, and from that date onwards, the smells to nearby residents increased markedly, especially as organic matter had had longer to decompose. The character of that Westmill neighbourhood had included quarrying and tipping for many years (over a decade), alongside residential areas. However, introducing pre-treated waste into an area with a history of quarrying and tipping, created additional discomfort sufficient to constitute a nuisance.

D's own activities. If D's own activities are taken into account when assessing the character of the locality, then it may be difficult for C to establish any private nuisance, because the locality would inevitably take its flavour from what D was doing. These concerns prompted the view, in *Coventry v Lawrence*, that D can point to his own activities as constituting part of the character of the locality, **only** where those activities do not constitute a nuisance – so that if D's activities 'could not be carried out without creating a nuisance, then they have to be entirely discounted when assessing the character of the neighbourhood' (per Lord Neuberger[141]).

Inevitably, as Lord Neuberger acknowledged in *Coventry*, this involves circular reasoning – the court has to ignore D's activities if they constitute a nuisance, where the very question that the court is seeking to determine (and to which the issue of locality is relevant) is whether D's activities are a nuisance at all. However, Lord Neuberger did not consider this to be a problem in the ultimate analysis. Whether that optimism is borne out remains to be seen. It does emphasise, however, that evidence as to what *others in the neighbourhood* do with their land and the uses to which their land is put, will be of great import, when judging the locality against which D's nuisance-making activities are to be judged.

The duration, intensity and frequency of the interference

§16.18 The duration, intensity and frequency of the interference caused by D is relevant to the balancing exercise required to assess whether D committed an 'unreasonable user'.

As noted previously,[142] both a one-off interference and a continuing state of interference are capable of giving rise to private nuisances, although the latter is more commonly found in the case reports.

Further, whether an interference is intermittent, continuous, short-lived or permanent, is relevant to the question of an unreasonable user. As stated in *Barr v Biffa Waste*, '[t]he duration of an interference is an element in assessing its actionability, but it is not a decisive factor; a temporary interference which is substantial can be an actionable nuisance'.[143] The frequency and intensity of the interference matter too. An interference which is finite, of short duration, or intermittent, can certainly give rise to an 'unreasonable user' and an actionable nuisance; but the balancing exercise is more likely to be in C's favour if the interference is of long duration, continuous, intense, or hard to escape from. It is a very fact-specific enquiry. Some cases may usefully be contrasted on this factor. In the following cases, an actionable nuisance was proven:

[140] [2012] EWCA Civ 312, [41]. [141] [2014] UKSC 13, [74].
[142] See pp 856–7. [143] [2012] EWCA Civ 312, [36].

In *Barr v Biffa Waste Services Ltd*, facts previously, the introduction of 'pre-treated' tipping by Biffa caused unpleasant smells on a fairly constant basis for five years (but always worse when the wind was blowing from a certain direction), until the site was filled up and the pre-treated waste area moved away from the Estate. In *Ruth v Jones*,[144] Mr Ruth, D, carried out renovation and extension works to his houses at 103 (adding an extension and a third storey) for four years, which caused Ms Lovegrove and Ms Jones, living at 105, to suffer from excessive and persistent noise, dust, pollution and vibration; also caused cracking in the walls of C's premises; affected Cs' privacy because of scaffolding erected for long periods; and D 'deliberately disregarded' Cs' peaceable enjoyment by allowing noisy building works at the weekend and permitting the builders to play radios loudly, and use heavy machinery with no warnings to C.

However, no actionable nuisance occurred in the following cases, notwithstanding that there was, undoubtedly, some interference of frequent occurrence:

In *Hirose Electrical UK Ltd v Peak Ingredients Ltd*,[145] facts previously, the evidence as to the frequency, intensity and effect of the odours reaching C's premises was not sufficient. The discomfort caused on an industrial estate, where persons concerned work on weekdays in the daytime, was not as great as would be caused to residential neighbours who simply could not have escaped from it. The odours were not noticed daily; or necessarily throughout the day; and the odour was stronger in the warehouse section of C's premises and in the back stairs, kitchen and toilet area, but was not nearly as noticeable in the working areas of C's premises, so it was not as noticeable in the most commonly-used areas of C's premises. In *Murdoch v Glacier Metal Co Ltd*, facts previously, the factory noise was a fairly constant drone, and affected C's sleep on an ongoing basis. The nuisance was also of intensity – the evidence was that the level of noise emitted from the factory was, at times, in excess of the level identified by the WHO as being capable of injuring health. However, the previous factor (locality) outweighed this factor in the balancing exercise.

These cases demonstrate just how difficult the factor is to predict, outcome-wise, and how it can be easily 'trumped' by the locality factor, in particular.

The public interest and utility of D's activities

§16.19 The fact that D's activities, while causing an interference, may carry a considerable public utility or community benefit, is not an outright defence to private nuisance. It is, however, a factor in the balancing exercise required to assess whether D was committing an 'unreasonable user'.

The importance of the public interest of D's activities under Element 2 has waxed and waned over the course of private nuisance litigation, with disagreement in the case law. Sporting clubs/activities operated by D commonly feature in this issue. In *Kennaway v Thompson* (1981),[146] re D's boat-club, public interest was held to be completely irrelevant when determining private nuisance claims; whilst in *Miller v Jackson* (1977),[147] re D's cricket club, the Court of Appeal split entirely – a majority (Lord Denning dissenting) held that public benefit was not relevant to liability (so that a nuisance was upheld), but a different majority (Lane LJ dissenting) held that it could be relevant to an assessment of remedy (in denying C injunctive relief to stop play at the cricket club, and leaving C to his remedy in damages). Much earlier, in *Adams v Ursell*

[144] [2010] EWHC 1538 (TCC) [77]–[78] (finding of nuisance not appealed: [2011] EWCA Civ 804). Anti-social behaviour by D towards C was also the subject of a claim under the Protection from Harassment Act 1997.
[145] [2011] EWCA Civ 987, [2011] Env LR 34 (CA). [146] [1981] QB 88 (CA). [147] [1977] QB 966 (CA).

(1913),[148] the public benefit provided by D's fish-and-chips shop 'to the poor people who get food at his shop', did not preclude a successful action in private nuisance because of the odours caused by cooking the fish.

The modern view is that the public interest provided by D's activities is not an outright defence to a claim of nuisance (per Lord Carnwath in *Coventry v Lawrence*[149]). However, it does appear to retain some relevance to the balancing exercise required for an assessment of 'unreasonable user', although its weighting may be very slight. For example, in *Barr v Biffa*,[150] the Court of Appeal stated that the factor has (at its highest) 'very little significance'; while, in *Transco plc v Stockport MBC*, the House of Lords held, in dicta, that it 'cannot be taken too far' as to the extent to which public interest could be taken into account in the balancing exercise.

Certainly, there have been some significant cases (below) in which D was carrying out an activity of public interest, and yet C succeeded in proving an actionable private nuisance against D – indicating that the factor does not have much influence in the assessment of what constitutes an 'unreasonable user'.

> In *Halsey v Esso Petroleum Co Ltd*,[151] re the noxious fumes from Esso's oil storage depot, Esso had turned their total through-put to fuel oil, expressly with Government encouragement, and it was this change which created the nuisance, because when the heavier grades of oil were heated, they produced more smell. In *Barr v Biffa Waste Services Ltd*,[152] re the odours arising from Biffa's waste treatment and tipping site, it was acknowledged that the activities of Biffa did 'provid[e] a necessary, indeed vital, environmental service', in treating and disposing of residential and industrial waste. However, an actionable private nuisance was still capable of being proven (said the Court of Appeal – whether that would ultimately be proven was a matter of referral back to trial, if the matter could not be mediated to a conclusion). In *Dennis v MOD*,[153] Mr and Mrs Dennis, C, owned a large country estate, Walcott Hall Estate, of 1,387 acres, adjoining the RAF Wittering airbase, which was the oldest operational RAF base in England. It was a training base for pilots for the Harrier Jump Jets, which entailed low-altitude noisy flying ('no-one convincingly suggested that there is a noiser [aircraft]'). The MOD's activities were a nuisance in law, notwithstanding the clear public interest in the training of pilots at RAF Wittering for the purposes of the national defence ('defence of the realm is ... to everyone's advantage').

However, in the most recent private nuisance case to go before the Supreme Court, the factor received some judicial support in dicta, in assisting to preclude any action for private nuisance:[154]

> In *Coventry v Lawrence*, Lord Carnwath gave the following hypothetical example: C buys a house beside a major football stadium. There is significant disturbance to his domestic life on match days, but the crowd and traffic control, etc, is subjected to proper measures by the public authorities, including the police, to ensure that the disturbance is contained as far as reasonably practicable. C could not sue for private nuisance, because society attaches importance to having places for professional football within urban areas, and the facility is regarded as being socially important. C could only sue if the organisation, or lack thereof, took the disturbance beyond what was reasonable.

148 [1913] 1 Ch 269 (Ch) 271.
149 [2014] UKSC 13, [193].
150 [2012] EWCA Civ 312, [31], [36] (Carnwath LJ).
151 [1961] 1 WLR 683 (CA) 695–96.
152 [2012] EWCA Civ 312, [31], citing: the trial judge, [2011] EWHC 1003 (TCC) [388] (Coulson J).
153 [2003] EWHC 793, [84], [91]–[92] (Buckley J).
154 [2014] UKSC 13, [185].

Malice

§16.20 Where D acts with malicious intent towards C, that factor points towards an 'unreasonable user' in the balancing assessment.

Malice on D's part will not be conclusive in proving an 'unreasonable user' – but it is relevant to the question of whether D has committed an actionable nuisance (per *Hollywood Silver Fox Farm Ltd v Emmett*[155]). Of course, malice will not be present in 'the vast majority of cases. All the same it is not inconceivable' (per Lord Cooke in *Hunter v Canary Wharf Ltd*[156]).

> In *Hollywood Silver Fox Farm v Emmett*, the owners of the farm, C, bred silver foxes. During breeding, and if agitated, the foxes tended to kill and eat their young. Mr Emmett, D, a neighbour, objected to the foxes, and fired his gun on his own land, but close to their pens, with the intent of disturbing them. This reduced their breeding numbers significantly. **Held:** an actionable nuisance. The malicious intent behind D's actions rendered his use of his land most unreasonable.

The effect of planning permission

§16.21 Where planning permission for D's activities has been granted, and D acts within the bounds of that planning permission, that does not provide D with an automatic defence against an action in private nuisance. The planning authority has no authority to license or to sanction a nuisance. However, the terms of that planning permission, and the extent of D's (non) compliance with those terms, is a relevant factor when assessing whether D was committing an 'unreasonable user'.

Where C's use and enjoyment of his land is adversely affected by D's acting in accordance with a planning permission, then D has no absolute defence; and where D has breached planning permission, C has no automatic claim for private nuisance. The legal position is far more nuanced than that.

Not a defence. Why is planning permission, granting D authorisation to commit the very nuisance now complained of by C, not an absolute defence? After all, in *Coventry v Lawrence*,[157] Lord Carnwath made the point that the system of planning permissions, issued according to local government law, 'exists to protect and promote the public interest', and that Parliament has, by virtue of modern planning legislation, established a statutory framework for planning permission. In the same case,[158] the Court of Appeal described how that framework delegates to the local planning authority the task of balancing the interests of the community against those of individuals, and of balancing the conflicting interests between individuals. C can object to proposals for planning permissions, and planning authorities make their decisions, acknowledging that granting planning permission for a particular use in an area may prejudice some local residents in the quiet enjoyment of their properties. (In *Coventry*, the local authority reports 1992–2002 showed that the officers had given 'careful consideration ... to the differing interests of those who lived in the locality' – from the need to protect residents close to the moto-cross track from undue noise disturbance, to the recognition that a motocross facility performed a valuable social function for 'young people whose skills were mechanical rather than academic or who needed to 'blow off' their energies away from public roads.') There was also rights of appeal and/or inquiry, and of judicial review from a Minister's final planning

155 [1936] 2 KB 468. Similarly: *Christie v Davey* [1893] 1 Ch 316.

156 [1997] AC 655 (HL) 721, and referring to both *Davey* and *Silver Fox Farm*, *ibid.*

157 [2014] UKSC 13, [193].

158 *Moto-land UK Ltd v Lawrence* [2012] EWCA Civ 26, [21]–[22], [53] (Jackson LJ), citing: *Planning System: General Principles* (Office of the Deputy Prime Minister, 2005) [29].

decision. Hence, the planning process already provides the aggrieved resident, C, with several avenues for self-protection.

Additionally, some cases certainly illustrate that, where D has complied with planning permission, there was a 'reasonable user' (and no actionable nuisance) – taking into account the steps *which had already occurred*, in the planning authority's decision-making process, in seeking to balance the competing interests of C and D.

> In *Hunter v Canary Wharf Ltd*,[159] re the complaints from residents in the London Docklands area that the large building, One Canada Square, interfered with their television reception: D had constructed their building in accordance with the planning permission which had been granted for the Docklands redevelopment. The Secretary of State had created an 'enterprise zone', of a scale to 'totally transform the environment', and '[a]lthough [the Canary Wharf Tower] did interfere with television reception, the Canary Wharf Tower must ... be accepted as a reasonable development in all the circumstances'.
> In *Hirose Electrical UK Ltd v Peak Ingredients Ltd*,[160] facts previously, both C and D conducted their businesses on the Crownhill light industrial estate precisely in accordance with the terms of their planning permission. 'The light industrial character of that Estate covered D's food additive manufacturing, which was permitted on both planning grounds and by the user covenant in its lease'.

However, the current position in English law is that, even if D adheres strictly to the terms of the planning permission, that does **not** constitute an absolute defence in private nuisance. An action in private nuisance is still available. The key reasons for this view are two-fold (per *Coventry v Lawrence*[161]). First, planning authorities have to take into account **many** considerations – the effect of the proposed development on neighbouring residents, the public interest, and the political and economic consequences of granting the application. The last-mentioned of these, however, is irrelevant to the question of an 'unreasonable user' under private nuisance claims, and hence, whatever the planning authority determines cannot be conclusive of C's rights in private nuisance. Secondly, a planning authority is entitled to make its decision on the assumption that residents in the area will still be able to pursue claims for private nuisance: 'it could not be expected to take on itself the role of deciding a neighbour's common law rights'. Earlier, in *Hunter v Canary Wharf Ltd* too, Lord Hoffmann noted that it would be 'wrong to allow the private rights of [C] to be taken away by a permission granted by the planning authority to the developer'.[162]

The principle does have the curious effect that planning permission may be granted by a planning authority, D complies with that planning permission in every particular, his development causes a substantial interference with the use and enjoyment of C's neighbouring property, C sues in private nuisance, and is then able to obtain damages and/or injunctive relief against D, thereby undermining the planning process.

Relevance. Even though it is not an outright defence, the grant of planning permission may be relevant to the balancing exercise required for the element of 'unreasonable user', in limited respects.

i. If the planning authority grants permission for the use/development, on the basis that D's activity is acceptable between certain hours, on certain days, or at certain maximum decibel levels, then that can assist with the assessment of whether an 'unreasonable user' has occurred: '[w]hile the decision whether the activity causes a nuisance to C is not for the planning authority but for the court, the existence and terms of the permission are not irrelevant

159 [1997] UKHL 14, [1997] AC 655 (HL) 722 (Lord Cooke).

160 [2011] EWCA Civ 987, [2011] Env LR 34 (CA), quote at [40].

161 [2014] UKSC 13, [95] (Lord Neuberger).

162 [1997] UKHL 14, [1997] AC 655 (HL) 710.

as a matter of law' (per Lord Neuberger in *Coventry v Lawrence*[163]). The various statements from members of the public, either in support of or against the planning application, may also be useful evidence as to what disruption might be caused by uses included in that planning permission.

In *Coventry v Lawrence*, facts previously, **held:** an actionable private nuisance. The levels of noise emitted from the stadium and track constituted a nuisance at intermittent times. The planning permissions granted in respect of the use of the stadium and track did not provide a defence for D. But those permissions were not entirely irrelevant either. The evidence of supporters and objectors to the planning application had properly been taken into account by the trial judge. An order should be made to limit the level of noise to a specified level (and not to shut the track and stadium down). The Supreme Court reinstated the trial judge's order (the CA had overturned his decision[164]), subject to a later decision to suspend the injunction until Fenland was restored and fit for occupation, given that the house was rendered uninhabitable by a major fire before the trial was heard.

ii. If D has **not** complied with any relevant terms of the planning permission, then whilst C does **not** have an automatic claim in private nuisance available to him, it is relevant to the question of an 'unreasonable user'. In *Biffa*, the Court of Appeal remarked that '[a]n activity which is conducted in contravention of planning controls is unlikely to be reasonable',[165] while in *Coventry*, the Court of Appeal noted that, if D either ignored a breach of condition notices issued by an authority, or conducted their business at noise levels above those permitted by the planning permissions, then C 'might have been able to make out a case in nuisance'[166] (an observation which was not adversely commented upon on appeal). However, both observations were dicta: neither D had contravened planning permissions in those cases.

§16.22 The status of the so-called '*Gillingham* principle' remains somewhat unsettled. That principle states that, once planning permission has been granted and the nature of the locality changes, then it is the *prevailing* nature of the locality, and not the *historical* locality (i.e., how the neighbourhood used to be, prior to permission being granted) which is the character against which D's interference must be judged. The changed character of the locality does not afford D an outright defence; but it will be relevant to an assessment of whether D's activities were an 'unreasonable user'. It is a question of fact and degree as to whether the character of the locality changed as a result of the planning permission.

The principle and its applications. The basis of the '*Gillingham* principle' (named after the decision of Buckley J in *Gillingham BC v Medway (Chatham) Dock Co Ltd*[167]) was that the effect of a grant of planning permission could not be ignored, when judging whether D's activities were truly beyond the 'give and take' expected of those living in that locality. However, if taken into account, then it could render C's task in proving an 'unreasonable user' much harder, because D's activities were being judged against that new character. Judicially, the principle was expressed (post-*Gillingham*) along the lines that planning permission which changes the use of land in an area may 'so alter the nature and character of the locality as to shift the standard of reasonable user which governs the question of nuisance' (per Morritt VC in *Watson v Croft Promo-Sport Ltd*[168]), or 'may render innocent the nuisance' (per Pill LJ in

[163] [2014] UKSC 13, [96]. [164] [2012] EWCA Civ 26. [165] [2012] EWCA Civ 312, [76].
[166] [2012] EWCA 26, [75]. [167] [1993] QB 343. [168] [2009] EWCA Civ 15, [31]–[32].

Hunter v Canary Wharf Ltd,[169] and approved by Lord Cooke on appeal[170]). However, whether that character had indeed changed as a result of the planning permission was always a question of fact and of degree.

The character of the locality **did** change as a result of planning permission, so as to render D's activities a 'reasonable user' (and not actionable in nuisance), in *Gillingham* itself.

> In *Gillingham BC v Medway (Chatham) Dock Co Ltd*,[171] planning permission was granted for the development of a commercial port on the site of the disused Chatham Royal Naval Dockyard in 1983. The only access to the port was by two residential streets. The permission was granted, over the objections of numerous residents, because the economic benefits of the port were adjudged by the planning authority to outweigh the disruption to local residents. However, it was realised that, to make it financially successful, the port needed to operate on a 24-hour basis, and that permission was granted in 1988. This resulted in heavy traffic at all hours of the day and night, seriously disturbing local residents. The Council then had a change of heart, and brought an action in public nuisance on behalf of the residents against the port operators (based upon a series of private nuisances being suffered by those Cs). **Held**: no actionable nuisance. The noise and lorry activity was the inevitable result of the planning permission granted in 1983, whereupon the nature of the locality had changed.

However, there are other post-*Gillingham* cases in which the court concluded that the character of the locality had **not** changed materially, notwithstanding that planning permission had been granted – so that when D's activities were judged against the standards of that locality, a nuisance was proven:

> In *Watson v Croft Promo-Sport Ltd*,[172] D used a WWII airfield for motor-racing. Permission had been granted in 1963 for that purpose, subject to conditions. The track was used about 10 times per year, and caused the local residents little disruption. However, in 1998, the local planning authority granted new planning permission for the motor-racing circuit, including a limit on the number of days' use (110 days) by reference to noise levels N1-N5, including noisier activities at levels N2-N4 on certain days per year which involved vehicle testing and high-speed racing all day. Local residents sued in nuisance, regarding the N2-N4 days of usage. An actionable nuisance was proven, because the introduction and intensification of motor-racing and the gradual development of the track, following the 1963 and 1998 permissions, had not altered the essentially rural character of the neighbourhood. D's activities were nuisance-making, when having regard to that rural locality.
> In *Barr v Biffa Waste Services Ltd*,[173] planning permission for tipping of industrial and household waste at Westmill was granted by the district council to D (Biffa) in April 1980. Tipping commenced in 1984, and was uncontroversial. Then, a Waste Management permit for tipping of 'pre-treated waste' was granted by the Environment Agency in 2003, and from that point on, the smells became much worse from the landfill site. An actionable private nuisance was again proven, and *Gillingham* was distinguished. The 2003 permit did not change the essential character of the neighbourhood, which had long included tipping, but it did introduce a more offensive form of waste, and a new type of smell emission, for nearby residents. That permit did not, and could not, authorise the emission of such smells, which were a new and offensive addition to the locality. In *Wheeler v JJ Saunders*,

[169] Cited at: [1997] AC 655 (HL) 669.

[170] [1997] AC 655 (HL) 722 (while 'compliance with planning permission is not in itself a defence to a nuisance act, it could change the character of the neighbourhood by which the standard of reasonable user fell to be judged').

[171] [1993] QB 343. [172] [2009] EWCA Civ 15, [35]–[40]. [173] [2012] EWCA Civ 312, [46(iii)].

JJ Saunders, D, obtained planning permission for two new buildings to be used on a pig farm, for intensive pig breeding. A bad smell from the farm affected a wide area of the neighbourhood. The farm was only 11 m from Mr Wheeler's, C's, house. According to Govt guidelines, there should have been 100 m distance from the nearest residence. An actionable nuisance was proven, and damages and an injunction awarded, to restrain the use of the new buildings for pig breeding. The grant of planning permission did not change the character of the 'neighbourhood'. This was 'not a strategic planning decision affected by considerations of public interest', because it was not authorising a new large-scale development (and hence, *Gillingham* was distinguished).

Hence, it by no means followed, from the *Gillingham* principle, that a claim in private nuisance was unavailable to C, even if the character of the neighbourhood had changed.

Doubts about the *Gillingham* principle. Nevertheless, there were some judicial doubts expressed as to the limits – and even the correctness – of the principle.

In *Wheeler v JJ Saunders Ltd*,[174] Peter Gibson LJ emphasised that the principle should **not** be taken to extinguish an action for private nuisance brought by aggrieved Cs – especially where planning permissions were 'as a result of administrative decisions which cannot be appealed and are difficult to challenge';[175] Sir John May said that, whatever *Gillingham's* authority may be, a court could not treat the grant of planning permission for D's activities as the equivalent of a statutory authority, 'even in a limited sense'; while Staughton LJ remarked that, to rely upon the *Gillingham* principle, D must point to 'a strategic planning decision [which was] affected by considerations of public interest' (and the permission for the pig farm building in *Wheeler* itself was not in that category, given that it concerned such a small area).

In *Barr v Biffa Waste Services Ltd*,[176] Carnwath LJ said that the scope of the *Gillingham* principle 'remains unsettled', but that it could not be applied, to protect D from the nuisance-causing activities associated with the Westfill tipping site, for several reasons. The aforementioned 'strategic planning decision' had not occurred here. The *Gillingham* principle could only apply when the *whole balance of uses* in the neighbourhood changed, but not when the permit concerned the regulation of *one particular activity* within the neighbourhood. In addition, *Gillingham* was distinguished, in that here, there had been no detailed consultation on the likely adverse implications of the planning permit in terms of odour, nor any balancing of the conflicting interests of the residents and the public interest in land-filling; and as a matter of law, there was no authority for extending the *Gillingham* principle to a waste permit granted by an Environment Agency, and not by the planning authority.

Hence, these decisions markedly circumscribed the scope and application of the principle.

The division in the Supreme Court. The current status of the *Gillingham* principle – and when the court can, or should, have regard to the change in uses, and the character of the locality, brought about by planning permission – has been left in a state of some uncertainty by the Supreme Court decision in *Coventry v Lawrence*. Although the separate members of the Supreme Court came to the same result (an actionable nuisance was proven), they were divided on this point.[177]

174 [1996] Ch 19 (CA) 30 (Staughton LJ), 35 (Peter Gibson LJ), 37–38 (Sir John May).

175 [1996] Ch 19 (CA) 35. 176 [2012] EWCA Civ 312, quote at [81], reasoning at [75] and [82].

177 [2014] UKSC 13, [223], [232] (Lord Carnwath), [84]–[97] (Lord Neuberger), [165] (Lord Mance), [156] (Lord Sumption). Whether Lord Clarke agreed with Lord Carnwath or with Lord Neuberger on this point is not entirely clear: [169].

Lord Carnwath thought that the *Gillingham* principle should apply **only** in 'exceptional cases', where there has been such a 'strategic' or 'major' development, altering the character of an entire neighbourhood, that it 'cannot sensibly be ignored in assessing the character of the area against which the acceptability of D's activity is to be judged'. On the facts, his Lordship did not regard the permissions granted to operate the motocross circuit and the stadium to be 'strategic planning decisions' of the type found in *Gillingham*, and hence, the principle did not apply, and the character of the locality had not changed by virtue of the planning permissions. There was an actionable nuisance.

On the other hand, Lord Neuberger (with whom Lords Mance and Sumption agreed on this point) plainly disapproved of the principle altogether, stating that its reasoning 'cannot stand', and that, 'the mere fact that the activity which is said to give rise to the nuisance has the benefit of a planning permission is normally of no assistance to D' in a private nuisance action. Lord Neuberger did not agree that distinctions should (or could) be drawn between 'strategic planning decisions' (where the principle would apply) compared to others (where it would not), or between permissions that related to large areas (where the principle would apply) compared to small areas (where it would not). Hence, under this view, the fact that a planning permission had been granted which facilitated D's activities would be almost irrelevant.

However, where all judges did agree was that the existence of planning permission for D's activity was pertinent to the remedy to be granted to C (whether damages or an injunction in lieu). This is discussed later, under 'Remedies'.

Thus, summing up: the fact that D was complying with planning permission can never operate as a complete defence. Even if planning permission has been granted to enable D's activities, the courts have shown a tendency not to hold that the character of the environment changed as a result, thereby making C's task easier in proving private nuisance. If the character of a neighbourhood has indeed changed as a result of planning permission (as one of Lord Carnwath's 'exceptional cases'), then the better view is that it can still only constitute one factor in the assessment of 'unreasonable user'.

'Coming to the nuisance'

§16.23 Where C moves to a locality where D's activity is already established, and C then complains that D's activity constitutes a nuisance, the fact that C has 'come to the nuisance' does not constitute a defence for D. However, where C changes the purpose for which his land is used, after D's nuisance starts, and then complains that D's activities constituted a nuisance, the defence could apply (at least where the nuisance causes C intangible interference rather than physical damage).

The general principle. Where C 'comes to the nuisance', i.e., moves to the neighbourhood in which D operates and which already had its noises, dust, smells, vibrations, etc, and then C complains that D's activities cause him inconvenience, D may still be found liable in nuisance – even though D was 'first in time' in the neighbourhood. Although such a result may seem unfair to D, English law is adamant – 'it is no defence that [C] came to the nuisance' (per Lord Goff in *Hunter v Canary Wharf Ltd*[178]).

That principle was evident in the leading 19th-century cases of *St Helens Smelting Co v Tipping*[179] and *Sturges v Bridgman*,[180] and was approved by majority in *Miller v Jackson* in 1977

[178] [1997] AC 655 (HL) 682. [179] (1865) 11 HL Cas 642. [180] (1879) LR 11 Ch D 852.

(but sustained a notable dissent by Lord Denning MR, in which that judge held blameworthy 'the thoughtless and selfish act of an estate developer in building right up to the edge of [D's existing cricket ground]'[181]). It remains the law today (per the 2014 Supreme Court decision in *Coventry v Lawrence*[182]).

The draconian effect of the principle has been borne out in the case law. It means that a business or activity of D which has historically been carried on in that neighbourhood can be stopped by injunctive order; or that D, who had improved his premises to provide more amenity for his customers, could be ordered to pay significant damages for the nuisance caused by those activities, where no complaint had been made before C elected to move to the neighbourhood. However, in *Coventry v Lawrence*,[183] the principle was justified on the bases that, as a property-based tort, C's right to complain about D's activities should 'run with the land'; and that whether D's activity constitutes a nuisance should not depend upon whether his neighbour changed. Hence, in the following cases, C who 'came to the nuisance' succeeded in making out the tort.

In *Sturges v Bridgman*,[184] Mr Bridgman, D, occupied a house in Wigmore Street, which he used in his business as a confectioner. In the kitchen of his house (at the rear), he used two large mortars in which meat and other materials were pounded. This carried on for over 20 years. Dr Sturges, C, a doctor, occupied a house in Wimpole Street, and his garden backed onto D's land. In 1873, C built a consulting room in his garden, and C's surgery shared a wall with D's premises. From that point onwards, the pounding of the mortars caused a level of noise and vibration which seriously inconvenienced C in the use of his consulting-room. D argued that he had acquired the right to carry out his nuisance-making activity, by prescription, by uninterrupted user for about 60 years before the litigation was brought. However, nuisance was found, and an injunction was awarded to stop the nuisance. In *Dobson v Thames Water Utilities Ltd*,[185] various residents, C, lived near to the Mogden Sewage Treatment Works in Isleworth, Middlesex, owned and operated by Thames Water, D. C sued in nuisance for swarms of mosquitoes attracted by the treatment works. The fact that C came to live there, with the treatment works already established, did not preclude a private nuisance from occurring: '[it] does not mean that the mere fact that [C's] houses have been built around the boundary of [D's established] sewage treatment works at Mogden means that odour from the sewage treatment works cannot be a nuisance'. In *Miller v Jackson*,[186] C's house was built at the edge of D's cricket ground, in a new housing estate, built in 1972. C was apprehensive of being hit by cricket balls emanating from the ground (players had hit balls out of the ground onto the housing estate about 8–9 times a season, which were 'like thunderbolts from heaven'). The cricket club had been established since 1905, i.e., over 70 years before C's house was built. Nuisance was proven. It was 'no answer to a claim in nuisance for D to show that C brought the trouble on his own head by building or coming to live in a house so close to D's premises that he would inevitably be affected by D's activities, where no one had been affected previously'.

Caveat. However, according to Supreme Court dicta in *Coventry v Lawrence*,[187] the principle is very dependent upon *timing*. Lord Neuberger observed that D cannot claim that 'C came to the nuisance', when C uses his land for essentially the same purpose as that for which it was used

[181] [1977] 1 QB 966 (CA) 976–78. [182] [2014] UKSC 13, [51] (Lord Neuberger). [183] *ibid*, [52].

[184] (1879) LR 11 Ch D 852. [185] [2011] EWHC 3253 (TCC) [946], and with quote at [689].

[186] [1977] 1 QB 966 (CA) 986–87 (Lane LJ, with Cumming-Bruce LJ concurring; Denning LJ dissented, holding that there was no nuisance, given that C had 'come to the nuisance', and was perhaps overly-sensitive).

[187] [2014] UKSC 13, [51].

before D's nuisance started. However, if C changes the use of his land, or builds something new on his land, *after* D's activities started, and then complains that D's already-established activities constitute a nuisance, Lord Neuberger suggested that a defence of 'coming to the nuisance' **should** apply for D's benefit.

However, were it to do so, that would also *prima facie* suggest that the older cases of *Sturges* and *Miller v Jackson* should have been decided differently – given that D's activities there (the pounding of the meat, and operating the cricket club, respectively) each started decades before C's change of use (i.e., constructing the consulting-room, and building a new house). On the basis of Lord Neuberger's caveat above, both Cs should have 'come to the nuisance'. However, Lord Neuberger sought to rationalise their outcomes, by specifying five criteria[188] as to when C could be said to 'come to the nuisance', thus providing D with a good defence – D's activity:

i. caused an intangible interference, affecting C's senses – nuisances which caused physical damage to C's land (as with the flying cricket balls in *Miller v Jackson*, or the vibration damage in *Sturges*) may not take advantage of the defence;
ii. was not a nuisance before C built something or changed the use of his land;
iii. was a lawful use of D's land;
iv. was carried out in a reasonable way; and
v. caused no greater nuisance or extent of interference than when C built the new thing or changed the use of his land.

However, whilst this dicta opens up the prospect of 'coming to the nuisance' as a successful defence, it has yet to be applied or tested in a directly-relevant scenario.

In *Coventry v Lawrence*,[189] facts previously, C purchased Fenland and 'came to the nuisance', in that D's motor-racing activities at the stadium and motocross track were already well established. However, any defence could not apply, as C used Fenland as a residence, which was exactly the same purpose to which the premises had been put since before D's activities had started.

The role of negligence

According to Lord Wilberforce in *Goldman v Hargrave*, 'the tort of nuisance ... may comprise a wide variety of situations, in some of which negligence plays no part, in others of which it is decisive'.[190] In fact, the scenarios in which negligence is relevant in the tort of nuisance are quite exceptional.

General rule

§16.24 Three points are generally pertinent to the relationship between private nuisance and negligence: (1) to prove an actionable private nuisance, C does *not* have to prove that D was negligent in carrying out his activities; an 'unreasonable user' can occur without any negligence at all; (2) absence of any negligence is ***not*** a defence on D's part; and (3) whether D committed any negligence in its activities is irrelevant to the balancing exercise required to assess an 'unreasonable user'.

In that sense, liability for private nuisance is said to be strict – an 'unreasonable user', and hence the tort, can be proven, without any negligence on D's part (per *Barr v Biffa Waste*

[188] *ibid*, [56]. If one of these failed, however, C's claim in nuisance would not be 'bound to succeed'.
[189] Although the point did not strictly need deciding, *ibid*, [55].
[190] [1967] 1 AC 645 (PC, on appeal from Australia) 657.

Services Ltd[191]). In *Transco plc v Stockport MBC* (in which a nuisance claim was rejected), Lord Hoffmann confirmed that: '[l]iability in nuisance is strict, in the sense that one has no right to carry on an activity which unreasonably interferes with a neighbour's use of land, merely because one is doing it with reasonable care'.[192] In the earlier case of *Read v J Lyons & Co Ltd* (in 1947), Lord Simonds said much the same: 'if a man commits a legal nuisance, it is no answer to his injured neighbour that he took the utmost care not to commit it. There the liability is strict'.[193] In *Cambridge Water v Eastern Counties Leather*, Lord Goff also affirmed the principle: 'if the user is not reasonable, [D] will be liable, even though he may have exercised reasonable care and skill to avoid it'.[194] The following cases bear out the point, where a private nuisance was indeed proven:

> In *Barr v Biffa Waste*,[195] facts previously, that D, the waste treatment operator, exercised reasonable care, and used 'the best practicable means' to stop the spread of odour, was no defence. In *Dobson v Thames Water Utilities Ltd*,[196] facts previously, D was not negligent in the way in which it dealt with mosquitoes which were present at, or bred at, its Modgen treatment works, and indeed, the court found that D exercised reasonable skill and care to deal with those mosquitoes.

Notably, a statutory nuisance claim may be brought by the local authority against D under s 79 of the Environmental Protection Act 1990 – and under that Act, D can rely on a defence that he employed 'the best practicable means' to combat the effects of the nuisance (per s 80(7) of the EPA). However, the *Biffa* case (in which both a s 79 suit and a private nuisance claim were brought) demonstrates that such provision has no effect on the common law position, if D is sued for private nuisance arising out of the same fact situation.

Exception: failure-to-abate nuisances

§16.25 Where D fails to abate the interference or escape of a naturally-occurring or man-made hazard onto C's land, then, exceptionally, proof of an actionable nuisance requires C to prove that D was negligent in not abating that hazard, according to 'the *Leakey* principle'.

In nuisance cases of this type, negligence is most certainly relevant: '[t]he tort is nuisance, and the test of liability is whether there was negligence, and the standard of care is to be shaped by the personal capabilities and circumstances of [D]' (per *Dobson v Thames Water Utilities Ltd*[197]). However, the scope of this exception, in which negligence on D's part is required, is narrowly-cast – it only applies to failure-to-abate hazards.

In this context, D owes C a 'measured duty of care' (to adopt the term used by Lord Wilberforce in *Goldman v Hargrave*[198]) – also called the '*Leakey* duty' in *Green v Somerleyton*,[199] after the eponymous case of *Leakey v National Trust for Places of Historic Interest or Natural Beauty*[200]). Breach of that duty will expose D to action by C in both negligence and nuisance (per *Delaware Mansions v Westminster CC*[201]). The scenario is one of the unusual instances in English law of a positive duty being cast upon D to do something to avert a hazard. The general rule that there is no duty to act to fix a mere omission (discussed in Chapter 3) is subject to this *Leakey* 'measured duty of care'.

191 [2012] EWCA Civ 312, [46(iv)]. 192 [2003] UKHL 61, [2004] 2 AC 1, [26]. 193 [1947] AC 156 (HL) 183.
194 [1994] 2 AC 264 (HL) 299. 195 [2012] EWCA Civ 312, [376], [382], [460].
196 [2011] EWHC 3253 (TCC) [948]–[949]. 197 [2011] EWHC 3253 (TCC) [944].
198 [1967] 1 AC 645 (PC, on appeal from Australia) 653, 662. 199 [2003] EWCA Civ 198, [52].
200 [1980] QB 485 (CA). 201 [2001] UKHL 55, [2002] 1 AC 321, [31].

§16.26 The *Leakey* principle requires C to prove that:

i. D knew of the hazard which did, or could, encroach onto C's land;
ii. D knew, or should reasonably have foreseen, that if he did not abate the hazard, then it could cause damage to C's use and enjoyment of his land (and D must have foreseen the extent of the damage to C too); and
iii. D was able to abate the hazard by taking reasonable measures – where the resources, capabilities and circumstances of D must be taken into account when deciding whether D acted reasonably.

These three principles, affirmed in *Holbeck Hall Hotel v Scarborough BC*,[202] require some teasing out, by reference to leading case law:

i. The hazard. The hazard can be natural or man-made. The *Leakey* duty has applied (or potentially applied) to tree-roots (*Delaware*), floodwater (*Green v Somerleyton*), fire (*Goldman v Hargrave*), a mound of naturally-occurring earth (*Leakey* itself) and a defective wall (*Birmingham Development Co Ltd v Tyler*).

There is no distinction drawn, for the purposes of the *Leakey* duty, between man-made and naturally-occurring hazards. This is for a practical reason, as much as for a legal one. The point was made in *Green v Somerleyton* (where the allegation was that C's marshes had flooded due to water encroaching from D's marshes and lake) that '[t]he landscape, as most English landscape, is man-made. The lake, although probably natural in origin, had its present extent and contours determined by peat extraction in the Middle Ages or earlier'.[203] Hence, what may seem like a naturally-occurring feature might, on closer historical or physical examination, turn out to be man-made, so that any distinction between 'natural' and 'artificial' 'is an inherently uncertain foundation on which to rest a decision as to the existence of liability in nuisance'.[204] It has been more satisfactory, legally-speaking, not to differentiate at all.

In *Green v Somerleyton*, Lord Somerleyton, and Trustees set up to administer his estate, D, were alleged to have breached the *Leakey* duty. Water emanated from a lake, flowing from their land Scale Marshes, through culverts under the A143 road, and onto Mr Green's, C's, lower land, the Priory Marshes. **Held**: the *Leakey* duty could apply to naturally-flowing water, and D owed the *Leakey* duty to C. However, there was no breach of the duty by D. Under a deed of agreement between the parties, they were both aware of the clear propensities of the marshes to flood, and of the need to drain Scale Marshes into Priory Marshes, and then to pump water into the river, and the agreement set out the respective responsibilities of C and D, re providing and operating the pumps. That was sufficient to discharge the *Leakey* duty, and D was not liable for the flooding.

The hazard may not have actually encroached, and yet, D can *still* be liable in private nuisance and negligence, under the *Leakey* principle. A dilapidated or unstable structure may simply exist on D's property as a hazard, and interfere with C's use and enjoyment of his land. In such a case, without any actual encroachment, C must prove that his fear of the danger was 'real' (i.e., 'well founded', requiring C to prove, on the balance of probabilities, that the threatened hazard presented a danger to C). A subjective belief on C's part is **not** sufficient to trigger the *Leakey* duty. If C's fear was about a non-existent danger (no matter how genuine and honest C's belief may have been), then D could hardly be expected to know of the danger, as the first element of the *Leakey* duty requires. Hence, no complaint of private nuisance can lie.

[202] [2000] QB 836, [39], [42], [46] (Stuart-Smith LJ). [203] [2003] EWCA Civ 198, [39]. [204] *ibid*, [81].

In *Birmingham Devp Co Ltd v Tyler*[205] Birmingham Devp Co, C, was apprehensive about two defects in a flank wall of Mr Tyler's, D's, neighbouring factory, which C felt was in imminent danger of collapsing. C (supported by its expert advisers) had an honest and reasonable fear that part of D's factory flank wall presented a danger to the safety of C's site, causing C to cease use of part of the site. **Held**: no actionable nuisance. This type of interference can be actionable if C has to 'live in the shadow of such a danger', or the interference prevents C from using part of his property 'for fear of what will happen, if there is a collapse', or it requires C to leave altogether. However, here – and regardless of C's genuine, subjective fear that the wall was dangerous – the wall never presented any actual danger at all; C's honest fears were unfounded. Hence, it was legally untenable that D should be answerable for C's concern, and should have to carry out, at his own expense, unnecessary works to make safe that which was already safe. C's concerns were 'caused by the jumping to wrong conclusions by BDC and the experts, not one of whom carried out a professional examination of the supposed problem'.

Also, it does not matter, for the purposes of the *Leakey* duty, that a man-made structure was not a hazard when it was built, but became so after a period. However, once the structure **has** become a hazard, there is a duty on D to abate the nuisance created by the structure.

In *Bybrook Barn Centre Ltd v Kent CC*,[206] Bybrook, C, owned a garden centre in Kent, but the premises were flooded and seriously damaged when Bockhanger Dyke burst its banks in 1996. A culvert built by the Council, D, as highway authority, was unable to take the quantity of water flowing down the dyke. When constructed in 1969, the culvert was adequate to carry the natural flow of water within the dyke, but with changes upstream in the catchment area (e.g., the construction of the M20 motorway), that had increased the amount, and rate of flow, of water in the dyke. D became aware, in 1990, that the culvert was no longer able to handle the quantity of water flowing down the dyke, but did not widen the culvert. **Held:** where D has constructed a culvert which was not a hazard when it was constructed, but becomes so through external factors beyond D's control, D is under a duty to enlarge the culvert: '[t]he highway authority had the means of preventing the flooding by enlarging the culvert at some cost, but basically without great difficulty'.

ii. Foreseeability of damage to C's property. The risk of damage arising from D's acts or omissions must have been known, or reasonably foreseeable. Otherwise, a reasonable D would not have done anything to abate the nuisance, to prevent the interference to C's use and enjoyment of his land. D's actual knowledge of the hazard and the risk that it posed has been proven in some cases (*Goldman v Hargrave* being one such example, below). However, more usually, the query will be whether the risk of damage was reasonably foreseeable, i.e., there was a 'real risk' of damage (per *Berent v Family Mosaic Housing*[207]).

Encroaching tree roots can cause particular legal (as well as building) problems, because D will not know of the actual interference being caused to C's premises from the encroachment, given that the danger is latent (i.e., below ground, and non-obvious). In that event, constructive knowledge of the hazards which the tree roots of particular trees may pose – gleaned from information that would have put a reasonable D on enquiry about a hazard being posed – will suffice (per *Berent v Family Mosaic Housing*[208]). It is not enough to fix D with sufficient knowledge, however, to point to a mature plane tree, on London clay soils, of larger-than-usual size,

[205] [2008] EWCA Civ 859, [54]. [206] [2000] EWCA Civ 299, [46].
[207] [2012] EWCA Civ 961, [15], [20]. [208] [2011] EWHC 1353 (TCC), aff'd: [2012] EWCA Civ 961.

and say that D is therefore on notice that there was a risk that the roots of that tree may have encroached upon the foundations of C's neighbouring property, and that D should be fixed with liability in nuisance: '[t]hat would be arguably an argument that is far too wide and would ... amount almost to strict liability' (per *Kirk v Brent LBC*[209]). Nevertheless, an absence of any knowledge of the hazard will preclude liability in nuisance. In this regard, at least, liability in private nuisance is not strict; D cannot be liable for interferences of which he has no requisite knowledge.

In *Berent*, Mrs Berent, C, lived at Highbury New Park, in an avenue lined with London plane trees. Her house suffered sudden and extensive structural damage in 2003–4. Apart from tree roots of three trees outside her property causing dehydration of the soil, there were other problems: the house was virtually adjacent to the Channel Tunnel; and the storm drainage system of the house was severely blocked until 2005. Islington LBC, D, received written report on 2 March 2010 that three London plane trees in its street could be implicated in the damage being done to C's house. Until then, there was no reason to say that D knew, or should have known, that there was a real risk that its street trees and their root system had caused damage to C's property, as nothing identified those particular trees as being a 'hotspot' that should have required some remedial action over and above D's usual regime of tree management. But, after March 2010, D knew, or reasonably foresaw, that the tree roots were a real risk, and they should have been immediately felled to abate the nuisance. D delayed for a year before doing this. **Held**: D was not liable in nuisance for the 2003–4 damage to C's house, but was liable in nuisance *after* March 2010, for not removing the troublesome trees forthwith. The co-D, the Housing Assn, was also liable in nuisance for the same period. Damages were only awarded for C's loss of amenity over that period. The risk of damage to C's house from the trees was **not** reasonably foreseeable to the Islington LBC, D, when the principal damage to C's house occurred in 2003–4. The court did not accept that D knew sufficiently of the geology of the area, and that clay-based soils are susceptible to shrinkage and swelling on changes in moisture content caused by tree root extraction of moisture, and desiccation. However, after receiving the report of March 2010, D knew, or reasonably foresaw, the dangers posed by the trees to the foundations of C's building from that point onwards. In *Willis v Derwentside DC*,[210] Mr and Mrs Willis, C, owned a house and smallholding for breeding animals and poultry on the floodplain of the River Derwent, adjacent to part of the West Durham coalfield, owned by D, with extensive coal seams. In certain atmospheric conditions, dangerous levels of carbon dioxide and stythe gas were emitted, and some of C's animals were asphyxiated in July 2006. D was aware of a significant gas escape from Burn Drift in April 2006. From then onwards, D came under an obligation to abate the nuisance and remedy the gas escape.

Furthermore, the measured duty of care requires that *the extent of the damage which eventuated* was foreseeable. It would not be fair, just and reasonable to impose a duty on D to abate a hazard, when the damage which occurred was more extensive than that which was foreseeable. This is undoubtedly a more pro-D legal principle than applies in negligence – in the latter cause of action, it will be recalled (from Chapter 9) that once D knows or reasonably foresees the type of damage suffered by C, then D is liable for the **full** extent of the damage which is actually suffered by C. However, in *Holbeck Hall Hotel v Scarborough BC*,[211] that modification

[209] [2005] EWCA Civ 1701, [29]. [210] [2013] EWHC 738 (Ch) [47]–[55].
[211] [2000] QB 836 (CA) [45]–[46], [49].

of principle in D's favour here in nuisance was justifiable, as a *quid pro quo* for the fact that D was liable for a non-feasance (or omission) wherever the *Leakey* duty applied.

In *Holbeck Hall Hotel*, a cliff owned by the Council, D, was known to be unstable, and remedial works to shore up the cliff were carried out negligently by D. C's hotel had to be demolished when a massive land slip on D's land caused loss of support for the hotel, rendering it unsafe. **Held**: no breach of the *Leakey* duty occurred. It was reasonably foreseeable that the defect in the cliff would, if un-remedied, cause slippages to parts of the hotel grounds, but the nearest slippage, prior to the massive slip, had been about 100 m from the hotel. However, it was not fair, just or reasonable to impose liability on D for damage which was greater in extent than anything that was foreseeable, especially where the defects existed as much on C's land as on D's. In that regard, this case was unusual, because the hazard existed on both sides of the boundary. Also, it was not expected that D would carry out expensive further geological investigations, or extensive and costly remedial works in this case. The scope of the measured duty was limited to D warning neighbours of risks that D was aware of, and sharing such information as D had acquired relating to the risk posed by the cliff.

iii. Abatement measures. What D must do in order to discharge the *Leakey* duty is assessed *subjectively*, not objectively. If the risk of damage caused by the encroachment could have been easily and cheaply abated, D will breach his measured duty of care if he does nothing, or nothing sufficient.

On the other hand, if the only remedy to abate the hazard required substantial and expensive works, D may do enough to discharge the duty if he gives C permission to come onto his land to do agreed works at C's expense, or offers to share the expense of remedial works with C, or warns C of the risks and shares what information he has about those risks with C (referred to in *Leakey* itself[212]). It is, after all, a 'measured duty'.

Of course, the usual principle is that whether D breached the standard of care should be judged objectively (Chapter 7). There are two reasons for the modification to that usual rule, according to Lord Wilberforce in *Goldman v Hargrave*:[213]

- there is a wide spectrum of nuisance-type interferences – some could be easily dealt with by D, but some 'may not be so simple' – and 'the law must take account of the fact that [D] has ... had this hazard thrust upon him through no seeking or fault of his own. His ... resources, whether physical or material, may be of a very modest character, either in relation to the magnitude of the hazard, or as compared with those of his threatened neighbour'. Hence, if the law required of D some sort of expense or physical effort of which he was incapable, then that 'would be unenforceable or unjust'; and
- C may have such resources and stakes at interest himself that more should be expected of C, compared with D who may be a 'small owner [who] does what he can, and promptly calls upon his neighbour to provide additional resources'. In *Leakey v National Trust*, Megaw LJ noted that, 'in arriving at a judgment on reasonableness, a[n] ...assessment may be relevant as to the neighbour's capacity to protect himself from damage, whether by way of some form of barrier on his own land, or by way of providing funds for expenditure on agreed works on the land of [D]'.[214]

212 [2000] QB 836 (CA) [54] (dicta; C failed because the extent of damage was unforeseeable).

213 [1967] 1 AC 645 (PC, on appeal from Australia) 663.

214 [1980] QB 485 (CA) 526.

In *Goldman v Hargrave*,[215] a Western Australian red gum tree on D's land was struck by lightning, and caught fire in its upper limbs. D had the tree cut down by a contractor, but took no reasonable steps to douse the fire with water to prevent it from spreading, believing that the fire would burn itself out. A hot wind picked up the next day, and the fire spread to C's neighbouring property and caused considerable damage. **Held:** D was liable in both nuisance and in negligence. D, as occupier, was under a general duty of care in relation to hazards occurring on his land, to remove or reduce such hazards to his neighbour. D should have taken simple steps to prevent the spreading of a fire caused by lightning striking a tree, such as dampening down the site with water. In *Willis v Derwentside DC*,[216] facts previously, **held:** D was liable in nuisance. Where the nuisance in question consists of the dangerous and frightening escape of potentially asphyxiating gas from disused mine workings, reasonable steps on the part of D include providing information (on C's request) about the causes of the escape, the levels of gas being emitted, and the design of the remedial works planned by D to abate the danger. D had that information, and should have made it freely available to C without their having to engage their own expert (calling to mind the dicta noted in the *Leakey* case description above). D re-housed C in a portakabin to allow them to care for their animals, but that was not sufficient to avoid liability under the *Leakey* duty, given that no arrangements were made by D to obtain a certificate of satisfactory completion of the remedial scheme.

This principle does not mean, however, that even well-resourced Ds – such as local authorities or government entities – are expected to do something to abate the nuisance. Even financially powerful D's may not have breached the *Leakey* duty. That is legally justifiable for two reasons:

- to hold D liable for not taking onerous steps pushes their liability towards strict liability, which the law is keen to avoid. In *Berent v Family Mosaic Housing*, the court made the point that, in an area like Highbury New Park in London, with established gardens, mature vegetation, tree-lined streets and Victorian houses, a responsible local authority 'could not reasonably contemplate the desertification of such a neighbourhood by wholesale tree felling to avoid a possible risk of damage. Such an approach it seems commended by [C] almost gives rise to strict liability'[217];
- in *Lambert v Barratt Homes Ltd and Rochdale MBC*,[218] the Court of Appeal took account of the limited resources for even well-resourced Ds. It did not expect the Council to do the work required to fix the flooding affecting C's land – 'it is well known that most local authorities are under a degree of financial pressure. Moreover their resources are held for public purposes and are not generally available for the benefit of private citizens. The likelihood is that as householders the residents were insured against damage to their properties by flooding and when considering their ability to carry out and bear the cost of the work required to safeguard those properties, we see no reason to ignore the possibility of their obtaining the necessary funds from their insurers'.

In *Lambert v Barratt Homes*, Mr Lambert, C, owned a house nearby to a school playing-field owned by the Rochdale MBC, D. There was a man-made drainage ditch along most of the western side of the field, draining into a culvert, and these drainage arrangements worked to everyone's satisfaction. Then, D sold the lower part of their playing field to Barratt Homes for housing development. While carrying out their housing development, Barratt filled in and blocked the lower part of the drainage ditch and culvert, which caused water from D's playing field to accumulate and then flood

[215] [1967] 1 AC 645 (PC) 646–47. [216] [2013] EWHC 738 (Ch) [67]–[69], [78].
[217] [2011] EWHC 1353 (TCC) [104], aff'd: [2012] EWCA Civ 961. [218] [2010] EWCA Civ 681, [21]–[22].

C's property. C sued D (and Barratt) in negligence and in nuisance. **Held**: D did not breach the *Leakey* duty of care. It was not under any duty itself to construct, and presumably pay for, the necessary drainage ditches on their retained land, to prevent the accumulation of water. 'The cost of that work was obviously likely to be considerable. This was not a case like *Sedleigh-Denfield v O'Callaghan*, where a simple and inexpensive act on the part of the occupier of the land on which the hazard arose could have abated the nuisance'. At most, D was under a duty to cooperate in a solution which involved the construction of suitable drainage and a catch pit on their retained land – e.g., assisting Barratt to obtain any council consents needed to enable the drainage to be laid. In *Thomas and Evans Ltd v Mid-Rhondda Co-op Socy Ltd*,[219] the Society, D, with planning permission, pulled down a river bank wall that had been built to protect shop premises, including C's shop, and highway, from flooding. The rebuilt wall was not as long, and small gaps were left at either side, which allowed flooding to occur. **Held**: D did not breach the *Leakey* duty. D had not acted unreasonably, given that the river flooded only occasionally. This was to be contrasted with where a stream ran through D's land, which was known to flood and spread to C's land every time it rained. The *Leakey* duty would then apply, so that if D failed to keep the stream free from blockage by flotsam or silt, something that would be easily done, then that would be a breach. That was not this case.

ELEMENT #3(A): CAUSATION

The legal principles governing the law of causation and remoteness of damage in private nuisance are analogous to, and closely-linked with, the relevant principles under a claim in *Rylands v Fletcher.*[220] That overlap is inevitable, given that, in *Transco plc v Stockport MBC*, Lord Bingham explicitly held that a *Rylands v Fletcher* claim was 'a sub-species of nuisance', and, as such, that both torts are 'directed, and directed only, to the protection of interests in land'.[221] Hence, the principles canvassed below are relevant to both private nuisance (re interferences) and *Rylands v Fletcher* (re escapes), unless otherwise stated.

Damage to land/interest in land

§16.27 The tort of private nuisance is not actionable *per se.* C, who is suing for the adverse effects caused by D's interference/escape of a dangerous thing from D's land, must prove damage, i.e., some compensable injury arising from damage to C's land or to his interest in the land.

Damage is an essential ingredient of the cause of action in private nuisance (per *Northumbrian Water Ltd v McAlpine Ltd*[222]). Nuisance, like negligence, was historically an action on the case, whereby neither tort was complete until C had suffered some damage from D's act or omission (per Lord Goff in *Cambridge Water*[223]).

When C sues under the rule in *Rylands v Fletcher*, he must seek 'a remedy for damage to land or interests in land' (per Lord Hoffmann in *Transco*[224]); and in *Hunter v Canary Wharf Ltd*, the same Law Lord decreed that nuisance is 'a tort against land' too.[225] The remedies available inevitably and necessarily reflect the fact that both are property-based torts. The types of damages recoverable for private nuisance (and under the rule in *Rylands v Fletcher*) are dealt with under 'Remedies', below.

[219] [1941] 1 KB 381 (CA). [220] (1868) LR 3 HL 330. [221] [2003] UKHL 61, [2004] 2 AC 1, [9].
[222] [2014] EWCA Civ 685, [12]. [223] [1994] 2 AC 264 (HL) 295. [224] [2003] UKHL 61, [2004] 2 AC 1, [39].
[225] [1997] AC 655 (HL) 702.

The 'but-for' test

§16.28 C must prove that, but for the interference/escape of the dangerous thing, the damage would not have occurred.

The causal link between D's interference/escape, and C's damage, must be established on the balance of probabilities. If the damage alleged by C probably would have occurred anyway, regardless of D's interference/escape, then the causal link will fail. If, however, absent the interference/escape, the damage to C probably would not have happened, then the interference/escape caused the damage.

D's interference/escape need not be the *sole* cause of C's damage – however, it must be 'an effective and substantial cause' of C's damage (per Chadwick LJ in *Loftus-Brighan v Ealing LBC*[226]).

In *Ellison v MOD*,[227] facts previously, **held:** no private nuisance or *Rylands v Fletcher* liability. The (accepted) expert evidence was that water which had accumulated in and around the heap of spoil did not play a causative role in the flooding of Cs' land. The natural rainwater which followed the heavy storm was the cause.

D may argue that the alternative causes of C's damage were attributable to one of two other sources, any of which may exculpate D, if the evidence so points:

i. C's own activities – so that D can prove that the interference/escape of which C complains was caused by C, and that there was no material contribution to that by D himself.

In *Birmingham Devp Co Ltd v Tyler*,[228] facts previously, where BDC, as C, sued for two defects in a flank wall of Mr Tyler's, D's, neighbouring factory, which C felt was in imminent danger of collapsing, **held**: causation failed. One of the defects was wholly caused by water flowing from a gutter on C's property, resulting in rotted wood, a rusted steel beam, and a defective gutter pipe on C's property over a number of years prior to 1999/2000. This, in turn, caused the defect in the flank wall. That was a latent defect so far as D was concerned. In *Hirose Electrical UK Ltd v Peak Ingredients Ltd*,[229] facts previously, employees C alleged that D's odorous manufacturing of food additives, and the noxious smells which emanated from D's premises, caused C's blocked sinuses and eye irritation and asthma. **Held**: causation failed. These symptoms were not, on the balance of probabilities, caused by D's operations. Although C's asthma was probably exacerbated by the smells, that condition was deteriorating well before D arrived next door and commenced its business.

ii. the acts or omissions of third parties, or naturally-occurring hazards, neither of which D is responsible for.

In *Berent v Family Mosaic Housing*,[230] facts previously, **held:** causation succeeded. Family Mosaic Housing, D, had argued that the London plane trees growing on its property were not the cause of the subsidence of neighbour C's house, and that the subsidence was due, instead, to a combination of: tunnelling works carried out in 2003, for the construction of the Channel Tunnel; the composition of the infill ground beneath the house; by the London plane trees growing on the co-D's,

[226] [2003] EWCA Civ 1490, [12]. [227] (1996) 81 BLR 101 (QB, Official Referees' Business, Judge Bowsher QC).
[228] [2008] EWCA Civ 859. [229] [2011] EWCA Civ 987, affirming: [2011] JPL 429, [72], [114].
[230] [2011] EWHC 1353 (TCC) [93], aff'd: [2012] EWCA Civ 961, although with some criticism about the lack of clarity in the trial judge's findings about causation.

Islington LBC's, footpath outside C's house; and by the Council's refusal to permit the removal of D's tree because of a Tree Preservation Order[231] which the Council would not amend. However, D's trees became the predominant and effective cause of the structural problems from 2005 onwards. The alternative causes, while they may have played a part, were not sufficient to break the causal chain between D's plane trees, and C's foundation subsidence, and structural damage.

ELEMENT #3(B): THE DAMAGE IS NOT TOO REMOTE

Type of damage

Reasonable foreseeability

§16.29 The type of harm suffered by C must have been *either* actually foreseen (known about) by D, *or* otherwise, it must have been reasonably foreseeable, at the time of the interference/escape, in order to render D liable under private nuisance and *Rylands v Fletcher.*

Neither private nuisance nor the rule in *Rylands v Fletcher* imposes liability for unforeseeable damage. The requirement of foreseeability under *Rylands v Fletcher* is discussed in Chapter 17. The section below focuses upon the tort of private nuisance.

In *Overseas Tankship (UK) Ltd v Miller Steamship Co Pty Ltd (Wagon Mound No 2)*, Lord Reid held that, in relation to private nuisance: 'although negligence may not be necessary, fault of some kind is almost always necessary, and fault generally involves foreseeability, [i.e.] the fault is in failing to abate a nuisance, the existence of which [D] is, or ought to be, aware as likely to cause damage to his neighbour [C]'.[232] In *Cambridge Water Co Ltd v Eastern Counties Leather plc*,[233] the House of Lords held that Lord Reid's opinion had 'settled the law to the effect that foreseeability of harm is indeed a prerequisite of the recovery of damages in private nuisance'. In *Transco plc v Stockport MBC*[234] too, it was recognised that D will only be liable for damage which was foreseeable, and that this was 'the general rule of liability for nuisance today'.

In that sense, liability in private nuisance might be strict, in that D can be liable even if not negligent – but it **cannot** be strict in the sense that D is liable for **all** damage resulting from the interference. Rather, liability to pay damages in private nuisance is limited to damage which was reasonably foreseeable. A lack of foreseeability of the type of damage suffered has certainly negated liability in some leading nuisance cases.

In *Cambridge Water Co Ltd v Eastern Counties Leather plc*,[235] Eastern Counties, D, a leather goods manufacturing company, used a chemical solvent (PCE) to degrease pelts, and over several years, some of it spilt onto its concrete factory floor. Employees believed that it would evaporate upon contact with the ground. Unbeknown and, with the expertise then reasonably available to D, unknowable, some of the spillage seeped into cracks in the concrete floor of its premises and entered the chalk aquifer beneath. The PCE then contaminated, by means of micro drainage channels, a borehole 1.3 miles away, which Cambridge Water, C, intended to use to provide water for Cambridge's inhabitants. **Held (HL):** no liability under *Rylands v Fletcher* (nor would be possible under private nuisance either). When the PCE was being used in the tanning process at D's factory, 'nobody could reasonably have foreseen the

[231] The TPO was made in July 2007, and the Council's consent was necessary to remove the tree, under s 211 of the Town and Country Planning Act 1990.

[232] [1967] 1 AC 617 (PC, in appeal from Australia) 639.

[233] [1994] 2 AC 264 (HL) 301, 304.

[234] [2003] UKHL 61, [2004] 2 AC 1, [26].

[235] [1994] 2 AC 264 (HL) 306.

resultant damage which occurred at [D's] borehole at Sawston'. Spillages of very small quantities were expected to evaporate. In *Network Rail Infrastructure Ltd v Morris (t/as Soundstar Studio)*,[236] Network Rail, D, installed a new signalling system on its rail-track in 1994. That caused electromagnetic interference to the recording of music created by electric guitars played in Mr Morris's, C's, recording studio 80 metres from that signal box. The noise that resulted when most of C's customers played their guitars for the purpose of making recordings was unsatisfactory. Over a period of two years, C steadily lost his customers, and claimed financial losses of more than £60,000. C complained to D about the problem in April 1995, and D tried to fix the problem, without much success. **Held:** no actionable nuisance. C could not prove that D should have foreseen that the installation of the signalling system might cause interference of this type. No other complaints about interference had been made, and no similar problem had been encountered nearby to signal boxes installed elsewhere. Otherwise, the interference would have been actionable. In *Northumbrian Water Ltd v McAlpine Ltd*,[237] facts previously, **held:** no actionable nuisance. D could not have known that the very old disused private sewer was on its site (the only plan showing its existence was in a museum), or that it was still connected with the public sewer, so D could not have reasonably foreseen that breaching the private sewer during pile-driving would allow concrete to flow from its site into the public sewer.

The critical time at which D must have known, or reasonably foreseen, the damage caused by an interference/escape is at the point that the thing invaded C's use and enjoyment of his land. If C cannot prove foreseeability of damage at that point, then D is not liable. It does not matter if D (and everyone else) knows about or can foresee the damage, after the thing has interfered with C's use and enjoyment, or escaped and is lost to the control of D – that is too late. Hindsight may be 'a wonderful thing', but it does not fix liability.

In *Cambridge Water Co*,[238] once the PCE chemical had seeped into the ground beneath the floor of D's tannery, pools of neat PCE still existed at the base of the chalk aquifer, and the PCE continued to slowly dissolve in the water in the aquifer, such that the escape was ongoing and continuing ('to the present day', the House of Lords noted). It was argued that, since it has become known that PCE, if it escapes, is capable of causing damage by rendering water available at boreholes unpotable and unsaleable for domestic purposes, D should be liable under *Rylands v Fletcher* for any damage occurring after the damage had become foreseeable. However, there could be no private nuisance or *Rylands v Fletcher* liability for any of the escape, either before or after the damage became foreseeable. The PCE had travelled well beyond the control of D at that point.

Hence, as *Cambridge Water* demonstrates, neither private nuisance nor the rule in *Rylands v Fletcher* provides any basis for successful claims based upon historical pollution, where the polluter did not know and could not foresee the prospect of that pollution damage, at the time of the interference/escape.

Directness

§16.30 Indirect losses caused by the interference/escape are not recoverable.

The division between direct and indirect damage may be fairly blurred at times (and it certainly does not feature any longer in negligence suits), but it has eminent authority in the context of these property-based torts.

[236] [2004] EWCA Civ 172, [2004] Env LR 41, [28], [37]. [237] [2014] EWCA Civ 685, [19].
[238] [1994] 2 AC 264 (HL), quote at 294, and see too, 306.

For the purposes of *Rylands v Fletcher*, any loss which C suffers as a result of the escape of a dangerous thing from D's land must be within the 'the proximate and direct consequences of [D's] wrongful acts' (per *Cattle v Stockton Waterworks*[239]). For the purposes of private nuisance, there is also authority that the damage must be 'direct physical injury to a neighbour's land' (per Lord Lloyd in *Hunter v Canary Wharf Ltd*[240]). In *British Celanese v AH Hunt* too, it was said that 'direct damage' occurs wherever C's 'property was injured by the operation of the laws of nature without any human intervention'.[241]

In the context of both torts, this proposition was affirmed in *D Pride & Partners v Institute for Animal Health*, where C had 'no real prospect of establishing that any physical injury was done to their land, still less that it was *direct* physical injury'.[242] Indeed, where C is claiming for relational pure economic loss (as was the case in *D Pride*, and a topic which is dealt with in the next section), the damage is irrecoverable in any event for policy reasons – but, additionally, it is too indirect to be recoverable. The farmers' claims in that case were caused by the effect of the government-imposed restrictions upon movement of livestock, which saved their livestock from risk of infection with foot-and-mouth disease (FMD), but which came at an economic cost. Tugendhat J remarked: 'the loss that the [farmers] suffered was ... indirect ..., and that is so whether the loss be physical injury or economic loss. Their farms were not polluted by FMD virus'.

The exclusionary rule

§16.31 Under the exclusionary rule, where D permits an interference/escape of a dangerous thing which causes damage to property owned by a third party (TP), C cannot recover any economic losses (e.g., lost profits) which he suffers as a result of that damage to TP's property. That *pure* economic loss is irrecoverable damage in English law – regardless of whether the claim is brought in private nuisance, under the rule in *Rylands v Fletcher*, or in negligence.

The exclusionary rule was considered in Chapter 4 in the context of negligently-inflicted pure economic loss. As discussed there, what C is seeking to recover in the abovementioned scenario is 'relational pure economic loss', which cannot be recovered in English law for policy reasons.

The problem has arisen equally in the context of private nuisance and under the rule in *Rylands v Fletcher*. It arose in the early *Rylands v Fletcher* case of *Cattle v Stockton Waterworks Co*,[243] and was applied more recently, within the realm of both private nuisance and *Rylands v Fletcher*, in the 2007 foot and mouth virus outbreak in *D Pride & Partners v Institute for Animal Health*[244] and in the context of the Buncefield oil depot explosion in *Colour Quest Ltd v Total Downstream UK plc*.[245]

In *Cattle v Stockton Waterworks*, Mr Cattle, C, a building contractor, entered into a contract with Mr Knight to build a tunnel under a turnpike road, to join up his land on each side of the road, from which C expected to make a profit. The water company Stockton, D, laid its main pipes under the road too. One was defective and leaked large quantities of water into the surrounding soil, forming a dam. During C's tunnelling, he accidentally breached that dam and Mr Knight's land was partly flooded.

239 (1874–75) LR 10 QB 453 (Div Ct) 457 (Blackburn J).

240 [1997] AC 655 (HL) 695.

241 [1969] 1 WLR 959 (QB) 966.

242 [2009] EWHC 685 (QB) [93]–[94], [97], [105], [108], [134]. See too: *Landcatch Ltd v Intl Oil Pollution Compensation Fund* [1998] 2 Lloyd's LR 552 (CSOH); [1999] 2 Lloyd's LR 316 (CSIH) (losses too indirect).

243 (1874–75) LR 10 QB 453 (Div Ct).

244 [2009] EWHC 685 (QB) [91].

245 [2009] EWHC 540 (QB (Comm)) [409], [471]–[472].

C's work had to stop, and C lost income while the pipe was repaired. C sued D to recover that sum, alleging that D allowed a dangerous thing (water) to escape and do mischief. **Held:** no *Rylands v Fletcher* claim possible. Mr Knight could have sued D for damage caused to his own land. Also, any of his workmen whose tools or clothes were destroyed could bring an action for those damaged goods (being consequential economic loss). However, C's lost profit on the contract was relational pure economic loss, and was irrecoverable. In *D Pride & Partners v Institute for Animal Health*, facts previously, various farmers, C, whose properties were **not** affected by the FMD virus, alleged that, because of the infection at other farmers' (TPs') properties, they lost the opportunity to take their livestock to market, had to keep feeding and maintaining that stock when otherwise they would have been sold; and some of the breeding stock had to be sold for meat at a lower price (hence, the claims were losses of sales or lower prices on sales). **Held:** no private nuisance or *Rylands v Fletcher* possible. This damage was the same as the lost profits claimed by the contractor in *Cattle v Stockton* – relational economic loss which was irrecoverable. Indeed, from one perspective (said Tugendhat J), this claim was weaker than in *Cattle*, because here, C had no contractual relations with the affected farmers – none of the claimant farmers (unlike Mr Cattle) was expecting to make any profit from their dealings with the affected TP farmers. In *Colour Quest v Total Downstream*, the explosions at the Buncefield Oil Storage Depot at Hemel Hempstead were caused by the ignition of an enormous vapour cloud that had developed from the spillage of some 300 tons of petrol from a storage tank. A subsequent fire engulfed a further 20 fuel storage tanks, and large volumes of black smoke remained visible over Southern England for several days. Total, D, owned the Buncefield site. One of the claims against Total, D, arising from the disaster was brought by oil company, Shell, C, which owned fuel tanks on the Buncefield site. Significant damage was done to the West London Pipeline System by the explosion. C did not own that pipeline, but used it to transport its aviation and ground fuels to customers, and could not use it for a period, except in reduced volumes and/or at increased costs. However, it was **common ground** that C's claim was for relational pure economic loss, and not pursuable in negligence, nuisance or *Rylands v Fletcher*.[246]

The scenario of these cases is summarised in the following Diagram (with the case detail italicised):

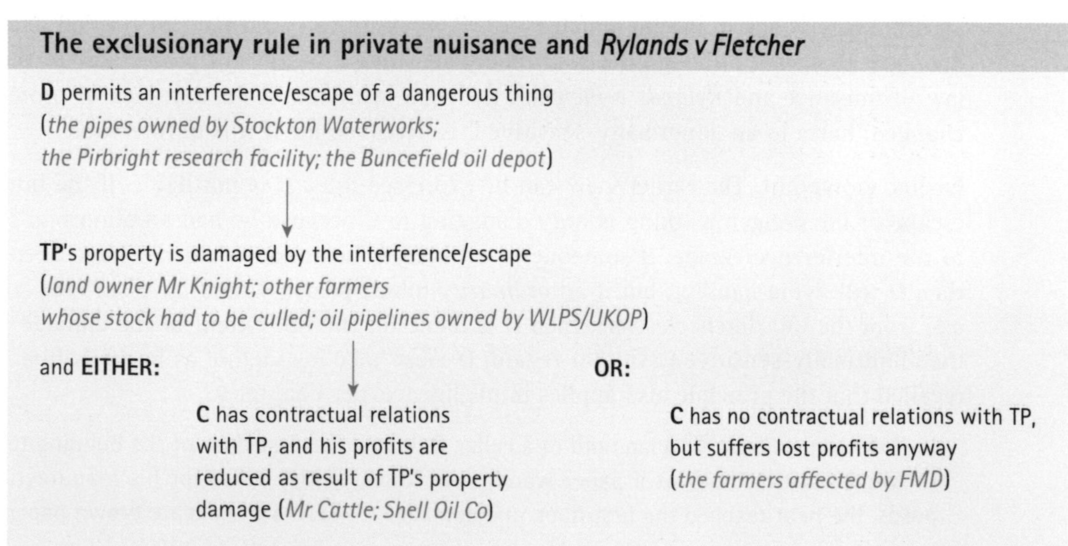

[246] After detailed analysis, these pure economic losses were not recoverable in negligence either (per Chapter 4).

Notably, the exclusionary rule only applies where C suffered pure economic loss, and not where C suffers some physical injury with consequential economic losses.

In *British Celanese Ltd v AH Hunt (Capacitors) Ltd*,[247] facts previously, where the metal foil strips flew from D's premises onto the electricity substation, the subsequent interruption in electricity supply then caused materials to solidify in C's spinnerets, which had to be cleaned off before they could be restarted. Although D argued that C only suffered pure economic loss in this scenario (invoking *Cattle v Stockton Waterworks*), Lawton J rejected that line of argument, preferring to hold that (as the claim was re-pleaded), C did indeed suffer physical injury, thereby avoiding the *Cattle* problem.

The exclusionary rule was described in *Cattle v Stockton Waterworks* (by Lord Blackburn, as he was then) as an example of the law being unable to deliver 'perfectly complete remedies for all wrongful acts'.[248] Imagine (said Lord Blackburn) that the claimants in *Rylands v Fletcher* had been 'every workman and person employed in the mine who, in consequence of its stoppage, made less wages than he would otherwise have done'. It would have been untenable to allow this type of claim to arise out of the *Rylands* scenario, so as to permit those workmen, C, to sue the owner of the reservoir, as D, for the damage which he caused to the colliery owner TP's mine, which ultimately caused those workmen's lost wages.

Significantly though, in the context of private nuisance and *Rylands v Fletcher*, this 'floodgates'-type policy reason has never been expressly challenged by posing the argument – what if the class of claimants was, not a large group of mine-workers, but small and finite? The exclusionary rule has, to date, been an immutable rule in the context of both private nuisance and *Rylands v Fletcher* (as it has been in the context of negligence too) – and regardless of the size of the class which suffered the relational economic loss.

Abnormal sensitivity

§16.32 According to earlier judicial views, an abnormally-sensitive C could not recover either in private nuisance or under *Rylands v Fletcher*, unless the interference/escape would have damaged an ordinarily-robust C too (in which event, C was entitled to recover for the full extent of his damage). However, although the abnormally-sensitive C is still not protectable in the modern law of nuisance and *Rylands v Fletcher*, the legal justification for that lack of protection has changed; harm to an abnormally-sensitive C is irrecoverable if it is unforeesable.

Earlier viewpoint. The earlier view can be expressed thus: D is not liable, if the interference/escape of the dangerous thing is only damaging to C because he had an abnormal sensitivity to the interference/escape. If someone of ordinary robustness would not have been affected, then D will avoid liability; but if an *ordinarily*-robust person would have suffered some damage from the interference/escape, then D is liable for the full extent of the damage caused to the abnormally-sensitive C. In that regard, D must 'take his victim' as he finds him. It will be recalled that the principle also applies in negligence, per Chapter 9.

In *Robinson v Kilvert*,[249] a landlord of a cellar, D, leased the first floor of the building to a tenant, C, who used that floor as a paper warehouse. D heated the cellar for his manufacturing purposes, the heat reached the first floor, and damaged C's stocks of delicate brown paper. **Held**: no

[247] [1969] 1 WLR 959 (QB) 966. [248] (1874–75) LR 10 QB 453 (Div Ct) 457, citing *Lumley v Gye* (1853) 2 E & B 216.
[249] (1889) LR 41 Ch D 88 (CA) 94, 97.

actionable private nuisance. That level of heat would not have prejudicially affected any ordinary trade carried on there: 'ordinary paper would not be damaged by what [D] was doing, but only a particular kind of paper'. Hence, '[a] man who carries on an exceptionally delicate trade cannot complain because it is injured by his neighbour doing something lawful on his property, if it is something which would not injure anything but an exceptionally delicate trade'. In *Eastern and South African Telegraph Co Ltd v Cape Town Tramway Co Ltd*,[250] the Telegraph Company, C, had a licence to lay a submarine cable along the seabed, and owned premises in Cape Town where the signals were received. The transmission of messages along the cable was interfered with by the escape of electricity from Cape Town Tramway's, D's, tramway system. C had to spend significant sums on measures to prevent the interference. **Held:** no liability in *Rylands v Fletcher*. The cable had a peculiar capacity to be affected by even minute currents of electricity. C could not 'create for themselves, by reason of the peculiarity of their trade apparatus, a higher right to limit the operations of their neighbours than belongs to ordinary owners of land who do not trade with telegraphic cables'.

This principle had been judicially-explained on a couple of bases. First, in *Network Rail Infrastructure Ltd v Morris (t/as Soundstar Studio)*, the Court of Appeal noted that the effects of *strict* liability for interferences/escapes could lead to unreasonable results from D's perspective, and the 'abnormally-sensitive C' principle was one way of *mitigating* the harshness of the strict liability tort.[251] Secondly, as the Privy Council noted in *Cape Town Tramway*, if C's property is so susceptible to damage from an interference/escape that he requires special protection against whatever his neighbour is lawfully doing, then 'that must be found in legislation ... A man cannot increase the liabilities of his neighbour by applying his own property to special uses, whether for business or pleasure'.[252]

Modern viewpoint. Doubts were expressed about the earlier principle, by the Court of Appeal, in *Network Rail v Morris*[253] – with Lord Phillips MR referring to **if** *Kilvert* and *Cape Town Tramway* 'remain good law', and with Buxton LJ stating that it was 'difficult to see any further life' in the precise principle of the abnormally-sensitive C not being protected by nuisance. Instead, both judges favoured that the sensitive creature be dealt with under the test of reasonable foreseeability of damage (as discussed previously[254]). If the damage was suffered by an abnormally-sensitive C when ordinary persons would not have suffered any damage from the interference/escape, then the appropriate legal answer is that the damage suffered by C was not, in law, reasonably foreseeable. That is how the case of *Network Rail v Morris* itself was resolved (noted above). The Court of Appeal reiterated that, since *Wagon Mound (No 2)*, foreseeability of the type of damage has become a criterion for the recovery of damages in private nuisance – a principle which did **not** apply at the time that *Kilvert* and *Cape Town Tramway* were decided.

Hence, the development of foreseeability, at the expense of the principle of abnormal sensitivity, is unlikely to change the outcomes in the key cases – peculiarly-sensitive Cs will **not** be protected under these property-based torts, regardless. As reiterated in *Pusey v Somerset CC*, '[a]bnormal sensitivity to noise or the other matters is not sufficient to found a cause of action'.[255]

[250] [1902] AC 381 (PC, on appeal from the SC of the Colony of the Cape of Good Hope) 392.

[251] [2004] EWCA Civ 172, [33]–[35] (Buxton LJ). [252] [1902] AC 381 (PC) 393.

[253] [2004] EWCA Civ 172, quotes at [19] and [35], respectively. [254] See pp 884–85.

[255] [2012] EWCA Civ 988, [19].

In *Pusey*, Mr and Mrs Pusey, C, owned Heathpoult Farm in Somerset, which was opposite to a lay-by owned by the Council, D, about 90 m long and wide enough to park lorries and cars. C took exception to the use of the lay-by by lorry drivers, car drivers, etc, and wrote to D to complain about overnight parking there, dropped litter, people urinating and swearing and vandalising the area, and making noisy turns, etc. **Held:** no actionable nuisance. The incidents had continued over many years, but most were relatively infrequent, the noise relatively isolated, and most would have gone un-noticed and remained invisible, 'had C not been in the practice of investigating almost any use made of the lay-by', and keeping a diary log of each and every event. Any particular sensitivities of these Cs had to be disregarded. The use of the lay-by was not an actionable nuisance.

Provided, though, that harm to C was indeed foreseeable under the *Cambridge Water* approach, the position remains the same: the full extent of C's damage (sustained because of his particular susceptibility to damage) must be compensated for by D. The Privy Council decision in *McKinnon Industries Ltd v Walker*[256] is still a good illustration of this principle.

In *McKinnon*, McKinnon, D, manufactured steel and iron products for the car industry, and operated a foundry on its premises for that purpose. William Walker, C, a neighbour, carried on the business of a commercial florist, and was the second-largest grower of orchids in Canada. The smoke vapours and noxious sulphur dioxide emanating from D's premises caused many of C's herbs and shrubs and orchids to die. **Held:** an actionable nuisance. The question arose whether the injunction granted in respect of the nuisance should in some way exclude damage to the orchids from its operation, because that was a 'particularly difficult and delicate operation' from a horticultural point of view. However, the damage to the orchids was properly subject to a remedy (because *any* horticulture would have suffered some damage from the noxious fumes).

DEFENCES

Some factors – that D had planning permission for its activities, and that D's activities had public interest or utility – are **not** outright defences to an action for private nuisance. They are simply part of the balancing assessment under Element #2. Whether C 'came to the nuisance' may possibly constitute a valid defence in limited circumstances, in light of recent dicta by the Supreme Court in *Coventry v Lawrence*, but normally will not do so. If the interference to C's premises is caused by a trespasser, that is no outright defence either – D will still be liable if he has adopted or continued the nuisance-making activity created by that trespasser (per *Sedleigh-Denfield v O'Callaghan*, and discussed earlier under Precondition #2). These various topics have been considered previously, and will not be re-canvassed.

Statutory authorisation

§16.33 Where D is undertaking an activity which has been authorised by statute, D has a good defence if two conditions are met: (1) the statute expressly or impliedly exempted D from liability for any private nuisance or escape under *Rylands v Fletcher*, which is attributable to that activity, and (2) D undertook the activity without negligence.

When Parliament has, either expressly or impliedly, authorised a nuisance-making undertaking to be carried out by D, that 'carries with it an authority to do what is authorised, with immunity

[256] [1951] UKPC 51 (on appeal from Ontario CA).

from any action based on nuisance. The right of action [in nuisance] is taken away' (per Lord Wilberforce in *Allen v Gulf Oil Refining Ltd*[257]). It follows that, if there is **no** express or implied statutory authorisation available to D as a defence, then D's activities 'must be exercised in strict conformity with private rights' – and that includes the obligation **not** to create a private nuisance (per *Allen*).

As the Court of Appeal explained in *Wheeler v JJ Saunders Ltd*:[258] 'Parliament is sovereign and can abolish or limit the civil rights of individuals ... Parliament cannot be irrational, just as the sovereign can do no wrong'. By contrast, a 'planning authority ... has only the powers delegated to it by Parliament', and that does not include the power 'to abolish or limit civil rights in any or all circumstances'. That is why statutory authority, and planning permission, are treated entirely differently in the law of private nuisance. The former is a defence; the latter cannot be.

Similar principles apply to the application of statutory authorisation for escapes which would otherwise be culpable under the rule in *Rylands v Fletcher* (which tort is the subject of discussion in Chapter 17). Hence, the defence will be considered, for **both** property-based torts, below. In many cases, C's interest in his land will have suffered the adverse effects of some utility (e.g., gas, electricity, water, sewerage) escaping from a pipe or other infrastructure. But what if the infrastructure necessary to provide these utilities has been laid down or constructed by D, pursuant to statutory authorisation? Did Parliament intend D to be strictly liable under the rule in *Rylands v Fletcher*? Again, the position depends upon a proper construction of the statute under which D acted.

Dealing with the two conditions necessary to confer on D an immunity from any action based on private nuisance or *Rylands v Fletcher*:

Express or implied authorisation

Parliament must either expressly or impliedly exempt D from liability, i.e., it must authorise the nuisance by D without compensation being payable to C. It can do this in several ways.

Parliament may choose to **impose** strict liability on D if some interference/escape of a public utility occurs which damages C's property, regardless of whether D was negligent. That will oust any defence of statutory authorisation, for any interferences/escapes, howsoever caused. As observed in *Anglian Water Services Ltd v Crawshaw Robbins & Co Ltd*,[259] such statutory provisions are fairly rare. Of much the same effect is where the statute provides that nothing contained in the statute should exonerate D from any liability in nuisance, in the event of any nuisance being caused by D. That sort of provision was at issue in *Midwood v Manchester Corp*, and was held to render D liable in nuisance, without protection. Matthew LJ noted that such a provision means, essentially, that Parliament granted D 'a right to carry on a dangerous business, to which latent risks may be incidental that cannot be prevented by any degree of care; and, that being so, it was thought reasonable that those who are empowered to carry on that business for their profit should have to bear the inevitable loss arising from such risks'.[260]

At the other end of the spectrum, Parliament may expressly **immunise** D from common law nuisance claims. This has occurred, e.g., for certain 'nationally significant' infrastructure

[257] [1981] AC 1001 (HL) 1011, citing: *Hammersmith and City Rwy Co v Brand* (1869) LR 4 HL 171, 215 (Lord Cairns).

[258] [1996] Ch 19 (CA) 28, 37. [259] [2001] BLR 173 (QB) [145]–[146] (Stanley Burnton J).

[260] [1905] 2 KB 597 (CA) 610.

projects, including hazardous waste sites (per the Planning Act 2008, s 158). No nuisance arising out of the flight of aircraft over property at reasonable height or given the 'ordinary incidents of such flight' can arise either (per the Civil Aviation Act 1982, s 76[261]).

Otherwise, a statute **impliedly** authorises a private nuisance if it 'authorises the user of land in a way which will "inevitably" involve a nuisance, even if every reasonable precaution is taken' (per *Barr v Biffa*[262]).

In *Allen v Gulf Oil Refining Ltd*,[263] Parliament permitted the construction of an oil refinery on Milford Haven harbour, near the village of Waterston, pursuant to the Gulf Oil Refining Act 1965. The permission also entailed jetties large enough to accommodate large crude oil tankers, and a railway to carry the products of the refinery overland. It caused considerable interference to the peaceful enjoyment of surrounding residents, including the Allens, C. **Held**: no actionable private nuisance. Parliament had impliedly authorised a dramatic change in the neighbourhood of the village, by encouraging industrial or trade activities. The statutory authority contained in the Act 'confers immunity against proceedings for any nuisance which can be shown ... to be the inevitable result of erecting a refinery upon the site'. In *Marcic v Thames Water*, Mr Marcic, C, suffered repeated flooding in his garden and house from the Thames Water's, D's, sewerage system (some pipes ran under his property), because the system had become unable to cope with increased demand. C alleged that D should build more sewers if sewer flooding to residential properties was occurring. However, that obligation was clearly not imposed on D by the Water Industry Act 1991. Rather, there was an 'enforcement scheme' in that Act: when flooding occurred, the Director, as the regulator of the industry, had to consider whether to make an enforcement order; and individual householders could bring proceedings in respect of inadequate drainage only when the sewerage services provider has failed to comply with an enforcement order. **Held:** no actionable private nuisance/*Rylands v Fletcher* action. D was subject to an elaborate scheme of regulation under the 1991 Act, and an authorisation to exempt D from common law liability in private nuisance was implied from that statutory regime. To permit a parallel action in nuisance/*Rylands* 'would set at nought the statutory scheme, and would effectively supplant the regulatory role that the Director was intended to discharge when questions of sewer flooding arise'. C's remedies were limited to the 'enforcement scheme' and judicial review.

Three factors that assisted to show that Parliament impliedly authorised a private nuisance (and any escapes under *Rylands v Fletcher*) were stated in *Marcic*.[264] First, where a statutory operator (like Thames Water), D, could not refuse to accept sewage from a new development and was under a statutory obligation to provide water and sewerage facilities to their customers, then D cannot operate simply as a commercial organisation with 'a complete commercial free hand'. Hence, the common law should not impose on D obligations (to pay compensation via private nuisance actions) which would be inconsistent with the statutory scheme; that would run counter to the intention of Parliament. Secondly, where D has to balance its commercial aims with its obligations to the general public, and it takes decisions involving a complex balancing exercise between expenditure/investment and profit/loss, this is not the type of balancing exercise that courts are qualified to undertake. Essentially, these matters are not justiciable.

[261] Both examples cited by Lord Neuberger in: *Coventry v Lawrence* [2014] UKSC 13, [28].

[262] [2012] EWCA Civ 312, [36(v)], citing: *Clerk and Lindsell on Torts* (20th edn, Sweet & Maxwell, 2010) [20-87].

[263] [1981] AC 1001 (HL) 1014.

[264] [2003] UKHL 66, [2004] 2 AC 42, [33]–[35] (Lord Nicholls), [64] (Lord Hoffmann). See too: *Barr v Biffa Waste* [2011] EWHC 1003 (TCC) [64], [228]–[232], [314]–[316].

Only D and the regulator can balance the need for investment with the level of services to be provided to customers as a whole. Thirdly, historically-speaking, whether more sewers should be constructed has been entrusted by Parliament to the Director-General of Water Services rather than to judges.

In *Transco*, Lord Hoffmann confirmed that a system of statutory regulation relating to the storage of a dangerous thing could create 'an exhaustive code of liability for a particular form of escape', thus excluding the property-based torts of nuisance and *Rylands* from operating.[265] It was suggested that statutory schemes covering certain discharges of water,[266] and escapes of waste[267] and radio-active matter,[268] could comprise such codes, in addition to the scheme under the Water Industry Act 1991 which was the subject of *Marcic*.

Nevertheless, there have been cases in which D could **not** refuse to accept those who relied upon their services – but who **were** liable in private nuisance, not being able to invoke the defence of statutory authority:

> In *Metropolitan Asylum District v Hill*,[269] the Local Government Board directed that District Managers, D, had to provide hospitals for the sick poor of cities in England, under the Metropolitan Poor Act 1867. D built a smallpox hospital in C's area. **Held**: an actionable private nuisance. The statutory authority to treat the sick and poor did not authorise a private nuisance, because the Act did not indicate that the statutory powers should be exercised 'at the expense of, or so as to interfere with, any man's private rights'. Although it could undoubtedly be difficult for D to find suitable sites to discharge their functions under the Act, that was a matter for the Legislature. In *Barr v Biffa Waste Services Ltd*,[270] facts previously, **held**: an actionable private nuisance. D did not have statutory immunity, express or implied, to create a private nuisance from its waste tipping site. D's case was a 'close parallel' with *Metropolitan Asylum*. It was for Parliament to provide statutory immunity from common law nuisance claims arising from waste sites, and Parliament chose not to do so. D then remained exposed to claims in private nuisance for smells and other interferences emanating from those waste sites.

An absence of negligence

In order to take advantage of the defence of statutory authorisation, D must exercise the statutory powers conferred upon it by the statute without negligence – where 'without negligence' means, in this context, that D conducted the activity 'with all reasonable regard and care for the interests of other persons' (*Allen v Gulf Oil Refinery Ltd*[271]). This is a particular construction of the negligence standard (a 'special sense' of the phrase) which is sometimes described as 'the *Allen* duty'.

When determining whether D had reasonable regard for C's interests, a court will consider matters such as: 'state of the art' scientific knowledge available to D at the time of the interference; and the practicability and expense of countervailing measures available to D to minimise the interference.

C bears the burden of proving that D acted with negligence, so as to remove the immunity conferred by the defence; and D bears the burden of proving that the interference was

[265] [2003] UKHL 61, [2004] 2 AC 1, [45]. [266] Per s 209 of the Water Industry Act 1991.

[267] Per s 73(6) of the Environmental Protection Act 1990. [268] Per s 7 of the Nuclear Installations Act 1965.

[269] (1880–81) LR 6 App Cas 193 (HL) 201 (Lord Selborne LC), 208 (Lord Blackburn), 212–13 (Lord Watson).

[270] [2012] EWCA Civ 312.

[271] [1981] AC 1001 (HL) 1011 (Lord Wilberforce), aff'd: *Marcic* [2002] EWCA Civ 64, [58]–[60].

inevitable because no reasonable measures could have been taken to minimise the interference (per *Dobson v Thames Water Utilities Ltd*[272]). Two cases may be usefully contrasted:

> In *Dobson v Thames Water*, facts previously, re the claim for nuisance by residents, C, who lived near the Mogden Sewage Treatment Works in Middlesex, Thames Water, D, sought to rely on the defence of statutory authority arising out of their duties under the Water Industry Act 1991. **Held:** an actionable private nuisance. D could not rely on the defence of statutory authorisation. D did not carry out the work and conduct the operation at the Mogden Works with all reasonable regard and care for the interests of other persons, including nearby residents. There were a number of breaches by D, in respect of the sources of odour, such as: failing to apply suitable chemical dosing; failing to maintain, operate or replace the system to clean the storm water tanks effectively; and failing to maintain or replace the necessary pumps, pipework and valves. In *Pearson v North Western Gas Board*,[273] an explosion occurred early New Year's Day in 1963 in Manchester. The home of the Pearsons, C, was entirely destroyed by the ignition of a mixture of coal gas and air. The coal gas had escaped from the Gas Board's, D's, gas main, and had accumulated under the floor boards of C's home. Mr Pearson died and Mrs Pearson was seriously injured in the explosion. The gas main, which was made of metal, had been laid in 1878, was in good condition, and had an expectation of useful life of at least 120 years. The fracture was probably caused by a shift in the soil from severe and continuous frosts for nine nights. **Held:** it was conceded that *Rylands v Fletcher* must fail. D was statutorily authorised to supply gas to the area, and it could not be liable for the escape of the gas, as there was no negligence on D's part.

Judicial reservations

Clearly, the defence of statutory authorisation has important ramifications for adversely-affected residents – and that, ultimately, how widely the defence is applied is a matter of judicial policy.

On the one hand is the view that the defence should be widely construed, because providers of public utilities (gas, oil, water, electricity, etc) should not be held to be insurers for every escape or interference which such essential services provide to society. Application of the defence may result in a harsh outcome, but that is the policy which English common law has generally favoured (per *Dunne v North Western Gas Board*[274]):

> Gas, water and electricity services are a necessity of modern life, or at least are generally demanded as a requirement for the common good, and ... are being ... despatch[ed] to every village and hamlet in the country, with either statutory compulsion or sanction. It would seem odd that facilities so much sought after by the community, and approved by legislators, should be actionable at common law because they have been brought to the places where they are required, and have escaped without negligence by an unforeseen sequence of mishaps ... Gas, water and electricity are capable of doing damage, and a strict or absolute liability for any damage done by them would make the undertakers of these services insurers.

On the other hand, according to the Court of Appeal in *Barr v Biffa Waste*, the defence should be kept within limits – '[t]he common law of nuisance has co-existed with statutory controls, albeit less sophisticated, since the 19th century. There is no principle that the common law

[272] [2011] EWHC 3253 (TCC) [688], [694], [1120], citing: *Allen v Gulf Oil Refinery Ltd* [1979] 1 QB 156 (CA) 171, aff'd [1981] AC 1001 (HL) 1013.

[273] [1968] 2 All ER 669 (Manchester Assizes).

[274] [1964] 2 QB 806 (CA) 832, 834.

should "march with" a statutory scheme covering similar subject-matter. Short of express or implied statutory authority to commit a nuisance, there is no basis, in principle or authority, for using such a statutory scheme to cut down private law rights'.[275] Further, as Lord Hoffmann noted in *Transco*,[276] if the defence applies whenever a public utility escapes and causes C damage (absent any negligence on D's part), then the end result is that C suffers a 'private loss for a public benefit'.

Clearly, the application of the defence can leave landowners who have suffered the most serious of damage (such as the Pearsons) with no compensation at all – a matter which has troubled jurists elsewhere.

The comparative corner: **The defence of statutory authorisation**

In *Union of India v Prabhakaran Vijaya Kumar*,[277] the Indian Supreme Court criticised the statutory authorisation defence, as applied in English law, on two bases:

- the outcome in *Pearson* was a prime example of 'the decline of the rule in *Rylands v Fletcher* [which] left the individual injured by the activities of industrial society virtually without adequate protection';
- the policy reason in *Dunne* was misconceived: 'the idea that a body which acts not for its own profit but for the benefit of the community should not be liable [in nuisance or under *Rylands v Fletcher*] ... is based on a misconception. Strict liability has no element of moral censure. It is because such public bodies benefit the community that it is unfair to leave the result of a non-negligent accident to lie fortuitously on a particular individual rather than to spread it among the community generally'.

Furthermore, under modern law, any statute which purports to provide D with statutory authorisation must be read in light of modern human rights legislation. As emphasised in *Thomas v Bridgend BC*,[278] the court has power to remedy any defect in legislation which is not Convention-compliant under s 3 of the HRA, by 're-interpreting' the provision; or failing that, to make a declaration of incompatibility.

A right of prescription

§16.34 To acquire a right by prescription to conduct an activity which would otherwise be a nuisance, D must have carried out that activity, uninterrupted – and with C's consent to the activity *as a nuisance* – for at least 20 years.

Where the defence applies, then D has the benefit of a prescriptive right to cause the nuisance, and C cannot prevent the nuisance being committed as of right. As Lord Neuberger MR stated in *Coventry v Lawrence*, '[p]rescription is a form of deemed grant and arises as a result of long use'.[279]

That case confirmed that the nuisance to which the defence applies can be either some tangible emanation or encroachment which physically damages/injures/affects C's land, or

[275] [2012] EWCA Civ 312, [46(ii)].
[276] [2003] UKHL 61, [30] (quote), [39], citing *Hammersmith and City Rwy v Brand* (1869) LR 4 HL 171, 196.
[277] [2008] INSC 802, [36], [41]. [278] [2011] EWCA Civ 862, [2012] QB 512, [28]. [279] [2014] UKSC 13, [29], [32]–[34].

intangible interferences (noise in that case, but also potentially embracing smells, smoke, dust, etc) which affect C's use and enjoyment of his premises. Judge Seymour QC had remarked, at first instance, that '[t]he concept of a prescriptive right to create a noise which is a nuisance is a rather challenging one',[280] and that this had been recognised academically and judicially – per the authors of *Clerk & Lindsell on Torts*[281] ('whether a right to commit a nuisance by means of smoke, smells, noise or vibration can ever be acquired by prescription is doubtful'); and per *Hulley v Silversprings Bleaching Co*[282] ('certainty and uniformity [are] essential for the measurement and determination of the user by which the extent of the prescriptive right is to be ascertained', which was difficult for a noise-based interference). Those particular concerns were put to rest by the Supreme Court.

In *Coventry*,[283] Lord Neuberger also affirmed that D's right to commit a nuisance by noise by prescription (or, more accurately, the right to transmit sound waves over the servient land) is *an easement* which runs with the land affected by the noise (i.e., the servient tenement) – a view which reflected the 'property-based nature of nuisance'.

The defence has three elements. Dealing with each in turn:

i. the nuisance was carried out by D with the requisite degree of knowledge or acquiescence/tolerance by C (per *Sturges v Bridgman*[284]). This is an objective assessment, and depends upon whether a reasonable person in C's position (i.e., the owner of the servient tenement) was aware that a continuous right to enjoyment was being asserted by D (i.e., the dominant owner), and should be challenged if C resisted that assertion being made against his land (per *Coventry v Lawrence*[285]).

ii. the nuisance must have been carried out for at least 20 years – an arbitrary period, but which has a long pedigree for this defence. That 20 years does not need to be continuous (per Lord Neuberger in *Coventry v Lawrence*, approving of the proposition that 'an interruption of even seven years might not destroy the claim to have acquired a right by prescription over 20 years'[286]), and it does not even have to occur on every single day of the 20 years. Moreover, some significant interruption may mean that D's activities did not occur over the full 20 years at all – and yet, still, a prescription defence can be upheld, provided D's activities were consistent and significant enough over the whole 20 years for element (i) to be made out. That would be sufficient to establish the prescriptive right – rendering the defence slightly easier for D to prove.

In *Coventry v Lawrence*, facts previously, the stadium had been used for motor-racing activities for 20 years when C claimed that a nuisance existed. However, there was an interruption in use, especially in respect of stock car and banger racing, in 1991– 92. **Held (first instance):** that was fatal to any defence of prescription. **Held (HL):** an interruption of 2 years did not defeat a prescriptive right. The owners of Fenland ought to have appreciated what right was being claimed by D in operating the consistent and substantial motor-racing activities at the stadium for all but two of those 20 years.

iii. the activity being carried on by D must have constituted *an actionable nuisance* for the requisite 20 years. Hence, even where D's activities prompted some level of complaint (either from C or from

280 *Lawrence v Fen Tigers Ltd* [2011] EWHC 360, [214].
281 (20th edn, Sweet & Maxwell, 2010) [20–85], cited in *Lawrence, ibid*, [214] .
282 [1922] 2 Ch 268, 280–81. 283 [2014] UKSC 13, [29]. 284 (1879) LR 11 Ch D 852 (CA) 863–64.
285 [2014] UKSC 13, [142] (Lord Neuberger). 286 *ibid*, [37], citing: *Carr v Foster* (1842) 3 QB 581.

others) during that 20 years, if the complaint 'was of so trifling a character, that ... [D's] acts would not have given rise to any proceedings either at law or in equity' (per *Sturges*), or if there was a lack of complaint altogether for a significant period (per *Coventry*), then there is no basis for stating that the nuisance has continued for over 20 years. The activity may have, but a nuisance did not.

This third element may raise a considerable evidential difficulty for D. Whilst *Coventry* and *Sturges* at least recognise that, in principle, a right to create a nuisance by noise can be acquired by prescription, the difficulty is establishing *a level of uniformity and constancy* sufficient to amount to nuisance – the interference must be such that C could validly complain of it, for that whole period. Otherwise, if it was not a nuisance for some of that period, then how could it be said that C was accepting, rather than objecting to, the assertion of a right against his land? In that regard, 'time does not run for the purposes of prescription unless the activities of the owner (or occupier) of the dominant land can be objected to by the owner of the servient land', as Lord Neuberger put it in *Coventry* – albeit acknowledging that this element of the defence could well amount to a problem 'practical in nature', and make proof of the defence 'difficult'.[287] Both of the leading cases aptly demonstrated the problems which the element causes for D:

> In *Coventry v Lawrence*, facts previously, **held**: an actionable nuisance; and no defence of prescription applied. The evidence did not support that D's activities re the Stadium had caused a nuisance to Fenland for a continuous period of 20 years (even allowing for periods of no activity by D at all). The fact that motor-racing and associated activities were carried on was not enough; no complaints or witness statements showed that anyone objected to D's activities much before 1994, or that they constituted an interference with the use and enjoyment of Fenland or surrounding properties for much of that period. Hence, prescription could not be proven. In *Sturges v Bridgman*,[288] facts previously, **held**: an actionable nuisance; and no defence of prescription applied. D's activities were not a nuisance until C's consulting room was built. Hence, there could be no consent by C to any nuisance-causing activity for more than 20 years. There had been an 'invalid lady' who had lived in C's house before his occupation, who about 30 years before, had requested D 'if possible to discontinue the use of the mortars before 8.00 am', plus there was 'some evidence of the garden wall having been subjected to vibration', but both of these were so slight that they did not point to any nuisance, or any nuisance being consented to.

The defence cannot be taken too far. If D's nuisance-making activities exceed the scope of the prescriptive right to commit a nuisance, then C may successfully sue for the tort. The defence of prescription does not permit **all** manner of noises, or pollution, or smells, but only permits interferences to the extent of the nuisance which has been agreed to or tolerated for the 20-year period (per *Coventry v Lawrence*[289]).

The independent contractor/non-delegable duty defence

§16.35 If a nuisance was caused by an independent contractor (X) who was engaged by D, then D is entitled to rely on a defence that an employer (i.e., D) is not liable for the torts of his independent contractor. The defence is subject to two exceptions: D is strictly liable for the nuisance caused by his independent contractor X: (1) where X undertook ultra-hazardous activities when committing the nuisance; and (2) under the 'dividing structures' exception. Where either exception applies, D is liable for the nuisance committed by his independent contractor X.

[287] [2014] UKSC 13, [37], [43]. [288] (1879) LR 11 Ch D 852 (CA) 863, 865. [289] [2014] UKSC 13, [39].

The principle of 'no liability of an employer for the acts of an independent contractor' applies just as much to claims in private nuisance as it does to claims in negligence (per *Tinseltime Ltd v Davies*[290]).

In *Tinseltime Ltd v Davies*, part of a building, 'The Old Creamery', owned by the Welsh Assembly Government, D, was demolished by Mr Davies, and his employed labourer, Mr Roberts. Fountain of Youth (FOY), C, used part of the Old Creamery for its tinsel-making business. When Mr Roberts was cutting concrete blocks, large amounts of dust were produced, which entered C's premises and clogged up its machinery, causing significant damage. The machinery had to be repaired and, until repairs could be completed, C lost production and sales. **Held**: an actionable private nuisance; but D could rely on the independent contractor defence.

There are two exceptional circumstances in which D will be liable for the private nuisance caused by X – because D, as employer, has a non-delegable duty to C in the following circumstances:

Exception #1: Ultra-hazardous activities. According to the Court of Appeal in *Biffa Waste Services Ltd v Outokumpu Wenmac AB and Maschinenfabrik Ernst Hese GmBH*,[291] D, as employer, is liable for the negligence of his independent contractor, where the activities of the independent contractor are 'ultra hazardous'. This principle was established much earlier, in 1934, in *Honeywill v Larkin*.[292] In *Tinseltime Ltd v Davies*, it was clarified that, although *Biffa* was only concerned with an allegation in negligence, the ultra-hazardous exception applied to private nuisance as well as to negligence, so that the scope of the exception was precisely the same in nuisance as it was in negligence.[293]

The *Biffa* court was not enamoured of the exception, describing it as 'so unsatisfactory that its application should be kept as narrow as possible'.[294] Indeed, the exception has since proven difficult to rely upon, in the context of private nuisance.

In *Tinseltime Ltd v Davies*, facts above, **held**: the ultra-hazardous exception did not apply. There was nothing that could be regarded as 'exceptionally dangerous' about the dust-creating activity of cutting concrete blocks in the open, adjacent to FOY's premises.

Indeed, this explanation – that D owes a non-delegable duty to C, where the independent contractor conducted a hazardous activity – is analogous to (but separate from) the principle in *Rylands v Fletcher*, where D is strictly liable for the wrongdoing of his independent contractor in permitting a dangerous thing to escape from D's land onto C's land. That analogy between *Rylands v Fletcher* and a non-delegable duty is explored further in Chapter 17.

Exception #2: Dividing structures. According to *Alcock v Wraith*,[295] where D has a legal right to carry out work on a wall or dividing structure between two properties, and that work (carried out by independent contractor X) involves a risk of damage to the adjoining property, the law imposes on D a non-delegable duty to ensure that the work is carried out carefully. This exception applies to nuisance claims as well as to negligence claims.

In *Tinseltime Ltd v Davies*,[296] **held**: the exception could not apply. The work being done for the cutting of the blocks was going to provide part of the outside wall of the Old Creamery. However, it was not a case of D (or Mr Roberts) working on one-half of the building, causing damage to FOY's

[290] [2011] EWHC 1199 (TCC) [51]–[55]. [291] [2008] EWCA Civ 1257, [63]. [292] [1934] 1 KB 191.
[293] [2011] EWHC 1199 (TCC) [50]. [294] [2008] EWCA Civ1257, [78]. [295] (1991) 59 BLR 20 (CA).
[296] [2011] EWHC 1199 (TCC) [54] (Stephen-Davies J).

part. There is no warrant for taking into account the extent of the works as a whole – otherwise it would follow that where a completely new building is erected next to an existing building, the mere fact that the works forming part of the erection of the new building involve some shoring up of the foundations of the old building would mean that the employer would be under a non-delegable duty for all of the works, even those undertaken on the other side of the site from the existing building. That would be far too onerous.

The 'common enemy' doctrine

§16.36 The 'common enemy rule' permits landowner, D, to erect barriers, the effect of which will be that water, which would otherwise have flowed onto his land, may be diverted onto his neighbour's, C's, land.

The so-called 'common enemy' doctrine arises from a long line of authority, dating back to the 18th century – specifically, 'the rule was first recognised in the Court of Session in 1741 in *Farquharson v Farquharson*'.[297] The defence provides that 'an owner or occupier of land is entitled to use or develop his land so as to prevent flood waters coming on to his land. If, in times of flood, waters which would have entered his land, in consequence damage another's land, that does not provide a cause of action in nuisance' (per *Arscott v Coal Authority*[298]).

In *Arscott*, the land of Mr Arscott, C, flooded, after the Coal Authority, D, made improvements (anti-flooding works) to its own land to prevent it from flooding. The flooding of C's land was an unforeseeable result of those defensive works designed to protect D's own land from flooding. **Held**: no actionable nuisance. D was entitled to act as he had, by reason of the 'common enemy' doctrine.

Estoppel by acquiescence

§16.37 C may lose the legal right to sue for nuisance, because of the defence of estoppel by acquiescence, whereby D was encouraged or allowed by C to believe that he was entitled to commit the nuisance, to D's detriment.

The defence of estoppel by acquiescence is 'an encouragement or allowance of a party to believe something to his detriment' (per *Jones v Stones*[299]). In the context of nuisance, it has three requirements:

i. C encouraged D to believe that he was entitled to commit the nuisance-making interference;
ii. that encouragement caused detriment to D; and
iii. in all the circumstances, it was unconscionable for C to assert his legal rights.

Jones v Stones was a trespass, rather than a nuisance, case, but the defence is analogous in both torts. The Court of Appeal considered that, although the estoppel usually applies where D has acquired some right over C's property which C cannot then object to because of acquiescence, the defence is equally applicable where D is alleged to have committed an act of nuisance. In both types of cases, C's conduct 'relates to his property interests, and the estoppel operates to bar the enforcement of [C's] legal rights' (per *Lester v Woodgate*[300]).

[297] Courts of Session (1811) vol 29–30, 12779, cited in: *Arscott v Coal Authy* [2004] EWCA Civ 892, fn 11.
[298] [2004] EWCA Civ 892, [4], [32], approving trial judge: [2003] EWHC 1690 (QB) [27].
[299] [1999] 1 WLR 1739 (CA) 1744–45. [300] [2010] EWCA Civ 199, [43].

This defence, where applicable, extinguishes C's right to pursue damages for the tort, so that D's interference cannot constitute an actionable nuisance. It bars common law damages, let alone an equitable discretionary remedy such as an injunction. (By contrast, the defence of laches (delay) is a general equitable defence which only bars the grant of equitable injunctive relief, when C has been guilty of passivity and undue delay in asserting his rights, but does not extinguish C's legal right to sue for the tort, nor does it prevent the award of damages for C's claim in nuisance.)

In *Lester v Woodgate*, Mr Mees, predecessor of Woodgates, D, destroyed part of a steep ramp on Mr Lester's, C's, land, and built a carparking space at the foot of the ramp. This work by Mr Mees made C's ramp unusable. D then bought the land off Mr Mees, and used the carparking space built by Mr Mees (thereby adopting Mr Mees' nuisance). C's predecessor, Mr Chitty, had objected to Mr Mees throwing some rubble from the works onto C's land, but did not complain about or challenge Mr Mees' destruction of part of the ramp. C sought a mandatory injunction for the re-instatement of the ramp, as well as an injunction to prevent parking. **Held**: the defence of estoppel by acquiescence applied. Mr Chitty had complained about the dumping of the rubble, but had accepted the destruction of the ramp. This amounted to an assurance or encouragement, that Mr Mees could use the carparking space, necessary to found an estoppel, and it would be unconscionable for C to now seek to reinstate the ramp. Mr Chitty had been in a position to object to Mr Mees about the carpark (as he did about the dumping of spoil), and chose not to, which allowed Mr Mees to sell the property to D, with the apparent benefit of these parking places. That defence precluded C from claiming any injunctive relief or damages (the sum of £10 awarded for the loss of use of the ramp was overturned on appeal, and C recovered nothing).

Acts of God

§16.38 D is not liable for interferences or escapes caused by natural events, or 'acts of God'.

Some event amounting to an 'act of God' is a typical defence used in relation to torts of strict liability, and relates to the lack of causal connection between D's conduct and C's damage, as the House of Lords pointed out in *Transco plc v Stockport MBC*.[301]

In the context of private nuisance, in *Ellison v MOD*,[302] an allegation that the flooding of C's land was an 'inevitable accident' was not considered, given that no nuisance arose; and in *Sedleigh-Denfield*,[303] the potential for the defence to apply was judicially recognised, but the rainfall was not so heavy or exceptional as to amount to an act of God.

The defence seems to have arisen more extensively in the context of escapes of dangerous things under *Rylands v Fletcher*, and hence, will be deferred to Chapter 17.

Contributory negligence/*volenti*

§16.39 D has a complete defence if C consented to the interference with full knowledge and without duress; and has a partial defence if C contributed to the damage suffered by D's interference.

It was suggested in *Leakey v National Trust*[304] in dicta that *volenti* could be a possible defence to private nuisance, where C, 'knowing of the danger to their property, by word or deed, had

301 [2004] 2 AC 1 (HL) 24–25. 302 (1996) 81 BLR 101 (QB).
303 [1940] AC 880 (HL) 888–89. 304 [1980] QB 485 (CA) 515.

showed their willingness to accept that danger'. However, a successful case of its application has not been found.

The partial defence of contributory negligence also applies to nuisance, given that s 4 of the Law Reform (Contributory Negligence) Act 1945 defines 'fault' as 'other act or omission which gives rise to a liability in tort'. That encompasses an interference amounting to a private nuisance, and the defence's application to the tort has been uncontroversial, if somewhat unusual.

In *Khan v Harrow LBC*,[305] a dispute arose between neighbours, Mrs Kane, D, and Mr and Mrs Khan, C, about encroaching tree roots. D was not liable in nuisance. **Held:** had CN applied, 15% would have been allocated against C. Ramsey J noted that it was a 'surprising aspect of this case that there was no communication between C and D directly concerning the trees and, in particular, the damage caused to their property by the tree roots from D's trees'. Given that there is a 'concept of reasonableness between neighbours', it would have been reasonable for C to have communicated with D.

REMEDIES

Where a nuisance is proven, C will seek compensatory damages for the consequences of the past nuisance. In the event that D's interference is liable to continue, C will also seek an injunction to restrain D from committing that nuisance in the future, or alternatively, an injunction may be refused but damages awarded in lieu of that injunction. In addition, this section will briefly consider the availability (if any) of other remedies: abatement; and restitutionary, aggravated, and exemplary damages. The remedies canvassed here are equally applicable under the rule in *Rylands v Fletcher*, given that both are property-based torts.

Compensatory damages

§16.40 C may recover damages for (1) physical damage to the land; (2) consequential chattel damage; (3) consequential economic losses; (4) special damages for outlays to deal with the nuisance; and (5) loss of amenity (albeit controversial).

Dealing with each briefly in turn:

Physical damage to the land

Injury to things growing on the land will clearly constitute damage to the land sufficient to base a private nuisance or *Rylands v Fletcher* claim (see, respectively, the damage to fruit trees and hedges/herbage from acid rain in *St Helen's Smelting Co v Tipping*,[306] and damage to plants and shrubs from creosote fumes in *West v Bristol Tramways Co*[307]).

Injury to buildings/structures affixed to the land (e.g., the house damage sustained by the claimant when his neighbour's LPG-fuelled car exploded because of a spark from the freezer in *Coxhill v Forward*[308]) will constitute compensable damage under both torts too.

C will seek the usual measure of damages in tort, which is to put C in the position as if the tort committed by D (i.e., the interference/escape) had not occurred. Where the interference/escape causes injury to the fabric of C's land, then the basis of damages may comprise one of two measures (per *Bartoline Ltd v Royal Sun Alliance Insurance plc*[309]). First, it may be the

[305] [2013] EWHC 2687 (TCC) [91]–[92]. [306] (1865) 11 HLC 642, 11 ER 1483. [307] [1908] 2 KB 14 (CA).
[308] QB, McNeill J, 19 Mar 1986 (available via Lexis). [309] [2006] EWHC 3598 (QB (Mercantile Court)) [48].

reinstatement value – calculated by the cost of doing remedial works on the land, so as to remove or repair the effects of the interference/escape (e.g., to remove the effects of pollution). Secondly, it may be calculated by the diminution in value of the land – brought about by the interference/escape and its effects ('a landowner may not think it worth the trouble and expense of cleaning up his land and may be content simply to seek damages from the wrongdoer for any diminution in value or interference with the use of the land', as the court put it in *Bartoline*[310]). In *Hunter v Canary Wharf*, Lord Lloyd pointed out that these two measures will often (but not necessarily) be the same.

Consequential chattel damage

Damage to washing, cars, or toys, resulting from an interference/escape can found a claim in private nuisance or in *Rylands v Fletcher*, where such damage is consequential upon damage to the land itself.

In *Halsey v Esso Petroleum Co Ltd*,[311] facts previously, noxious acid smuts from the chimneys were deposited onto Mr Halsey's, C's, car, damaging its paintwork, and also damaged some clothes which had been hung out to dry in his garden. **Held:** claims in nuisance and *Rylands v Fletcher* both succeeded, and this damage was recoverable. In *Hunter v Canary Wharf Ltd*,[312] residents, C, around the construction site for the Limehouse Link Road complained about excessive amounts of dust created by the construction. C claimed damages for the dirty washing, and dusty furniture and cars, as part of their claim in private nuisance. **Held:** the claim in *Rylands v Fletcher* was abandoned, and private nuisance failed because of standing difficulties (discussed previously).

In *Hunter*,[313] the House of Lords appeared to accept, in dicta, that consequential chattel damage *could* be recoverable in nuisance (and presumably also in *Rylands v Fletcher*) – Lord Hoffmann referred to scenarios where, 'in addition to damages for injury to his land, [C] is able to recover damages for consequential loss ... if the land is flooded, [C] may also be able to recover damages for chattels or livestock lost as a result'; whilst Lord Cooke remarked that C, 'should be entitled to recover in nuisance for damage to chattels', giving the example of C's car, being damaged by spray from D's land.

Consequential versus pure economic loss

Economic losses (e.g., lost profits) sustained by C as a result of the interference/escape of the dangerous thing are recoverable in private nuisance and under *Rylands v Fletcher*, if they are consequential upon injury to the land. The standing rules require that C has a proprietary or possessory interest in the land which suffered the damage. (It will be recalled that pure economic losses are irrecoverable, according to the 'exclusionary rule'.)

In *Hunter v Canary Wharf Ltd* (re a private nuisance claim caused by excessive dust), Lord Hoffmann stated that C, whose property is damaged, 'will be entitled to loss of profits which are the result of inability to use the land for the purposes of his business'.[314] In *Bartoline Ltd v Royal Sun Alliance Insurance plc* too (a *Rylands v Fletcher* pollution-of-waterways case), it was acknowledged that C, who has suffered from the effects of pollution, 'might well be able

[310] *ibid*, [48]. [311] [1961] 1 WLR 683 (QB). [312] [1997] AC 655 (HL) 719.

[313] [1997] AC 655 (HL) 706 (Lord Hoffmann). Although Lord Cooke dissented on the question of standing to sue, he did not dissent on chattel damage.

[314] [1997] UKHL 14, [1997] AC 655 (HL) 706.

to recover damages for any consequential loss resulting, for example, from interference with his business activities'.[315]

In *Cambridge Water Co Ltd v Eastern Counties Leather plc*,[316] facts previously, both torts failed, due to lack of foreseeability of damage (contamination by PCE) to the borehole at Sawston Mill which was owned by Cambridge Water, C. Had the claim succeeded, C could have claimed damages for the damage to the borehole and water itself, and consequential economic losses arising because C had to take the Sawston supply out of action, develop a new source of water supply until carbon filtration technology could be trusted to treat and remove PCE from the Sawston Mill water, and supply its customers from that different source.

As discussed previously under 'Remoteness', relational pure economic loss is not recoverable under either private nuisance or *Rylands v Fletcher*. Indeed **no** pure economic loss suffered by C is recoverable under these torts (per *D Pride & Partners v Institute for Animal Health*[317]). Although the distinction which the law draws between consequential economic losses (which are recoverable) and pure economic losses (which are irrecoverable) is long-standing, identifying precisely what is pure or consequential economic loss, where an interference or escape has occurred, can be quite contentious and finely-drawn. Essentially, consequential economic loss accrues from C's **damaged** property, machines, etc. Pure economic loss, on the other hand, results where there is **no damage** *per se*, but C's premises or activities are shut down, idle, or inactive, due to D's interference/escape. (Alternatively, the types of relational economic losses in *D Pride* and *Cattle v Stockton*, discussed under 'Remoteness', are also 'pure' in type.) C must therefore prove that his economic losses were consequential, because of the 'cold face' which the law turns towards pure economic losses under these torts. The following cases are to be contrasted on this very important point:

In *GT Gilbert (t/as Woods Farm Christmas Trees) v British Waterways Board*,[318] the Gilberts, C, were brothers who, in partnership, built up a successful business selling Christmas trees (the largest in the country). British Waterways, D, operated a canal, which ran across C's land, and which leaked persistently from 1997–2005. This caused plantations 18 and 19 to become waterlogged, the roots of the Norway Spruces growing in those plantations were affected, and a substantial number died or were damaged beyond use. **Held:** both private nuisance and *Rylands v Fletcher* succeeded. This was not a case of 'pure' economic loss, since C's loss of business profits arose from the direct physical damage to their trees. C was entitled to claim consequential losses of the lost profits on those trees which would otherwise have been sold, less the costs of production and of harvesting. In *British Celanese Ltd v AH Hunt (Capacitors) Ltd*,[319] facts previously, re the metal foil strips which flew off D's premises, causing a power failure, and damage to C's machinery when the electricity supply was cut, **held**: claims in *Rylands v Fletcher*, negligence and nuisance succeeded, and D was liable for the damage to the machines, plus the consequential loss of profit whilst they were being repaired. By contrast, in *Spartan Steel and Alloys Ltd v Martin & Co (Contractors) Ltd*[320] (facts previously in Chapter 4 under the 'exclusionary rule' in negligence), where D's negligent act of severing an electricity cable cut electricity supply to C's factory, C suffered physical damage in the form of one metal 'melt' which had to be thrown out (worth £368), otherwise it would have solidified and caused damage to the furnaces; and C also suffered consequential economic losses, *viz*, lost profits on that melt (worth £400). Both were recoverable. However, the furnaces themselves were not damaged by the

[315] [2006] EWHC 3598 (QB) [48]. [316] [1993] UKHL 12, [1994] 2 AC 264 (HL). [317] [2009] EWHC 685 (QB) [55].
[318] [2005] EWHC 3094 (TCC) [62]. [319] [1969] 1 WLR 959 (QB). [320] [1973] QB 27.

electricity cut; and hence, whilst the furnaces remained idle, and C waited for power to be restored, the melts which could not be done in that time and the lost profits from those melts were pure economic losses, and were not recoverable.

Special damage

C may be compensated for outlays for any expenses required to overcome the effects of the nuisance.

In *Dobson v Thames Water Utilities Ltd*,[321] special damages were awarded for de-odourisers and fans which C had to install, to abate the smells emanating from D's sewage treatment works.

General damages for loss of amenity

Where C contends that the nuisance-making activity of D causes C personal physical discomfort, then loss of amenity damages may be awarded. However, their basis, and quantum, in private nuisance has been controversial, given that damages in nuisance are purportedly for an injury to C's land, and **not** to C's person. Personal discomfort, in this context, may entail, say, not being able to sit out in the garden, invite friends over, leave windows and doors open, or leave washing and other chattels in the yard, for fear of contamination.

According to the House of Lords in *Hunter v Canary Wharf Ltd*,[322] damages in nuisance are for *injury to the land* – but where the land's utility has been diminished by the nuisance, then 'it is for the diminution in such utility that [C] is entitled to compensation'. Key principles governing damages for loss of amenity are principally derived from *Dobson v Thames Water Utilities Ltd*[323] and from *Hunter*:

i. Damages in nuisance for personal discomfort are *prima facie* assessed on the basis of the diminution of the amenity value of the land (whether in its capital value or rental value), rather than damages for the personal discomfort itself. However, it is not strictly necessary, for an award of 'loss of amenity damages', that it can be shown that C's property would sell or rent for less (per *Bone v Seale*, and approved on this point in *Hunter v Canary Wharf Ltd*).

   In *Hunter*, Lord Hoffmann remarked[324] that, 'diminution in capital value is not the only measure of loss ... the value of the right to occupy a house which smells of pigs must be less than the value of the occupation of an equivalent house which does not. In the case of a transitory nuisance, the capital value of the property will seldom be reduced. But [C] is entitled to compensation for the diminution in the amenity value of the property during the period for which the nuisance persisted. To some extent, this involves placing a value on intangibles'. A large measure of imprecision is 'perhaps inevitable', but the court will be assisted by real estate agents putting a value on those 'intangibles', by taking account of the experience of those who live at the affected premises (that is 'likely to be the best evidence available of how amenity has been affected in practical terms', per *Dobson*[325]).

ii. A court cannot make separate awards of damages for distress in cases of nuisance, because whatever personal distress or discomfort C suffers as a result of the smells, noise, etc, will form part of the assessment of C's loss of amenity (per *Raymond v Young*[326]).

[321] [2011] EWHC 3253 (TCC) [1016]. [322] [1997] AC 655 (HL) 706 (Lord Hoffmann).
[323] [2011] EWHC 3253 (TCC) [1027]–[1032], and earlier: [2009] EWCA Civ 28 (an appeal in the same case) [31]–[36].
[324] [1997] AC 655 (HL) 706. [325] [2009] EWCA Civ 28 [33] (Waller LJ). [326] [2015] EWCA Civ 456, [28].

iii. Damages for diminution of amenity value may depend upon the size and value of the affected property, but it will not depend upon the number of occupiers. Loss of amenity damages cannot be inflated, simply by the number of people who live there (whether or not they have the requisite standing to sue). Damages are awarded, under this head, for 'damage to the land', and loss of amenity will have to be divided among them (per *Hunter v Canary Wharf Ltd*,[327] and applied recently in *Raymond v Young*[328]). Hence, there is 'one potential cause of action for each home' (per Lord Lloyd in *Hunter*[329] – if D operated a factory which produced vast quantities of smoke over neighbouring properties, then the same damages would be awarded to a bachelor as to a family with two children).

In *Bone v Seale*,[330] D was a pig farmer, and Cs were the owners and occupiers of two adjoining properties who objected to the smell from the pig farm, over a period of 12 years. **Held (first instance):** an actionable nuisance; and damages of >£6,000 awarded to each C to reflect the loss of amenity. **Held (CA):** damages reduced to $1,000, to reflect loss of amenity to the properties as a whole. No evidence was adduced of any diminution in market value of either of the properties. In *Dobson*,[331] Waller LJ gave the example of where amenity damages will be totally inappropriate, i.e., where a house was unoccupied throughout D's nuisance-making activities, e.g., where C was working or living elsewhere, or keeping the house empty awaiting renovation. There can be no impact upon the occupier, necessary to prove loss of amenity, in these scenarios.

iv. Damages for loss of amenity are just as relevant to transitory nuisances which interfere with C's comfort and enjoyment of the land, as they are to nuisances which cause permanent injury to the land (per *Dennis v MOD*[332]).

Loss of amenity damages are only 'intended to provide modest, not generous, compensation' (per *Berent*[333]). The sample of cases in the Table below bears out that view (where 'pa' means 'per annum for the duration of the nuisance').

Quantum of damages

Case	Nutshell	Outcome
Watson v Croft Promo Sport Ltd[a]	noise from a motor-racing circuit (C accepted use of the track for 40 days pa; it was used for 140 days pa; the damages reflected non-consent to a noise nuisance for 100 days pa)	£2,000 pa, for a more expensive home of £720,000; $750 pa awarded for a lesser-value home of £400,000
Milka v Chetwynd Animal By-Products (1995) Ltd[b]	smells arising from a meat-knackers/ animal rendering plant	£1,000 pa
Anthony v Coal Authority[c]	flooding (duration of the past nuisance about 4 yrs)	£3,500 pa for each property

[a] [2008] EWHC 759 (QB, Newcastle-upon-Tyne District Registry) [107], [110].
[b] (Carmarthen CC, Case No 19100) [555]–[556].
[c] [2005] EWHC 1654 (QB) [117], [163].

[327] [1997] AC 655 (HL) 692–93. [328] [2015] EWCA Civ 456, [27]–[28].
[329] [1997] AC 655 (HL) 698–99. [330] [1975] 1 WLR 797 (CA). [331] [2009] EWCA Civ 28, [34].
[332] [2003] EWHC 793. [333] [2012] EWCA Civ 961, [40].

Case	Nutshell	Outcome
Dobson v Thames Water Utilities Ltd[d]	smells from waste treatment plant (duration of the past nuisance about 10 yrs)	up to £630 pa, for the worst-affected house
Jones v Ruth[e]	renovation works at D's premises, creating noise and lack of privacy for C	£30,000 awarded for loss of amenity
Berent v Family Mosaic Housing[f]	subsidence and cracking to C's house due to tree root damage caused by D's trees	£150 for gross inconvenience and loss of amenity
Barr v Biffa Waste Services Ltd[g]	odours emanating from D's landfill and waste treatment site	£1,000 pa for each household affected by the nuisance

[d] [2011] EWHC 3253 (TCC).
[e] [2011] EWCA Civ 804, [37].
[f] [2012] EWCA Civ 961, considerably reducing the £5,000 awarded at trial: [2011] EWHC 1353 (TCC) [141].
[g] [2011] EWHC 1003 (TCC) [556].

Personal and psychiatric injury

§16.41 The weight of appellate authority is that C cannot claim for personal, or psychiatric, injuries sustained as a result of D's interference/escape of the dangerous thing, either in private nuisance or under *Rylands v Fletcher.*

Personal injuries. Interestingly, insofar as private nuisance is concerned, the House of Lords was somewhat mixed on the issue of damages for personal injuries in *Hunter v Canary Wharf Ltd*,[334] albeit that anything said on this topic was dicta only. Some seemed to leave the door to personal injuries being recoverable ajar (e.g., Lord Cooke remarked that personal injury has been recoverable in public nuisance, and that 'it would be hard to see any sensible difference between public and private nuisance'). The majority were of the view, however, that '[s]o far as the claim is for personal injury ... the only appropriate cause of action is negligence' (Lord Hoffmann, with Lords Lloyd and Hope making statements to same effect).

Since then, the Court of Appeal has definitively stated that damages for personal injuries are **not** recoverable in private nuisance (a principle 'clearly established', per *Corby Group Litigation v Corby BC*[335]), because the tort is 'based on the interference by one occupier of land with the right in or enjoyment of land by another'. Hence, there is no place for recovery for personal injuries arising from that interference. That principle has been applied by the Court of Appeal since.

In *Ruth v Jones*,[336] Ms Jones, C, alleged that she witnessed damage to her property at no 105, as a result of the nuisance-causing activities of D at no 103, and that, as a result, she suffered from severe back pain brought on by anxiety and depression. It was held at trial, and not appealed against,

[334] [1997] UKHL 14, [1997] AC 655 (HL) 692 (Lord Goff), 719 (Lord Cooke), 696 (Lord Lloyd, emphasis in original), 724 (Lord Hope), 707 (Lord Hoffmann).
[335] [2008] EWCA Civ 463, [2009] 2 WLR 609, [13].
[336] [2011] EWCA Civ 804, [13].

that it was not possible to award damages for personal injury based on a claim in private nuisance. In *Hirose Electrical UK Ltd v Peak Ingredients Ltd*,[337] the claim in nuisance was, in part, based upon employees' complaints that the garlic/curry odours emanating from D's premises caused those employees breathing difficulties, e.g. asthma, sinus problems, severe headaches, feelings of sickness and nausea, and dry throats. The claim in private nuisance failed for other reasons, but even had it succeeded, damages could not have been awarded for personal injuries *per se*.

By contrast, personal injury damages **are** recoverable in public nuisance (per 'Public nuisance', an online chapter).

The House of Lords has also confirmed that damages for personal injury cannot be recovered under *Rylands v Fletcher*. In *Transco plc v Stockport MBC*,[338] Lord Bingham held that a *Rylands v Fletcher* claim 'cannot include a claim for death or personal injury, since such a claim does not relate to any right in or enjoyment of land', and that, as 'a sub-species of nuisance', both torts are 'directed, and directed only, to the protection of interests in land'; Lord Hoffmann explained the reasoning in two steps: *Cambridge Water* was a decision of the House which held that *Rylands v Fletcher* is a special form of nuisance, and *Hunter* decided, a few years later, that nuisance is a tort against land: 'It must, I think, follow that damages for personal injuries are not recoverable under the rule'; and Lord Hobhouse observed that personal injuries are covered by other torts, such as negligence, but not by *Rylands* (or under private nuisance). Although these statements in *Transco* were, strictly speaking, obiter dicta (no personal injury from the burst water-pipe occurred), that position had already been adopted in *Read v J Lyons & Co Ltd*.[339] Lord Macmillan categorically said that the rule in *Rylands* 'has nothing to do with personal injuries', and Viscount Simon pointed out that Lord Blackburn himself never alluded to personal injuries being recoverable under the rule either.

Given the above, some earlier authority in which C sued successfully under private nuisance and/or *Rylands v Fletcher* for personal injuries must now be taken not to be good law:

In *Malone v Laskey*,[340] it was assumed that Mrs Malone, C's wife, could recover in private nuisance for the personal injuries she sustained, when a bracket fell on her head. This would now be impossible. In *Hale v Jennings Bros*,[341] Ms Hale, C, was the owner of a shooting-gallery at a fairground, and Jennings Bros, D, were amusement proprietors who occupied the adjoining land on which they conducted a chair-o-plane fair ride. A rider in one of the chairs swung it around and bounced in it, causing it to become loose, and both chair and rider separated from the rest of the apparatus, sailed through the air, and crashed into C, causing her very serious injury. *Rylands v Fletcher* succeeded, and those personal injuries were recoverable. In *Perry v Kendricks Transport Ltd*,[342] Trevor Perry, C, was severely burnt on Kendrick's, D's, premises, from the explosion of a petrol tank of a bus, into which two boys had thrown a lighted match. *Rylands v Fletcher* failed, due to a valid defence being available to D, but it was accepted that personal injuries could be recovered for in *Rylands v Fletcher*.

The capacity to recover damages for personal injuries is one advantage which negligence offers over private nuisance/*Rylands v Fletcher* – prompting some courts to focus specifically on negligence.

[337] [2011] EWCA Civ 987.

[338] [2003] UKHL 61, [2004] 2 AC 1, [9] (Lord Bingham), [35] (Lord Hoffmann), [52] (Lord Hobhouse), and cited in: *Corby* [2008] EWCA Civ 463, [13].

[339] [1947] AC 156 (HL) 173 (Lord Macmillan), 169 (Viscount Simon).

[340] [1904–6] All ER Rep 304 (CA) 306.

[341] [1938] 1 All ER 579 (CA) 586 (Scott LJ).

[342] [1956] 1 WLR 85 (CA).

In *Ribee v Norrie*,[343] Mrs Ribee, C, and Mr Norrie, D, owned neighbouring terraced houses. D's house had been converted into a hostel, with a number of individual bed-sits let to tenants, who shared communal kitchen and living areas. Due to a smouldering cigarette dropped in one of the communal areas by someone living or visiting the hostel, a fire started, and spread to C's property one night. She was awoken by her pet dog, and was rescued by the fire brigade. C suffered smoke inhalation, and some property damage. **Held:** negligence was proven against D for failing to control his tenants' actions. Although the case was pleaded in nuisance, negligence and *Rylands v Fletcher*, the court deliberately did not deal with private nuisance/*Rylands*, given the considerable doubt that existed as to whether C's personal injuries could be recovered under those causes of action.

Psychiatric injuries. Unusually, it may be claimed that an accident which caused the interference/escape of a dangerous thing gave rise to, not physical injuries, but psychiatric injuries. The predominant view is that the latter cannot be claimed for either, under these property-based torts.

As noted above, a claim for depression arising from D's alleged interference failed in *Ruth v Jones* in 2011. Earlier, in 1996, in *Crocker v British Coal Corp*[344] (where Ms Crocker was 11 when, as a pupil, she witnessed the Aberfan tip disaster in 1966, when a massive amount of moving sludge escaped from the Aberfan tip and buried and killed some of her school mates), Mance J did not rule out the possibility of recovery for psychiatric injuries under a *Rylands v Fletcher* claim, but suggested, in dicta, that, in light of *Cambridge Water*, it would be necessary to prove reasonable foreseeability of psychiatric injury. However, in light of the dicta statement by Lord Bingham in *Transco* in 2003, that damages for death or personal injury cannot be claimed for (although psychiatric injuries were not explicitly referred to), it seems clear that a claim for damages for pure psychiatric injuries would not now be permissible under *Rylands v Fletcher* (or, by analogy, in private nuisance).

However, under both torts, C may recover damages for discomfort, under 'loss of amenity' damages, as discussed above.

Injunctive relief

§16.42 C may seek an injunction which restrains D from causing/continuing the interference/escape, either at certain dates/times, or at all.

The Supreme Court recently reiterated, in *Coventry v Lawrence*,[345] that where it is likely that, unless restrained, D's interference/escape of a dangerous thing will continue, the remedy to which C is *prima facie* entitled is an injunction, to restrain D from committing the nuisance in the future. That means that the burden is on D to prove why an injunction should not be granted, and why D should be able to continue the activity, leaving C to his remedy in damages in respect of any future interferences/escapes. An award of damages, in lieu of injunctive relief, is colloquially called, 'Lord Cairns' Act damages', and will be considered shortly. In fact, whether C should be entitled to an injunction, or damages in lieu, is one of the most contentious aspects of nuisance litigation – and given that each is a discretionary remedy, the outcome is notoriously hard to predict.

343 [2000] EWCA Civ 275, [29]–[30] (Ward LJ).

344 (1996) 29 BMLR 159 (QB). The case turned on whether the claim was statute-barred.

345 [2014] UKSC 13, [101] (Lord Neuberger).

Certainly, an injunction will **not** be granted if there is no continuing nuisance (as in *Merthyr Tydfil Car Auction Ltd v Thomas*,[346] where an injunction was originally sought by C, but was dropped when D amended the conduct of their car auctions, so as to diminish the interference to C; C recovered damages for past nuisance only); or if the wording of the proposed injunction is so unclear that breach of the injunction by D would be difficult to ascertain or to enforce.

Crucially, injunctive relief will not necessarily be granted so as to stop D's activities altogether. The purpose of such relief is only to stop the *nuisance-causing* aspect of D's activities, and hence, the terms may be very specific and tailored.

In *Coventry v Lawrence*, facts previously, the Supreme Court reinstated the trial judge's injunctive relief, that D be restrained from carrying out motor-racing activities which emitted more than a specified level of noise at the track; there should be a lower specified level permitted at evening and at night; but that D were permitted to emit somewhat higher levels of noise on 12 weekends a year. In *White v Lynch*,[347] Mr White, C, owned a building in Biggin Hill, with retailers (and Mr Lynch's, D's, restaurant, Madison's) on the ground floor. Residents in flats on upper floors complained about the intrusive noise from C's restaurant, especially late at night. C successfully sued D in nuisance. C was entitled to a permanent injunction that the measured noise level in the restaurant (measured at a point 1 m from the dance floor and midway between two speakers) did not exceed 85 dBA. In *Watson v Croft Promo-Sport Ltd*,[348] facts previously, an injunction was awarded to prevent the use of D's motor-racing circuit for more than 40 days pa at specified decibel levels. There was no question of the stadium/track, restaurant, or motor-racing circuit being closed down, however.

Nonetheless, there are certainly some rare cases in which the award of an injunction has had the draconian impact of ceasing D's activities – and livelihood by that means – altogether.

In *Sturges v Bridgman*, facts previously, the doctor was entitled to stop the working of the confectioner/kitchen which had been long-established, because of the noise and vibrations caused in his consulting room. In *Tetley v Chitty*,[349] a local council granted planning permission to a go-kart club to develop a go-kart track on land owned by the authority, and had granted the club a 7-year lease to use it for that purpose. The council was liable in nuisance in its capacity as landlord, for the noise arising from the use of the track, and go-karting was injuncted. In *Adams v Ursell*,[350] facts previously, D's fish shop was closed down by injunction. The Chancery Court sought to ameliorate that hardship by stating that 'it does not follow that D cannot carry on his business in another more suitable place somewhere in the neighbourhood'.

Some factors will mitigate against injunctive relief. For example, where D is a public authority, an injunction will be refused if it would conflict with a statutory scheme under which D operates.

In *Dobson v Thames Water Utilities Ltd*,[351] facts previously, the odour and mosquito infestation from the Mogden Sewage Treatment Works operated by Thames Water, D, were a nuisance. However, an injunction to restrain D from causing or continuing that nuisance to the nearby residents was not appropriate because: the exception in the proposed injunction for 'nuisances which are the inevitable consequence of the Works [at Mogden] being operated without negligence' introduced further uncertainty, which made breach difficult to ascertain and enforce; and any injunction could

346 [2013] EWCA Civ 815. 347 [2011] EWHC 1664, [106], [109], [112].
348 [2008] EWHC 759 (QB) [64]–[66], aff'd: [2009] EWCA Civ 15, [53]–[55], [87]. 349 [1986] 1 All ER 663 (CA).
350 [1913] 1 Ch 269 (Ch) 271–72 (Swinfen Eady J). 351 [2011] EWHC 3253 (TCC) [1118].

potentially conflict with the statutory scheme under which D operated, especially if compliance with the injunction required D to carry out major capital works or projects at the Mogden Works.

Additionally, if D was operating under planning permission which expressly or impliedly authorised D to carry on that activity in such a way as to cause a nuisance, then that can be a factor in favour of refusing an injunction, and leaving C to his remedy in damages. It will be recalled, from discussion under Element #2, that the existence of planning permission does **not** provide D with an outright defence. However, in *Coventry v Lawrence*,[352] **all** members of the Supreme Court held that it was directly relevant to the question of remedy, and injunctive relief. The reasoning was explained by Lord Neuberger: 'the grant of planning permission for a particular activity ... may provide strong support that the activity is of benefit to the public ... This factor would have real force in cases where it was clear that the planning authority had been reasonably and fairly influenced by the public benefit of the activity, and where the activity cannot be carried out without causing the nuisance complained of'. In such cases, injunctive relief would be less likely.

In *Miller v Jackson*, facts previously, **held (2:1):** injunctive relief refused. The cricket ground had enormous benefit to the village residents, and they should not 'be deprived of their facilities for an innocent recreation which they have so long enjoyed on this ground' (per Cumming-Bruce LJ), and 'the public interest lies in protecting the environment by preserving our playing fields in the face of mounting development, and by enabling our youth to enjoy all the benefits of outdoor games, such as cricket and football' (per Denning MR). The dissenter (Lane LJ) considered that damages would not be an adequate form of relief, and that C should not have to 'submit to the inevitable breakage of tiles and/or windows, even though D has expressed their willingness to carry out any repairs at no cost to C'. In *Dennis v MOD*, facts previously, **held:** injunctive relief refused. Even though a nuisance by noise was established, 'the public interest clearly demands that RAF Wittering should continue to train pilots', it would be enormously expensive and inconvenient to relocate the RAF Wittering base, it was likely that Harriers would be phased out by 2012, and the training of pilots for the replacement fighter aircraft was likely to be undertaken by British pilots in the US. C was left to his remedy in damages (£950,000).

The injunction may also be suspended or postponed, whether to give D time to put measures in place to rectify the nuisance-making aspect of its activities (the dissenter in *Miller v Jackson* would have permitted a suspension of the injunction for 12 months to look elsewhere for an alternative cricket pitch); or until C re-occupies the affected premises (in *Coventry v Lawrence*,[353] C's house, Fenland, was badly damaged by fire – with the 'suspicion' that someone in the locality who supported the continuation of D's motocross track and stadium had deliberately started it – and had not been rebuilt by the time of trial).

Any injunctive relief granted to C must be necessary, proportionate, and ECHR-compliant.

In *Olympic Delivery Authority v Persons Unknown*,[354] where protestors undertake nuisance-making activities, their rights under Art 10 (the right to freedom of expression) and Art 11 (the right to freedom of assembly) are engaged, and any injunctive order granted must be both necessary and proportionate, otherwise, damages will be considered an adequate remedy. An injunction was granted, and continued, on the basis that it was proportionate, in that it did not prevent or inhibit lawful and peaceful protest by D re the Olympic venue.

352 [2014] UKSC 13, [125] (Lord Neuberger), [157] (Lord Sumption), [166] (Lord Mance), [169] (Lord Clarke), [240] (Lord Carnwath).

353 See: [2014] UKSC 46, [5]–[9].

354 [2012] EWHC 1114 (Ch).

Finally, a *quia timet* interim injunction may be awarded, if damage arising from D's nuisance has not yet happened, but is threatened or apprehended, and if C can show a 'good arguable case' that the feared damage will in fact occur (per *Shebelle Enterprises Ltd v The Hampstead Garden Suburb Trust Ltd*[355]).

Damages in lieu of an injunction

§16.43 A court has jurisdiction to award damages in lieu of an injunction, to compensate C for the loss of his property rights caused by a private nuisance.

The court has a discretionary jurisdiction, under s 50 of the Senior Courts Act 1981[356] (formerly Lord Cairns' Act 1858 (the Chancery Amendment Act 1858)), to award 'Lord Cairns' Act damages', instead of an injunction. This reflects the common law principle that the award of an injunction, by way of discretionary equitable relief, may be supplanted by an award of damages to C instead.

According to the long-standing, if controversial, '*Shelfer* principle' (per *Shelfer v City of London Electric Co*[357]), damages should be awarded, in substitution for an injunction, where ('as a good working rule'):

i. the injury to C's legal rights is small;
ii. the injury is capable of being estimated in money;
iii. the injury is one which can be adequately compensated by a small money payment; and
iv. it would be oppressive to D to grant an injunction.

> In *Shelfer*, the operations of City of London Electric Co, D, caused noise and vibrations, leading to structural damage to Mr Shelfer's, C's, pub, for which he had a 19-year lease. C successfully sued in nuisance. **Held:** an injunction was awarded. It was not an appropriate case for damages to be awarded in lieu, notwithstanding that D would be required to either cease operations to supply electricity to the area, or take steps to abate the nuisance. The injury to C, caused by the nuisance, was not small (e.g., effects on long-term leasing, illness in the family, cracks in the house), and were not capable of being estimated in money, nor adequately compensated by a small money payment.

The status of the four *Shelfer* requirements has been the source of much dispute. On the one hand, it has been said that **all** four requirements must be satisfied (and especially the fourth), and that 'damages in lieu of an injunction should only be awarded under very exceptional [or special] circumstances' (per *Watson v Croft Promo-Sport Ltd*[358] and *Regan v Paul Properties DFP No 1 Ltd*[359]). On the other hand, it has been said that 'the judgments establish a willingness on the part of the courts to depart from the strict requirements of the four requirements set out in *Shelfer* in an appropriate case', and to award damages in lieu of an injunction (per *Midtown Ltd v City of London Real Property Co Ltd*[360]).

More recently, in *Coventry v Lawrence*,[361] the Supreme Court generally favoured a 'less mechanistic' application of the *Shelfer* criteria, and a 'more open-minded approach' to an

[355] [2013] EWHC 948 (Ch) [23].

[356] Also known as the Supreme Court Act 1981, per the Constitutional Reform Act 2005, ss 59, 148 (as of 1 Oct 2009).

[357] [1895] 1 Ch 287 (CA) 316–17, 322–33. [358] [2009] EWCA Civ 15, [53]–[54].

[359] [2006] EWCA Civ 1319, [28]–[32]. [360] [2005] EWHC 33 (Ch) [73].

[361] [2014] UKSC 13, [115], [123] (Lord Neuberger), [161] (Lord Sumption), [239] (Lord Carnwath).

award of damages, i.e., whether to award an injunction or damages in respect of future interferences was a 'classic exercise of discretion which should not be fettered' by guidelines. Hence, even if one of those *Shelfer* criteria failed, damages (rather than an injunction) could still be awarded if the circumstances warranted it. The strong presumption in favour of an injunction for private nuisance should be abandoned, and there was 'much to be said for the view that damages are ordinarily an adequate remedy for nuisance', at least where D was complying with planning permissions. Although a strict (or 'slavish') application of *Shelfer's* criteria was heavily-criticised by the Supreme Court in *Coventry*, that was not the appropriate case to consider the issue, as the trial judge had not been asked to award damages in lieu of an injunction. Hence, the precise scope of the *Shelfer* principle, in the context of private nuisance, remains to be determined by the Supreme Court on another occasion.

However, in the interim, it would appear that *Watson* and *Regan* are two examples in which, according to the Supreme Court, judges may have been too willing to grant injunctions without considering damages in lieu. Neither was cited with much favour by the Supreme Court.

The contrasting and difficult assessments re Lord Cairns' Act damages

Case	Verdict	Reasoning
Regan v Paul Properties Ltd[a] (re disruption of light to C's living room)	at first instance: damages should be awarded to C in lieu of an injunction; on appeal: decision reversed, and an injunction awarded (so as to force a change in the construction of the building)	• if the whole of D's building was erected, this would seriously disrupt C's enjoyment of natural light in his living room; • C's injury was capable of being estimated in money; • however, the injury was not adequately compensated by 'a small money payment', because if the light was disrupted, valuers said that a reduction of value of around £5,500 was appropriate – 'not a small figure'; • C had protested against the infringement of his right to light 5 months before the development reached the fifth floor level (the penthouse), so D had taken a calculated risk in proceeding with the development after C's complaint – 'they had continued with the construction with their eyes open' – Ds 'who took and acted on the wrong advice [that there was no nuisance being caused to C] must take the consequences'
Watson v Croft Promo-Sport Ltd[b] (re noise nuisance from a motor-racing circuit)	at first instance: damages should be awarded to C in lieu of an injunction; on appeal: decision reversed, and an injunction awarded	• there was substantial injury to C in the enjoyment of their properties; • the public interest served by D's activities did not preclude an injunction, and did not serve to establish oppression if an injunction were awarded; • there was no oppression here, especially if the injunction still allowed D to carry out their 'core activities' of other physical recreational activities

[a] [2006] EWCA Civ 1391, [71], [74].
[b] [2009] EWCA Civ 15, [53]–[54].

As the cases show, whether C will be able to obtain an injunction, or will be left to his remedy in damages, has often been very difficult to predict – and this uncertainty is only likely to continue, given the fact that injunctive relief is discretionary and hence no case is binding on another as to how the discretion should be exercised; and the Supreme Court has, in *Coventry v Lawrence*, cast the authority of *Shelfer* into considerable doubt. In any event, it is important to remember that D is not entitled to ask the court to sanction his wrongdoing by 'buying off' C's rights with damages in lieu of an injunction, and that wrongs should not be permitted to continue simply because D is willing and able to pay damages. However (according to *Regan*[362]), this argument should not be 'overdone' – injunctive relief is discretionary, and there are going to be some cases where C will need to be content with damages for the ongoing interference/escape.

Restitutionary damages

§16.44 The availability of restitutionary damages in private nuisance (whether as an account of profits or 'user damages') has not been definitively determined. However, it has been judicially stated that the remedy, if available, may be awarded only in 'exceptional circumstances'.

Suppose that D is conducting an activity which constitutes a private nuisance, and from which D has made a profit which exceeds any loss caused to C from the activity. Whether C can seek a disgorgement or transfer of that profit from D to himself has yet to be definitively decided. In *Forsyth-Grant v Allen* (2008),[363] the Court of Appeal noted that there had been **no** decided case in which an account of profits had been ordered, as an alternative to damages, in an action for private nuisance, but that any such award would only be awarded in 'exceptional circumstances'. The Court declined to award an account of profits against D who was found liable in nuisance, whilst it was also noted that a private nuisance 'does not involve the misappropriation of [C's] rights in the same way, even, as in a case of trespass'.[364] Patten LJ cast considerable doubt as to whether an account of profits for private nuisance can *ever* be awarded, and Toulson LJ also left the point open.

However, in *Coventry v Lawrence* (2014),[365] there was some interest in, but no agreement about, the question. Lord Clarke stated that he would 'leave open the question whether it may, in some circumstances, be appropriate to award what have been called gain-based damages in lieu of an injunction ... it does seem to me that, where C is seeking an injunction to restrain the noise which has been held to amount to a nuisance, it is at least arguable that there is no reason in principle why a court ... should not be able to award damages on a more generous basis than the diminution in value caused by the nuisance'. Lord Carnwath, however, was notably less-enthused, observing that 'I would be reluctant to open up the possibility of assessment of damages on the basis of a share of the benefit to D'.

The concept of 'user damages' is a particular type of restitutionary damage – whereby damages are awarded by reference to the fair value of a right of which D has wrongly deprived C, even where C would not himself have sought to use that right and so incurred no loss. This type of damage has seemingly received somewhat stronger appellate support. In *Stoke-on-Trent Council v Wass*, Nourse LJ stated that, in some cases of private nuisance, the court may award user damages, albeit that to award such damages 'would revolutionise the tort of nuisance by

[362] [2006] EWCA Civ 1391, [61]. [363] [2008] EWCA Civ 505, quotes and reasoning at [31]–[33].
[364] *ibid*, [32]. [365] [2014] UKSC 13, [173] (Lord Clarke), [248] (Lord Carnwath).

making it unnecessary to prove loss'.[366] Further, in *Devenish Nutrition Ltd v Sanofi-Aventis SA (France)*, Arden LJ held that, by virtue of *Allen*, the possibility of a claim for user damages for nuisance was 'not ruled out', and 'might be made, though on a more limited basis than a full account of profits in equity.'[367] More recently in 2013, Arnold J remarked, in *Couper v Albion Properties Ltd*,[368] that even if C did not make use of the land (or intend to) at the time that D interfered with his proprietary interest, it is possible for C to recover for that interference – in such cases, '[t]he measure of damages is the price which would be agreed in a hypothetical negotiation between two reasonable persons for the use of the land'.

Aggravated and exemplary damages

§16.45 Awards of aggravated and/or exemplary, damages are technically available for the tort of private nuisance, although difficult to identify in practice.

Aggravated damages compensate C 'where the manner in which D has committed the nuisance, or his motives in so doing, or his conduct subsequent to the nuisance, has upset or outraged C' (paraphrasing the English Law Commission[369]). Hence, to be available, D must have committed some acts which were in aggravation of the nuisance or escape.

Of the three categories of exemplary damages posed by Lord Devlin in *Rookes v Barnard (No 1)*[370] (and canvassed in Chapter 11), it is only the third – D's conduct was 'calculated by him to make a profit for himself which may well exceed the compensation payable to [C] ... with cynical disregard for [C's] rights' – which will have any potential relevance to a nuisance scenario.

In *Coventry v Lawrence*, C's claim for aggravated and exemplary damages failed at first instance.[371] Either the circumstances pleaded were not aggravating; or if they were, there was no clear identity as to who committed them. Ultimately, C succeeded in their claim of nuisance on appeal, but the availability of these damages was not re-addressed by the Supreme Court.

Abatement

§16.46 The remedy of abatement is a self-help remedy, by which C may remove the source of the interference himself.

Abatement is a common law remedy, which enables C to take reasonable steps to remove the occurrence or repetition of D's interference. Whilst the remedy itself may be 'beyond question' (per Lopez LJ in *Lemmon v Webb*[372]), it has been treated, judicially, in fairly lukewarm terms at times (with Lord Atkin remarking, in *Sedleigh-Denfield v O'Callaghan*, that the remedy 'inevitably tends to disorder, and has been on many occasions spoken of with discouragement'[373]). Although the right to abate was said by Viscount Maugham, in *Sedleigh-Denfield*, to arise 'in most cases of private nuisance', its scope has been cut down in modern times, with the Court of Appeal noting, in *Burton v Winters*, that it is 'only justified in clear and simple cases, or in an

[366] [1988] 1 WLR 1406 (CA) 1415. [367] [2008] EWCA Civ 1086, [81]–[82].

[368] [2013] EWHC 2993 (Ch) [527] (Arnold J).

[369] EWLC, *Aggravated, Exemplary and Restitutionary Damages* (Rep No 247) [2.1].

[370] [1964] AC 1129 (HL) 1226–27.

[371] Called, at first instance: *Fen Tigers Ltd v Lawrence* [2011] EWHC 360 (QB) [309].

[372] [1894] 3 Ch 1 (CA), aff'd: [1895] AC 1 (HL). [373] [1940] AC 880 (HL) 890.

emergency'.[374] The remedy is particularly relevant in providing a common law right to C to remove overhanging branches and tree roots encroaching from D's land (per *Davey v Harrow Corp*[375]).

There is no question of C having to choose between damages and abatement; the remedies are cumulative (per *Lemmon v Webb*,[376] and affirmed in *Sedleigh-Denfield*[377]). However, failure to exercise the remedy of abatement correctly can result in C *himself* being liable in tort (e.g., for the tort of trespass to land if he enters D's land without permission; or for conversion of goods if he keeps the thing he has removed for himself, per *Mills v Brooker*[378]).

There are some pre-requisites for the defence to be effective for C:

- the remedy must be exercised promptly, and without undue delay – and whilst that does not necessarily require an emergency, it must be shown that C needed to remove the source of the interference more quickly than the litigious process would provide (per *Burton v Winters*[379]);
- if C can abate the nuisance without entering D's land, then notice of the intention to abate is not required (per *Lemmon v Webb*[380]); otherwise, notice will be required to enable C to take advantage of the remedy (per *Delaware Mansions Ltd v Westminster CC*[381]);
- C must do the minimum to remove the source of the nuisance (i.e., he may remove the offending branches, but not cut down the tree entirely, per *Perrin v Northampton BC*[382]). Whatever C does to remove the interference cannot be out of all proportion to the damage suffered by C, otherwise the benefit of the defence will be lost (per *Burton*[383]) and;
- the remedy only permits C to abate an *existing* nuisance; it does not permit C to take steps to prevent a nuisance from coming into existence (per *Perrin*[384]).

THE IMPACT OF THE HUMAN RIGHTS ACT 1998

§16.47 Where D, as a public authority, causes an interference with C's use and enjoyment of his land, then (in addition to a claim in private nuisance) that may constitute an infringement of C's Art 8 rights. If so, an award of general damages in C's favour *may* be awarded by a domestic court, if necessary to afford just satisfaction under s 8(3) of the HRA.

Article 8 of the ECHR provides a qualified protection for C's private and family life and his home. Where available, a suit pursued under the ECHR confers one immediate advantage over a common law action. Those who do not have the requisite standing to sue at common law (because they lack the necessary proprietary or possessory interest) may bring an action under Art 8, because according to the Court of Appeal in *Dobson v Thames Water Utilities Ltd*,[385] 'a person with an interest in the property [has] an Article 8 claim' – and that includes any person living in a house affected by the nuisance.

Proof of a violation

A high threshold of damage has to be sustained in order to trigger an infringement of Art 8. According to *Lopez Ostra v Spain*,[386] there must be 'severe environmental pollution', and in

[374] [1993] 1 WLR 1077 (CA) 1082. [375] [1958] 1 QB 60 (CA).
[376] [1894] 3 Ch 1 (CA) 24 (Kay LJ), aff'd: [1895] AC 1 (HL).
[377] [1940] AC 880 (HL) 893–94 (Viscount Maugham), 899–900 (Lord Atkin). [378] [1919] 1 KB 555.
[379] [1993] 1 WLR 1077 (CA) 1081. [380] [1895] AC 1 (HL) 2–3. [381] [2001] 3 WLR 1007 (HL) [12] (Lord Cooke).
[382] [2006] EWHC 2331 (TCC) [37]. [383] [1993] 1 WLR 1077 (CA) 1082. [384] [2006] EWHC 2331 (TCC) [37].
[385] [2009] EWCA Civ 28, [18]. [386] (1995) 20 EHRR 277, [51], [58].

Barr v Biffa Waste Services Ltd,[387] the first-instance court remarked (with no adverse comment on appeal) that Art 8 'does not guarantee any right to freedom from transient odour or noise nuisance, particularly one with no impact on health'. That high threshold could not be met in *Sec of State for the Environment v Downs*.[388]

In any event, Art 8 does not accord absolute protection to C's property – it only requires a reasonable balance to be struck between C's interests, and the interests of the wider public. Where Parliament has struck a proper balance between the rights of the community as a whole, and those of individuals (including C) who might be put to inconvenience by D's activities, and where it has provided feasible remedies in the statutory regime under which D operates, C will not have a HRA claim (per *Marcic v Thames Water Utilities*[389]).

However, the fact that D has statutory authority to conduct its works, and is complying with that statute, will not necessarily save D from liability under Art 8, where D failed to have all reasonable regard and care for the interests of other persons (per *Dobson v Thames Water Utilities Ltd*[390]).

Actions for alleged violations of Art 8, in connection with the law of nuisance, have been brought against a range of public authorities, with fairly mixed success:

Private nuisance claims under Art 8

Case	The interference	Breach of Art 8?	Reason
Dobson v Thames Water	odours from Mogden Sewage Works	yes	D failed to respect the rights of nearby residents, by allowing odour/mosquitoes to emanate from Mogden
Marcic v Thames Water	sewage flooding in C's house and garden	no	a proper balance was struck between people whose homes were prone to sewer flooding, and the interests of the wider public who have to meet the cost of building more sewers; and other remedies were available to C: the right of complaint; enforcement orders; judicial review
Arscott v Coal Authy	flooding from D's land	no	neither D's actions, nor the common enemy doctrine, contravened Art 8
Downs v State	crop-spraying	no	no 'severe environmental pollution' to invoke Art 8
Dennis v MOD	military aircraft noise	yes	persistent and high-level noise over C's estate

Damages under the HRA

Damages awarded under the HRA serve a different purpose from common law damages for private nuisance. These quite distinguishable features were described by Lord Woolf CJ in *Anufrijeva v Southwark LBC*[391] (and endorsed in *R (Greenfield) v Sec of State for the Home Dept*[392]), to include:

[387] [2011] EWHC 1003 (TCC) [310]. [388] [2009] EWCA Civ 664.
[389] [2003] UKHL 66, [2004] 2 AC 42, [40]–[46]. [390] [2011] EWHC 3253 (TCC) [1069].
[391] [2003] EWCA Civ 1406, [2004] QB 1124 (CA) [55]. [392] [2005] UKHL 14, [2005] 1 WLR 673 (HL) [9].

Damages under the HRA:	Damages for a tort:
• the court has a discretion to make an award, only where it is 'just and appropriate' to do so, per s 8(1) – hence, damages are a remedy of last resort	• upon proof of the elements of the tort, C has a right to common law damages – they are an as-of-right entitlement
• the award must be necessary and appropriate to achieve 'just satisfaction', and are generally lower than awards of damages at common law	• C is entitled, so far as money can achieve it, to be restored to the position he would have been in if the tort had not been committed
• when awarding damages under the HRA, C's interests must be balanced against the interests of the public as a whole – the ECHR serves public law aims, and the principal objective of any suit for breach of the ECHR is to declare an infringement and to stop it – any award of damages is 'ancillary and discretionary'	• when awarding damages at common law, the interests of the individual are not just 'part of the equation', they are the **only** interests which the court takes into account. The interests of the wider public in having the behaviour stopped is not an explicit part of the function of compensatory damages

The principles governing an award of damages under the HRA, where the gist of the complaint is in private nuisance, are still evolving – especially where there are both 'common law claimants' and 'HRA claimants' living in the one household, and all of whom have been affected by D's nuisance. However, some key principles have emerged from the Court of Appeal's judgment in *Dobson v Thames Water Utilities Ltd.*[393] Damages may be awarded to a HRA claimant for 'inconvenience, mental distress and physical suffering', taking into account factors such as C's age, state of health and the duration of the nuisance. However, if C has recovered damages for private nuisance, then that common law award will be relevant to the question of whether an award of HRA damages is necessary to afford just satisfaction under Art 8, to others living in that same household (say, a spouse or children) but who lack standing to bring a nuisance action. If the common law damages are sufficient to 'do the job', then no separate HRA damages will be awarded at all. A declaration that Art 8 rights have been infringed will suffice. The reality is that 'top-up damages' under the HRA claim will be unlikely where C has recovered common law damages for nuisance, because any award for 'loss of amenity' damages awarded to C covers the inconvenience suffered by *the whole household*. In that light, 'it is highly improbable, if not inconceivable, that Strasbourg would think it appropriate or just or necessary to award a further sum on top for breach of Art 8' (said *Dobson*).

In *Dobson*,[394] the effects of the odour and mosquitoes upon Thomas Bannister, *viz*, in not being able to have friends stay over, finding exam study difficult, suffering from incessant mosquito bites, etc, were taken into account in assessing the damages awarded to his parents in nuisance. In *Dennis v MOD*,[395] the estate's damages for loss of amenity, caused by the aircraft noise, afforded just satisfaction to Mrs Dennis, who did not have a proprietary or possessory interest in the land affected by the military aircraft noise. Neither Master Bannister nor Mrs Dennis was awarded further damages for D's violation of Art 8.

393 [2009] EWCA Civ 28, [12], [41]–[53], [226]. 394 [2011] EWHC 3253 (TCC) [1088]–[1090], [1100].
395 [2003] EWHC 793, [91]–[92].

17

The rule in *Rylands v Fletcher*

DEFINING THE RULE

§17.1 Where D deliberately accumulates something on his land which amounts to a 'non-natural user' of his land, and which is likely to do damage to C's land if it escapes, D is required by law to prevent its escape, and is liable for all the direct and foreseeable consequences of its escape.

The classic statement of the rule was articulated by Blackburn J in *Rylands v Fletcher*:[1]

> the person who for his own purposes brings on his lands and collects and keeps there anything likely to do mischief if it escapes [and it is a non-natural use], must keep it in at his peril, and, if he does not do so, is *prima facie* answerable for all the damage which is the natural consequence of its escape.

D is free to use his land as he chooses, but if he creates a risk of harm to C, by deciding to use his land to accumulate a dangerous or mischievous thing, then he should bear the consequences if that thing does damage to C as adjoining or nearby landowner.

The framework for the tort of *Rylands v Fletcher* can be summarised as follows:

Nutshell analysis: The rule in *Rylands v Fletcher*

Preconditions for the tort to apply:

i Capacity of C to sue
ii Capacity of D to be sued

Elements of the tort:

1 A dangerous thing escaped from D's land
2 D deliberately accumulated that dangerous thing
3 The accumulation was a non-natural user of the land
4(a) The escape caused C the requisite damage
4(b) The damage is not too remote to be recoverable at law

[1] (1865–66) LR 1 Exch 265 (Exch Chamber) 279 (Blackburn J delivered judgment on behalf of Willes, Keating, Mellor, Montague Smith, and Lush JJ). Blackburn J's statement was approved by the House of Lords. The text at [...] was added by Lord Cairns (at 339), and later accepted as correctly part of the rule: (1868) LR 3 HL 330.

Defences to the tort:

- The escape was caused by an Act of God
- The escape was caused by a *vis major*
- The escape was caused by a stranger
- The accumulation was consented to by C
- D's activity was permitted by statutory authorisation or codification
- Contributory negligence

Miscellaneous matter:
Fire: Is it a scenario to which the Fires Prevention (Metropolis) Act 1774 applies?

Before considering the issues outlined in the framework, it is useful to consider briefly the history of the rule and the reasons for its emergence, and its coalescence with other causes of action.

PUTTING THE RULE INTO CONTEXT

A strict liability tort – but in a limited sense only

§17.2 Liability under *Rylands v Fletcher* can arise, even if D has committed no negligence, and has exercised the greatest of care to prevent the thing from escaping. However, the rule does *not* give rise to *automatic* liability for all damage caused by ultra-hazardous activities or operations on D's land.

C does not need to prove any culpability or wrongdoing on the part of D to prove the tort. In that sense, it is a strict liability tort.

As the Court of Appeal stated in *Bedfordshire Police Authy v Constable*, '[t]orts of strict liability are based on *the concept of responsibility* ... the land owner in *Rylands v Fletcher* ... is to be strictly answerable because of the responsibility inherent in [his] position',[2] i.e., he deliberately accumulated something that was likely to do mischief if it escaped.

In *Rylands v Fletcher*, Mr Rylands, D, a mill-owner in Lancashire, employed a contractor to build a reservoir to supply water to the mill. The contractor failed to take care to block up five disused shafts under the site of the reservoir, which led to old coal mines below the land. On adjoining land was an operating colliery, owned and operated by Mr Fletcher, C. Unknown to D and the contractor, those shafts and tunnels connected the disused coal mines under the reservoir to C's colliery. It was negligent of the contractor not to ascertain the position of the shafts. After the sizable reservoir was filled (a capacity of over 4 m gallons, covering 1.5 acres), the water broke through some of the shafts, and flooded the mine. **Held:** D was liable, notwithstanding that he was unaware that the shafts existed, and was not himself guilty of any negligence.

As a strict liability tort, it is *never* a pre-requisite, under *Rylands v Fletcher*, for C to point to some negligence/lack of care on D's part in using the land as he did and for allowing the thing to escape. However, the reality is that negligence will often arise in the scenario. Lord Hoffmann

[2] [2009] EWCA Civ 64, [27] (Longmore LJ) (emphasis added).

noted, in *Transco plc v Stockport MBC*,[3] that 'the cases in which there is an escape which is not attributable to an unusual natural event or the act of a third party [both defences under *Rylands v Fletcher*] will, by the same token, usually give rise to an inference of negligence'. In that case, negligence may actually offer some advantages over *Rylands v Fletcher*:

In *Margereson v JW Roberts Ltd*,[4] Mrs Margereson, C, suffered from mesothelioma (cancer of the pleura, or outer lining of the lungs), and alleged that her condition had been caused by environmental exposure to asbestos dust emitted from Roberts', D's, asbestos-processing factory in Leeds. **Held:** negligence succeeded; *Rylands v Fletcher* raised, but not decided. There was a clear breach of the duty of care; unchallenged evidence said that emissions of asbestos dust could have been reduced by 85%. In that light, any claim under *Rylands v Fletcher* was disadvantageous to C, given: she had to prove *locus standi* under *Rylands*; she would have to prove a non-natural user of the land by D, with the problem of whether a factory engaged in production for the war effort was indeed non-natural; and damages for personal injury could not be recovered under *Rylands*.

However, even though *Rylands v Fletcher* is treated as a strict liability tort (the 'other end of the spectrum from negligence', as the court put it in *Bartoline Ltd v Royal & Sun Alliance Insurance plc*[5]), it is not an immutably 'strict' rule at all. As discussed later,[6] it excludes damages for personal injuries caused by an escape; there are a number of useful defences upon which D can rely; there must be an escape; and the type of damage must have been foreseen or reasonably foreseeable in order to render D liable.

It follows, from the aforementioned carve-outs, that the rule in *Rylands v Fletcher* does *not* equate with any general principle of strict liability for damage caused by ultra-hazardous activities/operations on D's land. English law does not recognise any such widely-drawn legal principle. This was confirmed by the House of Lords in three significant *Rylands v Fletcher* cases – in each of which C's person and/or property was harmed by dangerous and hazardous activities being conducted on D' land, but where *Rylands v Fletcher* failed:

In *Read v J Lyons & Co Ltd*,[7] Lyons, D, operated an ordnance factory where shell cases were filled with high explosives during WWII. Ms Read, C, an employee of the Ministry of Supply, visited the factory in August 1942 under her employment duty to inspect the filling of the shell cases. While in the shell-filling shop, an explosion occurred, killing one man and seriously injuring C. No negligence was claimed or proved against D. At trial, *Rylands v Fletcher* had been applied, as a rule of strict liability for carrying out ultra-hazardous activities which injured persons, whether on or off the premises. **Held (on appeal):** liability under *Rylands v Fletcher* failed.

In *Cambridge Water Co Ltd v Eastern Counties Leather plc*,[8] Eastern Counties, D, had conducted the business of a tannery on their land since the 1960s, and stored large quantities of industrial solvent, perchloroethene (PCE), on site. PCE was applied to the animal pelts to degrease and clean them. For several years, this solvent spilled from time to time onto the tannery floor from the 40-gallon drums in which it was transported around the tannery. Unknown to D, the solvent percolated through cracks in the concrete floor and into a chalk aquifer which ran below the tannery. Via very small drainage channels, the solvent travelled downstream approximately 8–9 yards a day, and in 9 months, reached and polluted the borehole owned by Cambridge Water, C, at Sawston Mill, 1.3 miles from the tannery.

[3] [2003] UKHL 61, [2004] 2 AC 1, [39].

[4] [1996] EWCA Civ 1316, [1996] PIQR P358 (the alleged breach by D here occurred during WWII).

[5] [2006] EWHC 3598 (QB), [2008] Env LR 1, [41].

[6] See pp 928–29, 933–35, 946–53, 959.

[7] [1947] AC 156 (HL).

[8] [1994] 2 AC 264 (HL).

C used that borehole to supply water to domestic customers, *viz*, some 275,000 people in the Cambridge area. The PCE so contaminated the water that it did not pass UK regulations on 'wholesome water'. C had to take the Sawston supply out of action, and develop a new source of water supply, until carbon filtration technology could be trusted to treat and remove PCE from the Sawston Mill water. **Held (at trial):** C lost on negligence, nuisance, and *Rylands v Fletcher*. **Held (CA):** *Rylands v Fletcher* succeeded, and C was awarded almost £1.1m. **Held (HL):** liability under *Rylands v Fletcher* failed.

In *Transco plc v Stockport MBC*,[9] a multi-storey block of 66 flats was built by Stockport MBC, D, who also supplied the water for residents' domestic use, via a 3-inch asbestos cement pipe, from the water main to tanks in the basement of the block. The pipe's capacity was much greater than the capacity of a pipe supplying a single dwelling, but was a 'normal' pipe. The pipe fractured at some point (which was not attributable to any negligence on D's part). The leak went undetected for a long period, and a lot of water escaped. It percolated to an embankment which supported Transco's, C's, high-pressure gas main. The weight of the sodden soil caused the embankment to collapse, leaving the gas main exposed and unsupported, and with a serious risk of rupture. C undertook urgent remedial works, and sued D for those costs. **Held:** liability under *Rylands v Fletcher* failed.

These cases failed under *Rylands v Fletcher* for entirely different reasons, which will be discussed under the pertinent elements of the tort which each C could not satisfy. However, their very failure demonstrates the absence of any general no-fault liability for the conduct of hazardous activities by D on his land (a proposition recently applied by the Court of Appeal in *Northumbrian Water Ltd v McAlpine*[10]).

A brief history of the rule

Why did the rule in *Rylands v Fletcher* emerge in the mid-19th century? Blackburn J himself stated (in *Ross v Fedden*[11]) that he did not create a new rule: 'I wasted much time ... in *Rylands v Fletcher*, if I did not succeed in showing that the law held to govern it had been law for at least 300 years'. That is, it was an instance of private nuisance, but exceptional because the water's incursion was isolated and not continuing. However, in *Transco plc v Stockport MBC*,[12] Lord Bingham remarked that many of those early cases lacked the 'mischief or danger' test, that the thing had been accumulated for non-natural purposes, while Lord Hoffmann remarked that none of those early cases permitted recovery for an escape which was unforeseeable (which, at that time, *Rylands v Fletcher* permitted).

In any event, many reasons have been suggested for the new rule's emergence:[13]

- with the advent of industrialisation, courts were inclined to compensate the public for incidents which could give rise to accidental, and widespread, damage in the pursuit of industrial wealth;
- the rule provided the landed aristocracy (which, at that time, included many judiciary) with the opportunity to maintain some ascendency over rich industrialists;
- as a matter of policy, entrepreneurs should pay for ('internalise') the consequences of whatever risks eventuated as a result of their commercial enterprise by the payment of damages (whether by their own means, or by taking out insurance);

[9] [2003] UKHL 61, [2004] 2 AC 1, [9]. [10] [2014] EWCA Civ 685, [24]. [11] (1872) 26 LT 966.

[12] [2004] 2 AC 1 (HL) [10] (Lord Bingham), [24] (Lord Hoffmann).

[13] As argued in: B Simpson, 'Legal Liability for Bursting Reservoirs: The Historical Context of *Rylands v Fletcher*' (1984) 13 *Leg Stud* 209, cited in *Transco plc v Stockport MBC* [2003] UKHL 61, [28]–[29] (Lord Hoffmann).

- public anxiety about the safety of reservoirs was rife. The Bradfield Reservoir, near Sheffield, burst on 12 March 1864, shortly before *Rylands* was heard, killing almost 250 people;
- other torts were proving, at the time, unhelpful. Private nuisance required a 'continuing state of affairs' and could not handle isolated escapes; trespass to land required a direct and immediate encroachment (which did not occur in *Rylands* itself); and a non-delegable duty of care on the part of an employer, casting liability upon that employer for the negligence of its independent contractor for allowing the thing to escape from the employer's land (precisely what happened in *Rylands* itself), had not yet been developed (that occurred a decade after *Rylands*, in *Bower v Peate*[14]). Hence, a new rule was required.

It is fair to say that *Rylands v Fletcher* has received a mixed judicial reception in English law. In *Dorset Yacht Co Ltd v Home Office*,[15] the House of Lords hailed the decision, along with *Donoghue v Stevenson*, as one of the 'landmarks in the common law'. Not all, though, have considered the rule in such a positive light. *Rylands v Fletcher* was famously described as a 'mouse' of a rule by Lord Hoffmann in *Transco*,[16] and that, insofar as flooding was concerned, it was 'perhaps not surprising that counsel could not find a reported case since the Second World War in which anyone had succeeded in a claim under the rule'. As pointed out later in *LMS Intl Ltd v Styrene Packaging and Insulation Ltd*,[17] there **have** been successful applications of the rule over that period, apart from flooding – albeit that English courts had manifested a 'generally restrictive approach to the rule'.

In recent times, the rule has continued to feature. It was relied upon (ultimately, unsuccessfully) in respect of the escape of the foot and mouth disease virus from the Pirbright animal research facility in 2007, which had such a devastating impact upon the English agricultural industry (*D Pride & Partners v Institute for Animal Health*[18]). It also formed part of the litigation arising out of the Buncefield Oil Storage Depot explosion at Hemel Hempstead (in *Colour Quest Ltd v Total Downstream UK plc*[19]), the largest-ever peacetime explosion to have occurred in Europe, which measured 2.4 on the Richter scale, was heard 200 km away, and gave rise, allegedly, to some £750m in damages to surrounding commercial and residential claimants. Liability under *Rylands v Fletcher* was conceded in the Buncefield litigation in respect of those claimants *outside* the perimeter fence of the Buncefield depot site (whereas those *within* the perimeter fence failed under the tort). Hence, *Rylands v Fletcher* continues to resonate in modern English law.

In *Union of India v Prabhakaran Vijaya Kumar*,[20] the Indian Supreme Court undertook a very useful discussion of the history of the rule in English law, and this is summarised in the Table below.

The comparative corner: The rise, fall, and rise again of *Rylands v Fletcher*

The key stages of the rule's development and application can be summarised thus:

Pre-1866

- until *Rylands*, landowners could only be liable for fault-based damage to their neighbours (fault being predicated upon either intention or negligence), which was consonant with the then-prevailing *laissez-faire* theory;

[14] (1875–76) LR 1 QBD 321. [15] [1970] AC 1004 (HL) 1059 (Lord Diplock). [16] [2003] UKHL 61, [39].
[17] [2005] EWHC 2065 (TCC) [14]. [18] [2009] EWHC 685 (QB). [19] [2009] EWHC 540 (Comm).
[20] [2008] INSC 802, especially at [18]–[30], [37].

- as industrialisation emerged, so did the theory of 'the welfare state', and the *laissez-faire* theory diminished;
- this period marked a shift 'from positivism to sociological jurisprudence'.

The emergence of strict liability

- the rule in *Rylands* took the view that there were certain activities in industrial society which, though lawful, were so fraught with the possibility of harm to others that the law had to treat them as permissible, but only if the public was insured against injury caused by those activities, irrespective of who was at fault – and if the worst happened, and injury was caused, then compensating those harmed was a cost of undertaking that activity;
- although Blackburn J professed to draw on analogies to existing law, *Rylands v Fletcher* in fact created a new legal principle of strict liability in the case of hazardous activities;
- the point of *Rylands v Fletcher* liability was to focus upon the *nature* of D's activity, rather than on the manner in which it was being conducted – shown by the fact that, even conducting it without fault will lead to liability;
- as with any strict liability doctrine, part of the ethos behind it is that it is preferable for D to bear the loss (via compensation) and then distribute that loss among society via insurance and by raising the prices of the products or services generated by that activity;
- *Rylands v Fletcher* 'gave English law one of its most creative generalisations which, for a long time, looked destined to have a successful future'.

Post-*Rylands v Fletcher*

- the rule was 'progressively emasculated, until subsequently it almost became obsolete in England';
- its concept of strict liability may have been ahead of its time; it was not until the 20th century that 'the concepts of social justice and social security, as integral parts of the general theory of the welfare state, were firmly established';
- the rule was progressively narrowed in its interpretation, e.g., by the application of defences, by removing personal injuries from its ambit, and by defining a 'non-natural user' as an 'abnormal use of the land';
- all of this gave rise to the view[21] that the rule 'has hardly been taken seriously by modern English Courts'.

Modern jurisprudence

- the injustices of not applying the rule, and leaving individuals who have been harmed by industrial activities uncompensated, is of concern;
- however, there is now a movement back to favouring strict liability – especially given the Bophal gas tragedy, the *Exxon Valdez* oil disaster, and the Chernobyl nuclear accident, which 'have shocked the consciences of people all over the world, and have aroused thinkers to the dangers in industrial and other activities, in modern society'.

[21] As stated in: *AG v Geothermal Produce (NZ) Ltd* [1987] 2 NZLR 348 (CA) 360.

Attention now turns to the requirements of the tort, as outlined earlier in the framework.

PRE-REQUISITES FOR THE TORT

Precondition #1: Capacity of C to sue

§17.3 As property-based torts, private nuisance and the rule in *Rylands v Fletcher* share the same restrictive rules of standing, i.e., that C had a proprietary or possessory interest in the land.

As Neuberger J stated in *McKenna v British Aluminium Ltd*,[22] 'in order for a claim to be brought in *Rylands v Fletcher*, [C] must have an interest in the land which would be sufficient to justify his bringing a claim in nuisance'. In *Transco plc v Stockport MBC*,[23] Lord Hoffmann affirmed that the standing rules are analogous under each of these property-based torts. The relevant rules governing C's standing to sue for private nuisance are discussed in Chapter 16.

In *Bodo Community v Shell Petroleum Devp Co of Nigeria*,[24] C were individuals and communities who had no relevant proprietary or possessory interest in land, but who suffered inconvenience because of oil pollution to land, fishing ponds, etc, in the Niger Delta which C used. The pollution occurred as a result of oil spills from pipelines allegedly caused by Shell Petroleum's lack of security in permitting illegal bunkering (i.e., criminal gangs who drilled and broke into the pipelines to extract crude oil). **Held:** the court reaffirmed that, without a relevant interest in the land, there could be no action in *Rylands v Fletcher*.

Hence, some earlier authority in which *Rylands v Fletcher* either succeeded or was held to be at least potentially applicable to the facts would now fail, on the basis that C lacked standing.[25]

In *Perry v Kendricks Transport Ltd*,[26] Kendricks, D, owned and operated a garage with an adjoining yard, in which was parked a disused bus. D had removed the petrol from its tank and screwed the cap on, and the business owners regularly told children to stay away from the yard. However, one day, two young children removed the cap, and threw a lighted match into the petrol tank. Vapours in the tank exploded, and another child, Trevor Perry, C, walking nearby on waste ground outside the yard, was dreadfully burned as a result of the explosion. **Held:** *Rylands v Fletcher* liability failed, due to the availability of the act-of-stranger defence (discussed later). However, that C had sufficient standing to sue was not doubted.

Under the rules espoused by *Hunter v Canary Wharf* (discussed in Chapter 16), C could not maintain any action under *Rylands* now.

Precondition #2: Capacity of D to be sued

The usual rule

§17.4 The appropriate defendant in *Rylands v Fletcher* is one who owns or occupies the land from which the thing escapes.

[22] [2002] Env LR 30 (Ch) [21]. [23] [2003] UKHL 61, [2004] 2 AC 1, [47].

[24] [2014] EWHC 1973 (TCC) [144(b)] (Akenhead J).

[25] See too: *Shiffman v The Hospital of St John of Jerusalem* [1936] 1 All ER 557 (KB) 561 (visitor to fair hit by falling flagpole; *Rylands* potentially available); *Powell v Fall* (1879–80) LR 5 QBD 597 (CA).

[26] [1956] 1 WLR 85 (CA), [1956] 1 All ER 154 (CA).

As Bray J explained in *Charing Cross Electricity Supply Co v Hydraulic Power Co*, it is not crucial that D does not *own* the relevant land, provided that he has the right or permission to occupy the land for a certain purpose – then, 'it is equally his, for the purpose of this principle [in *Rylands v Fletcher*]'.[27] Similarly, in *Transco plc v Stockport MBC*, Lord Bingham described an appropriate D in *Rylands v Fletcher* as being 'an occupier of land [who] has brought or kept on his land an exceptionally dangerous or mischievous thing in extraordinary or unusual circumstances'.[28]

There are some dicta comments which expand the notion of 'an occupier', in the context of *Rylands v Fletcher*, as widely as applies under the law of occupiers' liability (discussed in Chapter 12). That is, whether D occupied the property from which the dangerous thing escaped depends upon, not actual control, but whether he had the *right to exercise control* over those premises, according to dicta in *Ribee v Norrie*: '[i]t arises from a judgment as to whether he was in a position to exercise such control, should he wish to do so'.[29] Although Miss Ribee, C, did not ultimately recover under *Rylands v Fletcher* (instead, Mr Norris, as landlord, owed a non-delegable duty of care to C for the negligence of his tenants), the comments by Evans-Lombe J, as to who constitutes an occupier for the purposes of strict liability, bear noting.

Escapes from a highway

§17.5 Where D permits a dangerous thing to escape from a highway, waterway or other public thoroughfare, some English authority confirms (in dicta) that D has a sufficient interest in that land to be capable of being sued under *Rylands v Fletcher*.

English courts have been, at least, willing to entertain the possibility of a *Rylands v Fletcher* action, where the thing which escaped emanated from D's vehicle or other property which was situated on a public road. In *Rigby v CC of Northamptonshire*,[30] Taylor J considered that what really mattered was D's *control over the dangerous thing*, not necessarily over *the land* from which the thing escaped – provided that D had, at least, a licence to be on the highway: 'I can see no difference in principle between allowing a man-eating tiger to escape from your land onto that of another, and allowing it to escape from the back of your wagon parked on the highway.'

In *Powell v Fall*,[31] the farm of Mr Powell, C, adjoined a highway. Mr Fall's, D's, steam-powered traction engine was being driven along the road, when some escaping sparks set fire to a haystack on C's land. There was no negligence in either the construction or operation of the engine. **Held:** liability under *Rylands v Fletcher* proven. No point was taken about the fact that D had no proprietary interest in the highway. In *Rigby v CC of Northamptonshire*,[32] a psychopath, Mr Porter-Harris (PH), broke into a gunsmith's shop, owned by Mr Rigby, C. PH armed himself, fired shots indiscriminately out of the shop, and the police, D, laid siege to the shop for several hours. Eventually, from the highway, the police fired in a canister of CS gas to 'smoke out' PH. The canister set the shop ablaze, burning it

[27] [1914] 3 KB 772, 785. [28] [2003] UKHL 61, [2004] 2 AC 1, [11].

[29] [2000] EWCA Civ 275, [11], [42], citing: *Wheat v E Lacon & Co Ltd* [1966] AC 552 (HL).

[30] [1985] 1 WLR 1242 (QB) 1255.

[31] (1879–80) LR 5 QBD 597 (CA). At first instance, Mellor J noted that the 'principle which governs this case' was *Rylands*; and on appeal, although there was no explicit reference to *Rylands*, Bramwell LJ explicitly affirmed Mellor J's judgment. Further, in *Stannard (t/a Wyvern Tyres) v Gore* [2012] EWCA Civ 1248, [115], *Powell* was treated as a *Rylands v Fletcher* case.

[32] [1985] 1 WLR 1242 (QB) 1255.

out (and, as it happened, this incident occurred during a strike by the fire brigade). C sued the police, D, for the loss and damage to the premises and contents. **Held:** *Rylands v Fletcher* ultimately failed; but D was capable of being sued for the action.

This reasoning has even been extended to waterways. In *Crown River Cruises Ltd v Kimbolton Fireworks Ltd*,[33] Potter J noted that there were scenarios in which the rule in *Rylands v Fletcher* had been extended to cover dangerous things brought upon a highway which caused injury to adjacent property owners, and hence, there were strong arguments to extend the rule to such things which D brought onto a vessel in a navigable river (the Thames, in that case) – provided always that D had an express or implied licence to use the waterway for the purpose for which he was there. Ultimately, however (and as discussed shortly), *Rylands v Fletcher* did not succeed in that case.

ELEMENT #1: THE ESCAPE OF A DANGEROUS THING

'Things' which have escaped

§17.6 The types of things which have based a plea in *Rylands v Fletcher* have ranged from the animate to the inanimate, from the visible to the invisible, and from the natural to the man-made.

Some examples, in the Table below,[34] serve to illustrate the range of entirely mundane and sometimes rather bizarre 'escaped things' which have founded a plea in *Rylands v Fletcher* (albeit that not every case succeeded, for reasons explored later under other elements of the tort):

'Escaped things' under the rule in *Rylands v Fletcher*

The 'thing'	Case example
water	*Rylands v Fletcher* (a reservoir); *Transco plc v Stockport MBC* (water pipes); *Rickards v Lothian* (overflowing lavatory); *Charing Cross Electricity Supply Co v Hydraulic Power Co* (water main under a city street); *Superquinn Ltd v Bray UDC* (artificial lake); *Ellison v MOD* (culverts on land)
an industrial chemical solvent	*Cambridge Water Co Ltd v Eastern Counties Leather plc*
foot and mouth virus in a lab	*D Pride & Partners v Institute for Animal Health*
electricity	*Eastern and South African Telegraph Co Ltd v Cape Town Tramways*
spoil/mounds of waste/sludge	*A-G v Cory Bros and Co Ltd* (mineral waste on a hillside)
acid smuts belched from chimney stacks	*Halsey v Esso Petroleum Co Ltd*
metal foil strips blown by wind	*British Celanese Ltd v AH Hunt (Capacitors) Ltd*
caravanners and their horses	*AG v Corke*

[33] [1996] 2 Lloyd's Rep 533, [1996] CLC 1214 (QB) 1232.

[34] Each of the cases mentioned herein, and in other Tables in the chapter, are cited elsewhere in this chapter.

The 'thing'	Case example
a violent explosion on D's land, causing debris/materials/ vapour to escape to C's land	*Rainham Chemical Works Ltd v Belvedere Fish Guano Co Ltd* (chemical components exploded); *Miles v Forest Rock Granite Co* (explosives in a quarry caused rocks to escape); *Coxhill v Forward* (leaked LPG gas exploded); *Colour Quest Ltd v Total Downstream plc* (oil/petroleum exploded)
a hormonal herbicide	*Hamilton v Papakura DC*
fire	*LMS Intl Ltd v Styrene Packaging and Insulation Ltd*; *Mason v Levy Auto Parts of England*; *Hobbs (E) (Farms) Ltd v Baxenden Chemical Co Ltd*; *Coxhill v Forward*
one of the chairs of a chair-o-plane fairground ride	*Hale v Jennings Bros*
vibrations (caused by pile-driving)	*Hoare v McAlpine*
fireworks and sparklers	*Crown River Cruises Ltd v Kimbolton Fireworks Ltd*
fumes and gases emanating from D's premises	*West v Bristol Tramways Co* (creosoted wooden blocks); *Midwood v Manchester Corp* (escape from pipes)

Despite the wide range of possible 'dangerous things', not all escaped items 'fit' *Rylands v Fletcher*:

> In *Bolton v Stone*,[35] Miss Stone, C, was hit by a cricket ball as she exited from her house onto the pavement. The cricket ball flew from the adjacent cricket ground. C sought to advance her case on the doctrine of *Rylands v Fletcher*, arguing that a cricket ball was a dangerous thing which the cricket club had brought onto the cricket ground, and it had 'escaped' by being hit by a batsman. **Held:** no *Rylands v Fletcher* liability proven. A cricket ball was not a 'dangerous thing' within the meaning of the rule.

Perhaps the most novel case was the caravanners in *AG v Corke*,[36] and the finding that they could be 'dangerous things', for which the landowner who had granted them a licence to occupy his disused brickworks site could be liable for the damage which they caused. The case has been judicially criticised. For example, in *Smith v Scott*,[37] it was remarked that *Corke* had never, to that point, been applied against a landlord who had let his property to undesirable tenants as to render the landlord liable under *Rylands v Fletcher*. Pennycuick V-C considered that, given that a landlord parts with possession of the leased property in favour of his tenant and 'could not in any sense known to the law be regarded as controlling the tenant upon property still occupied by himself', this landowner should not have been liable for failing to prevent the 'escape' of the licensees/caravanners. Rather, a more elegant solution (according to Pennycuick V-C) would have been to hold that Mr Corke, the landowner, was in possession of the property, and was himself liable in nuisance for the acts of his licensees.[38]

35 [1951] AC 850 (HL) 867 (Lord Reid). 36 [1933] Ch 89.
37 [1973] Ch 314, and also discussed in: *Lippiatt v South Gloucestershire CC* [2000] QB 51 (CA).
38 *ibid*, 321.

An 'escape' is necessary

§17.7 'Escape', for the purposes of the rule in *Rylands v Fletcher*, means escape from premises over which D has legal ownership or control, to premises which are ***outside*** its legal ownership or control.

The rule does **not** cover an escape that occurred *within* D's premises. The enquiry is solely directed to whether the dangerous thing escaped the physical *boundaries* of the premises over which D had ownership or control.

The 'no escape' scenarios

§17.8 The rule in *Rylands v Fletcher* does not apply where *either* the thing always remained within the physical boundaries of D's land *or* the thing was always situated upon C's land where it caused the damage.

If the dangerous thing never 'escaped' from D's land, but at all times remained within the boundaries of D's land, *Rylands v Fletcher* **cannot** apply, as shown in the following cases:[39]

> In *Read v J Lyons & Co Ltd*,[40] facts previously, Mrs Read, C, was injured in the shell-filling shop, on D's premises. There was no escape of the explosive material from Lyons' factory, the explosion occurred entirely within its confines. (Similarly, if C had left her car parked in D's factory car-park, and the car had been damaged by the shell explosion, she could not have recovered under *Rylands v Fletcher*, as there would have been no escape from Lyons' premises.) In *Yorkshire Water Services Ltd v Sun Alliance and London Ins plc*,[41] Yorkshire Water Services, D, owned and operated a waste tip on the bank of the River Colne, the Deighton Tip, which was used for sewage sludge. Early one day, an embankment of the Deighton Tip failed, and a vast quantity of sludge surged into the river, blocking it, and also spreading across the river into the Deighton Works, also owned by D. The blockage of the river meant the possibility of riverside properties being flooded, including works belonging to ICI, C, which owned a factory upstream. C sued *under Rylands v Fletcher*, for the economic consequences of the slip. No *Rylands v Fletcher* liability was proven, as the sludge slip had never extended beyond the boundaries of D's property, and had not therefore directly affected C's property.

It was strongly argued in *Read* that it would be a 'strange result' if D was liable under *Rylands v Fletcher* for damage which occurred just outside the boundary, but not for an injury a foot inside. Nevertheless, the House of Lords considered it 'undesirable' to extend the rule, given that if it 'were extended as far as strict logic might require, it would be a very oppressive decision'.[42] (In any event, as discussed later,[43] Mrs Read's case would not be able to be framed under *Rylands v Fletcher* now, given that personal injuries are excluded from the ambit of the rule.)

[39] See too: *Transco plc v Stockport MBC* [2003] UKHL 61, [2004] 2 AC 1, [77], where Lord Scott considered that the water that leaked from the fractured water pipe had never 'escaped' from Council D's land. 'The water flowing from the fractured pipe accumulated in a part of the old landfill site and then made its way to the embankment. It began its "escape" on the council's property, accumulated on the council's property and eventually damaged the embankment, also the council's property.' Hence, a *Rylands v Fletcher* claim was barred by *Read v Lyons* (the other members of the House denied the claim on different grounds).

[40] [1947] AC 156 (HL), with the bracketed example given in *Transco plc v Stockport MBC* [2003] UKHL 61, [2004] 2 AC 1, [78] (Lord Scott).

[41] [1997] 2 Lloyd's Rep 21 (CA). [42] [1947] AC 156 (HL) 167. [43] See p 959.

The comparative corner: Non-escapes under *Rylands v Fletcher*

Australia: In *Perre v Apand Pty Ltd*,[44] Apand, D, was a potato crisp manufacturer. Negligently, Apand introduced a form of potato disease onto the land of one of its potato growers in South Australia. The disease itself was not shown to have spread, but the Western Australian potato authorities imposed a ban upon the import of potatoes from South Australian farms which were within a certain distance of the affected farm. Mr Perre, C, owned one of these neighbouring farms, and he suffered significant economic losses (from lost sales) because of the ban. **Held:** C was unable to sue in *Rylands v Fletcher*, because the disease itself did not escape from the affected farm onto C's farm.[45]

Moreover, if the thing which is dangerous *was always posited on C's land* (not D's), and that dangerous thing happens to cause damage to C's land, then again, *Rylands v Fletcher* cannot apply, because nothing 'escaped' onto C's land – the danger was always there.

In *AG v Cory & Co Bros Ltd*,[46] colliery company, Cory Bros, D, deposited about 500,000 tons of colliery spoil on the side of a steep hill belonging to a public housing authority, C, without making it stable. After heavy rains, a landslide occurred, causing damage to many houses belonging to C. C had granted D a licence for the deposit. **Held:** D was liable in negligence, but *Rylands v Fletcher* was not relied upon.[47] There was no escape – both the tip and the houses had been on C's land.

Additionally, if a thing (say, fire) starts on X's land, spreads or passes through or over D's land (burning some flammable material on the way), and thence onto C's land, that is not technically an escape from D's land, and will not satisfy the rule (per *Harooni v Rustins*,[48] in dicta).

The 'no encroachment' scenarios

§17.9 If the thing escapes from D's land, but did not actually *encroach* upon C's land, but nevertheless caused C to suffer loss and damage, then whether C can sue for *Rylands v Fletcher* remains somewhat unsettled.

It will be an unusual scenario where the thing does escape from D's land, did not actually *encroach* upon C's land, yet still caused C loss and damage. However, if this occurs (and it will be more likely when a threatening disease means that Government-imposed emergency measures are put in place), then although the decisions are not all one-sided, it appears from more recent authority that no action in *Rylands v Fletcher* will lie.

In *D Pride & Partners v Institute for Animal Health*,[49] the live foot and mouth disease virus escaped from the Pirbright animal research facility due to a defect in the effluent system (this allegation was assumed to be correct for the purposes of the strike-out application). Farmers from various parts of England, C, were affected by either being prohibited from moving their cattle and from

[44] [1999] HCA 36, (1999) 198 CLR 180.

[45] A point noted by Briggs J in *Calvert v William Hill Credit Ltd* [2008] EWHC 454 (Ch), [152].

[46] [1921] 1 AC 521 (HL) 539.

[47] Although interpretations of this case differ. See, e.g., *Anthony v Coal Authy* [2005] EWHC 1654 (QB) [123], which considered that both negligence and *Rylands v Fletcher* were made out against Cory Bros.

[48] [2011] EWHC 1632 (TCC) [67].

[49] [2009] EWHC 685 (QB).

bringing them to market, or by having to slaughter infected animals under emergency measures, but their land was not affected by the spread of the virus. C alleged that they lost the opportunity to take their livestock to market at the most profitable time; had been required to feed and maintain livestock when otherwise that livestock would have been sold; and some of the stock that would have been sold for breeding had to be sold for meat at a lower price. C alleged that the research company, D, had brought onto the Pirbright site quantities of live foot and mouth disease virus, that this constituted a non-natural user of land, and that the virus was a dangerous thing likely to cause damage if it escaped. **Held:** *Rylands v Fletcher* could not succeed, and was struck out. None of C's livestock was actually infected with FMD. Hence, nothing from the Pirbright facility encroached on any land of these particular farmers, C.

Some earlier authority differed. Where the thing which escaped from D's land did not fall onto C's land, but instead, fell onto a third party's land, which in turn caused damage to C's property, that fact was not deemed to be fatal to a *Rylands v Fletcher* claim in *British Celanese Ltd v AH Hunt (Capacitors) Ltd.*[50] Here, Lawton J stated that there was 'nothing in Blackburn J''s dictum which says that the escape must be on to a plaintiff's land ... Once there has been an escape ..., those damnified may claim. They need not be occupiers of adjoining land or indeed of any land'.[51] The view was obiter dicta, as the claim failed for another reason:

In *British Celanese*, British Celanese, C, and Hunt (Capacitors), D, occupied sites about 150 metres apart on a trading estate. D manufactured electronic components, and kept mounds of strips of metal foil, which were light enough to be blown about in the wind. The factories on the estate received light and power from a substation of the electricity board, about 100 metres away. Three years prior to this incident, some strips had blown away and fallen onto the substation, causing power outages. As a result, D had been warned, by letter from the electricity board, about the dangers of a flash-over and power failure if the strips came into contact with the substation's equipment. However, D did not cover the strips, and again, a large number of strips of metal foil from D's premises were blown away, fell onto the substation, and caused a power blackout. As a result, C's machinery stopped, materials in certain machines solidified and had to be cleaned out, and lost profits during the period totalled almost £10,000. **Held (preliminary issue):** no *Rylands v Fletcher* liability proven. The storage of the metal strips was a natural user of the land by D, not an abnormal user. However, the rule could potentially apply, regardless that the thing which escaped encroached upon a third party's (the electricity substation's) land.

Later, in *Anglian Water Services Ltd v Crawshaw Robbins & Co Ltd*,[52] it was questioned whether this aspect of *British Celanese* was correct. Stanley Burnton J remarked that, 'one of the crucial elements of that case was that the metal foil did not escape on to any land of the plaintiffs, but to an electrical substation owned by the electricity supplier ... Lawton J's judgment in the *British Celanese* case has frequently been approved in so far as it dealt with liability in negligence. With one exception, his judgment on liability *in nuisance* appears to have been judicially overlooked'.[53]

Hence, although the matter is not entirely free from doubt, it seems that some encroachment of the dangerous thing onto C's land *is* a pre-requisite to the application of *Rylands v Fletcher*.

[50] [1969] 1 WLR 959 (QB). [51] *ibid*, 964. [52] [2001] BLR 173 (QB).

[53] *ibid*, [130]–[131] (emphasis added). References to nuisance herein are taken to include the rule in *Rylands v Fletcher*. The exception was *SCM (UK) v WJ Whittal & Son Ltd* [1970] 1 WLR 1017, which did not explicitly address this question.

The fire scenario

§17.10 Where fire escapes from D's land, the rule in *Rylands v Fletcher* requires modification, because the 'thing' brought onto the land which then caught fire did not *itself* escape.

Fire was not actually referred to by Blackburn J in *Rylands v Fletcher* itself, but subsequent cases, as referred to in the Table above, have been prepared to apply the rule to the escape of fire. However, in a further sign of the rule being narrowly construed to the point of emasculation, the Court of Appeal held, in *Stannard (t/as Wyvern Tyres) v Gore*[54]), that the spread of fire will *rarely* fall within *Rylands.*

Ward LJ remarked, in *Gore*, that '[o]ne simply cannot say that there is no liability for fire damage under the *Rylands v Fletcher* rule, because the very man who established the rule said there was: see *Jones v Festiniog Railway Co*,[55] [where C's] haystack had been fired by sparks from a railway engine. Blackburn J held, "[t]he general rule of common law is correctly given in *Fletcher v Rylands*, that when a man brings or uses a thing of a dangerous nature on his own land, he must keep it in at his own peril; ... if sparks escape and cause damage, [D] are liable for the consequences though no actual negligence be shown on their part"'.[56]

However, the modern rarity of the rule applying, insofar as the spread of fire is concerned, was justified by Ward LJ on three bases. First, it is the 'thing' brought or collected by D on his land that must escape, and not the fire which was started or increased by the 'thing' being present there. Secondly, to fall within the rule, the fire itself must have been *started by D*, which means that he either deliberately or negligently started it. Thirdly, starting a fire on D's land may well be an ordinary user of that land, which would render the rule inapplicable in any event.

How, then, to rationalise the earlier escape-of-fire cases, in which C **did** succeed under *Rylands v Fletcher*? Various attempts were made in *Stannard* to do so, but (as Etherton LJ put it), 'with no clear consensus as to how the principle should be restated' in light of that previous case law. However, two scenarios where the rule in *Rylands* had applied to fire were as follows:

i. where the fire's escape was due to D having started it himself (or by a person for whom D is responsible), either deliberately or negligently. It was then that D had brought fire onto his land (per *Mason v Levy Levy Auto Parts of England Ltd*);
ii. where D had brought onto his land things which were likely to cause and/or catch fire, and then kept them in such a condition that, if they ignited, the fire would be likely to spread to C's land (per *LMS Intl v Styrene Packaging*). Hence, this would apply where the thing was flammable, enhancing the risk of danger to C's land via the spread of fire (per *Musgrove v Pandelis*).

Which of these approaches should be preferred, so as to render the rule of *Rylands v Fletcher* applicable in the context of fire, is not entirely clear from the *Stannard* decision.[57] Ward and Etherton LJJ appeared to favour (i), whilst Etherton and Lewison LJJ also accepted (ii). Lewison LJ would have favoured excluding fire from the operation of the rule in *Rylands v Fletcher* altogether, but neither of the other judgments seemed prepared to go that far. Of course, the modified version of the rule, above, clearly introduces some degree of wrongdoing on D's part, which rather flies in the face of the strict liability nature of the tort. However, it

[54] [2012] EWCA Civ 1248, [2014] QB 1, [48] (Ward LJ). [55] (1868) LR 3 QB 733, 736.
[56] [2012] EWCA Civ 1248, [36]. [57] *ibid*, especially at [48] (Ward LJ), [66] (Etherton LJ), [169]–[170] (Lewison LJ).

was evident that the Court of Appeal did **not** exclude fire from the ambit of *Rylands v Fletcher*, and considered that it could not do so, in light of the House of Lords' analysis of the rule in *Transco*. Although that case concerned an escape of water from water pipes, the principles of a *Rylands v Fletcher* claim espoused by the House were considered, in *Stannard*, to be just as applicable to cases involving an escape of fire (otherwise, the House of Lords would have taken care to exclude fire damage from the ambit of rule).

However, even if the modified principle applies, if the 'thing' stored by D, which ultimately caused or increased the fire, was a natural user of D's land, then no liability under *Rylands v Fletcher* will be proven (discussed later, under element #3). Two cases may be contrasted:

In *Stannard v Gore*, Mark Stannard, D, ran the business of Wyvern Tyres supplying and fitting tyres, at a trading estate in Hereford. Over 3,000 tyres were stored in and about buildings and chimneys on the premises. An electrical fault started a fire in a storeroom, and the tyres caught alight. It became very severe, and spread to Mr Gore's, C's, premises next door, destroying both premises entirely. No negligence could be proven; the wiring was competently checked, and the electrical fault was entirely accidental. **Held (at trial):** D was liable under *Rylands v Fletcher*, for the spread of the fire from his premises. The fire escaped within the meaning of the rule. Storage of such a large quantity of tyres in a haphazard manner gave rise to a special risk of fire which would be difficult to control, so as to amount to a non-natural use. **Held (on appeal):** liability under *Rylands* failed. The 'thing' brought by D onto his premises was a large quantity of tyres. The tyres did not escape. Rather, the fire escaped, and its severity was heightened by the tyres. However, the tyres were not exceptionally dangerous or mischievous. They were not likely to catch fire, as they were not in themselves flammable, and were not easily set alight. Hence, the modified principle for escape of fire was not satisfied. Moreover, keeping a stock of tyres on the premises of a tyre-fitting business on a light industrial estate, even a very large stock of tyres, was not, for the time and place, an extraordinary or unusual use of the land either.

In *LMS Intl Ltd v Styrene Packaging and Insulation Ltd*,[58] Styrene, D, made polystyrene blocks for insulation and polystyrene mouldings for use in packaging. A fire started in a factory unit which D occupied, which spread to the three adjoining neighbours', including C's, premises, causing substantial damage to their stock and premises. D's manufacturing process involved expanding polystyrene beads (EPS) with pentane as a blowing agent, and then cutting the resulting polystyrene blocks with a hot wire machine. A wire in this machine broke, causing an electricity spark, which caused a polystyrene block to catch fire. The high quantity of flammable materials in the factory unit quickly caught fire. **Held:** *Rylands v Fletcher* liability proven. The EPS beads, the pentane blowing agent, and the hot wire cutting machines, all posed a clear risk of fire. D had brought onto his land the EPS beads which were highly flammable, and these were likely to cause/catch fire when the pentane blowing agent was used, or if one of the blocks on the cutting machine caught fire. The blocks were not compartmentalised, so that if they ignited, the fire would be likely to spread to C's premises next door in the trading estate.

The mischief or danger test

§17.11 The escaped thing must be likely to be dangerous or do mischief, *should it escape*. It does not need to be inherently dangerous to give rise to *Rylands v Fletcher* liability, nor present any perils while sitting benignly on D's land.

[58] [2005] EWHC 2065, [2006] BLR 50 (TCC).

Blackburn J originally proposed that the thing was 'likely to *do mischief* if it escapes' or was 'something *dangerous*'.[59] In modern parlance, danger or mischief will do. The thing does *not* have to be dangerous to human health. Rather, it must be something that could damage C's land, or his interests in that land, if it escapes. In *Transco*, Lord Bingham observed that, given the historical origins of the rule, and also the strict liability nature of the tort, 'I do not think the mischief or danger test should be at all easily satisfied'.[60]

Of course, the acid smuts in *Halsey v Esso Petroleum Co Ltd*,[61] the foot and mouth virus in *D Pride & Partners v Institute for Animal Health*,[62] and the leaking LPG gas in *Coxhill v Forward*,[63] were inherently-noxious or dangerous things, even to D.

However, the water in the reservoir in *Rylands* itself and the chair-o-plane ride in *Hale v Jennings Bros*[64] which was in proper working order when the accident happened, were noted to pose no dangers while contained on D's land, and yet, liability could still arise. Hence, it is the mischief *upon escape* that is a pre-requisite for the rule to apply.

What D must know or have reasonably foreseen

Requisite knowledge on D's part

§17.12 If D does not know that the dangerous thing is on his land, then no liability under *Rylands v Fletcher* can arise.

Although it will undoubtedly be a very rare instance in which D does not know that the dangerous thing is on his land, if that scenario should occur, then no liability in *Rylands v Fletcher* can arise. D has to know of the existence of the thing in order to be liable under the rule – that is implicit in Blackburn J's statement in *Rylands* that D 'brings the peril onto his land and keeps it there'.

In *Dempsey v Waterford Corp*[65] (an Irish case), the Dempseys, C, had lived in their home since 1984. In March 2000, sewage water flowed into their home, through the living room floor, from an old sewage culvert beneath the floor. The culvert was actually positioned in Council's, D's, land. The culvert had been blocked, and the inflow to C's home, had been caused by redirection of sewage as a result of D's sewage repair works. D was unaware of the culvert, it did not appear marked on any maps in D's possession. **Held:** no liability under *Rylands v Fletcher* could possibly arise where D did not know that the dangerous thing, the sewage, was on its land.

The escape versus the damage: what must be foreseeable?

§17.13 The *type of damage* caused by the escape must be foreseeable, in order for a *Rylands v Fletcher* claim to lie. The *escape itself*, however, does *not* have to be foreseeable. D is strictly liable for the escape.

Escapes are likely to be unforeseeable, legally speaking, in three circumstances: (1) if the thing had never escaped previously; (2) the thing had escaped, but only as an isolated, one-off incident; or (3) the thing had escaped previously, but no scientific or other available knowledge would have alerted D to that possibility. Nevertheless, C's action can still succeed, because it is not the escape which needs to be foreseeable.

[59] (1865–66) LR 1 Exch 265, 279 (emphasis added). [60] [2003] UKHL 61, [2004] 2 AC 1, [10].
[61] [1961] 1 WLR 683 (QB). [62] [2009] EWHC 685 (QB). [63] (QB, 19 Mar 1986).
[64] [1938] 1 All ER 579, 82 Sol Jo 193 (CA). [65] [2008] IEHC 55.

Indeed, the leading case itself proves that. In *Transco plc v Stockport MBC*, Lord Hoffmann noted that *Rylands v Fletcher* was 'an innovation, in being the first clear imposition of liability for damage caused by *an escape which was not alleged to be either intended or reasonably foreseeable*'.[66] In the litigation arising out of the Buncefield explosion, *Colour Quest Ltd v Total Downstream UK plc*, Steel J remarked that '*Rylands v Fletcher* is concerned with non-natural or extraordinary user leading to *an escape, whether foreseeable or not*'.[67] In fact, liability was proven in each of the following cases, where the escapes were unforeseeable:[68]

> In *Rylands*, neither mill-owner nor his contractor who built the reservoir had any knowledge of the fact that tunnels under the mill-owner's land joined up to the adjoining colliery, nor were there any maps and plans in existence that could have drawn their attention to that linkage. Nevertheless, the mill-owner was strictly liable, even for an escape which he could not possibly foresee. In *West v Bristol Tramway Co*,[69] poisonous fumes emanated from creosoted wooden blocks laid by the tramway company, D, between the rails of the tramline. Those fumes wafted to C's neighbouring property, damaging plants and shrubs in C's nursery garden. This escape/emanation of fumes had never been known to have occurred previously, but damage occurring from that toxic source was very foreseeable.

Hence, the escapes themselves may be unforeseeable, but that does not preclude a *Rylands v Fletcher* claim – provided that the type of damage then sustained was reasonably foreseeable.

However, where **both** the escape, **and** the type of damage which resulted, were unforeseeable, then no liability under *Rylands v Fletcher* can be established. The latter requirement is considered later, under Element #4(b).

> In *Cambridge Water Co Ltd v Eastern Counties Leather plc*,[70] no reasonable supervisor at the tannery, D, could have foreseen that repeated spillages of small quantities of solvent would escape into an underground aquifer. The court accepted that D expected (from their knowledge at the relevant time) that any spillages of the solvent onto the tannery floor would be expected to evaporate rapidly into the air, and that the only foreseeable harm was that someone would be overcome by fumes from a significant spill in the tannery. It was unknown, and unforeseeable, to D, that the solvent could percolate through cracks in the concrete floor and into a chalk aquifer which ran below the tannery. That, being unforeseeable, would **not** have precluded liability. But the damage itself, i.e., the pollution of the water supply 1.3 miles away by the solvent, was also unforeseeable, and that **did** preclude liability from arising.

The principle under consideration is why *Rylands v Fletcher* has an advantage over private nuisance (where the interference to C's peace and enjoyment of his land must have been foreseeable for D, the nuisance-maker, to be liable). As *Rylands* does not require the escape of the dangerous thing to be foreseeable, the tort is particularly useful for isolated escapes (as the owner of the drowned mine demonstrated in that case). A one-off escape from D's land may well prove to be unforeseeable, yet C can recover for it. As Lord Hoffmann noted in *Transco plc v Stockport MBC*, *Rylands* changed the law in that important respect:

[66] [2003] UKHL 61, [2004] 2 AC 1, [27] (emphasis added).

[67] [2009] EWHC 540 (Comm), [2009] Lloyd's Rep 1, [411] (emphasis added).

[68] See too: *Rainham Chemical Works Ltd (in liq) v Belvedere Fish Guano Co Ltd* [1921] 2 AC 465 (HL) 471–72 (explosion of two chemicals ignited by flame never occurred previously; explosion; liability proven).

[69] [1908] 2 KB 14 (CA) 21–22 (Lord Asverstone CJ). [70] [1994] 2 AC 264 (HL).

> repeated escapes such as the discharge of water in the mining cases and the discharge of chemicals in the factory cases do not raise any question about whether the escape was reasonably foreseeable. If the Defendant does not know what he is doing, the Plaintiff will certainly tell him. It is the *single escape* which raises the question of whether or not [the escape] was reasonably foreseeable and, if not, whether the defendant should nevertheless be liable. *Rylands v Fletcher* decided that he should.[71]

Intentional versus accidental escapes

§17.14 If D *intended* for the dangerous thing to escape its land, and C's property was damaged as a result, then whether C can claim under the rule in *Rylands v Fletcher* remains unsettled.

In most *Rylands v Fletcher* scenarios, D never intended the water, fire, explosions, chair-o-plane, acid smuts, etc, to escape his land at all. The fact that they did was unintended, and indeed, in some cases, unforeseeable.

But what if D *did* intend for the dangerous thing to escape his land (e.g., by deliberately setting off fireworks), and C's property was damaged as a result? Does *Rylands v Fletcher* apply in this scenario too? The authorities appear to be inconclusive on this point:

> In *Rigby v CC of Northamptonshire*,[72] facts previously, **held:** the claim in *Rylands v Fletcher* failed. Taylor J stated that he was 'inclined to the view' that *Rylands v Fletcher* does not apply to escapes amounting to a deliberate, intentional or voluntary release of a dangerous thing, and if the escape was caused by an intentional act, the correct cause of action was trespass to land, not *Rylands*.

> In *Crown River Cruises Ltd v Kimbolton Fireworks Ltd*,[73] Kimbolton, D, set off fireworks from a barge on the Thames, to celebrate the Battle of Britain anniversary in 1990. Falling embers of fireworks ended up causing Crown River Cruises', C's, barges, moored in the Thames, to smoulder and then catch fire. **Held**: negligence proven; but not *Rylands v Fletcher*. Potter J considered that 'there was no good reason' (and respectfully disagreed with Taylor J on this point) for limiting the rule in *Rylands* to an accidental escape, as opposed to an intentional release – at least where the release was not deliberately aimed in the direction of C or with the intention of affecting his property. However, given the uncertainty as to whether intentional acts were caught by *Rylands*, it was better not to base the decision on that claim, when negligence was already proven against D.

Significantly, the outcomes in *Crown River Cruises* and *Rigby* were both decided in Cs' favour, in *negligence*, but not under *Rylands v Fletcher* – partly because of the courts' concerns that the rule should not be extended beyond its limits. Given the aforementioned judicial difference of opinion, and the lack of ratio on the point to date (as far as can be ascertained), the application of *Rylands* to intentional releases appears to be still open.

ELEMENT #2: DELIBERATE ACCUMULATION

§17.15 D must deliberately create some accumulation, by either bringing something dangerous onto his land or by deliberately containing something that was already on his land. The escape of some naturally-occurring feature or matter from D's land does not found any action in *Rylands v Fletcher*.

[71] [2003] UKHL 61, [2004] 2 AC 1, [27] (emphasis added). [72] [1985] 1 WLR 1242 (QB) 1255.
[73] [1996] 2 Lloyd's Rep 533, quote at 547, [1996] CLC 1214 (QB) 1232.

Many things noted in the abovementioned Table – fireworks, water, rocks, metal foil strips, etc – are entirely 'harmless to others, so long as [they are] confined to [D's] own property', as the rule in *Rylands v Fletcher* requires. The decision to deliberately accumulate a thing is never wrongful on its own, whether the thing is innately dangerous (such as explosives) or benign (such as water), but it is the escape of the thing which constitutes the danger.

The rule requires (according to Lord Hobhouse in *Transco plc v Stockport MBC*[74]):

> the creation or preservation of the dangerous user by bringing something dangerous onto the land or keeping it there ... Natural features of the land do not satisfy this criterion, even if they constitute a danger to adjoining landowners, e.g., rivers which are liable to flood ... there will not be a duty of care simply to protect one's neighbour from natural hazard.

Hence, if some natural feature of the land breaks away or wafts off D's land, such an escape does not base any claim in *Rylands v Fletcher*, as the following cases demonstrate:[75]

> In *Pontardawe Rural DC v Moore-Gwyn*,[76] the Council, D, owned land on which there was an outcrop of rock overhanging a steep slope, from which a 5-ton portion of rock broke away, rolled down the slope, and crashed into Mr Jenkins', C's, house. No *Rylands* liability arose, because the accumulation of rock was natural; the escape was due to natural causes, such as weathering; and D had used the land in an ordinary way, without any mining or quarrying operations. In *Willis v Derwentshire DC*,[77] Mr and Mrs Willis, C, owned a house and smallholding for breeding animals and poultry on the floodplain of the River Derwent. Next to the property was part of the West Durham coalfield, owned by D, with extensive coal seams. In certain atmospheric conditions, dangerous levels of carbon dioxide and stythe gas were emitted, leading to the evacuation of C, and remedial works. The gases were not accumulated, but were released naturally, or by the natural reactions of oxygen with carboniferous strata.

Water can accumulate on land either through deliberate action or naturally. Only the former (if that water escapes) invokes the rule in *Rylands v Fletcher*. Hence, if rainwater is collected on D's land (via a dam or artificial lake), then the rule applies; if the rainwater streams off D's land onto C's land according to the contours of the land, or a river floods on D's land and spreads to C's land without any interference having been made to the course of that river, then it does not.

> In *Ellison v MOD*,[78] the MOD operated the RAF Greenham Common Airbase, built during WWII. The Ellisons, C, lived at the foot of a valley near the airfield, and provided engineering services for agriculture. The other two Cs ran a sawmill and a motor cycle club. On 10 August 1986, a very intense storm occurred. At the time, 4 x 5,000 cubic metre bulk fuel storage tanks, plus pipelines and pumphouses, were being constructed, and the excavated spoil was tipped in piles at the edge of the base. After the storm, a vast amount of water flowed from the airbase into the valley, causing serious damage to Cs' property (cars, caravans, and whole sheds, moved; possessions were swept more than a mile away). C alleged that the MOD's positioning of the spoil interfered with the natural drainage of their land, whereas, before the spoil was deposited, the natural rainwater flow passed safely along the course of gullies and culverts on the airbase. **Held:** no *Rylands v Fletcher* claim proven. What escaped from the MOD's land was natural rainwater. The only artificial (contained) water on

[74] [2003] UKHL 61, [2004] 2 AC 1, [63].

[75] See too: *Healy v Bray UDC* [1962–63] Ir Jur Rep 9 (rock rolled down Bray Head, injuring C; *Rylands* claim failed; D had not brought the rocks onto land).

[76] [1929] 1 Ch 656. [77] [2013] EWHC 738 (Ch) [45]–[46]. [78] (1996) 81 BLR 101 (QB).

the MOD's land was that contained in front of the spoil heaps, but *that water* did not cause the flood, according to expert evidence.

Hence, if C complains of some *natural* hazard spreading to his land from D's neighbouring land, then the appropriate cause of action is either nuisance or negligence. As discussed in Chapters 16 and 7, respectively, and according to a trio of decisions – *Leakey v National Trust for Places of Historic Interest or Natural Beauty*;[79] *Sedleigh-Denfield v O'Callaghan*;[80] and *Goldman v Hargrave*[81] – D owes a duty (a 'measured duty, subject to qualifications not usually found in tort', per *Vernon Knight Associates v Cornwall Council*[82]) to take reasonable care to prevent damage to his neighbour's property as a result of a nuisance spreading from his land to his neighbour's land. It is, however, not a scenario that invokes *Rylands v Fletcher.*

ELEMENT #3: A NON-NATURAL USER OF THE LAND

This is undoubtedly the most difficult element of the cause of action, both legally and historically.

A dramatic change over time

The requirement that D must have put the land to a non-natural use, to be liable, did not appear in the original rule articulated by Blackburn J in *Rylands v Fletcher.* It was introduced by Lord Cairns when the case reached the House of Lords.[83] Lord Cairns intended it to mean that D was using the land for something that was 'artificial', or did not exist naturally ('in or by nature') on the land. Obviously, the reservoir was a non-natural user under that concept. Had that construction of the rule continued – encompassing all things artificially there – then the rule would have a much wider application than it has today.

However, in 1913, in *Rickards v Lothian,*[84] the Privy Council modified the meaning of a non-natural user significantly. Lord Moulton stated that a non-natural user 'must be some special use bringing with it increased danger to others, and must not merely be the ordinary use of land, or such a use as is proper for the general benefit of the community'. This amendment had two consequences. First, the tort was much-narrowed – because many things artificially on land can still be 'ordinary uses' of that land. Secondly, it introduced a marked degree of complexity and vagueness into the rule, because what seemed like extraordinary and hazardous activities on land (commercial, industrial, even wartime, activities) could be deemed to be ordinary uses of that land. No claim under *Rylands* could be established in the following, under the amended construction of 'non-natural user' – the thing may have been artificially there, but it was 'natural':

In *Rickards v Lothian*, Mr Lothian, C, leased the 2nd floor of a building in Melbourne from Mr Rickards, D. D occupied the rest of the building, and a toilet on the top floor was used by the other tenants of the building. Some unknown person blocked the waste-pipe, and turned the water full-on, causing flooding to the floors below, which damaged some of C's stock. D was putting his land to

[79] [1980] QB 485 (CA). [80] [1940] AC 880 (HL).
[81] [1967] 1 AC 645 (PC) (on appeal from the HCA). [82] [2013] EWCA Civ 950, [38].
[83] See n 1 above. [84] [1913] AC 263 (PC) 280 (on appeal from the HCA).

> a natural use (*viz*, properly providing piped water for sanitation to his tenants), even though the thing on his land (piped water) was artificially there. Proper sanitation also benefited hygiene and public health. In *Read v J Lyons & Co Ltd*,[85] facts previously, where a factory was filling shell cases with high explosives during WWII, the factory owner was putting the land to its ordinary natural use. According to Lord Macmillan: 'I should hesitate to hold that in these days, and in an industrial community, it was a non-natural use of land to build a factory on it and conduct there the manufacture of explosives'.

The House of Lords has since approved Lord Moulton's view of a 'non-natural user', with Lord Goff describing it, in *Cambridge Water Co v Eastern Counties Leather plc*, as 'the most authoritative statement of the principle of natural use of land'.[86] The Indian Supreme Court has since remarked that:

> the expression 'non-natural' was later interpreted to mean 'abnormal', and since in an industrial society, industries can certainly not be called 'abnormal', the rule in *Rylands v Fletcher* was totally emasculated in these subsequent rulings. Such an interpretation, as Prof Newark writes, 'would have surprised Lord Cairns and astounded Blackburn J'.[87]

The modern articulation and application of the test

§17.16 To be a non-natural user, D must have accumulated the thing in such unusual circumstances as to amount to an extraordinary and unusual use of the land, and which created a special hazard to C's neighbouring property, should it escape.

In modern parlance, the use to which D put his land – which, in turn, has resulted in the accumulation and escape of the dangerous thing – must 'create a special hazard, such as to be an extraordinary use of land' (per *Lambert v Barratt Homes Ltd (Manchester Division)*[88]), or 'some inherently dangerous thing which poses an exceptionally high risk of damage' to C (per *Gavin v Community Housing Assn*[89]). In *Transco plc v Southport MBC*,[90] the judges used a variety of expressions: D's use must give rise to an 'extraordinary risk to neighbouring property, if an escape occurs' (Lord Walker); D must have brought or kept on his land 'an exceptionally dangerous or mischievous thing, in extraordinary or unusual circumstances' (Lord Bingham); and it is the 'creation of a recognisable risk to other land owners which is an essential constituent of the tort' (Lord Hobhouse). Such a danger cannot arise 'by an everyday element of modern life, like [a] domestic water pipe' (per *LMS Intl Ltd v Styrene Packaging & Insulation Ltd*[91]).

It is fair to say that these descriptions have not always resulted in a bright-line distinction between natural and non-natural users. Examples of non-natural users in the following Table bear out the view of Laws LJ, in *Arscott v Coal Authority*, that the distinction is 'diminishing' and 'by no means self-evident'.[92]

[85] [1947] AC 156 (HL), with quote at 174, although Lord Bingham questioned, in *Transco plc v Stockport MBC* [2003] UKHL 61, [2004] 2 AC 1, [11], whether this was correct.

[86] [1994] 2 AC 264 (HL) 299.

[87] *Union of India v Kumar* [2008] INSC 802, citing: 'Non-natural Use and *Rylands v Fletcher*' (1961) 24 *MLR* 557.

[88] [2009] EWHC 744 (QB) [65].

[89] [2013] EWCA Civ 580, [25].

[90] [2003] UKHL 61, [2004] 2 AC 1, with quotes at [103] (Lord Walker), [11] (Lord Bingham), [64] (Lord Hobhouse).

[91] [2005] EWHC 2065, [2006] BLR 50 (TCC) [227].

[92] [2004] EWCA Civ 892, [27].

Non-natural users (i.e., abnormal or extraordinary uses of land)

- D created, on his land, an artificial reservoir (*Rylands v Fletcher*) or a dam (*Superquinn Ltd v Bray UDC*)
- D operated a thrilling fairground ride (*Hale v Jennings Bros*: 'the purpose [was] to whirl heavy objects around in reliance upon the combined strength of the various parts of the structure')
- D stored substantial quantities of chemical PCE for use in its factory work in cleaning animal skins (*Cambridge Water Co Ltd v Eastern Counties Leather plc*: 'the storage of substantial quantities of chemicals on industrial premises should be regarded as an almost classic case of non-natural use', per Lord Goff). That view was dicta, but significant, given that the trial judge had held that storage of PCE was a natural user of the land, commonly used in the tanning industry (the claim ultimately failed because the contamination of the borehole was not foreseeable)
- D granted licences to caravan dwellers to take up a site on his land (*AG v Corke*: 'collected together in large numbers, on a comparatively small parcel of land')
- D, a vehicle reconditioner, stacked spare motor parts and engines in crates, and stored combustible materials, near C's boundary fence, and close to a high laurel hedge and trees (*Mason v Levy Auto Parts of England Ltd*)
- D kept in his garage, a car with an LPG fuel supply system which had a history of spontaneous leaks, and a thermostatically-controlled freezer which could throw off sparks when starting up (*Coxhill v Forward*); also, storage of >200,000 litres of flammable products on D's premises (*Harooni v Rustins*, dicta)
- D, a factory owner, operated a hot wire cutting machine, igniting flammable polystyrene blocks (*LMS v Styrene Packaging*: 'I can see no substantive difference between the storage of the chemicals for the purposes of a tanning process, as in *Cambridge Water*, and the storage of EPS, with pentane, in and around the hot wire cutting machine')
- D made munitions; two chemical compounds, nitrate of soda and dinitrophenol, were stored in close proximity; on fire breaking out, they violently exploded (*Rainham Chemical Works Ltd v Belvedere Fish Guano Co*)

The Table below, on the other hand, sets out examples of natural, ordinary uses of land, for which D was **not** liable under *Rylands v Fletcher*:

Natural users (i.e., ordinary and natural uses of land)

- D, a developer, built a housing development on a disused school playing field, resulting in the surface water not draining away as previously, but flooding adjoining premises (*Lambert v Barratt Homes Ltd (Manchester Division)*)
- D, a munitions factory, manufactured explosives as part of the war-time effort in 1942 (*Read v J Lyons & Co*, dicta only – it will be recalled that there was no escape in this case)
- D, owners of a military air base, constructed bulk fuel tanks for aviation purposes. At the time of a severe storm and flooding, the tanks under construction contained no fuel whatsoever, and hence, 'did not bring with them any increased danger to others' (*Ellison v MOD* – it will be recalled that there was no accumulation of water either)
- D's storage of flammable or highly-flammable products in a domestic context (a can of turpentine or of paint, petrol in a car) does not engage the rule at all (*Harooni v Rustins*, dicta)

- D, a council, laid a 3-inch asbestos cement water pipe between its water main and holding tanks in the basement of a block of flats (*Transco v Stockport MBC*: this was quite different from the substantial reservoir created by Mr Rylands – just because the piping was larger than the usual domestic or commercial plumbing did not render it unusual enough to make the use of the land 'non-natural')
- D, a council, laid a pipe in a natural ditch to carry off rainwater, but the pipe became choked with leaves, causing flooding to the adjoining property: *Sedleigh-Denfield v O'Callaghan* (the claim was framed in nuisance; the HL confirmed that it was not a *Rylands v Fletcher* case, because this was 'an ordinary use of the land')
- D, a landlord, is not liable for spills from sewerage or soil pipes from common areas, into C's leased premises (*Gavin v Community Housing Assn*: these pipes resemble pipes for domestic water supply – a very natural use)
- D, engaged in mining activities, engages in a natural user of land with that mining (*Willis v Derwentshire DC*)
- D, operating a tyre-fitting business in a light industrial trading estate, stored large quantities of tyres (over 3,000) (*Stannard v Gore*)
- D, a factory, stored metal foil strips on its premises to be incorporated in electrical conductors (*British Celanese Ltd v AH Hunt (Capacitors) Ltd* – the business estate was properly-planned and laid out to accommodate manufacturers such as D, D properly used it for manufacturing purposes, and manufacturing electrical and electronic components using metal foil was not a special use, these were goods of a common type)
- D, a construction company, was redeveloping a site in Newcastle's city centre, which required large foundations to be sunk. During those excavations, a private sewer, not shown on any public plan (but only on a 1908 plan held in the Newcastle Discovery Museum), was breached, and concrete ran through that gap, into the public sewers – redevelopment of a city centre site was a natural user of that land by D (*Northumbrian Water Ltd v McAlpine Ltd*)
- D, a houseowner, lit a fire in his grate which then spread to adjoining premises (*Sochacki v Sas*: it was 'an ordinary, natural, proper, everyday use of a fireplace in a room. The fireplace was there to be used'), and applied in *Johnson (t/as Johnson Butchers) v BJW Property Developments Ltd* – *Rylands v Fletcher* was inapplicable to domestic fires started within grates and fireplaces

The blurred lines between a natural and a non-natural user is one of the most unsatisfactory aspects of the rule in *Rylands v Fletcher*. Although, in *Cambridge Water*,[93] Lord Goff expressed the hope that the element would come to have 'a more recognisable basis of principle' if a requirement of foreseeability was introduced into the tort (thereby putting less pressure on this element #3 to circumscribe the ambit of *Rylands*), the precedents in the above Tables confirm that it is very difficult to identify clearly a natural, or non-natural, user.

In *Mason v Levy Auto Parts of England Ltd*,[94] Mackenna J articulated **three** factors which tend to point towards a 'non-natural user' by D. These may include (but are not limited to): where D accumulated large quantities of the thing; where D accumulated the thing in a specific way that created danger to C; or where D accumulated the thing in a way that compromised the character of the neighbourhood. Although parts of *Mason* were overruled recently in *Stannard*,[95] the three factors were not adversely commented upon. They may provide some assistance in a given fact scenario. Briefly dealing with each in turn:

[93] [1994] 2 AC 264 (HL) 309. [94] [1967] 2 QB 530 (Winchester Assizes) 542.
[95] [2012] EWCA Civ 1248, [2014] QB 1, [164] (Lewison LJ).

i. The quantities of the dangerous thing which D has accumulated. Things stored in bulk are more likely to attract *Rylands v Fletcher* liability than things stored in just-sufficient quantities for ordinary household use and the 'comfort and convenience of life', as Lord Wright noted in *Collingwood v Home & Colonial Stores Ltd*: 'these dangerous things were being handled in bulk and in large quantities: they were being carried in mains ... [and] undoubtedly come within the principle of *Rylands*, but they seem to be very different in principle, and in result, from the case of the ordinary domestic pipes for gas or water or for wiring electricity'.[96]

   This factor operated to significant effect in *Cambridge Water*, re the 'substantial quantities' of solvent used by the tannery; in *LMS v Styrene Packaging*, re the quantity of polystyrene blocks stored on the factory premises; and in *AG v Corke*, re the large numbers (200–300) of caravanners occupying D's site.

   Nevertheless, the factor is by no means conclusive. LPG gas stored for domestic purposes was a non-natural user in *Coxhill v Forward*, while water transported in larger pipes to a block of flats was a natural user in *Transco*. This factor is certainly no firm indicator of the outcome of the question of non-natural user.

ii. The manner in which the dangerous things were stored. It must be kept in mind that the court is, notionally, not concerned with negligence on D's part in *Rylands v Fletcher*. Hence, the fact that the heap of metal foil strips were stored negligently by Hunt did not render them liable to British Celanese under *Rylands v Fletcher*. However, the fact remains that the way in which the thing was stored by D may render it dangerous enough to be a non-natural user.

   By way of example, as pointed out in *Anthony v Coal Authority*, '[t]o lay a spoil heap would be an ordinary use of land for the purpose of considering liability for escape – unless the manner in which the spoil is heaped creates a danger to others'.[97] In *Mason v Levy Auto Parts of England* itself (in which *Rylands v Fletcher* succeeded), Mackenna J noted that the flammable materials were placed by D in close proximity to C's fenceline, despite the large block of land which the vehicle reconditioning business occupied.

iii. The character of the neighbourhood in which D carried on its activities. Provided that D was using his land precisely for the purposes which would be expected within that particular neighbourhood, the use will be a 'natural' one, and will not give rise to *Rylands* liability.

   In *Transco*, piping water to a residential neighbourhood was exactly the type of activity which Stockport Council would be expected to carry out on its land, just as the storage of the metal foil strips by Hunt was exactly what would be expected on a trading estate for manufacturers in *British Celanese* (both natural users). Similarly too, in the purely domestic setting of the fire which spread in *Sochacki v Sas*,[98] the fire grate was being used for 'proper, everyday' purposes.

   However, again, the factor has inconsistently arisen, emphasising the problematical task which the 'non-natural user' element presents in the *Rylands v Fletcher* analysis. In *LMS v Styrene Packaging*, the 'specific manufacturing process' which Styrene carried out in its factory unit (which was a non-natural user) had a very considerable in-built risk of fire to those businesses surrounding Styrene – although Styrene's activity was precisely one which the industrial estate had been zoned for. Similarly, in *Colour Quest v Total Downstream*,[99] the storage of oil

[96] (1936) 56 Lloyd's Law Rep 105 (CA) 112 (Lord Wright MR). [97] [2005] EWHC 1654 (QB) [124] (Pitchford J).
[98] [1947] 1 All ER 344 (KB) 345. [99] [2009] EWHC 540 (Comm) [395].

and petroleum by Total Downstream in bulk on the Buncefield industrial site was a non-natural user (Total conceded that it was liable in *Rylands v Fletcher* to businesses and residents outside the perimeter fence of the Buncefield site), even though the locality was an important fuel storage site for a number of fuel companies.

Hence, none of the three factors mentioned above is determinative, but in this author's view, each provides some valuable assistance, albeit that element (ii) tends towards a fault-based analysis, contrary to the nature of a strict liability tort.

A time-specific enquiry

§17.17 'Non-natural users' must be judged according to contemporary, and not historical, standards.

In *Transco*, Lord Walker made the point that some activities (such as railway locomotion) which were once dangerous are no longer so, whereas some relatively modern users (such as the generation of nuclear energy) are very dangerous.[100] Whereas, in 1919, storing a motor vehicle with a tank full of petrol in a garage was a non-natural user in *Musgrove v Pandelis*,[101] less than 20 years later, it was suggested, in *Collingwood v Home and Colonial Stores Ltd*, that garaging a car was an entirely ordinary and proper use of land.[102] Recently, the Court of Appeal reiterated (in *Stannard (t/as Wyvern Tyres) v Gore*[103]) that *Musgrove* would most definitely be decided differently today, and that the case should 'simply be relegated to a footnote in the history of *Rylands v Fletcher*'. Furthermore, in *Read v J Lyons & Co Ltd*,[104] Lord Porter remarked that what is a natural user during a war effort (in that case, making shells in a factory) may be a highly abnormal and non-natural use of land during peacetime.

In summary, it is difficult to avoid the impression that, although *Rylands v Fletcher* is supposed to comprise a strict liability doctrine – attributing liability without proof of fault on the part of D – a finding of 'non-natural user' strays distinctly into fault-based territory at times, particularly when considering the way in which the thing was stored. In line with the theme that *Rylands* is kinder to the 'innocent' defendant than to the careless defendant, the former also has a wider range of defences to rely upon (discussed shortly).

Benefit to the community

§17.18 D's use of its land might provide the wider community with valuable employment opportunities; or the products or utilities supplied by D may be necessary for the convenience of modern life. Such a 'community benefit' does not prove conclusively that D's activity was a natural user, but may assist towards that finding, thereby refuting any liability under *Rylands v Fletcher*.

In *Rickards v Lothian*,[105] the Privy Council suggested that the use to which D put his land could not be a non-natural user (and could not give rise to liability in *Rylands v Fletcher*), if it was 'a use as is proper for the general benefit of the community'. The high-water mark of this principle undoubtedly occurred in *Read v J Lyons & Co Ltd*, but reference to this factor *still* continues to be made in more modern case law, to support natural users, so that the claims in *Rylands v Fletcher* failed:

[100] [2003] UKHL 61, [2004] 2 AC 1, [107].
[101] [1919] 2 KB 43 (CA) 47–48, 50.
[102] [1936] 3 All ER 200 (CA) 209 (Romer LJ).
[103] [2012] EWCA Civ 1248, [2014] QB 1, [49] (Ward LJ).
[104] [1947] AC 156 (HL) 176, citing: *Musgrove v Pandelis* [1919] 2 KB 43 (CA).
[105] [1913] AC 263 (PC) 280 (on appeal from the HCA).

In *Read v Lyons*, the manufacture of explosive munitions could be treated as an activity necessary for national security during wartime. In *Ellison v MOD*,[106] the construction of the bulk fuel tanks at the RAF Greenham Airbase was of benefit to the 'national community as a whole', given the national security provided by the activities carried out at the airbase. In *British Celanese*,[107] '[t]he metal foil was there for use in the manufacture of goods of a common type which at all material times were needed for the general benefit of the community'.

However, in *Transco*,[108] substantial doubt was cast upon the utility of the factor: Lord Bingham said that little assistance was to be gained ('and unnecessary confusion perhaps caused') by considering whether the use to which D put his land was of benefit to the community; Lord Hoffmann regarded the test of community benefit as 'reasonably unhelpful', noting that its application to commercial enterprises had produced different case outcomes, with 'distinctions being sometimes very hard to explain'; and Lord Walker remarked that a court 'cannot sensibly determine what is an ordinary or special (that is, especially dangerous) use of land by undertaking some utilitarian balancing of general good against individual risk'.

It is also plain, from various modern authorities, that a user which has 'benefit to the community' can **still** give rise to liability under *Rylands v Fletcher*, as the following cases demonstrate:

In *LMS v Styrene Packaging*,[109] Styrene's representative argued that, 'it would seem grossly unfair if I am found to be strictly liable for a heavily regulated manufacturing process, which provides benefits to the community'. In *Cambridge Water*,[110] Lord Goff noted, of the tannery which stored large quantities of chemical solvents, that 'sawston contains a small industrial community which is worthy of encouragement or support'. Significantly, this factor had convinced the trial judge that the tannery's use of the solvent in its leather business rendered it a natural user, outside the reach of *Rylands v Fletcher*, but that was ultimately overruled (to no avail, as the claim ultimately failed because C's damage was unforeseeable).

Hence, although community benefit has been an oft-cited consideration in the case law, both its weight and relevance, when assessing the question of non-natural user, appears to be much diminished.

The availability of insurance

§17.19 If C could have insured his property against the damage caused by the escape of the dangerous thing from D's land, the law is unsettled as to whether the availability of that insurance suggests that D's activity was a natural user, refuting any liability under *Rylands v Fletcher*.

If C, whose property was damaged by the escape of the dangerous thing from D's land, could have taken out insurance to cover that particular damage, the issue has arisen as to whether the availability of that insurance provides a pointer that D's use is therefore a natural one.

In *Transco*,[111] members of the House of Lords disagreed on this question (and also upon the policy considerations that underpin *Rylands v Fletcher*):

[106] (1996) 81 BLR 101 (QB). [107] [1969] 1 WLR 959 (QB) 963.
[108] [2003] UKHL 61, [2004] 2 AC 1, with quotes at [11] (Lord Bingham), [37] (Lord Hoffmann), [105] (Lord Walker).
[109] [2005] EWHC 2065 (TCC) [230]. [110] [1994] 2 AC 264 (HL) 309.
[111] [2003] UKHL 61, with views respectively at [49] (Lord Hoffmann) and [60] (Lord Hobhouse).

Lord Hoffmann's view: If insurance against the particular property damage which C suffered is readily available and relatively cheap (and property damage is all that is recoverable in a *Rylands v Fletcher* claim), then C has the opportunity to protect himself against the harm, and it will point to a natural user. Given that most domestic and commercial property is insured in England, it is preferable for C's property insurer to bear that loss (provided that the claim falls within the scope of the insurable event) via a low-transactional-cost insurance claim, rather than for D (or its liability insurer) to be held strictly liable for a non-natural use of land, pursuant to *Rylands v Fletcher* litigation which has huge transactional costs. Hence, the availability of insurance for C pointed to no liability under *Rylands v Fletcher*.

Lord Hobhouse's view: The purpose of the rule in *Rylands v Fletcher* determines **which** of the insurers who are inevitably standing behind the litigation should bear the burden – C's property insurer whose property was damaged by the escape, or D's liability insurer who will be seeking to avoid any strict liability against its insured who allowed the dangerous thing to escape. If C were unable to bring a *Rylands v Fletcher* claim, simply because insurance was available for his loss, then that would be analogous to saying that a driver who has taken out a comprehensive car insurance policy should never be able to sue a negligent driver in negligence, if he is hurt. Just because insurance is available does not remove the function of the law of tort, which is to allocate responsibilities among insured parties.

In *LMS v Styrene Packaging*,[112] the court noted the disagreement which had emerged in the House of Lords on this point, and tentatively preferred the view of Lord Hobhouse: 'the existence or otherwise of insurance in favour of [C] should not, of itself, be determinative of that party's right of action in law'. Nevertheless, the question must be regarded as being unsettled at this juncture.

Profit-making purposes

§17.20 Where D does not accumulate the dangerous thing on his land for his own commercial (i.e., profit-making) purposes, the law is unsettled as to whether D can be liable under *Rylands v Fletcher*. However, the better view is that D must have accumulated the thing for some profit-making endeavour, to be liable.

In *Rylands v Fletcher* itself, Blackburn J noted that D must bring or keep the thing 'for his own purposes' in order to be liable. Should that be taken to mean, for his own *profit-making, commercial* purposes?

Early case law, such as *AG v Corke*, adverted to D being liable where he deliberately accumulated something on his land 'for his own profit'.[113] In that case, D owned disused brickworks, and was liable in *Rylands v Fletcher* for the activities of caravanners on that site. The court referred to the fact that, in granting licences to the caravanners and by charging them weekly sums to camp there, D had benefited financially from the accumulation of people on his land. On the other hand, some defendants clearly had no commercial endeavour in mind in keeping the dangerous thing on their land, yet were liable in *Rylands v Fletcher*. The car owner in *Coxhill v Forward*,[114] who stored LPG gas to power his domestic motor vehicle, is one such example.

More recent House of Lords' authority suggests that some profit-making enterprise on the part of D, who accumulated the thing and allowed it to escape, *is* a pre-requisite for liability

[112] [2005] EWHC 2065 (TCC) [228]. [113] [1933] Ch 89, 94–95. [114] (QB, 19 Mar 1986, McNeill J).

to arise. In *Transco*,[115] Lord Hobhouse said that a 'salient feature' and a 'constituent element' of the rule in *Rylands v Fletcher* was 'the self interest of the landowner'; while Lord Hoffmann pointed out that there is an underlying rationale as to why D must have been operating for his own profit in order to be liable under *Rylands v Fletcher*, and to exclude the claim if D has no profit-making endeavour in mind when accumulating the thing:

> To exclude domestic use is understandable if one thinks of the rule as a principle for the allocation of costs; there is no enterprise of which the risk can be regarded as a cost which should be internalised. That would at least provide a fairly rational distinction [between natural and non-natural user].[116]

It will be recalled[117] that one of the supposed justifications of *Rylands v Fletcher* strict liability was that entrepreneurs should pay for ('internalise') the consequences of whatever risks eventuated as a result of their commercial enterprises, by considering any compensatory payouts (or insurance premiums to cover such damages) as a cost of conducting that business. When viewed in that light, then accumulation for some profit-making purpose naturally and reasonably becomes a pre-requisite to liability under the rule.

Hence, on the basis of modern authority, the better view is that D must have accumulated the dangerous thing for commercial purposes, in order to be liable under *Rylands v Fletcher.*

ELEMENTS #4(A) AND 4(B): CAUSATION AND REMOTENESS

Given that, in *Transco plc v Stockport MBC*,[118] Lord Bingham explicitly held that a *Rylands v Fletcher* claim was 'a sub-species of nuisance', and that both torts are 'directed only to the protection of interests in land', there is a large overlap in the treatment of causation and remoteness for both torts. Hence, readers are referred to Chapter 16, and its discussion of causation and remoteness in the context of private nuisance.

On the topic of foreseeability, Lord Goff, who delivered the leading judgment in *Cambridge Water Co Ltd v Eastern Counties Leather plc*,[119] remarked categorically that, 'foreseeability of harm of the relevant type by [D] should be regarded as a prerequisite of liability in damages in nuisance and under the rule [in *Rylands v Fletcher*]'.[120] In *Transco plc v Stockport MBC*[121] too, it was recognised that D will only be liable for damage which was foreseeable, and that this was 'the general rule of liability for nuisance today', where *Rylands v Fletcher* was regarded as a subspecies of nuisance in that case.

> In *Cambridge Water*,[122] facts previously, **held:** the claim in *Rylands v Fletcher* failed. The problem for C was not that the escape of the solvent from the tannery premises was unforeseeable (which it was); the real problem was that, having escaped, the type of damage actually sustained – pollution of a borehole some 1.3 miles away by that solvent – was unforeseeable. 'To impose strict liability on Eastern Counties Leather, in these circumstances, ... under the rule in *Rylands v Fletcher*, on the ground that it has subsequently become reasonably foreseeable that the PCE may, if it escapes, cause damage, appears to me to go beyond the scope of [the rule].' In *Rylands* itself, the damage was foreseeable once the escape of the water occurred, as the flooded coal-mine was

[115] [2003] UKHL 61, with quotes at [54], [66] (Lord Hobhouse). [116] *ibid*, [37]. [117] See pp 921–23.
[118] [2003] UKHL 61, [2004] 2 AC 1, [9]. [119] [1994] 2 AC 264 (HL) 307.
[120] [1993] UKHL 12, [1994] 2 AC 264, 307. [121] [2003] UKHL 61, [2004] 2 AC 1, [26].
[122] [1993] UKHL 12, [1994] 2 AC 264, quote at 306–7.

next door, but Cambridge Water's borehole was some distance away, and D could not foresee that the chalk aquifer and its micro-channels could provide a courseway for the solvent to travel over that distance. In *GJ Hamilton v Papakura District Council*,[123] Mr and Mrs Hamilton, C, claimed that their cherry tomato crops were damaged in 1995 by hormone herbicides which were present in their town water supply. That water was obtained from Watercare Services, D, the main bulk water supplier for the Auckland area. C argued that D brought hormonal herbicide onto its land in the catchment area which, if it escaped, was likely to cause damage; and that the herbicide did escape by entering the reservoir from which contaminated water was supplied to C. **Held:** the claim in *Rylands v Fletcher* failed. D could not have reasonably foreseen any harm occurring to C's tomatoes, from the occasional occurrences of herbicide in the very low concentrations which tests had historically shown.

It had always been a requirement, from the judgment of Blackburn J in *Rylands*, that D's damage had to flow 'naturally' (directly) from the escape of the dangerous thing. However, D's liability to pay damages is now limited to the type of damage which was reasonably foreseeable. Essentially, Lord Goff postulated three reasons in *Cambridge Water* for this principle.[124] First, in Blackburn J's judgment, one could discern a 'general tenor ... that knowledge, or at least foreseeability of the risk [of mischief as a result of the escape] was a prerequisite to the recovery of damages'. Secondly, since *Rylands v Fletcher* was handed down, the House of Lords had shown a desire (e.g., in *Read v J Lyons & Co Ltd*) to limit the scope of liability under the rule. Hence, it was appropriate to adopt the foreseeability test – a somewhat narrower test than the 'direct connection' test – as a pre-requisite for liability under the rule. Thirdly, liability under *Rylands v Fletcher* should be regarded as 'essentially concerned with an extension of the law of nuisance to cases of isolated escapes' (that was how Blackburn J himself saw it, not as any 'revolutionary decision'), and in that regard, since foreseeability of damage was a pre-requisite to recovery of damages in nuisance, then 'it would lead to a more coherent body of common law principles' if *Rylands v Fletcher* was treated in the same way.

Hence, *Rylands v Fletcher* is **not** such a strict liability tort that it renders D liable for damage which he does not know, or reasonably foresee, could result from the escape. However, it remains a strict liability tort in the sense that D will be liable, even if he acted with all reasonable care to prevent the escape.

Interestingly, there has been subsequent judicial reservation about a requirement of foreseeability of damage being necessary for an action in *Rylands v Fletcher*. In *Harooni v Rustins*,[125] Akenhead J said that such a requirement 'is more consonant with negligence'. Nevertheless, the law has been definitively set by the House of Lords in both *Cambridge Water* and *Transco*.

DEFENCES

Several defences circumscribe D's liability under *Rylands v Fletcher*. These serve as 'control mechanisms'[126] or 'excusing factors'[127] for D's liability, for allowing the escape of a dangerous thing from his land. Indeed, the range of defences available to D considerably 'water down' the

[123] [2002] UKPC 9, [40], [47] (on appeal from New Zealand: [1999] NZCA 210).

[124] [1994] 2 AC 264 (HL), with the reasoning at 283, 297, 300–4, 306 (Lord Goff).

[125] [2011] EWHC 1632 (TCC) [66].

[126] *Transco plc v Stockport MBC* [2003] UKHL 61, [2004] 2 AC 1, [66] (Lord Hobhouse).

[127] *Superquinn Ltd v Bray UDC* [1998] IEHC 28, [1998] 3 IR 542, [131].

supposedly strict liability doctrine – perhaps precisely because it is notionally a strict liability tort. From mischievous third parties to one-off natural events, D has considerable scope to avoid *Rylands v Fletcher* liability.

Nevertheless, whether through lack of use, or in light of their own limitations, the defences have not had a particularly frequent application in *Rylands v Fletcher* jurisprudence to date.

Act of God

§17.21 D is not liable for escapes caused by natural events, or 'acts of God'.

In *Transco plc v Stockport MBC*,[128] Lord Hobhouse usefully defined an 'act of God' to require the following: (1) the event was due to *natural causes*, directly and exclusively; (2) the event involved no human agency or human intervention; and (3) it was not realistically possible for a human to reasonably guard against or prevent the event by any amount of foresight, pains and care. The defence typically involves storms, floods, earthquakes, and the like.[129] The *natural* cause which gave rise to the exceptional nature or severity of the event in question is what distinguishes this defence from that of *vis major*, which entails some human act (discussed below).

In the following cases, D could not have prevented the escape due to acts of God, and so the escapes caused by such events were outside the scope of *Rylands v Fletcher*:

> In *Superquinn Ltd v Bray UDC*,[130] Superquinn, C, owned and operated a supermarket on a riverside block in Little Bray along the River Dargle. Coillte Teoranta, D, was the owner and occupier of an artificial lake known as Paddock pond, located upstream of the Dargle. One night in August 1986, a storm known as 'Hurricane Charlie' occurred, and the River Dargle burst its banks and caused extensive flooding. The dam at Paddock pond failed. C claimed that the waters released by the dam's failure joined the Dargle, increased the river level, and caused/contributed to the flooding in Little Bray, and its business. The storm could not reasonably have been anticipated or guarded against by D, as the storm fell within the category of the most extreme natural phenomena. In *Nichols v Marsland*,[131] Mrs Marsland, D, owned a property with ornamental pools containing large quantities of water, the pools having been formed by damming up a natural stream which flowed through D's land. Due to a period of extraordinary rainful one day in 1872, flooding occurred, the artificial banks were carried away, the water in the pools escaped, and the water washed away four county bridges downstream. The county surveyor, C, brought an action for escape of a dangerous thing. A jury had found that there was no negligence in the maintenance or construction of the pools. There could be no *Rylands v Fletcher* liability either, because the flood was so great that it could not reasonably have been anticipated or guarded against.

However, the defence appears to have been applied fairly infrequently and restrictively. Although, in *Sedleigh-Denfield v O'Callagan*, it was stated (obiter) that a rainfall or a storm could be 'so exceptional that it should be regarded as an act of God',[132] some courts have clearly not been enamoured of the defence. In *Dockeray v Manor Park Homebuilders Ltd*,[133] the Irish High Court was not prepared to find that even a 20-year heavy rainfall event of 'extraordinarily high

[128] [2003] UKHL 61, [2004] 2 AC 1, [59].

[129] Noted, e.g., in: *Oxford Dictionary of Law* (6th edn, Oxford University Press, 2006) 11.

[130] [1998] IEHC 28, [1998] 3 IR 542 9. [131] (1876–77) 2 Ex D 1 (CA). [132] [1940] AC 880 (HL) 886.

[133] Irish HC, O'Hanlan J, 10 Apr 1995, cited in: *Superquinn* [1998] IEHC 28, [1998] 3 IR 542, [134].

proportions' constituted an act of God for the purposes of *Rylands v Fletcher*, while in *Greenock Corp v Caledonian Rwys*,[134] the Lord Chancellor remarked that, 'floods of extraordinary violence must be anticipated as likely to take place from time to time', and that the rain which occurred could hardly have been said to be unprecedented in Scotland.

In *Greenock*, D interfered with the course of a stream, by constructing a culvert that acted as a new 'channel' for the water to travel through a valley. After an event of extraordinary rainfall, C's property was damaged. **Held:** the defence of act of God could not apply, where 'if damage results from the deficiency of the substitute which [D] has provided for the natural channel, he will be liable. Such damage is not in the nature of [an act of God], but is the direct result of the obstruction of a natural water-course by [D's] works, followed by heavy rain'. *Nichols v Marsland* was distinguished, on the basis that the course of a natural stream was not interfered with there – the ornamental pools merely dammed up the course of the stream.

Hence, this defence is a little like the rule to which it attaches – ameliorated to the point of being of very doubtful utility, even when it seems, on the facts, that it could feasibly apply.

Act of *vis major*

§17.22 D is not liable for acts of *vis major*.

An act of *vis major* means some 'irresistible force', some 'interposition of human agency which from its nature is absolutely uncontrollable' (such as the acts of an invading army, or a violent robbery).[135] The acts of such persons will relieve D from any liability under *Rylands v Fletcher* (although the author's searches have been unable to elicit any example of the defence in operation in this context).

Act of a stranger

§17.23 D is not liable for the acts of a stranger which cause the escape of the dangerous thing – provided that (a) D had no control over the stranger, and (b) the acts of the stranger were unforeseeable.

D can escape liability under *Rylands v Fletcher* if the escape was caused by the acts of a stranger – whether those be intentional, malicious, negligent, or mere errors of judgment.

In *Rickards v Lothian*,[136] facts previously, where some unknown person blocked the waste-pipe in Mr Rickard's, D's, premises on the top floor, turned the water on full, causing flooding to the floors below, damaging Mr Lothian's stock, D was not responsible for the escape of the water from the top floor, given that a jury had found that the plugging up was done by some unknown and maliciously-minded person. In *Perry v Kendricks Transport Ltd*,[137] facts previously, the bus company, D, was not liable for escape of metal shards and debris from its premises, caused by the acts of strangers (*viz*, the two children). In *Fallows v Crossley*,[138] Mr Crossley, D, a farmer, had created two ponds on his

[134] [1917] AC 556 (HL) 557. [135] JE Penner, *The Law Student's Dictionary* (Oxford University Press, 2008) 308.
[136] [1913] AC 263 (PC, on appeal from the High Court of Australia). [137] [1956] 1 WLR 85 (CA).
[138] CA, Balcombe and Beldam LJJ, 29 Oct 1993.

land in a boggy area, by building up the banks so that water could collect there. The higher pond was breached; that allowed the escape of water into the lower pond, and caused that pond to overflow and discharge water into the stream. The property of Mr Fallows, C, next door was flooded. It was arguable (without deciding) that the escape of water from D's pond did not cause the damage to C's land; the stream flowed into a culvert which had become blocked and overgrown because of *others'* failure to maintain it properly.

Although the acts causing the escape in *Rickards* and *Perry* were malicious and intentional, respectively, and although Singleton LJ suggested, in *Perry*,[139] that the defence depended upon the 'deliberate and conscious act of a stranger', there is considerable authority to the contrary. In *Perry* itself, Jenkins LJ remarked that, 'I see no necessity to confine the exception ... to acts which proceed from the conscious volition or the deliberate act of the stranger',[140] while more recently in *Bodo Community v Shell Petroleum Devp Co of Nigeria*,[141] Akenhead J noted that a stranger's act does not need to be malicious to attract the defence under the tort. Moreover, the defence has arisen for consideration, at least, in cases (e.g., *Hale v Jennings*, *Northwestern Utilities*, *Fallows*) in which the stranger's act in causing the escape was non-intentional – and the defence did not fail for that reason. This suggests that any type of act can potentially raise the defence – but it is subject to the two caveats below.

Caveat #1: Control of the stranger. The point of the defence is that the person who did the harm was one over whom D had no power of control. That renders that person 'a stranger'. Of course, some strangers may truly be unknown to D (e.g., trespassers, unknown parties who do mischief), but some may well be known to D, but over whom D has no control. Either will suffice.

Whether D *actually* controlled the activities of the 'stranger' is not to the point – the correct question is whether D had that *power of control*. If so, then the acts of those whom he had the right to control were **not** the acts of strangers, and D will remain liable for the acts of that third party in permitting the escape (per Ward LJ in *Ribee v Norrie*[142]).

In *Ribee v Norrie*, Mrs Ribee, C and Mr Norrie, D, owned neighbouring terraced houses. D's house had been converted into a hostel, with a number of individual bed-sits let to tenants, who shared communal kitchen and living areas. Due to a smouldering cigarette dropped in one of the communal areas in D's premises, by someone living or visiting the hostel, a fire started, and spread to elderly Ms Ribee's, C's, property during the night. She suffered smoke inhalation, and some property damage. Negligence was proven against D for failing to control the actions of his tenants. Although the case was pleaded in *Rylands v Fletcher*, that was not dealt with, given the doubt as to whether C's personal injuries could be recovered under *Rylands*.

Hence, whatever was said about *Rylands v Fletcher* in *Ribee* was dicta only. However, on the question of control of whoever dropped the cigarette in the communal area which started the fire in Mr Norrie's premises, Ward LJ concluded that, 'clearly the landlord [D] had the power to exercise some control. He could, by terms of the licence or by prominent notices in the premises, regulate the smoking as he thought fit, to ensure that the premises were safely used'.[143] Hence, it is unlikely that any *Rylands v Fletcher* could have been defended.

139 [1956] 1 WLR 86 (CA) 87. 140 *ibid*, 90. 141 [2014] EWHC 1973 (TCC) [55].
142 [2000] EWCA Civ 275, [2001] PIQR P8, [24], and for case description, [29]–[30].
143 *ibid*, [24].

Recently, in *Stannard (t/as Wyvern Tyres) v Gore*,[144] the Court of Appeal confirmed that D was liable for escapes of dangerous things that were caused by his employees (presumably when acting within the scope of that employment), his independent contractor, or 'anyone else who was on his land with his leave and licence'. Each of these parties acted under D's control – they were not strangers.

Caveat #2: Lack of foreseeability of the stranger's acts. The stranger's act of interference, in allowing the thing to escape, must have been unforeseeable. If it was foreseeable, and should have been guarded against by D, then the defence will fail. Mischievous children, and foolish high-spirited adults, may be something that should have been anticipated. This caveat has rendered the defence difficult to prove, as demonstrated by the cases below:

> In *Shiffman v Hospital of St John of Jerusalem*,[145] the hospital, D, was asked by the police to erect a casualty tent in Hyde Park, on a day which was the 25th anniversary of the death of King Edward VII (who died in 1910). D erected a flag pole, 30 yards from the tent, which was supported only by four guy ropes. An attendant repeatedly told children who came to play round the pole, and to swing on the rope, to keep away. However, while the attendant was assisting a casualty inside the tent, the pole fell and injured Mr Shiffman, C, causing serious head injuries. **Held:** Negligence succeeded, but it was said that *Rylands v Fletcher* would have been an alternative claim. The defence that the flagpole fell due to the acts of strangers (children) swinging on the ropes could not succeed, because their high spirits and the allurement that the pole represented ought to have been foreseen and guarded against by D. In *Hale v Jennings Bros*,[146] where the chair-o-plane flew off, the fairground operators, D, were liable under *Rylands v Fletcher*. The stupidity of rider Mr Crampton, in bouncing about in the chair, was precisely the kind of danger that D should have guarded against, given that '[p]eople go there in a spirit of fun. Many of them are ignorant, and many of them are wholly unaware of the dangers incidental to playing with the chairs in that sort of way, and they cause a danger that they do not in the least realise'. Riders could interfere with the safety of the machine, which was wholly to be expected.

In *Transco plc v Stockport MBC*,[147] Lord Hoffmann criticised the act-of-a-stranger defence, stating that '[n]o serious principle of allocating risk to [D's] enterprise would leave the injured third party [C] to pursue his remedy against the vandal. But early cases on *Rylands v Fletcher* quickly established that ... acts of third parties excluded strict liability'.

Occasionally, the third party who caused the escape will be a public or corporate body – the other end of the spectrum from a free-spirited or malicious person. Even then, D who kept the dangerous thing may be liable for the escape caused by the public body, if D did not guard against and anticipate what could happen:

> In *Northwestern Utilities Ltd v London Guarantee and Accident Co Ltd*,[148] the Corona Hotel in Edmonton, Alberta, owned by London Guarantee, C, was destroyed by fire. The fire was caused by the escape and ignition of natural gas, which had percolated through the soil and penetrated into the hotel basement from a fractured welded joint in a gas main that ran below street level. Northwestern, D, a public utility company which supplied natural gas to consumers in Edmonton, owned the main. The rupture was due to the City of Edmonton council constructing a storm sewer immediately beneath the gas main. **Held:** D was liable under *Rylands v Fletcher*, for the loss of C's hotel. D could

[144] [2012] EWCA Civ 1248, [2014] 1 QB 1, [34] (Ward LJ), citing: *H&N Emanuel v GLC* [1971] 2 All ER 835 (CA).
[145] [1936] 1 All ER 557 (KB). [146] [1938] 1 All ER 579 (CA). [147] [2003] UKHL 61, [2004] 2 AC 1, [32].
[148] [1936] AC 108 (PC) (on appeal from the SCC), with quote at 127.

not rely on the act-of-a-stranger defence, because it failed to foresee and guard against the consequences to their works of the City's operations, when the work had been ongoing, conspicuous and in full public view. If D 'did not know of the City works, their system of inspection must have been very deficient. If they did know, they should have been on their guard: they might have ascertained what work was being done and carefully investigated the position, or they might have examined the pipes likely to be affected so as to satisfy themselves that the bed on which they lay was not being disturbed. Their duty to [C] was, at the lowest, to be on the watch and to be vigilant: they do not even pretend to have done as much as that'.

Consent (including common benefit)

§17.24 If C consented, expressly or impliedly, to D either bringing a dangerous thing onto D's land or to its accumulation there, that can constitute a defence to a claim in *Rylands v Fletcher*. Consent may, but need not, arise from a common benefit or undertaking with D. If the escape was caused by D's negligence, however, the defence of consent is vitiated.

According to the House of Lords in *Transco*, this defence is based upon the principle of reciprocity or mutual benefit, 'give and take, live and let live'.[149]

Consent is typically proven by the fact that the accumulation was for the *common benefit* of C (whose property was injured by the escape) and D (who allowed the escape). However, a common benefit is not strictly required, in order for consent to be present. Hence, consent and common benefit cannot be strictly equated as defences. Consent can exist without common benefit; but common benefit will impute consent. The defence applied, for D's benefit, in the following cases:

In *Peters v Prince of Wales Theatre (Birmingham) Ltd*,[150] the theatre company, D, leased a shop and six rooms to Mr Peters, C. Situated over C's premises was D's rehearsal room. C knew that there was a sprinkler system installed there as a precaution against fire, and that extended to his own shop. The sprinkler heads were attached to water pipes, and each head contained a ball which easily melted if a fire occurred. Unknown to C, if ice formed in the sprinkler head during frost, that could shift the ball so that, when a thaw followed, the sprinkler system might allow water to escape. This happened in January 1940, damaging goods in C's shop. **Held:** *Rylands v Fletcher* failed. C must have been taken to have consented to the sprinkler system *in situ*, when he took the lease from D; it was not a condition of the lease that D had to remove the system in his shop, C 'took the place as he found it for better or worse'. If a common benefit was required (which it was not), then theatres were generally regarded as being exposed to higher risk of fire, so the sprinkler was for C's benefit too. In *Carstairs v Taylor*,[151] Mr Carstairs, C, rented a warehouse ground floor at Liverpool to store rice. Mr Taylor, D, the landlord, occupied the upper floor where he stored cotton. The water from the roof was collected in gutters, which discharged into a wooden box resting on a wall, and from there, into a pipe and drain. The gutters and box were examined by D's employee on 18 April, and were sound. Sometime between then and a heavy storm on 22 April, a rat gnawed a hole in the box, and water poured out of the box into the warehouse, and damaged C's rice. **Held:** *Rylands v Fletcher* failed. The guttering and box was part of a drainage system which was for the common protection and joint benefit of both occupants of the building. There was no negligence in the way in which

[149] [2003] UKHL 61, [2004] 2 AC 1, [61] (Lord Hobhouse), citing *Bamford v Turnley* (1862) LR 3 B&S 62 (KB) 84.
[150] [1943] KB 73 (CA) 79–80. [151] (1870–71) LR 6 Ex 217.

the wooden box was constructed, nor in the maintenance of it, nor in the fact that rats were in the vicinity of the warehouse.

The defence has a distinct limitation, however. Where the escape of the dangerous thing is caused by D's negligence, then any consent given by C is negated. In that event, a claim for *Rylands v Fletcher* can be maintained (per *Biffa Waste Services Ltd v Maschinenfabrik Ernst Hese GmbH*[152]). D's negligence may be systemic, or may constitute an isolated instance of lack of reasonable care. Either way, the defence will fail:[153]

In *Colour Quest Ltd v Total Downstream UK plc*,[154] facts previously, Total, D, the joint venturer which owned the Buncefield site, denied liability to businesses *inside the fence* (ITF), C, which included fuel companies such as BP and Shell who owned fuel tanks on the site, on the basis that C consented to oil products being stored at the Hemel Hempstead site. However, the defence of consent could not apply, because D's negligence in over-filling the bulk fuel tank the night before the explosion occurred vitiated any consent on the part of C to the dangerous oil products being accumulated onsite.

Statutory authorisation

This defence also applies to the tort of private nuisance (as discussed in Chapter 16), and readers are referred to that discussion for its analogous application under *Rylands v Fletcher*.

Volenti/contributory negligence

§17.25 If C was partly responsible for the escape of the dangerous thing, then D may rely upon the defences of *volenti* or contributory negligence.

In *Rylands v Fletcher* itself, Blackburn J stated that D, from whose land the thing escaped, 'can excuse himself by shewing that the escape was owing to [C's] default'.[155] This terminology equates with that of *volenti*, and unsurprisingly (given that defence's unsympathetic judicial reception) has been scarce to find in practice.

In *Crompton v Lea*,[156] Mr Crompton, C, was lessee of a coal mine. Another mine owner, Mr Lea, D, threatened to work coal seams by sinking and making shafts, which would have the effect of letting in a river and flooding D's mine, and through that, C's mine. C sought to restrain D from working his mine without putting up walls or dams sufficient to keep out the water. **Held:** *Rylands v Fletcher* proven, and an injunction granted. D argued that it was C's own fault that the water would enter his mine, because he might have erected a barrier, and he had also partly worked out his mine. However, while the defence was potentially available, it did not apply on the facts.

Contributory negligence is also technically available to D, given that the definition of 'fault' under s 4 of the Law Reform (Contributory Negligence) Act 1945 can encompass the strict liability arising from an escape on D's part (as it can also encompass private nuisances, discussed in Chapter 16).

152 [2008] EWHC 6 (TCC) [285].

153 See too: *A Prosser & Son Ltd v Levy* [1955] 1 WLR 1224 (CA) 1225 (water leak in apartment building due to D's negligence, damaging C's flat; even if C knew of plumbing deficiencies, no consent).

154 [2009] EWHC 540 (QB (Comm)).

155 (1865–66) LR 1 Exch 265 (Ex Ch) 279–80.

156 (1874–75) LR 19 Eq 115 (Ch).

The comparative corner: The defence of contributory negligence

In the Australian case of *Burnie Port Authy v General Jones Pty Ltd*:[157]

- per McHugh J (dissenting), a reason why *Rylands v Fletcher* should **not** be subsumed into negligence was that contributory negligence could not be a defence to a *Rylands v Fletcher* action – other defences to *Rylands v Fletcher* 'go to the issue of causation. The occupier is not liable under those defences because the act of God or the act of a stranger is a *novus actus interveniens*' – those defences could not be equated with contributory negligence;
- the *Burnie* majority, on the other hand, appeared to accept that contributory negligence could apply to a *Rylands v Fletcher* action, but cited no authority for that view.

MISCELLANEOUS

Relationship with other actions

A claim in *Rylands v Fletcher* is often pleaded, in the alternative, with claims based upon private nuisance; and the breach of a non-delegable duty of care. The tort's interaction with these warrants some mention.

Private nuisance

§17.26 While *Rylands v Fletcher* and private nuisance had different geneses, the law has evolved, such that the same scenario can conceivably give rise to both claims.

In *Transco plc v Stockport MBC*,[158] the rule in *Rylands v Fletcher* was recognised by the House of Lords to be a 'sub-species', 'aspect', or 'special case' of nuisance. The relationship between the two torts is not entirely straightforward. Three aspects will illustrate.

Reasonable foreseeability. It will be recalled that the key difference between the two torts is that, under *Rylands v Fletcher*, the escape of the dangerous thing does not need to be foreseeable, whereas in private nuisance, the interference with C's peaceable enjoyment of his land must be foreseeable. Thus, as the Court of Appeal noted recently in *Northumbrian Water Ltd v McAlpine Ltd*,[159] escapes/interferences which are unforeseeable are not recoverable at all, **unless** they can be brought within the scope of *Rylands*.

In *Northumbrian Water Ltd v McAlpine Ltd*, facts previously, D, a construction company, was redeveloping a site in Newcastle's city centre, which required large foundations to be sunk. The pile-driving breached a private sewer not shown on any public map. Concrete ran through that gap, and into the public sewers owned by Northumbria Water, C, which put C to considerable expense in fixing the blocked sewer. **Held:** *Rylands* could not succeed, because the redevelopment of a city centre site was a natural user of that land by D. Nuisance could not succeed either, because the interference (the escape of the concrete into the public sewer) was unforeseeable (that would not have mattered for *Rylands v Fletcher*). Both torts also failed because the damage, partial blockage of the public sewer, was unforeseeable too.

[157] (1994) 179 CLR 520 (HCA) [30] (McHugh J).

[158] [2003] UKHL 61, [2004] 2 AC 1, [9] (Lord Bingham), [52] (Lord Hobhouse), [92] (Lord Walker), respectively.

[159] [2014] EWCA Civ 685, [18].

Isolated escapes. When it emerged, *Rylands v Fletcher* was intended to apply to 'isolated escapes', whereas the tort of private nuisance could only arise from a 'continuing state of affairs'. The flooding of Mr Ryland's colliery mine was the result of an isolated escape, and not from a continuous or recurring interference, and hence, it did not fall into any recognised category of actionable nuisance at that time. As Lord Bingham noted in *Transco*, it 'seems likely' that the House of Lords in *Rylands* 'regarded it as one of nuisance, novel only to the extent that it sanctioned recovery where the interference by one occupier of land with the right or enjoyment of another was *isolated and not persistent*'.[160] Lord Goff too, in *Cambridge Water*, considered that it would 'lead to a more coherent body of common law principles if the rule were to be regarded essentially as an extension of the law of nuisance, to cases of isolated escapes from land'.[161]

Nevertheless, the dividing line between the two torts has blurred, and they clearly have considerable room nowadays to overlap. *Rylands* can cover repeated escapes and is not limited to isolated occurrences; while nuisance can cover isolated escapes. It was emphatically stated, in *Colour Quest v Total Downstream*,[162] that the two torts are **not** mutually inconsistent, and can indeed arise on the one fact situation. David Steel J noted that it was a scenario of *repeated* escapes that could more feasibly give rise to both *Rylands v Fletcher* and nuisance. Earlier, in *British Celanese v AH Hunt (Capacitors)*, it was also noted that, while most nuisance actions 'do arise from a long continuing condition; and many isolated happenings do not constitute a nuisance, ... an isolated happening by itself can create an actionable nuisance'.[163]

Unreasonable user and non-natural user. What of private nuisance's requirement for an 'unreasonable user', and *Rylands v Fletcher's* requirement for a 'non-natural user'? According to Lord Goff in *Cambridge Water*,[164] both principles are intended to reflect a relationship of 'give and take' as between neighbouring occupiers of land. Claimants are expected, by law, to 'put up with' natural users (in *Rylands v Fletcher*) and reasonable users (in nuisance). But will they necessarily correlate in outcome, on a given fact situation?

A non-natural user (under *Rylands*) can still amount to a reasonable user (in nuisance), according to Lord Bingham in *Transco*.[165] For example, in *Rylands* itself, the storage of the huge volume of water in the reservoir (a hazardous use) was a non-natural user of the land – yet it was a reasonable use of the land by a mill-owner. However, judicial opinion on this issue seems to vary. In *Arscott v Coal Authority*, Laws LJ expressed the view (obiter) that if D is using his land for an activity that is classified as a non-natural use (i.e., an extraordinary use), then he will **not** be able to prove, in a nuisance action, a reasonable user.[166]

On the other hand, plainly D whose use is classified as a natural user for the purposes of *Rylands v Fletcher* could still be guilty of an unreasonable user in private nuisance, if the quality or extent of his use of that land was unreasonable, or if, in other words, his natural user was 'pursued excessively' (Laws LJ in *Arscott*[167]). Noisy neighbours, bad smells and disagreeable smoke, may all constitute private nuisances (as discussed in Chapter 16) – but with no suggestion that the land from which these inconveniences emanate is being put to an abnormal or non-natural use.

[160] [2003] UKHL 61, [2004] 2 AC 1, [3] (emphasis added). [161] [1994] 2 AC 264 (HL) 306.
[162] [2009] EWHC 540 (Comm), [2009] ICLC 186, [409], [412]. [163] [1969] 1 WLR 959 (QB) 969 (Lawton J).
[164] [1994] 2 AC 264 (HL) 299. [165] [2003] UKHL 61, [2004] 2 AC 1, [11].
[166] [2004] EWCA Civ 892, [26]–[29]. [167] *ibid*, [29].

Breach of a non-delegable duty of care

§17.27 Where an employer/landowner, D, engages an independent contractor to do work on its land, and the negligence of that independent contractor causes a dangerous thing to escape from D's land to C's adjoining premises, then C may bring an action against D in *Rylands v Fletcher*, for allowing something dangerous to escape (it is irrelevant if D himself played no role in allowing its escape, he is strictly liable for the negligence of his independent contractor). Alternatively, C may sue the employer/landowner, D, for breach of a non-delegable duty of care owed to C, for the negligence of D's independent contractor, if the contractor was carrying out an ultra-hazardous activity and permitted the escape of a dangerous thing during the course of that activity.

Under the tort of *Rylands v Fletcher*, D is strictly liable for the wrongdoing of his independent contractor in permitting a dangerous thing to escape from D's land onto C's. This scenario is precisely what occurred in *Rylands v Fletcher* itself – and, had the non-delegable duty of care 'been around' in 1866, the case conceivably could have been decided in that way instead. A non-delegable duty owed by the landowner to his adjoining landowner may have been implicit in *Rylands v Fletcher* (as noted by Lord Sumption in *Woodland v Essex CC*[168]), but it certainly was not the ratio of Blackburn J's judgment at that time. The reason for imposing that non-delegable duty of care on D was explainable on two alternative bases (per *Woodland*) – that the independent contractor was engaged in hazardous operations; or that, regardless of the nature of the wrongful act, the duty arose from 'the antecedent relationship between the parties as neighbouring landowners ... it attached to [D] in his capacity as the occupier of the neighbouring land from which the hazard originated'.

The Diagram below illustrates the key cases (with the parties' names in italics):

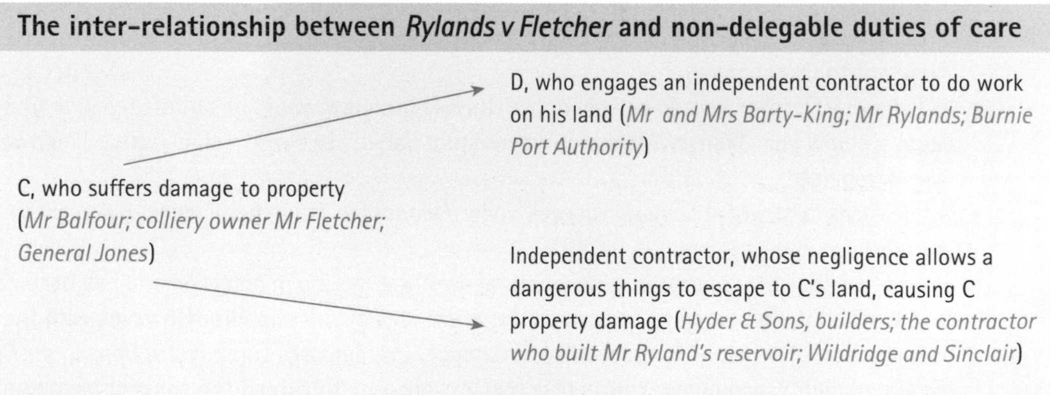

In the following case, C proceeded on the basis that it was owed a non-delegable duty of care – rather than in *Rylands v Fletcher* – and succeeded:

> In *Balfour v Barty-King*,[169] Mr and Mrs Barty-King, D, owned a house within a large converted mansion, and their pipes froze. Mr Balfour, C, owned an adjoining house in the mansion. D arranged for representatives of Hyder & Sons (Builders) to thaw their pipes. To do this, the workmen applied the flame of a blow-lamp to the pipes. Most of the pipes were lagged with felt, and the use of a

[168] [2013] UKSC 66, [2013] 3 WLR 1227, [8]–[9]. [169] [1957] 1 QB 496.

blow-lamp caused the lagging to catch alight, which in turn ignited other flammable material in the loft, causing an extensive fire which spread to C's premises. C sued D for the damage caused by their independent contractor. The builders were insolvent at the time of trial. **Held:** D was liable to C for the negligence of their independent contractor, given the 'highly dangerous operation' carried out in the loft. The court remarked that it would not consider the plea in *Rylands*, and the case was decided without reliance on that cause of action.

Given that the legal outcome of a non-delegable duty of care mimics that of *Rylands v Fletcher*, the question has arisen as to whether there is any need to retain *Rylands* in English law. In both *Transco* and *Cambridge Water*, the relevant defendants invited the House of Lords to abolish the *Rylands* rule – and, on both occasions, the House of Lords declined to do so. In *Transco*,[170] the House of Lords (per Lord Walker) explicitly refuted the idea that the *Rylands v Fletcher* rule should be 'recast' as a non-delegable duty of care. Given the controversy surrounding the rule, however, it is worth summarising the views expressed by the senior English appellate court, as to why the tort continues to have resonance and should be retained:

The case for retaining *Rylands v Fletcher* – per *Transco* and *Cambridge Water* (HL)

- there is a potentially small category of cases in which D should be liable, without any proof of fault (and, had there been foreseeability of damage, *Cambridge Water* may have been such a case);
- 'common law rules do not exist in a vacuum'. Some statutory schemes regulating liability in the event of the escape of a dangerous thing have been implemented by Parliament, on the assumption that *Rylands v Fletcher* would continue to apply. Had that assumption not existed, Parliament may have drafted the schemes differently;
- having said in *Cambridge Water* (1993) that the rule would not be abolished, but should be better articulated and applied, *Transco* (2003) should abide by that; 'stop-go' developments in the law were not to be endorsed;
- if *Rylands v Fletcher* were to be abandoned, then English law would be out of step with Continental legal systems (e.g., France, Germany), where strict liability between neighbouring landowners was also recognised;
- while cases exist where C would succeed under *Rylands* but fail in negligence, *Rylands* had a useful purpose;
- it was true that the concept of a 'non-natural user' was lacking in precision and had become vague, and this had the potential to undermine the whole idea of strict liability. However, with the explicit introduction of a test of foreseeability of damage, that imposes some restrictions upon *Rylands v Fletcher* liability, and hence 'courts may feel less pressure to extend the concept of natural use ...; and in due course it may become easier to control this [concept], and to ensure that it has a more recognisable basis of principle' (per Lord Goff in *Cambridge Water*);
- unless and until English law saw fit to introduce some compulsory public liability insurance scheme for all landowners who used their land for dangerous purposes (a most unlikely scenario), the common law rule in *Rylands v Fletcher* would continue to have *some* application, albeit that the rule had become somewhat narrowly drawn.

170 [2003] UKHL 61, [2004] 2 AC 1, [109] (Lord Walker).

Alternative views

The Australian view

The close parallel between *Rylands v Fletcher* and a non-delegable duty of care was one key reason as to why the Australian High Court (by a 5:2 majority) decided to abolish the rule in *Rylands v Fletcher* from that country's common law, such that *Rylands v Fletcher* should be assimilated into ordinary negligence principles.

> In *Burnie Port Authority v General Jones Pty Ltd*,[171] the Burnie Port Authority, D, extended its building to install further cold storage facilities at Burnie, Tasmania. General Jones, C, occupied part of that building, to store large quantities of frozen vegetables. Wildridge and Sinclair Pty Ltd carried out insulation works on behalf of D, which involved welding. This was carried out close to cardboard cartons which contained an insulating material called Isolite, which burnt fiercely if brought into sustained contact with flame. Wildridge negligently allowed sparks to cause the Isolite to burn. The fire spread to the area of the building occupied by C, and destroyed its frozen vegetables stock. **Held:** a non-delegable duty of care was owed to C by D, as employer. That duty of care was breached by Wildridge's failure to prevent the Isolite from being set alight as a result of the welding activities.

The majority's reasoning was predicated upon several key points, described below. A differently-constituted Australian High Court has subsequently noted[172] that, by abolishing *Rylands v Fletcher* and drawing it within the folds of negligence, the *Burnie* decision 'showed the disfavour with which strict liability is viewed'.

The case for abolishing *Rylands v Fletcher* – per *Burnie Port Authority* (HCA)

- if a defendant landowner (D) engages in some hazardous activity that would attract liability under *Rylands v Fletcher*, C, the party injured, is already protected by negligence, because the magnitude of the harm, should it occur, will be very high – thus, the *degree of precaution* expected of D as a reasonable landowner, in order to avoid a finding in negligence, will also be very high. Indeed, the standard of care in negligence may involve 'a degree of diligence so stringent as to amount practically to a guarantee of safety';
- if D engages an independent contractor to do work on his land, and that independent contractor engages in some extra-hazardous activity (precisely as happened in both *Burnie* and in *Rylands*), then ordinarily an employer is not liable for the torts of his independent contractor – but where that contractor is carrying out hazardous operations, then exceptionally, the employer is liable, on the basis that the employer owes a non-delegable duty of care – a development in negligence since the days of *Rylands v Fletcher*. The mill-owner in *Rylands*, as one who engaged an independent contractor to carry out a hazardous activity of constructing the reservoir, owed a non-delegable duty of care to the adjoining colliery owner, Mr Fletcher. Hence, most who are entitled to succeed under *Rylands v Fletcher* would succeed in a claim for negligence in any event – and if not that, then in nuisance or trespass to land;
- the non-natural user element of *Rylands v Fletcher* has come to depend on all the circumstances surrounding the introduction, production, retention or accumulation of the relevant thing. Whether D negligently dealt with the substance often conflated with the decision as to whether D's use of

[171] (1994) 179 CLR 520 (HCA). [172] *Scott v Davis* [2000] HCA 52, (2000) 204 CLR 333, [250].

land was 'abnormal', 'extraordinary', and 'non-natural'. This intertwining of negligence with a supposedly strict liability tort was increasingly unsatisfactory;

- strict liability of any sort was better left to legislative enactment than to case law;
- the rule in *Rylands v Fletcher* had been subject to much 'progressive weakening', especially via its numerous defences and erosions, as to render it of very limited application. With its difficulties of interpretation and application, the rule required 'an essentially unprincipled and *ad hoc* subjective determination'.

In addition to Australia's rejection of the principle, *Rylands v Fletcher* forms no part of Scottish law (per *Graham & Graham v Re Chem Intl Ltd*[173]). Indeed, in *RHM Bakeries (Scotland) Ltd v Strathclyde Regional Council*,[174] Lord Fraser described the rule as 'a heresy which ought to be extirpated'.

In *Transco*, however (and despite the *Burnie* judgment being described as a '*tour de force*'), the House of Lords considered that the *Burnie* approach should **not** be followed in English law.

Law reform consideration

There have been two law reform considerations of the rule in *Rylands v Fletcher* to date.

The law reform corner: **Liability**

- Lord Pearson, *Royal Comm on Civil Liability and Compensation for Personal Injury* (1978):[175] the rule in *Rylands* should be replaced by a statutory regime that imposed strict liability 'on the controllers of things or operations [which either] by their unusually hazardous nature require close, careful and skilled supervision [or] are likely, if they do go wrong, to cause serious and extensive casualties'.
- EWLC, *Civil Liability for Dangerous Things and Activities* (1970):[176] the rule in *Rylands* is 'complex, uncertain and inconsistent in principle' and should be replaced by a statutory liability for the conduct of hazardous activities.

Judicial consideration

A statutory basis for hazardous activities has also been judicially favoured. In *Cambridge Water*,[177] Lord Goff reiterated that he did not favour an extension of *Rylands v Fletcher* liability, by rendering D liable for unforeseeable damage arising from an escape, and that if that was the direction which English law should pursue, then it was preferably a matter for legislation:

> it is more appropriate for strict liability in respect of operations of high risk to be imposed by Parliament than by the courts. If such liability is imposed by statute, the relevant activities can be identified, and those concerned can know where they stand. Furthermore, statute can, where appropriate, lay down precise criteria establishing the incidence and scope of such liability.

However, any suggestion for a generalised statute imposing strict liability for ultra-hazardous activities which cause C damage has never been taken up by Parliament (although some

[173] [1996] Env LR 158 (QB) 160. [174] 1985 SC (HL) 17, 41. [175] (1978, Cmnd 7054-1) 342–43.
[176] (1970, Rep 32), with quote at [20(a)]. [177] [1994] 2 AC 264 (HL), with quote at 305.

scenario-specific statutes are noted in Chapter 16). The dangerous spread of fire was one early statutory incursion (considered below).

Remedies

Given the House of Lords' view, in *Transco plc v Stockport MBC*,[178] that the tort in *Rylands v Fletcher* is 'a sub-species of nuisance, which is itself a tort based on the interference by one occupier of land with the right in or enjoyment of land by another occupier of land as such', certain consequences follow, insofar as remedies are concerned. The damages recoverable should only compensate for injuries to that land, and will exclude damages for death or personal injury. Although these were recoverable in *Shiffman v Order of St John of Jerusalem*,[179] they were disapproved in dicta in *Read v Lyons*,[180] and recently, the Court of Appeal emphatically stated, in *Northumbrian Water Ltd v McAlpine*,[181] that '[d]amages for death or personal injury are not recoverable'. Secondly, the remedies available for private nuisance (discussed in Chapter 16) are equally as applicable to this tort (and those principles will not be repeated herein).

ESCAPE OF FIRE: STATUTORY REGIME

§17.28 Under the Fires Prevention (Metropolis) Act 1774, a landowner/occupier, D, has a good defence against any claim brought against him by C, if a fire 'accidentally begins', and then escapes, from D's property to C's, with no fault on D's part.

The 1774 Act is expressed (in its long title) to be 'an Act ... for the more effectually preventing Mischiefs by Fire within the Cities of London and Westminster and the Liberties thereof'. Despite the impression created by that long title, and its age, the Act applies still throughout England and Wales (per *Richards v Easto*[182]).

s 86 No action to lie against a person where the fire accidentally begins

no action, suit or process whatever shall be had, maintained or prosecuted against *any person* in whose *house, chamber, stable, barn or other building*, or on whose estate any fire shall ... *accidentally begin*, nor shall any recompence be made by such person for any damage suffered thereby, any law, usage or custom to the contrary notwithstanding; ... provided that no contract or agreement made between landlord and tenant shall be hereby defeated or made void.

Reason for the Act

At common law, if a fire escaped from D's land and damaged C's land, D was strictly liable for the damage caused, per the doctrine of *ignis suus*. This ancient custom, since Anglo-Saxon times, imposed a duty upon householders to keep their fires safe,[183] reflecting the dangers posed by timber and thatch construction. As Lord Goddard CJ pointed out in *Balfour v Barty-King*,[184]

178 [2003] UKHL 61, [2004] 2 AC 1, [9] (Lord Bingham). 179 [1936] 1 All ER 557 (KB). 180 [1947] AC 156 (HL).
181 [2012] EWCA Civ 1248, [2014] QB 1, [22]. 182 (1846) 15 M & W 244 (Exch) 251, 153 ER 840 (Parke B).
183 *Filliter v Phippard* (1847) 116 ER 506 (KB).
184 [1957] 1 QB 496 (CA) 502, referring to the *Oxford Dictionary* and to *Encyclopaedia Brittanica* for the origins and purpose of a 'curfew'.

the 'curfew bell's origins were actually to call householders indoors to make sure that their fires were doused for the night, rather than with any purpose of preventing criminal conduct, or political repression, and the like'. Also, in the early days before insurance, the loss fell at the door of the person on whose property the fire had started, no matter that he was entirely blameless in permitting it to start or to spread (per Lewison LJ in *Stannard v Gore*[185]).

The purpose of the 1774 Act (which endures to this day) was to ameliorate the effects of that common law. Hence, D has a good defence under the statute, if a fire spreads accidentally from his property with no fault on his part. The Act has been said to have resulted from the Great Fire of London in 1666, whereby the terrible losses from that fire 'fuelled the growing belief ... that it was anomalous that a man should be liable for fire damage that had not been caused by his fault' (per *Johnson Butchers v BJW Property Devp Ltd*[186]). Notably, s 86 only applies where the fire begins on D's land or property; hence, fire which spreads from a highway and damages C's land is not covered by the Act's protection (per *Powell v Fall*[187]).

Protection lost through negligence

§17.29 Under the Fire Prevention (Metropolis) Act 1774, the fire will not begin 'accidentally' (and D cannot take advantage of the statutory defence) if D (or his independent contractor) was negligent in beginning, or spreading, the fire.

According to the statutory wording, the fire has to 'accidentally begin', in order to provide a good defence. That phrase has given rise to some uncertainty. Indeed, in *Goldman v Hargrave*,[188] the Privy Council noted that its 'simplicity is deceptive'. Its meaning has been variously remarked upon as 'never authoritatively settled' (*Johnson Butchers*[189]), 'obscure' (*Mason v Levy Auto Parts of England Ltd*[190]), and demonstrating 'a proof of our love of old things, rather than a tribute to ... drafting skill' (*Mason* again, noting that the 1774 Act re-enacted a statute from Queen Anne's era[191]).

Modern jurisprudence has provided some assistance, however. According to *LMS v Styrene Packaging*, the term had 'always been given a narrow construction, and effectively been taken to mean "non-negligent"'.[192] According to *Johnson Butchers*,[193] it is also not fatal to the defence if the fire is started deliberately by D on his land (e.g., by lighting a fire in a grate) – so long as the fire then *escapes accidentally* without any fault on D's part. Even if the fire has been started deliberately, the fact that it spreads without fault means that, for the purposes of the 1774 Act, the fire 'accidentally begins'. The defence applies.

However, there are some significant scenarios in which D will lose the effect of this statutory defence. The fire will not 'accidentally begin', and liability will apply to D, in the following cases:

- D's negligence loses him the defence: 'the Act does not cover a fire which begins or is spread by [his] negligence' (per *H & N Emanuel Ltd v GLC*[194]). In the following cases, the Act did not apply so as to provide any effective defence:

185 [2012] EWCA Civ 1248, [2014] QB 1, [75]. 186 [2002] EWHC 1131 (TCC), [2002] 3 All ER 574, [20].
187 (1879–80) LR 5 QBD 597. 188 [1967] 1 AC 645 (PC) 664 (Lord Wilberforce).
189 [2002] EWHC 1131 (TCC) [22]. 190 [1967] 2 QB 530 (Winchester Assizes) 537.
191 *ibid*, 543, referring to s 6 of the Fires Prevention (Metropolis) Act 1707 (6 Anne, c 31).
192 [2005] EWHC 2065 (TCC) [27]. 193 [2002] 3 All ER 574 (TCC) [21]–[22].
194 [1971] 2 All ER 835 (CA) 839 (Lord Denning MR).

In *E Hobbs (Farms) Ltd v Baxenden Chemical Co Ltd*,[195] a fire started in Hobbs', D's, barn, due a spark from a grinding machine falling onto combustible material/debris below the machine. The fire spread into, and destroyed, the adjacent hanger owned by Mr Gerber, C. D was not able to rely on the defence in the 1774 Act, because D had been negligent in allowing combustible materials to be positioned below the machine. In *Coxhill v Forward*,[196] Mr Forward, D, had a car which was converted from petrol to LPG fuel. This required LPG cannisters and a valve supply system to be kept in his garage with the car. The fuel system had a history of spontaneous leaks, which D did not have rectified. In the garage was also kept a thermostatically-controlled freezer. Sparks from the freezer when it turned on, ignited some leaked LPG gas. There was an explosion and fire, which seriously damaged Mr Coxhill's, C's, adjoining premises. D could not rely on the defence in the 1774 Act, because he was negligent in failing to properly maintain his car's LPG fuel supply, and to detect the leakages. In *Ribee v Norris*,[197] facts previously, the fire started in the common area of the property as a result of the negligence of one of the occupants, and was not 'accidental'.

- if the fire spreads from D's land, due to the negligence of an independent contractor employed by D, then the fire did not 'begin accidentally' either, and the protection of the 1774 Act does not apply. D, as employer, is liable for the damage caused by that fire, under a non-delegable duty of care. According to *Johnson Butchers*,[198] the employer's liability in this scenario 'was the last vestige of the ancient strict liability for the escape of *ignis suus*'. Not only can the employer not take advantage of the 1774 Act if his independent contractor is negligent in allowing a fire to spread, but the employer will be liable, even if it is contrary to the 'general development of the law of negligence against the imposition of vicarious liability for the negligence of an independent contractor'.

In *Johnson (t/as Johnson Butchers) v BJW Property Devp Ltd*, BJW, D, engaged Mr Young, an antiques dealer, to replace a fireplace in the party wall between its property and Mr Johnson's, C's, property next door. Mr Young removed firebricks and replaced them with a thin layer of plaster, causing timber fillets to smoulder. Fire broke out, and spread to C's premises, causing extensive damage. It was held that Mr Young's workmanship had been negligent. **Held:** the 1774 Act did not apply to protect D. Rather, D was liable for the escape of fire resulting from the negligent acts of his independent contractor, such as Mr Young.

- if the fire started accidentally on D's land, but D negligently did not extinguish it, when he had a reasonable chance to do so, then the fire did not 'begin accidentally', and he will lose the protection of the Act. It is sufficient if the fire was 'begun or continued negligently' (per *Stannard v Gore*[199]):

In *Musgrove v Pandelis*,[200] Mr Musgrove, C, occupied rooms over a garage. Part of the garage was let to Mr Head for the purposes of storing his car. Mr Coumis, D, Mr Head's chauffeur, who knew little about cars, started it up, and for some unexplained reason, and without any negligence on D's part, the petrol in the carburettor caught fire. If D had promptly turned off the tap leading from the petrol tank to the carburettor, the fire would have harmlessly burnt itself out, but D set off to look for a cloth, and the fire took hold, burning the car, the garage, and C's rooms and furniture. In *Goldman v Hargrave*,[201] lightning struck a tree in an upper fork on D's land on 25 Feb, and it was felled,

[195] [1992] 1 Lloyd's Rep 54. [196] QB, 19 Mar 1986. [197] [2000] EWCA Civ 275.
[198] [2002] 3 All ER 574 (TCC) [39]. [199] [2012] EWCA Civ 1248, [71].
[200] [1919] 2 KB 43. [201] [1967] 1 AC 13 (PC).

and left by D to burn out. Hot winds blew up on 28 Feb, and fire spread to C's land on 1 Mar. **Held (in both cases):** the 1774 Act did not afford D any defence. While both fires began accidentally, they *spread* via D's negligence in not promptly turning off the petrol tap, or dousing the tree with water, respectively.

Interplay of s 86 with *Rylands v Fletcher*

§17.30 If a fire spreads via some non-natural user of D's land (but without negligence on D's part), the law is currently somewhat unsettled as to whether that fire begins 'accidentally' (which affords D protection from liability under the 1774 Act), or does not 'begin accidentally' (in which event the Act's protection is not available to D).

Once a fire starts (and then spreads to C's property) due to a non-natural user of D's land, then it is a fire to which *Rylands v Fletcher* applies. However, whether the protection of the 1774 Act is lost in those circumstances is not clear, in light of the recent decision of the Court of Appeal in *Stannard (t/as Wyvern Tyres) v Gore*.[202]

On one view, where D allows a fire to escape which gives rise to *Rylands v Fletcher* liability, that is not an 'accidental' fire, and the 1774 Act does not exclude D's liability for that escape. This was the view expressed by Etherton LJ:[203] that liability under *Rylands v Fletcher* 'is not exonerated by s 86'; that '[i]t still remains a principle of statutory interpretation that, in cases of doubt, there is a presumption against interference with the common law'; and that 'accidentally-started' fires for which D is protected do **not** include either negligently-started fires, or fires which arise from a non-natural use and which give rise to *Rylands* liability against D.

On the other hand, Lewison LJ preferred the view that any liability for the spread of fire which may arise under *Rylands v Fletcher* still affords D the defence in s 86 of the 1774 Act, where that fire has started and spread without anyone's negligence, because that is still an 'accidental' fire.[204] He based this view, in part, on the wording of s 86, that it expressly exempts a person from liability for accidental fires, 'any law, usage or custom to the contrary notwithstanding' – which meant that 'accidentally' must be read as meaning 'without negligence; the custom of the realm giving rise to D's liability for strict liability under '*ignem suum*' was overruled by s 86; and any other common law basis for D's strict liability (whether, say, under *Rylands v Fletcher*, nuisance, or under the traditional 'innkeeper's liability') was also overridden by s 86. This latter view of Lewison LJ's obviously affords D protection in **any** non-negligence scenario, a wide view indeed.

Some previous case law has, however, certainly supported the former view that a fire that is caused by a non-natural use and which exposes D to *Rylands v Fletcher* liability is not 'accidental', and that the protection afforded by s 86 is lost to D in those circumstances:

In *Mason v Levy Auto Parts of England Ltd*,[205] Captain Mason, C, owned and occupied Mill Cottage, next door to the car dealer, Levy, D. D stored large quantities of combustible materials (paints,

[202] [2012] EWCA Civ 1248, [2014] 1 QB 1.

[203] [2012] EWCA Civ 1248, [69]–[71]. Also: *Transco* [2005] EWHC 2065 (TCC) [30], aff'd [2003] UKHL 61 (dicta; not a fire case).

[204] *ibid*, [126]–[129], [170]. The third member, Ward LJ, did not explicitly deal with this issue.

[205] [1967] 2 QB 530 (Winchester Assizes). Lewison LJ preferred to overrule this case in *Gore v Stannard* (at [164]), but the other two members of the Court of Appeal did not do so.

petroleum products and acetylenes used in the course of its business) in their yard up to its common boundary with C's property. One day, a severe fire of unknown cause started in D's yard, and could not be brought under control. It spread to C's property, causing extensive damage. **Held:** *Rylands v Fletcher* succeeded; and D could not rely on the 1774 Act as a defence. The statute does not apply to a fire which arises through the storage of large quantities of combustible materials which amount to a non-natural user under *Rylands*. In *E Hobbs (Farms) Ltd v Baxenden Chemical Co Ltd*,[206] and in *Coxhill v Forward*,[207] facts previously, both Mr Hobbs (the factory owner) and Mr Forward (the owner of the LPG-powered car) could not take advantage of the 1774 Act's protection because of their respective negligence. In addition, they were both liable for escape of fire from their premises under *Rylands v Fletcher* because of their respective non-natural users, and again, the 1774 Act did not avail them of a defence for that cause of action either.

To the extent that D was negligent in permitting the spread of the fire (which lost him the protection of s 86), then anything said in these cases about the interplay of *Rylands v Fletcher* and s 86 was dicta only.

[206] [1992] 1 Lloyd's Rep 54. [207] QB, 19 Mar 1986.

Part IV

Miscellaneous

18

Vicarious liability

INTRODUCTION

§18.1 Vicarious liability is a legal doctrine whereby a person who is *not* personally at fault is legally required to bear the burden of another's tortious wrongdoing. It is, hence, a form of strict liability.

Vicarious liability is 'on the move' – and (sadly!), it has become more difficult to identify the criteria governing the area now than it was 50 years ago, said the Supreme Court in 2012 in *Catholic Child Welfare Socy v Institute of the Brothers of the Christian Schools* (*Child Welfare Socy*).[1]

The word, 'vicarious', is derived from the Latin *vicarius*, 'substitute'.[2] This aptly describes the legal substitution of an innocent party for the wrongdoer. In that respect, the notion of vicarious liability 'is at odds with the general approach of the common law [which is to] ... impose liability on the wrongdoer himself' (per *Majrowski v Guy's and St Thomas's NHS Trust*[3]), and so 'should not be too readily impose[d] on D' (per *Maga v Archbishop of Birmingham*[4]).

Where vicarious liability applies, the wrongdoer is not exculpated from his wrongdoing – strictly speaking, C has the option of suing the wrongdoer, or the vicariously-liable D, or both – although, from a practical point of view, the vicariously-liable D will have the 'deeper pocket' with which to satisfy a judgment.

The vicariously-liable employer: some general concepts

§18.2 An employer may be vicariously liable for the tortious acts or omissions committed either: (1) by an employee, whose torts are committed during the course of that employee's employment, or (2) by a wrongdoer who shares with the 'employer' a relationship which is merely 'akin to employment', and whose torts are connected to that relationship. As a general rule (to which there are exceptions), an employer will not be vicariously liable for the torts of an independent contractor.

[1] [2012] UKSC 56, [2013] 2 AC 1, [21].

[2] *Oxford Dictionary of English* (2nd edn, revised, Oxford University Press, 2006) 1963.

[3] [2006] UKHL 34, [2007] 1 AC 224, [7]–[8] (Lord Nicholls). [4] [2010] 1 WLR 1441, [52] (Lord Neuberger).

The employment scenario (or some relationship which is 'akin to that between an employer and an employee', as noted in *Child Welfare Socy*[5]) remains the most common type of legal relationship giving rise to vicarious liability. (Other scenarios to which the doctrine may apply, apart from the employment-type context, are discussed later in the chapter, online.) The legal requirements in the employment scenario are outlined below:

In a nutshell: The three elements of vicarious liability

1 The wrongdoer committed a tort
2 The wrongdoer was an employee (or his relationship with another was sufficiently 'akin to employment' to render that other vicariously liable), but he was not an independent contractor
3 The wrongdoer committed the tort within the course, or the scope, of his employment (or, where the relationship was 'akin to employment', there was a close connection between that relationship and the wrongdoer's tort)

Elements 2 and 3 have given rise to a great deal of litigation around the common law world (per the Irish Supreme Court in *O'Keeffe v Hickey*[6]) – albeit that this chapter will focus predominantly on English jurisprudence. Those two elements also 'synthesise' to a certain extent, due to the scrutiny of the particular relationship between employer and employee under both elements (per *Child Welfare Socy*[7]), which adds to the difficult analysis of this topic.

The types of torts

Although vicarious liability on an employer's part arises, principally, from the acts or omissions of the *negligent* employee, this form of strict liability can apply across a wide spectrum – in respect of torts which entail intention or malice on the employee's part, and at the other end, those in which the employee is not even negligent. It may also arise from non-tortious culpability (e.g., equitable fraud).

Additionally, just because the employee commits, and is punished for, a criminal offence, does not preclude vicarious liability from being imposed on the employer D. The torts of conversion, assault and battery, may all attract criminal liability – but all are capable of giving rise to vicarious liability in tort too (per Lord Nicholls in *Majrowski*[8]).

To illustrate via a small selection of torts:

In *Racz v Home Office*,[9] Mr Racz, C, alleged that, while a remand prisoner, he was assaulted by prison officers, forcibly strip-searched, his food deliberately tipped onto the floor and was then told to 'clean it up'. **Held**: the Home Office could be vicariously liable for acts of prison officers that amounted to misfeasance in public office. In *Lloyd v Grace Smith & Co*,[10] Mrs Lloyd, C, a widow, was induced by the managing clerk of a law firm to execute deeds transferring her title in two cottages to the clerk, via his deceit (fraudulent misrepresentation). The clerk then sold the properties for his own benefit. The principal solicitor, D, was highly respected and innocent of any involvement in or knowledge of the fraud. **Held:** D was vicariously liable for his clerk's fraud. In *Lister v Hesley Hall Ltd*,[11] a group of men including Mr Lister, C, sued Hesley Hall Ltd, D, which ran a school, Wilsic Hall

[5] [2012] UKSC 56, [47]. [6] [2008] IESC 72. [7] [2012] UKSC 56, [21]. [8] [2006] UKHL 34, [26].
[9] [1994] 2 AC 45 (HL), overturning the CA on this point. [10] [1912] 1 AC 716 (HL) 742.
[11] [2001] UKHL 22, [2002] 1 AC 215.

School, and a boarding annexe, Axeholme House, as a commercial enterprise. Boys with emotional and behavioural difficulties were sent to the school by local authorities, and the boarding annexe was to provide care to enable the boys to adjust to normal living. Between 1979–82, D employed a warden, Mr Grain, to run the boarding annexe and to care for the boys who lived there. During this time, the warden systematically sexually abused the boys, and he was sentenced to 7 years' imprisonment. **Held**: D was vicariously liable for the torts of assault and battery committed by its employed warden.

Particular issues arise in vicarious liability, under the statutory tort of the Protection from Harassment Act 1997 (where Parliament did not expressly provide for the employer to be sued vicariously or directly for an employee's harassment of C), and under the tort of breach of statutory duty (where a statute confers a civil right of action upon C to recover for damages in the event that a wrongdoing employee breaches that statute, but it may not expressly impose any statutory duty or vicarious liability upon the *employer*, when it would have been easy enough for Parliament to do so). These issues are discussed, respectively, in 'The statutory tort of harassment' and 'Breach of statutory duty' (which are both online chapters).

Distinguishing between vicarious and direct liability on the employer's part

§18.3 Where C is injured by the negligent acts or omissions of an employee, not only may the employer be vicariously (strictly) liable for that negligence, but alternatively, the employer may be directly liable to C in negligence because of some personal (systemic) negligence on that employer's part. Direct liability can *only* arise where the employer owes a *personal* duty of care to C. C may sue the employer concurrently for vicarious liability and for systemic negligence, notwithstanding that the bases for the claims are entirely different.

To reiterate: where found, vicarious liability imputes no fault on the part of the employer – that party is simply bearing a substituted responsibility for the misdeeds of its employee. However, direct (personal) liability of the employer arises from a claim for *systemic* negligence, or 'corporate failure'. This latter means that the employer owed C a *personal* duty of care, and that the employer's systems or procedures were systemically flawed and fell below the standard of care expected of a reasonable employer. In this context, it is often said that the employer owes a non-delegable duty of care to C – the duty was to provide a safe system, and the duty cannot be precluded by pointing the finger at an employee and saying, 'it was his fault'.

In an appropriate scenario, the injured C may seek to bring claims for *both* vicarious and direct systemic liability against the same employer – even though the conceptual bases for each claim are quite different. If both claims succeed, then C's damages are, of course, recoverable only once.

This possibility of bringing a vicarious liability claim, in addition to a direct negligence suit, against D, can apply in **any** scenario where employer D's employee committed some negligence against C. On the one hand, C may be another employee of D's who was injured by a negligent co-worker in D's workplace (in that regard, an employer's liability towards an employee, C, including the four subduties owed directly by an employer to an employee, was analysed in 'Employers' liability', an online chapter). On the other hand, C may be some external third party who is negligently injured by D's employee (say, a patient receiving treatment from a doctor who is employed in D's hospital).

Possible suits for both vicarious and direct liability against the one Employer

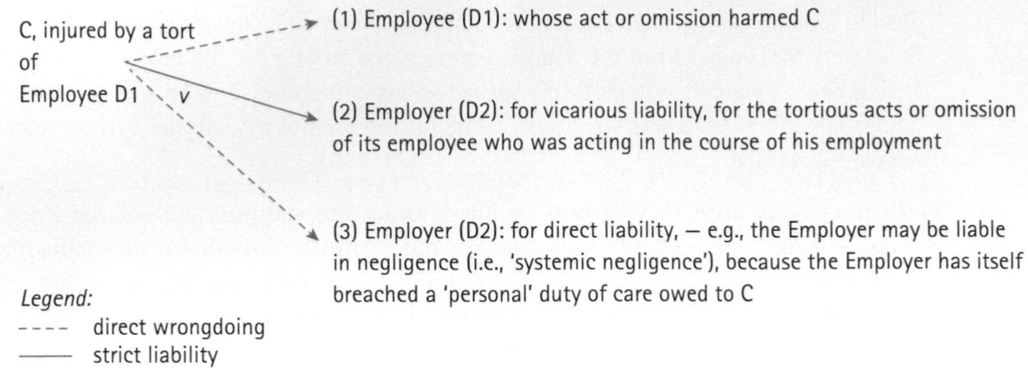

To illustrate, both direct negligence and vicarious liability claims were brought by C in the cases below:

Vicarious versus direct liability: some examples

- ***an educational institution, sued by its pupils*** – in *Lister v Hesley Hall Ltd,*[a] facts previously, the group of abused Cs recovered against Hesley Hall, D, for vicarious liability (for the acts of abuse of the warden). However, their claim for direct negligence against D, based on a personal duty of care owed by a school to its pupils to properly select and supervise the warden, and to take up references, was rejected at trial, and was never appealed. In *Maga v Birmingham Archdiocese,*[b] it was noted that a school would not normally be vicariously liable for sexual abuse committed by the school gardener against a school pupil, but if the school had received previous allegations against that gardener of sexual abuse against pupils and failed to deal with those complaints appropriately, then that would potentially give rise to a direct negligence suit against the school;
- ***a local authority, sued by vulnerable children in its care*** – in *Phelps v Hillingdon LBC,*[c] C, a school pupil, alleged that she suffered dyslexia and other learning difficulties, and that her school referred her to a psychologist employed by the local education authority for an assessment, which was negligently performed. C could proceed with her claims for vicarious liability against the education authority (for the alleged negligence of the psychologist), and for direct negligence by the authority (for failing to provide competent advice through its educational psychology service);
- ***a health authority, sued by its patients*** – in *Bull v Devon AHA,*[d] an Exeter hospital operated as a 'split-site' hospital, constructed over two campuses. Mrs Bull was admitted to the maternity wing, and baby Darryl was delivered safely – but unfortunately, there was no doctor attending at the relevant time, the student midwife did not realise that it was a double birth and pulled the umbilical cord, and there was then a 68-minute delay until the birth of second twin Stuart, C, because attempts to summon the obstetrician by pager, etc, at the other campus failed. The Devon HA was

[a] [2001] UKHL 22, [2002] 1 AC 215.
[b] [2010] EWCA Civ 256, [74].
[c] [2001] 2 AC 619 (HL).
[d] (1993) 22 BMLR 79 (CA) (judgment 2 Feb 1989). See also: *Gold v Essex CC* [1942] 2 KB 293 (CA) 301–2; *Cassidy v Ministry of Health* [1951] 2 KB 343 (CA); *Roe v Ministry of Health* [1954] 2 QB 66 (CA).

vicariously liable (for the negligence of the student midwife employee); and was also directly liable in negligence (it owed its patients a personal duty of care, and failed to ensure that an adequate or efficient system was in place for summonsing medical staff from one site to the other);

- ***a police force, sued by members of the public*** – in *AG (British Virgin Islands) v Hartwell*,[e] the only police officer stationed on Jost Van Dyke island in the British Virgin Islands was having relationship difficulties with his girlfriend. He abandoned his post, took a police-issued revolver to another island, fired shots in a crowded bar where his girlfriend was working, and shot and seriously injured Mr Hartwell, C, a British tourist. The Govt, as the police officer's employer, was not vicariously liable for its employee's act (for reasons discussed later); but it was directly liable in negligence (a personal duty of care was owed to the public to ensure that a police officer was suitably selected, trained and entrusted with a firearm).

[e] [2004] UKPC 12, [2004] 1 WLR 1273 (on appeal from the CA of the British Virgin Islands).

The role of the wrongdoing employee in vicarious liability

The employee's legal exposure

§18.4 A wrongdoing employee and a vicariously-liable employer are jointly and severally liable for the damages to which C is entitled (i.e., each party is fully liable for the damages). The employee is not legally entitled to an indemnity from his employer – although, in practice, such an indemnity is usually forthcoming as a 'gentlemen's agreement' between the litigants' insurers. Further, even if the wrongdoing employee remains unidentified, that does not preclude a suit against the employer for vicarious liability.

In practice, it is the vicariously-liable employer (or its insurer) – and not the wrongdoing employee – who bears the burden of paying the requisite damages to C. The strict legal position of the wrongdoing employee is as follows (per *Jones v BBC*[12]):

i. As between employer and employee, there is no implied term in their employment contract that the employee is entitled to be indemnified by the employer in respect of any vicarious liability incurred as the result of that employee's negligence. This was established, as a matter of common law, in 1957:

   In *Lister v Romford Ice and Cold Storage Co Ltd*,[13] Martin Lister, 27, was employed by Romford Ice as a lorry driver. One day, while accompanied by his father, C, he drove his lorry into a slaughterhouse yard to collect some waste, and reversed and accidentally knocked down his father. C successfully sued Romford Ice for vicarious liability for the negligent driving of Mr Lister Jnr, and was awarded £1,600 in damages. The insurer of Romford Ice (who had paid out the damages claim to C, acting without the consent of Romford Ice, the insured) claimed an indemnity from Mr Lister Jnr in respect of those damages. **Held** (3:2): Romford Ice (and its insurer, by subrogation) was entitled to recover from Mr Lister Jnr damages for breach of contract in failing to carry out his duties with reasonable care and skill. There was no implied term in the employment

[12] [2007] All ER (D) 283 (QB) [139]–[141]. [13] [1957] AC 555 (HL).

contract that Mr Lister Jnr was entitled to be indemnified by Romford Ice, his employer, for his negligent driving.

ii. Quite apart from *Lister v Romford Ice*, under the Civil Liability (Contribution) Act 1978 (under which liability between culpable defendants is apportioned, discussed in 'Multiple defendants', an online chapter), the strictly-liable employer is entitled to a 100% contribution (i.e., an indemnity) from the employee wrongdoer. Hence, as between employer and employee, liability to pay the damages may properly fall upon the *employee*;
iii. However, this harsh position has been substantially moderated in practice. As described in *Jones v BBC*, the consequences of *Lister* for employment relations 'led, ultimately, to employers' liability insurers entering into an agreement whereby they would not institute claims against employees of insured companies in respect of death or injury of fellow employees, unless the weight of evidence indicated either collusion or wilful misconduct. The agreement seems to have operated satisfactorily'.[14] Hence, the so-called 'gentlemen's agreement', as between the employers' insurers, has mitigated against the employee having to pay out the damages personally, even where the employee is the one who was at fault;
iv. Nevertheless, the right to recover from the wrongdoing employee may be claimed by a vicariously-liable employer in some scenarios, as *Jones* itself demonstrated:

In *Jones v BBC*, Mr Jones, C, was working as a sound recordist/freelancer for the BBC. Whilst sound-recording the lowering of a windmill mast for a TV programme, and while C was passing under the inclined mast, the heavy windmill rotor fell onto C, breaking his back and causing paraplegia. **Held:** liability was apportioned between the BBC (65%), the owners of the farm where the accident happened (25%) and a cameraman, Mr Rees, an employee of the BBC who was assisting C at the time (10%). The BBC told the court that it intended to seek an indemnity from Mr Rees, its employee, in respect of Mr Rees' negligence. Judge Hickinbottom noted, in dicta, that, '[w]hatever the realities of accident litigation in an industrial setting might be, the BBC have made it clear in this litigation that ... they intend to seek an indemnity from Mr Rees in respect of any liability borne by them vicariously ... one can only assume that, before adopting this approach, the BBC very carefully considered these issues and the potential consequences of the stance they have taken'.

Recently, it was observed, in *Bell v Alliance Medical Ltd*,[15] that the decision in *Lister v Romford Ice* seemed to emanate from a bygone era, and that in the modern industrial relations landscape, employers have ample measures available to them against wrongdoing employees (e.g., disciplinary sanctions, the right of dismissal), without resorting to the recovery of damages from that wrongdoing employee – and that it would hardly heighten the employee's sense of responsibility either, to be exposed to that liability. In any event, *Lister v Romford Ice* still theoretically remains good law – and the 'gentlemen's agreement', which virtually nullifies *Lister's* effect, continues to apply.

Given the potential exposure of an employee to personal liability for C's damages, not all jurisdictions have been content to leave the reversal of *Lister v Romford Ice* to the province of a 'gentlemen's agreement'.

[14] [2007] All ER (D) 283 (QB) [139(iv)], quote in case description at [140]–[141].
[15] [2015] CSOH 34, [107]–[110].

The law reform corner: Reversing *Lister v Romford Ice*

In *Employees' Liability*,[16] the NSWLRC noted that the UK Minister of Labour appointed a committee to study the implications of *Lister*, but it did not recommend its legislative reversal. Rather, 'it was preferable for insurers to agree not to exploit their legal rights against negligent employees. Members of the British Insurance Assn subsequently entered into a "gentleman's agreement" [the *Lister v Romford Ice Agreement*] ... One commentator has doubted "whether on general grounds, this rather peculiar method of law reform should be encouraged"'.

The UK committee identified some important limitations to the gentlemen's agreement, e.g.:

- it only applied to insurers, and hence, employers could still sue negligent employees for breach of an implied term in the contract of employment to exercise reasonable care;
- it only operated to prevent the insurer from suing a negligent employee who killed or injured his co-employee, and hence, injuring a person who was not a co-employee, but rather, was some external third party, C, meant that the insurer could sue that negligent employee to recover the damages paid out to C. (That proposition was also suggested, in *Morris v Ford Motor Co Ltd*,[17] to be a narrow reading of *Lister*.)

The NSW Commission preferred a reversal of *Lister* by statute, as 'a more direct and effective way' of dealing with the issue.[18] This was eventually implemented, by virtue of the Employers' Liability Act 1991 (NSW):

s 3 (1) If an employee commits a tort for which his or her employer is also liable:

(a) the employee is not liable to indemnify, or to pay any contribution to, the employer in respect of the liability incurred by the employer; and

(b) the employer is liable to indemnify the employee in respect of liability incurred by the employee for the tort (unless the employee is otherwise entitled to an indemnity in respect of that liability).

Unidentified wrongdoing employees

In most cases, the culpable employee will be easily identifiable. Rarely, though, C will be unable to nominate the wrongdoer – but C will still be able to sue the relevant employer for vicarious liability.

For example, English authorities have supported vicarious liability against the Chief Constable or Home Office, for the wrongdoing of their unidentified officers. In *Racz v Home Office*,[19] mentioned previously, only one of the relevant prison officers could be identified; and in *Flavius v MPC*,[20] a police officer who unlawfully broke C's leg was never identified. Vicarious liability was not precluded in either case.

[16] Report to the AG (May 1988) [3.11]–[3.12], citing G Gardiner, '*Lister and Romford Ice and Cold Storage* (Report of the Inter-Departmental Committee)' (1959) 22 *MLR* 652.

[17] [1973] 1 QB 792 (CA) 798–99.

[18] See too: Queensland LRC, *Vicarious Liability* (Rep No 56, 2001), ch 5, 'Indemnity and Contribution', which also concluded the rule in *Lister v Romford Ice* should be abrogated by statute: [5.1]–[5.3].

[19] [1994] 2 AC 45 (HL). [20] (1982) 132 NLJ 532 (QB).

RATIONALES FOR VICARIOUS LIABILITY

§18.5 A consistent rationale which underpins the doctrine of vicarious liability is difficult to elicit. Rather, a number of different rationales have been proposed, which can conveniently be divided into two categories: those that impose strict (no-fault) liability on the employer; and those that impute some low degree of fault to the employer.

Plainly, overarching the doctrine are the concepts of policy and pragmatism, as a sample of judicial comments over the years demonstrates:

> in the common law world generally, there is a pragmatic element involved as to when and where vicarious liability is imposed (*O'Keeffe v Hickey*, per Hardiman J[21]).
>
> The theoretical underpinning of the doctrine is unclear ... the doctrine cannot parade as a deduction from legalistic premises ... The danger is that in borderline situations, and especially in cases of intentional wrongdoing, recourse to a rigid and possibly inappropriate formula as a test of liability may lead the court to abandon the search for legal principle (*Lister v Hesley Hall Ltd*, per Lord Millett[22]).
>
> The doctrine of vicarious liability has not grown from any very clear, logical or legal principle, but from social convenience and rough justice (*Imperial Chemical Industries Ltd v Shatwell*, per Lord Pearce[23]).
>
> Over the years, the tests ... have developed in a way which has gradually given precedence to function over form (*Viasystems (Tyneside) Ltd v Thermal Transfer (Northern) Ltd*, per Rix LJ[24]).
>
> [to say that] 'it must seem just to place liability for the wrong on the employer' ... seems to me utterly lacking in rigour, and perhaps even in meaning. It is utterly useless as a predictive tool. [It is] a modern version of the 'Chancellor's foot', an old legal metaphor for an uncontrolled highly subjective discretion (*O'Keeffe* again[25]).
>
> Though its roots go back to ancient days, its present form was fashioned in the 18th and 19th centuries as a matter of social expediency and general justice (*Uddin v Assoc Portland Cement Manufacturers Ltd*, per Lord Pearce[26]).

A number of different justifications for vicarious liability have been judicially mooted. These rationales can be conveniently divided into those which accept that the employer is entirely *innocent* of any responsibility, but should, for reasons of justice and fairness, bear liability; and those which impute some *responsibility* to the innocent employer.

Notably, in *Child Welfare Socy*,[27] Lord Phillips endorsed several of the rationales below, but prefaced them with the overarching requirement that it must be 'fair, just and reasonable to impose vicarious liability on the employer.' That is, perhaps, the most important rationale in modern English vicarious liability law.

Strict (no-fault) rationales

There are **three** rationales of interest (but with strong counterpoint arguments, noted below):

i. The 'deep pocket'. Given that the essence of tort is to achieve compensation, liability should 'follow the deep pocket'. The employer (or its insurer) will be more capable of satisfying a

[21] [2008] IESC 72.
[22] [2001] UKHL 22, [65]–[66], citing: Fleming, *Law of Torts* (9th edn, Law Book Co, 1998) 410.
[23] [1965] AC 656 (HL) 685.
[24] [2005] EWCA Civ 1151, [2006] QB 510, [55].
[25] [2008] IESC 72.
[26] [1965] 2 QB 582 (CA) 593.
[27] [2012] UKSC 56, [2013] 2 AC 1, [34]–[35].

judgment than an individual wrongdoing employee will be. Hence, as the eminent scholar Glanville Williams said, 'the master is liable because he has a purse worth opening',[28] and vicarious liability is concerned with 'the search for a solvent defendant'.[29] This rationale cannot be overstated. Where D is not vicariously-liable, then it will leave an often seriously-injured C with no compensatory redress at all, 'save against an assailant who was unlikely to be able to pay full compensation' (per *Mohamud v WM Morrison Supermarkets plc*[30]).

To the contrary, in *O'Keeffe*,[31] there was a strongly-worded criticism by the Irish Supreme Court of this rationale, in that 'even if the pocket is genuinely deep, that fact cannot in ordinary justice support the imposition of liability on such a person where it would not be imposed on a poorer person ... A finding of vicarious liability for perhaps very serious or gross injuries is not a light thing for a company, an institution, the State, or an individual – it has an effect quite separate from its consequences in damages – it may have a chilling effect on state, private or charitable initiatives, or create defensive practices, or convey some stigmatisation for the paying party, or entail some "reputational loss". Plus it will impact upon the cost of insurance'.

ii. Protecting an employee from financial ruination. As Staughton LJ noted in *X (Minors) v Bedfordshire CC*, '[t]he great expansion of tortious liability over the last 150 years has had the remarkable feature, that the direct financial consequences almost invariably fall on someone whose purse is assumed to be bottomless, such as an insurance company or a large commercial concern or an organ of central or local government. It is, I imagine, rare for a private individual [employee] to find himself paying substantial damages for negligence'.[32]

iii. Loss distribution. The employer is in a better position than the wrongdoer employee to absorb and distribute the loss (the damages payout) by either pricing measures (i.e., the employer can increase the price of its product or service to recoup the damages or the increased insurance premium), or through liability insurance (*Lister v Hesley Hall Ltd*[33] and *Dubai Aluminium Co Ltd v Salaam*,[34] per Lord Millett, who called vicarious liability 'a loss distribution device' for this reason).

Fault-based rationales

There are **four** rationales which are, essentially, fault-based – or, at least, reflect that the employer's *responsibilities* in the workplace warrant its bearing the burden of legal liability. However, not all appellate courts in other jurisdictions consider these rationales to be tenable, and the differences of opinion are interesting:

i. The enterprise benefit argument. The employer has engaged the wrongdoing employee for the former's benefit. That employee advances and promotes the employer's business enterprise via the employee's profit-making endeavours. Hence, an appropriate *quid pro quo* for that benefit is the burden of vicarious liability (per Rix LJ in *Viasystems (Tyneside) v Thermal Transfer (Northern)*[35]).

[28] G Williams, 'Vicarious Liability and the Master's Indemnity' (1957) 20 *MLR* 220, 231.
[29] *State of NSW v Lepore* [2003] HCA 4, (2004) 212 CLR 511, [303], citing Williams, *ibid.*
[30] [2014] EWCA Civ 116, [51] (Clarke LJ). [31] [2008] IESC 72 (per Hardiman J).
[32] [1994] 2 WLR 554 (CA) 583. [33] [2001] UKHL 22, [65].
[34] [2002] UKHL 48, [2003] AC 366, [107]. See too, [155]. [35] [2005] EWCA Civ 1151, [2006] QB 510, [79].

ii. The enterprise risk argument. The employer's enterprise created the risk that the employee would commit a tort, causing harm to third parties. Hence, the employer should bear the burden, should those risks manifest (per *Bazley v Curry* per McLachlin J,[36] and *Bernard v AG (Jamaica)* per Lord Steyn[37]). According to the Canadian Supreme Court in *Jacobi v Griffiths*, the employer should justifiably be liable, where it 'introduced the seeds of the potential problem into the community, or aggravated the risks that were already there, but only if its enterprise materially increased the risk of the harm that happened'.[38]

However, in *O'Keeffe*, the Irish Supreme Court was very critical of the two abovementioned rationales.[39] For one thing, they apply exclusively to commercial ventures – it is nonsensical (said that court) to speak of 'risk creation' and 'enterprise benefit' in the case of a State providing free primary education, and hence, a rationale that lacked universal application also lacked theoretical strength. Another criticism was that the risk of sexual abuse of pupils by teachers was not one which was inherent in the nature of the business of providing primary education – just because there had been notorious cases of sex abuse involving teachers, that did not demonstrate that things had reached the stage where abuse was an inherent risk of schooling.

iii. The selection argument. The employer selects the employee, so it is only fair that the employer should bear the burden of his poor choice of servant, one who carelessly or intentionally engages in wrongdoing (per *Reedie v London and North West Rwy Co*, per Rolfe B[40]).

However, in *State of NSW v Lepore*,[41] the Australian High Court criticised this rationale for two reasons. First, to impute vicarious liability with the hope of achieving better selection and recruitment practices was, 'at best ... speculative and remote'. Secondly, the reason that vicarious liability was being pursued was that the employer had **not** itself been negligent, whether in selecting or supervising its staff (otherwise a direct action in negligence would likely succeed).

iv. The deterrence argument. Vicarious liability serves a deterrent purpose, by encouraging better practices by the particular employer, and also among similarly-situated employers whose employees may be minded to engage in similar wrongdoing (see, e.g., Lord Millett's reference, in *Lister*,[42] to the prospect of indecent assaults on the vulnerable in boarding schools, prisons, nursing homes, old people's homes, geriatric wards, and other residential homes for the young or vulnerable by those who are placed in positions of trust or authority over them – a finding of vicarious liability against Hesley Hall provided a deterrent effect).

However, in *Leichhardt MC v Montgomery*,[43] the Australian High Court did not favour this rationale either. For example, if the sanctions imposed by the criminal law could not deter the employee from engaging in criminal acts, then imposing vicarious liability on the employer would hold little extra deterrent value. In any event, to shift the economic cost of negligence to an employer would only have an indirect, remote and speculative effect upon the wrongdoing employee, and might even have 'the potential to impede the deterrence of the person whose

[36] [1999] 2 SCR 534, (1999) 174 DLR (4th) 45, [41].
[37] [2004] UKPC 47 (on appeal from the CA of Jamaica) [23].
[38] [1999] 2 SCR 570, 174 DLR (4th) 71, [65]–[79] (Binnie J, for the majority).
[39] [2008] IESC 72. [40] (1849) 4 Exch 244, 250, 154 ER 1201, 1205.
[41] [2003] HCA 4, [219] (Gummow and Hayne JJ). [42] [2001] UKHL 22, [82]–[83].
[43] [2007] HCA 6, (2007) 233 ALR 200, [113] (Gleeson CJ).

conduct is most in need of influence' (given that the very operations of the employer could be compromised by a finding of vicarious liability).

Summary. Evidently, judicial opinion about the rationales underpinning vicarious liability differ enormously. Furthermore, even though vicarious liability is said to be a doctrine of strict liability, some judges have determinedly sought to imbue the doctrine with a fault-based (or, at least, responsibility-based) flavour.

Turning now to the two elements of the doctrine:

THE 'EMPLOYMENT RELATIONSHIP' LIMB

As a general rule, an employer is vicariously liable for the tortious acts or omissions of its *employees* (or for those in a relationship 'akin to employment'), but not for those of any *independent contractor/s* hired to undertake work for it.

Essentially, in order to **defeat or reduce** vicarious liability under this element, the employer D has three possible legal avenues open to it:

Three ways of defeating the 'employment relationship' element:

1. The wrongdoer was D's independent contractor – **not** D's employee (nor someone 'akin to D's employee')
2. The wrongdoer was someone else's employee at the time of the relevant tort (i.e., the employee was 'on loan' to a temporary employer), thereby shifting vicarious liability to that temporary employer
3. The employment of the wrongdoer was **shared** between D and another employer, giving rise to dual vicarious liability (which will reduce, rather than preclude, any damages payable by the principal employer)

Dealing with each of these legal possibilities in turn:

Employee or independent contractor?

Traditionally, wherever one person works for another, a differentiation has been drawn between 'a contract of service' and a 'contract for services' (see, e.g., *Simmons v Heath Laundry Co*[44]). Employees enter contracts *of service*. Independent contractors, and those employed on their own account, enter into contracts *for services* to undertake a particular job or task. Hence, if a passenger pays a taxi driver to drive him from A to B, and the taxi driver negligently hits a pedestrian, the passenger cannot be vicariously liable, for the driver was the passenger's independent contractor, and not his employee – but in the case of a full-time chauffeur, a contract of service may be established such that the passenger is vicariously liable.[45]

However, it can be difficult to assess just which side of the line the wrongdoer falls. A variety of legal tests have been developed by which to answer the question, 'is the wrongdoer an employee?'. Before canvassing these, two caveats are worth noting.

[44] [1910] 1 KB 543 (CA) 549 (Fletcher Moulton LJ).

[45] An example given in: E Martin and J Law, *Oxford Dictionary of Law* (6th edn, Oxford University Press, 2006) 270; and *JGE v Portsmouth Roman Catholic Diocesan Trust* [2012] EWCA Civ 938, [65].

Employment in different contexts

Several of the leading cases, to which these tests are sourced, do not concern vicarious liability at all. Rather, they arose in other contexts, which required some assessment of the litigant's employment status (re, e.g., rights to sue for unfair dismissal, or entitlements to holiday pay, or ownership of the copyright of material produced during an engagement, or liability to pay PAYE income tax and National Insurance contributions).

It is highly debatable whether the principles governing who an 'employee' is for the purposes of vicarious liability *can*, or *should*, be translated *holus-bolus* from these other contexts. The policy considerations underlying the reasons for finding for, or against, employee status may be quite different.

In *Cairns v Visteon UK Ltd*,[46] the Employment Appeal Tribunal (EAT) declared itself 'attracted' by the notion that the 'concept of employment' for the purpose of unfair dismissal proceedings may require a different approach from that which the concept means for vicarious liability – e.g., the policy underlying vicarious liability is to protect C's ability to obtain compensation from an insured defendant; whereas, in unfair dismissal claims, the policy is to regulate relations between employer and employee. Indeed, the Australian decision of *Hollis v Vabu Pty Ltd*[47] is illustrative. According to a taxation decision,[48] all couriers who worked for a courier company were taxed as if they were independent contractors – yet, when one of those same cycle couriers hit and injured a pedestrian, the courier was treated as an employee for the purposes of vicarious liability! Recently, in *Child Welfare Society*,[49] Lord Phillips cited the view in *JGE v Portsmouth Roman Catholic Diocesan Trust*[50] (without comment) that it was **not** appropriate to apply tests of employment which were developed in cases involving unfair dismissal, taxation, or discrimination.

However, it is submitted that cases from these other contexts – whilst requiring some caution – do continue to provide helpful assistance to the law of vicarious liability, when determining whether the wrongdoer was D's employee under a contract of service, or D's independent contractor under a contract for services. The fact scenarios, and the factors which they throw up on each side of the balancing scales, are informative, when determining the question which vicarious liability's 'employment' limb entails. In any event, it is plain that some of the tests which were developed in those other contexts (e.g., the control test, the integration test, the common mission/purpose test) were nevertheless confirmed in *Child Welfare Socy* as being directly relevant to vicarious liability, which confirms a significant degree of cross-pollination of jurisprudence. Furthermore, the difference in outcomes in *Vabu* does not render the vicarious liability outcome wrong – as the EAT noted in *Cairns*, the policies underlying vicarious liability are likely to be quite different from those which underpin the statutory regimes. Hence, in this author's view, the cases emanating from other contexts offer some guidance on the types of factors (illustrated shortly) to which a court should properly have regard, when deciding a vicarious liability dispute.

The modern employment environment

Another factor that impinges upon vicarious liability is that the employment world is becoming increasingly complex, and judicial tests to determine employee status have had to develop (and struggle) accordingly.

[46] [2007] ICR 616 (EAT) [10]. [47] [2001] HCA 44, (2001) 207 CLR 21.

[48] *Vabu Pty Ltd v Federal Commr of Taxation* (1996) 33 ATR 537 (NSWCA).

[49] [2012] UKSC 56, [49]. [50] [2012] EWCA Civ 938, [59] (Ward LJ).

Agency-supplied workers, zero-hours contract workers, part-time workers, casual or intermittent workers, franchisees, members of religious orders who do not serve under contracts of employment but under vows of chastity and obedience – all, and more, are a feature of the modern workplace. Many of the traditional common law rules governing just who an employee is at law emanated from a different and bygone era (as the old terminology, 'a master is liable for the torts of his or her servant', itself suggests, per *Bell v Alliance Medical Ltd*[51]). Consistently with this, the Court of Appeal frankly admitted, in *Brook Street Bureau (UK) Ltd v Dacas*,[52] that there was considerable confusion in the workplace, and in the law, about the status of individuals who obtained work through employment agencies, for example.

Hence, as the employment environment has changed, so too, it has become clear that no one judicial test of employment status will fit all circumstances in vicarious liability either.

The contractual wording used by the parties

§18.6 Whether a party is, on the one hand, an employee, or someone in a relationship 'akin to employment' (both of which are sufficient for vicarious liability) – or, on the other hand, an independent contractor (which generally is not sufficient) – is determined by all the surrounding circumstances. Whatever the parties expressly provided in their contract (assuming that one exists) is not conclusive.

Insofar as any written contract between employer D and the wrongdoing worker is concerned, Henderson J usefully set out the governing principles in *Dragonfly Consultancy Ltd v HMRC*[53] – and whilst these were not said in the context of vicarious liability, they are nevertheless helpful:

i. in a borderline case, the parties' written intentions should be taken into account, and although the weight to be attached to such statements may be minimal, they may help to tip the balance one way or the other;
ii. in most cases, however, the contractual wording will be of little, if any, assistance in properly characterising the relationship between the parties;
iii. where the worker is placed by an employment agency, then whatever statements of intention may be contained in the contract between worker and agency are unlikely to shed any light on the proper characterisation of the status of that worker who is placed with a client.

In some cases, there may be **no** contract between D and the worker at all, wherein the parties could have stated their intentions. Nevertheless, that does not preclude a finding of vicarious liability. This scenario has especially arisen in the context of relationships which are 'akin to employment'. For example, in *JGE v Portsmouth Roman Catholic Diocesan Trust*,[54] there was no contract of employment between the Trust and a priest who committed sexual abuse against C (i.e., no terms and conditions, no remuneration, no right of dismissal except through the church in Rome) – and in *Cox v MOJ*,[55] there was no contract of employment between the MOJ and a prisoner who assisted in the prison kitchen either. Yet these relationships were sufficient to give rise to vicarious liability on the part of the Trust and the MOJ, respectively, given the surrounding circumstances and indicia.

[51] [2015] CSOH 34, [105]. [52] [2004] EWCA Civ 217, [2] (Mummery LJ).
[53] [2008] EWHC 2113 (Ch) [32], and [52]–[57] (omitting internal authorities).
[54] [2012] EWCA Civ 938. [55] [2014] EWCA Civ 132.

Relevant judicial tests

It is preferable, for the sake of clarity, to deal with strict employer–employer scenarios separately from those which are merely 'akin to employment'.

§18.7 The decision as to whether the wrongdoer was an employee or an independent contractor may be indicated by a variety of tests, the principal one of which is the control test, *viz*, that the wrongdoing employee agrees, expressly or impliedly, that he will provide his own work and skill in the performance of some service for another, and that, in the performance of that service, he will be subject to that other's control to a sufficient degree to make that other an employer. Additionally, other tests to determine whether a contract of service existed include: the common mission test, the substitution test, the business-on-one's-own-account test, and the integration test.

The meaning of a 'contract of service' in the principle above is taken from the judgment of McKenna J in *Ready Mixed Concrete (Southeast) Ltd v Minister of Pensions and National Insurance*,[56] and represents perhaps the most widely-cited passage in English law regarding employment status. Since then, however, several other tests (set out below) have been posed/applied (and referenced subsequently in *JGE v Portsmouth Roman Catholic Diocesan Trust*[57]), in order to provide greater guidance and to cope with different scenarios. Some of them overlap, and none is decisive:

The various judicial tests for employment status

The test	Description	Leading authority
The control test	Does the employer have the immediate direction and control of the relevant work? Is the employer entitled to tell the worker what work is to be done, and when and where to do the work? If so, the worker is likely to be an employee. Given the high degree of specialist employment these days, it is not necessary for the employer to control the *way* (or method, or manner) in which an employee is to do the work	Per May LJ in *Viasystems (Tyneside) Ltd v Thermal Transfer (Northern) Ltd*[a] and *Child Welfare Socy*[b]
The common mission test	Does the employer have a common mission or purpose with the worker, so that the essential purpose of the worker's activities was to further the employer's objective – and their very relationship was directed to achieving that joint 'apostolate' or mission? If so, then it points to an employee, or to a relationship 'akin to employment'	*Child Welfare Socy*[c]

[a] [2005] EWCA Civ 1151, [2006] QB 510, [16].
[b] [2012] UKSC 56, [36].
[c] [2012] UKSC 56, [59].

[56] [1968] QB 497, 515.

[57] [2012] EWCA Civ 938, [2013] Ch 722, [72] (Ward LJ), citing: R Kidner, 'Vicarious Liability: for Whom should the "Employer" be Liable?' (1995) 15 *Legal Studies* 47.

The test	Description	Leading authority
The substitution test	If the worker is free either to do the job himself, or to arrange (at his own expense) for another person to do the job instead, then that ability to substitute is inconsistent with a contract of service – although a limited or occasional substitution (falling short of a blanket licence to supply the contractual services through a substitute) may be permissible for an employee to arrange	*Byrne Bros (Formwork) Ltd v Baird;*[d] and *Dragonfly Consultancy Ltd v HMRC*[e]
The business-on-one's-own-account test	Did the worker provide his own equipment, or hire his own assistants? Did he take a degree of financial risk, plus a degree of responsibility for investment and management of his work? Does he have an opportunity of profiting from the task, apart from a basic salary? If so, these are inconsistent with a contract of service	*Market Investigations Ltd v Minister of Social Security;*[f] and *Lee Ting Sang v Chung Chi-Keung*[g]
The mutual obligations test	Was there an 'irreducible minimum of mutual obligation' on both sides of the contract (i.e., on the employee's side, an obligation to undertake the work, and on the employer's part, an obligation to pay)? If so, it points to a contract of service	*Nethermere (St Neots) Ltd v Gardiner;*[h] and *Carmichael v National Power plc (HL)*[i]
The integration test	Was the worker's task an integral part of the employer's organisation and business, so that the worker was fully integrated into the set-up? Or was the work (while of benefit to the employer) merely an accessory to the employer's organisation and business? If the former, then a contract of service is more likely	*Stevenson Jordan & Harrison Ltd v MacDonald & Evans;*[j] and *Cox v MOJ*[k]

[d] [2001] UKEAT 542, [25]–[29].
[e] [2008] EWHC 2113 (Ch).
[f] [1969] 2 QB 173.
[g] [1990] UKPC 1, [1990] 2 AC 374, [374]–[375] (on appeal from the CA of Hong Kong).
[h] [1984] ICR 612 (CA).
[i] [1999] 1 WLR 2042 (HL) (Lord Irvine).
[j] [1952] 1 TLR 101 (CA).
[k] [2014] EWCA Civ 132, [45].

At least in the context of the strict employment-versus-independent-contractor decision, the control test has proven to be the most significant test, for some degree of control over the manner in which the work is done will be 'an essential ingredient of a contract of employment' (per *Dragonfly Consultancy Ltd v HMRC*[58]) – albeit that, for very highly-skilled workers (such as doctors, engineers and IT specialists) who are performing complex tasks, the degree of control will be very light-handed. Indeed, in many cases, the employer will not have sufficient knowledge or expertise to be expected to order the manner in which these workers should exercise their professional skills (that is why the employee has been hired!). Hence, in *Market Investigations*, Cooke J observed that 'control will always have to be considered, although it can no

[58] [2008] EWHC 2113 (Ch) [41].

longer be regarded as the sole determining factor'[59] – of which the Privy Council said, in *Lee Ting Sang v Chung Chi-Keung*[60] that 'the matter had never been better put'.

Clearly, the determination of whether the individual wrongdoer was an employee or an independent contractor may be a very imprecise exercise in legal semantics. As the court put it in *Hall (Inspector of Taxes) v Lorimer*, the task is to 'paint a picture from the accumulation of detail. The overall effect can only be appreciated by standing back from the detailed picture which has been painted, by viewing it from a distance and making an informal, considered qualitative appreciation of the whole'.[61] Further, there is no exhaustive list of relevant factors, and 'nor [can] strict rules be laid down as to the relative weight which the various considerations should carry in particular cases' (per *Dragonfly Consultancy v HMRC*[62]).

This picture of imprecision is confirmed by considering how finely balanced were some of the leading cases, as the Table below shows (Emp'ee = employee; IC = independent contractor):

Leading cases on employee status

Case	Factors pointing towards Emp'ee	Factors pointing towards IC	Verdict
Market Investigations Ltd v Minister of Social Security	Mrs Irving was a member of a panel of part-time interviewers of a company engaged in market research, and undertook market research for the company from time to time		
	– the company's 'Interviewer's Guide' gave detailed instructions as to the method in which interviews were to be conducted – could not be moved to another place without her consent – could not be dismissed in the middle of a survey	– during field trips, could be out of contact with her supervisor – free to work when she wanted, provided that she completed the work within the allotted time – could simultaneously undertake similar work for other firms – paid per interviewing job – no provision for time off, sick pay, or holidays	Emp'ee
Dragonfly Consultancy Ltd v HMRC	B, an IT tester, worked for the Automobile Assn almost exclusively for a period of over two years, testing three IT projects being undertaken by AA		
	– could not have substituted another person to perform his work – B's work was informally monitored as the work progressed	– highly skilled work, and not subject to any directions as to how to perform the work – expected to conduct tests, but not how to conduct them	

[59] [1969] 2 QB 173, 184–85. [60] [1990] 2 AC 374 (PC) 382.
[61] [1994] 1 WLR 209 (CA) 216. [62] [2008] EWHC 2113 (Ch) [42].

Case	Factors pointing towards Emp'ee	Factors pointing towards IC	Verdict
	– B attended weekly team meetings at AA – B had to complete tests within a specific time-frame set by AA – B subject to 'spot checks' or to requests for specific tests to be run	– no detailed or formal review of B's work – worked about 25% of the time from home for one project	Emp'ee
Hall (Inspector of Taxes) v Lorimer	H was a vision mixer who worked freelance under a series of short-term contracts		
	– performed the editing work at the studios of production company clients – used studio's equipment, not his own – production companies controlled the time, place and duration of any given engagement	– had discretion to charge in excess of union rate for his services – set up a home office – short-term contracts, could last one day – could substitute another worker for himself – did not share in the profits/losses of clients	IC
Carmichael v National Power plc	C and L worked from time to time as part-time guides at a power station – query arose as to their status when not working – employee or not?		
	– the guides were paid for their services	– no notice of termination – contract said nothing about when, or how often, work would be offered – sickness, holiday, and pension for regular staff, did not apply to C and L – grievance and disciplinary procedures also inapplicable – construing the contract, there was no obligation on the power station operators to provide casual work, nor on C and L to undertake it	IC

It is evident from these cases that there were, in fact, indicia pointing to *both* outcomes: contract of service *and* a contract for services. It all depended upon the weight which the relevant courts placed upon each indicium in the assessment exercise.

Relationships 'akin to employment'

§18.8 As an alternative to the traditional 'contract of service', vicarious liability is triggered where the wrongdoer had a relationship with D which was 'akin to employment'. Whether that type of relationship existed will be determined by reference to the same tests which apply when identifying a contract of service (identified in the preceding principle). A wrongdoer who is in a relationship 'akin to employment' is legally distinct from an independent contractor.

The extension. When Lord Phillips referred, in *Child Welfare Socy*, to the law of vicarious liability being 'on the move', it is in relation to this principle that his remarks were directed. Vicarious liability was extended, in that case, to cover those who were not, strictly speaking, D's employees, but with whom D had a relationship 'akin to employment'.

This principle has become particularly applicable in the context of those wrongdoers who are clergy or members of religious orders, and prisoners. Vows, and prison sentences, rather than the traditional indicia of the employment contract, bind those wrongdoers and the 'employers', respectively – but the latter are not necessarily beyond the reach of the modern vicarious liability doctrine.

Much of this case law has broken new ground. In *JGE v Portsmouth Roman Catholic Diocesan Trust*,[63] it was the first time that the defendant Church had challenged the allegation that it was the employer of its priests. Prior to that, litigation had been restricted to whether acts of abuse committed by priests and other religious clergy had been committed in the course of their employment. For example, in *Maga v Birmingham Archdiocese of the Roman Catholic Church*,[64] the archdiocese was vicariously liable for the sexual abuse committed by one of its priests – the employer–employee limb was actually conceded, and the sole focus was whether the 'in the course of employment' limb was proven. Additionally, in *Cox v MOJ*,[65] whether a prison authority was vicariously liable for a prisoner's negligence was another case of first impression.

It is evident that the same tests (e.g., the integration test, the control test) which applied when determining whether the wrongdoer was an employee under the 'contract of service', and not an independent contractor, have also been used when determining whether the wrongdoer was in a relationship 'akin to employment'. That is **not** to say that such a wrongdoer was an independent contractor of D's – the distinction between someone 'akin to employment' and an independent contractor remains good law (as noted, e.g., in *Whetstone v MPS Ltd*[66]), despite the relaxation on vicarious liability which *Child Welfare Socy* instituted.

Relevant categories. The following categories have been held to be relationships 'akin to employment', capable of giving rise to vicarious liability:

- members of a worldwide religious order, and an unincorporated association of which they were members:

  In *Child Welfare Society*,[67] 170 men sued for sexual abuse committed by Brother James and other De La Salle teaching brothers of the Catholic Church. The brothers were members of the Institute, the 'Brothers of the Christian Schools', D. They taught at various schools, including St William's School, where this abuse occurred, but were not employed by the school, or by D either. The Institute, D, was vicariously liable for the sexual abuse committed by Brother James and others. D exercised a degree of control over the brothers, because of their lifelong vows of chastity, poverty and obedience, when becoming members of D. The teaching brothers were obliged to conduct themselves as dictated by D's rules and by those vows. D's structure was hierarchical, and it ran its activities like a corporate

[63] [2012] EWCA Civ 938, [5]. [64] [2010] EWCA Civ 256, [2010] 1 WLR 1441. [65] [2014] EWCA Civ 132, [45].
[66] [2014] EWHC 1024 (QB) [116]. [67] [2012] UKSC 56, [56]–[58].

body, akin to an employment relationship. All teaching within schools was taken at the direction of the head ('the Provincial'), and the brothers were sent where directed to carry out the mission or objective of D, *viz*, providing Christian teaching for boys (which was the brothers' common mission too, given their lifelong vows). The brothers were bound to D, not by contract, but by their religious vows. Also, they were obliged to transfer all their earnings to D, from which D catered for their needs. Hence, even though D was not strictly the brothers' employer, theirs was a relationship 'akin to employment'.

- a Roman Catholic priest, and the bishop (or diocesan trust) of the parish in which the priest provided his Catholic ministry:

In *JGE v Portsmouth Roman Catholic Diocesan Trust*,[68] C alleged that, aged six, she was sexually abused by a Roman Catholic priest when she was at a children's home. The priest was appointed by the Trust, D, which was in an equivalent position to a diocesan bishop. The relationship between the priest and D could give rise to vicarious liability. Although there was an absence of strong control by D over the priest (the priest was subject to Canon law and hence, owed the bishop obedience, but he was free to conduct his ministry as he saw fit without interference from the bishop, whose role was advisory, not supervisory), the priest was appointed in order to do D's work in the parish. He was provided with the premises, the pulpit and the clerical robes to do the bishop's ministry; was accountable to the bishop, because he could be dismissed from office in the event of gross breach of his duties under Canon law; was integral to the Church's mission to spread the Catholic faith; was wholly integrated in that mission, by virtue of his vows; and was not carrying on the ministry of the Roman Catholic faith on his own account, but rather, on behalf of the Church (and the 'regional office' of the bishopric). Hence, the relationship of priest and D was 'akin to employment'.

- a prisoner, and the owners/operators of the prison:

In *Cox v MOJ*,[69] a prisoner, Mr Inder, assisted in the prison kitchens on a paid basis (£11.55 pw), undertaking various tasks to help prepare the meals for 400 prisoners. On this occasion, he ignored instructions from Miss Cox, C, a prison catering manager, to stop transporting heavy bags of rice and foodstuffs whilst a split bag of rice was cleaned up. In an ensuing mishap, he negligently dropped a heavy bag onto C's back, injuring her. The MOJ was vicariously liable for the prisoner's negligence. Assisting in the prison's kitchens to prepare meals for the prisoners gave rise to a relationship 'akin to employment'. Mr Inder's work was 'clearly part of the venture, enterprise or business ... of the [MOJ] in running the prison'. The integration test was met, in addition to the degree of supervision and control exercised over Mr Inder during his activities in the kitchen and beyond.

Cox should be distinguished from the scenario in *Home Office v Dorset Yacht Co Ltd*[70] (see Chapter 3), where the Home Office could be vicariously liable for the torts of its correctional officers employed at the Borstal institutions, but **not** for the Borstal youths who had escaped custody from Brownsea Island, and whose actions extensively damaged C's yachts during that escapade. Those youths were neither acting under the direction of the prison, nor integrated into Borstal's organisational structure. The scenarios were entirely different.

[68] [2012] EWCA Civ 938 (Ward and Davis LJJ, Tomlinson LJ dissenting).
[69] [2014] EWCA Civ 132, [45]. [70] [1970] AC 1004 (HL) 1057.

- an associate (consultant) dentist, working in D's dental practice:

  In *Whetstone (t/as Whelby House Dental Practice) v MPS Ltd*,[71] Mrs Lelliott, C, was negligently treated by Mr Sudworth, S, as a dental patient. S was an associate in Mr Whetstone's, D's, dental practice. D was vicariously liable for S's negligence. Their relationship was 'carefully constructed' to ensure that they were not in an employment relationship – but their mutual obligations were too close for S to be an independent contractor. If S was an independent contractor, one would not expect that he should hand over his patients' books and records to D, not have any goodwill in relation to his own patients, and not be able to treat his own patients wherever he liked: 'provisions of those types are normally only found in contracts of employment'. D exercised a high degree of control over S's activities. S was bound to follow D's policies, to provide his services at times prescribed by D, and to charge fees fixed by D. S participated in D's organisation and was integrated into it. He was provided with equipment and support staff to provide dental services. Their relationship 'was as "akin to employment" as one could get in a relationship deliberately structured by contract to avoid an employment relationship'.

- the elders and ministerial servants in the hierarchical structure of Jehovah's Witnesses:

  In *A v Watchtower Bible and Tract Socy*,[72] C was sexually abused by Peter Stewart, a Jehovah's Witness 'ministerial servant', between the ages of 4 and 9. A ministerial servant had a role of 'great importance', essential to many of the activities of Jehovah's Witnesses, deputising for an elder in the absence of an elder, assisting elders, and helping with teaching if necessary. Hence, 'a ministerial servant is part and parcel of the organisation, and integral to it', and 'the relationship between elders and ministerial servants and the Jehovah's Witnesses is sufficiently close in character to one of employer/employee that it is just and fair to impose vicarious liability'.

By contrast, the following relationship was **not** 'akin to employment', triggering no vicarious liability:

- foster parents, and the local authority social services which placed child C with those parents:

  Pre-*Child Welfare Socy, in H v Norfolk CC*,[73] a child, C, was placed by a local authority, D, into the care of foster parents, and was then abused by one of the foster parents. D was not vicariously liable for the wrongs of the foster parent. This was affirmed, post-*Child Welfare Socy*, in *NA v Nottinghamshire CC*.[74] Foster parents do not provide family life on behalf of D, so the integration test failed. D promoted the child's welfare by placing that child in a home where he/she could be expected to benefit from family life, but D did not, itself, provide family life as part of its activities and business. Also, the foster parents were not, to any material degree, under the control of D – rather, the whole concept of foster parenting was that D should not have that degree of control.

Is the employee on loan to another employer?

§18.9 Exceptionally, a Temporary Employer may bear the sole burden of vicarious liability for an employee's wrongdoing – and the Permanent Employer bears no vicarious liability at all – if, at the time at which the employee committed a tort, his employment had been transferred temporarily to the Temporary Employer, to complete a specific task or for a certain time period.

[71] [2014] EWHC 1024, [123]. [72] [2015] EWHC 1722 (QB) [69], [71].
[73] [1997] 2 FCR 334 (CA). [74] [2014] EWHC 4005 (QB) [177].

Whether the loaned employee's employment was transferred largely depends upon whether the Temporary Employer exercised the requisite degree of control over the loaned employee, and whether the employee was sufficiently integrated into the Temporary Employer's business.

A 'loaned employee' is sometimes termed an employee *pro hac vice* (for an occasion). Difficult issues arise where such an employee commits a tort during the period of secondment.

According to the leading case of *Mersey Docks and Harbour Board v Coggins & Griffith (Liverpool) Ltd*, the burden of proof rests on Permanent Employer to shift the responsibility for the employee's tort to Temporary Employer, which burden 'is a heavy one'.[75] Subsequently, in *Biffa Waste Services Ltd v Maschinenfabrik Ernst Hese Gmbh*, the Court of Appeal reiterated that 'exceptional facts are required'.[76] More recently, in *Child Welfare Socy*,[77] the Supreme Court noted that the *Mersey Docks* scenario of transfer of vicarious liability was 'so stringent as to render a transfer of vicarious liability almost impossible in practice' – and yet, the technique was not overruled, and hence, still adds another 'bow' to D's attempts to shift vicarious liability elsewhere.

Achieving a transfer of liability will be especially crucial to C, where Permanent Employer is insolvent or otherwise unable to satisfy any judgment, given that the wrongdoing employee himself will probably be uninsured (see, e.g., *Hawley v Luminar Leisure Ltd*[78]). Temporary Employer may be the only 'deep pocket' from which C can realistically recover. Alternatively, Permanent Employer (or its insurer) may well be able to satisfy a judgment, but may argue that liability is properly to be borne by the firm which was benefiting from the employee's services when the tort was committed.

The leading authorities

The scenario (together with the parties involved in leading cases shown in italics) is described below:

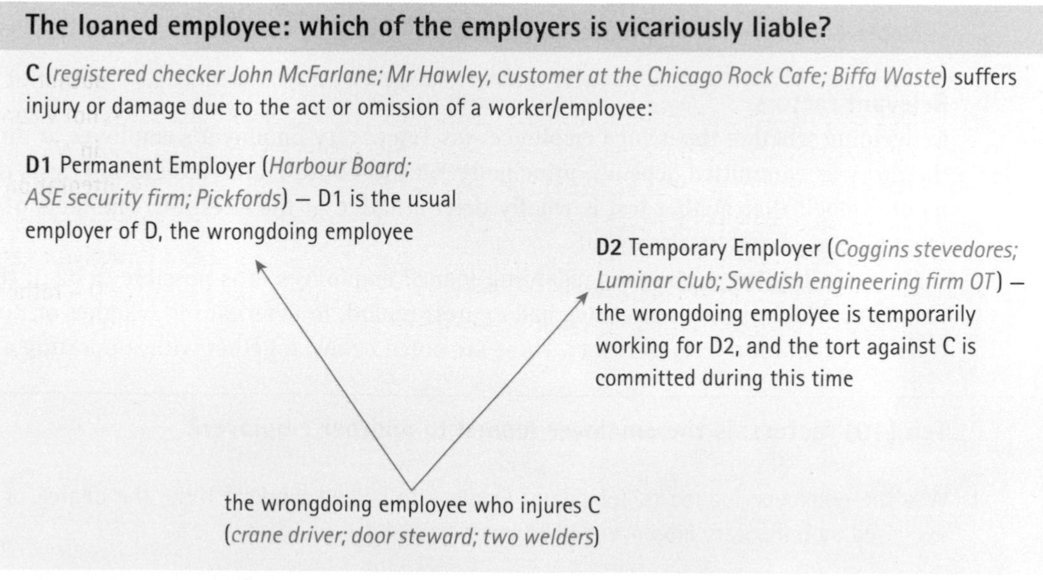

[75] [1947] AC 1 (HL) 10 (Lord Simon). [76] [2008] EWCA Civ 1257, [2009] QB 725, [59]. [77] [2012] UKSC 56, [37].

[78] [2006] EWCA Civ 18, [2006] PIQR P17. Although ASE went into liquidation prior to trial and had no assets, it did carry a public liability insurance policy.

Two of the cases of 'loaned employees' unsuccessfully attempted to shift responsibility to Temporary Employer – reinforcing that Permanent Employer has a tough legal job to escape vicarious liability:

In *Mersey Docks v Coggins & Griffith*, the Harbour Board owned a number of mobile cranes, each driven by a skilled crane-driver. Cranes plus drivers were regularly hired out to stevedoring companies to load/unload cargo at Liverpool Docks. The Harbour Board paid the drivers at all times, but the hiring contract provided that stevedores 'must provide all necessary slings, chains, and labour for preparing the article to be lifted, and for unshackling the same. They must also take all risks in connexion with the matter'. The Harbour Board hired a crane-plus-driver to stevedores, Coggins, to load a ship at dock. The crane-driver seriously injured Mr McFarlane, C, who was checking the load, by trapping C with the crane. **Held:** the Harbour Board, as Permanent Employer, was vicariously liable for the crane driver's negligence. Vicarious liability did not shift to Temporary Employer, Coggins. In *Hawley v Luminar Leisure Ltd*, bouncer, Mr Warren, was employed by ASE Security Services, and worked at Luminar club at Chicago Rock Café at Southend-on-Sea for two years. During an incident outside the club, Mr Hawley, C, was punched by Mr Warren, and suffered severe facial injuries, fractured skull, and serious brain damage. Mr Warren was convicted of grievous bodily harm. C sued ASE as Mr Warren's employer (but ASE was in liquidation, and played no part in the proceedings), and C also sued Luminar. **Held:** Luminar, as Temporary Employer, was vicariously liable. There was no vicarious liability on the part of the Permanent Employer, ASE. In *Biffa Waste Services*, Biffa Waste, C, had a contract with the Leicester CC to collect, recycle and dispose of Leicester's domestic waste. C had to build a recycling plant and install a Ball Mill, a large rotating drum that pulps waste. Engineering firm, OT, was subcontracted to design/supply/install the Ball Mill, and some work was subcontracted by OT to Pickfords Vanguard. Partly due to negligence by two Pickfords' welders in not wetting down the welding, combustible materials caught fire, and the Ball Mill and other parts of the recycling plant were badly damaged. **Held:** Pickfords, as Permanent Employer of the welders, was vicariously liable (but it was insolvent). Vicarious liability did not shift to OT as Temporary Employer, so C was unable to recover its losses.

Relevant factors

In deciding whether the loaned employee was Temporary Employer's employee at the time that the tort was committed depends, principally, on the 'control' and 'integration' tests of employment – albeit that neither test is wholly determinative of the question. The facts of each case must be considered 'in the round'.

From the leading authorities regarding loaned employees, it is possible to distil **ten** specific factors to which those courts have had express regard, in determining whether or not the control and integration tests were met. These are noted below, together with supporting authorities:

Ten (10) factors: is the employee loaned to another employer?

1 Was the employee loaned to Temporary Employer a **skilled worker**? If so, the degree of control exercised by Temporary Employer will be much lessened.

In *Biffa Waste*, the welders were skilled individuals who had a Pickfords' foreman on site to supervise them, so that OT did not exercise control over the manner in which they welded. On the other hand, as Parker J observed in *Garrard v A E Southey & Co*, if what has been loaned is 'a matter of labour only and, perhaps, labour which is not very highly skilled, it seems ... much more easy to infer that the hirer should not merely control in the sense of being able to tell the workman what he wants doing, but control the manner of doing it as well'.[a] The bouncer's activities in *Hawley* fell into that category, hence a shift of vicarious liability.

2 Was the employee using Permanent Employer's **own equipment/property** to undertake the work for Temporary Employer? If so, then the degree of control by Temporary Employer will be much lessened.

In *Mersey Docks*, the crane always remained the property of the Harbour Board. Lord Macmillan noted that the stevedoring firm 'were entitled to tell [the crane driver] where to go, what parcels to lift and where to take them, i.e., they could direct him as to what they wanted him to do; but they had no authority to tell him how he was to handle the crane in doing his work [which was] the [Harbour Board's] property confided to his charge'. Also, the welders in *Biffa Waste* used their own welding equipment, gas cylinders and weld rods. As Denning LJ said in *Denham v Midland Emp Mutual Ass Ltd*, a transfer of vicarious responsibility 'rarely takes place, if ever, when a man is lent with a machine, such as a crane or a lorry: ... In such case the parties do not contemplate that the temporary employer shall tell the man how to manipulate his machine'.[b]

3 Does it remain the responsibility and the right of Permanent Employer to **pay and dismiss** the employee, respectively? If so, the Temporary Employer will not exercise much control over the employee.

In *Mersey Docks*, both payment and dismissal remained within the ambit of the Harbour Board's responsibilities. The degree of control of ASE in *Hawley* was much less marked, as ASE nominated who should work on a particular night, and who should replace somebody who did not turn up, but Luminar could stipulate that any particular bouncer should not work at the club, without any reason being given.

4 **How long is the secondment** to Temporary Employer? The shorter it is, the less integration is likely.

The welders in *Biffa Waste* worked on OT's site for a weekend (and vicarious liability did not shift to OT); whereas the bouncer in *Hawley* worked at the club for two years (and vicarious liability did shift).

5 **Who trained** the employee? If the Permanent Employer, that is where control/integration is more likely.

The training of the crane-drivers in *Mersey Docks* rested with the Harbour Board; whereas in *Hawley*, the training provided to Mr Warren principally came from Luminar, where the club manager stipulated where bouncers should be stationed, who should be admitted, and how to deal with noisy customers.

6 Which employer was in the superior position to have **prevented the employee from committing the tort**? The greater the power of prevention, the greater the degree of control over the employee.

In *Biffa Waste*, Pickfords' foreman was responsible (in part) for ensuring that safety requirements were complied with. OT itself had no employees on site, or even in the country, when the negligence occurred.

[a] [1952] 2 QB 174, 179.
[b] [1955] 2 QB 437 (CA) 444.

7 **Whose uniform** did the employee wear (if indeed one was worn)? That impacts on integration.

The bouncer in *Hawley* wore the Luminar uniform, and in that sense, the public could not distinguish door staff (supplied by ASE) from bar staff (Luminar's own employees).

8 Did the employee **sign any document** of Temporary Employer which indicated that control over the way in which the employee was to do his job was vested in Temporary Employer?

In *Hawley*, bouncers signed job descriptions with Luminar, which contained terms about codes of behaviour expected of door stewards. This was a significant factor to shift vicarious liability to Luminar.

9 Was the employee **integrated within Temporary Employer's organisation** to such extent that the public, management, etc, viewed the visiting employee in the same light as the permanent employees?

In *Biffa Waste*, Pickfords' welders were not integrated into the business undertaking of OT at the recycling plant. However, in *Hawley*, senior management said that they 'saw everybody working at the club as operating as a team', and that 'the door staff were equally part of the Luminar staff as were the bar staff'.

10 Are there any **miscellaneous factors** which indicated that Temporary Employer exercised control over the way in which the employee worked?

In *Biffa Waste*, Temporary Employer OT had requested that two Pickfords' employees attend the site to rectify the Ball Mill works, but four Pickfords' employees were involved in the work. When more employees came to do the job than the Temporary Employer was expecting, the Court of Appeal rhetorically asked: how was the law to decide over which two did OT exercise control? Was it the two who happened to perform the welding work negligently, or the other two? Such difficulties precluded vicarious liability from shifting to OT at all. Further, Pickfords' employees started work on their first day onsite before any supervisors engaged by OT arrived – negating that their work was controlled by OT.

The terms of the parties' contract

§18.10 As between Permanent Employer and Temporary Employer, the parties' express contractual intention is not conclusive on the legal question, 'whose employee?'. However, any transfer of vicarious liability from Permanent Employer to Temporary Employer requires, as a pre-requisite, that the employee consented, expressly or impliedly, to the transfer of his employment. Further, a contractual term that seeks to transfer vicarious liability to Temporary Employer must satisfy the Unfair Contract Terms Act 1977, otherwise it will be void.

In *Mersey Docks*, reg. 6 of the hiring contract between the Harbour Board and stevedores Coggins provided that, 'The drivers so provided shall be the servants of the Applicants [the stevedoring company, Coggins]'. Nevertheless, the crane driver who caused C's injury remained the Harbour Board's employee at all times, notwithstanding that contractual statement. Whether vicarious liability shifted was not to be determined by the parties' agreement, said the House of Lords, 'but depends on all the circumstances of the case'.[79] Hence, even if the employers have contracted *between themselves* (a) that the Temporary Employer must completely indemnify the Permanent Employer in respect of any tortious liability incurred by the employee, or (b) as to

[79] [1947] AC 1 (HL) 10 (Lord Simon).

which of them should insure against the risk of liability to third parties caused by the conduct of the employee, that is not conclusive as to which of them is the employer (per *Biffa Waste*[80]).

Moreover, no transfer of an employee's services can occur without the employee's consent. That consent may be express (which is unlikely – as Denning LJ noted in *Denham v Midland Employers' Mutual Ass Ltd*, usually Permanent Employer 'has simply told him to go and do some particular work for the temporary employer, and he has gone'[81]) or it may be inferred from all the circumstances (per *Biffa Waste*[82]).

Finally, it will be recalled that, in *Mersey Docks*, the hiring contract provided that the stevedores were required to 'take all risks in connexion with the matter'. Any modern-day attempt by the parties to include in their contract a clause to the effect that Temporary Employer 'alone shall be responsible for all claims arising in connection with the operation of the [loaned] Plant by the [loaned employee]' – as an attempt to exclude or restrict Permanent Employer's liability for the employee's negligence – may not satisfy the requirement of 'reasonableness' under s 2(2) of the Unfair Contract Terms Act 1977. If it does not, then such a clause which seeks to protect Permanent Employer will be void (as occurred, e.g., in *Phillips Products Ltd v Hyland*[83]).

Dual vicarious liability

§18.11 Where Temporary Employer 'borrows' an employee from Permanent Employer, and the right to control that employee is shared between both Employers, then vicarious liability for any tort committed by that employee may be shared between the Employers, via dual vicarious liability. The relevant test is whether the employee was integrated into the organisation of both Employers.

So far in this section, it has been an all-or-nothing outcome. The responsibility for the wrongdoing employee either rested with the employer, or it did not. However, since 2005, another option – *viz*, dual vicarious liability – has been recognised in English law.

> In *Viasystems (Tyneside) Ltd v Thermal Transfer (Northern) Ltd*,[84] *Viasystems*, C, wanted its factory air-conditioned, and engaged Thermal Transfer to do the installation. Thermal Transfer subcontracted the ducting work to Darwell Ltd, and CAT Metalwork Services provided Darwell with their employees, Mr Megson, fitter, and Mr Strang, fitter's mate, on a labour-only basis. Due to Mr Strang's negligence, the ducting fractured the fire protection sprinkler system, and C's factory was flooded, causing extensive damage. The question was which of Darwell or CAT Metalwork was vicariously liable for Mr Strang's negligence. **Held:** dual vicarious liability 'provided a coherent solution to the problem of the borrowed employee' here. Both Darwell (as Temporary Employer who had hired Mr Strang as fitter's mate) and CAT Metalwork (his Permanent Employer) were obliged to control Mr Strang, to stop his negligent act, so both bore vicarious liability.

The concept has been utilised since, e.g.:

> In *Child Welfare Society*,[85] it was held at trial that the Middlesborough Ds, which managed St William's school, and which employed Brother James and other brothers to teach at that school under contracts of employment, were vicariously liable for the acts of abuse committed by the brothers at

[80] [2008] EWCA Civ 1257, [53]. [81] [1955] 2 QB 437 (CA) 443. [82] [2008] EWCA Civ 1257, [49].

[83] [1987] 1 WLR 659 (CA). Cf: *Thompson v Lohan (Plant Hire) Ltd* [1987] 1 WLR 649 (CA) (on different facts, a similar clause was reasonable).

[84] [2005] EWCA Civ 1151, [77]. [85] [2012] UKSC 56, [56]–[58].

that school – but the Middlesborough Ds claimed that the Institute, D, should be vicariously liable too. **Held:** dual vicarious liability applied there.

Dual vicarious liability: can both employers be vicariously liable?

C suffers injury due to the act or omission of an employee (*Viasystems; abused boys at St William's school*):

D1 Permanent Employer (*CAT Metalwork Services; Middlesborough Ds*) – D1 is the usual employer of D, the wrongdoing employee

D2 Temporary Employer (*Darwell; the Institute of Brothers*) – the wrongdoing employee is temporarily working for D2, and the tort against C is committed during this time

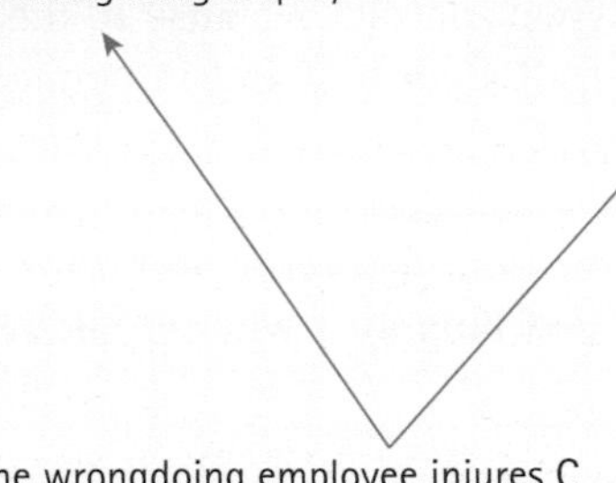

the wrongdoing employee injures C (*Mr Strang, the fitter's mate; Brother James et al.*)

The change of view represented in *Viasystems*

Prior to *Viasystems*, there had been a long-standing assumption, since 1826 in *Laugher v Pointer*,[86] that dual vicarious liability was not possible in English law. Littledale J had stated that the negligent coachman must be 'the servant of one or the other, but not the servant of one and the other; the law does not recognise a several liability in two principals who are unconnected.' This reflected the adage, 'a servant cannot serve two masters'.

However, in *Viasystems*, the Court of Appeal upheld a different view in the modern era:[87]

i. the *Laugher v Pointer* rule was truly a rule of convenience, in order to prevent a multiplicity of defendants from being joined in the one action, but that rationale does not unduly trouble modern litigation – and, even under the all-or-nothing *Mersey Docks* principle, more than one D is likely to be sued in one action;
ii. *Laugher's* views were dicta only, and not binding on the Court of Appeal. *Mersey Docks* did not preclude dual vicarious liability either, as the point was not argued there. Mr Strang's wrongdoing, and the flood of Viasytems' factory, squarely raised the possibility for a determination which had not arisen previously;
iii. other jurisdictions, such as Australia, Canada and the United States, recognised the legal possibility of dual vicarious liability (although it had been rejected in Ireland);
iv. sole vicarious liability had long centred upon the right to absolutely control the employee's method of doing his work, but May LJ remarked, in *Viasystems*, that '"entire and absolute control" is not, at least since *Mersey Docks*, a necessary precondition of vicarious liability'.

In fact, whether the relevant legal test for dual vicarious liability should be the *degree of control* which both Permanent Employer and Temporary Employer exercised over the employee, or the *extent of integration* of the employee into both Employers' business, was an unsettled issue in

[86] [1826] 5 B&C 547, 108 ER 204, 209. [87] [2005] EWCA Civ 1151, [21], [39], [40], [46]–[49] (May LJ).

Viasystems. As noted by differently-constituted Courts of Appeal subsequently (in *Hawley v Luminar Leisure Ltd*[88] and *Biffa Waste*[89]), the two members of the Court of Appeal in *Viasystems*[90] did not agree upon the legal test which should govern an award of dual vicarious liability. May LJ relied on the control test (i.e., which employer had responsibility to prevent the negligent act from happening? Which one was entitled, or obliged, to give orders as to how the work should be done?). However, Rix LJ considered that the control test was only *one* factor in determining whether Permanent and Temporary Employers should share vicarious liability, and that the integration test was very important in the analysis (is the employee 'so much a part of the work, business or organisation of both employers that it is just to make both employers answer for his negligence?').

Applying May LJ's test, neither Darwell, the ducting contractors, nor CAT Metalwork Services who supplied Mr Strang and the fitter who was supervising him, had absolute control over Mr Strang, but both could exercise control over his negligent act (crawling through the duct when he should not have). Both the fitter (CAT's more senior employee) and Darwell's foreman who was supervising the installation of the ducting could have instructed Mr Strang as to where to move while the ducting work was ongoing. Also, Mr Strang was answerable to both his senior co-employee and to Darwell's foreman in his day-to-day routine. Applying Rix LJ's test, Mr Strang was both part of Darwell's team under the supervision of the foreman, and part of CAT Metalwork's small hired squad. Under both tests, dual vicarious liability for what happened at Viasystems' factory was appropriate.

However, in *Child Welfare Socy*,[91] Lord Phillips noted a clear preference for Rix LJ's adoption of the 'integration test' for dual vicarious liability – albeit that control will always be *a* factor in the analysis.

Some scenarios will suit dual vicarious liability better than others, as Rix LJ posited in *Viasystems*:[92]

The spectrum of possibilities for dual vicarious liability

no shift of VL possible ↑	it was 'tempting to think that liability will not be shared' in a *Mersey Docks*-type case – crane-driver was skilled, using the Harbour Board's crane, and it was a limited-duration secondment – i.e., Harbour Board was always the employer of the crane-driver
dual VL possible	where the employee is contracted-out labour, selected by a Permanent Employer, trained and hired out by that Employer, but employed at Temporary Employer's site, using Temporary Employer's equipment, and subject to Temporary Employer's directions, the situation will be borderline (e.g., *Timeplan Education Group Ltd v NUT;*[7] *and Child Welfare Socy*)
shift of VL very likely ↓	for a longstanding secondment – where an employee is seconded for a substantial period of time to Temporary Employer, 'to perform a role embedded in that employer's organisation' – VL is likely to shift entirely (as in *Hawley v Luminar Leisure Ltd*)

[88] [2006] EWCA Civ 18, [29]–[33]. [89] [2008] EWCA Civ 1257, [51]–[54].

[90] [2005] EWCA Civ 1151, [77]–[80] (only two members heard the case: May and Rix LJJ, oddly for such an important case, as noted in *Child Welfare Socy* [2012] UKSC 56, [39]).

[91] [2012] UKSC 56, [45]. [92] [2005] EWCA Civ 1151, [80].

A sparse usage of the dual vicarious liability doctrine was predicted in *Viasystems*, with May LJ stating that: '[a]n equal measure of control will not often arise.'[93]

> In *Hawley v Luminar Leisure Ltd*,[94] it was argued that the bouncer, Mr Warren (W), was shared between ASE Security Services (as Permanent Employer) and the Luminar club (as Temporary Employer) to such an extent that dual vicarious liability should apply. **Held:** only Temporary Employer was vicariously liable for the assault on C. Applying May LJ's control test, ASE had no immediate or effective control over the activities of W. If anyone was going to prevent W's behaving badly, it was Luminar's manager. ASE's sole role was to employ W in the first place, provide him as a doorman at the club, and pay his wages for as long as Luminar were happy to use his services. In all other respects, W answered to Luminar for his conduct at the club. Applying Rix LJ's integration test, the answer was the same. W was seconded to Luminar's club for as long as Luminar wanted: 'he had become embedded in Luminar's organisation ... He was no longer recognisable as an employee of ASE.'

Nevertheless, in *Child Welfare Socy*,[95] Lord Phillips noted that, 'arguably', *Hawley* could have justified a finding of dual vicarious liability. However, it is suggested that the result in *Hawley* was entirely correct. Even the integration test did not warrant a different outcome in the circumstances.

Allocating vicarious liability between each employer

§18.12 English law favours an equal division of liability between vicariously liable Employers, where dual vicarious liability applies.

On one view, a just and equitable division of liability between two vicariously liable employers, under s 1 of the Civil Liability (Contribution Act) 1978, must be equal. This division between Darwell and CAT Metalwork was applied in *Viasystems*[96] – May LJ called it 'close to a logical necessity', while Rix LJ emphatically stated that 'the responsibility of each employer, for the purposes of contribution, must be equal'.

Two reasons were given. First, since vicarious liability is a strict liability doctrine to transfer the burden of the wrongdoing from a culpable employee to an employer who is not personally at fault – how could two vicariously-liable employers be *innocent to different extents*? Secondly, if the relationship between the employers yields dual control, then 'it is highly likely that the measure of control will be equal, for otherwise the court would be unlikely to find dual control' (per May LJ).

Not every jurisdiction sees this result in the same way, however.

The comparative corner: A Canadian perspective

In *Blackwater v Plint*[97] (a 'residential schools' case, re alleged physical and sexual abuse at an Indian residential school in British Columbia in the 1940s–1960s), the SCC held that the Govt of Canada was 75% vicariously liable, and the United Church of Canada was 25% vicariously liable. Some of the Aboriginal children were taken from their families pursuant to the *Indian Act*, sent to the school, and repeatedly and brutally sexually assaulted by an

[93] [2005] EWCA Civ 1151, [47]. [94] [2006] EWCA Civ 18, quote at [85]. [95] [2012] UKSC 56, [46].
[96] [2005] EWCA Civ 1151, [50]–[53] (May LJ), [81]–[85] (Rix LJ).
[97] (2005), 258 DLR (4th) 275, [69]–[71] (McLachlin CJ, for the court), delivered 11 days after *Viasystems*.

employed dormitory supervisor. The uneven apportionment of vicarious liability was justified for two reasons: (1) notwithstanding that it is a no-fault doctrine, vicarious liability implies fault, and employers can display different levels of fault; and (2) the Govt employer was 'more senior' and had more control of training and supervision, and was in a better position than the Church to supervise the children and to prevent the abuse.

THE 'IN THE COURSE OF EMPLOYMENT' LIMB

The relevant tests

§18.13 An employer is only vicariously liable for the tort of his employee, where that tort was committed during the course of, or in the scope of, his employment. Either the *Salmond* test (whether the employee engaged in authorised work in unauthorised modes) or the *Lister* test (whether the tort of the employee was so closely connected to his employment that it would be fair, just and reasonable to hold the employer vicariously liable) may be applied.

The *Salmond* test

The *Salmond* test (named after the distinguished academic who proposed it[98]) has long been utilised under this element of vicarious liability. To paraphrase the test:

An employee's wrongful conduct is in the course of his employment where it consists of either:

i. a wrongful act authorised by the employer; or
ii. an improper and unauthorised mode of doing an act which the employer has authorised.

As Auld LJ observed in *Majrowski v Guy's and St Thomas's NHS Trust*,[99] category (i) is not vicarious liability at all, but rather, primary liability – if an employer authorises or ratifies a tort of an employee (or, indeed, of an independent contractor), then that employer has committed *its own wrong*, giving rise to *direct* liability (discussed later in the chapter). Only category (ii) is true vicarious liability.

At face value, were that second test to be applied to the abhorrent acts committed by the abusive warden in *Lister v Hesley Hall Ltd*,[100] then the employer ought not to have been vicariously liable – for the systematic serious sexual assault upon pupils within that warden's care could **never** have been an improper mode of doing what Hesley Hall, D, authorised as being part of the warden's duties at Axeholme House. Indeed, this was precisely the view adopted earlier by the Court of Appeal:

In *Trotman v North Yorkshire CC*,[101] a deputy headmaster sexually assaulted a mentally-handicapped student during a school field trip to Spain, during which they shared a bedroom. The council which operated the school, D, was sued for vicarious liability. **Held:** no vicarious liability. The assault was not an unauthorised mode of carrying out the teacher's duties on D's behalf; it was 'far removed' from any unauthorised mode for which D could have been vicariously liable.

[98] J Salmond, *Law of Torts* (1st edn, 1907) 83. [99] [2005] EWCA Civ 251, [28]–[29].
[100] [2001] UKHL 22, [2002] 1 AC 215. [101] [1999] BLGR 584 (CA) 591 (Butler-Sloss LJ).

However, in *Lister*, Hesley Hall *was* vicariously liable, *Trotman* was overruled, and the House of Lords propounded a new test of assessing whether an employee was 'acting in the course of his employment'.

The *Lister* test

The *Lister* House of Lords proposed the following 'close connection' test:

> The question is whether the [employee's] torts were so closely connected with his employment that it would be fair and just to hold the employer vicariously liable ... [and whether the tort was] inextricably interwoven with the carrying out by the [employee] of his duties.[102]

Adopted from the Canadian Supreme Court case of *Bazley v Curry*,[103] also concerning sexual abuse of a child by an employee, the result is that strict liability can be imposed on an employer – even when an employee's acts are criminal, and could not possibly have been, even impliedly, authorised. *Lister* was subsequently called a 'radical change' in the law's direction, by a differently-constituted House of Lords in *A v Hoare*.[104]

There were several reasons put forward in *Lister* for adopting this test.[105] First, the second limb of the Salmond test was ill-fitting to intentional wrongdoing by an employee. Secondly, the close connection test was intended to avoid 'terminological quibble' about 'unauthorised modes', and to allow for an 'intense focus' on the connection between the nature of the employment and the employee's tort. Thirdly, it was also necessary to ask, as a policy-driven enquiry, whether 'it is *just and reasonable* to hold the employers vicariously liable'. Finally, the deterrent rationale of vicarious liability would be supported by a positive finding against D to which the 'close connection' test gave rise – especially for those who conducted boarding schools, prisons, nursing homes, old people's homes, geriatric wards and residential homes for the young or vulnerable – because a finding of vicarious liability would encourage better employee management among those employers.

Certainly, in holding that heinous acts of sexual abuse were within the warden's course of employment, the House of Lords adopted an extremely 'broad approach'[106] to that question. It follows that pre-*Lister* decisions which adhered to the Salmond test may not be entirely safe indicators of whether the wrongdoing employee was acting in the course of his employment, were those particular scenarios to arise now.

Interestingly, the wider basis of recovery permitted by the 'close connection' test found vociferous opposition with the Irish Supreme Court which, in *O'Keeffe v Hickey*,[107] considered that invoking the *Lister* view should be left to the Irish legislature, and that the *Lister* test was judicially insupportable in any event:

The comparative corner: An Irish perspective

In *O'Keeffe v Hickey*, at least 21 girls were sexually abused by the principal at a Catholic school near Kinsale in County Cork. The principal pleaded guilty to sexual abuse in a criminal prosecution. **Held (4:1):** the State (which operated the school) was not vicariously liable.

[102] [2001] UKHL 22, [20], [28] (Lord Steyn), [41]–[42] (Lord Clyde), [82] (Lord Millett).

[103] [1999] 2 SCR 534, (1999) 174 DLR (4th) 45.

[104] [2008] UKHL 6, [2008] 1 AC 844, [22] (Lord Hoffmann).

[105] *Bernard v AG of Jamaica* [2004] UKPC 47, [18] (Lord Steyn).

[106] The term used in *Lister* [2001] UKHL 22, [42] (Lord Clyde, citing: *Trotman*, at [32]).

[107] [2008] IESC 72. By a 4:1 majority, the State employer was not vicariously liable (Geoghegan J dissented).

The following criticisms of the 'close connection' test were made by Hardiman J (a majority judge):

- the outcome in *Lister* was guided by a need to find for the abused victims, rather than by any clear policy or logic; and it is 'lacking in fundamental justice to impose liability on D simply because [he has a deep pocket]';
- *Lister* conflated personal and vicarious liability, by referring to vicarious liability together with a non-delegable personal duty, per Lord Hobhouse, e.g., 'The employers are liable for the employee's tortious act or omission because it is to him that the employers have entrusted the performance of their duty. The employers' liability to C is also that of a tortfeasor' – and yet, Hesley Hall was vicariously, not personally, liable;
- contrary to Lord Steyn's sentiment, the *Salmond* test was not the 'germ of the close connection test'; the only resemblance is that the word 'connection' is used in both tests;
- reliance upon *Rose v Plenty* to support the 'close connection' test was inappropriate, because, the milkman's wrongdoing there was done to further the employer's business, whereas the sexual abuse was an act of self-gratification, in no way performed in furtherance of Hesley Hall's business;
- the 'close connection' test lacked a principled basis, as reflected in the contrasting outcome in the two 1999 Canadian Supreme Court decisions of *Bazley v Curry* and *Jacobi v Griffiths* (from which the *Lister* court derived the 'close connection' test), which turned on very fine factual distinctions.

Further, Hardiman J considered that any change in the common law, of this significance, should be implemented by legislation, and not by judicial determination, for the following reasons:

- the changed test was 'entirely inconsistent with the established common law basis of liability';
- some of the policy considerations underlying the 'close connection' test (e.g., 'enterprise liability' and 'risk creation' on the part of public entities such as schools and voluntary associations) involved fundamental social and political questions, which were for Parliament to resolve;
- the changed test could represent an enormous burden to enterprises, charities and individuals, and possibly a 'terminal blow to voluntary charitable associations';
- it also moved the law towards 'universal insurance, whose merits were fundamentally a political question'; and
- the State would, in many cases, be the ultimate insurer of the vicariously-liable D.

Notably, the *Salmond* test has not lost its utility. However, it has been displaced, where the wrongdoing on the employee's part adopts an intentional and criminal flavour.

Tests which do *not* apply

§18.14 Vicarious liability will not be proven, merely because either: (1) some benefit accrued to the employer as a result of the employee's tort; or (2) the opportunity for the employee to commit the tort was created by the employment offered by the employer. Something more (i.e., some connection between the employee's tort, and what it is that the employee was engaged to do) is required.

In the 1867 case of *Barwick v English Joint Stock Bank*,[108] Willes J stated, as a necessary ingredient of vicarious liability, that 'the master is answerable for every such wrong of the servant or agent as is committed in the course of the service *and for the master's benefit*'.

However, in 1912, in *Lloyd v Grace Smith & Co*,[109] the House of Lords determined, in a 'breakthrough' case,[110] that an employee **could** act within the scope of his employment, even if the employer received no benefit from that employee's wrongdoing. The employer solicitor was innocent of any involvement in his employee clerk's fraud, and certainly derived no benefit from it, but was vicariously liable, nevertheless.

The modern position is thus set: whether the employer derived some benefit from the employee's wrongdoing is only one factor in the matrix. Some benefit to the employer may be 'cogent evidence' (per *Irving v Post Office*[111]) or a 'valuable indication' (per *Kooragang Investments Pty Ltd v R&W Ltd*[112]) that the employee was acting in the course of employment – but it is certainly not a pre-condition for vicarious liability in English law. There may be no benefit to employer D, and yet, still vicarious liability will be found.

Furthermore, an opportunity for the employee to commit the wrongdoing which was offered by the employment with D is not enough, *on its own*, for vicarious liability either. This point was reiterated in *Lister*, where Lord Millett said:

> the warden's duties provided him with the opportunity to commit indecent assaults on the boys for his own sexual gratification, but that in itself is not enough to make the school liable. The same would be true of the groundsman or the school porter [who worked where the boys resided]. But there was far more to it than that.[113]

In fact, a mere opportunity to commit the tort, provided by the employment, had never been sufficient to base vicarious liability in English law:

> In *Heasmans v Clarity Cleaning Co Ltd*,[114] Clarity Cleaning Co, D, had a contract to provide Heasmans, C, with office cleaning services. D's cleaner, Mr Bonsu, ran up a telephone bill of £1,400 on C's account by making unauthorised international calls. **Held:** D was not vicariously liable. Some nexus other than mere opportunity to commit the tort (conversion) was required between the act and his employment. In *Deatons Pty Ltd v Flew*,[115] a barmaid threw a glass of beer at a customer, C, who was rude to her, and the customer lost his eye. **Held:** the hotel owner, D, was not vicariously liable. The barmaid's action was 'an act of passion and resentment ... a spontaneous act of retributive justice', and that '[t]he occasion for administering it and the form it took may have arisen from the fact that she was a barmaid, but retribution was not within the scope of her employment as a barmaid'.

However, *Heasmans* would likely be decided differently today – if the cleaner was employed to clean the phone, and misused that property in some way, then that is likely to be viewed as a wrong that was committed in the course of the cleaner's employment (per Moore-Bick LJ in *Brink's Global Services Inc v Igrox Ltd*[116]).

[108] (1867) LR 2 Ex 259, 265. [109] [1912] AC 716 (HL).
[110] The term used by Lord Steyn to describe *Lloyd's* case in *Lister* [2001] UKHL 22, [17].
[111] [1987] IRLR 289 (CA). [112] [1982] AC 462 (PC) 473 (Lord Wilberforce).
[113] [2001] UKHL 22, [82], and also [45]. [114] [1987] ICR 949 (CA).
[115] (1949) 79 CLR 370 (HCA) [9] (Dixon J), which received explicit approval in *Irving v Post Office*.
[116] [2010] EWCA Civ 1207, [31].

In *Brink's v Igrox*, Brink's, C, contracted to transport 627 bars of silver, packed into wooden crates, from London to India, on behalf of a bank. (As bailee of the goods, C had a sufficient interest to sue for their loss.) The wooden pallets required fumigating for pests, prior to transport. The task was undertaken by two employees of Igrox, D. One of those employees, R, returned to the container during the fumigation, and stole 15 bars of silver, which were never recovered. **Held**: D was vicariously liable for the theft of the silver by R. That theft was committed by R during the course of employment. If a TV repairman can be acting in the course of employment if he steals the TV he is repairing (an example approved in *Lister*), then R was acting in the course too, when stealing the goods that were in a container that he was fumigating. He had to deal with the goods, secure them, access them, and seal them up again. There was a sufficiently close connection between R's theft of the silver and the purpose of his employment, to make it fair, just and reasonable that D should be vicariously liable for R's actions.

Some difficult scenarios

Whether the employee's wrongdoing is to be regarded as being within the scope of his employment – or a 'frolic of his own'[117] for which the employer will not be vicariously liable – can be difficult to assess. Pedantic distinctions and inconsistencies abound. It is hard not to agree with the comment of one judge that '[o]ne is constantly surprised at reading the facts of a reported case and jumping ahead, as one will, to guessing the answer that the court gave; in no field has it proved more surprising than in this' (per *Harrison v Michelin Tyre Co Ltd*[118]). Even the House of Lords ('many of the reported cases are decisions which have turned essentially upon their own circumstances'[119]) and the Privy Council ('these cases have given rise to a number of fine distinctions, the courts in some cases struggling to find liability, in others to avoid it'[120]) have admitted that drawing a coherent thread from the decisions can be difficult.

This section canvasses some of the scenarios which pose particular difficulties in vicarious liability under this limb, 'in the course of employment'.

§18.15 An employee may (depending upon all the facts and circumstances) be acting within the scope of his employment, even where the employee:

- was specifically instructed by the employer as to what was prohibited or disallowed conduct – and the employee deliberately disobeyed those instructions, injuring C;
- acted with gross negligence;
- committed some intentional criminal wrongdoing;
- committed the tort during a meal or other break from work;
- committed the tort whilst travelling to/from his place of employment;
- committed a one-off prank and engaged in skylarking behaviour – although personal malevolence and maliciousness by an employee toward C will usually preclude any finding of vicarious liability on the employer's part;
- committed the tort remotely in time and place from the employer's premises.

[117] An expression used by Diplock LJ in *Morris v CW Martin & Sons Ltd* [1966] 1 QB 716 (CA) 733.

[118] [1985] ICR 696 (QB) 699 (Comyn J).

[119] *Lister v Hesley Hall Ltd* [2001] UKHL 22, [41] (Lord Clyde).

[120] *Kooragang Investments Pty Ltd v Richardson and Wrench Ltd* [1982] AC 462 (PC) (on appeal from HCA) 473.

Dealing briefly with each in turn:

Acting contrary to an employer's express prohibition/instruction

However counter-intuitive it may seem, an employee's acts or omissions which directly contravene or disobey an employer's instructions and commands may still render that employer vicariously liable.

In some cases, vicarious liability only attached where the employee's contraventions of express prohibitions or instructions promoted the interests of his employer, or advanced or assisted the employer's business. However, given the relaxation on that requirement (per *Lloyd* in 1912, discussed above), the search for some benefit accruing to the employer is no longer strictly required. Nevertheless, it may assist a finding of vicarious liability – whereas if the employee ignored an instruction, and his act garnered for the employer no benefit at all, then vicarious liability may fail:

> In *Rose v Plenty*,[121] Mr Plenty was employed by a grocery company, D, as a milkman, to distribute milk, collect the money, and bring back the bottles. D's notice at the milk depot stated: 'Children and young persons must not in any circumstances be employed by you in the performance of your duties'. However, Mr Plenty allowed Leslie Rose, C, 13, to ride the float, take the milk bottles up the customers' doors, collect the money, and bring the empties back to the float. Mr Plenty paid C to assist him with his round. Whilst riding on the float, C broke his leg when Mr Plenty drove the float too close to the kerb. **Held:** D was vicariously liable. C was doing the precise duties of the milkman himself, and hence, Mr Plenty's wrongdoing furthered D's business: '[t]he decisive point was that it was not done by the servant for his own purposes, but for his master's purposes'. In *Irving v Post Office*,[122] Mr and Mrs Irving, C, who were Jamaican, were neighbours to their postman, Mr Edwards. The postman's duties included sorting the mail, and he was authorised by the Post Office, D, to write upon letters to ensure that they were properly dealt with, but forbidden from writing on mail for any other reason. The neighbours did not get on, and had a history of (parking and other) disputes. Mr Edwards saw an envelope addressed to C, and wrote on the back of the envelope, 'Go back to Jamaica Sambo', and added a cartoon of a smiling mouth and eyes. C were highly upset by the offensive communication, and sought damages from D for Mr Edwards' racial abuse. **Held:** D was not vicariously liable, even though the postman did it while on duty, during work hours, and at D's premises. Among other things, the misconduct was not done for D's benefit.

However, the cases are difficult to reconcile. Even if the employee was assisting the employer's enterprise, in contravening a prohibition, the employer may not be vicariously liable:

> In *Iqbal v London Transport Executive*,[123] Mr Carberry was a bus conductor, and was forbidden by his employer, London Transport Executive, D, from driving a bus under any circumstances. Mr Iqbal, C, a bus driver, was preparing to head off on a run, but exit from the garage was blocked by another bus. Mr Carberry was requested to find an engineer to move the offending bus, but instead, he hopped on board and attempted to move the bus himself. He had never driven a bus before, and was unable

[121] [1976] 1 WLR 141 (CA) 143 (Denning LJ). Also: *Limpus v London General Omnibus Co* (1862) 158 ER 993 (Exch) 999–1000; *Ilkiw v Samuels* [1963] 1 WLR 911 (CA).

[122] [1987] IRLR 289 (CA) (decided under s 32(1) of the Race Relations Act 1976, but on this point, the common law is consistent). Also: *Conway v George Wimpey & Co Ltd* [1951] 2 KB 266 (CA) 276; *Twine v Bean's Express Ltd* [1946] 1 All ER 202 (CA) 204.

[123] (1973) 16 KIR 329 (CA).

to stop the bus moving forward. C was crushed between buses, and was seriously injured. **Held:** D was not vicariously liable for the conductor's negligence, because he acted outside the course of employment: 'driving buses was no part of his work as a conductor'.

Given that Mr Carberry was attempting to help out D's interests by getting the bus underway, Denning LJ noted later, in *Rose v Plenty*, that *Iqbal* 'seems to be out of line, and should be regarded as decided on its own special circumstances'.[124] In any event, as noted above, searching for some benefit accruing to D's business is no longer strictly necessary, for vicarious liability to apply.

Acting with gross negligence

Where the employee commits some gross negligence (in the sense of both (i) a grave departure from the standard of reasonable care, and (ii) imputing recklessness to the employee as to the consequences of his actions), that does not necessarily take his conduct outside the scope of his employment.

The following employers were vicariously liable for the grave carelessness of their employees:

In *Kay v ITW Ltd*,[125] employee Mr Ord had to return a fork-lift truck to the warehouse where he worked for ITW, D. A delivery lorry was in the way, situated on a ramp, and was left in reverse gear because of the slope. To move the lorry out of the way, Mr Ord got into the lorry cabin, and started its engine, without giving any warning to those behind. The lorry rolled backwards, seriously injuring D's chief storekeeper, C. This employee's behaviour was 'most blameworthy conduct', but it was not 'so gross and extreme as to take the act outside what he was employed to do. It is perhaps a question of degree'. In *Century Ins Co Ltd v Northern Ireland Road Transport Board*,[126] employee Mr Davison, a petrol tanker driver, lit a cigarette and threw away the lit match, whilst the petrol was flowing from the tanker to the garage's storage tank. When a fire erupted at the manhole to the storage tank, instead of turning off the tanker's stopcock as urgently requested, Mr Davison jumped into the tanker and drove off, causing petrol to escape from the tanker and delivery hose. The fire followed the petrol trail, the tanker itself violently exploded, and a car and several nearby houses were damaged. The case was later judicially cited as an example of no matter how 'improper the manner' of the employee's negligence, vicarious liability may ensue for the employer,[127] and as an instance of 'where the word "frolic" is an understatement: I would have thought [that the employee was engaged] on a "madness" of his own'.[128]

Torts that amount to criminal wrongdoing

Prior to *Lister*, it had already been established that an employer could be vicariously liable for an employee's criminal wrongdoing, e.g., the fraud in *Lloyd v Grace, Smith & Co*,[129] and the conversion in *Morris v CW Martin & Sons Ltd*.[130] As a result (and notwithstanding the decision in *Trotman*), Lord Steyn noted, in *Lister*, that English law 'no longer struggles with the concept of vicarious liability for intentional wrongdoing'.[131]

However, the 'close connection' test proposed in *Lister*, 'tells one nothing about the nature of that connection' (as Lord Phillips put it, in *Child Welfare Socy*[132]). It requires the court to

[124] [1976] 1 WLR 141 (CA) 144. [125] [1968] 1 QB 140 (CA) 154 (Sellers LJ). [126] [1942] AC 509 (HL).

[127] *Hilton v Thomas Burton (Rhodes) Ltd* [1961] 1 WLR 705 (Manchester Assizes) 707 (Diplock J).

[128] *Harrison v Michelin Tyre Co Ltd* [1985] ICR 696 (QB) 700–1 (Comyn J).

[129] [1912] 1 AC 716 (HL). [130] [1966] 1 QB 716 (CA). [131] [2001] UKHL 22, [20]. [132] [2012] UKSC 56, [74].

scrutinise the relevant connection between the employee's tort, and the nature of the employee's duties of employment. So, legally speaking, how **does** C establish the test? In *Lister*, the following factors were used to establish a close connection between the warden's employment and his torts of battery and assault, and so establish vicarious liability on the part of Hesley Hall, D:

i. **The time and place when the employee's tort occurred:** the acts of sexual abuse were committed during the hours for which the warden was responsible for the boys, and on D's premises (Lord Steyn);
ii. **The particular duties entrusted to the employee:** D entrusted the care of the children in Axeholme House to the warden (e.g., allocating pocket money, arranging outings, supervising school work, acting as a *loco parentis* figure to the boys), and the sexual abuse was inextricably interwoven with the carrying out by the warden of those duties (Lord Steyn). The warden abused the 'special position' in which the school had placed him to enable it to discharge its own responsibilities for the care of the boys (Lord Millett). The opportunity to be at the boarding house (say, as a gardener or a porter) would not, in itself, constitute a sufficient connection between the warden's abuse and his employment, but the very position of warden, and the close contact with the boys which that work involved, created a sufficient connection between the acts of abuse and the work which Mr Grain had been employed to do (Lord Clyde);
iii. **Creation of inherent risks in D's business:** where the employee's torts fell precisely within the inherent risks of wrongdoing that D's business created, then that 'enterprise risk' assisted a finding of a close connection. It was known, via experience, that boarding schools, along with prisons, nursing homes, old people's or children's homes, etc, carried an inherent risk that indecent assaults on the residents could be committed by those who exercised authority in those establishments – and the warden's assaults fell precisely within that band of known inherent risk (Lord Millett);
iv. **The employer itself owed a duty of reasonable care to C:** D fell into that class of case (together with prisons, hospitals, and occupiers of land) where the institution itself was in a special relationship with C directly, such that it owed C specific duties of care. Here, D had to take reasonable steps to safeguard pupils in their physical, moral and educational development. In that scenario, said Lord Hobhouse,[133] '[t]he liability of the employers is a *vicarious* liability because the actual breach of duty is that of the employee. The employee is a tortfeasor', but D's vicarious liability, 'derives from their voluntary assumption of the relationship towards [Lister, as pupil] and the duties that arise from that relationship and their choosing to entrust the performance of those duties to [warden Mr Grain].' (Note, however, the strong condemnation of this reasoning in *O'Keeffe*, as confusing vicarious liability with personal non-delegable duties of care owed by an employer, discussed above.)

Various post-*Lister* cases have thrown up extra factors that also assist to prove the 'close connection' test:

v. **The employee's act (albeit undesirable) was expressly contemplated by employer D:** Where contractual terms between employer D and its wrongdoing employee envisaged that the wrongdoing might occur, then when it does, and C is injured, it is one factor pointing to a 'close connection' between the employee's tort and the nature of his duties.

133 [2001] UKHL 22, [55] (original emphasis).

In *Gravil v Redruth Rugby Football Club Ltd*,[134] second-rower Mr Carroll threw a punch at prop forward Mr Gravil, C, following a scrum in a rugby union match. As a result, C suffered a blow-out fracture of the right orbit; the injury required extensive reconstructive surgery. **Held:** Mr Carroll's employer, the Redruth Rugby Club, D, was vicariously liable. The contract between Mr Carroll and Redruth Rugby Club provided that he should 'abide by the rules of the game', and should not physically assault an opponent, and what the ramifications of a yellow or a red card might be. These contractual terms helped to show the requisite close connection.

vi. The opportunities for assault arose frequently during the course of employment: Again, in *Gravil*, it was held that the melee involving Mr Carroll and Mr Gravil was 'of the kind which frequently occurred during rugby matches', the 'kind of thing that both clubs would have expected to occur', and which 'can fairly be regarded as an ordinary (though undesirable) incident of a rugby match'.[135] It was by no means a unique, odd, or unforeseeable event. This assisted with a finding of 'close connection'. Similarly, if the employee's job is to 'keep order', then the risk of a tort being committed is higher than if the employee's interaction with the customer is much more restricted. It will be a matter of fact and of degree:

In *Mattis v Pollock (t/as Flamingo's Nightclub)*,[136] Mr Cranston was a doorman employed at a nightclub in London, owned and operated by Mr Pollock, D. One night, Mr Cranston ejected various people from the club, was hit with a bottle and assaulted by patrons, and then chased by 4–5 patrons. He went back to his flat nearby, and returned armed with a knife. He stabbed patron Mr Mattis, C, in the upper left back, severing his spinal cord and causing paraplegia. **Held:** D was vicariously liable for the assault. The doorman was employed to keep order and discipline at the nightclub, and D encouraged and expected him to perform his duties in an aggressive and intimidatory manner, which could include the physical manhandling of patrons. In *Mohamud v WM Morrison Supermarkets plc*,[137] Ahmed Mohamud, C, of Somali descent, visited Morrisons, D's, petrol station in Birmingham, and asked D's employee, Mr Khan, K, whether he could print off some documents from his USB stick at the kiosk which served as a small convenience store attached to D's petrol station. K abused C, and then followed him out and viciously attacked him on the petrol station forecourt. **Held:** D was not vicariously liable. K was not engaged to enter into any form of confrontation with a customer, angry or placid. This was distinguishable from *Mattis*, as there was an additional element there, *viz*, to maintain order. That was not K's role within D's organisation – and the law had not reached the stage where the 'mere fact of contact between a sales assistant and a customer, which was plainly authorised by an employer' D, could fix D with vicarious liability.

vii. At the time of the tort, the employee represented that he was acting as an employee: If the employee's assaults on C were committed at a time when that employee was ostensibly acting in his capacity as D's employee, using the accoutrements of that employment (e.g., uniform, equipment, etc), then that will assist with a finding of 'close connection'.

In *Bernard v AG of Jamaica*,[138] Mr Bernard, C, had an altercation with a police officer, PC Morgan, about the use of a phone at the central sorting office in Kingston, Jamaica. PC Morgan pulled out his service revolver and fired at C, rendering him unconscious. When C awoke in the hospital casualty department, he was arrested by PC Morgan for allegedly assaulting a police officer, and handcuffed

[134] [2008] EWCA Civ 689, [24] (also known as: *Gravil v Carroll*). [135] *ibid*, [4], [23].
[136] [2003] EWCA Civ 887, [2003] 1 WLR 2158. [137] [2014] EWCA Civ 116, [37], [49].
[138] [2004] UKPC 47.

to his bed. Criminal charges against C were later withdrawn. **Held:** the AG was vicariously liable for PC Morgan's assault, false imprisonment and malicious prosecution. The shooting followed immediately upon his announcement that he was a policeman, which created the impression that he was on police business when demanding the use of the phone; and in the hospital, he claimed that C had interfered with his execution of his duties as a policeman. In *Weir v CC of Merseyside Police*,[139] an off-duty policeman assisting his girlfriend to move house was told by her that youths, including Mr Weir, C, were rummaging amongst her belongings outside her new flat. The policeman told C to leave. When he did not, the police officer assaulted him, threw him down the stairs at the block of flats, and locked him in the police van he had borrowed to help with his girlfriend's move. **Held:** the CC was vicariously liable for the police officer's assault. The policeman had been apparently exercising his authority as a police officer, confirmed to C that he was a police officer, and said to C that he was taking him to the police station in the police van – which meant that he was acting in the course of employment, 'albeit one who was behaving very badly'. In *Maga v Trustees of the Birmingham Archdiocese*,[140] the abusive priest wore his clerical garb when he met C, a young boy who assisted the priest in cleaning and other activities in the presbytery, as part of a youth work programme, etc. **Held:** vicarious liability proven. The moral authority conveyed by the clerical garb assisted to prove a close connection. Also, D had encouraged the priest to engage in community youth work, as part of the evangelical purpose of the Church, to bring the gospel to non-Roman Catholics (of whom C was one). C came to a disco which the priest arranged on Church premises, and helped to clean up afterwards, drawing C into a relationship via a Church-organised function.

However, this factor is not conclusive (as a policeman's conduct in *N v CC of Merseyside Police*,[141] discussed below) demonstrated. Even where ostensibly acting in his capacity as an employee, by wearing the uniform and by stating that he would take C to a police station, no vicarious liability attached there.

viii. **The known vulnerability of C, which the employee could exploit:** The children in *Lister*, of course, were highly-vulnerable and with educational and emotional needs – but it was in *Child Welfare Socy* that this factor was really emphasised, as assisting to prove the close connection test: 'Living cloistered on the school premises were vulnerable boys. They were triply vulnerable. They were vulnerable because they were children in a school; they were vulnerable because they were virtually prisoners in the school; and they were vulnerable because their personal histories made it even less likely that if they attempted to disclose what was happening to them they would be believed'.[142] Similarly, in *JGE*, the fact that C was a girl of 6 who was placed in a children's home for two years away from her family, helped to find a close connection between the organisation which was responsible for the abusive priest, and the torts which he committed against C.[143]

ix. **A benefit accrued to the employer from the wrongdoer's tort:** It will be recalled that proving some benefit to employer D from the employee's tort is not a pre-requisite for vicarious liability. However, where the wrongful act may have advanced D's aims as employer, then this factor may assist to find a close connection.

In *Cox v MOJ*,[144] facts previously, **held:** the MOJ was vicariously liable for the prisoner's negligence. The work carried out by prisoners, in assisting with the preparation of meals for other prisoners,

139 [2003] EWCA Civ 111 (also known as: *Weir v Bettison*).
140 [2010] EWCA Civ 256, [45].
141 [2006] EWHC 3041 (QB).
142 [2012] UKSC 56, [92].
143 [2012] EWCA Civ 938, [74].
144 [2014] EWCA Civ 132, [45].

relieved the MOJ from engaging employees at market rates of pay, and their assistance in the kitchen was clearly done for the MOJ's benefit, to defray the expense to the state caused by prisons. In *Mohamud v Morrisons*, facts previously, **held:** no vicarious liability applied. Mr Khan's confrontation with C did not advance D's aims at all, because it was no part of K's duties to maintain order or to pacify customers.

Meal and other breaks

Obviously the employee is not actually engaged in work during meal or smoking breaks, but is usually paid by the employer for that time nevertheless. It is difficult to draw any bright-line rule in this scenario. Inconsistencies again abound. Any wrongdoing slightly out of the break may not amount to 'acting in the course of employment', even if it happened on employer D's premises –

In *R v Industrial Injuries Commr, ex p Amalgamated Engineering Union (No 2)*,[145] a fitter in a factory, C, went to a smoking booth during the tea-break (10.30–10.40 am) to have a cigarette. It was occupied, so he squatted down beside the booth to wait, chatted to a colleague, and at 10.45 am, was struck and seriously injured by a fork-lift truck being negligently driven. C claimed injury benefits, which depended on his being injured 'in the course of his employment'. **Held:** C had taken himself temporarily out of the course of his employment because he stayed smoking 'long after' the tea-break had ended. His 'casual behaviour' in extending the tea break, so as to make it at least half as long again, could not be seen as within the scope of his employment.

– whereas a tort during a meal break, remote from the employer's premises, *can* be 'in the course':

In *Harvey v RG O'Dell*,[146] Mr Harvey, C, and Mr Galway were engaged by their employer, D, a building firm, to repair a fence. For their lunch break, they drove to Maidenhead to get a meal. On their way back to the site, and due to G's negligent driving, G was killed, and C was seriously injured. **Held:** G was acting in the course of his employment, during the meal break, as the journey to get lunch was fairly incidental to their work. It was an all-day repair job; no instructions were given by the employer that the men should take food with them; and the travelling time to/from Maidenhead counted as working time.

Journeys to/from, or between, work premises

In *Smith v Stages*,[147] Lord Lowry stated that the 'paramount rule is that an employee travelling on the highway will be acting in the course of his employment if, and only if, he is at the material time going about his employer's business. One must not confuse the duty to turn up for one's work with the concept of already being "on duty" while travelling to it'. Paraphrasing some of his Lordship's propositions as follows:

i. an employee travelling from home to his regular workplace, and then back again, even if the transport is provided by the employer, is not on duty and is not acting in the course of his employment – but if he is *required* by his contract of employment to use the employer's transport, the position is normally reversed;
ii. travelling in the employer's time between workplaces (one of which may be the regular workplace), or in the course of a roving job, will be in the course of the employment;

[145] [1966] 2 QB 31 (CA) 48. [146] [1958] 2 QB 78. [147] [1989] AC 928 (HL) 955–56.

iii. the fact that the employee may have discretion as to the mode and time of travelling will not take the journey out of the course of employment;
iv. an employee travelling in the employer's time from his home to a workplace other than his regular workplace, or to the scene of an emergency (such as a fire, accident or mechanical breakdown of plant), will be acting in the course of his employment;
v. any detours or interruptions of a journey undertaken in the course of employment may take the employee out of the course of his employment.

Again, though, the relevant cases show mixed (even irreconcilable?) outcomes, sometimes turning on the most pedantic of distinctions. Some trips to work will give rise to vicarious liability, but some may not, even where the journey was on the employer's land itself. To provide a small sample:

In *Compton v McClure*,[148] a factory employer, D, imposed a speed limit (5 mph) on a road leading from the factory gates to a workers' car-park. An employee was running late for his afternoon shift, and to try to clock on in time, he drove over 5 mph and on the wrong side of the road. He hit Mr Compton, C, whose leg was injured. **Held:** D was vicariously liable. By entering the gates to clock on for work, its employee was there for the purposes of D's business: the factory gates were 'the least artificial place at which to draw the line'. It would have been different if, say, the employee was returning for the purposes of collecting a forgotten coat. In *Smith v Stages*, Mr Machin, C, and Mr Stages were employed by Darlington Insulation Co Ltd, D, to install insulation at power stations. They usually worked on a power station in the Midlands, but were sent to carry out an urgent job on a power station in Wales. They were paid eight hours' pay for the travelling time to Wales and back, as well as the equivalent of the rail fare for the journey (although no stipulation was made as to the mode of travel). They worked for 24 hours straight without a break at the end of the week, in order to finish the job. On the return journey to the Midlands, their car, driven by Mr Stages, crashed, and C was seriously injured (and died prior to trial). **Held:** D was vicariously liable. Since the employees had been paid by D while driving back to the Midlands, which was their usual place of employment, they had been travelling in D's time. In *Meek v British Rwys Board*,[149] Mr Meek, C, a train driver employed by D, saw a figure on the tracks ahead of him (which turned out to be his colleague, Mr Murray). Despite applying the emergency brake (at 55 mph), C hit Mr Murray, and subsequently found dismembered parts of Mr Murray along the track. C suffered depression after the accident. **Held:** D was not vicariously liable for Mr Murray's negligence (in not wearing a high visibility vest, or having his torch with him, and for being in the path of the train in an unauthorised spot on the main line). Mr Murray had finished his shift early and was authorised to leave work, and was crossing the track about 40 yards from the authorised short-cut route for rail-workers. He was using an unauthorised deviation (albeit on D's land, and albeit only a matter of yards from the designated safe-route), and was on a 'frolic of his own', with tragic consequences.

Employees 'skylarking' around

It will be evident from 'Employers' liability' (an online chapter) that there is a personal duty on the employer to provide competent staff. If an employee engages in repeated skylarking and practical jokes upon co-employees, including C, then the employer may be in breach of that personal duty of care, and hence, be *directly* liable to C (as occurred in *Hudson v Ridge*

[148] [1975] ICR 378 (QB) 379, quote at 388. [149] QB, Park J, 15 Dec 1983.

Manufacturing Co Ltd[150]). Whether that employer can also be *vicariously* liable for any skylarking which its employees engage in towards each other is, of course, a different question.

Behaviour that constituted one-off instances of 'pranks' or 'practical jokes' and which injure C has given rise to cases that are difficult to reconcile, and again, seems to turn on pedantic distinctions. Sometimes 'wicked' acts were **not** done in the course of employment, meaning no vicarious liability was possible –

> In *Smith v Crossley Bros*,[151] a young apprentice employee of D's approached Master Smith, C, 16, another apprentice, from behind, in D's workroom, and placed a compressed air pipe near his bottom and signalled to a third apprentice to turn on the compressed air. C's colon was ruptured, causing serious injury. The wilful misbehaviour of these two 'wicked' and 'malevolent' apprentices constituted a 'frolic of their own'. In *McCready v Securicor Ltd*,[152] Mr McCready, C, an employee of Securicor, D, got into a trolley (usually used to transport coinage and banknotes from D's security vans into D's vaults) as a joke, whilst a fellow employee pushed him around the office in it, and then into the vault. C's hand was crushed by the door of the vault during the skylarking. C argued that his colleague's task was to close the vault door at night or if an emergency arose during the day, so the fact that he closed it at an inappropriate time onto C's hand did not mean that he had gone outside the course of his employment, but that did not prevail; this skylarking was a 'frolic of their own'.

– whereas some pranks and practical jokes *have* been held to be in the course of employment:

> In *Harrison v Michelin Tyre Co Ltd*,[153] an employee, S, was pushing a truck at Michelin's, D's, tyre factory, when as a joke, he turned his truck deliberately into Mr Harrison's, C's, machine. C fell off the duck-board, and was injured. This horseplay by S was not 'a frolic of his own'. In *Chapman v Oakleigh Animal Products Ltd*,[154] Master Chapman, C, 16, was employed by Oakleigh, D, during his school holiday to assist in the grinding shed. As a practical joke, co-employee G and others asked C to put his hand into the spout of a mincing machine to clear an alleged blockage, his hand being smaller than theirs. The idea was that ground ice would be sprayed at C through the spout as a surprise, but when C's hand was up the spout between the rotor blades, G accidentally turned on the machine, and C's hand was badly injured. G's act in pressing the switch was not done to further the practical joke, but was accidental, so it was within the scope of his employment.

However, where D's conduct has gone well beyond skylarking – in that it was motivated out of real spite or malevolence – then English case law has fairly consistently precluded vicarious liability, on the basis that the act was not 'in the course of employment':

> In *Irving v Post Office*,[155] where the postman drew a racially-offensive message and cartoon on Mr and Mrs Irving's mail, there was no vicarious liability, because it was an 'act of private spite'. In *AG of British Virgin Islands v Hartwell*,[156] where the police officer abandoned his post, improperly took a police revolver, travelled to another island, and fired indiscriminately into the bar in which his girlfriend worked, injuring Mr Hartwell, that could not give rise to vicarious liability, because he was on a 'vendetta of his own'. In *Weddall v Barchester Healthcare Ltd*,[157] a senior health assistant at D's care home was telephoned at home by Mr Weddall, C, the deputy manager, and asked to fill in for a night shift because someone had called in sick. He took the request badly, thinking that C was

[150] [1957] 2 QB 348. [151] (1951) 95 SJ 655 (CA).
[152] [1991] NI 229 (CA). Also: *Hunter v Dept for Regional Development for Northern Ireland* [2008] NIQB 88.
[153] [1985] ICR 696 (QB). [154] (1970) 8 KIR 1063 (CA). [155] [1987] IRLR 289 (CA) 292 (Sheldon LJ).
[156] [2004] UKPC 12, [2004] 1 WLR 1273, [17] (Lord Nicholls). [157] [2012] EWCA Civ 25, [45].

mocking him because he was drunk, and rode his bicycle to the care home and violently attacked C. No vicarious liability arose, as the attacker was acting personally for his own reasons, and he used the request for him to fill in as a pretext for an act of violence against C.

Outside working hours and/or remote from the employer's work premises

A tort committed outside of work hours and/or remote from the employer's premises may contribute to a finding of no vicarious liability. As Lord Clyde remarked in *Lister*, '[t]hat an act was committed outside the hours of employment may well point to it being outside the scope of the employment'.[158]

In *N v CC of Merseyside Police*,[159] N, a nightclub patron, was carried out of the club very drunk. T, a probationer police constable, was sitting in his own car outside the club, still wearing his full uniform. He had been off-duty for two hours, and was out of the area where he worked. T told the club's concerned personnel that he would take N to the police station, and identified himself to N as 'the police'. Instead, he took N to his own home, and raped and indecently assaulted her while she was unconscious, and filmed those assaults. **Held**: T's employer was not vicariously liable. T was 'on the prowl', to find a vulnerable woman near a club, whilst off-duty, and he had merely used his uniform and position as a police officer as the opportunity to commit the assaults. In the **Canadian** case of *Jacobi v Griffiths*,[160] an employee (the programme director) of a non-profit Boys' and Girls' Club (a children's club) sexually abused a brother and sister. **Held** (4:3): the employer was not vicariously liable. In all but one instance, the abuse occurred in the employee's home – remote from the club itself – and outside working hours. That established a much weaker connection than in *Bazley v Curry* (where a close connection had been met). The employee was able to establish his own 'bait' of home attractions, away from the club itself.

On the other hand, remoteness in time or place from one's employment may *still* render one's employer vicariously liable, depending upon all the circumstances:

In *Weir v CC of Merseyside Police*,[161] facts previously, where an off-duty policeman was assisting his girlfriend to move house when he assaulted C, vicarious liability did attach, and the 'close connection' test was proven.

Hence, no bright-line dividing line is possible to draw in this category either.

It is evident that, quite apart from the difficulties associated with an employee's committing a criminal wrongdoing against C, there are numerous other instances where the courts have struggled to maintain a clear concept of what it means to 'act in the course of one's employment'.

EXCEPTIONAL CASES: AN EMPLOYER *CAN* BE VICARIOUSLY LIABLE FOR THE TORTS OF ITS INDEPENDENT CONTRACTOR

The general rule that an employer is vicariously liable for the torts of its employees, but not for those committed by its independent contractor (or by the employees of that contractor), is rooted in policy. The employer has no control over the manner in which its independent

[158] [2001] UKHL 22, [44]. Also: *Kay v ITW Ltd* [1968] 1 QB 140 (CA) 154. [159] [2006] EWHC 3041 (QB).
[160] [1999] 2 SCR 570, (1999), 174 DLR (4th) 71, delivered the same day as the companion case, *Bazley v Curry*.
[161] [2003] EWCA Civ 111, [2003] ICR 708, 712.

contractor carries out his work, and hence, it would be unfair to impose vicarious liability upon that employer (per *Rowe v Herman*[162]).

However, there are some *exceptional* circumstances where the employer **will** be liable – either directly or vicariously – for the torts committed by an independent contractor. The diagram illustrates:

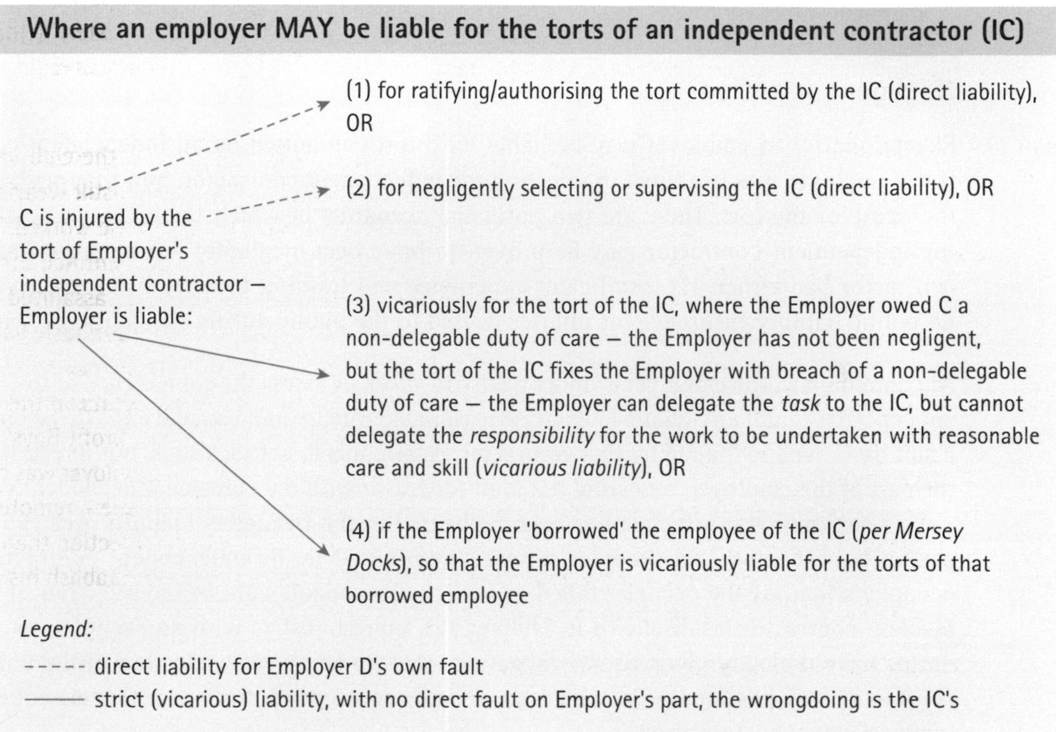

Dealing with each exceptional case in turn:

Ratification or authorisation

§18.16 Exceptionally, an employer may be liable for a tort committed by an independent contractor if the employer expressly authorised or ratified that tort.

Ratification/authorisation imputes direct liability on the employer's part. Both employer and independent contractor will be joint tortfeasors if that occurs (per *Ellis v Sheffield Gas Consumers' Co*[163]).

This basis for liability tends to be extremely fact-specific, and strong evidence that employer D knew of the act of the independent contractor, and authorised it, is necessary, to render D liable.

In *Jolliffe v Willmett & Co*,[164] Mr Jolliffe had separated from his wife, and Mrs Jolliffe was represented by solicitors' firm Willmett & Co. Mrs Jolliffe wished to sue for divorce, and required (in those days, 1968) evidence of adultery on her husband's part. Willmett & Co instructed Mr Hearne (H) as

[162] (1997) 58 Con LR 33 (CA) 38. [163] (1853) 17 JP 823, 118 ER 955 (KB). [164] [1971] 1 All ER 478 (QB).

the enquiry agent. H visited the flat where both Mr Jolliffe and his part-time secretary lived, to seek corroboration of adultery, gained access to the flat, and became involved in a fight with Mr Jolliffe. Mr Jolliffe alleged that H had trespassed on his property and assaulted him, and that his wife's law firm had authorised and ratified these torts by H as independent contractor. **Held**: no ratification occurred. The solicitor had told H not to visit Mr Jolliffe's premises, did not know H was going to the flat, and would never have condoned entry to the flat (having already written to H that: 'a direct approach would be useless, as only stealth and cunning ... are likely to serve in this case').

Negligent selection

§18.17 Exceptionally, an employer may be liable for a tort committed by an independent contractor, if the employer was negligent in selecting the independent contractor, and that negligence was the cause of the tort. There are two particular scenarios in which the employer's selection of the independent contractor *may* be proven to have been negligent – where the independent contractor had either: (1) insufficient experience and training to carry out the activity; or (2) no public liability insurance for injuries caused to the public during the course of the activity.

At common law, the employer is under a duty to check or assess the competence of the independent contractor; and any failure to exercise reasonable care in doing so will expose the employer to a suit by C, who is injured by that contractor. Again, this is not vicarious, but direct, liability on the part of the employer, rendering it a joint tortfeasor with the culpable independent contractor.

This common law principle has been replicated in the Occupiers Liability Act 1957, by imposing liability upon **an occupier** for torts committed by its independent contractor on the occupier's land, if the occupier failed to exercise reasonable care in the selection of the independent contractor (as discussed in Chapter 12). Indeed, just as with an occupier, two key scenarios have typically given rise to allegations that an employer's selection of the independent contractor was negligent, *viz*, where the independent contractor was either ill-equipped and inexperienced; or uninsured.

The allegation: 'the independent contractor had inadequate training/experience'

§18.18 A breach on the part of the employer, by engaging an independent contractor who had inadequate training/experience, will be easier to establish where the particular activity was hazardous or posed a real risk of harm to the public.

To defeat this type of allegation, the employer may point to the following sort of evidence – that it:

i. checked up on the quality and reliability of the independent contractor by word of mouth enquiries – e.g., in *Jolliffe v Willmett & Co*,[165] the law firm was not negligent in selecting Mr Hearne as enquiry agent, as he had come recommended by their usual enquiry agents, who themselves were very competent and reputable;
ii. followed up references about the independent contractor, and/or was justifiably reassured by prior experiences with that independent contractor – e.g., in *Naylor (t/as Mainstreet) v Payling*,[166] the employer nightclub owner had selected the contractor who provided security services at its nightclub with reasonable care, because the employer had satisfied itself that the contractor's security men were properly accredited under a local authority's licensing scheme, plus the employer

[165] [1971] 1 All ER 478 (QB) 485. [166] [2004] EWCA Civ 560.

had used these security contractors for 18 months, had no reason to consider their work unsatisfactory before C's incident, and had good references about them from the previous owner;

iii. chose the independent contractor from a phone book, without further enquiries about competency, but had no reason to doubt the competency of their staff – e.g., in *Gwilliam v West Hertfordshire Hospital NHS Trust*,[167] where the hospital engaged Club Entertainments to set up a 'splat-wall' at its fair, the hospital was not liable as employer, for it had selected Club Entertainments as its independent contractor with reasonable care (in the case, C did not dispute that Club Entertainments was competent).

A breach on the part of the employer, in selecting the independent contractor, will be easier to establish for hazardous activities being undertaken by that contractor (e.g., as in *Bottomley v Todmorden Cricket Club*,[168] where Chaos Encounter, a two-man stunt team, had been engaged by the cricket club, as independent contractors, to conduct a pyrotechnic and fireworks display) – and harder to establish where the independent contractor is engaged for more benign activities (e.g., as in *Naylor (t/as Mainstreet) v Payling*,[169] where, as Waller LJ said, 'the job of acting as a bouncer does not ... fall within the type of hazardous activity which was under consideration in *Bottomley*').

In any event, where an independent contractor is engaged to undertake an 'ultra-hazardous' activity, then the employer will be liable for injuries caused by the negligence of the independent contractor in performing that activity – because ultra-hazardous activities is one of the common law categories in which an employer will owe C a non-delegable duty of care. This is an entirely *separate* basis for an employer's liability (discussed below).

The allegation: 'the independent contractor had no public liability insurance'

The position of an employer, when its independent contractor lacks any, or any current, public liability insurance, reflects that of an occupier (and readers are referred to Chapter 12 for analysis of the relevant principles).

To reiterate: as a general rule, there is no 'freestanding duty' owed by an employer to check that its independent contractor carried public liability insurance. If the independent contractor causes injury to C, and lacks any public liability insurance cover, then a direct action in negligence by C against that contractor will likely go unsatisfied. Despite C's hopes of reaching the 'deep pocket' of the employer under the 'negligent selection' route of direct liability, C cannot claim that, as a general rule, ascertaining that the independent contractor had insurance cover was part and parcel of the employer's duty to assess the competence of the independent contractor either. Notably, in *Gwilliam v West Hertfordshire Hospitals NHS Trust*,[170] Waller LJ seemed to suggest that such a free-standing duty did exist on the employer's part, but later clarified, in *Naylor (t/as Mainstreet) v Payling*,[171] that this is **not** what he intended.

However, there are exceptions. The employer would be acting unreasonably and negligently if it arranged for an independent contractor to carry out ultra-hazardous activity without first checking that the public would be as protected, as if the employer had carried out the activity itself (per *Bottomley v Todmorden Cricket Club*[172]) – whereas if the activity was not hazardous, then no enquiry about the independent contractor's insurance will be legally required (per *Naylor (t/as Mainstreet) v Payling*[173]).

167 [2002] EWCA Civ 1041, [2003] QB 443. 168 [2003] EWCA Civ 1575, quotes at [16] and [17] respectively.
169 [2004] EWCA Civ 560, [58]. 170 [2002] EWCA Civ 1041, [2003] QB 443.
171 [2004] EWCA Civ 560, [55]–[59]. 172 [2003] EWCA Civ 1575, [48]. 173 [2004] EWCA Civ 560, [57].

Even if the activity by the independent contractor was hazardous, there is no breach on the employer's part if it properly enquires as to the independent contractor's insurance position, and then omits to ask to see the terms of the policy, so as to verify whether the contractor's answer was correct (per *Gwilliam*[174]).

Non-delegable duties of care

§18.19 Exceptionally, an employer may be liable for a tort committed by an independent contractor, if the employer was able to delegate the task, but could not, by law, delegate the *responsibility for the work to be undertaken with reasonable care and skill.* In such cases (which are narrowly construed), the employer owes a non-delegable duty of care to C.

Where a non-delegable duty of care is owed by the employer to C, then the tort of the independent contractor constitutes a *breach* by the employer of that non-delegable duty of care.

In practical terms, reliance on non-delegable duties of care owed by the employer are particularly useful where the independent contractor itself is insolvent, uninsured, or otherwise unable to satisfy any judgment which may be obtained against it.

A number of judicial viewpoints have been expressed, about the theoretical basis which underpins the non-delegable duty on D's part. On the one hand, this scenario is seen as a form of strict liability, because (unlike in the previous two scenarios), there is **no** direct wrongdoing on the employer's part. The wrongdoing is by the independent contractor, but the employer is strictly liable for it. In the words of Lord Sumption in *Woodland v Essex CC*, '[n]on-delegable duties of care are inconsistent with the fault-based principles on which the law of negligence is based, and are therefore exceptional.'[175] On the other hand, theoretically speaking, this is **not** a case of vicarious liability, because the employer owes a direct duty to C 'to see that care is taken [which] rests upon the employer throughout the operation [of the independent contractor]' (per *Salsbury v Woodland*[176]). As pointed out in *Ship Chandlers v Norfolk Line Ltd*, if the employer's liability were truly vicarious, then the employer would owe no duty of care to C, but 'merely bear the burden of the independent contractor who did. However, non-delegable means something else'.[177] Non-delegable duties, as Lord Bridge explained in *D&F Estates Ltd v Church Commrs for England*, 'are dependent upon a finding that the employer is, *himself*, in breach of some duty which he personally owes to C. The liability is thus not truly a vicarious liability, and is to be distinguished from the vicarious liability of a master for his servant'.[178]

In *Woodland*,[179] Lord Sumption noted that the categories of non-delegable duties tend to divide into two categories – those where the employer D employs an independent contractor to perform some function which is, or is likely to become, inherently hazardous; or those where the employer D shares some antecedent relationship with C, whereby D owes an affirmative duty to protect a particular class of persons (including C) against a particular risk, and where that duty is personal to D ('the work required to perform such a duty may well be delegable, and usually is. But the duty itself remains D's').

[174] [2002] EWCA Civ 1041, [2003] QB 443. [175] [2013] UKSC 66, [2013] 3 WLR 1227, [22].
[176] [1970] 1 QB 324 (CA) 337. [177] QB, Judge Hicks QC, 10 Apr 1990 (paraphrased).
[178] [1989] AC 177 (HL) 208 (emphasis added). [179] [2013] UKSC 66, [6]–[7].

A few leading scenarios giving rise to non-delegable duties of care are noted in the Table:

Non-delegable duties of care

Scenario	Leading case example
Duties of safe system of work, etc, owed to employees – the independent contractor is working for the employer and, by some tortious act, injures C (one of the employer's *own employees*) – the employer is put in breach of a direct duty of care to its own employee (to provide a safe system of work, etc)	*McDermid v Nash Dredging & Reclamation Co Ltd*[a] – Mr McDermid, Nash's employee, was working aboard a tug, when he was injured because of the negligence of the captain of the tug. Captain Sas was not Nash's employee, but its independent contractor. **Held:** Nash owed a non-delegable duty of care to Mr McDermid, as its employee, and the captain's negligence put Nash in breach of that non-delegable duty of care.
Withdrawing support to neighbouring land – the independent contractor is working on employer's land, and withdraws support to a neighbour's (C's) land – the employer will be liable for breaching a non-delegable duty of care owed to that neighbour not to withdraw support	*Bower v Peate*[b] – Mr Bower and Mr Peate owned adjoining houses. P wished to pull down his old house and build a new one on the same site, and engaged Mr Rae, an independent contractor, to do the work. During Mr Rae's works, and because of defective underpinning and lack of support to the adjoining walls, B's property was badly damaged. **Held**: P was liable for the damage caused by Mr Rae's negligence.
Public nuisances to road-users by hazards on a highway – when doing work for employer on a highway, if the independent contractor causes a public nuisance by creating a danger to road-users (C) on the roadway, then the employer will be liable for breaching a non-delegable duty of care to those road-users	*Holliday v National Telephone Co*[c] – independent contractors were laying telephone wires in a highway on behalf of the Telephone Co, the employer, and negligently immersed a defective blow-lamp in a pot of solder which was on the footpath. The blow lamp blew up and C, a pedestrian, was injured. **Held:** the Telephone Co was liable for the contractors' negligence, as the source of danger was sufficiently on the highway to qualify. It would be ridiculous if there was liability because the pot of solder was on the highway, but no liability if it was two feet off the highway.
Escapes of dangerous things from the land – where the independent contractor is working on the employer's land, and allows a dangerous thing (such as fire) to escape, per *Rylands v Fletcher* liability, for which the independent contractor is strictly liable, then the employer will be liable for breaching a non-delegable duty of care to C who was harmed by the escape	*Balfour v Barty-King*[d] – Mr Balfour lived next door to the Barty-Kings. A pipe in the loft of the Barty-King's premises became frozen, and they engaged Hyder & Sons (Builders) Ltd, as independent contractors, to unfreeze the pipe, which the workmen did negligently, by thawing the pipe using a blow-lamp (highly dangerous, given that most of the pipes in the loft were lagged with felt). Fire spread to Mr Balfour's house, causing extensive damage. **Held:** the Barty-Kings were liable for the negligence of the two workmen of their independent contractors.

[a] [1987] AC 906 (HL).
[b] (1875–76) LR 1 QBD 321 (Civ Div).
[c] [1899] 2 QB 392 (CA).
[d] [1957] 1 QB 496 (CA).

Scenario	Leading case example
Ultra-hazardous activities – where the independent contractor, working for the employer, is engaged in ultra-hazardous activities[e] which give rise to special danger to others (including C), then the employer will be liable for breaching a non-delegable duty of care to C who is harmed by the independent contractor's ultra-hazardous activity	*Honeywill & Stein Ltd v Larkin Bros Ltd*[f] – acoustic specialists Honeywill installed a new sound system in a cinema, wished to take photos of it for their marketing, and engaged Mr Larkin (L), as independent contractor, to take the photos. The stage curtain caught fire from the flash which L used, and the cinema was badly damaged by fire. The question arose as to whether Honeywill would have been legally liable to the cinema owners if sued. **Held**: Honeywill was liable to the cinema owners for the negligence of L, as independent contractor engaged in ultra-hazardous activity.
Duties by a school to its pupils, for teaching and supervision – where the independent contractor, working for the employer, undertakes some activity which is integral to a school's teaching function, and causes harm to pupil C, then the school, as employer, will be liable for breach of its non-delegable duty of care to C. Key to this category is the vulnerability of the child, and the antecedent relationship between school and pupil of custody, charge and care of C	*Woodland v Essex CC*[g] – school pupil C, 10, had swimming lessons (part of the national curriculum), which were taken by independent contractor, 'Direct Swimming Services'. The lessons were in school hours, at other premises. C got into difficulty in the pool, due to the alleged negligent supervision by employees of Direct Swimming, and suffered brain damage. **Held**: the education authority was liable to C for the negligence of Direct Swimming. Swimming lessons were an integral part of the school's teaching function, the contractor was exercising custody and care of the vulnerable pupil, C, and it had a distinct element of control over how the lessons were conducted.

[e] Also termed extra-hazardous or 'inherently dangerous' activities in relevant case law.
[f] [1934] 1 KB 191 (CA).
[g] [2013] UKSC 66.

However, attempts to expand the categories of non-delegable duties of care have been judicially resisted. For example, the meaning of 'ultra-hazardous activities' has not been widely construed – and activities by an independent contractor 'near' to (rather than on) a highway are not sufficient to constitute an exceptional scenario rendering the employer liable.

In *Salsbury v Woodland*,[180] Mr Woodland wanted to have a large hawthorn tree near the road removed from his front garden, and engaged Mr Coombe, as independent contractor, to fell and remove the tree. Unfortunately, due to the way it was felled, it broke a pair of telephone wires running across the front garden, and these wires fell onto the road, causing an obstruction. Mr Salsbury, C, a neighbour, watching the operation, went onto the road to remove the wires. A car which was being driven too fast approached, and C, realising that a collision between car and wires was inevitable, threw himself onto the grass verge to avoid injury. This fall ruptured a tumour in his spine, and the bleeding and damage to the spinal cord caused C paralysis. **Held:** Mr Woodland, as employer, was not liable for the negligence of his independent contractor, Mr Coombe. The general rule that an

[180] [1970] 1 QB 324 (CA).

employer of an independent contractor was not responsible for his contractor's acts or omissions applied here, and none of the exceptions applied. Removal of the tree was not ultra-hazardous work. Nor was this work carried out *on* the highway. The exceptional categories would **not** be extended to work carried out *near* to a highway.

The category of non-delegable duty arising out of the independent contractor's performance of ultra-hazardous activities also drew criticism in *Biffa Waste*:

> the doctrine enunciated in *Honeywill* is so unsatisfactory that its application should be kept as narrow as possible. It should be applied only to activities that are exceptionally dangerous whatever precautions are taken ... the principle in *Honeywill* is anomalous. It is important that it is understood that its application is truly exceptional.[181]

Biffa Waste represented another unsuccessful attempt by C to allege a non-delegable duty of care – this time, in the context of property damage rather than of personal injury.

In *Biffa Waste*,[182] one of the claims brought against the contractor OT by Biffa Waste, C, whose recycling plant was badly damaged due to the negligence of Pickfords' welders, was based upon a non-delegable duty of care owed by OT, because the welding work carried out by Pickfords was ultra-hazardous. **Held:** no non-delegable duty of care was owed by OT. Arc welding near combustible material was ultra-hazardous – but *not* if appropriate precautions were taken (i.e., keeping the area free from flammable or combustible materials, wetting down the area, and monitoring the work for an hour afterwards). The CA noted that much of what happens in the construction industry is hazardous and dangerous, unless suitable precautions are taken (and crossing the road falls into that category!). It also remarked that the Australian High Court had held, in *Stevens v Brodribb Sawmilling Co Pty Ltd*,[183] that the doctrine was inherently flawed and should form no part of Australian law, and that the English Court of Appeal in *Bottomley* had already invited the House of Lords to do the same.

Moreover, the concept of non-delegable duties of care owed by employers is circumscribed, in that the employer is not liable for any 'collateral negligence' on the part of the independent contractor. Collateral negligence arises from acts which were 'coincidental', and which were not central to the work which the independent contractor was engaged to do (per *McDermid v Nash Dredging & Reclamation*,[184] where the actions of Captain Sas, in putting the engine of the tug into operation before it was safe to do so, were **not** collateral negligence – rather, employer Nash was liable for the negligence of Captain Sas, its independent contractor, because operating the tug safely was precisely what he was engaged by Nash to do).

Borrowing employees from the independent contractor

§18.20 Exceptionally, where the employer has 'borrowed' an employee of the independent contractor, and it is the employer, and not the independent contractor, who controls how that employee does his work, then under the *Mersey Docks* principle, the employer is vicariously liable for the torts of that 'loaned employee'.

181 [2008] EWCA Civ 1257, [2009] QB 725, [78], [85].

182 *ibid*, [75]–[77], citing: *Bottomley v Todmorden Cricket Club* [2003] EWCA Civ 1575, [50] (the House of Lords might 'prefer to avoid subtle distinctions between what is and is not "extra-hazardous" and follow Mason J (in *Stevens v Brodribb*)').

183 (1986) 160 CLR 16 (HCA) [77].

184 [1987] AC 906 (HL).

This is an instance of strict liability on the employer's part, discussed previously in the chapter.[185] The wrongdoing is by the employee of the independent contractor – but it is the Temporary Employer, and not the independent contractor, who will bear the burden of that employee's tort, via the doctrine of vicarious liability. However, as mentioned previously, the burden of shifting vicarious responsibility to the Temporary Employer is a heavy one.

In *Biffa Waste*,[186] it will be recalled that Biffa Waste, C, claimed that the contractor OT, who had engaged Pickfords to perform some work on a construction site, were liable to C, because two Pickfords employees, fitter and fitter's mate, were borrowed by OT. **Held:** the control of these Pickfords' employees never shifted to OT, and so, Pickfords remained vicariously liable for the fitter's mate's negligence in causing C's factory to flood.

[185] Cross cite pp 986–91. [186] [2008] EWCA Civ 1257.

Index

This index is for the print book only, and does not incorporate the online material.